The COMPLETE BOOK OF EVERYDAY CHRISTIANITY

AN A-TO-Z GUIDE TO FOLLOWING CHRIST IN EVERY ASPECT OF LIFE

EDITED BY
Robert Banks & R. Paul Stevens

InterVarsity Press
Downers Grove, Illinois

InterVarsity Press® is the book-publishing division of InterVarsity Christian Fellowship®, a student movement active on campus at hundreds of universities, colleges and schools of nursing in the United States of America, and a member movement of the International Fellowship of Evangelical Students. For information about local and regional activities, write Public Relations Dept., InterVarsity Christian Fellowship, 6400 Schroeder Rd., P.O. Box 7895, Madison, WI 53707-7895.

Cover photographs: Michael Goss

ISBN 0-8308-1450-7

Printed in the United States of America ♾

Library of Congress Cataloging-in-Publication Data

The complete book of everyday Christianity : an A-to-Z guide to following Christ in every aspect
   of life / edited by Robert Banks & R. Paul Stevens.
      p.   cm.
   Includes bibliographical references and index.
   ISBN 0-8308-1450-7 (alk. paper)
      1. Christianity—Dictionaries.   I. Banks, Robert J.
II. Stevens, R. Paul, 1937-   .
BR95.C65   1997
248'.03—dc21
                                                                                        97-11776
                                                                                              CIP

22   21   20   19   18   17   16   15   14   13   12   11   10   9   8   7   6   5   4   3   2   1

15   14   13   12   11   10   09   08   07   06   05   04   03   02   01   00   99   98   97

INTRODUCTION

Everyday life is a complex affair. Most of it is made up of familiar situations, responsibilities, frustrations, pressures, conflicts, obligations, dilemmas and demands. In the midst of these we entertain hopes and expectations and meet satisfactions and disappointments. But sometimes crises, public or private, intrude on the regular rhythms of our lives. New opportunities come our way; long-standing certainties are replaced by newly discovered ambiguities. The world around us changes, and it is hard to keep pace with all that is happening. If we are able to deal with portions of what is happening, the big picture often eludes us. Life easily becomes confusing, and the messages we pick up are often contradictory.

There are two further complications. First, those of us who are committed to connecting our faith with every part of our lives are not always sure how to do so. If it is true, as the major Christian traditions have always insisted, that our religious convictions and values should be reflected in all that we do—the way we eat and drink, work and play, worship and vote, the quality of our parenting and friendships, our involvement with neighbors and colleagues, our engagement with popular or high culture—then there is much to consider. All these activities need to be related to our understanding of God, and whatever we learn must be incarnated in our behavior. How else will others know that God makes a distinctive claim on their lives? This is a daunting task, one we cannot handle alone but only with help from others.

Second, it would be easier for us to deal with these matters if there were a deposit of accumulated wisdom on which we could draw. Down through the centuries some impressive groups have developed an integrated approach to life. In such groups, everything was viewed through the lens of faith, hope and love. If the early monastic movements and medieval Christian orders did this for the few, the early Anabaptists and Puritans did it for the many. In the intervening years we have lost some of the breadth of such visions. We have compartmentalized life and either separated ourselves too much from the world or accommodated ourselves too much to it, generally without realizing what we are doing.

There is little to help us over this gap. Sermons are often too general, small groups avoid sensitive subjects, Christians magazines mainly deal with personal or relational issues, theological writings rarely address everyday concerns. This book seeks to provide what we are lacking. We have tried to make it as comprehensive, accessible and substantive as possible. While we have sought to make it practical, it is more than a self-help book because it analyzes wider issues, peers beneath the surface of the subjects it treats, and identifies some of the connections between them.

You can use *The Complete Book of Everyday Christianity* in a number of ways.

1. You may have a particular interest you wish to pursue (such as developing a simpler lifestyle) or a felt need on which you require help (say, the issue of workaholism). All you have to do is look up such terms in the subject index, find the entries you want, and then follow any cross-references to related articles.

2. You may be passing through a troublesome period in your life (such as a midlife crisis) or facing a specific set of concerns (perhaps family problems). In such cases the Life Experience Index is especially helpful, since it lists a range of entries under various life stages and situations.

3. You may be preparing a talk, study, sermon or workshop. As you do so, you may profitably consult entries directly in the dictionary itself. Alternatively, many entries in this volume would lend themselves to being part of a series for small-group or class discussion. You might develop a series with the help of the Life Experience Index, or create your own with the help of group cross-references in a major entry. For instance, a series on redeeming our daily routine might be based on articles about washing, chores, reading newspapers, commuting, office politics, coffee drinking, shopping and television.

4. You may wish to use the volume as a textbook for a church or parachurch-based class or a college or seminary course. With regard to the first of these, you could consult the Life Activities, Interests & Concerns Index and take one of its main divisions and construct a series out of it, or choose a theme (such as community) that crosses several divisions. With regard to the second, we ourselves will be using the volume in courses on lifestyle ethics, marketplace ministry and the spirituality of everyday life.

5. You may simply prefer, at times, to browse through the book when and where you have opportunity, moving from topic to topic as your interest takes you.

Throughout the volume you will find numerous cross-references in *see* or *see also* listings. Articles are also frequently cross-referenced through the use of asterisks(*) at the ends of words on which there are separate listings in the dictionary. Sometimes the exact listings may use slightly different forms of the words; thus "homosexual*" points to an article entitled "homosexuality," and "greetings*" points to an article entitled "greeting."

For the two of us, working on this volume was an adventure that has developed a growing friendship and appreciation of one another. Through its hundred or so contributors, the book has also introduced us to a wide range of thoughtful practitioners who share some common interests. From the outset InterVarsity Press took a keen interest in the project and, with the help of Rodney Clapp, brought our "concept" into being. We are also grateful to the secretaries and research assistants who helped us at various points on this journey. Above all, we are thankful to God, for all the encouragement and sustenance that came to us along the way, and whose vision for all people and every part of creation is so astonishingly inclusive, vibrant and glorious.

LIST OF
CONTRIBUTORS

Dr. Carol Anderson, physician: **Conception; Birth; Breast-Feeding; Pregnancy; Miscarriage; New Reproductive Technology**

Dr. Stephen Anderson, psychiatrist: **Dreaming**

Dr. David Augsburger, professor of pastoral counseling, Fuller Theological Seminary: **Chocolate; Conflict Resolution; Confronting; Emotions; Grieving; Love; Secrets**

Dr. Thena Ayres, assistant professor of adult education, Regent College: **Singleness**

Dr. Stuart Barton Babbage, author: **Aging; Retirement**

Dr. Judith K. Balswick, professor of marriage and family, Graduate School of Psychology, Fuller Theological Seminary: **Family Goals; Family Problems**

Julie Banks, homemaker: **Family History; Pets; Simpler Lifestyle; Weddings**

Robert Banks, executive director, De Pree Leadership Center; Homer L. Goddard Professor of the Ministry of the Laity, Fuller Theological Seminary: **Authority, Church; Automobile; Blessing; Chores; Church; Church in the Home; Church, Small; Coffee Drinking;**
Community; Compromise; Conversation; Daydreaming; Denominations; Examinations; Fences; Freedom; Gardening; Gossip; Home; Individual; Letter Writing; Megachurch; Mobility; Neighborhood; Noise; Ownership, Private; Part-Time Employment; Privacy; Public Spaces; Public Transportation; Service, Workplace; Shiftwork; Shopping; Shopping Malls; Simpler Lifestyle; Stress, Workplace; Suburbia; Teaching; Telephone; Time; Visiting; Walking; Washing; Watch; Weddings; Work Ethic, Protestant; Workplace; Worship

Dr. Roy D. Bell, emeritus professor of family ministries, Carey Theological College: **Conflict, Church; Empty Nesting; Grandparenting**

Iain Benson, constitutional lawyer, lecturer, author; senior research fellow, Centre for Renewal in Public Policy, Ottawa: **Rights; Values; Virtues**

Dr. Ken Blue, pastor, author: **Abuse; Discipline, Church**

Dr. Lynn Buzzard, professor of law, Campbell University School of Law: **Justice; Law**

Dr. Jonathan Chaplin, lec-
turer in politics, Plater College, Oxford: **States/Provinces**

Rodney Clapp, senior editor, InterVarsity Press: **Church-Family**

Dr. John Court, director of Psychological Clinic, Fuller Theological Seminary: **Homosexuality**

Derek Creighton, municipal lawyer, City of Vancouver: **Zoning**

Stephen W. Crowe, journalist: **Newspapers**

Ron Dart, professor of political science, social activist: **Poverty; Social Action**

Dr. Peter Davids, sessional lecturer, Regent College; pastor: **Hate**

Dr. John M. Dettoni, president, Chrysalis Ministries: **Adolescence; Faith Development; Life Stages; Nondenominational**

William Diehl, consultant, author: **Competency; Conflict, Workplace; Firing; Negotiating; Office Politics; Promotion**

Dr. John Drane, professor of religious studies, Scotland: **Evangelism; Witness**

Paddy Ducklow, pastor, psychologist: **Affirming; Emotions; Family Communication; Family Systems; Marriage**

Dr. William A. Dyrness, dean and professor of theology and culture, Fuller Theological Seminary: **Art; Beauty**

Dr. Gordon Fee, professor of New Testament, Regent College: **Spiritual Gifts**

Donald E. Flow, president, Flow Automotive Companies: **Profit**

Dr. Cheryl Forbes, assistant professor of writing and rhetoric, Hobart and William Smith Colleges: **Imagination**

Sharon Gallagher, editor, *Radix* magazine; associate director, New College Berkeley: **Movies**

Dr. Craig Gay, assistant professor of interdisciplinary studies, Regent College: **Consumerism**

Dr. David Gill, professor of applied ethics, North Park University: **Power, Workplace; System; Technology**

Robert Girard, pastor, author: **Failure**

Vernon Gleddie, farmer: **Community, Rural; Farming**

Dr. Julie Gorman, professor of Christian formation, Fuller Theological Seminary: **Small Groups**

Dr. Michael Green, evangelist: **Baptism; Communion; Fellowship; Sacraments**

Dr. Donald Gray, professor of sociology, Eastern College: **Crime; Crowds**

Angus Gunn, emeritus professor of education, University of British Columbia: **Education; Homework**

Pete Hammond, director, InterVarsity Marketplace: **Accountability, Relational; Partying**

Dr. Maxine Hancock, author, television journalist; sessional lecturer, Regent College: **Reading**

Dr. Archibald D. Hart, professor of psychology, Graduate School of Psychology, Fuller Theological Seminary: **Anxiety; Depression**

Dr. Young Lee Hertig, professor of crosscultural ministry, School of World Mission, Fuller Theological Seminary: **Sugar/Sugary**

Richard Heyduck, graduate student, Fuller Theological Seminary: **Reasoning**

Dr. Alexander D. Hill, Joseph C. Hope Professor of Leadership and Ethics, Seattle Pacific University: **Business Ethics**

Simon Carey Holt, graduate student, Fuller Theological Seminary: **Eating; Home**

Dr. Edwin C. Hui, associate professor of medical ethics and spiritual theology, Regent College: **Abortion; Addiction; Contraception; Euthanasia; Healing; Health; Sickness**

Dr. Robert K. Johnston, professor of theology and culture, Fuller Theological Seminary: **Play; Pleasure**

Patricia Kerr, teacher, Buenos Aires Bible Institute, Argentina: **Hospitality**

Susan Klassen, storyteller: **Storytelling**

Dr. John Kleinig, professor of philosophy; director, Institute for Criminal Justice Ethics, John Jay School of Criminal Justice: **Law Enforcement**

Patricia Lane, lawyer/mediator; past director of Consultation for the Ontario Fair Tax Commission: **Taxes**

Dr. Patrick Lattore, director of corporate and foundation relations, Children's

Hospital Los Angeles Foundation; adjunct assistant professor of leadership, Fuller Theological Seminary: **Leadership**

Paul W. Lermitte, registered financial planner: **Allowances**

Kathryn Lockhart, homemaker, humorist: **Dress Code, Workplace; Humor; Laughter**

Ken Luscombe, director, Office of Urban Advance, World Vision International: **City**

Dr. David Lyon, professor of sociology, Queen's University, Kingston: **Society**

Dr. Paul Marshall, Institute of Christian Studies: **Civil Disobedience; Nationalism; Politics; Power**

Dr. Michael Maloney, physician: **Contraception**

Thomas H. McAlpine, director of urban evangelism, World Vision International: **Sleeping**

Jenny McDermit, quilt shop owner and craftsperson: **Quilting**

Dr. Alister E. McGrath, research professor, Regent College; principal, Wycliffe Hall, Oxford: **Creation**

Al McKay, InterVarsity staff; training director of B.C. Pioneer Camps, Vancouver: **Camping**

Dr. Michel Mestre, professor, Faculty of Business and Economics, Trinity Western University: **Unemployment**

Dr. Robert P. Meye, retired professor of preaching, Fuller Theological Seminary: **Gardening**

Hal Miller, software engineer: **Computer; Computer Games; Information Superhighway; Suc-**

cess; **Virtual Reality**

Peter Mogan, lawyer: **Contracts**

David J. Montgomery, assistant minister, Stormont Presbyterian Church, Belfast: **Forgiveness; Sports**

Dr. Richard Mouw, president, Fuller Theological Seminary: **Civility**

Dr. Nancey Murphy, associate professor of Christian philosophy, Fuller Theological Seminary: **Reasoning**

Mike Nichols, pastor, counselor: **Habits; Masturbation; Self-Esteem**

Ed Norman, organist; adjunct professor of music, University of British Columbia: **Music; Music, Christian**

Susan Norman, homemaker: **Homemaking**

Kathleen Norris, author: **Small Towns**

Ruth Oliver, Volunteer Bureau, Vancouver: **Volunteer Work**

Dr. William Pannell, professor of preaching, Fuller Theological Seminary: **Racism**

Valerie Pyke Parks, student, Regent College: **Menstruation**

Dr. Richard Peace, professor of evangelism, Fuller Theological Seminary: **Discipleship; Spiritual Formation**

Dr. Richard W. Pollay, professor of marketing, University of British Columbia: **Advertising**

James Postlewaite, minister of Christian education, First Baptist Church, Vancouver: **Christian Education; Sunday School**

Gordon Preece, chaplain and lecturer in ethics and lay ministry, Ridley College, Melbourne, Australia: **Work**

Dr. Peter Quek, director, Educational Initiatives, Regent College: **Competition**

Dr. Elaine J. Ramshaw, associate professor of pastoral care, Luther Seminary: **Godparenting**

Dr. John H. Redekop, professor of political science and media critic, Trinity Western University: **Lobbying; Pluralism; Political Parties, Joining**

Ron Reed, actor, playwright, artistic director, Pacific Theatre Company: **Theater, Live**

Dr. John E. Richardson, associate professor of management, Pepperdine University: **Discrimination, Workplace; Whistle-Blowing**

Dr. Robert Roxburgh, pastor, author: **Church Renewal**

Dal Schindell, director of publications, Regent College: **Architecture, Urban; Comics**

Gerry Schoberg, lecturer, Theological College of Central Africa, Zambia: **Greeting; Structures; System**

Celeste Snowber Schroeder, dancer, lecturer: **Body; Femininity**

Dr. Quentin J. Schultze, professor of communications, Calvin College: **Entertainment; Mass Media; Televangelism; Television; Home Video**

Dr. Calvin Seerveld, professor of philosophical aesthetics, Institute of Christian Studies: **Adornment; Games**

Dr. James Skillen, director, Center for Public Justice: **Citizenship; Voting**

Graeme Smith, carpenter, craftsman: **Craftsmanship**

Dr. Howard A. Snyder, professor of missiology, Asbury Theological Seminary: **Mission; Missions; Parachurch Organizations**

Dr. Brian F. Stelck, missionary; principal, Carey Theological College: **Ethnocentrism; Multiculturalism**

Gail C. Stevens, homemaker: **Death; Menopause and Male Climacteric**

R. Paul Stevens, professor of applied theology, Regent College: **Advertising; Ambition; Anniversaries; Blessing, Family; Boredom; Calling/Vocation; Camping; Career; Clergy; Clubs; Cohabiting; Conscience; Credit Card; Dating; Death; Divorce; Drivenness; Equipping; Family; Family Values; Farewell; Financial Support; Friendship; Gift-Giving; Global Village; Guidance; Hobbies and Crafts; Insurance; Investment; Laity; Leadership, Church; Leisure; Listening; Membership, Church; Menopause and Male Climacteric; Ministry; Organization; Organizational Culture and Change; Organizational Values; Parenting; Photography; Prayer, Corporate; Preaching; Principalities and Powers; Professions/Professionalism; Promising; Recreation; Rest; Sabbath; Sexuality; Soul; Speaking; Spiritual Conflict; Spiritual Disciplines; Spiritual Gifts; Spiritual Growth; Stewardship; Structures; Talents; Tentmaking; Trades; Traveling; Unemployment;**

Vacations; Vocational Guidance; Waiting; Wealth; Weather Watching; Will, Last; Worship

John R. Sutherland, professor of management and business ethics, Trinity Western University: **Credit; Debt; Strikes; Unions**

Wilber Sutherland, director, IMAGO: **Immigration**

Dr. Siang-Yang Tan, associate professor of psychology, Graduate School of Psychology, Fuller Theological Seminary: **Counseling, Lay**

Dr. Yiu-Meng Toh, psychologist, Surrey and Vancouver, B.C.: **Counseling, Lay**

Dr. John F. Van Wicklin, professor of psychology, Houghton College: **Drugs**

Dr. Brian J. Walsh, university chaplain, University of Toronto: **Worldview**

Dr. Tony Walter, lecturer in sociology, Reading University, England: **Need**

Dr. Bruce Waltke, professor of Old Testament, Regent College: **Circumcison**

Jude Tiersma Watson, instructor in urban mission, Fuller Theological Seminary: **Inner City**

Dr. Loren Wilkinson, professor of interdisciplinary studies, Regent College: **Backpacking; Culture; Ecology; Pollution; Wilderness**

Mary Ruth Wilkinson, homemaker/hearthkeeper: **Fairy Tales; Meal Preparation**

Dan Williams, pastor,

author: **Allowances; Church Structures; Committees; Planning; Vision**

Rodger Woods, architect: **Church Building**

David Worley, radio station owner: **Radio Listening**

Dr. Walter Wright, president, Regent College: **Accountability, Workplace; Integrity; Loyalty, Workplace; Management**

Scott Young, campus minister, UCLA: **Networking**

Dr. John C. Zimmerman, Charles Bentall Professor of Pastoral Studies, Carey Theological College: **Pastoral Care**

Martha Zimmerman, author: **Birthdays; Festivals—Christmas; Festivals—Easter; Festivals—Thanksgiving**

ABORTION

Abortion has been with us throughout the ages. While first accepted as a necessary measure or "therapy" in saving the life of the mother, it has also been accepted in many countries as a means of population control, "quality of life" control (in the case of deformed fetuses) and reproductive control. It is often a choice for teens and women in economic hardship who do not have the resources to care for a child, as well as for women who are victims of rape and incest. In modern Western culture the justification and acceptance of this practice has widened as women's rights and reproductive rights have come to the forefront. Often a woman's request for abortion is justification enough for the procedure.

Medical Considerations

Abortion is termination of a pregnancy. It can be classified as either *spontaneous* or *induced*. A spontaneous abortion is a miscarriage, that is, the pregnancy ends usually due to various chromosomal or congenital defects, diseases or infections— of fetal or maternal origin. Unlike spontaneous abortion, an induced abortion is not a natural process of the body and involves a medical intervention. This intervention is of two types—therapeutic or elective— depending on the reason for the abortion. If the mother's life is in danger, as in the case of cardiovascular and hypertensive diseases, an abortion might be per-

formed for therapeutic reasons. An elective or voluntary abortion, on the other hand, is requested for reasons other than maternal health and is the most commonly performed type of abortion in the West today. It is estimated that approximately 25 percent of all pregnancies in the world are terminated by elective abortion, making this the most common method of reproduction limitation.

The method chosen for an abortion is commonly determined by factors like the duration of the pregnancy, the patient's health, the experience of the physician and the physical facilities. The methods include (1) suction or surgical curettage; (2) induction of labor by means of intra- or extraovular injection of a hypertonic solution or other oxytocic agent; (3) extraovular placement of devices such as catheters, bougies or bags; (4) abdominal or vaginal hysterotomy and (5) menstrual regulation. About 75 percent of induced abortions in the United States are performed by suction curettage for a pregnancy of twelve weeks' duration or less; these are usually performed in abortion outpatient clinics. There are, however, medical concerns about this spreading practice.

The two major medical reasons for limiting abortion today are fetal viability (which changes with technological capabilities) and medical consequences to the mother. Viability, the point at which a fetus can survive outside the mother's womb, now stands at twenty-four weeks and can often be easily defined. Yet the consequences of an abortion procedure to the mother are debated and controversial. While most abortions, especially those done in the first trimester, are safe for women physically, the psychological sequelae have gone undocumented. Some reports deny serious psychological effects of abortion, but most cite overwhelming statistics indicating dire long-term negative effects, including guilt, shame, depression,* grief,* anxiety,* despair, low self-esteem,* distrust and hostility. Women with previous histories of psychiatric illnesses tend to be affected to a greater degree.

Both the Canadian Medical Association and the American Medical Association recognize abortion as a medical procedure available under the law. Recently, the Accreditation Council for Graduate Medical Education called for compulsory abortion training for students of obstetrics (McFarland, p. 25). In contrast, the Christian Medical and Dental Society (CMDS) opposes the practice of abortion.

Prolife Versus Prochoice

It is most unfortunate that the abortion debate is divided into two clearly opposing camps: the prolife and the prochoice, each entrenched in its respective uncompromising positions. The prolife stance holds the view that the fetus is a developing human being with intrinsic values* and inviolable rights.* She is as much a human being as the mother. So the sanctity of the fetal life in the womb, however developed, should have priority over the reproductive freedom of the woman. Abortion should be considered only when the life of the mother is in jeopardy. The basis of the prolife position is largely, but not exclusively, grounded on divine authority and the belief that human life is a gift of God.

The prochoice position does not see the fetus as possessing rights independent of the mother, who alone has the right to decide the fate of the fetus. This maternal right is in turn grounded in the principle of autonomy or self-determination, which provides the mother with freedom to make reproductive choices. The prochoice position also views access to abortion as necessary for women's complete social equality. They see reproduction as the major obstacle to women's competing successfully with men, and hence control of reproduction, including abortion, is necessary for equality. Any restriction of the availability of abortion is interpreted as coercing women to carry pregnancies to term against their will.

Personhood

While it is seldom disputed that a conceptus or a fetus is human, there is hardly a consensus as to when a human person begins. Personhood is still a crucial and practical issue, since modern society accords a person certain moral rights, such as the right to life. General philosophical criteria for personhood include any one, a few or all of the following: rationality, consciousness, self-consciousness, freedom to act on one's own reasons, capacity to communicate with others and capacity to make moral judgments. Some hold that only when one or all of these qualities have been actualized should a human being be considered a person (actuality principle). Others feel that these qualities of personhood only emerge gradually in the course of fetal and early childhood development, so what counts in defining personhood is the potential that the human life possesses (potentiality principle). In this view fetuses and infants are recognized as having different degrees of personhood and therefore are given different measures of right to life.

The Bible does not use specifically the

words *person* or *personhood,* but a biblical view of personhood can be established on the basis of a Christian doctrine of the image of God. Genesis 1:26-27 reads: "Then God said, 'Let us make man in our image, in our likeness, and let them rule.' . . . So God created man in his own image, in the image of God he created him; male and female he created them." Because God exists as three persons in communion, we also believe that human persons are created in his image to live in community.* The most fundamental attribute of being in the image of God and human personhood, therefore, is relationality. God creates every single human person in order to relate to him or her. In response, every created human person seeks to relate to the Creator and other fellow creatures. Since each human being is created uniquely by God, every single human being is God's image bearer. This is the ground for personhood, uniqueness and the right to life. Life is sacred because God creates a particular life for a unique relationship between him as the Creator and us as his creatures. This relationship begins when a conceptus is formed as God permits a human sperm and ovum to unite in the creation of a new unique life. How that life unfolds and whether all the inherent potentialities are actualized or not do not take away the intrinsic value of that life as God's image bearer, a human person.

A Christian Response

Such a Christian understanding of personhood undergirds the proper attitude toward abortion. The sixth commandment in the Bible (not to kill; Ex 20:13) carries the positive mandate of stewardship* of all lives as sacred to God. This means not that the value of life is absolute (Mt 24:9) but rather that no life is to be taken without an absolutely and unequivocally justifiable reason. As the Creator and Giver of life, it is God who ultimately has the sovereign right to take away life. So any attempt to terminate life, as in an abortion, must be done with the fullest sense of accountability before the sovereign God. For this reason the CMDS, both in the U.S. and Canada, in contrast to its secular counterparts, opposes the routine practice of abortion. Four main points are maintained in their position: (1) CMDS opposes abortion, yet supports alternatives; (2) CMDS believes abortion is in opposition to the Word of God, to respect for the sanctity of life and to traditional, historical and Judeo-Christian medical ethics; (3) CMDS believes that the Bible espouses principles that oppose the interruption of pregnancy (the sovereignty of God, the value of life over quality of life, moral responsibility in sexual conduct); (4) in the face of rights arguments put forth by patients and physicians alike, CMDS adheres to the final authority of Scripture, which teaches the sanctity of human life.

But resolving the dilemma of abortion takes more than ardently defending the sanctity of life in the unborn, for there is sacred life to embrace, though tragically unwanted, when abortion is opposed and denied. As a community that espouses Christian teachings and opposes abortion, we must be prepared to parent any children, not just our own, as a shared obligation. This means taking concrete steps to receive unwanted children into our families as a gesture of taking seriously the sacred lives God has created and exercising stewardship.

As a community of grace, Christians must, in addition to exercising the stewardship of life, honor our obligation of love.* Love sees a woman seeking abortion as a neighbor in need of compassion. Regardless of whether abortion is given or denied, the pregnant mother, father and other members of the family will likely feel wounded. The Christian community must live out its spirit of *koinonia* by developing various forms of care and support during such a difficult time and by providing a context in which repentance, reconciliation, healing* and nurturing may take place.

Finally, the Christian community must not abdicate its responsibility in the prevention of abortion in our society. This must be achieved through education of our teenagers and young adults with regard to moral sexual conduct and responsible family planning. Sexual abilities are given to human beings to experience in part on earth what God is fully in eternity—love. Children, as a product of the love between husband and wife, are gifts from God to deepen the experience of love. No sex or childbearing outside the institution of marriage* fulfills this divine intention. Christian education in the form of counseling is also important, and participation with a Christlike humility and patience in organizations such as Pregnancy Crisis Center enables a Christian community to resolve and persevere with the abortion dilemma.

See also PARENTING; SELF-ESTEEM; SEXUALITY.

References and Resources
T. Beauchamp and L. Walters, eds., *Contemporary Issues in Bioethics* (Belmont, Calif.: Wadsworth, 1989) 181-239; S. McFarland, "The Abortion Rotation," *Christianity Today* 39, no. 4 (1995) 25; F. Mathewes-Green, *Real Choices: Offering Practical, Life-Affirming Alternatives to Abortion* (Sisters, Ore.: Multnomah, 1994); M. L. Pernoll, ed., *Current Obstetric and Gynecologic Diagnosis and Treatment,* 7th ed. (Stamford, Conn.: Appleton & Lange, 1991); P. Ramsey, "Morality of Abortion," in *Life or Death: Ethics and Options* (Seattle: University of Washington Press, 1968) 60-93; D. C. Reardon, *Aborted Women, Silent No More* (Westchester, Ill.: Crossway Books, 1987); N. Stotland, "Psychiatric Issue in Abortion, and the Implications of Recent Legal Choices for Psychiatric Practice," in *Psychiatric Aspects of Abortion,* ed. N. Stotland (Washington, D.C.: American Psychiatric Press, 1991) 1-16; J. R. W. Stott, "The Abortion Dilemma," in *Issues Facing Christians Today* (Old Tappan, N.J.: Fleming H. Revell, 1984) 2:187-214.

Edwin Hui

ABUSE
There has been a dramatic increase in the public's awareness of and concern about various forms of abuse, primarily family* abuse. Most of this is physical and sexual assault as well as psychological and emotional abuse against women and children. According to the Federal Bureau of Investigation one out of every two American women is beaten during her marriage; 28 percent are battered at least once a year. A woman is battered every fifteen seconds. Battering is the single greatest cause of injury to women in the U.S., more than accidents, rapes and muggings combined. Over 70 percent of men who batter their wives also physically or sexually assault their children. The vast majority of women who are beaten, raped or murdered are assaulted by someone with whom they are intimate. By contrast, men who are beaten or murdered are assaulted by total strangers. The FBI estimates that less than 10 percent of domestic violence is reported to authorities.

Understanding Abuse
Abuse is a buzzword today. One way of overcoming this is to view abuse on a continuum. At one end of the continuum we place brutal, systematic exploitation and oppression. Here power abuse is often premeditated, and the perpetrator knows full well that the abuse hurts others. At the opposite end of the continuum we place relatively mild and sporadic social manipulation. Here the abuser does not intend harm but blindly pursues personal desires and hurts others in the process. Many such abusers are

curiously naive about the damage they do to others. This naiveté is usually a factor when abuse occurs in the church.*

Abuse of any type occurs when someone has power* over another and uses that power to hurt. Physical abuse means that someone exercises physical power over another and causes physical wounds. Sexual abuse means that someone exercises sexual power over another and causes sexual wounds. Spiritual abuse means that someone in a position of spiritual authority* uses that position to inflict spiritual wounds. And so, social, political and psychological abuse occurs when those in power use that power to cause unjust suffering to those around them.

The Silent Epidemic
The American Medical Association refers to physical and sexual abuse against women and children as the "silent epidemic" of the 1990s. The AMA tells physicians to be on the lookout for symptoms of abuse and then to go beyond just treating those symptoms. Once doctors see evidence of abuse they are urged to report it to authorities. If necessary, doctors are to assist in pressing charges against the perpetrators of the abuse. This new activism on the part of physicians is one indication of society's alarm over abuse.

Is there a real increase of abuse today, or are we just reporting it and talking about it more? The answer to both questions is yes. There is a documented increase of child abuse in the home and sexual abuse in and outside the home. For instance, twenty-year-old women are reporting nearly twice the instances of sexual assault against them as their mothers had experienced at the same age.

Also, abuse has become a less taboo topic. For years Americans maintained a virtual silence on the issues of child abuse and sexual violence against women in the home. The church was most reticent of all to discuss these concerns, but now they are out in the open. The Roman Catholic Church, for example, is dealing openly with child sexual abuse by its priests. Some leaders estimate that by the year 2000, the Catholic Church will have paid out over one billion dollars in settlements to victims of clergy sexual abuse.

Spiritual abuse happens when a leader with spiritual authority uses that authority to coerce, control or exploit a follower, thus causing spiritual wounds. Unlike physical abuse, which often results in bruised bodies, spiritual abuse leaves scars on the psyche and soul.* Counselors report that those wounded by spiritual abuse share many symptoms seen in victims of childhood sexual abuse, including deep fearfulness, depression,* anxiety* and an inability to trust. They are often too ashamed to talk openly about it. Some who do talk about their experiences are called "divisive" or "troublemakers" or are told that *they* are the problem.

Spiritual abuse is as widespread today as it was at the time Jesus spoke the words which contain the Bible's clearest teaching on the subject. Jesus points out that abusive spiritual leaders demand authority for themselves, based on title and office (Mt 23:6-7), whereas healthy leaders rely on their demonstrated servanthood to exercise influence. Abusive leaders oppress and manipulate people by heaping on people loads of legalism, guilt and shame (Mt 23:4), while nonabusive leaders lift those burdens off, directing their followers to Jesus Christ for rest and for "yokes" that are light and fit well (Mt 11:28-30).

Spiritual abuse occurs on a continuum from minor and sporadic to heavyhanded and systematic. Some abusers are easy to identify by their obviously immoral behavior. Others are much more subtle, but equally damaging. They may officially embrace an orthodox theology and present a polished, respectable public image. But in reality they practice "another gospel" which undermines adult reasoning* and personal relationship with God in favor of unbalanced submission to an authoritarian church leadership.* Such people subtly coerce their congregations through skillful use of language of intimacy and trust. When these types of leaders pretend to be a friend representing the heart of God and use this illusion to dehumanize and manipulate people, they inflict deep spiritual wounds.

Exploring the Reasons

Many factors contribute to the increasing incidence of abuse: sociological, political, cultural and spiritual. People in the Western world feel an increasing sense of powerlessness, pressured as they are by an increasingly automated, depersonalized and globalized society. One way of responding to powerlessness is by violence, and persons closest at hand frequently are the targets of this frustration. Further, society in general is decaying. Increasingly we hear our culture* described as "post-Christian." One symptom of this is that what is right and wrong from a biblical perspective is taught and understood less and less. Since there no longer exists a moral consensus among us, people increasingly do what is right in their own eyes.

The breakdown of the family also contributes to the increase of abusive behavior in children. Children who grow up in broken and otherwise dysfunctional homes often suffer from poor emotional health and tend to be less psychologically stable. Statistically they are also more likely to be the victims of abuse. Add to this their anger* and frustration over being neglected and their efforts to survive under oppressive living

conditions, and it is easy to see why disadvantaged children often act out and tend to become abusive toward others. Abusive parents today were very likely victims themselves of parental abuse. This creates a dismal generational view of the problem.

Sadly, there is little difference between the moral performance of the general public and churchgoers. Frequency of all kinds of abuses is more or less the same for the "Christian" and non-Christian population—the abuse of power among church leaders approximates the abuse of power among leaders elsewhere. Power always brings privileges, and all too frequently these privileges are abused.

Using and Abusing Power

The idea of power is complex. Every living human being possesses power. That is to say, every living person has some capacity to act on the environment and effect change—some more, some less. Some people are strong physically, intellectually, spiritually, politically, socially and so on. They have more power. Others are weak. They obviously have less power. Society* dictates how certain kinds of power are distributed. Some people are awarded more power, some less. That means that some are dominant and others must defer. In most societies police officers are assigned power. In business bosses are assigned power. In religion pastors and priests are assigned power. In all our social arrangements, power is unequally distributed.

This unequal distribution of power is not the problem so far as the Bible is concerned. "Everyone must submit himself to the governing authorities, for there is no authority except that which God has established" (Rom 13:1). The problem arises when those with power use that power to hurt others. When the power arrangements in church and society produce injustice, then God comes *against* the power abusers and *to* the aid of the victims. As God's people, we must have the same attitude.

The Old Testament prophets spoke frequently on God's behalf against the political and religious power abusers of their day: "For three sins of Damascus, and even for four, I will not turn back my wrath. Because she threshed Gilead with sledges . . ." (Amos 1:3). When those who were abusing power did not repent of their sin, God stepped in to judge them and work justice* for the victims. "The Sovereign LORD says: I am against the shepherds and will hold them accountable for my flock. I will remove them from tending the flock. . . . I myself will search for my sheep and look after them" (Ezek 34:10-11).

Jesus continued God's justice work as he spoke out against the ecclesiastical power abusers of his day and offered help to their victims: "Woe to you, teachers of the law and Pharisees, you hypocrites! You shut the kingdom of God in men's faces" (Mt 23:13). "They tie up heavy loads and put them on men's shoulders" (Mt 23:4). "Come to me, all you who are weary and burdened, and I will give you rest" (Mt 11:28).

God not only distributes power and allows society to make power arrangements but also demands that those in power act responsibly. Specifically, God calls those in power to use it to serve those subject to them. Isaiah says to the power brokers of his day, "If you do away with the yoke of oppression . . . and if you spend yourself in behalf of the hungry and satisfy the needs of the oppressed . . . the LORD will guide you always" (Is 58:9-11). That is to say, those in power with the ability to serve the needy are obliged to do so. Jesus put it this way: "You know that the rulers of the Gentiles lord it over them. . . . Not so with you. Instead, whoever wants to become great among you must be your servant" (Mt 20:25-26). Jesus has no problem with someone becoming powerful so long as the power of greatness is exercised in servanthood.

Healing Abuse

Anyone with power over others is a potential abuser. Parents have power over children, husbands over wives, bosses over workers, police over citizens, pastors over church members. Before God, these positions of authority, privilege and power come with obligations. Jesus himself models how to carry out these obligations. Jesus exercised authority and power over his followers by washing their feet and laying down his life for them. He was among them as one who served. Paul says that if we possess power and authority of any kind we are to follow Jesus' example. "Your attitude should be the same as that of Christ Jesus: Who, being in very nature God, did not consider equality with God something to be grasped, but made himself nothing, taking the very nature of a servant" (Phil 2:5-7).

Abuse should not become the next cause or the witch-hunt of the nineties. We must be careful to discern patterns of abuse from incidents of mistakes. However, Jesus was certainly not silent on this issue, and we should, as always, follow his example. Any type of abuse continues because of ignorance and silence. As we responsibly discuss it, we can identify and stop it. As we learn to spot and correct abusive leaders and systems,* we can also identify and support healthy, nonabusive leaders and systems. In addition, we can bring understanding and healing to many who remain shamed and wounded by past abuse.

The cure for abuse is spiritual healing. This begins with knowing the truth. "You will know the truth, and the truth will set you free" (Jn 8:32). The truth is that God is angry at abuse perpetrated in the divine Name. God stands ready and able to heal the effects of such abuse and to turn bad family and church experiences into wisdom and power in our lives.

References and Resources

K. Blue, *Healing Spiritual Abuse* (Downers Grove, Ill.: InterVarsity Press, 1993); P. R. Gaddis, *Battered but Not Broken: Help for Abused Wives and Their Church Families* (Valley Forge, Penn.: Judson Press, 1996); Bruce A. Chadwick and Tim B. Heaton, eds., *Statistical Handbook on the American Family Violence* (Phoenix: Onyx, 1992); Linda Schmittroth, ed., *Statistical Record of Children Crimes* (Washington, D.C.: Gale Research, 1994).

Ken Blue

ACCOUNTABILITY, RELATIONAL

It used to be popular to say, "No one is an island," reflecting a cultural understanding of connectedness and responsibility between people. But it is different today. Simon and Garfunkel's plaintive 1960s folksong preached, "I am a rock; I am an island," reflecting the extreme of our society's rugged individualism.* It is in this environment that accountability has almost disappeared and loneliness has become dominant.

Designed for Accountability

Rugged individualism goes against God's design for human society. We were designed to be interconnected and complementary to each other. Even though the word *accountability* does not occur in most Bible translations, the concept is foundational. Male and female were designed to "become one flesh" (Gen 2:24). People of faith are to answer to one another (Acts 15:1-4; Jas 5:14-20).

A very clear picture of accountability is presented by Paul in his letter to the Corinthian church. Here he uses the image of a builder to describe all people of faith. He then describes how what we build will be measured and the quality or lack of it will bring either reward or loss. He clearly explains how responsible we are to God for all we are and do (1 Cor 3:10-23).

Meaning of Accountability

What does accountability actually mean? Some contemporary definitions include the following:

Reckoning. Computation. A statement explaining one's conduct. *(Webster's Dictionary)*

Accounting denotes certain theories, behavioral assumptions, measurement rules and procedures for collecting and reporting useful information concerning the activities and objectives of an organization. *(Encyclopedia Britannica)*

Accountability looks back to some deed done or attitude held. Obligation looks forward to moral demands that need to be met in relationships. (Cole, pp. 734-35)

Our cultural understanding suggests that accountability is best designed when it encourages desirable performance. This process is served by the disciplines of bookkeeping or the classifying of data and activities in order to measure them against agreed-upon standards and expectations.

But in the community of faith it is much more. Accountability for believers is more dynamic. It is organic in nature and expressed through relationships, networks* and systems.* It is developed through visibility as in commissioning or storytelling, reporting and case-study processes. Further it is developed through strong relationships and creating a "confessing" environment among congregational or small-group leaders, thereby encouraging it among others (Jas 5:16). Reflection questions can be used in small groups* to help people self-audit and mutual friends inquire of each other. Finally, accountability is demonstrated through stewardship* and audit rhythms through annual reports, budgets, building upkeep, staff reviews and so on that are magnetic, enriching and clarifying.

Accountability in Scripture

There are examples of accountability in Scripture. Jesus exhibited accountability to his Father as he prayed and reviewed his work in his high priestly prayer (Jn 17:1-25). He illustrated our accountability to particular kinds of people by his concern for "the least of these" (Mt 25:40). Ananias and Sapphira were held accountable for their manipulation of money and reputation in the early church and were punished for their violation of the group's integrity (Acts 5:1-11).

Paul and Barnabas demonstrated their understanding of accountability when they voluntarily reported to the Jerusalem council regarding the controversy about non-Jews coming into the faith through their new work in Antioch (Acts 15:1-35). Paul declared, "Each of us will be accountable to God" (Rom 14:12 NRSV). Rewards and penalties will be administered in light of whether we construct our lives on the foundation of Jesus Christ or something less (1 Cor 3:9-17). James held his churches accountable for their treatment of widows, the poor, the wealthy and sinners (Jas 1:9-11, 18; 3:12-18; 5:7-8, 17-18). John demonstrated that evil will be judged and recompensed in absolute and final ways (Rev 20:1-5).

Outcomes of Accountability

Accountability is essential to healthy living. Herein we find protection from our worst tendencies. Sin has given us the terrible ability to misuse every good thing. Belonging to a body of faithful believers shields us from the worst manifestations of this condition. Living in relationships that call for responsibility to others brings balance and complementarity in our areas of weakness and encourages love, forgiveness, insight, protection and care. We are designed for and are called to this, and herein we thrive. Being held responsible to each other in the faith is a human demonstration of our creation nature as those who belong to God and who delight in that relationship.

See also ACCOUNTABILITY, WORKPLACE, CHURCH IN THE HOME; CONFRONTING; DISCIPLESHIP; FELLOWSHIP; FRIENDSHIP; NETWORKING; SMALL GROUPS; SPIRITUAL GROWTH.

References and Resources

G. A. Cole, "Responsibility," in *New Dictionary of Christian Ethics and Pastoral Theology*, ed. D. J. Atkinson et al. (Downers Grove, Ill.: InterVarsity Press, 1995), pp. 734-36; D. L. Watson, *Covenant Discipleship: Christian Formation Through Mutual Accountability* (Nashville: Discipleship Resources, 1991).

Pete Hammond

ACCOUNTABILITY, WORKPLACE

Accountability is not a new concept. Deeply ingrained in the prophetic mind of the Old Testament was the understanding that God holds the leaders of Israel accountable for the care and nurture of his people. For example, God says to the shepherds of Israel, "who only take care of themselves! . . . I am against the shepherds and will hold them accountable for my flock" (Ezek 34:2, 10). Where there is expectation, there is also accountability. This is true for family life, for church membership,* for volunteer work,* in organizations* and in business.

How am I doing? Am I going anywhere? Am I growing? Am I learning? These are the questions of accountability. The expectation of progress, change or movement carries with it the element of accountability.

Accountability and Mission

Accountability therefore rests on a corporate purpose. Without a goal, objective, mission* or expectation, there would be no need for accountability. It comes into play as soon as someone desires to change from the status quo to a new level of reality, experience or accomplishment, a future against which the present is compared. Accountability accepts responsibility for movement from the present in line with the purpose and measures progress toward the mission. It does this whether the responsibility is a self-expectation or the expectation of others.

Accountability and Responsibility

Accountability is in fact the flip side of responsibility. While we often use the concept of accountability to refer to the measurement of specific action or behavior in pursuit of the mission or objectives, it might be more appropriate to keep accountability closely linked with responsibility. It is only when a person is understood (and understands himself or herself) to be responsible for a particular action or progress that he or she is accountable. So accountability measures the progress or growth for which a person has accepted responsibility. It assumes that we want to grow, that we expect some movement which we want to measure, unless of course we want to stay in a steady state, in which case accountability seeks to measure that we have not lost ground!

While it is possible to be held accountable by another for a responsibility assigned, accountability and responsibility are most powerfully linked when they are owned. *Ownership* is the intentional internalizing of responsibility so that a person holds himself or herself accountable.

When responsibility is owned, when accountability is internalized, it becomes a personal commitment and a powerful motivating force within the person.

Accountability and Commitment

Peter Block, in his excellent book *The Empowered Manager,* calls attention to the difference between commitment and sacrifice. When responsibility is imposed from outside and not owned by the person responsible, it requires sacrifice. The individual must sacrifice his or her personal vision to pursue a vision owned by someone else. This is neither satisfying nor motivating. Responsibility is assigned by someone else, and accountability is measured by someone else. On the other hand, ownership of responsibility leads to commitment. When the individual owns responsibility for the purpose, accountability flows from personal commitment. This is the highest form of motivation. The individual is accountable to himself or herself to fulfill the accepted responsibility as an expression of his or her own personal vision.

Accountability and Power

This distinction becomes painfully important in organizational settings where responsibility is given (and accepted), where accountability is expected, but the authority or resources necessary to fulfill the responsibility are not provided. This is the classic definition of powerlessness and leads to a significant loss of motivation and performance. It is critically important that the appropriate authority and resources be available to enable the person to fulfill the responsibility. Otherwise accountability is personally frustrating and organizationally meaningless.

In an organizational setting it is important to distinguish between accountability for results and accountability for tactics or strategies. Responsibility is best shared when it focuses on results and allows the individual to invest himself or herself in the determination of the best way to achieve those results in line with the organization's mission and values.* If too much specificity is involved in this, there is little responsibility given and thus little accountability. The assumption here is that responsibility can and should be shared, recognizing that this does not release those drawn into its exercise from responsibility and accountability.

Whether in business or volunteer church work, accountability structures need to be clearly defined. This can be one to one in spiritual friendships,* through small groups,* by means of performance reviews and through formal accountability groups, such as those outlined in David Watson's book *Covenant Discipleship*.

Accountability at its best is the ownership of responsibility for results with self-evaluation and self-correction as one moves toward the accomplishment of a purpose or the living of a vision. It assumes personal integrity* and organizational trust and loyalty.*

See also ORGANIZATION; ORGANIZATIONAL CULTURE AND CHANGE; ORGANIZATIONAL VALUES; PLAY.

References and Resources
P. Block, *The Empowered Manager* (San Francisco: Jossey-Bass, 1987); D. L. Watson, *Covenant Discipleship: Christian Formation Through Mutual Accountability* (Nashville: Discipleship Resources, 1991).

Walter Wright Jr.

ADDICTION

In the past the term *addiction* was reserved for the compulsive and uncontrolled use of certain psychoactive substances, notably alcohol, cocaine, narcotics and other mood-altering drugs.* In recent times the term has been used as an overall label for a set of diverse addictive behaviors to objects, people, relationships, ideas or pursuits. So we now talk about addictions to food, work,* sex, perfection, religion, ministry,* gambling and even computer games.* It is commonly believed that there is an underlying similarity among the entire spectrum of addictive behaviors—that all addicts desire a sense of well-being, a temporary heightening of self-esteem, a transient experience of ecstasy, a state of oblivion or some measure of relief from pain or tension.

The Addictive Process
The first step in a potentially addictive process is the individual's encounter with the addicting "object" and the mood-altering experience it produces, the so-called peak experience. This affects different people in differing degrees. Those who are more susceptible to addictive behaviors tend to seek repetition of the peak experience until they become mentally obsessed by this emotional craving and preoccupied by the euphoric recalls, often fed with fantastic imaginations. Because of the mental obsession, the individual begins to lose contact with self and the environment; this is most obvious in the person's denial of his addictive relationship to the peak experience by saying, "I am not an addict." Other forms of denial may present themselves as a tendency to minimize the problem, to find an excuse for the preoccupation or to blame others for it.

The next stage in the addictive process is a loss of control. This is manifested not only in the frequent mental recall of the peak experience but also in an escalation of the frequency of acting out. In this stage, seeking peak experiences has become a behavioral obsession, and the individual usually develops observable personality changes, becoming defensive and irritable. Although the addictive behavior may still be within socially acceptable limits, the individual begins to feel shame and remorse and may make repeated resolutions and compulsive attempts to control his or her own thought patterns and behaviors. There is a need to create an illusion to oneself and to others that he or she is still in control.

Nevertheless, repetitions of the peak experience require an increasing amount of the addictive object (for example, alcohol) to be established and maintained. (This process is known as *tolerance*—a form of physiologic habituation in which the nerve cells become less sensitive and responsive to repeated stimuli so that an increase is required in order to produce a similar level of satisfaction.) When this stage is reached, the addicted individual's loss of control becomes obvious, as it is accompanied by personal and social breakdowns. Often the addicting behaviors have to be interrupted abruptly due to a number of possible reasons, including financial exhaustion or repeated troubles with the law leading to incarceration. The individual will experience a state of withdrawal that can be mentally, emotionally and physically terrible. The physical withdrawal from some substances can be life threatening.

Psychosomatic Interpretation of Addiction

Throughout the last century, a number of theories have been advanced to explain the causes of addiction. One approach starts from the observation that addicted persons commonly exhibit one or all the following attributes: (1) exaggerated emotions* and inability to deal with them, (2) difficulty with forming and/or maintaining normal relationships, (3) inability to look after oneself and (4) low self-esteem. A psychodynamic interpretation following the Freu-

dian tradition suggests that the addicted person may be seeking to counterbalance an unfulfilled need* experienced in infancy or a developmental defect due to either a physical or a psychological deficiency; in this view an addictive behavior serves as an affective prosthetic designed to strengthen the individual's self-esteem. In this sense, addictive behavior is seen as a form of self-medication.

Disease Model of Addiction

While the psychodynamic model is valuable in explaining certain psychological aspects of addiction, it tends to disregard any biological factors as possible determining forces in addictive behaviors. In contrast, the biologic/disease model views addiction as a form of physiologic-genetic abnormality more or less beyond the control of the individual. This has been proposed since 1933 as a cause for alcoholism, with the result that hospitals were opened to treat alcoholics. The biological basis of addiction has since been corroborated by an enormous amount of neurophysiological and genetic research.

One of the most fascinating and significant studies was undertaken by James Olds and Peter Milner, who accidentally discovered in 1954 that stimulation of certain parts of the brain in experimental animals was able to elicit a pleasurable response. When allowed to self-stimulate through an electrical device, a variety of animals would seek these stimulations until they collapsed from exhaustion.

These brain areas are now referred to as *reward centers* or *pleasure centers,* and the activities within these centers are mediated by neurotransmitters such as serotonin, GABA and a number of opioid peptides. It is postulated that defects in these centers are linked to a loss or impairment of the sense of well-being and induce in the animal or human a craving for a substance(s) or activity that will relieve the feeling of dysphoria. Heroin, cocaine and amphetamines are known to interact with these centers, making them good candidates for substance abuse. Studies have also shown that activity-related elations and mood upswings associated with physical exercise, such as jogging, are related to an increased release of certain opioid/peptides (for example, endorphins known to be active in these brain centers), thus making health-conscious compulsive joggers classic addicts.

Addiction and Heredity
Furthermore, to some extent deficiencies and imbalances in the pleasure centers have been shown to be inheritable. A degree of heredity in addictive behavior was postulated as early as the 1940s, when studies showed that the children of alcoholic parents often underestimated the amount of alcohol they consumed and usually drank considerably more than others before sensing any effect. Recent genetic research has shown that children of alcoholics have an unequal and increased susceptibility to alcoholism or other addictive behaviors when compared to their peers, even if they are raised by a nonalcoholic family.

In a thorough study based on the statistical analysis of the families of 2,651 alcoholics and 4,083 nonalcoholics, parental alcoholism was correlated specifically to alcohol problems in the children. Other adoption studies have shown a high incidence of alcoholism among the children of alcoholic parents, even if they are raised in a nonalcoholic home. These and other studies strongly suggest a possible genetic predisposition for addictive disorders, although the biological mechanism has yet to be elucidated. While the biologic/genetic model is scientific and rational and provides clear explanations for a relatively complex phenomenon, it is too much influenced by a modern paradigm of biomedicine and as such is reductionistic. Specifically, it overlooks social context and personal responsibility in health and sickness.

The Sociocultural Context of Addiction
The sociocultural/behavioral model emphasizes the impact of the social and cultural environment upon the behavior of the individual and its role in the development of an addiction. This approach regards addiction as a socially acquired habit* carried to the extreme. Because family plays the most significant role in one's psychosocial well-being, the stability of the family and particularly its interactive patterns, between parents and between parents and children, may be regarded as the main psychosocial determinant for addictive susceptibility. On the whole, research has shown that a family in which adolescents are living with both biological parents represents a low-risk family environment because it allows secure attachment patterns to be established; children growing up in such an environment are less susceptible to addictive behaviors than those living with single parents or stepparents. High-risk family environments are those in which anxious and fearful parents are extremely protective and restrictive, emotionally abusive parents are contradictory and misleading in communication, or parents are physically and emotionally abusive. Marital and psychiatric problems or conflicts with the law on the part of the parents are also factors in promoting addictive behaviors in children. Outside the family, societal values* and worldviews* also contribute to a person's sociocultural milieu and thus play crucial roles in causing addictive behaviors. An example of the influence of social values is seen in the spread of eating disorders, which is correlated to the idealization of slimness in modern society.

Spiritual Basis of Addiction

Finally, there is the moral/spiritual model. This interpretation takes into consideration the importance of human desire as a basic determinant of human life. It views human desire as created by God and for the purpose of relating to God (Gen 1:26; Ps 42:1-2; Jn 17:5). Saint Augustine's prayer "You have made us for yourself, and our soul is restless until we find rest in you" testifies to this basic human desire. But this desire has been distorted by our sinful nature. When we are disengaged from desiring God, our proper desire is derailed. Turning away from the Creator, we look for created things, objects and relationships to replace God (Ex 20:3-5; Rom 1:18-32; 1 Cor 8:4). We seek peak experiences and tend to indulge in them even when they are harmful to ourselves and others. Ultimately, human desire is corrupted to lust, worship to idolatry, devotion to addiction. This model views all addictions as sinful and all sins as addictive. A true test of grace is, therefore, freedom from all our addictions. The Christian life is a pilgrimage from lust to desire and from addiction to freedom.

It is unlikely that an adequate theory of addiction will be provided by any one single model. To the extent that humans are created and redeemed to be whole (*see* Healing; Health), any satisfactory analysis of addictive disorders must include biological, psychological, social and spiritual dimensions.

Recovery

The first step to recovery is to overcome the denial of addiction, not only by the addict but also by the significant others, who often act as codependents. This may involve painful but necessary confrontations, for which prayer, education and counseling are useful preparation. Next, a modification of one's sociocultural milieu by avoiding addictive environments (for example, bars, casinos) and joining a specifically antiaddiction group (for example, Alcoholics Anonymous) is important. There is also a need to develop new skills and activities to fill the void after addictive behaviors are removed and to relearn to attend to such basic needs in life as relationships, family, physical health, housing, work and finances. At the same time, one needs to develop new skills to cope with stress,* tension and inner hurts involved in feeling one's true self, which has been masked by the addictive process in the past.

The popular Twelve Steps is a powerful and indispensable program in addiction recovery. Christians may recapture its Christian roots and put the biblical foundation back into this program. Many have witnessed it to be a life-transforming spiritual journey in which they have met God. Admission of one's powerlessness and surrender to God (steps I, II, III; Prov 3:5-6; Rom 12:1) is followed by an honest self-examination and a taking of one's personal moral inventory (step IV; Ps 139:24-25; Lam 3:40). Confession of wrongdoings and asking for forgiveness ensue (steps V, VI, VII; Ps 37:4-5; Jas 4:10; 5:16; 1 Jn 1:9), which also includes making restitution to those who have been harmed (steps VIII, IX; Lk 19:8). Ongoing recovery involves an ongoing journey of sanctification by continuing personal inventory and confession whenever necessary (step X; 1 Jn 1:7-8), and this means daily prayer and meditation to maintain conscious contact with God and to seek his will and power to carry it out (step XI; Col 3:16). Having been visited by grace and set free, one also tries to share the good news with others who are in bondage and reach out to others who may need help (step XII; Gal 6:2).

See also DRIVENNESS; DRUGS; HEALING; HEALTH; SPIRITUAL CONFLICT; SPIRITUAL

DISCIPLINES; SPIRITUAL GROWTH.

References and Resources
G. May, *Addiction and Grace* (San Francisco: Harper & Row, 1988); J. E. Royce, *Alcohol Problems and Alcoholism* (New York: Free Press, 1989); *The Twelve Steps—A Spiritual Journey* (San Diego: Recovery Publications, 1988).

Edwin Hui

ADOLESCENCE

Adolescence is the period of life between childhood and adulthood in which life-affecting changes occur. Many academics have called adolescence an invention of modern society.* They claim that people in more primitive and earlier times, even as late as the nineteenth century, did not view people between the ages of fifteen and twenty-five as being in a special time of growth and development. Certainly this time period was not filled with the stresses and struggles that we often associate with contemporary adolescence. While there is some truth to their assertion, one can find many historical references to the fact that the period we call adolescence is significantly different from childhood and adulthood. Some references go back as far as Socrates, who decried the behaviors of youths in his day. It would be worthwhile for us to acknowledge these changes and work with them to facilitate the growth and development of youths from childhood to adulthood.

A Time of Inner and Outer Change

Adolescence is a special time of development in all areas of a young person's life. Development occurs as youth grow from less to more mature in all areas of their lives within their own social and cultural environment. Because of their development in several domains, adolescents sense new powers, abilities, interests and processes at work in them. Exploring these new avenues leads to new creations both *internally* within the adolescent and also *externally* between the adolescence and his or her world.

Internally, adolescents restructure and develop values,* and ultimately a new understanding of the self, of "who I am." This occurs in the six domains of human development: physical—growing from a child's body to an adult body; cognitive—developing the ability to think abstractly (perform formal operations); social—learning to recognize and accept adult social and sex roles; affective—gaining control of one's emotions*; moral—moving from making egocentric moral judgments and actions to those that are other-centered, then principle-driven and ultimately agape-based; spiritual—forming a personally owned, examined and internalized faith.

Externally, adolescents make many changes in their relationships with others. These changes take the forms of new processes by which adolescents relate to their entire world, new modes of behavior, new relationships and experiences, and new feelings and meanings about others and the external world.

These internal and external processes and relationships produce *intrapersonal* disruptions, changes, stresses and at times turmoil, as well as *interpersonal* conflicts between self and parents, relatives, friends, siblings, teachers and many other authority figures.

In short, adolescent development is the process within the total personhood from approximately age twelve through twenty-five by which various structural and development changes occur at identifiable stages along the way.

Adolescent development is manifested in various forms of behavior, some of which are socially acceptable. Other forms are questionable, and some are socially and personally destructive.

Culture* and Adolescence
The world of adolescence in both West-

ern and non-Western societies is composed of major dimensions or factors that are characteristics of any subculture. The astute youth worker or parent will want to keep in mind that youth subcultures go through dynamic changes. What might be in vogue today may be out tomorrow; something new will become all the rage for anywhere from a few weeks to a few years or even longer. Only one thing is certain. Youth culture does not remain static; it is in a constant state of flux.

How can one address the needs of youth when the subculture is constantly changing? By becoming a social anthropologist, that is, one who studies youth culture and seeks to understand what is going on. All cultures have certain common factors, but particular subcultures exhibit them in unique ways.

Consider these major dimensions (for 1-8 see Sebold):

Values and norms. These are the basis for decision-making and behavior. They are usually unique to youth and are often not understood by adults.

In-group language, their argot. Youths have their own words and language to communicate with each other that are unique to their own culture and time. This language is not shared by children or adults. In this way adolescents keep their secrets and keep out nonadolescents from their world.

Distinct channels of mass communication. MTV is their station. Rock music radio stations* are also theirs. They have their own magazines, Internet pages and forums. This is how they communicate with each other and how the subculture of adolescents is made more homogenous worldwide.

Unique styles and fads. Adolescents have distinct hair and clothing styles, mannerisms and so on. These styles are usually fads that change often within a year or two.

Sense of solidarity. Adolescents feel like they are in their own clan, and they are correct to a large degree. They are segregated into schools, offered low-paying after-school jobs and generally kept separate from the adult world. They hang out together because they are pushed by social institutions.

Status criteria. They have developed a way of measuring successful achievement, ownership and use of their subcultures' status symbols—language, fads, values, channels of communication and identification with their subculture. People who do not measure up are often shunned or treated badly because they do not confirm to the criteria.

Influence and power of leaders. Adolescents are influenced by heroes and charismatic leaders, especially those that are disdained by adult cultures.

Subcultural institutions. Specialized institutions meet the needs that the main culture cannot, or does not, desire to meet; the entertainment/recreational industry caters to teens by offering youth-oriented magazines and electronic malls.

Geography. This is where adolescents reside and, almost equally important, where they go to learn, hang out, work, have fun, recreate, be entertained and play.* They have their own locations, be it a street corner, someone's house or a mall.* It is their own bit of turf. Almost all American high schools have particular sections on their campuses where various subgroups assemble.

*Use of technology.** Mechanical and electronic technology allows adolescents to escape (or leave) their immediate surroundings and go somewhere else literally or figuratively. Teens escape by means of cars, bikes, skateboards, body/surfboards, radio and TV stations (MTV), youth-oriented movies,* video games, amusement parks and concerts.

Of great and increasing importance to adolescents are the Internet and other electronic means of communicating with those of like mind.

In many ways adolescents today are in their own world. They are a subculture to themselves. This world is only more complicated by the fact of the irregular but sure development from immature to more mature persons. What youth need today, as in any other day, is loving acceptance of them as real human beings, not some sort of otherworldly creatures that have to be tolerated until they "grow up." Adolescents are people *now.* They are people whom God loves, for whom Christ died and in whom the Holy Spirit may dwell. Christian teens are spiritually gifted people called into ministry just as are adults.

Jesus as an Adolescent

Jesus was a teenager! For many, this might be a revelation. Luke 1 and 2 tell of his conception,* birth* and growth as a normal human being. This does not denigrate Jesus' divinity; he was entirely God. Luke is careful, however, to tell us that Jesus was also very much a total human being. Hebrews 2:17,18; 4:15 also state explicitly that Jesus was just like any other human being. In fact, the writer of Hebrews makes it very clear that Jesus had to be human. If he were not, then he could not identify with us, and his reconciling act of redemption would not be complete.

What is most amazing is that Jesus' adolescent behaviors in Luke 2:51-52 are similar to those that many teenagers evidence today—and with the same reactions from their parents as Jesus had from his! So the temple narrative provides parents with a great deal of encouragement that their own adolescents, whether they are twelve or twenty-two, are quite normal. Adolescents themselves can find comfort in this story if they recognize that the problems Jesus encountered are similar to their own, and that he can be a model for how to handle similar ones today.

The age of twelve was critical for a Jewish male. This age was the transition from childhood to adulthood, much like modern adolescence is for today's youth. In Jesus' day life was less complex, temptations were less prevalent, and society was of one mind in how to raise up children into adulthood, so adolescence may have been less turbulent than now. Yet it was at the age of twelve that Jesus went to the temple, full of the excitement that anyone his age would have contemplating the holy city and the temple rituals associated with the Passover feast.

The narrative of Jesus in the temple illustrates all six of the previously stated major developmental domains or areas.

Physical development. Jesus was evidently a physically mature person, enough for him to take care of himself alone in the capital city of Jerusalem for at least three and perhaps up to five days. Perhaps he even looked older than the normal twelve-year-old.

Luke states: "Jesus grew in wisdom and stature" (2:52; see also v. 40). Jesus grew up physically just like any other human, and just like young people today. This verse along with Hebrews 2 and 4 suggests that Jesus' physical body went through the same growth and development as any other adolescent. If this is so, then we can assume that he developed structurally and muscularly like any other teenager. His body proportions changed from a boy to a man. He began to grow body hair and develop sexually just like any normal youth. His voice changed from a child's to that of an adult. He developed hand-eye coordination so that he could pound a nail in the carpenter shop in Nazareth without destroying either the wood or his fingers. He could run and play and had lots of energy. He probably ate as much as possible so that his parents wondered if he had a bottomless pit for a stomach.

Cognitive development. According to Jewish custom, Jesus would at this age begin to study the Law (Talmud) and to take on the responsibilities associated with the Law. His parents evidently felt he could be trusted to make informed judgments about what to do. They had to have allowed him much unsupervised time in Jerusalem, otherwise how could he have been left behind? Jesus evidenced independence from his parents, seeking out his own interests and concerns. He knew enough about himself and what he was about to begin to enter into dialogue with the teachers in the temple.

Mary and Joseph did not seem to understand Jesus. First they thought he was with the pilgrims on the return trip; then they looked for him all through the city. Seemingly in exasperation and not without some sense of hopelessness, they finally went to the temple, not really expecting to find him there. We can almost hear one of Jesus' earthly parents saying to the other, "Well, we've searched everywhere and can't find him. Let's start where we last saw him and go from there." And surprise of all surprises, there he was!

Why did Jesus go back to the temple? He was like any other cognitively growing adolescent. He had questions about life, about his experiences in the temple, about what he saw and heard as he went through the feast of the Passover. One wonders what he might have been thinking if he recalled the words of Isaiah 53 and of the suffering servant of other parts of Isaiah. His parents found him among the teachers in the temple, listening to them and asking them questions. He was using his mind to inquire and learn. One can only speculate as to his questions. It would seem natural that he

had questions about the Feast of the Passover which they had all just experienced. Whatever he asked and said, he amazed those around him with his understanding, insights and replies. The teachers and other adults present treated him as a person on a par with themselves. They did not dismiss him as some little child. They allowed him to interact with them. Adults are amazed when a younger person today, like Jesus, listens carefully, asks thoughtful questions and offers responsible answers. So Jesus surprised those teachers in the temple.

In typical adolescent fashion, he was developing a sense of self-identity and mission that would eventually lead him to Calvary. But in the temple, he knew that he was not just the son of Mary and Joseph. He, like adolescents today, had begun to distinguish self from others, to know what he was not and what he wanted to become, and to articulate that self-identity even though in only partial ways. His reply to Mary is instructive about his self-identity. He distinguished between Joseph and his heavenly Father and the need to be in his Father's house, and by implication, to be about his Father's instead of his father's business.

In one sense, Jesus demonstrated what many adolescents want to demonstrate, namely, that they are growing up; they do not want to be considered children any longer; they are searching for new and exciting experiences to test their own sense of identity and development. Jesus' young life was awakening to his mission and to the very essence of his being.

Social development. Jesus' parents evidently thought he was a "social" person, that he was somewhere with the crowd of friends and family on the return trip to Nazareth. They must have considered other occasions when Jesus would be gone for a long part of the day and had no great concern for his safety. They probably thought, *He's probably with his friends.* Jesus, however, wasn't with his usual associates; he was holding his own with teachers and priests. Evidently, he could talk and interact socially with many people in such a way that they did not think to consider his young age and his apparent lack of supervision.

Today's youth are similar to Jesus. They are increasingly socially adept in various situations. With the advent of the first totally TV* generation already in history, and now a second and even third TV generation, adolescents around the world are ever more sophisticated in situations that would have totally discomforted their grandparents of the 1950s. Today's adolescents surprise many adults when given a chance to ask questions and state their thoughts or insights. The problem many adolescents face is not that they lack social skills but that adults will not carry on a serious conversation* with them. Often most of the communication from adults to youth is in the form of commands or prohibitions. The "Just Say No" campaign is a good example of well-meaning adults' failure to recognize the social and cognitive development of today's youth and the temptations surrounding them. Merely telling youth not to do something without giving them a chance to talk, share, inquire and question is a recipe for failure.*

Affective development. Both Jesus' parents and Jesus himself showed affective, emotional development in the incident in Luke 2 (*see* Emotions). His parents showed their astonishment and exasperation, if not even panic. Upon finding him in the temple, seemingly calmly interacting with the teachers, his mother let out a typical "Jewish mother" shout. She exclaimed, "Son, why have you treated us like this? Your father and I have been anxiously searching for you." She was emotionally upset. It is no won-der: Jesus had been missing for three or more days, depending on how one counts the days in the text. There had been no hint of where he could be. They were upset, and rightly so. They did not understand why he had done what he had done.

This is a common plight of just about every parent in the world when it comes to their adolescent sons and daughters. Parents continually ask the emotionally laden question "What have you done and why did you do it?" The often-asked question of parents is "What has become of our little boy/girl? You used to be so good. Now look at you. We don't understand what is happening to you."

Jesus, on the other hand, showed typical adolescent lack of thought about what consequences his actions might have for other people's feelings. He was looking for new experiences; he was caught up in the emotion of the event, finding great personal satisfaction by being in his Father's house. There is no suggestion that "the devil made him do it" or that he was driven to stay in the city by the Holy Spirit. It was his free choice, flowing from his decision to encounter more of the great delight that he found at the temple. Undoubtedly he was excited by the big city of Jerusalem compared to the small town of Nazareth. The activities of the Feast of the Passover with its sacrifice and meals stirred his heart, mind, and soul to reflect on the lamb that was slain. His response would be similar today to an adolescent who attended the Super Bowl and then sneaked his way on the team airplane.

Moral development. Moral development focuses on the way one decides what actions to take and which actions are considered good or bad. Children usually make moral judgments based on what is best for themselves. If they are punished, they know something is bad. If they like what they are doing and there is no punishment associated with it, then it must be good. In the temple story we see Jesus making a moral judgment that it was fine for him not to tell his parents where he was, to remain in Jerusalem without permission, and not to be accountable to any earthly person except himself. He was focused on his own needs, identity, and desire to interact in the temple. He did not think about his parents and their needs. This should sound familiar to parents worldwide. Jesus evidenced typical moral judgments of a twelve-year-old. He may have been physically mature, precocious in intellectual or cognitive development, and well adept at social relationships, but he was typical of early adolescence when it came to moral development.

When Mary rebuked him by her comment, Jesus responded with mild rebuke to her in the form of a question: "Why were you searching for me? . . . Didn't you know I had to be in my Father's house?" Regardless of Jesus' sinlessness, he responded typically of someone at his stage of moral development. Unfortunately, that response is often taken by authoritarian parents as being disrespectful, insolent and therefore offensive.

If we understand Jesus' developmental stage, we would not see it this way. Jesus' response to his mother's question should be taken as it is meant to be understood: a statement of a well-meaning young person who cannot understand why his parents were all upset by what appeared to him as innocent behavior. They should have know where to look for him. Why? Because Jesus knew what he was doing and where he was. He assumed, like most adolescents, that his parents would somehow know what he was thinking if he was thinking it. It takes a higher level of moral development for a young adolescent to be able to switch places with others to learn how they might understand a particular moral

situation. Jesus was not mature enough at this point to do so and therefore responded in a typical way to his mother's excited question and statements.

Jesus demonstrated the way many adolescents make their moral choices. They view things only from their limited moral viewpoint: it takes time for normal adolescents to move from their immature egocentrism to a more mature stage.

Jesus, however, willingly submitted to his parent's authority. Though he had just alluded that Joseph was not his father, yet he went with his parents to Nazareth and was obedient to them. He recognized that they had authority over him and that his role was to obey that rightful authority. Jesus' sinlessness comes to the fore at this point. Although all adolescents are tempted and often succumb to defying their parents' authority, Jesus, being tempted to do the same at the temple, did not. This is where Jesus' actions differ from those of adolescents: he did not consider his parents' lack of understanding of him, his actions and motives as sufficient grounds to disobey them. Parents would very much like to see Jesus' behavior copied by their own adolescent children.

Spiritual development. Jesus' faith development was evidenced in several ways in the narrative. He was in the temple with the teachers, obviously interested in the faith of his parents and nation. His cognitive and social development helped him to be comfortable asking questions, listening and processing the teachers' comments. He also was seemingly quite at home in his "Father's house." It seems by implication that he had spent a good amount of the days separated from his parents in the temple. His developing sense of who he was and what he was to do was growing on him. One can imagine the intense look on his face and the thoroughness of his questions as he sought to understand what was being taught.

Like all adolescents, Jesus had a genuine interest in religious things, more so since he grew up in a society that enculturated the Jewish faith from infancy through adulthood. To be Jewish meant believing in the one true God of Abraham and the law of Moses. Today the vast majority of adolescents have a sense of religion and a high interest in spiritual matters. Few are truly atheists, especially younger adolescents. Not until young people arrive in university or college classes do they begin to "lose their faith," or at least begin to have serious doubts about what they have been taught.

Because Jesus was human, likely he had doubts about many things as he grew up. His faith development, however, continued and did not waver. Luke states, "And Jesus grew . . . in favor with God and men." His strong identification of himself with his Father's house indicated that his faith development was more mature than that of most adolescents his age. Yet while he was precocious in faith development, he was not totally off the normal faith development scale. He had questions to ask about his faith. Many youth have a strong identity with God and do not waver into unbelief even though they may have doubts from time to time. Many youth have a strong spiritual sense that continues to cause them to seek God and to keep on growing. It is not until the "cares of this life" in adulthood come upon them that they begin to lose some if not much of their enthusiasm for spiritual things. More than one adult has commented on the spiritual enthusiasm of youth by saying, "Just wait until they get to be adults and they see how difficult it is to be a Christian in the world. They'll not be so excited about Christ then." If we as-

sume that spiritual and faith development get thwarted by the cares of this world, perhaps these adults are correct. The message of Jesus' own life and the teachings of the Epistles suggests that while lack of continual spiritual development may not be too unusual, it is by no means the biblical norm. Jesus showed us that a young adolescent could be actively engaged in his own faith development and that such action is normal and welcomed.

Adolescence is a normal part of human development, as Jesus' example shows. Adults need to recognize the signs of normalcy in the lives of all the adolescents with whom they have contact. Adults should help adolescents along their developmental paths so they may continue as smoothly as possible in their growth and development into more and more mature adolescents and then adults.

See also FAITH DEVELOPMENT; FAMILY; LIFE STAGES; PARENTING; SPIRITUAL GROWTH.

References and Resources

D. P. Ausbel et al., *Theory and Problems of Adolescent Development* (New York: Green and Stratton, 1977); M. Brake, *The Sociology of Youth Culture and Youth Subcultures: Sex, Drugs and Rock 'n' Roll* (Boston: Kegan Paul, 1980); J. M. Dettoni, *Introduction to Youth Ministry* (Grand Rapids: Zondervan, 1993); D. Elkind, *All Grown Up and No Place to Go: Teenagers in Crisis* (Reading, Mass.: Addison-Welsey, 1984); T. Lickona, *Raising Good Children: Helping Your Child Through the Stages of Moral Development* (New York: Bantam, 1983); D. Offer, E. Ostrove et al., *The Teenage World* (New York: Plenum, 1988); S. Parks, *The Critical Years* (New York: Harper & Row, 1986); L. Parrott, *Helping the Struggling Adolescent* (Grand Rapids: Zondervan, 1993); Q. Schultz, R. M. Anker et al., *Dancing in the Dark: Youth Popular Culture and the Electronic Media* (Grand Rapids: Eerdmans, 1991); H. Sebold, *Adolescence: A Social Psychological Analysis* (Englewood Cliffs, N.J.: Prentice-Hall, 1984).

John M. Dettoni

ADORNMENT

Adornment is a mark of humanity. Seashells and lilies of the valley do not need decoration, and it is an affectation to clothe animals, who are never naked. Clothing is a gift of God to humankind.

Adornment Initially Provided by God

In the beginning husband and wife were at ease with one another and naked before God without shame (Gen 2:21-25). After the original sin, Eve and Adam felt exposed and tried to cover themselves with makeshift aprons of fig leaves (Gen 3:7). God's first act of mercy was to provide the man and woman with leather coats so they would be less vulnerable in God's good world to the cursed thorns, the heat, the cold and the violence and decrepitude that humankind now would be busy resisting (Gen 1:26-31; 3:14-21). To this day clothing is a blessing that protects the privacy peculiar to us human creatures made in God's image.

Adornment and Celebration

When a person is grieving or depressed, you feel like Job that being stripped down to your nakedness is somehow elementally appropriate (Job 1:21). But when it is time to be happy, married or festive, or time for a song about Christ's victory over sin, you want to be dressed up (compare Is 61:10-11; Rev 7:9-17). The Old Testament reports extensively on the splendid finery prepared for the high priest Aaron to don after he was ritually purified (Ex 28—29). The elaborate vestments and perfuming oils certified that Aaron's official "naked purity" and the priests who mediated God's forgiveness to God's people were covered over by the holy glory of God (Ex 39:27-31). Such attention to careful adornment is probably behind the practice of praising God on the Lord's Day in "your Sunday best," since all God's people are now priests, thanks to Jesus Christ's mediatorial sacrifice (1 Pet 2:1-10; Rev 1:5-6).

Adornment as Temptation

Any of God's gifts to humankind can be perverted by our vanity. The show of a leg, a hairstyle or the jewelry of women and men is evil if it supplants hope in the Lord's mercy or distracts us from heartfelt love of the neighbor. Then adornment stinks in God's nostrils (Ps 147:10-11; Is 3:16-26; 1 Pet 3:1-12). It is typical of false leaders, said Jesus, to wear elaborate suits (Mt 23:1-12).

Adornment and Joy

It is significant that Christ mentions clothing in the same breath that he says our heavenly Father knows we need food and drink but advises we not chase it down the way godless people do (Mt 6:19-34). If a person follows secular fashions in order to put himself or herself on display as a conspicuous consumer* or simply dresses in a humdrum manner for all occasions, the clothes betray the man and disclose where the woman's heart is. Both aesthetes who are dressed to kill and ascetics who reject the God-given opportunity of adornment to enhance our bodily lineaments go wrong. Humans are called upon to thank God for clothing, to use cotton, flax, wool and animal fur and skin to protect ourselves from evil, and to reflect that we are corporeally a good-looking godly man or boy or a glorious girl or woman of God—in short, that we are beautiful. Homespun, imaginative ethnic apparel can often be more normative and comely in the Lord's eyes than reigning secularized Western couture if the dress brings an ordinary, peaceful joy of nuanced glory to one's neighbor.

See also BODY; CULTURE; DRESS CODE, WORKPLACE.

References and Resources
J. Craik, *The Face of Fashion: Cultural Studies in*

Fashion (London: Routledge, 1994); A. Lurie, *The Language of Clothes* (New York: Random, 1981); M. Starkey, *Fashion and Style* (Crowborough, U.K.: Monarch, 1995).

Calvin Seerveld

ADVERTISING

Years ago Marshall McLuhan said, "Ours is the first age in which many thousands of our best trained minds made it a full-time business to get inside the collective public mind . . . to manipulate, exploit, and control" (p. v). Given its pervasive and persuasive character, advertising is without doubt one of the most formative influences in popular culture,* shaping values* and behavior and telling people how and why to live. It is estimated that the average North American is subjected to over one thousand advertisements daily in one or other of the media (television,* radio, magazines, newspapers, billboards, direct mail) covering everything from perfume to automobiles, from fast food to insurance.

Advertising is simply any paid form of nonpersonal presentation to promote products, services or ideas, sometimes, but not always, in a way attractive to the person the advertiser wishes to influence. In a market economy, advertising can supply information needed for the people to make an informed choice. But on the other hand, advertising is frequently used to persuade people or even seduce them to believe that what they want is what they need and that consuming a particular product will in some way change them. In other words, advertising tinkers with identity and values.

Not a Recent Invention

While many people think advertising was invented on Madison Avenue in New York City during the post-World War II boom, advertising is as old as civilization. Ironically one of the oldest pieces of advertising from antiquity that can be viewed today is an inscription of a woman in the pavements of ancient Ephesus (modern Turkey) advertising the nearby brothel. But even before this, in ancient Egypt (3200 B.C.) the names of kings were stenciled on temples, and runaway slaves were "advertised" on papyrus. Advertising took a giant step forward with the invention of movable type and the printing of the Gutenburg Bible (A.D. 1450). It could then be endlessly repeated and mass-produced. Not long after this, an English newspaper advertised prayer books for sale, a forerunner of the newspaper ad. While it can be argued that people have always been trying to persuade others to do, buy or experience something—from town criers to preachers—it is unquestionable that rapid industrialization, urbanization, the proliferation of media and now the information superhighway* have escalated advertising to a central role in culture formation, perhaps even in spiritual formation, since it is a major player in establishing values and defining meaning-giving experiences.

As a form of communication, advertising has some good intended effects, some recognized by commentators on the Third World scene, where advertising has found almost virgin territory. Besides sometimes giving people information to make choices when there is more than one product or service offered, advertising is often used to promote desirable social aims, such as savings and investment,* family planning, health-promoting products (such as antimalarial drugs), lifestyles that will reduce AIDS and fertilizers that will enhance crop production (MacBride, p. 154). Advertising helps the media to be autonomous from politics*—not a small matter in some countries. But when we consider the overall impact, it is less clear to most observers that the effects of a highly commercialized culture are beneficial. Nowhere is this more evident than in the West.

The Not-So-Subtle Message

The intended effect of advertising is not merely to make a sale but to awaken or produce predispositions to buy an advertised product or service (Britt, p. 195). To advertise "Coke Is It" is not simply to sell a brand, but to have us think of branded, packaged goods when thirsty, not just plain water. It also alters our perceptions so that when we experience that branded beverage, we will see it a certain way, associating fizziness with youthfulness and joy. The total effect of advertising is to preoccupy society* with material goods and services as the path to happiness and the solution to virtually all problems and needs. Commercial persuasion appears to program not only our shopping* patterns but also the larger domain of our social roles, language, goals, values and the sources of meaning in our culture.

Advertising does this very effectively for several reasons. It is (1) pervasive, appearing in many modes and media; (2) repetitive, reinforcing the same and similar ideas relentlessly; (3) professionally developed, with all of the attendant research sophistications to improve the probabilities of attention, comprehension, retention and/or behavioral impact; and (4) delivered to an audience that is increasingly detached from traditional sources of cultural influence like families,* churches* or schools. A stunning example of the deceptiveness of advertising is the story of American cigarette ads in the 1960s. Backed by massive television budgets, they implied that filtered brands were good for our health. Smoking rates among teenagers continued to grow even after the famous report of the surgeon general in 1964.

Unintended Consequences

Not surprisingly, such an intrusive and all-pervasive system of communication has been negatively critiqued by academics and social scientists who are concerned with the effects of advertising on role-modeling, child development, social behavior and even religious belief. A Yale psychologist confessed, "Advertising makes me miserable" by an intensified pursuit of goals that would not have been imagined save for advertising (Dollard, p. 307). People are induced to keep productive in order to keep consuming, to work in order to buy because we are always in need of more. This has the serious (unintended) side effect of displacing feelings from people to objects and an alienating effect in which the self is perceived not as a child of God or as a person in community, but as an exchange commodity. Life is trivialized, not dignified, when someone becomes evangelistic about mundane material objects like mayonnaise.

Nowhere may interpersonal relations be more affected than in the home* as the roles of both women and children as consumers get expanded and redefined. Advertising has become an insolent usurper of parental function, "degrading parents to mere intermediaries between their children and the market" (Henry, p. 76). Relations with neighbors, the proverbial Joneses we strive to keep up with, are increasingly based on envy, emulation and competition.* Advertising works on the tension-arousal and tension-reduction (with the use of the product) process. In the case of the poor and marginalized, the inaccessibility of the products being offered "may create in some viewers feelings of frustration sufficient to make them engage in antisocial acts" (Myers, p. 176).

Advertising, for almost as long as it has existed, has used some sort of sexual sell, sometimes promising seductive capacities, sometimes more simply attracting our attention with sexual stimuli, even if irrelevant to the product or the selling point. While less graphic than pornography, advertising is more of a tease than a whore, for sexual stimulation is moderated and channeled. Nevertheless, the overall effect represents a challenge to standards of decency, a devaluing of women and a revaluing of the body.* Erik Barnouw notes that we now see women caressing their bodies in showers with a frequency and reverence of attention that makes "self-love a consecrated ritual" (p. 98).

Advertising also affects the credibility of language. S. I. Hayakawa notes that "it has become almost impossible to say anything with enthusiasm or joy or conviction without running into the danger of sounding as if you were selling something" (p. 268). Advertising is a symbol-manipulating occupation. For example, "Christmas and Easter have been so strenuously exploited commercially that they almost lose their religious significance" (Hayakawa, p. 269). Because virtually all citizens seem to recognize this tendency of ad language to distort, advertising seems to turn us into a community of cynics, and we doubt the advertisers, the media and authority in all its forms. Thus we may also distrust other received wisdoms from political authorities, community elders, religious leaders and teachers of all kinds. But without trustworthy communication, there is no communion, no community,* only an aggregation of increasingly isolated individuals,* alone in the mass.

Religious Significance

Some anthropologists view advertising in terms of rituals and symbols—incantations to give meaning to material objects and artifacts. Advertising defines the meaning of life and offers transcendence in the context of everyday life.

Our commercial-religious education begins early with jingles, slogans and catch phrases, the total commercial catechism, so that children learn the "rite words in the rote order." So direct exhortations are employed, literally a series of commandments, a secular litany that Jacques Barzun identified as "the revealed religion of the twentieth century" (p. 53). "You get only one chance at this life; therefore get all the gusto you can!" is a theological claim and a moral injunction. Toward this end advertising appeals to the traditional seven deadly sins: greed, lust, sloth, pride, envy and gluttony, with anger only infrequently exploited or encouraged. Since these words are frowned upon in the advertising community, they must be given a different spin. Lust becomes the desire to be sexually attractive. Sloth becomes the desire for leisure.* Greed becomes the desire to enjoy the good things of this life. Pride becomes the desire for social status (Mayer, p. 128). In this way advertising cultivates what Paul called "the works of the flesh" (Gal 5:17-23; 6:8 NRSV). Morality is subverted; values are revised; ultimate meaning is redefined.

The Ethics of Persuasion

All this happens largely without the viewer knowing it. Those who defend the present state of the advertising art claim that the most far-reaching advertising campaign cannot force someone to buy something he or she does not want. The citizen is supposedly immune to persuasion. But advertising is by definition intrusive, so intrusive that the real message communicated on television or in magazines is often the commercials. This successful commanding of attention makes the attempt to concentrate on the remaining content of media "like trying to do your algebra homework in Times Square on New Year's Eve" (Hayakawa, p. 165).

Such intrusion, first into our consciousness and then into our inner voices, distracts us from the serenity of solitude and thereby inhibits self-awareness. The repetitive, fantastic, one-sided and often exhortative rhetorical styles of advertising combine to blur the distinction between reality and fantasy, producing a state of uncritical consciousness, passivity and relative powerlessness. Nonwants becomes wants; wants become needs.* Advertising would never have taken hold the way it has without the American (and ultimately the Western) psyche having undergone a change in the direction of viewing itself therapeutically. We need help; advertising offers it. Not only this, but morals and values get adapted to the message: indulge, buy, now and here. As Barnouw observes, "The viewer's self-respect requires a rejection of most commercials on the conscious level, along with some ridicule. Beneath the ridicule the commercial does its work" (p. 83).

It does this work in ways that are ethically questionable. Advertising is advocative through giving incomplete information, half-truths or careful deceptions, by being insistent, exhortative and emphatic. It appeals essentially to emotions,* seducing people to indulge themselves now rather than defer gratification, reducing life to the here and now, if not the moment. It reinforces social stereotypes, aggravates sexism, racism* and ageism. In idealizing the "good life" advertising makes us perpetually dissatisfied. Can it be resisted?

Battling Seduction

The myth of immunity to advertising's inducements is clearly a delusion for some or perhaps many or even most of the public, including Christians. So the first thing we need to do is admit that we live in an advertising environment. Then what?

First, Christian organizations and churches need to repent of their own seductive advertising. The end never justifies the means. Keeping the televangelist* on the air does not justify half-truths and appeals to the flesh. Many relief organizations use rhetorical devices and selected "truths" to get money* for their great cause. A good first step would be for Christian organizations to establish an ethical code for their own advertising to be published along with their financial statements.

Second, the church or groups of people can lobby* or use legitimate channels of political expression to press for the closer regulation of advertising. Some obscene ads have been effectively banned by consumers boycotting certain suppliers, although an unintended side effect is sometimes more publicity for the product itself, as happened with some of the Calvin Klein ads (Faltermayer, p. 64).

Third, Christians working in the advertising industry need the prayerful support of their church as they are stewards of the culture and shapers of morals. There is no place in the world where it is easy to work as a Christian (even the church), but there is no place so demonized that a Christian might not be called to work there. The well-known novelist and apologist Dorothy Sayers worked for many years in advertising and turned the experience to good literary and theological effect.

Fourth, individually we can become more critical of advertising, reflecting on what we see and hear and discussing the intended and unintended consequences as families and groups of friends. One of the most important facets of Christian education in the family is to learn how to more than survive in the world. This will normally involve limiting time watching television, deliberately excluding commercials where possible and discussing the values implicit in advertising.

Fifth, in place of the seven deadly sins, which are often cultivated by the advertising industry, we should cultivate the seven cardinal virtues*—wisdom, justice, temperance, courage, faith, hope and love (*see* Organizational Values; Values). Spiritual conflict* is a fact of life in this world, but if we live in the Spirit and are firmly rooted in a genuine community of the Spirit we can battle the world, the flesh and the devil victoriously. Paul said, "Live by the Spirit, and you will not gratify the desires of the sinful nature" (Gal 5:16 NRSV).

Sixth, the recovery of solitude, sabbath* and spiritual disciplines* are crucial to regaining and keeping our true identity. Most people in the Western world need to reduce the input they receive from the media, take periods of fasting from television, magazines and advertising, in order to regain perspective. If we get over a thousand messages each day to buy and consume, we need equally to hear God speak through Scripture and the stillness of our hearts. The advertising world cultivates discontentment; true spirituality leads to contentment whether we have much or little (Phil 4:12). By recovering God at the center through worship,* we are protected from both being manipulated and becoming manipulators.

Seventh, we need to recover shopping as a spiritual discipline: not shopping impulsively, not shopping thoughtlessly, not buying on the strength of advertisements but doing our own research on products and services with the help of others and objective surveys.

Advertising is clearly not an omnipotent master, nor is the consumer a helpless puppet. But the cumulative effect of an advertising environment cannot be avoided. The analogy of rain is appropriate. Individual raindrops are benign and have little noticeable impact, like individual advertisements inducing us to consume. But when heavy rains come, defensive gear is needed. In a deluge individuals become preoccupied, and in extreme conditions, overwhelmed. Advertising has such influence not only because of its saturation impact but because it normally addresses many of life's common issues, while other institutions, especially the church, have all too often neglected everyday life—eating,* sleeping,* playing,* working,* relating, washing* and so on. The issue posed by advertising today is simply who will become the social and spiritual guide.

See also CONSUMERISM; CULTURE; NEED; SHOPPING; SIMPLER LIFESTYLE.

References and Resources

E. Barnouw, *The Sponsor: Notes on a Modern Potentate* (New York: Oxford University Press, 1978); J. Barzun, "Myths for Materialists," *Chimera* 4, no. 3 (1945) 52-62; S. Britt, "Advertising," in *Encyclopedia Americana* (Danbury, Conn.: Grolier, 1989) 1:195-206; J. Dollard, "Fear of Advertising," in *The Role of Advertising*, ed. C. H. Sandage and V. Fryburger (Homewood, Ill.: Irwin, 1960) 307-17; C. Faltermayer, "Where Calvin Crossed the Line," *Time,* 11 Sept. 1995, 64; S. Fox, *The Mirror Makers: A History of Twentieth Century American Advertising* (New York: Morrow, 1984); E. Griffin, *The Mind Changer: The Art of Christian Persuasion* (Wheaton: Tyndale, 1976); S. I. Hayakawa, *Language in Thought and Action* (New York: Harcourt, 1964); J. Henry, *Culture Against Man* (New York: Random, 1963); S. MacBride, *Many Voices, One World: Communication and Society, Today and Tomorrow* (New York: Unipub-UNESCO, 1980); M. Mayer, "The American Myth and the Myths of Advertising," in *The Promise of Advertising*, ed. C. H. Sandage (Homewood, Ill.: Irwin) 125-33; M. McLuhan, *The Mechanical Bride* (Boston: Beacon Press, 1951); J. G. Myers, "Advertising and Socialization," in *Research in Marketing*, ed. J. Sheth (Greenwich, Conn.: JAI Press, 1978) 1:169-99; R. W. Pollay, "The Distorted Mirror: Reflections on the Unintended Consequences of Advertising," *Journal of Marketing* 50 (April 1986) 18-36, portions quoted with permission; R. W. Pollay, "On the Value of Reflections on the Values in 'The Distorted Mirror,'" *Journal of Marketing* 51 (July 1987) 104-9.

Richard Pollay and R. Paul Stevens

AFFIRMING

The Boston Marathon is among the world's best-known races. One of the most infamous portions of the 26-mile, 385-yard course is "Heartbreak Hill." Thousands of spectators gather there to cheer on the near-collapsing runners. During one race a young man was near total exhaustion as he approached the foot of Heartbreak Hill. Halfway up the hill an older man, in better shape, came alongside the younger man, put his arm around him and spoke quietly to him. Together step by step, they painstakingly made their way to the top. This is a picture of affirmation. To *affirm* is to endorse someone who needs consolidating or firm up what is crumbling. The writer of Hebrews calls us to "strengthen your feeble arms and weak knees" (Heb 12:12). We do this primarily with words, but sometimes through actions.

The Bible not only encourages us to affirm but also contains stories of how people were affirmed. For example, the story in Exodus 17:8-13 is a picture of enormous struggle and the weariness that comes from striving to reach up to God. Certain destruction is averted by coming alongside of committed family and friends. When the Amalekites attacked Israel from the desert, Moses sent Joshua into battle. Moses withdrew to the mountain for the labor of oversight and intercession with God. He discovered that when he held his hands and staff up to the Lord, Israel prevailed in the battle, but when he let his hands down, the Amalekites prevailed. Soon Moses' hands were so heavy that he could no longer raise them in victory. His brother and brother-in-law moved him toward a resting stone and helped him lift his hands to the Lord. As a result, Joshua defeated Amalek. Moses' action was affirmed in a very practical way.

In the New Testament mutual affirmation is one of the normal ways of ministering love to one another in Christian fellowship.* Paul himself is a wonderful example of this in the way he endorses those to whom he writes, always encouraging them in the opening lines of his letters, even those who were not affirming, but criticizing him (as, for example, the Corinthians).

Affirming Others in Daily Life

In a survey parents were asked to record how many criticisms versus affirming comments they made to their children. The results were alarming: they criticized ten times for every affirming comment. In one Florida city teachers revealed that they gave 75 percent more criticisms than verbal blessings.* The Institute of Family Relations reports that it takes four affirming statements from a teacher/parent to offset the effects of one criticism to a child. William Barclay comments:

> One of the highest duties is the duty of encouragement. It is easy to pour cold water on . . . enthusiasm; it is easy to discourage others. The world is full of discouragers. We have a Christian duty to encourage one another. Many a time a word of praise or thanks or appreciation or cheer has kept a man on his feet. (p. 95)

We should also affirm each other in the church. Knowing some of the difficulties our church leaders* would be facing in the beginning of the new year, I wrote the following blessing for them:

Enough joy to keep you pure.
Enough slings and arrows to keep you courageous and watchful.
Enough anguish to keep you vulnerably human.
Enough hope to keep you faithful daily.
Enough failure to keep you humble.
Enough sleep to keep you rising early pray.
Enough wealth to keep you generous

to others whom few are generous to.
Enough confusion to keep you won-
dering and dreaming.
Enough success to keep you eager.
Enough friends to keep you encour-
aged.
Enough enthusiasm to keep you
expectant.
Enough hardihood to keep you
willing.

In this way I sought to affirm in advance the work they would do and struggles they would have.

Practical Ways to Affirm Others

In intimate relationships, we can lose intimacy by overfamiliarity. Often it is good to return to treating each other as we did when we first met. We are polite, affirming and interested. Our conversa-tion is more focused on the other than on ourselves. For married couples who find their affections broken and in need of affirmation, this idea can help.

Ask to see what God is doing and comment on it. Seeing others through our Lord leads to discernment. We can affirm others and be there for them in their hour of need. Seeing another's need in the light of God's love for him or her frees us to respond in that love, mak-ing us safe, giving and serving.

Understand that seeing the good in someone is a spiritual discipline!* It is uncreative and lazy to find a person's weaknesses. This is probably why we do it so often. However, to see the good in another and to make comment are a great encouragement.

Practice "positive gossiping" (see Gos-sip). Exchanging positive affirmations about our family, friends and colleagues distributes warmth to all. A couple who did this each night about their children allowed the children to fall asleep hear-ing their parents brag about them. Some-times it is awesome to overhear your name spoken well of.

Observations are always more power-ful than compliments. Compliments can make you feel worthless and are often discarded before they are fully enjoyed. A therapist, after giving an affirmation, wanted his client-friend to remember it. Upon hearing the dismissive thank-you, the therapist said, "This is not a compli-ment; it is an observation." This is more likely to be valued as being true and authentic.

Catch someone doing "good." When my daughter was four years old and quite proud of her long brown hair, she was observed by the church grouch stroking her locks during worship. Wanting to protect her from a reprimand, I leaned over, but heard, to my surprise, "Christine, you have beautiful hair and are a beautiful girl. I love how you sing." Later, my daughter said, "That nice lady caught me doing good!" That is affirma-tion!

Dump the "yes, buts." A "yes, but" is a hidden criticism behind a halfhearted compliment. Drop them both. Also, evaluating and comparing one person with another is almost always unaffirm-ing. Address people on their own merits.

Recognize that affirmation is a chal-lenge. When someone is well affirmed, it often is psychologically upsetting! Peo-ple are not used to the straightforward challenge of an affirmation. Affirma-tions challenge how a person thinks about himself or herself; it confronts dis-crepancies in how one views life.

Affirmation is a friendship* skill. It warms both the giver and the receiver to the relationship. Friendships are built and sustained by affirmation. So too are good marriages* and parenting.* Author Lawrence Peters (The Peter Princi-ple, p. 82) has noted that you can tell a real friend by the fact that when you have made a fool of yourself, he or she does not feel you have done a permanent job. Affirmation is the ability to maintain a relationship with a friend who has failed.

When we affirm each other, God too is there affirming us: "The LORD your God is with you, he is mighty to save. He will take great delight in you, he will quiet you with his love, he will rejoice over you with singing" (Zeph 3:17). The ultimate affirmation is from God at the end of the race: "Well done, good and faithful servant" (Mt 25:23 NRSV). But even before the end of the race, God affirms us in the context of everyday life through God's servants—whether knowingly or not—and through the hug of the Spirit within.

See also BLESSING; BLESSING, FAMILY; FAMILY COMMUNICATION; FRIENDSHIP; LOVE.

References and Resources

W. Barclay, *The Letter to the Hebrews: The Daily Study Bible* (Edinburgh: St. Andrew Press, 1955); R. F. Capon, *The Parables of Judgment* (Grand Rapids: Eerdmans, 1989); X. Leon-Dufour, *Dictionary of Biblical Theology* (London: Geoffrey Chapman, 1970); B. Manning, *The Ragamuffin Gospel: Good News for the Bedraggled, Beat-Up and Burnt-Out* (Portland, Ore.: Multnomah, 1990); L. Peters, *The Peter Principle* (New York: Morrow, 1969).

Paddy Ducklow

AGING

Every species has a definite life span, and human beings are no exception. Aging is an inevitable concomitant of life. As the preacher put it: "For everything there is a season, and a time for every matter under heaven: a time to be born, and a time to die" (Eccles 3:1-2 NRSV). Human beings age rapidly. The human body attains its peak of efficiency early. The rate of scar formation begins to decrease as early as age fifteen. Eventually, there are inescapable signs of physical decline: failing eyesight, impaired hearing, shortness of breath, high blood pressure; often associated with these is a measure of mental deterioration: memory lapses (an inability to remember the recent past while retaining intact older memories) and frequent repetitiveness. The final stage of the aging process is that of second childhood: when a semiliquid diet replaces solid food, the digestive function becomes the focus of attention, and one becomes increasingly dependent on the care of doctors and nurses.

The aging process, being biologically determined, is part of God's providence and is to be accepted with grace. Somerset Maugham, the Nobel Prize-winning novelist, was obsessed with the matter of his longevity and sought desperately to arrest the aging process. During the last twelve years of his life he regularly submitted to a series of rejuvenation treatments (involving life-preserving injections) at a clinic in Switzerland. It is doubtful whether they extended his physical life. What is not in question is the moral and intellectual deterioration that was such a sad feature of his final years.

Not everyone resorts to such desperate expedients; more popular is cosmetic surgery. Medical science suggests, however, that self-acceptance is the best antidote and cure for the discomforts that are inseparable from growing old.

Aging from a Sociological Point of View

Sociologists note the significant involvement of older people in politics* and religion as well as their active membership in clubs,* lodges and auxiliaries. Golden-age clubs and senior-citizen groups, which provide recreational, educational, health and welfare services, cater to an aging population and have an important role to play. There are also widely read magazines for seniors, such as *Modern Maturity*.

The older people are, the fewer the social roles open to them. Older people retire from work, their children leave home, their peers die, and their contacts with others tend to contract and lessen. Social activity, however, remains greatest among those who are in good health and who come from a higher, rather than a lower, socioeconomic background. For those with a living spouse, the marital relationship continues to be of central importance, making possible a variety of joint activities. Shakespeare speaks of the seven ages of humankind. He paints a sad and poignant picture of human beings in their dotage: "sans teeth, sans eyes, sans everything." Though the aging process is often sad, it can also be strangely beautiful, for Christians believe that "at evening time there shall be light" (Zech 14:7 NRSV).

The extraordinary advances in medical science, together with the availability of new drugs, have had a dramatic effect on such things as life expectancy. An increasingly aging population is a social challenge. Most of the elderly are women. Furthermore, there is a growing disparity between the age of retirement* and the time when all biological effects of aging begin to make themselves felt.

Aging from a Biblical Perspective

The classic description of the aging process is that given by the preacher in Ecclesiastes 12. He provides a beautiful and poetic description of progressive fading and failing in each of the several faculties of the body. It is a picture of sad and ineluctable deterioration and decay.

We are exhorted to remember our Creator in the days of our youth "before the sun and the light and the moon and the stars are darkened," before "the day when the guards of the house tremble, and the strong men are bent, and the women who grind cease working because they are few, and those who look through the windows see dimly; when the doors of the street are shut" (Eccles 12:2, 3-4 NRSV). The marvelous beauty of the imagery cannot disguise the fact

that what is being described is the painful loss of one's capacity to work,* walk,* eat,* see and hear. The exhortation then is to look beyond all earthly vanities, to face the fact of our coming mortality: when "the silver cord is snapped, and the golden bowl is broken, and the pitcher is broken at the fountain, and the wheel broken at the cistern, and the dust returns to the earth as it was, and the breath returns to God who gave it" (vv. 6-7 NRSV). So, in matchless language, the remorseless decay of all our faculties and their final dissolution are portrayed.

Other passages of Scripture highlight additional facets of aging. The psalmist describes divine companionship in the green pastures and by the still waters and also in the valley of the shadow of death (Ps 23). The apostle Paul uses the image of a tent to speak of the body*: a time is coming when the tent must be pulled down, to be replaced by "a building from God, a house not made with hands, eternal in the heavens" (2 Cor 5:1 NRSV). In the meantime, those who are aging know that their times are in God's hands (Ps 31:15). Each age has its own glory. If the young are given the privilege of seeing visions, the old are given that of dreaming dreams (Joel 2:28). If there is the happy remembrance of things past, there is also the joyous anticipation of what is yet to be: "No eye has seen, no ear has heard, no mind has conceived what God has prepared for those who love him" (1 Cor 2:9).

See also BODY; CHURCH-FAMILY; EMPTY NESTING; GRANDPARENTING; RETIREMENT; SICKNESS; SOUL.

References and Resources

R. Blythe, *The View in Winter: Reflections on Old Age* (Baltimore: Penguin, 1981); S. M. Chown, ed., *Human Aging* (Baltimore: Penguin, 1972); N. Coni, W. Davison and S. Webster, *Aging* (Oxford: Oxford University Press, 1992); D. Hobman, ed., *The Impact of Aging* (London: Croom Helm, 1981); R. A. Kenney, *Physiology* of Aging (Chicago: Year Book Medical Publishers, 1989); P. Tournier, *Learning to Grow Old* (London: SCM, 1972).

Barton Babbage

ALLOWANCES

Many people believe that the best way parents can give their children a financial education is to give them practical experience through an allowance, "a sum regularly provided for personal expenses" (*Webster's New Collegiate Dictionary, 1974*). As you cannot learn to read without books, you cannot learn how to handle money* if you never touch it.

The Bible contains much about training up children in the way of the Lord (for example, Deut 6:6-7; Eph 6:4), and personal finances are as important an area in which to lay down a godly life pattern as any other. There are many general references to handling money in the Scriptures, and many of these can be applied to the raising of godly and wise children. For example, insights such as "Whoever loves money never has money enough" (Eccles 5:10 NRSV) and Jesus' comment on the sacrificial generosity of the widow's offering (Mk 12:41-44) are vital parts of a child's home "curriculum." The specific commandments against stealing and coveting that, according to Deuteronomy, are to be impressed upon children are certainly to the point. The passages in Proverbs about money are also applicable (for example, Prov 1:19; 3:9; 13:11, 22; 15:16; 28:8). Certainly handling personal finances is one of the key ways in which a child needs to be trained. In our increasingly complicated and stressful economic world, as much practice with money as possible before adolescence* is particularly essential.

Two Kinds of Allowances
We must be clear on terminology: some parents apply the word *allowance* only to regular money given to a child that is not tied to any chores* but just reflects the child's membership in the family.* Most families expect contributions by the child to the cleanliness of his or her own body and bedroom and usually encourage some participation in household work, but the allowance is never seen as a direct reward for any duties. It is never removed as a punishment for "sins" of omission or commission in the area of chores or personal responsibilities. With this approach, which we might call the *true allowance*, additional funds can still be received by the child for assignments in the household that they take on voluntarily (for example, grass cutting).

Other families downplay or eliminate the type of allowance just described in favor of a pay-for-work approach. While the parents with this mindset agree that personal hygiene, tidying one's closet and doing school assignments should be their own reward, they arrange (often in dialogue with the child) regular, age-appropriate duties that are real contributions to the household (for example, dusting, laundry and gardening) to which all or most of the allowance is directly linked. This approach, which could be called the *cooperative family economy*, clearly puts emphasis on the Scriptures that teach against laziness (for example, Prov 10:4; 2 Thess 3:11-12) and about the dignity of work.*

For at least two reasons those taking this approach should not give up on some expression of the true allowance: (1) to avoid turning childhood into a job and caregivers into managers and (2) to help regularize and control the inevitable gifts of money (for small treats) that flow from parent to child during a week. Why not collect these "gifts" into a simple, true allowance and eliminate a lot of bother? On the other hand, for the biblical reasons already stated, true-allowance parents should also pay attention to the value of "money for work," recognizing that even young children can make a significant contribution to a family economy. In practice the two approaches often come together in child rearing, with a true allowance being emphasized in the earlier years and working directly for a share of the family income being stressed more with teenagers.

Guidelines

There are many specific systems used by parents to manage the distribution of family income. The following common-sense guidelines can be applied by all parents.

Progressive. Increase weekly money as the children get older, with consequently more responsibility for making purchases for themselves (for example, teenagers purchasing clothes, personal grooming products and entertainment). One rule of thumb suggests a number of dollars each week equal to half the child's age, but each family needs to decide for itself what is realistic and reasonable.

Consistent. It is extremely important to give the allowance regularly, in full and at the same time each week (consider how adults would respond to an employer who operated any differently). Wisdom can be applied to the best timing (Sunday or Monday evening avoids the temptation of Saturday shopping sprees), and extending advances should be kept to a minimum (having to save for a costlier purchase is usually a better discipline).

Independent. The benefit of an allowance as a training tool is maximized if the "allowance" part includes freedom* in spending. Though it is difficult to see children "wasting" money on sweets or trinkets, there is no better way for them to learn to make decisions, plan ahead and determine value. Parental guidance or caution is not

thereby eliminated, but parents must be prepared to let their children grow through mistakes.

Positive. The temptation to use an allowance as a bribe or punishment ("Do this or else no money") should be avoided. The important thing is not to change the rules midstream and unilaterally and thus begin to create a negative image around what should be a gift (true allowance) or compensation (cooperative family economy). Other strategies to change a child's behavior unrelated to the allowance should be used (for example, removal of privileges for breaking curfew).

There will always be differences of opinion about how to handle allowances. For example, some people create complicated ways to distribute the allowance over several categories (tithing, a family "tax" for group outings, long-term savings and personal spending). The most important thing is to involve children as much as possible in setting up the system and the amounts in the context of an appreciation of the overall state of family finances, to embody the practice in wider teaching about God's will for money and stewardship,* and to establish good attitudes and behaviors from the earliest age: "If the groundwork has been correctly laid, there's little cause to worry" (Weinstein, p. 89).

See also FAMILY GOALS; FAMILY VALUES; GIFT-GIVING; MONEY; STEWARDSHIP.

References and Resources
J. R. Peterson, *It Doesn't Grow on Trees* (Crozet, Va.: Betterway Publications, 1988); G. W. Weinstein, *Children and Money* (New York: Charterhouse, 1975).

Paul W. Lermitte and Dan Williams

AMBITION

Ambition is normally associated with the ardent desire to have high position or a place of influence though it can, simultaneously, be a passion for excellence and improvement (Schnase, pp. 10-11). The passion for personal advancement, so widely cultivated in the secular world, places the Christian in an ambiguous situation. In the workplace* there is wide acceptance of the creed that one should be challenged at all times and keep "moving up." In professional ministry the call to a bigger church is generally understood to be God's will. Is ambition positive, neutral, destructive or fallen but redeemable? When General Booth spoke of the founding of the Salvation Army as prompted by the "urgings of an undying ambition" (see Schnase, p. 11), was he simply using the wrong word? This everyday issue touches people at many critical points in their lives—considering a new job, coping with discontentment at home, developing new friendships,* struggling with comparisons made with others on a rising career* trajectory and wondering why enough is never enough (*see* Drivenness).

The Biblical Data

The word used for "fleshly" or "selfish" ambition in Galatians 5:20 is *eritheia*. Originally this meant "work done for pay" and came to mean accepting position and office, not from motives of service, but for what one can get out of it. It is related to the word *jealousy*, which started out well—as "the desire to attain to nobility"—but came to mean "the desire to have what someone else has" (Barclay, pp. 47-48). Since *zelos* is the word from which our English word *zeal* comes, jealous, self-seeking ambition may be thought of as "zeal gone bad." James speaks of "selfish ambition" as earthly, unspiritual and demonic "wisdom" (Jas 3:13-16). The Lord himself warned against seeking first place (Mt 20:26-27), desiring power, prestige and wealth (Lk 14:10). Jesus called his disciples to a life

of self-sacrifice that gives priority to God's kingdom and righteousness (Mt 6:33).

Since Scripture is somewhat ambiguous on the subject of ambition, it is not surprising that many Christians are confused. Paul warned against unbridled appetites (Phil 3:19) and the danger of loving money (1 Tim 6:10). But there are also positive statements like the one approving those who set their hearts on being an elder—a godly ambition (1 Tim 3:1). While Paul counseled against being conformed to the mindset of the world (Rom 12:2) and rejoiced to see his enemies preach the gospel even though they wanted to make life more difficult for him (Phil 1:18), he was ambitious to have a harvest among the Romans (Rom 1:13) and to evangelize Spain. It has often been suggested that when Paul got converted, so was his ambition: "What Paul can teach us is that there is a gospel-centered way to speak about competitiveness, a way to be ambitious for the sake of Christ, a way to raise the desire for success above the level of self-interest or ideology" (Kuck, p. 175).

The Old Testament is rich in examples of both unholy and holy ambition. These are often given to us without comment, leaving us to read between the lines for their positive or negative effects. Joseph's dreams* were not simply an expression of a subconscious superiority complex; they were a part of his having a legitimate vision of greatness under God. Though at first Joseph wrongly used his dreams as weapons against his brothers (Gen 37:1-11) and only later learned to let God be the architect of their fulfillment, his dreams were a powerful motivating factor in his life. Jacob, in contrast, was rightly ambitious to have the Lord's blessing but resorted to stealing and subterfuge to get it (Gen 25:19-34; 27:1-40), thus fulfilling his prophetic name (which means "heel-grabber").

Gideon had the holy ambition of wanting to save Israel, Joshua of conquering the land, Nehemiah of restoring the kingdom and Paul of planting a self-propagating church in every major center of the Roman Empire.

Unfortunately passages like Matthew 6:33 that encourage holy ambition are usually applied exclusively to Christian service roles in the church and evangelistic activity in the world rather than to the promotion of kingdom values in the home,* workplace and community.* Having an ambition to provide extraordinary service* to customers and to provide fair compensation packages to employees can be as holy as desiring to plant a new church in a presently unreached area. Indeed, selfish ambition may be easily disguised in a Christian service career and praised as godly zeal.

Any consideration of ambition must take into account the function of personality. More important, however, is the way ambition becomes an expression of our spirituality and therefore an important dimension of self-knowledge and self-discipline in everyday life.

Bad and Good Ambition

As a work of the flesh, selfish ambition is present when we define ourselves by our achievements, rather than by our character. For many men, and increasingly for women, the choice of career represents an "idealized fantasy of who one is or might become . . . the medium through which these dreams are enacted and judged" (Ochberg, p. 3). Defining our identity by achievement is, in the end, self-defeating as it leads either to a frenzied, driven life spurred by diminishing returns of past successes or to despair when we realize we can never become that wished-for self. Because our motives are so mixed, the search for a satisfying and challenging career is less like fitting a peg into its slot and more like compressing an unruly spring into a container and wondering how long it will stay (Ochberg, p. 4).

At the root of this spiritual pathology is the autonomous self trying to find meaning in life by its own action rather than as a child of God. Symptoms of this selfish ambition are relentless striving with an inability to rest,* discouragement at the lack of recognition obtained for one's hard work, predatory competition* (even in Christian leadership), use of the present situation (and people) as a stepping stone and an "endless itchiness for other possibilities" (Schnase, p. 17). The Bible leaves little room for exalting human achievement and constantly points us in the direction of exulting in God's achievements. But our motives are always mixed, and a theology of grace accepts humanness just as it is. At the same time it points to something better. Because ambition is not uniformly evil, it is a risk worth taking.

Life without ambition would be largely passive and complacent, victim to the latest manipulating persuader or discouraging turn, rather than directed toward a goal. As a redeemed passion, ambition gives force to a life direction of seeking God's purposes in family,* workplace, church* and community. Ambitious people take initiative and are future oriented and consistently motivated: "Ambition gives color to our dreams and places before us an appetite for the possibilities of life. Ambition gives us strength of character to turn aspirations into reality through muscle and sweat, mind and imagination" (Schnase, p. 14). Ambition can be redeemed through *orthopathy,* that is, the conversion of our passions to line up with God's *pathos,* what God cares about. A truly Christian conversion is concerned not only with orthopraxy (true and right action) but also with orthopraxy (true and right affections).

Converting the Passions

As the Galatians 5:16-26 passage makes plain, simple trust in Jesus does not immediately eliminate the battle within. Ambition is a reflection of this inner struggle.

Ongoing reconquest. After initial conversion the Christian normally experiences an ongoing reconquest of the person through walking and living in the Spirit (Gal 5:15, 25) and maintaining a crucified perspective on our fallen human nature (the flesh; Gal 2:3; 5:24; 6:14). The latter is not self-crucifixion, mortifying one's bodily life, or self-hatred but fully and continuously agreeing with God's judgment on our autonomous self-justifying life. Since such a life puts God to death and crucifies Christ in our hearts, it is worthy of death. Negatively, walking according to the Spirit means not setting the mind on or doing the deeds of the flesh (Rom 8:5; Gal 5:19-21) nor doing the deeds of the flesh, but putting these desires and deeds to death by the Spirit (Rom 8:13; Gal 5:16-18, 24-26). Also, the one who walks by the Spirit does not boast in human achievement (Phil 3:3-6), human wisdom (1 Cor 2:1-6) or righteousness (Rom 2:17-19; Gal 2:15-21). Thus, walking according to the Spirit means a renunciation of the desires and deeds of the flesh, including the temptation to define our identity and self-worth by "getting ahead." In a positive statement, walking according to the Spirit implies that the Christian "keeps in step" (Gal 5:25) with what the Spirit is already doing. This involves setting one's mind on the things of the Spirit (Rom 8:5) and allowing the Spirit to produce character fruits (Rom 12—14; Gal 5:19-21) and to empower works of holiness (Rom 12:9-21; compare Is 58).

Inside godly ambition. Several life patterns in the New Testament surround and illuminate the process of the conversion of our ambitions: self-control, contentment, faithfulness, neighbor love and praise. *Self-control* is bringing one's whole self into harmony so that we are in charge of our own life—thoughts, feelings, appetites, drives and bodily needs. Some people claim they want Christ to take control of their lives, but this may be something less than the full dignity of being a self-controlled child of God. Self-control is the fruit of the Spirit (Gal 5:23), a byproduct of a life lived in harmony with God's purposes and for God's glory. Ironically we are most likely to be freed from compulsive ambition and addictions* when we give up trying to accomplish the conversion of our passions by self-justifying self-discipline and focus on following Jesus and glorifying God.

Contentment is not antithetical to godly ambition, but it is incompatible with selfish ambition. Ambition and contentment must coexist peacefully in the Christian soul (Shelley, p. 3). Paul was able to confess that he had "learned the secret of being content in any and every situation" (Phil 4:12). He gained this through trust in God (Phil 4:13) and the practice of continuous thanksgiving (Phil 4:6). Paul claims he had "learned" contentment; it was not something automatically gained through conversion or by an ecstatic Spirit-filling. It is sometimes argued that we should be content with what we have but not content with what we are. This seems to shortchange the full conversion of our passions, a conversion involving the pruning of unworthy ambitions to encourage godly ambitions. This is best done in the company of other believers who can hold us accountable and, when necessary, name the lie in our stories. In this way we can be released from the slavery to more, better and bigger.

Faithfulness feeds the godly ambition and is complementary (Gal 5:22). Eugene Peterson described the faithful life as a "long obedience in the same direction," a life neither passively quiet nor frantically busy. In the marketplace ambition can be good if it is used for the common good and is harmonized with the advancement of others (Troop, p. 25), a life pattern I call *neighbor love*. In 1 Corinthians 3—4 Paul raises the crucial question of evaluation, or *God's praise*, in the context of a congregation that compared its leaders and prided itself on spiritual advancement. He argues that "each will be rewarded according to his own labor" (1 Cor 3:8), stressing that any difference in work will be for God to reward and judge at the final judgment (1 Cor 3:10-15; compare Mt 25:21). No one else is capable of finally evaluating a servant of God: "Even the servant's own self-evaluation means nothing. Only one opinion matters—that of the Lord" (Kuck, p. 179), a factor that is relevant not only for Christian service workers but Christians tempted to unholy ambition in the workplace or political realm.

Self-control, contentment, faithfulness, neighbor love and praise all contribute to the redemption of ambition, for they liberate ambition from paralyzing self-centeredness. J. S. Bach had it right. He wrote over every manuscript what we can write over balance sheets, sermons and shopping lists: "SDG," which means *soli Deo gloria* (to God alone be the glory). Coupled with this should be the statement by the playwright Anton Chekhov: "One would need to be a God to decide which are the failures and which are the successes in life" (Kuck, p. 174).

See also CALLING; CAREER; DRIVENNESS; SPIRITUAL CONFLICT; SPIRITUAL GROWTH; SUCCESS; WORK.

References and Resources

W. Barclay, *Flesh and Spirit: An Examination of Galatians 5:19-23* (London: SCM, 1962); J. Epstein, *Ambition: The Secret Passion* (New York: Dutton, 1980); D. Kuck, "Paul and Pastoral Ambition: A Reflection on 1 Corinthians 3—4," *Currents in Theology and Mission* 19, no. 3 (1992) 174-83; R. L. Ochberg, *Middle-Aged Sons and the Meaning of Work* (Ann Arbor, Mich.: U.M.I. Research Press, 1979); R. Schnase, *Ambition in Ministry: Our Spiritual Struggle with Success, Achievement and Competition* (Nashville: Abingdon, 1993); M. Shelley, "From the Editors," *Leadership* 11, no. 3 (1990) 3; J. Troop, "High Hopes," *Christianity Today* 30, no. 14 (1986) 24-25.

R. Paul Stevens

ANNIVERSARIES

Remembering significant events on an annual basis is something as old as humankind. Even before calendars were invented, people used the annual cycle of seasons and the rhythms of the work year—planting, cultivating and harvest—to recall significant marker events. Israel celebrates Passover (the annual remembrance of deliverance from Egypt; Deut 16:6), and the church* celebrates the festivals* of Easter, Christmas and Thanksgiving. Nations celebrate their day of independence, the queen's birthday or the day the constitution was approved. In the same way each individual life is annually marked with significant events, the most obvious being one's birthday.* Married people celebrate their wedding* anniversaries. Some pastors celebrate the anniversary of their ordination. Christians sometimes celebrate the day of their baptism.* All these are happy occasions.

Most people have anniversaries inscribed in their souls that are difficult to celebrate: the anniversary of a spouse's, parent's or child's death,* the day one was raped or fired or the date that the decree came through on the divorce.* Even if these dates are not written on the wall calendar, they are inscribed on the calendar of the heart. Most people have an annual emotional cycle that forms the seasons of the soul, both summer and winter. These too are worthy of theological and spiritual reflection.

Sacramental Events

Celebrating important marker events in one's life serves the yearly cycle in the same way as sabbath* serves the weekly: it gives perspective to the rest of the time* and points us godward. It invites contemplation. It focuses affirmation.* It is a way to redeem time. So having a birthday party* or a special anniversary dinner for one's beloved is a way of remembering the significance of the original event and deepening the meaning. This is especially so if it is an occasion of corporate prayer* and recounting the mercies of God. Parents may use the anniversaries of a child's marriage to express and deepen their "letting go" of son or daughter in order to "cleave" (Gen 2:24 KJV), as well as to express and welcome the entry of a daughter- or son-in-law into the family.* Some people with a radical conversion celebrate the anniversary of their new birth or the day they stopped drinking.

In the Hebrew way of living, remembering is not simply digging back the past; it is making something from the past present to us now. This is the real meaning of remembering the Lord's death until he comes (1 Cor 11:25-26; see Communion). So there is sacramental significance in remembering. It becomes a means of grace both to the person or relationship so honored, as well as to those who honor them. Families, as part of their family traditions, do well to establish a few significant anniversaries that will become the means of recounting the goodness of God and reinforcing family values.* Why not keep an anniversary of the day you moved into your home* or the day Dad came home from the hospital for good? But what can we do with our negative anniversaries?

Healing Painful Memories

Some misguided Christians think that denying painful anniversaries is a mark of advanced spirituality. They never talk about the loss and pretend that it is "all over." But like a cork pushed down in water, such painful wounds surface in compensatory behavior: inappropriate emotions, depression, withdrawal from situations that bring back memories, conspicuous lack of reference to deceased people, unwillingness to risk being loved again or rebound relationships. Often this happens around the date written on the emotional calendar. Most commonly an unhealed past leads to a wall of defense built around the person. Grieving,* as we know, is a long-term process, and it is literally true that we never really get over a significant loss; we adjust to it. But the adjustment cannot happen if there is denial. So anniversaries can help expound this part of our soul life as well.

Significantly Israel's "church" year included painful memories and a remembrance of the bitter experiences in Egypt (see Sugar/Sugary), just as the modern remembrance of the Holocaust and the birth of the state of Israel has an edifying function. In the same way people can find creative ways to celebrate painful anniversaries. They do this not to keep the pain alive and nurture the root of bitterness (Heb 12:15) but to put it into perspective and allow God to heal. For example, the annual remembrance of a death can become an occasion for a family to recall the contribution of that person, telling stories, thanking God for their lives, and when unforgiven sins are remembered, to "let go." A meal is a great time to do this. The mixture of tears and laughter* on such occasions is emotionally healing* and spiritually edifying. Some people find it constructive to write a letter to a dead or divorced spouse expressing thoughts, regrets and gratitude, a letter that will afterward be burned.

Extremely painful marker events, such as a rape or unjust dismissal, may require continuing counseling and inner healing with an experienced friend or counselor. But even these extremely bitter experiences can be healed, especially if they are not cocooned in a cloak of secrecy and denial. Having dinner and conversation with an intimate friend each year at "the time" can be a healing sacrament of remembrance. There are some wounds and events that in this life will never be forgotten, but they can be forgiven and substantially healed. And the process of getting there is part of God's agenda for our spiritual growth* and maturing.

Celebrating anniversaries as individuals is based on good theology. God is sovereign and has a wonderful purpose (not a plan) for our lives. Nothing has happened to us that cannot be incorporated into his good purpose for us. He is a saving and healing God. We are not a bundle of accidents or a victim of fate. God's grand purpose, not the stars or horoscope, defines our life path. Each person is a unique creation (Ps 139), and celebrating the marker events of our unique life path is a way of celebrating creation and Creator at the same time.

Not only is celebrating anniversaries good theology; it is good spirituality. It helps us find God at the center of our lives. True spirituality is gained, as Dietrich Bonhoeffer once said, "by living unreservedly in life's duties, problems, successes and failures, experiences and perplexities. In so doing we throw ourselves completely into the arms of God" (Bonhoeffer, p. 15).

See also BIRTHDAYS; FESTIVALS; PARTYING.

References and Resources

D. Bonhoeffer, letter from Tegel Prison in 1944, quoted in M. Morrison, "As One Who Stands Convicted," *Sojourners* 8, no. 5 (May 1979) 15-19; M. E. Hazeltine, *Anniversaries and Holidays: A Calendar of Days and How to Observe Them*, 2d ed. (Chicago: American Library Association, 1944).

R. Paul Stevens

ANXIETY

"Don't Worry—Be Happy" was the title of a song that swept the pop charts in 1988. Why was it so popular? I suspect because this phrase expresses one of the deepest yearnings of the human heart—to be free of all anxiety. Is such a yearning realistic? Is all anxiety bad for us? Thirty years in the psychologist's chair has taught me one important lesson: anxiety is intricately interwoven with the essence of living. You cannot expect to live and be free of all anxiety.

"Don't be anxious; anxiety is the exact opposite of faith"—so reads a tract, written by a popular preacher, that I came across recently. How realistic are such admonitions? Are these writers attacking all forms of anxiety or just some?

How is it possible for some to see anxiety as an essential emotion* while others see it as a sign of spiritual failure?* The answer lies in the fact that there are many forms of anxiety. When Jesus tells his disciples not to be anxious (Lk 12:25), he is referring to that form we commonly call *worry anxiety*. It is that form of anxiety that incapacitates and serves no useful purpose. Unfortunately, there are other afflictions we also call *anxiety* that are not so easy to dispose of. Before we pass judgment on anyone for being anxious, therefore, we need to know what form of anxiety we are talking about and understand how it differs from the neurotic form we call *worry*.

Why Should We Be Free of Anxiety?

Is it because God does not like anxious people? Is it because anxiety is synonymous with a lack of faith and is thus sinful? Is it because anxiety serves no useful function in the human psyche? These are provocative questions. The fact is that anxiety is an enigma. It has many faces, and while we can effectively treat some of its symptoms, we still do not fully understand its function or purpose in human experience.

While worry anxiety is clearly an undesirable disorder, anxiety's very presence in human experience seems to point us to some larger and useful purpose. To many, including this author, some forms of anxiety are necessary and can be purposeful. Take the mother's anxiety over her newborn baby. Is it breathing normally? Is it getting enough milk? These anxious thoughts help the mother to care for the baby.

Like pain, therefore, some anxiety is an important emotional "warning system" that alerts us to potential danger. Just as pain is necessary to the body to warn of disease and damage (though we may not deliberately seek it), so anxiety serves to send important messages of impending threat or danger to our emotional well-being. Without it, we would become emotional lepers and be constantly harming ourselves by not heeding emotional danger. To put it in a nutshell: people who have no anxiety are dangerous, tend to be sociopaths and feel no guilt. This is hardly a desirable set of traits!

Such a model of anxiety, however, assumes a perfect world and a mind that has been trained to respond only to healthy anxiety. In reality this wonderful warning system can all too quickly go astray very early. For many, then, too much anxiety is the problem, and their anxiety becomes a painful and debilitating experience. Furthermore, there is now ample evidence to show that the high demands and stress of modern life are taking their toll on and distorting our anxiety warning systems. Natural brain tranquilizers, produced within the brain to keep us at peace when there is no real threat or to enable us to act constructively when in danger, become depleted in our overworked brains. The result is a high incidence of incapacitating, purposeless anxiety disorders. This, as well as purposeless worry, is what Jesus warns us to avoid!

Battling Anxiety
Despite our high level of sophistication and technological expertise, anxiety and its related manifestations remain a major psychological and medical challenge today. The treatment of severe anxiety disturbances puts many at risk for addiction* to the medications used. It is no wonder that many Christian leaders are concerned about how this problem is approached today.

Intuitively we know that prescribing massive doses of artificial tranquilizers is not a satisfactory solution. We also know that the incidence of severe anxiety disorders is on the increase. According to the National Institute of Mental Health, panic anxiety disorder is now the number-one mental-health problem in women (Hart, p. 56). It is second in men only to substance abuse. Distress, restlessness, nervousness, fear and panic, competitiveness,* crowded living conditions and too much stress make matters worse, not better. The stress of twentieth-century living affects everyone, and part of the price we pay for it is an increase in general anxiety.

And what will the twenty-first century bring? Better and less addicting tranquilizers? Perhaps! Certainly not less anxiety. With problems such as polluted air, contaminated food, the greenhouse effect and nuclear waste (to name just a very few) already staring us in the face, a person would have to be awfully naive not to be anxious about the future.

The Anxiety Picture Today

As a result, scores of people in every neighborhood suffer from persistent anxiety-related problems: difficulty in sleeping,* stomach problems and generalized stress. They worry themselves into an early grave or fret away their precious life seeking an escape in alcohol, drugs* or shopping.*

The anxiety-related disorders we suffer from today include the following: *worry anxiety* (excessive rumination on imagined or unlikely fears, expectation of the worst and a bracing for an imagined catastrophe), *fear anxiety* (anxiety over real fears, threats or demands; overconcern about a particular happening that may only have some basis in reality), *existential anxiety* (anxiety over lack of purpose or nonbeing, awareness of the inevitability of death* leading to concern for a meaningful life), *panic anxiety* (chemical imbalance in the brain due to the lack of natural tranquilizers, causing all systems to become hyperactive and easily panicked; can lead to agoraphobia), *phobic anxiety* (exaggerated and persistent fears, avoidance of certain places, people or projects), *generalized anxiety* (unfocused and generalized anxiety that becomes free-floating, often changing its object of concern), and *separation anxiety* (originating in an insecure childhood, this anxiety arises whenever a person is cut off from home or loved ones).

How Common Are Anxiety-Related Disorders?

Millions of Americans experience incapacitating anxiety every day. For most it lasts long enough, is severe enough and causes sufficient dysfunction to disturb their everyday living and warrant psychological therapy and/or medical treatment. Just how many suffer from some sort of anxiety problem? No one really knows. One estimate puts it as high as forty million (15 percent of the popula-

tion). According to a recent news report, thirty-five million Americans suffer from periodic panic attacks alone, and this is only one form of anxiety disorder (Hart, p. 3). And while we now know a lot about how to treat the more severe anxiety disorders, there is still much confusion about the best form of treatment.

Many other emotional problems also have their roots in anxiety. Several studies have shown that those who suffer from depression* also have severe anxiety symptoms. Clinically, the close connection between anxiety and depression has been known for many years. The problem is further complicated by the fact that some of the medications used to treat anxiety will aggravate depression symptoms and vice versa. This can be perplexing, even to professionals.

Getting Help for Anxiety

Few emotional problems are more common or more debilitating than anxiety. Most of us realize, on the basis of personal experience as well as observation of fellow humans, that anxiety is a pervasive and profound phenomenon in our society. As we approach the end of the twentieth century, its devastation seems to be on the increase. We are anxious as individuals, and an air of anxiety hangs over everything.

Medications that calm the nerves or relax the muscles are helpful and absolutely essential in panic and generalized anxiety. Sufferers from these forms of anxiety disturbance need to seek immediate professional help because the sooner they are treated, the less likely the problem will become permanently entrenched.

But medications are useful only if they buy the time needed to bring one's life under control—to master fears, reduce stress and susceptibility to anxiety. In the end the problem with all anxiety is a problem of lifestyle, a matter of goals and priorities. No matter how effective treatment is, the problem will recur if major life changes are not made.

Faith and Anxiety

How does one's faith in Jesus Christ interface with anxiety? It would be grossly irresponsible to say that all anxiety is a sign of spiritual failure. While stress underlies panic anxiety and can therefore be susceptible to the choices we make, separation and generalized anxiety have roots that go way back to early childhood and possibly even have genetic influences. These forms of anxiety need very careful handling, and it usually takes the skill of a well-trained professional to help. Inept help can significantly increase anxiety problems.

Whatever the type of anxiety being experienced, however, the resources of the Christian life are profoundly designed to help us cope with it. Achieving a balanced life is the ultimate goal. Whether or not medication is used, we ignore to our loss the profound effect that spiritual dimensions can have on our emotional well-being. Prayer and Scripture are more than just spiritual resources. They influence how we feel, our values* and priorities. Humans are more than physical organisms, and nowhere does a balanced spiritual life affect us more than in the realm of our anxieties.

I am convinced that one reason so many people suffer from acute anxiety in our society is that they fail to make this important connection. Not even our most sophisticated technology, medical or psychological, can free us from an important but painful facet of our existence—our built-in need to be reconnected with our Creator. This need overrides all others, and when it is unmet, there is much cause for anxiety. Because most researchers and therapists ignore this reality, they tend to place too much emphasis on the physical world as a cause of anxiety and fail to address deeper spiritual needs.

Christians are by no means free of the problem of anxiety. Many are even at greater risk than the general population because trying to live a holy life in an unholy world where fragmentation is the norm is not easy. The words of Peter are a strong medicine even today, and we ignore them to our detriment: "Cast all your anxiety on him because he cares for you" (1 Pet 5:7 NRSV).

See also DEPRESSION; DRUGS; EMOTIONS; FAILURE; HEALTH; STRESS, WORKPLACE.

References and Resources

S. Agras, *Panic: Facing Fears, Phobias and Anxiety* (New York: W. H. Freeman, 1985); A. D. Hart, *Overcoming Anxiety* (Waco, Tex.: Word, 1989).

Archibald D. Hart

ARCHITECTURE, URBAN

The first arresting image of urban architecture in Scripture is the tower of Babel—hardly a great beginning for a biblical view of the built environment. Starting with the tabernacle (in the wilderness wanderings) and later the temple, we see a much more positive approach. God gave the children of Israel the design for these structures, not just providing the overall size and shape but detailing such items as blue pomegranates as part of the decoration. In fact, we learn in the New Testament that the tabernacle was "a copy and shadow of what is in heaven" (Heb 8:5; 9:24). The vision of the heavenly city at the end of history also contains many specific materials and measurements (Rev 21:9-21).

Modernism

Modern urban architecture is set in a very different world. In the early twentieth century, philosophy shaped buildings more than functional concerns did. Mies van der Rohe, Adolf Loos, Walter Gropius and Charles Edouard Jeanneret (better known as Le Corbusier) remade the world. With technical advancements, the elevator and skeleton construction (resulting in nonweight-bearing walls), combined with a morally superior, utopian outlook, this small handful of architects left their image on modern cities worldwide. Their ideas on town planning and design have made close kin of downtown Boston, Brasilia and Beijing.

A number of basic doctrines drove these changes (these owe much to Brent Brolin, *The Failure of Modern Architecture*):

*Inventive technology.** New building materials, like glass, steel and reinforced concrete, brought forth new forms.

Worship of change. New processes made stylistic traditions irrelevant. Modernism "has never been presented as a style; it has been considered a movement of truths for so long that we are unable to think of it as a set of arbitrary, systematized aesthetic choices" (Brolin, p. 13).

Simplicity. With modernism the inevitable result of design would be something reductive, pared down, simplified. In a way, modernist building shape was inspired by minimalist painting and sculpture. Decoration on a building was equated with crime.* Simplifying a building meant getting rid of nonessentials. In this way function was stressed over ornamentation.

Antihistorical. Modernists turned their backs on tradition in favor of a Darwinian idea of progress. In 1923 Le Corbusier declared traditional architecture to be a lie. Materials had to be "honest," and architects were to be true to themselves rather than just mirror the past. According to Adolf Loos: "The time is nigh, fulfillment awaits us! Soon the streets of the city will glisten like white walls. Like Zion, the holy city, the capital of Heaven. Then, fulfillment will come!"

(Brolin, p. 17).

Standardization. Hand in hand with new materials was mass production. The modernists wanted to rationalize the industry so that wherever buildings were built, the same principles would apply. The impersonal look of concrete would replace hand-shaped local materials. "Wherever western civilization has penetrated, impersonal forms intrude upon the traditional profiles of cities, towns and villages" (Brolin, p. 12).

Planning. To Le Corbusier, Manhattan was a mess. The buildings were getting big, to be sure, but it was all muddled. He preferred "La Ville Radieuse," the radiant city, an urban arrangement of large skyscrapers in parklike settings connected by rapid transit to other areas of the city containing different functions. Le Corbusier spoke of humankind's need for "greenery, sunlight, fresh air and space. All very true; but man's primary yearning, it seems, is not for great expanses of open space, but for other men, women and children" (Blake, p. 88).

The automobile* was crucial to this ideal city. "We watched the titanic rebirth of the traffic—cars, cars! speed, speed! One is carried away, seized by enthusiasm, by joy . . . enthusiasm over the joy of power" (Hughes, 188). Ironically, what they eliminated was the life of the street. In the Radiant City—the Vertical City—the elevator ruled, not the sidewalk (*see* Public Spaces). (And you know what it's like on an elevator for relationships of even the most basic type.) The inhabitants of such a modern city go to the old town center, where there are shops, cafés, people. When you travel to a city as a tourist, you end up on the same crowded streets, maybe medieval, probably meandering, rubbing shoulders with people—all miles from the rational park settings of the high-rise with its "machines for living" (Le Corbusier).

All that the well-intentioned planning tended to produce was ghettos. "The finest public housing projects to be found anywhere in the world, and designed according to the noblest precepts, are turning into enclaves of rape, murder, mugging and dope addition, with the only way out a change of dynamite to reduce those noble precepts to rubble" (Blake, p. 11).

In St. Louis in 1972, this came true quite literally. The Pruitt-Igoe development blew up a number of their buildings after continued vandalism. The buildings were impersonal and not in keeping with the needs of the inhabitants.

More could be said about modernism as a world- and city-shaping philosophy, but where does this leave us? Most people who live in cities, anywhere in the world, see the same glass and steel high-rise shapes. What do these mean? The message they send: human beings don't matter; elevated aesthetic views about esoteric minimalist designs *do*.

This modernist architectural dictatorship seems to be near its end. What concerns should we as Christians have as we think of its demise?

Concerns and Directions

An appreciation of history. Whatever was built in the past does not need to be rejected or superseded automatically without much thought. Let us learn from its richness, its shapes, its decoration.

A sensitivity to locale. Instead of dropping in a specific setting the same vertical, glass and steel, right-angle building, let us relate what we construct to what is there, in terms of buildings, natural setting, mix of functions and so on.

A willingness to conserve. Don't destroy just to be up-to-date. The wholesale clearing of our cities' historic districts is a sad legacy. Tearing down what is too old-fashioned, too small or too whatever needs to be looked at seriously.

The richness of different scales. The visual intricacy of hand-done ornamentation on traditional buildings presents a rich vision, from varying distances. The closer you get, the more you see and learn. The fascination with minimalist art made modernist buildings that give the same information whatever distance you are from them. The fascination with speed also led to the omission of detail—you go by too fast to see or appreciate it.

Attention to local concerns. What kind and size of buildings should be built? With what materials? What traditions need to be respected?

The importance of street life. People need to be with each other. Streets with their shops, churches and parks need to be retained for human contact, places where people can talk about life. In the wake of the destruction caused by the automobile, we need to remember the pedestrian and the variety of sensations available on a walk (*see* Walking).

A mix of functions. Planning shouldn't mean segregating uses and placing them tidily in separate areas around a city. A variety of housing types (*see* Home), public spaces* and appropriate commercial facilities should coexist within neighborhoods.

Architecture is the one art form that touches us all. We may not visit art galleries or go to concerts, but we do live in buildings, whether forty stories high or only one with a large backyard. What the city looks like, therefore, concerns us. The view expressed by Philip Johnson, that "architecture would improve people, and people improve architecture until perfectibility would descend on us like the Holy Ghost, and we would be happy ever after" (Hughes, p. 165), sounds like idolatry.

Instead, the architect should give up his or her semidivine pretension to be Creator and Judge, and aspire, as Vincent Scully says, to "the more humane and realistic role of healer, of physician" (Katz, p. 224). No other profession leaves such large and permanent reminders of its ideas. It is crucial that Christian architects and planners think and work together to design buildings and communities that respect the God-given dignity of people. Let us shape homes and places of work where people flourish, jobs are done creatively and healthy relationships are encouraged.

Ultimately, let us look forward to that "city with foundations, whose architect and builder is God" (Heb 11:10).

See also CITY; NEIGHBORHOOD; PUBLIC SPACES; ZONING.

References and Resources
P. Blake, *Form Follows Fiasco* (Boston: Little, Brown, 1977); B. Brolin, *The Failure of Modern Architecture* (New York: Van Nostrand Reinhold, 1976); R. Hughes, *The Shock of the New* (New York: Knopf, 1991); P. Katz, *The New Urbanism* (New York: McGraw-Hill, 1994).

Dal Schindell

ART

For the Christian all of life is meant to glorify God. This fact has been used both to encourage and to discourage the use of art by Christians. Historically, of course, Christianity (and religion in general) has provided the most important motivation and sources for the development of art.

The Church and Art
After the conversion of Constantine in 312, the church became the primary patron of the arts, especially in the building and decorating of churches. During the Middle Ages, in addition to architecture,* drama, sculpture, music* and painting were all developed vigorously for purposes of worship and instruction. Painting in particular was stimulated by an important change in the church's liturgy. In the thirteenth century the priest began to face the congregation as he performed the Eucharist. This necessitated moving the table forward from the back wall of the sanctuary, thus leaving an empty space that soon was filled with beautiful altar pieces. Drama as we know it today likewise had its birth in medieval morality plays that acted out various parts of the gospel for the people, who were mostly unable to read Scripture for themselves. In the case of music it is difficult to imagine any form of Christian life and worship in which this does not play a central role (*see* Music, Christian). As we will see, music goes back to the biblical period, but it was given special impetus by the medieval Gregorian chants and the Reformation chorales.

The desire to glorify God with the whole of one's life also served to discourage the development of certain kinds of art. At the Reformation, for example, John Calvin was convinced that the use of images (in both painting and sculpture) had begun to distract people from hearing the truth of God's Word and tended to become idolatrous. As a result the Reformed tradition has often focused on the verbal arts of music and drama, rather than the visual arts, as safer vehicles for communicating the gospel. Meanwhile the Catholic tradition, with its emphasis on the visual drama of the Eucharist and its sacramental view of reality, has continued to place a high value on the visual arts.

As society gradually became more secular and the influence of the church and Christianity declined, the connection between art and Christianity was lost. By the end of the nineteenth century most leading artists prided themselves on their independence, not only from Christianity but from any mythological framework. Art became a medium for the expression of a personal vision rather than the means of communicating common values. And since most artists were raised without any Christian influence, what they expressed was not only antagonistic to Christianity but often alarming to Christians.

It is not surprising that at the beginning of the twentieth century Christians looked at the arts more as a field for evangelism* than as an ally in expressing and living out their faith. Becoming an artist was not considered to be a viable option for the serious Christian, and those Christians who did manage to go to art schools encountered an environment that was not encouraging to their faith. The result is that outside of music (mostly classical or Christian) and an occasional drama, Christians do not typically give much thought to the arts in their everyday life.

Biblical Perspectives on Art

In support of this negative attitude, Christians typically point out how little emphasis the Bible gives to the arts. The Old Testament appears to forbid the making of graven images, and the New Testament obviously has more important things on its mind.

Like the Reformation, the Old Testament seems clearly to favor music and poetry over the visual arts. Beauty was surely included when God judged the work of creation to be very good, but at the Fall the devil was able to use this very beauty to tempt Adam and Eve to doubt God's word (Gen 3:6). The prohibition against graven images in the Ten Commandments probably had more to do with the temptation to idolatry than with the fear of images as such. In support of this view, notice the careful and detailed instructions given for building the tabernacle and temple as places where beauty is brought into the service of worship (Ex 31). In this respect God's people seemed almost profligate in their use of art. The temple used materials and motifs from

all over the ancient world, and Psalms and Proverbs actually embody poetic forms to praise Israel's God that were used elsewhere in the ancient Near East. So while nothing, not even beauty, should be allowed to share the honor due God, all the works of human hands (and hearts) could be employed to promote that honor.

In the New Testament Paul's reaction to the classical beauty and paganism of Athens is perfectly consistent with this reading of things (Acts 17). When he rose to speak on Mars Hill, he could easily see the splendid frieze of the Parthenon (known to us as the "Elgin Marbles" in the British Museum); there too was the Temple of the Wingless Victory and the vast statue of Athena Promachus. Like the prophets before him, "his spirit was provoked within him as he saw that the city was full of idols" (Acts 17:16 RSV). Was this his only reaction to such splendor? That Paul was no philistine is clear from his quoting no fewer than two Greek poets in that same Mars Hill sermon. No, he was not insensitive to beauty, but he saw that art taken out of the service of God could become a snare and that God's kingdom mattered more than humankind's achievement—even in the realm of beauty. The error of pagan artists was not their view of art but their view of God, though the former showed the latter as surely as water flows downward.

Likewise the thronelike altar to Zeus on the acropolis of Pergamum moved God to say through the apostle John to the church at Pergamum, "I know where you dwell, where Satan's throne is" (Rev 2:13 RSV). So John could rightly urge: "Little children, keep yourself from idols" (1 Jn 5:21). It would be as much a mistake to read all of this as an absolute denunciation of art as it would be to see Christ's statement about hating one's father and mother (Lk 14:26) as a denunciation of the family.* Rather, we are seeing a biblical vision of a higher order of things in which both family and art should find their right and lovely place—an order in which all things find their relation to God, who in Christ is calling out a people for his name.

But like Ezekiel and Isaiah, the New Testament not only contains warnings about the false use of imagination but draws on imagery throughout the Bible and puts it in the service of its view of the last things in the book of Revelation. In our concentration on the literal meaning of that book, we often overlook the more immediate emotional impact of these images.

Art in Everyday Life

All of this suggests that the use of the arts in our ordinary life should not be treated lightly. On the one hand, we need to understand the ways in which beauty* and aesthetic forms generally move us. Beauty can seduce us to evil, as David learned, but ugliness can also tempt us to turn away from human need. So we cannot ignore the working of art and music in our lives, even if they have not figured prominently in our Christian conversation and training. Popular music, movies* and television* are important parts of the modern environment in which aesthetic forms are put in the service of worldviews* that may conflict with or sometimes support Christian values.* If we believe that all of life is to be brought under the lordship of Christ, we must learn to develop a Christian discernment in our use of contemporary media, for one way or another it will influence us.

On the other hand, we can positively seek to make even ordinary events of our lives into vehicles for honoring Christ. If God has given particular talents in the arts, these need to be developed and put in God's service—whether in the church or in the larger world of culture. But even if we do not feel a particular call or interest in the fine arts, we can still seek to make our lives into vehicles for God's own beauty. As well as our treating people with dignity and respect, this involves making our homes places where family and visitors can relax and know something of the peace and loveliness that God's reconciling grace has brought into our lives. The biblical record clearly implies that salvation will have a visual and aesthetic dimension as the Holy Spirit manifests God's grace throughout the fabric of our lives together—in our meals, conversations* around the fire and the flowers we place around.

Art and Spirituality: Glimmers of the Heavenly Kingdom

Art and beauty are important not only as nice additions to our lives but because there is a close relationship between the experience of these things and our worship of God, that is, between art and spirituality. While our chief calling* is to love God with all we are, art can train our sensitivity to people's pain and joy, both of which Scripture mandates. It can move us to a more profound praise of God and a deeper understanding of God's work in our lives, as our experience of a Bach chorale or a lovely Communion service testifies. Exposure to and involvement with great art make us better able to feel the heights and depths of human experience and so to become agents of God's love in a broken world. For all these reasons it is no accident that the connection between art and worship* has been so strong throughout the history of God's people.

There is another reason why art should play a central role in our lives as Christians. The imagery of the book of Revelation pictures the heavenly kingdom in terms of a great chorus or, better still, a great opera in which God and the redeemed from all the ages are involved. Revelation 5:11-14 and 6:9-10 picture people from every tongue and nation gathered around God's throne singing (and shouting) praise to God for the Lamb that was slain. It is no accident that the culmination of all history is described in terms of a great religious drama filled with both music and visual imagery. All of this gives us ample grounds for featuring arts prominently in our present lives. In fact, we might be justified in seeing all we do as a kind of grand rehearsal for that heavenly chorus. If the forms of art and music will honor God throughout all eternity, they can certainly be used now to point people to the source of all that is good and beautiful. Our goal should be to write over the whole of our lives the words that J. S. Bach put over each of his chorales: *soli Deo gloria*—"to the glory of God."

See also ARCHITECTURE, URBAN; BEAUTY; IMAGINATION; MUSIC; MUSIC, CHRISTIAN; VISION; WORSHIP.

References and Resources
D. Apostolos-Cappadona, ed., *Art, Creativity and the Sacred* (New York: Crossroad, 1984); J. S. Begbie, *Voicing Creation's Praise* (Edinburgh: T & T Clark, 1991); J. Dillenberger, *Style and Content in Christian Art* (New York: Abingdon, 1965); F. Gaebelein, *The Christian, the Arts and Truth* (Portland, Ore.: Multmomah, 1985); H. Rookmaaker, *The Creative Gift: Essays on Art and the Christian Life* (Weschester, Ill.: Cornerstone Books, 1981); E. Schaeffer, *The Art of Life* (Wheaton, Ill.: Good News Publishing, 1987).

William Dyrness

AUTHORITY, CHURCH

Authority is a major issue in the church today, as it is in society at large. Although the older generation tends to accept and respect authority in most spheres of life, members of the dominant baby-boom generation have constantly questioned it in their private and public lives. In place of standards and institutions they prefer to assemble their own values* from a range of sources or replace those in authority with people who have similar views to themselves. This is partly why public life is presently in such turmoil. There is less deference toward those in authority in the institutions of government, law* and education* and increasingly in science and medicine. The same is true in religion, both at the denominational level and in the local church.*

This distrust of authority is even more pronounced among the "buster" generation. Though the younger members of this group, teenagers, have often rebelled for a time against various forms of authority, among those who are older in this group is a more nuanced approach. They believe in a more egalitarian, participatory view of authority. For them authority has to be earned, and this has more to do with who a person is than with the position the person holds or what he or she has achieved. If this group encounters problems with authority, it is less likely to confront it or seek to change it directly. Its members will tend to sidestep it or sometimes create new structures for doing what they feel is important.

In an important book on the subject, sociologist Richard Sennett describes the fear of authority that many people have, often because they have been deceived by it too often. The main difficulty today is that we want to believe in strong figures, but we are not sure about their legitimacy. What complicates matters is that often in rejecting illegitimate authority, we remain tied to it in some way: we substitute complaining for doing something about it, allow our view of authority to be negatively defined by it or entertain illusions about life without authority. Two illegitimate forms that authority often takes are *paternalism*, the authority of false love, in which some make others dependent on them for meeting their needs, and *autonomy*, authority without love, in which some operate without recourse to others but in fact exercise disguised power over them. We need to renounce these false forms of authority, not only by disengaging from their power over us but also by refusing to define ourselves in terms of being their victims. The question then is to understand, respond to and practice authority in ways that are legitimate.

The Meaning and Types of Authority

The word *authority* is frequently misused or misunderstood. In common speech it is often identified with *authoritarian*. The latter refers to the illegitimate use of authority involving coercion or lack of justification. Some simply identify authority with the exercise of power, but they overlook the fact that authority is granted to people—through the traditions of a society, the casting of a vote or giving of voluntary allegiance—not just claimed or seized. Authority is a characteristic not just of the person exercising it but of those upon or with whom it is being exercised. It implies some degree of trust between the two that it will be duly accepted and responsibly used. In a quite genuine sense authority is entrusted by followers to leaders and held in trust by leaders for followers.

Discussions of the different types of authority owe much to the seminal writings of the sociologist Max Weber. Authority is generally classified according to three types.

Traditional authority. This is accorded to people or structures by the conventions, laws and accepted procedures of a society or organization.* Such is the case with the authority that parents have over their children, for they are entrusted with this by the society or extended family. In time this is transferred to children as they grow up to adulthood. In the church this is primarily the kind of authority that the pope has in the Roman Catholic Church.

Rational authority. This is accorded people or structures* by reasoned agreement. In the wider society this happens in the political arena through the ballet box or in a voluntary association through elections held at an annual meeting. In some denominations moderators are chosen as a result of the considered vote of a general assembly or council, and in some church polities senior pastors are called as a result of the careful deliberations of a selection committee.

Charismatic authority. This is accorded to certain key figures because of the beneficial influence they have or impressive results they achieve. A positive example of this in American society is Billy Graham, who is revered as a national, not merely religious, figure. In many newer congregations and denominations leadership* emerges and is recognized on charismatic grounds, as, for example, with John Wimber in the Vineyard movement.

These three types of authority are all what sociologists call *ideal types;* that is, they are ways of analyzing authority rather than exact descriptions of actual figures or structures. The present pope, for example, also has a degree of charismatic authority and for those persuaded by the logic of his encyclicals, rational authority as well. In time, all of these types of authority tend to become institutionalized or *routinized,* as with the decision by Billy Graham to pass over his evangelistic association to his son Franklin.

A Biblical Approach to Authority

The early church was interested in the way power* was interpreted and communicated, including the issue of authority, though it was not a major preoccupation for the early Christians. Paul, for example, really uses the word *authority* only in connection with one local church where he happened to be under challenge (2 Cor 10:8; 13:10; see in a different sense 1 Cor 9:4-18; 2 Cor 11:7-10; 2 Thess 3:9). Occasionally, however, issues did arise concerning what kind of power in the church was legitimate, how this was practiced and discerned, and who exercised it. The chief authority was, of course, God. Acknowledgment of God and obedience to God were paramount for every believer and congregation, and this took precedence over everything else. This does not settle the issue of authority, however, for while divine authority is sometimes opposed to all human authority (as the apostles said with regard to political leaders, "Judge for yourselves whether it is right in God's sight to obey you rather than God"—Acts 4:19), it is mostly mediated through human figures (even unbelieving rulers if they act rightly, since a ruler "is God's servant to do you good"; Rom 13:4). This is also the case in the church. The basic Protestant principle that each individual (or each congregation) owes basic allegiance to God should not be defined to mean that they can ignore all other forms of authority. The basic issue, then, is when, how and by whom does divine authority come to us through other people?

The best place to begin in deciding this is to look at the person of Christ, who is the image of the invisible God (Col 1:15). Christ at one and the same time exercises the Father's authority (Jn 5:19, 36; 10:36-38), yet Christ also is an authority for those who believe in him. Like the Father Jesus does not exercise authority in a coercive way. Although the church has sometimes forced people to become Christians or do what it wants, this is not the way Jesus operates (Rom 15:7, Gal 6:1). He desires our full-hearted assent and love. It is similar with the Holy Spirit, who operates with the consent of the minds and wills of the people of God, not, as in pagan worship, in ways that compel people to say or do something over which they have no control (1 Cor 12:1-3; 14:26-28). In other words, though divine authority is forceful, it is not forced on people. The basic reason for this is that it is based on love,* which courts and woos rather than compels, and is based on truth, which seeks to convince and persuade rather than dogmatically insist on its acceptance. This is the way the gospel came to us, and we received it. It was God's love, Christ's sacrifice and the Holy Spirit's drawing us that led us to embrace the gospel and give ourselves to it.

In the church this divine authority is mediated through all the members, but through some more than others. Whenever God speaks through any person in the church or works through some action they perform, that word and action have authority, as also does the person through whom they come. Sometimes it is a particular group in the church who represents the mind and character of Christ in a fuller way than others, though no group ever represents it entirely. Sometimes particular individuals in the church will demonstrate over a long period of time that much of what they say and do is reflective of God's nature and purposes, but God always remains operative through coworkers and other people in the congregation. This is why giving authority to just one person or to a group in the congregation is wrong. Paul is a good example here, for even though he brought the gospel to the churches, they should not listen to him—not even to an angel—if he departs from that original message (Gal 1:8-9). In other words, his authority is derived from God and obtains only so long as he is faithful to God's message. In another place, even though Paul is confident how a disciplinary case should be handled, he does not decide the issue himself but insists that the whole church come together to face the issue and deal with it (1 Cor 5:1-5). At the root, authority resides in the whole congregation: in this respect the early churches were a precursor of a democratic attitude toward politics,* with the exception that they were to come to a common mind on important matters, not to make decisions by a majority vote (2 Cor 13:11).

False ways of exerting authority come before us in the New Testament. These include people boasting about their preeminence, dazzling others with eloquence, or manipulating and controlling the church (2 Cor 10:12; 11:5-6, 16-19; compare 2 Cor 1:24). Another instance is people using authority to tear down good work God has done rather than to further build on it (2 Cor 10:8; 13:9). It is only those seeking to disrupt that good work whose arguments and actions ought to be destroyed (2 Cor 10:4). Genuine authority uses the language of persuasion (1 Cor 14:6) rather than command, as Paul himself does on almost every occasion (for a rare exception see 1 Cor 14:37), and rests upon love rather than a desire to control (Phil 8). Genuine authority also works with, rather than lords over, people (2 Cor 1:24) and comes to them primarily with "a gentle spirit" (1 Cor 4:21), only in extreme circumstances with a stern word. None of this means that the authority exercised is weak or lacking in power: lacking in the exercise of worldly power, yes, but of divine power, no (2 Cor 10:1-3).

This approach to authority is normative for us today. All too often it is the world's view of authority, and way of practicing it, that rules in the church. It has been vested in the hands of one person or a small group rather than in the whole congregation within which certain individuals and groups have considerable respect and influence. In relation to people in the church it has had more to do with controlling and submission than with equipping* and empowerment. It has operated most often according to a chain of command and prior decision rather than through argument and persuasion in search of the mind of the Spirit. Where this is the case, it is time things changed, not only because from a biblical point of view it is wrong but because current changes taking place in society make it unacceptable. Not only among the young but in the business world as well, echoes of biblical insights into authority are reappearing as credibility, not formal power, becomes the centerpiece of leadership and as collaborative approaches to leadership take the place of solo performers.

See also CHURCH CONFLICT; CHURCH DISCIPLINE; EQUIPPING; LEADERSHIP, CHURCH; LOVE; ORGANIZATION; POWER; SERVICE, WORKPLACE; STRUCTURES.

References and Resources

T. Adorno, *The Authoritarian Personality* (New York: Wiley, 1964); R. Banks, "Church Order and Government," in *Dictionary of Paul and His Letters,* ed. G. F. Hawthorne, R. P. Martin, D. G. Reid (Downers Grove, Ill.: InterVarsity Press, 1992) 131-37; R. Banks, *Paul's Idea of Community: The Early Churches in Their Cultural Setting* (Peabody, Mass.: Hendrickson, 1994); E. Best, *Paul and His Converts* (Edinburgh: T & T Clark, 1988); H. Doohan, *Leadership in Paul* (Wilmington, Del.: Michael Glazier, 1984); R. A. Heifetz, *Leadership Without Easy Answers* (Cambridge, Mass.: Belknap, 1994); R. Sennett, *Authority* (New York: Vintage, 1980); H. Von Campenhausen, *Ecclesiastical Authority and Spiritual Power in the Church of the First Three Centuries* (London: A. & C. Black, 1969).

Robert Banks

AUTOMOBILE

Along with the clock, the automobile has had a more profound effect on modern life than any other invention. Its impact is arguably greater than that of any idea or movement during the last century.

Most people are aware of its benefits; that is why the automobile remains so popular. Increasing concern has been expressed about its social costs through road deaths, pollution and urban sprawl. Studies have also been undertaken of its, sometimes deleterious, psychological effects on drivers. But little attention has been paid, especially in Christian circles, to its impact on individual attitudes and behavior, our sense of time and place, our significant relationships and our contact with the poor and needy.

Spread of the Automobile

The first gasoline-powered horseless carriage was sold in France in 1887. Sales followed in other countries, including the United States in 1896, soon thereafter. By 1910 almost half a million cars were on the road in America. In Europe cars tended to remain a sign of social status. North America became the leading automobile culture. Registration had already begun in 1901, and by 1902 the American Automobile Association (AAA) was launched. The decisive factor in the democratization of the car was the introduction from 1908 onward of the Ford Model T. Other giant car manufacturers, such as General Motors, rapidly emerged. Within two decades over half the families in America owned cars. In other countries this took longer, and everywhere the process was slowed by the Great Depression.

But during the thirties the automobile remained the major unifying force in America. By the end of the decade public preference for it was resulting in the attrition of public transportation,* which was a harbinger of the future. Though World War II curtailed the use of the automobile, at its end the car-propelled exodus to the suburbs, modestly begun twenty years before, received a massive impetus. Spurred by the example of the autobahns in Germany, in 1956

Congress passed the ambitious Interstate Highway Act. By the late seventies interstate highways were largely in place. By then two-car, and then three-car or more, families became the norm. Traffic density increased despite more roads, insurance* costs soared, and road deaths continued to mount. During this whole period in turn the home,* job, shopping,* leisure* and church* all became automobilized. Increasingly these revolved around the automobile as it played a key role in determining where suburbs, workplaces,* malls, entertainment* centers and churches were located. People also based their decisions on where to reside, earn a living, shop, play* and meet for worship on the basis of the automobile.

Advantages of the Automobile

In the early days the car was seen to have many advantages. It was cleaner than the horse, eliminating the problem of great quantities of manure and urine that were daily deposited on streets (2.5 million and 65,000 tons respectively in New York City). Despite all the initial concerns about speed, automobiles were also considered safer. They were not only more reliable but more convenient than horses and horse-drawn public transportation. As well they opened up the benefits of the countryside and seashore to harried city* dwellers. In particular they offered greater flexibility and choice, were held to keep the family together and could cover increasingly larger distances in shorter time.

Automobiles are still largely valued for the same reasons, even if there is now more realism attached to their ownership. There are other reasons people appreciate them so much. They enable many to live away from suburbs and city in more pleasant surroundings. They open up new opportunities for study or work. Indeed, as the idea of the mobile office complete with telephone,* fax machine, word processor and printer catches on, a growing number of people now work out of their cars. The automobile turns the whole city into a huge mall and enables people to call on a large number of services and enjoy a diverse range of leisure opportunities.

Significance of the Automobile
People have always valued the automobile apart from these practical advantages. Many of the reasons touch on deep chords in the human psyche. The car is often a symbol of status and wealth,* a way of informing others of our place on the social and economic scale. It is a symbol of individual freedom and independence, one of the reasons car pools are so difficult to get off the ground. The car is a symbol of identity; for men of masculinity, an expression of our actual or fanciful self-image. It is a symbol of adulthood and citizenship,* since it is in having a car rather than gaining the vote that a young person becomes a full participant in modern society. It is also a symbol of reward and punishment, for being grounded is the ultimate punishment for a teenager, and having your car repossessed is the ultimate deprivation for an adult.

The automobile is also an embodiment of personal priorities and dreams, as advertisements* and movies* constantly remind us. It is a place where we can play out many of our fantasies about exercising power, confronting danger and overcoming fear. The car ushers us into a private, climate-controlled, technological world that increases our withdrawal from the environment as well as from neighborliness and community*: children especially become conditioned to this from an early age. At the national level the automobile is a barometer of economic well-being and progress—as the saying goes, "When Detroit sneezes, the country catches a cold." With the spread and merger of the largest automobile manufacturers and the advent of the "world car," the automobile has become a key indicator of the globalization* of business. Keeping supply lines of fuel open can be a major—in the case of the Gulf War perhaps *the* major—cause of war.

Disadvantages of the Automobile
In view of the ambiguous role of the car, it is not surprising that already by the late 1920s some people were beginning to have second thoughts about it. The automobile seemed to be dividing the family more than uniting it, congesting cities as much as decentralizing them, generating regulations as well as increasing freedom and downgrading public transportation instead of complementing it. The American humorist Will Rogers once remarked, "Good luck, Mr. Ford. It will take us a hundred years to tell whether you helped or hurt us. But one thing is certain: you didn't leave us where you found us." Serious criticism of the car surfaced again through Ralph Nader and others during the fifties. Increasingly psychologists and others noticed the strange effect upon people of getting behind the wheel. Drivers tend to become one with their machine, an extension of it. As David Engwicht says, "Metamorphosis takes place as the driver is transformed from homo-sapiens to homo-machine; both hearts of steel united in their drive for efficiency, speed, and power. The driver becomes the driven" (p. 118). How else do we explain the greater than usual competitiveness, rudeness and carelessness so many otherwise equable people exhibit (*see* Commuting)?

During the last decades of the twentieth century, the emergence of the Green movement has resulted in other protests. A photographic exhibition from West

Germany entitled *Automobile Nightmare* visually documented the century-old impact of the car on many aspects of modern life. The evocative captions and text accompanying various collections of photographs told the story: "from life in the streets to danger to life," "cutting up the land and killing off the forests," "the escape from weekday traffic jams to weekend traffic jams," "from pretty roads to superhighways," "smelling the gas instead of the flowers," "animal slaughter and human sacrifice," "paving over the city," "the new forest of concrete posts and traffic signs," "the long commute to distant suburbs," "where have all the front gardens gone?" "pedestrians last," "give us our daily car." One of the key victims of the automobile is the experience of local neighborhood.* Since people drive to and from their homes, they do not see, greet or talk with each other much anymore; since they go greater distances to shop and relax, the corner store disappears, and the neighborhood park empties, so removing the chief hubs of local neighborhood life; since residents are somewhere else during the day, crime* increases as houses become easy pickings for burglars. Even where people stay at home, as traffic density on streets increases, the number and quality of relationships people have with others on the block dramatically decline.

The high social cost of the automobile has now begun to register on middle-class citizens. (1) The automobile is the largest cause of smog. In most places the average car puts into the air each year the equivalent of its weight in pollutants. Automobile emissions are wasting the forests of Europe, are degrading marine life in the Atlantic coastal areas and are the major contributor to the overall greenhouse effect. An estimated loss of between $2 billion and $4 billion affects four of the main cash crops in the United States. (2) Automobiles kill and maim forty times as many people per miles traveled as do planes and buses and eighty times as many as travel on trains. The number of people killed by the automobile worldwide per year is somewhere between 300,000 and 500,000, and in Europe and North America alone there are more than 3,000,000 injuries annually. It is estimated that 30,000 people die in the United States each year from the carcinogenic gases that rise from the automobile excreta. (3) Through the building of roads, parking lots, garages, median strips and gas stations, at least one-third of the land area in major cities is now given over to the car. In some places, for example Los Angeles, this rises to over one-half. (4) Freeways, once so full of promise, now move during rush hours at the pace of a bicycle or, in some cities, at little more than walking pace. The car discriminates against the old, the infirm, the handicapped, the poor—all those who cannot afford to buy one or who are frightened to cross busy roads. Automobiles and roadside vans are increasing congestion in major national parks to urban proportions and threatening their delicate ecological balance.

Sanctification of the Automobile

Most serious thinking about the automobile assumes that it is a morally neutral object that is sometimes used by individuals or manufacturers in adverse or destructive ways. The basic task is to reduce its moral ill effects. On an individual basis, this involves educating drivers to have different attitudes and improved skills and punishing intentional or drink-driven abuse of the car. At the institutional level, it involves compelling manufacturers to produce safer and cleaner cars and pressuring urban planners and federal agencies to provide better and ecofriendly roads. Very little thinking has focused on the morally ambiguous character of the automobile itself, on its inherent shadow side. All significant technological* inventions have this two-sided character and possess an inbuilt capacity to do both good and harm. An example is this: given their speed, it was inevitable that cars would kill animals crossing roads. There may be ways in which this can be lessened, but there is no way it can be prevented.

We must seek to make the automobile more a servant than a master, more an instrument than an idol. Rather than our allowing it to captivate us, we need to bring our attitudes and use of it fully captive to Christ (2 Cor 10:5). Instead of conforming to its demands and possibilities, we need to be "transformed by the renewing" of our attitudes toward it (Rom 12:2). We need to work out ways of loving our neighbor and caring for the creation in and through our automobiles. What does this mean in practice? It involves more than driving safely in a way that conserves energy, more than using our cars to get people to and from church, to visit the old or needy and to service worthy causes. For most people, it involves less than giving up the car altogether. There are times—as for over ten years in our own family—when it is right to go without a car. For some people this may even be a kind of prophetic calling.

Our basic starting point is this. We are not the owners of our automobiles but stewards of them. They are one of several ways of getting around granted us by God. As such, they are a gift from God for our own benefit and for the benefit of others. From this we may extract some practical guidelines: (1) Since we are able to walk, use bicycles (the most energy-efficient form of transportation) and take public transportation, we should use the car only when it is more appropriate to do so. Speed and convenience are not the only issues here. Other

considerations are fitness, tension levels, enjoying company and opportunity to reflect or pray. (2) We should buy cars that will be more economical in use of gas and other basic materials, most appropriate for the number of people traveling and least damaging to the human and created environment. (3) Given that cars absorb approximately a quarter of people's weekly or annual budget (it now costs around fifty cents a mile to travel by car, which is more expensive than by taxi or airplane), we should purchase and use cars that will result in as little drain on our financial resources as possible. (4) Combine journeys to different locations in the same or adjacent areas so that one longer trip takes the place of several shorter ones, and choose places to live, work, shop, relax and worship that require the minimum of car use.

Here are some more radical ways of understanding and utilizing the automobile. (5) Where possible we should lessen rush hour frustrations and increase community by car-pooling to work, as well as explore ways of car-pooling to shops and church. (6) Examine whether it is really necessary to have more than one car in the household, or consider the possibility of sharing a car with a fellow resident or friend so that financial costs are shared. (7) If the opportunity arises, consider replacing commuting* with telecommuting by working some or most of the time at home. (8) Fast occasionally from the car, perhaps one workday each week or one day each weekend or month, breaking our dependence on it and supporting public transportation, on which the poor and needy are dependent.

Congregations also have a contribution to make here. They can give instruction on the responsible Christian use of the car, encourage car-pooling of members, provide congregational cars or buses where multiple staffs or needy members are involved and decentralize larger churches into regional ones so that people have less distances to travel. Those who work in transportation-related occupations have other things to offer. They can keep up the pressure for manufacturers to provide vehicles powered by alternative sources of energy, encourage more effective rapid transportation systems, give inducements to firms that reward employees for carpooling or leaving the car at home, develop computerized transportation controls to improve efficiency and safety, experiment with dial-a-ride vans and buses in local areas or to busy destinations.

Putting the car in its proper place ultimately requires a combination of individual, group and institutional responses to an incredibly complex but increasingly urgent area of modern life. Difficult though it may be, we must make the effort. In this respect we should "not be conformed to this world," as for the most part we are, "but transformed through the renewing of [our] minds" (Rom 12:2 NRSV). If we were to follow through on this, then one day we might begin to see a reflection of the idyllic urban situation pictured in the book of Revelation. In the "holy" and "faithful" city, "once again old men and women, so old that they use canes when they walk, will be sitting in the city squares. And the streets will again be full of boys and girls playing" (Zech 8:3-5 GNB).

See also COMMUTING; ECOLOGY; MOBILITY; TECHNOLOGY.

References and Resources

T. Bendixson, *Instead of Cars* (London: Temple Smith, 1974); M. L. Berger, *The Devil Wagon in God's Country: The Automobile and Social Change in Rural America* (Hamden, Conn.: Archon, 1979); D. Engwicht, *Reclaiming Our Cities and Towns: Better Living with Less Traffic* (Philadelphia: New Society, 1993); J. J. Flink, *The Car Culture* (Boston: MIT Press, 1975); D. Lewis and L. Goldstein, eds., *The Automobile and American Culture* (Ann Arbor: University of Michigan Press, 1983); J. McInnes, *The New Pilgrims* (Sydney: Albatross, 1980); Organization for Economic and Cultural Development, *The Automobile and the Environment* (Boston: MIT Press, 1978); A. J. Walter, "Addicted to Mobility: The Morality of the Motor Car," *Third Way,* 21 January 1985, 21-23.

Robert Banks

B

BACKPACKING

Backpacking is carrying the necessities of food and shelter from one place to another. In some form this has always been a human necessity: the first men and women had no choice but to carry their few belongings when they traveled. Much that we call *progress* consists in our development of ways of avoiding such work. Through taming animals (beasts of burden), building boats, inventing the wheel, then (more recently) harnessing the energy of fossil fuels, we have nearly escaped the necessity of carrying our own burdens.

Ironically, it is only as the need for backpacking has vanished that its attractiveness as a recreation* has emerged. As a popular recreation, backpacking is only a few decades old (though the roots of modern backpacking go back as far as nineteenth-century romanticism in both Europe and America).

What is the point of backpacking? Certainly one of the most obvious reasons for the popularity of the activity is that it is the only means of access into the few remaining wilderness areas. The value of *wilderness* (which, in the words of the U.S. Wilderness Act of 1964, is a region where "man is a visitor and does not remain") has also increased significantly in recent times. Both the popularity of backpacking and the new value placed on wilderness—the places where most North American backpacking takes place—can be traced to a disillusionment with, and a reaction against, the alienating consequences of modern (and increasingly urban) civilization.

From a biblical viewpoint, the appeal of backpacking can easily be understood. We were made for relationship: with creation,* with each other and with our Creator. One need only look at rush hour on a modern city highway (with thousands of speeding cars, most carrying one person) to realize how profoundly our preferred modern transportation technology* has distanced us from each other and (most obviously) from the sounds, scents and textures of creation. Less obvious, but just as important, is the way in which the ease of modern transportation distances us from our own bodies,* which were made to be used (a fact that the proliferation of exercise and fitness centers makes plain).

The overall thrust of modern technology is to make things easy for us, to remove from us the created limitations of space and time. On the most profound level, then, backpacking—and the respectful experience of creation that it enables—is an attempt to recover the fact that we are *creatures* and are made for relationship.

Backpacking requires that we strip down what is needed for living to the bare necessities of food, water and shelter. It reminds us that we are finite, limited and that we depend ultimately on God and the Creator's gifts for our life.

It also opens for us the inexhaustible sensual richness of the created world. Motorized travel* limits our appreciation of creation almost entirely to the visual. But in backpacking all the senses are awakened. Thus it restores our relationship not only with creation but with our physical body.

Some also feel that the solitude and vulnerability that backpacking invites make them more open to the Creator. Indeed, many who have turned their backs on all organized religion find wilderness backpacking an intensely spiritual experience. The importance of wilderness sojourns in the Bible—whether of the Israelites, David, Elijah or Jesus—underlines the spiritual importance of that recovery of the value of solitude, creation and physical work.* That value is caught in the significance of words like *pilgrim, journey* and *sojourn,* words which are deepened in their meaning by the ancient experience of backpacking.

Modern equipment—formfitting packs, good rain gear, lightweight stoves and waterproof tents—can take some of the hardship and danger out of backpacking. (Though another danger is that the fascination with equipment turns backpacking into another excuse for being a consumer.) Persons—and families—who are new to the activity might be wise to make their first trip with someone who has more experience.

See also CAMPING; CREATION; ECOLOGY; LEISURE; RECREATION; SABBATH; TRAVELING.

References and Resources

S. P. Bratton, *Christianity, Wilderness and Wildlife: The Original Desert Solitaire* (Scranton, Penn.: University of Scranton Press, 1993); H. Manning, *Backpacking: One Step at a Time* (New York: Vintage Books, 1986); R. Nash, *Wilderness and the American Mind* (3rd ed.; New Haven, Conn.: Yale University Press, 1982).

Loren Wilkinson

BAPTISM

As one of the two sacraments* ordained by Jesus, baptism has a direct relationship to the theology and spirituality of daily life because (1) it takes a simple everyday experience—washing,* bathing or cleaning—and elevates it to a special means of grace, thus giving us a lens through which we can see God's love for us; (2) it brings meaning by symbolizing and certifying that we are not alone but are truly members of the people of God, God's true laity*; (3) as a special means of grace, baptism introduces us to the realm of the Spirit by which we are empowered to live extraordinary lives in ordinary situations. This article will consider the confusing testimony of the church on the matter, the examples of Jesus and John, a Christian understanding of baptism, the vexed question of its administration and, finally, the significance of baptism with the Holy Spirit.

One Baptism or Three?

There is one baptism (Eph 4:5), but you would never guess as much from the way Christians talk about it. For the Catholic, it was his baptism as an infant that brought him into the church and made him a Christian. For the Baptist, her baptism was by immersion, administered after profession of faith. For the Pentecostal, baptism was in or by the Holy Spirit, normally accompanied by the gift of tongues: this Spirit baptism eclipses all else. All three are saying something important. All three are stressing an important aspect of Christian baptism.

Churches in the Catholic tradition see baptism as the way of gaining membership* in the people of God. Just as you entered the old covenant people of Israel by circumcision, so you enter the new covenant people of God by baptism (Acts 2:40-41; Gal 3:27-29). This noble view, strong on God's act of incorporation, is weak on response. If we think of it as the only strand in Christian initiation, it degenerates into magic.

Churches in the Baptist tradition see baptism as a seal on the profession of faith, and that is clearly the emphasis in Acts 16:31-33. The church is the company of believers. This view is strong on response, but very individualistic. It makes human commitment almost more significant than divine initiative. Moreover it is very cerebral: it makes little room for those too young or too handicapped to make a decisive response.

Churches in the Pentecostal tradition see baptism very differently. The church is not so much a historical entity (which may well be apostate), not a company of believers (which may mean little more than intellectual assent). No. Reception of the life-giving Spirit of God is the authentic mark of the church. Baptism with the Holy Spirit is the only baptism worth having (Rom 8:9). Important though this emphasis undoubtedly is, it too is deficient. Cut off from historical continuity it can be, and often is, very divisive. Cut off from any serious emphasis on the content of the faith, it can easily go off the rails in doctrine or morals. There is such a thing as church history and Christian doctrine. The Spirit of God, the Word of God and the people of God need to walk hand in hand.

These different strands belong together. We find them all in Acts, where baptism is sometimes seen as the agency of salvation (Acts 2:38), sometimes as the seal of faith (16:31-33) and sometimes as the sovereign anointing of the Holy Spirit (10:44-48). The Catholics are right to see baptism as the objective mark of God's great rescue achieved on Calvary, to which we can make no contribution or addition. The Baptists are right to see in baptism a personal response, in repentance and faith, to the grace of God. The Pentecostals are right to see baptism as the

way we are ushered into the world of the Spirit. Baptism is as deep and broad as the salvation of which it is the sacrament.

What Can We Learn from the Baptism of John?

John's baptizing caused an immense stir. It was a mark of repentance. No pedigree, no good deeds, could bring one into the coming kingdom of God: the only path lay through the baptismal waters of repentance. And that was very humbling.

Moreover, the baptism of John pointed ahead to the forgiveness of sins and the gift of the Spirit that Jesus, the Messiah, would bring. It was also a very public and a very humiliating act. Never before had Jews been baptized: baptism was one of the initiation ceremonies for Gentiles joining the people of God.

And finally, the baptism of John was decisive. A person either went through the waters of God's judgment in the Jordan or else would have to face it in stark reality later on. In all these ways, John's baptism, a landmark in Judaism, was an advertisement of the main feature: Christian baptism.

What Can We Learn from the Baptism of Jesus?

In his baptism Jesus identified with sinners, something which even John the Baptist found scandalous (Mt 3:14). It was an anticipation of Calvary, when his cross was to be his baptism—in blood (Lk 12:50). We cannot enter with Jesus into the unspeakable agonies of bearing the world's sin, but we can and should share in other aspects of his baptism.

The baptism of Jesus was an assurance of sonship (Mt 3:17). So it is with the Christian, adopted into the family of God (Rom 8:15-16). It was a commissioning for costly service. The voice from heaven at Jesus' baptism, "You are my Son; in you I am well pleased," was a combination of two significant Old Testament texts (Ps 2:7; Is 42:1). Jesus, the Son of God, is also the Servant of God. Those servant songs in Isaiah, culminating in Isaiah 53, sketch the path of ministry* and suffering. For the Christian, ministry and suffering are also inescapable: baptism points inexorably to that calling.*

Christian baptism embraces us in the threefold baptism of Jesus—the baptism of repentance in the Jordan, the baptism of rescue on the cross and the baptism of power in the Holy Spirit. In our own baptism we see these same three realities. It calls us to repentance. It shows us where pardon is to be had. And it offers us the power of the Holy Spirit.

How Are We to Understand Christian Baptism?

In the light of these precedents of John and Jesus, how are we to understand Christian baptism? It is no optional extra: Jesus solemnly enjoined it upon us at the climax of his life on earth (Mt 28:18-20).

1. Christian baptism embodies God's challenge to repentance and faith. It cannot be conducted without some expression of both. Baptism says to us, *You are unclean. You need washing. I can do that for you. But you must change your ways.* It takes us to the heart of the gospel.

2. Christian baptism offers us the blessings* of the new covenant. God approaches us in utterly unmerited grace. We respond in repentance and faith. And baptism signs over to us the blessings of the new covenant: forgiveness, adoption, servanthood, the Holy Spirit, the new birth, justification and the promise of life after death.*

3. Christian baptism plunges us into the death and resurrection of Jesus. We are brought to the point of death to the old life, which had little room for God, and the dawning of new life as the Holy Spirit enters our hearts. This dying and rising life is the essence of Christianity. It

is what we are called to—and empowered for. It has a profound impact on the way we behave. So baptism is the gateway to a complete revolution in morals and lifestyle, even though we shall never achieve perfection in this life. It embodies our aim to live out the life of Christ in our own daily circumstances.

4. Christian baptism initiates us into the worldwide church. It is the adoption certificate into the family of God. It is the mark of belonging, the badge of membership. That may not always be obvious in traditionally Christian lands. But if your background is in Judaism or Islam, your baptism is the Rubicon. It is the essential dividing line.

5. Christian baptism appoints us to work for the kingdom of God. It is God's appointing for service in this world. For baptism is indeed a sign of the kingdom. It shows that we have surrendered to our King, and it is the uniform we wear as we go about the King's business. Through our baptism, then, we are commissioned to engage in active ministry for Christ wherever we find ourselves—in our homes,* neighborhoods,* workplaces,* leisure* activities and cities.*

6. Christian baptism does something! This New Testament emphasis is often overlooked by Protestants, many of whom prefer to think it symbolizes something. But the New Testament uses some strongly instrumental language about baptism. It is through baptism that we enter the "name" of the Trinity (Mt 28:19) and thus are saved (1 Pet 3:21), regenerated (Jn 3:5), united with Christ in his death and resurrection (Rom 6:3-8; Col 2:12) and incorporated into his body (1 Cor 12:13). To be sure, several of these references mention the Holy Spirit (the divine agency) or faith (the human agency), but there is an undeniably instrumental flavor about the language used by the biblical writers. This should not surprise us. Justification, re-

generation, incorporation into Christ, baptism—these are all different images of the way God makes us his own.

Baptism, then, is an efficacious sign of the new life. But of course it is not unconditionally efficacious, any more than a wedding ring is! It was not efficacious with Simon Magus (Acts 8:13, 21-23) nor with some at Corinth (1 Cor 10:1-6). But it is intended to bring about what it symbolizes. It is a palpable mark of belonging, like the wedding ring or the adoption certificate. Luther grasped this clearly. When he was tempted to doubt his own faith, he recalled the standing emblem of God's faithfulness marked upon him as an infant. He cried out in confidence, *Baptizatus sum,* "I have been baptized," realizing that God's faithfulness was even more important than his faith.

How Was Baptism Administered?

Whether the early Christians sprinkled or immersed candidates for baptism is not a matter of supreme importance. They insisted on baptizing in water in the name of the Trinity, but the amount of water is nowhere specified. It is not a matter that should divide Christians. Sometimes a river was at hand, and they would doubtless immerse. Sometimes it would take place in a home, like that of the Philippian jailer, where immersion was not possible. One of the early murals in the Catacombs shows John the Baptist and Jesus standing waist deep in the Jordan with John *pouring* water over the head of Jesus: both methods are depicted!

But does not the word *baptizō* mean "immerse"? Not necessarily: it can mean "wash" (Lk 11:38). The early Christians seem to have been very relaxed about the mode of baptism. The very early *Didache* says, "Baptize in the name of the Father and of the Son and of the Holy Spirit, in running water. But if thou hast not run-

ning water, baptize in other water. And if thou canst not in cold, then in warm. But if thou hast neither, pour water three times upon the head in the name of the Father and of the Son and of the Holy Spirit" (*Didache* 7:1).

Who Received Baptism?

Adult believers certainly received baptism, and they are primary in any theological reflection about baptism. But probably children, wives and slaves in the household were also baptized when the head of the household professed faith (Acts 16:31, 33). Children were sacramentally admitted to the Old Testament church (Gen 17); whole families of proselytes, including children and slaves, were baptized into the Jewish faith. The attitude of acceptance that Jesus displayed to tiny children would have helped (Mk 10:13-16). Infant baptism does emphasize the objectivity of the gospel: what Christ did for us at Calvary is marked upon us, whether we choose to respond to it or not. And it emphasizes the initiative of God, reaching out to us before we ever think of reaching out to him. But it is a practice open to gross abuse if it does not take place in the context of faith. It should not be administered indiscriminately, but only with careful teaching of the obligations it calls for and the blessings it offers. And it requires personal reaffirmation on behalf of the candidate when he or she is confirmed.

Believer's baptism stresses that baptism is the Christian badge of belonging, not a social ceremony for the very young. It gives a clear, datable time of commitment. It produces far less in the way of fallout than infant baptism does, and it is a powerful evangelistic occasion. My prayer is that Baptists and pedobaptists may grow in mutual understanding of the strength of the other's position and respect, rather than criticize, one another.

Can You Repeat Baptism?

No. Baptism is as unrepeatable as justification or adoption, of which it is the sacrament. The early Christians were clear about this. There is an ambiguous longing for rebaptism today. People very often feel that their baptism as an infant was deficient. There was too little faith around, too little water, too little feeling, too little chance for public confession of faith. The desire to do it again, and do it properly, often springs from the modern cult of feelings. But baptism cannot be done again, any more than birth* can. It is ever to be remembered but never to be repeated. Baptism may be reaffirmed. It may even be reenacted: "If you are not already baptized, I baptize you . . ." But it cannot be repeated.

What Is Baptism with the Holy Spirit?

There are seven references to baptism with the Holy Spirit in the New Testament: Matthew 3:11; Mark 1:8; Luke 3:16; John 1:33; Acts 1:5; 11:15-16; 1 Corinthians 12:13. The first six of these draw the distinction between John the Baptist's baptism which was looking forward to Jesus and the baptism Jesus would himself give "in" (or "with" or "by") the Holy Spirit. These six point forward, then, to Christian initiation. It is the same with the seventh, where Paul reminds the Corinthian charismatics and noncharismatics alike that they had all been baptized by one Spirit into the one body. So none of the New Testament references points to a second and more profound experience. That is not for a moment to deny that such subsequent experiences may and do occur. Sometimes they are the most momentous spiritual experiences in our lives. But it simply causes confusion to call them baptism. As we have seen, the Pentecostals are right about the importance of having the Spirit to come and flood your life; they are wrong to call that experience "baptism in the Holy Spirit" in contrast to "baptism in water." The Bible never speaks of it that way.

Although there are not many references to baptism in the New Testament, it was clearly critically important to early Christians as the sacrament of initiation. It sealed for them their unrepeatable incorporation into Christ. It pointed them to the dying and rising life that Christians are called to live. It joined them to brothers and sisters throughout the world. And it released in them the power of the Holy Spirit so long as they claimed in faith the gift God so generously offered them.

See also COMMUNION; MEMBERSHIP, CHURCH; SACRAMENTS; SPIRITUAL GROWTH.

References and Resources

P. R. Beasley-Murray, *Baptism in the New Testament* (Grand Rapids: Eerdmans, 1962); D. Bridge and D. Phypers, *Waters That Divide: The Baptism Debate* (Downers Grove, Ill.: InterVarsity Press, 1977); G. W. Bromiley, *Children of Promise* (Grand Rapids: Eerdmans, 1979); M. Green and R. P. Stevens, *New Testament Spirituality* (Guildford, U.K.: Eagle, 1994); P. K. Jewett, *Infant Baptism and the Covenant of Grace* (Grand Rapids: Eerdmans, 1979); L. H. Stookey, *Baptism: Christ's Act in the Church* (Nashville: Abingdon, 1982); W. Ward, "Baptism in Theological Perspective," *Review and Expositor* 65, no. 1 (1968).

Michael Green

BEAUTY

Often when we're standing before a breathtaking sunset or after we've heard the final notes of a great symphony, the word *beautiful* springs naturally to our lips. What exactly do we mean by this, and what is the place of beauty in our lives as Christians? Some would argue that our discipleship should be difficult and we should not seek ease or beauty, while others believe that beauty is a snare that can lead us away from God (*see* Art). Yet most Christians sense in their hearts that beauty—especially seen in creation*—is somehow a gift from God, and that we should enjoy this gift in ways that honor God. Where did our ideas of beauty come from, and how can we think about this in God-honoring ways?

The Earliest Ideas of Beauty

Most of our ideas about beauty, at least in Europe and America, have been formed under the influence of Greek philosophy. In the field called aesthetics beauty was, at least before the eighteenth century, the dominant idea, more central even than consideration of what we call today art. As this was first expressed in the work of Plato (especially in his dialogue *Philebus*), beauty is a property of particular objects—specifically ordered in a balanced way with an internal unity—that can be known by the mind. In Plato's view this order is a reflection of a reality existing independently of our knowledge, whether or not the order is precisely comprehensible. Plotinus, a follower of Plato, included a spiritual dimension in beauty, defining it as that which "irradiates symmetry rather than symmetry itself" (Enneads, 7) and so moves us. This added the important idea that beauty involves the whole of the object or event and so cannot be defined only by reference to particular qualities.

Modern ideas of beauty did not come to expression until the eighteenth century. There, as a result of the empiricism of John Locke, beauty was described not as something inherent in the object but as an experience of the observer. Since it was understood as a subjective (rather than objective) quality, the way was open to include ideas like "sublime" (that which arouses amazement or even horror). Beauty no longer played the central role in aesthetics, and it took its place alongside other aesthetic qualities. Art objects that were successful were no longer required to be beautiful in any traditional sense but could move viewers by their ugliness or simply the power of their imagery. It is this development in what we call modern art that leaves many Christians (and many non-Christians for that matter) puzzled and unsure about the role of art and beauty in their lives.

A Biblical Approach to Beauty

What does beauty mean in the Bible? Can we find there some help in sorting out this modern difficulty? In the Old Testament there are as many as seven different word groups that refer to events and objects that are beautiful or splendid. What strikes one at once is that these words almost never refer to separate experiences that we might call "aesthetic experiences" in the modern sense. Rather, various facets of Israel's life are termed beautiful. In people and nations beauty often is associated with what is honorable or what sparks admiration: "Babylon [is] the jewel [beauty] of kingdoms" (Is 13:19 RSV). There is a word for splendor that is used of the beautiful robes of the priests (Ex 28:2) and is associated with the pomp and display of the king (Esther 1:4) or even with God's acts of deliverance (Is 63:12). This beauty God strips from his people during the exile (Ps 78:61), though it will characterize them again in the last days (Jer 33:9).

Other words refer to "delight" or "desire" and speak of the attraction of beauty and often the greed or lust that beautiful things can inspire in us, just as Achan coveted gold (Josh 7:21). Or beauty can be simply what is fitting, in the sense of suitable to the situation. For example, a word for beauty describes an old man's gray head (Prov 16:31) and a young man's strength (Prov 20:29). In this sense praise "suits" the righteous (Ps 33:1), the feet of the evangelist are "lovely" (Is 52:7), words spoken appropriately are "seemly" or "lovely" (Prov 16:24), as is bread eaten in secret (Prov 9:17). This last reference underlines the fact that aesthetics and ethical qualities are inevitably interrelated; the Bible knows nothing of beauty that is not integrated into the larger purposes of God for his people.

This integration of beauty into the whole of life and its (ultimately) moral purposes is seen clearly in the virtual absence of the idea of ugliness from the Bible. The nearest equivalent is the notion of a blemish or defect, which can be physical or moral (*see* Pollution). A blemish is what keeps anything from being what God intended it to be. This integration of the aesthetic, the ethical and the religious can be seen most clearly in the application of words related to beauty to God's presence in Zion or Jerusalem (Ps 50:2), the place or experience of worship* (Ps 93:5; compare "Holiness is the beauty of thy house" NEB), and especially to God's people when in the last days they dwell with him and reflect his character (Is 44:23; compare RSV and 46:13; Ps 16:11; Rev 21:24). These last verses imply that the very process of redemption, focusing on the death and resurrection of Jesus, has as a part of its purpose a restoration of the integrity of the created order wherein it will again be characterized by beauty and wholeness.

So while we are not encouraged to seek beauty for its own sake, it is clear from Scripture that obedience to God and God's Word leads to a life which is meant to display beauty as well as goodness. Good works (the Greek word used in the New Testament can also mean "beautiful works") are to characterize our lives so that people will glorify the Father who is in heaven (Mt 5:16). It is in this context that we may understand Paul's advice to the Philippians: "If anything is excellent or praiseworthy—think about such things" (Phil 4:8).

A Christian Perspective on Beauty

This biblical material gives us a perspective in which we can understand modern subjective notions of beauty. We might put this in terms of three comments.

First, it is clear that God's purposes for the Christian embrace the entirety of our existence. Just as our lives should show the righteousness of God's character, they also ought to reflect God's beauty. Our brief study makes it clear that this is meant to be in and through our ordinary world of work* and play.* While experiences of art in concert halls and museums may play a part in our "training in righteousness," their impact is to be felt in how we dress, the way we decorate our home (*see* Adornment), even (or especially) in how we treat one another from day to day (*see* Love). As Calvin Seerveld says, for example, in his treatment of the calling of beauticians: "Not every person can be 'beautiful'— whatever that means; but everyone has the capacity, even duty, to be groomed, and that includes aesthetic enhancement as well as hygienic care" (p. 28). All of these dimensions of life can certainly be characterized as lovely or beautiful if they are done in sensitive and God-honoring ways, because God made the world to show his glory and redemption, and we are to retrieve some of that splendor.

Second, the Bible makes it clear that beauty, for the believer, focuses ultimately on our experiences of corporate worship and especially on our life with God. It is for this reason that Christians through the centuries have built beautiful buildings (*see* Church Buildings), painted altarpieces and composed chorales (*see* Music, Christian) both as expressions of their faith and as symbols of God's own glory. Paul's advice about making our worship orderly (and decent) when placed in the larger biblical context implies that our church* and community life ought to reflect what the Bible calls the "beauty of holiness."

And third, we must remember that our life together, even as believers, is still "defective." As John puts this in his letter to the early church, though we are already God's children, it does not yet appear what we shall be. We only know we will be like God (1 Jn 3:2). For this reason we are not surprised at the ugliness that our sin causes, though we are often made to suffer because of it. But at the same time we can take the moments of joy and beauty that God gives us as an anticipation of what life will be like when God wipes away every tear from our eyes. It is for this reason that beauty, while not as important to the Christian as faith, hope or love, can be a bearer of all these gifts and thus help draw people to worship the Lord.

References and Resources
M. Beardsley, *Aesthetics: Problems in the Philosophy of Criticism* (New York: Harcourt Brace, 1958); W. Dyrness, "Aesthetics in the Old Testament: Beauty in Context," *Journal of the Evangelical Theological Society* 28 (December 1985) 421-32; T. Howard, *Splendor in the Ordinary* (Wheaton, Ill.: Tyndale, 1976); H. R. Rookmaaker, *The Creative Gift: Essays on Art and the Christian Life* (Westchester, Ill.: Crossway, 1981); E. Schaeffer, *Hidden Art* (London: Norfolk Press, 1971); C. Seerveld, "Beauty and the Human Body: Reflections on Cosmetology," *Christianity Today* 15 (11 September 1961) 27-28.

William Dyrness

BIRTH

To attend a birth is to be awakened with unimaginable wonder as you begin to rediscover the world with your child. Following conception* and pregnancy,* birth is the definitive moment that a new life enters fully into the family* and community to be blessed and named. It is a precarious passage we have all at one time navigated and may revisit in the agony and ecstasy of birthing our own children. Metaphorically, labor represents a form of "redemptive suffering" as a mother creatively brings a child into light and love,* a transition analogous to the salvation and new identity claimed in spiritual "rebirth." The physiological processes of labor and delivery can be described in terms of the four elements common to the understanding of the natural world by the biblical ancients: the cosmos of water and fire (experienced through labor), (with delivery to) air and earth.

The Wonder of the Elements
During earthquakes, volcanoes, floods and forest fires and no less during a birth, we feel the power and mystery of the elements—their exhilaration and danger. The elements were believed by the ancients to be the essential energy forces that sustained the world. Water, fire, air and earth were seen as vital components of the human body. The maintenance of health* was a matter of keeping a balance between them.

The human mind expands in the attempt to overwrite chaos with order by classifying, categorizing and defining the ineffable. *Wonder* always outgrows our organizing principles and is the essential element we bring to the mysterious and natural event of birth. According to Albert Einstein, experiencing awe "is at the center of true religiousness" (Konner, p. 383). It is wonder, says Oswald Chambers, "that keeps you an eternal child." Our faith and wonder can be reawakened when we become parents.

While birth is a normal physiological process of which we have only a superficial understanding, it is painful and incurs risks to both mother and child. Mortality, although rare today, has been well documented over the course of history. Isaiah 43:1-2 reassures us at this time: "Fear not, for I have redeemed you; I have summoned you by name; you are mine. When you pass through the waters, I will be with you; and when you pass through the rivers, they will not sweep over you. When you walk through the fire you will not be burned; the flames will not set you ablaze."

Traditionally cloistered in the privacy of a tent or home and attended by sisters, mothers and midwives, birth is now charted with the technological assistance of modern medicine in hospitals and, more recently, well-equipped birthing centers that offer more family-oriented care. Home deliveries and licensing of midwives have created unfortunate divisions between health care workers but are motivating necessary changes. Controversies arise when the physician's imperative to intervene on behalf of the unborn child conflicts with a mother's right to be autonomous in an experience that she wishes to be as positive, private and natural as possible.

Waters of Passage

Water symbolically shares many features with amniotic fluid in the labor process. The fetus swims in a fluid-filled sac that acts as a protective cushion and assists the fetal lungs in their development. When the water "breaks" and the salty fluid gushes or dribbles, there is marked point of no return, a boundary between pregnancy and birth. Literally "the bath is over" and "it's time to get out!" Although labor pains may not have begun, the breaching of the baby's sterile environment signals that birth needs to be imminent. Rivers and streams represent boundaries between worlds and countries, the inexorable flowing of time, and are conduits for passage and communication (Is 26:17). Because the fetus drinks and excretes (primarily water) into the amniotic fluid, the characteristics of this bath water communicate

important details about the baby's health. Through examining the fluid for clarity and color, the presence of bile, prematurely passed bowel movements and infection, fetal illness can be detected. Genetic integrity is determined by examining sloughed skin cells present in the amniotic fluid, sampled by an ultrasound-guided abdominal needle.

When the attending physician, in an attempt to initiate or accelerate labor, breaks the waters or enters the womb and sac during cesarean section, it is not unlike a baptismal spring that douses through all layers of emotional protection. It washes the image anew and allows the doctor to see this birth as if it were the first.

With courage and humility, physicians attend a delivery struggling in the currents, weighing all the odds, and waiting with Hypocrites' words echoing all the way back from the fifth century B.C.: "One must assist nature in effecting the cure. Life is short and the art long. The right time is an instant, the treatment precarious and the crisis grievous."

The physician strives to achieve balance between being overly impatient, taking the child too soon from the mother, or being indecisive with the resultant danger of allowing the mother to become exhausted or the child to be asphyxiated. Above all, physicians need to be attentive to the patient, tuning their ears to the cries of the laboring mother. As one can be trained to listen only for the oboe out of the whole orchestra, so one may need to strain to hear the voice of the patient in the thin reed of her crying. Tears are shed not just in response to pain but in frustration, helplessness and suffering, sending out a message and cleansing the mind.

Fiery Birth Force

Labor is a baptism not only of water but by fire. The fury and energy of labor is intense and transformative. The rhythmic contracting of the uterus is like the relentless pounding of the surf against the rocks as a storm breaks. The birth force rises, swells as a great wave, peaks and recedes—the tempo ever quickening. Pain can be overwhelming but is mercifully interspaced with pauses of quiet and rest.* The intermittent relaxations of the uterus allows blood to perfuse the placenta again. It may be a brief, intense laboring, or it may be a marathon of physical and mental exertion lasting days. Essential is the support of others who focus the mother in purposeful concentration on her own breathing. The perception of distress and pain can be diminished by the neurochemical effects of relaxation.

Physiologically, pain and heat usually warn us of impending danger or harm. Although unpleasant, these sensations have vital protective value. Most, however, would agree hours that turn into days seem to serve little purpose. A woman languishing in prolonged labor tires in her breathing and cannot expect that the mind will forever be master over the body so wrung in pain. Fortunately, modern medicine offers analgesics that are increasingly safer to both mother and child while miraculously maintaining consciousness—humanizing what has been for millennia a time of torturous pain or in the last century "twilight sleep."

Paul Harvey says, "A father is a person who is forced to endure childbirth without an anesthetic." Only recently have fathers been welcomed or persuaded to participate in labor support and observe the birth of their children. Having attended prenatal classes, he is equipped to rub the mother's back and salve her dry mouth, help her focus on breathing and at the pushing stage cheer and encourage her. Even his nervous jokes offer needed levity. Being a warrior and advocate for his wife can mean ensuring the highest care and the clearest communication of her wishes and expectations. The physical presence and touch of her husband can be of inestimable comfort at this time of *extremis*. In reminding her of the anticipated reward, his vision and optimism can transform her suffering beyond pain into parenthood. Some mothers prefer alternative or additional persons to support them, and some fathers prefer to have the option of leaving the room at any time they feel the need. Very few husbands faint, and most report the event as highly traumatic but worthwhile as they sense the full mystery of their child's entrance and share those often precious first moments. He has renewed respect for his wife's strength and is more understanding about her wishes for future children. Inclusion of husbands acknowledges the renewed priority of fathering and exemplifies how men have been liberated to enter into what has historically been a woman's world.

In some cultures a man may be so sympathetic toward his wife that he can develop an enlarged abdomen during pregnancy (pseudocyesis) and retire to bed while his wife is squatting in labor in the fields. Without experiencing firsthand the tangible bodily metamorphosis during pregnancy, the father has fewer cues with which to anticipate his imminent fatherhood. These cultural idiosyncrasies may impart preparatory wisdom not only to fathers but to modern medicine.

Archaeological evidence of women birthing seated or squatting, even in biblical times (Job 3:11-12, "knees to receive me"), has proven mechanical advantages that are noteworthy considering the increasing rates of interventions such as cesarean section, the use of forceps and episiotomy since the reclining position was adopted as a convenience for physicians. When the mother is seated upright, her pelvic outlet diameter is maximally widened, and the path the baby takes is a smooth "C" shape. Conversely, the inverted "S" course taken in the reclining position often causes the baby's head to become obstructed against the pubic bone, particularly when the baby starts its journey "posteriorly," in a more awkward back dive rather than front dive. Gravity in the preferred upright position is solicited as an accomplice. The deliveries a physician dreams of attending are the kind that can occur spontaneously in the dark under a chair. Perhaps physicians can show their versatility and in humility bend down with a flashlight, at least until it is clear that their services are necessary.

In all fairness, the rising rate of intervention is multifactorial. Several generations of medical assistance may have affected the hereditary ability of women to birth naturally. Women who were obstetrically disadvantaged never survived, and neither did their babies. Bad genes died out. Better nutrition, larger babies and the socially encouraged attractiveness of slight women may not be conducive to natural childbirth. Complicating a physician's judgment is the threat of lawyers who attempt to blame every inexplicable tragedy on a physician's reluctance to intervene early enough.

Midwives are advocates for self-control in labor and have restored confidence in the body's resources. Working in a spirit of teamwork like the disparate members of the body of Christ, we should be able to assist birthing women in unity with one another. Most seasoned midwives are aware of their limitations and choose to practice within the hospital setting where vital equipment is available within seconds to minutes in those critical situations when a baby is asphyxiated or a mother is bleeding. Birthing in the private, familiar atmosphere of one's home with the "guarantee of an intact perineum" is not worth the price of life or health. Nurses, physicians and midwives alike need to relinquish disparaging condemnation and join together in the common goal of bringing children into the world in greatest safety, with least intervention and greatest respect to the laboring mother and family. At the root of mistrust is a kernel of truth: technological medicine has lost its humanity. The compassionate physician, who waiting at the bedside centuries ago, unable to do anything but observe, predict, wait and comfort had more respect than the technological wizardry that has immunized whole populations, treated most infections successfully and, through surgery, rescued mothers and babes from death.* The current use of epidural and spinal anesthetics allow both parents to participate fully awake in the joyful event of a cesarean delivery of their child. However, the postoperative pain and recovery is an odyssey that requires additional support and compassion transcending technology's* limitations.

Pain intensifies to a state of suffering when it seems to serve no purpose and in that sense has no meaning. Rachel sacrificially died in childbirth (Gen 35:16-17), naming her surviving child "Son of My Trouble." Redemptively, his father renamed him "Son of My Right Hand." Paul reminds us, "We know that the whole of creation has been groaning as in the pains of childbirth. . . . We . . . groan inwardly as we wait eagerly for our adoption as sons, the redemption of our bodies" (Rom 8:22).

Labor pain is naturally one of the most tangible examples of how pain and suffering are translated into creative efforts. As birth tears through a woman cruciform in labor, so we pass in life and in death through a tunnel to light, love and reconciliation. We make an heroic exit through our wounds—birthing not only child, but mother and father, sister and brother. Jesus' birth has been recalled poetically by R. Paul Stevens:

Remember another watery invasion
incising this peaceless world
with indomitable love.
A child's cry exegetes Father,
earthed world, birthed maker
glorified flesh. (unpublished,
    December 1988)

Birth is the supreme effort of a mother to bring a child through water and fire to air and earth. Spiritual rebirth, although natural and intended, is no less miraculous.

Rebirth to Air and Earth

Birth is that moment when the baby enters air and is infused with the breath of life, now belonging fully in blood and body to earth and in spirit to sky. Birth is an awesome mountaintop experience—where heaven and earth meet, symbolizing our communion with God as we are reborn into the divine family because Immanuel ("God with us") was born into humanity. The child's first gutsy cry recalls the image of God breathing into red clay our very life (Gen 2:7). Sometimes when breathing does not occur spontaneously, medical efforts of resuscitation make the child centered in the calm eye of a hurricane of activity. These evocations of breathing are epitomized by the Chinese character for "love"; literally a composite of breathing into one's heart. "The breath of the Almighty . . . gives him understanding" (Job 32:8). The mind emerges from out of the waters; a babe's breath is a warm miraculous mist, like a whale's surfacing, anticipated and celebrated.

Reverence for life is steeped in acknowledgment of the source of our blood and breath: rebirth also involves testimony of the source of our inspiration, direction, life and joy (Jn 3:3). At the transition of birth, oxygen will now be derived from the baby's lungs. Through a series of detours, with vessels constricting and opening, blood shared between the baby and placenta is channeled away from the cord and toward the inflating lungs. As the pulsations cease in the three-vesseled cord, it can be clamped and cut painlessly like fingernails or hair. Once a lifeline, this cord of three strands is not easily broken (Eccles 4:12).

The placenta or afterbirth is the incredible organ that until now has been hidden like the fruitfulness of earth. During pregnancy it allows the fetal and maternal circulation to interface across a selectively permeable membrane. The placenta actively pumps antibodies into the fetal bloodstream, renews fetal blood with oxygen and nutrients, and takes away wastes and carbon dioxide, functioning for the fetus as lungs, kidneys, intestines and immune system. In rebirth, as in birth, we take on new responsibilities, and there is a full actualization of all our potentials that have lain in wait.

Blood and earth share a rich rust color that is the result of the common element of iron. In the red blood cells it is the iron held in hemoglobin that carries oxygen from the lungs to the tissues for use as fuel. The fetal blood circulation contains many "detours" where mixing of used (venous) blood and fresh (arterial) blood occurs. There is less clear distinction between the spent blue blood and the renewed red blood in the fetus as one melds into the other. Soon after birth different paths of circulation are established; the new order of the bloodstream distinguishes clearly between the soiled and the pure. Similarly in rebirth the conscience is awakened and begins actively closing doors on old habits and opening new patterns of flow and relatedness. For example, grounded as we are in our earthiness and granted a renewed sense of the wonder of creation,* we may find a new respect for the elements of air and water and the cleansing and healing of the earth (*see* Stewardship; Ecology).

Throughout the world red has been traditionally used as a sacred color symbolizing mysterious life energy. Bodies were buried in the fetal position in Paleolithic graves, and funeral furnishings were reddened with ocher for a closer resemblance to the womb from which the dead could be born again. Blood has been inextricably linked with healing through the sacrificial blood of atonement shed on Hebraic altars or by shamans cross-culturally. Bloodletting practices were popular in medicine throughout the ages. The life-giving blood of the mother is a hope marked monthly at menstruation.* Jesus' blood given to humankind is remembered at the Eucharist. Rituals are steeped in blood and celebrate the numinous in the ordinary, the hope inherent in death as in life.

The description of the foundling in Ezekiel 16 is a metaphor of the newly birthed and abandoned Jerusalem—cold, wet, bloody and crying. The description suggests that claimed newborns were treated ritualistically much as they are now, usually bathed, dried, rubbed with salt (with antibacterial properties now targeted around the cord stump and as ointment in eyes) and swaddled in comfort, like the enclosing womb left so recently. Even in the early moments the baby receives consolation by nursing away the anxieties of the new world on the breast, an intimate, interpersonal event (*see* Breast-feeding). Newborns across the planet are welcomed, blessed and named, brought blinking into the light to be beheld and to behold the world. They are also introduced into, and from the start nourished by, the community of the church,* especially where they receive strong spiritual and relational sustenance and guidance (*see* Membership; Godparenting).

The news of a new baby's arrival travels in great expanding waves through newsprint, phone calls, faxes and e-mail, and across neighbor's fences passing from person to person in songs of praise. "On the day you were born gravity's strong pull held you to the earth with the promise" that you belong here with a measurement to boast and the "sun sent up towering flames" to celebrate your arrival in light from dawn till dusk (Frasier, pp. 9, 11).

The seal of the human spirit is wonder, no less apparent on a newborn's wrinkled face. The human infant for the first few months is unfathomable eyes and ears—actively receptive at this, the dawn of awe. The newborn's mind has a fine sense of novelty of pattern, favoring symmetry and even beauty. A splash of red on a tie, a shadow on the ceiling or the sound of rain may evoke rapt attention. Newborns within one to two weeks will recognize their parents' voices. Like a child newly born who has heard parents' voices long before having seen them, so too in rebirth we have often heard God's whisperings before the divine Presence is fully and most personally revealed. Often it is the pain and light of fire that brings revelation, a sense of being carried through the waters of affliction.

For some people that sense of birthed wonder diminishes with time, becoming peripheral to everyday life. For some it becomes their central, moment by moment, reason for being—analytically as scientists, contemplatively as artists and worshipfully as children of God and parents of children.

If a child is to keep this inborn sense of wonder, he or she needs the companionship of at least one adult who can share it, rediscovering together the joy, excitement and mystery of the world we live in (Rachel Carson, quoted in Ward, p. 23).

One of the most reassuring concepts in rebirth, as illustrated metaphorically through the physical birth process, is that it is a revelation, refinement and redirection of what is already innate. It is an uncovering and releasing of our inherent good and wonderment despite our persisting shadows, perhaps even clearer now in the daylight. Salvation does not mean we become unrecognizable, perfect or pawnlike. Instead, we discover the source of our true identity with the Creator that began from conception. As part of the community of the church and in the intimacy of our immediate families, God reveals himself palpable as father and mother and Christ as brother. Though ultimately we will be in some way orphaned by our earthly families, this deprivation only draws us homeward, where we are claimed and healed by our Creator.

See also BREAST-FEEDING; CONCEPTION; GODPARENTING; PREGNANCY.

References and Resources
E. J. Cassell, *The Nature of Suffering and the Goals of Medicine* (New York: Oxford University Press, 1991); P. Teilhard de Chardin, *Hymn of the Universe* (New York: Harper & Row, 1965); D. Fontana, *The Secret Language of Symbols* (San Francisco: Chronicle Books, 1993); D. Frasier, *On the Day You Were Born* (San Diego: Harcourt Brace Jovanovich, 1991); P. Harvey, in *Promises to Parents* calendar (Bloomington, Minn.: Garborg's Heart and Home, 1990); M. Helewa, "Birth Positions: Historical, Mechanical and Clinical Considerations," *Journal of the Society of Obstetrics and Gynaecology of Canada,* May 1992, 47-54; M. Hoffman and J. Ray, *Song of the Earth* (London: Orion, 1995); M. Konner, "The Tangled Wing" in R. Reynolds and J. Stone, *On Doctoring* (New York: Simon & Schuster, 1991); A. S. Lyons, *Medicine: An Illustrated History* (New York: Harry N. Abrams, 1978); J. M. Ward, *Motherhood: A Gift of Love* (Hong Kong: Running Press, 1991).

Carol Anderson

BIRTHDAYS

"This is the day which the LORD has made; Let us rejoice and be glad in it" (Ps 118:24 NASB). The day, and the annual anniversary of the day, on which any person is born calls for a celebration. The Bible proclaims that everything God has made is good, which includes you! God's view of you is true and unchanging. You are a unique, unrepeatable creation; you are understood fully and beloved. This good news is important to remember on your birthday and every day.

A birthday celebration provides a special time to appreciate the unique gifts each family member or friend brings into our lives. Before making specific plans, think about your purpose. As you remember age, hobbies and talents, consider what would best suit the individual you are wishing to honor.

In many families the birthday person selects the menu for the celebration meal. Traditionally, a favorite kind of cake with an appropriate number of candles is the highlight of the party. When the cake appears, it signals the start of the "Birthday Song." The second verse is not as familiar but is an excellent addition to family traditions: "We love you, we do; We love you, we do; We love you, dear _____; We love you, we do." This simple verse provides an opportunity for family members to verbalize the words "I love you." Cards, gifts* and various expressions of caring attention help to make it a special day.

Looking Back
"And we know that all that happens to us is working for our good if we love God and are fitting into his plans" (Rom 8:28 LB). At a family dinner retell the story of your child's birth. When and where did it happen? What was the weather* like? Describe the joy! Everyone who remembers joins in

the telling, filling in special details.

As a way to reflect on the verse from Romans, let an older birthday person share important decisions that became turning points, changing his or her life. What are the special memories from the year or years? Others may want to speak of activities and events from the past that caused the friendship* to grow.

Experiencing something together builds relationships. This is a time to share positive developments that have been observed in your loved one. Simple words of affirmation* will mean so much. Bring out the baby books, slides, movies,* home videos* and scrapbooks that help to retell the birthday person's life story. Be sure and take a birthday picture!

Looking Ahead
"In everything you do, put God first, and he will direct you and crown your efforts with success" (Prov 3:6 LB). Encourage the guest of honor to share goals, hopes and dreams for the coming year. Thankful for benefits received, joyfully dedicate all of the days ahead to the service and worship* of God.

In conclusion, offer a prayer asking God's blessing on your loved one. Invite everyone present to place a hand on the honoree. To bless* someone is to address God in prayer,* calling for mercy, assistance, happiness and protection. This simple ritual is a powerful way to affirm a life and for family and friends to declare their faith in God.

See also AGING; BLESSING; FAMILY HISTORY; GIFT-GIVING.

References and Resources
G. Gaither and S. Dobson, *Let's Make a Memory* (Waco, Tex.: Word, 1983); S. W. Shenk, *Why Not Celebrate!* (Intercourse, Penn.: Good Books, 1987).

Martha Zimmerman

BLESSING

In recent times the word *blessing* has gone out of favor. For many outside the church, the word does not seem congruent in a secular world; *luck* is the preferred alternative. The word still turns up occasionally in certain conventional responses, such as "What a blessing!" "Well, bless me!" or, after someone has done a good deed or just sneezed, "Bless you." Even the parting "God bless" retains some general currency, but it often is little more than a kindly farewell. Greeting card messages about having a "blessed Christmas" echo language that for many has only a nostalgic ring.

Even believers who regard the word as having real meaning rarely use it. They look for other ways of saying something similar. Those who continue to use the word tend to be older, more conservative or charismatic Christians, some of whom use it quite habitually.

Blessing in the Bible and Beyond
Blessing is a central theme in the Bible, second only to its emphasis on deliverance. These two great themes speak of the main ways God relates to the world—through dramatic intervention into it and through regular participation within it. Hebrew and Greek words for blessing are associated with other terms, such as presence, peace, success.* At its root, a blessing refers to God's friendly approach to those who are open to receiving divine generosity. When a blessing is given, either by God to us or by us in God's name to one another, there is a specific recognition of the person being addressed and a recognition that this person is directly affected by the content of the blessing. While blessing is similar to thanking, it goes further in the direction of appreciation by acknowledging the character of the one blessed and therefore strengthening the bond between them.

As any concordance demonstrates, the biblical passages containing the word *blessing* are too numerous to list, but the following questions and answers summarize what is central to them.

What is a blessing? Blessings include such things as the gift and enhancement of life, fertility and other forms of tangible reward, the experience of salvation through Christ and the deepening growth of the believing community.

Who blesses? In the Bible blessings are conveyed mostly by God, either directly or by request, occasionally by Christ but also by human beings, such as priests and then increasingly any of God's people.

Who is blessed? Those blessed are especially the chosen people (including children and all human beings through the people of God—even those who revile and curse the chosen ones) and food and drink (both good gifts of God).

How does a blessing come? It can be conveyed in either a conventional or a fresh way, by either word or action, and can occur in a wide variety of settings, private and public, alone or with others.

When is a blessing given? Blessings are conveyed on various occasions, but they notably come at the beginning of someone's lifework or reign, at the conclusion of public worship,* at the exchange of greetings* or farewells, during a wedding* and just before dying.

Over the next few centuries of the early church and beyond, additional forms of blessing developed: for example, rituals for blessing people at different stages in their lives, the blessing of various objects and activities in the church building* and the blessing of key ventures, objects, seasons and anniversaries* in the wider community.* The chief innovation here, somewhat doubtful in view of the biblical focus, was the blessing of inanimate objects other than food and drink. Ceremonies involving blessings also became more elaborate, and the conveying of blessings increasingly fell into clerical hands.

Blessing in Church and Daily Life

Although even Christians use the word *blessing* less today, we still experience it and should give expression to it in various ways. For example, we should joyfully acknowledge and value God for choosing us to become sons and daughters of the kingdom, for redeeming us in Christ and justifying us despite our sinfulness and unworthiness and for promising us both personal and cosmic transformation in the last days. But life is full of other kindly actions on God's part, large and small, surprising and regular. We should be aware of these and regularly remind others of them. God is generous day after day, year after year, making good things available to those open to receiving them.

We can bless others as well as God. We should do this when others show us special kindly actions reminiscent of the ones God directly showers upon us. At such a time we can respond by passing on some blessing to them on God's behalf or by giving them some tangible evidence of our appreciation for them, a blessing or gesture that will evoke a response in them similar to the one their action has evoked in us. We have a deeper obligation to do this to those whom God has placed in greatest proximity to us, for example, members of our immediate family,* long-standing friends, members of our communal church group and close colleagues.

We do not have to wait on a priest or clergyperson to pass on these blessings to others. Under the leading of God's Spirit, any of God's people can perform this function in church or outside it. Likewise the blessing over bread and wine connected with the Lord's Supper (*see* Communion) can be conducted by any respected member, couple or family in the congregation. This is also true of the blessing that concludes a Christian gathering, for this is only a corporate version of the common blessing by Christians of one another at the end of any significant time they are in each other's company and, as such, is a clear reminder of the close continuity between what happens in church and ordinary life.

Using the word *blessing* itself is not essential to the giving of one. It is not a magical term whose absence causes God to withhold divine favor. Often the content and manner of the blessing speaks for itself. At other times synonyms can be used, as in the Bible, where the word is part of a wider language field. The word *happy*, frequently used in modern translations of Jesus' blessings, or beatitudes, in the Sermon on the Mount, is not a good alternative. It focuses too much on the subjective well-being of the believer rather than the objective endorsement of God. A New Testament scholar wrestling with the best translation of the word in the Sermon on the Mount concluded that the English term closest in meaning and spirit to it was *Congratulations!* This was an excellent choice.

There is something for unbelievers in this whole phenomenon too. In sharing news about God with them, we should be careful to do so in a way that comes to them as a blessing rather than as a duty or demand. This will be helped if we associate the special blessings of the gospel with the wider blessings God showers on all people day after day, of which they are occasionally aware. After all, the good news is essentially an invitation, and although this entails repentance, people should realize that accepting it is something for which congratulations are in order. Fortunately, even those who reject the word *blessing* because of its religious associations are themselves sometimes looking for the gracious real-

ity of which the word speaks. For it is a fact that most people, whatever their religious convictions or lack of them, deep down long to be blessed. This desire is basic to who we are as human beings and, as such, is implanted in us all by God.

See also BLESSING, FAMILY; FAREWELL; FELLOWSHIP; GREETING; MINISTRY; PLEASURE; WORSHIP.

References and Resources
R. Guelich, *The Sermon on the Mount: A Foundation for Understanding* (Waco, Tex.: Word, 1982); G. Vann, *The Divine Pity: A Study in the Social Implications of the Beatitudes* (London: Collins, 1945); C. Westermann, *Blessing in the Bible and the Life of the Church* (Philadelphia: Fortress, 1978).

Robert Banks

BLESSING, FAMILY

Blessing* is one of the most powerful ways human beings can express love,* especially in a family context. Indeed it is conspicuous when absent because children hunger for the approval and goodwill of their parents, parents long to be blessed by their children and spouses need to nourish each other in the covenant relationship. To give a blessing is to use speaking* in a powerful way to express positive goodwill toward, to bestow favor upon and to offer some benefit to another person. Blessing can be given without words through a gift* or action, but such material blessings have greatest meaning when accompanied by words. Take the situation of the parent who "blesses" her child by giving multiple presents but never verbalizes her love, respect and goodwill. Blessing is more than, though not less than, affirmation.* In this article the older meanings of bless as "consecrate" or "sanctify by a religious rite" will not be explored though, as we shall see, blessing is a holy relational ministry* that takes us to the very heart of God.

Blessing in any context, but especially

in the family, is good for three reasons. First, it is one of the fundamental ways God relates to the world. God relates through dramatic intervention (deliverance) and through regular positive participation in it (blessing; *see* Blessing). Second, blessing is an expression of one's person at a very deep level so that through words or actions an individual communicates presence, peace and goodwill to another. The words are fraught with unavoidable consequences. When an Israelite pronounced a blessing, he or she did not merely offer good wishes for the future. Rather, the soul was offered and something happened (Pedersen, 1:200; compare Gen 48:15). For example, Isaac could not recall the blessing he gave to Jacob, even though it was accomplished by deception, because Isaac had put himself into it. To withdraw his blessing would be to destroy himself, and he intuitively understood the hand of God in it all (Gen 27:27-40; *see* Promising). Third, to bless and be blessed is a fundamental need of every human being, created as we are for love and to love.

Family Blessings in the Bible and Beyond
In biblical times, and in all older cultures, blessing the children was something expected; it was often attended with certain rites and ceremonies. French Canadian fathers used to bring in the New Year with their hands of blessing on their children. Israelite fathers were expected to give their blessing to their children before their own death (Gen 27:4). This was not a fully egalitarian act. These blessings often involved appointing the future leadership of the family or tribe (the first-born male usually took over) and passing on the inheritance (again the first-born male would get twice as much as the others). Occasionally the birthright could be sold, as was the case when Esau exchanged his family leadership for a bowl of stew (Gen 25:29-34).

Parental blessing was like an unwritten last will* and testament. Job was conspicuously different from other ancients in this matter, for he gave his daughters an inheritance along with his sons (Job 42:15). Normally women were provided for through the bride price and dowry, a system repugnant to most modern Western people but containing more social security than is normally understood. Blessing the children in ancient times was, however, not merely a legal and financial act. It was a ministry that involved speaking a prayer for health, abundance, protection and peace (Gen 27:28-29). Sometimes the father would speak prophetically about the future of each child, as Jacob did in Genesis 49. Remarkably, the author of Hebrews selects this very last act of Jacob's blessing his children as his supreme act of faith (Heb 11:21). For parents, blessing our children is an act of faith in which we trust them to God, pray for God's blessing upon them, discern God's unique gift to them (including talents* and spiritual gifts*) and release them to fulfill God's purpose in their lives. There is an important principle involved in this ancient and almost universal practice.

The Importance of Family Blessings
From the earliest age children crave the approval and favor of their parents and will do almost anything to get it. The less-favored son Esau pathetically tried time and again to get his parents' blessing (especially his mother's) by marrying women he thought they might approve of, only to find out the wives brought more bitterness to them (Gen 26:34-35). Paradoxically, the parents who withhold affirmation from their children because they fear making the children proud may assist in producing pride and self-centeredness as the children try to prove themselves. Bless children, and they will

grow up with good self-esteem* and will experience freedom from organizing their life around the need for approval. They may gain a measure of humility and will be more free to think about others.

Blessing a child's marriage* is another crucial ministry of parents, since the freedom to leave one's father and mother (something both husband and wife must do) is partly, though not totally, facilitated by the parents' letting go. This blessing includes support, goodwill and expressed love; it means that the parents will never undermine the marriage even if, at an earlier stage in the relationship, they feared the choice was not a good one. As with forgiveness, and sometimes because of it, the parents will put the past in the past when they bless. The parents' blessing frees not just the children but paradoxically frees the parents to release their children to form a new family unit while still remaining connected to the parents in a revised way. When this is not done, the parents may still be bound to their children even though the children want nothing to do with them. The parents may cling to their married children in a codependent way, a phenomenon that usually leads to a tragic emotional triangle of husband, wife and in-laws.

In healthy families, blessings of children and marriages are not part of a one-time, deathbed drama but are something woven into the warp and woof of everyday life. Daily expressions of appreciation, with or without the actual word *bless* and not always tied to performance at school or around the house, reinforce that people are valuable for themselves, not just for what they do. Parents who only reward excellent achievement at school are contributing to drivenness* and workaholism.

When Blessing Is Hard

When parents are not able to bless their children regularly, it is often for reasons that signal the need for growth in the parents themselves. God gives children to parents to help the parents to grow up! Perhaps the parents were not affirmed, never had their parents' approval for their marriage or did not choose a career* acceptable to their parents. Much deeper than these factors is the possibility that the parents do not themselves enjoy a profound acceptance with God.

Paul speaks to this in Ephesians 6:1-4. Parents are not to exasperate their children; this is exactly what they do when they make demands without blessing, requiring performance without acceptance and approval. Instead, Paul says, parents are to raise their children "in the training [nurture] and instruction [admonition] of the Lord" (Eph 6:4). This is commonly misunderstood to mean that parents are to deliver Christian education* to their children. In fact, it speaks about the context in which both parents and children grow—while they both experience the nurture and instruction of the Lord.

Have the parents experienced the unconditional love of Jesus? Do they know existentially that there is nothing they can do to make the Lord stop loving them? Are they aware of the Lord's instruction, discipline and nurture in their lives in such a way that even the parents have limits and are held accountable? Do they delight in the Lord's approval and the certainty that they have a future with promise? We give what we get. If parents did not get such blessing from their parents, they must seek it from the Lord. If children cannot get such blessing from their earthly parents, they must find it with their heavenly Parent. If parents do not receive the blessing from their children, they too must find this in their relationship with God. Fortunate are those who experience such compensatory blessings from God through parents and children in the Lord as part of their involvement in a familial small group or house church in the congregation.

Not only do children need blessings from parents, but parents need their children's blessing. Husbands and wives need blessing from each other, as do brothers and sisters and members of the extended family. The wife of noble character described in Proverbs 31 receives an invaluable gift: "Her children arise and call her blessed; her husband also, and he praises her" (v. 28). Such blessing cannot be contrived or demanded. When it is, it is no blessing at all since it does not come from the heart. The words fall to the ground. But when a blessing is freely given, it nourishes the soul. Few children and few spouses understand the power at their disposal to nurture their closest neighbors in life.

See also AFFIRMING; BLESSING; FAMILY; GIFT-GIVING; PROMISING; SPEAKING; WILL, LAST.

Resources and References
J. Pedersen, *Israel: Its Life and Culture*, 4 vols. (London: Oxford University Press, 1963); M. H. Robins, *Promising, Intending and Moral Autonomy* (Cambridge: Cambridge University Press, 1984); L. B. Smedes, "The Power of Promising," *Christianity Today* 27 (January 21, 1983) 16-19; H. W. Wolff, *Anthropology of the Old Testament*, trans. M. Kohl (Philadelphia: Fortress, 1964).

R. Paul Stevens

BODY

God is the author and creator of our bodies. The well-known passage in the first chapter of Genesis powerfully portrays the creation of man and woman in the Maker's own image. Bearing that image, they are living persons, clothed in all the intricacies of the body: organs, blood, muscles, flesh, bones and body language. The body is integral to being human. Even the simplest of tasks requires numerous and complex bodily systems to be working: circulatory, auditory, muscular, nervous, glandular, sensory, kinesthetic and respiratory.

And God Breathed: Spirit and Body
God is the most superb craftsperson, as Psalm 139 so aptly describes, "For you created my inmost being; you knit me together in my mother's womb. . . . I was woven together in the depths of the earth" (Ps 139:13, 15). Who but God could weave this body-spirit? The body has been woven by a proficient artist, and the finest architect or biologist cannot duplicate what God has created. The metaphor of a weaving vividly captures the body's connection with the spirit. In weaving, the warp threads run vertically, and the weft threads run horizontally. Both are needed: they can be spoken of as separate, yet the weaving can only "be" a weaving if the warp and weft are both there.

God breathed into man and woman the breath of life; bones and flesh became enlivened with spirit. The creation story tells us that God made us from the dust of the ground, the humus of the earth, and breathed life into our very bones: "God breathed in the nostrils the breath of life, and the human became a *nephesh* [soul]" (Gen 2:7; translation mine). The passage does not say that the human was supplied with a soul* as some other attachment to the body, but that by the breath of God, the human became a living body-soul, a living human being. The body (weft) connected with spirit (warp) makes us human.

Breath is a physical reminder to us that we were "inspired" into being by God. The Hebrew understanding of the breath is closely associated both with the soul and with human desire. The psalmist proclaims, "Let everything that breathes praise the LORD!" (Ps 150:6 NRSV).

The Body in the Old Testament

Old Testament anthropology in general reveals a close relationship between the soul and body. The Hebrews regarded the person as a totality: body can be spirit, and spirit can be body. Though they could differentiate between various aspects of a person, the Hebrews believed that human beings operate as integrated, connected and embodied people. Nowhere is this more apparent than in the interchangeable Hebrew terminology for the words *heart, breath, soul, flesh, bones* and so on. We see a language that is bodily and gutsy, one in which the flesh can cry out or long (Ps 84:2; 63:1), bellies can grieve (Ps 31:9), bowels groan (Jer 31:20) and bones can proclaim, rejoice and tremble (Ps 35:10; 51:8; Jer 23:9). Body parts are constantly used to express the innermost yearnings, the heartfelt prayer to God.

Given this, it is understandable that Jewish prayer* was expressed through bodily gestures and postures. In the Old Testament we find crouching movements of lament (Ps 44:25), bowing and kneeling (Ps 5:7; 95:6), acts of falling prostrate (Dan 8:17-18), lifted hands (Ps 63:4) and jubilant leaps of celebration (2 Sam 6:14-16, 21). Inward grace was made visible through physicality—theology was transformed to doxology.

The Body in the New Testament

Physicality is the same in the New Testament. Lifting hands was encouraged by Paul (1 Tim 2:8); kneeling was demonstrated by Jesus (Mt 26:39; Lk 22:41); and dance was used to celebrate the return of the prodigal son (Lk 15:11-31). God came to bring salvation not only to the soul but to the whole person. The word for salvation itself, *sōzō*, is sometimes rendered "save" and sometimes "heal." Both senses show that God is concerned with the physical dimension.

The highest affirmation of the physical is in the incarnation of Jesus Christ. As the Gospel of John says, "The Word became flesh and dwelt among us" (1:14 RSV). God became a living body and made a home among us: living, breathing, eating,* celebrating and mourning with women, men and children. God became known through human flesh, breathing and pulsing with all the limitations and capabilities we have, miracle and mystery twined together. Jesus fulfilled his earthly vocation through his body: walking among the poor, kneeling in prayer, eating with sinners, washing* feet, healing* the sick. Jesus' hands became a living extension of the heart of God; his bodily touch was central to loving and transforming people while on earth.

Christianity's regard for the body is stated so well by C. S. Lewis: "Christianity is almost the only one of the great religions which thoroughly approves of the body—which believes that matter is good, that God himself once took on a human body, that some kind of body is going to be given to us even in Heaven and is going to be an essential part of our happiness, our beauty, and our energy" (Lewis, p. 91). The centrality of the incarnation and resurrection affirms the body as part of God's intentional design, not only for our creation* but also for our re-creation. We are our bodies, and if God can honor the body enough to be revealed through it and to redeem us in flesh, we need to take the body seriously.

The Body in Everyday Life

Our bodies are very much like breath—so much a part of us we don't recognize them unless they are distressed or ill. Our bodies remind us of a paradox: they are filled with wonder but have limitations. They are also fragile: Paul reminds us that "we have this treasure [God's power] in clay jars" (2 Cor 4:7 NRSV). Bones, like clay, can be broken and cracked. Bodies succumb to everyday annoyances of colds, stress, fatigue and disease. Bodies are not perfect but can be a spiritual reminder of the One who created and will transform us.

Our bodies are also the place of delight. They enable us to feel the wind on our faces, the warmth of a hug, the joy of moving. Many of us experienced this far more when we were children, in the days when we were not as self-conscious about "body image." Children engage physically in their world, rejoicing that they can skip, run and hop to a dance of their own. Arms reach, knees bend, legs climb, torsos slide, and bodies swing with sheer joy as children play.* But it does not take long for them to "learn" that being a bodily being has more to do with appearance than how one engages in the world. The emphasis on body image stresses the split between body and heart, relegating the body to a shell or container. In contrast, many of the subjects taken up in this volume are bodily activities that can be expressive of true spirituality: eating, sleeping,* washing, walking,* adornment,* dressing and sexuality.*

It is not surprising that as adults we find it difficult to put body, soul, mind and heart in balance. At times we emphasize the body to the point of neglecting the heart. Physical exercise and toning can never ultimately bring about toning of the spiritual life, and neglect of the body can wreak havoc with the wholeness that God intended for us. We divide ourselves as if we were two separate organisms, each unaffected by the other. Western culture is bombarded with images from the media that reveal a fragmented attitude toward the body. This has seeped into core attitudes toward the body, self-concept and relating to each other and God. These dualistic attitudes are nothing new and have been an ongoing theme in Western culture for centuries.

Western philosophy was loosely built upon this dualism. In classical Greek thought the body was equated with irrationality and viewed as an obstacle to seeking the higher attributes of truth and beauty. Plato refers to the body as a prison of the soul, defiling it and inhibiting its ability to know the divine. Such thinking affected the fathers of the early church. Scripture was eventually read through "dualistic world view glasses" (Walsh and Middleton, p. 109). This leaves little room for the human being to feel at home with his or her body or for embracing the reality that our bodies are a gift from God through which we can fulfill our God-given vocation.

In contrast, the biblical realities of creation, incarnation, redemption and resurrection affirm that we were masterfully designed as complete and complex creatures—the physical and spiritual intertwined. The biblical concept of the body celebrates this interconnection. We honor God and ourselves when we affirm the goodness and wholesomeness of God's work in us.

See also ADORNMENT; BREAST-FEEDING; CIRCUMCISION; HEALING; HEALTH; JOGGING; MENSTRUATION; SICKNESS; WALKING; WASHING.

References and Resources

P. Brand and P. Yancey, *Fearfully and Wonderfully Made* (Grand Rapids: Zondervan, 1987); J. W. Cooper, *Body, Soul & Life Everlasting: Biblical Anthropology and the Monism-Dualism Debate* (Grand Rapids: Eerdmans, 1989); C. S. Lewis, *Mere Christianity* (New York: Macmillan, 1943); C. S. Schroeder, *Embodied Prayer: Harmonizing Body and Soul* (Liguori, Mo.: Triumph Books, 1994; portions quoted here with permission); B. J. Walsh and J. R. Middleton, *The Transforming Vision: Shaping a Christian World View* (Downers Grove, Ill.: InterVarsity Press, 1984); D. Willard, "Spiritual Life: The Body's

Fulfillment," chap. 6 in *The Spirit of the Disciplines* (San Francisco: Harper & Row, 1988).

Celeste S. Schroeder

BOREDOM

Charlie Chaplin's film *Modern Times* expounds the dilemma of boredom in the workplace: routine, meaningless, repetitious, mindless work that results in fatigue. Such boredom at work* has not been alleviated by increased technology or by the introduction of the information society—a cultural shift that may have escalated the problem by overloading people with information. Not even a challenging career* can guarantee freedom from boredom. Executives reach the top and, with nowhere else to go, ask, "What is it all for?" Culturally North America is "bored to death," "bored stiff," "bored to tears," "bored silly" and even "bored out of one's skull." Surveys indicate that up to half of North Americans are either temporarily or permanently bored (Klapp, p. 20), a trend that is all the more disturbing for a society that is saturated with fun industries. Perhaps that is part of the problem. Being "amused to death," to quote Neil Postman's penetrating analysis, does not seem to offer anything more than a cultural placebo. Klapp (p. 30) suggests the analogy of aspirin: frequent usage means not the absence but the presence of extreme pain. "Bored? How could you be bored when there is so much to do?" the exasperated father shouts at his teenagers. And for the Christian hardly any more damning comment can be made at the conclusion of a worship service than "It was boring."

Though this article will focus on boredom at work, we will explore boredom as a social and cultural problem that affects everything from relationships to church life. People are bored with their marriage partners, bored with school, bored with sex, bored with work, bored with television, bored with church, bored with prayer, even bored with the thought of going to heaven. A Catholic philosopher once said, "Heaven did not seem to me worth going to." While among the French aristocracy boredom was once considered to be the lot of being a courtier, it is now the privilege of the common person. Popular culture, high culture, literature, music and philosophy all witness to it. Indeed boredom is not merely a personal problem; it is systemic to the culture, incarnated in the icons, norms and communication patterns of everyday life. It is also one of the most pressing questions for the theologian today, perhaps overshadowing guilt and finitude (Dean).

Types of Boredom

The church has traditionally named boredom—under the Latin title *acedia*—as one of the seven deadly sins. Frederick Buechner describes it as a voluntary form of death. Boredom is an absence of feeling, emotional flatness, passivity to life, lack of interest in anything. All these states are covered by the French word *ennui*, which was used in England before the word *bore* was invented in the eighteenth century and its derivative *boredom* a few decades later.

Some boredom (we could call it *basic boredom*) is surely not sinful: to lapse into daydreaming at the concert because one is not engaged with the music at that moment is harmless, possibly even a sign of health since leisure* requires the freedom to move in and out of consciousness. Some boredom theorists argue that there is a holy boredom implicit in life in this world because nothing in this age can fill the God-shaped vacuum in our souls. This inspired boredom keeps reminding us, as C. S. Lewis once said, that if we find nothing in this world that completely satisfies us, it is a powerful suggestion that we were made for another life, another world—for heaven.

But boredom that is alienating from God and destructive of human relationships becomes, as Buechner suggested, a form of voluntary suicide. It is an oversimplification to say, as some do, that this is the boredom we choose over against the boredom that overcomes us. This terrible boredom is part of the human predicament. As Blaise Pascal said, "Man is so unhappy that he would be bored even if he had no cause for boredom, by the very nature of his temperament." Not only is this boredom endemic to fallen human nature, it is now embodied in the cultural forms and institutions of society, part of the principalities and powers* that shape our life in this world and that must be overcome by cultural stewardship and spiritual warfare. Boredom is both a personal and a systemic problem.

Since medieval times two deadly sins were almost always considered together: boredom and sloth. Sloth is the inability to fulfill one's religious duties or secular responsibilities. In addition, sloth is the inability to enjoy leisure (who thinks of this as sloth today?). In other words, sloth is the rejection of interest in both work and leisure. Paradoxically, workaholism (see Drivenness) is a form of moral sloth, since it involves the neglect of certain basic duties. But boredom is the rejection of interest in life itself, being emotionally flat, passionless. It is, as Byron said, "that awful yawn which sleep cannot abate." How are sloth and acedia related? For Kierkegaard sloth was not the source of boredom. Boredom itself was the root of all evil. In contrast, Richard Baxter, in his Puritan exposition of sloth and idleness, considered sloth the source of most other sins, citing, for example, the idleness of David watching Bathsheba bathe when he should have been out at war; sloth in this case led to lust, adultery,

lying and murder. With great wisdom the church has always considered sloth and acedia together as capital sins (*caput* from "head," which is the source of other sins; Healy, p. 17). In reality they are interdependent, each influencing the other and feeding on the other.

Many Puritans did not have an adequate doctrine of leisure; neither have we. But Baxter made a substantial contribution to thinking and acting Christianly by understanding both sloth and boredom as sins against our calling: "Suffer not your fancies to run after sensual, vain delights; for these will make you weary of your callings" (p. 382). He could have just as easily said, "When nothing interests you at all, ask whether you are responding to the call of God in your life." Every person (and not just ministers and missionaries) is called of God to live purposefully for God and the common good. Sloth and boredom are vocational sins, living as though one had not been summoned by God to a holy purpose (Eph 4:1). It is an immensely challenging, venturesome, interesting vocation. Kierkegaard did not use vocational language but witnessed to the same truth in relation to acedia: we are summoned by God to live wholeheartedly and joyfully for God. Acedia for Kierkegaard was the "despairing refusal to be oneself."

Overcoming Boredom
How then does one agree to be oneself? Final healing will come with the Second Coming of Christ, the resurrection of the body, and the new heaven and the new earth. But substantial healing of boredom in this life is a matter both of receiving grace and harmonizing our lifestyle to the purpose and call of God. We can approach this by asking what is the opposite of boredom—joy? playfulness? passion? contentment? If joy, then we are dealing with the fruit of the Spirit. If playfulness, we are dealing with an in-

spired freedom from the compulsion to produce. If passion, we are dealing with that internal energy that comes from simultaneously getting the heart of God and willing one thing. If contentment, we are dealing with the grace that is "learned" (Phil 4:12) through constant thanksgiving. Like many spiritual maladies, boredom is not healed by attacking the problem directly; it is healed by the expulsive power of the infilling and liberating love of Christ, a greater passion.

Turn boredom into prayerful waiting. As mentioned above, boredom serves as a symptom of something in our inscapes, our soul life. It is a sign that life in this world will not fully satisfy. While waiting* can be boring, it can be made contemplative. It can be transformed into an active questioning of God (as it was for Job), longing for insight and meaning, waiting for God. Both the bored preacher of Ecclesiastes and the psalmist looked to God, the preacher by considering the question of meaning beyond the framework of this age—"under the sun"—and the psalmist by hearing the Word of God: "My soul is weary with sorrow [boredom?]; strengthen me according to your word" (Ps 119:28). Waiting for God is not like waiting for Godot in Samuel Beckett's play by that name. Godot never comes; God does. But as Job found out, waiting for God is a holy war in which, like Abraham, Jacob and Jesus in the Garden of Gethsemene, we refuse to take boredom (in this case) as God's last word.

Gain an eternal perspective by keeping sabbath.* Most Christian moralists equate boredom with idleness and recommend work as its cure. It is true that retirees (and others) engaging in an orgy of leisure* need the balance of purposeful work,* whether volunteer* or remunerated. Where a choice of jobs exists, we should choose those that best fit our motives, personality and talents (*see* Vocational Guidance). But boredom is not simply an absence of activity. One can be busy and bored at the same time, even in Christian service. Contrary to the advice of many well-meaning Christian leaders, and most parents, the answer is not simply to work harder. Most bored people need to work less and learn how to keep sabbath, which is God's deepest provision for a restless spirit. The world offers work and leisure (with no sabbath); the Bible offers work and sabbath (with some leisure). I am making the unpopular proposal that we probably need less leisure than we are told we need (by those who market leisure) and more sabbath.

Develop a contemplative lifestyle. Get into the meaning of what you are doing. Attend to people, things and situations in a more complete way that includes their aesthetic and spiritual meaning. Michael Raposa describes it this way:

> For example, having become bored with all the useful things that I can do with a given object, I may suddenly begin to contemplate its aesthetic qualities. Bored with the conversation at a party or meeting, I may suddenly become playfully enthralled with people's voices and with the sounds of their accents. Having grown weary with carefully observing an object for some specific purpose, I may suddenly begin to "see" it in a new way. And, having become bored with someone that I love, I may suddenly fall in love with that person all over again, but not simply "again," because here something new has been added to that love and to the relationship. (p. 87)

Become aware of the systemic nature of the problem. Our society trivializes leisure, reduces entertainment* to a consumer item and offers placebo solutions. Being titillated with the latest soap opera, fashion, concert or hit song can only divert us for a moment. As Orrin Klapp says, "Without significance, variety is not the spice of life. It can be as dull as monotony when it has nothing to say— becomes noiselike" (p. 81). Especially information about which we can do nothing (like the news) adds to boredom and learned helplessness (p. 89). Some Christians must work in the leisure and advertising worlds as cultural stewards, bringing depth and hope into the media and entertainment. All of us must do spiritual battling, discerning, praying, exorcising, interceding. As a practical (though unpopular) measure, we must reduce the amount of stimulation we receive, control the information overload and see that we choose leisure that edifies.

Boredom, in the end, is not so much subdued as it is expelled by recovering our passion for God, what some people call "being centered." Boredom is not so much a sin as a symptom of sin, a sign that our fundamental relationship with God, life and ourselves has been broken. In Romans 1 the fundamental sin is failure to reverence God or give thanks to him (Rom 1:21). From this fundamental sin come all the sins to which God gives people up (1:24, 26, 28), including futility (1:21), which is close to boredom. The human predicament, as Kierke-gaard said, is a failure to be our (true) selves— creatures in love with God and therefore in love with life. Pascal, out of his own struggle, claimed the answer to boredom lies in an act of faith, or rather a visitation of grace: "Happiness is neither outside us nor inside us; it is in God, both outside and inside us."

See also ENTERTAINMENT; IMAGINATION; LEISURE; PLAY; VOLUNTEER WORK; WAIT- ING; WORK.

References and Resources

R. Baxter, *The Practical Works of Richard Baxter,* vol. 1 (Ligonier, Penn.: Soli Deo Gloria Publications, 1990); M. Csikszentmihalyi and R. E. Robinson, *The Art of Seeing: An Interpretation of the Aesthetic Encounter* (Malibu, Calif.: J. Paul Getty Museum and Getty Center for Education in the Arts, 1990); W. Dean, "Theology and Boredom," *Religion in Life* 47 (Spring 1978) 109-18; H. Fairlie, *The Seven Deadly Sins Today* (Notre Dame, Ind.: University of Notre Dame Press, 1979); S. D. Healy, *Boredom, Self and Culture* (Cranbury, N.J.: Associate University Presses, 1984); O. E. Klapp, *Overload and Boredom* (Westport, Conn.: Greenwood, 1986); D. W. McCullough, "Anything but Boredom," *Christianity Today* 35 (August 19, 1991) 30-32; N. Postman, *Amusing Ourselves to Death: Public Discourse in the Age of Show Business* (New York: Viking, 1985); M. L. Raposa, "Boredom and the Religious Imagination," *Journal of the American Academy of Religion* 53 (March 1985) 75-79.

R. Paul Stevens

BREAST-FEEDING

Usually a newborn babe is brought to the breast as soon after birth* as possible. For the infant it is their first experience of eating* and drinking, and for the mother it is a privilege to provide sustenance for which there is no chemical or immunologic substitute. Breast milk is a vital, natural resource available in almost unlimited supply, provided demand feeding is encouraged. Breast-feeding is the most cost-effective and health-promoting activity mothers can undertake during their children's early years of life. Through this intimate, everyday act bonding is solidified, forming the essential foundation for relational and family health. Early feeding patterns that respect the child's needs require parental altruism and stamina. Suckling at the breast is the beginning of a trusting and nurturing relationship, forming the primal context in which we understand God's constancy and love: "Yet you brought me out of the womb; you made me trust in you, even at my mother's breast. From birth I was cast upon you; from my mother's womb you have been my God" (Ps 22:9-10).

As an exclusive dyad, mother and child together weave a new cord to replace the one that was severed at birth. Fathers and siblings contribute their own colorful threads, which become more significant as the infant gradually leaves the breast to explore the world independently at longer intervals. Parenting* is a lifelong task that seeks to balance dichotomous needs—drawing together and pulling apart, offering nourishment and protection as well as affirming independence.

There are only two lasting bequests we can hope to give our children. One of these is roots; the other, wings (Carter, in Hodgson, p. 82). Breast-feeding secures the first, making the second procurable. With well-established self-esteem* and secure spiritual identity, we have the freedom to climb, putting our feet in high places where the wind invites our wings (Ps 18:33).

Breast-feeding as Affection

Bonding is not an instantaneous event, but a gradual process of claiming each other and establishing understanding, love* and loyalty. Bodily contact—the skin-to-skin exploration of the scent of babe and mother's milk—is vital for animals in recognizing each other and no less so for humans. Unique among mammals, the human mother and child nurse within distance of the eye's focal range. Like marsupials, human offspring are born "prematurely," that is, almost a year before they can eat or move independently. The almost continuous contact required during early months of breast-feeding can be regarded as a continuation of gestation. In the delivery room the breast helps to bridge the abrupt change of worlds. Arriving cold and wet into blinking brightness, the babe can be soothed against the warm breast. Breast-feeding accomplishes not only nutrition but vital communication of caring and affection through touch. Institutionalized infants who are seldom held fail to thrive despite seemingly adequate nutrition, indicating that as we hold babies we feed their souls.* There are volunteers who visit neonatal hospital units specifically to hug needy babies. "The eternal God is your refuge, and underneath are the everlasting arms" (Deut 33:27).

Touch starts as a reflex, a little fist grasping around your finger and the instinct to draw the child to your breast. It becomes a healing language we all understand, smoothing the furrows in our hearts. Softening the ripples of anxiety, a mother's hand traces over her newborn's face, wrinkled and covered in greasy vernix—the ointment acquired in the womb. Common sense tells us that what we crave as infants, what is the source of our earliest sensations, is a need that continues throughout our lives, be it the healing touch of a physician, the handshake of a brother or the embrace of spouse or child.

Nutrition and Immunity

Parenting, like breast-feeding, involves not only protection but a translation of nutrients and information from the world to the child. Parents actively select enriching experiences and assist their children in defining emotions* and in guiding responses. Interpreted and refined by the parent, nourishment and immunity are presented in an easily digestible or understandable form.

In keeping with the baby's needs, breast milk is differentiated. "Foremilk," received when the infant begins to suckle, is dilute and thirst quenching. For the reward of a hungry baby's persistent suckling there is the richer "hindmilk." In contrast to consistently composed formula, breast milk prevents excessive caloric intake; if the baby is simply thirsty he can stop with the foremilk. The advantages of less readily digestible formula is that its use prolongs the interval between feedings. This may be convenient for the mother, but it ignores the infant's need for apt milk and frequent interaction. Breast milk is easily digested, leaving soft stool without an offensive odor. Likewise regurgitated breast milk is not unpleasant like formula vomitus. Diapering and laundry duties have a sweeter air about them when the infant is breast-fed.

Breast milk is ordered to human neurological growth. One of the most species-specific characteristic of human milk is the unique biochemical composition that assists the cerebral cortex to double in size in the first postnatal year. The breast also synthesizes neural chemicals that resemble placental hormones thought to influence sexual development and gender formulation. No doubt at this time we have only an infantile understanding of all that breast milk contains.

During pregnancy* and through breast milk, a mother confers to her child the wisdom of her years, an immunologic heritage. The memory of countless victories fought against viruses and bacteria are passed on as antibody artillery and houndlike white blood cells that have been programmed to act on a specific scent of a past offender. Vaccines impart immunity by presenting a harmless invader that has the same scent as its dangerous cousin, arming the immune system for future attacks. Breast-fed babies have documented healthier, more allergy-free childhoods. In addition, some forms of cancer and diabetes are rarer in children who have been breast-fed as infants, presumably through immune-mediated protection. The Scriptures, analogous to breast milk, not only nourish our souls, bodies and minds but also provide us with armor and arms (Eph 6:17).

Indications and Support for Breast-feeding

In the Third World, where illiteracy is significant, as in the growing poverty-stricken areas in North America, the cost, the possible contamination and the complexities of accurately measuring and mixing concentrated or powdered infant formulas make breast-feeding the only safe alternative. Unfortunately, formula companies adeptly market their products by providing free samples to hospitals and doctors' offices. By distributing these gifts, the medical profession communicates the fallacy that "formula feeding is as good as breast-feeding." The suggestion of supplementation undermines the confidence of the nursing mother and becomes a self-fulfilling prophecy. The breast acts by a supply-demand quotient. As the mother removes the baby from her breast to the bottle, the breast responds to decreased stimulation by producing less milk. Bottle feeding both causes and "cures" the apparent lack of milk, replacing nature with technology.* To increase lactation one needs only to allow increased nursing time.

Breast-feeding need not be discontinued in situations of maternal or infant illness. Even in cases of infections of breast or gastrointestinal tract, breast-milk continues to provide vital immunological resources and rehydration fluid with antidiarrheal properties. Care must be taken with regard to medication usage during breast-feeding. Chemicals in the mother's bloodstream, including alcohol and nicotine, appear in breast milk and are absorbed from the baby's intestines. Because an infant's immature liver and kidneys have difficulty metabolizing and eliminating chemicals and because few medications have been formally tested in pregnant women, nursing mothers or infants, few reassurances can be given with certainty.

In recognition of the outstanding benefits of breast-feeding, the Canadian Paediatric Society recommends that infants be *exclusively* breast-fed for four to six months and weaned during the second year. The World Health Organization and the United Nations International Children's Education Fund (UNICEF) have outlined specific directives to be incorporated into hospital maternity care in order to assist mothers in their attempts to breast-feed. La Leche League International began in 1956 as a pioneering group of mothers who had the courage to breast-feed despite widespread formula use and prior to the discovery of the immunological properties of breast milk. Today it provides a network of experienced mothers who assist with the practicalities of breast-feeding in almost every community.

Vital to the success of breast-feeding is the proper positioning of the baby and breast and the principle of feeding at the request of the baby (on demand) to encourage adequate milk supply. The baby can be weighed before and after feeding to reassure the mother of adequate milk ingestion. Documenting the progression of the baby's weight gain is important especially after the anticipated weight loss in the early weeks. We are challenged by the mid-eighteenth-century philosopher Jean-Jacques Rousseau's words "Would you restore all to their primal duties, begin with the mothers; the results will surprise you."

Bottles, Laughter and Time

A mother with a babe at the breast appears as a closed circle—two people existing only for each other. This dependency is celebrated at satisfying reunions after even brief separations are felt in swelling breasts, a hungry tummy or anxious wondering. Mother and child yearn for another, not unlike God's zeal for us or our thirst for him (Ps 42:1-2). This circle opens, allowing a father to burp, bathe and change the newborn and a sibling to bring a diaper or toy, sing a song or sit for a story while Mother nurses. As weeks pass into months and breast-feeding is well established, the father and siblings can experience the satisfaction of giving a bottle on a daily basis. This creates an opportunity for a mother to occasionally exit without being anxious that the infant's needs cannot be met by another caregiver. Ideally a small amount of expressed breast milk in a bottle, given daily in the evening, will not appreciably alter milk supply, especially if it is part of the routine. Later if the mother chooses to work outside the home, the infant will already be familiar with the bottle and will have fewer adjustments to make. The mother can still nurse in the morning and after work, maintaining her unique identity with the child despite the presence of secondary caregivers. Later, as the baby becomes interested in family foods, exploring tastes and fingerpainting with textures, family members participate by holding the spoon or offering the spoon to the child.

If "mommy" means primarily comfort, "daddy" means predictable fun. Laughter* becomes as tangible as food passed between father to child. Sounds and words become invested with personal meaning even from birth, and little jokes are carried across the decades. "My little sparrow" became a term of endearment for a newborn who almost died from birth asphyxia; this reminded the new father that if God knows even when a sparrow falls, then his children are worth even more to him, so much that even our hairs are numbered (Mt 10:29-31). During feeding parents can observe their children, drinking in their beauty*—the unique curve of their ears and the pattern of hairs on their head.

Time* is also a food that passes reciprocally between parent and child, persisting long after weaning in the form of reading* aloud and jointly engaging in activities like running errands, walking,* making crafts,* building projects, cooking, learning computer* skills, playing sports* and gardening.* Breast-feeding may involve extra time, but it means time with the baby and less time mixing formula and sterilizing bottles. All the positive interactions that occur with breast-feeding occur also with bottle feeding, provided the bottle is not propped up and the baby left alone. Breast-feeding is not a guarantee of good mothering, nor does bottle feeding rule it out.

The Case of Adoption

Adoptive mothers with sufficient motivation and support can breast-feed. Knowing the baby's approximate due date, the receiving mother can actually induce lactation, even if she has never been pregnant or nursed a child before. If she faithfully expresses her breasts several times a day with a hand-held pump for two to six weeks before the baby's arrival, her breasts will respond by producing milk, although perhaps only in small quantities. When the baby arrives, the adoptive mother can use a nursing supplementer—a small tube taped to the breast that adds formula by gravity while the baby is nursing. The breast still receives stimulation and is encouraged to make more milk while the child receives additional nourishment. Thus it is possible for an adopting mother to experience the intimacy and naturalness of breast-feeding, which may compensate her in some way for the missed experiences of pregnancy and birth.

Whether the birth mother breast-feeds in those early days of hospital recovery is a highly personal decision. As discussed in Miscarriage,* completing the recognition of what she is about to lose may assist her in grieving,* even though the intimacy of breast-feeding may reawaken ambivalence about her decision that must be legally finalized soon after birth. "Can a mother forget the baby at her breast, and have no compassion on the child she has borne? Though she may forget, I will not forget you! See, I have engraved you on the palms of my hands" (Is 49:15-16). "Her gift is of inestimable worth; her secret genetic talents are passed on to the child, and the child falls like a star into the arms of longing parents. "Praise the LORD. . . . Who is like the LORD our God? . . . He settles the barren woman in her home as the happy mother of children" (Ps 113:1, 9).

For the adoptive parents who carry the torch of life onward, it is a task of claiming, naming, and protecting the flame. By comforting, nourishing and investing all of themselves they complete the love that others began. "Nothing is precious save what is yourself in others and others in yourself" (Teilhard de Chardin, p. 62). Spiritual and emotional nurturing establishes a heredity that is eternal—not transient like the legacy of DNA (see Conception), which alters or is lost as a branch of a genealogy comes to an infertile end. In welcoming and attending to the needs of children it is as if we are ministering to Christ himself (Mk 9:37).

Breast-feeding as Pleasure

Cross-culturally there are remarkably different attitudes toward the breasts' function and value—nutritively and sexually. It is a curious commentary on our own society that we tolerate all degrees of explicitness in our literature and mass media with regard to sex and violence, but the natural act of breast-feeding is taboo. There is a whole generation of women who as children never observed their own mothers nursing and consequently have invested their breasts with exclusively sexual value. Without the necessary modeling they find themselves embarrassed with even the thought of breast-feeding and often are unable to overcome their modesty even in private settings.

Nursing mothers need to be sensitive to the potential embarrassment of observers. Discretion can be the better part of valor. It may be easier and less offensive to others in the room to retire to a private place to get the baby started and possibly return with a lightweight blanket draped over a shoulder to conceal what might embarrass someone. Many mothers can nurse successfully with no one even surmising what is happening.

Although breast-feeding can be initially painful, over time and with proper latching of the baby breast-feeding becomes a pleasurable experience. This is mediated by two hormones. Oxytocin is released during the "letdown" or milk-ejection reflex and is experienced as a "pulling sensation" as the milk ducts contract. The "supply-demand" hormone prolactin is released in proportion to the duration of suckling. These hormones facilitate a meditative focus that for mothers who are usually whirling dervishes provides the necessary calm to hold their little one close in rapture.

Breast-feeding as Service
Breast-feeding is an act of service as the mother respects and responds to the baby's needs, putting aside her own agenda and enduring discomforts, interruptions, inconveniences and sleep deprivation. What is natural may not be uncomplicated or effortless. Despite all the sentimental expectations one may have of the breast-feeding experience, there can be many hurdles to overcome

as mother and babe settle into the early weeks and months. Until the nipples become tougher and desensitized, breast-feeding may be initially uncomfortable. Excess milk leaking out of both breasts during feeding or spontaneously at night may require breast pads. The initial engorgement of the breasts that occurs in the early days as the milk comes in can be uncomfortable and presents a hard, stiff surface, making it difficult for the baby to latch successfully. After expressing by hand, the pressure is relieved and the breast softens. With time the breasts settle down and produce milk only at designated feeding times without the exaggerated responses of the early weeks. Time and maturity also dampen the oscillations of parental reactions, reflecting God's constancy with us.

Many circumstances can make breast-feeding difficult to initiate. Operative deliveries, separation of mothers and babies during hospital confinements and overzealous supplementation with formula have been identified as major obstacles to well-established breast-feeding. Although babies will instinctively turn toward a breast, latch and suckle, successful feeding depends on appropriate positioning. To maintain the baby's body and head toward the breast often requires supporting the baby on a pillow and using a hand to guide the baby's head and shoulders. Breast-feeding is a learned skill, and solutions to problems that have been gleaned over generations are passed on through the "doulas" of La Leche League and lactation consultants.

Infants instinctively know when to stop, and they should be allowed to feed as long as they wish. Babies will spontaneously let go of the breast when satisfied. The first breast should be emptied before offering the second to prevent milk stasis and infections. In addition, if the babe exclusively drinks the thin, sugary "foremilk" by being switched prematurely to the other breast, colicky gas and hunger pains can be exacerbated. Routine supplementation is unnecessary, and especially in the early weeks it takes away from the infant's time on the breast, resulting in decreased milk production. Also, early supplementation and use of pacifiers can result in "nipple confusion." Infants use quite distinctive techniques to suckle on a breast versus an artificial nipple.

Early frequent feeding at the request of the baby is exhausting but essential for establishing the milk supply, if breast-feeding is to be successful. Usually a harmonious routine evolves over the first few months.

Adhering to a strict schedule by day, then forcing a baby to "make it through the night" resembles military training under spartan conditions of deprivation. There is no medical or psychological rationale for parent-controlled feeding. It is unethical for newborns to wait in hunger while the mother looks at the clock to determine if it is time for feeding. These infants cry but are unheard, their stomachs distending with swallowed air, their emotions* utterly confused. Failing to meet the moment-by-moment needs of infants undermines the foundation of their trust in the world.

Consider God as he comforts and satisfies his children: "For you will nurse and be satisfied at her comforting breasts; you will drink deeply and delight in her overflowing abundance . . . be carried on her arm and dandled on her knees. As a mother comforts her child, so will I comfort you" (Is 66:11-13).

The rhythm of "hunger-crying-response-satiety" reinforces the child's confidence about his bodily sensations and the just and predictable world. Militant, rigid feeding schedules are a harbinger of the eating disorders that plague North American women. Anorexia nervosa is a life-threatening illness that occurs when a young woman denies sensations of hunger and derives masochistic pleasure from the control inherent in fasting.

The rigors of breast-feeding are not to be underestimated. Responding to a newborn's needs results in sleep deprivation and exhaustion. As months pass, however, it is possible by feeding at more frequent intervals during the day that nighttime feeding will lessen. Ideally the baby should be in a nearby but separate room so that mothers do not inadvertently respond to every little noise. Making the clear distinction between day and night feedings can be accomplished by keeping lights low, voices quiet and saving play* and talk for daytime. If night feedings draw a very minimal response, the nocturnal creature will change shifts, adjusting his activity pattern to match that of the family. Sudden prolongations between-feeding intervals in the early months are unwise. As in weaning, gradual changes are the least traumatic for everybody.

Weaning: Taking Wing from the Breast
Weaning is a milestone in the child's development, an achievement of independence and the differentiation of self from mother. It is a transition that should be made in gradual steps to avoid not only engorged breasts, but inconsolable babies, and it should not be perceived as a time of punishment. It can be very satisfying if it progresses at the pace of the slowest member of the pair. Often children lose interest in the breast before a mother is ready to wean. Sometimes children are still very attached to the breast, relying on specific nursing times for reassurance, more so than for nutrition. Often a thumb or a soft toy becomes a more easily acquired source of comfort. It is possible to allow a toddler to breast-feed discreetly, as they are at an age when they can understand the

need to wait for an appropriate time and place. Alternate forms of attention through interacting in play, reading or sharing chores* should gradually replace the time spent feeding. "Instant availability without continuous presence is probably the best role a mother can play" (Bailey).

Breast-feeding is not incompatible with pregnancy. The birth of an additional child does not necessarily mean abrupt weaning is indicated. Nursing two children at once is possible and egalitarian, defusing sibling rivalry. Usually the older child needs very little attention at the breast; perhaps the option to nurse is enough. Holding on to our children longer than necessary can thwart their growth, just as can prematurely pushing them out into the world before they have the necessary confidence and skills.

When considering the motivations for weaning, one needs to examine societal pressures and the need for time away as a couple. In 1 Samuel, Hannah sensitively considers the needs of her toddler when she stays back from the temple, delaying the fulfillment of her promise because he is not yet ready to wean. Pediatrician William Sears states, "Early weaning is an unfortunate practice in western society. We are accustomed to thinking of breast-feeding in terms of months and not years. I have a little sign in my office which says early weaning is *not* recommended for babies" (La Leche, 250). We can experience God in "the ever-present now" as his love permeates daily life, flowing from breast and spoon, through laughing mouths, sparkling eyes just learning to read and in the taste of a child's tears kissed into oblivion.

Strengthened and equipped by adequate nurturing, our children are released into the world to feed each other with the fruits of their daily work,* sharing monetary wealth* and the gifts of health and education* with the nations of the world

(Is 58:10-11). As breast-feeding is a paradigm for the spiritual rooting of our identity and the nourishment we receive in God's family and by Scripture, so weaning is analogous to being launched by the strength of our own wings, lifted by love, to explore and enrich the world.

See also BIRTH; PARENTING; PREGNANCY.

References and Resources
L. Bailey in *Promises for Parents* calendar (Bloomington, Minn.: Garborg's Heart and Home, 1990); B. T. Brazelton, *What Every Baby Knows* (Reading, Mass.: Addison-Wesley, 1987); P. Teilhard de Chardin, *Hymn of the Universe* (New York: Harper & Row, 1965); H. Hodgson, *When You Love a Child* (Minneapolis: Deaconess Press, 1992); La Leche League International, *The Womanly Art of Breastfeeding*, 5th ed. (New Market, Ont.: La Leche League International, 1991); V. H. Livingstone, "Protecting Breastfeeding: Family Physician's Role," *Canadian Family Physician* 38 (August 1992) 1871-76; V. H. Livingstone, "Too Much of a Good Thing: Maternal and Infant Hyperlactation Syndromes," *Canadian Family Physician* 42 (1996) 89-99; J. M. Vickerstaff-Joneja, "Breast Milk: A Vital Defense Against Infection," *Canadian Family Physician* 38 (August 1992) 1849-55.

Carol Anderson

BUSINESS ETHICS

Business is often compared to a poker game. Both, it is argued, require nondisclosure and distrust in order to succeed, with only the naive showing their true intentions. Mark Twain's observation that "an ethical man is a Christian holding four aces" reflects a notion still in vogue today—that ethics and competitive environments like business or winner-takes-all games rarely mix.

A Separate Business Ethic?
The poker metaphor serves to legitimize business behavior that would be considered immoral in the personal realm—bluffing, deception and contributing to

another's harm. All of these behaviors are justified in the name of their "real world" contexts.

Advocates of dual morality, that is, applying one set of ethics in the marketplace and another in the home* and church,* expect employees to lay aside personal values* and to focus solely on generating corporate profits. Everything possible, except perhaps breaking the law,* must be done to enhance the bottom line. Subordinates have no right to interject personal values, such as environmental protection, fairness to fellow workers or contempt for dishonest sales techniques, into corporate matters. A century ago businessman Dan Drew, founder of Drew Seminary, smartly summed up this philosophy: "Sentiment is all right up in the part of the city where your home is. But downtown, no. Down there the dog that snaps the quickest gets the bone. I never took any stock in a man who mixed up business with anything else" (quoted in Steiner and Steiner, p. 333).

A soul mate of Drew was oil baron John D. Rockefeller. Influenced by his devout Baptist mother, he developed on the one hand a strong personal religious ethic. His shrewd father taught him on the other hand to win at any cost in business, once boasting, "I cheat my boys every chance I get. I want to make them sharp." Rockefeller resolved this contradiction by compartmentalizing his life into two separate realms. Ruthless in business, he gave kickbacks to railroads, violently suppressed labor unrest and bribed competitors' employees to give him inside information. However, in his personal life he donated nearly half a billion dollars to a countless variety of worthy causes. One writer concludes that "Rockefeller was a conscientious Christian who struggled to end the livelihood of his every rival" (Steiner and Steiner, p. 27).

Such a segmented ethical system is inherently unchristian because it ignores the twin doctrines of creation* and sovereignty. The apostle Paul argues that no realm of life is beyond the lordship of Christ. Indeed, all things were created "through him, "in him" and "for him." His authority sustains the created order, extending over "thrones, or dominions, or principalities, or powers" (Col 1:16 KJV).

As such, Christ has power over all beings and institutions. No human activity—including the practice of business—falls outside of his lordship. To argue otherwise is to denigrate his authority. The sacred-secular split embodied by Drew and Rockefeller must be rejected because Christian ethics cannot be relegated to part-time status, applied only on evenings and weekends. On the contrary, Martin Luther correctly asserted that Christian vocation is best expressed in life's most common experiences.

It must also be noted that business is no mere poker game but a major social institution. To compare it to a game* is to trivialize its importance. Further, not all of its so-called players understand the unwritten dog-eat-dog rules. Many, including immigrants,* family members, the elderly and the young, do not have their guards up and are easy prey. Finally, to argue that employees must turn off their consciences when they enter their workstations is to ignore the lessons of Nuremberg and My Lai (Konrad, pp. 195-97).

God's Character and Human Nature

How then should Christians, having rejected dual morality, behave in the workplace?* Simply put, we are called to imitate God. But what does this mean? Three divine characteristics repeatedly emphasized in Scripture are holiness, justice* and love.* Of course, such imitation is easier said than done. Despite our noblest intentions, we regularly exaggerate, break promises and hide our errors. Why? We do so because we are sinners whose moral grip is weak and whose moral vision is clouded. This is particularly problematic in the hothouse of the marketplace where financial stakes are high, career destinies are decided and the temptation to rationalize is strong.

Even as sinners, however, we generally aspire for wholeness and regret when we fall short. Our consciences, though less reliable than originally designed, are still operative. Personal redemption and the guidance* of the Holy Spirit also contribute significantly to our efforts.

Holiness in Business

During the Middle Ages *holiness* was construed to mean separation from ordinary life in order to pursue otherworldly contemplation. Hence business—perhaps the most fleshy of all human enterprises— was viewed as being "dirty," even antithetical to holiness. Fortunately, this is not an accurate definition of biblical holiness.

Holiness has three primary attributes: zeal for God, purity and accountability.* The first attribute, zeal for God, requires that all human concerns—material goods, career* goals and personal relationships—be considered of secondary importance. As Jesus observed, only one master can be primary (Mt 6:24). Does this mean that God is opposed to business success?* No, the crucial point is that holiness is fundamentally about priorities. As long as business is a means of honoring God rather than an end in itself, the concept of holiness is not violated. What holiness prevents is making business, or any other human activity, an idol.

The second attribute of holiness is purity. Ethical purity reflects God's moral perfection and separation from anything impure. Jesus beckons his followers to "be perfect . . . as your heavenly

Father is perfect" (Mt 5:48), and Paul encourages believers to be "holy and blameless" (Eph 5:27). In business such purity means being morally different from one's peers. This includes, but is by no means limited to, purity in communication (not skewing financial reports, not manipulating contract language and not using innuendo to undercut others) and purity in sexuality* (not making lewd comments, not engaging in flirting and not participating in sexual discrimination).

The third attribute of holiness is accountability. Scripture abounds with illustrations of righteousness being rewarded and of sin being punished. The analogy may be rough, but accountability is not solely a theological concept. It is an economic principle as well. For while the market neither credits righteousness nor sanctions sin per se, it does tend to reward companies that keep promises and are honest while punishing enterprises that regularly miss deadlines and produce substandard products.

Many false perceptions of holiness exist. J. I. Packer writes, "Partial views abound. Any lifestyle based on these half-truths ends up looking grotesque rather than glorious; one-sided human development always does" (p. 163). Three such misguided views of holiness are legalism, judgmentalism and withdrawal. Legalism reduces holiness to rule keeping. Like the Pharisees of Jesus' day, legalistic managers tend to be procedurally rigid, emphasizing policies and petty rules over employee welfare. Judgmentalists justify themselves by pointing out even greater moral lapses in others, having long memories of subordinates' errors. Ironically, they are doomed to lives of hypocrisy because of their inability to measure up to their own standards. Finally, those who define holiness as withdrawal from society are guilty of confusing moral separation, which Scripture endorses, and physical separation, which it generally does not. Judging from the company Jesus and Paul kept, they would feel quite comfortable mingling with today's stockbrokers, IRS agents and sales representatives.

Justice in Business

On his conversion to Judaism, entertainer Sammy Davis Jr. commented, "Christianity preaches love your neighbor while Judaism preaches justice. I think that justice is the big thing we need." Fortunately, he was only partially correct. Christianity also emphasizes justice. Four key concepts are procedural rights, substantive rights, meritorious justice and contractual justice.

Procedural rights focus on fair processes. Scripture requires a decision-maker to be impartial, having neither preexisting biases nor any conflict of interests. Nepotism is a classic violation of this principle. Another example occurs when a corporate board member fails to disclose her personal financial interest in another company with which the board is negotiating. Procedural justice also mandates that adequate evidence be marshaled and that each person affected by a decision be afforded the opportunity to tell his or her side of the story. Thus, auditors must be thorough and able to authenticate all findings. In like manner, supervisors should hesitate before dismissing employees for theft, disloyalty or incompetence solely on the word of a coworker or circumstantial information. In the New Testament both Jesus and Stephen were denied such simple due process (Mt 26:60; Acts 6:13).

Substantive rights are ones such as the right to own property, to physical safety, to prompt payment for work completed and to be told the truth. Hence employees must steal neither time nor material, because such behavior violates their em-

ployer's property rights. Likewise, employers must neither deceive nor discriminate against their employees, because this would infringe on their right to be told the truth and to be treated with dignity. When parties fail to respect substantive rights, the government is often called in to remedy the harm (Rom 13:1-7).

Meritorious justice links the concepts of cause and effect. Good choices (for example, working hard or selecting trustworthy business partners) bring success, while bad choices (for example, hiring a mediocre manager or expanding too rapidly) produce failure. Merit earns its own rewards. Proverbs concurs: "He who works his land will have abundant food, but the one who chases fantasies will have his fill of poverty" (28:19). Similarly, Jesus states, "With the measure you use, it will be measured to you" (Mt 7:2), and Paul advises: "A man reaps what he sows" (Gal 6:7).

Contractual* justice recognizes that individuals may agree to take on additional duties vis-à-vis each other. This may be as simple as a seller and buyer transferring title to a house or as sophisticated as the merging of two multinational corporations. Each party's performance is conditioned on the performance of the other. Examples of such expanded duties include business partners who agree to divide their earnings. By contrast, neighbors* assume no such obligations. Likewise, while employers pay* their workers and retain the right to bring disciplinary action against them for poor performance, friends* possess no such rights. The difference is that contractual justice permits the creation of additional duties. Similarly, God's covenant with Israel extended extraordinary rights to Abraham's progeny but also imposed additional responsibilities. Compliance was rewarded by peace and prosperity; breaches were met with severe sanctions (Lev 26:3-39).

As central as justice is to the core of Christian ethics, it must, however, never be separated from holiness and love. Isolated, it becomes harsh, permitting no second chances for those who fail. None of us cherishes working for a company that fires staff for minor breaches of corporate policy or that reacts in knee-jerk fashion with a lawsuit for every noncompliance by a supplier or dealer. Of course, the problem is not with justice or holiness, but with us. We stumble over their high standards due to our moral imperfections (Rom 7:1-25). A third characteristic—love—is therefore vital to complete our picture of Christian business ethics.

Love in Business

Many consider love to be the apex of Christian ethics. Paul identified it as the greatest human virtue, and Martin Luther thought it best described the essence of God's character (Bloesch, p. 42). Jesus ranks love for God first and love for neighbor second. It is important to note that his definition includes both holiness (making God our highest priority) and justice (always taking the interests of others into account).

Love's primary contribution to the holiness-justice-love mix is its emphasis on relationships. By way of example, imagine an embezzler who now regrets what she has done. While holiness causes her to feel unclean and justice creates a fear of getting caught, love produces a sense of grief over the harm caused to others. Breaching relationships causes such pain.

While it is tempting to define *love* as a "soft" virtue, concluding that it has no place in the rough and tumble of the marketplace, we need only note that business history is littered with companies ruined by fractured relationships. Indeed, commercial ventures depend more upon cooperation than competition. To be successful, partners must get along with each other; supervisors must engender loyalty among their subordinates; and suppliers must be brought into a supportive network.

Love has three primary characteristics: empathy, mercy and self-sacrifice. *Empathy* is the capacity to celebrate others' joys and shoulder their burdens, that is, to sincerely feel what others feel. Of course, it would strain credibility to argue that modern capitalism operates primarily on the basis of empathetic love. Backs are scratched to mutual advantage, and perhaps achieving reciprocal respect is the best that can be expected. Christian empathy goes far beyond this, however, encouraging corporate executives to demonstrate concern for the less fortunate, to take personal interest in the fate of deathly ill associates and to sympathize with sales staff who miss quotas due to unexpected personal problems.

Mercy is empathy with legs. It takes the initiative in forgiving, redeeming and healing.* Christian mercy seeks reconciliation, even to the extent of loving one's enemy (Mt 5:38-44). Other ethical systems refuse to go so far. Aristotle and Confucius, for example, taught that the duty to love is conditioned on the other person's response. The Christian position demands much more, requiring us to live not according to the golden rule but beyond it (Bloesch, p. 33).

Self-sacrifice means that love willingly sacrifices the very rights that justice bestows. For example, an employee motivated by love may voluntarily relinquish her office in order to accommodate a disabled peer. Or a spouse may consent to move so that his wife's career is enhanced. Saint Francis of Assisi was so sacrificial in giving his clothes to the poor that his disciples had difficulty keeping him dressed. Sacrificial love frightens us because it appears to be a blank check with no limits. While soldiers who jump on hand grenades to save the lives of their comrades and Jesus' sacrificial death are admired, business leaders understandably balk at such extreme vulnerability.

Are there any limits to such love? Clergyman Joseph Fletcher, author of *Situation Ethics,* thinks not. He contends that love is Christianity's sole ethical principle and that holiness concepts (for example, zeal for the truth, ethical purity and concern for right and wrong) are to be cast aside when they impede love. Fletcher's approach provides minimal guidance as to what actions should be taken in a morally unclear situation. Does love really provide moral cover for falsifying a document in order to protect a fellow worker? Does an executive's concern for shareholder wealth and employee job security justify his bribing government officials? For Fletcher, "altruistic sinning" is the order of the day. This emasculated definition of love not only ignores holiness but flouts justice as well. What good are the rights of property ownership* and due process if they can be willy-nilly disregarded in the name of love? Justice prohibits such behavior by providing a base line set of rights—dignity being primary—that can neither be given or taken away in the name of love.

Love places limits upon itself. Is it really loving to lie for a peer who is using drugs? Serving as a doormat in such situations may actually cause more long-term harm to the person being "helped." King David's slavish devotion to his son Absalom resulted in a selfish, and ultimately self-destructive, personality (2 Sam 15). Biblical self-love calls us to love our neighbor as ourselves (Lk 10:27). The ethical rule of thumb regarding self-love is an inverted golden rule: if we would feel ethically uncomfortable asking another to do a particular act, then we ought not consent to do it for others. Christian self-love does not condone abuse* or servility. Rather, incorporating the concepts of holiness, justice and love, it produces healthy reciprocal relationships.

Holiness, Justice and Love in Business

A balanced view requires that holiness, justice and love be respected equally. Without holiness, love degenerates into permissiveness. Nearly anything can be justified in the name of love—defamation, price fixing, industrial espionage. Conversely, holiness without love produces unforgiving perfectionism. Who would want to work for a supervisor who embodies such an ethic? But holy love produces the highest and purest form of integrity and compassion.

Likewise, love without justice lapses into favoritism and a short-term perspective. Imagine an employee being given a day off with full compensation without regard to the perception of partiality by other staff. Justice without love is equally unacceptable. To twist the facts of the prior example, what do we think of supervisors who always go by the book, never acknowledging exceptional individual circumstances? Such a harsh approach leaves us feeling cold. Only when combined do justice and love form "tough love," a disciplined balancing of long-term interests.

Finally, holiness without justice drifts toward withdrawal from the marketplace and a privatized form of religion. Conversely, justice without holiness results in an amoral form of procedural fairness that lacks moral substance. Decision-makers become absorbed in procedural details (for example, time lines, required signatures, waivers) and fail to focus on the deeper rights and duties involved. Only through holy justice can ethical integrity and procedural justice both be ensured.

The ultimate goal is to produce practitioners who imitate God's holy, just, loving character in the marketplace. This is the true character of biblical business ethics.

See also ACCOUNTABILITY, WORKPLACE; BUSINESS; COMPROMISE; INTEGRITY; JUSTICE; LOVE; NEGOTIATING; POWER, WORKPLACE; PRINCIPALITIES AND POWERS; PROFIT; SUCCESS.

References and Resources

T. Beauchamp and N. Bowie, *Ethical Theory and Business,* 4th ed. (Englewood Cliffs, N.J.: Prentice-Hall, 1993); D. Bloesch, *Freedom for Obedience: Evangelical Ethics for Contemporary Times* (San Francisco: Harper & Row, 1987); R. Chewning, *Biblical Principles and Business,* vols. 1-4 (Colorado Springs: NavPress, 1989); R. Chewning, J. Eby and S. Roels, *Business Through the Eyes of Faith* (New York: Harper & Row, 1990); J. F. Fletcher, *Situation Ethics: The New Morality* (Philadelphia: Westminster Press, 1966); A. Hill, *Just Business: Christian Ethics in the Marketplace* (Downers Grove, Ill.: InterVarsity Press, 1997); A. Hill, "Colossians, Philemon and the Practice of Business," *Crux* 30, no. 2 (1994) 27-34; A. Konrad, "Business Managers and Moral Sanctuaries," *Journal of Business Ethics,* 1 (1982): 195-200; J. Packer, *Rediscovering Holiness* (Ann Arbor, Mich.: Servant, 1992); L. Smedes, *Mere Morality* (Grand Rapids: Eerdmans, 1983); G. Steiner and J. Steiner, *Business, Government and Society* (New York: Random House, 1983); J. Stott, *Christian Counter-Culture: The Message of the Sermon on the Mount* (Downers Grove, Ill.: InterVarsity Press, 1978); O. Williams and J. Houck, *Full Value: Cases in Christian Business Ethics* (San Francisco: Harper & Row, 1978).

Alexander D. Hill

C

CALLING/VOCATION

The English word *vocation* comes from the Latin *vocatio,* which means "calling"; they are the same thing, though this is not obvious to the people who use these words. Experiencing and living by a calling provides a fundamental orientation to everyday life. But most of the world today has strayed from this and defines calling as a self-chosen career,* usually a professional* one that involves keeping appropriate standards and norms.

The fact that many people speak of their jobs as their "vocation" while pastors and missionaries speak of "being called" shows how inadequately we have grasped the universal call of God to every Christian. As Os Guinness says, calling means that our lives are so lived as a summons of Christ that the expression of our personalities and the exercise of our spiritual gifts* and natural talents* are given direction and power precisely because they are not done for themselves, our families, our businesses or even humankind but for the Lord, who will hold us accountable for them. A calling in Scripture is neither limited to nor equated with work. Moreover, a calling is to someone, not to something or somewhere. This last statement is sublimely significant but missed in this postvocational world.

Misunderstanding Calling

There are many indications that we are living in a postvocational world, one which views human beings as determining their own occupations and roles. Some difficulties arise from a secular approach, others from a distorted religious understanding.

Secular misunderstanding. In the secular mindset, a calling has been reduced to the occupation a person chooses. But "choosing a vocation" is a misnomer. To speak of a calling invites the question "By whom?" It is certainly not oneself! In line with this, vocational guidance* has been reduced to *career selection.* As a secular perversion of calling, careerism invites people to seek financial success, security, access to power and privilege, and the guarantee of leisure, satisfaction and prestige (Donahue, p. 318). Some young people despair of finding a career and wrongly assume they lack a vocation. When people retire* or become unemployed,* they think they have lost their vocation.

One consequence of reducing a calling to an *occupation* is that work and ministry* easily become professionalized,* introducing a dangerous distortion. Without a deep sense of calling many people drift into a toxic mix of drivenness* expressed in workaholism and the compulsive pursuit of leisure,* a debilitating substitute for the freedom of the called life and the experience of sabbath.* But if the secular world has missed the meaning of a calling, the people best positioned to teach it seem also to have misunderstood it.

Ecclesiastical misunderstanding. In most churches the average Christian has a job or profession, which he or she chooses. The minister, however, has a calling. The professional ministry has been elevated as the vocation of vocations and the primary work to which a person should give evidence of a call. Martin Luther was eloquent on the tragic results of this two-level view of vocation, stemming as it did from medieval monasticism, though now extending into modern Christianity:

> Monastic vows rest on the false assumption that there is a special calling, *a vocation,* to which superior Christians are invited to observe the counsels of perfection while ordinary Christians fulfil only the commands; but there simply is no special religious vocation since the call of God comes to each at the common tasks. (Bainton, p. 156)

As we will see, this profound misunderstanding is partly responsible for the widespread difficulty of relating Sunday to Monday and translating Christian faith into everyday activities. Unfortunately the Reformation introduced another distortion.

Reformational misunderstanding. Following the Protestant Reformation, a calling became equated exclusively with the personal experience of the providence of God placing us in a "station," or "calling," where we were to serve God as ministers. Called people live in harmony with their gifts and talents, discerning circumstances and accepting their personalities and life situations as God's "call." The Reformers did not universally teach this.

On the basis of 1 Corinthians 7:17 ("Each one should retain the place in life that the Lord assigned to him and to which God has called him"), Luther opposed the prevailing idea that in order to serve God fully, a person should leave his or her previous way of life and become a member of the priesthood or of a religious order (Kolden, pp. 382-90). This is the one place where Paul, or any other New Testament writer, seems to use call language for the "place in life" or "station" we occupy (for example, slave, free, married, single, etc.). It is complicated by the fact that in verse 17 Paul speaks of the situation as that "to which God has called him" and in verse 20 of "the situation which he was in when God called him." Though such life situations get taken up in God's call and are transformed by it, the call of God comes to us in these situations (1 Cor 7:20) and is much more than occupation, marital status or social position. Although Paul comes very close to seeing the setting in which one is called as *calling* itself, he never quite makes that jump. At most, *calling* refers to the circumstances in which the calling took place. This does not mean that a person is locked forever in a particular situation: "Rather, Paul means that by calling a person within a given situation, that situation itself is taken up in the call and thus sanctified to him or her" (Fee, 309-10).

This Reformational overemphasis on staying where God has placed us has led to reducing mission, suspecting charismatic gifts and, ironically, downplaying nonclerical ministry. But there is a half-truth in this distortion. The purpose of God is revealed in our personality and life path. Elizabeth O'Connor says, "We ask to know the will of God without guessing that his will is written into our very beings" (O'Connor, pp. 14-15).

Reasons for the Loss of Vocation

Several factors have converged to produce the contemporary postvocational society. First, medieval monasticism, based ultimately on Greek dualism, contributed a two-level approach to Christian living: the ordinary way (in society) and the spiritual way (in the monastery or priesthood). This distinction is now thoroughly embedded in all strands of Christianity, including evangelical Protestantism.

Second, the Protestant Reformation, in part because it was a reaction, failed to liberate the laity fully. In medieval monasticism Christians elected a superior religious life by embracing the evangelical counsels of poverty,* chastity and obedience. Against this, Luther and the Reformers restored the central place of the Ten Commandments as God's direction for the whole of life and exalted the civic vocation of the ordinary Christian: "true Christianity" is now located in the everyday life and work of the layperson. "The real 'saint' is the 'secular saint'—not the one who withdraws from society" (Bockmuehl, p. 30). Luther said his milkmaid was potentially more holy than the monks on pilgrimage. The emphasis on a "secret" call taught by John Calvin, however, produced a ministerial elite, and the long-term result was the reestablishment of an unbiblical clergy-lay distinction. The Protestant preacher replaced the priest.

Third, in one sense Martin Luther's famous "Here I stand" speech expressed the emerging individualism of the Western world, an individualism antithetical to the corporate nature of calling. It is primarily in North America that Calvin's fears of the lawlessness of the "believers' churches" were realized, namely, that people would claim to be "guided by God" (for example, in adulterous relationships or immoral business deals) even though the path led to a transgression of God's commandments (Bockmuehl, p. 33). In contrast, biblical vocation involves mutual accountability, membership within the people of God and ethical living for the common good.

Fourth, with the increasing secularization of Western society, a biblical perspective on work* was lost. Work is commonly regarded as a curse from which we should seek deliverance or an idol through which we should find ultimate satisfaction.

Fifth, consumerism,* the compulsive pursuit of leisure, the loss of sabbath, the alienation of workers from management typified in the complex union* movement and increasing organizational* complexity in society (Almen, p. 136) all have contributed to the loss of vocation. The Western world is now oriented toward individual self-fulfillment in the pursuit of career and profession. The recovery of biblical vocation is desperately needed.

Call Language in the Bible

Call (*qara*) language in the Old Testament is used primarily for the people of God who are summoned to participate in God's grand purpose for the world. It is a call to salvation, a call to holiness and a call to service. In the New Testament it is the same. The word *call* (*kaleō* and *klēsis*) is used for the invitation to salvation through discipleship to Christ, the summons to a holy corporate and personal living and the call to serve. All Christians are called. All are called together. All are called for the totality of everyday life. What does biblical theology teach us about the meaning of being called?

The one and the three. In the Bible there is only one call of God that comes to God's people, but there are three dimensions in that call: to belong, to be and to do.

First is the call to belong to God, to become persons who have their identity as children of God and members of the family of God (Hos 11:1-2; Mt 9:13; Mk 2:17; Lk 5:32; Acts 2:39; Rom 1:6-7; 8:28; 9:24; 1 Cor 1:24, 26; 7:17, 20; Eph 1:18; 4:1; Phil 3:14; 1 Thess 2:12; 5:24; 2 Thess 2:14; 1 Tim 6:12). Second is the call to be

God's people who exist for the praise of his glory as we live out our true identity in all aspects of life in the church and world. This is expressed in holiness or sanctification (1 Cor 1:9; 7:15; Gal 5:13; Eph 4:4; Col 3:15; 1 Thess 4:7; 2 Tim 1:9). Third is the call to do God's work, to enter into God's service in both the church and the world. This involves gifts, talents, ministries, occupations, roles, work and mission (Ex 19:6; Is 41:2, 4; 42:6; Mt 4:21; Mk 3:13-14; Eph 4:1; 1 Pet 2:9-10). In this way Christian vocation fulfills the human vocation mandated in Genesis 1:27-28, a vocation also with three (parallel) parts: (1) the call to enjoy communion with God (belonging), a communion lost through sin; (2) the call to community building (being) and the mandate to build a family; and (3) the call to cocreativity (doing), through which humankind expresses stewardship of the earth and makes God's world work.

Unfortunately, most discussions of the human vocation center on the third dimension exclusively. In reaction to this Christians normally focus on the Great Commission (Mt 28:18-20) without understanding that Christ's work of salvation enables people to recover their full humanity and embrace the threefold creation mandate. A truncated understanding of vocation as merely relating to the Great Commission has resulted in the tragic loss of dignity to persons working in various so-called secular occupations. Thus teachers, lawyers, doctors and homemakers have been tacitly placed in a subordinate rank to pastors, evangelists and missionaries, these last being designated as *ministers*. The gospel involves us in serving God's purposes in the world through civic, social, political, domestic and ecclesiastical roles. All three dimensions of the human vocation are fulfilled by the single command to love: loving God (belonging in communion), loving our neighbor (being a community builder) and loving God's world (doing God's work on earth).

The many and the few. In the Old Testament the people as a whole were called to fulfill Adam's vocation in the context of being a chosen nation: (1) to belong to God as a chosen people and so to enjoy God; (2) to live as a covenant community in holiness, justice and mercy; and (3) to serve God's purposes in the world through missionary outreach (Jonah) and winsome living (Zech 8:23), thus being a "light for the Gentiles" (Is 42:6) and a "kingdom of priests" (Ex 19:6). That is the call to the *many*. But within the people of God under the older covenant, some people were called individually to special roles of service as prophets, priests and kings: Moses (Ex 3:4), Samuel (1 Sam 3:10-14), David (1 Sam 16), Isaiah (Is 6), Jeremiah (Jer 1:4-19), Ezekiel (Ezek 2), Amos (Amos 7:15). This is the call to a *few* for special anointed service.

Under the new covenant the call of God is both individual and corporate. Individually we are called to belong to God through adoption, live holy lives and serve God. The individual experience of the call of God means that each person is led by God and invited so to live, work and minister in the light of the wisdom and Spirit of God. While it may be appropriate to speak of one's daily work or specific ministry initiatives as included in the calling, the New Testament does not normally do so! This individual call also has three dimensions, which Greg Ogden outlines in these terms: (1) we experience an inner oughtness; (2) it is bigger than ourselves; and (3) it brings great satisfaction and joy (p. 209). You have a sense that you were "born to this."

Corporately, the call of God brings into existence a people that belongs to God (1 Pet 2:9-11) with members belonging to one another. Together we live a community life that bears witness to our true identity and serves God's purposes of humanizing the world until Christ comes again. This call of God is comprehensive (Eph 4:1) and embraces work, service in the church, family life, civic and creational responsibilities, mission in the world and personal spirituality. The call of God engages us totally and not merely in the religious sector of our lives.

The general and the particular. The distinction between a general calling to salvation and discipleship and a particular calling to a specific context for discipleship was elaborated by the Puritans. William Perkins, the only Puritan author to describe callings in a systematic way, emphasized calling as "a certain kind of life ordained and imposed on man by God for the common good" (p. 46), though Perkins himself often spoke of callings as though they were simply occupations, some of which were not lawful callings. It seems Perkins fused the two ideas of duties and occupations. In time the Puritan movement lost this synthesis that reflects the biblical balance of calling to salvation expressed in the concrete everyday contexts of our life (family, nation, city, etc.).

In summary, God's call is primarily soteriological rather than occupational—we are called more to someone (God) than to do something. Luther "extended the concept of divine call, vocation, to all worthy occupations" (Bainton, pp. 180-81), but he meant that the Christian is called to be a Christian in whatever situation he or she finds himself or herself, rather than equate vocation with occupation (Kolden, pp. 382-90). Further, there is no authority in the Bible for a special, secondary call from God as a prerequisite to enter the professional ministry. The call to leadership in the church comes from the church! While a special existential call may be given by God in some cases, the primary biblical basis upon which a person may enter pastoral leadership is character (a good reputation and ethical behavior) and God-given gifts of leadership (1 Tim 3; 1 Pet 5:1-10). There is no status difference between leaders and people, so-called clergy* and so-called laity,* and only in some areas is there a functional one.

In the same way there is no need to be called through an existential experience to an occupation or other responsibilities in society. God gives motivation and gift; God arranges circumstances and guides. Through God's leading, work, family, civil vocation and neighboring are encompassed in our total response to God's saving and transforming call in Jesus. Misunderstanding on this point has been promoted by the overemphasis of 1 Corinthians 7:17, mentioned previously. Focusing on this one text has had several side effects: (1) it minimizes the corporate, people-of-God aspect of vocation, (2) makes too much of the specific place one occupies in society as though the place itself were the calling, and (3) focuses on task, or *doing,* to the exclusion of *being.* Nevertheless, one should regard the various contexts of life—marriage* and singleness,* workplace, neighborhood,* society*—as taken up into the call of God and therefore expressed in terms of holiness and service rather than arenas chosen for personal self-fulfillment. Thus vocational guidance is not discerning our call but in the context of our call to discipleship discerning the guidance of God in our lives and learning how to live in every dimension in response to God's call. (For an investigation of the process of making occupational and life decisions in light of the above, *see* Vocational Guidance.)

Living as Called People

Understanding and experiencing calling can bring a deep joy to everyday life. Paraphrasing Os Guinness, I note several fruits of living vocationally rather than simply yielding to careerism, occupationalism or professionalism. First, calling enables us to put work in its proper perspective—neither a curse nor an idol but taken up into God's grand purpose. Second, it contributes to a deep sense of identity that is formed by whose we are rather than what we do. Third, it balances personal with public discipleship by keeping our Christian life from becoming either privatized or politicized. Fourth, it deals constructively with ambition* by creating boundaries for human initiative so that we can offer sacrificial service without becoming fanatical or addicted.* Fifth, it equips us to live with single-mindedness in the face of multiple needs, competing claims and diversions—the need is not the call. Sixth, it gives us a deep sense of integrity when living under secular pressures by inviting us to live in a counterculture and a countercommunity—the people of God—so we can never become "company people." Seventh, it helps us make sense of the brevity of our lives, realizing that just as David "had served God's purpose in his own generation, [and] fell asleep" (Acts 13:36), we can live a meaningful life even if our vision cannot be fully realized in one short lifetime. Eighth, the biblical approach to calling assures us that every believer is called into full-time ministry—there are no higher and lower forms of Christian discipleship.

See also AMBITION; CAREER; DAYDREAMING; MINISTRY; PROFESSIONS/PROFESSIONALISM; SERVICE; SUCCESS; TALENTS; TRADES; VOCATIONAL GUIDANCE; WORK.

References and Resources

L. T. Almen, "Vocation in a Post-vocational World," Word and World 4, no. 2 (1984) 131-40; R. Bainton, Here I Stand: A Life of Martin Luther (Nashville: Abingdon, 1978); K. Bockmuehl, "Recovering Vocation Today," Crux 24, no. 3 (1988) 25-35; L. Coenen, "Call," in New International Dictionary of New Testament Theology (Exeter, U.K.: Paternoster, 1975) 1:271-76; J. A. Donahue, "Careerism and the Ethics of Autonomy: A Theological Response," Horizons 15, no. 2 (1988) 316-33; W. Dumbrell, "Creation, Covenant and Work," Crux 24, no. 3 (1988) 14-24; D. Falk, "A New Testament Theology of Calling with Reference to the 'Call to the Ministry,' " M.C.S. thesis, Regent College, May 1990; G. D. Fee, First Corinthians, New International Commentary on the New Testament (Grand Rapids: Eerdmans, 1987); O. Guinness, "The Recovery of Vocation for Our Time" (unpublished audiotape); M. Kolden, "Luther on Vocation," Word and World 3, no. 4 (Fall 1983) 382-90; P. Marshall, "Calling, Work and Rest," Christian Faith and Practice in the Modern World, ed. M. A. Noll and D. F. Wells (Grand Rapids: Eerdmans, 1988) 199-217; E. O'Connor, Eighth Day of Creation: Gifts and Creativity (Waco, Tex.: Word, 1971); G. Ogden, The New Reformation: Returning the Ministry to the People of God (Grand Rapids: Zondervan, 1990); W. Perkins, The Work of William Perkins (Appleford, U.K.: Sutton Courtenay, 1969); K. L. Schmidt, "καλέω," in Theological Dictionary of the New Testament, ed. G. Kittel, trans. G. W. Bromiley (Grand Rapids: Eerdmans, 1965) 3:487-91.

R. Paul Stevens

CAMPING

Camping is the experience of moving from a familiar environment into a new one, usually simpler and almost always in the out-of-doors or wilderness. It is done for fun, rather than work, and is a form of play.* As challenge, as exploration, as experimenting with new skills without the compulsion to make or produce something, camping is a renewing form of recreation* and leisure.* It is also one of many creative ways we put ourselves into a more receptive mode to hear, observe and respond to our God.

When children ask if they can sleep in the backyard on a summer's night, they have taken a step toward untangling themselves from the complexities of their world and discovering a simpler way to live, even for a night. Camping gives us the opportunity to be around the "stuff" that our God has created. When we are immersed in God's creation instead of our humanly made environment, we are confronted with "God's invisible qualities—his eternal power and divine nature—[which] have been clearly seen, being understood from what has been made, so that men are without excuse" (Rom 1:20). Whether it is a family trip or a residential program, camping is an important vehicle to get away from it all, to challenge our abilities and to be more in tune with who God is and what God says.

Life on Life

There is more to relating to the physical environment than mere brawn. For the solo camper it provides opportunity for meditation and for developing self-control. Solo campers must confront themselves. But most commonly families and groups of people camp, thereby providing an opportunity to relate not only to God's physical creation but also to God's human creation in life-on-life experiences. Not only did God create us to live in and care for the created world, but God has also invited us into community (Gen 1:27). It is difficult to role-play on a camping trip when we are reduced, as we usually are, to the bare essentials and cannot merely slip into our occupational lifestyles. Whether on a weekend retreat or fishing trip, a formal residential program or an informal weekend venture with a group of friends, campers usually return to their normal life refreshed with a new perspective, sometimes with a new perspective on themselves.

I once took a group of boys on a three-night camping trip around the Gulf Islands of British Columbia. When we left our base camp, we looked painfully awkward trying to maneuver the large voyager canoe as a team when we were not yet a team. In our struggle we learned a great deal about ourselves and one another as we paddled all day and arrived at the campsite in the pouring rain. No one wanted to help get a fire going to cook dinner, and we could not simply go to our favorite fast-food restaurant. We had to put our selfishness aside and look after each other. On the ocean by day and on the shore by night, we learned survival skills. We also learned how to work together as a team. And when we arrived back at camp three days later, our cooking had not improved very much, but *we* had! We also had wonderful stories to tell the others in the camp. In contrast to the highly competitive environment in which most live today, camping draws out cooperation and invites community.

Sometimes lifelong friendships* result from camping together. Relationships are central at camp because our God is a relational God. Before anything else was, God was and is three persons: Father, Son and Holy Spirit. Therefore when we camp together, we enjoy a double divine context: creation, which declares the glory of God, and community, which declares the relational nature of God. Making friends often happens because we have allowed ourselves the leisure to be relaxed and open, a form of wasting time profitably.

The benefits of camping are numerous. Not only do we get a chance to work together and make friends, some which may prove to be lifelong, but there is time to observe God's creation and see how it functions, to sit around the fire, to look at the stars and talk significantly about the One who created this earth. The order and sometimes the seeming chaos of God's physical creation, the awesome power and unpredictability of the weather* point us godward, inviting us to be creatures dependent on God's provision and care rather than autonomous beings attempting to control everything. A camp environment is a great place to explore the teachings of Jesus and to discuss issues that really matter: Is there a God? What is the purpose and meaning to life? What is the future of our planet? What happens when we die? Both children and adults may entertain questions at camp that they have difficulty discussing at home.

Informal Learning

In addition to being a good place to ask questions, camp is a great place to seek answers, learn new skills and become a more mature person. All of this happens without a classroom, indeed partly because there is none! Informal learning is the kind that happens when we do not think that we are learning. It happens by repetition, mimicking the actions of others and solving problems, in contrast to more intentional methods of instruction. How to light a fire when it has just rained, how to make a meal for ten people when you have one pot, how to set up a tent and make a campsite comfortable, how to climb a steep slope when you need to be roped to others, how to paddle a canoe or sail a boat, how to put together a campfire skit are skills that are learned by doing them rather than by mastering manuals and doing simulations. Camping is an enriched learning environment for crucial life skills: cooperation, leadership, caring for God's physical creation and caring for God's human creation.

According to anthropologists, those things we have learned informally stay with us longest and are the hardest to change. This is certainly true of things learned informally outside of the camping context, including what we have learned about God both negatively and positively. Often people need to live in a temporary Christian community—which is what Christian camping offers—to change their negative attitudes about God and the Christian life. Tragically, many people have difficulty associating play, enjoyment and hilarious pleasure* with the Christian faith. But the informal learning environment of camping can lead to a paradigm shift, a changed worldview* and sometimes even a personal conversion.

When people have an exhilarating backpacking* adventure in the mountains, get up in the middle of the night to go swimming under moonlight, race with the wind down a channel in a small sailboat, dress up for a hilarious skit, play a wide game that takes all day, they are learning all the time. Often their lives are transformed as they come to know God and experience the beginning of abundant life. And the process of transformation continues long after. It need not stop. The Christian faith is about joy, and camping is one way of entering into that joy. By the way, what are you doing this weekend? Let's go camping!

See also BACKPACKING; CREATION; LEISURE; PLAY; RECREATION; SIMPLER LIFESTYLE; VACATIONS.

References and Resources
C. Nicoll, This Could Be Your Life Work, (Imageo, 1992), videocassette; H. Nouwen, In the Name of Jesus (New York: Crossroad, 1993); T. Slater, The New Camping Book (Sydney: Scripture Union Ministry Resource, 1990); T. Slater, The Temporary Community (Sutherland, N.S.W.: Albatross, 1984).

Al McKay and R. Paul Stevens

CAREER

A career is an occupation for which people train and in which people expect to earn their living for most of their working years. It is part of one's calling* but must not be equated with vocation. A calling, or vocation, is the summons of God to live our whole lives for his glory;

a career is part of that but not the whole. A job is work* that is simple toil out of necessity. In one sense Joseph could think of himself as having the career of a shepherd (following in his father's path), a job as a slave in Potiphar's house (something he did for survival) and the vocation or calling of saving the lives of God's family of promise and the Egyptians (Gen 45:5).

In the modern Western world the idea of a career is profoundly challenged on several fronts: (1) The possibility of spending one's whole life doing one kind of work has been eroded except perhaps for the professions.* Even there, people make career changes within their profession or into other professions. (2) Often one trains for an occupation but must learn to transfer the skills to other occupations. In-service training and lifelong learning are replacing the idea of up-front education for a lifetime career. (3) The notion of stability and security implied in a career is increasingly threatened by the exponential change taking place in the modern world largely fueled by the technological* revolution. Workers in the Western societies are scrambling to stay on top of this change.

In a penetrating reflection, Walter Kiechel III asks three questions about the emerging trend: "Can technology help make service jobs as productive as manufacturing jobs have been, in ways that are high-paying to the worker and enriching to society? How many Americans have the basic education and the flexibility to become technical workers or new-style service workers? How many of us are ready for the changes in the very nature of work that the emerging economy will bring with it?" (p. 52). His last question hints at the coming redefinition of work* from repetitive task to intervention in a programmed process, a relocation of the workplace* from factory/office to multiple locations including the home, a rescheduling of the workday from regular to adjustable hours and a rethinking of work life from dealing with tangibles to dealing with intangibles.

Change is something Christians should especially welcome because of their conviction of the sovereignty of God, the certainty of our identity as children of God (not just plumbers or university professors) and the biblical insight that Christians live at the intersection of the kingdom of God and fallen human society—always a place of ferment and change. Because Christians have a sense of vocation, they are able to encompass several career changes within the larger purpose of their lives to serve God and God's purposes in the church and the world. The shift in modern society from producing products to offering services provides new career opportunities for Christians who are called to be servants (Mt 20:26). The challenge to be a lifelong learner fits perfectly the vocation of being a disciple, for the education of a disciple never ends.

With the escalation of information and communication capabilities, and careers associated with them, the deeper questions of what we are communicating will surface. Over a century ago Henry David Thoreau wrote: "We are in great haste to construct a magnetic telegraph from Maine to Texas; but Maine and Texas, it may be, have nothing important to communicate." Speaking to this, Kiechel asks, "Information for what purpose? Knowledge to serve what human aim or itch? Where's the juice?" (p. 48). Followers of Christ will have many opportunities to bring meaning to the secular world as they take their place in so-called secular careers. Pastoral ministry may offer new opportunities to address the soul needs of human beings, though it is debatable whether in the strictest sense the ministry* should ever be a career (*see*

Financial Support; Tentmaking). With escalating stress* levels, antistress professions (including counselors, therapists and exercise advisers) will take on a new importance. Christians will not be immune to the anxiety-producing dimensions of postmodern society,* but they have resources to find rest within the pressures (Mt 11:28).

As free time becomes more important than pay as the currency in negotiating lifestyle, Christians will need a theology and spirituality of leisure.* Sabbath,* the threefold rest of God, humankind and creation, is fundamental to gaining perspective on life, to discovering each day and each week why one is working and for whom, and to learning to approach our work as justified by faith rather than performance. Without a spirituality of careers, and sabbath in particular, we could miss the opportunities afforded by information technology and find ourselves deeply enslaved to our own technological creations. Our identities all too easily become attached exclusively to our careers when they should be founded more deeply (and with more freedom and personal health) on our God. Years ago Augustine said that if you want to know who people are, do not ask them what they do for a living. Ask them whom they love.

See also AMBITION; CALLING; MINISTRY; SERVICE; SUCCESS; VOCATIONAL GUIDANCE.

References and Resources
J. A. Bernbaum and S. M. Steer, *Why Work? Careers and Employment from a Biblical Perspective* (Grand Rapids: Baker, 1986); W. Diehl, *Thank God It's Monday* (Philadelphia: Fortress, 1982); R. M. Grant, *Early Christianity and Society* (New York: Harper & Row, 1977); L. Hardy, *The Fabric of This World* (Grand Rapids: Eerdmans, 1990); W. Kiechel III, "How We Will Work in the Year 2000," *Fortune* 127, no. 10 (1993) 39-52; P. Marshall, "Calling, Work and Rest," in *Christian Faith and Practice in the Modern World*, ed. M. Noll and D. Wells (Grand Rapids: Eerdmans, 1988) 199-217; R. Slocum, *Ordinary Christians in a High-Tech World* (Waco, Tex.: Word, 1986); R. P. Stevens, *Disciplines of the Hungry Heart: Christian Living Seven Days a Week* (Wheaton, Ill.: Harold Shaw, 1993); R. P. Stevens, *Liberating the Laity* (Downers Grove, Ill.: InterVarsity Press, 1985).

R. Paul Stevens

CHOCOLATE

The mysterious and mystical *theobromine* (literally, "the food of the gods"), which is commonly called *chocolate,* is a substance deserving of thoughtful and tasteful theological analysis. As one of the primary motivators of human behavior (hunger, thirst, pain, pleasure, self-esteem, sexual desire and chocolate), it is a force deserving ontological, theological, historical, ethical and relational reflection.

Ontologically, chocolate raises profoundly disturbing questions: Does not chocolate offer natural revelation of the goodness of the Creator just as chilies disclose a divine sense of humor? Is the human born with an innate longing for chocolate? Does the notion of chocolate preclude the concept of free will? If chocolate is a foretaste of heaven, what does it mean that chocolate is freely available to all?

Theologically, the creation of chocolate demonstrates both the unity and the diversity of humanity. Wherever you taste it, in every country of the world, it is immediately recognizable. Other things, in every cuisine, are just food, but chocolate is chocolate. At the same time each country, or culture, makes its own distinctive chocolate: French chocolate has a bitter bouquet; Belgian, a whisper of hazelnut; Swiss, a hint of condensed milk; English, a slight burnt-sugar finish; American, an undertone of peanuts; Dutch, a silken waxy texture; Indian, a trace of spices; Japanese, a touch of soy; Russian, a rumor of cabbage. Yet wherever chocolate is made, chocolate is chocolate. And any month that contains the letter *a, e, i, o* or *u* is the proper time to share it with others.

Historically, the discovery of chocolate by the Mayans and Aztecs dates to the dawn of time. The drink they made from the beans of the cacao tree, called *xocoatl,* was the queen of nutrients, medications, aphrodisiacs and social lubricants. Hernán Cortés, the sixteenth-century Spaniard wrote, "One cup of this precious drink permits one to walk a whole day without taking nourishment." Its introduction to Europe by the Spanish invaders in 1528 began the worldwide spread of *cho-co-LAH-tay.* By 1615 it was served at a royal wedding in France. By 1662 it was reported in England as *chocolata* (Stubbs), and in 1669 as *jocolatte* (Depys). By 1700 it had become an almost universal common denominator.

Ethically, chocolate is meant to be shared. Its essential purpose is the creation of community, of joint experiences of joy, of celebrating the goodness of creation. Chocolate is a primary means of strengthening the human will. *Willpower* is the ability to break a piece of chocolate into four pieces with your bare hands and then eat only one of them.

Relationally, chocolate has been widely touted as a substitute for love. Phenyl-ethlamine (its magical stimulant) is identical to the substance manufactured in the brain during infatuation, so the sweet stuff is nothing more than a counterfeit affection. Is chocolate only a self-medication for loneliness, or does the true chocolate lover sometimes substitute love and affection for the real joy of chocolate?

The central issues we face in confronting this essential substance of the life force, this elixir of existence, are, How shall we maintain the courage of our confections? How shall we live a life worthy of the glory of this good gift of God? and How shall we confront those who see chocolate as a symbol of wickedness and guilt? (I refer to all those desserts named "Chocolate Decadence" and "Chocolate Sin" and to those references to "devil's food" that defame this means of healthful living, this virtuous vital force that can carry us through the light and dark, the bitter and the sweet of life.)

See also ADDICTION; COFFEE DRINKING; EATING; SUGAR/SUGARY.

David Augsburger

CHORES

Chores are responsibilities, generally of a manual and regular nature, that are basic to our everyday operating. The first biblical reference to such activities occurs in God's injunction to "work . . . and take care of" the Garden of Eden (Gen 2:15). The word most commonly brings to mind household duties such as washing, cleaning, tidying, ironing and putting out the trash, as well as a wider set of tasks such as lawn mowing, shopping,* running errands and, in rural areas, work around the farm.* Sometimes we use the word in other settings, for example, the workplace* or voluntary service,* sports or cultural events, generally referring to unglamorous and repetitive activities.

Chores as Burden and Education

Often we feel that chores are a burden we could do without, an intrusion into other more important responsibilities. Few people actually like to do chores, though some find them easier than others and occasionally a person approaches them obsessively. Where do chores fit into the divine scheme of things, including our ministry?* What should be our attitude toward them, and how should we undertake them? Should they be mainly assigned to certain people while those who have more important functions to perform are exempted?

According to common wisdom, at least until recently, household chores were also undertaken by children so that they could learn responsibility and contribute to the full life of the family. Increasingly, when people can afford it, someone is hired—often a person from a minority group and frequently a woman—to look after these. Chores in the workplace are mainly undertaken by juniors so that senior employees or employers themselves are set free for more significant tasks. In mixed company on the job, women are still often expected to make coffee or convey messages.

Generally Christians with important responsibilities view chores as mundane and as peripheral. That is, chores should be gotten out of the way as quickly as possible, or left in the hands of someone else, to fulfill the work of ministry. In this case, chores are done when there is nothing more significant on the agenda or when it is imperative they be completed. They should be left as long as possible and done as quickly as possible. In other words, chores are an unfortunate, or at best second-order, necessity. Rather than being part of the Way, they only get in the way. From a biblical and theological perspective, there is much to question in this view.

Chores as a Privilege and Service
We should view our chores as opportunities to cooperate with God in the divine work of caring for the world. God is active in providentially sustaining, preserving, ordering and otherwise blessing human life. Chores are part of the way we join hands with God in this divine enterprise and are instruments through which the world is maintained and benefited. Because of their repetitious, mundane and sometimes demanding character, chores are undoubtedly a labor and are not always particularly enjoyable. But they are also vehicles for the

maintenance of life and the service of others.

Just as weeding is necessary for growing flowers or vegetables, cleaning house is essential for maintaining a healthy environment and exercising hospitality,* and washing* clothes is required for dressing* presentably and interacting with others, so chores in general are integral to a range of central functions in life. They are not just a preliminary to these but an essential part of them. If the chores are not attended to, we cannot undertake these other activities. Chores are more than a prelude to engaging in ministry, they are an aspect of ministry itself.

Chores are often a more acceptable service to God than other tasks that appear more spiritual and onerous. According to Martin Luther, "it looks like a small thing when a maid cooks and cleans and does other housework. But because God's command is there, even such a small work must be praised as a service of God far surpassing the holiness and asceticism of all monks and nuns." According to William Tyndale this is even true of the most important tasks connected with the work of the kingdom: "If thou compare deed and deed, there is a difference betwixt washing of dishes and preaching of the Word of God: but as touching to please God, none at all."

Chores are also a vital service to one's fellow Christians, to the wider society and to the environment. Our household chores are a tangible way in which we show our care for others in the family. They are concrete expressions of our love* for them and of our commitment to a common life. In this area, as the saying goes, "little things mean a lot." They are far more the touchstone of our devotion and concern than the larger, often easier, expressions of love and commitment that we make in conjunction with anniversaries* and birthdays.*

As we offer our chores to God, view them as part of our service of Christ and undertake them in the Spirit, they become a school or spiritual discipline* through which we are further shaped into the image of Christ. In other words, they are one of the key ways in which spiritual formation takes place. We do well to remember that Jesus was one who waited upon his disciples as a servant, so modeling to them the way they should be willing to perform even menial services for one another (Jn 13:1-17). As we do our chores, from time to time God will speak through them to us, so turning them into a parable of some aspect of the priorities, values* and dynamics of the kingdom. This was why Jesus was able to illustrate his teaching with such menial and routine tasks as sweeping the floor, putting lamps on a stand or getting up in the middle of the night to deal with a caller in order to illuminate God's ways of operating in the world.

Toward a Spirituality of Chores

I have already drawn attention to the way in which the Reformers perceived the connection between chores and the ongoing work of God. Their approach, as well as that of the early Puritans who succeeded them, has much to offer here, especially in view of more compartmentalized evangelical approaches to ministry and spirituality. In the writings of such people, we are reminded that God spends a good deal of time doing the spiritual equivalent of weeding, cleaning, washing, preparing, in our own lives and in the church so that the divine purposes may bloom and bear fruit in the world.

The Celtic tradition of spirituality likewise has much to offer. Consider the attitude to the routine but essential household chore of stirring to life the fire banked down the night before. Through the crooning of a simple prayer

and the familiar gestures that accompany it, this everyday action is transfigured into a deeper significance.

I will kindle my fire this morning
In the presence of the holy
    angels of heaven.
God, kindle thou in my heart within
A flame of love to my neighbor,
To my foe, my friend, to my kindred
    all . . .
From the lowliest thing that liveth
To the name that is highest of all.

In this way a simple chore becomes a sacramental activity, a parable of all activities and relationships through the day. The extraordinary breaks through into the ordinary; the mundane is suffused with heaven.

See also ALLOWANCES; BOREDOM; GARDENING; VALUES; WASHING.

References and Resources
D. Adam, *The Edge of Glory: Modern Prayers in the Celtic Tradition* (London: Triangle/SPCK, 1985); E. Dreyer, *Earth Crammed with Heaven: A Spirituality of Everyday Life* (New York: Paulist, 1994); C. Forbes, *Catching Sight of God: The Wonder of Everyday* (Portland, Ore.: Multnomah, 1987); Brother Lawrence, *The Practice of the Presence of God* (Albion Park, Penn.: Hadidian, 1989); K. A. Rabuzzi, *The Sacred and the Feminine: Toward a Theology of Housework* (New York: Seabury, 1982).

Robert Banks

CHRISTIAN EDUCATION

The average churchgoer views the terms *Christian education* and *Sunday school** as being synonymous. Such is not the case. Christian education is a learning function of the church,* which is tied with worship* and mission* in a climate of fellowship.* These functions are interrelated and supportive of one another. As I learn more about my faith, I am motivated to worship my God more fully. As I worship, I am in turn motivated to learn more about my Christian faith. Likewise, as I learn about my faith, my desire to share that faith with others in witness and service increases. And as I share my faith and serve others, my desire increases to learn more. Learning, worshiping and mission overlap in a fluid manner. The balance of growth between these functions is what discipleship* is all about. Sunday school, on the other hand, is a tool or program that helps the church accomplish the goal of Christian education—which is to educate for growth (Col 1:9-11). To better understand this essential function of the church, we must explore several characteristic themes.

A Lifelong Process

Too often the association of Christian education with the Sunday school has linked our impression of it in our minds with the school model. As a result, we think of our education in the church coming to a conclusion in much the same manner as a student finishes a course or program. In addition, we tend to view the educational ministry in the church as a ministry for children. But education and spiritual growth* for the Christian take place throughout one's whole life. While lifelong learning has enjoyed rising popularity in continuing education programs at community colleges, it remains a new idea in many churches.

More than a Classroom Process

Along with the false idea that education in the church is tied to a school model, there is the view that educational ministry is primarily a classroom experience. In the book of Deuteronomy (6:4-9), we see that parents were encouraged to teach their children the truths of God in the midst of everyday situations. Likewise, much of Jesus' teaching used everyday occurrences as a springboard to an important truth. Our classroom mentality can greatly limit the learning process.

Little behavioral change in Christians takes place through the use of classroom lectures or discussions. In contrast, the discussion of a biblical truth in real-life situations seems to have a more lasting impact on the learner. Foundational beliefs of our faith can be easily shared within the walls of the church, but real application and growth usually take place in the home* and workplace.* The Christian educators' task is to breach this created gap.

Several years ago a teacher of twelve- and thirteen-year-olds in our church took these young people on "walk-talks" on Sunday mornings. The group would walk several blocks to different locations near the church where the teacher would begin asking questions related to the walk. For example, a visit to the local courthouse prompted questions about how a person decides what is right and wrong and, in turn, how God decides what is right and wrong. Another walk to the nearby hospital led to a discussion about sickness* and why God allows suffering. Another walk down a busy street prompted a discussion about why people do and do not attend church. Christian education is much more than classes and programs; maturing in Christ is a dynamic process.

Interaction with Truth

A primary purpose of the educational function of the church is to teach the truth of Scripture (2 Tim 3:16-17), communicating this knowledge to others so they can teach others (2 Tim 2:2). While the methodology of this process may vary, the focus of this endeavor, as seen in Paul's encouragement to Timothy, is to pass along a true understanding of God. This giving of information includes not only the facts and principles of Scripture but other related insights that enable Christians to better live their faith in their society, insights that do not contradict the truth of Scripture.

Information transmission, however, should not be an end in itself. It may only be the initial stage in a process of growth. The learner must interact with truth. Alongside *information* for the learner, *formation* of the learner must take place. This, in turn, leads to a *transformation* through the learner of what they are involved in. When Moses was at the burning bush, he did not just listen to God, but he interacted with what God was telling him. Through his questioning of and discussion with God, Moses began to assimilate God's truth into his own life. He was then able to begin fulfilling the lifework God had for him. Oftentimes in the church we are content with merely passing along truth, never knowing whether the learner has grasped the truth for his or her own life. Wise leaders, teachers and parents allow those we teach to wrestle with the truth we share in order to promote living that truth.

Interaction with Others
God designed the church to be a community (Acts 2:42-47). The strength of a community rests on its members' ability to learn from one another through modeling, encouragement and rebuke. Healthy settings for interaction, such as classes, small groups, committees, work groups, mentoring relationships and friendships, can be a tremendous asset to enabling believers to share and learn from one another. What one is learning often needs to be refined through the input of others. This refining can come through both encouragement and loving rebuke. Encouragement can enable one to apply what is known to be true. Loving rebuke can keep one from distorting scriptural truth.

In the church we often fail to provide this important dimension of learning, as when we rely too heavily on the lecture approach, even with some added small-group discussion. When people hear a new truth, they often lack the experiences to help them turn knowledge into wisdom of life. In-depth interaction is essential for this. The ultimate interaction takes place when modeling truth is included in interaction. Paul reminds the Thessalonians of this involvement when he writes, "We loved you so much that we were delighted to share with you not only the gospel of God but our lives as well, because you had become so dear to us" (1 Thess 2:8). Effective Christian education in the church must go beyond providing programs to providing a climate for nurturing relationships to be formed and encouraged.

The Learning Climate of the Church
Research by the Search Institute of over five hundred congregations has indicated that a primary factor in the spiritual maturity of Christians is their involvement in the Christian education ministry of their church. Though the technical aspects of this study are debatable, the general findings demonstrate the importance of the educational function of the church. Continuous spiritual growth can be stimulated if leaders in the church promote a positive educational climate empowering learners, whether children or adults, to use their gifts for the benefit of the community. In this way learners grow in teachableness. This growth will be seen in ongoing worship, mission and fellowship of the church.

An openness to learning leads us beyond the six to eight traditional Christian education programs in the church. It, instead, leads the church to endless dynamic possibilities for accomplishing the education of Christians. The church itself becomes a learning fellowship. The whole life of the church becomes the curriculum through which all members grow into full Christian understanding and maturity. So while the shape of the educational ministries may need to change constantly in order to be effective in a changing society, the educational function of transforming Christians into believers who know what they believe and who are growing up in Christ (Eph 4:14-16) is essential for every nurturing and growing church.

See also CONVERSATION; DISCIPLESHIP; EDUCATION; SPIRITUAL GROWTH; SPIRITUAL FORMATION; SUNDAY SCHOOL; TEACHING.

Resources and References
E. A. Daniel, *Introduction to Christian Education* (Cincinnati: Standard Publishing, 1987); M. Harris, *Fashion Me a People* (Louisville, Ky.: Westminster/John Knox, 1989); P. J. Palmer, *To Know As We Are Known: A Spirituality of Education* (San Francisco: Harper & Row, 1982); E. C. Roehlkepartain, *The Teaching Church: Moving Christian Education to Center Stage* (Nashville: Abingdon, 1993); D. S. Schuller, ed., *Rethinking Christian Education: Explorations in Theory and Practice* (St. Louis: Chalice Press, 1993); J. Wilhoit, *Christian Education and the Search for Meaning* (2nd ed.; Grand Rapids: Baker, 1991).

James Postlewaite

CHURCH

We use the word *church* in a number of different ways. The word can refer to a building, the members of a congregation, worship services, a denomination, the church as an institution and the worldwide body of believers. It has also been used as a name by a rock group and by a chain of fast-food stores. In some parts of the world non-Christian religious groups call themselves churches in order to take advantage of tax breaks.

Even when we focus on the ways in which church members most often use the word—*church* as the full range of activities in a congregation—questions arise. Those activities vary greatly in character. They may include the congregation's corporate worship, committees, small groups, programs, organizations, events and action groups. How can the

one word encompass all these activities and their different constituencies?

What is its basic meaning? How did it come to have so many uses? What is the primary purpose of church? How can this be given the most effective contemporary expression? These are the main questions I will consider below. Other important issues are dealt with in related entries (*see* Authority, Church; Mission).

The Developing Meanings of Church over Time
The word *church* comes from the Greek word *ekklēsia*, from which we derive our word *ecclesiastical*. It was a common word in first-century Greek and meant simply "meeting" or "assembly." It was used widely of all kinds of formal and informal gatherings, such as the regular meeting of citizens to discuss the affairs of a city, the gathering of an army or the spontaneous assembling of a crowd. The Hebrew word *qahal* was used in similar ways. We find several examples of this ordinary meaning of the word in the New Testament (Acts 19:39, 41).

The word *ekklēsia*, then, was not a religious term. It only gained this meaning by the attachment of other words to it, such as "of God" (1 Cor 1:2; 2 Cor 1:1) and "in God the Father" and "in the Lord Jesus Christ" (1 Thess 1:1; 2 Thess 1:1). In early Christian usage it referred basically to the regular gathering of God's people in a particular place. Luther and other early translators understood this perfectly well when they rendered it "congregation," that is, "those who come together." It refers to the weekly coming together of believers—or to the people of God as regularly reconstituted through their meetings—rather than just the members of a church in a more abstract sense, including those who do not, or hardly ever, gather.

The word *ekklēsia* refers to both the smaller gatherings of believers, "the church that meets at their house" (Rom 16:5; *see* Church in the Home), and the larger gatherings of several such groups, "the whole church" (Rom 16:23). When the believers in several places are in view, the word is consistently used in the plural (Gal 1:2, 22), again indicating that it is a local affair involving actual gatherings, not a generic term for believers everywhere.

Because of its basic meaning, *ekklēsia* is never used in the New Testament to refer to the worldwide church, though in some of the later writings it does refer to the heavenly church in which all believers also share. Just as the local church can exist at two levels, the church in the house and the larger congregation, so do congregations exist in two dimensions, on earth and in heaven. Each local church is a manifestation in time and place of the heavenly church to which all believers presently belong (Eph 1:22; 3:10; 5:22-30; Col 1:18, 24). This is because we are raised with Christ and seated with him in the heavenly places (Eph 2:6; Col 3:1) as a result of his death and resurrection. Here again the sense of "gathering" is present.

As disputes arose in subsequent centuries about who were the most orthodox believers, some began to draw distinctions between those who were the true church and those who were not. This gradually led to the word being used of the people of God more generally rather than of those who regularly gathered and interacted with one another in particular places. As the idea of the catholic church emerged, a worldwide fellowship of true believers distinguished from other believers who did not have the full truth, the word *church* began to gain a universal sense.

When, in the fourth century, Christians gathered for worship began to move out of homes into special buildings constructed on the pattern of pagan basilicas or temples, the word began to refer to the buildings themselves. This association of the word *church* with a building placed the emphasis on where people met rather than on the quality of their fellowship* with God and one another. As the church grew in political power, it became defined institutionally over against the state and so became representative of the sacred over against the secular arena. It is only in more recent times, with the development of the program-oriented church, that the word has been applied to the whole range of activities in which a congregation is engaged.

The Basic Marks of the Church

Down through the centuries various theologians have sought to determine what distinguishes a church from other forms of gathering. The medieval Catholic church emphasized two elements in particular. First was the celebration of the sacraments,* among which were included marriage,* ordination and the last rites as well as baptism* and Communion. Second was the transmission of authority by the Spirit from the original apostles, especially Peter, through an unbroken line of bishops associated with the church at Rome. The medieval Catholic Church placed special importance on the ceremonial and hierarchical character of the church and viewed church tradition as playing a determining role.

During the Protestant Reformation this view of the church was challenged in part. The Reformers placed chief emphasis on preaching the Word of God, followed by celebration of the sacraments, which were reduced to those instituted by Jesus: baptism and the Lord's Supper.* While the Reformers exercised due care in the choosing of ministers to preside over these, they redefined the idea of apostolic succession as a preserving of biblical teaching in the church through a line of people raised up by the Spirit. The Protestant Reformation placed special importance on the homiletical and sacramental nature of church and gave Scripture more weight than tradition.

The so-called Anabaptist movement, or left wing of the Reformation, wanted to go further. To preaching of the Word and celebration of the sacraments, the Anabaptists added a third mark of the church. Since the church was a society of people in relationship, its members were responsible to both disciple and discipline* one another more deeply into Christ. While excommunication had often been practiced in the ancient church, it had mostly functioned as a marker of who was in and out of reach of the church's saving sacramental grace. The Anabaptists placed more emphasis on the responsibility of members to be accountable to one another for the quality of their Christian life. This view of the church stresses its voluntary and relational character and sets Scripture more fully against tradition.

The Pentecostal, and subsequent charismatic, movement has in effect added a further mark of the church, namely, exercising the gifts of the Spirit. The early Anabaptists had begun to move in this direction by opening up the preaching of the Word to a wider range of people in church than just the minister. But Pentecostals sought to reclaim the full range of spiritual gifts,* including those, like healing* and miracles, that are primarily nonverbal. In this view of the church, while preaching generally remains important, celebrating Communion tends to become secondary, and the presence of the Spirit is more central overall than the exposition of Scripture.

From a biblical point of view, there is something to be learned from each of these views. It is hard to deny a place among the marks of the church to sharing the Word of God or to the gifts of the Spirit, but it would be better to see these as all stemming from the same source, so that prophetic speaking and teaching by any member qualified in the Spirit are also regarded as charismatic gifts. It is also impossible to deny the role of love* as involving both mutual discipling and mutual discipline, and perhaps we would do best to view the sacrament of Communion as the highest expression of this rather than as a different mark of the church. Consider the following as a concise, yet also complete, definition of the marks of the church: the church is truly present wherever the people of God associate to share and live by the gifts and the fruit of the Spirit, both of these being centered on the Word of God and expressed in the sacrament of Christ's death and resurrection.

Community as the Basic Purpose of Church

As outlined above, the word *church* acquired the range of meanings associated with it today. Does it really matter? Words are always changing their meanings, and surely we should feel free to employ them. While this is true, problems arise if the theological content attached to a particular use of the word is inappropriately transferred to the derived meaning or if that content is diminished because the original sense of the term is diffused.

For example, according to the New Testament, relationships between members of the church are to be governed by love (Rom 13:8-10; 1 Cor 13:4-8; Eph 5:1-2; Col 3:14). This word has a profound and concrete meaning when it refers to a group of people in close relationship who are regularly meeting together. That was the case in the early Christian communities, both at the smaller and larger level, for even the whole church was able to gather in a house. But when the word *church* is used of a building, of a huge number of people most of whom are unknown to one another or to the universal church scattered throughout the world, the meaning of *love* changes and weakens. This is compounded if the meaning of the word is determined by modern rather than biblical usage, stressing the role of emotions* more than actions and mutual attraction rather than sacrificial service.

The same is true of other injunctions in the New Testament, such as "be kind and compassionate, . . . forgiving," "be devoted to one another . . . honor one another," "bear with each other" as well as "pray for each other" and "carry each other's burdens" (Eph 4:32; Rom 12:10; Col 3:13; Jas 5:16; Gal 6:1), and of other dimensions of Spirit fruit, such as patience, gentleness, goodness and faithfulness (Gal 5:22-23). According to the New Testament, the smaller and larger gatherings of Christians should embody, or incarnate, mutual Christlike and Spirit-transformed behavior.

We come to the same conclusions when we consider the link between instruction, or other gifts of the Spirit, and the church. It is clear from the New Testament that what happened in smaller ecclesial meetings involved a high degree of participation on the part of everyone present. In passages that have house churches in view, believers are encouraged to share the gifts of the Spirit with one another (Rom 12:6-8) and to "teach and admonish one another" (Col 3:16). The limited size of such gatherings presented an opportunity for all believers to take part with their particular gift.

Participation by all believers was basically true of the larger church gathering also. Paul notes that when the whole church came together in Corinth "everyone has a hymn, or a word of instruction,

a revelation, a tongue or an interpretation" (1 Cor 14:26). Though some members played a more prominent part in the meetings than others (1 Cor 14:27-33), especially apostles or their associates when they were in the vicinity (2 Tim 4:2), once again the relative size and— on occasions at least—leisurely length of the meetings (Acts 20:6-12) provided the opportunity for a large measure of mutual ministry* to take place.

At the center of both gatherings for church was a common meal (Acts 2:46; 1 Cor 11:20-34). As a full meal, not just a token, this was a highly social and joyous occasion, centered on the ongoing significance of Jesus' sacrificial death and future return (1 Cor 11:23-34). Perhaps the basic criterion determining whether a smaller unit in the congregation is a house church or just a small group,* and the largest size of a congregation before it divides into two, is whether the members can eat and drink the Lord's Supper regularly together.

All this suggests that the primary purpose of church is genuine community* with God, one another and others who come in range, in which everyone has the opportunity to participate toward building up its common life, both in the church in the house and in the whole congregation. Understood this way, church is community, community in progress, interactive community that is building community among its people and extending community to others.

Church understood as "community" includes worship* but is not exhausted by it, for worship is something that believers should be engaged in wherever they are and whatever they are doing during the whole of their lives (Rom 12:1-2). It involves mission* to those who drift into the church (1 Cor 14:24-25) and also generates, supports and monitors mission to those who remain outside (Acts 13:1-3; 14:27-28; Phil 4:18), but most of this is the largely independent work of some of its members or the overflow of members' lives into their daily activities in the home,* workplace* or wider community, rather than something that takes place on church property or is organized by the church itself.

We would do best to reserve the word *church* for gatherings of the community to fellowship with God and one another and to use other terms for the additional meanings the word has acquired. For example, *meetinghouse* and *church building** are better terms for the place where Christians gather; *denomination** or *network of churches,* for wider groupings of congregations; *worldwide people of God* or *community,* for the so-called universal church; and *religious and civic or political institutions,* for what we refer to as church and state. Events, programs or action groups stemming from the congregation to reach out to the wider community have more to do with mission than with church and should be described accordingly. They join with a whole range of activities engaged in by Christians individually or with members of other congregations in their neighborhoods,* workplaces or voluntary organizations and other interdenominational or ecumenical endeavors that have a similar intent.

Reshaping the Structures of Church

A more discriminating use of language would help prevent inadequate or even false notions of what the church should be doing and would encourage the church to focus on what is most essential. The prime aim of the church, as many are now beginning to say, is to actually *be* the church—that is, to become a counterculture kingdom community in the midst of a world that mostly has a set of different priorities and operates mostly by different values. The church should be a window through which anyone coming into contact with it can visualize, in advance of its full coming, the quality of life that characterizes the kingdom. They should be able to see something of the motivation of the kingdom revolving around giving and receiving in life, the relationships of the kingdom (people of different sexes, classes and races operating without regard to gender, class or racial differences), the economics of the kingdom (mutual sharing of goods) and the politics of the kingdom (decision-making to reach a common mind).

At the very least this view of the church emphasizes the necessity of small familylike groups in larger churches where people do not all know one another, so that the biblical injunctions can be lived out by subunits of the congregation. But the view also raises questions about the optimum size of a congregation. Once this grows larger than eighty or a hundred people, including children, it becomes impossible to put into practice these injunctions as a whole body of God's people, especially if general gatherings are relatively formal and short and subgroups are highly compartmentalized by age, gender and interest. In contrast, once a home church gets too large, it multiplies into two groups, thus increasing the presence of groups of Christians in parts of the neighborhood or suburb where they can be in closer contact with the particular needs of the people around them.

Interestingly, most churches down through history have tended to be no larger, and often smaller, than this. Indeed, even in as churchgoing and size-oriented a country as the United States, the average-sized congregation is still around seventy-five adults plus children. Elsewhere it is often less. While this is generally regarded as a liability, if the purpose of church is properly understood, then a smaller size might be a genuine advantage (*see* Church, Small).

It is worth taking note that adult Sunday-school classes in larger churches, if children were added to them, are often around a similar size.

The basic character of church also suggests that meetings of the congregation should be no larger than what enables everyone to have some knowledge of other members, including the children, so that there is a tangible experience of the wider community. Such a size also enables those whose gifts transcend the smaller home-church groups to have an opportunity to exercise them. Once the meeting of the congregation gets too big, there is room up front for only a few people to engage in ministry of this kind. An appropriately sized congregation also opens up the possibility of each of the home-church groups to contribute in some way, something that becomes impossible once numbers get too large. The advantage of dividing a congregation into two once it reaches a certain size is that it plants a church in another part of the town or city and so strengthens the presence of the church in particular districts or neighborhoods.

Alongside the regular, though not necessarily weekly, gathering of the whole congregation for fellowship with God and one another, other wider groupings of Christians belonging to it will take place. These need not be numerous but should certainly include a pastoral meeting for the core people in the home-church groups and congregational leaders, occasional meetings for prayer as particular needs arise and require attention, and perhaps other meetings for specific groups in the congregation (again not necessarily weekly) who would benefit from coming together across home-church boundaries.

Where a congregation has multiplied or decentralized into two or three congregations, there is still value in retaining a common link, periodically meeting together and undertaking certain things in common. But such a link becomes more like a minidenominational rather than congregational one. For example, its prime purpose should be to provide services and resources to the congregations and home churches. Meetings, which could be held in a rented space or sometimes in the open, would be held less often, monthly or quarterly or during the main festivals of the church year, and would have the character of celebrations and times for seminal instruction rather than developing community through the exercise of the gifts and fruit of the Spirit. Such centers need not be people- or capital-intensive, but they could provide training and education for members of the congregations and home churches which they are unable to supply themselves. This would take the pressure off such congregations from trying to provide the full range of services and ministries that they see present in larger churches but do not have the capacity to develop.

Further, a recognition of the difference between church and mission, along the lines suggested, would reduce the temptation for ecclesiastical structures to enter into time-consuming and cost-consuming territory that can best be occupied in other ways. For example, saying that "the church" should have a presence in business or in politics,* or among the poor and marginalized, implies that this will be mainly carried out through the congregation or denomination. But by virtue of their daily occupations and voluntary work, Christians are already present in industry and politics and working among the poor and marginalized. While now and again it may be appropriate for a congregation or denomination to make a distinctive contribution in these or other areas, their main responsibility is to provide resources for these people and to encourage them to cooperate across congregational and denominational boundary lines so that resources are not fragmented but used most effectively.

What we have, then, whether we look at the Bible or at the challenges facing Christians today, is the possibility of reshaping the church in a way that frees it to fulfill its basic goal of becoming a kingdom community at both home-church and congregational level, as well as through ancillary meetings of equipping and commissioning all its people to extend the lines of the kingdom out into every aspect of society. The church is not merely an instrument to this end; it is an end in itself. But it is not an end for itself: it is an end for another end, the transforming of the lives, structures and culture of the surrounding world. Strangely, if the church focuses too much on mission, it runs the danger of losing community and all that centrally powers the mission. On the other hand, the more the church focuses on becoming a kingdom community, the more it tends to generate mission as its members' lives overflow into the world. This is the paradox or mystery of the church, yesterday, today and tomorrow.

See also CHURCH IN THE HOME; CHURCH, SMALL; COMMUNITY; DENOMINATION; FELLOWSHIP; NONDENOMINATIONAL; SMALL GROUPS.

References and Resources

R. Banks, *Paul's Idea of Community: The Early House Churches in Their Cultural Setting* (Peabody, Mass.: Hendrickson, 1994); R. Banks and J. Banks, *The Church Comes Home: Redesigning the Congregation for Community and Mission* (Peabody, Mass.: Hendrickson, 1996); E. Brunner, *The Misunderstanding of the Church* (London: Lutterworth, 1952); V. Eller, *The Outward Bound: Caravaning as the Style of the Church* (Grand Rapids: Eerdmans, 1980); C. N. Kraus, *The Community of the Spirit: How the Church Is in the World* (Scottdale, Penn.: Herald, 1993); H. Küng, *The Church* (London: Search, 1968); L. Mead, *The Once and Future Church: Re-inventing the Congregation for a New Mission Frontier* (Washington, D.C.: Alban Institute, 1991); J. Moltmann, *The Open Church: Invitation to a Messianic Lifestyle* (Philadelphia: Fortress, 1978); C. Smith, *Going to the Root: Nine Proposals for Church Reform* (Scottdale, Penn.: Herald, 1992); E. Trueblood, *The Company of the Committed: A Manual of Action for Every Christian* (San Francisco: Harper & Row, 1961).

Robert Banks

CHURCH BUILDINGS

The English word *church** is derived from the Greek adjective *kyriakos* implying a place of Christian worship. In the New Testament, however, church is translated for *ekklēsia,* which means "a local congregation" and not a building. In the earliest manifestations of *ekklēsia* there was no confusion, for there were no special buildings designated as places of Christian worship.* In the first century early Christians met in the most immediately available structures, that is, their own homes. The earliest-known extant Christian sanctuary was a private house in Dura, Syria, dated in the early third century.

A case can be made for maintaining this arrangement today. Churches that do not own real estate are often able to invest their resources in ministry more effectively and extensively. The lack of permanent facilities also combats the debilitating illusions of comfort and permanence, which might otherwise be realized. Without a building the *ekklēsia* is composed of "living stones" rather than bricks and concrete. Currently there are many examples of congregations who function effectively without a building. These congregations without buildings are often innovative and well targeted to the ministries to which they feel called. The house church movements in many parts of the world are examples of this approach.

Origins of Church Buildings

As early churches grew and liturgy developed, the homes in which *ekklēsiai* met were adapted to suit the congregation's use. By the fourth century buildings were being separately constructed for Christian worship, adapting the basilica form used in pagan worship. After the Reformation, *meeting houses* provided an alternative form. The model of *auditoriums* has provided an alternative in the twentieth century. Until the twentieth century, church structures have dominated the landscapes of Western civilization. In recent times the university, the hospital and the shopping mall* have come to more accurately represent the priorities of our culture.

A majority of contemporary congregations are accommodated in buildings built for the purpose. These buildings have a powerful influence on the life of the local church. The building determines to a large extent the activities in which the congregation will engage, its perception of itself and the allocation of its resources. The lack of flexibility in many church designs actually prevents congregations from activities to which they feel called. It is important for the *ekklēsia* to examine its essential nature and its mission, as the building that accommodates it is a powerful influence capable of reinforcing or frustrating the expression and perception of the life of the congregation.

Meaning of Church Buildings

What our buildings say about the congregations they accommodate and the way they shape us needs careful examination. Many of the current trends in church design have a relatively recent history and are borrowed from secular building types that may be based on inappropriate assumptions about the nature of the activities they accommodate.

An impartial examination of the main gathering space of many church designs would indicate that the life of the *ekklēsia* is primarily one of individuals consuming live entertainment* or educational services. Many are designed to facilitate the production of electronic entertainment as well. This assumption extends to the buildings of most Christian traditions, with the performance of the presider at the altar the focus of observation in sacramental churches and the preacher in the pulpit or worship team and overhead projector seen on the stage in others. The building form determines the nature of the activity within it and forms the expectations and self-image of those who attend. The fact that many structures will be used no more than a few hours per week implies that this type of building is exempt from the criteria of effective stewardship* of financial and physical resources, which we would apply to most other enterprises.

The use of pews is a relatively recent custom in the history of the church. This type of permanent seating usually means that only one type of activity can take place in the room. The permanence of the arrangement ensures that the possibilities of variation even within the broad category of worship will be limited. Many congregations are finding new life in apparently obsolete church buildings by removing this type of seating in favor of individual, movable seats. There is a growing trend for new churches to be equipped with movable seating. In some cases this seating is arranged in a semi-wraparound form rather than in serial rows, allowing more participation to take place and some interaction between the members.

In our culture communications are increasingly influenced by symbols. Church buildings are symbols that need to be used carefully. For many in the community, a church building is the primary source of information about the congregation within. It has been said that some *ekklēsiai* are private clubs* run for the benefit of its members. The building can communicate this by insensitivity to its surroundings, lack of adequate parking, uninviting and difficult-to-find entrances and other features that indicate it is closed to nonmembers. It is alternatively possible to indicate to the local community the existence of a welcoming, open-ended, serving, hospitable worshiping community that is active and open for the business of the kingdom of God.

Spaces Within Church Buildings
Christians have been endowed with powerful and corporate actions such as baptism* and Communion.* The character of these symbols is often not exploited in our buildings. Many traditions are becoming aware of the power of Christian worship as practiced in the ancient church of the third and fourth centuries.

Baptism was usually carried out on Easter eve. The baptistery was often a pool in the entry courtyard of the house in which the congregation met. The candidate would go down into the water (identifying with Jesus in his death) from the street-entry side of the pool and rise out on the other side of the pool (a participant in Christ's resurrection) to enter directly into the meeting room of the *ekklēsia* as a full member of the company of the redeemed. The association of the baptistery with the entry to the sanctuary has a number of symbolic possibilities.

Similarly the Lord's Supper was seen as a community event in which the presider hosted the celebration with the congregation as active participants. The simple expedient of arranging seating so that worshipers can see one another's faces can emphasize the nature of a congregation as a group related to one another because of their being guests at the same meal.

If the function of a local congregation requires the development of a building, it presents a great opportunity to understand and express the *ekklēsia*'s nature, function and values. The building will help them remind themselves and communicate it to others.

See also CHURCH; CHURCH IN THE HOME; CHURCH STRUCTURES; FELLOWSHIP; MISSION.

References and Resources
R. Bowman, *When Not to Build* (Grand Rapids: Baker, 1992); M. Mauck, *Shaping a House for the Church* (Chicago, Ill.: Liturgy Training Publications, 1990); R. Messner, *Building for the Master* (Wichita: RAM Media, 1987).

Rodger Woods

CHURCH CONFLICT

Susan M. Heitler makes the simple and clear assertion "The health of any given system, be it an individual, couple, or group, can be seen as a function of its ability to negotiate conflict" (p. 47). This statement identifies a critical concern about church life. All churches are vulnerable to conflict, perhaps especially evangelical ones because of their independence and emphasis on the individual's personal relationship to God. Conflict itself should not be seen as spiritually bad news. It is similar to conflict in marriage. The difference between good and bad marriages, like the differences between healthy and unhealthy churches, is not the amount of conflict but the way in which it is processed. Indeed any local church that takes its mission seriously will generate all kinds of conflict; absence of conflict may be evidence of spiritual lethargy rather than health.

Nevertheless, Heitler's statement is challenging. If the capacity to negotiate conflict is a sign of health, evangelical churches are, by and large, unhealthy.

Indeed it has been argued by some that evangelicals are by nature schismatics. That may be more extreme than is justified, but there is enough truth to be taken seriously.

Learning from Secular Sources

There is much to be learned from secular sources. For example, the idea that the best solution is when both parties emerge feeling they have both won is highly desirable. Interestingly it seems often to have been Paul's technique, the letter of Philemon being a conspicuous example. It may not always be possible to attain this, but it is a good ambition. If we love and care for our brothers and sisters in Christ, we will want to work it out in a way that everybody feels satisfied with the resolution.

Another helpful technique is a timeout. This happens when a local church debating a very contentious issue calls a meeting not to decide but to discuss. One ground rule is the avoidance of personality issues. By removing the possibility of a vote, people will be relaxed and heard. A further meeting can be held to make the decision. A variation of this is to call a meeting to brainstorm on the issue. All suggestions are listed. There is permission to include both the sublime and the ridiculous. No decision needs to be made yet.

Conflict in the New Testament Churches

The churches in the New Testament were very familiar with conflict, for example, the Corinthian church, and the classic case recorded in Acts 15. Paul and Barnabas were drawn into a serious debate over the Gentile converts who had been won to Christ during their missionary journey. The argument was ostensibly over circumcision.* Some of the believers "who belonged to the party of the Pharisees stood up and said, 'The Gentiles must be circumcised and re-

quired to obey the law of Moses'" (Acts 15:5 NRSV). This was no minor discussion. Circumcision was at the heart of Judaism. The passage speaks of "sharp dispute and debate" (Acts 15:2 NRSV) and "much discussion" (Acts 15:7 NRSV). The tone, comment and content affirm that the discussion was radical and emotional.

But it does not appear to have been personal. There was clearly lots of mud that could have been thrown. The issues were very important to the individuals debating them, to the community* and to the future of Christianity. Nevertheless, there was an underlying goodwill, and they did not debate personalities. Without this and a significant willingness to hear what the Spirit had to say (Acts 15:8), no agreement could have been made.

Here was a church debate that could have been polarized ethnically, even with "biblical justification." But they reached a unanimous conviction that transcended so many of the attitudes that divide many churches today. This classic model to resolve disputes within the local church reveals the following principles: (1) a willingness to discuss things openly and with a high degree of candor, without putting each other down or introducing personality differences; (2) a willingness to identify the issue clearly, that is, to clarify the matter under dispute; (3) a concern to understand not only what God has said but any fresh truth found in Scripture that applies to the situation; (4) a willingness to negotiate, recognizing that the compromise process does not necessarily produce an inferior Christianity.

It was obviously worth the debate because out of that discussion the whole Christian church has prospered down through the years. The whole Christian cause was liberated to reach the world for Christ. What a wonderful and constructive way to resolve conflict. It is not always so straightforward, though the lessons learned are applicable to all times.

Incidentally, Acts 15 goes on to record the clash between Paul and Barnabas over John Mark. The church seemed to have little patience with them and essentially told them to choose other partners and go about the Lord's work. There appears to be a distinction here: personality conflict has a much lower priority, especially as this was a mission team rather than a local church. There could be no question of their being in fellowship even if they would not work together as a team in leadership. The situation was different for Euodia and Syntyche in Philippi (Phil 4:2), two church members out of fellowship with each other.

Levels of Conflict

Another way of looking at church conflict is to determine how serious it is becoming by discerning levels of conflict. An example of level 1 conflict is disagreement over some proposal that is designed to move the church into a more active role. Not a significant amount of the church's resources is involved. Often what is needed is clarification and a nondefensive attitude by the leadership. A more intense, level 2, conflict is a recurring issue over which strong feelings have been expressed and arguments about Scripture are advanced. A current example of this would be a debate over the role of women in the leadership of the church. A level 3 conflict has persisted with constant escalation for a period of time without resolution. An example is an ongoing debate about a charismatic style of worship in an otherwise emotionally withdrawn congregation. A level 4 conflict is one in which a significant group in the church is determined to have its way whether or not there is a church split and regardless of who gets hurt. There is no goodwill left in the system.

All of these find an example in 1 Corinthians. A level 1 conflict is manifest in 1 Corinthians 16 regarding "the collection for God's people" (1 Cor 16:1). All Paul had to do was to clarify. Level 2 is illustrated by the debate over meat offered to idols in 1 Corinthians 10:23—11:1; this debate has become more serious. The preoccupation with worship in chapters 11—14 was threatening the very existence and unity of the church and had the potential to escalate without hope of being resolved. It is a level 3 conflict. An examples of level 4 conflict forms the lead issue in 1 Corinthians: " 'I follow Paul'; another, 'I follow Apollos'; another, 'I follow Cephas'; still another, 'I follow Christ' " (1 Cor 1:12). A similar level of conflict is found in the debate about expelling from the fellowship the immoral brother (1 Cor 5).

In a healthy church level 1 would almost go unnoticed. Level 2 would create vigorous debate, hard feelings and some losses depending on the ability of the leadership to hold the people together and be responsive. Level 3 would be much more difficult and would probably require some kind of outside mediation, but it is reconcilable. Level 4 in modern church life would demand outside help; it has reached the stage at which a spirit of reconciliation has been altogether lost.

A local church needs to examine the level of conflict and be willing in more serious cases to call in someone, either an individual or a team, who can help them. Paul functioned as a conflict resolver in Corinth. What one looks for in such a team is critical. Eddie Hall cautions the church:

> Listening and mediation skills are great, he says, and understanding personalities and social systems is also helpful. However, skills are not enough. I once was part of a team that had excellent skills, but we couldn't

pray together. That visit produced the least satisfactory outcome of my experience with conflict-resolution teams. (p. 69)

Destructive church conflict is a spiritual issue involving spiritual warfare. It cannot and should not be processed as if the church were General Motors. It is appropriate to discipline individuals who, like Diotrephes in 3 John, are notorious and unrepentant troublemakers. A healthy church will seek the gift of discernment to know how to discipline such individuals. This too is part of conflict resolution.

Out of all of this the local church and the church universal can emerge stronger, more resolute and more effective, occasionally bloodied but focused again on its mission and, more important, focused on its Lord.

See also CONFLICT RESOLUTION; FORGIVENESS; PASTORAL CARE.

References and Resources
R. D. Bell, *Biblical Models of Handling Conflict* (Toronto: Welch, 1987); C. M. Cosgrive and D. D. Hatfield, *Church Conflict: The Hidden Systems Behind the Fights* (Nashville: Abingdon, 1994); E. Hall, "The Conciliation Calvary," *Leadership* 14, no. 1 (1993) 66-72; S. M. Heitler, *From Conflict to Resolution* (New York: Norton, 1990).

Roy D. Bell

CHURCH DISCIPLINE

Church discipline is the traditional term for how the church corrects sinful behavior in the congregation or removes a sinful person from the assembly. The term *church discipline* has largely fallen into disuse in the West because, for the most part, the practice itself has. Anyone familiar with church history should be surprised at this.

Through the centuries the church has shown vital concern about how to discipline its members. Discipline has been one of the most hotly debated and divisive issues. In the fifth century, even an emperor was excommunicated from the church. The Protestant Reformation overthrew many aspects of Roman Catholic polity but sharpened the historical church's concern for congregational discipline. Luther and Calvin made church discipline central to their doctrine and practice of church government. The Anabaptists went so far as to place church discipline alongside preaching* and the sacraments* as one of the three marks of the church.

Why Has It Died Out?
One reason for the decline of church discipline is past abuses of it. Church discipline is abusive when it is used by church authorities as a tool of suppression and manipulation. When this occurs, the church, in time, decides that the price of church discipline is too dear, and it is allowed to die out.

Another reason is that the church is always affected by, even co-opted into, the dominant culture. Western culture is now more permissive than ever and has become increasingly tolerant of what we used to call sin and less tolerant of those who oppose that sin. It is no longer fashionable, and in some cases permissible, to challenge a person's values or behavior.

A further reason for the scarceness of church discipline today is because the church has traditionally defined the focus of discipline too narrowly. In the past it has been carried out primarily to purge the assembly of sin or doctrinal error. This singular concern for congregational purity has led leaders to allow drastic and even cruel measures against those judged to be impure. This often has inflicted more damage on the church* than it has corrected. As a result, churches consciously or unconsciously decided the price of practicing discipline was too high and let it drop from its central place of importance.

How Can It Be Reintroduced?

The church could receive benefits of discipline, and the above-mentioned problems connected with it would be avoided if we followed Jesus' clear instruction in Matthew 18:15-17:

> If your brother sins against you, go and show him his fault, just between the two of you. If he listens to you, you have won your brother over. But if he will not listen, take one or two others along, so that "every matter may be established by the testimony of two or three witnesses." If he refuses to listen to them, tell it to the church; and if he refuses to listen even to the church, treat him as you would a pagan or a tax collector.

Jesus began his instruction by making everyone in the congregation responsible to everyone else for the ministry* of discipline. Church discipline is neither the exclusive responsibility nor the prerogative of church leaders.* This should keep discipline from becoming a weapon of control wielded by autocratic leaders.

According to Jesus, the first disciplinary approach is to be made in private. This prevents the poison of gossip.* No one should talk about another's alleged sin behind his or her back. The person who is suspected of sin must be the first to hear about it.

Jesus' teaching on discipline follows his story of the return of the lost sheep (Mt 18:10-14). Accordingly, the person who has sinned is the lost sheep, and discipline is analogous to rescue. Discipline does not first push the contamination out of the church but rather draws the erring brother or sister back into it. Jesus says in verse 15, "If he listens to you, you have won your brother over." Successful church discipline is not the upholding of some abstract notion of congregational purity but the restoration of broken fellowship.* It is the welfare of the person that is of primary importance.

Everything said about the motive of the first private approach is true of subsequent more public meetings. Whether one or two others are taken along or whether the matter is taken to the church, the purpose of discipline is to persuade the offender to be reconciled to the assembly by repenting of sinful behavior. If the community fails in reconciling the sinner to itself and the lost sheep insists on remaining lost, the church will then "treat him as you would a pagan or a tax collector" (Mt 18:17). In this, we would follow Jesus in his own treatment of pagans and tax collectors. While he did not have an ongoing close relationship with them, he did keep mixing with and talking to them in hopes that they would repent and believe and follow him.

Our first task, however, is to develop churches in which people really know and care for one another. Without that there is no context in which discipline makes much sense. It is interesting to note that Paul's approach to discipline (1 Cor 5:1-5; Gal 6:1-5) is very similar to Jesus' approach. Then if our churches follow Jesus' and Paul's practice, our discipline will have teeth—it will be binding. But it will be above all an expression of pastoral care* in its motive and effect.

See also ACCOUNTABILITY, RELATIONAL; AUTHORITY, CHURCH; CONFLICT RESOLUTION; DISCIPLESHIP; FELLOWSHIP; MEMBERSHIP, CHURCH; PASTORAL CARE.

References and Resources

K. Blue and J. White, *Discipline That Heals* (Downers Grove, Ill.: InterVarsity Press, 1992).

Ken Blue

CHURCH-FAMILY

The meaning and value of *family* may

seem like one of the most obvious things in the world. After all, most of us are born into a family, grow up under the care and tutelage of parents and spend our lives answering (happily or unhappily) to an array of grandparents, siblings, aunts, uncles and other kin. In so many ways, family is the ground we stand on. Small wonder we want to call it "natural" and believe it to be as final and unchanging as the law of gravity.

But in fact the meaning and value of family have shifted constantly from time to time and from place to place. It is well known, for instance, that the ancient Greeks considered homosexual* practice natural, presenting little or no problem for their families. In some places and times, polygamy has been considered as (or more) natural than monogamy. Customs of inheritance, the gender roles of spouses, conditions for marriage and child rearing practices are just some of the aspects of family life that vary from culture to culture.

Contemporary Christians are perhaps more aware of the varieties of family than their ancestors. The late twentieth century is widely acknowledged as a time of rapid and epochal change, as a period of extraordinary diversity and widespread conflict. So Western Christians dwell in societies in which the very definition of family is debated. Do we best understand family as a man, a woman and their biological (or adopted) offspring? Or is a society better off if we widen the definition of family to include two men or two women living together, with or without children? Is lifelong fidelity, heterosexual or homosexual, at all realistic or even ideal? However *marriage** is defined, why do married people have children? In a world of burdened resources, *should* they have children?

All this may be unsettling and even frightening. But in some ways it is a beneficial development. It is only after we

have admitted that the family takes many shapes and forms that we can ask what a *Christian* shape and form is and dream about how to better embody it here and now.

Church as First Family

Modern Christians have often assumed the Bible offers a detailed, once-for-all blueprint and definition of family. But the God of the Bible is not a philosophical construct, not an impersonal force to be dissected and manipulated. The God of the Bible is the living, dynamic source and sustainer of all that is, who deigns to enter history and relationship with the people Israel and the man Jesus.

So the Bible itself is not a list of abstract, timeless formulas providing technical guidance on such things as family life. Instead, the Bible is centrally and first of all the *story* of Israel and Jesus. To create and live in truly Christian family, then, the church* in every generation and culture must read the biblical story anew. It must attend closely to the poetry and prison letters (and other genres) to see how the pioneers of the faith responded to the story in light of the particular challenges and privileges of their cultures. Then, without assuming it can simply mimic the pioneers (declaring, for instance, that all good Christians must wear sandals like Peter or that women will cover their heads in worship like the early Christians at Corinth), the church must respond to the story of Israel and Jesus in the light of the particular challenges and privileges of its day.

Turning to the Bible for clarity of vision rather than technical guidance, we are quickly reminded that Jesus called his followers to live in the light of the arrival of God's kingdom: "The time is fulfilled, and the kingdom of God has come near; repent, and believe in the good news" (Mk 1:15 NRSV). The coming of God's kingdom was in many ways shocking. Not least was it shocking because in its train came a revolutionary understanding and practice of family.

Jesus creates a new family. It is the new first family, a family of his followers that now demands primary allegiance even over the old first family, the biological family. Those who do the will of the Father (who, in other words, live under the reign of God) are now brothers and sisters of Jesus and one another (Mk 3:31-35). Jesus can speak even more challengingly: he forthrightly declares that the advent of the kingdom means brother will turn against brother, children against parents and parents against children (Mt 10:21-22). So far as biological family is concerned, "I have not come to bring peace, but a sword" (Mt 10:34 NRSV). Those who love father or mother more than Jesus, this Jesus says, are not worthy of him (Mt 10:37).

The consequences for the early church were real, visible and disturbing. A Roman family might, for instance, worship a number of popular gods—especially those in favor with the ruling elite at the time. It could be financially and politically costly to worship a single, imperious god, such as the God of Israel and Jesus. So if a Roman son became a Christian, the entire family fortune and heritage were endangered. The resulting conflicts were severe. Families were actually divided.

At the same time, it is important to notice that Jesus did not destroy the biological family. He did create a new first family and call for allegiance to the kingdom to precede the biological family. Yet he also spoke strenuously against divorce* (Mt 19:3-12) and welcomed and blessed children (Mk 10:13-16; Lk 18:15-17). So Jesus did not expect the biological family to be denied or eliminated. What he did was decenter and relativize it. He did not see it as the vehicle of salvation. He expected the first family,

the family of the kingdom, to grow evangelistically rather than biologically (Mt 28:19-20). Entrance to the kingdom in fact required a second birth, this time of water and the Spirit (Jn 3:5-6). For those who would follow Jesus, the critical blood, the blood that most significantly determines their identity and character, is not the blood of the biological family. It is the blood of the Lamb.

The sense of *church* as the first family is also clear in the letters of Paul. His most significant language for describing the church is the language of family. For Paul, Christians are children of God and brothers and sisters to one another (see, for instance, 1 Thess 1:4, 6). The phrase "my brothers" occurs more than sixty-five times in his letters. Paul can also call members of a church "my children" (as in 1 Cor 4:14; Gal 4:19). Both the number and the intensity of these familial phrases make Paul's letters remarkable in their time and place.

Such greetings* were not merely pious niceties. The church Paul knew met in households. Paul expected and depended on Christians' opening their homes (and thus their biological families) to Christian brothers and sisters (Rom 16:5; 1 Cor 16:15; Col 4:15; Philem 2). Such hospitality* extended to a wide network of Christians, including missionaries and those on business trips (2 Cor 8:23). By so opening their homes, these Christians in effect recognized and welcomed "relatives" near and distant.

On a more basic level, Paul crucially links familial language with baptism. The Gospel of John, as we have noted, recognizes a need for the disciples of Jesus to be born again, to know a second birth that redefines identity and admits the disciple to a family-community that will nurture the new identity. Paul has similar concerns but addresses them with the language of adoption rather than birth (Rom 8:15-17; Gal 3:26—4:6). He reminds believers that they have a new identity because they have been baptized into Christ. When children are adopted, they take on new parents, new sisters and brothers, new names, new inheritances. And those who have been baptized into Christ, according to Paul, have been adopted by God. This new baptism* means that Christians' new parent is God the Father ("Abba," cries Paul). Their new siblings are other Christians. Their new name or most fundamental identity is simply "Christian"—one of those who know Jesus as Lord and determiner of their existence. And their new inheritance is freedom, community* and resources provided a hundredfold (Mk 10:28-31; Gal 3:26—4:6).

New Testament scholar N. T. Wright affirms in dramatic terms the centrality of what is here called *first family*. Noting that "from baptism onwards, one's basic family consisted of one's fellow-Christians," he writes:

> The fact of widespread persecution, regarded by both pagans and Christians as the normal state of affairs within a century of the beginnings of Christianity, is powerful evidence of the sort of thing Christianity was, and was perceived to be. It was a new family, a third "race," neither Jew nor Gentile but "in Christ." (Wright, pp. 449-50)

Single in First Family

One of the immediate and down-to-earth effects of Jesus' creation of a new family is that single, or unmarried, people are very much a part of family. Perhaps it is not too strong to say that there is at least one sure sign of a flawed vision of the Christian family: it denigrates and dishonors singleness.*

It was in the light of the kingdom come that Paul could write, "He who marries his fiancée does well; and he who refrains from marriage will do better" (1 Cor 7:38 NRSV). How could single-

ness be better than marriage? Paul recognized that the age of the kingdom does not come painlessly. Jesus announced and embodied God's kingdom; the church after him witnesses to this Lord and his kingdom. But this means all false gods and idols are challenged. The rule of the principalities and powers*—the undue, overreaching claims of governments, markets, fashions, cultures,* educational and other institutions—is revealed to be illegitimate and ultimately destructive. So the false gods are not friendly to Jesus and those who would worship only the God he called Father. And so we live in awkward times. A new age has arrived but is not here in its fullness; the old age drags on with more than a little effect and efficiency. Because the powers of the old age remain real and often malignant, Christians can survive only with hope—the hope of Jesus' return and the complete manifestation of God's loving, just rule. In these circumstances, Paul notices that the married person may sink more deeply into the affairs of the passing world, or the old age, than singles (1 Cor 7:33). With spouse and children, the married person takes on additional responsibilities and anxieties. The single person can live and serve in less complicated "devotion to the Lord" (1 Cor 7:35).

For our day, Paul's awareness of the advantages of singleness can serve as a reminder that in Christian (or first) family singleness and marriage are complementary. And this complementarity has some quite practical effects. Christian parenting,* for instance, is a task for the entire church. It is a responsibility (as baptismal ceremonies in many traditions imply) even for those who have never conceived or legally adopted a child. This is not to dispute the primacy of biological or adoptive parents. But in Jesus' and Paul's first family, Christian parents are agents of the church. And they are engaged in a task too big and important for them alone. Single Christians should not be exempt from either the joys or the responsibilities that children bring. Singles are significant role models. In a transient society where many children are separated from biological relatives by hundreds of miles, singles can serve invaluably as surrogate grandparents or aunts and uncles. (A service most important, of course, to the parent without a spouse.)

Serving the church's mission,* singles also have the advantage of mobility.* On balance it is simpler for the single, should it seem right, to move to a new situation, to make do with less money or even to confront potentially dangerous circumstances. This is not something for married Christians to exploit: no Christian, married with children or not, is exempt from moving, giving up possessions or facing danger. Yet singles can affirm a unique missionary advantage and take it seriously.

Married in First Family
If singles have the missionary advantage of mobility, married Christians may possess the missionary advantage of hospitality. Christians are peculiar people with a long tradition of welcoming strangers. God called the Israelites to love and care for strangers, since they were strangers themselves in the land of Egypt (Lev 19:33-34; Deut 10:17-19). Jesus welcomed strangers or outsiders of many sorts, even to the point of inviting them to table with him. So too the early church put hospitality at the center of its life. As we have noted, Christians generously opened their homes to fellow believers. Christians are called to be hospitable within both the first family of the church and the second, or biological, family, and Paul effusively praises families whose homes are the hub of the church in several cities (Rom 16:5, 23; 1 Cor 16:15;

Col 4:15; Philem 2).

Among the significant strangers Christian parents must welcome are their own children. Our children are strangers to us in many ways: they come to us as aliens and have to learn to live in our world; they ask awkward questions ("If Christians are supposed to love each other, how can they kill each other in wars?" "Why is God letting my little sister die of cancer?") that remind us how strange we ourselves are. Christian parenthood, then, is practice in hospitality, in the welcoming and support of strangers. Welcoming the strangers who are our children, we learn a little about being out of control and about the possibility of surprise (and so of hope). Moment by mundane moment—dealing with rebellion, hosting birthday* parties, struggling to understand exactly what a toddler has dreamed and been so frightened by in the night—we pick up skills in patience, empathy, generosity, forgiveness. And all these are transferable skills, skills we can and must use to welcome other strangers besides our children. We become better equipped to open ourselves to strangers who are not our children but our brothers and sisters in Christ. Thus the Christian home can be a mission base in many ways.

The Christian Home as Mission Base
The Christian home is a mission base when Christians live in intentional community, such as Chicago's Jesus People U.S.A. or Washington's Sojourners Fellowship. But the Christian home is also a mission base when Christians who happen to live in the same neighborhood enjoy meals together, share a lawn mower and tree-trimming tools or "exchange" kids for an occasional evening.

The Christian home is a mission base when members of a church move into the same apartment complex, sponsor

Bible studies and organize supervision of the playground. It is a mission base when it opens its doors to missionaries on furlough, friends marooned between apartment leases, someone out of work or a family that has lost its home to a fire. It is a mission base providing us resources and encouragement from which to launch into new mission endeavors—whether across town or across the world.

The point is simple. In a world that offers less and less nominal support for Christian practices, in a world increasingly fragmented, hostile and lonely, there is no end to ways the Christian home can serve as a mission base. The limit, quite literally, is our imagination.

In sum, Christian family is first and finally the life of the church. It includes singles and marrieds, those with and those without biological or adoptive children—all called to exercise unique but complementary missionary advantages. Its purpose is to witness, through its shape and practice, to the kingdom of the God met in Israel and Jesus. Christian family is where we live not so much in a "private" haven from the world as in a mission base to the world. The Christian home is where we strain and labor and sometimes weep in service to the kingdom. But it is also where we learn to "do" mission as rest* and play,* where welcoming friends and reading novels and planting gardens and making babies are among our most noble moral endeavors. It is where we do our most strenuous and refreshing work—for what could be more strenuous and more refreshing than rearing children?

See also CHURCH; CHURCH IN THE HOME; FELLOWSHIP; GODPARENTING; HOSPITALITY; LOVE; PARENTING; SINGLENESS; WITNESS.

References and Resources
R. S. Anderson and D. B. Guernsey, *On Being Family: A Social Theology of the Family* (Grand Rapids: Eerdmans, 1985); B. Berger and P. L. Berger, *The War over the Family* (Garden City, N.Y.: Doubleday, 1983); R. Clapp, *Families at the Crossroads: Beyond Traditional and Modern Options* (Downers Grove, Ill.: InterVarsity Press, 1993); D. E. Garland and D. R. Garland, "The Family: Biblical and Theological Perspectives," in *Incarnational Ministry: The Presence of Christ in Church, Society and Family,* ed. C. D. Kettler and T. H. Speidell (Colorado Springs: Helmers & Howard, 1990) 226-40; S. Hauerwas, *A Community of Character* (Notre Dame, Ind.: University of Notre Dame Press, 1981) 155-95; W. H. Willimon, *The Service of God* (Nashville: Abingdon, 1983) 170-86; N. T. Wright, *The New Testament and the People of God* (Minneapolis: Fortress, 1992).

Rodney Clapp

CHURCH IN THE HOME

According to some leading observers of the Christian scene, the two fastest growing forms of church life today are the very large church, including the megachurch,* and the church in the home. The latter is found under various names, for example, house (or home) church, basic Christian (or basic ecclesial or small faith) community and street (or neighborhood) church. What is this form of church life? How does it justify itself? What are some of its main operating principles? Why is it growing in so many places today?

What Is the Church in the Home?
The terms *house church* and *church in the home* conjure up different pictures in people's minds. In some Protestant circles they describe any regular meeting in homes by members of a congregation for any religious purpose whatsoever, for example, for prayer, study, support or mission. These meetings are often in small groups.* In many Catholic circles these terms often refer to the family* as it seeks to live out the gospel and as it prays and listens to Scripture together. In certain

charismatic circles these terms refer to the emergence of newer independent groupings of congregations that began but may no longer center in homes.

None of these captures the full sense of a house church or church in the home. This is essentially a group of adults and children meeting in a house, apartment or other convivial space, who have covenanted to meet together regularly as an extended Christian family. In doing this they engage in all the functions of a church gathering—praying and praising God, learning and teaching God's Word, eating and drinking together in God's name—as well as share their life together, take responsibility for one another, become mutually accountable and assist each other to be involved in ministry* and mission* to the wider community.

Generally those involved in a house church also meet regularly, though not necessarily weekly, with a larger group of Christians for fellowship with God and one another. This may take the form of a cluster of home churches that have combined meetings or a congregation that is part of an existing denominational* or nondenominational* grouping. However this takes place, participants experience church* at two levels, both as a smaller phenomenon and as a larger (though not necessarily big) one, each of which has a unique value.

What Is the Basis for the Church in the Home?
In Old Testament times, believers met for corporate worship and fellowship primarily in their homes* on the sabbath* and in the temple for major festivals. One of the main festivals, the Passover, was itself centered on the home and included children in a significant way (Ex 12). From the day of Pentecost, the first Christians in Jerusalem met in both homes and in the temple, in the former

dining together and praising God and in the latter hearing the apostles' teaching and participating in the wider fellowship* (Acts 2:42-47).

As the apostles preached the gospel, communities of faith were formed throughout the ancient world. These also operated at two levels—the church in the home (Rom 16:5; 1 Cor 16:19; Col 4:15; Philem 2; compare Acts 16:40; 18:7; 20:8) and the church in a town or city (1 Cor 1:2; 2 Cor 1:1; 1 Thess 1:1; 2 Thess 1:1). Though in some places the believers were not all able to gather together (even a century later this did not happen in Rome), where possible they seem to have met both as extended Christian families in an apartment or house and as a gathering of such groups in the house of a significant member (Rom 16:23).

Based on what is said in passages mentioning the smaller gatherings for church in the home, or in letters where one is mentioned, meetings involved exchanging greetings* and the kiss of peace (1 Cor 16:19-20), giving mutual encouragement (Acts 16:40; compare Heb 10:25), teaching and admonishing one another, singing psalms and hymns and spiritual songs to God (Col 3:16), contributing gifts of prophecy, financial aid and practical help (Rom 12:6-8), showing love,* mercy and hospitality* (Rom 12:9-13) and, as mentioned before, eating the Lord's Supper (Acts 2:46; see Communion).

Though traces of the church in the home disappear at certain points in church history—partly because such gatherings do not leave much in the way of records—evidence for their existence, or the existence of groups sharing many of their features, is present. Archaeological evidence shows that for most of the first three centuries Christians met in their own homes or converted homes to wider church use. In the following centuries, small communal and ecclesial (churchlike) groups regularly surfaced, especially in times of major reform or renewal: the earliest monastic groups in late antiquity, the non-Catholic Waldensians in the Middle Ages, the Anabaptists during the Reformation, the Quaker meetings and Methodist classes in the early modern period, the conventicles or "little churches within the church" among the German Pietists, and such later groups as the Scottish Covenanters and early Plymouth Brethren.

During the twentieth century the church in the home has taken various forms, for example, the underground churches in Eastern Europe prior to the fall of the Iron Curtain, basic ecclesial communities in Latin America and Asia, house churches in India and mainland China, new independent Christian movements in various parts of Africa, and house churches in the West. Some of these arose for practical reasons such as too few clergy,* some as a response to political oppression or social injustice, some because of impersonal, disempowering or hierarchical encounters with church structures.* On the whole, house churches have had a strong emphasis on laity,* frequently combined with a commitment to linking faith with everyday life and a desire to have an enhanced presence and witness in their local neighborhoods.*

The movement toward the church in the home tends to avoid any formula-driven approach to church life. Not only do individual groups develop their own unique identity, one which may change over time, but clusters or networks of such groups also develop their own distinctive character. Some are more charismatic than others, some more structured; some are more concerned with social action, some with evangelism*; some have a greater ecological commitment, some a stronger cultural one; some are more interested in restoring biblical patterns, others in finding contemporary expressions of biblical intentions. There may also be theological, cultural and denominational differences.

What Are the Marks of the Church in the Home?

In contrast to typical small groups in the local church, or larger meetings of a congregation, home churches tend to have the following characteristics:

1. Giving quantity as well as quality time to one another and God as participants meet for several hours a week. This includes praying, singing, eating,* sharing, learning, planning* and—especially with children—playing* together.

2. Churching together as an expression of being a community,* not simply reproducing a smaller-scale version of what happens on a Sunday. This provides an opportunity for members to share whatever gifts they have to offer and to develop a common life.

3. Making decisions about all major matters affecting the group by consensus. This involves seeking to reach a common mind under God rather than a democratic process of agreement or abiding by a majority vote.

4. Recognizing children and teenagers as equally important as adults and integrating them in as many activities as possible. This leaves room for activities especially designed for them, as well as time with an adult apart from the main group.

5. Incorporating a sacramental dimension through combining the Lord's Supper with a common meal. This is introduced by a member or household with readings and prayer, and Christ's sacrifice is held out as a model for, as well as a basis for, the group's life.

6. Building strong relationships in the group between the members, including the children. This involves members' be-

ing willing to care for others in practical ways and making themselves accountable to others in major areas of discipleship.

7. Integrating Sunday and weekday, private and public responsibilities. This takes place as people bring their ordinary concerns to the group for processing by Scripture, experience and prayer and as they celebrate their family, work and social life.

8. Developing leadership* organically rather than through top-down appointment. This takes place as a core group of men and women with pastoral capacities emerges. These members are then recognized and encouraged in some way by the group.

9. Assisting each member to identify his or her unique ministry to the group, to the larger church and to the wider community and world. Support for these ministries takes place inside and outside the group through interest, prayer and sometimes financial aid.

10. Looking for new members to invite into the group and multiplying the group when it becomes too large and unwieldy. The latter normally takes place by commissioning a few members of the existing church in the home to go out and bud a new one.

How Do Home Churches Differ from a Cell Church?

Both approaches to renewing the church recognize the central place occupied by the home in the ministry of Jesus and in the early Christian movement. In the cell-church model, converts are grouped into home cells, and several home cells are grouped to form a congregation. Cell churches stress the role of every believer in these meetings and the character of leadership as nonspecialist and nonhierarchical. Each home cell has a servant-leader or deacon; in time—after two years perhaps—a cluster of five

home churches would have a servant-elder; a congregation of some twenty-five groups would have a pastoral leader. There are also the citywide apostles, prophets, evangelists and teachers whose main function is to equip the churches within their region. Though the language of servant leadership is used, all positions of responsibility are described as "offices." This people-based design for the church is set over against the program-based design of most congregations, which is built up in a corporate managerial fashion around the hierarchy of specialists, committees and organizations.

There are a number of key differences between the cell-church model and the one I am advocating. First, the structure of the early church is interpreted too much in terms of the present practice of cell churches. While to some extent we all tend to read into the biblical accounts our own ideas and frameworks, the precise numbers and organizational grid attached to the cell-group reconstruction do this in an observable, somewhat managerial way. While the model moves away from a hierarchical view of leadership, the role of the leader (always singular) in the individual cells, cluster of cell groups and cell-group church suggests top-down, chain-of-command elements that sit uneasily with the side-by-side, spheres-of-influence approach that is more in keeping with the early church. Congregational meetings are also larger than what would allow them to operate in a sufficiently interactive way.

Second, there are also a number of important differences between the way cell groups and home churches work. Cell groups normally meet for around an hour and a half, not three or more hours, and appear more task-oriented. Since they are to grow new groups every four months, they change more rapidly and so allow little time for deep relationships to build. When there is a sufficient number of cell groups to form a congregational network, they are often redistributed, thus further weakening communal bonds. Children and teenagers in cell groups are regarded more as witnesses to what takes place than as full participants, or they have separate cell groups altogether. Indeed, cell groups can be relatively homogeneous rather than being as much as possible a microcosm of the whole church. So while there are some similarities between the cell church and interactive congregations based on home churches, there are also some fundamental differences.

Why Is This Form of Church Life Growing?

There are several reasons why house churches are growing in popularity. In these groups people experience together the reality of God in ordinary settings and relationships of life rather than mainly in a separate, sacred space and time.* God becomes present, vivid, intimate in the familiar setting of a living room, around the dining-room table, in washing dishes and cleaning up, in playing with children. God becomes present in the midst of discussion, prayer and learning about everyday pressures, responsibilities and challenges. In other words, the reality of God appears in the midst of everyday realities.

In such groups many people are discovering for the first time a sense of genuine family* life or the value of the extended family. Believers who come into such groups from broken or dysfunctional families often are reparented. Others start to appreciate the benefit of belonging to an extended family as opposed to just the nuclear family. All gain the opportunity of a place to belong, the experience of acceptance, a setting in which they can gradually make themselves

vulnerable and share as well as test out their personal and vocational dreams. As in a good family, in time members of the group also begin to develop fresh rituals for celebrating the ordinary and special events that come their way.

As the common life of members in the group deepens and expands, they begin to see ways in which more holistic forms of Christian education* are taking place, both for themselves and for their children. The ethos of the group plays a highly formative role in shaping the priorities and values* of its members. Parents learn from observing the way other parents in the group parent children, relate, develop their lifestyle, make decisions, deal with work,* face difficulties, endure illness or suffering. More focused learning opportunities within the meeting are always practical as well as instructive.

The church in the home increasingly becomes a safe house for members and newcomers who are often on the margins of our society. Unmarried people, those who have been widowed, the physically or mentally challenged, single parents, overseas visitors, lonely people or social misfits—all these can find a home and support. In an increasingly busy, mobile and fragmented society, the church in the home becomes ever more important as a form of available and relevant community for those who seek it.

None of this is intended to downplay the difficulties sometimes encountered in belonging to such a group. It requires a deeper commitment than participation in most small groups* or membership* in larger congregations. Belonging can lead to more open conflicts between members than what transpires in more anonymous settings. It may take longer to develop forms of leadership or servanthood within the group. On the other hand, commitment develops through people's being voluntarily drawn and loved into such a community, not through its being a demand imposed on them. If properly handled, conflict is one of the primary ways of moving forward into a deeper experience of divine and human community. Leadership becomes a corporate reality, shared among the whole group as well as embodied in core people within the group who model God's faithfulness, love and vision. Among the growing number of Christians who belong to a church in the home, there is a conviction that the widespread growth of these groups is the next stage of the small-group movement and that their reappearance in the church is fundamental to its renewal and expansion in our day.

See also CHURCH; COMMUNITY; FELLOWSHIP; HOME; SMALL GROUPS.

References and Resources

R. Banks, *Going to Church in the First Century* (Beaumont, Tex.: Christian Books, 1990); R. Banks and J. Banks, *The Church Comes Home: Redesigning the Congregation for Community and Mission* (Peabody, Mass.: Hendrickson, 1996); A. R. Baranowski, *Creating Small Faith Communities: A Plan for Restructuring the Parish and Renewing Catholic Life* (Cincinnati, Ohio: St. Anthony Messenger, 1988); L. Barrett, *Building the House Church* (Scottdale, Penn.: Herald, 1986); B. J. Lee and M. A. Cowan, *Dangerous Memories: House Churches and Our American Story* (Kansas City, Mo.: Sheed & Ward, 1986); C. Smith, *Going to the Root: Nine Proposals for Church Reform* (Scottdale, Penn.: Herald, 1992).

Robert Banks

CHURCH RENEWAL

Renewal is difficult to define. It can mean different things to different people. Even the dictionary suggests several options, from "restore to original state" (as in a painting) to "replenish with a fresh supply" (as in recharging a dead battery). Church renewal has encompassed both of the above, that is, a desire by churches to rediscover the life and form of the early church and to restore its "Pentecostal" power.

Ecclesiastical and Charismatic Renewal

In England the late David Watson (*I Believe in the Church*) and in North America Howard Snyder (*Community of the King*) are but two authors among many who have tried to share a vision of church life that is more vital and effective. This ecclesiological emphasis on renewal stressed the priesthood and giftedness of all believers and that the role of church leadership* was to equip* God's people to do the ministries so long designated as "clergy*" roles (Eph 4:11-16; see Stevens).

Alongside of, and vital to, ecclesiological renewal has been the charismatic movement. Controversial, multifaceted and at times schismatic, it has nevertheless brought new life to most denominations. Not all charismatics have exactly the same theology. Some believe that the baptism of the Holy Spirit (accompanied by the gift of tongues) is a distinct and special experience that launches a believer into a new life of power and spiritual giftedness.* Others, while strongly affirming that all the gifts of the Spirit exist today, do not believe that the baptism in the Spirit is a special (or second) work of grace. They believe that the command to be filled with the Spirit (Eph 5:18) is given to God's community as the norm that establishes the full operation of all of the Holy Spirit's gifts in the church. In the early 1960s the charismatic movement (what some call the "renewal in the Spirit") was in full force. In the United Kingdom Colin Urquhart's *When the Spirit Comes* and in North America Dennis Bennett's *Nine O'Clock in the Morning* were early editions of scores of books, Catholic and Protestant, explaining what some have called *neo-Pentecostalism*.

The marriage of both the ecclesiological and the pneumatological has been typical of most churches that declare they are being renewed. For a good theological analysis of this blend, read J. I. Packer's *Keep in Step with the Spirit*.

Renewal and Small Groups

In Britain this duality was seen in the so-called house church movement. Some Christians took on radical anti-institutional church positions at first, but by and large they were believers experiencing the new wine (the power of the Spirit) in new wineskins (simpler New Testament forms). Many mainline churches in England, particularly Anglican and Baptist, took on much of the ethos of the house churches while remaining within and loyal to their denominations. There was an emphasis on the three *C*'s: cell, congregation, celebration. This means that the primary unit of life in a church is the small cell, consisting of about a dozen people who meet weekly for worship, study, fellowship and outreach. A number of cells come together periodically to form a congregation, when the same experiences on a broader scale can be expressed. They can meet geographically in an area of a town and be more localized in their ministries than the church at large meeting in a regular church building. The celebration is the meeting of all the cells for praise, worship and public teaching. ICTHUS Fellowship of London, led by Roger Forster and Graham Kendrick (who writes many of Britain's renewal songs), is among the most well-known expressions of this renewal.

The largest church in the world, the Oida Full Gospel Church of Seoul, South Korea, led by David Yonggi Cho, has attained phenomenal statistical growth through its emphasis on the role of cells, that basic concept that has been championed by Ralph Neighbour in his book on the cell church, *Where Do We Go from Here?*

The cell-church model differs from the North American metachurch model advocated by Carl George, which encourages many kinds of cells and interest groups within a church that also has many programs. The "pure" cell-church model emphasizes that the cell *is* the church and that by intentional evangelism* it will keep growing and multiplying. Most cell churches have some form of the three *C*'s.

In North America and elsewhere, the Vineyard churches (whose chief early leader was John Wimber) are similar and have brought to the fore an emphasis on the church displaying the power of God's kingdom in our society* (read *Power Healing* and *Power Evangelism* by Wimber and Springer).

An early model of renewal in North America was the Church of the Savior in Washington, D.C. (clearly explained by E. O'Connor in *Call to Commitment*). In what has been called a post-Christian and postmodern time, this model of church renewal, while contrary to the present trend of megachurches,* may yet prove to be one of the most feasible and effective as we enter the twenty-first century. Its emphasis on mission groups (cells) and high commitment to community life (though not monastic), which is mobilized to affect the world with care and evangelism, is highly relevant and suggestive.

Renewal, Revival and Evangelism

Contemporary renewal movements are similar to earlier ones, for example, to John Wesley's emphasis on the class meeting (cells) and bands (mission groups). Each renewal also brings a fresh emphasis on music* and worship* with new and simple songs in the popular idiom of the day.

Historically, renewals have seen a fresh emphasis on evangelism. This was not at first true of the current renewal, but now it is becoming a major aspect among all churches. Many not in the charismatic movement have found renewal in churches through evangelism and have realized that reaching out to others with the gospel was at the heart of the first Pentecostal visitation (Acts 1:8). Leaders such as Bill Hybels of Willow Creek Community Church near Chicago have invited us all to contextualize our gospel and find effective means of growth in order to reach unchurched peoples; seeker-sensitive services are but one aspect of a growing renewal in evangelism.

Renewal is seen by some as the forerunner to revival—getting the church back on track so that God can bless it fully. Renewal is not revival, but it carries the seeds of revival, especially as such renewal relies on God's Spirit to produce by his power what our human effort cannot. Renewing churches rediscover prayer, particularly intercessory prayer, so they can do warfare against dark principalities and powers.* Members of renewing churches will be sensitive to the presence of God's Spirit in all aspects of their lives, and empowered by the Spirit, they will express and demonstrate the power of the gospel through reaching out to those without Christ. Renewal without evangelism is simply not renewal but self-centered indulgence in quasi-spiritual things.

No church can say it is renewed but rather that it is being renewed. But the process has begun with the confession of need, both personal and corporate, as expressed in the ancient prayer "Lord, revive your church, beginning with me."

See also CHURCH IN THE HOME; EVANGELISM; SMALL GROUPS.

References and Resources
D. J. Bennett, *Nine O'Clock in the Morning* (Plainfield, N.J.: Logos International, 1970);

R. Neighbour Jr. and L. Jenkins, *Where Do We Go from Here? A Guidebook for Cell Group Churches* (Houston: Touch, 1990); E. O'Connor, *Call to Commitment: The Story of the Church of the Savior* (New York: Harper & Row, 1963); H. A. Snyder, *The Community of the King* (Downers Grove, Ill.: InterVarsity Press, 1977); H. A. Snyder, *Signs of the Spirit: How God Reshapes the Church* (Grand Rapids: Zondervan, 1989); R. P. Stevens, *Liberating the Laity* (Downers Grove, Ill.: InterVarsity Press, 1985); C. Urquhart, *When the Spirit Comes* (London: Hodder & Stoughton, 1979); D. C. K. Watson, *I Believe in the Church* (Grand Rapids: Eerdmans, 1979); J. Wimber and K. Springer, *Power Evangelism* (San Francisco: Harper & Row, 1986); J. Wimber and K. Springer, *Power Healing* (San Francisco: Harper & Row, 1987).

Bob Roxburgh

CHURCH, SMALL

Small congregations are of different kinds—rural, fringe and urban. By virtue of their integration into and reputation within the community, some are still the dominant church in their area. In some places it is their denominational profile that stands out. Others have developed a distinctive identity and style. Normally they are known for the quality of their communal life rather than of their corporate worship. They are more likely than large congregations to resist change and innovation. They tend to give more attention to continuity, their place of meeting and a social agenda. Most small churches have a relatively stable or declining membership.

In a growing number of places it is very easy for small churches to feel second-rate compared to larger ones. Since these days success is mostly measured in numbers, members of small churches—especially in cities—can easily feel they are lacking. Yet in most parts of the world the majority of congregations are small. This is not only true in relatively unchristianized countries like China or post-

Christian societies such as Europe. Even in the United States, about half of all Protestant congregations average fewer than seventy-five people. In fact nearly one-fifth of all United Methodist churches, one-seventh of all Presbyterian churches and one-tenth of all Baptist and Episcopal churches in the United States have fewer than twenty-five members.

Their History and Extent

Historically, for the most part, churches have not been large. The earliest Christian gatherings were small enough to fit into a home or apartment. Though this changed when Christianity became the state religion in the fourth century, most churches were not that large, particularly in rural areas where the majority of the population lived. The large cathedrals built during the Middle Ages mostly supplemented the life of local churches in a particular region. While the Reformation reinvigorated church life and attracted larger congregations in some cities, most people still lived in the countryside and attended small churches. Later renewal movements, such as Methodism, were originally also strongest in villages and towns. Most congregations in North America began their institutional life as small churches. Also, the main models for congregations until recently included only one paid staff, one part-time staff or one volunteer-led staff, all of which are oriented to small churches.

As the Industrial Revolution expanded the size of cities and evangelicalism effected renewal in many places, larger preaching houses began to appear. This became easier with the advent of streetcars and automobiles. As the driving population has increased (see Automobile; Commuting), some very large churches have appeared in newer

suburbs and cities where freeways converge. Now megachurches* of several thousand members have become a fixed feature of the religious scene. Even so, these still serve about one-sixth of the total churchgoing population. About one-half attend medium-sized or larger congregations, and the remaining third are in small churches. Increasingly people are preferring to attend a church not too far from where they live, at least in their region if not in their locality.

Some Advantages and Disadvantages

In principle, though not always in fact, small churches have many advantages. They tend to be less impersonal, giving members and their children a better chance of knowing and supporting one another. As a recent survey of Southern Baptist congregations indicated, they tend to generate greater commitment: people in them give more of their money and time than members of large congregations. Since in smaller churches there are fewer people to undertake the work of the church, members develop a greater sense of responsibility and leadership. They tend to be more missionary-minded: proportionally they give more to, and offer themselves more to train for, Christian work overseas.

Small churches also have potential disadvantages. While members of small churches may know one another more, for this reason they may also have stronger conflicts. Unless resolved, these can easily become long-lasting feuds between different factions in the church. While in small churches there is more opportunity for people to take responsibility and exercise leadership, sometimes it is also easier for them to hold the reins too long and restrict the contribution of others. Unless the church is made up of people who are relatively mobile, new members can sometimes find it more difficult to become fully accepted. Also, in a small congregation unhelpful gossip* may exercise a strong sway.

None of these need to happen. They are not inherent in the small size of a church. They are simply the reverse side of the advantages just mentioned. For despite the widespread perception that small churches are more likely to be in-centered and cliquish, often this is far from the case. Whether a congregation is inward-looking or outward-looking has little to do with size: it depends on people's—and the pastor's—attitude. In fact, strong mission-oriented denominations like the Mennonites and committed socially conscious ones like the Quakers have generally been made up of smaller congregations. There is also a widespread belief that larger churches with well-known teacher-pastors produce members who know more about their faith and apply it more consistently to their lives. Surveys across a range of denominations by the Search Institute in Minneapolis show that this is just not the case.

Their Possibilities and Challenges
There is no doubt that some small churches are at risk, especially those made up of first-generation immigrants, those who no longer have a resident pastor and new mission churches that never grow beyond around forty people. But small churches are not vulnerable in general. While it is often felt that small churches cannot serve their members or communities as well as large churches, in most respects this is highly doubtful. Where it is the case, there are ways of dealing with the situation. We do well to remember that down through the centuries the small church has been a highly effective instrument for producing mature believers and Christian leaders. There is no reason to believe that this

cannot be the case today. God managed to do this without the array of buildings, organizations and programs that most congregations today feel are necessary. Where parents take the primary responsibility for educating their children in the Christian faith, where strong relationships are built with adults in the congregation as well as with peers, where intergenerational small groups replace groups segmented by sex, age and interest, the nurture and equipping of church members is at least as strong as that in the largest program-oriented congregations and in many cases is actually stronger.

Limits on what a small church can achieve can be overcome through working cooperatively with other local churches or by participating in wider community activities. For example, some small churches combine forces to feed the hungry, shelter the homeless, help unemployed people find work, teach literacy skills and so on. It is also possible for small churches to organize occasional common services or a combined youth program, evangelistic outreach or vacation Bible school. Also, members of a small church can join local community movements involved in service, bringing justice or protecting the environment rather than feel they must create their own structures to fulfill such objectives. Small churches can also partner with particular local institutions and also encourage members to become involved in community choirs, societies or other cultural activities rather than set up parallel church-based ones. Too many churches unnecessarily duplicate what is being done elsewhere or could be better done collaboratively.

In spite of all this, small churches are in for an increasingly difficult time. With the trend towards megachurches on the one hand and house churches on the other, small churches may find themselves caught in the middle. This would be a great pity. Megachurches might be more effective if they multiplied smaller congregations throughout a city and held only occasional huge meetings, that is, if they turned themselves into a constellation of smaller churches. House churches can be fully effective only if they cluster together in congregations, still relatively small, that meet regularly, perhaps monthly.

In the coming years small churches will need to find ways of opening up more to new members, without feeling that numerical growth is the only criterion of fidelity to the gospel. To remain vital, they should continue focusing on what they do best: building community, especially among the lonely and unchurched, and serving their immediate neighborhoods,* which sometimes are increasingly multicultural. They have much to offer families, mature adults and lifestyle enclaves. One possibility for them is to develop house churches so that they can attain greater relational depth and collaborate more systemically with other small churches in evangelism, education, youth work and mission, thus having access to larger resources and having a more concerted influence on their neighborhoods and cities. In some rural areas small congregations could almost turn themselves into home churches within their denomination and so be less dependent on itinerant pastors or costly buildings. Looked at as a challenge rather than a problem, the present uncertainty surrounding small churches can lead to very creative experiments and opportunities.

See also CHURCH; CHURCH IN THE HOME; FELLOWSHIP.

References and Resources
S. R. Burt and H. A. Roper, *Raising Small Church Esteem* (Washington, D.C.: Alban Institute, 1992); M. Breen with S. Fox, *Growing the Smaller Church* (London: Marshall Pickering, 1992); C. S. Dudley and J. M. Walrath, *Develop-ing Your Small Church's Potential* (Valley Forge, Penn.: Judson, 1988); L. Schaller, *The Small Membership Church: Scenarios for Tomorrow* (Nashville: Abingdon, 1994).

Robert Banks

CHURCH STRUCTURES

John Alexander says, "If you are a leader who believes in structure, brace yourself to receive criticism as a carnal stifler of freedom, creativity and the Holy Spirit" (p. 11). Any conversation* about structure* in Christian settings, especially church* structure, must contend with the attitude suggested in this quotation—as prevalent today as it was twenty years ago. At the very least, there is a warning here about the care needed in approaching structure in the church. How can structure enhance rather than inhibit freedom*? How can structures advance the cause of the church?

The term *church structures* in this article refers not to "hard" architecture, that is, church buildings,* but rather to the "soft" architecture that is reflected in how a church is organized—though no doubt there ought to be a link between the two types of architecture (for *structure* as an overarching way of dealing with reality, *see* Structure; System). The focus will be on how a local congregation is organized, as opposed to a house church on one end of the ecclesiastical spectrum and a denomination on the other. In one sense the house church is a structure all by itself, whereas denominations* have a number of local congregations, and sometimes regional associations, as building blocks (*see* Church in the Home; Denominations). By focusing on the traditional local church, this article deals with the level of organization that has the greatest impact on most believers. Rather than examine the internal workings of a local church in detail, the article will overview the variety of structures and how they relate to one another (*see* Church Leadership; Committees; Small Groups; Sunday School).

The Purpose of Structure and Structures
Structure is a rather modern, abstract way of talking about the intentional, purposeful subdivisions of a local church and the linkages between them. There is the ushering team, home groups, Sunday-school* classes, the church board and congregations that gather for worship.* Structures are one of the three major components that make up the system of a local church. The other two are *resources*—all of which are limited in some way (for example, member gifts, staff, building, time together, money* and communication "platforms," such as pulpit and publications)—and *culture* (the traditions and unspoken assumptions about the life and mission of the congregation). This *systems theory* approach to understanding the biblical idea of the body has been creatively explored by R. Paul Stevens and Phil Collins in *The Equipping Pastor.*

To what purposes should resources be applied under the influence of the culture of the church and through the structures in the church? The obvious answer is New Testament purposes. As we will see, however, this simple approach provides a powerful basis for evaluating the organization of a church. Although the New Testament is key, it is true that there are some clues about structures found in the Old Testament. A classic example is Exodus 18, where Moses, overburdened by caring for the Israelites in the desert, delegates responsibility for judging in minor matters to officials set over very specific subunits, right down to groups of ten. Another oft-cited example is the construction and security teams set up by Nehemiah that allowed the wall of Jerusalem to be rebuilt in fifty-two days (Neh 6:15).

In spite of these stories, the central Old Testament *system components* were left behind under the new covenant; in particular these were the three central elements of the Mosaic covenant—sacrifice, priesthood and tabernacle. As Howard Snyder reminds us, "The amazing teaching of the New Testament, especially in the book of Hebrews, is that Jesus Christ is the fulfillment of sacrifice, priesthood and tabernacle" (p. 57). This is why we should not speak of "going to church" on Sunday (for Jesus is accessible all the time through his once-for-all sacrifice) or of attending Pastor So-and-So's church (for every believer is a member of the priesthood under the Great High Priest) or of "meeting at the church" (for Jesus is present everywhere and especially where two or three are gathered—regardless of the building in which they sit). According to Snyder, "The great temptation of the organized church has been to . . . turn community into an institution. Returning to the spirit of the Old Testament, she has set up a professional priesthood, turned the Eucharist into a new sacrificial system and built great cathedrals" (p. 58). Note how the soft and hard architectures often become intertwined, one reflecting the other and both reflecting a theology. Thus, from a structures point of view, the New Testament requires abandonment of the long-standing clergy* and laity* subdivisions in the church. It also may mean that building development committees are out of a job!

Structural thinking, however, must include more than knowing what to avoid. What are the positive New Testament purposes that should shape and evaluate structures (and all other aspects of local churches)? The most succinct description of these purposes, although anticipated by Jesus' life beforehand and interpreted by Paul later, is found in reference to the earliest days of the church in Acts 2—3. There we find the perfect fulfillment of the so-called Great Commission of Matthew 28:19-20: Go out and enroll (baptize) disciples or learners and then teach them to obey everything I have commanded ("the apostles' teaching"; Act 2:42). The key "obedience points" according to Acts 2:42 are loving one another (service and fellowship*) and communion,* offering praise, thanksgiving, worship and prayer. The conclusion, then, is that all structures in a local church should serve one or more of these five purposes: going/enrolling and discipling, which lead to "one-anothering," worshiping and praying. Furthermore, none of these purposes should be neglected or out of balance.

Variety of Structures
What structures are appropriate to fulfill these purposes? Traditional subdivisions in a congregation have included the clergy-laity one criticized above, as well as age-and-stage groups, in either graded Sunday-school classes or midweek communities like "college and careers." However, the latter groupings can be evaluated (and found somewhat wanting) in light of the benefit of intergenerational approaches to learning and relating. Are there any other useful structures? Indeed, two dividing lines have arisen with strong modern expression but also a good pedigree: group size and group purpose.

First, many students of ecclesiology are claiming that it is wise to have both large and small structures in a local church, typified by congregational meetings, such as worship services, and home meetings, such as Bible studies. This claim arises because it seems logically impossible to fulfill the fivefold purpose of the church without both kinds of experience. On one hand, how much prac-

tical and consistent loving of one another can happen in large meetings? On the other hand, how can the worship life of eight believers compare with the praise of one hundred or one thousand? Interestingly, though "the Bible is relatively silent regarding organizational and administrative patterns" (Getz, p. 185), it does seem to support the rhythm between large and small structures, as the meeting in the temple courts and in homes suggests (Acts 2:46). Based on the Bible and church history, Snyder is convinced that this rhythm is normative: "Whatever other structures may be found useful, large-group and small-group structures should be fundamental" (p. 164).

One modern finesse of this principle that has arisen out of the church growth movement is the addition of a medium group (sometimes—confusingly—referred to as "congregations" and numbering anywhere from fifty to two hundred people). These may form on an ad hoc basis (special equipping or evangelistic events) or be permanent (several small groups joining together for worship and teaching). In practice, though they may be of benefit in some settings, such medium groups represent the size of the average church—which returns to Snyder's essential large-small rhythm.

The other distinction that leads to structures is that of group purpose or the wisdom of banding together to fulfill certain functions in a focused way. Thus, there is a place for the evangelism* group and the fellowship group and the discipling group and the prayer group. These groups may be large or small; for example, evangelism took place in both settings (Acts 5:42). The point is that these groups focus gifting and other resources on certain purposes and peoples. Is this focus permitted? Or does every small group and large gathering have to cover all the purposes of the church all the time, with inward and outward emphases perfectly balanced?

Some argue strongly for this latter view. The Bible, however, seems to suggest otherwise. One of the most famous examples is the occasion in Acts 6 when the apostles preserve their own sense of purpose around prayer and teaching by appointing seven leaders to focus on practical fellowship needs in the body. This illustration also shows that the two favorite structures of local churches, namely, committees* and leadership boards (elders, deacons, councils, staff teams), can function as purposeful small groups (sometimes called mission groups) if they are rightly designed and have been careful to gather the appropriate leadership gifts together to fulfill their mandate.

Losing and Choosing Structures

The ideas just promoted—design and care—suggest an element of freedom in the way a church is structured. This is the "scandal" of the local church: each one is free to choose its own way when it comes to how it is organized. Such diversity can be unsettling, but if it is true that the New Testament paints only broad strokes concerning church structure, then a diversity of organization seems inevitable. The first choice of church organizers may be to eliminate some structures; the second choice may be to add some new wineskins. Before any such plans for change are made, seven final provisos are in order.

1. All structures must be tested against the only critical measure: Are they advancing the cause of New Testament purposes in the unique life and mission setting of a particular church?

2. Structural thinking must extend beyond polity, that is, issues of church government or order and debates between congregational, episcopal and presbyterian forms. The whole body, not just decision-makers at the top, is to be equipped* and mobilized through appropriate structures.

3. Any structure in place, including the specific large- and small-group models being tried, must be seen to be humanly created and temporary and therefore held on to with humility and an openness to change. A church not willing to change or even eliminate any structure is risking paralysis.

4. The substance always must come before the structure: "The church's essential characteristic is life. . . . Its life is an organized life, to be sure; but this organization is secondary and derivative. It is the result of life. The church is, first of all, a spiritual organism, which may, secondarily, have some organizational expression" (Snyder, p. 157). The hard question that must be asked is, How much effort is being put into forming structures and how much into making sure those structures express New Testament life?

5. This is not to say that church structures are in the end somehow optional, even in churches that stress the charismatic over the institutional. Snyder refers to "phantom churches" that pride themselves on having little structure and impromptu gatherings. These may have highly individualistic members and yet be vulnerable to the first strong personality that comes along (Snyder, p. 77).

6. In this day of accelerated social change and increasingly flat hierarchies (with lots of lateral rather than vertical communication) in organizations outside the church, it is more important than ever for churches to have simple, flexible structures. If people walk into a church having experienced the organizational revolutions in the workplace* and social institutions of today, they should not feel like they have stepped back three decades into the past.

7. However, one should be sure that

any changes are truly necessary. Change should not be dictated by the latest fashion in church management or by some ideology about grassroots versus top-down initiatives or by an artificial struggle between people and programs. The adage "If it ain't broke, why fix it?" applies. One must heed the warning attributed to Petronius Arbiter (c. A.D. 66), who was project manager to Emperor Nero for the Roman games:

> We trained hard—but it seemed that every time we were beginning to form into teams, we would be reorganized. I was to learn later in life we tend to meet any situation by reorganizing, and a wonderful method it can be for creating the illusion of progress while producing confusion, inefficiency and demoralization.

See also CHURCH; CHURCH STRUCTURES; EQUIPPING; ORGANIZATION; ORGANIZATIONAL CHANGE AND CULTURE; STRUCTURES.

References and Resources

J. W. Alexander, *Managing Our Work* (Downers Grove, Ill.: InterVarsity Press, 1975); J. D. Anderson and E. E. Jones, *The Management of Ministry* (San Francisco: Harper & Row, 1978); G. Getz, *Sharpening the Focus of the Church* (Wheaton: Victor Books, 1984); R. Neighbour Jr., *Where Do We Go from Here?* (Houston: Touch Publications, 1990); H. A. Snyder, *The Problem of Wineskins: Church Structure in a Technological Age* (Downers Grove, Ill.: InterVarsity Press, 1975); R. P. Stevens and P. Collins, *The Equipping Pastor: A Systems Approach to Congregational Leadership* (Washington, D.C.: Alban Institute, 1993).

Dan Williams

CIRCUMCISION

Circumcision refers to the practice of removing the prepuce of a male. Historically it has been practiced in a variety of societies for cultural and religious reasons. Jews and Arabs continue to circumcise their sons in keeping with their religious traditions. Some groups in Africa and the South Pacific also practice the ritual, though the origins of these practices are sometimes obscure. Sometimes it is performed as a rite of passage from puberty to manhood. The procedure has never been common in Europe.

Circumcision in the Old Testament: A Metaphor for Holiness

In the Old Testament God adopted this West Semitic rite, depicted on statues of warriors from the early third millennium B.C., to show that the organ of procreation was consecrated to him.

Moses complained that he had "uncircumcised lips," by which he meant his speech was not fit to participate in God's program (Ex 6:12 KJV). God remedied the situation by giving him speech that made him as God to Pharaoh (Ex 7:1). Jeremiah speaks of uncircumcised ears, that is, ears unfit to hear God's word (Jer 7:10). When Israel entered the Promised Land, they were to regard its fruit as uncircumcised for three years, but in the fourth year "all its fruit will be holy, an offering of praise to the LORD" (Lev 19:24). A circumcised heart (Lev 26:41; Deut 10:16; 30:6; Jer 4:4; 9:25-26) refers to the human intellectual-emotional-spiritual forum, where decisions are made, as able to participate in God's covenant.

The Practice of Circumcision in Old Testament Times

According to Genesis 17:9-14 Abraham was obliged to circumcise himself and his household to make the organ of procreation symbolically fit to produce seed fit to participate in God's covenant. Some cultures circumcise their children at puberty as a rite of passage from childhood to manhood in the community. God employed the sign for infants eight days old to show that they are "holy" (see Rom 11:16; 1 Cor 7:14).

The extension of the sign to all of Abraham's physical seed, not just Sarah's, shows it included nonelect children. Physical circumcision could not be equated with the circumcision of the heart, the essential covenant requirement (Deut 6:5; 10:16; 30:6). The granting of the sign to those bought with money, however, shows that the covenant relationship could include Gentiles. An uncircumcised male will be cut off by God (that is, he might die any day; Gen 17:9-14).

Two Old Testament stories about circumcision have received considerable discussion. After the Lord threatened Pharaoh with the announcement that unless he let Israel go the Lord would kill Pharaoh's firstborn son, God met Moses to kill him, or more probably Moses' firstborn son, for failing to circumcise him (Ex 4:24-26). Moses' narrow escape validated God's threat against Pharaoh's household (compare Prov 11:31; 1 Pet 5:18).

Two explanations have been proposed for God's command to Joshua to circumcise the Israelites again (that is, a second time; Josh 5:2-3). On the one hand, that portion of the united militia who were forty years and older may have had to be circumcised again because the Egyptian circumcision was an incomplete slit, unlike the Israelite complete circumcision. This interpretation best explains the emphasis on flint knives, which were plentiful in Palestine but not in Egypt, and the reference to the reproach of Egypt (Josh 5:9). On the other hand, that older portion may have been reckoned as the first circumcision, and those under forty, who were not circumcised in the desert, the second. This interpretation best suits verses 4-7.

Circumcision of the Heart: The New Testament

Without circumcision of the heart, circumcision is uncircumcision (Rom 2:25-

29). The outward sign fades into insignificance in comparison with keeping the commandments (1 Cor 7:18-19). The circumcision in Christ entailed the putting off of the whole, not only part, of the sinful nature (Col 2:11). Paul vehemently opposed the notion that Gentiles had to accept circumcision and thus become Jews before they could belong to God's chosen people. Christians are justified by faith in Christ alone (Acts 15:1; Gal 2:3; 5:12). Since both circumcision and uncircumcision are nothing (1 Cor 7:19), if Jews wished to continue the practice, they could (Acts 16:3).

Circumcision in North America

In the United States over 60 percent of males are circumcised (62.7 percent in 1994; Hill). In addition to religious tradition, it is practiced for cosmetic, precedential (that is, "like father, like son") and hygienic reasons. Its popularity is somewhat puzzling since many physicians say it is unnecessary. Advocates of the practice, however, claim it might serve to prevent penile and cervical cancer, and there is fear that delayed circumcision will be more risky and traumatic (about 5 percent of uncircumcised infants require the operation later in life). Christians, be they ethnic Jews or Gentiles, may elect to circumcise their children for these reasons but not for spiritual advantage.

See also BODY; SACRAMENTS.

References and Resources
R. de Vaux, Ancient Israel: Its Life and Institutions (London: Darton, Longman & Todd, 1961); George Hill, "U.S. Circumcision Statistics," http://www.gepps.com/circus.htm, 3 Apr. 1997.

Bruce Waltke

CITIZENSHIP

To be a citizen is to hold a political office: not an elected office, to be sure, but an important office of public responsibility nonetheless. But what is citizenship? Where does it come from? And what, if anything, does it have to do with Christian faith? What is the connection between one's earthly citizenship and citizenship in God's kingdom? Or is there none?

The History of Citizenship

The idea and practice of citizenship originated in ancient Greece, not in Israel. But biblical religion had a big influence on the development of the meaning of citizenship in the West. The citizen in certain Greek city-states was someone who had a voice in shaping the common life of the community,* especially in making its laws* through a deliberative process. Most people in those city-states were not citizens. Citizens gained their status by virtue of their education, wealth or leadership prowess. The role of the citizen came to be distinguished from other affiliations and classes of people, such as cultic officials, tradespeople, warriors, farmers and slaves. Citizenship meant having the responsibility and privileges of membership in what was thought to be the highest form of human community, namely, the political* community.

The children of Israel exercised many responsibilities similar to those exercised by citizens of Greek city-states and in early republican Rome. However, Israel was structured not as a city-state but as the covenanted people of God, living under a legal order handed down by God to a nation made up of many family clans. Human responsibility for the common laws that governed Israel as a whole belonged to judges, arbiters, conciliators, courts and eventually kings. But everyone of the children of Israel was a member of God's covenanted people through whom God was revealing his will for all nations. The community of which they were a part was more profound and historically far-reaching than a Greek city-state.

Israel, as we know from the Bible, was conquered by Assyria and Babylon more than five hundred years before Christ. Between about 400 B.C. and A.D. 300 the independent Greek city-states and republican Rome also came to an end. Massive empires took their place and essentially smothered the earlier meaning of citizenship and Israelite clan membership. Most people became mere subjects, which is to say, they became subject to an imperial authority and were required simply to obey.

Several important developments between about A.D. 300 and the Protestant Reformation (which began in the 1500s) led to new understandings of citizenship. First, the early church,* which had no political authority in the first centuries after Christ, gradually grew to become the most influential institution in the collapsing Roman Empire and in the feudal period that followed. The Roman Catholic Church gained so much moral and legal authority that it succeeded in subordinating political authority to the church and to the church's canon law—a law that functioned not merely as internal church law but in many respects as public international law for all the lands where the church's authority extended. Consequently, an important distinction was drawn between higher ecclesiastical authority and lower political authorities.

For the most part, until the time of the Reformation, a top-down conception of political authority dominated in this church-led culture, which reached its height in the twelfth through fourteenth centuries, called the High Middle Ages. The Roman Catholic Church absorbed the hierarchical pattern from imperial Rome. The idea was that God granted authority to the church (eventually to the leading church official—the bishop of Rome), and the church then delegated political authority to lower, nonecclesiastical officials. However, beginning late in the Middle Ages, a rediscovery of ancient Greek and Roman documents led to a renewed interest in the work of Aristotle, the Stoics and other ancient philosophers. One consequence was a revival of the idea of citizenship.

Both inside the church and in wider political circles a number of people began to argue for a bottom-up origin of authority. In one way or another, officials—whether in the church or the empire—ought to be accountable to the people. From this point of view, God delegated authority to the whole church, not just to priests, and to the body politic, not merely to the rulers. Great battles ensued, both intellectual and military, between those claiming the divine right of kings and those arguing for some kind of popular or national sovereignty. These battles contributed to the breakup of the Holy Roman Empire and to the splintering of the church,* neither of which could withstand the impact of Reformation theology and the increasingly volatile campaigns for national independence. By the 1700s new political entities had come into existence—the first versions of modern states. In some cases these states refused to subordinate themselves to the Catholic Church. And inside many of them, various efforts were made to redefine the state as a limited, law-bound trust in which the rulers would have to be accountable to the people.

One line of argument for citizenship in the new states was deeply rooted in Christian faith. Its advocates continued to believe that God is the source of all authority on earth, but they also believed that God's grant of authority to governments, for example, should be recognized as having the purpose of establishing justice rather than perpetuating

autocracies or monarchies. People should not merely be subject to authority but should be free to participate in holding governments accountable to God. Furthermore, there is nothing sacred about a monarchy, and there is no reason why political authorities should be subordinate to church authorities. Different officeholders have different kinds of authority from God, and each one should exercise that authority in a way that is accountable to the people—whether those people are members of the church or citizens in the state.

The Secularization of Citizenship

At the same time that many Christians were trying to rethink (and reform) politics away from the hierarchical patterns that had dominated the church and most lower governments, another stream of thought was also emerging. Many thinkers during the Renaissance and on through the eighteenth-century Enlightenment wanted to recover political authority entirely for "the people." From this point of view, God and the church were part of the problem, not part of the solution. Political freedom* and responsibility of citizens would be impossible to achieve as long as people appealed to God or the church for help. Citizenship would have to arise from the people themselves. Sovereignty would have to be grounded originally in the people and then delegated in limited amounts to the rulers chosen by citizens. Rulers—governments—would have to be subject to citizens, not the other way around.

It should be clear to anyone in our day that this line of argument for citizenship won out over the milder form of argument proposed by many Christian reformers. Today, in most democracies and modern states,* the belief is that political sovereignty originates with the people, that rulers are subject to the people and that citizenship is an entirely secular affair, unrelated to God. Even in the United States, which was greatly influenced by Puritan and other Christian immigrants, the Constitution grounded political authority in the people. The Declaration of Independence may trace our inalienable rights and freedoms back to the Creator, but the American system makes government entirely accountable to the people, not to God.

Recovering Christian Citizenship

What then shall we say, from a Christian point of view, about the meaning of citizenship today? First, I would urge Christians to try to understand all of life as directly accountable to God. Perhaps most of our employers, government officials and leaders in science, art* and the media* will not agree with this judgment, but there is no alternative from a Christian point of view. Not only does the apostle Paul say that governments are ordained by God (Rom 13), but the whole of biblical teaching makes this clear. It is not just the church, the people of God, who are dependent on God; the entire creation depends on the Creator, and all human authority comes from God.

Some Christians interpret the passage about Caesar in Mark's Gospel (12:13-17) to suggest that Jesus was separating human civic obligations from the obligations owed to God. But when Jesus says, "Give to Caesar what is Caesar's and to God what is God's" (12:17), he does not say that what belongs to Caesar does not belong to God. Instead, we should interpret this passage as we would the passage in Ephesians where Paul writes, "Children, obey your parents in the Lord, for this is right" (6:1). Children should obey their parents, but obedience to parents is part of what children owe to God. So also in political life: citizens owe honor and taxes* to government (Caesar), but

they do so as part of their total obligation to God. Or, to put it another way, Caesar deserves taxes from citizens, but both Caesar and the citizens together owe all of their political/governmental responsibilities to God. Caesar deserves taxes, but God deserves everything, including the dutiful service we render to Caesar when we pay Caesar our taxes. This is why the apostles were bold, when push came to shove, to say, "We must obey God rather than men!" (Acts 5:29), even when some of those men happened to be government officials.

The error of modern secularism, therefore, is not in affirming the distinction between church and state, but rather in trying to disconnect ordinary life from God. The error is not in the revival of citizenship and the demise of top-down hierarchicalism. Rather, the mistake is in believing that government's accountability to citizens can be sustained only if both government and citizens disconnect themselves from God.

Staying in tune with biblical revelation about God's diversified creation (including diverse kinds of human responsibility in marriage,* family,* agriculture, government, industry, commerce, the arts and more), Christians have every reason to accept the differentiation of modern society. Family life may legitimately be distinguished from various professions,* as may science from art, politics from church life and so forth. This great diversity of social life holds together under God as a single creation from God; it need not be organized hierarchically under an all-powerful emperor or church. Citizenship is different from parenting or engineering or pastoral ministry. Christians may accept the distinct, distinguishable responsibility of citizenship without imagining that it must be disconnected from the all-embracing allegiance owed to God.

Citizens of Two Realms

Citizenship in two realms is where the important connection between earthly citizenship and citizenship in God's kingdom comes in. Another analogy might be helpful. Christians should have no difficulty recognizing that a family member—a child in the Smith family, for example—can at the same time be a child in God's family. The two are not incompatible. In fact, biblically speaking, the earthly family is supposed to be an image of the family of God. The same can be said about citizenship in the United States of America or in any other country. Fulfilling one's earthly civic responsibilities is a duty owed to God as well as to fellow citizens. Believers who recognize God's supreme rule in Jesus Christ and, by faith, thereby accept citizenship in God's kingdom are people who must learn to perform their civic duties as unto the Lord.

There are correct ways and wrong ways to act as a citizen, just as there are good and bad ways to act as a child in one's home. Christians must be willing to obey God rather than earthly rulers if the rulers seek to compel an obedience that radically conflicts with obedience to God. But very often the challenge to believers is to perform their civic responsibilities constructively in ways that demonstrate their obedience as citizens in God's kingdom. God has called us in Christ to pursue justice,* to seek to live at peace with all people and to love our neighbors.* In a complex society such as ours, one of the most important ways to live by this faith as a citizen in God's kingdom is to pursue justice for all neighbors in the political community in which we hold citizenship.

If we now turn to examine the nature of citizenship in the country in which we live, we will discover all kinds of important resources in the biblical tradition to help us. Part of what is good about most constitutional governments today is that they were created over centuries by citizens who were trying to define them as limited authorities. Thankfully, Christians do not stand alone in rejecting totalitarian government, but Christians should recognize that every form of earthly totalitarianism is a mistake because God alone holds total authority over the earth.

As soon as citizens seek to define government's limits, they ought to confront the question about the nature of other types of human authority, outside government. This is often a difficult task for those who reject biblical revelation. Most often they recognize only the authority of individuals and the state. Christians can hold a high view of citizenship in the state while also recognizing that family life, business, church life and other arenas of human responsibility are not reducible to either individual autonomy or a department of state.

When it comes to trying to hold government accountable to its own calling* before God, citizenship in a modern state becomes an extremely important calling for the average Christian citizen. Certainly one important way to hold government accountable is through voting* in regular elections. Another is to make sure that governments are held accountable to a basic law, a constitution, which government may not abrogate autocratically. The fact that these means of accountability have been built into most democratic states should be accepted with thankfulness, and we should recognize that Christian influences had something to do with their implementation.

Christians should be at the forefront of citizen actions that seek to secure accountable governments through constitutional limits and protections and through regular elections and court reviews. They should also take their civic responsibilities much further than this. Not every Christian is called to be a full-time political activist or government official. But the office of citizen gives one important responsibility nonetheless. Part of that responsibility is somewhat passive: stopping at stoplights, paying taxes and essentially heeding the laws that exist. But good citizenship, from a Christian point of view, must go beyond mere obedience to the law. Laws are not always just; times change, and reforms are required even of good laws. To serve God with heart, soul, strength and mind means to offer up all of life, including one's civic responsibility, to God in service. To do that, Christians must do more than merely go along with the expectations and demands of fellow citizens (even the majority of fellow citizens). Instead, Christians should pursue justice by seeking to influence government through elections and other means, by seeking to revise unjust laws and by helping governments make the proper distinctions among state, church, family, school, business enterprises and other institutions responsible to God. Citizenship is one of the important callings Christians have in a highly differentiated social order, which in its entirety is called to accountability before God.

See also LAW; LOBBYING; POLITICS; PRINCIPALITIES AND POWERS; STATES/PROVINCES; TAXES; VOTING.

References and Resources

R. Beiner, ed., *Theorizing Citizenship* (Albany: State University of New York Press, 1994); *The Public Justice Report*, published six times a year by the Center for Public Justice, Washington, D.C., seeks to develop mature Christian insight into the responsibility of citizens; T. R. Sherratt and R. P. Mahurin, *Saints as Citizens: A Guide to Public Responsibilities for Christians* (Grand Rapids: Baker, 1995); J. W. Skillen, *Recharging the American Experiment: Principled Pluralism for Genuine Civic Community* (Grand Rapids: Baker, 1994); J. W. Skillen, *The Scattered Voice: Christians at Odds in the Public Square* (Grand Rapids: Zondervan, 1990).

James W. Skillen

CITY

The city is a fascinating, complex and dominating fact of contemporary life. An increasing number of the world's population are city dwellers. It would be rare to find someone who has not had firsthand experience of the city, and impossible to find someone whose life is beyond the reach of the city and its influences. But what are we to make of the city? And what is the city to make of us?

The City in Western Culture

The city has provoked a range of attitudes and commentaries. On the one side, the city has been celebrated as the seat of civilization and the crucible of high culture.* It is associated with enlightened minds, innovation and social progress. On the other side, the city has been portrayed as promoting social pathology and moral disorder, the very antithesis of community,* kinship ties and family values.* Invariably, the city is contrasted for better or worse with the culture of the countryside (*see* Community, Rural; Towns).

The language of the city in Western culture draws deeply on the legacy of the Greco-Roman world. The English word *city* derives from Latin terms having to do with membership of the citizenry (*civitas*) and with the individual citizen (*civis*). Concepts such as freedom, public citizenship and political democracy lean heavily on the philosophy and polity (*polis*) undergirding the ancient Greek city-state. The latter was broad enough to incorporate the city and its hinterland as a political unit, but over time the concept of citizenship in the polis became associated with the public life of the *urbs*, the city, and the urbane qualities of the free citizen of good taste and sound judgment. These qualities of city life seem today to be lost in the fog of a past era. We are more accustomed to the pejorative language of "blight," "decay," "problem" and "crisis." As goes our language, so go our perceptions. What are we to make of the urban social upheaval that is transforming our cities?

A Matter of Perspective

It is a remarkable experience to fly into any major city at night. One gets a sense of the city as a whole, without distraction. Benign as it appears from such a height, however, what we observe is already filtering through the lens of what we think, judge, want and expect the city to be. Once at street level, we can grasp the whole city only with an act of the imagination.* Our imagination is fueled by reports of events that lie outside our immediate field of observation. Such external reports collude with our hopes and fears, dreams and aspirations, needs and desires. They help shape our image of the city. This is true also when it comes to the attitudes and judgments we make about other people and places in the city based on our limited personal experience. Experience is never unmediated or free of the assumptions and biases of the interpreter. However, as we open ourselves to the experiences of the city with a view to encountering its rich diversity, so we receive wisdom and insight from surprising places, causing us to shift our perspective and our accustomed ways of thinking and acting. Since we possess the city as a whole only in our imagination, we must remain open to the experiences and observations of others, especially to the "other," the strange and the stranger.

City living is the art of constructing mental maps by which to integrate and order the myriad impulses of the city. These maps enable us to negotiate our way in a complex and constantly changing environment. We scan the city as a landscape, and translate it like a text. City living is like learning a language, replete with cultural nuances and the collective wisdom and experience of generations.

Received Wisdom About the City

The biblical images of the city demonstrate the range of attitudes noted above. On the one hand the city is depicted in the Bible as the center of apostasy, injustice and self-aggrandizement, characterized by Babylon, a city of rampant evil. On the other hand, the city is characterized as Jerusalem, a place of God's dwelling, governance, protection and promise of a future full of hope and healing.* In reality, the biblical vision of the city incorporates both characterizations. It is the home of sinner and saint, of grit and grace. Above all, it is the primary locus within which the biblical drama unfolds. As has often been noted, the biblical journey begins in the garden, moves to the city, spreads from city to city and culminates in the vision of a garden transformed into a city.

The city in our times differs in fundamental ways from the cities of the Bible, from ancient Greece and Egypt, and from those of medieval Europe. One important difference is the degree of visibility of the whole as noted above. The modern city is in fact a composite of many worlds. Increasing specialization of function brought about by modern technology* underlies the wealth of individual worlds found in the modern city. We construct our lives in the city in unique ways out of the many options that the city provides.

It is common wisdom to characterize the modern industrial city by the metaphor of the machine. In the modern city the person is more nearly a part of a machine than a whole personality, fitted to fulfill a particular task with the appropriate frame of mind. This specialization of the person prompts the observation that the modern person is fragmented. We meet in the city the fragments of persons rather than whole persons. Not only is the city fragmented through the intense differentiation of human affairs, but the city dweller is fragmented by a thoroughgoing specialization in which each brings to their specialized activities only the fragment of themselves, the part which is needed for the efficient performance of that activity.

As we move steadily into the postmodern, postindustrial stage of urban society, cities are themselves becoming specialized institutions within a broad network of cities. The increased capacities of information technology to span space and time* in nanoseconds undermines the tendency of bygone cities to determine the entire round of life of its inhabitants. Cities are integrated into a much larger complex, national, regional and global (*see* Global Village). Paradoxically, the globalizing of the city has also seen a resurgence in localism and the investment by people in the life of the neighborhood.

Can the biblical treatment of the city make sense in the postmodern city of our times? Without a doubt we are all familiar with the sinfulness of our cities, etched into the very fabric of our corporate culture, and menacing the well-being of individuals,* families* and communities. This much has not been changed. But the gospel message sounded in the city, to the city and through the city remains the same: where sin abounds, the grace of God abounds all the more. This is a challenge for us to recover a spirituality adequate to the needs and opportunities of our times.

An Urban Spirituality

What does it mean for us to live in the city as disciples of Jesus Christ? What is the good news for everyday life? How does the city build our humanity as creatures before God?

At his conversion, Saul was instructed to "get up and enter the city, and you will be told what to do" (Acts 9:6 RSV). A spirituality adequate to the challenge of urban discipleship today will make a similar metaphorical journey of conversion. This spirituality has the elements of liturgical celebration, where liturgy fulfills its literal meaning as "the work of the people."

To begin with, we are challenged to get moving, to arise and step toward the city. Let me suggest that this is not a movement so much from outside to inside the city as from passivity to activity within the city appropriate to the invitation of God. And what is this invitation? It is the gracious beckoning to step into the place of pain and temptation in the struggle for the soul of the city. It is not the call to either precipitate our own action in response to a deep sense of guilt and culpability over our participation in the injustice and brokenness of the city, nor to attempt to break through the feeling of powerlessness by an aggressive activism. Rather, it is the invitation to "follow Jesus," through liturgical identification, into the very place of action where the full force of evil assails us, threatens to destroy us, but is forced to yield to the resurrection power of new life.

This movement of paying attention to the invitation of God will enable us to "enter" the city, that is, to enter into a profound awareness of the mysterious presence of God as grace active in all our dealings and relations within the city. To enter is to become aware and more keenly discerning of the movement of God in and through the city.

Then we are ready to hear the voice of God which addresses us in the very act of paying attention—to God, to the city, to the community and to ourselves. As we move in concert with God in the city, we are told what we are to do. As we do what we are told, we discover again and again the grace of God's transforming passion for the city, and the sustaining power of the divine life in our own lives and communities. And out of this spirituality of engagement and discernment we are led to celebrate the festival nature of the kingdom of God in the city. We rejoice that God is in the business of transforming urban culture and celebrate the anticipations of the future city in our present cities. We celebrate the gifts of creativity* and the imitations of the presence of the Creator in moments of justice* for the powerless, hospitality* to strangers, equality for the underprivileged and recovery of dignity for the degraded. For such is the city of God.

References and Resources

R. Bakke, *The Urban Christian: Effective Ministry in Today's Urban World* (Downers Grove, Ill.: InterVarsity Press, 1987); D. Callahan, ed., *The Secular City Debate* (London: Collier Macmillan, 1966); D. Clarke, *Cities in Crisis: The Christian Response* (New York: Sheed and Ward, 1960); H. G. Cox, *The Secular City: Secularization and Urbanization in Theological Perspective* (London: SCM Press, 1965); K. B. Cully and F. N. Harper, eds., *Will the Church Lose the City?* (New York: World Publishing, 1969); J. Ellul, *The Meaning of the City* (Grand Rapids: Eerdmans, 1970); C. S. Fischer, *To Dwell Among Friends: Personal Networks in Town and City* (Chicago: University of Chicago Press, 1982); P. S. Hawkins, ed., *Civitas: Religious Interpretations of the City* (Atlanta: Scholars Press, 1986); L. Mumford, *The City in History: Its Origin, Its Transformations and Its Prospects* (New York: Harcourt Brace and World, 1961).

Ken Luscombe

CIVIL DISOBEDIENCE

Civil disobedience means breaking the law* nonviolently for conscientious reasons. The term is a recent one, probably coined in the nineteenth century by Henry David Thoreau, but the practice is an old one, found in ancient Greek drama, in the life of the prophet Daniel and, arguably, in Israel's exodus from Egypt. More recent noteworthy examples include the campaigns against slavery and the slave trade, the fight for women's suffrage, Gandhi's campaigns against the British in South Africa and India, and Martin Luther King's campaigns for civil rights in the United States. Tactics can include sit-ins, illegal marches, tax boycotts and blockades. Should a Christian be involved in such actions? Are there situations in which it would be wrong not to be? After defining the term, this article will explore options, ethics and cautions.

The Meaning of Civil Disobedience

The term *civil disobedience* is not a terribly precise one, for it attempts to bring together two ideas. One describes an action: *disobedience,* usually meaning disobeying someone in authority. The other describes the manner of disobeying: *civil,* that is, it is not just any kind of disobedience. The notion of civility* can be understood in two ways: (1) as the disobedience of civil, that is, political,* authorities and/or (2) as disobedience carried out in a civil manner. To say disobedience is carried out in a civil manner can also be understood in two ways: (1) the disobedience is carried out in a respectful way, and/or (2) the one disobeying recognizes the legitimacy of the authority being opposed. We shall look at each of these in turn.

Types of Civil Disobedience

Disobedience is different from rebellion, revolution or any other attempt unconstitutionally and violently to overthrow a government, a regime or a political order. It is an attempt not to overthrow an order but to dissent from it in some way and to show that dissent in actions more than words. In some cases, for instance, in blocking a logging road, a nuclear plant or an abortion* clinic, it is an attempt to impose an outcome by nonviolent means. It is not merely a symbol or a statement, though it will have these overtones as well, but an active attempt to stop something from happening or to start something. In other cases it is simply a collective, or an individual, act of conscientious refusal to pay a tax* or to obey a law or an order because people believe that they cannot morally carry out a particular directive from a government. They have no wish to start a political movement; they just will not violate their conscience.

Some say that civil disobedience is not restricted to opposition to the government, that it includes actions such as blocking an entrance to support or protest women priests. Since there is no official definition of what civil disobedience means, this usage cannot be faulted. However, the fact that the state* is usually recognized as the only body authorized to use coercion in public life means that opposition to it has a particular edge. With other bodies in society we may be not so much disobeying as dissenting: they have fewer means to compel us. Also, if we do cause problems for other bodies by physical disruption, it is usually the state as the enforcer of last resort with whom we must deal eventually.

Disobedience can be carried out against an entire regime, against only a particular law or against only a particular government action. If the disobedience is against a particular law or action, typically those involved continue to accept the overall legitimacy of the government as such. People who protest certain types of logging do not (usually) deny all legitimacy to government or deny the validity of other laws. They think that in one or more instances government has overstepped its bounds. One common manifestation of this is a protester's calm acceptance of being arrested and fined or imprisoned. Sometimes fines are refused as a matter of conscience, whereas prison cannot really be refused. So the government is both opposed and accepted at the same time, hence the common sight of people being carried away from demonstrations by police. The demonstrators will not cooperate in their own arrest, but they will not run away from or actively oppose the police. Civil disobedience always contains this duality of rejection and acceptance.

The situation in which a regime as such is opposed is a little more complicated. A person may oppose a regime in its entirety but, for practical reasons, disobey only certain of its commands. Hence in countries such as the Netherlands during World War II, some people took up arms against the occupying Nazi regime, whereas others obeyed most laws except those, for example, requiring that Jews be handed over. The latter group would be practicing civil disobedience; the former, rebellion. The basic view of the legitimacy of the regime might have been the same, but the strategies were different.

Civil Disobedience and Christian Ethics
One of the major elements that distinguishes civil disobedience from other forms of opposition is civility. It neither casts all discretion to the winds nor demonizes its opponents. It is carried out with a modicum of respect; it grants a certain legitimacy to those whom it fights. Gandhi developed this into a view of *satyagraha*, or "truth force," wherein the disobedience must be carried out without hatred* or anger as an act of love*; this is the core of its essential power.

Civil disobedience's duality of acceptance and refusal has commended it to Christian ethicists, especially to those, such as Anabaptist and other pacifist theologians, who reject the notion of violent opposition to government. Civil disobedience forswears violence. At the same time it denies certain things to Caesar all the while respecting Paul's stricture that the powers that be are God's ministers (Rom 13:1-8) and also Peter's claim that "we must obey God rather than men" (Acts 5:29; compare 1 Pet 2:13-14). Obedience to God and God's ministers are combined in Jesus' admonition to give to God the things that are God's and to Caesar the things that are Caesar's (Mk 12:13-17). Hence civil disobedience has won the respect and support of people in many Christian communions as an avenue of Christian action, though of course they disagree on when it is appropriate. It is practiced by groups as divergent as Operation Rescue on abortion and Sojourners on refugees or nuclear arms. Even Christian groups who do not think of themselves as politically active engage in widespread acts of civil disobedience, such as smuggling Bibles into closed countries, making contacts with underground Christians in countries such as China or conducting evangelism in areas where it is forbidden.

Cautions About Civil Disobedience

The notion of civil disobedience has become accepted so widely, particularly among Western Christians, that it would be wise to be more careful than we often are in advocating it. In particular we should beware of reducing the Christian tradition of civil disobedience to the American tradition of individual rights against government. The gospel emphasizes not so much a *right* of disobedience as a *duty* of disobedience. It is not a matter of personal discretion but a matter of Christian obligation.

This necessarily raises the vexed question not only of the legitimacy of a ruler but also of the legitimacy of an opponent. Who has the authority to say that the government is wrong and that a law should be disobeyed? The anarchic idea that any individual Christian (or congregation) should just decide simply to "obey God rather than men" is a manifestation of Western individualism more than biblical insight. What is necessary is some form of legitimate authority within the Christian community, something that Protestants especially are loath to face. In addition, what we loosely call *democracy*—the growth of representative government, the division of political powers and the legitimizing of legal opposition—raises these questions to a higher pitch. If a government has been constitutionally elected by most of the members of a state (including most of the Christian members), who has the authority to challenge its laws and why?

It might be useful to apply the criteria of a just war to civil disobedience. In particular, we need to ask whether it is a last resort. Have all legal avenues been exhausted? Are the actions appropriate to the cause and proportionate to the outcomes? Is there a specific and achievable end? The growth of democracy means that there are a wide variety of legal means available to oppose bad laws or a corrupt government as a whole. This is not to say, of course, that a democracy guarantees right government. "The people" are no more inherently righteous than their rulers and are quite capable of supporting genocide: Nazi Germany was a "democracy." But there are legal means of opposition: elections, lobbying, media and party organizations. Within a democracy, however, Christians—especially younger ones—may find civil disobedience more attractive because it is easier and more glamorous than the often boring day-to-day work of politics.* If we have not yet campaigned, organized, voted,* lobbied* long and strenuously and found it utterly futile, we should not quickly leap to civil disobedience, which, by alienating people, can sometimes hinder more than help.

Despite these caveats, civil disobedience should be seen in principle as an important and authentic expression of the gospel of Jesus Christ. Karl Barth once said, "To clasp the hands in prayer is the beginning of an uprising against the disorder of the world."

See also CIVILITY; JUSTICE; LAW; ORGANIZATIONAL CULTURE AND CHANGE; POLITICS; POWER; PRINCIPALITIES AND POWERS; STRUCTURES.

References and Resources
H. Bedau, ed., *Civil Disobedience: Theory and Practice* (New York: Pegasus, 1969); J. F. Childress, *Civil Disobedience and Political Obligation* (New Haven, Conn.: Yale University Press, 1971); L. Rasmussen, *Dietrich Bonhoeffer: Reality and Resistance* (Nashville: Abingdon, 1972); J. H. Redekop, *The Christian and Civil Disobedience* (Hillsboro, Kans.: Kindred Press, 1990).

Paul Marshall

CIVILITY

To be civil is to be courteous and respectful. While we sometimes employ the concept in describing rather intimate relationships, as in "They are still living together, but they are barely civil to each other," it more accurately applies to more public interactions. Originally civility had a direct connection to how people behaved in cities.* The word comes from *civitas,* Latin for "city." It was in the ancient urban center that a person was most likely to encounter strangers. The public square was a space in which people interacted on a basis other than kinship or friendship.*

Cities are still very impersonal places today—even more so than in ancient Athens or Rome. But contemporary human beings typically encounter strangers in many other contexts as well: in air travel, over the phone lines, on E-mail networks, on interstate highways and in national parks. Modern means of transportation and communication have made civility an even more complex challenge in contemporary life.

Civility ranks high as a positive trait in many philosophical systems. Aristotle insisted, for example, that we do not fully actualize our human potential until we learn to be civil. While experiencing the intimacies of family bonds and friendship is necessary to our development, we reach a higher stage of human awareness when we can treat other persons with courtesy and respect, not because we love them and know them, but simply because we recognize the common humanity that we share with them in spite of tribal or linguistic differences. This pattern of thought was taken over by many Christian thinkers who incorporated an emphasis on civility into Christian systems of thought.

Biblical Civility
Civility is not a biblical term as such, but the idea is certainly present in the Scriptures. Indeed, taken as a way of describing respect for strangers, civility is a rather prominent biblical motif. In the Old Testament God regularly encouraged the people of Israel to show courtesy to those who were different from themselves. For example, the chosen people are reminded that they received God's mercy even when they were still strangers: "for you were aliens in the land of Egypt" (Lev 19:34). This theme is repeated in the New Testament: Christians are called to "speak evil of no one, to avoid quarreling, to be gentle, and to show courtesy to everyone" (Tit 3:2 NRSV).

The Christian community has often been rather uncivil. This has usually been due to a failure to live up to biblical standards. To be a Christian does not mean that all the vestiges of human fallenness automatically disappear. Like pride and greed and lust, intolerance is not an easy sin to purge from human relationships. Unfortunately, Christian incivility has often seriously hindered the witness* of the Christian community, as when Christians have actively persecuted those with differing convictions or when Christian thought and practice have been distorted by racism,* ethnocentrism* and other forms of prejudice and bigotry.

But not all instances of Christian incivility can simply be dismissed as blatantly sinful. There are special challenges associated with the obligation to cultivate civility within a biblical framework. The Scriptures also call us to maintain strong convictions. Christians are commanded to stand firm in the faith, to resist being "tossed to and fro and blown about by every wind of doctrine" (Eph 4:14 NRSV). This means that civility may never be elevated above other virtues,* nor may it be treated in isolation from other demands in the life of discipleship.*

The Christian sociologist John Murray Cuddihy chose his words wisely when he entitled his book on this subject *The Ordeal of Civility.* The element of *ordeal* is never absent from Christian efforts to cultivate a civil attitude toward those with whom they differ on important questions. The writer to the Hebrews counsels us to "pursue peace with everyone" (Heb 12:14 NRSV), clearly implying that the pursuit will sometimes be a very strenuous exercise.

Pluralistic Settings
The challenges of civility take on various forms in different historical periods. In some settings Christians have been a persecuted minority. In others they have controlled the patterns of power* and wealth.* For many Christians in recent times the challenges have emerged in the context of *pluralistic* settings. Pluralism, as such, is not a negative thing. The body of Christ is intentionally pluralistic, with a membership drawn "from every tribe and language and people and nation" (Rev 5:9 NRSV). In the context of Christian community,* then, pluralism is not a pattern to be avoided or even merely tolerated; it is to be encouraged as a means of exhibiting the manifold riches of God's creating and redeeming purposes.

The appropriate patterns of Christian civility become especially difficult to sustain, though, in a larger culture* in which relativistic themes are very prominent. The question, Who is in a position to tell other people what is right and wrong for them? is typically meant to be rhetorical. Each person is taken to be his or her own reliable guide to the basic issues of life. But from a Christian perspective, the question has a definite answer: *God* is in a position to tell us how we ought to think and act. The divine Creator has fashioned us in accordance with wise purposes and has given us instructions for living that, in Lewis Smedes's apt phrase, "fit life's designs." Christian civility can never rightly align itself with an anything-goes relativism.

This does not mean, however, that Christians should simply impose their beliefs and convictions on others. One important ingredient in God's wise design for humankind is that human beings are created with the capacity for free choice. God does not want grudging service from us—God wants our freely offered obedience. Christians best witness to the truth of God's revelation when they *invite* others to consider the convictions and values that are associated with the way of discipleship: "O taste and see that the LORD is good; happy are those who take refuge in him" (Ps 34:8 NRSV).

Theological Reference Points

There are no simple, fail-safe rules for cultivating and sustaining civility. It is helpful, however, to coordinate our efforts at civility with some practical theological reflections. To be sure, becoming civil persons requires more than our having the right kind of theological thoughts. But attempting to think clearly about the demands of civility can provide us with guidance for this important spiritual exercise.

One important reference point for a practical theology of civility is God's creating purposes. All human beings are created by the Maker of heaven and earth. By virtue of this created status, each human being is greatly valued in the sight of God. One reason why we ought to be civil toward people, even those with whom we disagree significantly, is that they are valuable products of a special creation.

This emphasis is an important counterweight to the Christian tendency to see our non-Christian opponents primarily in terms of their fallenness, especially when we are caught up in heated debates with them. Fallen human beings are nonetheless *created* persons. The biblical reference to humankind as created in "the image of God" is a much-debated theological topic. Whatever our specific interpretation of this theme, the Genesis account clearly implies that God created human persons with special—and highly valuable—capacities. It is also true, of course, that the creation story is immediately followed in Genesis 3 by the sad tale of human rebellion against the will of God. But Christian theologians, even ones who have given special emphasis to the devastating effects of the Fall for the human condition, have typically insisted that some glimmerings of God's creating design shine through the gloom of original sin.

Human beings can be thought of as precious works of divine art.* Even those products that have been seriously bruised and vandalized by human rebelliousness are still greatly valued by the divine Artist. Every human being, no matter how sinful he or she has become, deserves to be treated with the reverence that is appropriate to a creature who has been lovingly fashioned by God.

A second theological reference point is the redemptive ministry of Jesus Christ. The Incarnation is, in an important sense, the model for Christian civility. God did not wait for human beings to earn the love of their Creator by first of all cultivating pleasing beliefs and actions: "But God proves his love for us in that while we still were sinners Christ died for us" (Rom 5:8 NRSV). Jesus explicitly described his earthly ministry in these terms when he answered those who criticized him for associating with disreputable characters: "I have come to call not the righteous but sinners to repentance" (Lk 5:32 NRSV). To be sure, Jesus also on occasion used rather uncivil language ("hypocrites," "whited sepulchers"—Mt 23:27) against some of the people he encountered. But these judgments were usually unleashed against religious leaders who took a condescending attitude toward the poor and outcast of society.

A third reference point for developing a practical theology of civility is the sanctifying mission of the Holy Spirit. The indwelling Spirit has been sent by Christ to cleanse us so that we might live the kinds of holy lives that are appropriate for the demands of discipleship. The contours of Spirit-filled holy living, as spelled out in the "fruit of the Spirit" characteristics in Galatians 5, have direct links to the cultivation of civility: "love, joy, peace, patience, kindness, generosity, faithfulness, gentleness, and self-control" (Gal 5:22-23 NRSV).

Most of these characteristics are primarily other-directed, having to do with the Christian's attitudes and behaviors toward other persons. When we think of how this fruit applies to fellow citizens and coworkers whose beliefs and values differ significantly from our own, the relevance to civility is obvious. We must be loving toward them, striving to live at peace with them. They should expect us to be kind and gentle toward them, exhibiting a generous spirit in our relationships.

Some of the other fruit characteristics are primarily inner-directed: they have to do with traits within ourselves that we have cultivated by the power of the Spirit. Patience and self-control are especially crucial for the nurturing of civility since they are linked, in the Christian life, to our sense of what God is doing in history.

God's dealings with rebellious creatures are regularly portrayed in Scriptures as *long-suffering*. We are living, to use a Mennonite phrase, "in the time of God's patience." In accordance with a wise and mysterious plan for the creation, God has chosen not to rush to judgment. The arena of human activity, as we presently experience it, is one wherein people are relatively free to follow through on their basic life choices, for good or for ill. This state of affairs will not continue forever. Divine judgment is coming.

Nurturing Civility

Two lessons in particular are important for the nurturing of Christian civility. First, it is for God to decide when the final accounting will take place. Until that decision is revealed, Christians must share in the divine patience, tolerating the beliefs and values that people have chosen as their framework for living. In such a context, the primary Christian obligations are to demonstrate, to all who will pay attention, what it means to live in obedience to God and to invite others to join in that way of life through faith in Jesus Christ. The second lesson is that God alone will do the final judging. The decisive verdict as to who is "in" and who is "out" is for the Lord alone to make. On that day no one will be saved except by sovereign mercy. To absorb these supremely important lessons is to learn humility, which is foundational to Christian civility.

To repeat: none of this can be taken as an excuse to conform to an anything-goes permissiveness. Christian civility can never be divorced from sound biblically based convictions. The relationship between a civil spirit and a love of the truth is stated succinctly by the apostle Peter: "Always be ready to make your defense," he encourages, "for the hope that is in you"; then he quickly adds, "yet do it with gentleness and reverence" (1 Pet 3:15-16 NRSV).

See also CITIZENSHIP; CIVIL DISOBEDIENCE; LOVE; WITNESS.

References and Resources
J. M. Cuddihy, *The Ordeal of Civility: Freud, Marx, Lévi-Strauss and the Jewish Struggle with Modernity* (New York: Basic Books, 1974); R. Mouw, *Uncommon Decency: Christian Civility in an Uncivil World* (Downers Grove, Ill.: InterVarsity Press, 1992); L. Smedes, *Mere Morality: What God Expects from Ordinary People* (Grand Rapids: Eerdmans, 1983).

Richard Mouw

CLERGY

In common speech *clergy* is a term used to describe a religious official, certain members of a religious order or a pastoral leader of a church or denomination. Its counterpart is *laity*—the untrained, uneducated, common members of the church. This two-people approach to the church is anachronistic and unbiblical (see Laity). We look in vain in the Bible for laypersons in the sense of untrained, unequipped and not-called. Those words available in the ancient world to describe laypeople (in the common sense)—*laikos* and *idiōtēs*—were never used by inspired writers to describe Christians. Instead we are introduced to the whole people of God—designated by the word *laos* (the people)—who including leaders together are the true ministers. The Greek word for *clergy* (*klēros*) is used to describe the dignity and appointment of all the people to ministry. So paradoxically the church has no laypeople in the usual sense of that word and yet is full of clergy in the original meaning of that word.

We will examine how the tragic division between clergy (used henceforth in the normal and unbiblical sense) and laity appeared within the people of God and discover what we can do about it. The problem is almost universal, even among denominations* that began with a vision for every-member ministry. Nothing can happen without the clergy's presence; *ministry* is defined by "what the minister does"; pastors are called "the ministers" of the church. The clergy give the ministry, and the laity receive it. Four dimensions seem to be implicit in the modern concept of clergy: (1) the *vicarious* function, that is, service is rendered not only on behalf of, but instead of, the people; (2) the *ontological* difference, that is, a person becomes a priest or clergyperson by virtue of ordination, not character, and therefore cannot resign from ministry (I "am" a minister, rather than I "do" ministry); (3) the *sacramental* function, that is, generally the clergy alone are qualified to administer baptism* and the Lord's Supper (see Communion); and (4) the *professional* status, that is, the clergy represent an elite group with specialized functions that they can perform better than others.

Clergy in the Bible

According to the Old Testament the entire people were called to belong to God, to be God's people and to serve God's purposes (Ex 19:6). But within that people only a few—prophets, priests and princes—experienced a special call to give leadership to God's people, to speak God's word and to minister on behalf of God (for example, Is 6:8). Old Testament saints looked forward to the day when a new covenant would be inaugurated, when God's law would be written on the hearts of all the people (not just in a document), when "all know [God], from the least of them to the greatest" (Jer 31:34) and when the Spirit would "move [people] to follow [God's] decrees and be careful to keep [God's] laws" (Ezek 36:27). The apostles firmly believed that the promised day came with the coming of God's Son, Jesus, and the outpouring of God's Spirit on the day of Pentecost (Acts 2:14-21). For this reason the apostles used the Greek word *kleros* (clergy) to describe a whole new reality: the dignity, calling* and privilege of every member of the family of God.

Remarkably the Greek word *klēros,* a word from which *clergy* is derived, means "assigned by lot or inheritance." It is used in the New Testament for the privileges and appointment of all the people of God (Gal 3:29; Eph 1:11; Col 1:12). When we step into the world of the New Testament, we meet a single people (*laos*) marked by universal spiritual giftedness,* universal priesthood, universal empowerment by the Spirit of God, universal call or vocation and universal ministry.* All are *klēros* in the sense of being appointed by God to service and dignity. The ministry belongs to the people. *Layperson* then is a term of incredible honor. A pastor can rise to no greater honor than to be a layperson. Indeed, one searches in vain in the New Testament for a theology of the laity in the usual sense. As the Catholic historian Alexandre Faivre observes, "Neither laymen nor priests can be found in it" (pp. 7-8).

The New Testament, however, has many references to *leaders* being set aside to exercise their gift of ministry within God's *laos*, but these are not described and do not function in ways that resemble the modern idea of clergy: they are not vicarious leaders; they are not ontologically different from other laypersons; they do not perform a sacramental function; and they are not a professional class. Not even the call of Saul to be an apostle can be used to justify a special call to the clerical ministry, as some maintain, since the apostle never offers his own unique call to be an apostle to the Gentiles as a model for the special, "secret" call to become a pastor, missionary or priest.

The Clerical Captivity of the Church

In the second and third centuries a clergy-lay distinction arose in the church. Four influences can be discerned: (1) the attraction of secular "management" structures in the Greco-Roman world (the magistrates and the *plebs,* the common people), (2) the transference of the Old Testament priesthood model to the leadership of the church (church elders are the same as Old Testament priests), (3) the influence of popular piety elevating the Lord's Supper to a mystery that required priestly administration and (4) political and theological pressures in the church calling for more control from the top. The last influence requires more explanation.

In the face of heresy threats (Docetism, Gnosticism and Judaizing), Ignatius of Antioch (A.D. 50-110) appealed for the necessity of having a single bishop as the focus of unity. In the works of the lawyer Tertullian (A.D. 160-220), we are given a structure for the church in which the laity is identified with the *plebs,* or ordinary people, and is distinguished from the priestly, or ecclesiastical, order of bishops, presbyters and deacons, though for him the laity is still the privileged and endowed people from whom the hierarchy emerges (Faivre, p. 46). Clement of Alexandria also used *laikos* for ordinary believers, but in sacralizing the hierarchy of the church, he also relativized it because he envisioned human deacons and presbyters as mere imitations of and steps toward the heavenly *episkopos* (Faivre, pp. 58-59). Origen, himself a layperson, complained about how difficult it now was for a lay teacher to bring a homily in the presence of bishops but also gave priests power to purify laypersons at the penitential level. So by the beginning of the third century, the term *clergy* was used to describe a special class within the church, and *laity* the rest (sometimes not even including women) who were not bishops, presbyters or deacons. The layperson's function was "to release the priest and levite from all his material concerns, thus enabling him to devote himself exclusively to the service of the alter, a task that was necessary for everyone's salvation" (Faivre, p. 69).

Cyprian, bishop of Carthage (A.D. 249), made it clear that a member of the clergy was not a layperson. Using the analogy of the Levites, he argued that clergy must not become involved in the world in order to properly attend to the ministry of the altar (Faivre, pp. 106-7). He was convinced that a bishop was accountable to God alone (Rademacher, p. 565) and modeled his church order on the civil orders of the rulers of the city of Carthage. As shown by Rademacher (p. 59), Cyprian's influence on the church has been substantial: (1) He made a clear distinction between the *ordo* of bishops and the laity. (2) He sacralized the priesthood according to the Old Testament model of sacrifice priesthood. (3) He linked ministry to sacrifice, again in the image of the temple priesthood. (4) He shaped the church as a clearly defined institution of salvation. (5) He modeled the bishops on the image of Roman senators, thus excluding women. (6) He consolidated the ruling powers of bishops through numerous episcopal conclaves and established a monolithic episcopate.

From the fourth to the sixteenth centuries the clergy-lay distinction deepened. The laity ranked on the bottom of the clerical ladder. After his conversion (A.D. 312) Constantine appointed civil magistrates throughout the empire, organized the church into dioceses along the pattern of Roman regional districts and consistently used *clerical* and *clerics* to denote a privileged class (Rademacher, p. 60). Under the Gregorian reform (A.D.1057-1123), the ministry of the entire Western church was shaped by Roman law. So in the period prior to the Reformation: (1) The bishop of Rome came to be regarded as the head of the church on earth. (2) The language of worship had ceased to be the language of the people. (3) The clergy dressed differently and were prepared for ministry in an enculturating seminary. (4) Ordination became an absolute act so that congregations were no longer needed for the celebration of the Eucharist. (5) The clergy became celibate and thus removed from the normal experiences of the laity. (6) The cup was removed from the laity in the Eucharist.

In due course the clergy-lay distinction became institutionalized in religious orders, priestly ordination and the seminary system.

The Incomplete Reformation

Even the Protestant Reformation with its call to recover "the priesthood of all believers" did not succeed in recovering laity as a dignified people. How this happened—from the time of the Reformation itself and through the succeeding centuries—is a fascinating and important story. Factors in the incomplete Reformation follow.

Protestant replacement for priests. The substitution of the sermon for the sacrament as the central act of Protestant worship may have set the church up to give the preacher-expositor the same clerical standing as the priest-officiant at the Mass. Thus, the preacher replaces the priest. It tended to keep interpretation of the Bible out of the hands of the layperson again and confine it to the ordained person. In the evolution of Western society from A.D. 500 to 1500, laypersons lost access to top culture and learned traditions. An educated church leadership perpetuated the division.

Inadequate structures for renewal. The Magisterial Reformation did not provide an ecclesiology comparable to its rediscovered soteriology. Though this developed more among the Anabaptists, in time even denominations stemming from the so-called Radical Reformation gravitated from their founding vision of every-member ministry to the old clergy-lay distinction.

Lay theology lost. A theology of and by the laity was only partially attempted and largely lost. Though during the Reformation and in later periods there was a flurry of pamphlets and short books by laypeople, these rarely survived in the following centuries and, until recently, were mostly ignored by theologians and other scholars. The story of ministry and theology itself has almost always been written by clergypersons for clergypersons. Parallel to this is the written history of the church—which is from the perspective of the clergy and councils rather than the laity.

Eclipse of the kingdom. There has been a preoccupation with ministry in the gathered life of the church (or in its expansion through evangelism) rather than the totality of life under the rule of God. Kingdom ministry has been mostly eclipsed by church ministry. Ministry is viewed as advancing the church rather than the kingdom. The Epistles are the primary guide; the Gospels have been eclipsed.

A two-level call. Calvin's "secret call" to the ministry of the Word perpetuates a two-level call to the ministry: a general call to all and a special call to the few. Even in denominations claiming to proceed from the Radical Reformation, ordination councils still require a testimony of the secret and special call to the professional ministry.

Laity unrecognized. Ordination is still retained almost universally for the full-time supported church worker; no adequate recognition of lay ministries exists. Most denominations still regard ordination as conferring a distinctive status rather than recognizing a specific function. No denomination ordains people to societal careers and missions (see Ogden, pp. 188-215).

Theological education. The Catholic seminary system was eventually adopted. While important exceptions still exist, by the end of the nineteenth century the seminary system became the universal model for equipping a generation of pastors, thus guaranteeing their enculturation into the clerical culture. With a few exceptions, theological education remains, by and large, the exclusive preoccupation of those intending a career in the clergy.

Spirituality. An adequate lay spirituality has rarely been developed. While the Reformation rejected the two-level spirituality of the monastery and the common Christian, and some of the Puritans developed a spirituality for the whole life, most Protestant spirituality has had a clerical cast with emphasis on the deeper life of outstanding Christian leaders or, occasionally, on the mystical. Thus, most Protestant spirituality has ignored exploring the holiness of the ordinary Christian in the totality of his or her life in the world. The church in the West has never become free of Greek dualism, which relegates bodily life to a lower level.

Influence of the world. As in the past, cultural and social forces at work in the wider society (secular management models, professional-lay analogies, increasing centralization of government) have influenced the shape of the world. The church must continuously fight the fleshly predisposition to distinguish between clergy and laity. Each generation must enter the renewal of ministry in Christ. The priesthood of all believers can be lost in a single generation. What will it take to liberate the church from its clerical captivity?

Liberating the Clergy

The trinitarian basis of understanding the people of God (*laos*) is crucial. As in the interpenetrating relationships between Father, Son and Spirit, the members of God's people coinhere, pour life into one another, without coalescence and merger. Different spiritual gifts and various leadership functions can be expressed in a unified way without hierarchy. Those in a mutually other penetrating, cohering and functioning community can have submission to one another without subordination because that is the way it is in God, when the church reflects. The submission of the Son of God to the Father is not subordination but the quality of the way the Son relates to the Father. No hierarchy is implied. It is the whole Godhead, not just the Father, who rules. In the church it is the same: leadership is vested through mutual submission and rich diversity in the whole community without hierarchy. So, as Leonardo Boff says, being a people like God "produces a vision of a church that is more communion than hierarchy, more service than power, more circular than pyramidal, more loving embrace than bending the knee before authority" (Boff, p. 154).

What can be done to live out this biblical and theological vision of the people of God, a people who at one and the same time are without laity and full of clergy? First, theological education should be provided for the whole people of God in the context of both church and societal ministry (congregation, academy and marketplace learning). It is too important to be restricted to a few. A reformation in theological education institutions is sorely needed. Clergy and laity must study side by side in the same environment.

Second, every Christian should undertake lifelong theological education with the goal of becoming mature in Christ (Col 1:28) and participating in God's grand purpose for the universe. That is, every Christian person should become a theologian—reflecting biblically and culturally on one's life and service in the church and the world.

Finally, those in church leadership should form a gracious conspiracy with the rest of God's laity to bring an end to unbiblical clericalism. Equipping* the saints (Eph 4:12) is a corporate task. Clergy must be liberated by laity from having the impossible task of representing the entire ministry of the church. Laity must be liberated from becoming clergy assistants to discover and embrace their own ministry. Pastors then become assistants to the rest of the people of God. This mutual liberation must be a ministry of love, not rebellion. As Jan Grootaers said, it will take the remainder of the twentieth century "to move towards this balance of revising the status of laity within the institutional Church.... One part of the Church can never move forward without the other, for both are subject, in common obedience, to one and the same Lord" (quoted in Rowthorn, p. 46).

See also EQUIPPING; LAITY; LEADERSHIP, CHURCH.

References and Resources
L. Boff, *Trinity and Society,* trans. P. Burns (Maryknoll, N.Y.: Orbis, 1988); A. Faivre, *The Emergence of the Laity in the Early Church* (New York: Paulist, 1990); G. D. Fee, "*Laos* and Leadership Under the New Testament," *Crux* 25, no, 4 (1989) 3-13; R. Kimelman, "Judaism and Lay Ministry," *NICM Journal* 5, no. 2 (1980); 32-53; S. C. Neill and H. Weber, *The Layman in Christian History* (London: SCM, 1963); G. Ogden, *The New Reformation: Returning the Ministry to the People of God* (Grand Rapids: Zondervan, 1990); W. J. Rademacher, *Lay Ministry: A Theological, Spiritual and Pastoral Handbook* (New York: Crossroad, 1991); A. Rowthorn, *The Liberation of the Laity* (Wilton, Conn.: Morehouse-Barlow, 1986); C. A. Voltz, *Pastoral Life and Practice in the Early Church* (Minneapolis: Augsburg, 1990); M. Warkentin, *Ordination: A Biblical-Historical View* (Grand Rapids: Eerdmans, 1982); J. H. Yoder, *The Fullness of Christ: Paul's Vision of Universal Ministry* (Elgin, Ill.: Brethren Press, 1987).

R. Paul Stevens

CLUBS

My first exposure to clubs was through my mother. Born in Newfoundland (now a province of Canada but then a colony of England), my mother joined the Toronto chapter of the Old Colony Club. They gathered weekly to talk about life back on "The Rock," as Newfoundland was affectionately called, and performed many services to needy Newfoundlanders in Toronto. I remember especially her weekly visits to the tuberculosis sanatorium to bring gifts and cheer to the people interned there. Belonging to a club never seemed to her to be anything other than a practical expression of her commitment to follow Jesus. But it was many years later that I began to reflect on why she joined at all or why I should join a photography club.

Clubs Past and Present

Clubs are usually small, voluntary societies that people elect to join for the purpose of pursuing an interest or service* with people of like mind and heart. Most clubs meet periodically, have tests or standards for membership, collect annual dues, have an elected hierarchy of officers and sometimes have their own building as a meeting place. The word *club* is sometimes used for the building that houses a club ("Let's go down to the golf club"), for a building that houses a random group of people (a night club) or for an association of nations (such as the European Economic Club), but these senses of the word will not be considered in this article.

Today one faces an extensive array of clubs: social clubs, dinner clubs, hobby clubs, ski clubs, Christian clubs on the university or college campus, badminton clubs, racial clubs (like the Old Colony), rifle clubs, political clubs, women's clubs, rowing clubs, Bible clubs, sewing clubs, yacht clubs, fitness clubs and book clubs, to mention a few in which the word is actually used. Then there are societies with membership and selective interests that are clublike without using the name *club,* such as professional societies, Rotary (a service club), trade unions* (occupational clubs), the Masons (a service club with secret rituals), fraternities (select student clubs), writers' groups (art clubs), volunteer orchestras (musical clubs), groups of people who regularly enjoy recreation together (mountain climbing clubs or kayak clubs), Morning Out for Moms groups in churches (a mothers' club) and buddies who go to the same tavern at the same time (a drinking club). Gangs are really street clubs with initiation rites, codes of behavior and a common identity. It is some-

times argued, wrongly though not without reason, that even the local church* is a club since it involves membership* with people having a common interest and is a voluntary society in which persons can know and be known by others as they pursue a common interest. We will return to this later. The list above is not exhaustive, but it shows how club life permeates everyday life. But it is not just a modern phenomenon.

Men have always gathered in small groups outside the home, a privilege only recently accorded women. There is evidence of club life in earlier periods of civilization, for example, the social, athletic, occupational, political, philosophical and religious collegia or societies that were so characteristic of the first-century Greek and Roman world. Membership in the guilds proved to be a terrible dilemma for the Christian tradespeople in the seven churches of Asia since, as evidenced in the last book of the Bible, these were associated with pagan religious rituals and sexual orgies (Rev 2:20-25). The problem was that believers often could not find work without belonging to these guilds, a situation not unlike the almost universal requirement to belong to a trade union in some parts of the world today. Other kinds of gatherings, such as the regular banquets in pagan temples referred to in 1 Corinthians 10, posed other problems such as eating meat offered to idols.

In modern times clubs for eating, drinking and conversation similar to what are commonly found today developed in England around the emergence of coffeehouses following the introduction of coffee in 1652. Samuel Pepys referred to gatherings in the Coffee Club Tavern as *clubbing.* This intimate environment afforded an opportunity for free speech. With the spread of coffeehouses customers began to associate with particular clubs. Gradually older and more important customers dominated, and the coffeehouse speakeasy gave way to a class or professional group, which during the nineteenth century became even more specialized: clubs for travelers, diplomats, university graduates, agriculturalists, artists and cyclists. Not until 1883 did women in England have a club of their own. Nor did working-class people have clubs until 1862 when the Reverend Henry Solly founded the Working Men's Club and Institute Union, which promoted adult education,* provided indoor and outdoor activities and brought dignity to laboring people. Throughout this period political discussion was a crucial component of club life, from the earliest coffeehouses to the clubs that met for parliamentary reform. Clubs spread to continental Europe and North America, the first American club being established in 1732—the Fish House Club of Philadelphia. A plethora of social, professional, college and service clubs followed.

The emergence of private sporting* clubs in England in the nineteenth century provided a way for the wealthy and elite to separate themselves from the crowd. This is club life at its extreme, but clubs do not normally exist to promote egalitarianism. They exist to express difference, pluralism, distinctiveness, not sameness and uniformity. They exist because people have something in common with only *some* other people. In one sense they are necessarily exclusive. A common characteristic of clubs throughout history is selectivity of membership. It is always a club for *certain* kinds of people or for a *certain* interest.

The secret society ratchets the selectivity factor a notch higher, since the members pledge not to divulge what actually happens in their initiation or their meetings. Membership in the Masons, a club that originated in Egypt several centuries prior to the coming of Christ, is especially problematic for Christians, who, because they are followers of Christ, are liberated to live open and transparent lives (2 Cor 3:18), allowing others, especially those outside the faith, to observe fully "what makes them tick" (compare 2 Tim 3:10). Throwing "your pearls before swine" (Mt 7:6 NRSV) relates to showing discretion in telling everything about the kingdom of God to those unwilling to respond, not to having secrets.

Toward a Theology of Joining

It is significant that most clubs have a meeting house where the members meet, talk, share a beverage, swap stories and display their trophies. This incarnates the two dimensions of club life: pursuit of an interest and relationship with others who share that interest. Club life is not a private pleasure.* Clubs meet a fundamental human need to belong to and relate to other people, a need written into our construction by the Creator. We are "hard-wired" for relationships. These are essential to our dignity and growth and intended for our enjoyment as well as profit.

Many clubs offer a concrete opportunity to serve, which again is a fundamental human need and calling.* It cannot be emphasized too often that the Greek word for *ministry** is simply the word for *service*. So service clubs are ministry opportunities. But not all clubs exist to serve; nor need they. Leisure* is the freedom to do anything or even nothing. So clubs that allow us to cultivate ourselves in the company of others are legitimate and worthwhile even for people who are members of a church. One should not expect the local church to meet all these needs, and the provision of multiple-interest clubs within the church (often as a way of keeping people involved or protecting them from secular society) may be a negative thing in isolating Christians from the world.

Often the richest fruits of club life are byproducts of meeting with a very select group: the stimulation of interchange that takes place for the sheer joy of sharing a common passion with others. The Inklings was a literary club that provided rich inspiration for people like C. S. Lewis, J. R. Tolkien, Charles Williams, Dorothy Sayers and others. The Clapham sect in England was a group of prominent evangelical Christians, among them people like William Wilberforce, who met from 1790 to 1830 in members' homes and churches. These wealthy Anglicans believed in the preservation of ranks in society and appealed to the rich as the Methodists appealed to the poor. But the Clapham sect also gave themselves unstintingly to helping the poor and disadvantaged and was almost single-handedly responsible for abolishing the slave trade in England. This is as it should be. Reform in all of its forms comes from nurturing the inner life, often without the pressure to produce.

All clubs (even church clubs) are something less than family* and less than the church. Clubs are, by and large, a good place to meet people and to meet them on the basis of a common denominator—interest, race, language, hobby, sport. They are associations rather than communities, even if they often contain a genuinely communal dimension. This is why they are always something less than the full experience of the people of God, the church. The church was not intended to be a club of like-minded people from the same socioeconomic group, even though many local churches have gravitated in that direction. Constitutionally the church is a crosscultural, international, interethnic community in which Jew and Gentile (two irreconcilably separated peoples in the ancient world) are included in something that transcends both: a new humanity (Eph 2:14-16). It is also an entity that seeks to develop a common life, not just a common interest (even religious interest), one marked by long-term commitment, mutual care and accountabilities and deep sharing of personal and physical things (see Church; Community).

So paradoxically, Christians may be encouraged to join clubs for personal enrichment, service and (best as a byproduct) evangelism,* but the church itself must never become a club. While it has a voluntary membership and offers face-to-face fellowship,* the church must never become selective. That has always been the church's scandal: slaves shared the Lord's Supper in the ancient world with philosophers and wealthy merchants. Today the church scandalously takes all comers. But it is also the church's glory: the one society on earth whose constitution requires accepting everyone. So Christian growth* involves not only associating like with like in clubs but associating with those we have not selected and probably would not want to join except for Jesus.

See also CHURCH; COMMUNITY; HOBBIES AND CRAFTS; LEISURE; PLAY; SOCIETY.

References and Resources
D. Christen, *How to Survive Belonging to a Club* (Appelton, Wis.: Tolvan, 1979); J. Friguglietti, "Clubs," in *The Encyclopedia Americana* (Danbury, Conn.: Grolier, 1989) 17:123-25; W. Rybczynski, *Waiting for the Weekend* (New York: Viking Penguin, 1991); E. E. Wolfers and V. B. Evanson, *Organizations, Clubs, Action Groups: How to Start Them, How to Run Them* (New York: Penguin, 1982).

R. Paul Stevens

COFFEE DRINKING

Coffee is more than a beverage, more than the most popular hot drink consumed throughout the world and more than a major industry that affects the economies of many Third World countries. Drinking coffee is integral to our way of life, a significant social and cultural phenomenon.

The Origins and Spread of Coffee

Around A.D. 600 coffee was found growing in Ethiopia. Initially it was rolled with fat into little balls and eaten. Several centuries later it appeared in Arabia under the name *quawha,* meaning "that which enables you to do without something." Steeped in water, it was regarded as a tasty drink and as possessing recuperative powers. For a long time its attractions were kept relatively secret. Mocha was the first port where it became more freely available.

By the early seventeenth century coffee had spread eastward to India and beyond, and westward to the Caribbean and Latin America. The first coffeehouse in England was set up in 1637. It was patronized by the elite of society and within thirty years had many imitators. The Dutch introduced coffee to America, though it was only after the Boston Tea Party that it became the preferred drink there. As a result of mass production and the invention of instant coffee in the twentieth century, coffee became the most popular drink in most Western countries. The growing, harvesting, processing and distributing of coffee is now a huge industry. It is dominated by global corporations that often exploit workers in Third World countries, influence their economies in ways that are not always beneficial and effect cut-price deals for affluent nations with very large markets.

The Benefits of Coffee

Already in the seventeenth century coffeehouses became known as "penny universities," where, for the payment of a relatively small sum, a person could take part in interesting social, intellectual and political discussion. In nineteenth-century Europe such places were often the seedbeds of democratic or revolutionary change. Coffee shops have long been a favorite haunt of artists and creative people. They have also been the setting for a great deal of business and commercial activity.

Offering someone a drink of coffee is also a mark of hospitality* and helps create an atmosphere that puts people at ease. Why else do we so often offer or accept a cup of coffee even though we may not need anything to drink? In his poem "White with Two Sugars Please" the English poet Steve Turner refers to other functions or dimensions of this drink. Coffee, he says, can give you a legal shot of energy when you are feeling drowsy. It can help you pass time* when waiting for the weather* to clear. It is "something you can dangle your lips in when conversation is scarce." It helps friendships* develop and is always a good excuse to stay longer. Coffee is a universal language, a kind of multiracial, multilingual, multicultural Esperanto enjoyed by people of all ages. "Yes," he concludes, "there's something quite religious about coffee."

At the personal level, people generally find that coffee enhances concentration and boosts energy. This is because caffeine is a mild central nervous stimulant. A 1994 study demonstrated that caffeine intake improved performance on semantic memory, logical reasoning, recall and memory recognition tests. For some tasks it gave people more energy than eating breakfast. On the other hand, there is no proof that it enhances creativity, and its effects are only temporary. Its stimulant effect leads many people to avoid it or drink it before bedtime only in a decaffeinated form. Others, however, find that coffee helps them relax, even sleep.* This may have more to do with its warmth or with the fact that it signals a time to unwind. Caffeine can also help minimize the discomfort of migraine headaches and overcome dizziness in those who have low blood pressure by raising its level.

The creation of places specifically for drinking coffee has many benefits. They provide a welcoming, convivial space alongside or between the home* and the workplace.* Though not alone in doing this—bars, diners, beauty parlors and to some extent shopping malls* play a similar role—they are less expensive and avoid the problems created by alcoholism or consumerism* in some other so-called third places. Coffee shops provide an inclusive and level playing ground for people who are otherwise typecast by position, class, race or gender. In them people can shrug off their main domestic and work-related responsibilities, let go of some of their inhibitions and relax. They can socialize with others in spontaneous ways undetermined by a set agenda. In these places spirits are generally lifted—on average people laugh nine times as much in such a setting as elsewhere during the day—which means they have therapeutic value. Over time, long-term relationships involving real acceptance of others have been built up among those who visit the same coffee shop on a regular basis.

The Disadvantages of Coffee

Unfortunately, largely because of its caffeine content, coffee drinking can become addictive (*see* Addiction). Like chain-smokers, some people drink coffee continuously throughout the day. Also, depending on certain physiological conditions, coffee can sometimes have adverse effects. For example, people with high blood pressure can become overstimulated and should therefore limit their intake to two cups a day.

Since there is a proven link between imbibing caffeine and difficulty in conception,* women wishing to become pregnant should minimize or eliminate coffee intake. There is also a link between very high coffee intake and an increased risk of miscarriage.* Breast-feeding* mothers should drink little coffee so that they do not overstimulate their babies. Anyone suffering from anxiety* or panic disorder problems should cut back on coffee, as should those with ulcers, coronary artery disease or high cholesterol levels.

Some medical opinion specifies the number of cups of different kinds of coffee people should drink a day—generally somewhere between three to six caffeinated drinks a day. As mentioned above, the difficulty is that people's toleration of caffeine depends on other factors and that caffeine appears in many other beverages, such as tea, soda, candy and even some over-the-counter medicines. The secret seems to be developing a less pressured lifestyle (*see* Busyness), an awareness of the way our body* and nervous system react and, as in so many other areas, taking things in moderation.

See also ADDICTION; EATING; HOSPITALITY; SUGAR/SUGARY.

Resources and References
R. Hattox, *Coffee and Coffeehouses: The Origins of a Social Beverage in the Medieval Near East* (Seattle: University of Washington, 1985); C. Katona and T. Katona, *The Coffee Book* (San Leandro, Calif.: Bristol, 1992); R. Oldenburg, *The Great Good Place: Coffee Bars* (New York: Paragon Place, 1989); S. Turner, *Up to Date: Poems 1968-1982* (London: Hodder & Stoughton, 1982).

Robert Banks

COHABITING

The phenomenon of a man and woman living together under the same roof as though they were husband and wife, yet without a solemnized wedding and without regarding themselves as married, is a pervasive trend in North American society. Some researchers predict that in a few years almost all young adults will live together before marriage and that this will soon be considered the normal way of courting (*see* Dating) and the equivalent to engagement. This phenomenon is not unique, however, to the Western world, since many societies have *marketplace marriages*—that is, a couple simply decide to live as married, raise a family and avoid the expense and hassle of a huge wedding.*

Frequently the church in these countries faces a difficult challenge—whether to recognize this couple as married or to treat them as living in sin and therefore in need of church discipline.* Some well-meaning church leaders, anxious to get these people married, rush them to the altar, only to find that the relationship, while reasonably stable when the two were living together, sometimes becomes fragile after marriage. Sometimes the marriage ends in divorce.* This raises a profound theological question: When are two people married? Are they married when they have sexual intercourse? when they cohabit and share life fully? when they make their marriage official in a public ceremony? It also raises a spiritual question, for many declared Christians have adopted this pattern either secretly (by spending weekends in each other's apartments) or openly (all the while retaining their membership in a church).

Cohabiting as Marriage Preparation

Many people think of cohabitation as a trial marriage, without using those words per se, since it simulates fully married life and is preferable to the alternative of dating.* The problem, however, is that marriage* cannot be simulated. It is an unconditional covenant of belonging that is made by vows and promises,* by public approval and consent (leaving one's father and mother), and that is sealed and consummated with sexual intercourse. The only way to try marriage

is to get married. Karl Barth insightfully notes that a person who enters marriage must renounce the thought of ever leaving it, which is the very thing cohabitation keeps open. So a couple is either married, unmarried or pretending. It is the pretense that makes cohabitation so illusory a way of assessing marriageability.

Living together is an unwritten contract to meet each other's needs and to make each other happy. It is a convenient relationship without mutual cross bearing and self-sacrifice. There is always the freedom to break the contract if one does not meet the terms. What often happens when a couple who has lived together gets married, especially if they have not been prepared through adequate counseling, is a shocking change in the dynamics and politics of their relationship. A comfort factor sets in. They really belong to each other now and therefore relax some of their efforts to hold on to their live-in companion. On a deeper level, many begin to realize that they are not just lovers but husband and wife, and revert to models they have learned from their families of origin. The problem is not marriage—as is often alleged—but poor preparation for marriage through cohabitation.

Research indicates that couples who have lived together before marriage, in comparison with those who have not, express higher levels of uncertainty and assertiveness and lower levels of conflict avoidance, marital satisfaction and sharing. Rosanne Lyster notes that the absence of a true honeymoon is a significant loss to the marriage. One purpose of the honeymoon is the establishment of positive memories that can hold a marriage together through difficult times. Though most cohabiters take a trip after their wedding, it is not a time of unique sexual pleasure and mutual discovery. Neither were their first few

169

days of living together a honeymoon, since so often moving in was not a concrete decision but just seemed to happen. Further, since most cohabiting couples believe that they are already prepared for marriage, they are more resistant to premarital preparation, even though they may need it as much as others who approach marriage by dating.

The quality of the living-together arrangement has also been the subject of research. Its conditional nature opens the door to exploitation, with the intimacy of short-term gains making it too easy to rationalize one's behavior, to overlook or minimize things that are important to building a permanent relationship or to disregard the long-term welfare of oneself or the other person. Experience has shown that women are more easily exploited than men when it comes to living together. When conception occurs, the couple is often then faced with the decision of whether to keep their child (see Abortion) or whether to marry and give the child a permanent family shelter. As a young boy in a cartoon said to his pal, "First my mom and dad were living together. Then I came along. Now all three of us are living together."

Are They Married?

From a biblical perspective, cohabiting rather than marrying is a stolen covenant. It is not stolen because the couple has failed to register their marriage in the town hall or pay for an expensive wedding in the church. These are important but not essential. The covenant is stolen because the benefits of marriage are being enjoyed without the presence of all three constituent parts of the full covenant, which are found in Genesis 2:24, Matthew 19:5 and Ephesians 5:31—leaving (public wedlock), cleaving (social unity and friendship) and becoming

one flesh (sexual consummation). The abiding absence of any one of these three dimensions means that the couple is not married. They may be pretending, but there is something missing.

Marriage is a mystery (Eph 5:32), and Scripture raises as many questions as it answers on this issue. Jesus, when pressed on the divorce question, said, "Therefore what God has joined together, let man not separate" (Mt 19:6). This raises the question of whom God joins together: those who have had a church wedding? those who live together? those who have had sex? If the last option were true—namely, that one is married to every sex partner—many people are polygamists or have had multiple divorces. Though Paul warns that a person who has sex with a prostitute has become one body with her—there is a transcendent bond—he does not say they are married in 1 Corinthians 6:16. Sex before and outside of marriage is a marriagelike experience but still less than marriage itself.

Marriage is essentially a covenant marked by unconditional relational belonging ("I take you to be . . ."). Christians do not have a monopoly on covenant making, and many not-yet Christians, stumbling on God's plan of leaving, cleaving and becoming one flesh, have unknowingly enjoyed the divine blessing.* Some Christians, in spite of their church wedding, have never really made a covenant. They may have been manipulated into the marriage, may refuse each other sex or may fail to bless their spouse, and so they are not actually married by God. On this point Karl Barth gives wise counsel that we should always cling to God's yes and not quickly conclude that our relationship lacks the divine blessing. So it is a mystery. As such, marriage is to be treated not thoughtlessly but reverently and in the fear of God. It is a matter of worship and faith.

Marriage is a spiritual discipline.

Marriage is also a process. We err in reducing *getting married* to an event: the pronouncement by the pastor ("I declare them husband and wife"), the signature in the book (a legally binding agreement), the first act of intercourse (which may have occurred before the wedding or on the wedding night), the end of the honeymoon (which could have been a disaster), the conception* of the first child (which might not even be physically possible). Each of the three constituent parts of the marriage covenant is a progressive and continuing challenge. Leaving one's father and mother is a lifelong process and is rarely fully accomplished on the wedding day, even if the parents "give" their son or daughter away. Cleaving is a dynamic process, because a marriage relationship is always changing and partners find over time that their spouse is not the same person they married. Becoming one flesh is also a process, since the line between heavy petting and penetration is fine indeed and mere physical touching may lack the gift of self which is the essence of the sexual act.

So it is the intent, willingness, personal capability and action on all three dimensions of the marriage covenant—whether or not the persons acknowledge God—that makes a couple married. The abiding absence of any one of these, such as exists in cohabiting arrangements, means that the couple is not married. In the Western world, the ideal order is cleaving (friendship*), leaving (formal wedlock) and becoming one flesh (full sexual union). Under the arranged-marriage system in the East, the usual order is leaving, becoming one flesh and cleaving (see Gen 24:67). In the living-together arrangement, provided it leads to marriage, the order is cleaving, becoming one flesh and leaving. God's grace may work through each of these arrange-

ments, and for the couple living together there is hope for a good marriage, provided there is repentance and a willingness to prepare properly for full marriage. Some churches have found the discipline of a couple's separating publicly for an extended period of time prior to a church wedding to be a constructive step for the couple and the church.

In conclusion, living together is not a good way to try marriage, because marriage cannot be tried. Neither is living together good marriage preparation. So the church has a unique opportunity to speak prophetically regarding a major trend in the Western world, enfolding couples living together in constructive pastoral care,* all the while confessing that legal marriage or a mere church wedding does not guarantee that God has brought two people together. Marriage is a mystery (requiring faith) and a process (requiring continuous intentionality), something much more than living together.

See also DATING; MARRIAGE; PROMISES; SEXUALITY.

References and Resources

R. Anderson and D. Guernsey, *On Being Family: Essays in a Social Theology of the Family* (Grand Rapids: Eerdmans, 1985); R. F. Lyster, "Implications of Research on Cohabitation for Marriage Preparation," *Marriage Education News* 8, no. 1 (Spring 1995) 1-2; J. H. Olthius, *I Pledge You My Troth: A Christian View of Marriage, Family, Friendship* (New York: Harper & Row, 1975); W. R. Schrumm, "Sex Should Only Occur Within Marriage" (Department of Family and Child Development, Kansas State University, 1984); R. P. Stevens, *Married for Good: The Lost Art of Remaining Happily Married* (Downers Grove, Ill.: InterVarsity Press, 1986).

R. Paul Stevens

COMICS

What part of the newspaper do you turn to first? Sports, finance, food? For many the most important item in the daily paper is the comics section. In fact, during the first half of the twentieth century 60 percent of readers surveyed admitted that this was their number-one reading priority. We want to know what horrible trick Garfield has pulled on Jon. It matters to us that Calvin is having trouble with the school bully, Moe.

Definitions

A few definitions are in order. *Comics* refers to an ongoing series published in newspapers of narrative cartoons with a regular set of characters. *Cartoons* were originally drawings used as the basis for paintings. By Victorian times cartoons referred to humorous single drawings in the newspaper. *Comic books* are booklets of comic strips. Originally they were collections of the weekly colored comics.

Why do we care about these little drawings? Pictures are important as signs to communicate in any culture.* We doodle when we are thinking or bored. International highway signs use shorthand symbols to allow everyone to understand important information quickly.

History

Human beings have created narrative picture sequences for thousands of years. Egyptians combined painted images with hieroglyphics. The Assyrians carved low-relief stories of lion hunts in long, horizontal strips. The Bayeux tapestry, finished in the late eleventh century, described the Battle of Hastings in a band 20 inches high and 230 feet long! And in European Gothic churches stained-glass windows served as "reading" for illiterate peasants, communicating biblical truths through pictorial means.

In the Reformation, art met the new technology* of printing. Printed on paper from engraved wood, and later from metal, these cheap prints at first were commonly used as propaganda for or against the Catholic Church. Both sides

had their graphic artists. Hogarth, in eighteenth-century England, painted narrative sequences, which were quickly reproduced as engravings to be sold cheaply by unscrupulous dealers. Political satire became popular, mostly as single images printed in newspapers.

The first comics were developed in the last half of the nineteenth century in England. *Funny Folks* came into being as the first weekly comic tabloid, half text and half pictures. The first regular comic strip hero was Ally Sloper, going weekly in 1884, in *Ally Sloper's Half Holiday*. Sloper had first appeared seventeen years earlier in *Judy,* an imitation of *Punch. Comic Cats* appeared in 1890. Often thought to be the world's first regularly appearing comic, *Comic Cats* introduced a new element—competition.* It cost a halfpenny, which was half the price of the other comics at the time.

In the late nineteenth-century United States, newspapers were divided into sections. From 1892 they included color, and comics lent themselves readily to this. By 1894 strip-sequence cartoons were appearing in the *Sunday World Comic Weekly,* a section of the *New York World. The Yellow Kid* first appeared in 1895 as one of the kids of *Hogan's Alley.* A creation of Richard Felton Outcault, *The Yellow Kid* was part of the lower-class, immigrant population that was new to the United States. The comic strip first appeared as a single-panel cartoon and later developed to a series of panels and used balloons to indicate dialogue between characters. *The Yellow Kid* has gone down in history as the first comic strip (at least in North America).

Competition was already cutthroat by 1895 with William Randolph Hearst, Joseph Pulitzer and other publishers outbidding one another for popular cartoonists, either buying the rights for the comic series or luring cartoonists to their newspaper. At first a cartoonist's work would show in only one newspaper, but over the years, as publishing empires grew, comic strips were syndicated, appearing in newspapers across the country and around the world.

Comics as Entertainment and Propaganda

What are comics about? Right from the beginning they were conceived as entertainment.* The ability to laugh* at oneself and one's surroundings, in good times and bad, is a healthy thing. Early on in the history of comics the colored Sunday comic supplements were called *funnies,* an abbreviation of *funny papers.*

Though the majority still are concerned with humor, or are trying to be, comics are not only funny. Comic heroes include those drawn from literature: Hercules, King Arthur, Tarzan. Various characters have had an effect on popular culture—for example, Popeye and spinach, Dagwood sandwiches and Buster Brown shoes. Batman has gone from comics to television* and movies.* Mickey Mouse has ended up with theme parks and a communications empire.

There is also satire: *Li'l Abner, Pogo* and *Doonesbury.* Adventures include *Tarzan, Flash Gordon* and *Terry and the Pirates.* Soap operas hit the comics long before television in *Mary Worth; Rex Morgan, M.D.;* and *Judge Parker.* And humor reigns in all of its slapstick, sarcastic joy in *Beetle Bailey, Garfield, Bloom County* and *Calvin and Hobbes.*

Comics have been used as propaganda (especially at the time of the world wars) and in advertising.* They have made learning information more palatable. Reading teachers have used them for students who have been unable to learn to read. It has been found that the student is led from comics to books, something like reading *Howards End* after seeing the movie.

Telling the Story

At the heart of comics' strength is narration. Comics tell stories. They can deal with important human issues in humorous ways, in a disarming fashion. Though comics are a rarity in biblical dictionaries and commentaries, publications like *Christianity Today* and *Leadership* often use cartoons with telling effect. Some comics illuminate some spiritual as well as human issue, and that with telling effect.

Calvin and Hobbes often deals with important religious issues, usually while our heroes are rattling toward the edge of a ravine in their wagon, talking about the meaning of life. *B.C.* and *Peanuts* are more explicit in their inclusion of biblical material. The former often presents Scripture in the comic strip at Christmas and Easter without apology. *Peanuts* has used the Bible for inspiration for over thirty years, sometimes just quoting a verse or two, but often grappling with spiritual issues in a deeper way. When Linus finds out that his sister, Lucy, wishes he had never been born, he confesses to Snoopy, "Why, the theological implications alone are staggering." Though this has been a regular feature in *Peanuts,* such thoughtful additions appear less frequently nowadays. But humor in comic strips remains an effective way of introducing biblical truth to a wide audience in a disarming manner.

But should we, as Christians, be involved with the comic? Is it not a distraction? Frivolity? Comic art is mostly positive and reinforces traditional Christian values of right and wrong. Morality is underlined: "Comedy implies an attitude towards life, an attitude that trusts in man's potential for redemption and salvation" (Inge, p. xxi). This is the comic in the larger sense of Chaucer and Dante, a look at all of life, from hell to heaven. And those who can laugh are secure.

See also CULTURE; HUMOR; LAUGHTER; STORYTELLING.

References and Resources
D. Gifford, *The International Book of Comics* (London: Hamlyn, 1988); M. T. Inge, *Comics as Culture* (Jackson: University Press of Mississippi, 1990); J. O'Sullivan, *The Great American Comic Strip* (Boston: Bulfinch Press, 1990); G. Perry and A. Aldridge, *The Penguin Book of Comics* (London: Penguin, 1971).

Dal Schindell

COMMITTEES

You'll find in no park or city
A monument to a committee.
(Victoria Pasternak)

The ambivalence of some people with regard to committees can be summed up in the cartoon that shows a minister reading a story to his child, with his paraphrase going like this: "And when the pastor cut down the beanstalk, the giant committee came tumbling down, and the church lived happily ever after." This sentiment was echoed by another pastor who described committees as one thing the devil really loves. Of course the church* is only one context in which committees exist. They are present in every sphere of life, for example, workplaces,* community organizations,* voluntary associations and so on. Committees intersect with two social phenomena: leadership* and group or meeting dynamics. Christian hesitations about the appropriateness of committees arise from both spheres.

Leadership often appears to happen in the absence of or in spite of committee work. It is true that the biblical record is weak on the role of the committee in leadership. Leadership is overwhelmingly an individual affair in the Old Testament, being regularly mediated through three types of individuals: prophets, priests or princes. This reality reaches a climax when all three roles are summed up in Jesus. We hardly think of Jesus as setting his plans by committee. In fact, he sometimes had to resist the will of the potential committee represented by his disciples (Mt 16:21-23). Likewise, when Paul received wisdom from the majority in an ad hoc committee, he chose to ignore it (Acts 21:10-14), though this is an exceptional example. As we will see, the Bible does support the idea of setting and accomplishing goals through groups. In the New Testament especially we see people working in teams: plural eldership, Paul's normal practice of team ministry and shared ministry in local churches.

The other hesitation comes from the actual functioning of committees, especially committee meetings. Because of sin or ignorance, meetings sometimes are very unprofitable and frustrating: time is wasted, conflict goes unresolved, decisions are not reached or implemented, people are not heard, or people are heard too much. Better, it seems, to forget committees (and especially committee meetings) and just let someone get on with the job at hand.

The Value of Committees
In the end, the deep theological rationale for committees comes less from proof texts in the Bible and more from an overall sense of the biblical plan for salvation. The plan is simply to form a people for God, a body made up of cells, individual people who have all received the Spirit. Spiritual gifts,* including any gifts of leadership, are not concentrated comprehensively in individuals, whether prophets, priests or princes. Instead, the metaphor of the body suggests connection, one gift reinforcing and supplementing another, so that the whole body "grows and builds itself up in love, as each part does its work" (Eph 4:16).

This idea is the basis for using committees: the whole is greater than the sum of the parts, whether in making decisions or dividing up the tasks of a project. The latter notion is probably generally accepted: using teamwork to conquer an obstacle or exploit an opportunity makes sense. However, we are more comfortable with the model of a coach deploying the players than with the model of the players deploying themselves according to an agreed-upon strategy. Thus, we are back to the idea of a singular leader. For example, we might think of Moses dividing up the job of judging the children of Israel or Nehemiah parceling out the job of rebuilding the wall of Jerusalem. In the end, however, this does not represent committee work. Committees represent a commitment to forming policies, plans or strategies within a group. In other words, leadership is shaped and directed by a group process, in the belief that ten heads are better than one.

There are dangers in committees: an individual's hiding behind the group to avoid personal responsibility or the group lapsing into such complex processes that decisions are never made. As a wit once observed, a committee is a group of people who individually can do nothing but as a group decide that nothing can be done. On the other hand, committees can also be very effective in avoiding dangers: manipulative leaders and foolish plans. The output and impact of a good committee are threefold: good decisions, good relationships and good leadership. The only way to make sure that these results happen is to make sure that good decisions, relationships and leadership are also the basis of every committee.

The Effective Committee

A committee is a species of small group.* Like every small group, an effective committee must be based on a strong sense of what it is trying to accomplish. How will the committee know when it is doing (or has finished) its job? To what precise external end is the committee committed? The clearer the sense of purpose, and the more it shapes every meeting agenda, the more satisfying and successful the committee will be. Every committee should give more time to clarifying purpose and procedures than is usually set aside.

The purpose may be set by the group, as in the case of the "nominating committee" in Acts 1:15-26, or it may be mandated by a higher authority, as in the appointment of the Seven to manage charity toward widows in Acts 6:1-6. The latter is instructive in two other ways. First, it shows that the members of the first committee in the church, the apostles, knew they had to protect their agenda from distractions. Every group of elders in a local church today needs to take this to heart. Second, it shows a group moving beyond an advisory or animating role to actually accomplishing the plan that it formulated. A committee may be constituted to advise some external leader or animate some of its members toward action, but the most effective committee is probably the one that seeks to implement its plan together as a group. A plan worked by the owners of the planning is usually worked best.

Setting and accomplishing a purpose require a process of communicating ideas and coming to a consensus about the idea that will prevail. This requires a good base of positive relationships. Committee members need to be committed to one another as much as to their purpose. This bond is strengthened by good group dynamics: honoring the gift of each member, listening* to every contribution, submitting to one another and fighting fairly. See Em Griffin's book *Getting Together* (pp. 134-56) for help with conflict resolution.* Good dynamics during committee meetings help to forge

175

the sorts of relationships that produce good teamwork when the committee moves into action mode. The story of the "committee of Jerusalem" in Acts 15 provides a healthy model for a group process; note especially the careful listening.

Finally, committees need good leadership if they are to be effective. Leaders must focus on maintaining purpose and maintaining relationships. If one person cannot handle both these functions, then there should be two official leaders: one to manage the agenda and one to facilitate communication. Emphasizing one or the other aspect of committee work leads to imbalance. Most commonly, task supplants relationships. Roberta Hestenes has written a good corrective for this in *Turning Committees into Communities*. Good, balanced leadership during a committee meeting will release good leadership after the meeting. This is what Paul hoped for in Acts 20: he not only reminded the Ephesian elders of their purpose but also took part as they prayed, wept and embraced him.

Even though they sometimes seems to keep minutes and waste hours, committees are here to stay, both in the church and in the wider world. Christians have an excellent opportunity to help them be a true expression of the body of Christ and a positive force for kingdom purposes.

See also COMMUNITY; CONFLICT RESOLUTION; LEADERSHIP; ORGANIZATION; SMALL GROUPS.

References and Resources
E. Griffin, *Getting Together* (Downers Grove, Ill.: InterVarsity Press, 1982); R. Hestenes, *Turning Committees into Communities* (Colorado Springs: NavPress, 1991).

Dan Williams

COMMUNION
Baptism* is the sacrament* of Christian initiation; the Lord's Supper (also called Communion or the Eucharist) is the sacrament of Christian growth and development. Both are vital. The early Christians were well aware of this and valued both highly, including regular gatherings to eat and drink in remembrance of Christ. Here again we are often impoverished by our own tradition. The very names used for it in Scripture hint at the breadth of meanings in this most wonderful sacrament. The *Lord's Supper* takes us back to the upper room (1 Cor 11:20). The *breaking of bread* alludes to the familiar action of beginning and having a meal (Acts 2:42). *Holy Communion* indicates a joint participation in the body and blood of Christ (1 Cor 10:16). *Eucharist* (meaning "thanksgiving") speaks of blessing God for all that Jesus has done for us (1 Cor 11:24; *Didache* 9.1). (*Mass,* though somewhat obscure in etymology, probably means dismissal of the congregation into the world for ministry* and mission.* *Mass* is not a New Testament term, though the idea of sending out certainly is.)

Communion in the Early Church
Most early Communions did not take place in a church* at all but in a home* (*see* Church in the Home). People would begin to appear in the early evening with materials for a potluck supper. They greet* one another. They are happy and relaxed; work* is over. All are on one level here, men and women, Roman citizens and commoners, slaves and free. Lamps are lit. Couches are set. Feet are washed. They have a meal, reclining around a courtyard or squashed into a room. They share news. Someone produces a musical instrument, and they begin to sing. Indeed, they create new songs, snatches of which are to be found in the New Testament, like "Wake up, O sleeper, rise from the dead, and Christ will shine on you" (Eph 5:14) or "Holy, holy, holy is the Lord God Almighty, who

was, and is, and is to come" (Rev 4:8).

Meanwhile someone brings out the church box, which contains their most precious Christian belongings: some sayings of Jesus or perhaps a letter from an apostle. The praise is heartfelt. Speaking in tongues might well follow. There could be prayer for a healing* or a specific need of one of the members. Certainly prayer, the reading of an Old Testament Scripture, the recitation of a story about Jesus and some words of encouragement from members of the community, along with joyful singing, will all feature. And as the evening comes to an end, they tell again the story of Jesus' passion and break bread and drink wine in remembrance of him. Every scrap is finished. The prayer that Jesus taught them is recited. They move around and embrace one another with a holy kiss and then go home. All very simple. No service books. No priests. No altars. Every eye is on the unseen Lord, the bread, the wine and each other. And then—out into the night, spiritually refueled for the journey of the coming week.

What Is This Meal?

There have been many speculations. Some have seen the meal as a *haburah,* a special religious meal held by a group of friends. Others have sought to show that it derived from a *kiddush,* a Friday-evening family gathering to prepare for the sabbath.* Still others have looked to pagan sources for this meal. But the clue to understanding this meal lies in the Passover of the Old Testament, as 1 Corinthians 5:7-8 makes plain: "Christ, our Passover lamb, has been sacrificed. Therefore let us keep the Festival."

A Passover with a Difference

The biblical scholar Joachim Jeremias persuasively demonstrated this Passover background to the Communion in his book *The Eucharistic Words of Jesus,* and all

subsequent scholarship on the subject has been beholden to him. He points out eleven elements in the account that substantiate this Passover background. For example, the Last Supper took place in Jerusalem; it extended into the night; it was a small, intimate gathering; the participants reclined instead of sitting; a dish preceded the breaking of bread; wine, an essential at Passover, was drunk; the words of institution are an adaptation of Passover *haggadah;* Judas went out, ostensibly to give to the poor—a Passover custom—and so on.

Jeremias piles up the evidence that the meal was an anticipated Passover. He then deals with ten objections. There are two he does not handle. One is the absence of any mention of a lamb. Was this due to the compression of the account as Christians recited what was special about that Passover? Was it because they saw Jesus as the Passover lamb? We may never know. The other of Jeremias's omissions was an explanation of how the annual Passover celebration turned into the weekly (or even more frequent) Christian celebration. The frequency was probably due to the well-remembered fact that the Master had made a point of eating* regularly with his disciples. They had regular common meals, but all subsequent communal meals were impregnated with the meaning of this awesome night, repeated often, at his express command.

All four Gospel accounts, despite their different nuances, are agreed that Jesus took bread, blessed and broke it, spoke interpretative words over it and gave it to his disciples. It is beyond the scope of this article to study in detail this meal that gave rise to the Holy Communion, but the following factors are of great importance.

First, this complete meal extended for a long time. Our accounts cover only the special Christian differentia in this

Passover meal; the bread and wine were only selections from a much fuller mealtime together.

Second, the annual Jewish Passover was not a sacrifice but the memorial of the first Passover, which certainly was a sacrifice when the lambs of Israel died and their blood was painted on the door lintels to avert the angel of wrath. Equally, the Christian Eucharist is not a sacrifice but the memorial of that great sacrifice when the Lamb of God shed his blood to avert judgment on a sinful world.

Third, the words *body* and *blood,* clearly a pair, lead us back in Aramaic to the only pair that Jesus could have used: *bisra udema.* Both are sacrificial words. Each denoted violent death. They point to Jesus' sacrificial death on the morrow.

Fourth, by giving his disciples the bread and the wine, Jesus gives them a share in the benefits of his atoning sacrifice, just as the Israelites who ate the Passover lamb shared not in making the sacrifice but in its benefits—rescue from bondage and death in Egypt. This is how sacrificial language came to be applied to the Communion. Properly speaking, it is not a sacrifice but a dramatic, concrete fresh appropriation of Jesus' atoning sacrifice and a means of enjoying its benefits.

Fifth, the change in the explanatory words about the Passover is truly amazing. Normally the presider would (in obedience to Ex 12:25; 13:8) take bread and say, "This is the bread of affliction which your fathers ate in the wilderness." Imagine the electric atmosphere when Jesus, presiding, says, "This is—my body, given for you." In Aramaic the saying would have gone like this, "This—my body . . . ," leaving it open whether representation or identity was intended (an issue that has divided Catholics from Protestants for centuries). Then Jesus said, "Do this in remembrance of me."

The word *anamnēsis,* "remembrance," does not mean mere mental recollection, as we Westerners would interpret it. To the Semitic mind it meant re-presentation. The Jews were accustomed to saying at Passover, "This the Eternal did for me when I went out of Egypt." They saw the past as in some way made contemporary. Similarly, Jesus seems to have intended his disciples at the Eucharist to see his death as in some way made contemporary, however many years ago it happened. Here in this service I see afresh before my very eyes what the Eternal did for me to bring me out of a bondage and a doom far worse than those which befell the Jews in Egypt. The broken bread and the poured-out wine not only dramatically reminded the early Christians of what Jesus did for them on the cross; it also showed them that this historical event has present power and relevance. They could enter into the experience to which it referred, sharing in the benefits of his death and resurrection for them.

The blood is as significant as the bread. The Passover blood was originally applied to the houses of the Israelites and brought salvation, rescue from the destroying angel who killed the firstborn of the Egyptians. That is why wine (to recall the blood) was an essential part of Passover. The benediction before the "cup of blessing" in the Passover specifically praises God for that deliverance from Egypt and the covenant with his people. The praise that followed had Psalm 116 as its core, a psalm that spoke of gratefully receiving the cup of salvation. So profound associations were combined here: the blood, the covenant, the exodus, the vicariousness, the cup and the appropriation.

Sixth, the shocking language was intentional and was remembered. To eat human flesh and to drink blood were expressly forbidden in Judaism.

We need to take seriously both the metaphorical and the realistic significance of this language. We feed on Christ in our hearts, really feed on him. But we do so by faith.

The Meaning of the Meal

Set in this way against the backdrop of the Passover, both historically and theologically, the depths of the Lord's Supper begin to become apparent.

The Passover had a *backward* orientation. The first Passover was a sacrifice. Indeed, it was the sacrifice that constituted Israel as a people. Succeeding Passovers were not sacrifices, though they might loosely be called such, and they had no expiatory significance. Their purpose was not to take away sins. But they brought that original sacrifice powerfully before the worshiper. It is like that with the Communion. Not a sacrifice in itself, it is the representation of Jesus' sacrifice, and we feast on the benefits he won for us through it.

The Passover has a *present* orientation. The first Passover had been a meal to strengthen the Israelites for their march from the land of bondage to the land of promise. This element was reenacted annually. The theme of God's constant care and provision for them is prominent in the account of God's mighty rescue, recounted at the meal. The eating and drinking formed a sacred bond between the worshipers; one can see from Psalm 41:9 how heinous was the breaking of such table fellowship. It was the same with the Lord's Supper. It too has the effect of binding together all its participants into one (1 Cor 10:17). Its fellowship* cannot be violated without the most heinous sin and disastrous consequences (1 Cor 11:19-20, 27-30). And the Lord's Supper too strengthens pilgrims for the journey, for it feeds them on the body of Christ (1 Cor 10:16), and he is their nourishment and sustenance (Jn 6:51).

The Passover had a *future* orientation. It prefigured the ultimate feast of salvation as well as being the re-presentation of deliverance from Egypt. Passover would be the night when the Messiah would come. "On this night they were saved, and on this night they will be saved," mused the rabbis. This forward look is integral to the Christian Passover, the Eucharist. In Luke's account (Lk 22:7-23) it is stressed almost to the exclusion of all else. It is also there in Matthew and Mark and in the allusive language about the "true" bread and vine in John's Gospel. It is notable in 1 Corinthians 11:26, and the cry *Maranatha* ("Our Lord, come"; 1 Cor 16:22 NRSV) was probably used at the Lord's Supper, as we learn from the post-New Testament writing the *Didache* (10.4). Just as the Passover was the pledge of the coming of the messiah, so the Eucharist is the pledge of Jesus' return and of the messianic banquet toward which every Communion points.

The Significance of Regular Communion

No wonder this is the central meal for Christians, the service important beyond all others. For it is the archetypal symbol of our redemption, past, present and future. We will grow deeper and deeper in its appreciation until we taste it new in the kingdom of God. This is especially the case if we ensure that our gatherings for the Lord's Supper are regular, contain all the features that characterized the early Christian celebrations and, when appropriate, have the form of an actual meal (*see* Church in the Home; Eating). Our Master knew what he was doing when he left just two sacraments to his church—baptism and the Lord's Supper. Both are incandescent with all the colors of salvation's rainbow. The one points to its once-for-allness and its need to govern the dying and rising life of Christians. The other calls and empowers for persistence on the journey, as pilgrims climb the upward path. It lifts our eyes to the Lord, our bread and vine, and it points us toward God's wedding banquet, when Christ will marry his bride, the church, forever, and there will be no more sorrow, no more crying, no more death.* We shall see his face and share his likeness.

See also BAPTISM; CHURCH IN THE HOME; EATING; FELLOWSHIP; SACRAMENTS; WORSHIP.

References and Resources

R. Banks, *Going to Church in the First Century* (Beaumont, Tex.: Christian Books, 1990); W. Barclay, *The Lord's Supper* (London: SCM, 1967); M. Green and R. P. Stevens, *New Testament Spirituality* (Guildford, U.K.: Eagle, 1993), portions quoted with permission; J. Jeremias, *The Eucharistic Words of Jesus* (London: SCM, 1970).

Michael Green

COMMUNITY

The word *community* is on many people's lips today and is used in many different ways. It can, for example, refer to

□ any grouping of people, small or large, that springs out of organic, rather than organized, links (for example, a group of friends or people who regularly enjoy vacations* together)

□ a cluster of people who are in some kind of kinship relation with one another (such as an extended family* or clan)

□ a group of people in a locality who over time have formed some common bonds, interests or concerns (for example, a rural community* or town*)

□ an intensive, emotional shared experience between a group of people (such as a camping* community or encounter group)

□ a longer-term, face-to-face gathering of people seeking to develop mutual bonds and obligations (such as a small group* or house church; *see* Church in the Home)

□ a group of people who live together and have a common mission* (for example, a religious order or community house)

□ a larger body of people who meet regularly and engage in common artistic, intellectual or religious activities (such as a synagogue or local church)

This wide range of meanings reminds us that we always need to be clear on how we or others are using the term. Here I shall focus on the first meaning, which has the longest history among thinkers about community, and the last meaning, which has the longest continuing usage in the church.* A major article on church takes the view that community is the basic purpose of the church. The remaining meanings of the word listed above can be explored elsewhere in this volume, as indicated by asterisks.

Understanding Human Groupings

Over a century ago the German sociologist Ferdinand Toennies published his groundbreaking *Community and Society* (1887). He was building on a distinction, which had a long history in both Western and Eastern philosophy, between the kinds of groups to which people belong. In some cases there are *natural* links, forged through belonging to the same family or living in the same place, where people simply share a common life. In other cases they are *rational,* creating through joining an enterprise or club, where people are pursuing a particular purpose. The first type of relationship, a community, is an end in itself, even if other things spring out of it. The second, an association or society, is a means to some other end: it is task-oriented rather than existing for its own sake.

Other thinkers have similarly distinguished between *mechanistic* and *organic* (Émile Durkheim), *familistic* and *contrac-*

tual (Pitirim Sorokin), *primary* and *secondary* (C. H.Cooley) groups. Both kinds of groups exist in every society. But a dramatic shift occurred in the West after the Industrial Revolution, when more natural communities were broken up or weakened in favor of more planned ones. While this introduced more possibilities for achieving certain purposes, it came at the loss of close links that bound people together. This is why so many people lament the loss of community today and look back nostalgically to earlier times or rural settings when it was experienced more fully.

Community includes the home,* craft guilds and the church, though over the course of time each has tended to take on board more elements of an *association*. For example, for many people marriage* has become a contractual arrangement that can be easily broken if certain goals are not met; the workplace* has become governed by contracts* and regulations rather than by family links or vocational commitment; and the church in places is becoming a kind of corporation, emphasizing programs rather than the body of Christ experiencing fellowship.* The communal element in family, work* and church life has been further diminished through the intrusion of bureaucratic procedures and regulations.

Misunderstanding Christian Community
The distinction between community and association is also useful in differentiating between various kinds of Christian groups. It helps us understand the well-known distinction drawn between modalities (congregations) and sodalities (mission groups), between the local church and parachurch* organizations, and between support groups and mission.

Failure to recognize the many differences between a community and an association has led many Christian enterprises

to become confused as to their own purpose or to misunderstand what other groups are doing. Some examples of this follow:

☐ When something organic such as the formation of communal groups or small groups in the church is approached in too organized, contrived or programmed a way, the experience of community is undercut rather than enhanced.

☐ When the decision-making processes and leadership* of a task-oriented enterprise are too dependent on everyone's participation and feeling good about the outcome, inefficient management* of the organization results.

☐ When congregations and parachurch organizations remain suspicious of one another or trespass on the limits proper to each, they generally fail to see that one is primarily about nurture for its members and outreach to its immediate community and the other primarily about mission to a diffused constituency, with the nurturing element only to that end.

☐ When the leaders of a program, say in Christian education,* do not see that it must be both people- and task-directed, forming people spiritually and relationally as well as enhancing learning and practice, they fail to understand which category particular activities fall into and end up confusing the two.

In all these ways the distinction between community and association helps us to understand what community is and is not about. Its meaning is deepened when we see community as an expression of the communal life of our trinitarian God. We are called upon to express to God and one another the same unconditional faithfulness, self-sacrificing love and visionary hope we find in Christ. None of this is possible without the presence, gifting and fruit of the Spirit. The articles indicated by asterisks above indicate the ways in which Christians are to express and develop community.

See also CHURCH; CHURCH IN THE HOME; CHURCH, SMALL; CHURCH STRUCTURES; CLUBS; COMMUNITY, RURAL; FELLOWSHIP; NEIGHBORHOOD; NETWORKING; SMALL GROUPS; SOCIETY.

References and Resources

P. M. Cooey, *Family, Freedom and Faith: Building Community Today* (Louisville, Ky.: Westminster John Knox, 1996); R. A. Nisbet, *The Quest for Community* (New York: Oxford University Press, 1953); G. Tinder, *Community: Reflections on a Tragic Ideal* (Baton Rouge: Louisiana State University Press, 1980); F. Toennies, *Community and Society* (New York: Harper & Row, 1957).

Robert Banks

COMMUNITY, RURAL

The lights of rural communities and villages flicker and die as farm families desert the countryside and those remaining drive past to the larger centers. Rugged individualism seems to be replacing the traditional cooperative spirit. But earth keeping and community* are still mutually essential (Gen 2:15-18; Lev 25—26; Bryden and Gertner, pp. 72, 211).

The Setting

Rural *out-migration* began after World War II (Riedel and Wefald, p. 108). Stimulus was provided by unprecedented mechanization and other technological* development, which continues unabated today. Therefore people with acquisitive attitudes were and still are able to accumulate ever larger units of primary food production (Connick, Connick and Keating, pp. 57-61; Kneen, p. 76). The prophet Isaiah described well the situation: "Woe to you who add house to house and join field to field till . . . you live alone in the land" (Is 5:8). The sparsely populated countryside we see today does not conform to the Lord's decree to fill the earth (Gen 9:7) nor to his scattering the people over the earth (Gen 11:8).

A significant remnant of social support remains in rural community. In Canada, for example, 57 percent of rural people are directly involved in support networks from which 90 percent benefit (Apedaile et al., pp. 8-9). These involvements still provide some local vigor and stability (Apedaile et al., p. 22). Women, through their volunteer work* and social networking,* are the glue that holds rural communities together (Apedaile et al., pp. 7-8). Though most have off-farm jobs (Apedaile et al., p. 11), women remain the major producers of household goods for consumption and provide on-farm support and labor (compare Prov 31:10-31). In the Canadian province of Saskatchewan, traditionally a grain-growing rural economy, off-farm income of farm families exceeded net farm income by a substantial margin in 1991 (Apedaile et al., p. 11). Sixty percent of farm women and 30 percent of farm men had off-farm jobs.

The Decline

Rural people have sought out urban amenities of shopping,* entertainment* and recreation.* Other less-edifying city attractions are the possibilities of anonymity, glitz, fast living and unmitigated materialism. Farm income cannot fulfill the desire for the luxuries available to city people. That, in combination with other factors including government encouragement, has resulted in the great exodus of country folk to the city (Freudenberger, p. 81).

Not only is the number of farmers and villagers small, but they are fractionalized by social and political differences. Therefore there is diminishing contact between rural neighbors,* with little reason remaining to bring neighbors together, especially when rural commuting* to a fifty-mile range is common.

Individualism, fueled by greed, is a big factor in the depopulation of the countryside. Individualism is not biblical (1 Cor 12; Marshall, p. 142; Walsh and Middleton, p. 86). In the Bible direction from the Lord is usually toward a people, not individuals (Rom 12:3-5; Eph 4—5; Col 3:5-17; 1 Pet 2:9-10). The strength of community is the complementary nature of unique gifting to individuals.

Rural Vulnerability

With the industrialization of the farm and depletion of the rural population has come considerable loss of connection to the earth. A rural life keeps one in touch with the land on which we all depend for sustenance. Knowing where food is grown lends one credibility. There is wisdom derived from knowing how the weather* makes the production of food an uncertain matter. Above all, we hear from God through creation (Ps 8; 19; Rom 1:20). Too many people live an aseptic, naive, disconnected-from-creation-and-its-reality existence to be good for society as a whole (Connick, Connick and Keating, pp. 235, 242).

With the current trend toward bigger farms, residents are becoming increasingly vulnerable. Obviously, personal and farm safety is a concern. Moreover, since farmers are now between 3 percent and 4 percent of the population, they have lost political significance (Freudenberger, p. 82). This small voting bloc is the one most in touch with the land from which we all receive our food and is ignored, therefore, at the peril of the nation (Riedel and Wefald, p. 109; Kneen, p. 83; Connick, Connick and Keating, p. 235; Bryden and Gertner, p. 73). Finally, when independence is the hallmark of a society, can social, government, health and school problems be far behind?

Alternatives: The Amish and the French

The Amish are well known for their counterculture. To give their young people a reprieve from the perceived degrading influence of the predominant culture,* they have devised a lifestyle that keeps their children in the community (Dobson, p. 52; Goering, Norberg and Page, p. 59). The Amish have been successful in providing a place for their children in a rural setting, in part by resisting the use of motorized vehicles. They are committed to each other, and that has a remarkable socioeconomic impact. For instance, neighbors and family gather to raise a new barn. Insurance* is not needed because the community is there to help.

In his book *Global Dust Bowl*, C. Dean Freudenberger describes how France, beginning in the 1960s, turned the nation back to traditional agriculture. The result has been a revitalizing of the rural community, growing rural-urban solidarity and an improved "health of its countryside" (Freudenberger, pp. 94-98).

Renewal

Near large cities there has been a recent in-migration of city workers to the country (Connick, Connick and Keating, p. 69). This has been a disruptive influence on farming, hastening the demise of the very best agricultural land through country residential development. Any plan to reverse the population shift in favor of rural areas must be approached carefully. The introduction of industrial development from outside only creates problems of commuting workers and resentment from local residents over outsiders' taking jobs. Any project must be done from within the community with careful planning and education involving local residents and government (Riedel and Wefald, p. 113; Connick, Connick and Keating, p. 250).

An international group of researchers, the Agriculture and Rural Restructuring Group (the Group), has proposed that current government aid to a depressed rural economy be replaced with a system of direct payment for rural development and sustainability by something like a tax on food (Apedaile et al., p. 23). Most urbanites are willing to help the dwindling rural population maintain roads, sustain the countryside for the enjoyment of all and provide food. Another recommendation from the Group is that, given the consolidation of farms, there is need for growth in nonagricultural activity in rural areas to help stabilize the rural economy. The context of the proposal is "re-integration of family with business interests" (Apedaile et al., pp. 24, 27). Also proposed is a change from an emphasis on the diversification of on-farm enterprise to farmer and community diversification into nonagricultural pursuits.

Conclusion

A growth in rural population coming from an increase in the number of farms and rural businesses will benefit a nation. Any such move must take into account that the country offers a different set of benefits and experiences than does the city. While some might consider it a sacrifice to live in the country, there is substantial compensation to be living where true community is more likely and where ties to creation can be renewed.

See also CITY; COMMUNITY; GOSSIP; HOSPITALITY; NEIGHBORHOOD; SMALL TOWNS; VISITING.

References and Resources

P. Apedaile et al., *Towards a Whole Rural Policy for Canada* (Brandon, Man.: University of Brandon, Canadian Agriculture and Rural Restructuring Group, 1994); J. Bryden and M. E. Gertner, *Towards Sustainable Rural Communities* (Guelph, Ont.: University of Guelph, 1994); D. Connick, N. Connick and N. C. Keating, *Alternative Futures for Prairie Agricultural Communities* (Edmonton: University of Alberta, 1991); R. V. G. Dobson, *Bringing the Economy Home from the Market* (Montreal: Black Rose Books, 1993); C. D. Freudenberger, *Global Dust Bowl* (Minneapolis: Augsburg, 1990); P. Goering, H. Norberg and J. Page, *From the Ground Up* (London: Zed, 1993); B. Kneen, *From Land to Mouth* (Toronto: NC Press, 1989); P. Marshall, *Thine Is the Kingdom* (Basingstoke, Hants, U.K.: Marshalls, 1984); R. Riedel and J. Wefald, "Strengthening Rural Communities," in *Farming the Lord's Land,* ed. E. Lutz (Minneapolis: Augsburg, 1980); B. Walsh and R. Middleton, *The Transforming Vision* (Downers Grove, Ill.: InterVarsity Press, 1984).

Verne M. Gleddie

COMMUTING

Commuting to work by private or public transportation is one of the daily realities of modern life. In previous times people generally worked in their homes or walked a relatively short distance to their place of employment. But with the advent of the train and tram, bus and automobile,* along with the spread of suburbia,* getting to and from work has become a more complex and time-consuming business.

A generation ago people were congratulating themselves that working hours were fewer, little realizing that in most cases these were taken up by extra time* commuting. Now that working hours are expanding again, and freeways are becoming more clogged, there is a danger that commuting hours will also rise. This is especially the case for those who are unemployed* and can find work only a long distance from home.

Commuting Times and Patterns

By far the greatest proportion of people commute to work by car. This varies from city to city and depends on climatic conditions, quality of public transportation and provision of cycleways. In most places, 90 percent or more of commuters travel by automobile, and somewhere between 5 percent and 15 percent travel by public transportation, mostly train or bus. Although improvements in public transportation, along with diversification of it and additions to it, in recent years have reclaimed some people from their cars, it is still used by only a small proportion of the commuting population. This is significant enough to ease some congestion on the roads, but not enough to make a wholesale difference in the quality of road or rail commutes.

On the whole, commuting time by car has remained surprisingly stable over the last couple of decades. At present the average length of car trips in the larger cities in North America is roughly equivalent. Older, denser metropolises in the East and Midwest lose what they gain by being more compact through the greater length of time it takes to traverse them. In newer, more sprawling metropolises in the South and West, traffic flows a little faster and so makes up for the longer distances between job and suburb. The majority of car trips, almost 40 percent, take about twenty to thirty minutes, 20 percent around ten to fifteen minutes less, 20 percent around ten to fifteen minutes more, and fewer than 10 percent up to an hour in length. A small but growing proportion of people—whether going by car, bus, train or ferry—travel two hours or more a day to work. There are also those who commute by plane.

Most people who commute by car travel alone. In North America car-pooling is usually defined as two or more passengers, in other countries three or more. Though the ratio of car-poolers to lone travelers varies from city to city, on average it is around one in seven but can vary from half to double that number. Those who travel by van or bus, less so by tram or train, often socialize with fellow commuters, especially in the western states. Such people build a modest level of community through regularly traveling at the same time with each other day after day. This is especially the case where

longer distances are involved.

The amount of stress* and frustration caused by some forms of commuting, especially traveling by car, is a matter of widespread complaint. Here and there some interesting responses to these expressions of dissatisfaction are beginning to emerge. For example, driving schools are beginning to include in their lessons to new drivers sessions on stress management as well as on how to deal with rudeness. Also, family members and neighbors intentionally or instinctively help those who are drivers among them to debrief at the end of the day, that is, to report on the dangers they have encountered, obstacles they have overcome and fatigue they are experiencing.

The amount of time people spend commuting, the fact that they mostly do it alone and, as roads get busier and trains become fewer, the tiring or frustrating nature of commuting generally raise many questions. These are worth asking in an effort to become more aware of what is at stake and what are the options with respect to commuting: When there is a choice, is it more important to live closer to work, schools and shops in less advantageous surroundings so that families and friends can have more time together, or is quality of location and residence more important? Are there additional ways in which commuting can become a more sociable, community-building activity or even a more reflective, educational one? Is it possible to handle commuting better so that it is less energy-taxing and anxiety-producing and so would give people more chance at the end of the day to socialize or engage in other worthwhile activities?

These are not the only questions. We could ask how we can improve people's capacity to drive safely and courteously on the roads so as to reduce traffic accidents. Or we might consider the impact of commuting long distances on those who find it difficult to find or keep work. Since our adoption of the automobile has led to the deterioration of public transportation, we might consider our responsibility to older, younger, poorer or disabled people who most rely on public transportation to get around. But it is the first, basic, set of questions that will be addressed here.

Commuting Practices and Possibilities
In recent ethical thought much has been made about the importance of developing a range of character-based practices that are genuinely virtuous. Insofar as people seek to acquire good driving habits, they are developing a standard way of operating that will serve them well on the road. But what other practices might be relevant in driving to and from work, ones more related to personal well-being, community building, educational or spiritual development? And what practices might be helpful for those who do not commute by car? Are there specific practices related to being a passenger rather than a driver?

Perhaps the first desirable practice with respect to commuting is that time spent traveling to and from work be decreased as much as is realistically possible. All forms of commuting, but particularly those undertaken by car, add to our already congested, polluted and often accident-ridden transportation situation. If the time people spent commuting could be decreased, morning rush hours of between five miles per hour (in London) and fifteen miles per hour (in many American cities) would be greatly aided. Pollution—in Los Angeles every car puts approximately its own weight into the air as pollutant each year—would lessen. The awful physical, psychological and economic toll of road injuries and deaths would be significantly diminished.

But how do people go about decreas-ing the amount of time it takes to travel to and from work? Fortunately there is a growing tendency for people to seek work closer to home, but perhaps they should also consider moving home closer to work. It is ironic that many people move to outer suburbs because of less cost and greater safety and then put themselves on the roads at even more expense, especially if they then need a second car, and at greater risk, due to the extra driving.

When decreasing the distance between work and home is not possible, and even when it is, more commitment to car-pooling would make some real contributions. It would help develop community* on the commute and so nurture an increasingly scarce yet absolutely basic resource in modern society. Many people can testify to both the short-term and long-term benefits of this. While it challenges our fetish about individual convenience and freedom of choice and requires some accommodation to others' schedules and rhythms, we could do much more in this direction than we attempt at present.

The same case can be made for making the move from commuting by car to traveling by public transportation. People complain that commuting by public transportation usually takes longer. Since someone else is doing the driving, however, the commuter has more time for profitable and sometimes enjoyable personal activities, such as reading,* reflecting, meditating, praying, keeping a journal and planning. Sometimes there can be other benefits, such as socializing with a more ethnically diverse, older and poorer range of people. (This, by the way, could help overcome some of the stereotyping and suspicion that so often go on between different racial or class groups who rarely meet.) Another benefit is increased educational possibilities. (One group of daily commuters between two large cities were instrumental in getting a continuing-education organization to conduct daily classes on the train and eventually to add a whole car especially for that purpose.) People are often surprised to find out that a move to commuting by public transportation also generally results in considerable financial savings.

Those who must commute a relatively lengthy period of time can take steps to minimize the degree of effort and anxiety involved in arduous daily travel: for example, making use of flextime arrangements so that travel to and from work can take place at other than rush hours or working a ten-hour day so that an extra day a week can be used for leisure* or being at home. When a car audio system is available, and so long as it is not just a tranquilizing substitute for a more radical change in commuting patterns, playing relaxing music can also be helpful, as an increasing number of people are finding. In places where a good and pleasant bicycle-path network is provided, people can bike to work. For a small percentage of people—almost 5 percent of the population—there is also the option of walking.* Another possibility, and not only for the 5 percent of people already telecommuting, is searching for ways of doing some work each week from home.

For the remainder, it is helpful to begin looking at the complexities, surprises, frustrations and delays of traveling by private or public transportation as opportunities in the Spirit to grow in patience and self-control, as well as in the creative use of time.

Conclusion

As well as individual changes, there are changes that political and urban authorities can implement to improve the commuting experience. In various cities* a number of these are already in opera-

tion. They include placing a tax on businesses if a certain percentage of their employees do not car-pool or travel by public transportation, providing more bus and car-pool lanes on freeways, introducing "smart" technology to improve travel conditions and reduce commuting time, and, where they have some likelihood of being effective, proposing new public-transportation initiatives.

Employers and supervisors can also help. As is already happening in some firms and agencies, they can pay employees extra to car-pool or travel by public transportation, since this costs less than providing parking spaces at work. Even churches* can make a contribution to commuting by encouraging their members to car-pool as much as possible to meetings, providing vans or buses for those who cannot or can little afford to use public transportation, siting themselves near well-served public-transportation routes, and decentralizing many of their activities to local centers or homes* so that people have less distance to travel.

See also AUTOMOBILE; CITY; MOBILITY; NEIGHBORHOOD; PUBLIC TRANSPORTATION; TIME; TRAVELING; WORK PLACE.

References and Resources
D. Engwicht, *Reclaiming Our Cities and Towns* (Philadelphia: New Society, 1993); J. McInnes, *The New Pilgrims: Living as Christians in a Technological Society* (Sydney: Albatross, 1980).

Robert Banks

COMPETENCY

In their places of work, families, communities and churches, Christians give praise to God by using their time and talents* as competently as they possibly can. Their competency is a fundamental service to the world.

The book of Genesis sets the tone. At the end of each day, God looked upon the work* he had done and saw that it was good. On the final day of creation

"God saw all that he had made, and it was very good" (Gen 1:31)—*very* good. That is the creation God gave us. And the very first command God gave to humans was "Be fruitful and increase in number; fill the earth and subdue it" (1:28). To *subdue* is to bring under one's control, not to destroy. The arena for this service to God is the whole of creation, not just church-related activities.

Our society is so complex and interrelated that we depend on the competency of many others to meet our needs. The airline pilot's competency is far more important to his passengers than whether he is a Lutheran or Roman Catholic. The competency of those schoolteachers who help educate our children is much more important to us than whether they also teach Sunday school. We depend on the competency of our auto mechanics to keep our cars safe; whether they attend church conventions is secondary. We depend on the competence of our surgeon; whether she sings in the choir is incidental. So, too, competency is crucial for farmers,* salespeople, bus drivers, custodians, politicians, pastors and lawyers. Each one, by doing his or her job with high competency, serves God by helping to keep creation *very* good.

In criticizing the church for not helping people see the importance of competency in their daily lives, Dorothy L. Sayers wrote, "The church's approach to an intelligent carpenter is usually confined to exhorting him not to be drunk or disorderly in his leisure hours and to come to church on Sundays. What the church should be telling him is this: that the very first demand that his religion makes upon him is that he should make good tables" (pp. 56-57). If our daily work is praise of God and service to God's creation, it is surely spiritual in nature. The term *spirituality of work* was first coined by Pope John Paul II in his encyclical *On Human Work*. In writing for the National Center for the Laity, Gregory Pierce says, "A spirituality of work necessitates orienting ourselves toward the divine through our daily activity of improving and sustaining the world" (p. 26). To see our work as spiritual compels us to execute it with the greatest of competency. No longer can a job be seen simply as a means of earning enough money with which to live.

The emphasis on total quality management in business in recent years is evidence that the American work force is not as competent as it could be. Incompetence can be found in all levels of an organization, from the CEO to the janitor. Total quality management recognizes this fact and addresses it. An example of what can be done to increase competency comes from the American automobile industry. During the 1980s Japanese and German cars got a larger share of the U.S. market due to better design, higher quality and lower prices. The trend was obvious. Either the American auto industry had to become more competent in its design, quality and costs or else it would die. Through massive changes at all levels of the industry, some of which resulted in many jobs' being lost, the carmakers began to reverse the trend. By the mid-1990s, American-built cars were equal to or better than their foreign competitors in design, quality and cost. Aided by the low value of the dollar in relation to the yen and mark, American car prices have become the lowest in the world market. This happened because a total industry became more competent.

Organizational competency is not confined to the for-profit sector of our society. Many human-service agencies operate far below their potential simply because of a philosophy that employees cannot be evaluated with respect to competency. This is the bane of the not-for-profit organizations. It is a serious misunderstanding of the nature of voluntary work.* Sometimes, in such organizations, when incompetence is recognized, managers are themselves too incompetent to deal with it. American churches* have relied on voluntarism to provide money* and assist in the programs and governance of congregations and judicatories. The personal involvement of competent church members is largely responsible for the greater vitality, attendance and feeling of ownership in American churches than in state-supported churches in other countries.

Not only service organizations but also educational institutions need to deal with competency issues. With colleges and universities facing reduced enrollments due to demographic factors, it is the competent educational institution that will survive. Long-time policies that rewarded seniority rather than competency in teaching are being changed in many schools.

Competency in one's daily life is not confined to one's paid job. A society needs competent parents* to raise our children and give them values.* Surely we serve God and maintain God's "very good" creation as we bring in new lives and, in turn, educate them to use their God-given talents. The challenge has become greater as the number of single-parent families has increased and as the pattern of double wage earners in the traditional family* has increased as well. Many parents are overcome with stress* as they try to balance the demands of the workplace and the home, with the demands of the paid job usually taking precedence over family needs. As a result, many have an uneasy sense that they are not as competent in their parenting as they should be. Churches need to help people with their priority setting here.

Competency is demanded of us in our community activities. Surveys and polls tell us that Americans are unhappy with the competency of their elected political leaders. Yet, strangely, less than half of those eligible to vote do so, and less than 1 percent of the public ever volunteers to help in political campaigns. Competent citizenship* calls for an active role in our political process, for government too can play a major role in keeping creation good. Furthermore, a unique characteristic of American society is the way in which people have volunteered their time and money for human services, the arts and other civic causes. Competent citizens are needed in order to maintain and improve our social fabric—God's creation.*

Competency in one's job, family, community and church—this is what is asked of us. To strike the right balance in accordance with the gifts God has given us drives us to meditation, prayer and dependence on the Holy Spirit.

See also AMBITION; DRIVENNESS; PROMOTION; SUCCESS; TALENTS; WORK; WORK ETHIC, PROTESTANT.

References and Resources
W. Diehl, *The Monday Connection: A Spirituality of Competence, Affirmation and Support in the Workplace* (New York: Harper & Row, 1991); W. E. Diehl, *Thank God It's Monday*, Laity Exchange Books Series (Philadelphia: Fortress, 1982); W. F. Droel and G. F. A. Pierce, *Confident and Competent* (Notre Dame, Ind.: Ave Maria, 1987); G. F. A. Pierce, "A Spirituality of Work," *Praying*, Sept.-Oct. 1983, p. 26; D. L. Sayers, *Creed or Chaos?* (New York: Harcourt Brace, 1949); E. F. Schumacher, *Good Work* (New York: Harper & Row, 1979); G. Tucker, *The Faith-Work Connection: A Practical Application of Christian Values in the Marketplace* (Toronto: Anglican Book Centre, 1987).

William E. Diehl

COMPETITION

Competition is a fact of everyday life. Students compete for academic honors by scoring high marks in examinations.*

Athletes compete in a race, and only the first three runners past the finish line receive prizes of recognition (*see* Sports). Businesses compete for a market share of their products and services. Churches* compete for the attention and voluntary support of adherents in the midst of a pluralistic, multireligious society. Nations compete for economic advantage in the global village.* But what do we mean by competition? Is it always, or normally, negative? Can we construct a theology of competition?

The negative consequences of competition in society are easily identified, especially in business. Competition in the corporate world forces companies to reengineer in order to survive, often leading to loss of jobs (*see* Firing). Unionized employees negotiate for better compensation, but the prospects for job security are increasingly jeopardized by demands for greater benefits. Consumers benefit from competitive pricing, but sometimes at the expense of small businesses unable to offer the volume discount promised by chain stores in their weekly advertisements.*

At the personal level, our children compete in examinations and sports. Students strive for a place at the university based on their academic achievements in high school. Undoubtedly these harsh realities affect our perspective on priorities and purposes in personal life. Should we pursue a "successful life" by embodying an unbridled competitive spirit (*see* Success)?

Beyond Definition?

The word *competition* has a history. As the *Oxford English Dictionary* notes, the root word *compete* derives from the Latin *competo*, which in its original sense means "to fall together, coincide, come together, be convenient or fitting, be due." But by the sixteenth century it took on a stronger sense of engagement with an-

other person, thus "to enter into or be put in rivalry *with,* to vie *with* another *in* any respect." Subsequently, it came to be used "to strive *with* another, *for* the attainment of a thing, *in* doing something." In order to achieve a certain end or goal, we strive with another person, and in the process we may overcome obstacles or challenges, whether personal or impersonal. But these definitions fail to account for the complex character of human competition as it involves biological, psychological, rational, voluntary and social factors.

A theoretical understanding of competition must consider the human situation. The field of sociobiology, represented by E. O. Wilson, distinguishes two modes of competition, scramble and contest. The former is exploitative, without universal rules of conduct governing the scramble for limited resources. The latter involves a conscious struggle for appropriating specific resources and thus permitting a winner in a contest competition. When a group of boys scramble for coins thrown on the ground, a contest ensures certain rules of behavior and predicts certain agreed-upon outcomes, such as winner-take-all. But an evolutionary model of competition that assumes the commonality of animals and humans competing for survival for limited resources appears to make some sense, but it is incomplete, especially with regard to the ambiguous motivation of human beings.

Competition has a moral character; individuals are able to exercise self-control in limiting or suspending pernicious kinds of aggressive competition. Often this is not done. Examples in the Bible of people striving with one another for personal advancement in unbridled sibling competition include Cain and Abel, Jacob and Esau, and James and John. The story of Joseph is especially illuminating. Joseph's brothers schemed to eliminate him as they competed for parental attention and acceptance. Joseph was both a victim and a victor. But the biblical account suggests that a higher purpose determined the outcome (Gen 50:20). Whereas the brothers' attempts at destroying Joseph's future seemed obviously malicious, the unintended consequence of Joseph's fortune pointed to a divine drama with significant benefits for the extended family.

Inside Competition

Why is it important for human beings to act in a competitive manner? Psychological explanations point to the need to gain recognition, approval and acceptance. Along this line public demonstrations of competitive behavior are often motivated by a desire to overcome weakness, helplessness and loss of individuality. So Stuart Walker concludes that "competitors think of themselves as being primarily motivated to develop, demonstrate, and enjoy competence" (p. 4). In other words, competitive behavior is largely about winning and about public awareness, regardless of the outcome. Walker has possibly overstated the case, since it is conceivable that an individual might run a race for the sake of proving to himself a level of achievement associated with the sense of excelling in a particular field of sport rather than merely winning public recognition.

The difficulty in determining actual motivations in competitive conduct may be due in part to the ambiguities and complexities of human behavior. There is more to motivation than the individual. Greek ideals exemplified in Aristotle's notion of human good and in Plato's articulation of timeless virtue illustrate the potential of personal actions. Values, standards and ideals are not created in a vacuum but are shaped by social and personal experiences. Therefore, competition and cooperation are not necessarily antithetical in a given society. In fact, anthropologists like Margaret Mead have described the relative significance of both types of behavior in tribal groups. Mead concludes that

competitive and cooperative behaviour on the part of individual members of a society is fundamentally conditioned by the total social emphasis of that society, that the goals for which individuals will work are culturally determined and are not the response of the organism to an external, culturally undefined situation, like a simple scarcity of food. (p. 16)

If we accept the *cultural* dimension without denying the *natural* disposition inherent in human behavior, then we can recognize how competition and cooperation may take place simultaneously. This happens when an athlete competes with others while cooperating with members of his or her own team to challenge their opponents. What is important here is the impact of cultural and structural factors in determining the outcome for a particular group of individuals. While some societies exhibit cooperative characteristics, others appear more competitive (Mead, p. 511).

The Protestant Work Ethic*

Not only culture but even religion influences competitive behavior. The classic explanation of competition was given by Max Weber. In *The Protestant Ethic and the Spirit of Capitalism,* Weber accounts for the impact of theological ideas on human behavior and social life. He sees the Reformation as leading ultimately to the emergence of a capitalist economy in Europe. Weber's basic hypothesis revolves around the notion of divine election as a key theological idea that influenced the moral and ethical outlook of Protestant Christians. In particular, he suggested that the believer needed concrete confirmations for his experience of salvation. Therefore, individuals took hold of the opportunities for work, investment and industrious activity in order to produce tangible rewards of achievement that could be interpreted as divine approval. In other words, divine blessing* in this life indicated positive assurance of salvation for eternity.

Participation in God's gift of salvation demanded a conscious performance in this world—hard work, prudence, frugal stewardship and productive output. Weber was careful to highlight the affinity between a certain work ethic and the emergence of a successful middle class. While he was not necessarily arguing for a direct cause-effect relationship between the Protestant work ethic* and the rise of capitalism in Europe, Weber persuasively demonstrated a strong correlation. His conclusion remains compelling: the emerging culture of capitalism was in a complex but significant way influenced by the religious idea of divine election and by the ethical orientation to competing for success in this world. In the Work Ethic article Weber's thesis is more completely critiqued. What is needed now is to develop a fully biblical approach. Thus far, we have considered the lexical, functional, biological, psychological, cultural and religious factors influencing our concept of competition. But how does the Bible speak of competition? Can we construct a theology of competition? When is competition good, even holy?

Competition in the Old Testament

The Bible is full of competitive activity. The Old Testament stories, ranging from the exodus to the exile, depict the struggle of God's people in the face of religious pluralism and political conflicts. The challenge of maintaining loyalty to the one true God was central to the story of covenant faithfulness. Recognizing the Old Testament drama of divine contention for Israel's allegiance, each narrative uncovers a competitive tension between Yahweh and the diabolical schemes of Satan. The life of Job reveals a cosmic competition in which Satan is granted limited jurisdiction over the circumstances of Job and his family. Israel had to choose, time and again, the one true God and to obey his revealed laws for holy living, to give up popular myths and religious idolatry in favor of the distinct lifestyle demanded by the God of Abraham, Moses and David.

Thus incidents like Aaron and the golden calf and David and Goliath illustrate the danger of competing ideas about God. On both occasions, the people were motivated by fear, helplessness and the need for security. These motivations were largely inspired by an inadequate view of God and an inflated view of the enemy. Moses and David contested for the people's allegiance to God as a prerequisite for competing against their enemies. Narratives such as the exodus and David and Goliath highlight the persevering character of God in demanding total allegiance in the midst of competing forces. In these instances competition in the religious life of Israel issued from this theological understanding.

Competition in the New Testament

In the New Testament Paul uses the metaphor of an athlete engaged in a race (1 Cor 9; Phil 3), and Jesus teaches with parables about the danger and potential of competitive behavior (Lk 16:1-8; 19:12-27). The parable of the shrewd manager focuses on the resourcefulness of an employee facing malicious accusations of impropriety and eventual dismissal. By turning his employer's creditors into friends, he transformed hostile circumstances into opportunities for survival. Competitive behavior in this instance was marked by a streetwise motivation to strive for economic security. Jesus commended the shrewd manager for his prudent actions. In the words of Eugene Peterson's translation,

The master praised the crooked manager! And why? Because he knew how to look after himself. Streetwise people are smarter in this regard than law-abiding citizens. They are on constant alert, looking for angles, surviving by their wits. I want you to be smart in the same way—but for what is right—using every adversity to stimulate you to creative survival, to concentrate your attention on the bare essentials, so you'll live, really live, and not complacently just get by on good behavior.

Not only does Jesus acknowledge the competitive nature of living in the world, but he recommends a streetwise approach to survival that overcomes the destructive potential of competition. For the Christian, this competitive advantage is gained by a circumspect awareness of the issues and the relationships affected by changing circumstances. Sometimes, cooperating with our competitors may produce positive results. In contrast hostile, predatory competition bent on destroying relationships and institutions often leads to unscrupulous actions. When a salesperson exaggerates the value of a product, an unwitting consumer might succumb to deceptive persuasion. However, when the product fails to deliver in performance, the reputations of both salesperson and company are greatly discredited. In the final analysis, competing for consumer confidence is more important than sales profits. Companies and employees succeed in a competitive economy by delivering quality products and services and thus ensuring customer satisfaction.

There is more in the parable of the ten minas (Lk 19:12-27) than stewardship of investments. Jesus deliberately draws attention to the character of each servant who was given a mina. The one who earned ten more was rewarded with responsibility for ten towns. Similarly, the servant who invested the operating capital and earned five more minas was recognized for his achievement. In turn, he also gained additional responsibility for five towns. Finally, the parable focuses on the servant who avoided the risk of investment. Out of fear, he opted to deposit the money in an unsecured and unprofitable place. The master condemned the foolish attitude of this servant and, in an unexpected manner, deprived him of the asset by transferring the money to the servant who gained ten.

While the narrative appears similar to the parable of the talents, what is unique about this parable is the circumstance surrounding the events. The master had to secure authorization from a distant ruler in order to return with legitimate governing powers over the region. The period of absence was marked by protests from the local citizens as well as tensions among the servants over the master's instructions. How should they deal with local resistance to the master's sphere of influence? At the same time, how would they invest the capital entrusted to them in the face of competition? The servants were competing with external uncertainties and with internal challenges. Each servant had equal opportunity to invest, but the social and economic circumstances were not necessarily favorable. High standards of achievement were demanded by the master, thereby increasing the pressure to perform. How do we explain the variable productivity of the servants despite equal capital investment opportunity? What accounts for the difference in results? Why did the master reward the servant with ten minas additional capital taken from the unproductive servant?

Good Competition

As the parable suggests, competition can bring out the best and the worst in each person, depending on the motivations. Jay Newman, in his study of competition in religious life, agrees with Simmel's sociological thesis that competition "not only provides the individual with the occasion for self-realization and self-respect, but simultaneously presents him with an incentive and an opportunity to contribute to social progress" (p. 48). In other words, competition enhances the value of human relationships by cultivating the best from each person. Unlike the destructive potential of conflict, one positive outcome of competition is excellence in character and in performance.

Sports and athletic activities are usually associated with the idea of competition. In a race, every runner aims for first prize. Apart from the first three places, all other contestants are not even recognized. Paul's metaphor of the athlete in the coliseum assumes the competitive spirit. However, he does not appeal to the unbridled side of aggressive competition. In 1 Corinthians 9:24-27, Paul compares himself to an athlete in training for the games, not unlike present-day sportsmen preparing for the Olympic marathon races. It seems Paul is urging for a competitive spirit in the Christian's life. But the metaphor of a race and the goal of winning the prize does not preclude the possibility of a marathon. In a race, only one person gets the prize. But the analogy of winning in a competition cannot be applied to the Christian in a simplistic manner. Surely Paul is not suggest-ing that only one Christian will complete the race and win the prize. Instead, the reference to disciplined training for the express purpose of gaining the reward points to a deep concern in Paul's life that he will not become disqualified at any point in his race toward the end.

Paul maintains a clear vision of the ultimate reason for his Christian endeavor: "Forgetting what is behind and straining toward what is ahead, I press on toward the goal to win the prize for which God has called me heavenward in Christ Jesus" (Phil 3:13-14). Every Christian, in Paul's estimate, is called to run in a race that has an eschatological purpose more profound and deeper than a hundred-yard sprint. We may assume that Paul exaggerates the point of winning the race in order to make the more important claim that each person "should run in such a way as to get the prize." Therefore Paul views the competition as more of a marathon than a sprint. The difference is that everyone who completes the marathon wins.

A Sprint or a Marathon?

In the context of daily life and organizations, we may choose to regard competition as a race or a marathon. Whereas in a race only a few winners enjoy recognition, everyone who competes in a marathon and finishes actually wins. Charles Handy, a management consultant, suggests that competition "is good news for everyone, but only if everyone can win" (p. 83). He recalls the feedback from several thousand managers in America who were invited to account for the occasions when they did their best: "they did not talk about competition, but about goals that were exciting and challenging, about autonomy and ownership, high visibility and accountability, and an exciting task" (Handy, p. 85). From our earlier discussion about the definitions of competition, we recognize the basic elements in Handy's observations that match Paul's concept of competing in a marathon.

The quality of our goals and the challenges of the tasks before us make for a positive engagement in work and daily life. We compete by pursuing goals of excellence. When work entails a sense of ownership and accountability, each worker is given the opportunity to prove their merits. Organizations that offer incentives and motivate toward realistic goals will cultivate a healthy work force. Whereas monopolies in a market economy tend to take their products and services for granted, and internal monopolies exist through isolating or removing external challenges, people become lazy. Handy observes,

> In tough competitive situations people like to be surrounded by people less competent than themselves because it gives them a better chance of winning. That is not good news for the organization. Nor do people always, or even often, take the risks or make the creative leaps which competition is supposed to encourage. The fear of failing is usually much stronger than the hope of winning, so people play safe. (p. 85)

Competition usually involves a positive effort to aim for a set of goals worthy of the individual or organization in the face of changing circumstances and varying opposition. One may do this with integrity and courage. Competition issues from a basic theological conviction that God calls each person to live out his or her full potential, which is not defined by human evolution but by what Christ has accomplished in each one (Phil 3:12). Furthermore, competition at the personal and social levels involves risks. The ethic of excellence can transform the destructive character of unbridled, unscrupulous competition into a creative spirit of true competition; of turning races into marathons. The Christian thrives in a competitive environment through a clear vision of the ultimate purpose for living and working.

References and Resources

C. Handy, *Inside Organizations: 21 Ideas for Man-* *agers* (London: BBC Books, 1990); J. Newman, *Competition in Religious Life,* editions SR vol. 11 (Waterloo, Ont.: Wilfred Laurier University Press, 1989); M. Mead, ed., *Cooperation and Competition Among Primitive Peoples* (New York: McGraw-Hill, 1937); S. H. Walker, *Winning: The Psychology of Competition* (New York: W. W. Norton, 1980); E. O. Wilson, *Sociobiology: The New Synthesis* (Cambridge, Mass.: Belknap/Harvard University Press, 1975).

Peter Quek

COMPROMISE

Compromise is generally regarded as a dirty word. It is something to avoid. To make a compromise, to be compromised, even to accept a compromise, is to settle for second best, at worst to be involved in a shady activity. Therefore ethically inclined, especially Christianly committed, people should steer away from compromise. The difficulty with this view is that there is scarcely any situation in life in which at some point compromise is not required. This is so when a group decision has to be made by a committee,* for example, since it is rare for several people to reach complete agreement. Or this is so, as in the case of social services or welfare, when limited resources mean that some have to miss out or get less than others. Or this is so in schools when conflicting opinions between parents and teachers mean that no decision is going to completely satisfy everybody. Even on the home front, juggling the sometimes competing options and demands in two-career families requires compromise—for example, when the whole family must decide to move so that one of its members can take up a job offer or promotion* elsewhere. Some Christians, especially those who are very idealistic, are troubled by having to abandon what they feel is God's will for them or in general so that they can adjust to the positions or aspirations of others. Since they are concerned to do God's will, anything less seems a departure from God's ideal plan for them or wider purposes.

This issue becomes particularly acute in connection with our work.* It is often thought to be especially connected to certain occupations. Politics,* for example, with its adversarial dynamics, is as well "the art of compromise" (a definition Luther would have found quite acceptable). This is why many people regard politics with suspicion, but nothing would take place in politics, even developing and implementing the best policies, without it. And according to the New Testament, politics is a task in which even unbelievers, if doing right, can be servants of God (Rom 13:4). It is not essentially different in the world of commerce, especially in the making of business deals. This is also the case in various professions,* especially in law.* In a world that is more and more culturally diverse and pluralistic, a whole range of activities inside and outside the workplace* require the various parties to make concessions to one another. But making compromises in any of these areas troubles many Christians, leading them to regard themselves as second-rate Christians or to develop a growing skepticism about the relevance of biblical ideals to everyday life.

Approaching the Issue of Compromise

What do we mean by the word *compromise*? Generally we use it in one of two ways. First, it is used for taking a middle way between two courses of action that may be based on different principles or on different possibilities derived from the same principle. Second, it is used for a decision or action that seems to involve a lowering of standards. I want to suggest that a situation such as the first usage has in mind certainly enables us to engage in a positive or legitimate compromise. Regarding the second usage, what some-

times appears to be a lowering of standards in making a decision may not necessarily involve that. But I also want to suggest that depending on the circumstances and the decision, the first situation can lead to a negative or illegitimate compromise as much as the second.

It is also helpful to distinguish compromise from two overlapping ways of operating: between compromising and strategizing and between compromising and negotiating. Strategizing involves working out a long-term, often complex, set of tactics for reaching a desired end. This may involve all kinds of moves and countermoves, unexpected demands and apparent concessions, which initially and for some time may obscure the goal of the exercise. Such strategies are means to an end, temporary positions that are part of the larger game being played. Strategizing is broader than compromising and may involve good or bad strategies as well as good or bad compromises. A subset of strategizing is negotiating.* While there may be legitimate and illegitimate, or more and less legitimate, ways of conducting negotiations, compromise is not necessarily involved here, though sometimes it is. A negotiator may make many proposals and responses in coming to an agreement without at any point yielding something basic, only appearing to do so. In the case of both strategizing and negotiating, a person may take into account people's sensitivities, particular circumstances or specific cultural contexts, without which a good agreement—or sometimes any agreement—cannot be reached. So, to the extent that compromising is sometimes confused with appropriate strategizing or negotiating, there need not necessarily be anything negative involved in it.

What then is compromise? Is it, as is commonly thought, betraying one's basic convictions for the sake of expediency, because it is opportunistic to do so, to relieve the pressure one is under or simply as a consequence of moral weakness? Or is it possible to make good compromises that are not a betrayal of principles so much as an appropriate, perhaps under the circumstances the most appropriate, response to them? If this is the case, how can we tell the difference between these two, and what practical steps can people take to ensure that they do not break faith with their own strongest convictions and standards or those of the institution they represent?

Toward a Positive View of Compromise
It is possible to compromise in ways that are positive and defensible from a Christian point of view. As always, the Bible provides a good place to start. There are many biblical stories in which people made decisions that seem to be acceptable to God or to even further God's will even though these did not express all of their basic beliefs or hopes. A clear example is the meeting in Jerusalem between Paul and Barnabas, on the one hand, and the apostles and elders, on the other, to discuss the validity of the Gentile mission. There was considerable debate, and the upshot was an agreement in which the Jewish Christians endorsed Paul's initiative in taking the gospel to the Gentiles and Paul's missionary team accepted the condition that they communicate certain restrictions on the behavior of Gentile Christians that could be interpreted as supportive of idolatry and promiscuity (Acts 15:23-29). Another example in Acts is Paul's apparently contradictory practice of, in one place, circumcising one of his coworkers and, in another place, refusing to do so. The first concerned Timothy, who was half-Jewish; Paul felt there was some ground for placating the scruples some Jewish Christians had about him. The second concerned Titus, a Gentile,

whose circumcision, no matter how strongly certain Jewish Christians may have desired it, would have betrayed Paul's basic convictions about Gentile Christians' freedom from keeping Jewish observances.

But elsewhere Paul is quite outspoken about his missionary practice of becoming "all things to all people" (1 Cor 9:22). When he preaches the gospel, he takes serious account of the religious and cultural convictions of his hearers. If they are Jews or observe the law, he accommodates them and speaks as one who respects the Jewish heritage and law himself. If they are "strong" and do not observe particular holy days or follow regulations concerning food and drink, he begins with the freedom in Christ he experiences in such areas despite being a Jew. On the other hand, if they take the opposite point of view, since he too sometimes feels "weak," he is willing to begin from that and proceed from there. This way of operating is not restricted to Paul's missionary endeavors; it is also his regular pastoral practice. When confronted by viewpoints at some distance from his own, unless they are being advocated in a proud, hardened or manipulative way, as much as possible he seeks some common ground and then articulates his own position and tries to draw people toward it (as with discussions on ascetic sexual and overly charismatic practices in 1 Cor 7 and 12—14). Though Paul has often been accused of compromise in the negative sense because he acted in all these ways, it is not difficult to defend him against this charge in the name of a higher consistency.

The Negative Side of Compromise
We also find in the Bible examples of poor or negative compromises that are condemned. In Paul's letters we find the classic case of the behavior of Peter in the controversy between Jewish and Gentile Christians at Antioch. Though Peter has

his own strong convictions on what is required of each group, convictions that are virtually identical with Paul's, he bends under pressure from certain people who have come down from Jerusalem and who were probably misinterpreting the position of his fellow apostle James. Peter urges the withdrawal of the Jewish Christians from the Lord's table because of the Gentile Christians' different eating habits (Gal 2:11-14). At principle here from Paul's point of view was the gospel's full acceptance of the Gentiles even though they did not observe all the regulations of the law of Moses. Though it was not his intention, Peter's position was a compromising one in a seriously negative sense. This is why Paul would not yield so much as an inch.

The story of Peter's rebuke indicates, as we know, that compromise can have serious negative effects. This is so, first and foremost, for the person who makes it. Acting in this way weakens a person's capacity to made good compromises or other good decisions in the future. It is also unfortunate for those affected by the compromise, all of whom, not only the ones allegedly being protected, will suffer from the result. The key then is how to know the difference between good and bad, or better and worse, compromises. At this point our moral terminology can often get in the way. So long as we think only in terms of black and white, only in terms of good and bad, we are limited in our capacity to deal with such situations as discerning when good compromises can be made, what they are, when we are in danger of making a bad compromise or when no compromise should be made at all.

We can be helped here by the language of the Old Testament Wisdom literature, which expands its moral vocabulary to judge actions according to whether they are wise or unwise, fitting or unfitting, appropriate or inappropriate. There are times when it is better not to press for something that is good simply because it would not be wise to do so and we would jeopardize any possibility of its happening later. Or sometimes it may be wise to engage in an action even if it is not what we would most prefer since it is the best that is likely to come out of the situation and is far better than other choices that could be made. Other words than compromise could be used in such cases. Depending on the nature of the decision and the surrounding circumstances, terms like adjustment, accommodation, concession or conciliation could apply, again demonstrating that compromise in the pejorative sense is not necessarily in view.

In such cases the theologian Reinhold Niebuhr tended to talk in terms of our having an attitude of "delayed repentance." That is, we make the best decision we can under the circumstances, which is often the "lesser of two evils," then later ask God to forgive us. But if such a decision is the best compromise we can make in that situation, while we may regret that it could not be otherwise, repentance does not seem called for. Does this not mean that it is the will of God for us in that circumstance? Given the circumstances, what more could be called for? For example, when Jesus is unable to heal in a certain place because people's faith was lacking, was it a compromise on his part? Helpful here is Dietrich Bonhoeffer's distinction between ultimate and penultimate realities, the latter constrained by events, situations and people in this world. Sometimes the latter, to use his words, require us to "sacrifice a fruitless principle to a fruitful compromise" (pp. 79-101). The latter, though not the ultimate, is still derived from it and points toward it.

Learning How to Make Good Compromises

A legitimate or, to use Bonhoeffer's

words, fruitful compromise, then, will seek to preserve our basic faith convictions, safeguard loving relationships and retain vision for the future. If it does, this will be an expression of the will of God in its particular time, place and set of circumstances. More specific criteria include the following: Does it generate good or bad effects? Is it likely to lessen evil and wrong? Does it extend justice, particularly to those who require it most? Will it exhibit a proper regard for all persons with a stake in it? Have those involved shown throughout a genuine concern for truth in what is under discussion? Is there a recognition of the choice involved and an avoidance of talk about "having to do it"? Do both the process and the decision display the virtue* of patience? Can the decision be altered if circumstances change and another decision becomes possible? Though these criteria are still very general, at least they provide a framework within which a proper decision can be reached and the appropriate compromises, if necessary, made.

What can we do to ensure as far as possible that we are in the best position to judge an issue by these criteria and work toward the best possible compromise? The following considerations are relevant whether we are dealing with issues between husband and spouse or parents and children in the family,* with issues arising between friends or neighbors, with issues that we encounter in the workplace or in voluntary associations, with issues that come before us in the church or church-related ministry, or with issues of a social or political kind on which we have to cast a vote. In all these situations we should (1) continue to give first priority to maturing in our relationship with God and others, for good compromises are more likely to proceed from people who are attempting with God's help to become increasingly good. (2) Keep the big picture in mind, never

letting go of our ultimate aims and purposes, so that we can preserve a proper perspective on the issues at hand. (3) Consult closely as much as possible with other people so that we have as much wisdom as possible in making decisions involving compromise. (4) Be prepared to give way on minor issues where a major issue is at stake; otherwise, we will tend to confuse the forest for the trees and win or lose small victories at the expense of big ones. (5) Aim at a win-win rather than a win-lose, or lose-win, situation, for which lateral thinking or seeing new possibilities is really required.

If we keep these factors in mind, are serious about bringing such matters to God in prayer and meditation, and have resort to a group of supportive people with whom we can sometimes talk over these issues, we can have every confidence that God will go with us into our decisions and help us discern how best to respond.

See also BUSINESS ETHICS; CONFLICT RESOLUTION; INTEGRITY; NEGOTIATING; VALUES.

References and Resources
D. Bonhoeffer, *Ethics* (New York: Macmillan, 1955); J. Calvin, *The Institutes of the Christian Religion*, ed. J. T. McNeill, 2 vols. (Philadelphia: Westminster, 1960); W. J. Diehl, *The Monday Connection* (New York: Harper Collins, 1991); K. E. Kirk, *Conscience and Its Problems* (London: Longman, 1933); H. R. Niebuhr, *The Responsible Self* (New York: Harper & Row, 1979); W. Temple, *Christian Faith and the Common Life* (London: Allen & Unwin, 1938); H. Thielicke, *Politics*, vol. 2 of *Theological Ethics* (Philadelphia: Fortress, 1969); W. Ury, *Getting to Yes* (Boston: Houghton Mifflin, 1981); H. F. Woodhouse, "Can Compromise Be the Will of God?" *Crucible*, January-March 1982, 22-30.

Robert Banks

COMPUTER

Humans have used computing devices

for millennia. The abacus is a common example, but the fact that we use a base-10 numbering system surely indicates that the fingers predated even that as a tool for computation. Through the years we have invented an amazing array of machines to help us compute things more rapidly and more accurately.

Basic Character

The digital computer (which is what we now mean by "computer") is not simply another computing device among these machines. Only a few decades ago International Business Machines estimated that the total American demand for digital computers was about a dozen. This estimate was not the result of a mere miscalculation but based on a very basic misunderstanding: IBM falsely thought that digital computers were just another computing device.

In spite of the fact that we routinely call these machines "computers," they only began their lives that way. They are not simply computing devices. Though computation is at the core of many operations that computers do, they are really not computers but "rememberers."

As never before, digital computers offer us devices to remember information. From the invention of writing and before, humans used the means at their disposal to record information in hopes that it would be remembered. But merely recording is itself insufficient. In order to remember and reuse information, it must be retrieved as well as recorded.

Computers have given us this capability to store information so that it can be easily retrieved and reused. Monthly credit card* bills are mundane examples of computers' role as rememberers. So are the reams of "junk mail" sometimes generated by attempts to recycle the information that computers remember for us.

As more and more information becomes available to us over computer networks, the role that computers play as rememberers will become ever more significant. Not only will they be the means by which we store and retrieve information; they will also be the tools that allow us to navigate around the world's enormous information stores to find just the knowledge we need.

Rapid Proliferation

Counting the embedded systems that control our automobile engines, VCRs and telephone systems, there are more computers in the United States than people. Even the number of recognizable computer systems like the one I am using to write this article numbers in the millions.

The demand for computers, and their power, seems to know few bounds. The state-of-the-practice computer from my college days, the IBM 370, cost a great deal, could be used only in a controlled environment and could be approached only from a distance, punched cards in hand.

One watershed came in the early 1980s when significant computing power could first be reduced to a small set of integrated circuits. These "personal computers" were first popular with hobbyists but came into more mainstream use when software such as Lotus 1-2-3 and WordStar made them capable of doing significant business tasks like budgeting and correspondence. This confluence of relatively inexpensive hardware and software that made it easier to do standard business tasks began to bring computers out of the laboratories and into everyday life.

As computers have become more powerful, most of that power has been expended making them more accessible. Cryptic commands, and before them setting control panel switches, have been replaced by icons that perform basic functions. The early personal computers responded to the command *pip* (peripheral interchange program) to copy a file. Now they respond to "dragging and dropping" a file icon onto a disk icon. Soon they will respond to the spoken command "Copy my file to the disk." This increasing ease of use has made computers more accessible and has itself contributed to their omnipresence in modern life.

Current Uses

If computers have become our chief rememberers, it should be relatively easy to list the tasks they perform. This is far from true. Any simple categorization of current uses of computers seems to leave out important segments of their domain. And even complete lists become rapidly incomplete as new applications for computing power are discovered. Consider, however, this list, which a mainstream business user might put together: numeric projection and accounting (spreadsheets); transaction and information tracking (database); communication and messaging (electronic mail); text editing and publishing (word processing); drawing and image manipulation (graphics).

This list is based on the content of software "suites" which claim to offer a well-rounded set of resources for business. Several aspects of this list are remarkable. First, only one of these functions has directly to do with computing narrowly defined. Spreadsheets are the contemporary number-crunching functions of computers. The other functions, although they may be highly numeric under the surface, have entirely to do with storing, manipulating and retrieving other types of information.

Second, the list leaves out one of the most widespread uses of computers—information presentation. This domain includes computer-based training but is much broader. Computers drive much "kiosk" information display, designed to communicate to casual passersby rather than dedicated students. In this case too, however, the intent is to inform and instruct, and computers do the job for us.

Social Impact

As digital computers have become ubiquitous, they have transformed social life in many remarkable ways. Of course one must be "computer literate" to be considered educated, but that is one of the least important social impacts of computers. The significant ways in which they are transforming society are often much more subtle.

First, consider the kinds of information we can easily communicate to each other using traditional means. The book you are now reading, like many books, is trying to communicate information. But books are very good at communicating only certain kinds of information. Information that is "linear," where one piece builds upon the previous piece, can be easily rendered in books. So can information that is hierarchical or layered.

What about information that is networked together arbitrarily? The only way books can render such information linkages is with cross-references. Most readers find cross-references annoying because they are so inconvenient to use. But when information is rendered using computers rather than printed books, hyperlinks allow readers to conveniently go back and forth across cross-references. This opens up whole worlds of information that, while they may have existed before, were virtually inaccessible because they were so inconvenient to use.

Second, computers make all information, whether we could easily communicate it before them or not, more available. When cashiers ask me for some sort of ID, as I let my wallet disgorge all the pieces of plastic and paper that tell who I am, I sometimes joke that I am one of the most thoroughly identified people in the world.

The truth of the matter is that the widespread use of computers has caused us all to be more thoroughly "identified" than we might like. Credit* history, affiliations and police records for each of us are all out there on computers. This wealth of information is far more available than ever before, even when it is kept relatively confidential. Computers have made our thorough identification what it is.

Third, because computers have made so much information available to so many people, we will soon be forced to use them to sort through all that information. This role is very different from the one they play now as rememberers. When information is relatively limited, storing and retrieving it is adequate. When it becomes relatively unlimited, as it is becoming today, we must begin to use computers to *filter* it.

Filtering is different from retrieval because when computers retrieve information for us they do so in response to our specifications. Filtering, however, requires us to train computers to do our specifying *for* us. The available information will soon be so vast that, in order to find anything at all, we will have to trust computers to sift through things for us and return with what we need.

From one point of view, a computer is just another tool that can be used for both good and evil. And so it is. Such tools, however, always put their stamp on our activities and change them whether we like it or not. As our computers remember more and more information, we ourselves suffer from acute information overload. What are we to make of the power that inexpensive computers put into the hands of many of us? Clearly,

they make many tasks easier; they also make some more complex. In some cases, they add a much-needed medium of personal communication, e-mail, that enables us to keep in touch with each other. In some cases, they add an impersonalness even to our personal communications. Now, after all, it's possible to get form letters from your family.

The challenge we face as Christians is to make use of our computers to enhance our communication with others and our abilities to negotiate our lives successfully. But enhancing life and communication is not part of the "out-of-box experience" of unpacking a new computer. We add that capability to the machine or allow the machine to take it out of the activities we use it for. Our task is to direct these resources in ways similar to the direction we give to writing by hand or any other tool we use for tracking and communicating. Computers do the same things so much faster, but they require the same deliberate management as do lower technologies. There are further Christian reflections on the mixed blessing of this technology in the article on Information Superhighway.

See also COMPUTER GAMES; PRINCIPALITIES AND POWERS; SYSTEM; TECHNOLOGY.

References and Resources

N. Negroponte, *Being Digital* (New York: Knopf, 1995); http://home.netscape.com/home/internet-search.html; http://www.yahoo.com/

Hal Miller

COMPUTER GAMES

Though most computers are actively used for relatively pedestrian activities like accounting and word processing, a remarkable amount of their resources is devoted to simple diversion. Games* and puzzles account for a significant portion of younger people's interactions with computers; indeed, supervisors of many adults who work with computers might be surprised at the amount of gaming that goes on with these "business machines."

The original computer games arose almost as soon as computers were powerful enough to do anything remotely "interactive" with humans. Though they were rudimentary, puzzles like Wumpus and forerunners of arcade games like Pong set the stage for the more sophisticated games of today. These games began to define the kinds of games computers could be "good at," that is, activities providing fun for their human companions. Computers quickly became both interesting playmates and challenging opponents.

The current generation of computer games may use dedicated hardware (the Sega and Nintendo units, or complex joysticks for input), but they can often be operated on general purpose machines with corresponding input devices. In these cases they are impressive for the sheer quantity of computing resources they require. A machine that will comfortably run the most demanding business software sometimes grinds to a halt when asked to run gaming software. Complex video and audio requirements that are standard for contemporary computer games have become an important factor in making increasingly robust computers available at a reasonable cost.

Similarities to Traditional Games

With some important exceptions, computer games fall into all the categories of traditional games. There are games of skill, usually called *arcade games* from their origins in pinball arcades. While these games are hardly aerobic, in other ways they are very much like traditional games of skill such as athletic contests or pocket billiards. Arcade games generally require speed and coordination in the use of input devices from their players. Current arcade games couple these demands with the color and sound distractions used to complicate pinball games for decades. Common examples of arcade-style games include various chase games and flight and driving simulations.

Related to arcade games are the *action games,* which require arcadelike skills but use those skills in a more or less continuous series of battles. The violence of these battles may be quite graphic at times. Indeed, the excesses in violence and gore of some action games led to the current system of voluntary rating of computer games by the industry.

A third category of computer game is *solitaire games* or puzzles. In these games, computers bring a fresh capability that revitalizes the game itself. Computers selflessly shuffle the cards or set up the pieces, leaving only the play to the human partner. Computer versions of crosswords allow you to erase the same word an unlimited number of times without making the paper illegible. In these cases, the difference of medium is an enhancement to the game itself.

We have also developed computer versions of *traditional games* that use boards or manipulatives. Chess and checkers, for instance, are based on relatively simple sets of determinate rules. But both games are endlessly rich in their strategic and tactical variety. In these cases, computer versions provide portable partners but also do something more significant. Here, computer games can become serious contests between people and machines. It is a point of pride that chess programs cannot at present consistently beat the best human players, although they can now do so with increasing frequency. How long we can expect this to continue is a matter of speculation, but the research behind development of these games has illuminated a great deal about the processes the best human players use.

A final category of computer game is *adventure games,* including the newer interactive story. These games have fewer counterparts among traditional games, although the scavenger hunt is a reasonably close analogy. Adventure games require players to follow a thread (or one of several threads) through a story. Along the way, problems arise that the players need to solve, often using materials they have gathered in the course of the adventure.

Adventure games run the gamut in their premises and plots. Some require fights of various kinds, some are set in magical fairy-tale worlds. The themes may be overtly sexual or romantic, or they may be dominated by black magic or warfare. Overall, adventure games are much like novels or movies* and cover the same range of themes. They also require similar guidance from parents.

Significant Differences in Computer Games

Although in most ways computer games are simply traditional games thrust into a new medium (with all the changes in speed and dimension that brings), they are qualitatively different from traditional games in three important ways.

First, computer games have strongly contributed to blurring long-standing distinctions between gaming and education.* In the past few years we have begun to hear this described by the neologism *edutainment.* Edutainment—and many computer games, especially those aimed at preteenagers, are excellent examples of edutainment—is shorthand for the loss of easy differentiation among the so-called content industries, such as schools, media companies and publishers.

Twenty years ago it was easy to distinguish music* from movies and learning from playing. Now MTV and video gaming have made those conventional distinctions less compelling. Skillful teachers have always known that their job was at least part entertainer. That knowledge is now mainstream in the sense that it is often difficult to tell which part of an activity is the instruction and which the entertainment.*

Edutainment presents information or drills on skills in the context of a game or, alternatively, creates a game which requires players to master certain information or skills to succeed. Contemporary analyses of edutainment are also hobbled by the fact that the widespread use of computers has revolutionized the types of skills required for success in the working world. In some sense just being "computer literate," a skill players on standard desktop machines often develop merely to tune their gaming environment, is itself an important educational achievement. The edutainment phenomenon has been driven in large part by the evolution of computer gaming, but its influence on traditional educational goals is far from complete.

A second way that computer games are qualitatively different from traditional games is the way they can transport the player's senses. Unlike almost all traditional games, many computer games give the player a change of scenery. Computer games give you travel* opportunities. The ability to explore strange buildings or cities or worlds is one of the novel fascinations of the computer game.

Of traditional games, only golf comes even remotely close to this aspect of computer gaming. But even in golf, the terrain you can explore is limited by such parameters of the game as the dimensions of the course and the other players on it. In a computer game, the cities of the world (Where in the World Is Carmen San Diego?), a fantasy island (Myst) or a postholocaust building complex (Doom) is yours to explore. Computer games allow, and often reward, simply "poking around" in unknown places. In this particular they correspond much more to other rewarding human endeavors like natural science than do any traditional games.

Third, computer games are qualitatively different from traditional games in their graphic portrayals. A most instructive comparison here is between traditional chess and a computer version called Battle Chess. Chess is of course about war, and war is about killing. Yet chess hides all that carnage behind stylized game pieces and their moves. When a pawn is captured by a knight, what has "actually" happened in the reality represented in the game is that the footsoldier has been slaughtered by the horseman. Yet in the game, the wooden pawn is bloodlessly removed from the playing surface. Battle Chess, however, does away with this antiseptic distance between the game and what it represents. When the queen captures the bishop in Battle Chess, you watch on the screen as she slips out a stiletto and slides it between his ribs. The other pieces are no less violent in their activities.

Part of the "realism" of computer games, and the violence and gore that sometimes come with it, is a mere change of aesthetic. Photorealism has its seasons in art* of all kinds, as do less representational forms. Traditional games were forced to stylize what they were portraying. With the computing resources currently available to games, this limitation is no longer in force.

Partially, however, the change from mere representation to more graphic realism is in the social role of the game. Traditional, less representational games are played at a distance of abstraction from their theme that computer games deliberately avoid. Chess may be about

war, but it is a very abstract kind of war. Many action games are simply about killing, and the closer they come to the sensory reality of killing (it seems) the better. This difference gives traditional games a refinement and finesse that many computer games do not even try to achieve.

This change in portrayal may be only a stage in the evolution of computer gaming, but it has the same net effect as the evolution from screen kisses to graphic sexual encounters in movies. When mysteries like these are unveiled, a certain innocence is lost that cannot easily be recovered. The ultimate effect this will have on computer gaming remains to be seen, but it is an important development to watch.

See also COMPUTERS; ENTERTAINMENT; GAMES; LEISURE.

Hal Miller

CONCEPTION

When a sperm and ovum unite, usually as the result of a loving embrace, they become "one flesh" literally as a unique conceptus "fearfully and wonderfully made" (Ps 139:14 KJV; see Ps 139:13-16; Eccles 11:5). New reproductive technologies* now allow conception to occur outside the confines of the human temple, creating ethical dilemmas and evoking the need to restore reverence to our idea of conception and dignity to personhood.

Evolving Ideas of Heredity and Origins
Biblically and anthropologically there is a rich tapestry of philosophies that dovetail with evolving science. When Genesis describes the creation of Adam, the material of his body is completely and utterly earthy (Ps 90:3; 103:14). This contrasts with other creation myths, where humankind is extrapolated from blood or tears spilled from the gods. In

the Bible, the first man is the result of clay formed by the hands of God and invested with spirit and life through the transforming breath of the potter. In life man works this soil in intimate relatedness, returning to it in death (Eccles 12:7). There is speculation and some evidence that humble clay crystals may have served as the original catalysts for the formation of the hereditary molecule of life, deoxyribonucleic acid (DNA), in the first simplest life forms.

DNA has the unique ability to replicate itself, dividing and preserving a blueprint from one cell division to the next that maintains the form and function of the cell and communally the organism. During replication the DNA spiral staircase cleaves equally, like a zipper parting. Components of the complementary ladder rungs reassemble based on strict *exclusive* pairing in a lock-and-key fashion analogous to male and female union in marriage (Gen 2:24). It is this monogamy that preserves the sequence and meaning of the code, ensuring the correct translation into the intended gene product and faithful replication from one generation to the next (Ps 100:5).

That moment of divine spark in which matter is brought to life is in no way demystified by progress in the understanding of origins. Science serves to enhance, not diminish, the wonder of God's signature in matter, be it the whorled pattern of a fossil shell, Bach's mathematical harmonies or a dandelion seed aloft in the breeze. Seeds are mentioned in Genesis 1:11 inextricably associated with the first living entities; plants created some three and a half billion years ago are wondrously capable of capturing the sun's energy for food, so providing nourishment and oxygen for animal life to follow. Genesis and evolution are integrated in describing the sequence of created life.

Biblically, *semen* and *seed* are used interchangeably and intersexually. Note the allusion to the female seed made in Leviticus 12:2, "to sow a seed," and in Hebrews 11:11, "Sarah received power to have [literally] a seminal emission."

Historically views were often opposing. The traditional notion that the mother was not the begetter but only the nurse of the newly sown embryo conflicted with observable patterns of heredity whereby children resembled both parents. In Job 10:10 we are given the image of human creation as the pouring out of milk that curdles into cheese: the development of a firm embryonic body from milky semen. From the sixth century B.C. women were known to possess ovaries, although they were referred to as testes. Pre-Socratic philosophers defended the view that female semen is also necessary for procreation, hence menstrual blood was regarded as the female contribution to embryogenesis.

There was also great debate concerning theories accounting for the sex of the child or the dominant resemblance to mother or father. Novel proposals having to do with which partner's semen was most abundant or emitted first at the time of coitus, or the influence of temperatures and the position of the seeds in the uterus, testified to the creativity and curiosity of the human mind. The ancient principle that the seed of either parent can be "overpowered" is preserved in modern understanding of sex determination and gene dominance over recessiveness.

The ovum and sperm each contain half of the genetic material necessary for human life. The male has two varieties of the sex-determining chromosome, designated X and Y. Thus there are two forms of sperm existing in the semen with regard to this one characteristic. Ovum, however, contain exclusively an X chromosome; the mother has a pair of X chromosomes from which to donate, one originating from each of her parents. It is the type of sperm, then, that engenders the sex of the conceptus. Either the Y "maleness" chromosome overpowers the X, resulting in a male offspring, or the presence of another X chromosome from the sperm complements the X that is already in the ovum to produce a female offspring. In Genesis the creation of Eve from the rib of Adam has been metaphorically linked to the taking of the X chromosome to create out of man "flesh of his flesh and bone of his bone."

Scientifically, the division of labor for directing characteristics as diverse as eye color, predispositions for disease, personality and even addictions* is a complex interaction of multiple genes. The conceptus carries half the genetic material of each parent, but any possible ratio of grandparents' DNA may be represented. The diversity that sexual reproduction offers, analogous to reshuffling a deck of cards, serves as fuel for gradual changes that occur in species over time, imparting incentive and wisdom to adapt generationally to changing conditions.

As the thread of life, the DNA molecule not only epitomizes the biologic link between form and function but suggests metaphors for contemplation. An impossibly simple molecule in the form of a spiraling staircase, DNA contains the language to flesh out such diverse creatures as the towering cedar tree spanning a millennium and the transient intricate mouse, attesting to the universality of a spiritual language that knows no bounds of race or religion. If DNA is the self-propagating molecule of life, then love is the expanding universal message of the spirit. Simple in concept, but indomitably extensive, it forms a genetic fingerprint that identifies paternity or even culpability for crime. From only one cell, a strand of unwound DNA would stretch to the moon and contains the equivalent of three billion bytes in a computer program.

The double helix of DNA spirals cyclically (or seasonally) but directionally counterclockwise in defiance of time's entropic and decaying forces. Life, with its increasing order and complexity, is a back eddy against the natural flow to disintegration and chaos. The Creator's nudgings are acknowledged even in the scientific community as "creative explosions" that occurred "against all odds" in the evolutionary saga. God's sovereign hand has prompted us toward mindfulness of Creator and is beneath us despite threat of extinction and genetic deterioration (Deut 33:27). The consequences of mutations (errors in replication of the DNA molecule as a result of radiation or toxins) is usually disease and only very rarely an improvement. Life as we know it is precariously balanced on the knife edge between order and chaos, a grand compromise between structure and surprise. "Too much order makes change and adaptability impossible; too much chaos and there can be no continuity" (Kaufman, in Nash, *Time* 95, p. 46). With increasingly specific knowledge about our genes and how they manifest themselves in sickness and in health, the wonder of our innate complexities magnifies as we attempt to discern "God's creative thoughts after him" (Isaac Newton).

Conception Evokes Consummate Wonder

Consider the sperm, an enveloped package of DNA that has a means to propel itself through the female reproductive tract. Its limited energy resources give it a decidedly finite time frame of several days to complete the task of navigation and penetration. The sheer number of sperm provided (five hundred million) demonstrates the magnitude of the undertaking and the competitive strain that ensures the best is rewarded with success.

If maleness has been associated sometimes pejoratively with that which is "set apart," we need to reaffirm these qualities that are the father's conception gift—metaphorically, as he provides a sheathing, an overcoat around the soul. This envelope comprises heroism, liveliness, impulse, intensity, incentive and a warrior's imperative for self-sacrifice whether defending the higher ethic or protecting his loved ones. For the adopting father they become, through modeling, a birth gift in parallel to that of a genetic father.

In contrast, the ovum is the nutritive home initially for the woman's genetic material, "frozen" in time from her own intrauterine life. Sensing the monthly hormonal prompting, it will ripen and be released. Having internal rhythms synchronized with a lunar calendar gives women a sense of constancy and connectedness to the natural world (see Menstruation). Once penetration by that first sperm has occurred, there is a miraculous change in the outer coating of the ovum. Instantaneously it changes its structure, preventing another sperm from entering even before the two nuclei have fused—a paradigm of betrothal and monogamy. Hence, the exact amount of genetic material necessary to make up a new human individual is present and preserved from the moment of conception as the two halves become a whole.

The parental genetic material has cleaved and unified, finding in its complementarity a wondrously unique potentiality: "male and female he created them" (Gen 1:27). The image of God is a composite of male and female. The female attributes of God were downplayed out of necessity, considering that Judeo-Christianity arose against the backdrop of fertility goddess worship that curiously resembles New Age spirituality with its mother-earth worship. It is interesting to explore symbolically the spherical ovum, roughly the size of the dot of an *i,* a hospitable planet for the sperm's delving, a refuge for the conceptus and the initial provider of nutrients to flesh out the designs held in the DNA. As the already fertilized ovum is propelled by hairlike cilia through the fallopian tube, it becomes a spherical clump of dividing and differentiating cells that plunges into the fertile soil of the womb. Putting down placental roots that absorb nutrients from maternal blood, the conceptus sends chemical messengers to lull the mother's immune system to accept its intrusion and signal the presence of the pregnancy, now detectable by lab tests. Even after birth* the nutritive and protective memory of the egg is visited in the domed hut or cathedral, the spherical breast (see Breast-feeding) and later the bowl.

God's provision and comfort is like that of a mother who hears the cries of her children and responds to their needs. We are reassured in Isaiah 63:9 that "shekinah" (the Hebraic female "presence of God") empathizes with us in our distress. "As a mother comforts her child, so will I [God] comfort you" (Is 66:13), mirroring our first experiences of tangible love as persons.

The Soul of Personhood

Although the exact definition of when personhood begins eludes us, the scientific knowledge we have confirms our deepest conjectures that soul,* spirit and body* are integrated in some wondrous way from the moment of conception of a genetically distinct individual, even prior to implantation, even prior to acquiring full consciousness and rationality. T. W. Hilgers is correct when he asserts that "once conception has occurred an individual human life has come into existence and is a progressive, ongoing continuum until death ensues" (quoted in Hui, p. 6).

Soul—that dimension of personhood that makes us God-conscious and expressive—and body (or physicality) are so interdependent that one cannot think of a person having a body without a soul or a soul without a body. Contrary to Greek philosophy, which created a schism between spirit and matter, the Judeo-Christian view is that we are fully integrated as ensouled bodies or embodied souls. Understood in this way, conception is not merely the formation of physical shells for persons but is the cocreation with God of a person.

The element of development and "unending becoming" is a distinctive quality of human experience throughout life. When children begin to grapple with the notions of death* and spirit, they find the concept of eternity as simple and understandable as the circles they draw in the sand—a universal symbol of infinity, no beginning and no end. Pointing to a wedding picture of their parents, children are very unsatisfied by a finite answer to the question of where they were when the picture was taken: "You weren't in Mommy's tummy yet."

"But where was I?" they press on, satisfied only by the reassurance that "you were still with God" until conceived.

We are more than DNA living on in our offspring. What is this pearl that persists beyond flesh's fragility, the élan, the part of us that smiles and sings, worships and loves? God has "set eternity in our hearts" (Eccles 3:11, author's trans.). In contemplating the infinite, there is the distinct possibility that spirit was in the form of sheer energy somewhere with God and after being transformed into matter and nudged into consciousness will some day (with all due respect to the theory of relativity) find itself again with the ultimate source of all energy, love and matter.

In contrast to these truths "revealed . . . to little children" and "hidden . . . from the wise and learned" (Mt 11:25), consider technology's fruition in controlling the origins of persons.

See also NEW REPRODUCTIVE TECHNOLOGY.

Resources and References

P. Teilhard de Chardin, *The Appearance of Man* (New York: Harper, 1965); Edwin C. Hui, *Questions of Right and Wrong* (Vancouver: Regent College, 1994); M. J. Nash, "How Did Life Begin?" *Time,* October 11, 1993, 42-48; M. J. Nash, "When Life Exploded," *Time,* December 4, 1995, 38-46; L. Nilsson, *A Child Is Born* (New York: Dell, 1993); P. van der Horst, "Did Sarah Have a Seminal Emission?" *Bible Review,* February 1992, 35-39; H. W. Wolff, *Anthropology of the Old Testament* (Philadelphia: Fortress, 1974).

Carol Anderson

CONFLICT RESOLUTION

Conflict is a natural part of life. Although many people think conflict means open controversy, a truer definition might be the absence of peace—which can be obtained in its most complete sense only from God. Whenever people interact with one another, there is a potential for a difference in opinion or purpose. Most people are able to deal with minor differences. When major conflicts arise, however, many people do not know what to do. They fear conflict, react defensively or have difficulty negotiating just agreements. As a result, valuable relationships are damaged or destroyed, time and money are wasted, and promising businesses and careers fail.

In American culture today, litigation in civil court has become a common substitute for direct personal interaction. As a result, conflicts may be resolved as to substantive issues but are almost never resolved as to personal relationships. A focus on satisfying individual rights has supplanted concern for the good of the whole community. In some other cultures there continues to be reliance on the judges at the gate (Ruth 4:1-12), but in America's increasingly anonymous society the perceived cost-benefit of resolving conflict between individuals amicably has been skewed in favor of keeping the conflict unresolved.

Popular Christian Attitudes Toward Personal Conflict

Some Christians are more vulnerable than other people to conflict, this vulnerability arising from a misunderstanding about what it means to be *Christlike*. For example, some Christians believe they always should "turn the other cheek," without realizing that unless one does so freely, without resentment, this is no true reflection of Christ's peacemaking character. Such actions are like the Pharisees' carrying out the letter rather than the spirit of the law. Further, giving in may be inconsistent with God's Word, which includes also the concepts of justice, restitution and personal accountability. Others imagine that they should carry out God's justice. They may appoint themselves as God's avenging angel, even though Jesus instructed us not to do so (Mt 7:1-2). Such an attitude is precisely the opposite of how God approaches discipline, which is with a loving and expectant heart (Heb 12:1-13). Finally, some Christians spend a great deal of energy on broader matters of peace and justice. Although these are important, such people sometimes pay scant attention to resolving their own interpersonal conflicts, failing to recognize the broader community implications of individual discord.

All these attitudes can lead to confusion, abuse* or pent-up anger. In contrast, to seek resolution of disputes according to biblical principles means seeking both personal reconciliation and the just settlement of substantive issues, not only for the purpose of human unity but also to bring praise and honor to God (1 Cor 10:31). Jesus specifically urged peacemaking among his followers as a personal attitude that brings blessing* (Mt 5:9).

God's Interest in Conflict Resolution

As well as giving us the ultimate model of reconciliation—Jesus Christ (Heb 10:10)—the Old and New Testaments are full of direction and action from God on the reconciliation of persons to himself. There are many pictures of unilateral forgiveness and provision for sacrifice as a substitute for judgment. It is obvious that complete, direct, personal reconciliation is one of God's major preoccupations (Heb 2:1-4). God's method of resolving conflict serves both as a model for our own behavior and as a reminder of our own utter dependence on God as the source of all good we hope to achieve.

By studying the ultimate conciliator at work, certain guidelines emerge for dealing with conflict in our daily lives:

1. Conflict allows us to grow to be more like Christ (2 Cor 12:7-10).

2. Peacemaking starts with our own personal attitude, which in turn comes from a focus not on the conflict but on God (1 Pet 3:13-15).

3. It is possible to reconcile oneself unilaterally, but only if the past is forgiven completely (Phil 4:2-9).

4. Resolving conflict may require different methods at different times and places (1 Sam 25:26-35; Esther 7:1-6; Prov 6:1-5; Acts 16:22-24, 22:22-23, 29).

5. Differences of opinion are inevitable and usually are acceptable (1 Cor 12).

6. Reconciliation does not necessarily require giving up or giving in, especially when someone is being hurt by ongoing conflict; loving confrontation may be

preferable (Gal 6:1-5).

7. God reconciled all to himself through sacrifice and forgiveness, but we must pass this gift on to others to realize its full benefits (Eph 4:29-32).

8. Resolving conflict God's way may require us to accept consequences and to alter our behavior (Eph 4:22-32).

9. Justice* is God's, not ours (Lk 6:27-39).

Biblical peacemaking involves an active commitment to restore damaged relationships and develop agreements that are just and satisfactory to everyone involved (1 Jn 3:18). A spirit of forgiveness, open communication and cooperative negotiation clear away the hardness of hearts left by conflict and make possible reconciliation and genuine personal peace. True biblical vulnerability, honesty and forgiveness can restore a person's usefulness, both to God and to others, and lead to complete restoration of relationships (Gal 6:1-3; Eph 4:1-3, 24).

Resolving Conflict as Believers

The Bible contains two basic messages about how believers should seek to resolve conflict in their daily lives. First, as with most things in life, God's Word contains promises, principles and practical steps needed for resolving conflict and reconciling people. Second, it is clear that peacemaking is an essential discipling ministry of the local church, not a task reserved for professional counselors or lawyers.

See it as an opportunity for obedience and witness. Sometimes we wonder why God has allowed a certain conflict to come into our lives. Instead of viewing conflict as a painful burden, Christians can learn to see it as an opportunity to please God and to draw attention to God's wisdom, power and love (1 Cor 10:31-33). God has promised to use even our conflicts for good (Gen 50:19-20; Rom 8:28). This

perspective allows for a positive and confident response to conflict as we ally ourselves with the most powerful peacemaker in the world.

Examine your own part in the conflict first. This includes not only your actions but also your attitudes, motives, acts and omissions. Because it reveals our sinful attitudes and habits and helps us to see where we need to change, conflict provides an opportunity for us to grow to be more like Christ (Ps 32:3-5; 139:23-24; 1 Jn 1:8-10). This growth takes place when we follow Jesus' command to accept responsibility for our own contributions to a problem before pointing out what others have done wrong (Mt 7:5).

Look for steps you personally can take. Few things in the Bible are as clear as the steps we are to follow when seeking to resolve conflict, particularly within the body of believers. Each of us is commanded to make the first move when in disagreement with another (Mt 5:24). One opportunity provided by conflict is to serve others. Sometimes this can be done through acts of kindness and mercy (Prov 19:11), but at other times it requires constructive confrontation (Mt 18:15). Recall that Jesus confronted people not simply by declaring their sins to them but by engaging them in conversation designed to make them arrive at the same conclusion on their own (Mt 7:12; Lk 5:27-28; Jn 4:7-26).

Accordingly, if someone is angry with you, go to them immediately (Mt 5:23-24), even if you believe the other's anger is unjustified. If you are angry with someone else, first ask yourself if the issue really is worth fighting about and check your attitude—are you actually looking forward to the confrontation? If an offense cannot be overlooked, go privately and express your concerns. But do not assume that the other knows or understands your feelings; explain what you are concerned about but also why (Mt

18:15). Be sure to affirm the relationship and your desire to work things out lovingly before launching into a discussion of the issues (2 Cor 2:5-8).

Making the first move does not mean that someone else has done something wrong or bad. An otherwise innocent word or act can cause an unexpected negative reaction in another, leading to serious disagreement (Jas 3:5-7). One can apologize for the trouble such miscommunication has caused simply because one regrets the result. Too often, however, our own sins have played a part either in creating the conflict or in escalating it (Jas 4:1-3).

Call on the church for help if necessary. Private confrontation is a preferable first step, so long as we can speak the truth in love (Eph 4:15). But if after sincere good-faith efforts to work things out you are unable to resolve the issue or mutually forgive each other (Prov 19:11; 1 Jn 3:16-20), then seek out the assistance of a few "witnesses" (Mt 18:16). These are present not to provide evidence or accuse the parties but to act as supportive advisers to both sides and help restore peace (Phil 4:3). This can be done informally with a respected relative, friend or other adviser trusted by both parties or more formally with a pastor, church-appointed committee* or trained conciliator.

If someone will not listen to you and the witnesses, then, as we are instructed, "tell it to the church" and allow it to decide the matter for the parties (Mt 18:17) as a matter of church discipline.* This is preferable to filing lawsuits in civil court (1 Cor 6:1-8). Today, as in Paul's time, our churches (and most believers) have abdicated this authority to the legal system, yet the courts do not focus on restoration of personal relationships, only on the disposition of tangible assets and liabilities. The church should model God's view that discipline is an act of love and shepherding (Heb 12:6).

Going to court is a possible last resort. Finally, if a party will not listen to the church, then we are commanded to treat the other as an unbeliever (Mt 18:17). Does this mean that now we are free to sue in court? Yes, but our decision to do so should depend on the nature of the dispute and the consequences to us or others in our care if we do not pursue our claims (Phil 2:3-4).

Even though Paul's admonition about lawsuits is directed at believers suing believers, it only makes sense to tie God's conflict-resolution principles back to witness through reflection of Christ's character. Christ's approach was to be merciful even while directly confronting a harmful attitude or act. Whatever the choice, our attitude needs to remain one of obedience to and reliance on God, and the aim should be peace with others, even unbelievers (Rom 12:17-18; 1 Cor 10:31—11:1).

Because Jesus loved and sought out unbelievers even as he tried to both correct and heal them, we can at least attempt to work out differences with unbelievers using the same progression of steps as we would with believers (1 Pet 2:12). Serving an angry lawsuit on an unbeliever, before trying to work out things another way, may not be the defendant's best introduction to God's redemptive plan!

Some believers use the steps in Matthew 18:15-20 as a substitute for civil legal processes but demonstrate the same vengeful zeal and advocacy as if in court. The key to effective use of Matthew 18 is to appreciate it as God's detailed direction to us on how to keep peace on earth—our attitude should be one of caution, prayerfulness and thanksgiving.

See also CHURCH DISCIPLINE; COMPROMISE; CONFLICT, WORKPLACE; FORGIVENESS; JUSTICE; LISTENING; NEGOTIATING.

References and Resources

E. Dobson et al., *Mastering Conflict and Controversy* (Portland, Ore.: Multnomah, 1992); R. Fisher and W. Ury, *Getting to Yes: Negotiating Agreement Without Giving In* (2nd ed.; New York: Penguin, 1991); J. Hocker and W. Wilmot, *Interpersonal Conflict* (3rd ed.; Dubuque, Iowa: Wm. C. Brown, 1991); Institute for Christian Conciliation, 1537 Avenue D, Suite 352, Billings, MT 59102, (406) 256-1583; B. Johnson, *Polarity Management: Identifying and Managing Unsolvable Problems* (Amherst, Mass.: HRD Press, 1992); S. Leonard, *Mediation: The Book—A Step-by-Step Guide for Dispute Resolvers* (Evanston, Ill.: Evanston Publishing, 1994); G. Parsons and S. Leas, *Understanding Your Congregation as a System* (Washington, D.C.: Alban Institute, 1993); K. Sande, *The Peacemaker: A Biblical Guide to Resolving Personal Conflict* (Grand Rapids: Baker, 1991).

David Augsburger

CONFLICT, WORKPLACE

Conflict is so common in the workplace that one can safely say, "It goes with the territory." But the types of conflict are varied.

Many Kinds of Conflict

The most commonly recognized workplace conflict is between labor and management. The dwindling power of American labor unions* has not lessened tensions between those who manage and those who produce, especially in those organizations that have retained a hierarchical structure. Management* wants to minimize unit costs; labor wants to maximize compensation and benefits. Finding creative ways to increase productivity can sometimes meet the wants of both groups. But when increased productivity is achieved by fewer persons doing the same amount of work in the same way, the physical and psychological effect on the work force can be devastating.

Pity those persons who daily work* at the interface of labor and management:

the first-line supervisors. These are the persons who are called upon to see that management's plans or directives are carried out—sometimes against their own convictions. These are the persons who are called upon by the work force to communicate its complaints and wants to a management that is sometimes not interested in listening.* To make matters worse, the highest-ranked labor representative, who gets paid on an hourly rate for overtime, can often have more take-home pay than the lowest-ranked management representative, who works the same number of hours but gets no overtime pay because he or she is a salaried employee.

There can be conflicts in the workplace when an employee whose style is collegial works in an organizational culture* that is very autocratic. For a long time there has been conflict over dress codes,* but that is changing as younger employees keep pushing back the boundaries. Even IBM, whose male executives and sales personnel always wore dark suits, black shoes, white shirts and a conservative tie, is starting to weaken. But observe the dress of most male business travelers at airports; they still are invariably clad in dark suits, black shoes and, perhaps, a colored or striped shirt.

A great source of workplace conflict arises from tensions between work and family.* The percentage of parents who are holding down a full-time job continues to climb. Approximately two-thirds of married American women are in the paid work force. Single parents, most of whom are women, have little choice about work: either enter the work force or be dependent on family or society for support. The need to care for family while holding down a full-time paid job creates tensions that spill over into the workplace.* And the demands of the workplace create tensions that spill over into the family. What does a working parent do when a child develops a sudden illness and will not be accepted by the normal caregiver? Or suppose an employee's aged parent falls at home and needs immediate help? Does the employee take a vacation day? call in sick? In either event, the employee's supervisor is confronted with an unexpected staffing problem. Work must be reassigned, and there is resentment among all affected. If the family emergencies happen too frequently, conflict develops.

Most employers have yet to find ways to reduce the work-family tensions that nag so many of their employees. In the case of the birth* of a child, U.S. federal law now mandates that employees be allowed to take unpaid leaves of absence. But companies do not look upon such leaves with favor. Early reports show that while mothers will take leaves beyond their employer's normal maternity policies, fathers seldom take any leave. Why? The workplace views an unpaid leave of absence as proof of the father's lack of commitment to the organization.*

In short, much of the American workplace is still not "family friendly." When an employee puts the family ahead of the job, there is conflict at the place of work.

Add to the family-work tensions the fact that many people are working longer hours, either by choice or by job demands. In her book *The Overworked American,* Juliet B. Schor deals with the strange fact that although the standard of living of the American worker has increased significantly since the 1950s, the per capita hours worked have gone up instead of down. From 1969 to 1987 the annual hours of paid employment in the American labor force increased 163 hours, equal to four extra weeks of work per year. Schor suggests that our insatiable desire for more material possessions may be the reason we choose to work more hours. A more likely cause,

however, is that the drive for greater productivity and the downsizing of the work force in many organizations have put greater demands upon a smaller number of people. Whatever the reason, when the workplace gets more time, the family gets less.

Conflict can break out as coworkers compete for promotions.* There is conflict when a boss takes credit for the ideas or contributions of his or her workers (*see* Office Politics). Conflict arises when an employee has been given an unfair performance appraisal (*see* Firing). When senior employees hog all the best weeks for vacations,* there is conflict.

Women in the work force bear additional burdens of conflict over those listed above. Women continue to be overrepresented in those jobs that are lower on the pay scale. Retail sales, fast-food outlets, nursing homes, clerical support for managers and professionals, child care and domestic services are all heavily populated by women, and they generally do not pay well. To make matters worse, women generally still receive less pay than men for the same job or one of equal value. It is unjust and makes for conflict in the workplace.

The advancement of women into managerial jobs, law partnerships, directorships and CEO positions has been very slow, despite more than a generation of highly capable women in the work force. To the term *glass ceiling* has been added an even more devastating term for women—the *sticky floor.* Not only is there an invisible barrier preventing women from ever reaching top positions, but many women are glued to jobs at the bottom of the pay scale. With more injustice, there is more conflict.

To top it all off, women at every level of the work force constantly must be alert to sexual harassment or discrimination.* It can be intentional and as blatant as being asked to trade sexual favors for job advancement. Or it can be unthinking, as when all the men in a work unit go out for a drink late on Friday afternoon but forget to invite the one female associate of equal rank.

What has been said about women in the work force applies also to African-Americans, Latinos and persons from Asia. Hard as it is to believe, Jews still suffer from discrimination in some sectors of the American work force. Conflict arises as minority persons constantly overhear jokes that demean their race, sex, color or religion.

A Christian Response

What is a Christian to make of so much conflict in the workplace? How is the Christian to deal with so much injustice and conflict? Several fundamental truths about conflict and work will help Christians answer these questions.

First, conflict is a part of life; it is not peculiar to the workplace. The Bible is filled with stories involving conflict. Jesus told his disciples that to follow him could result in conflict of fathers against their children and brothers against brothers (Mt 10:21). Conflict is a manifestation of humans' self-centeredness, that is, original sin.

Second, the place of work is part of God's creation and is just as much under God's care as the place of worship.* What goes on in the place of worship on Sunday is intended to help us deal with the place of work on Monday. Churches* can help their members deal with conflict by providing adult-education programs on conflict resolution, personal time management, discrimination and ways to bring about change. Some congregations encourage small groups* to meet regularly in order to share conflict issues in their daily lives and receive suggestions and support from other Christians. Many church judicatories have professional mediation resources available to assist in specific conflict situations.

Third, we need to recognize that the place of work is where we respond to God's call* in our lives. As baptized* Christians, we affirm that God calls all people into ministry.* We respond to God's call through faithful ministries in our places of work, our homes,* our communities* and our church. With the assurance of God's presence, we are confident in facing conflict wherever it is encountered.

Fourth, we use the gifts we have been given by God to deal with conflict in the workplace. Some types of conflict call for reconciliation between parties. Some types of conflict call for education and new ways of doing things. Where conflict is the result of injustice, we may have to immerse ourselves in deeper conflict in order to correct the injustice.

Finally, we need to remember that the place of work does not define us or own us. We are children of God and are owned by God. That is our identity*; our identity is not our job. It is difficult to remember this in the heat of daily work, but when we take the time to reflect on our lives, we will know that no matter how much conflict there may be in the workplace, it cannot separate us from a loving God.

See also CONFLICT RESOLUTION; LISTENING; JUSTICE; MANAGEMENT; MULTICULTURALISM; OFFICE POLITICS; POWER, WORKPLACE; STRESS, WORKPLACE.

William Diehl

CONFRONTING

Confrontation is giving a report on another person's behavior, offering feedback on the other's role or response, providing a second person's perspective on one's way of being, acting or relating. Its goal, in a counseling setting, is to bring the counselee face to face with avoided aspects of behavior or emotional life. In everyday life it less ambitiously seeks to offer an alternative experience of the person's self-presentation or actions. We shall look at (1) confrontation in biblical and theological perspectives, (2) methodology for effective confronting and (3) desired outcomes.

Confrontation in Biblical and Theological Perspectives

The Pauline letters describe the blend of confrontation and caring necessary in effective communication. The most cited passages are Ephesians 4:15, "Let us speak the truth in love; so shall we fully grow up into Christ" (NEB), and 1 Corinthians 13:5, "Love keeps no score of wrongs; does not gloat over other men's sins, but delights in the truth" (NEB). For Paul the balance and unity of love and truth are essential to wholeness in both personhood and community.* Truth (confrontation) and love* (support) should not be divided. The Gospel of John sees this balance as a central element in the self-presentation of Jesus: "So the Word became flesh; he came to dwell among us, and we saw his glory . . . full of grace and truth. . . . Out of his full store we have all received grace upon grace; for while the Law was given through Moses, grace and truth came through Jesus Christ" (Jn 1:14, 16-17 NEB).

Throughout the Scriptures the balance of support and judgment is visible in the prophets such as Jeremiah (the weeping prophet), whose confrontation is legendary, or Micah, who links doing justice,* loving mercy and walking humbly (Mic 6:8). Jesus, in the prophetic tradition, is moved by both compassion (Mt 9:36) and anger (Mk 3:5) to be caring to the offender and offended (Jn 8:1-12) as well as confrontative to the blind (Mt 23:1-39). The commitment to be both prophetic and priestly, just and loving, shapes a biblical theology. A con-

text of caring must come before confrontation; a sense of support must be present before criticism; empathy must precede evaluation; trust is needed before risk; understanding opens the way to disagreeing; affirmation undergirds assertiveness; love enables us to level with each other.

Methods for Effective Confronting

A person's ability to offer the necessary amount of information about his or her part in a relationship with no unnecessary threat to that relationship—the maximum data with the minimum threat—is a skill to be learned. Effective confrontation is invitation: it invites another to consider change but does not demand it. It is not diplomacy, tact or smoothness of tongue; it is simplicity in speech, empathy in attitude and honesty in response. General guidelines for confrontation follow.

Focus feedback not on the actor but on the action. Comment not on the person but on the behavior in question. To criticize the person stimulates feelings of rejection; to critique the behavior can affirm the other's freedom to change and offer options for future situations.

Focus feedback not on your conclusions but on observations. Comment not on what you think, imagine, hunch or infer but on what you have actually seen or heard. Statements of inference, whether conclusions or rumors, can be made by anyone at any time without any personal experience. But statements of observation, firsthand reporting, must be limited to what one has seen and can be made, obviously, by only the observer. Restricting oneself to personal knowledge grounds the feedback in a more mutual reality and opens potential understanding between giver and receiver. Focus the feedback not on judgments but on descriptions.

Focus feedback not on quality but on

quantity. Comment on the amount of feeling expressed, not the kind; on the degree of action taken, not the evaluative labels; on the extent of the behavior, not the categories or cubbyholes you might use to name it. Use adverbs that tell how much rather than adjectives that tell what kind; use terms denoting *more-or-less* rather than *either-or,* which says, "Case closed!"

Focus feedback not on advice and answers but on ideas, information and alternatives. Offer data, enrich with options, and open further possibilities, rather than narrowing the right way down to a single choice and offering advice on which direction should be taken.

Focus feedback not on the amount available in you the giver but on the amount that is useful to the receiver. Do not vent; contribute. Do not overload the emotional circuits or overtax the other's ability to listen and absorb.

Focus feedback not on the time, place, schedule or needs you feel but on the best time and the optimal situation for the receiver. You are not confronting for your own benefit, release or discharging of emotion.* Your goal is focused on the interests of the other and of the enduring relationship.

The focus, when placed on the action, on observations, on description, on quantity, on information, on alternatives, on the amount useful and on the best time and place, will invite both parties in the conversation to meet each other with the best degree of understanding possible in an anxiety-prone communication.

Desired Outcomes

The goal is to deepen understanding by increasing the shared information base, to move behavior that is largely unconscious into consciousness, to bring what was in the blind zone into the open arena

for conversation. When this is accomplished well, the risk taken deepens the trust, and the dialogue achieved grounds the relationship in actual, honest, lived experience. As this is practiced gently, caringly, constructively and acceptingly it enriches community.

See also ACCOUNTABILITY, RELATIONAL; CHURCH DISCIPLINE; CONFLICT RESOLUTION; JUSTICE; LISTENING; LOVE; SPEAKING.

References and Resources
D. Augsburger, *Caring Enough to Confront* (Ventura, Calif.: Regal, 1973); J. Powell, *Why Am I Afraid to Tell You Who I Am?* (Los Angeles: Argus Books, 1969).

David Augsburger

CONSCIENCE

Søren Kierkegaard once explained his attack on "Christendom" in this way: "There is something quite definite I have to say, and I have it so much upon my conscience that (as I feel) I dare not die without having uttered it" (Lowrie, p. viii). Conscience is not just evident at crucial turning points like this but is also a part of everyday life, though we seldom reflect on what we mean when we speak of it. We say things like "Let your conscience be your guide"; "My conscience is clear"; or "I was troubled in my conscience." When children exasperate their parents with forbidden behavior followed by remorse, the parents sometimes comfort themselves with the fact that "at least they have a conscience." Forensic psychiatrists sometimes deal with criminals who appear to have no conscience at all. What is our conscience? How does it work? Why does it sometimes deceive us? How is it possible to have a clear conscience?

Conscience in Contemporary Thought
Psychologists offer various theories to describe the almost universal experience

of having an internal monitor of thought and behavior. Profoundly influential in this matter has been the thinking of Sigmund Freud, who proposed that the conscience is a subsystem of the superego. This subsystem produces feelings of guilt when society's demands are not met and when the person does not conform to what he or she "should be." Social learning psychologists link conscience development to the parenting process. Behavioristic psychologists view conscience as a result of conditioning by rewards and punishments so that patterns of self-criticism develop and persist even when the punishers are no longer present.

In contrast to these theoretical frameworks, theologians propose that conscience is not socially developed but "built in" as a God-designed capacity to put human beings in touch with the moral code of the universe. The Bible itself does not expound on the concept. Words for conscience are almost completely absent in the Old Testament, and are infrequently used in the New.

Conscience in the Bible

Conscience became a popular concept only in the first century B.C. in the Greek world to describe "the judge or witness within" or "knowing oneself," both phrases translating Greek words for conscience. It was part of the Greek segmentation of the human person into sections, with the outer shell, the body, being the least valuable.

But the Hebrew view of the human person was different. Persons are integrated wholes. In the Old Testament there are only six instances of *conscience* in the English NIV, and in each case the word translates the general word for "soul" or "heart."

The word *conscience,* for example, is not used in the text of Genesis 3:7 when Adam and Eve sinned because their whole persons were alienated from God and filled with shame. When Job declares, "My conscience [literally, heart] will not reproach me as long as I live" (27:6), he is claiming his complete conviction that he is free from condemnation in relation to God; none of his sins can explain his suffering. It is not until the first Christians were called on to address the Greek world that biblical authors began to use a specific word for conscience. So in Acts and the New Testament letters we find references to "good" conscience (Acts 23:1), "weak" conscience (1 Cor 8:7), "clear" conscience (1 Tim 3:9), "seared" conscience (1 Tim 4:2), "corrupted" conscience (Tit 1:15) and "cleansed" conscience (Heb 10:22). In Romans Paul says that the Gentiles are inexcusable for not reverencing God and that on the day of judgment they will find their consciences bearing witness to this by either "accusing" them or possibly "even defending them" (Rom 2:15).

Significantly Paul tells the Romans that his "conscience confirms . . . in the Holy Spirit" that he is speaking the truth (9:1). This last witness is especially insightful because the New Testament authors used *conscience* to describe the whole person *in relation to God,* not an independent witness built into human nature with or without God. The author of the letter to the Hebrews elaborates on this profoundly. Human beings have a guilty and polluted conscience which cannot be cleansed by sacrificial offerings in the temple, and even the ritual of the Day of Atonement offered only temporary relief (Heb 9:9-10). But the "once for all" sacrifice of Jesus results in a permanent cleansing that empowers us to enter the presence of God and serve all the time and every day.

Misguided Conscience

Not all condemnation is the result of the

Spirit witnessing to our consciences that something is wrong. Satan "accuses" Christians day and night (Rev 12:10). Sometimes we serve Satan's purposes by doing our own accusing of ourselves. Worse still, we judge one another. Albert Camus once made the shrewd comment that he would wait for the final judgment by God resolutely because he had known something far worse: the judgment of human beings.

Sometimes our conscience is like a sundial operating under moonlight. It gives a reading, but the wrong one! Letting our conscience be our guide is usually bad advice. God is our guide, and conscience is only one dimension of witness to God's guidance, but not a witness in isolation (see Guidance). Conscience gives us a false reading when we experience socially induced shame (despising our very persons) and false guilt (feeling bad for things that were not actually wrong or were not our fault). Paul deals with this in 1 Corinthians 8:4, 7-8, addressing the problem of Christians who are inhibited from enjoying something for which they can truly thank God. In some cultures such shame is more pervasive than guilt. But it comes from people, not from God. Sometimes we feel no guilt for genuine sins of commission or omission. Or we condemn ourselves when God has already justified us. As John says, God is greater than our consciences. By dwelling in love "we set our hearts at rest in his presence whenever our hearts condemn us. *For God is greater than our hearts, and he knows everything*" (1 Jn 3:19-20).

A conspicuous blind spot of evangelical Christians has been our lack of social conscience. We have too easily been acculturated to a privatized religion that lacks the passion of the prophets and Jesus for social action and justice. This conspicuous omission shows how deeply our consciences are affected by social conditioning even in the church.

Once again Paul's statement that his conscience confirms in the Holy Spirit that he is speaking the truth (Rom 9:1) is significant. Self-consciousness is an accurate witness when we are in the Spirit, in right relationship to God. Luther rightly said, "My conscience is captive to the Word of God." It should not be captive to culture, to peer groups, to advertising,* to our judging brothers and sisters. Conscience is not a free-standing authority within us but rather dependent on and built up through capturing every thought and making it obedient to Christ (2 Cor 10:5), submitting to Word and Spirit, relying daily on the cleaning of Christ's forgiveness and daily feeding our souls on the revelation of God's Word.

We need the community of God's people not only for this essential mutual nurture of our souls but also to gain perspective when we feel falsely accused or when we have actually sinned. James says, "Therefore confess your sins to each other and pray for each other so that you may be healed" (Jas 5:16). When we have a guilty conscience we should turn to Scripture and seek prayerfully the mind and will of God in the company of God's people. But in their company we can also rejoice that we are spiritually alive, that our consciences are not "seared" (1 Tim 4:2) like scar tissue without any feeling and that we are wonderfully and gloriously forgiven.

See also FORGIVENESS; SOUL; SPIRITUAL FORMATION; SPIRITUAL GROWTH.

References and Resources

J. Coakley, "John Henry Livingston and the Liberty of the Conscience," *Reformed Review* 46, no. 1 (Autumn 1992) 119-127; J. A. Davis, "The Interaction Between Individual Ethical Conscience and Community Ethical Conscience in 1 Cor," *Horizons in Biblical Theology* 10 (December 1988) 1-18; W. Lowrie, trans., *Kierkegaard's Attack upon "Christendom"* (Princeton,

N.J.: Princeton University Press, 1944); C. A. Pierce, *Conscience in the New Testament* (London: SCM Press, 1955); C. Pinnock, "Conscience," in *Baker's Dictionary of Christian Ethics* (Grand Rapids: Baker, 1973) 126-27; C. Words-worth, *Bishop Sanderson's Lectures on Conscience and Law* (Oxford: James Williamson, 1877).

R. Paul Stevens

CONSUMERISM

The word *consumerism* is occasionally used to denote the consumer movement and advocacy on behalf of consumers vis-à-vis the producers of consumer products. The term is also infrequently used to refer to the economic theory that maintains the growth of consumption is always good for an economy. Normally, however, consumerism is lamented as a significant behavioral blemish in modern industrial society. It suggests an inordinate concern—some might say an addiction*—with the acquisition, consumption and/or possession of material goods and services. Consumerism implies foolishness, superficiality, triviality and the destruction of personal and social relationships by means of selfishness, individualism, possessiveness and covetousness. The prevalence of consumerism suggests a general contraction of the compass of modern culture.*

Interpreting Consumerism

It is often suggested that consumerism is simply the necessary complement, on the side of consumption, to the modern capitalist economy's dramatic expansion of production. Consumerism, from this first perspective, is largely engineered by the producers of products. It is the result of the artificial stimulation, principally by means of manipulative advertising,* of an ever-increasing need* for mass-produced consumer products. The ready availability of consumer credit* in modern society, often financed by manufac-

turers, buttresses the plausibility of this (principally neo-Marxist) interpretation.

Consumerism has also been interpreted as a principal means of defining class and status boundaries in modern industrial society. Thus an individual might identify himself or herself as a member of a particular group by consuming, as the term *status symbol* suggests, the requisite products and services. As new consumer products and services are constantly being introduced, however, the specific indicators of class and status are constantly changing, in effect forcing individuals to continually consume new and different products. From this second perspective, consumerism does not have to do with greed or manipulation so much as with the ratio of what one thinks one ought to possess relative to others against the backdrop of constantly changing shopping* opportunities.

A third interpretation combines the first and second perspectives to suggest that consumerism is simply the behavioral reflection of a fundamentally new kind of culture. Within this new culture need has, in effect, become a new religion, and advertisers and other specialists have become priestly mediators of new, and predominantly materialistic, virtues and values.*

Historians point out, however, that many of the features of modern consumer culture, including manipulative advertising and the deliberate stimulation of desire, had already begun to emerge in the eighteenth century and so antedate the modern revolution in production by almost a century. This has led British social historian Colin Campbell to suggest that the roots of modern consumerism may not lie in the advent of modern production techniques so much as in Romanticism's emphasis on heroic individualism and self-creation. Consumerism's relentless "desire to desire," in other words, is not simply foisted on consumers by producers of consumer products but stems ultimately from a romantic ethic in which the individual is bound to realize himself or herself in the experience of novelty and more or less immediate gratification. This ethic has been amusingly summarized in the quip "I shop, therefore I am." It was this romantic ethic, Campbell suggests, that stimulated subsequent developments in production. The emphasis on self-creation by means of the consumption of things and experiences continues to animate much of contemporary culture.

Religious Consumerism

The rise of denominational,* and now religious, plurality* in modern societies has led to a situation in which we are increasingly encouraged to "shop for," and so to be consumers of, religion itself. The consumption of religion, furthermore, suggests a fundamental change in the meaning of religious belief such that it has increasingly less to do with conviction and more and more to do with personal preference. Many churches and religious organizations have responded to the changing meaning of belief by obligingly repackaging religion to make it conveniently and easily consumable. Such trends have contributed to the emergence of a kind of religious marketplace in which modern consumers are faced with a veritable smorgasbord of religious options.

Christian Reflections on Consumerism

Understood as a preoccupation with the consumption of material goods and services, consumerism has little to commend it from a Christian point of view. In the first instance, it suggests a kind of mindlessness on the part of modern consumers. As essayist Wendell Berry observes in a provocative piece entitled "The Joy of Sales Resistance," the contemporary preoccupation with marketing, salesmanship and consumption could arise only in a society whose members are expected to think and do and provide very little for themselves. More seriously, exorbitant Western consumption habits* have undoubtedly contributed to the degradation of the natural environment and the rapid depletion of natural resources. Consumerism has also been blamed for the exacerbation of poverty,* both domestically and in the developing world.

As a behavior, consumerism betrays significant confusion about the nature of the human situation. More specifically, it discloses confusion about the dangerous logic of *need*. One of the desert fathers, Saint Neilos the Ascetic (d. 430), is said to have advised his disciples to remain within the limits imposed by our basic needs and to strive with all their power not to exceed them. "For once we are carried a little beyond these limits in our desires for the pleasures of this life," Neilos warned, "there is no criterion by which to check our onward movement, since no bounds can be set to that which exceeds the necessary." Neilos went on to outline the sorts of absurdities that inevitably result from attempting to satisfy material desires beyond the reasonable limits of need, and in so doing he described something very much like late twentieth-century consumer culture. And it is certainly the case that much of the dissatisfaction and disappointment that so pervade modern life owes to the insatiable logic of *need* in consumer culture. The "more is better" attitude of modern consumer culture makes it very difficult to say, "Enough is enough." Of course, from a Christian point of view, the logic of need is insatiable simply because such things as pride, covetousness, lust, gluttony, envy and sloth are unlimited in the fallen situation.

The preoccupation with consumption may also betray a fundamental misunderstanding of one's own identity before God. To identify oneself only by the things one is able to consume is, in effect, to lack a true sense of one's self. This is the point of Jesus' simple, yet penetrating, questions: "What good will it be for a man if he gains the whole world, yet forfeits his soul? Or what can a man give in exchange for his soul?" (Mt 16:26). To imagine that we can create or sustain ourselves by means of our possessions or consumption habits, Jesus suggests, is tragically mistaken. It is also stupid, for such things have no lasting future. If we stake our identities—our *selves*—to these things, then we will pass away with them.

Yet beyond folly, consumerism also tends toward idolatry. To the extent that we seek security in consumption, we in effect worship another god, thereby arousing the anger and jealousy of the God and Father of our Lord Jesus Christ. Recall, in this connection, the apostle Paul's equation of greed and idolatry (Col 3:5), as well as the prophetic warning that the fate of idolaters is to become just as worthless as the gods they worship (Jer 13:1-11). Of course, it is not difficult to trace the connection between the fragility and ephemerality of many people's sense of themselves and the essentially restless and ephemeral nature of the gods of consumption.

Responding Christianly to Consumerism

The Christian response to consumerism is already suggested in the theological criticism of this behavior, but it may also help to recall that the original meaning of *consume* is "to burn," "to exhaust" and "to destroy completely." The object of our response to consumerism is to try—with the Lord's gracious help—to avoid destroying ourselves in this behavior and to try to prevent our neighbor* from being destroyed by such behavior as well (*see* Simpler Lifestyle). Our first duty,

then, as Wendell Berry insists, is to "resist the language, the ideas, and the categories of this ubiquitous sales talk, no matter from whose mouth it issues" (p. xi).

It may also help to juxtapose the modern obsession with acquisition, grasping and possessing with the Christian virtues* of gratitude, generosity and hope. Far from encouraging us to accumulate or consume as much as we possibly can, the Scriptures exhort us to view our lives as a gracious gift from God for which we are to be grateful. We are further exhorted to express our gratitude by giving ourselves generously away in the love of God and in the love of our neighbor (1 Tim 6:18).

Finally, because the plausibility of consumerism depends entirely on the apparent permanence of life in this world, we must continually remind each other—and ourselves—that this world and its lusts are indeed passing away (1 Cor 7:30-31). "Sell your possessions and give to the poor," Jesus says to us. "Provide purses for yourselves that will not wear out, a treasure in heaven that will not be exhausted, where no thief comes near and no moth destroys" (Lk 12:33).

See also ADVERTISING; MONEY; NEED; PLEASURE; SHOPPING; SHOPPING MALL; SIMPLER LIFESTYLE; STEWARDSHIP.

References and Resources
W. Berry, "Preface: The Joy of Sales Resistance," to *Sex, Economy, Freedom & Community*, (New York: Pantheon, 1993) xi-xxii; C. Campbell, *The Romantic Ethic and the Spirit of Modern Consumerism* (Oxford: Basil Blackwell, 1987); A. T. During, *How Much Is Enough? The Consumer Society and the Future of the Earth* (London: Earthscan, 1992); J. F. Kavanaugh, *Following Christ in a Consumer Society: The Spirituality of Cultural Resistance* (Maryknoll, N.Y.: Orbis Books, 1991); L. Shames, *The Hunger for More: Searching for Values in an Age of Greed* (New York: Times, 1989); T. Walter, *Need: The New Religion* (Downers Grove, Ill.: InterVarsity Press, 1985).

Craig M. Gay

CONTRACEPTION

Contraception, unlike many everyday matters, has been a matter of theological and ethical debate, largely among Christians. There is good reason for this: it is concerned with something profoundly awesome, the conception* of a human being. *Contraception,* or birth control, is the voluntary prevention of the conception of a child by human intervention. In this article we will explore the matter scientifically, scripturally and theologically.

Methods of Contraception

Today there are a number of methods of contraception available to people. The most primitive method is coitus interruptus, in which the male withdraws before ejaculation. This method has a 20 to 30 percent success rate in avoiding pregnancy. Next are the barrier methods, which employ creams, foams, jellies, caps, diaphragms or condoms to prevent the sperm from reaching the ovum. These methods are about 75 percent effective in pregnancy prevention. Hormone-based contraceptives include oral contraceptives, which contain fixed or variable doses of synthetic estrogen and progestin, Depo-Provera injection, and Norplant, which is a sustained-release contraceptive system implanted under the skin that acts continuously for five years.

The hormonal contraceptives all work through one of the following mechanisms: (1) by thickening the viscosity of the cervical mucus, making it hostile to sperm, (2) by inhibiting ovulation via interruption of a crucial feedback loop between the pituitary gland and the ovaries, or (3) by making the lining of the uterus hostile to the implantation of any newly fertilized ovum that "breaks" through the first two lines of defense. The current low-dose pills most likely operate through this third mechanism, making them in fact *abortifacient* (that is, they achieve birth control through early abortion). Other examples of abortifacient methods are surgical abortion, IUDs and RU-486 (mifepristone); these are not considered contraceptive devices, because a new human life in the form of an embryo is being destroyed. The use of low-dose hormone pills does carry high moral risks. Hormonal birth control has a theoretical effective rate of 99 to 100 percent and a 97 percent user-effective rate.

Permanent sterilization procedures are often performed for contraceptive purposes. For the female, two procedures are available: (1) tubal ligation, in which the fallopian tubes are tied and severed so that the sperm will not reach the ovum, and (2) hysterectomy, which makes conception impossible by removal of the womb. For the male, the method of permanent sterilization is vasectomy, tying the vas deferens (a small tube that transports the sperm from the testes to the prostate gland) to block sperm from entering the ejaculate. Tubal ligation, vasectomy and hysterectomy have a 99 to 100 percent pregnancy prevention success rate. Tubal ligation and vasectomy can be surgically reversed with a 30 percent and 50 percent success rate, respectively, in achieving a subsequent pregnancy.

Recently a new educational approach to birth control called Natural Family Planning (NFP) has been advocated primarily by those who do not want to engage in pharmacological or surgical contraception. It is a day-to-day method based on self-diagnosing the day of fertility in the woman's cycle, giving the married couple the choice to abstain from or enter into sexual intercourse at that time depending on their intention with regard to possible pregnancy. This is considered a true method of family planning in that it can be used to achieve or to avoid pregnancy. Some couples report a recurring honeymoon effect with this method. Four studies in the United States and two in the Third World claimed a 96.4 percent and 99.2 percent effectiveness rate, respectively, in using these methods to postpone, delay and avoid pregnancy.

Attitudes Toward Contraception

Even though contraception was known in ancient Egypt and throughout the ancient world some four millennia ago, it was not widely practiced. Both the Hebrew and the Chinese cultures highly valued childbearing, and contraception had very little, if any, appeal. Greeks and Romans encouraged reproduction in order to populate the state, and contraception was specifically condemned by the Stoics. The question of the legitimacy of the use of contraception arose in the early church,* when Christian free women who married Christian slaves wanted to avoid pregnancy in order not to bring more slaves into the world. The church responded by condemning contraception as sinful while affirming the basic equality of all human beings in the eyes of God, in whose image every man and woman is created. Historically, opposition to contraception has basically been the position of the church until the twentieth century. Church leaders including Augustine, Aquinas, Martin Luther, John Calvin and John Wesley are all on record as condemning contraception. The Comstock Act of 1873 in the United States, prohibiting the distribution of birth control information, reflected the rejection of contraception by North American Protestants. These laws were not repealed until the 1960s.

The change in attitude toward contraception came at the same time that people gained better understanding of the physiological processes involved in reproduction. Prior to the nineteenth century most people thought that new life was transmitted in the male semen and the role of women was to receive and nurture it. The ovum was discovered in 1827, and the relationship between ovulation (the production of a fertilizable egg) and the menstrual cycle was completely worked out in the late 1920s. As a result, the calendar rhythm method was introduced in 1932. This coincided with the growth of the birth control movement, which grew due to the perceived imbalance between population growth and available resources. For some Christians the break with the traditional opposition to contraception began at the Anglican Lambeth Conference in 1930, when the bishops recognized a moral obligation to limit parenthood and allowed for the use of contraception in certain limited circumstances.

The Roman Catholic Church responded with "On Christian Marriage" (1930) and "Of Human Life" (1968). These affirmed that the *unitive* meaning of the sexual act (in which the married couple grows in love and fellowship) and the *procreative* meaning of the sexual act (in which the potential of childbearing is actualized) are both inscribed by God into the very act of sexual intercourse and cannot be separated without serious moral consequences. Periodic abstinence is the only permissible course of action for couples who wish to delay conception.

Protestant writers, on the other hand, see "the completion of marital fellowship" as the "first essential meaning" of sexual intercourse; from the standpoint of this fellowship, then, it may not be generally and necessarily required that it should be linked with the desire for or readiness for children (Barth, p. 269), and readiness for children should include both procreation and education* of offspring. Contraception is therefore acceptable as a means to achieve "responsible parenthood," especially in cases where the mother's physical and psychological welfare may be jeopardized as a result of getting pregnant or where other problems exist, such as an already overcrowded family. Such factors are held to preclude a decent environment to ensure a proper upbringing of the child as a gift from God.

Contemporary Responses of Christians
The first response, which we may call the majority position, accounts for 90 percent or more of modern Christian couples and favors the practices of temporary contraception and permanent sterilization. This response emphasizes the importance of human responsibility and takes stewardship* seriously. It tends to downplay God's sovereignty in this matter and clearly believes that the unitive and procreative meanings of the marriage covenant and act need not be maintained in every sexual intercourse.

A tiny minority, less than 1 percent of Christians (both evangelical and Catholic), rejects every form of contraception, sterilization and even Natural Family Planning. This second response we might call the minority or fundamentalist position. These Christians insist on God's sovereignty in procreative matters and do not accord human responsibility and freedom any significant role in procreation within the sexual/marriage act. They do not see the unitive and procreative meanings of the marriage covenant and act as two separable aspects.

Third, a small but growing number (3 to 4 percent) of Christians are learning and practicing Natural Family Planning. This approach is seen to combine respect for God's sovereignty and human responsibility, seeing that God's love and our stewardship are meant to be intertwined. It is an acknowledgment of God's gifts and our responsible stewardship of them. When sexual intercourse is expe-

rienced, it does not contravene the total openness of the marriage act but trusts in God's providence for any outcome. And when sexual intercourse is abstained from for good reasons, the couple's sacrifice and self-control are considered a gift of the Holy Spirit and an integral component of Christian life.

A Christian Evaluation of Contraception
Undoubtedly, contraception has brought many positive benefits. Many women have been able to relax during sexual intercourse without the fear of annual pregnancies. It has helped some couples take more responsibility for bringing children into this world. But there has been a downside as well.

Looking back at the promise being made for the different approaches to contraception, we must admit that they have not solved the population problems nor made happier marriages. In fact the divorce* rate skyrocketed from 25 percent in 1960 to approximately 50 percent in 1975, when contraception had reached saturation levels in North American culture. In contrast, the divorce rate for those practicing Natural Family Planning is said to be approximately 2 to 3 percent. Furthermore, contraception has not decreased the demand for abortion.* In fact, every country that has accepted contraception has had to pass abortion laws to take care of any failure in contraception, as there are no 100 percent effective contraceptive methods.

There are many factors involved in the alarming statistical trends we observe in today's Western world. Near-perfect and universally available contraception is certainly one. There has been an explosion of abortion from below 50,000 per year before 1960 to 1.5 million per year in the United States today. The reality of unwanted children has not been eliminated either, as child abuse statistics have also skyrocketed in this time period. It is well known that the advent of contraceptive technology coincides with the devastating social consequences of unleashed sex outside of marriage, promiscuity, adultery, sexually transmitted diseases, infertility, value-free sex education and teenage pregnancy. Furthermore, many believe that contraception, by separating the unitive and procreative dimensions of the marriage covenant and act, has managed to reduce women and men to mere objects, seen as means of giving pleasure rather than as total persons with their fertility intact. This objectification of women is at the root of the increased abuse* and violence against women in our society.

Toward Responsible Contraception
First, even if we do not agree with the Catholic Church's position on artificial contraception as intrinsically immoral, it must be admitted that contraception has contributed a great deal to the immorality of our society. Any Christian endorsement of the use of artificial contraception must be accompanied by an unequivocal condemnation of those immoral consequences that run against all fundamental Christian teachings on humanity, sexuality* and marriage. Teenagers especially must be taught that parental use of contraceptives does not amount to justification of premarital sex.

Second, even though the Bible does not directly address the subject of contraception, throughout the Old and New Testaments children are considered a great blessing* from the Lord. In the Old Testament barrenness is considered to be a lamentable state. In Genesis 1:28 the command to be fruitful and multiply is seen to be integral to the meaning and stewardship (responsible parenthood) of the marriage union in creation. Eve's statement "With the help of the LORD I have brought forth a man" (Gen 4:1)

reveals God as integral to the creation of each new life. In conceiving and bearing children we are cooperating with God. Every birth is a sign of God's ongoing commitment to creation, work in redemption and extension of the kingdom. At the dawn of salvation history, it is the birth of a child that is proclaimed as joyful news, and the joy that accompanies the birth of the Savior is seen to be the foundation and fulfillment of the joy that should be experienced as every child is born into the world.

Third, in the light of New Testament teaching that other concerns, such as service to God's kingdom, can take precedence over marriage and family (1 Cor 7), the biblical injunction to be fruitful and multiply (Gen 1:28) need not be interpreted to mean that parents always have to bear the maximum number of children. Rather, the objective of marital partners must include cultivating an environment that is conducive to the growth of partner-fellowship between the couple and an optimal number of children who may receive adequate nurturing, attention and education. If this involves the assistance of artificial contraception, we should use it responsibly and with caution.

Fourth, it is a different matter if a Christian couple decides at the beginning of their married life to be permanently childless by the use of contraceptive devices. Here caution must be exercised. Some argue that the decision to be childless is similar to the decision to be celibate in order to be freed for a higher calling and thus the use of contraceptives should be allowed. Others link sexual intercourse to the kingdom of God. "The line of reasoning goes this way: Families are for the Kingdom of God. Marriage is for families. And therefore, since sex is for marriage, sex is for the kingdom of God" (Smedes, p. 167). Even though we agree that the reproductive meaning of sexuality need not be fulfilled in every instance of the sexual act, the link between the unitive and procreative aspects of sexual intercourse should be respected by insisting that all marriages should be open to the hope of bearing children at some point.

See also ABORTION; BIRTH; CONCEPTION; FAMILY; MISCARRIAGE; PARENTING; SEXUALITY.

References and Resources
C. Balsam and E. Balsam, *Family Planning: A Guide for Exploring the Issues* (Liguori, Mo.: Liguori, 1986); Karl Barth, *Church Dogmatics* 3/4 (Edinburgh: T & T Clark, 1961); R. A. Hatcher et al., *Contraceptive Technology* (New York: Irvington, 1994); J. T. Noonan Jr., *Contraception: A History of Its Treatment by the Catholic Theologians and Canonists*, 3d ed. (Cambridge, Mass.: Belknap/Harvard University Press, 1986); Pope Paul VI, *Of Human Life (Humane Vitae)* (Boston: St. Paul Editions, 1980); M. Pride, *The Way Home: Beyond Feminism, Back to Reality* (Westchester, Ill.: Crossway, 1985); C. D. Provan, *The Bible and Birth Control* (Monongahela, Penn.: Zimmer, 1989); L. B. Smedes, *Mere Morality* (Grand Rapids: Eerdmans, 1983).

Edwin Hui and Michael Maloney

CONTRACTS

In a typical day, most of us enter into several contracts, usually without giving them much attention. When we buy a newspaper, get a haircut, take a ride on a bus or make a long-distance telephone call, whether we know it or not we are entering into a contract. Our contracts can be verbal or written. They may be direct or implied, simple or complex. The purchase of a carton of milk at the local grocery store is an example of a simple, implied and verbal contract. A person takes his or her purchase to the counter, the store clerk asks for a sum of money, and the customer tenders the required sum and takes the milk out of the store. It is understood by both the customer and the store owner that there is to be an exchange of money* and goods by which the customer will come to own the milk and the store will get to keep the money. A bus ride is a more complex transaction. Posted on the vehicle are lengthy written terms related to payment, risk and proper conduct. By entering into the bus, the passengers are assumed to have read and agreed to all of those written terms. Similarly, if we purchase goods using a credit card,* we are expected to have read and accepted all the terms set out in the agreement that accompanies the issue of the credit card.

At another level, the law* will imply certain terms and conditions into a sale of goods, such as "merchantability" and "fitness for description." The implied term of merchantability means that if the milk we purchase at the grocery store turns out to be sour, the store will be required to replace the carton or refund the purchase price. The implied term of fitness would give the patron of the hair salon the right to a remedy if she asked for an auburn tint and ended up with flaming orange hair.

Understanding Contracts
It is no accident that contracts are an everyday feature of our lives. Alongside covenantal forms of interconnecting, the contractual form of transaction is one of the basic forms of human interaction and relationships. Moreover, contract is the building block of our legal and social structures.* It is therefore important for the Christian to understand what contracts are all about, how and when to enter into contracts, biblical principles regarding contractual behavior, how to respond when contracts are broken, and under what circumstances and in what relationships the contractual model would be inappropriate.

Black's Law Dictionary defines a contract as "an agreement between two or more persons which creates an obligation to do or not to do a particular thing. Its essentials are competent parties, subject matter, a legal consideration, mutuality of agreement and mutuality of obligation." The above definition alludes to certain basic contract essentials, in the absence of which there would be no enforceable contract at law. Of course, we all enter into agreements that are not intended to be legally enforceable, such as an agreement with a child to read her a story if she helps set the table for dinner. Such an agreement would not be a contract at law because the child could not be considered "competent" as a minor. The first essential to contract is that the parties be legally competent, meaning of legal age and of sound mind. Undue influence or duress upon one of the parties can also defeat a contract.

A second contract essential is the existence of an offer and the acceptance of that offer by the person receiving the offer. An offer can be made in writing or verbally, directly or implicitly. Stores implicitly "offer" to sell their wares by displaying merchandise with a stated price, and customers "accept" the offer by tendering cash, check, credit card or debit card to the store clerk. At a garage sale, the buyer may make an "offer" to the seller to buy a particular object for a stated price, which may be "accepted" or rejected by the seller. In the earlier example of a bus ride, the transit company offers to provide a transportation service and sets out the terms of its offer in writing either at the bus depot or on the vehicle itself. The passenger "accepts" the offer by purchasing a ticket or by boarding the bus and paying the fare.

A third contract essential is the concept of "consideration": an exchange of rights and obligations between the contracting parties. While the law does not attempt to regulate the value or inherent fairness of what rights go back and forth, nonetheless if all of the rights flow only in one direction, there is no contract and thus nothing to enforce at law. By way of example, an agreement to sell an entire city block for a mere ten dollars is enforceable, whereas an unsolicited promise to give a stranger a free book is not enforceable.

Finally, it is important to have "certainty" about the contract. The basic terms of the contract must be sufficiently clear to allow for a common understanding of the rights and obligations between the contracting parties. An agreement to build a cabin for a specified amount may fail as a contract if there is nothing said about when the work is to be carried out or completed. There would also likely not be an enforceable contract if the owner and builder had failed to agree on the specifications of the cabin to be built. On the other hand, failure to specify the exterior color of the structure would not be considered fatal to the contract, as color is not an essential term of the contract.

Entering into Contracts

While some of our contracts are routine and even seemingly mindless, there are many times when we enter into contract as a result of negotiations. Negotiation styles and skills are acquired at an early age and often do not change in adulthood. We learn to negotiate positionally by determining what we want and assessing what we are prepared to give up in order to obtain what we want. If what we want overlaps with what the other party is prepared to give up and vice versa, then a bargain is achieved and a contract can be entered into. The problem with this negotiation strategy from the Christian's perspective is that it is inherently selfish. Christ commands us to love our neighbor as ourselves (Lk 10:27). Is it possible to live out Christ's Great Command as we enter into contracts? The answer is a definite yes.

There is an entirely different approach to negotiations, which is "interest-based" as opposed to positional. In interest-based negotiations, both parties look at each other's interests (consisting of wants, needs and fears), and together they attempt to create an agreement that meets as many of those interests as possible. Where interests are mutually conflicting, the parties attempt to find some external objective criteria to help them in choosing between those conflicting interests. Not only does this approach lead to collaborative and relationally healthful negotiating, but also it increases the likelihood that agreement will be achieved and that the agreement will be a mutually satisfactory one. Consider the following situation: Susan very much wants to buy John's car but can afford to pay only $2,000. John has his eye on another vehicle and needs to get at least $2,500 for his old car. Positional bargaining results in no deal and leaves both of the parties irritated with each other. However, if John and Susan had entered into interest-based negotiations, they may have discovered that Susan operated a daycare service and that John had been looking for an opening in a daycare facility for his son. By exchanging $500 worth of services, Susan and John could have reached an agreement on both the car and day care, and both would have been very satisfied with the result.

Christians should carefully consider their contract-negotiating style. There are a wealth of resources on interest-based negotiations. Consider Paul's admonition to the Philippian church: "Each of you should look not only to your own interests, but also to the interests of others" (Phil 2:4).

Conduct in Contracts

There are numerous examples in both the Old and the New Testament of God's people entering into contracts:

☐ the owner of the vineyard contracted with workers to buy their services (Mt 20:1-16);

☐ Joseph was sold by his brothers to Midianite merchants for twenty shekels of silver (Gen 37:28);

☐ the "shrewd manager" contracted with his master's debtors to greatly reduced their debts in exchange for early payment (Lk 16:1-9);

☐ Moses contracted with Pharaoh to pray to God for relief if Pharaoh released the Israelites (Ex 8:8).

While there are few direct references to contracts in scriptural teaching (Lev 25 perhaps comes the closest to articulating rules of contracting), there are many relevant scriptural principles to guide the Christian in contractual relationships. The Christian should be fair in agreements and not take advantage of others (Lev 25:14). Special consideration should be given to the poor (Lev 25:25, 35; Prov 28:28). Exhortations to honesty and integrity* in all business dealings appear frequently throughout the Bible. God's people are to use honest scales and measures (Lev 19:36; Deut 25:13; Prov 11:1). "Woe!" says the prophet Micah to those who act in a fraudulent manner (Mic 2:2). Isaiah laments the lack of integrity of his people (Is 59:4). The book of Proverbs contains several principles that would be applicable as Christian behavior in a contractual setting: generosity, restraint, special care for the poor, honesty, acting without deception and keeping the law (see also Rom 13).

Another common theme, especially in the Old Testament, is justice.* The Christian should not use contracts for unjust gain or to take advantage of those who are disadvantaged or disempowered. The law allows the courts to strike down contracts that are considered to be "unconscionable." How much higher, then, the standard for Christians who, in following Christ, are to act and live out of love* in all dealings and relationships.

When Things Go Wrong

In our imperfect and fallen world, commitments made in contract will from time to time fail to be carried out, sometimes intentionally and sometimes for reasons beyond the control of the defaulting party. How is the Christian to respond when others fail to carry out their contractual obligations? First, we are encouraged in Scripture to be patient and long-suffering. Indeed, patience is one of the fruits of the Spirit (Gal 5:22). Tolerance and a willingness to give others a second chance ought to characterize the Christian's response to broken contracts. We are also told not to repay evil for evil (Rom 12:17). Thus, our response to another's default ought never to be an act of vengeance or "evening the score."

But when the breach of contract is serious or repetitive, what is the Christian to do? Again, as with the process of entering into a contract, the normal choice is between a positional approach and an interest-based approach. A positional approach may be to confront in an attacking manner or perhaps to seek legal recourse in a court of law. An interest-based approach would be to deal directly with the other party in the manner described earlier, seeking to bring out the needs, wants and fears of the parties to the contract. This may be very difficult when the relationship has been strained through a breach of contract. Fortunately there are professional mediators skilled in interest-based negotiations who can assist the parties toward a collaborative resolution (*see* Conflict Resolution). The interest-based approach is appropriate for Christians both because there is a scriptural admonition against lawsuits (1 Cor 6:1-8) and because the positional adversarial approach is usually antithetical to the response of love commanded in the Gospels.

When the Contractual Model Is Not Appropriate

While there are no general or specific biblical prohibitions on contracting, there are situations and relationships where it would be inappropriate for the Christian to act or think in contractual terms. Our relationship with God is clearly not to be thought of in contractual terms. Such a view would lead quickly to a doctrine of justification through works: if one obeys God's commands, then one can earn God's love. But, argues Paul, "all have sinned and fall short of the glory of God, and are justified freely by his grace through the redemption that came by Christ Jesus" (Rom 3:23-24). God has chosen not to contract but rather to covenant with his people. Whereas a contract involves an exchange of rights and duties, the biblical notion of covenant involves a unilateral act of love and promise* on the part of God and a promise that all can appropriate. This results in a loving and grateful desire on our part to live according to God's purposes, priorities and values.*

The covenantal model of relationship is the New Testament standard not only for God but for his followers. We are instructed by Jesus to love our neighbor not on a contractual basis (an equitable exchange of one's rights and duties) but on a covenantal basis, out of response to being first loved by God. That is the point of the parable of the unmerciful servant (Mt 18:23-35). The best that the state can legislate is mutual tolerance toward each other: that is all that public law can accomplish. But God's call to love one another is a much higher standard. We understand this in our relationship with our children. Our love for them is not conditional upon their behavior. In our marriages* we make vows or covenants to behave in a certain way regardless of the response of our spouse. Now the challenge is for followers of Christ to act and behave covenantally in all of their relationships and bring his covenantal grace into our contractual relationships.

See also INTEGRITY; JUSTICE; LAW; PROMISING.

Peter Mogan

CONVERSATION

Conversation is basic to daily life. Throughout the day, in a wide variety of settings, we relate to others through talking informally with them. Originally the word referred to "a way of life"; now it means "a type of discourse." Conversation overlaps but can be differentiated from discussion. Though one can easily move into the other, discussion is generally more focused and structured.

The Complexity of Conversation

Though conversation appears to be a simple activity, it is actually quite complex. First, not all conversation is the same. It is governed by unwritten conventions or codes particular to the settings in which it is taking place. We talk about conversations as being *formal* and *informal, polite* and *frank, freewheeling* and *directed.* What we talk about with a friend,* and the way we talk, differs from the way we converse with a client or boss. Conversation at a party differs from what we talk about at a business lunch or over the dinner table at home. Face-to-face conversation differs in certain respects from that conducted over a telephone* or a modem.

Second, women and men tend to converse differently. Men tend to discuss matters more abstractly women more concretely. Women tend to discuss in order to connect with other people, men to express their point of view. Men tend to be more preoccupied with ideas about which they sometimes feel strongly, women with the cognitive content of their feelings. Women tend to listen* and ask questions better, men to give answers and cut off others, especially women. One should not make too much of these tendencies, because they also occur between members of the same sex, because most, if not all, may be socially conditioned, and because people all too quickly erect gender* stereotypes around such differences. In any case, all of these ways of talking are valid ways of conversing.

Third, cultures* as a whole have different conventions governing how people converse. Among Australian aborigines, members of a group wait to speak until the most respected person among them has spoken or indicated that others may do so; women will wait until the men have spoken or given them the permission to do so; and each one will pause before speaking to examine whether he or she has something worthwhile to say. Even between Western societies there are noticeable differences. Most Americans speak more loudly and in a more uninhibited way than most Canadians. Australians are more democratic and colloquial in their conversations than most British people. There are even significant differences within countries, as between southerners and northeasterners in the United States.

In spite of these various conventions, conversation is the most spontaneous, versatile and open-ended way of communicating that we have. We enter into conversations with our partners, children, relatives and friends, as well as with fellow car-poolers, colleagues, salespeople, counter clerks and total strangers, sometimes even ourselves! We do it one on one and in small groups, casually and by arrangement. We chat about trivial matters yet also about major personal or social concerns. In prayer we converse alone or in company with God.

The Importance of Conversation

Conversation is fundamental to social life. It is central to (1) acquiring the necessary information to help us find our way around places or carry out our daily activities; (2) relating to other people in order to develop an understanding of who they are and how they function; (3) resolving problems that we find difficult to deal with individually; (4) enjoying the company of others and, through the "play" of conversation, just having a good time; (5) helping to determine our basic worldview,* commitments and priorities. Conversation is so pervasive and common that it is easy to overlook its importance. This is especially true in relation to learning or teaching.

We seldom regard conversation as having educational value. We assume that serious or substantial learning can take place only in a formal teaching situation or in an educational institution. Interestingly, studies of lecturing suggest that a speaker is mainly effective when there is a conversational element or style in the address. In fact it is through conversation that infants primarily come to know and cooperate with others. Older children prepare for adult life by "playing grownups," whether through conversing with adults or talking to each other like adults. It is by spending large amounts of time* "hanging out" with their peers or talking over the telephone that teenagers formulate their views and develop their relationships. Popular television* and radio* programs—whether sitcoms or dramas, talk or talk-back shows—reflect life more than we acknowledge. As adults, many of our views

on work, social issues and politics* are formed by conversation with families, colleagues and friends. Studies suggest that the most effective evangelism* also flows from informally sharing our experience with people we know.

The importance of conversation has been gaining serious academic attention. As a result of monitoring staged conversations in laboratories, psychologists began to categorize and quantify the various components and consequences of conversation. Over the last twenty years conversational analysis of ordinary exchanges between people—which always contain some level of theatricality—has undergone considerable development. Such analysis can be undertaken by any competent person, not just experts, recognizing that every detail in a conversation, such as utterances, exclamations, expressions, gestures and stance, is important.

Conversation in the Bible and History

In the Bible, conversation is not only central to the way people relate to each other but also characteristic of the way we learn about God. The Old Testament contains a number of conversations between God and key figures in the divine drama. For example, God converses at length with Abraham (Gen 18:22-33), Moses (Ex 3:1—4:17), Jeremiah (Jer 14:1—15:2) and, in a more one-sided way, with Job (Job 38—42). These conversations range over a wide number of concerns—the fate of people involved in wrongdoing, the nature of a call* to ministry,* why difficult times have come upon the nation and the point of apparently innocent suffering.

In these writings conversation is also central to the way the people of God were to pass on their faith. For example, the people of Israel should not only memorize or recite the Ten Commandments to their children but "talk about them when you sit at home and when you walk along the road" (Deut 6:7; compare 6:20-25). At the Passover the meaning of this basic ritual was to be discussed with children during the meal (Ex 13:1-10). In fact, conversations were to take place within families about the whole range of God's instructions to Israel (Deut 6:20-21).

The Bible also contains numerous conversations that consciously or unconsciously reveal people's motives, attitudes and intentions; their beliefs, standards and practices; their problems, fears and longings. Others focus on God's character, actions and purposes. In many of the psalms—especially those that take the form of a conversation between the worshiper and God—we find a combination of the two (explicitly in Ps 32; 81; and implicitly in many others, for example, Ps 85; 89); sometimes we also come across the psalmist having a conversation with himself as well as God (Ps 42; 77). Elsewhere people fulfill God's wider purposes through engaging in conversations with influential people (compare Neh 2:1-8; Esther 5—7).

In the New Testament we often find Jesus talking with his disciples as they ate a meal together or journeyed from place to place. Sometimes outsiders generate a discussion on some important topic (Mt 19:1-12); sometimes one or more of the disciples generate it (Mt 20:20-27); sometimes Jesus himself generates the conversation (Mt 16:13-28). After Jesus' death we read of two disciples on the road to Emmaus whose conversation about the events of the past week Jesus joined, though it was only later that they realized how much their hearts burned within them as he "talked" with them and opened up the Scriptures to them (Lk 24:13-32).

In the early church purposeful conversation continued to play an important role. The only narrative we have of an early church meeting describes Paul as first dialoguing with (not preaching* to) the people at length and then conversing with them after their common meal (Acts 20:7, 11). In those days both the sermon and the Lord's Supper had a strongly conversational character, one that was lost in the following centuries as churches got larger and clergy* emerged as a separate group. Paul also trained people such as Timothy, Titus, Priscilla and Aquila for missionary service largely through working and talking with them on his various journeys, not through formal classes in an educational institution.

Although in subsequent Christian history more formal approaches to learning and teaching tended to predominate, key figures continued to affirm the role of conversation in Christian formation and education. In the third century Clement of Alexandria instructed his students through both informal conversation and more structured discussion. Augustine taught mainly through dialogue with his students in informal surroundings and sometimes even out of doors. Martin Luther's collected *Table Talk* shows how he supplemented his formal lectures with regular theological and practical conversations over meals. Dietrich Bonhoeffer followed a similar pattern at his underground seminary in Germany during the Nazi era, as reflected in a discussion of the ministry of listening and communicating in his book *Life Together.*

During the Reformation influential converts in the universities were won over to the Protestant cause initially through conversation in taverns and pubs. In the eighteenth century it was through conversations initiated in one household after another that John Woolman induced Quakers throughout America to abandon slavery, just as later in England regular and lengthy conversations over many years in the homes of William Wilberforce and other members of the Clapham Sect formed the basis for the antislave movement there. During and after World War II, the regular conversations among members of the Inklings group, which was made up of C. S. Lewis, J. R. R. Tolkien, Charles Williams, Owen Barfield and others, played a seminal role in shaping the books for which they have become famous. These are just a few examples of many that could be given.

The Demise of Conversation

For at least two main reasons conversation today has fallen on difficult times. It is a victim of the increased busyness and noise that afflict modern society. We have less and less time for others generally, whether extending hospitality* to them or visiting* with them, and so less time for simply talking together in a regular or leisurely* way. Settings where we could talk have become too noisy with traffic or Muzak. The individualism and fragmentation of people in the West are also a problem. A century and a half ago the French social commentator Alexis de Tocqueville commented that Americans do not so much converse as speak to one another as if they were addressing a meeting. Instead of conversation there is either a discussion with a particular shape and goal or a series of individual presentations by people more interested in expressing their own ideas than participating in a genuine group experience in which people take their cues from one another.

Busyness, noise, individualism and fragmentation make it all the more important to recover conversation in significant areas of life. In this matter we can learn from those who are marginal in our society. For different reasons African-Americans, women and children all seem to converse easily with one another: the first perhaps because they have become skeptical of discussions, the second because they are less linear and more person-oriented, the third because they are so unself-conscious. There are excellent examples of people conversing in literature—from Shakespeare's plays to A. R. Gurney's theater pieces. But these are carefully contrived artifices and therefore do not provide the best models of ordinary conversation.

Recovering Conversation

Restoring conversation to a central place in life has many advantages.

For repairing marriages and families. Psychologists suggest that the main problem in marriages* today is the lack of communication between the partners. This stems partly from people's inability to talk with and hear from one another, partly from issues arising in which highly emotive factors take control, and partly because people do not spend enough time talking with one another (less than twenty minutes a week in meaningful conversation, according to one Australian study!). Time spent by parents with their children has also decreased, as the preoccupation with spending *quality*, rather than *quantity*, time with children testifies.

Behind such problems lie poor modeling and training during people's upbringing, the overly volatile place financial matters occupy in our lives and the emphasis on achievement in both school and workplace at the expense of personal and relational growth. When couples and families reorder their priorities, and where necessary learn some communication skills, the threat of marriage breakdown and of the generation gap diminishes. One step in reordering is to restore the evening family meal to its rightful place, free from the intrusion of television and telephone. Also helpful are regular opportunities for partners, while walking or relaxing, to talk about their dreams and frustrations, ideas and feelings.

For understanding and relating the Christian faith. When people engage in conversation about an interesting book, a film or a program, they tend to become enthusiastically caught up in discussion. They talk about how wonderful, exciting, stimulating or moving it was, what part they liked most or least or just didn't understand, who or what they really identified with. They may also talk about the values* or ideas it was projecting and how it challenged or confirmed certain attitudes or convictions. The same degree of involvement and excitement can be generated in studying the Bible or learning about the Christian faith.

Though not as ordered an approach to learning as more formal study of the Bible, church history or theology, good conversation does lead to greater understanding and self-challenge. It can bring to life stories and figures from the Bible, as well as ones that come out of the pages of church history. Even the lives and writings of Christian thinkers, past and present, can come alive in people's minds and wills if they are approached in this way. Formal classes or structured programs are not necessarily the best way for most people to learn and apply the basic elements of the Christian faith.

For deepening and extending the church. Small groups* have brought into church life a more relational, supportive and practical dimension. But in comparison with early Christian meetings and our own contemporary needs, they are still too structured and limited. Most commonly these groups are led and directed by one person and thus do not provide opportunities for all to share with and care for one another according to their God-given gifts and experience. They generally meet for an hour or an hour and a half and do not provide time for extended interaction or in-depth bonding. If they met longer and focused on dialogue or Christian conversation, more holistic learning and community building would take place.

Part of the answer is building into such gatherings a full meal—preferably carrying the full significance of the Lord's Supper—during which conversation on a wide range of concerns, small and large, to individuals and to the group as a whole, can take place. But recovering the importance of a meal, this time with unbelievers rather than believers as guests, is central to the task of extending as well as deepening the church. The early church grew largely through the act of ordinary Christians extending hospitality to others in their homes.* It was around the dining-room table in a conversational way that the gospel was most effectively shared. This is a challenge and a direction for all Christians and churches that are serious about evangelism today.

Conversation is a multisided phenomenon with multiple uses. Though often familiar or standardized, and in turn both comfortable and comforting, it is also full of the most extraordinary possibilities and consequences. As Erving Goffman says, "The box that conversation stuffs into us [or that we present to others] is Pandora's" (p. 74).

See also FELLOWSHIP; GOSSIP; LISTENING; SPEAKING; STORYTELLING.

References and Resources

W. R. Baker, *Sticks and Stones: The Discipleship of Our Speech* (Downers Grove, Ill.: InterVarsity Press, 1996); E. Goffman, *Forms of Talk* (Philadelphia: University of Pennsylvania Press, 1981); R. Hattox, *Coffee and Coffeehouses: The Origins of a Social Beverage in the Medieval Near East* (Seattle: University of Washington, 1985). G. Lakoff and M. Johnson, *Metaphors We Live By* (Chicago: University of Chicago Press, 1980); C. Lasch, *The Revolt of the Elites and the Betrayal of Democracy* (New York: Norton, 1995) 117-28; D. Roger and P. Bull, *Conversation: An Interdisciplinary Approach* (Philadelphia: Multilingual Matters, 1988); D. Tannen, *You Just Don't Understand: Women and Men in Conversation* (New York: Ballantine, 1990).

Robert Banks

COUNSELING, LAY

The widespread use of paraprofessionals or lay counselors gained momentum especially during the 1960s. This occurred because of a shortage of professionally trained personnel to cater to a steadily increasing demand for mental health services, especially from the socioeconomically disadvantaged population (Tan 1991a).

Lay counseling has become a significant part of Christian ministries today, especially in the context of the local church, but it extends to other contexts like parachurch organizations and mission groups. Since lay-counseling services are usually offered free of charge, it is also an important means of delivering mental health services, particularly to those who cannot afford to see mental health professionals. In some states in the United States it may be necessary to use terms like *lay helping, lay caring, lay helpers* and *lay caregivers,* rather than *lay counseling* and *lay counselors,* because of particular licensing laws that limit the use of the term *counseling* or *counselor* to those who are professionally trained and licensed (usually with at least a master's degree). But can laypeople do this work effectively?

Effectiveness of Lay Counseling

Over the last twenty years several important reviews of the research literature have attempted to determine whether paraprofessional helpers are as effective as professional therapists (Tan 1991a; Toh and Tan). The results were somewhat equivocal, with no clear indication of which group appeared superior. The majority of studies, however, indicated that lay counselors are often as effective as professional therapists. What is not so clear is "the conditions under which their contributions can be maximized— the types of interventions and patients for which this resource is most appropriate" (Lorion and Felner, p. 763).

A similar observation was offered more recently by researchers in the area of therapeutic effectiveness (Lambert and Bergin, p. 171). An even more recent review found that more trained and experienced therapists tended to have better therapy outcomes than less trained and experienced therapists, but the differences were modest (Stein and Lambert).

In summary, the question of the comparative effectiveness of these two groups is still not fully settled. This outcome brings to mind a statement made by Jerome Frank in 1982 after reviewing the therapeutic components shared by all psychotherapies: "My own hunch, which I mention with some trepidation, is that the most gifted therapists may have telepathic, clairvoyant, or other parapsychological abilities. . . . They may, in addition, possess something . . . that can only be termed 'healing power' " (Frank, p. 31).

So while training and research are important, we need to perhaps pay attention to therapists' qualities that go beyond credentials. Paraprofessionals (that is, those without the training, education, experience or credentials required to be professional therapists) may also be therapeutic if they have been identified with this healing* power and trained to utilize this potential.

Given the empirical support behind the usefulness of lay or paraprofessional counselors, the idea of utilizing them as mental health providers has been accepted and championed by some mental health professionals* and researchers. The rationale for their position is sound: (1) their effectiveness has been regularly documented; (2) the need for mental health services cannot be met by professional therapists alone since current estimates suggest that only 20 percent of diagnosable mental disorders obtain treatment; (3) because managed health care is becoming more prominent in medical care in the foreseeable future and an estimated 37 million Americans do not have insurance coverage at all, a cost-effective treatment offered by paraprofessionals may be valid or appropriate with perhaps mild versions of a disorder or as adjuncts to professionally administered approaches; and (4) many people already consult nonprofessionals such as clergy and physicians (Christensen and Jacobson).

The Rise of Christian Lay Counseling

Several other studies involving Christian paraprofessionals have also begun to document the effectiveness of Christian lay counselors (Tan 1991a). The most recent and well-designed study to date was a controlled outcome study that evaluated the effectiveness of Christian lay counselors working at a church-based program (Toh and Tan). These lay counselors were selected and trained for one year by professionals. Supervision after the training was also provided by professionals. Incoming counselees were screened at intake, and only individuals with temporary adjustment disorders subject to short-term, solution-focused counseling were candidates for this lay-counseling program. Individuals with suggested diagnoses of character or serious personality disorders were referred to a network of professional counselors associated with the church. The treatment group comprised twenty-two subjects, who received ten sessions of individual lay counseling, while twenty-four subjects were in the no-treatment, waiting-list control group (the majority of these randomly assigned counselees were later found to be highly committed Christians who attended church often and regularly). The results indicated that the treatment group reported significantly more improvement than the control group on all outcome measures and maintained their therapeutic gains one month after termination.

For this reason, and given the increasing demand for affordable mental health services, Christian lay-counseling programs should also be considered as a viable mental health service to churches and the community at large. The potential for church-based counseling is enormous. The church is a large, benevolent community, with unique resources in prayer and the Scriptures for those who are open to the spiritual dimension, a facility often absent from secular approaches.

Starting a Lay-Counseling Ministry

The first step is to recognize the biblical basis for lay counseling (e.g., see Rom 15:14; Gal 6:1-2; Col 3:16; 1 Thess 5:14; Jas 5:16) and its therapeutic potential. In 1 Peter 2:5, 9, Peter affirms the priesthood of all believers: the work of ministry* is not only for the pastor and church staff but for all Christians (*see* Laity). In line with these and other passages that speak about the development and use of believers' spiritual gifts* to build up the church (for example, Rom 12; 1 Cor 12; Eph 4; 1Pet 4), there should be training of appropriately gifted laypeople in various church ministries, including lay counseling.

The second step is to choose an appropriate model of lay-counseling ministry. To do this, the goals of the ministry must be identified. Who are the people to be reached, and what resources are available to provide this service? The program subsequently would be enhanced if an ethos, or distinctive character, was established by giving it an appropriate name.

There are basically three major models of lay-counseling ministry (Tan 1991a): the informal, spontaneous model; the informal, organized model;

the formal, organized model. In the *informal, spontaneous model,* lay counselors may or may not receive any systematic training in counseling skills. Yet counseling may take place in spontaneous and informal interactions that already exist in natural settings, such as restaurants, homes, classrooms, neighborhoods and businesses, as well as in religious, social and community meeting places. In this model ongoing supervision or formal organization and direction of counseling attempts are not provided. In the *informal, organized model,* informal or natural lay counseling takes place but in the context of a well-organized, regularly supervised and intentional helping ministry or activity where training is provided for the lay counselors. In the *formal, organized model,* lay counseling is conducted in an organized and well-supervised way (including training of lay counselors) but in more formal settings, such as a church counseling center, community clinic, agency or hospital.

The third step is to obtain full support for the idea and model of lay-counseling ministry selected from the pastors, pastoral staff and church board. Such a ministry should be seen as an extension of pastoral care* and counseling in the church and as an essential part of the priesthood of all believers.

The fourth step is to screen and select appropriately gifted and qualified lay Christian counselors from the congregation. Important selection criteria should include the following: spiritual maturity; psychological stability; love for and interest in people (including empathy, genuineness, warmth and respect); appropriate spiritual gifts for helping relationships (such as the gift of encouragement mentioned in Rom 12:8); some life experience; previous training or experience in people helping (desirable but not essential); age, gender and ethnic/cultural background relevant to the clientele of the lay-counseling program; availability and teachability; and ability to maintain confidentiality (Tan 1991a).

Guidelines for screening potential lay counselors include (1) a brief written statement about his or her reasons for being interested in lay-counselor training and involvement in a religious context (this statement should also include agreement with the doctrinal positions or beliefs of the local church in order to function well in that context); (2) letters of recommendation from two or three people who know the potential lay counselor well; (3) an interview with the appropriate leaders of the lay-counseling program; and (4) psychological testing, if conducted by qualified and licensed mental health professionals (Collins). The fifth step is to provide an adequate training program for the lay counselors. The final step is to let the lay counselors see actual counselees, but with ongoing supervision and further training provided.

Training and Supporting Lay Counselors
Training programs vary widely in approaches (for example, Rogerian, psychodynamic, cognitive-behavioral, systems), modalities (for example, individual, couple, family or group) and length (from several weeks to several months). Most programs, however, include a minimum of twenty-four to fifty or more hours of training in basic listening* and helping skills (Tan 1992). The number of trainees is usually limited to relatively small numbers (for example, ten to fifteen) with regular training sessions (for example, weekly or biweekly for two to three hours each time).

In any good training program for lay Christian counselors, the following content areas should be covered: basic Bible knowledge, especially that which is relevant to people-helping ministries; knowledge of counseling skills (with opportunities for experiential practice); understanding of common problems (for example, depression,* anxiety,* stress* or spiritual dryness); awareness of ethics and dangers in counseling; and knowledge of the importance and techniques of referral.

A good training program also usually includes the following components: clear, practically oriented presentations; reading assignments; observation of good counseling skills modeled or demonstrated by the trainer or professional counselor; experiential practice, especially through role-playing. Most training programs emphasize basic counseling skills (for example, listening and relationship building), but some have also provided training in more specific counseling methods, such as cognitive-behavioral and problem-solving interventions, marriage* and family counseling and even insight-oriented skills (Tan 1992).

Lay counselors should receive ongoing and regular supervision after their training and once they begin seeing counselees in helping relationships. As far as possible, the supervisor should be a licensed mental health professional. If the supervisor is not a licensed mental health professional, he or she must have access to such a professional as a consultant.

Most supervision sessions occur weekly for at least an hour, either individually or in small groups.* The client load of counselors is also usually limited to only a few each week. An alternative supervision format that has been used involves biweekly supervision meetings of about two hours' duration for small groups of lay counselors, with individual supervision provided when necessary.

Good supervision includes both skill training (that is, the supervisor teaching or modeling specific counseling methods or interventions) and some discussion of process issues or dynamics (that is, focusing on what is happening internally in the lay counselor and interpersonally between the lay counselor and the counselee). Some observation of the lay counselor's actual counseling work is essential, whether it be through audiotapes or videotapes of counseling sessions, through direct observation through a one-way mirror or through cocounseling (where the supervisor and the lay counselor conduct the counseling together).

An awareness of legal and ethical issues related to both the supervision of lay counselors and lay counseling itself is crucial for those involved in these activities. For example, lay counselors should be taught to recognize the limits of their skills and knowledge and should know when and how to refer counselees to appropriate professionals. Lay counselors also need to obtain permission from their counselees, preferably by written consent, to share information from counseling sessions with their supervisors and others, especially if group supervision is used. Such information should be kept confidential by those involved in supervision sessions.

Christian lay counseling or people helping, including peer counseling (Sturkie and Tan 1992, 1993), has grown and mushroomed in recent years. It is a ministry that should be conducted in a Christ-centered, biblically based and Spirit-filled way, as well as ethically, effectively and efficiently, so that many lives can be touched and blessed, to the glory of God.

See also DISCIPLESHIP; EMOTIONS; HEALING; LISTENING; PASTORAL CARE; SPIRITUAL GROWTH.

References and Resources

A. Christensen and N. S. Jacobson, "Who (or What) Can Do Psychotherapy: The Status and Challenge of Nonprofessional Therapies," *Psychological Science* 5 (1994) 8-14; G. R. Collins,

"Lay Counseling Within the Local Church," Leadership 1, no. 4 (1980) 78-86; J. D. Frank, "Therapeutic Components Shared by All Psychotherapies," in *Psychotherapy Research and Behavior Change,* ed. J. H. Harvey and M. M. Parks (Washington, D.C.: American Psychological Association, 1982) 9-37; M. J. Lambert and A. E. Bergin, "The Effectiveness of Psychotherapy," in *Handbook of Psychotherapy and Behavior Change,* ed. A. E. Bergin and S. L. Garfield (4th ed., New York: Wiley, 1994) 143-89; R. P. Lorion and R. D. Felner, "Research on Mental Health Interventions with the Disadvantaged," in *Handbook of Psychotherapy and Behavior Change,* ed. S. L. Garfield and A. E. Bergin (3rd ed. New York: Wiley, 1986) 739-75; D. M. Stein and M. J. Lambert, "Graduate Training in Psychotherapy: Are Therapy Outcomes Enhanced?" *Journal of Consulting and Clinical Psychology* 63 (1995) 182-96; J. Sturkie and S. Y. Tan, *Advanced Peer Counseling in Youth Groups* (Grand Rapids: Zondervan/Youth Specialties, 1993); J. Sturkie and S. Y. Tan, *Peer Counseling in Youth Groups* (Grand Rapids: Zondervan/Youth Specialties, 1992) 431-40; S. Y. Tan, "Development and Supervision of Paraprofessional Counselors," in *Innovations in Clinical Practice: A Sourcebook,* ed. L. VandeCreek, S. Knapp and T. L. Jackson (Sarasota, Fla.: Professional Resource, 1992); S. Y. Tan, *Lay Counseling: Equipping Christians for a Helping Ministry* (Grand Rapids: Zondervan, 1991a); S. Y. Tan, "Religious Values and Interventions in Lay Christian Counseling," *Journal of Psychology and Christianity* 10 (1991b) 173-82; Y. M. Toh and S. Y. Tan, *The Effectiveness of Church-Based Lay Counselors: A Controlled Outcome Study* (forthcoming).

Siang-Yang Tan and Yiu-Meng Toh

CRAFTSMANSHIP

Craftsmanship is an attitude and a quality possessed by people enabling them to make things that give pleasure* to themselves and others. The work of their hands is the very best that they can do, and the fabricated objects possess both utility and beauty.* Those who make things, one of a kind or mass-produced, vast in scale or minute, permanent or temporary, for profit or for pleasure, are going to be judged on their craftsmanship. There are good reasons for this.

God as Craftsperson

One thing we know about God is that God makes things and is pleased with what he makes (Gen 1:31). Human beings made in the image of God are like God when they make things and are pleased with the results of their labor. If this logic holds, superior craftsmanship is a form of godliness. This is not a trivial observation. To understand the essence of craftsmanship, we must start with our Maker, whose image all craftspeople bear.

Perfect conception and supreme skill are the essence of divine craftsmanship. All who have marveled at the order, complexity and beauty of nature are giving tribute to the Master Craftsman, even when they obtusely credit it to the twin gods of adaptation and genetic mutation. We, as created beings (and fallen ones at that), possess neither God's omniscience nor his omnipotence. We lack the ability to conceive the perfect object and the skill necessary to craft it—even if we were given the blueprint. Fortunately God works with us, enabling us to be subcreators, or craftspeople, an ability that anthropologists have identified as one of the characteristics that sets humankind apart from the rest of creation.

The Bible and Craftsmanship

The Bible has little to say directly about craftsmanship. We can infer from Proverbs that many of the virtues extolled there are essential for craftsmanship. Diligence, discipline, patience, honesty, discernment, teachability and humility are just some of the qualities for which the true craftsperson strives. These qualities are what we might call the foundational qualities for true craftsmanship. Proverbs 22:29 offers a promise as well:

Do you see a man skilled in his work?
He will serve before kings;
he will not serve before obscure men.

In addition, the spiritual and moral principles of the Gospels and the Epistles are important, but they are conditions of godliness for everyone, whether craftsperson or not. But faith and closeness to God are not conditions of high craftsmanship; craftsmanship is not an exclusive preserve of Christians. Nevertheless, true spirituality ought to give the Christian a "leg up" when it comes to acquiring the foundational qualities of craftsmanship because pride has been put in its place. Unbridled pride found in a "maker-of-things" would almost certainly be unfertile ground for growth in the virtues mentioned in Proverbs and other Wisdom writings.

Inherent in the concept of craftsmanship is the idea of meaningful and joyful work.* This is not a simple matter. Solomon confessed,

My heart took delight in all my work,
and this was the reward for all my
labor.
Yet when I surveyed all that my hands
had done
and what I had toiled to achieve,
everything was meaningless, a
chasing after the wind;
nothing was gained under the sun.
(Eccles 2:10-11)

The craftsperson cannot ultimately be satisfied solely by making beautiful things, for he or she must find a place in the community.* So to establish a spirituality of craftsmanship, we must examine the role of "makers-of-things" in the story of God's redeeming love toward humanity.

Crafting Cities and Idols

Most references to tradespeople and craftspeople in the Bible occur in two contexts: on one hand, building cities* and making idols, and on the other hand, building a dwelling place for God and crafting articles of worship.* In the former, craftspeople aid and abet humanity's rebellion against God; in the latter, craftspeople build a place for communion with God. The tower of Babel, a collective task of tradespeople, was the result of a conspiracy to supplant God. From the biblical perspective cities (the spiritual descendants of Babel) and those who build them are always tainted with idolatrous motives. Throughout the prophetic writings all the great cities, centers of human power in the Middle East, are fated to be reduced to rubble by the jealous hand of God. In stark contrast to the city as a monument to human pride are the tabernacle (later the temple) and ultimately the church,* each of which successive "structure" is a dwelling place for God. These two opposing spiritual realities provide the biblical context for craftspeople, but they also pose the primary dilemma. Will the hands of the craftsperson make something for the glory of humankind or for the glory of God?

The first craftsperson identified in the Old Testament was Tubal-Cain, who "forged all kinds of tools out of bronze and iron" (Gen 4:22). This is all we know of him. But the story of two other craftspeople from the wilderness years of Israel's journey to the Promised Land is more revelatory. When the Lord gave Moses the Ten Commandments on Mount Sinai, he also gave him detailed instructions for sacrificial ceremonies and the structure and articles necessary to fulfill those rites. The Lord concludes these instructions with the following:

I have chosen Bezalel . . . and I have filled him with the Spirit of God, with skill, ability and knowledge in all kinds of crafts—to make artistic designs for work in gold, silver and bronze, to cut and set stones, to work in wood, and to engage in all kinds of craftsmanship. Moreover, I have appointed Oholiab . . . to help him. Also I have given skill to all the craftsmen to make everything I have commanded you. (Ex 31:2-6)

In fact, Bezalel is the first and only person in the Old Testament who is described as being filled with the Holy Spirit. Others received empowerment for specific situations, but the craftsman Bezalel and his coworkers were especially privileged with divine "in-Spirit-ation" to exercise their skill in the building of the tabernacle. Their empowerment foreshadowed Acts 1:8, where Jesus tells his disciples they will be empowered by the same Spirit to spread the gospel and in so doing to begin to build and craft the church (1 Cor 3:10-15; Eph 2:19-22).

The Spirituality of Craftsmanship

This empowering carried and still carries with it responsibilities, one of which is to keep pure bodies (1 Cor 6:19). If sexual immorality defiles our bodies, our eyes and hands will be equally violated by employing them for unworthy ends. The wilderness story is clear about this. Before Bezalel and his fellow craftsmen ever received their orders, at the instigation of the people Aaron made an idol in the shape of a golden calf. It was to be the first of many false gods made by misguided craftspeople throughout Israel's history. These craftspeople prostituted their skills in the making of all manner of idols: everything from simple wood and stone forms to elaborate bejewelled gods of gold and silver. Surely there is a strong note of sarcasm in Israel's identification of the makers of those idols as skilled craftsmen (Is 40:19-20).

Perversion akin to the Israelites' continues into the present day. Today nothing is more distinctive of Western society than an ability to craft things. Other cultures have equaled or exceeded ours in poetry, art* and literature, but none has come close to ours in the making of such a bewildering array of things. These things have become the idol form of materialism, the underlying philosophy of our culture.* The bumper sticker "He who has the most toys when he dies, wins!" is simply declaring the unspoken credo of the dominant religion of our time.

So the turn-of-the-millennium environment presents a special dilemma for Christian craftspeople. How do we remain pure and as dedicated as Bezalel when the products of our employment (to one degree or another) feed the same appetite as Solomon's?

> I denied myself nothing my eyes
> desired;
> I refused my heart no pleasure.
> (Eccles 2:10)

The making of Communion cups and church furnishings surely cannot define the scope of the Christian craftsperson's skills.

There is, of course, no simple answer. One of the things we must do is to keep reminding ourselves that our crafting of things is subordinate to the building of the holy temple of the Lord, the body of Christ. It is a great honor for craftspeople to be the metaphor for that greater reality. Our participation in that spiritual crafting is what will keep the metaphor of our material craftsmanship pure and vital.

The other thing we must do is to heed Jesus' promise "If you remain in me and my words remain in you, ask whatever you wish, and it will be given you" (Jn 15:7). "Walking in the footsteps of Jesus, the carpenter's son," is a phrase we accept as a Christian truism, but there is no question that the closer we keep ourselves to Jesus, the easier it will be to define the line between worthy tasks and unworthy tasks that we will not cross (easier, but never easy!).

An important lesson that Jesus can teach the craftsperson is that nothing is merely a means to another end. All things have some value as an end in themselves. Thus Christian craftspeople must always distinguish themselves from those for whom work and wages are simply necessary evils to procure the necessities of life (hopefully with enough left over for pleasure and material gain). Christian craftspeople must be continually asking Jesus whether the objects they are making can be made to the glory of God and, if they can, challenging themselves to craft them to the very best of their "in-Spirit-ed" skill.

Surely there is merit in Solomon's judgment that there is nothing better for a people than to "find satisfaction in [their] work. This too, I see, is from the hand of God" (Eccles 2:24). But this hope must be purged of Solomon's pessimism. In my experience crafting homes, boats and furniture, there is no better way to do that than to emulate the persona of Wisdom in Proverbs 8. Wisdom is at God's side at the creation of the world, a partner:

I was the craftsman at his side.
I was filled with delight day after day,
    rejoicing always in his presence,
rejoicing in his whole world
    and delighting in mankind.
    (Prov 8:30-31)

This is what it means for the craftsperson to walk in the footsteps of Jesus. True craftsmanship is subcreativity, indeed even cocreativity. That partnership produced the world we live in. Dare we expect some small measure of that divine fulfillment in the things we make?

See also ART; TECHNOLOGY; TRADES; WORK.

References and Resources

R. Banks, *God the Worker: Journey into the Mind, Heart and Imagination of God* (Valley Forge, Penn.: Judson, 1994); E. L. Smith, *The Stones of Craft: The Craftsman's Role in Society* (New York: Oxford University Press, 1981).

Graeme Smith

CREATION

One of the central themes of Christian theology is that God is the Creator of the world. This has a number of important implications for our understanding of the everyday world and our place in it, as well as for our experience of the environment.

God the Creator

Belief in God as Creator has its foundations firmly laid in the Old Testament (e.g., Gen 1—2). The continuing importance of the Old Testament for Christianity is grounded in the fact that the God of which it speaks is the same God revealed in the New Testament. The Creator and the Redeemer God are one and the same. In the past this has been challenged. For example, Gnosticism mounted a vigorous attack on both the authority of the Old Testament and the idea that God was Creator of the world.

Gnosticism, in most of its significant forms, drew a sharp distinction between the God who redeemed humanity from the world and a somewhat inferior deity (often termed the demiurge) who created that world in the first place. The Old Testament was regarded by the Gnostics as dealing with this lesser deity, whereas the New Testament was concerned with the Redeemer God. As a result, belief in God as Creator and in the authority of the Old Testament came to be interlinked at an early stage. Of the early writers to deal with this theme, Irenaeus of Lyons is of particular importance.

Another debate centered on the question of whether creation was to be regarded as ex nihilo ("out of nothing"). In one of his dialogues, the classical Greek philosopher Plato developed the idea that the world was made out of preexistent matter, which was fashioned into the present form of the world. As well as being taken up by most Gnostic writers, this idea was adopted by early

Christian theologians heavily influenced by Platonism, such as Justin Martyr. They professed a belief in preexistent matter, which was shaped into the world in the act of creation.

For these writers, creation was not ex nihilo; rather, it was seen as an act of construction on the basis of material that was already at hand, as one might construct a boat from wood, an igloo out of snow, or a house from stone. The existence of evil in the world was then explained in terms of the difficulties in working with this preexistent matter. God's options in creating the world were limited by the poor quality of the material available. The presence of evil or defects within the world is thus not to be ascribed to God but to deficiencies in the material from which the world was constructed.

In part, however, the idea of creation from preexistent matter was discredited by its Gnostic associations; in part it was called into question by an increasingly sophisticated reading of the creation narratives. Writers such as Theophilus of Antioch insisted upon the doctrine of creation ex nihilo, which became the received doctrine within the church* from the end of the second century. Believing in and relating to God as Creator has several major implications.

Created but Not Divine

We must distinguish between God and the creation. From the earliest times Christian thinkers have resisted the temptation to merge the Creator and the creation. This is clearly stated in the opening chapter of Paul's letter to the Romans, which criticizes the tendency to reduce God to the level of the world. According to Paul, there is a natural human tendency, as a result of sin, to serve created things rather than the Creator (Rom 1:25). A central element in a Christian theology of creation is to distinguish God from the creation while at the same time affirming that it is God's creation.

This process may be seen at work in the writings of Augustine and also in the works of Reformers such as Calvin. The Reformers were concerned to forge a world-affirming spirituality in response to the general monastic tendency to renounce the world that was evident in writings such as Thomas à Kempis's *Imitation of Christ*.

There is a dialectic in Calvin's thought between the world as the creation of God and the world as the fallen creation. In that it is God's creation, it is to be honored, respected and affirmed; in that it is a fallen creation, it is to be criticized with the object of redeeming it. A similar pattern can be discerned in Calvin's doctrine of human nature, where—despite his stress on sin and the Fall—he never loses sight of the fact that it remains God's creation and is to be valued for that reason. This encourages a critical world-affirming spirituality, in which the world is endorsed but not idolized or treated as if it were God.

The importance of this point has been stressed by more recent writers, including Lesslie Newbigin. Elements of creation can easily become demonic, through being invested with the authority and power* which properly belong to God alone. They can come to usurp a place to which they have no right, the place which belongs to Christ and to him alone. They can, as we say, become absolutized, and then they become demonic.

A proper understanding of creation prevents this process of demonization from taking place by insisting that creational elements may be good but are never divine. It thus provides a framework by which we are protected against the usurpation of divine authority by any aspect of the creation—whether it be a person, a set of values* or an institution.

Divine Ownership, Human Stewardship*

Creation implies God's authority over and possession of the world. As the Dutch Reformed theologian Abraham Kuyper once affirmed, "There is not one square inch of creation about which Jesus Christ does not say: 'that is mine.' " We are a part of that creation, with special functions within it. The doctrine of creation leads to the idea of human stewardship of the creation, which is to be contrasted with a secular notion of human ownership* of the world. The creation is not ours; we hold it in trust for God. We are meant to be the stewards of God's creation and are responsible for the manner in which we exercise that stewardship. This insight is of major importance in relation to ecological* and environmental concerns, in that it provides a proper foundation for the exercise of human responsibility toward the planet.

This has important consequences for our everyday behavior. We have been placed within God's creation to tend it and take care of it (Gen 2:15), as we do in gardening,* craftsmanship* and town planning. We may be superior to the rest of the creation and exercise authority over it (Ps 8:4-8), but we remain under the authority of God and so are responsible to the Creator for the way in which we treat the creation. We hold it in trust. There is a growing realization today that past generations have seriously abused that trust by exploiting the creation and its resources. There is a real danger that we will spoil what God so wonderfully created.

Reflecting on our responsibilities as stewards of God's creation is the first step in undoing the harm done by past generations. It matters to God that vast areas of our world have been made uninhabitable through nuclear or toxic chemical waste. It matters that the delicate balance of natural forces is disturbed by human carelessness. Sin affects the way we treat the environment as much as it does our attitude toward God, other people and society* as a whole. This article of the creed is the basis of a new—and overdue—attitude toward creation.

World-Affirming Spirituality

The doctrine of God as Creator implies the goodness of creation. Throughout the first biblical account of creation, we encounter the affirmation "And God saw that it was good" (Gen 1:10, 18, 21, 25, 31). The only thing that is not good is that Adam is alone. There is no place in Christian theology for the Gnostic or dualist idea of the world as an inherently evil place. This is not to say that the creation is presently perfect. The world as we see it is not the world as it was intended to be. Human sin, evil and death are themselves tokens of the extent to which the created order has departed from its intended pattern.

For this reason, most Christian reflections on redemption include some idea of restoring creation to its original integrity, so that God's intentions might find fulfillment. Affirming the goodness of creation also avoids the suggestion that God is responsible for evil. The constant biblical emphasis on the goodness of creation is a reminder that the destructive force of sin is not present in the world by God's design or permission.

Our Worldly Calling*

The doctrine of creation has important implications for our everyday living. It allows us to feel at home in the world. We are here because God wants us to be here. We are not alone but are in the very presence of the God who made and owns everything. We are in the presence of a friend who knows us and cares for us. Behind the apparently faceless universe lies a person.

This conviction calls into question the Western distinction between sacred and secular. To describe one area of our lives (such as teaching a Sunday school*) as sacred and another (such as working in an office) as secular implies that only part of our life is dedicated to God and that only part of the creation belongs to God. In contrast, the Protestant Reformers strongly affirmed the priesthood of all believers and as a corollary the idea of being called to serve God in the world. All Christians are called to be priests to the world, purifying and sanctifying its everyday life from within. Commenting on Genesis 13:13, Luther stated this point succinctly: "What seem to be secular works are actually the praise of God and represent an obedience which is well pleasing to him." Luther extolled the religious value of housework, declaring that although "it had no obvious appearance of holiness, yet these very household chores are more to be valued than all the works of monks and nuns" (see Chores; Homemaking).

Underlying this new attitude is the notion that God calls his people not just to faith but to express that faith in quite definite areas of life in the world. One is called, in the first place, to be a Christian, and in the second, to live out that faith in a quite definite sphere of activity within the world. Whereas medieval monastic spirituality generally regarded the idea of vocation as a calling out of the world into the seclusion and isolation of the monastery, Luther and Calvin understood it as a calling *into* the everyday world. The doctrine of creation thus leads to a strong work ethic,* in the sense that work in the world can be seen as work for God.

Not Our Final Home

Yet this attitude of being at home in the world needs to be qualified. We are to see ourselves as passing through the world, not belonging there permanently. We are, so to put it, tourists rather than residents. In his *Geneva Catechism* Calvin suggests that we should "learn to pass through this world as though it is a foreign country, treating all earthly things lightly and declining to set our hearts upon them." In other words, we are encouraged to enjoy, respect and explore the world—while realizing that it is not our home.

All things that are connected with the enjoyment of the present life are sacred gifts of God. If we abuse them, however, we pollute them. Why? Because we always dream of staying in this world—with the result that those things which were meant to help us pass through it instead become hindrances to us, in that they hold us fast to the world. So it was not without good reason that Paul, wishing to arouse us from this stupidity, calls us to consider the brevity of this life and suggests that we ought to treat all the things of this life as if we did not own them. For if we recognize that we are strangers in the world, we will use the things of this world as if they belong to someone else—that is, as things that are lent to us for a single day.

One of the finest statements of this attitude may be found in Jonathan Edwards's sermon "The Christian Pilgrim," in which he affirms that "it was never designed by God that this world should be our home." Speaking with the eighteenth-century situation in New England in mind, Edwards declared:

> Though surrounded with outward enjoyments, and settled in families with desirable friends and relations; though we have companions whose society is delightful, and children in whom we see many promising qualifications; though we live by good neighbors and are generally beloved where known; yet we ought not to take our rest in these things as our portion. . . .

We ought to possess, enjoy and use them, with no other view but readily to quit them, whenever we are called to it, and to change them willingly for heaven.

Conclusion

Today people speak of "nature" rather than "creation," thus suggesting that our environment is something free-standing to be "used" rather than a sacred trust bearing the stamp of the Creator. Further, many Christians without knowing it are profoundly influenced by Gnosticism. For them working with the stuff of this world, whether through farming* or dealing with stocks and investments,* is less "spiritual" than preaching* and evangelism.* Really "spiritual" people have as little as possible to do with this world. We are in a situation analogous to the one the great Reformers faced. Recovering a biblical view of God as Creator and the world as created will assist us to serve God wholeheartedly in everyday matters. While this world is not our final home, a new heaven and *a new earth* are our ultimate destiny. It has been wisely noted that Christianity is the most materialistic of all faiths.

See also CALLING; CULTURE; ECOLOGY; POLLUTION; WORK.

References and Resources

I. S. Barbour, *Religion in the Age of Science* (New York: Harper & Row, 1990); J. N. Hartt, "Creation and Providence," in *Christian Theology,* ed. P. Hodgson and R. King (Philadelphia: Fortress, 1982); P. J. Hefner, "Creation," in *Christian Dogmatics,* ed. C. E. Braaten and R. W. Jenson (Philadelphia: Fortress, 1984), 1:269-357; R. J. Lyman, *Christology and Cosmology: Models of Divine Activity in Origen, Eusebius and Athanasius* (Oxford: Clarendon, 1993); G. May, "Creatio Ex Nihilo: The Doctrine of Creation Out of Nothing" in *Early Christian Thought* (Edinburgh: T & T Clark, 1995); J. Moltmann, *God in Creation: A New Theology of Creation and the Spirit of God* (San Francisco: Harper & Row, 1985); A. R. Peacocke, *Creation and the World of Science* (Oxford: Clarendon, 1979);

M. Schmaus, *Dogma 2: Creation* (London: Sheed and Ward, 1969); L. White, "The Historical Roots of Our Ecological Crisis," *Science* 155 (1967) 1203-7.

Alister E. McGrath

CREDIT

"Having lost its value, money may no longer be the root of all evil: credit has taken its place." (Dalton Camp, *Saturday Night Magazine*).

Credit is a controversial topic and not just in Christian circles, as the quotation by Dalton Camp illustrates. Nevertheless, credit has become a way of life for most North Americans. In Canada, for instance, there are more VISA cards and MasterCards combined than there are adult Canadians. According to the office of Consumer and Corporate Affairs, credit cards in Canada in 1990 were used for more than a half billion transactions, with interest charges totaling approximately $1 billion.

Attitude Toward Credit

For most people the controversy lies in the *abuse* of credit, but there are some Christians who feel that credit is *inherently* wrong. Those who are strongly opposed to the use of personal credit might say that credit cannot be used wisely, but only with differing degrees of foolishness. A study of the typical criticisms of credit use raises many of the theological dimensions of financial life and stewardship.*

Credit is inherently wrong. One cannot come to a conclusion about the acceptability of credit without first determining the biblical teaching concerning debt. A brief summary follows (*see* Debt).

Two kinds of debt are discussed in Scripture: (1) consumer debt, which was usually associated with some kind of personal misfortune such as crop failure, and (2) commercial investments, where a well-to-do Israelite might get involved with a traveling merchant.

With respect to the first kind of indebtedness, God's people were to be generous in meeting the needs of covenant brothers and sisters (see, for example, Deut 15:7-10; Mt 5:42). Israelites with means were to lend whatever was needed to the poor to fend off temporary misfortune and to restore the borrower and his family to financial stability. No interest (usury) was to be charged, and insignificant collateral was to be demanded. Borrowers were obliged under normal circumstances to repay their debts. However, if a debt* remained unpaid by the sabbatical year, it was to be forgiven. As was typical with all aspects of the covenant relationship, no one's poverty* was to be taken advantage of by better-off Israelites (Is 5:8).

Commercial debt is hardly mentioned at all. Israel was an agrarian nation and little involved with commercial life. However, such transactions were permitted, and unlike the case of poor covenant brothers and sisters, interest could be charged. Israelites were warned of the dangers of being in debt to another who might well exploit them (Prov 22:7).

To summarize, debt was not inherently evil but could be dangerous if the moneylenders were unscrupulous, as they often were. The purpose of consumer debt was not to cater to self-indulgence but rather to ease a person through temporary misfortune and to restore the family unit to stability. Debts were forgivable at legislated intervals (that is, every sabbatical year) to achieve some higher purpose, such as the preservation of the family unit.

Credit is a temptation to materialism. A further criticism of credit is that its easy availability is a temptation to make purchases one cannot afford at this time, or do not really need at all. Businessman

and author Jake Barnett puts it very well: "Credit's main function is to serve materialism" (Barnett, p. 164). Doubtless this is an astute observation. North Americans have realized an increasing standard of living over the past many decades. But with that improving standard has come a greater readiness to take on a larger debt burden. Levels of consumer credit have exploded since the early 1950s. Much of this, of course, is attributable to population growth and inflation. But with these effects removed (in other words, when indebtedness is measured in *constant* as opposed to *current* dollars), we are still vastly more prepared than our grandparents were to use, and abuse, credit in larger and larger amounts. In Canada, for instance, per capita increase in the use of credit between 1950 and 1985 was fivefold using constant dollars.

An analysis of consumer bankrupts done by Consumer and Corporate Affairs of Canada in 1982 revealed much disturbing data about the abuse of credit. First, consumer bankrupts tended to be younger than the adult population generally. About 63 percent of these bankrupt individuals were under age 35, a disproportionate number as only 43 percent of Canadians were in this age group. Only 8 percent of consumer bankrupts were age 50 or older. Second, a disproportionate number of personal bankrupts lacked employable skills. Managerial and professional people represented 9.8 percent of the Canadian labor force, but only 2.9 percent of consumer bankrupts. At the other end of the spectrum, unskilled clerical, sales and service personnel and unskilled manual labor constituted 23.4 percent of employees but a whopping 38.8 percent of those who declared personal bankruptcy. Third, and most important for our purposes, the major cause of personal bankruptcy was consumer debt.

The median indebtedness of those in the study was $10,865, while median assets were about $400. A breakdown of their creditors is rather interesting. Finance and insurance companies were the major source of credit (74 percent of bankrupts owed these institutions at least one debt), followed by Canadian chartered banks (61 percent), department stores and other retailers (46 percent and 41 percent, respectively) and bank credit cards (30 percent of bankrupts reported money* owing on such cards).

A senior employee of an accounting firm specializing in bankruptcies addressed this issue of why younger people who lack good occupational skills and financial prospects are so prepared to burden themselves with consumer debt.

Bankruptcy is very much an attitudinal thing, a commitment to one's obligations. It takes very little to be technically in a situation of going bankrupt.... Many use bankruptcy as a tool to avoid paying debts, especially younger people who believe that they have the right to a certain standard of living without putting out for it. (Sutherland, p. 51)

In summary, we have fueled the rising standard of living with greater and greater amounts of consumer credit. Clearly we are not content to live at the level of previous generations, nor are we prepared to improve our standard strictly through earnings. While income levels have increased in recent decades, debt burden has increased even more. Being able to afford more material things has given many a hunger for an even greater accumulation of goods than can be provided through earnings. Credit as an impetus to materialism is wrong.

To be truly effective, a Christian must be debt free. While this statement sounds plausible, it does ignore the fact that for many, many North Americans the wise use of credit in its various forms has put them on the road to long-term stability and effectiveness in their families, careers, churches and communities. Had I not taken out student loans, I might have avoided a level of indebtedness for some time, but I would have never graduated from either university or seminary. Were it not for my mortgage, I would never have owned a home. Most businesses have relied at least in part on credit to get started or to meet short-term working capital and long-term expansion requirements. The careful use of credit can be a tool toward long-term effectiveness. But the many perils associated with the use of credit must be avoided.

We have established that while credit can be greatly abused, it is not inherently wrong. Used wisely, credit can be a highly effective tool in establishing long-term stability for a family or a business. The issue that remains then is how to use credit properly.

The Right Use of Credit

Incurring debt is a decision to pay for something you bought in the past, rather than saving in order to buy something in the future. Given the cost of credit charges, it usually makes better financial sense to save. However, there are important exceptions, such as purchasing a home or financing an income-producing asset. Therefore, principles concerning how and when credit should be used must be established.

Setting your own credit limits. Merchants are always happy for customers to use credit. Over half of retail sales are made this way. Credit often provides a tie between a merchant and a customer if a person is using the store's credit card, charge account or installment contract. Consequently, the last place to which you should look for advice in setting your own credit limits is the institution granting the credit. Lenders consider two things when granting any particular level of credit: your total earnings and your other debts. They never ask you what your personal financial objectives are. Unfortunately, many Christians have not taken the time to set such objectives either. This must come first! How is it done?

First, Christians must see their financial resources as gifts from God with which they have been entrusted (*see* Stewardship). Too many Christians assign this view strictly to the tithe (not that most Christians actually tithe, but that is another story). It is pointless to talk of financial objectives without first accepting that our resources are from God's hand and that we are accountable to God for their use. This attitude provides a check on materialistic impulses.

Second, calculate net family income, that is, total gross family income minus all the usual deductions plus other costs of earning that income, such as day care, necessary additional clothing, running a car and so on. Then basic necessities of life must be calculated, for example, mortgage or rent payments, utilities, groceries, clothing and so on. As Christians, we should consider a regular schedule of offerings to further the work of God's kingdom as part of these necessities. All long-term savings needs must be considered as well. These include investments and capital goods, such as a car or a down payment on a home. Noncapital purchases can be anticipated and saved for also, for example, property taxes, Christmas presents and this year's family vacation.

Finally, ask yourself how much money you can afford to take out of your net family earnings to pay back credit charges that will in no way hinder meeting your financial objectives. This constitutes your personal credit limit.

Deciding what kind of credit to use. This is a complex subject, and the reader is urged to consult the many fine books on the subject of personal finances, including those written from a biblical perspective. Such books are legion. A visit to any decent bookstore will reveal dozens of books on personal finance often tailored to specific situations. What follows are a few brief remarks about some of the most common forms of credit.

The most significant debt that most borrowers will ever experience is a mortgage. Aside from interest rates, features of mortgages vary greatly from lender to lender, for example, how much can be prepaid without an interest penalty. Do not limit your comparison shopping* to the interest charged. In addition to the purchase of a home, income-producing assets may rightly be purchased on credit, especially if the interest on the loan is deductible from the taxable income generated.

Items that do not appreciate in value offer fewer advantages as credit purchases. The consumer must weigh the advantages and disadvantages of purchasing via credit, in order to have immediate use of these goods, versus postponing the purchase until sufficient savings are accumulated.

As far as credit cards* are concerned, it is best to limit the number you possess because multiple cards only increase the credit limit your lenders have decided is yours and because their availability increases the likelihood of impulse purchasing. In addition, use them only when you can repay the charge within the interest-free period. If you are unable to do this, then you should resort to a cheaper consumer loan from your bank. As with mortgages, shopping around for bank loans is highly recommended. Terms differ greatly.

Conclusion

Credit is often wrong—when it is an impetus to materialism or when it undermines carefully thought through financial objectives. But like many other aspects of material life, credit is amoral. It can be used wisely, or it can be abused. The challenge to the Christian is to see credit in its proper context—as one way of utilizing the resources with which God has entrusted us.

See also CREDIT CARD; DEBT; INVESTMENT; MONEY; STEWARDSHIP; WEALTH.

References and Resources
J. Barnett, *Wealth and Wisdom: A Biblical Perspective on Possessions* (Colorado Springs: NavPress, 1987); J. R. Sutherland, *Going Broke: Bankruptcy, Business Ethics and the Bible* (Waterloo, Ont.: Herald, 1991).

John R. Sutherland

CREDIT CARD

More than half of North Americans have a credit card in their wallet or purse. It is a handy way to obtain consumer credit* for the purchase of goods or services without carrying cash or making payments instantly, especially while traveling. This American innovation became popular in 1938, when oil companies set up a national system to honor one another's cards for the purchase of gasoline. But it was not until the 1950s, with the development of the computer,* that credit cards became almost universal, since this new technology* permitted accurate and fast accounting. The *debit card,* a variation on this, instantly withdraws the money from one's bank accounts and does not extend the usual thirty-day credit. Credit cards produce profits to the institution granting them by direct user fees, by high interest rates on unpaid balances and through payments from retail establishments, or some combination of these. Many cards now offer further incentives by giving points that can be redeemed for airline travel (*see* Traveling) and penalizing, so

it seems, the use of cash or checks.

As with all forms of credit, the credit card is based on the trust expressed in an individual by a bank or lender. The word *credit* comes from a Latin root meaning "faith" or "trust." An individual's credit rating is a measure of trust placed in him or her by a financial institution. Thus, the process of getting and maintaining a credit card is a form of financial testing, proving that one is a reliable person who will pay his or her bills. As with all forms of credit, this one facilitates the transfer of money in a way that increases its productivity by placing it where it will work. At the same time it economizes on the use of currency.

As with many technological advances, the use of credit cards has changed the way we live and think. We now carry "plastic money." We can make large purchases quickly without a penny in our pockets or guarantee a hotel room halfway around the world by simply using our number. Instead of providing a large cash deposit to guarantee a car rental, we simply use the line of credit provided with the card.

But there are several disadvantages. It is well known that credit cards make theft and fraud quite simple. The more serious problems are less obvious. We no longer have to wait,* for we can buy it now, even if we are not carrying cash. We can "afford" it because we have thirty days to pay, even if we do not have the money in the bank ("It will come!"). It is undeniable that easy credit feeds consumerism* and stimulates impulse buying. Many people are tempted to live beyond their means, accumulating debt* beyond their ability to repay. Young people in particular are tempted to abuse credit and are filing for bankruptcy in distressing numbers.

So the use of a credit card is in one sense a test of our maturity. Put differently, it is an invitation to grow to an increasing maturity. We can do this by determining not to make purchases unless we actually have the money or a clear and workable plan for repayment of the debt (*see* Credit; Debt). We can reduce the number of credit cards we have to one or two to resist spreading credit—really debt—over multiple institutions. Further, we can take our credit-card invoices as statements not only of purchases made but values held and carefully reflect on how we should exercise stewardship* by preparing a budget and living by it. The last place we should look for help in setting our own credit limit is the institution granting it. Sometimes it is good to fast from credit-card buying, as my wife and I have done, and to use only cash. This gives us a more accurate experience of the flow of money through our hands.

The book of Proverbs speaks to the use of money and credit. It takes wisdom from God to possess money without being possessed by it (Prov 1:17-19). Without wisdom we can have wealth* but no true friends, food on the table but no fellowship around it, a house but not a home, the ability to buy things but no financial freedom. Without wisdom we will use a credit card to indulge ourselves (Prov 21:17) and still never be satisfied (Prov 27:20; 30:15-16). Credit card in hand, the unwise person "chases fantasies" (Prov 28:19) and so comes to ruin, but the wise, accumulating as stewards "little by little" (Prov 13:11), "will be richly blessed" (Prov 28:20). It takes wisdom to have a credit card and not be possessed by the power in our pockets.

See also CONSUMERISM; CREDIT; DEBT; MONEY; SHOPPING; SHOPPING MALL; STEWARDSHIP; WEALTH.

References and Resources
R. N. Baird, "Credit Card," in *The Encyclopedia Americana* (Danbury, Conn.: Grolier, 1989) 8:166-67; J. Barnett, *Wealth and Wisdom: A Bib-*

lical Perspective on Possessions (Colorado Springs: NavPress, 1987).

R. Paul Stevens

CRIME

It seems we cannot watch the local news without being confronted by some senseless act of random violence. A young child is killed in the crossfire of a gangland drug war. A number of people die, and others are seriously injured, when a lone gunman goes on a shooting rampage in a fast-food restaurant. A serial rapist strikes again. Is violent crime out of control in American society? Can such acts be explained, and if so, how? Is the public concern about crime justified or exaggerated? How can crime be controlled?

Extent and Cost of Crime
Based on police reports, the FBI estimates that about 14 million crimes in eight major categories were committed in 1993, over 85 percent of which were nonviolent. This amounts to about six crimes per 100 persons, up only slightly since 1975 after increasing almost threefold between 1960 and 1975. National surveys of crime victims suggest that the actual crime rate is about twice that recorded by the FBI. This would mean that the average person becomes a crime victim about once every eight years.

There are about 25,000 murders annually in the United States, and contrary to popular conceptions shaped by the media,* the overall murder rate has increased only modestly in recent years. In 1991 almost twice as many persons died from traffic accidents as from murder. The lifetime probability that you or I will be a murder victim is less than 1 percent.

Other statistics on violent crime give more cause for concern. The United States has the highest murder rate among industrialized countries, about four times the average. Violence is most prevalent among persons 15-25 years old, and a new "baby boomlet" generation promises to increase the ranks of this age category in the near future. Other forms of violent crime continue to be on the rise.

Estimates of the cost of crime vary widely, depending on what kinds of losses are considered. For example, estimates of the recent annual cost of personal street crime range from $17 billion by the FBI to over $90 billion when such things as medical expenses, lost wages, and pain and suffering are taken into account (Conklin, p. 77). The costs of more sophisticated types of crime seem to run considerably higher. Estimates related to various white-collar crimes, including embezzlement, fraud, antitrust violations and environmental pollution, range from $50 billion to over $200 billion annually. A similar range of estimates is available for the cost of various so-called victimless crimes, such as illicit drug* use, illegal gambling* and prostitution. Some estimates indicate that the cost of income-tax evasion by individual taxpayers may easily run in excess of $100 billion. The cost of running the criminal justice system at all levels exceeded $50 billion in the mid-1980s.

These estimates of prevalence and cost have some interesting implications. When the violent element of street crime is removed, the public seems to be more disturbed about personal property crime, such as burglary and auto theft, than about the much more expensive "crime in the suites," whose cost is hidden in higher taxes and the prices we all pay for goods and services in the marketplace. Moreover, as tragic as 25,000 murders a year may be, this statistic is dwarfed simply by the mayhem we commit on our highways. Yet we seem to want more capital punishment but higher speed limits. Our wants suggest the need for a better understanding of the problem we seem to fear so much.

Understanding Crime

The most popular explanations of crime seem to focus on the individual offender. Some hereditary factor, some type of psychological disturbance or some internalized tendency to respond to environmental rewards is seen as the major factor underlying the so-called criminal personality. Though I grant that some of these explanations have merit, they usually provide little hope for altering the behavior of criminal offenders. We do not yet possess adequate knowledge to alter a person's basic biological makeup. Psychological therapy is typically very expensive, and success rates are problematic. Reward or reinforcement theories may operate well in highly controlled environments like prisons but are impossible to implement fully in the broader context of a free society.

The appeal of most of these theories seems to lie in the assumption that the causes of crime are located within the individual offender. This gives the rest of us license to absolve ourselves from any responsibility for the crime problem and to support get-tough policies that offer illusory quick fixes.

Theories that rely on significant features of the social environment to explain crime offer more adequate explanations, especially for those crimes whose incidence varies considerably from society to society. One of these, known as strain theory, proposes that crime rates will be high in a society that instills strong aspirations of success in its members but does not provide adequate means for the attainment of these goals on the part of large segments of its population (Merton, pp. 185-214). Those who cannot achieve legitimately will be highly tempted to rely on illegitimate means, such as crime. One version of this theory, known as relative deprivation theory, contends that crime rates will be especially high in poor inner-city areas that are in close proximity to extremely affluent areas. When the poor in these areas are confronted with their deprivation on a daily basis, they become increasingly frustrated and hostile. A collective sense of injustice develops, which tends to direct the frustration into various forms of profitable crime, such as drug trafficking, and the hostility into various types of violence.

Control theory also considers the impact of the social environment, using the concept of an individual's bonds to society. Crime is more likely to occur when these bonds are weak, for then crime is usually a more efficient way to achieve one's ends. T. Hirschi identifies four major elements of the social bond as attachment to others, commitment to conventional pursuits, involvement in conventional activities and belief in the validity of moral rules. By making effective use of these bonds, a society can effectively keep crime under control. Typically this involves using multiple control mechanisms so that if one bond fails, other bonds can take up the slack. For example, an adolescent* who is doing well in school and sees the possibility of a bright future is unlikely to become seriously delinquent even if he or she has conflicts with parents.

Finally, cultural transmission theory is based on the thesis that criminal behavior is learned as people absorb cultural definitions (norms, values,* attitudes, etc.) that are favorable to crime from others with whom they identify. D. Cressey contends that imprisonment is an ineffective way to reform criminals because it puts a person in intimate contact with others who reinforce attitudes favorable to crime. An alternative would be to relocate the person into a group that upholds anticriminal values. Cressey is simply proposing that efforts at criminal reform would be much more effective if groups for criminals existed that functioned in a manner similar to the way Alcoholics Anonymous does for alcoholics. Unfortunately, such groups are few and far between.

Controlling Crime

Criminal justice has been one of our most innovative social institutions. One recent effort at crime control is based on a study by M. Wolfgang and associates, who studied arrest records of roughly 10,000 males born in Philadelphia in 1945. Seventy percent of serious felonies were attributed to only 6 percent of the sample. This has inspired some law enforcement agencies to develop repeat-offender programs that target chronic offenders for surveillance, apprehension and conviction using special police units. This effort may be accompanied by habitual-offender laws that allow life sentences to be given to repeat offenders ("three strikes and you're in").

Supporters of these programs contend that their slightly higher costs result in a significant drop in the crime rate as the most chronic offenders are incapacitated for long periods. Others argue that the sting operations that often accompany chronic-offender programs actually increase crime rates by providing more outlets for stolen or illegal goods. There are also dangers in habitual-offender laws. In particular, they are sometimes applied to amateur criminals who commit a series of minor offenses. Whether such potential injustices can be minimized by fine-tuning the programs is a matter of much debate.

Another recent development involves efforts to revive the biblical concept of restitution. C. Colson and D. Benson contend that under our traditional justice system victims are doubly exploited—first by the criminal offender and second by the additional tax* burden that finances expensive correctional programs. Restitution reduces this burden by requiring the offender to compensate the victim for losses. Compensated victims will in turn be more supportive of social policies designed to help offenders reintegrate into the community. Ideally, offenders will identify with their victims' losses as they suffer a similar loss through providing compensation. If restitution can accomplish these ends, reconciliation between victim and offender, perhaps even between offender and society, might eventually be possible.

Though restitution has a number of advantages, it is difficult to implement because of the low level of job skills and high unemployment* rates among the vast majority of offenders. Given these limitations, the use of restitution and other similar innovations (for example, work release) is not likely to increase significantly until more fundamental changes occur in our economic system.

In general, sociological theories suggest that prospects for reducing the overall crime rate through alterations limited to criminal justice itself are meager. Crime seems to be primarily a product of at least three trends:

1. The importance of materialism in a period when differentials in wealth* and income seem to be increasing. Youth from economically disadvantaged families typically lack opportunities to acquire the educational skills needed to compete successfully in the job market. Thus poverty* is easily transferred from one generation to the next.

2. The decreased effectiveness of traditional agents of social control. An increasing breakdown of family* life and the transient character of most urban areas are weakening major bonds of attachment that serve to deter crime.

3. A growing emphasis on value pluralism* that threatens the moral climate necessary for a free society. Key institutions, such as education* and the media, fail to take responsibility for promoting such a climate in the name of "value neutrality" and "adult realism."

It is easy to become pessimistic concerning the prospects for crime control when we consider what would be required to reverse such trends. We might, for example, try to deemphasize affluence as a social value so that deprivations felt by the poorer segments of American society would be less extreme. However, this is a difficult task at best given an economic system whose well-being is dependent on a continually expanding market. Any realistic efforts to deemphasize materialism, such as controls on media advertising,* would meet strong opposition from the "powers" of our age (Eph 6:12).

Still, there are many ways to ameliorate the crime problem. Families need to create stronger bonds of attachment with children as the basis for consistent, loving discipline. Churches can increase their efforts to strengthen and support the family by providing affordable daycare centers for single working mothers along with various youth activities that emphasize values as well as recreation. Corporations can indirectly support the family by allowing workers more options with regard to part-time employment,* family leave and telecommuting. They can also promote employment policies that do not discriminate against ex-offenders.

In general, American society needs to strike a better balance between punishment for criminal offenders and their reintegration into the community. While Scripture recognizes a need for punishment in order to control human lawlessness (1 Pet 2:14), it also recognizes the need to forgive and restore the penitent (Lk 17:3-4; 2 Cor 2:5-10; Gal 6:1). For all our talk about being "too soft on crime," in the final analysis our major problem may be that we are not soft enough. Certainly the message of the cross assures us that God's program for human redemption is designed not to condemn but to reconcile and restore (Lk 1:49-55; Heb 12:5-11). Out of thanksgiving for our own redemption, and guided by a faith that this promise will one day be fulfilled, let us seek to become instruments through which the vision can begin to become a present reality.

See also DRUGS; JUSTICE; LAW; LAW ENFORCEMENT; POVERTY; UNEMPLOYMENT.

References and Resources

C. Colson and D. Benson, "Restitution as an Alternative to Imprisonment," *Detroit College of Law Review* 6 (1980) 523-98; J. Conklin, *Criminology* (5th ed.; Boston: Allyn & Bacon, 1995); D. Cressey, "Changing Criminals: The Application of the Theory of Differential Association," *American Journal of Sociology* 61 (1955) 116-20; Federal Bureau of Investigation, *Crime in the United States, 1993: Uniform Crime Reports* (Washington, D.C.: U.S. Government Printing House, 1994); T. Hirschi, *Causes of Delinquency* (Berkeley: University of California Press, 1969); R. Merton, *Social Theory and Social Structure* (enl. ed.; New York: Free Press, 1968); M. Wolfgang et al., *Delinquency in a Birth Cohort* (Chicago: University of Chicago Press, 1972).

Donald Gray

CROWDS

In their attraction to so-called newsworthy events, modern mass media* have heightened our awareness of crowds and their unpredictable behavior. Mass fights at soccer matches, demonstrations that turn violent and riots in urban areas are some of the many contemporary examples of crowds gone out of control. But crowds are not a strictly modern phenomenon. They were instrumental in the events surrounding the birth of the New Testament church. Jesus viewed the crowds to whom he ministered as "sheep without a shepherd" (Mt 9:36). The Pharisees manipulated the fickle crowds in Jerusalem to coerce Pilate to crucify Jesus (Mt 27:20). Pentecost was also a crowd event, chosen by the Spirit as an occasion for the first public declaration of Jesus' resurrection (Acts 2). Crowds have played an important role in religious revivals throughout church history.

A crowd is simply a gathering of people whose attention is temporarily focused on a shared concern. Gustave LeBon believed that crowds possess a common mind and are highly emotional and irrational. In this state, the veneer of civilized restraints is easily peeled away, exposing our baser natures and creating a situation in which radical impulses are highly contagious. In reality, most crowds are peaceful and rational. Yet crowds exhibit a capacity for suggestibility that is very understandable when one grasps the essentials of how they differ from other social groupings.

Most permanent groups that interact face to face are small and tend to develop a rich variety of behavioral controls. Crowds are usually large, and this seems to create a critical mass of emotionality, especially when certain highly charged events that are either tragic (someone is killed) or joyful (your team wins) occur. Crowds also lack the density of restraints prevalent in other gatherings. Crowd members usually have not developed common expectations regarding behavior, except perhaps for vague notions of politeness and self-restraint. These weak norms are easily overwhelmed by the press of events. It is not difficult to see how crowds are easily provoked, swayed and manipulated.

H. Blumer has identified several types of crowds. *Conventional crowds,* such as concert audiences, are typically restrained because the events they experience are preplanned and include mechanisms (formal and latent) for crowd management. They can become *expressive crowds* when emotions* are aroused, resulting in unrestrained behavior that can take a destructive turn. Charismatic figures such as rock stars may generate the necessary spark. Most dangerous is the *acting crowd,* which has a goal beyond just celebrating the moment. Demonstrations of various types fall into this category. These can become violent when an extreme sense of urgency emerges or when the goals of the demonstration are denounced or threatened. Sometimes the ensuing events belie the values of the demonstrators, as when peace advocates throw rocks at police or a prolife sit-in results in the murder of a prochoice physician.

Christians who feel called to profess their faith through mass demonstrations need to be aware of the pitfalls of crowd behavior. Chances that these events will proceed "in a fitting and orderly way" (1 Cor 14:40) are maximized when organizers provide appropriate training for volunteers, screen out highly volatile elements, give sufficient attention to details and contingencies in planning, and cooperate with management efforts by public officials. In our times, such precautions might even be considered as an extension of our spiritual armor (Eph 6:11).

See also CIVIL DISOBEDIENCE; CIVILITY; PUBLIC SPACES; SPORTS.

References and Resources

H. Blumer, "Collective Behavior," in *Principles of Sociology,* ed. A. M. Lee (3d ed.; New York: Barnes & Noble, 1969) 65-121; G. LeBon, *The Crowd: A Study of the Popular Mind* (New York: Viking, 1976).

Donald Gray

CULTURE

Culture in the broadest sense is everything that people do with creation.* It refers to the little worlds we make (through our own creativity in work,* play* and daily relationships) out of God's creation. That broad sense of the word is almost too big to think about, but it overarches two other more common and restricted meanings.

High, Folk and Popular Culture

One of those other meanings is expressed in the term *high culture.* It is implied when we refer to going to the symphony as "taking in a little culture" or when we describe someone as "refined and cultured." High culture describes the most honored of the works and ways of a civilization, the sorts of things we enshrine today in concert halls and art galleries, or promote through liberal arts education.

The other way we use the word *culture* is to describe all of the unique patterns of behavior of a particular people or society.* We say that an American living in China for a year is likely to experience "culture shock" until becoming adjusted or "enculturated"; we speak of the value of preserving local cultures, and so forth. Culture in this sense refers not to the works of specialized producers of high culture (musicians, poets, painters, actors) but to the unique flavor of a particular people's way of life. Often this other meaning of culture is called *folk culture.*

So we would seem to be left with a clear distinction: *folk culture* refers to what everyone does simply by being human; *high culture* refers to what a relatively small number of practitioners—with unusual talent—produce for the enlightenment or entertainment of the rest. And *popular culture* is something midway between high and folk though overlapping with both.

But that distinction between high culture and folk culture breaks down after a little reflection. It is the product of a relatively recent tendency to fragment and specialize. Today we think of Shakespeare's plays as high culture, but in Queen Elizabeth's time they were also popular culture, appreciated by aristocrat and beggar alike. To go further back, today we regard the everyday product of a primitive people—say a decorated bowl or a woven carpet—as high culture and place it in a museum as an object for contemplation. For our own bowls and carpets, we buy mass-produced utilitarian items that seem to have little of culture about them. When we want culture we go to the museum.

In the same way music*—which once was a part of everyone's life—has become the specialized work of a few. When we want music we go to a concert or (much more often) turn on the radio* or play a tape or CD. (Christian worship* is a notable exception. Church* is almost the only place in our society where large numbers of average people make music together. But even that communal music-making is sometimes threatened by a tendency to regard church as a religious high-culture concert and, more recently, by the ease with which we can replace live singers and players with a taped "track.")

Much of what we today think of as high culture is, therefore, either the result of everyday works of skill and creativity taken from their place in normal life and elevated as objects of contemplation—or else the work of specialized practioners of "culture" who are isolated from, and in some tension with, the needs and tastes of the cross-section of people who (a few centuries ago) would all have appreciated a play by Shakespeare.

So although it is a good thing to admire, enjoy and learn from the high points of culture, a Christian reflection on culture must begin much closer to home. Culture is neither the high culture of an educated elite nor the folk idiosyncrasies of a particular people, but the whole world which we make, as a kind of secondary creation, out of creation.

Of all creatures, human beings are unique in their dependence on this cultural world. To be sure, other animals, and even insects (such as ants, bees and termites), build shelters and environments, even seem to have rudimentary rituals and traditions. But those animal premonitions of culture are dwarfed by the infinitely complex and constantly growing human world. Cooking, clothing, commerce, poetry, pottery, politics,* architecture,* astronomy, astrology—all of these, both frivolous and essential, are part of culture, and part of our humanity.

Considered from a strictly biological viewpoint, human culture makes up for the fact that human beings seem, physically speaking, curiously fragile and illprepared for the world. We lack the built-in protection of fur and feathers; we are not well armed with teeth and claws; we have neither the rabbit's speed, the wolf's keen nose, the eagle's acuity of sight, the spider's web-building instinct, nor the honeybee's built-in social organization. As Friedrich Nietzsche observed, man is "the unfinished animal," required, in a sense, to complete himself in order even to survive. That "completion"—in endless varieties of houses,* languages, governments,* forms of art* and entertainment*—is the world of human culture. Its necessity for human life is glaringly evident in the fact that whereas any other creature can function on its own in (at most) a matter of months, human babies require years of patient teaching and learning how to fit into the human world of language, manners, raincoats and street crossings, before they can even survive.

Biblical Perspective on Culture

The biologist considers human nature

mainly from the lowest level: what it shares with other organisms. From that viewpoint, culture is simply another of the endless variations allowing an organism to pass on its genes to the next generation. But what happens when we look at culture from the highest level—in light of God's revelation in Scripture, and in the whole Christian story and tradition?

Christian Scripture does not often speak of culture in itself. This silence should not be surprising; like water to a fish, culture is normally invisible. The human world of near-Eastern culture—and later the culture of the Greco-Roman world in the New Testament—is simply assumed as the setting for the story of God's works. We should no more expect the Bible to reflect on culture in itself than we would expect it to reflect on Hebrew or Greek vocabulary.

But Scripture is concerned with the story of God's purposes in creation, the way that human beings have set themselves against those purposes and the way God has provided for bringing us back to them. Since human culture is either a way to further God's purpose or a way to turn against it, the Bible has much to say about culture. When the cultural worlds we make become idolatrous or, on the other hand, when they further the glory of creation and Creator, the Bible is not silent. In such a setting it is no surprise that culture in itself is sometimes spoken of positively but also, at least as often, negatively. Nor should it be surprising that Christians in different times and situations have tended to stress one set of texts about culture at the expense of another, with the result that the Scriptural ambivalence about culture has manifested itself in a variety of Christian understandings.

The place to start in thinking about the Bible and culture is our place in creation. As important here as the obvious Genesis passages are those places in Scripture where we see a community of people using all its human gifts to worship God. The central clue to the purpose of culture is found as much in psalms like 148, 149 and 150 as in Genesis 1 and 2. For example, Psalm 148 makes clear that a central purpose of all creatures is praise, and *all* creatures—sun, moon, snow, clouds, mountains, cedars, birds—are told to "praise the Lord." In this creationly chorus, human beings—kings and nations, young men and maidens, old men and children—are invited to join in with their praise. The place of culture in this is more obvious in the next two psalms: we humans are to "praise God with dancing," to "make music to him with tambourine and harp." "Let everything that has breath praise the LORD," writes the psalmist, and he is explicit about many of the works of human culture—dance, song, harp, lyre, trumpet, cymbals, flute, strings.

Gerard Manley Hopkins, a nineteenth-century Catholic poet, reflected eloquently on the unique place human beings have in the creation's overall task to give God glory.

"The heavens declare the glory of God." They glorify God. *But they do not know it.* The birds sing to him, the thunder speaks of his terror, the lion is like his strength, the sea is like his greatness, the honey like his sweetness . . . but they do not know they do, they do not know him, they never can. . . . This then is poor praise, faint reverence, slight service, dull glory. Nevertheless, what they can do *they always do.* (*Sermons,* p. 239)

Human beings, though, says Hopkins, are different. They have a choice. They can praise God with their God-given selves or choose not to. "Man was made to give, and meant to give, God glory." This "meaning to give God glory" is a uniquely human task and privilege, and it is the *ideal* of human culture: a world of governments, music, families,* farms* and cities* which amplifies and articulates, through human will and purpose, creation's thanks to the Creator.

A great deal of Christian thinking about culture has been rooted in this ideal, as it appears in Genesis 1 and 2. In Genesis 1 the act of creation is described in its variety and goodness. Then humans, "male and female," are created "in the image of God" and given a task. In Genesis 1 that task is described with the words *rule* and *subdue*. They are harsh words, and they leave no doubt about the high place humans have in creation: we have the job of making a world out of God's earth. In the Reformed tradition this job has often been called "the cultural mandate," the basic agenda for human civilization.

Others (both within and without the Christian faith) have noted the deadly ease with which we interpret *rule* and *subdue* into *enslave* and *exploit*. The culturing, world-making powers which we have been given are, in sinful people, all too likely to be used to build up our own little kingdoms at the expense of all people and things outside them.

So it is important to understand the cultural mandate in terms not only of Genesis 1 but of Genesis 2 as well. Here God the Creator is described not only as the transcendent Voice but also as the immanent and involved One, molding the human being (Adam) from the dust of the earth *(adamah)*, that is, getting his hands dirty in creation. Out of this different picture of God's involvement with creation comes a different picture of human culture. Adam is placed in Eden to "keep" the Garden and to "care for" it (the Hebrew word also means "serve"). Whatever "rule" and "dominion" implies in Genesis 1 for the cultural mandate, it must be compatible with this "care" and

"keeping" in Genesis 2.

The first cultural task which human beings were given was thus gardening.* And gardening—nurturing other creatures with care and wisdom into their fullest flower and fruit—is perhaps the best metaphor for culture. But we are called to garden not only plants and animals but all things. (The word *culture* after all is also used to describe the skill of making things grow, a connection which still remains in "agri*culture*.")

These are only hints. They are spelled out more in the only job we see the unfallen Adam do, naming the creatures. God the Creator watches Adam with divine curiosity "to see what he would name them; and whatever the man called each living creature, that was its name." Naming is basic to culture. It is not mere labeling, but rather involves a sympathetic understanding, so that the human word becomes a kind of articulation of what the creature is. Human naming gives a voice to other creatures and thus is a kind of model for culture at large. Naming, language, lies at the foundation of both science and art.

Yet the human story is of sin. All too often our culturing is dominion only—for our sake, not for the sake of the garden, whether that "garden" be spouse, friend or forest.

Differing Christian Attitudes to Culture

So the history of human culture and of Christian thinking about it is a complex and checkered affair. A classic study of the attitudes toward culture is Richard Niebuhr's *Christ and Culture*. He lays out various ways Christians have thought about culture that are helpful in understanding where we have come from. Roughly, these are listed below in the order in which they have gained prominence historically; but each has been present in every age, and each (Niebuhr suggests) can be supported by Scripture and can tell us something about how we ought to be in the world.

The rejection of culture. From the beginning there have been those who have felt the radical difference between the kingdom of God and the kingdoms of this world. We are called, they say, to "come out from among them and be separate" and to "love not the world, neither what is in the world." Out of this attitude of radical separation have come, over the centuries, a variety of Christian traditions. The early church was deeply aware that its loyalty was to Christ, not Caesar, and refusal to bow to the might of Roman culture—and its prime symbol, the emperor—drew many Christians to a martyr's death. Later, the monastic tradition led many to turn their back on a corrupt and decaying culture and to seek a life of prayer or service. After the Reformation, many Christians felt that the Reformers had not gone far enough, had failed to recognize the degree to which the church was still an arm of government.* They rejected the idea that all people in a nation were Christians simply by virtue of their baptism* and argued for an adult baptism as a symbol of withdrawal from a culture which forced people into sin—such as service in the military. Their emphasis was on forming separate communities as witnesses to the "New Way," the gospel.

This Mennonite or Anabaptist tradition continues to have great appeal, although it is increasingly difficult to maintain a total separation from the surrounding culture. A more widespread tendency has been to regard certain cultural practices—dancing, movies, drinking, card-playing (the forbidden activities have varied from century to century)—as symbolic of the world, and loyalty to Christ has been equated with refraining from those activities.

When we look at the whole biblical story, it seems clear that a rich cultural life in a real world—of families, governments, farming, feasting, storytelling,* music and dance—is never rejected. It is assumed to be the substance of holiness, not its opposite. In his letter to Titus (2:11-14), Paul writes that "the grace of God that brings salvation . . . teaches us to say no." But the "no" is not to life in the world; it is rather to ungodliness and worldly passions. We are advised instead "to live self-controlled, upright and godly lives in this present age," lives which must clearly be involved in culture.

The uncritical acceptance of culture. In the fourth century A.D. the emperor Constantine became a convert to Christianity. Almost overnight it became fashionable to be a Christian. In the chaotic centuries that followed, as the political might of the Roman Empire declined, the church increasingly became the guarantor and preserver of culture. Baptism in infancy became admission into the culture as much as into the church. This close alliance between Christian faith and a particular culture, though it has taken different forms, has continued up to the present, often with tragic consequences. Sometimes it has been used to justify "holy" wars, in which both sides of a conflict assumed that in advancing a country's cause they were advancing the cause of Christ. In a different way, this sort of cultural Christianity has sometimes hampered the spread of the gospel. Christians from one culture have been so at home in their own culture—and so repulsed by the strangeness of other cultures—that they have assumed a correlation between accepting the gospel and accepting the host culture. (Fortunately, all over the world the gospel has proven to be greater than those who brought it, so Christian faith has never been exclusively associated with one particular culture.)

Despite its general assumption that

we can live godly lives within in the broader culture, the Bible speaks often of the need to be in some tension with that culture. Thus Paul exhorts the Romans (at the center of the world's great empires): "Do not conform any longer to the pattern of this world, but be transformed by the renewing of your mind" (Rom 12:2). Neither rejection nor affirmation, therefore, seems to be the model for the Christian's life in culture, but some kind of necessary tension.

The gospel as completion of a culture. One of the ways Christians have lived in the tension between faith and culture has been to acknowledge that human culture, good and necessary as it is, always falls short of God's purposes for people. Culture must thus be completed and fulfilled by God's special work. Or, as it is often put in Catholic thought, grace must fulfill nature. Thus in Dante's great medieval allegory *The Divine Comedy,* Virgil—a pagan, pre-Christian Roman poet—becomes the protagonist's guide through hell and purgatory. A symbolic representation of all that is best in human culture, he is a completely adequate guide to the soul's experience of sin. But when the travelers come to the threshold of heaven, Virgil—human culture—can go no further. He commits Dante to a new guide, Beatrice, who symbolizes God's grace and revelation. Yet it is Virgil (all that is best in culture) who has led the questing soul to salvation (which always comes from God, not culture).

Appealing as this picture is, it encourages an unbiblical separation between the sacred and the profane. The biblical pattern seems to be that nothing is too high or spiritual to be perverted by sin, and nothing is too low, human or earthly to be transformed by grace. God's grace always works through and in culture, not beyond it. Jesus was fully God and fully human, not just a good sample of humanity to be perfected by the addition of the divine. In the same way, the problem is not that culture falls short of God; it is rather that humans fail to respond to God within their cultures.

The gospel in tension with culture. Another of the ways that Christians have reponded to the tension between Christianity and culture is to see it as an inescapable consequence of the *betweenness* of our condition. As Christians, we are citizens of God's kingdom, yet in our humanity we necessarily participate with everyone else in the institutions required for a fallen culture. As citizens of the kingdom of God we should no: kill; however, as citizens of the state we might sometimes be required to take life—in defense of the life of others, for example, or in the carrying out of justice.* Likewise, Christians in government (whether vocationally, or simply as voters) might often be called on to make compromises,* for the good of civil society, which are a step below what they would expect in God's perfect order. Voters might inadvertently support the right of divorce* or abortion,* even though such practices clearly go against God's intentions for us. This approach has often been associated with Martin Luther, whose vision both of God's grace and of our fallen condition led him to say "sin boldly" in such compromised situations and depend on God's grace for forgiveness.

The idea appears again in the critique of culture developed by Jacques Ellul. In *The Meaning of the City* Ellul points out that "the first city-builder was Cain" (p. 1). Cities, perhaps the quintessence of human culture, have thus from the beginning (argues Ellul) been a sinful human response to God. We would rather live in our world (the city) than in God's world (Eden). Every aspect of human culture is shot through with our rebellion and sinfulness. Culture always becomes an attempt to live without God.

Yet in God's sight it is always worthless. This is nowhere more obvious than in trying to come to terms with modern life, in which we seem to have little choice but to participate—through a worldwide market, through pervasive media*—in things which often seem less than the best for creation.

This picture of inescapable compromise does often seem to describe much of our situation. But it still falls short of the biblical ideal. Forgiveness* in Christ, not perfection on our own, is our hope. But that forgiveness is presented as the basis for a life of holiness which ought to reach out into the culture, transforming it, not simply accepting it. Here the great words of the prophets remind us that God's concern is with the redemption of cultures and their practices as well as with individuals. In the context of a corrupt culture—whose corruption was spoken of as the improper use of markets and courts—God declares (rejecting the superficial "solemn assemblies" of a culturally separate religion): "Let justice roll on like a river, and righteousness like a never-failing stream." Immersed as we all are in fallen cultures, we nevertheless are to work to change their unrighteousness, not merely submit to it. Though there is indeed a paradox between God's grace and our works, it is not the paradox expressed in the attitude behind Luther's "sin boldly." It is rather the paradox of Philippians 2:12-13: "Work out your own salvation with fear and trembling, for it is God who works in you to will and to act according to his good purpose."

The Transformation or Renewal of Culture

Each of these attitudes expresses some truth about our condition, but each falls short of the biblical picture of culture as outlined above. That biblical understanding of culture is richer than any of

them. Perhaps it is best caught in the idea of *transformation* or *renewal*. The pattern of salvation is not the rejection of creation—and the cultural worlds we make from it—but rather their restoration. God's purposes in world-making men and women are restored, and through them, his purposes for the whole creation. It is not only individuals who are to be "made new." That personal renewal in Christ makes changes in the culture as well. This is the force of Jesus' words about being salt preserving the whole lump—or light illuminating all around. Likewise Isaiah speaks of personal righteousness reaching out into cultural healing, promising that God's people would "rebuild the ancient ruins and will raise up the age-old foundations" and "be called Repairer of Broken Walls, Restorer of Streets with Dwellings" (Is 58:12).

In our time it is all too easy to drift with a sinful, consumerist culture. Much in that culture is wicked and will pass away. Consider the lament over culture described by John at the passing of the greatest of human cities—clearly a symbol of certain aspects of human culture: "Woe! Woe, O great city . . . the music of harpists and musicians, flute players and trumpeters, will never be heard in you again. No workman of any trade will ever be found in you again. . . . Your merchants were the world's great men. By your magic spell all the nations were led astray" (Rev 18:19-23).

But will all of human culture thus be thrown down and lost? No. For in John's vision of the city of God there is still an open door to human culture: "The glory of God gives it light, and the Lamb is its lamp. The nations will walk by its light, and the kings of the earth will bring their splendor into it. . . . The glory and honor of the nations will be brought into it" (Rev 21:23-26).

Two things stand out in this picture of

263

the heavenly city. The first is that it is centered on Christ, the slain Lamb of God; it is not a monument to any human cultural greatness, collective or individual. The second is that it is full of the best of human culture: the "splendor of the kings" and the "honor of the nations." Thus we may conclude that the "new creation" in Christ does not exclude the worlds of human culture.

Conclusion

What does all this mean for our day-to-day life? Two principles stand out. The first is that our cultural worlds can indeed be "worldly" in the old ungodly sense, and we should not "let the world squeeze us into its mold." But the second is that we are redeemed *for* work in the world—in the words of the prophet, "to rebuild the ancient ruins" and "raise up the age-old foundations." Our strength in this is God's gift: "The LORD will guide you always; he will satisfy your needs in a sun-scorched land. . . . You will be like a well-watered garden, like a spring whose waters never fail" (Is 58:11).

Watered by the inexhaustible spring of our Creator and Redeemer, we can, in humility, pain and joy, go about our infinitely varied tasks of "gardening" God's earth into human worlds.

References and Resources
R. Banks, *God the Worker: Journeys into the Mind, Heart and Imagination of God* (Valley Forge, Penn.: Judson, 1994); R. F. Capon, *An Offering of Uncles: The Priesthood of Adam and the Shape of the World* (New York: Sheed and Ward, 1967); C. Dawson, *The Historic Reality of Christian Culture: A Way to the Renewal of Human Life* (New York: Harper & Row, 1960); J. Ellul, *The Meaning of the City* (Grand Rapids: Eerdmans, 1970); H. R. Niebuhr, *Christ and Culture* (New York: Harper, 1956); J. Pieper, *Leisure, the Basis of Culture* (New York: Mentor, 1963); B. J. Walsh and J. R. Middleton, *The Transforming Vision* (Downers Grove, Ill.: InterVarsity Press, 1984).

Loren Wilkinson

D

DATING

A recent article in a Canadian magazine entitled "Is Dating Dead?" observed that dating has surely changed. In the Western world a person tries a succession of sexual partners prior to cohabiting.* Understandably some refuse to use the word *dating* at all, preferring instead such an innocuous phrase as "going out." Even "having a relationship" unfortunately now connotes a sexual liaison. The much older English words *courting* and *wooing*—similar in meaning to the terms "speak to the heart" and "allure" found in the Hebrew Bible (see Is 40:2; Hos 2:14)—suggest the sensitive persuasion with which a man will plead to a woman's heart for her hand in marriage,* thus raising the crucial question of whether dating and mating should themselves be married!

Must dating be practiced with a view to finding a suitable marriage partner? Should Christians participate in recreational romance or romantic networking*—whether or not one has any interest in or calling* to marriage? Can dating be a ministry to not-yet Christians, a form of romantic evangelism*? Should dating be restricted to finding a spouse? Is there a place in dating for relationship enhancement, the enjoyment of other persons, a form of neighbor* love* without marriage in view? Is there an explicitly Christian approach to dating? Is there a place for dating after one is married? Are there initiatives a person can take, spe-cifically if one is female, when no dating prospects seem to be on the horizon?

Dating Through the Ages

All cultures have found ways of allowing people to meet members of the opposite sex with a view to finding a suitable marriage partner, though in most cases these have been tightly controlled by social taboos, such as "no dating without the presence of a chaperon," and in others there simply was no opportunity for relational experimenting. In most ancient societies marriages were arranged by parents, and there was virtually no social contact prior to engagement (except through observation in village life or shared survival activities) and no sexual contact until marriage.

In some cultures today it is assumed that a man or woman cannot be alone together without having sexual intercourse. So the arranged marriage survives in a few places, and where there is wisdom exercised by parents, family and friends, this system may be preferred to the romantic networking* of the Western world, which is usually focused on falling in love or infatuation—a phenomenon that is actually a temporary derangement. The Christian church has penetrated and transformed various cultures* all over the world, but where it has brought the Christian view of marriage, it has not always eliminated the system of arranged marriages. Sometimes the church has transformed the system. But one thing Christianity has always brought is the requirement of consent, which is based on theological reasons relating to God's covenant with God's people. No covenant can be formed without the willing heart agreement of the bride and groom—hence the questions asked in a Christian marriage ceremony ("Do you take this man to be . . ."). Consent is implicit in making promises* and vows.

Some African tribes offered socially acceptable ways for young people to explore relationships with the opposite sex by permitting limited sexual affection in a very controlled situation, especially for couples that were predisposed to marry each other. This was not unlike the *bundling* or *binding* (in bed for an exploratory night together with a physical barrier between!) practiced by some Christian sects until quite recently. Festivals and harvest celebrations were natural contexts in which people in agrarian societies would experimentally explore special relationships with others of marriageable age, sometimes indicating interest through socially learned signals such as making repeated eye contact.

The older systems could assume a stable social network of families,* clans, tribes and peoples in which the parents and the children knew each other. A young man and young woman would observe each other at work,* home* and community* activities over years. This prolonged exposure cannot easily be accomplished in the modern city,* especially in a mobile society (*see* Mobility). In fact, there is no possibility for prolonged exposure in most of the world, careening as it is toward global urbanization. Only a disciplined approach to the modern dating system can replicate the advantage of long-term relationships in the same social network.

Jewish Betrothal

The Jewish system at the time of Jesus did not allow for anything that could be called *dating*. There was simply *betrothal*—the arrangement, much more than the modern engagement, by which two people were pledged in troth to each other. Through the betrothal ceremony the couple formally belonged, so much so that betrothal could be broken only by divorce* (as the case of Mary and Joseph in Mt 1:19 poignantly illustrates). Betrothal was presexual marriage—covenant without covenant consummation—tion—and therefore Scripture views betrothal as an illuminating analogy for our relationship with Christ as we wait for his Second Coming when we will "know" as we are now known (1 Cor 13:12; 2 Cor 11:2). Until then we belong unconditionally, but we do not have full union.

In the Jewish context betrothal might last for up to a year and was concluded with the wedding feast, sometimes lasting a week, during which the couple would consummate the relationship. Both virginity before marriage (Deut 22:13-21) and regular intercourse within marriage were assumed. Indeed the Jewish Mishnah, the textbook on Jewish life, regulated for how long a man might withhold sexual affection from his wife for the purpose of studying Scripture or because of work pressures (an interesting reversal of what is stereotypically thought to be the politics of the matter). A man may withhold sex for up to three months if he is a camel driver traveling on long safaris but must engage in it every day if he is unemployed (*Ketubot* 5:6-7)!

Remarkably, the apostle Paul taught full mutuality of sexual pleasure, full mutuality of bodily "ownership" and full mutuality of decision-making on when refraining might be appropriate. Paul relegated the matter to an occasional and brief time of sexual fasting for purposes of prayer (1 Cor 7:1-7; Stevens 1989, pp. 107-17). The New Testament assumes the Jewish approach, at least in areas where Jewish Christians predominated, though it is obvious from Paul's correspondence that the church was forging new patterns in the Gentile world, where sexual permissiveness and relational promiscuity were the norm, hence the strong teaching of 1 Corinthians 6:12—7:40.

North American and Western Dating

Except in the baths and brothels of the ancient world, and the privileged courtly life of the rich in Europe in recent centuries (from which we have the pejorative term *courtesan*), there has never been a dating system like the modern Western one. At the same time there has never been a more fragile marriage system than the modern Western one. Indeed, researchers on family life suggest that the greatest problem in North American marriage may well be North American courtship, that is, the dating system (Sell). From the earliest age children are taught and socialized to prepare for an extended period of relational experimentation in which each presents his or her best self to potential girlfriends or boyfriends and marriage partners. Long before dating became industrialized through dating services, escort services, voice mail and newspaper advertisements, an entire industry supported this social expectation through providing dress (*see* Adornment), cosmetics, mass media* (especially Hollywood movies*) and endless environments in which to meet people such as singles bars. Obviously the system favors the young, the wealthy and the outward-going personality who thrives on entrepreneurial challenges and enjoys networking, but even they are not served well by a system that does not encourage honest self-disclosure and true friendship.*

Dating, as currently practiced, is a staged play in which each person presents his or her outer "ideal" self (he, a macho male; she, a gorgeous doll) to the other. Inside, both he and she are insecure and weak, but they each see in the other the external image of what they have always wanted in a friend/partner of the opposite sex. They fall in love, that delightful derangement in which judgment is suspended and people live in a dream world of ecstasy. Some research suggests that this delightful derangement is supported by natural drugs and hormones in the body, though eventually the chemical balance of the body is restored. Without revealing their private selves, couples become entangled sexually sometimes as early as the second or third night, believing that touch, feel and fondle are quick ways to intimacy, whereas in reality the conversation* they have shut down would better serve the purposes of intimacy.

This romantic relationship is promoted in ideal circumstances—restaurants, theaters, hotels, leisure* spots—with scant exposure to one's family or workplace* and with rare openness to being seen without being made up, dressed up and presentable. Psychologists call this a collective defense mechanism. This period often lasts for as long as two years. If two people marry at this point, they are doomed to disillusionment, as when he (in his insecure private self) realizes he has married not a Barbie doll but another insecure person who is also swapping an empty bowl and saying, "Please fill up my emptiness." Couples often divorce at this point, at the very moment when they could get married at a deeper level and when sensitive counseling (*see* Counseling, Lay) could serve them well. If they are cohabiting or just spending weekends together in each other's apartments, they will probably move on to another "ideal" relationship and fall in (and out) of love once again.

Can Dating Be Redeemed?

It is my conviction that both the arranged-marriage system and the dating system can be redeemed. People have found suitable partners and made lifelong companionship covenants through private arrangements. My wife and I have assisted some young people to start a relationship that could lead to marriage. We also know of people who have found very suitable partners by anonymous, computerized dating services (we also know of Christian couples who have found very suitable partners by this means). In the same way the dating system can be redeemed, but this will require deep and costly measures. Christians are not exempt from the need to rethink and relearn dating from a Christian perspective.

Shrinking from the to-bed-the-first-night culture, and sometimes reacting to a promiscuous past, some Christians refuse to date at all. In its place they enjoy fellowship* and pursue ministry* with people of the opposite sex, all the while praying that God will deliver that one special person in the world who is God's choice. Some of this amounts to group dating in a work context and has the advantage of mutual exposure to others in contexts that are not idealized. There are, however, severe drawbacks, especially since any resulting relationship can be founded exclusively on mutual interest in Christian service and is not a well-rounded friendship.

The advice not to marry until you find someone with whom you can better serve God together as married rather than as single people is problematic and probably dangerous. Marriage is for companionship (Gen 2:18), not to get God's work done on earth. Further, many Christians think that if they pray, God will magically deliver a spouse from heaven. But in reality there are only two ways to get married: have an arranged marriage (someone else does the arranging) or arrange one yourself! God can work through both, and the church has a crucial role to play in both.

What the Church Can Do

Arranging marriages. Elders and mature couples in a church could sensitively introduce people to each other. Such arrangement must be followed by a period of friendship and mutual self-disclosure in a variety of settings and assumes that a couple will not marry until they are substantially without reservations and are able to give their full consent. Romance will follow and usually does, contrary to the mythology of Hollywood. Marriage does not destroy romance but is the normal garden for its cultivation. As Walter Trobisch once observed, the Western system of marriage is like taking a hot bowl of porridge and letting it cool down on the table, while the arranged-marriage system is more like putting a pot of porridge on the stove to cook and turning up the heat (p. 56).

Arrangement is implicit, or at least envisioned as a possibility, in the promises and vows that ask "Will you love . . . ?" not "Do you love . . . ?" Arrangement is also consistent with the view of marriage as a vocation or calling. On this point Ray Anderson and Dennis Guernsey make an insightful observation:

> What we discover—almost, as it were by accident—in selecting a mate and in being selected is that God also participates in this selection by virtue of election. This is why the marriage vow is not itself capable of sustaining the relationship as an expression of human wisdom (I made the right choice) or of human endurance (I made the wrong choice, but I will see it through to the end). The marriage vow can only be a sign of the covenant, and those who make the vow can find lasting joy and love only in

being covenant partners—receiving each other as God's elect. (p. 43)

Two biblical examples of such arrangement are Abraham's servant finding a wife for Isaac (Gen 24) and Naomi's guiding Ruth to take the initiative with Boaz (Ruth 3:1-6), though Ruth may be one of the few biblical examples of a woman who took an initiative in finding a marriage partner (Stevens 1990, p. 32).

One point to note in passing is that psychologists now say that in one sense all of us have marriages arranged by our parents, since our families of origin to a large extent determine whom we choose to date and marry, even in a healthy home and especially in one that encourages fusion and codependence (*see* Family Systems). The process of leaving one's father and mother (Gen 2:24), which is so crucial to cleaving and becoming one flesh, turns out to be a lifelong process rather than a single wedding* event.

Developing a congregational dating and mating ministry. As well as offering sensitively and confidentially to make some matches, leaders in the church can teach and model a family style of dating by encouraging kinship relationships in the church and the development of significant friendships in the context of service. Couples can open their homes to young adults to let them discover models of marriage other than ones in their families of origin. An environment can be created in which young adults can meet one another in the context of hospitality,* perhaps even through a spiritual friendship weekend. The church should offer seminars on sexuality* to help people cope constructively with the sexual pollution of our culture.

As members of the church, we can encourage group dating to take the pressure off one-to-one pairing. We can encourage people to seek preengagement counseling with trusted older people in the Lord's family to discern the mar-riageability of the relationship (this is generally a more teachable moment than after the the engagement is announced and the wedding date is set). We can teach biblical love and help people learn how to love one another with all the languages of love (from practical caring to verbal affirmation). We can empower laypeople to be involved in marriage ministry by linking mature married couples with engaged couples to do marriage preparation in the context of a home. Above all we can work in the church to develop covenantal relationships, a for-better-or-worse type of church membership* that is implicit in house churches (*see* Church in the Home) and small groups,* and so to communicate and foster covenant formation in marriages. We should not yield to the tendency in the Western world to reduce church life (and the marriages within that church) to a contract* basis amounting to an exchange of goods and services for pay by agreed-upon terms. If the church can prayerfully assist in the redemption of the arranged-marriage system, it can also minister toward the redemption of the dating system.

Arranging Your Own Marriage

For Christians a number of significant strategies are implicit in preparing for marriage and redeeming the dating system: (1) put the Lord's kingdom first; (2) pray to know God's will, whether it is to be single or married; (3) develop friendship relationships; (4) make a success of singleness*; (5) become a marriageable person by developing the betrothal qualities of Hosea 2:19-20 (Stevens 1990, pp. 47-55); (6) be open to special relationships; (7) build these relationships on social and spiritual friendship, expressing minimal physical affection and avoiding sexual entanglement; (8) keep your ministry priorities but do not regard the building of a relationship as a diversion from ministry or the spiritual life; (9) go out for a long time, preferably one to three years, spending as much time as possible in the home and family of your friend; (10) seek the counsel of mature believers and your parents, who know you better than most others; (11) speak your heart to your beloved; (12) wait for marriage for intimate sexual expression, but prepare for it (see Stevens 1990, pp. 63-75). Indeed, this last point may reveal the need for sexual healing before one can anticipate a life of sexual companionship and mutual sexual enjoyment. While the Bible does not offer specific directions on dating, it does provide a theological context in which to rethink it.

Toward a Theology of Dating
Dating relates to two great theological themes: friendship and marriage. On the latter, dating serves as one, though not the only, way to discover your marriage partner and discern marriage readiness in both yourself and your friend. Therefore all the following theological dimensions of marriage call us to see that dating becomes a relational ministry to the glory of God.

Marriage is part of God's creational design (Gen 1:27; 2:24); dating, while culturally determined in its present form, is potentially a means of conforming to God's law written into creation. God's creational design is leaving, cleaving and one flesh (Gen 2:24), the experience of which led to the first hymn of praise in the Bible (Gen 2:23). Dating one's marriage partner after marriage can strengthen the cleaving and continue, albeit in a more mature and changed way, the romance that is meant to be lifelong. Because of the exclusivity of the marriage covenant, datinglike relationships with persons other than one's spouse are highly problematic, dangerous and usually an offense to the covenant.

Sexuality—and its call to relationality, complementarity and community—is part of what it means to be made in the image of God. Dating can be a way of experiencing Godlikeness—though not, of course, by experimenting with full marriage sexual communication. Each person dated is potentially someone else's marriage partner, so one must behave in a way that will not mark that person as one's spouse. Even an engagement can be broken.

Marriage is "Christian" through conformity to God's plan and intention in marriage (Gen 2:24; Hos; Mal 2:14; Mt 19:1-12), not simply because of the presence of two Christians or a church wedding; dating must be understood covenantally as a progressive preparation for covenant making and covenant filling. Marriage is an exclusive lifelong covenant in which there is total sharing of one's life; dating someone without faith is therefore highly problematic (though divinely ordained exceptions exist). A Christian should marry a person of the same faith (see 2 Cor 6:14-18, though it was originally written about a different subject).

Marriage has gone through the Fall; people in dating relationships will struggle with the tendency of men to rule and control and of women to revolt or comply, neither of which is a good basis for marriage. Under the new covenant the curse is substantially reversed as Christ empowers couples to live with mutual submission (Eph 5:21); couples enjoying a dating relationship will need the continuous infilling of the Spirit in their relationship to learn mutual submission (Eph 5:18, 21).

The mystery of covenantal marriage is that God, not the law of the country or the action of a clergyperson, joins a couple together (Mt 19:6). Couples preparing for marriage through dating are called to reverence, prayerfulness and humility. This raises the question of the spirituality of dating as a preparation for marriage.

Toward a Spirituality of Dating

Because marriage is a parable of Christ and the church (Eph 5:32), the experience of unity through difference links us with God and makes sexuality contemplative (Gen 1:27). Dating therefore is a process of learning to cultivate gratitude for unity through difference.

Marriage is a vocation or calling, an all-embracing investment of ourselves in response to the summons of God that involves realignment of our relationship with parents (leaving), exclusive focusing on one special relationship (cleaving) and a private celebration of the covenant (one flesh). Dating that prepares for this vocation or calling is a process of spiritual discernment about the call and leading of God, not merely a process of making the best choice.

Marriage is a ministry through which the priesthood of all believers becomes actualized in mutual husband-wife ministry and in which we touch God through our spouse (Eph 5:21-33). Dating that prepares for marriage will be regarded not as recreational romance but as a form of ministry, even in playing* together. Further, all the issues of ministry are raised by marriage and dating: accepting someone else's spirituality, affirming God's work, refusing to play God, being interdependent, being spiritual friends (which can happen only between equals), trusting a loved one or friend to God and interceding on behalf of another.

Marriage is a spiritual discipline, not merely an arena in which to practice disciplines. It is so because it invites us Godward by requiring a level of cooperation humanly impossible. Marriage calls us to lay down our life daily for our spouse as to Christ (Eph 5:21-33). It con-

stantly proposes that our spirituality has to be down to earth (paying bills, raising a family, trying to say "I love you" and having sex). Marriage raises the question whether we are truly justified by faith and not by works by calling us to enjoy our spouse and not merely work with him or her. It calls us to renounce power and control and to become "equippers" of our spouse through empowerment. Marriage forces us to come to grips with ourselves—a person cannot role-play a marriage for very long—for our spouse is a mirror! Because of all this, dating that prepares for marriage is a school of Christian living.

Dating Without Marriage in View

Earlier I said that even single people should be marriageable people, cultivating those qualities that make for both stability and quality in a marriage covenant: faithfulness, loving loyalty, compassion, justice and righteousness (Hos 2:19-20). Given the parameters outlined above, namely, that dating must be conducted in such a way that if one does not marry this person, no violation of the person sexually or emotionally would have taken place, then dating need not, in every case, be an active search for a partner. Indeed, some potentially vital friendships are spoiled by the pressure to head in the direction of marriage. Provided that both friends understand well the level of commitment (a very sensitive matter when one is anxious to find a mate), and provided that dating is not used for recreational sex, a series of dating partners may be a valuable way to learn about ourselves, the opposite sex and the ways of our God. As an environment of testing and temptation, especially in the sexual area, dating may even be an arena for the development of the Spirit fruit of self-control, thus inviting, if not encouraging, a maturity that might not come if one were never tested. Dating, like betrothal, can place us in a truly spiritual posture: learning, waiting,* expecting and growing toward covenant readiness.

See also COHABITING; FRIENDSHIP; GUIDANCE; MARRIAGE; PROMISES; SEXUALITY; SINGLENESS.

References and Resources

R. S. Anderson and D. Guernsey, *On Being Family: Essays in a Social Theology of the Family* (Grand Rapids: Eerdmans, 1985); A. Fryling and R. Fryling, *A Handbook for Engaged Couples* (2nd ed.; Downers Grove, Ill.: InterVarsity Press, 1996); J. Huggett, *Dating, Sex and Friendship* (Downers Grove, Ill.: InterVarsity Press, 1985); J. H. Olthius, *I Pledge You My Troth: A Christian View of Marriage, Family, Friendship* (New York: Harper & Row, 1975); C. M. Sell, *Family Ministry: The Enrichment of Family Life Through the Church* (Grand Rapids: Zondervan, 1981); R. P. Stevens, *Getting Ready for a Great Marriage* (Colorado Springs: NavPress, 1990); R. P. Stevens, *Marriage Spirituality: Ten Disciplines for Couples Who Love God* (Downers Grove, Ill.: InterVarsity Press, 1989); R. P. Stevens, *Married for Good: The Lost Art of Remaining Happily Married* (Downers Grove, Ill.: InterVarsity Press, 1986); C. M. Sell, *Family Ministry: The Enrichment of Family Life Through the Church* (Grand Rapids: Zondervan, 1981); R. P. Stevens and G. Stevens, *Marriage: Learning from Couples in Scripture,* Fisherman Bible Studies (Wheaton, Ill.: Harold Shaw, 1991); W. Trobisch, *I Married You* (London: InterVarsity Fellowship, 1971); E. L. Worthington, *Counseling Before Marriage* (Waco, Tex: Word, 1990); N. Wright, *The Premarital Counselling Handbook* (Chicago: Moody Press, 1992).

R. Paul Stevens

DAYDREAMING

Dreaming* is a normal part of life, even for those who cannot remember their dreams. Much has been written about this. Daydreaming is an equally familiar part of life, but only in the twentieth century and particularly in this generation has it received serious attention. A working definition of daydreaming is that it is a shift of attention or wandering of the mind from ongoing tasks that takes up past memories, present wishes or fears, and future plans or fantasies. Though daydreams can be momentary or last over a minute, their average length is about fifteen seconds, and they occur frequently through the day.

In our society daydreaming is generally frowned upon. Such an attitude goes back to Plato and was reinforced by Freud. Parents regard it as a diversion from more practical and helpful activities. Teachers view it as a distraction from the business of learning and may take disciplinary action. Employers consider it a waste of time* and, if it happens too often, as a basis for dismissal. Though daydreaming is often thought to be evidence of dysfunction or as an expression of the unconscious, there is no hard evidence to support either view. Psychologically healthy people daydream as much as, sometimes more than, others, and daydreams seem to be triggered mainly by what is just below the surface of our minds, for example, unmet goals or strong emotions,* rather than by the stirrings of our unconscious.

Daydreams usually occur when we have little to do, when little effort is required, when little is at stake, and when we have little interest in what is happening (*see* Boredom). They often correlate with the ninety-minute rhythms that affect our bodies throughout the day. Various types of content appear in daydreams: for example, personal aspirations deriving from activities during the day; scenarios of reversal, rehearsal or rationalization; planning goals or possibilities. Highly fanciful or sexual daydreams, or strongly anxious ones, account for only about 5 percent of all daydreams.

To some extent the content of daydreams seems to vary according to gender, disposition and personality type. For example, men engage in more achievement or fear-of-failure, and more past-oriented, daydreams than women, worriers report more negative daydreams than those who are less anxious, and narcissistic subjects experienced more heroic and hostile, self-revelatory and future-oriented daydreams than others. As for the frequency of daydreaming, there is evidence that children who have more isolated upbringings and children of parents who put value on this activity daydream more than others.

Some daydreaming is unhelpful, distracting and time-wasting. A recent survey showed that both men and women fantasize—in extreme cases several times daily—about potential sexual partners, impossible job promotions* or payback responses to people who have wronged them. Some argue that daydreaming of this kind is better than engaging in the actions imagined and makes it less likely that anything will be done about them. Others argue that people who have a very low esteem may through daydreaming gain confidence to undertake simple, affirming actions such as inviting someone on a date, asking for a raise or challenging some injustice. Still others suggest that fantasizing in the ways suggested is nothing more than a form of play.* While there is some truth in each of these approaches, daydreaming can sometimes be harmful. If its objects are primarily lustful, covetous or vindictive, it may harden or increase a person's attitudes in any of those directions. If it is engaged in too frequently or in an undisciplined way, it might establish unhealthy patterns of disengaging from reality.

Yet this activity also has its more positive side. Apart from sometimes putting us in a more relaxed mood, daydreams might well help us come to terms with some past experience. They may also spring from a part of our personality that is legitimately looking for greater expression. In our kind of society—which still suppresses many people through an overabundance of regulations, all-too-fixed gender roles and clock-dominated schedules—daydreaming is often indicative of a healthy personality refusing to be typecast or manipulated. Even the kinds of daydreaming mentioned above may contain within them longings for a deeper relationship with a person of the opposite sex or one's spouse, for a more satisfying type of work* or for a more mature capacity to empathize or interact with other people. Where daydreaming seems quite unrelated to our present life situation, it may point to some area we should explore more seriously. In such cases it may help us find a creative solution to a present difficulty, glimpse some vision of what God wants us to pursue and even help us move toward making some decisions.

All of this is simply a way of saying that our daydreams—like our thoughts, feelings or actions—may spring from a number of sources. They may be stimulated by illegitimate sinful desires, may be an expression of playful human possibilities or may be echoes of genuine divine possibilities. Often they will be a mixture of all three. What we need, as everywhere else in life, is spiritual discernment, not only our own but that of our friends and others whom we trust in our primary Christian community, to work out what they are saying to us.

See also BOREDOM; CALLING; DREAMING; IMAGINATION; PLAY; VISION.

References and Resources
E. Klinger, *Daydreaming: Using Waking Fantasy and Imagery for Self-Knowledge and Creativity* (Los Angeles: Tarcher, 1990).

Robert Banks

DEATH

My (Paul's) father died of pneumonia in my brother's arms after being unable to speak or eat for two years. He was not

afraid to die, but he seemed to be lingering, hanging on, for reasons we could
not discover. His wife had died months
before, and there was no unfinished
business known to us or admitted by him.
My brother embraced him and said,
"Dad, it's all right to go." And within
minutes he died peacefully, sleeping in
Jesus. But he left us wondering about the
mystery of death, its timing, its meaning
and the strange way that we are created
by God to hang on to life, sometimes
even longer than we need. It is difficult
to tell yourself to die.

This article considers death as an occasion for theological reflection and
spiritual contemplation and deals with
letting go of ourselves. Grieving is the
process of letting go of others (*see* Grieving). But the two are related; the experience of losing others can teach us how to
die and, because of that, how to live today
in the light of eternity, or as the Puritan
William Perkins put it, "the science of
living blessedly forever" (p. 177).

The Last Unmentionable Topic

Death is rarely discussed in polite company and has been tragically separated
from everyday life. Instead of dying at
home* surrounded by relatives and
friends, we normally die in a hospital
surrounded by machines. Death has become institutionalized. In older cultures
and before medical science became capable of prolonging life by two or three
decades, people expected death at any
time, if not from disease, than from
childbirth, famine, plague or war. But
now people do not expect to die. Few
people actually see someone die, except
for those in the medical profession, and
dying for them is often surrounded by a
sense of failure.

Death has also been sanitized. Instead
of washing the person's body and digging the grave themselves, something
still done in rural Africa, the family ar-

ranges for a mortician to prepare the
body to be as "lifelike" as possible and
displayed for all to see, though rarely in
one's home. The funeral service takes
place in a mortuary chapel, and the body
is delivered hygienically to the flames or
the soil. The cemetery is not likely to be
found in the courtyard of the family
church but in a place apart. It may never,
or only rarely, be visited. In contrast, my
dear friend Philip in Kenya walks past his
wife's grave mound every time he goes to
the maize field of his small farm. To gain
a theology and spirituality of death will
involve recovering the connection between this once-in-a-lifetime experience
and everyday living. To do that, we must
also try to understand just what death is.

When Is Someone Dead?

Clinically *death* is defined as "the cessation of heartbeat, breathing and brain
activity." At this point a physician pro-
nounces someone "dead." Yet it is widely
recognized that a person as a fully robed
body-soul-spirit being may have died
hours and perhaps even months earlier.
The ambiguity of the matter is highlighted by the intrusion of technology.*
Life can be artificially prolonged on machines, sometimes with the purpose of
"harvesting" organs for transplants from
a dead-yet-still-living being who will die
in all respects once the machines are
turned off. Or will he? Does the soul
remain near for a while to be reunited
should the person be resuscitated by
starting the heart and breathing again?
Did the person actually die when brain
activity ceased, perhaps in a traumatic
car accident, even though clinically the
person remained living? Is it possible
to die months before clinical death by
becoming incapable of giving and receiving love, perhaps through a debilitating disease that puts the person in a
"vegetative" state? If so, there are many
walking dead in this world. Such is the

ambiguity of the subject.

There were two trees in the Garden of Eden, the tree of life (presumably offering immortality; Gen 2:9) and the tree offering godlike knowledge of good and evil. Adam and Eve could live forever only if they accepted their creaturely limitations, eating from the first tree and refusing to eat from the second. If they took from the knowledge tree, they would die (Gen 3:3). But there were other dimensions of that than simply returning to the dust (Gen 3:19). They died to oneness with God (spiritual death), intimacy with each other (relational death) and trusteeship of the world (vocational death).

Could Adam and Eve, had they not sinned, have died of old age, perhaps in a transition like Enoch's that led to fuller life with God? We do not know. Significantly, the first death in the account was not God-inflicted, but brought by humankind on itself: the murder of Abel. Equally significant is the growing consciousness of sin-cursed death by the characters of the drama exemplified in Cain's plea for protection from a violent death (Gen 4:14-15) and Eve's plea for a replacement son to fill the emptiness left by death (Gen 4:25). So whatever might have been possible in Paradise before human sin, death has become something terrible, something fraught with spiritual consequences, something to be feared. It is more than mere physical annihilation.

One reason death is so terrible is that it is not easy to kill a human being. The Polish filmmaker Krzystof Kieslowski explores this subject in his film on the sixth commandment: thou shalt not murder. In *A Short Film on Killing* Kieslowski graphically conveys the enormous effort it takes for a sad young man to fully extinguish the life of a cab driver. Then the filmmaker shows the strenuous and violent effort taken by the Polish govern-ment to end the life of this young criminal through the hanging that followed his conviction. In a technological age when a city can be annihilated by pressing a button, when a bullet can be planted in a chest at a distance too great to make eye contact and when an unseen fetus can be vacuumed from the womb, this is an important statement. Life is almost irresistible. The will to live is almost indomitable. Who then could dare be an instrument of death?

The Right to Inflict Death
The judgment of Cain (Gen 4:1-16) shows that God does not want human beings to inflict death, either by taking the life of another through murder (Ex 20:13) or by ending life by one's own act through suicide. The time and manner of death are to be left in God's hands, whether death comes by disease, accident or some natural process. Consider the distinction between artificially prolonging a life and actively ending a life (*see* Euthanasia). While murder by an individual or group is prohibited in all of its forms, including physician-assisted death, execution by the state or nation (as a just penalty for a grievous sin) was prescribed by the Old Testament. Some Christians arguing from both testaments claim that capital punishment is state murder, though in contrast to this view, Luther maintained that even the hangman is God's servant bringing God's justice into this world.

On this vexed subject the existentialist Albert Camus made a telling point. He argued that capital punishment could be justified only where there was a socially shared religious belief that the final verdict on a person's life was not given in this life. To condemn a fellow human being to death in this context would not involve divine pretension since the human verdict could be overturned by the only perfectly competent judge, God himself.

But in a society that lacked such a religious framework, execution would be a godlike activity since it eliminated a person from the only community that indisputably existed (Meilaender, pp. 20-21).

We have much to learn about death from Jesus' own fate. It was a murder by the sinful religious establishment (expressing the violence in all human hearts against God); it was a state execution by the Roman government on the presumed charge of treason; but it was a voluntary death without being suicide. "No one takes it [my life] from me," he said, "but I lay it down of my own accord" (Jn 10:18). The voluntary aspect of his death is most deeply indicated by the statement that he committed his spirit to God (Lk 23:46) and "gave up his spirit" (Mt 27:50)—a powerful hint that while death is ultimately in God's hands, we may be permitted a part in relinquishing ourselves, something we observe happening with many people at the point of death. While Jesus' death has some unique dimensions as a sacrificial death for all, it is also "typical" in this way: it involved his whole person, not just his body.

Death of the Whole Person

The author of Hebrews says that Jesus tasted death for everyone (Heb 2:9), clearly indicating that whatever death has become through sin—in all of its psychological and spiritual consequences (Mt 27:46)—it was experienced by Jesus on the cross. Death is more than the mere stopping of the heart, breathing and brain activity.

Understood biblically, persons are not souls with bodily wrappings but ensouled bodies or embodied souls, a psycho-pneuma-somatic unity. The body does not "contain" a soul to be released through death—a fundamentally Greek notion that has permeated European culture. The body is the expressiveness

of soul, and soul the heart of body. But these are so interdependently connected, indeed interfused, that to touch either is to touch both—hence the seriousness of sexual sin. We do not "have" bodies and "have" souls but *are* bodies and souls. So death, to the Hebrew mind, cannot strike the body without striking the soul, a connection that is not clear in many translations that substitute "person" for "soul" or "body" (Pederson, 1:179). For example, "the soul that doeth aught presumptuously . . . shall be cut off from the people" (Num 15:30 KJV). However much we may qualify this in the light of passages like "today you will be with me in paradise" (Lk 23:43; see Cooper), we must still deal with death as death *of a person*, not just of a person's shell.

More than our bodies die: emotions, personality, capacity for relationships, for giving and receiving love. Do our spirits die or at least "taste" death? We simply do not know whether we enter into a "soul-sleep" until the day of resurrection or persist in some kind of intermediate state, as it is called in theological texts, until Christ comes again and the dead are raised. What we do know is that death is more than a merely physical phenomenon. The whole person dies. We are obviously dealing with a mystery, but it is a mystery with windows.

A Vanquished Power

In all of this we admit we are facing a formidable power. Death holds people in slavery to lifelong fear (Heb 2:15). The fear may have multiple sources: fear of pain, of the unknown, of having to experience something we cannot control or predict, of losing all that is familiar and dear to us. Many older people fear increasing withering, loss of dignity and loss of independence, all preludes to death. A profound fear we carry from our earliest infancy is the fear of being dropped; the fear of death is the anxiety* that when we can no longer hang on, we will be dropped and plunge into nothingness. Deeper still is the fear of unpredictable consequences after the grave if there is a God. We are ultimately accountable to God, and the happy continuation into the "next" life is contingent on our performance in this life. Death is fraught with eternal consequences.

The fact that human beings cannot simply treat death as a way of recycling people illustrates what Scripture proclaims: death is one of the principalities and powers.* Paul spoke of death as the last enemy (Rom 8:38; 1 Cor 15:26) because it seems death has a "life of its own," making its pretentious claims on human hearts and holding them captive to their mortality. This last enemy was destroyed by the death of Christ, this death of death being certified by the resurrection of Christ. Death has been killed! For the person found in Christ, death is not fraught with temporal fear or eternal consequences, as it is for those who have not yet heard the gospel. Yet we still must die.

Come Sweet Death
The epicenter of our hope for life through death is the resurrection of Jesus. Only one has come back from the dead to tell us about the other side. The Gospels record all we need to know about Jesus after his death: (1) he had a real body that could walk, cook, eat and speak—this was no mere phantom or angelic presence; (2) there is a continuity between the body in this life and the next, so much so that the disciples recognized him—a powerful hint that we may recognize one another in the New Jerusalem; (3) there were continuing evidences of things experienced in bodily life in this world, namely, the scars; (4) the scars were not now the marks of sin but a means of grace as Jesus invited

Thomas to touch and believe.

In other words, our works done in this life are transfigured rather than annihilated. Even the creation itself will not be annihilated but transfigured (this being quite probably the meaning in 2 Pet 3:10). Ezekiel envisions the land "radiant" with the glory of God (Ezek 43:2), a prophetic announcement that the earth will become "a new earth" (Rev 21:1) just as the psychological body (literal Greek; "natural" NIV) will be transfigured into a "spiritual body" (1 Cor 15:44). In other words, the Christian hope is not the survival of the spirit after the death of the body or even the continuation of immortal (but disembodied) soul in a nonmaterial "heaven" or the provision of another body, soul and spirit to be given us through reincarnation.

Christian hope promises a renewal not a replacement. Our bodies, souls and spirits are transfigured and "will be like his [Christ's] glorious body" (Phil 3:21). Christians see death in a sacramental way: a physical experience through which a spiritual grace is mediated. In this case the spiritual grace is located in the promise of resurrection. Even personality defects in this life get healed, but not by our becoming *different* persons. In Christ we more than survive the grave; we triumph over it. It remains to consider how to die well.

The Art of Dying
First, we must repudiate the death denial of contemporary Western culture. Deaths of relatives and friends provide good opportunities in a family context to discuss what death means and to declare the Christian hope. The thoughtful preparation of our last will* and testament helps us prepare for death and contemplate what inheritance, material and nonmaterial, we leave behind.

Second, living Christianly involves the idea of dual citizenship: living simultaneously in this world and the next. We are equidistant from eternity every moment of our life from conception to resurrection. We treasure life as good and really flourish on earth, but it is not the highest good. We resist death as evil, but not the greatest evil, because it is the way to a better world.

Third, we can number our days, as the psalmist said, not by calculating our expected life span by the latest actuarial tables and then squeezing all we can into the remaining years because there is nothing more (or because eternity is just more of the same). This view unfortunately treats time* as a resource to be managed rather than a gift. Rather numbering our days means treating every day as a gift, being aware that it may be our last yet investing ourselves, talents* and all in a world without end (compare Mt 25:1-13). We do not live "on borrowed time" but on entrusted time. So we live one day at a time, not bearing tomorrow's burdens and anxieties today (Mt 6:25-34), but trusting that God will be sufficient for each day that we live.

Fourth, everyday hardships give us an opportunity to learn to "die daily." Paul said that we are like sheep led daily to the slaughter. Through these pains, persecutions and weaknesses that we suffer, we are able to live in the resurrection power of Christ, dying to self, living in him (2 Cor 4:10-12, 16-18).

Fifth, we can practice progressive relinquishment. As we go through life, we relinquish childhood and youth, our friends and parents through death, our children as they leave home (*see* Empty Nesting) and eventually our occupations and health. Most people will discover the hard words of the marriage vow, "until death us do part." Ultimately we must relinquish life in this world. We are left with the one treasure of inestimable value—the Lord. One of the Ignatian

exercises invites us to contemplate our own death using our inspired imaginations and doing so prayerfully in the Lord's presence: people gathering around our bed, the funeral, the burial in the soil, the gradual decomposition of our body until all that we were as a person in this life has dissolved and we are ready for full transfiguration. Are we ready to die? Are there broken relationships to be mended, persons to be forgiven, debts to settle? Is there something we can do for someone that we have been putting off?

The philosopher George Santayana said, "There is no cure for birth and death save to enjoy the interval" (quoted in Jones, p. 30). This accurately expresses the practical theology of a generation that denies death, fails to believe in a new heaven and new earth and, therefore, is preoccupied with fitness, health* and pleasure.* But the Christian approach, as J. I. Packer once said, is to "regard readiness to die as the first step in learning to live" (quoted in Jones, p. 30).

See also AGING; BODY; EUTHANASIA; GRIEVING; MENOPAUSE AND MALE CLIMACTERIC; RETIREMENT; WILL, LAST.

References and Resources

C. D. Exelrod, "Reflections on the Fear of Death," *Omega* 17, no. 1 (1986-87) 51-64; J. W. Cooper, *Body, Soul & Life Everlasting: Biblical Anthropology and the Monism-Dualism Debate* (Grand Rapids: Eerdmans, 1989); O. Cullmann, *Immortality of the Soul or Resurrection of the Dead?* (London: Epworth, 1958); T. K. Jones, "Death: Real Meaning in Life Is to Be Found Beyond Life," *Christianity Today* 35 (24 June 1991) 30-31; G. Meilaender, "Mortality: The Measure of Our Days," *First Things* 10 (February 1991) 14-21; Jürgen Moltmann, *Theology of Hope*, trans. J. W. Leitch (New York: Harper & Row, 1967); J. Pedersen, *Israel: Its Life and Culture*, 4 vols. (London: Geoffrey Cumberlege, 1964); William Perkins, "The Golden Chain," in *The Work of William Perkins*, ed. Ian Breward (Appleford, U.K.: Courtney, 1970); E. Trueblood, *The Common Ventures of*

Life: Marriage, Birth, Work and Death (New York: Harper & Row, 1949).

Gail C. Stevens and R. Paul Stevens

DEBT

Ben Franklin once said that it was better to "go to bed supperless than run in debt for breakfast." In more recent times North Americans have failed to heed his advice. The result has been an explosion in personal debt—and bankruptcies! Though I will focus on the subject of debt, one cannot really talk about this without also considering the related topic of credit.*

While debt has been a subject of considerable discussion in Christian circles for a long time, it was probably the explosion of business and personal bankruptcies in the 1980s that brought unusual attention to the topic and even caused some Christians to doubt their standing before God. Over five million Americans filed for bankruptcy in the decade of the 1980s. Canada realized proportionately similar numbers. In fact, it was only in 1993 that bankruptcy statistics actually began to decline from the record total realized the previous year.

Many Christian commentators were quick to condemn Christians who took this avenue of escape from their debts. American businessperson and author Albert J. Johnson suggested that those considering voluntary bankruptcy to resolve debt problems should read Psalm 37:21, "The wicked borrow and do not repay." He argued that a person considering bankruptcy was in financial trouble because of past violations of scriptural principles (Johnson, pp. 82, 85). Widely published financial and business adviser Larry Burkett is similarly outspoken, as is evident in one of his taped addresses:

> Now isn't that amazing to you, that somebody would actually default on a debt that they created legally, morally,

ethically, and then they would default on it? See, it ought to never happen with Christianity, or it should happen so rarely that we would take that person, and we would admonish them according to Matthew 18, and bring them before the church to restore them back to the faith.

This hard-nosed attitude toward bankruptcy is sometimes held toward taking on debt generally. Some commentators have argued that debt is a substitute for trust in God and that to be truly effective a Christian must be financially free. Furthermore, debts are viewed as lifelong obligations, ruling out any possibility of their being forgiven via the bankruptcy process. Taken to its extreme, financial success is, in some circles, linked with divine favor and right standing before God, while debt problems are seen as an indication of a Satan-defeated life.

Given the fact that North Americans have taken so readily to consumer and business credit and that indebtedness has become a normal aspect of life for many Christians, it is crucial to know just what the Bible says, and does not say, about the topic of debt. This will enable us to come to sound conclusions about the use of credit.

Is Debt Evil?

If one were to adopt a proof-texting approach to this topic, confusion would assuredly be the result, for the biblical message concerning debt appears at quick glance to be a mixed one. On the one hand, many times God's people are urged to lend to the needy. Deuteronomy 15:7-10 is particularly forceful:

> If there is a poor man among your brothers . . . do not be hardhearted or tightfisted toward your poor brother. Rather be openhanded and freely lend him whatever he needs. Be careful not to harbor this wicked thought: "The seventh year, the year

for canceling debts, is near," so that you do not show ill will toward your needy brother and give him nothing. He may then appeal to the LORD against you, and you will be found guilty of sin. Give generously to him and do so without a grudging heart; then because of this the LORD your God will bless you in all your work and in everything you put your hand to.

Our Lord takes a similar view, not only with respect to one's brothers and sisters, but even with one's enemies: "Love your enemies, do good to them, and lend to them without expecting to get anything back. Then your reward will be great, and you will be sons of the Most High, because he is kind to the ungrateful and wicked" (Lk 6:35) and "Give to the one who asks you, and do not turn away from the one who wants to borrow from you" (Mt 5:42).

On the other hand, in the Bible we see borrowers, desperate to avoid the exactions of hardhearted creditors, attempting to persuade a third party to act as a guarantor for their debts. The Old Testament frequently warns against this practice (Prov 6:1-5; 11:15; 17:18; 22:26-27). In fact, being in debt is sometimes linked with being in a hopelessly vulnerable situation, as Proverbs 22:7 suggests: "The rich rule over the poor, and the borrower is servant to the lender" (see further Deut 15:6; 28:12, 44). We also have the Pauline injunction "Avoid getting into debt, except the debt of mutual love" (Rom 13:8 JB).

Given the many times that God's people are urged to lend, compassionately and generously, to the needy, it would be ridiculous to assert that borrowing, and therefore debt, is evil. However, it is realistic to conclude that incurring debt can be dangerous. This two-edged characteristic is typical of most aspects of material life from the biblical point of view. For example, wealth* and property can

be seen as gifts from God and even as a reward for obedient living (Deut 28:1-14). Their value is in the opportunities that they provide for increased service to humanity (2 Cor 9:11), rather than for self-indulgent use (Lk 8:14). But material wealth at the same time is one of the chief obstacles to salvation (Lk 12:13-21; 16:19-31; 18:24-25).

One cannot arbitrarily conclude, then, that debt is inherently evil. God would not command his people to proffer help that was wrong to receive. But debt, like so many other aspects of economic life, can be abused by the lender and borrower alike. Thus, care must be taken to use debt wisely.

What Was the Purpose of Debt?

Virtually all of the ethical teaching about debt is found in the Old Testament. In the economy of Pentateuchal times, Israelites were involved almost exclusively in agriculture. The most common commercial participant in those days was the traveling merchant or trader, called simply a "foreigner" (Deut 23:20) or sometimes a "Canaanite" (Zech 14:21). While Israelites were to lend to their fellow Israelite farmers interest free, making loans with interest to foreigners (or traders) was permissible.

It was with respect to the interest-free loans to covenant brothers and sisters that the lender was urged to be compassionate, taking minimal collateral and forgiving unpaid debts by the sabbatical year (more on this below). Loans would have typically been solicited not for commercial investment purposes but as a result of economic hardship, for example, crop failure or the devastation that resulted from enemy raids (Judg 6:1-4). Borrowing was an indication of serious financial trouble, imperiling the well-being of the family unit, which was the fundamental building block of society. Thus, while the debtor was to be treated with great compassion, he or she was usually in debt not because of self-indulgent motives but because of the inability to meet the basic needs of life.

Commercial debt is mentioned but with very little comment. Clearly it was not wrong for God's people to be involved in commercial investments. They had to recognize, of course, that a loan carried with it not only responsibilities but also dangers, whether of loss or of exploitation. (This is evident in the many warnings about unwise involvement with lenders which could bring a borrower to the point of losing personal independence.)

So we see two kinds of debt in the Old Testament: interest-bearing loans to foreigners and interest-free loans to fellow Israelites. It was with respect to covenant brothers and sisters that more well-to-do Israelites were enjoined to be generous and forgiving. So important was this principle to God that it even appears in the Lord's Prayer as the perfect example of godly forgiveness (Mt 6:12: "Forgive us our debts, as we also have forgiven our debtors"). Neither of these types of debt is condemned. But the former tends to be discussed within the context of risk and the need to avoid being exploited. The latter is found within the context of generosity and forgiveness and the requirement not to exploit.

Are Debts Forgivable?

According to biblical teaching, borrowers were obliged under normal circumstances to repay their debts. This responsibility to meet one's financial obligations is vividly illustrated by a provision recorded in Leviticus 25:39. Here a debtor in default could go so far as to sell himself into slavery. Obviously the responsibility to repay one's debts was taken extremely seriously. However, the possibility of those debts being canceled (or debt-slaves released) was not ruled out. In accordance with sabbatical-year legislation, debtors were automatically relieved of their obligations every seventh year, whether or not they deserved compassionate treatment.

Compassion of this sort—the setting aside of the legitimate rights of lenders—was typical of all economic relations envisioned in the covenant community. God's desire for his people was that they would enjoy economic stability and security as family units. Wealth was viewed as a divine blessing (Deut 8:11-18, 28). This blessing was associated with God's people living in obedience and was based totally on God's compassion. Such financial mechanisms as the poor tithe (Deut 14:28-29; 26:12), gleaning in the field (Deut 24:19) and interest-free loans (Ex 22:25-27; Lev 25:35-37; Deut 23:19-20) were tangible ways by which God's people could, in turn, show compassion for each other. Beyond income-maintenance programs, God provided for permanent mechanisms—such as the sabbatical year and Jubilee—to ensure that temporary misfortune barred no family from full participation in economic life (see Ex 21:2; 23:11; Lev 25:1-7; Deut 15:1-15).

It is important to keep two points in mind. The cancellation of debts in the Old Testament was done at legislated intervals, that is, every seventh year (sabbatical year) and every seven sabbaticals (Jubilee year), regardless of the performance of the debtor, good or bad. In addition, these borrowers were not involved in commercial life. They were usually poor farmers borrowing to preserve their ability to make a living and to feed their families. But the principle that can be legitimately extracted from the biblical model and applied to our modern free-market economies in North America today is that while debt is to be taken seriously, it could be canceled to achieve some higher purpose, such as the preservation of the family unit. No desirable goal is achieved when unscrupulous debtors are allowed to escape from their financial obligations. But the Old Testament did provide for the cancellation of debts as an act of mercy, with no stigma attached.

Conclusion

Debt, like so many other topics that Christians must evaluate in contemporary society, is a morally neutral concept. Never are God's people told that debt is wrong—quite the opposite! In fact, one of the reasons that God entrusts his people with material means is because "there should be no poor among you" (Deut 15:4). Loans were one way of restoring the poor to economic stability, especially if the lending was accompanied by a merciful and forgiving attitude. Well-off Israelites could also participate in commercial ventures provided that they made careful allowances for the risks involved. But access to loans brings with it all of the temptations associated with material life: self-indulgence, riskiness and exploitation. Debt is a two-edged sword, to be handled with care.

See also CONSUMERISM; CREDIT; CREDIT CARD; MONEY; SIMPLER LIFESTYLE; STEWARDSHIP.

References and Resources

L. Burkett, *God's Principles for Operating a Business* (Dahlonega, Ga.: Christian Financial Concepts, 1982), audiocassette; A. J. Johnson, *A Christian's Guide to Family Finances* (Wheaton, Ill.: Victor Books, 1983).

John R. Sutherland

DENOMINATIONS

There was a time, not so long ago, when if asked the question, What is your religion? people would respond by giving the name of their denomination. This assumed a society in which most of the population was associated with the Christian faith in some way and in which a person's identity was somehow connected to his or her denominational affiliation. At the time denominations were still a major force on the religious scene, and there was a fairly clear sense of what differentiated them from one another. All this is now changing.

What Are Denominations and Denominationalism?

A denomination is a legally constituted association of local churches that agree to work together according to a common polity for their mutual benefit. There is considerable variety within denominations concerning forms of leadership, the relative strength of the central body or member congregations and the degree of flexibility in belief and practice. A denomination differs from a national or state church, which is the public religious expression of a specific country, and from a looser affiliation of churches who have only fraternal bonds but no formal structure.

The word *denominationalism* is sometimes used to describe the whole phenomenon of a church divided into separate denominations in distinction from other forms of wider church associations in the past. There was a time when Christianity was largely made up of two large ecclesiastical movements, the Catholic and the Orthodox, and, after the Reformation, primarily of national churches following particular theological traditions. We could call this the *predenominational period* of the church. The period of church history from the seventeenth to the twentieth centuries, first in the West and then in the Two-Thirds World, can be properly described as *the age of the denominations*. I will suggest below that we are now moving into a time that could be rightly called *postdenominational*.

Denominationalism sometimes has another more evaluative and generally negative connotation. When used this way, it refers to the tendency to become so preoccupied with denominational distinctions that a narrow or judgmental attitude develops toward denominations other than one's own or toward nondenominational forms of Christianity in general. In this sense it is just another form of sectarianism. What follows mostly has the first sense of the word in view but at points also takes the second into account.

The Origin of the Major Denominations
Denominations began for variety of reasons. While it is often thought that particular theological convictions were uppermost, this was only sometimes the case or only part of the motivation.

On the edges of the Reformation, the Anabaptist movement gave birth to several networks of churches across political boundaries. Among the earliest of these were the Mennonites and the Moravians, denominations founded on certain ecclesial convictions about the voluntary and communal nature of the church, ethical convictions concerning simplicity and pacifism and missionary convictions about preaching the gospel inside and outside their own countries. In the following century the Quakers differentiated themselves by emphasizing the inner presence of the Spirit in each individual and a more participatory form of worship* and decision-making, while the Congregationalists insisted on the God-given responsibility of each congregation to determine its own affairs. In America, especially after the Declaration of Independence, some denominations began for quite different reasons. For example, offshoots of established churches, such as the Anglican, could no longer function as a state church and so were forced to operate in a denominational way. Later this also happened to the Lutherans.

In the eighteenth century, influenced by contact with the Moravians, Methodists—as they came to be called—developed a set of spiritual and communal disciplines for their members and instituted meetings with a high degree of accountability, while remaining, in most other respects, Anglican in doctrine. Throughout the nineteenth century, especially in America, many new Christian movements arose, such as the Disciples of Christ, which began as a renewal movement for the whole church but developed into denominations. Older ecclesiastical traditions developed parallel denominations among different immigrant or racial groups. Some newer and older denominations split into separate groups as a result of social and political differences, as during the Civil War, or because of minor or major theological and ecclesiastical differences.

Today there are several hundred denominations in the United States, many of them particular versions of a more generic denominational tradition. These are often broadly categorized as mainline, confessional and evangelical, alongside other nondenominational* networks or congregations. Denominationalism has taken deepest root in America in the fertile soil of its emphasis on individual decision and opposition to governmental influence in religion, which is characteristic of revivals and awakenings. Interestingly, this denominationalism often goes hand in hand with strong interdenominational interests expressed in parachurch* associations. The voluntary decision of the individual lies at the heart of this, along with a tendency toward cooperation fostered by the challenges of developing a new nation under difficult circumstances. On the other hand, the strong ecumenical interest sometimes displayed by mainline denominations goes hand in hand with an intolerant—actually sectarian or denominationalist in the negative sense—attitude toward more conservative or nondenominational Christian groups.

A Theological Basis for and Critique of Denominations

Some have argued, on both the theological right and the theological left, that denominations have no biblical basis. The first believe in the absolute autonomy and independence of the congregation, the second in the sinfulness of all separate groupings of Christians and in the ideal of one universal church. There are others who argue, or at least act as if, denominations are sacrosanct. Some of these believe that not only diverse but even contradictory ecclesiastical stances have a divine right to exist. Others believe that no matter what denominations do or fail to do, it is our duty to remain loyal to them.

A biblical approach would recognize the relative autonomy granted by apostles like Paul to each congregation and yet the importance of their being part of at least a loose network of congregations from whom they could learn, to whom they could occasionally give aid and with whom members could have fellowship.* Such an approach would also recognize the value of developing links with some evangelistic, church-planting and missionary work, both to give support and to gain wisdom. It also provides precedent, as at Corinth, for Christians whose churches in the one city stemmed from different founders to come together every so often to fellowship with God and one another.

We do not find here local churches under some kind of official hierarchy to which they must submit. Nor did the apostles encourage congregations to separate from one another on the ground of particular doctrinal practices.

So long as they did not cut across fundamental gospel convictions and behavior in accordance with those, there could be different attitudes in belief and practice within one community. So we cannot derive from early Christian practice either a centralized denominationalism or a radical congregationalism. Neither can we find a strict conformity in belief among all members of a congregation, nor a tolerance of convictions between congregations on issues fundamental to the gospel. The figure of James in Jerusalem apart, key figures in the early Christian movement do not appear in a hierarchical position above the churches in their constituencies but in a respected position as leaders of teams focusing on outreach alongside them. The picture we have is of a partnership between such teams and local churches, between key figures and local leaders, somewhat akin to the cordial, interdependent relationships that some congregations have established with parachurch organizations. Denominations are generally a fusion of these two entities in which, depending on whether organizational links are tight or loose, there is a subservience on the part of one or the other rather than a mutual giving and taking.

Though we are not bound to reproduce this early Christian approach, which itself contained certain variations, we should seek to honor the basic principles that it enshrined. For here we have a complex but practical working out of the freedoms and limits, relationship and responsibilities, unity and diversity, of local churches and wider groupings of such churches. Both history and experience confirm that no church can live or die to itself and that there are certain advantages in cooperating with other groups to pursue some common ends. On the other hand, no church can realize its potential unless it possesses sufficient freedom to make basic decisions about its common life and experiment with a wide range of possibilities. The way this works out today should take note of the different cultural circumstances under which we operate, while being careful to avoid simply mirroring the kinds of structures typical of our age, such as the corporation or the bureaucracy.

The Vocational Responsibilities and Limits of Denominations

What is the particular vocation or calling of denominational bodies? It is essentially to serve their constituencies, not lord over them, to enhance their life in ways they cannot do themselves, whether as individual congregations or as clusters of congregations. What local churches, on their own or in smaller groupings, can or ought do themselves, denominational bodies should let alone. Such bodies should always be seeking to enhance the growth of such churches to maturity, not expand their own influence at the expense of local churches. What local churches most appreciate is educational resources in certain areas, pastoral support for key people involved in ministry to the body and actual pioneering of new models of evangelism* and mission.* From the key figures in their denominational network, people look for practicing role models rather than public declarations and administrative initiatives. Too often denominational agencies and leaders are caught up in predominantly administrative matters and are in any case too removed from the grassroots to have any powerful influence. Less bureaucratic and more decentralized structures would make a big difference here.

With respect to the interface between church and world, the main role of denominations is not to build up an institutional apparatus with which to confront the world or to penetrate it. A lot of energy and money presently goes

into this, often in ways that the ordinary churchgoer finds difficult to identify with. Largely overlooked in all this is the fact that denominations already have a presence and contribution in almost every sphere of society through the daily work and life of ordinary church members. What denominational agencies would be far better doing is encouraging and assisting those members to be fully equipped for their various ministries of daily life and providing ways of networking them to do this. This would be far less costly and far more effective than what is mostly attempted at present.

Denominations also ought to cooperate more with one another in certain areas. For all the rhetoric about ecumenical relationships, it is rare to find denominations giving up their own vested interests to collaborate with others. Take current attitudes toward the mass media,* especially television.* What we find so often is a range of small, underfinanced, often semiprofessional, programs representing different denominational hobbyhorses or trendy concerns rather than a creative, joint approach bringing Christian convictions to bear on an increasingly unchurched culture.* The same is also true to some extent in the field of publications, though here economic forces are beginning to work toward less duplication and greater cooperation.

Toward a Postdenominational Christianity

Can denominations reform themselves in ways that will enable them to fulfill their basic responsibilities? It is very difficult for any institution to engage in radical self-criticism and acknowledge how often it operates in a secular rather than Christian way. It is also difficult for religious institutions to radically change themselves or to share their power or collaborate with others. There is always the temptation for them to become principalities and powers* that disable and disempower their members, rather than genuinely "servant institutions" that seek to resource and enhance them. It is always difficult for them to look to the margins, where new and highly relevant things are often happening, and bring these into the mainstream; it is far easier to criticize such efforts or take defensive measures against them. In our day some businesses have shown themselves more capable of doing this than denominations, being more likely to express institutional repentance, redistribute power and take risks for the sake of the future. God's response is sometimes to raise up new denominations to do the work, as was the case with eighteenth-century Methodism, or new informal affiliations of congregations, such as networks of Vineyard Fellowships, as is happening in various parts of the world today.

What we have been watching over the last few decades is the gradual withering of the denominations. Membership in denominational churches has been steadily declining, a pattern that shows little sign of abating. Denominational budgets are constantly being scaled back, and programs are being cut year after year. Many denominational seminaries have had to close or merge. Meanwhile newer churches and networks of churches are experiencing dramatic or steady growth. Alongside this, churchgoers are generally placing less emphasis on their denominational affiliation and are choosing churches on the basis of style of worship, quality of teaching and provision of services. The latest surveys even show the beginning of a trend toward multiple church connection, a kind of smorgasbord approach to church attendance. All this heralds the early phases of a new form of church connectedness and membership.* One of the first to talk about the emergence of a post-denominational Christianity was the American writer and speaker Elton Trueblood. This is not to predict the end of denominations. Many older ones will continue, but they will be smaller, leaner and less influential. One or two may even go through a period of renewal, as Anglicanism did in England during the nineteenth century in response to Methodism, and experience a new burst of life. Some newer networks and affiliations may develop into full-scale denominations.

But many churches and people involved in ministry are finding that connections across denominational boundaries with others in similar settings and with similar goals are more meaningful. Interdenominational movements and seminaries have grown in significance. Nondenominational churches are growing and seem to appeal especially to the younger generation. All this suggests that denominationalism, though by no means to be written off as a spent force, is definitely on the wane. For the many who still have hope for their denominations and sense the call of God to remain with them and work for change, the task is to become a critical, loyal opposition, one that both is supportive and holds them accountable.

See also CHURCH; NONDENOMINATIONAL; PARACHURCH ORGANIZATIONS.

References and Resources

R. Banks, "Denominational Structures," in *In the Fulness of Time: Biblical Studies in Honour of Archbishop Donald Robinson*, ed. David Peterson and John Pryor (Sydney: Lancer, 1992) 277-300; J. Dillenberger, *Protestant Christianity: Interpreted Through Its Development* (New York: Scribner, 1954); E. Jacoby, *The Bureaucratization of the World* (Berkeley: University of California Press, 1976); D. B. Knox, "The Church and the Denominations," *Reformed Theological Review* 23, no. 2 (1964); 44-53; H. R. Niebuhr, *The Social Sources of Denominationalism* (New York: World, 1957).

Robert Banks

DEPRESSION

Depression is the most common and often most misunderstood of all the painful emotions.* Despite the fact that Scripture presents some very clear examples of depression in its heroes (Elijah, Saul, David and Paul) and in the history of great preachers, many of whom suffered from severe bouts of melancholy (Luther, Wesley and Spurgeon), Christians have tended to hold to the belief that to be depressed is a sign of failure* or spiritual weakness. Some conservative preachers and Christian writers have even gone so far as to suggest that depression is a sign of God's punishment or rejection, leaving many feeling more confused and guilty.

We have failed to grasp the naturalness of depression and the fact that often it has biological origins. Even the severest of depressions can have healing benefits if we strive to understand its purpose and cooperate with it. Because so many do not understand the depressive process, they feel like spiritual failures. The time is long overdue for Christians to set the record straight on this common cold of the emotions!

How common is depression? One out of every eighteen adults—about ten million of us—suffers from a clinical depression at any one time. In a church of 250 members this means that at least fourteen parishioners could be suffering from an incapacitating depression. One in five adults will experience a severe depression at least once in their lifetime. This reality about the commonness of depression cannot be avoided. What people need is clear guidance on when it is a normal process that should be left to take its course, and when it is necessary to seek treatment.

Current Progress in Understanding Depression

We live in an era when fantastic progress has been made in providing relief for this debilitating condition. Even in my own professional lifetime we have gone from virtually no effective treatment for the biological depressions (electroconvulsive shock treatment was the only help available at the time I began treating depressions) to a rich armament of effective medications that are not addicting and have minimal side effects. Yet many Christians turn their backs on this help, fearing that they will be stigmatized by others, become drug* addicts or, worse still, find that their problem is spiritual and not psychological or biological. The result is unnecessary suffering by untold millions of Christians, as well as by family members who must stand by and try to cope with a dysfunctional loved one.

Why Is Depression So Common?

While the more serious depressions are essentially biochemical in origin with a strong genetic tendency, modern-day stress* seems to be a major aggravating cause. The frantic pace of modern life combined with a breakdown of traditional values* is causing many to feel hopeless, uncertain and disappointed. This stress aggravates the genetic factors that predispose to biological depressions. It also sets the stage for an appalling sense of loss, which is the primary cause of psychological depressions. Demoralization is rampant in our modern culture and can turn an even minor setback into a major depression in a body* overextended by stress.

Many losses in our modern world are tangible and material. More significant, however, in causing psychological depression are such losses as insecurity, uncertainty, rejection, lack of fulfillment in one's vocation, and a general sense of the meaninglessness of life. These are losses that were not as prevalent in earlier times. As a culture, we may well have entered our own emotional "Great Depression."

The Cost of Depression

The economic cost of being depressed in the United States is estimated to exceed $16 billion a year. Estimating the emotional and human costs of serious depression, in the lives of both those who are depressed and the family members and friends who must suffer alongside, is almost impossible, but we know it is considerable. Major depression always disrupts, and sometimes disintegrates, otherwise healthy families, families whose lives are turned topsy-turvy by the emotional devastation of one member who is not able to function normally. Should the depressed person commit suicide, the consequences can continue for the rest of a family's lifetime.

In times past, depression was always associated with a major mental breakdown and seemed to be restricted to a few poorly adjusted, usually anonymous persons. It was a concealed problem. Now it has assumed a common, real, familiar and very personal identity for all of us. It is found with frightening regularity in ourselves, our relatives and our friends. There is hardly a family today that is not touched by depression's tentacles.

Who Is at Risk?

Depression is no respecter of age, sex, socioeconomic status or occupation. We are seeing an alarming increase in childhood depressions. In fact, the dramatic increase in depression in both the very young and the elderly is among the most frightening features of modern-day depression.

Women, however, are significantly at greater risk for depression than men (a two to one ratio). The reasons for this are twofold. First, the reproductive biochemistry of the female body implicates depression more often. At various times during the menstrual cycle, as well as in the life cycle of reproduction, depression results from hormonal changes. Problems with depression just before menstruation*(premenstrual syndrome) as well as later in life (menopausal depression; *see* Menopause) are extremely common.

Second, it is very clear that women today are under greater stress than men. Mothers often have to work a full-time job in addition to taking care of family needs. Their resources for coping are therefore pushed to the limits. The result is a greater propensity toward fatigue and depressions caused by adrenaline exhaustion.

Dealing with Depression

Nothing is as tough to fight as depression. The depression itself robs you of the energy and motivation to do anything about it. Untreated biological depressions are often debilitating and can last up to three years during each attack.

For some the depression hits with an unannounced suddenness that is quite alarming. For others it stalks up insidiously and may go unrecognized for months or even years. When sufferers finally realize that they are in its grasp, it has already sapped their strength and fogged up their mind so that they don't believe anything can be done to help.

Alarmingly, only about one-third of those seriously depressed will actually seek treatment. Some don't know they can be helped. Some are afraid to admit they need help because it might stigmatize them. Some are callously told by their pastor or Christian friends that they should just pray harder or try to find the sin that is causing the depression. Most don't seek treatment because they're too depressed and feel too hopeless to believe they can get better; they try to "tough it out." Unfortunately, this can have serious consequences not only for the sufferer but for all those connected to him or her.

Among these untreated depressed persons are many Christians. They don't realize that with the right sort of treatment they could probably bounce back in a matter of weeks and, more important, prevent any recurring episodes of their depression later in life.

How Can You Tell If You Are Depressed?
One of the most unfortunate secondary effects of depression is that it often causes the sufferer to be oblivious to the depression. Depression eludes recognition, especially in the less severe types. Some people can be depressed for a long time, therefore, and not realize it. Depression can also mask itself in irritability, fatigue and workaholism.* Many who overeat do so as a form of "self-medication" to ease their dejected state. Even when someone vaguely knows he or she is depressed, there is a tendency to deny the depression. Depression is often mistakenly viewed as a weakness, and people fear that even acknowledging their emotional pain to themselves is an admission of defeat.

So a large percentage of people with depression don't get appropriate treatment because they don't recognize their depressive symptoms. Religious sufferers tend to spiritualize their condition and want to blame God, Satan or some spiritual failure for their malady. The first step, then, in getting help is to recognize the symptoms and acknowledge that one is depressed.

What Are the Symptoms?
The following are among the most common symptoms of depression: persistent sadness, anxiety* or an "empty" mood; a sense of hopelessness and pessimism; feelings of guilt, worthlessness, helplessness; crying at the slightest provocation; loss of interest or pleasure in ordinary

and pleasurable activities, including sex; sleep* disturbances such as insomnia, early-morning waking or oversleeping; eating* disturbances (either loss or gain in weight); decreased energy, fatigue, feeling slowed down; thoughts of death* or suicide; restlessness and irritability; difficulty in concentrating, in remembering and in making decisions; and physical symptoms (headaches, digestive disorders and chronic pain).

In all depressions fatigue is a prominent symptom. This is particularly true for the biologically based depressions that tend to drain energy. There is also a general lack of interest in normal activities. Sadness or crying may or may not be present. In some, sadness is the least important sign of depression.

Getting Help
How one copes with depression depends on its cause. Since all depressions fall basically into two categories, endogenous (or biological) and exogenous (or psychological), this discussion will focus on each in turn and provide some treatment guidelines.

Endogenous depressions. Endogenous literally means "from within." Since there are many biological causes for depression, treatment must be directed primarily at the underlying disease or biochemical disorder. Besides obvious serious illnesses* such as cancer or heart disease, disruption of the endocrine system is a particularly common cause of many depressions. So whenever a biological depression is suspected, a thorough evaluation of the endocrine system, particularly the thyroid gland, is warranted.

When endocrine dysfunction is ruled out, attention turns to the nervous system and the brain's chemistry. The cause of two of the most common forms of endogenous depressions—major depression and bipolar disorder (the sufferer alternates between mania and depression)—lies clearly in a deficiency of a neurotransmitter within the brain's nervous system. Fortunately, there are now very effective antidepressant medications available that can correct these deficiencies.

While a complete discussion of these medications is not possible here, the following important points need to be stressed:

☐ Not everyone benefits from the same antidepressant. Individualized treatment is therefore essential.

☐ Antidepressant medications do not act immediately; they take between two and four weeks, or even longer, after the appropriate level of treatment has been reached before relief is experienced. Persistence in treatment is therefore essential.

☐ Modern antidepressant medications have far fewer side effects than earlier ones and are perfectly safe when taken under supervision for long periods of time. Don't be in a hurry to stop them.

☐ Antidepressant medications are not addicting. They may be taken without fear of becoming dependent on them.

Exogenous or reactive depression. While these depressions are not usually as serious as the biological ones, they can be much more difficult to cope with. There is no medication to speak of that treats them. Besides, since they are a reaction to loss, medication is most times inappropriate. What is needed is the more painful work of grieving.*

Reactive depression is essentially a call to let go of whatever it is we have lost. God has designed us for grief, so that whether the loss is the death of a loved one, the departure of our first child to college, getting fired* from a job or a business venture that has gone bad, we have to face this loss with courage and allow ourselves to grieve. Ecclesiastes tells us that "to every thing there is a season" (3:1 KJV) and that there is "a time to weep" (3:4). This is what reactive depression is all about. It is a healing* time to help us cope with loss.

The grief work needed for a major loss can seldom be accomplished without talking it through with someone else. Consulting a professional counselor, preferably a Christian, is almost essential in more severe depressive reactions. However, an understanding pastor, lay counselor* or friend can also be tremendously helpful.

Whatever resource is used, the following important points must be kept in mind:

☐ Grief work takes time, so don't be hurried. The more significant the loss, the longer it will take to get over it and the deeper will be the depression.

☐ Don't try to "short-circuit" your depression by rushing to replace your loss. Sooner or later your mind will bring you back to complete your grieving for past losses.

☐ Invite God to be a part of your grieving. Don't blame him for your loss, and there is certainly nothing to be gained by getting angry at him. He knows your pain and longs to be your comforter, so don't turn your back on him.

☐ As the title of one of my books suggests, every cloud has a silver lining. This means that within every grief experience there is great potential for spiritual and personal growth. Embrace your experience with the full confidence that when you come out of the fire you will be a little better for it (Job 23:10).

See also ANXIETY; GRIEVING; HEALTH; ILLNESS; STRESS, WORKPLACE.

References and Resources

Dean Foundation for Health, Research and Education, *Depression and Antidepressants* (Madison, Wis.: Dean Foundation, 1995); A. D. Hart, *Counseling the Depressed* (Waco, Tex.: Word Books, 1987); A. D. Hart, *Dark Clouds, Silver Linings* (Colorado Springs: Focus on the

Family, 1993); U.S. Department of Health and Human Services, *Depression in Primary Care: Detection, Diagnosis and Treatment* (Washington, D.C.: U.S. Government Printing Office, 1993).

Archibald D. Hart

DISCIPLESHIP

To be a disciple of Jesus is an exciting venture. It is to enter into a lifestyle that brings wholeness and fulfillment. It is to maximize our potential, fulfill our destinies and discover our true selves because it is to live in the way God has designed for human beings. Discipleship, however, is not always understood in this way. To those outside the church, the word has an archaic ring. In a culture* that values individual freedom,* personal truth and unrestricted choice, the whole idea of trusting oneself to another is frightening. Those inside the church are not free from these same reactions. They often equate discipleship with words such as *discipline, obedience, constraint, self-denial, hardship, sacrifice* and *martyrdom*—all words that have negative connotations in a culture given over to self-satisfaction and self-fulfillment. Each of us needs to probe what the word *discipleship* feels like to us. Is the idea of discipleship a burden or a joy to us? What images do we have of disciples? Are these positive or negative? How we answer will affect how we read this article.

Discipleship in the First-Century World
In light of such reactions, it is important to investigate the biblical roots of the concept of discipleship. In the Old Testament, apart from a few references (for example, 1 Chron 25:8; Is 8:16; 50:4; 54:13), there is little explicit teaching about discipleship. However, it is evident that the relationship between prophets and their followers was often that of master-disciple, even though it is not specifi-

cally defined in this way (see 1 Sam 19:20-24; 2 Kings 4:1, 38; 9:1; Jer 36:32).

In the New Testament there is abundant discussion of what it means to be a disciple. This is not surprising since discipleship was a common phenomenon in the first-century world. Greek philosophers had disciples, as did the Pharisees (Mt 22:15-16), not to mention John the Baptist (Mk 2:18; Jn 1:35). The Jews, on occasion, referred to themselves as disciples of Moses (Jn 9:27-28). In these relationships, disciples were understood to be individuals committed to a particular person so as to learn that person's teaching or way of life and then to follow a particular pattern of life, whether by living in a certain way, passing on the teaching to others or engaging in political or religious activities. Jesus and his disciples shared this common understanding of the relationship between teacher and disciple. Thus to follow Jesus meant to do what Jesus did (replicate his ministry*; for example, Mk 6:7-13, 30; Lk 10:1-20) and to believe what Jesus taught (obey his word; for example, Jn 8:31-32; 17:6).

The same two characteristics hold true today for those of us who would be Jesus' disciples. First, to be a disciple of Jesus is to be involved in ministry. The nature and character of that ministry varies greatly: from voluntary ministry to tentmaking* ministry to ordained ministry. The important point is not what we do but that we understand our task in life to be one of ministry. This will mean that we engage in that task with a consciousness that we are called to it by God, that we seek to honor and serve God in this task and that we exhibit the characteristics of a disciple of Jesus while engaged in our task. Second, to be a disciple of Jesus is to engage in ongoing examination, analysis and application of Scripture. In this way we come to know who God is, what God requires of us and how to live as God's people. As we go about this task of developing and sharpening our Christian worldview, we will also investigate the whole range of knowledge, understanding that God is the God of truth and that all truth is God's truth.

Discipleship in the Gospels

It was also true in the first century that the nature of one's discipleship depended on the nature of one's master. It is the master who determines the content of discipleship. So while the relationship between Jesus and his disciples shared connections with traditional understandings of discipleship, it also had a unique character all of its own, which was derived from who Jesus was and what he taught. Hence it becomes important to examine the Gospels in order to define the special character of the discipleship to which Jesus called men and women.

First, it is clear that the original relationship between Jesus and his followers was understood to be that of master and disciples. The word *disciple* occurs some 269 times in the New Testament with almost all the references found in the Gospels and Acts.

Second, Jesus had various types of disciples, ranging from the Twelve who were appointed to be apostles (Mk 3:13-19), to the Seventy (-two) who were sent out on a specific mission by Jesus (Lk 10:1-20), to the others who followed him (Mt 27:57; Lk 6:17; 9:59-62; 23:49, 55), and including the crowds, some of whom eventually left when his teaching became too hard for them to accept (Jn 6:60, 66). It is significant that a number of women were counted as Jesus' disciples, even traveling with him at times (Lk 8:1-3), despite the fact that women generally were seen as second-class citizens in the Greek and Jewish culture of the time. Later on, as the church expanded, women become quite prominent in its growth, governance and development.

Third, the relationship between Jesus and the Twelve is the example of discipleship about which we know the most and provides the best place to discern the unique characteristics of Jesus' call to it. In fact, this is interesting more generally because it quickly becomes clear they were not spiritual giants. As far as we can tell, they were quite ordinary first-century Jewish laymen with traditional theological views.

Each of the four Gospels describes the discipleship of the Twelve. While there is much common material, each Gospel highlights different aspects of discipleship. In Matthew we find a manual on discipleship. In particular, the Sermon on the Mount gives explicit instructions for living a kingdom lifestyle: instructions that are often at odds with prevailing cultural attitudes (Mt 5:1—7:28). In Mark we find the concept of disciples as servants—those who give themselves for the sake of others (Mk 8:27—10:45). In Luke following Jesus is synonymous with discipleship, but to follow Jesus requires counting the cost (Lk 9:23-26, 57-62; 14:25-33): it is to give up other attachments (such as wealth*) and, instead, to love God and others (Lk 10:25-37). In John the key characteristic of discipleship is acceptance of Jesus' claims about who he is. Here the three marks of the true disciple are abiding in Jesus' word (Jn 8:31-32), love for others (Jn 13:34) and a fruit-bearing life (Jn 15:8).

So for those of us who seek to be Jesus' disciples today, we do well to ponder the (still) puzzling call in Matthew to a countercultural lifestyle in which the poor and the meek are called blessed; in which mercy, purity and peacemaking are commended; in which persecution is to be expected; in which murder and lust are shown to begin as attitudes of the heart; in which turning the other cheek and walking the extra mile are marks of discipleship; and in which we are called to love even our enemies. We learn from Mark that the characteristic of discipleship is sacrificial love for others, a love that demands no return. In Luke we are faced with the challenge of other loyalties. What, in fact, determines our behavior? Is it love for Jesus or love of money (power, possessions, sex, etc.)? From John we learn of the vital importance of accepting Jesus for who he is, not for whom we would like him to be. We are challenged to follow the one who is the Bread of Life; the Light of the World; the way, truth and life; the Good Shepherd; the resurrection and the life; and the vine (of which we are branches).

Fourth, the end result of being Jesus' disciples is friendship* with him. This is quite amazing and moves beyond traditional understandings of discipleship. In speaking to the Twelve Jesus said, "My command is this: Love each other as I have loved you. . . . You are my friends if you do what I command. I no longer call you servants. . . . Instead, I have called you friends" (Jn 15:12-15).

The Unique Character of Discipleship to Jesus

Taken as a whole, three distinct characteristics emerge that define the disciples of Jesus in addition to the general characteristics of first-century discipleship: (1) calling and following: to be Jesus' disciple is to hear his call and to heed it by following him; (2) counting the cost: to be Jesus' disciple means to bear our cross; and (3) commitment: to be Jesus' disciple is to enter into a relationship with him.

Calling and following. It was common in the first century for potential disciples to seek out a rabbi with whom they wished to study. In contrast, Jesus called people to himself (Mt 8:22; 16:24; 19:21; Mk 1:17). Furthermore, he urged his disciples to call others to follow him. "Make disciples" is the core command in the Great Commission (Mt 28:19).

Jesus' call was to enter into a new way of living. This is best defined by the Great Commandment: " 'Hear, O Israel, the Lord our God, the Lord is one. Love the Lord your God with all your heart and with all your soul and with all your mind and with all your strength.' . . . 'Love your neighbor as yourself.' There is no commandment greater than these" (Mk 12:29-31). Thus the disciples of Jesus are called to a threefold path of love: loving God, loving themselves and loving others. That love at the center of the commandment points to the significance of giving our full attention as disciples to all our relationships. That we are called upon to love God in this all-encompassing way points to the fact that nurturing our spiritual lives is at the center of our discipleship. We are to love God with our whole beings: with our hearts (from the center of our being, which includes thinking and feeling), with our souls* (which connotes physical and psychological energy), with our minds (intellectual activity) and with our strength (physical and material capabilities including our wealth). All aspects of life are meant to come under the lordship of Jesus.

Counting the cost. The cost of discipleship continues to be a challenge to all who would follow Jesus. It is Jesus who said, "Anyone who loves his father or mother more than me is not worthy of me; anyone who loves his son or daughter more than me is not worthy of me; and anyone who does not take his cross and follow me is not worthy of me. Whoever finds his life will lose it, and whoever loses his life for my sake will find it" (Mt 10:37-39). The importance of the final sentence in this statement is that it is the most frequently cited saying of Jesus in the New Testament. These are puzzling words, for we know that Jesus calls us to love others (and family* is a priority) and that he chastises the Pharisees for using religious excuses for failing to care for family (Mk 7:9-13). In his typical, hyperbolical way, Jesus may be telling us that we need to leave our dependence on family so as to be able to love them truly. These are also strong words that haunt us as we compare our comfortable, safe, fulfilling lives to the lives of the early Christians, who came to assume that to be a Christian was to be a martyr. How can we live with the stringent demands of discipleship?

In response, some speak of "radical discipleship." By this some mean living in an antimaterialistic way so as to serve the poor and fight injustice (Bonhoeffer; Sugden; Wallis). Others use this term in a more individualistic way, understanding radical discipleship to be a life of active ministry (preaching, teaching, evangelizing) and of a committed "walk" with Jesus (Ortiz; Bridges), that is, Bible study, prayer, worship.*

Counting the cost has to do with priorities as much as anything. To what do we give ourselves—affirmation and acceptance? reputation and power? sensual indulgence and pleasure? knowledge or leisure? We face a long list of options in modern life. To follow Jesus is to choose (no matter how imperfectly) to give Jesus priority in life over against all these other options.

Commitment. At the core of discipleship is relationship with Jesus. Jesus called his followers not just to his teaching but to himself (Jn 15). This will involve coming to know who Jesus is in the full sense.

Commitment to Jesus will also involve an active attempt to cultivate a vital relationship with him. One aim of the spiritual disciplines* is to help us develop just such a lifestyle. The devotional activities to which we give ourselves will involve, at least, the kind of Bible study and prayer that is an active dialogue with Jesus through which we experience the love, guidance and presence of the one we follow.

Living as a Disciple

On a practical level, discipleship is commonly understood within the Christian community to be a particular program of learning rather than a holistic way of life. But the contemporary challenge is not just to participate in schemes that seek to teach discipleship; it is to conduct our whole lives as conscious disciples of Jesus. In fact, one author defines discipleship as "living a fully human life in this world in union with Jesus Christ and growing in conformity to his image" (Wilkins, p. 42). If our whole life is meant to reflect our active discipleship, this will involve the following choices and activities.

The use of time. With the average adult American working longer hours and, in addition, watching an average of twenty-five hours of television* a week, time* has become our most precious commodity. Yet it takes time to cultivate a life of discipleship. We need to develop regular patterns of prayer, study and reflection that become an integral part of our schedules. In addition, we need to learn to use the gaps in our day for reflection and prayer: driving to work, waiting* in line, lunch, time before going to sleep* and so on. As well we need to master the art of openness to God while working, much as Brother Lawrence did in the monastery kitchen.

The use of means. Given our overwrought schedules, we must take advantage of those vehicles for growth that are open to us. In particular, small groups* that meet on a regular basis for the purpose of spiritual growth seem to fit with both our need for regular spiritual activity and our need for the support of others as we seek to be disciples of Jesus (*see* Church; Church in the Home; Community). We also need to engage with others in a church for the purpose of learning, fellowship,* celebration of the Lord's Supper and prayer—as was the practice of the first disciples (Acts 2:42). A church community also gives us opportunity for service.

The use of vocation. We need to learn what it means to consider our jobs not just as means of earning a living but as the area in which to minister as disciples of Jesus (*see* Calling).

The use of spiritual disciplines. We need to rediscover the practices of the church down through the centuries by which men and women sought to cultivate a life of discipleship: meditation, fasting, solitude, confession, worship, prayer, study, celebration, discernment and simplicity.

In all this there must be conscious intentionality, the willingness to engage in the process of growth rather than seek instant growth and to engage in life in community with others on the same path. To live in this way is to live as a disciple of Jesus.

See also ACCOUNTABILITY, RELATIONAL; CALLING; FELLOWSHIP; SMALL GROUPS; SPIRITUAL DISCIPLINES; SPIRITUAL FORMATION; SPIRITUAL GROWTH.

References and Resources

E. Best, *Disciples and Discipleship: Studies in the Gospel According to Mark* (Edinburgh: T & T Clark, 1986); E. Best, *Following Jesus: Discipleship in the Gospel of Mark* (Sheffield: JSOT, 1981); D. Bonhoeffer, *The Cost of Discipleship,* trans. R. H. Fuller, 2d rev. ed. (New York: Macmillan, 1963); J. Bridges, *The Practice of Godliness* (Colorado Springs: NavPress, 1983); J. Bridges, *The Pursuit of Holiness* (Colorado Springs: NavPress, 1978); A. Gill, *Life on the Road: The Gospel Basis for a Messianic Lifestyle* (Homebush West, N.S.W.: Lancer Books, Anzea Publishers, 1989); J. C. Ortiz, *Disciple* (Carol Stream, Ill.: Creation House, 1975); R. Peace, *Pilgrimage: A Handbook on Christian Growth* (Grand Rapids: Baker, 1976); C. Sugden, *Radical Discipleship* (Hants, U.K.: Marshall, Morgan & Scott, 1981); J. Wallis, *Agenda for Biblical People* (New York: Harper & Row, 1976); M. J. Wilkins, *Following the Master: Discipleship in the Steps of Jesus* (Grand Rapids: Zondervan, 1992); D. Willard, *The Spirit of the Disciplines: Understanding How God Changes Lives* (San Francisco: Harper & Row, 1988).

Richard V. Peace

DISCRIMINATION, WORKPLACE

As a term, *discrimination* can be understood in different ways. Historically it has meant the process of observing differences and making distinctions in our choices. Whenever we are hiring an employee or choosing an employee for promotion, the process of selection involves a form of discrimination. In this respect all judgments are discriminatory.

In recent decades, however, *discrimination* has taken on a negative connotation. Current usage most likely refers to *unjust* discrimination that is the result of improper judgments. Here discrimination means choosing for or against a person based on their group or class, or some characteristic (attribute) related to their group, and not on individual merit. This subjective judgment is the basis for giving an individual unjustifiably positive or negative treatment.

Discrimination in the workplace* is manifested in different forms. It can be seen in the selection, hiring and promotional practices of organizations. The most conspicuous forms of workplace discrimination are *sexism, racism** and *ageism.* It is naive to believe that Christians are not susceptible to workplace discrimination issues. Should a Christian manager* not promote someone because of moral issues (perhaps the worker is racist, makes crude jokes, is a practicing homosexual*), or should she or he consider only the employee's work* performance record? Should a Christian be promoted over a non-Christian? Or should a "nice" person be promoted ahead of a profane but more competent worker? Such questions suggest the breadth and complexity of choices involving discrimination. To answer any of these situations without being aware of the myriad variables that make up each set of circumstances would be both unfair and simplistic.

One business ethicist observes that at its core, workplace discrimination involves adverse decisions against employees based on their membership in a group that is viewed as inferior or seen as deserving of unequal treatment. This discrimination can be institutional or individual, intentional or unintentional (Shaw and Barry, p. 364).

Diversity and the Changing Workplace

Diversity and *multiculturalism** are two words often applied to today's work environment. Here are some facts about the changing workplace in the United States:

☐ Women, people of color and immigrants account for more than 50 percent of the present work force.

☐ By the year 2000, 85 percent of the those entering the job market will be female, African-American, Asian-American, Latino or new immigrants.

☐ Two million "older" workers, between ages fifty and sixty-four, are ready, willing and able to work but are not being utilized.

☐ Encouraged by the Americans with Disabilities Act of 1990, many of the forty-three million Americans with disabilities will seek equal opportunity in employment (Blank and Slipp, p. 3).

There is considerable agreement that an ethical organization operates on ground rules which encourage managers to communicate and treat the diversity and differences in their work force fairly. However, dealing with diversity in the workplace without practicing some

discriminatory behavior has become a more complex task today than it was a decade or two ago.

A comprehensive 1980s study done by the Hudson Institute, *Workforce 2000: Work and Workers for the 21st Century,* made significant predictions that are worth examining. It projected that of the twenty-five million people who would join the American work force between 1987 and 2000, only 15 percent would be white males; almost 61 percent would be women; and 29 percent would be minorities (minority women were counted twice; cited by Garfield, pp. 8-9). For companies committed to a corporate culture that will include groups besides white males, this raises two dilemmas: first, how to ensure a diverse work force without antagonizing either white males, whose support is critical for change, or women and minorities, who may resent efforts to win over white males; and second, how to correct historical discrimination without creating new forms of it (Galen and Palmer, pp. 50-52).

Sexism, Racism, Ageism and Other Forms of Workplace Discrimination

Sexism occurs when people are treated in a biased or prejudiced manner based on gender rather than on personal traits or abilities. Sexism can be blatant or subtle and is often complex. There are numerous accounts of how successful professional women today had to surmount serious sexist roadblocks to advance in their careers. It has only been in the last few decades that women have been able to make substantial inroads into such fields as medicine and law, for example.

Sexism can be subtle because people may interpret a particular behavior differently depending on whether it is exhibited by a man or a woman. Some may see a man as assertive but a woman as aggressive, a man as flexible but a woman as fickle, a woman as sensitive but a man as a wimp, or a woman as polite but a man as patronizing (Range, p. 791). Women frequently encounter a "glass ceiling" as they attempt the ascent to upper-management levels. Only about 3 percent of American women have gained high-level management positions. Furthermore, in the United States a woman earns only about 70-75 cents for every dollar earned by a man having the same job (Reder, pp. 23-25).

In the work arena, *racism* or *racial prejudice* occurs when there is an unfair or unequal valuation of persons on the basis of race. Racism assumes that hereditary biology determines the differences between groups, that cultural differences are predetermined and unchangeable, and that the identifying social and cultural features of the subordinate group are inferior (Thoms, p. 342).

African-Americans in particular have experienced discrimination at work. Their representation in management positions falls dramatically short of their overall representation in the work force. As of 1991, according to U.S. Labor Department statistics, fewer than 24 percent of African-American workers held managerial, professional or administrative jobs, compared to about 60 percent of whites (Reder, p. 31).

While diversity studies tend to focus on differences in gender, culture and ethnic background, the broadest definition of diversity will also encompass differences in *age*. As the American population ages, new concerns about staffing shortages, mandatory retirement* and age discrimination are arising. Ageism is a much more subtle bias than racism and sexism; therefore it often goes unrecognized.

Sexism, racism and ageism are not the only areas where discrimination occurs in the workplace. Individuals may also suffer discrimination because of religious beliefs, sexual preference, disability status, educational background and even physical appearance. For example, some qualified individuals may be passed over for extremely attractive, less qualified individuals who broadcast the "ideal" organization image.

Group Characteristics Versus Stereotypes

Managers must take time to get to know and appreciate an individual's unique qualities and not take the dangerous, ill-considered path of using stereotypes as a shortcut means for labeling people. Unfortunately, stereotyping happens too often—consciously or unconsciously—without any thought to its potentially adverse effects on others. The following are examples of common stereotypes:

☐ People with disabilities are unable to work regular hours.

☐ Women who are mothers are not committed to their jobs.

☐ White men are racist and sexist.

☐ Immigrants have no desire to learn English. (Blank and Slipp, p. 9)

Management must be aware of the difference between a group characteristic and a stereotype. For example, a legitimate characteristic of many people with disabilities—although not all—is that they need some accommodation to perform their jobs optimally. A stereotype is the belief that people with disabilities cannot work regular hours because it is too hard for them; such a stereotype may lead managers not to hire anyone with a disability.

Scripture and Discrimination

As Christians, when we make moral choices, we are involved in a type of discrimination because our intent is to select the best moral alternative over less favorable ones. However, when we use inappropriate criteria for making our moral judgments, we are practicing *unjust* discrimination. Richard Chewning astutely points out that unjust discrimination reveals an ungodly form of favoritism and rejection that violates biblical norms. Scripture reveals that God is not a respecter of persons and that unjust discrimination is an abomination to him (see Deut 10:17; 2 Chron 19:7; Acts 10:34; Rom 2:11; Gal 2:6; Eph 6:9; Col 3:25; Jas 2:1-9; 1 Pet 1:17). Christians need to be aware, Chewning says, that our "old nature" has a tendency toward becoming protective and defensive whenever our psychological comfort is threatened. Sadly, this perverted reflex is often at the root of discrimination and generally reveals personal insecurities and pride (Chewning, p. 277).

For Christians, unjust discrimination is morally objectionable not only because it is wrong and evil but also because it stands against the revelation of God, who loves all people and offers them reconciliation through Christ. Our worth is tied to the belief that men and women are created in God's image (Gen 1:27), that all people have sinned and come short of God's glory (Rom 3:23) and that God's love* for the world culminated in Christ's death on the cross, which covers the sins of those who put faith in him (Jn 3:16). This egalitarian ideal is also critical to Paul's conception of the church, where "there is neither Jew nor Greek, slave or free, male nor female, for you are all one in Christ Jesus" (Gal 3:28; compare Col 3:11). Paul's view was in juxtaposition to that of ethnic Jews who saw themselves as being a superior race because they were God's chosen people.

The Israelites were commanded to deal with people in a just and loving manner (Deut 1:17; 24:17-18); special consideration was to be given to the poor, the widow, the orphan and the needs of the alien, who did not have equal political and economic status with adult Israelite males (Ex 22:21-27; Lev 19:10; Deut 15:7-11).

Jesus' teaching and behavior exemplified the importance of dealing with others in an impartial way (Lk 20:21) by practicing love and justice. In so doing he collided with many discriminatory practices of his day. Jesus took a strong stance in his radical inclusion and acceptance of women and children (Mk 10:13-16; Jn 4:1-27; 12:1-11); he openly befriended social outcasts (Lk 5:27-31; 18:9-14; Jn 8:1-11); and he healed the sick and unclean (Lk 5:12-26; 17:11-19). Compassion, not correctness, was his guide.

One of the most important New Testament passages addressing discrimination is the parable of the good Samaritan (Lk 10:25-37). In this parable, a man who is robbed and left half dead is passed by "on the other side" of the road by both a priest and a Levite. Yet a Samaritan, despised by Jews as an unclean half-breed, takes pity on him, attends to his wounds, puts him on his own donkey, takes him to an inn, and generously gives the innkeeper enough money to provide for the man to stay for up to two months at the inn.

What makes this parable striking is that the most likely candidates for attending to the man not only ignore his plight but also deliberately pass by on the other side. The person Jesus commends in the parable was neither the religious leader nor the lay associate but a hated foreigner—the Samaritan. If anyone has a reason for passing the injured man by, it is the Samaritan, since Samaritans and Jews were openly hostile toward one another. In this parable, then, Jesus pointedly asserts that authentic love transcends national boundaries.

When Jesus asks, "Which of these three do you think was a neighbor to the man who fell into the hands of robbers?" the answer is "The one who had mercy on him." To this Jesus adds, "Go and do likewise."

The parable of the good Samaritan is given in response to the poignant question "And who is my neighbor?" Immediately preceding this question in verse 27—and in other passages (Mt 22:35-40; Mk 12:28-33; compare Lev 19:18)—Jesus succinctly provides guidance concerning our priorities and relationship to God and our neighbors.

> Jesus replied: "'Love the Lord your God with all your heart and with all your soul and with all your mind.' This is the first and greatest commandment. And the second is like it: 'Love your neighbor as yourself.' All the Law and the Prophets hang on these commandments." (Mt 22:37-40)

Christians are called to accept all persons, regardless of race, creed or sex, on equal footing as children of God. In the final analysis, the problem of discrimination (in its negative sense) finds a certain resolution for Christians in the attempt to fulfill God's law as given in the "new commandment": "If you really keep the royal law found in Scripture, 'Love your neighbor as yourself,' you are doing right. But if you show favoritism, you sin and are convicted by the law as lawbreakers" (Jas 2:8-9).

See also AGING; BUSINESS ETHICS; FIRING; MULTICULTURALISM; OFFICE POLITICS; ORGANIZATIONAL CULTURE AND CHANGE; POWER, WORKPLACE; RACISM.

References and Resources

R. Blank and S. Slipp, *Voices of Diversity* (New York: American Management Association, 1994); R. C. Chewning, *Biblical Principles and Business: The Practice* (Colorado Springs: NavPress, 1990) 272-84; M. Galen and A. T. Palmer, "White, Male and Worried," *Business Week*, January 31, 1994, 50-55; C. Garfield, "Embracing Diversity," *Executive Excellence*, October 1994, 8-9; D. J. Miller, "Discrimination," in *Evangelical Dictionary of Biblical Theology*, ed. W. Elwell (Grand Rapids: Baker, 1984) 320-21; L. M. Range, "Sexism," in *Ready Reference: Ethics* (Pasadena, Calif.: Salem, 1994) 791-92; A. Reder, *In Pursuit of Principle and Profit* (New York: G. P. Putnam's Sons, 1994); J. Richardson. ed., *Annual Editions: Business Ethics 96/97* (Sluice Dock, Guilford, Conn.: Dushkin, 1996); W. H. Shaw and V. Barry, *Moral Issues in Business* (Belmont, Calif.: Wadsworth, 1992); D. E. Thoms, "Racism," in *Encyclopedia of Biblical and Christian Ethics* (Nashville: Thomas Nelson, 1992) 342-43.

John E. Richardson

DIVORCE

Divorce is a tragic dimension of everyday life. With a significant percentage of marriages ending in divorce in the Western world, many people are skipping marriage* altogether and are simply cohabiting.* Others want to get married "until death us do part," as the vows state, but enter marriage with a deep fear that they may become a statistic. Still others, influenced by a culture of "throwaway" relationships, enter marriage with an emotional loophole, thinking (often unconsciously), *If it doesn't work out we can always get a divorce.* Rather than being a covenant for lifelong companionship, marriage today is frequently reduced to a contract* for the mutual meeting of needs.* "So long as we both shall live" has become "so long as we both shall love." Taken in its best light, divorce is regarded by many as part of the process of personal growth. But the negative consequences for children, families,* society,* morality, mental health and education* are documented over and over again in both popular and scholarly works.

Approaching the Divorce Question

It is not the purpose of this article to consider all aspects of divorce including the emotional stages of divorce that precede legal divorce, preparation for a divorceless covenant (Stevens 1990), strategies for turning a for-worse into a for-better marriage (Stevens 1986; Weiner-Davis), or the recovery process when one has been divorced (Wallerstein and Blakeslee; Weiss). Rather it is concerned with the theology and spirituality of divorce: how we are to think about it, how divorce affects our relationship with God, and how we are to relate to this phenomenon in the world today. It must be said at the outset that nobody likes divorce (except a few who profit financially from it) and almost nobody wants to get divorced. Further, those people who have been divorced have not committed the unforgivable sin and are in deep need of love and acceptance.

The fundamental assumption of this article is that a theology and spirituality of divorce must rest on the Bible rather than on statistics, social mores or expediency. When it comes to divorce, taking the Bible as authority is a complicated matter. The church has tried to understand the divorce question in at least three ways: (1) through a legal-like interpretation of Scripture to find the permissible grounds, (2) by interpreting Scripture through the lens of dispensational thinking to find out whether the hard passages are really for today or some other age and (3) through biblical theology that considers two realities— Scripture and contemporary culture. We will consider each of these in turn and then offer a spiritual reflection.

It is difficult to speak of divorce and marriage at the same time. That seems to have been Jesus' dilemma when he was pressed with questions about the legality of divorce by his contemporaries (Mt 19:3-4). In effect, he said, "I can't speak about divorce until I have brought you back to God's intention in Genesis, which takes us beyond culture into the paradise of God. When two are united by God, and have become one, you would

be tearing apart a God-given unity if you divorced them." To quote Jesus' actual words, "What God has joined together, let man not separate" (Mt 19:6). While Jesus does not say that divorce causes polygamy (or polyandry), he implies this by stating that "anyone who divorces his wife, except for marital unfaithfulness, and marries another woman commits adultery" (Mt 19:9). Simply put, someone who already belongs to someone should not, perhaps cannot, also belong to another. Whether the practice results in multiple wives simultaneously (as in some cultures) or multiple wives sequentially (as in our culture), the effect is the same. Modern practice and biblical truth require treating the divorce question as a case study in serial polygamy and polyandry, as unpopular as this might be.

The Textual/Legal Approach

Those who approach the subject of divorce from a legal perspective are concerned to find the correct grounds for permissible divorce. This necessitates dealing with the absolute statements against divorce in Mark 10:11-12 and Luke 16:18. These must be considered in light of the clause "except for marital unfaithfulness" found in Matthew 5:32 and 19:9. On the assumption that Mark and Luke knew of this clause, some argue that a person can be divorced if he or she is the innocent party of a marriage that has been destroyed by adultery. If death permits the physical survivor to remarry (Rom 7:3), adultery may permit the "moral survivor" to remarry.

Peter Davids argues, however, that when Jesus was asked for a rabbinic interpretation of Deuteronomy 24, Jesus rejected this passage as a permission for divorce. Davids's point centers on the argument that one cannot really divorce; that is, the divorce decree is a legal fiction. The parties involved have sinned, but they have not ended the marriage.

The relationship can be negative, distant and cold, but it has not been annulled. These two cannot be as they were before marriage. The Deuteronomy passage ceases to have relevance for us in Christ except in the case of a woman or man desiring to return to a former spouse after a remarriage to a second spouse had terminated, for that is what Deuteronomy 24 deals with. Even then, the full light of forgiveness in Christ might make us reconsider this as legislation applying to the Christian today.

A further problem Davids explores concerns the language found in Matthew 5:32 and 19:9: the Greek word *porneia* is used rather than the usual term for adultery, *moicheia*. This suggests that Jesus is dealing not with marital adultery but with premarital sexual sin. While the Old Testament called for stoning to death one who committed such sexual sin (*porneia*), divorce would have been more likely in the New Testament period. Joseph's predicament with Mary, and his intended righteous action, is a case in point. Frequently, those who try to uncover the legal grounds for divorce in the New Testament fail to notice that in the Gospels adultery is grounds for forgiveness, not divorce. They also fail to note that according to Jesus, the lustful eye—intending adultery—is as evil as the deed. This makes almost everyone divorceable.

What about the second ground for divorce in the Bible, that is, the case of desertion by an unbelieving partner: "But if the unbeliever leaves, let him do so. A believing man or woman is not bound in such circumstances" (1 Cor 7:15)? In this case one partner has become a Christian, and the other demands either renunciation of faith or the end of the marriage. Where one must make such a soul-wounding choice, Paul advises that the believer is not bound to his or her partner. But, he is careful to note, the believer does not deny his Lord (or defile the marriage) by remaining married to an unbeliever, if this is possible.

In fact, no sooner has Paul said that the believer need not restrain the unbeliever from leaving (though the believer is not to take the initiative) than he reminds the believer that a believing husband may even save the wife (1 Cor 7:16). Previously Paul had said that an unbelieving husband is already sanctified through his believing wife (7:14). The use of the term "not bound" in verse 15 emphasizes the freedom of the Christian spouse, and it is possible that Paul would give cautious permission for remarriage of the believer in those cases where the unbeliever has contracted another marital union. But it is highly unlikely that Paul is counseling divorce and remarriage for the believer when the unbelieving spouse remains unconnected with another marital partner.

One aspect is seldom noted by those who legislate on the matter of a marriage between a believing and an unbelieving spouse: the Christian spouse should not be such a nuisance to his or her partner, such an unpleasant believer, perhaps even a superspiritual believer no longer interested in sex, that the unbeliever simply can no longer tolerate living under the same roof. Just as it is difficult to locate absolutely the "innocent" party in the case of marital unfaithfulness, so it is difficult to locate the innocent party in the case of a deserting unbeliever. In both cases believers are not to end their marriages.

There is no New Testament legislation concerning persons divorced and remarried before becoming Christians. The gospel covers that possibility, and every other one as well, by proclaiming a new start in Christ. The New Testament simply does not deal with the situation of an abused woman (or man). Presumably

Paul, if he had ruled on this in the spirit of Jesus, would have said that a woman should not submit to abuse even if her husband, by not getting his own way, leaves her. But Paul would also say that while they may separate for peace, or even for personal emotional survival (assuming that all other means of dealing with it have temporarily failed), they are not thereby granted the right to divorce and find another partner. Grace holds out the hope of reconciliation and never gives up hope that the fractured covenant could be healed.

It is difficult to believe that Paul was more lenient than Jesus on the matter of divorce, even though Paul had to legislate whereas Jesus did not. The burden of Paul's teaching, as it was for Jesus, is the divorceless covenant, not the grounds for permissible divorce. As a realist within the grace of God, Paul dealt with the difficulties in which believers found themselves, but he refused to reduce marriage to a contract with terms that, through being violated, would annul it. It is impossible to legislate for every possible situation in extremely strained marriages by appealing to the teaching of either Jesus or Paul.

Does "sexual impurity" (*porneia*) in Matthew refer only to heterosexual intercourse? Does it include homosexual* acts? Would one homosexual act require divorce? Would *porneia* include the demand of a husband for sexual variations that are repulsive to his wife? or sexual abuse? or rape within the marriage? Would a wife or husband's unwillingness to consummate the relationship except to conceive children constitute sexual unfaithfulness? And what happens if the partner is unwilling to have intercourse because she finds her husband overbearing, demanding and manipulative, rather than loving? Anyone wishing to approach divorce from the legal point of view is well advised to read the postbibli-

cal Mishnah. That document prescribes in the most minute detail the conditions and variations that should guide a decision on the legality of divorce in almost every situation. The problem is that there will always be a situation for which the rule does not apply!

The Dispensational Approach
This view takes seriously the existence of different stages in the story of God's dealing with the human race. Christ taught the ethics of the kingdom and, as the King-in-person, introduced God's reign into this age. The new age of the kingdom overlaps with the old. And the ethic of the kingdom, it is argued, is too high to be lived out in a partially saved world. According to this view when Jesus spoke about divorceless marriage, he was speaking about life in his ideal kingdom, not about life in this mixed reality we now have of kingdom and flesh. So, for example, Dwight Small argues that we must balance Jesus' ideal teachings with the realities of the overlapping kingdoms (this age and the next age). While he does not call this *dispensational* thinking (different parts of the Bible deal with different seasons of God's saving activity), the effect is the same. It divides the New Testament into parts that apply now and parts that do not. The problem with Small's approach is that Jesus says it is the foolish person who does not build his life on obedience to his teaching now (Mt 7:24-27).

P. T. Forsyth takes a slightly different approach worth considering, arguing that the legislation for divorce regarding "hardness of heart" (Mt 19:8) is not a concession to individual weakness and human nature but a reflection on the incomplete development of God's society on earth. Even if we must recognize divorce as a reality, and perhaps even a gracious reality in the case of an innocent victim, we should never lose sight of

God's intention. God's design is a divorce-less covenant, and no marriage should be conceived on any other foundation. Forsyth notes, however, that a move from basing marriage on covenant to consent would change the very idea of marriage. This has now happened. What we are losing today are not marriages but marriage itself—the whole covenant idea.

While we must be realists, we must never accept divorce in a way that erodes the idea of a divorceless covenant. The Christian community is deeply challenged to do this in such a way that the divorced people among us are not made to feel like second-class citizens or marital lepers.

Biblical Theology

A third approach emphasizes the teaching of Jesus that "what God has joined together, let man not separate" (Mt 19:6). Until now I have assumed that God is normally pleased to join together those who will enter into a covenant, "as God's Word doth allow" (as the old marriage service stated), with all its dimensions: leaving, cleaving and one flesh (Gen 2:24) (*see* Marriage). But we must ask now whether God joins everyone who gets married. Are there people whose marriage is neither blessed nor founded in God (whether they believe in God or not), and for these people is divorce right, if not necessary? Perhaps no one has thought more comprehensively on this subject than Karl Barth in his work *Church Dogmatics*. The following discussion summarizes Barth's theology on the subject.

Marriage (covenant) is an indissoluble union. According to Barth, "the marriage which rests upon the command of God and therefore upon his calling cannot be dissolved by man even if he wishes" (Barth 1968, p. 34). Such a marriage, he argues, makes the indicatives "I am yours" and "you are mine" into impera-

tives. We must accept this until death us do part. The little key to the exit door is lost. Whoever would enter marriage must renounce the thought of ever leaving it.

Even a well-married couple should not presume on God's grace. Such a couple, he says, should not rely on the encouraging indications of their marriage but "can only hold fast the mercy of God without any merit of their own" (Barth 1968, p. 35). Beware if they think they stand by their own effort! This is an important corrective to the pragmatic approach today that if you go to enough marriage-enrichment seminars, you can guarantee a good marriage. It is God's gift!

Can you know for sure your marriage is not blessed by God? Barth says no. Even though there may be many indications of an unsuccessful marriage and people suspect that their marriage lacks God's blessing,* this blessing may simply be hidden from them for the moment. Barth calls them to consider "whether there may not be indications that its malady can finally be healed and its union given permanence" (1968, p. 36).

No matter what, we are to cling to God's yes. Covenant marriage is based not on external indications but on the call and provision of God. Therefore, since the Word of God is primarily a word of promise and only secondarily a word of judgment, a believer is called to cling to God's yes rather than his no. For "no negative indications, however bad, can engender the certainty that a particular marriage is without promise and stands finally under the judgment of God because [it is] not . . .'made in heaven' " (Barth 1968, p. 38).

But in an extreme case we may painfully conclude that a couple should not remain married. We must be cautious and unassuming in thinking that we can discern whether or not a marriage is blessed by God. The saying of Jesus cannot be reversed to say "what God has *not* joined together, let man separate." Divorce may be permitted where God has evidently condemned the marriage as a noncovenant. Divorce applies only to the legal institution of marriage and not the divine covenant, which is indissoluble. Therefore the covenant is not dissolved, because there never was one.

The church must show compassion to the divorced. Barth asks rhetorically, "May it not be that those who are joined in a 'good' marriage are supremely characterized by the fact that they can manifest toward those to whom this boon has not been granted something of the divine mercy which they themselves may enjoy in this respect?" (1968, p. 36). In passing it is worthy of note that often couples with "good marriages" tend to flock together and avoid those with "bad marriages," each group developing its own support network.

Divorced persons must not be refused remarriage. In Barth's view, divorced persons know themselves as judged by God in their (noncovenant) marriages, but the church "will not regard them as polluted, or scandalously . . . refuse them the church's benediction in the case of a second marriage" (1968, p. 41) if they turn in repentance to Christ and the gospel. After all, the ministry of the gospel is to create a new beginning, whether in a single life or to be married again.

The big question is not divorce but marriage. "Legal divorce," according to Barth, "is not part of the divine command concerning marriage; for this proclaims and requires its indissolubility. It belongs only to the institution of marriage. The human institution takes into account the possibility of marriages which have no divine foundation and constitution . . . and which therefore can be dissolved" (1968, p. 40). In other words, marriage is dissoluble (that is, marriage as a human institution), but

the covenant is indissoluble.

Divorce and the Spirituality of the Church

Barth's reasoning is an attempt to explore God's Word about divorce. But equally important is the question of what divorce does to our hearing (*see* Listening) of God's voice in Scripture and our knowing God's presence in everyday life. The pastoral approach to divorce has more than one dimension. There is the obvious pastoral concern of how to prevent divorce if possible and care for those going through a divorce. But what does easy and widespread divorce do to our spirituality?

First, the marriage covenant takes us to the heart of God, who is a covenant-making and covenant-keeping God. Second, if we cannot believe that God will work a miracle in our hearts to keep covenant with our spouse, even in a difficult marriage (indeed, what marriage is not?), how can we believe that God could work the greater miracle of raising Jesus from the dead? Like Hosea in the Old Testament, we may seek a solution to a difficult marriage beyond the institution of marriage itself. Hosea called his wife Gomer into court and spoke of her as divorced (and perhaps would have gone through a legal divorce) *in order to win her back!* Third, the essence of being a child of God—contrary to popular psychology—is obedience. If we obey what we already have from God, we can be given more. As we do the truth, God reveals more. Finally, a hard heart is both the cause and usual consequence of divorce (Mt 19:8). If we harden our heart to our nearest and dearest neighbor, our spouse, we will be dead to the voice of God.

A church where couples can exchange partners freely, where divorce is accepted as a normal growth experience, and where marriage is entered thoughtlessly and lightly as something less than a lifelong covenant is a church that will soon have no real spiritual power and vitality. Love without truth is deadening, but truth without love is deadly. When a church does not stand beside divorced people and offer grace and hope if they turn in repentance to Christ and the gospel but instead offers judgment, condemnation and exclusion, the church will soon not hear the voice of God. Of the three Christian virtues that should be offered by the people of God today, especially in relation to marriage, the one most urgently needed is hope. And hope is what the gospel of Jesus brings.

See also COHABITING; CONFLICT RESOLUTION; FAMILY PROBLEMS; FORGIVENESS; MARRIAGE; PROMISES.

References and Resources

K. Barth, *Church Dogmatics* 3/4, *The Doctrine of Creation*, trans. A. T. Mackay et al. (Edinburgh: T & T Clark, 1961); K. Barth, *On Marriage* (Philadelphia: Fortress, 1968); P. Davids, "Divorce: The Biblical Data" (Vancouver: Equippers, 1985, unpublished); P. T. Forsyth, *Marriage: Its Ethic and Religion* (London: Hodder & Stoughton, n.d.); D. H. Small, *The Right to Remarry* (Old Tappan, N.J.: Fleming H. Revell, 1975); J. H. Olthius, *I Pledge You My Troth: A Christian View of Marriage, Family, Friendship* (New York: Harper & Row, 1975); R. P. Stevens, *Getting Ready for a Great Marriage* (Colorado Springs: NavPress, 1990); R. P. Stevens, *Married for Good: The Lost Art of Remaining Happily Married* (Downers Grove, Ill.: InterVarsity Press, 1986); J. S. Wallerstein and S. Blakeslee, *Second Chances* (New York: Ticknor & Fields, 1989); M. Weiner-Davis, *Divorce-Busting* (New York: Simon & Schuster, 1992); R. Weiss, *Marital Separation* (New York: Basic Books, 1976).

R. Paul Stevens

DREAMING

Approximately one-third of a normal lifetime is spent sleeping,* and much of that time is devoted to dreaming. Although sleep and dreams are commonplace facts of life, they remain mysteries, and each generation has tried to determine the cause and meaning of dreams. In this article we will explore the various theories about dreaming, the history of dreaming including dreams in the Bible, psychoanalytic interpretation of dreams, and an examination of what is actually happening when we dream. Finally, some practical suggestions will be offered.

Basic Facts on Dreaming

At the time of this writing, there is no generally accepted theory as to the meaning of dreams. All that is known for sure is that dreaming is a universal phenomenon in humans. In the mid-1930s scientists began to describe separate and distinct electroencephalographic (EEG) stages occurring during sleep. In the mid-1950s scientists reported that bursts of conjugate, rapid eye movements (REM) periodically appeared, and they linked these periods to dreaming.

Basically, there are two very different kinds of sleep: nonrapid eye movement (NREM), or *orthodox,* sleep and rapid eye movement (REM), or *paradoxical,* sleep. Within NREM sleep, three stages are usually recognized. Stage 1 is a transition stage between full wakefulness and clear sleep when thoughts begin to drift and thinking is no longer reality oriented. Though short dreams often develop, most people feel that they are awake during stage 1 sleep. Stage 2 is the first bona fide sleep stage, and mentation during this stage usually consists of short, mundane and fragmented thoughts. Stage 3, delta sleep, is when deep sleep occurs and it is hardest to awaken someone.

REM sleep alternates with NREM sleep at about ninety-minute intervals. The EEG pattern resembles that of stage 1 sleep. However, during REM sleep muscle tone is also extremely low, and heart rate and respiratory rate are relatively high and variable. More than 80 percent of people who are awakened during REM sleep are able to recall dreams. The first period of REM sleep occurs approximately seventy to ninety minutes after sleep onset and usually lasts about five minutes. REM sleep alternates with NREM sleep, with REM periods becoming more intense (both physiologically and psychologically) and longer toward morning. Many people therefore awaken in the morning while dreaming. The amount of dreaming changes with age. REM sleep drops from 50 percent of sleeping time at birth to about 20 percent by puberty. From that time on, REM remains reasonably constant throughout life, although there seems to be a slight percentage increase during young adulthood and a slight percentage decrease, at least in males, during old age.

The meaning of these changes in REM sleep is unknown, but they have given rise to many speculations concerning the need to dream and the function of REM sleep. It is clear that dreaming is needed for proper functioning. When volunteers are awakened each time they start an REM period, REM pressure seems to build up, and upon falling asleep again, they usually start to dream more quickly. They also make up the lost REM-time as soon as they are permitted to do so. REM sleep becomes more intensive, and upon the volunteers' awakening certain behavioral changes occur. People who are REM-deprived seem to become more agitated, more impulsive and less able to control their actions, whereas people deprived of delta sleep do not show these signs. It should be noted that many drugs and substances affect REM sleep and therefore may affect mood and behavior.

History of Dreaming

In ancient and primitive societies, dreams were usually thought to be the work of gods or demons, appearing to mortals with messages of hope or despair. The ancient Egyptians and Babylonians attached great importance to dreams and to oneiromancy, or dream interpretation. Such interpretation was already an advanced technique by the time of the earliest records.

The oldest of the thousands of dream books is found in the Chester Beatty Papyrus, which comes from Thebes in Upper Egypt and incorporates material probably dating back to 2000 B.C. In these writings a distinction is made between "good" and "bad" dreams. Some two hundred dreams are preserved in that papyrus, and various interpretations are given. For example, it records that it was good to dream of sawing wood, for this foretold of the death of enemies. The Egyptians also had a strong belief in *incubation,* which meant that sick persons were brought to sleep in the temple, where they fasted, or took potions, to induce beneficial dreams. There are examples of incubation dreams given throughout the Old Testament. First Kings 3:4-9 describes how Solomon went to Gibeon to offer sacrifices, "for that was the most important high place." There he had a dream in which God said, "Ask for whatever you want me to give you." Samuel's dream in the temple is another example of an incubation dream (1 Sam 3:1-14).

Most of the symbolic dreams in the Old Testament happen to Gentiles. For the Jews there was only one God; God alone could be the source of divine revelations in dreams and was expected to speak clearly to them. Such messages, however, might seem garbled or unclear to a Pharaoh or Nebuchadnezzar. Pharaoh's dreams were interpreted by Joseph (Gen 41:25-32). Though Pharaoh may have been consciously or unconsciously aware of climatic factors that could lead to a seven-year period of rich harvest followed by seven years of famine, the awareness broke through dramatically only in the form of a dream allegory of seven fat and seven thin cows. Joseph himself had a dream regarding his brothers (Gen 37:5-7) in which suddenly his sheaf stood upright, while their sheaves gathered around his and bowed down to it. This may have revealed his understanding of both his talents* and the ambition* that would carry him to great eminence.

The fact that several Jewish prophets gave warnings against false dreams and false interpreters suggests that there was a systematic effort to sharpen the distinction between divine and significant dreams and those that were either evil or without significance. In Jeremiah 23:25-28 (compare Deut 13:1-5) God says,

I have heard what the prophets say who prophesy in my name. They say, "I had a dream! I had a dream!" How long will this continue in the hearts of these lying prophets, who prophesy the delusions of their own minds? They think the dreams they tell one another will make my people forget my name, just as their father's forgot my name through Baal worship. Let the prophet who has a dream tell his dream, but let the one who has my word speak it faithfully. For what has straw to do with grain?

Some basic principles of the meaning of dreams can be seen in the Old Testament writings. In addition to being divine revelations, dreams provided a means for understanding one's innermost thoughts and feelings as well as for working through problem areas in one's life. For example, Daniel indicated that he would be interpreting Nebuchadnezzar's dream so that the king "may understand what went through your [the king's] mind" (Dan 2:30). Job 33:14-18 describes how God may speak in a dream "to turn man from wrongdoing and keep him from pride." In Psalm 16:7 it is writ-

ten, "Even at night my heart instructs me." However, dreams may not always carry special meaning or significance. As it says in Ecclesiastes 5:7, "Much dreaming and many words are meaningless."

In the Gospels there are only seven references to dreams or dreamers. All occur in Matthew, and none come from Jesus. The dreams are all prophetic. An angel tells Joseph in a dream to take Mary as his wife (Mt 1:20), and the Magi are warned in a dream not to go back to Herod but to return to their country by another route (Mt 2:12). Joseph also has other dreams (Mt 2:13, 19-20). Pilate's wife has a dream regarding Jesus and sends a message stating, "Don't have anything to do with that innocent man, for I have suffered a great deal today in a dream because of him" (Mt 27:19).

The only other reference to dreaming in the New Testament is a citation used for illustrative purposes in Acts 2:17. Words are quoted from the prophet Joel, who stated, "In the last days, God says, I will pour out my Spirit on all people. Your sons and daughters will prophecy, your young men will see visions, your old men will dream dreams."

Something related to dreaming occurred during the missionary journeys of Paul. Acts 16:9-10 notes that Paul had a night vision of a man from Macedonia begging Paul to come and help. The exact content of the dream and the identity of the Macedonian man have been the subject of much conjecture. The incident, however, reveals some important principles of how dreams and visions may fit into a larger experience of guidance from God. John Stott notes that the dream was preceded by two negative prohibitions (not to go to Asia and Bithynia). So the experience was not only negative but positive, not only circumstantial but rational (Paul and his companions discussed the vision), not only personal but corporate (they came to a common mind about the direction in which they should move; Stott, p. 261). We must now ask how dreams have been understood.

Psychoanalytic Interpretation of Dreaming

In 1900, when Sigmund Freud published *The Interpretation of Dreams,* the book provoked hostile criticism. The subject itself, let alone Freud's serious treatment of it, seemed ludicrous not only to other medical men but also to many intellectuals trained in a rationalist tradition. Dreams were seen by Freud as the royal road to the unconscious. Whereas modern philosophy really began when Descartes said, "I think, therefore I am," modern psychology began when Freud said in effect, "I am, therefore I dream."

Freud believed that dreams represented unfulfilled, and often unacceptable, wishes, most of which referred to instinctual impulses originating in the dreamer's early childhood. He believed that repressed infantile sexual wishes provided the most frequent and strongest motivating forces for the construction of dreams. Such wishes did not appear directly in dreams but were disguised in various ways in order to make them acceptable to the dreamer. Hence, the dream required interpretation. What the dreamer recalled was only the *manifest content;* the *latent content,* or the true meaning of the dream, could only be discerned after a lengthy process in which the dreamer's association to all the images in the dream had been subjected to trained analytical scrutiny.

Although dreams are under the control of the unconscious mind and are therefore not couched in language of everyday speech, there is certainly no evidence that all dreams are concealing unacceptable or unfulfilled wishes or urges. Freud himself recognized this when he considered the recurrent dreams of patients who had been subject to traumatic incidents in which the incidents occur in an undisguised form. This commonly occurs in persons who are suffering from posttraumatic stress disorder. Repetitive dreaming may be a way of working through feelings and coping with the trauma.

Carl Jung, as described by psychiatrist Anthony Storr, took a very different view of dreams from that given by Freud (Storr, p. 46). First of all, he did not consider dreams to be concealments. Rather, according to Jung, dreams were expressed in a symbolic language that may or may not be difficult to understand. Other similar forms of expression in which metaphors and symbolism occur include poetry and music.* Second, Jung believed that dreams may possess all sorts of meanings, not merely the imaginary fulfillment of repressed wishes. Dreams may contain memories, wild fancies and goodness knows what else. Third, Jung described the human psyche as being a self-regulation system. The unconscious and conscious parts of the mind were conceived as operating in a reciprocal relationship. For example, a celibate person may have an overabundance of sexual-laden dreams. Jung cites instances in which men who had consciously overestimated their own powers had dreams indicating that their limits had actually been reached (Storr, p. 46).

What Are Dreams?

Scientists continue to provide different answers to the question "What are dreams?" One recently suggested that dreams may have no function at all! REM sleep seems to have functions, but dreaming and REM sleep are not the same thing. However, it seems clear that dreams have been used throughout the centuries by people to help understand various problems as well as to receive guidance* and messages from God. We seem to dream mainly about issues that concern us at the present time, such as fears, wishes, plans, hopes and worries. Thus, dreaming that a friend is dead does not necessarily signify a latent death wish but might well mean that one is concerned for the friend's health. Dreams often relate to unsettled business stirred up during the day. But the language of dreams is often symbolic and distorted. Disentangling the so-called real meaning of the dream often requires intimate knowledge of both the dreamer and dream mechanisms in general.

Storr describes four basic functions of dreaming (pp. 46-47). (1) Some dreams certainly can represent wishes, very often of a sexual or ambitious kind, just as do daydreams.* An example of an ambitious dream would be the dream of Joseph described in Genesis 37:5-10. (2) Dreams often seem to serve as an outlet for impulses that have been impossible to express or that are partially unrecognized by the dreamer. Examples of these would include aggressive impulses towards employers, parents and other authority figures or sexual impulses towards people whom the dreamer desires but who, for social or religious reasons, are inaccessible. (3) Dreams often have a compensatory aspect. Dreams frequently bring out some feeling of affection towards people we thought we wholly disliked or, vice versa, some feeling of dislike towards those we thought we wholly liked. The atheist may discover a religious side to himself, or the scientist may discover that she is not as rational as she had supposed. (4) Dreams often relate to problems with which the dreamer is struggling but which he or she has not yet resolved. Dreams often seem to bring out problems of which the person may only be half aware. This problem-solving aspect of dreaming is illustrated by those dreams of scientists and other creative people in which solutions are found.

One of the most significant of such discoveries was the dream that revealed the ring structure of benzene to the scientist F. A. Kekule. He had tried for years to find a graphic means of representing the molecular structure of trimethyl benzene. Eventually its ring structure was revealed when he dreamed of a snake with its tail in its mouth.

Practical Suggestions

Though dreams are not material that allows dogmatic interpretation, they are often valuable indicators pointing towards emotional preoccupations of which, perhaps, the person was not consciously aware. They are couched in the language of the unconscious, and their interpretation should not be taken literally any more than poetry. Interestingly, one of the greatest of English prose works, John Bunyan's *Pilgrim's Progress*, is cast in dream form. Bunyan's allegory is so much a spiritual and psychological pilgrimage that the dream form must have been deliberately chosen to express the inner experiences that had deeply changed the author.

Various symbols occur frequently in dreams and in poetry. For example, the image of the snake, which is never consciously associated with that of the phallus, is one of the most constant and invariable symbols in primitive religions. Another example is the image of teeth (see Song 4:2), which often is symbolically related to childbirth, a connection that is hardly ever made consciously. It was due to such recurrences that Jung, going far beyond Freud, developed his theory of the collective unconscious, from which he believed such fundamental symbols as the circle and the cross, the trinity, the hero, the wise old man and the dragonlike, devouring mother ultimately sprang. However not all symbols have a universal meaning. For example, dreaming of a fire may bring feelings of warmth and comfort to one person but feelings of terror to another who has suffered from a significant burn injury.

Dreams continue to fascinate us. Practical suggestions for understanding them are as follows: (1) It is important to record your dreams. It is best to write them down immediately upon awakening. Because dreams occur in the unconscious mind, we soon lose memory of them. You should also record what was occurring during the day prior to dreaming. Dreams often relate to unsettled business stirred up during the day. (2) Dreams are often symbolic and distorted. They frequently appear illogical and should not be interpreted in a literal manner. (3) Discuss your dreams with another person who has a close understanding of your personality, needs and conflicts and who has a good understanding of your spiritual life. It is difficult to be objective enough to interpret your own dreams completely. (4) Before deciding whether the dream is a message from God, try to understand whether the message agrees with Scripture and leads one to a closer relationship with God. It is also best to wait for other forms of confirmation before changing your life drastically.

In summary, dreams can be extremely useful for understanding ourselves and for providing an impetus for change. God may also communicate with us through our dreams. However, dreams only make sense against a person's background and past, and most dreams require a detailed and intimate knowledge of the dreamer and his or her circumstances. Although a good deal of research has been carried out, especially about REM sleep, we are still far from knowing all there is to know about dreams. We do know that dogmatic interpretation of dreams is inappropriate and that, like works of art, dreams must often be allowed to speak for themselves. A

quote from the seventeenth-century physician Sir Thomas Browne shows that our understanding of dreams has not changed significantly in over three hundred years:

However dreames may bee fallacious concerning outward events, yet may they bee truly significant at home, and whereby wee may more sensibly understand ourselves. Men act in sleepe with some conformity unto their awaked senses, and consolations or discouragements may bee drawne from dreames which intimately tell us ourselves.

See also GUIDANCE; SLEEPING.

References and Resources

C. G. Jung, *Memories, Dreams, Reflections,* ed. A. Jaffe (New York: Vintage Books, 1965); J. Opmeer, "Dreams and Visions: God's Picture Language," in *Those Controversial Gifts,* ed. G. Mallone (Downers Grove, Ill.: InterVarsity Press, 1983) 51-78; A. Storr, *The Art of Psychotherapy* (2nd ed.; New York: Routledge, 1980) 43-55; J. R. W. Stott, *The Spirit, the Church and the World: The Message of Acts* (Downers Grove, Ill.: InterVarsity Press, 1990).

Stephen A. Anderson

DRESS CODE, WORKPLACE

In the book of Genesis people began to wear clothes when they first become aware of their sin: since the day Adam and Eve covered themselves with fig leaves, clothing has been a blessing and a curse—a cursed blessing to be exact (Gen 3:7). In the New Testament we are assured that God will provide us with the necessities of life, including clothing (Mt 6:28-30), and not just any old hand-me-downs but perhaps even designer labels, as Matthew claims the lilies of the field surpass "Solomon in all his splendor." Although we know intellectually about God's promise to care for us, many of us still fret about what to wear when we get up each morning. Moreover, while daily work* can be a blessing, it is interesting that in Genesis 3 God also declares that people will be cursed by daily toil as a result of their sin (Gen 3:17, 19).

The Corporate Image

On a basic level a dress code may be crucial to ensure an employee's safety (or at least to protect the company legally in case of worker injury). A dress code may also function to increase an employee's efficiency or to provide customers with easy identification of helpful staff. On a higher level, however, a company uses uniforms or a dress code to communicate a certain image to the public—a promise to get the job done right. While a dress code may indicate a company's lack of trust in its employees' judgment, it is useful in that it removes any ambiguity about what an employee should wear to work. To the extent that the employees themselves perform their jobs as professionally as they are dressed, the dress code serves a purpose.

Humans: Made in God's Image

We have all had experiences in which a professionally dressed salesperson does not give us the service promised. It is then that we realize how superficial worldly image can be. We are warned in the Bible that appearances may be deceiving: some people are merely wolves in sheep's clothing (Mt 7:15). We cannot fool God simply by putting on the right clothes (1 Sam 16:7), for God looks straight into our hearts and knows our true character. A Christian's daily struggle is to discern how God wants him or her to behave and to allow the inner character to shine through to the outside. As Christians, our true image comes from God (Gen 1:27), who created us to have a relationship with him such as no other living creature does, one so loving that it led to his Son's paying the ultimate

sacrifice for our sin (Jn 3:16). Therefore, it is important when we report for work that we not only dress the part but do our best work, for, as the apostle Paul exhorts the Colossians, "Whatever you do, work at it with all your heart, as working for the Lord, not for men, since you know that you will receive an inheritance from the Lord as a reward. It is the Lord Christ you are serving" (Col 3:23).

The Christian Image Paradox: Looking Good Matters

Christian workers have a double duty as ambassadors for both their earthly employers and their heavenly Father. In movies* and television,* Christians are often portrayed as prim and strait-laced with no style or adornment* (except a large cross pendant), wearing either paramilitary uniforms or ill-fitting, drab-colored, mismatched garments. The contrast between the joyous good news they are supposed to be spreading and their dowdy, lackluster appearance is laughably unattractive. Although this is a media caricature, it pinpoints a paradox: Christians need to have a healthy concern for what is on the surface even though God can see straight through it. This is because judging others by the way they look is a basic human characteristic. Even in biblical times dishevelment and dirtiness were considered a sign of mental derangement or demonic possession! In terms of a Christian witness, therefore, we need to work with this tendency rather than to ignore it.

Non-Christians are already convinced that to become a Christian means to adopt a life of restriction and mindless conformity. But when Christians present an attractive image, it is not to deceive but to demonstrate a healthy self-respect and to celebrate that each person is a unique creation of God. At the same time, when Christians are confronted with an office culture* in which other employees spend extraordinary sums of money to compete for the best image, the Christian may consider being countercultural without being unattractive or obnoxious.

Dress Code as Authority

The dress code is a company rule that must be obeyed. Unfortunately, humans have a natural tendency to rebel against authority of any kind (Eph 2:2). An obvious incentive for obeying a company dress code is to avoid being fired! But an even better reason is to show proper respect for authority when that authority is acting reasonably. Paul commands the Ephesians, "Slaves, obey your earthly masters with respect and fear, and with sincerity of heart, just as you would obey Christ" (Eph 6:5). When our bosses are acting unreasonably, however, it might be right to rebel, such as when a dress code regulation is humiliating or discriminatory. For example, in the United States during the 1980s a female airline employee who was fired because she refused to wear makeup took her employer to court. Her grievance was that her employer valued her more for the way she looked than for the high caliber of work she performed. In the book of Acts the apostle Peter justifies disobedience to earthly authority in cases where it is clearly superseded by God's authority (Acts 4:19-20). But ultimately we cannot go wrong if we adhere to God's own dress code as itemized by the apostle Paul: "Put on the full armor of God, . . . the belt of truth, . . . the breastplate of righteousness, . . . the shield of faith, . . . the helmet of salvation and the sword of the Spirit" (Eph 6:13-17).

See also ADORNMENT; WORKPLACE.

References and Resources

"Business Etiquette: Dress," in *Merriam-Webster's Secretarial Handbook* (Springfield, Mass.: Merriam-Webster, 1993); J. Martin, *Miss Manners' Guide to Excruciatingly Correct Behavior* (New York: Atheneum, 1982); A. Sterk and

P. Scazzero, "Self-Image," in *Christian Character* (Downers Grove, Ill.: InterVarsity Press, 1985); R. P. Stevens and G. Schoberg, "Work: Curse or Blessing?" in *Satisfying Work: Christian Living from Nine to Five* (Wheaton, Ill.: Harold Shaw, 1989).

Kathryn E. Lockhart

DRIVENNESS

Drivenness is behind one of the most respectable of all addictions*—workaholism. But it is also expressed in a wide variety of addictive behaviors not covered in this article: chemical abuse, religious zeal, sexual addiction, perfectionism and fitness, which are all subject to the law of diminishing returns as people try to meet their deepest needs in these ways. The condition of drivenness usually arises from sources deep within the human personality, as well as systemic problems in our society. Drivenness reveals a spiritual dysfunctionality usually associated with a failure to accept the unconditional love of God. Driven people tend to focus all their energies on an activity that feeds their inner dysfunction, and this activity becomes an addiction.

Workaholism: The Respectable Addiction

The now commonplace term *workaholism* was coined by Wayne Oates, an American minister and psychologist, in 1968. In that year he wrote a humorous and insightful confession in an article entitled "On Being a 'Workaholic' (A Serious Jest)" in *Pastoral Psychology*. Comparing himself to an alcoholic, Oates says that he started with "social" working, boasting about how much work he could "hold" and how he could work others "under the table." But then it progressed to a true addiction. He was hooked. Drawing on his own experience, Oates describes the progression. Workaholics "pass out" (become emotionally dead) either on the job or at home, usually the latter. Whereas formerly they attained social approval for working addictively, now they are besieged by well-meaning advice to slow down, though friends and family expect them to be too busy to attend to them. If they try to slow down, they suffer "withdrawal symptoms" and fight a terrible battle when they leave the office, factory or church, resolving it by taking some work home or by doing a "weekend binge" of work. Christmas, other holidays and family vacations* are terrifying experiences, and workaholics can only tolerate them by taking work with them.

Workaholics dread thinking about retirement,* and when they finally retire, they may die prematurely. Work is their love, and they may even feed this love by planning another report or sermon while making love to their spouse! In this seminal article Oates recognizes that the problem is profoundly theological and spiritual: the workaholic has made an idol of work. Salvation depends on work: "Far from thinking of God as someone who loves us whether we produce or not, this is unthinkable to workaholics. Acceptance is pay for work done" (Oates 1968, p. 17).

Since Oates's initial contribution, an extensive study has been undertaken by Barbara Killinger of what she calls the "respectable addicts." A workaholic is "a person who gradually becomes emotionally crippled and addicted to control and power in a compulsive drive to gain approval and success" (Killinger, p. 6). She describes the typical workaholic family of origin: one is born in a home where love* is conditional on good performance and behavior. Instead of communicating the value of a child for who he or she is, parents in such homes communicate only the value of the child's accomplishments. Thus the child does not learn to separate doing and being, performance

from personhood. Instead of hearing, "The grass you cut looks terrific; you must be proud of yourself!" they hear, "You did a great job cutting the grass; you are a good boy" (Killinger, p. 21). In the words of Killinger, "conditional love teaches a child to be dependent on others for approval; unconditional love encourages independent appraisal, objectivity, and self-affirmation in deserved pride" (p. 22). Many children raised in such environments become chronically overinvolved with work, usually as a way of avoiding anxiety or emotional pain.

Workaholism is the condition of persons whose self-worth is linked to what they do rather than who they are. The result of this orientation is that work moves from being an other-centered to a self-centered activity, defining every aspect of their existence. Workaholics do not work because they have a desire to be gainfully employed; they work to prove something to themselves. Though they keep trying by working harder, working better or trying to find the perfect job, they can never do enough to give full meaning to their lives. With some women workaholism takes a unique form in compulsive motherhood. The workaholic housewife has been well researched. Less recognized is the phenomenon of some women who become pregnant repeatedly for largely unconscious reasons: the inability to enjoy sexual relations apart from impregnation, being unhappy with any child except a new and helpless one, needing to control her husband or other children. The end result of this repeated "labor" is the martyred wife and mother, usually perfectionist and depressed (Oates 1971, p. 72).

Understanding Workaholism

The workaholic does not normally come from the ranks of the nine-to-five workers but more likely comes from a self-employed, small business, professional* or homemaking* background. All these people decide for themselves whether they should be working more or less (Oates 1968, p. 20). While this helpfully targets the part of our population that may be most likely to exhibit workaholism, it does not help us make an important distinction. Not all people who work hard or work long hours are workaholics. Indeed, some studies indicate that people highly involved in their work may indicate little or no sign of personal problems and may function in a healthy way on the job (Naughton, p. 181). Such persons typically find a lot of satisfaction in their work, more than they find in nonwork-related activities. Thus in developing a typology of workaholism for career counselors, Thomas Naughton distinguishes between the *job-involved workaholic,* who has high job satisfaction and performs well, and the *compulsive workaholic,* whose work reflects a ritualized pattern of thoughts and behaviors that are destructive to himself or herself and colleagues. In this latter case workaholics are not good workers, not an asset to a company or a church.* They have nothing to give their families and friends. Like the idlers in 2 Thessalonians 3:10-12, they are sponging on the goodwill of their family and friends.

There are signs of workaholism. Workaholics typically (1) keep excessively long workdays, (2) talk a lot about their accomplishments, (3) are unable to say no and (4) cannot rest* or relax (Minirth et al., pp. 29-31). Frank Minirth and his colleagues note how the deeply reflective words of Ecclesiastes 2:17-23 are applicable to the workaholic: "All his days his work is pain and grief; even at night his mind does not rest" (v. 23). In contrast, the godly person finds enjoyment in eating,* drinking and work (vv. 24-25).

There are substantial effects of this addictive behavior: disruption of family life, neglect of spiritual growth,* diminishing returns for work, physical tension, loss of perspective on life and misdirected resentment in which others are blamed for the pain they experience (Walters, pp. 103-4). The children of workaholics are especially disadvantaged. Sons may recall very few moments when their father (or mother) attended a sporting event with them. They may be preoccupied with getting good grades. Daughters of workaholic fathers have special problems. Speaking to this, therapists note: "Their fathers are apt to totally ignore them because of a feeling that females are less productive in terms of work than are males. . . . This can be devastating for the daughter and she may go to extreme lengths to gain her father's attention . . . [including] drugs and/or sexual misconduct" (Minirth et al., p. 46). Not only do the children of workaholics suffer direct effects in the circumstances of their lives, but the workaholic pattern gets ingrained in the children, thus passing the sins of the fathers (and mothers) to the children, sometimes for three or four generations (Ex 20:5).

Reflecting on Drivenness

Earlier I used the word *idol* in a description of a workaholic. *Idolatry* is a misplaced devotion; it is simply making something one's ultimate concern other than the One who is ultimate. The apostle Paul was a driven person until he experienced the call of God on the Damascus road. But perhaps this observation does not go deep enough. Was he obsessed and compulsive or ambitious* and determined?

Prior to meeting Christ, Paul was determined to find acceptance and righteousness with God through Jewish legalism and performance and was simultaneously compelled to eliminate Christians as a threatening sect. What happened at Damascus was not the changing of Paul's personality from one type to another. Rather, Paul was released from the self-justifying paralysis of his personality by an empowering and liberating experience of grace through which he knew himself to be unconditionally accepted by God. Since the great resources of his personality were liberated by his meeting with Christ, he was able to devote himself in an entirely healthy way in a magnificently liberating passion—his passion to love God and love his neighbor as himself. Paul confessed, "To this end I labor, struggling with all his energy, which so powerfully works in me" (Col 1:29).

It is tempting to say that the driven person and the called person may appear to be very similar to an outside observer. But this is too superficial an observation. The driven person has an obsession that destroys him and those around him. The called person is a liberated person who empowers and liberates others. Having a different source results in a different expression.

What is seldom mentioned in any discussion of addiction is that we were made for an all-consuming passion, love for God and love for our neighbor. The comparison Paul makes between being intoxicated with alcohol and being filled with the Spirit in Ephesians 5:18 is intentional. Canon Stanley Evans once described a Christian as "a controlled drunk, purposively intoxicated with the joy of the life which is perpetually created in God himself" (quoted in Leech, p. 103). "Be filled with the Spirit" (Eph 5:18) is in the imperative mood (it is not an option), in the present tense (it is an ongoing continuous experience) and in the plural number (it is something we experience in the community of faith). The similarity of this experience of completeness and profound pleasure in God with the sexual experience is a subject often noted.

Workaholism provides an alternative ecstasy. In an insightful section on "erotica," Killinger compares work experiences with sexual orgasms: "When there is a passionate obsession with work, erotic feelings can be expressed towards the accomplishments or products of work. The senses are aroused and alive when a coveted contract is signed, a record becomes a hit, or a sought-after degree is conferred" (p. 34). Failing to find the divine source of legitimate ecstasy, people find unsatisfactory substitutes. But how do people move from a debilitating compulsion to a magnificent obsession? In establishing a theology and practice of self-control, we must observe that self-control is not a human accomplishment, not even a religious work, but a fruit of the continuous inundation of the Holy Spirit (Gal 5:23). How can we become accessible to such an indirect grace?

Toward Substantial Healing

Self-knowledge. The deepest sources of drivenness may be understood and resolved only through professional counseling, but a beginning can be made through reflection on why you as an individual work so hard and why praise is so important to you. Getting in touch with your own story and understanding the influence of one generation on another may be especially helpful. One aspect that is frequently neglected is simply listening to your own body-talk. Sometimes a specific illness serves as a reminder of the need for the seventh day of rest and for relief from the demands of work (Oates 1968, p. 20).

While choices can be made by a workaholic, a profoundly addicted person is not likely to gain freedom simply by making resolutions or decisions. Just as alcoholics must come to the place of recognizing that they are unable to free themselves, so workaholics must recognize their helplessness. The theologian Reinhold Niebuhr once said that to be a sinner is our distress, but to know it is our hope. To come to the end of self-deception, excuses, alibis and hiding is a profound moment of hope. God can help the helpless. Because Western society, and most of the industrialized world, sees nothing wrong with a person's wanting "to get ahead," the workaholic is tragically often permitted to remain in denial much longer than with substance abuse.

Many workaholics are helped with a personal inventory, such as that used by Alcoholics Anonymous and other self-help groups. These inventories deal with self-centeredness (my workaholism is driven by my narcissistic need to prove that I deserve to exist or to be loved or . . .), aggressiveness (my aggressiveness is really a self-centered expression of my need to be in control or to rebel against a parent or . . .), anger and resentment (I have put the following people on my grudge list, and I am affected by my anger in this way: . . .) and fear (behind my anger and resentment is my fear that I will not be loved by . . . or that I will lose control of . . .). As we take off the mask that covers our resentments, we usually discover that our adult drivenness is a desperate attempt to outrun our fear of abandonment. The deepest answer to our self-preoccupation is not through deprivation or condemnation but experiencing the unconditional love of God (Hemfelt, Minirth and Meier, pp. 263-64). But this liberating process is often complicated by the fact that those closest to us may not want us to change!

Coconspiracy for health rather than codependence in drivenness. People making a transition out of job-involved workaholism may encounter social pressures that make change very difficult. Recovering workaholics may experience shame, guilt and fear as they continue to relate to peers and employers whose work styles require long hours and who communicate social disapproval for people who fail to conform (Naughton, p. 186). Controlling workaholics need to learn to trust others and to share power.

If you are a recovering workaholic, it is most desirable that you ask colleagues and peers to hold you accountable for reasonable work hours and to ask them for feedback (and listen to it!). The same holds true for your spouse and children. Instead of playing the nurturing "fixer" who compensates for the effects of workaholism, invite your spouse to verbalize how you can take greater responsibility for your lifestyle to help diversify your interests. Those responsible for shaping the environment of a workplace* have the privilege of creating organizations* based on grace, celebrating who people are and not just remunerating their performance, and giving people a second chance (Oates 1971, p. 108).

Lifestyle changes. You should "give yourself the freedom to live each day well" (Killinger, p. 209). To do this, a driven person needs to stop rushing, to enjoy play,* to learn to say no, to put energy into a wide variety of baskets. Killinger advises making a regular date with your spouse and a regular special outing with each of the children. Regarding your job, it is sometimes wise to ask whether you are in the right job and whether you should reduce your responsibilities rather than to seek another promotion (Killinger, pp. 208-21). Big changes in lifestyle are enormously difficult, but they can be accomplished through a succession of little changes in the right direction.

*Experiencing sabbath.** Some addictions, such as to pornography, require complete cessation, while others, like workaholism, require a balance of work, play, activity and rest, not unemployment.* To achieve this balance, recovering a Christian experience of sabbath is essential. People who are on a treadmill of working harder and harder to support a particular lifestyle, or, in the case of the academic world, to publish more and more to justify tenure, desperately need sabbath. Our society offers work and leisure.* While leisure is often a good thing, it is not contemplative; it does not direct us to reflect on the meaning of our lives and what God's view of our lives really is. Sabbath is not merely stopping work or resting. It is getting God's big view of the meaning of our lives and playing heaven.

Personal spirituality. Workaholics frequently doubt their own salvation. Not having felt unconditionally accepted as a child, they can hardly believe that the one who comes to Christ will not be cast out (Jn 6:37). To overcome workaholism, a person needs to deeply internalize the gospel and then to express it confidently in concrete everyday life. Experiencing gospel confidence is not like having one continuous spiritual orgasm; we were not made for continuous excitement. Practical steps for dealing with lust for more excitement all concern a deepening spiritual journey: (1) begin by reordering your spiritual values and beliefs about the root of pleasure (Prov 21:17); (2) accept a "deficit in excitement" as normal as being overcome by pleasure; (3) watch where and how you get your excitement; (4) come to appreciate *satisfaction* over *excitement* (Hart, pp. 60-63).

This last point hints at the seven dimensions of the fruit of the Spirit (Gal 5:22-23), especially joy. We were made for a magnificent and liberating passion—the constant, continuous filling of the Holy Spirit. But Spirit-filling is primarily not for ecstasy but for redeemed living, for submissive and loving relationships (Eph 5:21) and for joy. Thus being in a community of faith, reading* the Bible, practicing a life of prayer and inviting the Holy Spirit to inundate us continuously constitute the deepest answer for drivenness. This answer is not an alternative to dealing with the masks of denial, but without it we would be powerless to discover the intended content of the God-shaped vacuum in our souls.

Saint Augustine once said that God is always trying to give good things to us, but our hands are too full to receive them. Often our hands are full of the results of our drivenness. Gerald May suggests we may not be able to empty our hands by sheer willpower (p. 17). But we can relax them a little and admit that God's strength will be demonstrated in our weakness (2 Cor 12:9), for "sooner or later addiction will prove to us that we are not gods," thus becoming to our extreme amazement a kind of good gift (May, p. 20). A German philosopher enigmatically expressed this same thought: "My burden carries me!" (A. A. Schröders, quoted in Thielicke, p. 238).

See also ADDICTION; CALLING; LEISURE; REST; SABBATH; TIME.

References and Resources
S. Arterburn and J. Felton, *Toxic Faith* (Nashville: Nelson, 1991); A. D. Hart, *Healing Life's Hidden Addictions: Overcoming the Closet Compulsions That Waste Your Time and Control Your Life* (Ann Arbor, Mich.: Servant, 1990); R. Hemfelt, F. Minirth and P. Meier, *We Are Driven: The Compulsive Behaviors America Applauds* (Nashville: Thomas Nelson, 1991); B. Killinger, *Workaholics: The Respectable Addicts* (New York: Simon & Schuster, 1991); K. Leech, *True Prayer: An Invitation to Christian Spirituality* (San Francisco: Harper & Row, 1980); G. G. May, *Addiction and Grace: Love and Spirituality in the Healing of Addictions* (San Francisco: Harper, 1988); F. Minirth et al., *The Workaholic and His Family* (Grand Rapids: Baker, 1981); T. J. Naughton, "A Conceptual View of Workaholism and Implications for Career Consoling and Research," *The Career Development Quarterly* 135, no. 3 (1987) 180-87; W. E. Oates, *Confes-*

sions of a Workaholic: The Facts About Work Addiction (London: Wolfe Publishing, 1971); W. E. Oates, "On Being a 'Workaholic' (A Serious Jest)," *Pastoral Psychology* 19 (October 1968) 16-20; A. W. Schaef, *When Society Becomes an Addict* (San Francisco: Harper & Row, 1986); H. Thielicke, *Und Wenn Gott Ware* (Stuttgart: Qwee Verlag, 1970); R. P. Walters, *Escape the Trap* (Grand Rapids: Zondervan, 1989).

R. Paul Stevens

DRUGS

When you think of drugs, what comes to mind? Do you think of heroin, cocaine, marijuana—the hard, illegal drugs? Do you think of more commonly used, legal drugs like alcohol, nicotine and caffeine? What about prescribed drugs like Valium, Ritalin and lithium and nonprescription drugs like laxatives, sedatives, analgesics and weight-control agents? Do you think primarily of drug use or abuse? Do your images of drugs emphasize a particular age, gender or ethnic grouping?

What Are Drugs?

Many believe that drugs like heroin and cocaine are at the heart of the drug problem because they are illegal, powerfully addictive and personally ruinous. Yet their use is minor compared to legal drugs like alcohol and tobacco. Millions of Americans are problem drinkers, and tens of thousands of deaths* are directly attributed to alcohol each year. Furthermore, alcohol is considered a factor in most fatal car accidents, homicides, suicides and child abuse* cases. Consider as well the harmful effects of tobacco with over 50 million smoking Americans, many of whom will succumb to lung cancer, emphysema or other ailments. One should also consider the negative effects resulting from prescription and nonprescription drugs that are sufficient to hospitalize over 1.5 million Americans each year.

A drug is any substance that can influence one's mind, body* or emotions* and, when misused, can harm oneself or others. Most people use drugs for some purpose, and given that our bodies manufacture drugs like endorphins and adrenaline, everyone is a drug user. Our society* clearly has a love-hate relationship with drugs—sending mixed messages of benefit and harm. We advertise* the potential harm of drugs and the importance of just saying no. Yet we glorify celebrities and sports* figures who model drug use as a means of popularity and success.* One segment of society seeks to ban cigarette vending machines. Another segment rushes to paste colorful cigarette posters and decals at children's eye level near elementary and junior-high schools. Drug abuse shakes the very foundations of our society by negatively influencing our homes,* our schools, our political and law enforcement* systems, and our economy.

Who Uses Drugs?

Although everyone uses some form of drug, use and abuse vary by such factors as gender, age, and cultural and ethnic background. For example, men of all ages are more apt to use and abuse alcohol and most illegal drugs. Women are more apt to use prescription and nonprescription drugs—especially sleeping pills, tranquilizers and analgesics. Late childhood and adolescence* are the time for experimenting with tobacco and alcohol. Indeed, if a person reaches age twenty-one without experimenting with alcohol or tobacco, he or she is unlikely ever to use them or other dangerous drugs (Kandel and Logan). Although the elderly represent 10 percent of the population, they account for 25 percent of the use of prescribed drugs. Racial, ethnic and socioeconomic factors are associated with particular forms of drug use. For example, Native Americans have higher rates of alcoholism than do Asian-Americans. White college students are more apt to use cocaine, marijuana and hallucinogens than are black or Hispanic students. Whereas cocaine is the drug of choice for the affluent, problem drinking reaches its highest levels among shiftworkers* and the unemployed.*

Why Do People Use Drugs?

Attempts to seek a single cause for drug use and abuse are futile. The causes of drug abuse vary with the type of drug and involve interactions of biological, psychological, sociocultural and spiritual conditions. However, four major reasons or risk factors for substance abuse have been identified: personality, family,* friends and crises (Newcomb, Maddahian and Bentler).

First, those who are angry, impulsive or depressed or who have achievement problems are more apt to abuse drugs. Second, individuals whose family relationships are distant, hostile or conflicted, whose parents use or abuse drugs or whose parents are permissive, ignoring or rejecting will more often abuse drugs. Third, those who abuse drugs have friends and peers who use or tolerate the use of drugs. Finally, a person is more apt to abuse drugs when in transition or crisis, for example, when experiencing problems with school, family or romantic relationships or during times when questioning values or religious commitment.

What Can Be Done to Limit Drug Abuse?

Strategies to curtail drug abuse generally focus on limiting supply or demand. It is popular to wage supply-side war on the sale and distribution of illegal drugs. However, strategies that focus on the demands of users are more promising. If we consider the factors that put people at risk for drug abuse, there are several logical strategies. For example, as we raise an individual's self-esteem,* promote meaningful achievement, improve family life and provide safer alternatives for gratification, escape or relief, we help to mitigate drug abuse. Also, prevention is definitely preferable to intervention or postvention. Children need to receive helpful skills and information before they develop drug habits and dependencies that are difficult to break.

Thinking Christianly About Drug Use and Abuse

A Christian should view drugs in the context of God's creation of human persons affected by the Fall, redeemed by Christ and patiently sanctified by the Holy Spirit. This involves integrating a comprehensive biblical view with what God enables us to learn through inquiry and observation.

In Genesis 1:28-31 we read that God blessed woman and man in connection with the created order and called the whole relationship "very good." In other words, God created us with needs* and created elements in our environment to meet those needs. Undoubtedly our human capacities to explore and develop drugs like analgesics, allergy relief agents, antibiotics and laxatives are part of God's creational design. Yet we must struggle to discern proper and improper uses for the drugs we discover. Some drugs should not be used at all, some are good only in moderation, some should not be used too early in life, and some are intended for good but produce great harm (for example, thalidomide). One might also question whether instant chemical relief is preferable to building character through exploring and coping with root causes of anxiety,* depression* or pain.

The major goal of the Christian is not the pursuit of self-interest but the well-being of all people and the glory of God.

Short of complete abstinence from drugs, perhaps a good general principle is to consider the personal results of drug-related activities in light of the works of God's Spirit and the works of the flesh. The work of the Spirit is to produce such qualities as love,* joy, peace, patience, kindness, goodness, faithfulness and self-control (Gal 5:22-23). Does a particular form of drug use help to develop or maintain such qualities, not just as transitory personal emotions but as concrete actions in our relationships? Does another form of drug use associate with works of the flesh such as fornication, uncleanness, enmity, strife, jealousy, wrath and envy (Eph 5:19-20)? We are to love God with all our heart, mind, soul and strength (Mk 12:30). Does drug use open a person's heart to God, clear her mind, deepen her relationships with others and increase her strength? Or does the use of a given drug harden a person's heart, cloud his thinking, close him in on himself or dull his reactions?

A Personal Account

Drugs are allegedly involved in 60 percent of all child abuse cases. During the summer I direct a Christian camp for six- to twelve-year-old children who have been removed from their homes due to life-threatening conditions of abuse, abandonment or neglect. In my work with social welfare administrators, case-workers, foster parents and children, I see many ways in which child abuse and neglect are linked with drug use.

Victimization for many of these children begins in prenatal life when indiscriminate use of drugs and alcohol during pregnancy condemns some children to a "bio-underclass"—children whose physiological damage and underprivileged social position may doom them to a life of inferiority (Rist). Some children are removed from their families and placed in foster care because one or both parents are incarcerated for drug-related crimes.* Drug abuse may shatter the lives of some parents to the extent that effective supervision of and provision for their children are severely compromised. Parents under the influence of alcohol or other drugs may torment, batter or sexually exploit their own children. A cigarette may ease a parent's frustration but may also be used to inflict telltale circular burns on a child's arms, legs or buttocks.

I see "parentified" children, that is, children who have not been allowed to have a childhood because they are prematurely exposed to adult activities or because they are left to supervise and protect their younger siblings. One such child I know drinks straight black coffee four times each day because it "helps me with my worries." As many as half of the children who come to camp take prescribed medications for hyperactivity, depression and anxiety and for forms of withdrawal, dissociation and psychosis. And of course, the stress of working with these troubled children sends many a counselor or staff person to the nurse in search of an aspirin. Child abuse is just one example of how the consequences of drug and alcohol abuse reach deep within the fabric of Western society.

Summary

One child may be devastated by her father's indiscretions while under the influence of too much alcohol. Another child's aberrant development is greatly assisted by regular use of a prescribed drug. One may consume a moderate amount of a fine wine at a wedding* reception while remaining clear-headed and deeply appreciative of God's gifts of love, friendship* and commitment. Another individual's hallucinogenic trip may lead her to think of herself *as* God. The drunken stupor that clouds one's perception and judgment, taxes one's liver and alienates one from family, friends and work* is anything but a proper state for any human being, let alone a follower of Christ. There are no simple answers that hold for all forms of drug use and abuse. We must use biblical truth and the minds God gives us to discern proper from improper forms of drug use.

See also ADDICTION; ADVERTISING; DRIVENNESS; HEALING; HEALTH.

References and Resources

D. Kandel and R. Logan, "Patterns of Drug Use from Adolescence to Young Adulthood: I. Periods of Risk for Initiation, Continued Use and Discontinuation," *American Journal of Public Health* 74 (1984) 660-66; M. Newcomb, E. Maddahian and P. Bentler, "Risk Factors for Drug Use Among Adolescents: Concurrent and Longitudinal Analyses," *American Journal of Public Health* 76 (1986) 525-31; M. Rist, "The Shadow Children," *The American School Board Journal,* January 1990 19-24; J. Van Wicklin, "Substance Abuse," in *Christian Perspective on Social Problems,* ed. C. DeSanto, Z. Lindblade and M. Poloma, 2d ed. (Indianapolis: Wesley, 1992) 376-97.

John F. Van Wicklin

E

EATING

"Tell me what thou eatest, and I will tell thee what thou art." It was French gastronomer Jean Authelme Brillatt-Savarin who penned these words a century and a half ago. His argument is that what and how we eat say much more about us than our constant need of physical sustenance. But today eating is an activity so taken for granted that to seek after any deeper significance, especially from a spiritual perspective, would seem to most an odd pursuit. Yet the very fact that more of us do not take advantage of the wonders of modern science—not being content with meeting our nutritional needs with pills—is evidence that our eating habits have to do with much more than simply our digestive system. What significance does eating have from cultural and biblical perspectives? What do these perspectives say to us as we live out our Christian faith in the midst of ordinary life?

Eating from a Cultural Perspective

Eating and Culture. Anthropologists argue that when one knows what, where, how, when and with whom a person eats, one can understand the nature of his or her society. Eating is a transmitter of culture.* Much of who we are as social beings is determined through repetitive participation in this common event. Such basic matters as who sits where at the family table, who prepares the meal, who serves, who is served first, what is served and what is not, who dominates or directs communication and who cleans up after the meal communicate a wealth of information about social obligations and customs, authority structures and gender roles. It is also true that a society as a whole expresses its uniqueness and personality through its eating habits. Identity, passions, biases, prejudices, history, priorities and convictions are all expressed through how and what it eats.

Eating and Relationships. In all societies of the world, ancient and modern, eating is a primary way of entering into and sustaining relationships. In fact, the English word *companion* is derived from the French and Latin words meaning "one who eats bread with another." Eating plays an important, if not central, role in almost every social and family gathering. Restaurants from East to West are open and thriving night after night, playing host to the fostering of human relationships. Intimate dinner parties at home communicate a welcome into the life of the host. Family dinners express solidarity with a group of people to whom we are inextricably linked—business, collegial and family relationships, friendships* both intimate and casual, romantic ties, political alliances—all these and many more are recognized, ritualized and celebrated through the sharing of food. If life revolves around relationships, then it would be true to say that food and drink lubricate the cogs.

Eating and Covenant. Much has been made of the significance of the meal in the ancient Near East, where, traditionally, sharing food with a guest was equivalent to establishing a covenant. Certainly the host was obliged to offer protection and shelter to a guest who had eaten at his table. This concept of food as the seal of covenant is not confined to days gone by. Even today the Bantu of southern Africa regard exchanging food as the formation of a temporary covenant between individuals. They call it a "clanship of porridge." In Chinese society, the giving and sharing of food is considered to give flesh to relationships. And in the West, most major business deals are sealed with the mandatory business lunch. Negotiations begin, deals are made, and contracts are signed while the parties eat and drink.

Eating and Celebration. Celebration is incomprehensible within any society without the activity of eating. So central is it that certain food items are associated with particular rites of celebration. To a North American, Thanksgiving would not be Thanksgiving without the turkey, cranberry sauce, giblet gravy and pumpkin pie. For the English, a Christmas without plum pudding is hard to imagine, as it is for the Danes without the traditional rice dessert with almonds and whipped cream. For the Russians, a baked pascha is essential to an Easter celebration, as the moon cake is to the autumn festival for the Chinese. In the West, weddings* are celebrated with an elaborately decorated cake, and a birthday* requires a cake with candles. Formal good wishes are made with a glass of wine or champagne. Wedding anniversaries,* retirements,* special awards, engagements to be married, graduations and promotions* are often the cause for a celebratory feast. Even funerals are marked by the sharing of food and drink. It would be true to say that almost every significant rite of passage in every society is linked in some way to eating.

Eating in Time. While those of us who live in technological or informational societies can be drastically out of touch with the agricultural rhythms of the earth, the majority of people in the world are controlled by the foods that they produce and eat. The crops that they cultivate and the livestock that they nurture set the rhythm of their lives. Thus the farmer does not set the pace of life. Rather, he or she works to the pace set by the growth and harvest of the crops. Our habits of eating also give form and rhythm to our days and weeks. Breakfast, lunch and dinner set the pattern for each day that goes by. Each household marks the passing of certain days of the week with the eating of particular foods and the rhythms of formality and informality that surround the sequence of meals. In fact, our meals structure our year. As we move from January to December we pass through seasons, feasts and celebrations that dictate the foods we eat and enjoy.

Eating as a Spiritual Experience. Food has long been a popular and significant medium through which the human family experiences, communicates with and touches the divine. Detailed dietary rules are a part of all the major, and most minor, religions of the world. By keeping dietary rules, a devotee will summon the blessing and protection of the targeted divinity. Appeasing a god's wrath often calls for the sacrifice of animals, or perhaps vegetables, depending on the nature and tradition of the god being honored. Annual or more regular religious celebrations commonly center around the themes of sacrifice and consequent indulgence in a celebratory feast.

Eating from a Biblical Perspective

In the majority of cases, when the biblical ties between eating and Christian faith are discussed, it is the subjects of fasting and gluttony that rise to the surface. While the Bible has much to say on both issues, our canvas must be much broader to appreciate the real significance of eating from a Christian perspective.

Eating in the Old Testament. It is difficult to avoid the subject of eating as one wanders through the pages of the Old Testament. In the story of creation,* God's role as the Creator and Sustainer of life culminates in the provision of food for "everything that has the breath of life in it" (Gen 1:30). Of course this provision came with restrictions (Gen 2:16-17), and it was the disobedience of eating what was prohibited (Gen 3:1-6) that resulted in God's words of judgment, "Cursed is the ground because of you; through painful toil you will eat of it all the days of your life" (Gen 3:17), and the subsequent eviction from the Garden.

In the world of the Old Testament, eating was an important step in the establishment of covenant. As two parties sat down at table together, their common meal indicated reconciliation, enabling oaths and agreements to be entered into (Gen 26:28-31). It was by God's initiative that covenant relationship was established with Israel (Gen 12:1-3; 15:9-21; 35:9-15). The complex rites and rituals of sacrifice (Lev 1—7), and later establishment of feasts that played host to these sacrifices (Lev 23), were essential to the establishing and periodical renewing of this covenant relationship. Sacrifices and feasts were moments in which God and the people would sit at table together.

Throughout the Old Testament the imagery of eating signifies the presence, promises and blessings of God. As the people of Israel wandered in the desert after fleeing the Egyptians, it was God who rained down manna from heaven every day for forty years (Ex 16). As the people gathered the manna each morning and ate it, their eating served as a daily reminder of God's presence with them. The Promised Land itself was repetitively described as "a land flowing with milk and honey" (Ex 13:5; Num 13:27; Deut 6:3). For the people this description came to symbolize the richness of what lay ahead of them. It was a promise they could almost taste! The Old Testament imagery of blessing* and judgment is often tied to food. Satisfaction in eating was a picture of God's blessing (Deut 6:11; 8:10-12; 11:15), as lack of satisfaction was a picture of judgment (Lev 26:26; Is 9:20; Hos 4:10). Just as these more temporal of God's blessings were tied to eating, so the ultimate deliverance of the people is described in terms of God's invitation to an open table laden with an abundance of good food (Ps 23:5; 36:7-9; Is 25:6; Joel 3:18; Amos 9:13-14).

Eating in the New Testament. Around almost every corner of the Gospel accounts, Jesus can be found eating and drinking. He was labeled by some as a "glutton and a drunkard" (Mt 11:19). It was not so much the fact that he appeared to enjoy eating that riled his critics, but where and with whom he chose to do his eating. In a society that drew very clear and precise social and religious boundaries through the customs of the meal table, Jesus demonstrated a blatant disregard for protocol and tradition. His willingness to eat with anyone, regardless of class, race, profession or moral record, was deeply threatening to those who saw it as their duty to enforce such customs. One commentator has even suggested that Jesus got himself crucified by the way that he ate! Through time influential Jewish groups had constructed a complex set of rules and regulations designed to protect their racial and religious purity. Jesus' habit of sharing his meals with "tax collectors and sinners" (Lk 5:30) was threatening, for it demonstrated that his new kingdom order had little to do with religious customs and regulations. The kingdom of God was now symbolized by an open table to which all were invited to come and feast, an invitation without boundary or exclusion (Lk 14:15-24; 15:11-32; Mt 25:1-13). This imagery was later reinforced by a vision that God gave to Peter (Acts 10) in which it was made clear that the Levitical laws regarding clean and unclean foods were to be set aside. This signified the beginning of the early church's mission* to take the invitation to God's table to the Gentile community, who had long been considered "unclean" and outside the community of faith.

Jesus also used eating imagery to define his own mission. He calls himself the "bread of life" (Jn 6:35-59) and the "living water" (Jn 4:10-14). As he met with the disciples for the last supper he established that until the kingdom of God is fully come, his presence will be made tangible through the shared meal. Jesus established this meal as a time of remembrance when he said, "This is my body given for you; do this in remembrance for me" (Lk 22:19; cf. Mt 26:26; Mk 14:22), a time of covenant renewal; "This cup is the new covenant in my blood, which is poured out for you" (Lk 22:20; cf. Mt 26:28; Mk 14:24), and an anticipation of the messianic banquet that is to come, "For I tell you, I will not drink again of the fruit of this vine until the Kingdom of God comes" (Lk 22:18; cf. Mt 26:29; Mk 14:25).

As we move on into the life of the early church, the community of believers found their identity as followers of Christ most profoundly and most tangibly in their eating together. It was through the breaking of bread (*see* Communion), as part of an ordinary meal, that the church expressed its unity, identity and destiny as the people of God (Acts 20:7, 11; 1 Cor 11:33; 2 Pet 2:13; Jude 12).

Eating as a Christian

In the light of these cultural and biblical perspectives, how do we allow our Christian faith to affect and inform our eating habits?

Eating and Providence. Central to the prayer that Jesus taught his followers is the petition "Give us this day our daily bread" (Mt 6:11). As we break bread, whether in an overtly religious ritual or in the daily routine of breakfast, we are gathered up into the mystery of God's providence. Food is, indeed, the stuff of life, and the creation and sustaining of life are God's business. But dependence on God as our Provider is not altogether obvious for the majority of people in the developed world. In the United States, only 3 percent of the population is needed to produce more than 100 percent of the required agricultural products. If food is lacking on our table, no longer do we look heavenward. A quick trip to the supermarket solves our problem. And yet, for those who still plough the earth, await the rains, milk the cows, cast nets into the ocean and nurture the grapevines, their dependence on a power outside of themselves is a daily experience. But whether we are aware of it or not, every time we eat we express our complete dependence on a power outside ourselves. As we spoon more potatoes on our plate, butter the bread and pour the water, we handle the grace of God. For those who bow to pray before eating, dependence is articulated; those who do not so pray are still unavoidably dependent.

Those of us who are urban dwellers in the Western world need to get back in touch with our immediate dependence on the God-ordained rhythms of the earth. Perhaps growing our own vegetables, baking our own bread or being less dependent on convenience foods are good ways to begin. We could also work at being less preoccupied with convenience and the economy of time*—the law of the microwave oven—and more involved in the process of preparation and creation.

Eating and Sacrament. As Jesus broke bread and shared it with his fellow travelers on the road to Emmaus, "their eyes were opened and they recognized him" (Lk 24:31). While every meal we participate in is not overtly religious in nature, each time we sit down to a meal God is present. It is an expression of the principle of incarnation. We discover God in the midst of the ordinary. When we sit down to a meal, we sit down to a God-ordained part of life in which God is made manifest.

In the celebration of the Lord's Supper, we articulate a spiritual truth: life is dependent on death. In order that we might enter into the fullness of life, life had to be surrendered. Jesus surrendered his life to death in order that we might live. In a sense, that same principle of "life for life" is at work in every meal we eat. Every time we swallow we enact that principle. Whether we are eating a bowl of porridge, devouring a sirloin steak or sipping a glass of orange juice, life had to be laid down for us. It is part of the order of things. It is so ordinary, and yet in this ordinariness is mystery.

Nurturing a conscious awareness of God's presence at the meal table—a daily discipline in a fragmented and fast-paced world—is crucial if we are to develop an integrated spirituality. It will call for a degree of creativity as we seek to establish mealtime rituals that make God's presence a daily experience. It will mean consciously watching for incarnational moments when God's presence and purposes can be named and celebrated.

Eating and Community. It has been said that to be human is to belong. The need to belong is a need that has been central to our humanity from the beginning. As we have already discovered, Jesus extended the boundaries of belonging to the community of God's people. He proclaimed God's kingdom open to and inclusive of all those who respond to God's invitation to eat with him.

Wendy Wright has written, "When we break bread together, we symbolically enact the basic truth that we are most complete when we are together." A family* is that group of scattered individuals who come together at the end of the day, most commonly around the meal table. They may or may not be related, but every time they meet there, they acknowledge their identity as a family and reaffirm together their sense of belonging. There is a sense in which our meal table defines the boundaries of our community.* Occasionally, or regularly, an outsider is invited to the table. In welcoming them we communicate that, for the period of the meal at least, this person is no longer a stranger. They belong with us.

In a society that increasingly values individualism,* where families are sacrificing their common identity in pursuit of individual interests, the common mealtime is disappearing or shared around the television set. Our task is to reinvent the household mealtime as a time to value relationships, listen to each other, extend welcome to the outsider and reaffirm our need for community. Guarding the sanctity of the shared mealtime is crucial. Finding ways to make meal-preparation* a communal event will only deepen the experience.

Eating and Service. Through his words and actions, Jesus painted a picture of a kingdom in which love* and self-giving are central. His proclamations were, and still are, radical. For Jesus, genuine power can be experienced only in the laying down of personal ambition.* It is in the kingdom distinctive of service that we discover the greatness for which we were created. Jesus' example shows that there are few places where this can be so demonstrated as at the meal table.

Whether a ministry of compassion or of simple hospitality,* it is clearly a ministry of service that is offered at the table.

Ernest Boyer Jr. calls what we offer at the meal table "the sacrament of care." Care is offered most often in the routine and the ordinary activities of the day—washing dishes, peeling vegetables, making beds and so on. Is the one who selflessly prepares meals for a family, week in and week out, year in and year out, conscious of it as a sacrament of care? Probably not. It is routine, instinctive, second nature and ordinary. Yet if we take Jesus' words seriously, then what this provider offers to the family day after day is as significant and valued in God's kingdom as any glorified act of service offered by prophet, priest or king.

As a church we should be looking for ways and opportunities to recognize and celebrate these "sacraments of care" being offered daily by often unrecognized members of our communities. As household members we can nurture those who serve us by regularly voicing our thanks for revealing to us more of God's nature and character. We could even construct simple liturgies and rituals together which give voice to our mutual dependence.

Eating and Mission. In a sense, Jesus' eating habits embodied his mission.* His sitting at table with the despised, the disenfranchised, the closed-out was a clear indication that the kingdom of heaven is a place of welcome, refuge and healing for all. It indicates that the mission of the church is not merely proclamation of the "good news" to those outside the kingdom, nor is it limited to the clothing and feeding of the outcasts. It is a mission which calls for both of these, and yet more. It calls for intimate investment in the lives of those we call to the table. Jesus could have limited his ministry to the proclamation of the kingdom from the mountaintops and the synagogues. Instead, such moments were the exception. More commonly, Jesus was to be found brushing up against all manner of people in the most domestic settings and very often eating with them. The mission of the early church clearly reflected this pattern. Mission for Jesus and the early church involved initiating relationships and clearly demonstrating the nature of God's inclusive kingdom. According to Jesus, welcome into the kingdom will be extended to those who extend to others the same open hospitality of the table: "For I was hungry and you gave me something to eat, I was thirsty and you gave me something to drink, I was a stranger and you invited me in" (Mt 25:35).

Being invited into a private home for dinner is becoming the exception in American society. As a friend commented, "To invite me into your home is to invite me into your life." Increasingly today such an invitation of intimacy and commitment is avoided. If we are intended to model the inclusive nature of God's kingdom and yet fail to invite even those who are like us to the dinner table, then how in the world do we begin to address the call to the stranger and the alien? The mission of the church is about more than a distant proclamation or a free handout at the soup kitchen. It is about intimate investment in the lives of those around us. It is about securing our identity as a family and then opening the table to those who need the open embrace of Jesus.

While our eating may always be a very routine and ordinary part of our lives, essential to keeping us physically healthy and whole, it should not be forgotten that it is significant at much deeper levels. As those concerned to work out our discipleship* in the midst of all the ordinariness of life, it is helpful to remember that the announcement of the gospel is

327

like the ringing of a gong before the evening meal and the words "Dinner is served!"

See also COMMUNION; HOSPITALITY; MEAL PREPARATION.

References and Resources
S. S. Bartchy, "Table Fellowship," in *Dictionary of Jesus and the Gospels*, ed. J. B. Green, S. McKnight and I. H. Marshall, (Downers Grove, Ill.: Inter-Varsity Press, 1992); E. Boyer Jr., *Finding God at Home: Family Life as Spiritual Discipline* (San Francisco: Harper, 1991); J. A. Brillat-Savarin, *The Physiology of Taste* (London: Penguin, 1970); A. C. Cochrane, *Eating and Drinking with Jesus: An Ethical and Biblical Inquiry* (Philadelphia: Westminster, 1974); S. C. Juengst, *Breaking Bread: The Spiritual Significance of Food* (Louisville: Westminster/John Knox, 1992); R. J. Karris, *Luke: Artist and Theologian* (New York: Paulist, 1985); J. MacClancy, *Consuming Culture: Why You Eat What You Eat* (New York: Henry Holt, 1992); M. Visser, *Much Depends on Dinner: The Extraordinary History and Mythology, Allure and Obsessions, Perils and Taboos of an Ordinary Meal* (New York: Grove, 1986); W. M. Wright, *Sacred Dwelling: A Spirituality of Family Life* (New York: Crossroad, 1990).

Simon Holt

ECOLOGY

Ecology in its narrowest definition is the study of the relationship between living things and their environment. More broadly, ecology has come to refer to the way natural systems operate. Sometimes the word *ecology* (or the phrase "the environment") is used in the same way *nature* was a century ago.

Why Ecology Is Important

For all who believe that "the earth is the LORD's," the study of ecology is an important discipline, for it seeks to explain in detail the way the earth's systems function. Since human civilization (both deliberately and accidentally) is altering, in profound ways, the makeup and functioning of those systems (*see* Pollution), it is crucial for all people—and Chris-

tians in particular—to develop an ecological understanding. As Aldo Leopold (whose book *A Sand County Almanac* was influential in increasing popular understanding of ecology) puts it, "To keep every cog and wheel is the first precaution of intelligent tinkering" (p. 190). Increasingly, we are "tinkering" with the earth. Ecology is the study of the healthy functioning of living systems when all the parts are present and in good working order.

The word *ecology*, coined in the nineteenth century by the German biologist Ernst Haeckel, is made up of two Greek words: *logos*, meaning the "study of," and *oikos*, the "household" of living things. It is very closely related, at least in its origin, to the word *economy*, which referred originally to the stewardship* or human management of individual households. In fact, in the New Testament the Greek word *economy* is usually translated "stewardship."

Ecology therefore deals with the way the household of life on earth works, whereas economy describes the workings of the human household—industry, markets and technology*—that both depends on and affects that larger household of God's creation* which it is the purpose of ecology to describe.

Sometimes Christians have acted as though their only concern were the forceful domination and subjugation of that earthly nonhuman household, turning it all to exclusively human purpose. One could perhaps conclude that from a narrow reading of Genesis 1:28: "Fill the earth and subdue it. Rule . . . over every living creature." But a more careful reading of Scripture shows that this world of human economy must be understood within the larger earth of God's good creation, and that *stewardship* rather than *domination* best describes the human relationship to creation. This is the clear implication of the words describing Adam's task in Eden (Gen 2:15): "The LORD God took the man and put him in the Garden of Eden to work it and take care of it." The Hebrew word for "work" usually means "to serve," and the word for "take care of" is often translated "keep," as in Aaron's priestly blessing on the Israelites: "The LORD bless you and keep you" (Num 6:24).

Caring for Creation

This understanding that a main human task is to "keep" the good creation is consistent with the biblical witness of God's own intimate "keeping" of creation. Psalm 104, which has been called the ecologist's psalm, goes into considerable detail about the way the earth's systems work: "He makes springs pour water into the ravines. . . .They give water to all the beasts of the field. . . . He makes grass grow for the cattle, and plants for man to cultivate. . . . The trees of the LORD are well watered. . . . There the birds make their nests" (vv. 10-11, 14-17).

The same kind of divine delight in ecological complexity appears in God's answer to Job (Job 38—41). If God cares in this way for the created complexity of ecosystems and the whole great ecosphere or household of the earth, it is imperative that Christians develop an ecological understanding.

Ecological Principles

The serious study of ecology is endlessly complex. Yet a few principles of particular importance for human living in this created household can be highlighted.

1. *Everything is connected to everything else.* This sounds overstated, but it is not. The rapid cycling of winds and waters (and even the vastly slower crustal movements of the earth's surface) means that we cannot act as though our actions—making a species extinct, dumping waste in a river or even driving a car and releas-

ing exhaust gases into the atmosphere—will not ultimately have at least a tiny effect through the earth. The truth of this apparently extreme principle has been brought home to us as we have been able to measure in the fatty tissues of arctic animals the appreciable accumulations of chemical residues from local industrial civilization's activities thousands of miles away from the Arctic. We see the principle even more ominously in the ozone-destroying effect of chemicals we all use.

2. *Everything comes from somewhere and goes somewhere.* An ecological understanding shows us that because the earth is an interconnected system,* we cannot simply regard it as an inexhaustible storehouse of raw materials for our economy. We need to be aware of the consequences of our consumption of food, trees, oil and metals for the ecological systems disturbed by their extraction. At the same time, we need to be aware that there is, in God's creation, no "away" for things to be thrown to. There are no dumps or sanitary landfills in God's good creation.

3. *There is no free lunch.* This is a crude way of putting a profound truth which on one level is expressed as "the second law of thermodynamics"—that is, in the physical world, things move from order to disorder. Living things seem to contradict that physical principle, since life continually orders, and even reproduces. Unfortunately, even in living creatures that order is bought at the expense of other things—usually other living creatures. At the biological level, the principle is expressed in the aphorism that "ecology is the study of who is eating whom."

4. *Generally, in earth's ecosystems, complexity equals stability; and human activity reduces, and hence destabilizes, ecological complexity.* Even a casual study of creation reveals its astonishing complexity. This

complexity is creation's insurance against changes of environmental conditions. In a cold, wet spring certain species of plants will prosper and others won't; in a hot, dry spring the situation may be reversed. But the total is a healthy system. Likewise, among the great variety of species and subspecies, some will be resistant to certain predators and diseases, and others will not. The overall effect is one of a flourishing balance. Most human activity—such as when we replace the vast diversity of prairie wild plants with a wheat field sprayed with herbicides to ensure a weed-free return—reduces this life-giving complexity.

An ecological understanding helps to undo some of the damage done by several centuries of thinking of the earth as nothing more than a kind of biological machine which we could learn to manipulate for our benefit. Study of ecology ought to bring home to us principles that we learn from the Christian gospel: that life, in every sense of the word, depends on *community** and *relationship;* that living is necessarily costly; that agape, self-giving love,* is the way by which the tragedy of life is redeemed into the joyful purpose of God's great story. These things we ought to know, who are called to be stewards of creation, the ecosphere, which holds together in the self-giving life of the One "through whom all things were made."

See also CREATION; POLLUTION; STEWARDSHIP; SYSTEM; TECHNOLOGY; WORK.

References and Resources

A. Leopold, *A Sand County Almanac* (New York: Oxford University Press, 1949); G. T. Miller, *Living in the Environment* (Toronto: W. B. Saunders, 1980); L. Wilkinson, ed., *Earthkeeping: Christian Stewardship of Natural Resources* (Grand Rapids: Eerdmans, 1980).

Loren Wilkinson

EDUCATION

Education, or schooling as it is better known for those under twenty, is at a new height of popularity because of the information age. Individual successes in life and national destinies are being increasingly linked to the quality of educational experiences. In a parallel outlook the New Testament emphasizes the necessity of instruction. Paul, for example, talks about counseling and teaching everyone with all wisdom in a way that is similar to preparing students for a final exam (Col 1:28).

Despite their common concern for education, Greeks and Christians in the first century A.D. saw their educational philosophies as irreconcilable. Many asked, "What has Jerusalem to do with Athens?" Athens, the center on which most of our present-day educational traditions are based, espoused a morality and a concept of God totally unacceptable to Christians. This led to a rejection of all that emanated from that source. Some still think that way today, as will be seen when home schooling is discussed.

In fact, the so-called polarization between Jerusalem and Athens was not as clear-cut as it might seem at first glance. The early apologists, including Paul, sought to find common ground between Christian values* and the secular world of Greece. Today this concurrency is more visible; secular and Christian educators alike espouse many of the same timeless and universal ideas and values. Wilfred Wees, a Canadian educational leader, touched on this idea in a speech delivered at the Ontario Institute for Studies in Education in 1965. He described love* as the only lasting principle in education, one that, in his words, "would be as true two thousand years hence as it was two thousand years ago in the life of Christ."

Contemporary debates over educational goals arise from the different values that people bring to them. These values are evident whenever educational plans are made, when overall goals are stated or when content and methods of curricula are defined. At one time H. I. Marrou's definition of education received widespread acceptance: "Education is a collective technique which a society employs to instruct its youth in the values and accomplishments of the civilization within which it exists" (p. xiii). This is no longer acceptable in our multicultural society of today. As a result, there is a range of opinions on the values that ought to undergird educational programs.

Education in Values

Everything that happens in a school is value-laden. The notion of value-free education is a myth: every choice of teaching materials, every mode of instruction and every action by the teacher carries a set of values. These values can be seen most clearly in a school's overall goal, be it character formation, academic success,* social responsibility or some combination of these. Behind each goal lies a distinct view of human nature and destiny. If character formation is a primary goal, then morality will dominate the curriculum; if it is academic success, then intellectual prowess will get top priority. A Christian goal would lean heavily toward character formation, including the recognition of right and wrong (Heb 5:13-14).

Historically almost all education in our Western world is rooted in a Christian view of life. Christians and Christian organizations responding to particular needs, often of the neglected poorer members of society, established private schools. Christian values governed these schools, just as Jewish and Muslim values governed the schools of those religions. Only in modern times, particularly in the United States, has the myth of separate

secular and religious schools surfaced. Only in the narrowest sense of religious practices, like baptism,* is it possible to separate secular and religious values. For many parents, however, the two are indivisible because they see their religion as that dimension of culture* that deals with the meaning of life and humanity's place in the universe.

Many North Americans say that children exposed to the world's religions are more tolerant of other viewpoints. Yet in multiethnic Britain during the 1980s, a very different value prevailed. The government decided to make traditional Christianity the basic value system of the schools. Strongest support for the decision came from Muslims, Jews and representatives of several other religions, all of whom felt that a society ought to be true to its roots. Giving equal place to each of the world's religions would, they argued, confuse rather than help the young.

The primacy of the parental role is at issue in discussions over values, and this priority is fully recognized only when religious values are taken into consideration. This parental role stems from age-old traditions rooted in Jewish and Christian history. In many countries it has been retained throughout the centuries. In the United States, by contrast, the past 150 years witness the dominance of Greek and Roman traditions in which the state holds direct responsibility for the education of its citizens. The debate over primary responsibility for education is ongoing and lies behind the present popularity of private Christian schools.

Private Christian Schools

There are three common types of Christian schools, each representing a different level of accommodation with public education. All of them are costly, because while public financial assistance is sometimes available, families have to pay school fees while continuing to contribute to the costs of public education. At one end of the scale are parents who want only the teachers to be Christian. The teaching materials and procedures may be the same as are found in the general system.*

A second type goes further and insists that teachers be Christian and all teaching materials be supportive of Christian values. Books that teach evolutionary theory, for instance, are either banned or linked with biblical descriptions of the origins of life. For parents who choose this type, the school is seen as modeling Christian society; children are aggressively persuaded to choose Christian belief and demonstrate the application of their faith in everyday living. Paradoxically, it was a similar approach that destroyed John Dewey's famous progressive education movement. He sought to create a model democratic society within the school walls, one that would challenge and, in time, transform the surrounding society.

The third type, the home-schooling movement, is the most radical. In many ways it is reminiscent of the most extreme views of the early church. Parents take their children completely away from school and educate them at home* or in places where small groups can share the work. It is a demanding task, particularly in homes in which both parents work. Supporters of home schooling consider it to be the only true biblical education because the Bible has so many references to home-based education. A classic illustration is found in the early part of the Old Testament: "Impress them on your children. Talk about them when you sit at home and when you walk along the road, when you lie down and when you get up. Tie them as symbols on your hands and bind them on your foreheads. Write them on the doorframes of your houses and on your gates" (Deut 6:7-9). There are similar injunctions in the New Testament, particularly those that relate to fathers (Eph 6:4). Many public education systems now recognize home schooling as an approved method of learning.

Technological advances provide one reason for the success of home schooling. Parents need not be proficient in the content of school subjects. Television,* computers* and a host of related resources are readily available. In addition, departments of education provide textbooks and self-help study guides for students. Thus a parent's responsibility can be focused on a Christian perspective in the learning process, stressing responsible behavior and awareness of God at all times.

In ancient Israel only home schooling existed. Parents held an enormous range of influence that could be brought to bear on the education of the child. In many ways that range of influence parallels the plethora of factors that affect learning today (Cremin, p. viii). At the same time, changes over the centuries, partly due to the influence of Christians and partly to a response to societal conditions, have opened the door to Christian involvement in public education in a way that could not have been envisaged two thousand years ago.

Successful Schools

Reports of recent findings of educational research on successful schools illustrate these opportunities for Christian involvement. Researchers conclude that students' attitudes and achievements are powerfully influenced by teacher expectations, by what the teacher models, by consistency of values throughout the school, by students' home background, by a community spirit, by curriculum tied to stated goals and by experience of high success in routine exercises. Most of these characteristics rely on good relationships, student to teacher, teacher to teacher, student to student, and rely most of all on the teacher as a model of the school's values.

A healthy community spirit is possible when these relationships are intact, when every student has some level of acquaintance with every teacher, and conversely. It is quite a different atmosphere from that found in institutional life. Institutions have rules; communities have histories. Christians can readily relate to schools with these kinds of relationships because they resemble the exemplary Christian communities described in the early history of the church (Acts 2:44).

Given the characteristics of successful schools, the Christian can find endless opportunities for influencing public education. Consider, for example, the characteristic of home influence. People once assumed that progress in school derived entirely from the teacher and child. Now we know better, recognizing the tremendous educational value of the home. Children from homes in which parents show love and care and in which interest in good books is encouraged do better at school than those who come from deprived homes. Furthermore, since children are at home for the first four or five years of life, the period of time when critical attitudes and values are acquired, the home influences remain influential throughout life.

Armed with this new information, parents have sought to influence the curricula and methods of their schools. In New England during the 1980s school districts and groups of parents who shared common values forged partnerships. Parents could then select the school that met their values and, at the same time, met their curricular interests. In other settings children from impoverished homes found little success in public schools. Those children's parents persuaded their political leaders to allow a voucher system. In Milwaukee, for example, parents received vouchers for half the per capita cost of regular schooling. With this money they sent their children to Catholic schools prepared to accept them at the cost level represented by the vouchers. This new method of parental involvement succeeded: attendance and standards of achievement rose dramatically.

Christians in Public Schools

Educational research findings enable Christians to relate to many other aspects of public education. The motto "All truth is God's truth" must be kept in mind alongside our understanding of the differences between Christian worldviews* and those of others. John Dewey, though indifferent to Christian values, saw the necessity of relating all learning to the immediate world of the student. This emphasis is similar to Paul's stress on salvation's benefits being immediately relevant to life (2 Cor 6:2). Many opportunities for participation exist because of the new research findings, but mainstreaming provides perhaps the best place for significant Christian involvement.

Students with physical or mental impairments and those who have extremely high ability do not fit easily into regular classrooms. This is especially true for those who have low intelligence quotients, who would previously have been segregated and taught in special schools. Today the popular solution is *mainstreaming*, the inclusion of these children in normal classrooms. Not everyone agrees that the change is for the good. Teachers complain that too much time* must be devoted to these exceptional students, with the result that the others are ignored. Some describe the whole move as a money-saving scheme, particularly when inadequate support is provided. Debate rages around the borderline cases, those children who cannot be ac-

333

commodated in a classroom without seriously interfering with the activities of other students. There is general agreement that extremely handicapped children, those who need continuous care at all times, have to be looked after in special institutions, but there is difficulty defining the boundary between the ones who can be accommodated and those who cannot.

Rarely are the facilities completely adequate for the needs of severely disadvantaged children. Parents are expected to provide some help, and teachers are called upon to make special efforts beyond what they would normally be expected to give. Thus there is always an open door for volunteers*—someone to drive the child to school, to care for him or her at break times, to be around when an emergency occurs. It is a selfless task, an ideal opportunity for demonstrating Christian values. It is also an occasion when the benefits of mainstreaming can be shown.

The story of one quadriplegic student, who suffers from spastic cerebral palsy but has normal intelligence and can speak, illustrates the positive role of mainstreaming (Gunn, p. 8). Despite the student's physical impairments, she learns within a regular classroom. Her teacher argues that the value to the other students far outweighs the problems of integration. Regular students can learn to appreciate the enormous amount of energy she must expend to do what must seem to them quite simple things. The so-called handicapped, she says, can become models of humanity for the rest of us, leading to a society in which every individual has equal worth. In a letter to the Corinthian Christians, Paul once voiced a similar sentiment, describing how God accords exceptional worth to those who seem to be the least important members of the community (1 Cor 12:24-25).

Conclusion

Education has never been more important than today, both for the general community and for Christians. While some Christian parents reject secular school systems for their children's education, many parents believe that their children are well cared for in public schools. In either case enormous opportunities exist for all Christians to influence our schools, both directly and through the many agencies locally and worldwide that shape the lives of young people.

See also CHRISTIAN EDUCATION; DISCIPLESHIP; EQUIPPING; PARENTING; SPIRITUAL GROWTH; SUNDAY SCHOOL.

References and Resources

J. Bremer and M. von Moschziker, *The School Without Walls* (New York: Holt, Rinehart & Winston, 1971); L. A. Cremin, *Popular Education and Its Discontents* (New York: Harper, 1990); A. M. Gunn, "Champion of the Disadvantaged," *B.C. Catholic* 64 (30 May 1994) 8; H. I. Marrou, *A History of Education in Antiquity*, trans. G. Lamb (London: Sheed & Ward, 1956); P. Perkins, *Jesus as Teacher: Understanding Jesus Today* (New York: Cambridge University Press, 1990); K. Sidey, ed., *The Blackboard Fumble* (Wheaton, Ill.: Victor Books, 1989); G. H. Wood, *Schools That Work: America's Most Innovative Public Education Programs* (New York: Penguin, 1993).

Angus M. Gunn

EMOTIONS

The Bible is an emotional book, and the church* is an emotional community.* Relationships have a highly emotive content. Teachers and preachers know that emotions are the power behind effective communication. Parenting* involves the emotional education of children. In fact, there is no area of human life that excludes the powerful thrust of emotions. They travel with us wherever we go, and they affect whatever we do. It is not too much to say that without emotions we are detached and mechanical, subhuman and not as God intended.

The Good of Emotional Expression

The Christian faith is an emotional faith. Jesus Christ endured the cross "for the joy that was set before him" (Heb 12:2). The apostle Paul was a man who was "sorrowful, yet always rejoicing." It was said of Jonathan Edwards that "he deeply savored the sweet sovereignty of God." C. S. Lewis insightfully remarked that the Lord "finds our desires not too strong but too weak."

In life we observe that *interest* energizes learning, creativity and innovation; *anger* mobilizes energy for taking action against frustration, irritation or invasion; *joy* releases both celebration and stress* as it increases social exchange; *shame* assists us in discerning what is good and in making responsible choices; *guilt* motivates restoration of relationships and reparation of injuries; *fear* protects us by warning of imminent danger. The dysfunctions of each of these arise from exaggeration of the emotion and overload and overwhelming of the controls. But basically emotions are good.

Emotional expression serves several basic social functions. Our emotions signal the inner state of feeling; they request some response in thought or act by other participants; and they report when the trigger of the emotion is some event, person or situation in the context. In the expression of emotion we experience the intensity of both love and hate, acceptance and rejection, apathy and anger.

How We Feel About Our Feelings

Some people approach their emotions as being bad; they are the "stuffers." They treat their emotions as if they should never be expressed, repressing their own emotions and suppressing emotions in others. Such people say, "I feel fine" or "I'm okay." But these are not really feelings. They are judgments about their feelings. Or they play one feeling most of the time (for example, anger or happiness) like a trombone with a stuck slide. The note may be pure, but there is more to a symphony than this.

Others approach their emotional states as if they had a right to express them in every conversation*—they are the "gushers." These people feel that emotions are "who you really are." Bad temper for such people becomes a form of public littering in which others pick up the pieces. Unlike the stuffers, these people play all the emotions of the symphony, sometimes at the same time. Stuffers are afraid of gushers about as much as gushers are angry with stuffers.

There is a wondrous group of people who take responsibility for their feelings and see them as goal directed and purposeful. They are not dominated by their emotions, nor are they afraid of them. They see their emotions as useful. We will call these people the "emotional pragmatists." Living as an emotional pragmatist may sound boring (to a gusher), but to a stuffer it must sound like heaven!

The Value of Emotions

Emotions serve four essential functions. First, they are an instrument of rationality. Gerhard Frost says that "the hungers of the heart outrun the reaches of the mind." Our emotions enable us to learn. They provide direction for what it is that we need to know. Emotions provide instant rewards and punishments for truths held and values* broken.

Second, emotions are vital sensors to imbalance. They tell us if we are doing okay in social situations. Without emotions we would become like the leper who has no nerve endings and cannot know if he is breaking his leg or burning his arm. Emotions allow us the opportunity to respond, to ask for forgiveness,* to pursue a winsome glance.

Third, emotions enable us to know if we have achieved genuine human contact with another. Without emotions we would be bionic automatons. Marital intimacy would become mere mating. Cherishing our children would be reduced to technological parenting, providing the correct punishment and reinforcement. Emotions answer the question, Have I made contact with this person?

Fourth, emotions give us the possibility of embracing another's experience. Without emotion we would not have the privilege to count another's experience as our own. As such, it is emotions that permit us to enter genuinely into human community and covenant.

What Are Emotions?

The word *emotion* originates in the Latin *emovare,* meaning "to move." We sometimes say, "That worship service moved me." That is, it motivated us in some way. We also say we are "moved to anger," as when we are cut off in traffic. The anger was in response to a frightening stimuli and resulted in a form of self-protection. As we understand emotions, we need to know that they are affective responses to some sort of stimuli—they occur in response to some idea, cue or influence.

There are thought to be a small number of *primary emotions,* of which all others are derivatives. René Descartes describes six primary emotions (what he calls "primitive emotions") that he believes encompass all human emotional responses: admiration, love, hate, desire, joy and sadness. Robert Plutchik sees the primary emotions as four bipolarities: destruction versus protection, incorporation versus rejection, reproduction versus deprivation and orientation versus exploration. However we define them, they are probably limited in number.

The developmental process of growth from infancy to adulthood begins with the emergence of the primary emotions of anxiety, basic fears, trust and mistrust, followed by anger, shame, self-doubt, guilt and inferiority, as well as joy, pride, self-confidence, curiosity, interest, grief, sadness, love and forgiveness. As we move through the life stages,* the periodic ascendance of particular emotions supports us during particular passages, transitions, losses, as well as empowers us to make discoveries and accomplish meaningful life projects. But where did emotions come from?

The Origin of Emotions

As early as 1872 in the first widely accepted work on expressive emotions, Charles Darwin argued that certain emotional expressions are innate and universal. These fundamental emotions, which are recognized and labeled similarly across cultures, have been researched in multiple studies and include interest, joy, surprise, anger, sadness, disgust, contempt, fear and shame. Although the interpersonal meanings of these vary from one cultural context to another, the basic spectrum of emotional possibilities is similar among humans of every group. While this describes emotions common to humankind, we can account for emotions by considering the intention of the Creator.

In our original creation we were "naked and . . . felt no shame" (Gen 2:25). Our creation emotions include trust, joy and love.* We have these wonderful emotions because we are human beings created in the image of God. Through these feelings we express our fullest humanity and godlikeness. They are the emotions of worship.* John Piper in his book *Desiring God: Meditations of a Christian Hedonist* begins with the statement "This is a serious book about being happy in God." He argues that the "chief end of man is to glorify God By enjoying him forever" (p. 14). God is an experiencing Being and needs to be encountered in personal and feeling ways. So we approach God in trust, joy and love. We do this boldly and directly because as Hebrews 4:15-16 says, "We do not have a high priest who is unable to sympathize with our weaknesses, but we have one [Jesus] who has been tempted in every way, just as we are—yet was without sin. Let us then approach the throne of grace with confidence, so that we may receive mercy and find grace to help us in our time of need."

Our basic emotional needs as we grow are fundamentally related to healthy emotional expression. These needs include belonging; achievement or success; economic security; self-respect; freedom from fear; love and affection; freedom from feelings of guilt; understanding and being understood. As these basic needs are substantially met, especially in relation to God, we express trust, joy and love.

Not all feelings, however, are as wonderful as these. Some emotions are directly related to our sinful state. Genesis tells us Adam's experience after his rejection of God: "I was afraid, because I was naked; and I hid myself" (Gen 3:10 NRSV). The feelings associated with this behavior are shame, fear and guilt. Some feelings relate to the inevitable consequence of living in a fallen world and with the disfigurement of God's image in our lives—as described in Genesis 3:16-19. These feelings are sorrow, disappointment, grief,* despair, frustration, depression* and anger.

Thinking and Feeling

To understand the naturalness of our emotions, we must also consider the difference between thinking and feeling and how the two are related. Virtually all research supports the conclusion that there are separate processes and systems for cognition (thinking) and emotion (feeling). There has been a long debate with some scholars supporting the primacy of emotion to feeling (in other words, the mind is a rational faculty that creates reasons for what the heart wants to do) and others supporting the prior existence of perceptions (cognitions) to emotions (in other words, inside every feeling there is a perception; in fact, emotions are simply the energy for experiencing and expressing our perceptions). The current theories see the two as equal processes with distinct neural pathways that interact, influence, motivate, shape and direct each other.

The primacy of feeling in infancy and early childhood yields to the dominance of thinking in youth and adulthood, but both processes occur and control, trigger and interpret, the other. Some counseling approaches interrupt the cycles of thought and feeling by working with cognition; others enter through the enhanced and clarified emotional world. Affective therapists employ ventilating, flooding, learning the language of feelings, developing new patterns of experiencing and expressing these feelings; cognitive therapists utilize restructuring the cognitive programs of old self-instructions and learning new ways of perceiving, organizing, naming, thinking and controlling thought processes. Either process may be selected as a more appropriate point of entry in facilitating change. Both assume we have responsibility to deal with our own feelings.

Responsibility for Feelings

The role of theology in relation to emotions is to assure us of the goodness of our emotional creation and to point toward emotional wholeness as we claim the full range of human possibilities in work, play, worship and relationships. Theology also helps account for the complexity of our emotional life by explaining what has gone wrong with human life, including our emotions. Further Christian theology directs our emotional energies to service beyond ourselves. The role of ethics lies in the guidance of appropriate expression of emotion.

In the original garden Adam and Eve tried to transfer their responsibility to each other and to God. The New Testament, however, states: "When tempted, no one should say, 'God is tempting me.' For God cannot be tempted by evil, nor does he tempt anyone; but each one is tempted when, by his own evil desire, he is dragged away and enticed. Then, after desire has conceived, it gives birth to sin; and sin, when it is full-grown, gives birth to death" (Jas 1:13-15). Also, in Ephesians 4:26 Paul says, " 'In your anger do not sin': Do not let the sun go down while you are still angry."

By making us responsible, God confers a great compliment upon us. God says that we have what it takes to handle our most powerful emotional experiences! Indeed, if we do not take responsibility for our feelings, they can be corrupted. Love can degenerate into lechery; or joy, when not taken responsibility for, can degenerate into indolence and inactivity, as figure 1 indicates:

Love	Sacrificial pouring out	Lust and lechery
Anger	Power to right wrong	Hatred and violence
Guilt	Stimulus to repentance	Despair, depression, suicide
Peace	Presence of God	Indolence, inactivity
Joy	Intense experience of being alive	Intemperance, intoxication
Hunger	Drive for nurture	Gluttony, obesity

Figure 1. Feelings—Responsible and Irresponsible

Control of Emotions

Not all emotions should be expressed. A reliable gauge of maturity is whether an individual knows what emotions are to be expressed and what ones should be limited or unexpressed. The *ventilationist* view of emotions is that unexpressed emotions corrupt the person's inner life. This may not be always true. Expressing lust, anger or fear may be a rehearsal of more dangerous expressions for future times. A child enraged should not be encouraged "to get it all out," for if he is, he will be "doing time" for his venting when he is an adult. How does one go about limiting and controlling unwanted but intrusive emotions?

First, we should recognize our emotional states. Unpleasant emotions such as sorrow, fear, anger, jealousy, shame, disgust, pain, confusion and emptiness need to be acknowledged. Many people do not even know they are angry or happy. This comes as a surprise when they get "in touch" with their feelings. As well, some people convert their feelings into experiences that they consider to be more desirable. When they are afraid, they may withdraw into depression. So the first stage is to accept that there are uncomfortable emotions that are causing some upset.

Second, we should anticipate events so that we can avoid situations that are likely to produce undesirable emotional stress or approach the situations differently. We should determine the time and place to challenge our emotions. This stage of anticipation gives the person freedom to choose.

Third, we should care for our physical condition. An exhausted business executive confronting his overstressed wife about their problems with money will have a less than wonderful evening. Maximal physical resources are required to deal with difficult emotions. Church leaders* tell me that they are able to deal with the stresses and fears of their work when they regularly take a sabbath* each week.

Fourth, we should exercise some restraint in the overt expression of undesirable emotional states. Expression can quickly lead to venting of the undesirable emotion.

Fifth, we should expend the undesirable emotion in some socially approved manner. Paul advises the angry person in Ephesians 4:28 to work* rather than steal: "He who has been stealing must steal no longer, but must work, doing something useful with his own hands, that he may have something to share with those in need." This is often called "relating in the opposite spirit" and is a reliable way of handling strong emotions as long as it does not become a technique to avoid all feelings.

Sixth, we can set a deadline for the solution of emotional problems. *Bracketing* problems is quite helpful. Mature individuals have the ability to postpone negative emotions until some decided time later on. It is possible for everyone to limit the ongoing expression of emotions. Finally, we can avail ourselves of a transformative resource.

Worship as Emotional Healing

C. S. Lewis wrote that "worship is inner health made audible." This is true of the Christian filled by the Spirit who sings and makes melody in her heart. All worshipers, whatever their emotional makeup, have the same needs. The two most essential are the need to be accepted for who we are (approval) and the need to change to become who we can be (transformation). These seemingly opposing needs are both met in worship. The call to worship implies approval. To enter God's courts with praise is different from entering the courts of an austere monarch who will judge and reject us. So we anticipate acceptance and approval. But we are also transformed.

Popular psychology says that we are what we eat; life makes clear that we become what we worship. We need to be very careful about whom or what we worship. We will become like the object of worship, both good and bad (Ps 115:8). To worship Christ is to become like him. Personalities and emotions do not change in worship; they become transfigured. The anger of an easily irritated person is transfigured into right advocacy. The kind of thing that makes Jesus fashion a whip causes the choleric to petition politicians. The phlegmatic's passivity is transformed into empathic compassion. Gentleness is empowered through being transfigured. If through Christ we may come to God just as we are, we also dare not go away just as we have come, even in our emotional life.

See also ANXIETY; DEPRESSION; GRIEVING; LAUGHTER; LOVE; PLEASURE; WORSHIP.

References and Resources
D. Burns, *Feeling Good: The New Mood Therapy* (New York: Arbor House, 1976); J. Cook with S. Baldwin, *A Few Things I've Learned Since I Knew It All* (Dallas, Tex.: Word, 1989); L. Crabb, *Inside Out* (Colorado Springs: NavPress, 1988); J. MacMurray, *Persons in Relation* (London: Faber & Faber, 1961); J. MacMurray, *Reason and Emotion* (London: Faber & Faber, 1935); B. Narramore, *No Condemnation: Rethinking Guilt Motivation in Counseling, Preaching and Parenting* (Grand Rapids: Zondervan, 1984); S. Peck, *Further Along the Road Less Traveled* (New York: Simon & Schuster, 1993); J. Piper, *Desiring God: Meditations of a Christian Hedonist* (Portland, Ore.: Multnomah, 1986); C. Tavis, *Anger: The Misunderstood Emotion* (New York: Simon & Schuster, 1982); D. Viscott, *The Language of Feelings* (New York: Arbor House, 1976).

David Augsburger and Paddy Ducklow

EMPTY NESTING

An expression that pinpoints the moment when grown children are out of the home* and the parents face a new lifestyle, *empty nesting* is the time in a marriage* between launching the children and retirement.* Even in intact marriages it is a time of crisis, for it is usually the lowest point of marital satisfaction. The good news is that if the marital partners reinvest in their marriage, there is a dramatic upswing in their sense of joy.

Understanding the Transition
One reason why empty nesting is a high-stress* time, especially at its immediate onset, is that it marks the completion of a couple's investment in what they may have seen as the primary purpose of the marriage, the rearing of children. There are additional reasons.

> There is a tendency for men and women to be going in opposite directions psychologically at the point where their children move out into their own lives. Men, perhaps realizing that they have missed most of the intimacy of their children's development, may begin to seek closeness whereas women, after years of focusing on caring for others, begin to feel energized about developing their own lives—careers, friendships outside the family, and other activities. (Carter and McGoldrick, p. 52)

At this point the marriage is often viewed by both partners as sterile. There is often a switching of roles: the distancer becomes the pursuer, and the pursuer becomes the distancer. Further, in the more traditional marriage, the man has invested his life in his career,* and the woman in her children. Even if he is successful, the career seems less attractive. For the woman her reason for living, as she perceives it, has disappeared. The danger is that they will both blame the marriage for their dissatisfaction when it is not the prime culprit. Indeed, if they reinvest in the marriage, they will gain back some, even all, of the intimacy they have lost. Sadly, many couples who are unaware of the dynamics of the marriage give up on the marriage at a time when a minimum reinvestment could pay significant dividends.

If there are complications for intact marriages, there are greater ones for those for whom divorce* and remarriage have been a reality. Complications generated by the unhealed wounds of spouses and children affected by the divorce or divorces are a considerable challenge emotionally and spiritually. A support/accountability system is not just desirable but is a vital necessity. There is a further complicating factor. The empty nest is experienced mainly by the "sandwich generation." During this time the marital partners are torn between the demands of their adolescent children and those of their elderly parents, to say nothing of their own urgent needs.

Even if the children (young adults) have physically left home, their psychological, spiritual and financial demands often do not cease. They can continue to dominate the marriage unless the couple have agreed on how to handle their young adult offspring. When the increasing needs of elderly parents are added to this, the pressures of life can easily affect the quality of the couple's marriage. They will need to make space for their own relationship and for themselves and see this as a legitimate Christian decision.

Coping with the Transition
How any couple negotiates this point in their life cycle will be a function of how they have handled their relationships over the previous years. If they have empowered their children and each other, they will come into this period feeling good about the family and the marriage and themselves. If they have a deepened spiritual life individually and together, there will be a high degree of intimacy.

If their church relationship is significant, they will not need the kind of emotional support from their children that encourages unhealthy dependence.

Empowered children and parents, deep spiritual lives and strong church ties are particularly important if the children decide to return home, a not uncommon event in our day. Parents who are not good at setting healthy boundaries will find this a major crisis. It is imperative that if it is acceptable for children to land in the nest again, there is a clear understanding of how this is to be managed. Issues such as privacy, financial contributions, responsibility for chores,* presence or absence from meals and general use of the premises need to be clearly spelled out so that all parties empower one another.

Betty Carter and Monica McGoldrick maintain that the key emotional process at this stage in the life cycle is "accepting a multitude of exits from and entries into the family system" (p. 15). They go on to list what they describe as "Second Order Changes in Family Status Required to Proceed Developmentally" (Carter and McGoldrick, p. 15): (1) renegotiation of the marital system as a dyad, (2) development of adult-to-adult relationships between grown children and their parents, (3) realignment of relationships to include in-laws and grandchildren and (4) dealing with disabilities and death of parents (grandparents).

Each of these tasks is daunting. It is little wonder that this period is seen as one of crisis and change. Some Christian writers note that this is the reason why there are so many midlife sexual affairs: "People can't cope with all the pressing changes, so they try to cope with surface issues" (Minirth et al., p. 162).

Preparing for the Transition

The time to get ready for empty nesting is long before it arrives. Marriages and families that are built on what Jack Balswick and Judith Balswick propose as a theological basis will do much more than survive; they will thrive. The Balswicks argue for four biblical themes on which family should be based. First, commitment is to be based on a mature (that is, unconditional and bilateral) covenant. Second, family life is to be established and maintained within an atmosphere of grace that embraces acceptance and forgiveness. Third, the resources of family members are to be used to empower, rather than to control, one another. Fourth, intimacy is based on a knowing that leads to caring for, understanding, communicating with and communing with others. The Balswicks see these as a continual process. Each feeds on and reinforces the other. The result of so building one's family is that each member has a sense of worth along with "deep levels of communication and knowing" (Balswick and Balswick, p. 33).

Empty nesting is a deeply challenging period for marriages and families. The good news is that if the couple come into it with a healthy and godly commitment, it will bring them a deeper bonding and contentment. For David in the Old Testament it was an unmitigated disaster. It can be the opposite for those who, unlike David, have cultivated good marriages and families and see them both as an adventure in service of the kingdom.

See also AGING; GRANDPARENTING; MENOPAUSE AND MALE CLIMACTERIC; PARENTING; RETIREMENT.

References and Resources
J. O. Balswick and J. K. Balswick, *The Family: A Christian Perspective on the Contemporary Home* (Grand Rapids: Baker, 1991); B. Carter and M. McGoldrick, *The Changing Family Life Cycle* (2nd ed.; New York: Gardner Press, 1988); F. Minirth et al., *Passages of Marriage* (Nashville: Thomas Nelson, 1991).

Roy D. Bell

ENTERTAINMENT

In advanced industrial societies *entertainment* is virtually synonymous with *leisure,** since entertainment is the major form of leisure. People seek entertainment as a means of relieving boredom,* as a diversion from the hardships and difficulties of everyday life and as a vehicle for courtship or friendly socializing. Most entertainment has two characteristics: (1) it is offered at a financial cost, and (2) it is consumed or used up by the people being entertained. In other words, entertainment is a leisure-oriented commodity produced by industry and used by consumers.*

Electronic Forms of Entertainment

Entertainment is increasingly an electronic activity related to consuming one or another form of media product. Since World War II one form has increasingly dominated entertainment time—television, which includes broadcast and cable TV, satellite television, the videocassette recorder and video games. In the United States, for instance, television represents more leisure time than all other entertainment activities combined. Adult females view over five hours daily, while males watch four hours and children average approximately three and one-half hours. The phenomenal popularity of TV is undoubtedly partly the result of the medium's seemingly low cost to consumers, who often bear the indirect expense through the cost of advertised products, government subsidies or monthly cable-TV charges.

Many other popular forms of entertainment are also influenced by electronics. Radio,* for example, is combined with sophisticated audio circuitry for higher fidelity and greater realism. Musical concerts often rely on electronic sound reproduction and rely increasingly on high-tech visual "effect." Movies* also take advantage of special effects created by electronic fabrication of image and sound. New amusement parks are even started in conjunction with the entertainment industry, which creates exhibits and rides based on successful movie, television, computer* or musical products.

It appears that the electronic revolution in entertainment products may be affecting the perceived value of other forms of leisure. Reading,* exercise sports, participatory sports,* companionship (e.g., conversation* and socializing) and some hobbies* are not as appealing to many people in a high-tech world. Some of these low-tech activities are being combined with electronic technologies (e.g., reading computer files or conversing via computer bulletin boards), but the overall shift in industrial societies is toward electronic entertainment.

Entertainment as a Public Event

One of the unfortunate impacts of electronic entertainment is the decline of valuable public events. Electronics tend to make entertainment an individual and private activity instead of a social and public event. Electronic reproduction enables industry to manufacture inexpensive copies of entertaining products, thereby permitting individual consumers to enjoy the entertainment whenever and wherever they wish. Videotape, for example, delivers movies and even some plays and musical concerts directly to the individual consumer at home. Why should a consumer bother with the effort or expense involved in attending a public performance?

The answer, of course, is that public events generally provide greater opportunity for social interaction and collective discernment. When small groups attend concerts or movies, for example, they typically discuss the quality and content of the entertainment. At home individual consumers shift almost effortlessly from one entertainment product to another, whereas at public events the entertainment is connected to the shared relationships of the attending groups. As a result the public event is selected more carefully, taken more seriously, enjoyed more deeply and discussed more fully.

Christians can avoid the loss of public entertainment in two ways. First, they can spend more leisure time attending public events and less time consuming personal entertainment products at home. Alternatively, Christians can practice hospitality* (1 Pet 4:9) by inviting friends and relatives to their homes* to enjoy entertainment together. This type of event-oriented hospitality has considerable potential in a media-oriented society, in which so many people live relatively shallow, insignificant lives. Post-entertainment discussion and fellowship* are appealing to relationally hungry consumers. Even among families,* this kind of media event can help break the cycle of personal, selfish entertainment use, as well as enhance familial discernment about the broader culture.*

Producing Our Own Entertainment
Another disadvantage of the overindulgence in consumer-oriented electronic entertainment is people's underdeveloped gifts and talents. Nearly all of the personal satisfaction from modern entertainment comes from the act of consumption, and very little of it comes in the joy of production. In other words, industrialized entertainment tends to disenfranchise the public, which is relegated to the status of audience, viewer or purchaser. Industry becomes the playground of professional entertainers, while the public is transformed into a fickle, often irrational market. People may spend much time watching professional sports on television, for example, but little or no time themselves participating in entertaining sports activities.

The church can encourage people to experience the joy and satisfaction derived from producing entertainment for their family and friends, including their church family. One possibility is for local congregations to sponsor more of their own homegrown entertainment. Some of this entertainment can be integrated into worship services in the form of dramatic presentations, music and readings. This technique certainly has its limits, given the appropriateness for worship, but it also has the advantage of transforming entertainment into something more than relief from boredom or diversion from the hardships of life.

Another use of gifts and talents* in Christian circles is service-oriented entertainment. Comedy, drama and music* can help people inside and outside the church who are suffering from the stress* of their lives or the fears and pains attendant to physical illnesses. Some parachurch organizations* and a few churches and denominations* support small groups of traveling entertainers who perform for people in hospitals and special schools. Entertainment can also help individuals to see more clearly the spiritual dimensions of their lives. A handful of parachurch ministries work from this broader mandate, traveling in troupes from church to church or college to college.

Even within the family or neighborhood, however, there are possibilities for teaching children to exercise gifts and talents as entertainers. We should encourage children to make their own games* and not just to rely on commercial products for entertainment. We should similarly invite our offspring to participate in the planning of social events, including family vacations,* birthday* parties, holiday celebrations and neighborhood* gatherings. It might be helpful for some children if parents simply limit the availability of manufactured entertainment during particular hours or on given days. Especially for children, spontaneous play is often the most entertaining, creative activity.

Family Entertainment

Unless parents consciously promote family-oriented entertainment in their homes, the marketing of popular products will tend to isolate family members. The vast majority of entertainment products are sold to particular taste groups represented largely by demographics such as age. Teenagers, for example, tend to consume television shows, movies and music that are marketed to their own generation. An age difference of even five years can make an enormous difference as to which radio stations and movies teenagers prefer.

Parents would do well to offset this generational segmentation with cross-generational, family-oriented entertainment. It may require a bit of give-and-take on the part of each family member, but there are worthwhile entertainment products and events that all ages can enjoy. Local theaters and video-movie stores are among the best options. In order to attract local patrons, theater groups frequently perform musicals and accessible classics of the stage. Many video shops cater to families, providing special store areas designated for family-oriented films.

Family-oriented entertainment also gives parents an opportunity to transcend some of the highbrow versus lowbrow distinctions that separate many children and adults. Unless parents provide interesting fine-art entertainment for their offspring, children will gravitate almost exclusively toward popular art. And many parents will not appreciate any of their children's popular art unless they take the time to view and listen with their offspring. Therefore, parents should be encouraged to share entertainment time and money with children, especially adolescents.

Entertainment and Identity

Finally, contemporary entertainment frequently becomes a status symbol for people of all ages to establish a meaningful identity. Like other consumer products, entertainment says much about the individuals who purchase and display it. Entertainment often has a status value which transcends the mere entertainment value.

Teenagers are most susceptible to this type of identity formation. They wear shirts, for example, that publicly advertise their favorite rock music groups. Also, they compare themselves on the basis of who has seen the most popular movies or been to the biggest musical concerts. Stereo music systems are not just a means of listening to music, but for many teens they are also a symbol of cultural power and personal cultural relevance. In fact, access to adult-oriented video movies, such as R-rated films, is an important sign of a teenager's coming of age in many communities.

In contemporary consumer cultures, however, the identity value of entertainment extends across the generations. Individuals and even entire families define their social standing partly by access to entertainment products and, increasingly, by the purchase of entertainment technologies. Every new technological frontier, from personal miniradios to enormous television screens, advances the requirements for membership in the electronic status clubs. As soon as one identity is "purchased," the status frontier has shifted to a new arena, casting a shadow over the old identity. Even young children play this status game, comparing themselves on the basis of personal TVs, video games, VCRs and audio systems.

From a Christian perspective, the

whole concept of consumption-oriented identities is problematic, and entertainment-based status competitions may be among the most troubling of all. Christ looks not at our external consumption—what we are pretending to be by what we purchase and display—but at the heart of the individual believer (1 Sam 16:7). When our hearts are focused on acquiring entertainment products and technologies, we are defining our value by the standards of the world, not by the heavenly standards of the kingdom of God. In some cases, this misplaced identity actually represents the love of entertainment rather than the love of God and neighbor. Moreover, the love of self is contingent upon the acquisition of entertainment; the image of God is replaced by the identity of entertainment-derived social status.

The Discernment of Entertainment
Entertainment is an important area of life for Christians to exercise discernment (Ps 119:125). Such discernment should take three forms: (1) stewardship* of one's time, (2) wise selection of entertainment and (3) critical use of entertainment.

Godly use of entertainment first requires a stewardship of leisure time. It is too easy to fill nonwork time with personal entertainment, thereby living without deep and rewarding relations with God, family and friends. Entertainment should have an important but carefully limited place in the lives of Christians.

In addition, it is imperative that Christians select the most valuable or worthwhile entertainment to fill this limited time (Phil 4:8). Because of the entertainment glut especially in industrialized societies, people often feel the need to consume entertainment with a kind of thoughtless frenzy, for fear they will miss out on enjoyable products. Video stores, record shops, cable TV, broadcast TV and movie theaters encourage this frenzy by regularly changing their products. Instead of being duped easily by the consumerist onslaught, Christians should seek helpful, critical information about entertainment products before investing time or money.

Finally, Christians are called to be on guard against the false prophets of every age, even as those prophets are represented in the seemingly benign forms of entertainment (2 Pet 2:1). Popular art is never culturally neutral but is instead an expression of values* and beliefs usually forged by audience-minded entrepreneurs. Our task is not to enjoy this entertainment uncritically, but to help ourselves, our children and our communities see it for what it really is. Then we may truly celebrate the best and the most entertaining of the lot.

See also COMPUTER GAMES; GAMES; HOBBIES AND CRAFTS; LEISURE; MASS MEDIA; PLEASURE; REST; SABBATH.

References and Resources
A. M. Greeley, *God in Popular Culture* (Chicago: Thomas More Press, 1988); K. A. Myers, *All God's Children and Blue Suede Shoes: Christians and Popular Culture* (Westchester, Ill.: Crossway Books, 1989); N. Postman, *Amusing Ourselves to Death: Public Discourse in the Age of Show Business* (New York: Viking, 1985); Q. J. Schultze, *Winning Your Kids Back from the Media* (Downers Grove, Ill.: InterVarsity Press, 1994), also available in a five-part video series with Gospel Films; Q. J. Schultze et al., *Dancing in the Dark: Youth, Popular Culture and the Electronic Media* (Grand Rapids: Eerdmans, 1991).

Quentin J. Schultze

EQUIPPING

Equipping involves preparing people for service, empowering them to serve and creating the context in which their ministry* will thrive. In the New Testament the Greek word *equip* (*katartismos/katar-*

tizō) means "to set things in order," "to prepare," "to form and shape" and "to point to the final goal of one's faith." The primary function of church leaders* is to equip the saints (all the people of God) for ministry (Eph 4:11-12). But, as we shall see, equipping is not exclusively a clerical or leadership activity. Christians serve one another in the family of God: all should seek to draw out the ministry of others and make it thrive. Equipping is done in families through parenting* and in businesses by management.* This article concentrates on equipping in the church by asking three questions: "How come?" (the theology of equipping), "How to?" (the methodology of equipping) and "For what?" (the purpose and goal of equipping).

How Come?

God—the ultimate equipper. A theology of equipping starts with the liberating truth that God is the ultimate equipper. J. I. Packer says, "Equipping is an ongoing divine operation whereby God through the ministry of his word and the power of his Spirit fits his people for the living of servant-lives that commend the gospel and bear fruit for his praise" (lecture, Regent College). God does this in the church by profound self-giving, by supplying spiritual gifts* so God's own work can be done through God's people and by leading the church with Christ as the head to its destination—a people that will glorify God in life and throughout the universe (Eph 1:12; 4:10). So God graciously orchestrates, nurtures, supplies and guides, giving us everything needed to do what needs to be done in this world. Biblically the laity,* the people of God as a whole, are an empowered people, a gifted people, a priestly people, a servant people, and continue God's own ministry on earth. In the light of this, it would be arrogant for church leaders to think of themselves as any-

thing more than underequippers.

Ministry in and through the church. Most of the metaphors used in the New Testament emphasize that the church exists for the kingdom, not itself. The church is a body that serves, a building that grows, a colony that points people to the homeland, an army that fights, ambassadors for Christ, and a bride that loves and serves the groom. The body of Christ is not the body beautiful that admires itself in a mirror but a body for service—to itself and to others. Equipping liberates the people of God from all that paralyzes service—whether theological, structural, relational, emotional or demonic—anything that restrains the full mature growth and loving impact of God's people on earth.

God's goal—growth and unity. God desires a fully equipped church as the centerpiece of a renewed creation. To this end the church must grow and be united. According to Ephesians 4:1-16, church growth has the following characteristics: unity in Christ, not in a charismatic personality (Eph 4:3); demonstrated interdependence of leadership gifts (4:11); being built primarily as an organism (4:12); experiential knowledge of Jesus by every member (4:13); maturity as a community and as individuals (4:13); corporate experience of the fullness of Christ (4:13); doctrinal discernment by all the members (4:14); relational integrity, that is, truth spoken in love (4:15); mutual dependence on the Head and interdependence with one another (4:15-16); and continuous mission (4:10). How far this diverges from the Western fascination with church growth in terms of simple numbers should be patently obvious. Unity and love are not mere means to an end to get the job done; they are the goal. The mysterious social unity of the people of God is like the unity of God the Father, Son and Holy Spirit. It includes Jews and

Gentiles (as well as others) in a new international, multicultural community characterized by unity and peace (Eph 2:14-18). This complex social unity is the mystery of God's secret redemptive purpose now revealed in Christ (Eph 3:4). So God, the ultimate equipper, is at work growing the people in unity.

Mature people—character development. God is also interested in equipping individual people in and through everyday life. James is eloquent on this subject: "Consider it pure joy, my brothers, whenever you face trials of many kinds, because you know that the testing of your faith develops perseverance" (Jas 1:2-3). God works through hard times, transforming life experiences into sacraments so that believers may receive the ultimate gifts of wisdom (Jas 1:5) and the crown of life (Jas 1:12). Testing removes the dross of our spirituality and develops perseverance—the missing virtue in an instant-gratification Christianity and a culture that despises waiting.* The ultimate end of divine equipping is that we will not lack anything in our characters, not that we will have well-honed ministry skills or heads stuffed with information. But God's interest in equipping is larger than our personal development.

A glorified universe. Two books of the New Testament—Revelation and Colossians—especially proclaim God's intention of ultimately renewing everything under the headship of Christ (Col 1:20; see also Eph 1:22). The goal is not that we will escape from earth and its materiality to live in heaven as rarefied spirits but that we will enjoy a new heaven and a new earth in fully resurrected bodies (Rev 21—22). Equipping prepares people for the new heaven and the new earth by finding God in the earthiness and materiality of everyday life. Equipping also aims at bringing renewal to the world around us through all legitimate spheres of work* and service.*

How To?

Having considered the "How come?" question, we turn to the question of methodology.

Equipping the people as a whole. While pastors and other church leaders have the special responsibility and privilege of working with the whole congregation, even those who have only a small sphere of influence in the church can have a significant equipping impact by following the direction suggested here. This is sometimes called the *systemic,* in contrast to the *programmatic,* approach because it assumes that the church is a living system rather than a group of organizations. It is a body with interdependent members in which any desired effect is likely to be the result of multiple causes and factors. Every element of a system, like each member of the body, can influence all the others, like movement in a mobile. But the health of the whole system is critical, and the first thing to consider in equipping the saints. Simply put, a live, thriving and healthy church draws out the ministry of the members. A dying, stagnant and sick church cannot squeeze ministry out of people through a myriad of good programs. Instead of functioning as the body, some churches are more like a bouquet of believers (all different but without unity), a melting pot (merged into unity but with diversity lost) or, worse still, a seed package (with neither unity nor diversity). The problem is not solved with a well-packaged program.

The principles of working systemically with the whole church and caring for the subsystems within it have been explained elsewhere in detail (Collins and Stevens; Stevens 1992). Here I offer four analogies to help visualize equipping the people of God as a corporate unit rather than as a cluster of individual Christians.

First, encourage communication with

Jesus, the head of the church, and with one another. The body of Christ has a common nervous system, and we should all be wired into it. Getting people to depend on the Lord, to seek God for themselves, to listen to the voice of God and to listen to one another are strategic equipping ministries. God gives gifts, vision and passion. Our work as equippers is to help people get in touch with the movement of God in their lives and in the church. Sometimes a church leader can ask people to indicate what they would really like to do if time,* talent* and training were not barriers. Time can be found; talent usually follows motivation; training is the easiest thing to arrange. The results may provide months of equipping work.

Second, encourage Bible learning and not mere Bible preaching. This is sometimes called the digestive system, since we are what we eat and the equipper is concerned with nurture and nourishment. For people to come to the end of their lives having heard two sermons a week but still not knowing how to open the Bible for themselves and hear God speak is a terrible tragedy. Some churches have found it useful to link the passage of Scripture to be taught on Sunday with the same passage studied in advance in small groups,* thus encouraging learning in multiple settings. Others encourage their members to develop a conversational approach to Bible study, so freeing them to talk about the Bible the way they talk about everything else and to relate it naturally to their daily lives. Equipping pastors are sensitive to learning moments in congregational life when theological education can and should be done in the middle of a crisis or when a major decision must be made.

Third, cultivate an experimental culture. This is sometimes compared to the circulation of the blood that creates the climate of health for the body. We know that nonverbal symbols and clues communicate more powerfully than spoken messages. People discern almost immediately and often intuitively whether this is a congregation in which ministry is done by the experts and professionals or whether every member is prized and appreciated.

Fourth, develop structures that evoke ministry. This is like the bone-muscle system in the human body, providing structure for stability and movement. In the local congregation small groups and home churches provide one of the best structures to facilitate the development of every-member ministry. In face-to-face relationships, when people share their life journeys week by week, people equip one another. Committees* also have potential for becoming equipping structures.

Equipping one another. Equipping is the responsibility of every Christian to draw out the ministry of others. We do this by sharing our journeys, confessing our needs to one another and being willing to receive the ministry of others. We also do it by fanning the coals of someone else's interests, by affirming one another and by giving honest feedback. According to Ephesians 4:16 equipping takes place at the joints (RSV) or the ligaments (NIV). This does not mean that certain members, like the pastors, have the responsibility of making all the connections. Rather this means that real growth, personally and corporately, takes place at the point of real connection with other members.

In the New Testament Christian discipleship* is corporate by nature (*see* Church Membership). There is no such thing as an individual Christian. Life together in the body of Christ is designed to be one of mutual blessing* and mutual equipping. We do this by forgiving grievances (Col 3:13) and loving (Col 3:14), as well as by teaching and admonishing one another (Col 3:16), carrying "each other's burdens" (Gal 6:2), looking out "not only to your own interests, but also to the interests of others" (Phil 2:4), "speaking the truth [about God] in love" to one another (Eph 4:15), "building others up according to their needs" through affirming, helpful speech (Eph 4:29) and encouraging "one another and build[ing] each other up" (1 Thess 5:11).

So a methodology based on biblical theology takes seriously the truth that God is at work among his own people. Leaders work to create God-dependence among them and to encourage health in the body of Christ. Members draw out this ministry from other believers in this coequipping partnership with God. God gives the ministry. But what is it all for?

For What?

John Wesley once claimed that he feared most the situation of the "almost Christian." In the same way we should be concerned for the almost-equipped Christian. This almost-liberated layperson is usually aided and abetted by clergy* more than willing to accept the layperson's help but not really committed to the layperson's complete liberation to become a ministry colleague. The purpose of equipping is that the whole people of God should be empowered for service both in their gathered life as *ekklēsia* and their dispersed life as *diaspora* living twenty-four hours a day for God.

There is a spate of conferences, videos, books, journals, seminars and courses on equipping the saints, all designed to help the pastor mobilize the laity for his or her ministry. Why has there been so little substantial gain? There may be four reasons for short-circuited equipping today.

Beyond discretionary-time ministry. It is a good thing to release all the people of God for every-member ministry in the local church. But if we define *ministry* in terms of evangelizing the lost and edifying the found, the laypersons will only be doing ministry during their free time and will fail to be equipped for ministry in the workplace,* home,* neighborhood* and public arena. Unfortunately, we have largely relegated ministry to the layperson's discretionary hours, the five to ten hours per week he or she may give to church work. Roman Catholic author Leonard Doohan notes, "Ironically with the increase of lay ministry in Church positions, we run the risk of diminishing lay transformation of the world" (p. 60). But the church is a rhythm of gathering and dispersion, like the gathering and dispersion of the blood from the heart in the human body. Elton Trueblood once said, " 'Church-goer' is a vulgar, ignorant word and should never be used. You cannot *go* to church. You *are* the church wherever you go."

Beyond tokenism. It is a good thing for pastors and Christian leaders to learn how to recruit and manage volunteers. But this may easily be tokenism through which pastors use laypersons to accomplish their own goals by means of their people. In contrast, equipping pastors make as their primary concern learning what can be done to release laypersons to engage in their *own* ministries, not recruiting and training people to help pastors with their ministries. The layperson is not called to assist the pastor: the pastor is called to assist the layperson.

Beyond the technology of equipping. It is a good thing for pastors and lay leaders to develop programs and activities through which individual laypersons will be released in ministry. But unless the church is equipped as a whole in its total life (environment, goals, communication patterns and structure), it may counteract the effect of the programs. An unequipped laity is a systemic, not a

349

programmatic, problem. It is the church itself as an organism that must be equipped and prepared for ministry. Take, for example, the situation of a pastor who preaches a high view of married life and runs marriage-enrichment programs but finds his own marriage destroyed by the idolatrous, addictive life of the local church. If we equip the church, then the church will equip the saints under the headship of Jesus.

Beyond pop theology. It is a good thing to develop a theology for laypersons, to market the fruit of the theologian's study on the level of the nonscholar. But a theology of the laity must start with the assumption that the whole people of God (the *laos*) are called by God to live out their vocation through service and mission in the world. What is needed is a lay theology that takes the ordinary Christian's dignity and calling in the world with utter seriousness. Much that passes for a theology *for* the laity amounts to pop theology, watering down heavy theological tomes so that people unschooled in the language of the experts may nevertheless get a few drops. But the drops people get are relatively unrelated to their real life in the world.

A theology of and by the laity must concentrate on what the Bible says about the layperson's life and calling—doing theology "from above." But a theology of and by the laity must also concentrate on the questions being asked by ordinary Christians in the context of their work—doing theology "from below." Samples of questions raised in the marketplace include the following: Is persuasion a legitimate and God-pleasing field of work? Can a Christian rightly be ambitious?* Is it right to negotiate for the highest salary? When we do this, are we bartering for self-worth or for our needs? Is it possible to function with complete integrity within the capitalist system? Is it possible to humanize an impersonal workplace?

Is leaving the only way to cope with the idolatrous demands of a corporation? What is it that makes our work pleasing to God—the quality, the excellence, our zeal, its intrinsic value, its function in meeting real needs or the life of prayer that undergirds it? These questions call for a theology of everyday life, a theology of and by the laity that must be written in each generation by a partnership of biblically thoughtful Christians with life experience and theologically trained leaders seeking relevance to life.

In their classic work *God's Frozen People*, T. Ralph Morton and Mark Gibbs make a stunning comparison: they say that thawing out "the frozen assets of the Church would be for us like the discovery of a new continent or a new element" (p. 158). Equipping has this lofty goal. Fortunately God is more concerned to liberate God's own people than we are.

See also DISCIPLESHIP; LAITY; LEADERSHIP, CHURCH; MINISTRY; PARENTING; MANAGEMENT; SPIRITUAL GIFTS; TALENTS.

References and Resources

P. Collins and R. P. Stevens, *The Equipping Pastor* (Washington, D.C.: Alban Institute, 1993); L. Doohan, *The Lay-Centered Church: Theology and Spirituality* (Minneapolis: Winston, 1984); M. Gibbs and T. Ralph Morton, *God's Frozen People* (London: Fontana Books, 1964); B. Hull, *The Disciple-Making Pastor* (Old Tappan, N.J.: Fleming H. Revell, 1988); G. Martin and L. Richards, *Lay Ministry: Empowering the People of God* (Grand Rapids: Zondervan, 1981); G. Ogden, *The New Reformation: Returning the Ministry to the People of God* (Grand Rapids: Zondervan, 1990); J. H. Ok, *Called to Awaken the Laymen* (Seoul, Korea: Tyrannus Press, 1984); W. J. Rademacher, *Lay Ministry: A Theological, Spiritual and Pastoral Handbook* (New York: Crossroad, 1991); A. Rowthorn, *The Liberation of the Laity* (Wilton, Conn.: Morehouse-Barlow, 1986); R. E. Slocum, *Maximize Your Ministry: How You as a Lay Person Can Impact Your World for Jesus Christ* (Colorado Springs: NavPress, 1986); M. J. Steinbron, *Can the Pastor Do It Alone? A Model for Preparing Lay People for Lay Pastoring* (Ventura, Calif.: Regal, 1987); R. P. Stevens, *The Equipper's Guide to*

Every-Member Ministry (Downers Grove, Ill: InterVarsity Press, 1992); R. P. Stevens, *Liberating the Laity* (Downers Grove, Ill.: InterVarsity Press, 1985); H. W. Stone, *The Caring Church: A Guide for Lay Pastoral Care* (San Francisco: Harper & Row, 1983); F. R. Tillapaugh, *Unleashing the Church* (Ventura, Calif.: Regal, 1982); J. H. Yoder, *The Fullness of Christ: Paul's Vision of Universal Ministry* (Elgin, Ill.: Brethren Press, 1987).

R. Paul Stevens

ETHNOCENTRISM

Ethnocentrism has to do with how people define themselves and how they view others unlike themselves. It is a learned behavior that presumes one's own culture is the standard for measuring others' values and assumptions. It is the way each of us views the world, a perspective, which like patriotism, may be legitimate provided it does not involve prejudice *against* others who are different. Often, however, ethnocentrism becomes racism* and is accompanied by a belief that "our" culture is better than "their" culture. This unhealthy elitism usually extends to linguistic, religious, racial, cultural and national prejudice.

Ethnocentrism can take a variety of forms. It may refer to the monocultural Chinese looking at the Tibetan, the Iranian viewing the American or the Zairian looking at the African-American. Specialized forms of it include Eurocentrism, which in the past viewed and interpreted the world through colonizing eyes. The colonized had their own lenses, such as Afrocentric, Indocentric, Sinocentric and so on. In many nations, where immigration* has been the dominant mode for population increase, there may be a wide variety of views, each conflicting with other isolated positions. These are often identified by such hyphenated descriptions as Japanese-American, African-American, Native-American, French-Canadian and Ger-

man-Canadian. Ethnocentrism generally assumes one's own group is the standard and norm.

Issues Surrounding Ethnocentrism
Ethnocentrism can be defended as a response to the desire for survival of the human species. Children begin life demanding that their biological needs be met, and as they grow, they learn to trust and depend on their family for food, shelter, clothing and physical protection. This trust expands to include neighbors and by extension the entire cultural group. Protection of the family, clan, tribe or ethnic group may depend on preservation of tradition, territory and/or linguistic integrity. Directly or indirectly the child's education teaches it what must be done to protect the group's survival. This usually includes story, myth and experience that warns against those who are different from the norm. Children are taught what is and is not socially acceptable, whom to trust and not to trust.

There may also be national pressures that assume loyalties will extend to the nation-state. In areas of the world where the nation-state is composed of ethnically and linguistically similar peoples, these loyalties are rallied by a call for self-preservation. Many political boundaries, however, have been drawn so that similar people groups are divided and groups with ethnic or linguistic differences are combined into one nation. This brings the challenge of ethnocentrism much closer to home.

If at its best ethnocentrism assists in identity formation and social survival, at it worst ethnocentrism involves xenophobia, fear or hatred of another race. When "others" are judged as inferior, as outsiders or as physical threats, then intolerance quickly develops. With the hardening of the belief that one's group is legitimate and other groups are not goes an increasing probability of violent conflict. In some extreme cases these conflicts have escalated to genocide or "ethnic cleansing," as this form of mass murder is euphemistically called. People are classified in a hierarchical way. The farther away someone else is from "my own group," the greater the probability of being judged inferior and treated unequally. As the notion of superiority becomes entrenched, oppressive and discriminatory behavior appears to be the "normal" way of doing things. This in turn becomes learned behavior for other group members.

Factors in Escalating Ethnocentrism

Ethnocentrism is most often characterized by monoglotism—knowledge of only one language. Monolingualism severely limits the full understanding of other cultures. Ethnocentrism is further fed by isolation. This generally results in stereotyping "other people." Studies show that most stereotyping is based on hearsay and learned attitudes rather than on actual experience (Todd). This is the source of such common judgments as these: those people are not clean; their food smells; they dress strangely; they don't believe what we believe; they are lazy; they want our jobs; they are violent; and they should go back where they came from (even if here is home). Such derisory statements escalate ethnocentrism.

The expressed character of ethnocentrism varies with the perceived threat of the "enemy at the gate." At times of national crisis, such as real or perceived economic or military threat, exaggerated stereotypes are often created as a rallying point to focus common resolve. For several generations the West focused its attention against the "evil communist bloc" with its brutality, lack of democracy and desire to rule the world. The stereotypical equating of the word *Islamic* with *extremist* or *terrorist* is an example of ethnocentrism abused for political advantage in a way similar to the use of the phrase "America the great Satan." The desire to find a scapegoat is a common human response.

Dealing with Ethnocentrism

Understanding people who are different takes discipline and invites personal growth. When people are confronted with new cultural concepts, it is difficult not to be judgmental. Our worldview* provides a given framework for making assessments of our world. For example, if we understand time* as linear, moving from the past through the present to the future, then we have difficulty understanding others for whom it is cyclical. In East Africa attendance at a social event, like a wedding,* is not measured by time. Participants go to visit, to be seen and to become part of the lives of the people. There is no start time or end time. It is a social occasion with its own rhythm. In North America people expect a wedding to begin and end "on time." Time is treated as a scarce or limited commodity. It is not difficult for these divergent views of time to create conflict.

Ethnocentrism can be overcome through several strategies. First, there must be increasing opportunities for intercultural, rather than monocultural, education. Second, individual relationships must become more and more multicultural as we extend friendship* to those who are different from us. Third, government policies must become less discriminatory. In North America 250 years of sociopolitical history have shaped attitudes and racism, which will be overcome only with concerted efforts from all parties. The church* has a role to play in this.

The church needs to confront its own ethnocentrism concerning the gospel message. Does it preach the message in a way that contextualizes across cultural boundaries? Do we read the Bible with a sinful bias? There is no hierarchy among the peoples God created, even though many have attempted to distort Scripture in this direction. Though the gospel was given initially to a group of Jewish followers, it rapidly spread into Africa, Asia and Europe. Today there are more Christians south of the equator than north of it; yet many of the dominant worship styles and church structures come from the north. To reduce ethnocentrism in the church, we must learn to understand other cultures in terms of their own assumptions and values and to view their members as fellow humans who bear the image of God.

See also CULTURE; MULTICULTURALISM; PLURALISM; RACISM; SOCIETY.

References and Resources
A. Bonnet, *Radicalism, Anti-racism and Representation* (London: Routledge, 1993); W. Connor, Ethnonationalism: *The Quest for Understanding* (Princeton, N.J.: Princeton University Press, 1994); P. G. Hiebert, *Cultural Anthropology*, 2d ed. (Grand Rapids: Baker, 1988); C. McCarthy and Warren Crichlow, *Race Identity and Representation in Education* (New York: Routledge, 1993); K. A. Moodley, ed., *Beyond Multicultural Education: International Perspectives* (Calgary: Detselig Enterprises, 1992); R. Todd, *Education in a Multicultural Society* (London: Cassell, 1991).

Brian F. Stelck

EUTHANASIA

Euthanasia, which literally means "good death," is the intentional and voluntary taking of a patient's life either by omitting necessary medical treatments or by taking direct action such as an overdose of drugs. The omission of life-saving treatments intending to kill is to be distinguished from withdrawing or forgoing medical treatments when such interventions are clinically determined to be futile. The latter is not euthanasia

and is generally accepted as permissible, possibly even desirable under circumstances in which continuing such treatments amounts to artificially prolonging the dying process through medical technology. The omission of an otherwise life-saving treatment, however, in order to end a life deemed not worth living (for example, surgical relief of intestinal atresia in a Down-syndrome baby) is euthanasia. This is also an example of *involuntary* euthanasia, since the request is made by someone other than the infant patient, as opposed to *voluntary* euthanasia, which is requested by the patient. Whether voluntary or involuntary, euthanasia implies the assistance and/or participation of another person, usually medical personnel, for its consummation.

Arguments Supporting Euthanasia
One of the main arguments advanced to support euthanasia appears to arise from a misconception that terminally ill patients (for example, those suffering from cancer) usually die a painful and technologically prolonged death.* Euthanasia in this sense is seen as a form of mercy killing. But this concern is well addressed by the established right of patients or their surrogates to refuse such medical treatment. As for excessive pain, there are very effective drugs for just about all conceived illnesses. Underutilization of drugs is the main reason for failure to control pain and suffering. With more attention to pain management, together with supportive care of patients' emotional needs, almost all terminally ill patients should be able to function at a manageable level and to die relatively free of suffering. Unbearable pain and suffering are not a sufficient argument for euthanasia.

Another major argument in support of euthanasia is the autonomy of the patient: each person has intrinsic rights* and freedoms* to control his or her own destiny, including the timing and the manner of death. There are several problems with this. First, since euthanasia requires the assistance of another person, it is not an autonomous and private act, but a public action. Even if self-determination includes decisions of one's own death, it does not follow that it includes the right to require someone else to kill. Second, there is always doubt as to whether the patients are in fact making an autonomous decision when they request euthanasia. Most dying patients experience mental anguish through the loss of human relationships and loss of control. They have feelings of helplessness and fear death. Such psychological factors lead one to question the rationality of a patient's request for euthanasia.

Studies of suicide suggest that there is a correlation between suicide and emotional instability or disorders. Pleas of the terminally ill to be put to death may be anguished pleas for help and love rather than genuinely rational and autonomous choices. Medical personnel often fail to recognize despair and depression* in the terminally ill, sometimes because of their own fears about aging,* sickness* and death. Requests from competent terminally ill patients cannot always be assumed to be rational and therefore autonomous. Furthermore, individual autonomy must always be balanced with and, if necessary, limited by communal goals and values.* Individual desires, no matter how justifiable, must not be satisfied at the expense of societal interests. Unfortunately, our culture* favors individual rights against the common good.

One of the possible negative social consequences of legalizing euthanasia is the fear that it will gradually lose its voluntary character. This means that patients may be euthanized without their consent or that they may be subtly ma-nipulated and pressured to choose euthanasia to spare the family financial and emotional strain and society's limited resources. Groups of patients, particularly among the disadvantaged or minorities, are particularly vulnerable. Another fear is that, once legalized, euthanasia may be extended to incurable but not terminally ill patients, such as those with senile dementia or Alzheimer's disease. This "slippery slope" effect may then be extended to infants born with mental retardation and/or severe physical abnormalities, such as Down syndrome and spina bifida, all in the name of sparing the infant an intolerable and undignified existence. The possibility of infanticide as a social reality must be kept in mind whenever euthanasia is being seriously considered.

The Physician's Perspective

The trust and respect that are foundational in the patient-physician relationship are seriously compromised by any physician participation in euthanasia. The public has become confident that a doctor will do everything in his or her power to help and would never consciously do anything injurious. When patients realize that their doctors are prepared to either heal* them or kill them at their request, the medical profession will never again be worthy of full trust and respect as healer, comforter and protector of life in all its frailty. In our time both society in general and the medical profession* have betrayed an unwillingness to accept suffering and death as part of life and have believed that they need to control both.

Insisting on prolonging life with modern technology* and, failing that, consenting to patients' requests to foreclose on life through euthanasia are expressions of the sterile spirit of our society. What we need is a genuine spirit of candor, compassion and care in the physician-patient relationship. Euthanasia would become superfluous if the fear and anxiety* of a terminally ill patient were relieved by the assurance of a caring and compassionate physician who is prepared to acknowledge the limits of medical technology and is committed to help patients face death with dignity and humility. There is ample evidence to show that well-cared-for terminally ill patients have no desire to hasten their own death. They die a good death, naturally and with comfort and dignity.

Christian Response

Christians understand each human being as created out of the boundless love of God in his image (Gen 1:27). Thus each person has a God-given source of value and dignity beyond any mere physical well-being and social utility. Life is the fundamental and irreplaceable condition for the experience of all human values, and we have an obligation to nurture, respect and promote the integrity of life, rather than harm or destroy it. Not only is our life given by God, but it is God's property and not our own: "The earth is the LORD'S, and everything in it" (Ps 24:1). This means that God has sovereignty over life and death. To choose death is to illegitimately assume authority in an area that has not been assigned to our control.

Further, our existence rests entirely on the Father's loving decision to provide and to care; we are created to be dependent creatures. Much of the euthanasia movement is rooted in the modern idea of autonomy and independence. The right to die represents an escape from helplessness and dependencies on others. But the doctrine of creation establishes the link between our creatureliness and dependence as appropriately human. Dependency in time of serious illness and dying should not be repellent to the Christian. To accept one's depend-

ency is not to suffer indignity if care from others is accepted in humility and gratitude as a gift from God. As John Paul II says, "The Christian who thus accepts his own death and, recognizing his own condition as a creature . . . and confidently surrenders himself into the merciful hands of the Father, . . . reaches the height of his own human and Christian identity and achieves his ultimate destiny" (p. 106).

We also believe that God has invited us into a new covenant community of faith, hope and love established by the coming of Jesus Christ. Faithfulness to the covenant is established when we love our neighbor as we love God. Within this covenantal framework of human relationships, decisions and actions relating to life as well as death ought to be made. So we need to pay attention on the communal context of the bonds that exist between patients, family, health-care providers and the community at large. Moral evaluation of human activity should always include concern for the good in the social dimension. Critics of the slippery-slope arguments against euthanasia contend that each act must be judged right or wrong primarily in itself, thus betraying their lack of perception of the interdependent connections between society and individual acts. In opposing euthanasia, Christians are living out the Pauline image of the community as the body of Christ (1 Cor 12), in helping to convert society "from an aggregate of individuals pursuing their self-interests to an interdependent covenantal community" (Gula, p. 25).

As members of a Christian community, we have an obligation to care for the sick and the dying. To receive care and hospitality* is a privilege. In the process of giving care, providers, family and friends will be able not only to face their own death but to receive and participate in the final event of the patient's life. It is this spirit of giving in love and receiving in humility that renders euthanasia pointless. Euthanasia threatens the trust and solidarity that must prevail between us if we claim to belong to a community with a Christian character. Killing is incompatible with the character of Christians. Persistent opposition to euthanasia is rooted in our living as a redeemed community of compassion, trust and care that sustains life and reflects the true character of the triune God.

See also DEATH; HEALING; SICKNESS.

References and Resources
R. Gula, " The Virtuous Response to Euthanasia," *Health Progress* 70, no. 10 (December 1989) 24-27; Pope John Paul II, "To Recover the Meaning of Life," *The Pope Speaks* 35, no. 2 (1990) 102-7; R. N. Wennberg, *Terminal Choices* (Grand Rapids: Eerdmans, 1989).

Edwin Hui

EVANGELISM

One of the terms used most frequently in the New Testament to describe the Christian message is the Greek word *euangelion*, which means "good news." The English word *evangelism* is derived from that and simply means "sharing the good news." When Jesus visited the synagogue in his home village of Nazareth, he declared, quoting from the Old Testament book of Isaiah, that his purpose was "to bring good news to the poor . . . to proclaim release to the captives and recovery of sight to the blind, to let the oppressed go free, to proclaim the year of the Lord's favor" (Lk 4:18-19 NRSV). Hence evangelism can be defined as "ways to awaken or reawaken personal faith in Jesus Christ, and to proclaim to the nations the character and will of God" (Fung, *Isaiah Vision*, p. viii).

Evangelism is at the very heart of the Christian faith. By definition, to be a Christian is to share the good news with others. Paradoxically, however, evangelism is not always experienced as "good news." For many unchurched people, it is the exact opposite. Having been targeted by earnest believers as the objects of their evangelizing efforts, they go along to missions* and crusades out of a sense of curiosity, only to find themselves feeling conned and trapped by well-meaning church people whose main concern seems to be to process everyone to be like themselves. Even Christians have mixed feelings about evangelism. For some, the constant round of revival meetings has become a way of life. Others—perhaps the majority—find themselves afflicted by a mixture of embarrassment and guilt whenever the subject comes up. On the one hand, evangelism is something they would never do to their dog, let alone their best friends; yet on the other, they know their best friends should hear the good news, but they have no idea how to tell them.

One thing that is common to all these people, Christian and non-Christian alike, is that they identify evangelism with a particular style of Christian activism. It is about holding missions, crusades and revivals in order to recruit people for the church.* Even when it happens on a more intimate level, maybe in the context of a home group, evangelism can still look like a scaled-down version of the mass crusade, with Christians giving a summary statement of their belief and then inviting others to accept it and come into the life of the church.

Evangelism and Church
In reality, church often presents more questions than answers for unchurched people, who find there are just too many barriers to be negotiated. "Church is not for people like me," they say. Church members seem to be from a different social class or have a different lifestyle or live in different kinds of homes* and

families.* Church members also often seem to have no problems, or if they do, they have them stitched up in a way that seems unreal. Hence many people take it for granted that Christians are, by definition, hypocrites. The church's image barrier is a major obstacle to effective faith sharing.

The church also presents a cultural* barrier. The unchurched can find it threatening just to cross the threshold of a church building (or a cinema or stadium turned into a church for the period of a crusade). Even those who make it find that what happens in church, and the way it happens, is far removed from everyday life in the ordinary world. Where else do people engage for so long in procedures that are almost exclusively book-oriented? Where else do people sit passively listening to one person speaking for even as long as fifteen or twenty minutes? Where else does all the action happen invisibly, as it were, in mental abstractions within the mind? And how can anyone possibly fathom when to stand up, when to sit down, when to kneel, when to be silent and when to speak? When people say, "Church is boring," they usually mean, "This is not the way I normally do things."

If it is difficult to get people into churches to hear the good news, then logic suggests evangelism will begin when those who are already in church move out in order to share their faith in other contexts. But it is no easier to move Christians out than it is to get other people in. Some Christians regard themselves as spiritual consumers: the church is a place where their own spiritual needs can be met. They like everything the way it is, and the last thing they will allow is change, especially for the benefit of the unchurched. Others say, "My faith is my own business, part of my private life"—not realizing that this assumption is one of the major building blocks of secular-

ism and that the church's acceptance of it is arguably one of the primary reasons for its present lack of evangelistic success.

Of course, there are many Christians who want to share their faith with others. They are the activists. The church depends on them to give their time and talents to its work—and they do with great courage and at personal cost. But in the process, they find themselves sucked into the organization, and the bureaucracy uses up all their creative energy. Consequently they may easily be the most frustrated of all: they see the urgent need for evangelism but have no effective way of accomplishing it.

Evangelism and Lifestyle

Surprisingly, the New Testament contains very little overt advice about how to evangelize. The apostles recognized that some people might have special talents* in sharing their faith, and the role of "evangelist" is listed as one of the foundational gifts of Christ to the church (Eph 4:11). But the earliest Christian communities did not generally think of evangelism as some special activity to be delegated to experts, who then needed special training. Sharing the good news was the natural outcome of Christians being Christians.

As Christians live the Christian life, they share their faith naturally and unself-consciously and in the process invite others to follow Jesus. To appreciate the importance of this can bring a great sense of freedom in evangelism—as well as an even greater challenge to scrutinize carefully what is being communicated. "The medium is the message," said Marshall McLuhan. Whether Christians realize it or not, everything that they do is communicating something about their faith to those who are as yet not Christians. The World Council of Churches document *Mission and Evangelism* expresses it eloquently: "God leaves us free to choose how to share our faith. But our options are never neutral—every methodology either illustrates or betrays the gospel we announce" (sec. 28).

In John's Gospel the "new commandment" is a central feature of Jesus' teaching: "Just as I have loved you, you also should love one another. By this everyone will know that you are my disciples, if you have love for one another" (Jn 13:34 NRSV). Christians have often assumed that this teaching must be "domestic policy," related only to the internal workings of the church. Jesus identified it, however, as "foreign policy" and the starting point for effective sharing of the gospel. Could it be that evangelism is so difficult for many Christians today because they are failing to take all this seriously? The New Testament suggests it is not events and techniques that are the central features of effective evangelism but integrity in spirituality and lifestyle (see Witness).

Evangelism and Theology
Christians sometimes imagine that God is powerless unless they themselves are active—and so evangelism is about doing things on God's behalf. This can lead to great pessimism: either a defeatist pessimism in which the evangelistic task seems so great that it will inevitably overwhelm us or a triumphalist pessimism that assumes everything is in the control of the devil and evangelism is, therefore, about hostile confrontation with the world. Ultimately, our views about evangelism stem from our understanding of who God is. A defective view of God produces dysfunctional evangelism.

In Scripture, evangelism is not about Christians doing things on God's behalf. God is actually the first and primary evangelist, and authentic evangelism starts with the conviction that God is at work in the world. Christians are called to recognize what God is doing and to get alongside it. To invite God to come alongside our efforts is to put the cart before the horse.

In stories about Jesus, the New Testament actually provides a model for how this style of evangelism might work: "As the Father has sent me, so I send you" (John 20:21 NRSV). What then can be learned by taking Jesus as a paradigm? What do Christians need to learn in order to be sent in the same way as Jesus was?

First, for Jesus, evangelism was holistic, reflecting the all-encompassing nature of the gospel. Jesus had a broad understanding of the human condition. He saw people not just as sinners but also (even primarily) as sinned against. Modern evangelism sometimes begins by putting people down: you are a sinner, responsible for your sin or pain, but you can choose to follow Christ instead. But not everyone does have the freedom to choose, especially not the marginalized and oppressed. The message of the gospel is "You can be responsible," and for those who are wounded, this is really good news. Much Western Christianity has a shallow view of sin as something people do, rather than as a cosmic universal reality from which people suffer. As a result there is often little compassion in evangelism. Jesus always affirmed and lifted people up. It is never good news to do otherwise.

Second, Jesus took his message into other people's territory. He did not invite people to come to places where he felt safe and they felt threatened. He went to the beach, to the market, to the city streets. And he did not set up evangelistic events when he got there. He was simply there, sharing in the life of whatever was happening—and listening.* Even when it was obvious what people needed (for example, at the pool of Bethesda in Jn 5:2-9), Jesus asked questions in order to empathize more effectively with other people. Effective evangelism begins not when Christians speak but when they listen. In response to what he heard, Jesus most often told stories. Stories do not present ready-made (and maybe irrelevant) answers. They create a space in which people can interact and respond in their own ways. Evangelism is about creating a space for God to work in people's lives.

Third, Jesus issued a simple invitation: "Follow me." There was no organization* to join, and he laid down no preconditions. He accepted anyone who would follow—and in the process often caused offense to religious people, who felt he was too easygoing. Different people responded and followed in different ways, but Jesus accepted them all. There was no single stereotyped pattern for discipleship.* The only requirement was a willingness to be open to the good news and to respond to its challenge whenever and wherever that might come. In William Temple's words, it was about "as much as I understand of myself responding to what I know of God" (quoted in Neill, p. 45). As a consequence, following Jesus was not a static once-and-for-all experience but an evolving and growing relationship that demanded the whole of life.

Fourth, Jesus' style exemplified weakness in action. At the heart of the gospel story is the fact that in Jesus, God became a child. It is significant that God did not become a full-grown adult. Adults, especially evangelists, like to be in control of things, and they dislike being vulnerable. This is why many Christians feel they can never be evangelists—because they do not have this kind of dominant, extrovert personality. Judged by these standards, Jesus would not be regarded as a successful evangelist either.

Christians have something to share with others, not because they are differ-ent but precisely because they are no different. Their concerns and struggles are the same as other people's; the difference is that in the midst of struggle Jesus is also present. Understanding this, and taking it as a model for evangelism, might easily be costly. But it really will be good news—for Christians as well as for those who are not yet following Christ.

See also DISCIPLESHIP; FRIENDSHIP; HOSPITALITY; MINISTRY; MISSION.

References and Resources

W. J. Abraham, *The Logic of Evangelism* (Grand Rapids: Eerdmans, 1989); J. Drane, *Evangelism for a New Age: Creating Churches for the Next Century* (San Francisco: Harper, 1994); R. Fung, *Evangelistically Yours* (Geneva: World Council of Churches, 1992); R. Fung, *The Isaiah Vision* (Geneva: World Council of Churches, 1992); M. Green, *Evangelism Through the Local Church* (London: Hodder & Stoughton, 1990); B. Hanks Jr., *Everyday Evangelism: Evangelism as a Way of Life* (Waco, Tex.: Word, 1986); *Mission and Evangelism: An Ecumenical Affirmation* (Geneva: World Council of Churches, 1982); S. Neill, *The Unfinished Task* (London: Lutterworth, 1957).

John Drane

EXAMINATIONS

In this article the word *examinations* refers to written tests since that is the form examinations most frequently take. Very few people go through life without undergoing a number of written examinations. Preparing for these and taking them is often demanding and stressful. Not only do exams cast a shadow backward over the whole course to which they are attached, but sometimes they also cast a shadow forward over a person's whole future. While written tests are no longer as central in intelligence and skills testing as in the past, they remain a standard feature of modern education.* Indeed, from a purely numerical point of view, the greater number of people in school today means that more people are subject to examinations than ever before. Given this, it is surprising there is so little Christian reflection upon them.

The Widespread Use of Examinations

For most of human history, people's understanding of key areas of life, and their capacity to function within them, has been assessed in ways other than written exams. This is especially true of their ability to talk sensibly about various aspects of life or to practice them successfully. This is why Socrates debated so much with his students and why Jesus not only did the same but insisted so strongly on behavior as the ultimate test of understanding. Over the centuries, and particularly in recent times, written examinations largely replaced these forms of evaluation. In the East these were introduced to evaluate those training for administrative office; in the West they multiplied with the growth of public education.

Today written exams take many forms: multiple-choice questions, book reviews, reflective exercises and essays. Some test memory alone, others are open-book, and there are also take-home exams. Many questions about exams surface: What are their alleged value? Whom do they benefit or impede? Why do so many people have difficulty with them?

The Limited Value of Examinations

The value of written tests was once relatively undisputed. Advocates argued that exams showed whether students had understood and learned what they had been taught, could organize and evaluate their responses and displayed evidence of independent thought and quality of argument. The formal and anonymous character of exams was held to prevent favoritism and provide objective evaluation. Exams, it was said, motivated students to learn and offered them a way of judging their progress. Some viewed exams as preparing students for the rigors and pressures of real life. In a system of mass education, often with large classes, exams also offered teachers and judicatories the least exhausting and most practical means of assessing students.

Though reservations about exams go back to the institution of formal schooling, these were broadened and deepened earlier in the twentieth century by liberal educators in the progressive school movement and by new left and countercultural critics in discussions about education in the sixties and seventies. Liberal critics focused largely on the validity of written tests: they were too narrow in scope, competitive in style and impersonal in character. Learning should be more holistic, assignments more cooperative and the bond between teacher and student less judgmental. Educational critics in the sixties and seventies amplified these doubts, criticizing written examinations for their

☐ dependence on the "banking" approach to education, in which the teacher is the font of all knowledge;

☐ unsuitability for areas in which knowledge is not easily quantifiable and failure to take sufficient account of the subjective nature of much grading;

☐ artificiality of the conditions under which knowledge is tested;

☐ exclusion of such variables as the quality of teaching, predictability of questions, physical state or monthly rhythms of the students;

☐ inability by a simple grade to pinpoint strengths and weaknesses or help students improve their learning;

☐ discrimination against persons with different kinds of intelligence;

☐ tendency to categorize and socially stratify people in too rigid a way;

☐ contribution to abnormal levels of stress and even suicide for some students.

Meanwhile, doubts about the practical usefulness of written examinations have surfaced as some educators have begun to challenge their ability to predict both further academic potential and future vocational performance.

The Proper Role of Examinations

There is nothing at fault with examining or being examined per se. Words like *examine, test* and allied terms occur frequently in the Bible. About half of these passages speak of God's examining us. God tests all creatures (Ps 11:4-5), groups as well as individuals (Jer 46—51), in a continuous way (Job 7:18) and in heart as well as mind (Ps 26:2). This testing lasts through our whole lives; compare the stories of Abraham, Joseph, Moses, David, Jesus and Paul. Central to the way God evaluates people is suffering (Rom 5:3; Heb 2:18; 1 Pet 4:12). But some matters will not be judged until the last day, when everything will be revealed and everyone will know if their work has passed the test (1 Cor 3:4-15).

Most of the remaining passages speak of God's people corporately examining themselves. Are we holding rightly to the faith (2 Cor 13:5), displaying a proper attitude to other members of the community (1 Cor 11:28), serving others faithfully (2 Cor 8:2) and fulfilling our God-given obligations (Gal 6:4)? Many passages speak of individuals examining other members of God's family with respect to their integrity (Joseph of his brothers), moral behavior (Ezra of the Jerusalemites), perseverance in ministry (Paul of his coworkers) and basic allegiance to God (Jeremiah of the people of Judah). Other passages speak of God's people testing particular persons to see whether they are false apostles (Rev 2:2), valid prophets (1 Cor 14:29) or genuine workers (Phil 2:22). Indeed they are to "test everything" and "hold fast to what is good" (1 Thess 5:21 NRSV). In a few places God even invites the people to test him (Mal 3:10)!

Such passages remind us of the broader and deeper, long-term and eternal, examination that we are undergoing as members of God's covenant people. Though we will be judged by what we say and write, this is basically a life rather than a written exam. This puts schooling-type examinations in proper perspective. It helps us see that any assessment at this level, even within a seminary or Christian college, is secondary. Indeed these passages raise questions about whether educational forms of assessment, especially in such colleges and seminaries, should be broader and deeper than they are and based on far more than written responses under controlled conditions.

The ongoing nature and varied forms of assessment talked about in these passages are also indicative. They suggest that it is better to have a range of ways for evaluating people's development and performance and to engage in a regular, rather than once only, appraisal. The shift to continuous assessment in schools and universities, whatever inadequacies it might have or stresses it might induce, is a move in the right direction, especially if it contains diverse ways of evaluating performance. There are at least twenty proven ways in which this can be conducted, so there is no excuse for resting assessment purely on written examinations. Where appropriate, a written test can be one option among others, though all forms should primarily seek to improve the students's capacity to learn, not just judge how much learning has taken place. Testing, of whatever form, should be formative, not just evaluative.

The formative goal of testing raises two wider issues. First, it is important that both learning and assessment of learning take place in groups as a cooperative rather than competitive venture. In this way those who are stronger can help those who are weaker academically, and those who are weaker can sometimes help the academically stronger to develop more than their cognitive skills. Second, it is important to give greater room to learning by doing as well as by memorizing, discussing or researching. While learning by doing has always played some part in education, even in some written forms of assessment, it has rarely been given the place it deserves.

See also CHRISTIAN EDUCATION; EDUCATION; SPIRITUAL GROWTH; STRESS, WORKPLACE.

References and Resources

R. Dore, *The Diploma Disease: Education, Qualification and Development* (London: Allen & Unwin, 1976); B. Hoffman, *The Tyranny of Testing* (New York: Macmillan, 1962); J. Holt, *Why Children Fail* (London: Pitman, 1964); J. Kleinig, *Philosophical Issues in Education* (New York: St. Martin's, 1982); D. Mechamic, *Students Under Stress: A Study of the Social Psychology of Adaptation* (Glencoe, Ill.: Free Press, 1962); R. Montgomery, *A New Examination of Examinations* (London: Routledge & Kegan Paul, 1978).

Robert Banks

F

FAILURE

No one is immune to failure. Human weakness, ignorance and the effects of sin promise that failure will be a familiar companion, even to people who walk with God. The Bible accepts the idea of failure as a part of life. Solomon observed, "Though a righteous man falls seven times, he rises again" (Prov 24:16). Famous Bible failures who rose again include Moses, Samson, David, Peter, John Mark and Jesus Christ.

In Western culture, success* is often judged on the basis of the visible accomplishment of such things as wealth* and security, public appearance and notoriety, power and influence, physical beauty and talent.* Accordingly, failure is judged on the basis of the lack of these things. Even Christians, reflecting the culture, tend to evaluate persons and work on these cultural grounds. A closer look at Scripture, however, reveals that God's view of success and failure is quite different.

Neither the Old nor the New Testament uses words that coincide exactly with *success* or *failure* as we understand the terms. In the languages of the Bible the words that most nearly approximate the concept of success are ones that mean "blessed."* In Hebrew the word is *barak;* in Greek the work is *makarios.* Both convey ideas of success, prosperity, happiness and enviably abundant life.

In the Old Testament the key issue in

success, or blessedness, is to live in right relationship with God and to obey his instructions (Deut 11:26-28; Ps 1:1; 5:12). In the New Testament Jesus describes success in terms of personal transformation. The Beatitudes (Mt 5:3-12) indicate that the changed person, not his or her measurable accomplishments, is the key to blessedness. A definition of success quickly emerges by reading the Beatitudes and substituting the word *successful* for "blessed," as in "Successful are the poor in spirit." Success as Jesus defines it has nothing to do with worldly wealth, power or honor. True success is the inner riches of personal character conformed to God's character. According to the Beatitudes, success is in the riches of inner qualities like vulnerability, brokenness, gentleness, craving for righteousness, compassion, single-mindedness, reconciliation and joy in suffering for Christ's sake.

In the Old Testament the word that stands opposite "blessed" and most closely approximates "failure" is the word *cursed* (Deut 11:26-28). *Cursed,* as the Bible uses the term, does not represent something magical, such as casting spells or being under a hex. Lawrence Richards interprets the Old Testament word for curse as "the loss or absence of the state of blessing" (1985, p. 208). To fail is to have God's blessing withdrawn, lose the esteem of God, shrivel up spiritually, become small-souled. Obedience to the commandments of the Lord is the secret of success, and disobedience is the pathway to the withdrawal of God's blessing, reduced position, reduced power, reduced wealth, reduced honor and a broken relationship with God, which is the substance of failure (Richards, 1985, p. 207). To fail is to exist in a state of separation from God; to try to live without God is to die (Deut 30:19). The New Testament updates this fundamental concept to include a person's response to the revelation of God in Jesus Christ. According to Jesus, the ultimate failure is to fail to be recognized as belonging to Christ (Mt 7:21-23).

Success, Failure and Material Prosperity
The Bible encourages the expectation that if things are right between people and God, material abundance will follow. However, in Deuteronomy 8:12-20 the promise of material blessing is immediately followed by a warning: If, after God has made them rich, his people become proud and think they have won prosperity by their own strength and hard work and if they forget the Lord and give allegiance to other gods, they will be destroyed! This same destiny awaits any nation that refuses to obey the Lord. The link between material prosperity and a relationship with God is unmistakable. But sometimes other issues are at stake.

The biblical portrait of success is often a picture of people surviving amid harassment, poverty,* disaster and famine. Merely amassing material wealth and the power* that goes with it is not success. Many wealthy, powerful people are in rebellion against God. God declares them of slight value (cursed). Indeed David composed a song against people who "succeed in their ways, when they carry out their wicked schemes" (Ps 37:7).

The plutocracy of which David sings did not gain its power because of God's promises to bless the obedient. The people he describes have climbed to power and wealth on the backs of the oppressed and possess their wealth and power while the righteous have little (Ps 37:16-17). They flourish "like a green tree in its native soil" (v. 35), but they have no future (vv. 9-10, 15, 17, 38). The wealthy and powerful will be brought down in full view of the righteous poor whom they have oppressed (v. 34). The secret of the resilience of the righteous is that they trust God (v. 3). He is their delight (v. 4); their way is committed to him (v. 5); they are waiting for his justice* (v. 6). The righteous are promised a home (v. 3), security (vv. 3, 27), heart's desire (v. 4), justice (v. 6), peace (v. 11), protection (vv. 14-15, 28), support (vv. 17, 24), plenty to eat (vv. 19, 25), enough to share with others (vv. 21, 26), blessing-success (v. 22), confidence (v. 23), God's love (v. 28), deliverance (v. 33), a future (v. 37), salvation (v. 39), a refuge from the wicked (vv. 39-40) and the Lord's help (v. 40)—an inventory of success with God in the midst of circumstances that, in the world's view, constitute failure. Psalm 37 promises spiritual abundance more than material prosperity. Believers are led to expect that basic necessities will be supplied, not that trusting and obeying will lead to a cushy life.

Worldly Success Is Failure Waiting to Be Exposed
In the last book of the Bible a great city called "Babylon the Great" is destroyed by the judgments of God. This Babylon is the symbol of worldly wealth, power and success that, according to the description given in Revelation 18, is measured in terms of profits made from commerce in everything from gold to "the bodies and souls of men" (v. 13). The destruction of this symbolic Babylon is a picture of "the inevitable judgments of God upon . . . the worship of false gods, which include riches, power and

success" (Phillips, p. 516). The world's success story concludes with God's disclosure of the ultimate failure of worldly success (vv. 14-24). It is not that it is intrinsically wrong to succeed in commerce or business, but it is a serious mistake to look to these things as true security and prosperity or the source and meaning of life. The real world of commerce and business is a system riddled with injustice and greed, which will finally fall to God's judgment. Those who have built their lives on it will be left impoverished and broken.

Where Is Prosperity When You've Lost Everything?

Success and blessing do not depend on material prosperity; they are found in the joy of knowing God as Savior. In the days of the prophet Habakkuk, the righteous remnant of Judah was overrun by the Babylonian war machine and carried into captivity along with those who deserved God's wrath. Everything was taken away from them. As Babylonian hordes bore down on Jerusalem, Habakkuk composed a prophetic poem (Hab 3). At first he writes of God's sovereignty and mighty acts: "Suddenly Habakkuk is shown overwhelming waters of judgment, rushing like some Genesis cataclysm . . . to burst over the prophet and his people" (Richards, 1987, pp. 414-15). He trembles with fear; his knees buckle (Hab 3:15-16). He knows God's faithful will not escape the bitter disaster coming on their rebellious nation. How will those who trust God find hope and see God's promise of prosperity when starvation, deprivation and defeat are the orders of the day? Habakkuk knows:

> Though the fig tree does not bud
> and there are no grapes on the
> vines,
> though the olive crop fails
> and the fields produce no food,
> though there are no sheep in the pen

> and no cattle in the stalls,
> yet I will rejoice in the LORD,
> I will be joyful in God my Savior.
> The Sovereign LORD is my strength;
> he makes my feet like the feet of a
> deer,
> he enables me to go on the
> heights. (Hab 3:17-19)

Because he knew God, Habakkuk experienced spiritual success-blessing even as everything he possessed was swept away in the judgment of the condemned society in which he lived.

The Therapeutic Effects of Failure

For the person who believes God, failure is not fatal. The Bible affirms that failure will come, but when it does, it cannot destroy the believer (see Mic 7:8-9). The grace of God meets us at the point of failure.

Pressure produces sterling character (Rom 5:2-5). The Greek word for suffering means "pressure, distress of mind and circumstances, trial, affliction." The restoration in us of the likeness ("glory") of God takes place through a process involving pain and pressure, which produce perseverance, refined character, hope and the experience of God's love.

Jesus emerges through our struggles (2 Cor 4:7-18). Normal Christian experience includes reversals, inadequacies and failure. God distills positive results from such experiences: (1) Jesus is seen living in us (vv. 10-11); (2) spiritual blessing touches other people through us (v. 15); (3) even though outwardly we fail, our inner self is being thoroughly renovated (v. 16); (4) we learn to see from God's perspective (vv. 17-18).

God's power is visible in weak people (2 Cor 12:7-10). The apostle Paul could not get rid of a troublesome personal weakness he called his "thorn." It undermined his self-confidence and kept him from being the strong leader people expected. Three times he prayed about it. His prayer failed to make any difference. As he nursed his stinging disappointment, he heard God say, "My grace is enough for you. My strength is demonstrated as effective through your weakness" (see v. 9). It gave him a new perspective on failure. If God could demonstrate his strength through human weakness, Paul, instead of feeling embarrassed, would make his failure a focus of rejoicing and hope.

Difficulties move us toward destiny (Rom 8:28-29). No matter what happens, what we try and fail to accomplish, what opposition we face, what mistakes we make, what weaknesses plague us, what pressure, distress or pain we suffer—all of it has a sign over it that reads "God at work!"

Through failures people move from bragging to brokenness. Peter is one of the world's most famous failures. Before Jesus was arrested, Peter bragged, "I will lay down my life for you" (Jn 13:37). He miserably failed. A few hours later, Peter cowardly denied three times that he knew Jesus (Lk 22:54-62). After the resurrection, Jesus met him and asked three times, "Do you love me?" (Jn 21:15-19). The Greek New Testament reveals that the first two times Jesus used the word for perfect love. But Peter's swagger was gone. He responded with a word meaning "friendship."* "I would like to be able to boast that my love for you is perfect," he seemed to say, "but my failure has taught me the truth about myself. The best I can do is tell you that I love you as a dear friend." Peter could never have been the useful instrument he became had he not gone through his humiliating collapse at the point where he felt strong.

Based on Peter's experience we can see that failure accomplishes several things. First, failure enables us to more accurately assess ourselves and our situation. Second, failure helps us to see our weaknesses. Third, failure takes the wind out of our spiritual boasting. Fourth, failure provokes us to find answers. Fifth, failure shows us how dependent we are on God and others. Sixth, failure frees us to love genuinely and honestly.

See also AMBITION; BLESSING; DRIVENNESS; FORGIVENESS; SUCCESS.

References and Resources
R. C. Girard, *When the Vision Has Vanished* (Grand Rapids: Zondervan, 1989); J. B. Phillips, "Introduction to the Book of Revelation," in *The New Testament in Modern English* (New York: Macmillan, 1960); L. O. Richards, *Complete Bible Handbook* (Waco, Tex.: Word, 1987), L. O. Richards, *Expository Dictionary of Bible Words* (Grand Rapids: Zondervan, 1985).

Robert C. Girard

FAIRY TALES

For some, the term *fairy tales* conjures up visions of wand-waving ballerinas; for others, the term is simply a catch-all for any fanciful story that couldn't be true. But though traditional fairy tales, with their "once upon a time," edge us into "another world" of wonder and magical possibility, that world can open us to truths we have forgotten—or refuse to see in our own world. "These tales," writes G. K. Chesterton, "say that apples were golden only to refresh the forgotten moment when we found that they were green. They make rivers run with wine only to make us remember, for one wild moment, that they run with water" (*Orthodoxy*, p. 257).

Since the umbrella of "fairy tale" spreads so widely that at times it covers everything from ancient myths and legends to Saturday-morning cartoons, we do well to get a good grip on its handle—the traditional fairy tales. These stories, such as "Cinderella," "The Fisherman and His Wife," "Little Red Riding Hood" and "The Frog Prince," not only contain the basic patterns—story types and motifs—of literature but also help us understand the ability of literature to move us in profound ways. As Christopher Morley has often been quoted as saying, "When you sell a man a book, you don't sell him just twelve ounces of paper, ink, and glue—you sell him a whole new life."

The power of great literature, of stories, to change our lives—to shake heart, mind and soul* to the core of our being—is itself embedded in traditional fairy tales.

Characteristics of Fairy Tales

"Once upon a Time"—Agelessness. These stories are sometimes called "nursery tales," implying, to a twentieth-century audience, that they are best read to toddlers. While many of the stories can, at least in some form, be appreciated by very young children, the prime age for most fairy stories is anytime from ages six to seven and up. The bare bones of plot are there for all, including the very young, but these bones are a sturdy skeleton for the whole human story. As we grow older, we flesh them out more and more with our own experience, and we clothe that flesh with interpretations and understandings that we weave with the warp and woof of our own needs and longings.

These bones of human story in fairy tales have the ability to hold the flesh of our own stories—no matter how old we are or who we are—because they have weathered the storms of historical and cultural change. The story of Cinderella, for example, comes in over fifteen hundred versions from sources as spread out over time and place as Egypt's first-century B.C. "Rhodopis," China's ninth-century A.D. "Yeh-shen," North America's Algonquin Indian "Rough-Face Girl" and Germany's "Aschenputtel." And the German and English names reflect the tales' inherent universality of both character and theme, for *Cinderella* and *Aschenputtel* describe a very lowly state—a

"girl in ashes"—rather than a distinguishing name.

Through all the variations of detail and development in these versions of "Cinderella," the essential story of a young maid's rise from ashes to royalty has remained remarkably intact—complete, in most cases, with a focus on footwear. As G. K. Chesterton points out: "The lesson of 'Cinderella' . . . is the same as that of the Magnificat—*exaltavit humiles* ['he exalted the humble']" (p. 253). The great truth underlying the story of Cinderella can be a door to the scriptural truth of Mary (herself another such humble handmaid) and of her song (the Magnificat), and of the Gospels—the good news: our God "has lifted up the humble" (Lk 1:52).

Fairy tales have a habit of making heroes of the humble: the rejected daughter becomes a princess, the youngest son becomes a king, the ugly duckling becomes a graceful and beautiful swan. George MacDonald's answer to the query (which most of us have) "But, Mr. Author, why do you always write about princesses?" was to assure his reader that "every little girl is a princess, and there would be no need to say anything about it, except that she is always in danger of forgetting her rank, and behaving as if she had grown out of the mud" (p. 9).

A woman brought up with a Chinese heritage once read the German version of "Cinderella" and ended it crying for joy: "That is *my* story," she wrote. "*I* am the third unloved child who had to do all the menial chores—this story gives me hope!" These old stories can cut through our despair and disillusionment to the heart and bone of human life, enabling us to remember that we can be, each one of us, a son or daughter of the King and that through his life-giving love we look forward to the great end-celebration of hope we call heaven.

"Don't Stray off the Path"—Moral Truth-

fulness. "The Ethics of Elfland" is the title G. K. Chesterton gave to his fine and deeply Christian treatise on fairy tales. There he claims that a great principle of the fairy philosophy is "the Doctrine of conditional Joy" (p. 258). In these old stories, he goes on to point out, "happiness depended on *not doing something* which you could at any moment do and which, very often, it was not obvious why you should not do" (p. 260).

The condition is usually simple obedience to a seemingly arbitrary command. As Robert Farrar Capon puts it in *The Third Peacock,* his book on the problem of evil, "After entering the garden go straight to the tree, pick the apple and get out. Do not, under any circumstances, engage in conversation with the third peacock on the left" (p. 27). We all remember the childhood lessons of Little Red Riding Hood: "Stay on the path; don't talk to strangers."

Nevertheless, the heroes and heroines of these tales are reassuringly like us—they fail to meet the condition, sometimes over and over again. As Chesterton reminds us, in the biblical story "an apple is eaten, and the hope of God is gone" (p. 259). And so these tales teach us the lessons of character we need to pick up and keep on going. They teach us persistence and faithfulness, the ability to keep trying against all odds and in spite of repeated failure*; they teach us kindness and compassion, the ability to forgive* others' failings and weaknesses; and, above all, they teach us love,* the willingness to sacrifice our own happiness for someone else's. In fairy tales, the burden of these lessons for living is lightened by the wings of story.

"And They Lived Happily Ever After"—Good (and Bad) Endings. The greatest wonder of the fairy-tale world is the "happily ever after." Yet the hope that is offered to Cinderella, and vicariously to us, is more and more rejected as wishful

thinking. But to endure the ups and downs of life we *need* hope, and these tales offer hope of a perfect end. These good endings are not cheap grace: as Chesterton makes clear, "in the fairy tale an incomprehensible happiness rests upon an incomprehensible condition" (p. 259). The scales of justice* tip on this "if" from which hangs the balance between gloom and glory, between death* and life, between dancing to death in red-hot shoes and a wedding celebration of great splendor. The good endings are glorious intimations of heaven; the bad endings are sometimes so harsh and hellish that fairy tales are accused of both black-and-white rigidity and violence that is too much for children.

Yet we need these tales to clear our clouded consciences* and sharpen our moral sensitivity. "For children are innocent and love justice, while most of us are wicked and naturally prefer mercy" (Tolkien, p. 66). Mary's Magnificat promises that God lifts up the humble, but, as both the Magnificat and the Cinderella story remind—warn—each of us, he also brings down "those who are proud in their inmost thoughts" (Lk 1:51). The good ending of a fairy tale is, like the good ending of all time, always bought with a price. In his great essay "On Fairy-Stories," J. R. R. Tolkien affirms that familiar refrain "and they lived happily ever after": "The Evangelium has not abrogated legends; it has hallowed them, especially the 'happy ending.' The Christian has still to work, with mind as well as body, to suffer, hope, and die; but he may now perceive that all his bents and faculties have a purpose, which can be redeemed" (Tolkien, p. 89).

Some Suggestions for Reading Fairy Tales

1. We should begin reading these stories in the nursery, in other words, with young children, but we must not leave

them there. *All* of us need these stories. Perhaps, however, the prime time for them is ages seven to ten. During these years the doors of the soul can start to swing shut on the possibility of that larger world—the heart of Faerie—that includes not just the realities we see and touch every day but the spiritual realities of God and of that "Perilous Realm" of the human soul where choices lead to heaven or hell. Fairy tales can keep the door open to belief in "another world" that includes and is much larger than the visible world.

2. We should remember that fairy tales were originally told, not read, and that much of their value comes from the embellishments we add with our mind's eye. Illustrated or extensively rewritten versions often fill blanks best left open to the imagination* and perceptions of the listener.

3. We must try to resist finding allegories and lessons in these old stories. And we must certainly resist pointing such possibilities out to children. They will grow into a continually richer and fuller understanding on their own—as they need to. George MacDonald wisely observes that children find out what they are capable of finding, and more would be too much. Sometimes our interpretations can block out what children (or adults!) need to discover on their own. We must, however, listen to their interpretations. Through the connections they discover and tell us about, we may learn much about the concerns of our children (or of our friends).

4. We need to avoid worrying that our children will confuse the "other world" of Faerie with the world of the biblical story—or with the everyday world. Recently this fear has escalated into a panicky association of these old tales with the New Age movement, leading to a rejection of not only fairy tales but also, in extreme cases, such imaginative litera-

ture as the Narnia books of C. S. Lewis. As Lewis points out in his fine essay "On Three Ways of Writing for Children": "About once every hundred years some wiseacre gets up and tries to banish the fairy tale" (p. 28). We are in such a period now: fairy tales are accused of being nightmarishly scary, of leading to fantasizing and unreal expectations and longings, or, increasingly, of being remnants of ancient satanic rituals. The truth here is that fairy tales, like all stories, rise from longings to know who we are and what we are about—and these are spiritual questions. Any good literature is dangerous and often frightening, because it forces us to deal with these questions—and thus more deeply with spiritual issues.

But by far the greater danger is a wooden flatness of our world, whether spiritual or physical, that can come if we "protect" ourselves—or our children—from either the heights of the glory or the depths of the gloom to be found in imaginative literature. Lewis defended the true world of the fairy tale: "I think no literature that children could read gives them less of a false impression. . . . I never expected the real world to be like the fairy tales. I think that I did expect school to be like school stories" (p. 28). The superficial concerns of such school stories and of much of our lives often cover up truths of self-giving love and ultimate justice which form the bedrock of the fairy-tale world. In *The Voyage of the Dawn Treader* by C. S. Lewis, the great Aslan, who is there both lamb and lion, both love and justice, says to Edmund and Lucy, "This was the very reason why you were brought to Narnia, that by knowing me here for a little, you may know me better there" (p. 247). The "other world" of fairy tales tells us truths that help us recognize patterns of spiritual truth—and even God *himself*—better in our own everyday world.

5. We *must* immerse our children and ourselves in the "other worlds" of C. S. Lewis's Narnia, J. R. R. Tolkien's Middle Earth and George MacDonald's "Princess" books. We should read them out loud and read them often. Their worlds were created by a wide reading of both fairy tales and the biblical story.

But we need to keep coming back, all our lives, to the old, traditional tales. Fairy tales that insist on wonder and magic can enrich our reading of the biblical story—for deep through that ocean of fairy tale runs the warm, rich current of God's full and final truth.

See also IMAGINATION; READING; STORY-TELLING.

References and Resources
R. F. Capon, *The Third Peacock* (New York: Image Books, 1972); G. K. Chesterton, "The Ethics of Elfland," in *Orthodoxy*, vol. 1 of *The Collected Works of G. K. Chesterton* (San Francisco: Ignatius, 1986); M. T. Donze, *Touching a Child's Heart* (Notre Dame, Ind.: Ave Maria, 1985); R. Haughton, *Tales from Eternity: The World of Fairy Tales* (New York: Seabury, 1973); C. S. Lewis, "On Three Ways of Writing for Children," in *Of Other Worlds* (New York: Harcourt Brace Jovanovich, 1966); C. S. Lewis, *The Voyage of the Dawn Treader* (New York: Harper, 1980); G. MacDonald, *The Princess and the Goblin* (New York: Books of Wonder, 1986); I. Opie and P. Opie, *The Classic Fairy Tales* (New York: Oxford University Press, 1974); J. R. R. Tolkien, "On Fairy-Stories," in *The Tolkien Reader* (New York: Oxford University Press, 1974).

Where to Begin
P. C. Asbjornsen, I. D'Aulaire and E. P. D'Aulaire, eds., *East of the Sun and West of the Moon* (New York: Viking, 1969); W. Gag, ed., *Tales from Grimm* (New York: Coward, McCann & Geoghegan, 1981); W. Gag, ed., *More Tales from Grimm* (New York: Coward, McCann & Geoghegan, 1981); V. Hamilton, *The People Could Fly: American Black Folktales* (New York: Knopf, 1985); A. Lang, *The Blue [Gray, Purple, Red, Pink, Brown, etc.] Fairy Book* (New York: Airmont, 1969); M. Twain, *The Arabian Nights* (New York: Grosset and Dunlap, 1981).

Mary Ruth Wilkinson

FAITH DEVELOPMENT
Faith is not just a single act, though faith often begins with a single act. Nor is it only a body of doctrine to which one gives assent, though what one believes can be described in statements of faith. Faith is an action, a commitment of one's life to Jesus Christ. "To faith" (Fowler, *Faith Development*) is a process of continual growth, development and Christian nurture from less to more mature stages. Faithing is as much a verb or action as it is a noun. The concept of spiritual growth* and development is found throughout Scripture. The disciples ask for an increased faith (Lk 17:5). Faith continues to grow (1 Cor 3:1-6; 2 Cor 10:15). Luke describes Jesus' childhood development as growing "in wisdom and stature, and in favor with God and men" (Lk 2:52).

Fowler's Stages of Faiths
James Fowler, probably the foremost researcher on faith development in the last twenty years, has provided useful perspectives on faith and faith development. Fowler states that a person comes to the activity of faithing through one's community.* For children that community is at first their parents. The community expands to include their churches' teachers and pastors, their denomination* and eventually a community of committed believers regardless of denominational affiliation. According to Fowler, community consists of three parts: the persons themselves, their faith community and the object of their faith community's faith, namely, God. Fowler describes six stages of faith:

Stage One: Projective Faith. This faith development stage is based on the authority of one's family and/or primary caregivers. People in this stage imitate their authority figures and copy what they do. Ultimate reality for stage one persons is whatever the authority figures say is true and ultimate. Children believe what their parents tell them to believe about God, Jesus, the Bible, heaven and so on.

Stage Two: Mythic-Literal Faith. Authority in this stage is based on an enlarged community of faith, usually one's own church* and its teachers and pastors. The enlarged community helps define the content and object of faith. Ultimate reality is what one's church teaches.

Stage Three: Synthetic-Conventional Faith. The person synthesizes and identifies with a larger group of believers beyond his or her immediate church and accepts their explanation of ultimate reality. This is the stage when catechism, church membership* and the like are important. People in this stage accept the standard doctrines and other teachings of their church and of people in their denomination. Hence the word *synthetic-conventional.* At the earliest this stage usually occurs in the young adolescent* years and can continue throughout adulthood. Probably most adults are in this stage and will never become more mature. They hold tenaciously to their faith and clearly identify with the larger faith community beyond their family, friends and local church.

Stage Four: Individuating-Reflective Faith. Persons at this stage begin to evaluate and self-consciously reflect on the issues and problems associated with their faith commitments. This is the stage when one clearly internalizes one's faith. Ultimate truth is understood not just because it was taught by one's faith community and acceptable doctrines of the church, but because it has been critically examined and accepted as one's own. There is a strong commitment to this. This stage usually begins in late adolescence or adulthood, but many adults never develop this far. People at this stage think through the issues of their faith. Much thinking, talking and critical

examination take place during this stage. Long discussions occur regarding seemingly paradoxical issues such as human free will versus the sovereignty of God and other theological conundrums.

Stage Five: Paradoxical-Consolidated Faith. This is clearly a stage of faith development that even few adults achieve. People at this stage recognize the validity of others' beliefs yet clearly internalize their own. Their own faith is clearly and consciously held together with the recognition that "all truth is God's truth." A person at this stage goes beyond the clearly defined theological formulas and continues to probe deeper, higher and broader to discover more of God's revelation. They live in the tension of having accepted clearly defined truth for oneself and yet recognizing that one has glimpsed only a small part of the ocean of God's truth. There is more to be known of God than the creeds and church can teach us. We are responsible to search more to know the God of our own faith.

Stage Six: Universalizing Faith. This stage is very rare. The paradoxes and complexities of one's faith that have been wrestled with in the previous stages become less important compared to being swept up into the oneness of being in Christ. Ultimate truth is perceived not just as propositional but as relational. This stage calls forth a radical commitment to the ethics of the kingdom and an active participation in working out the righteousness of the kingdom of God in this present age.

One of the problems with Fowler's approach to faith development is that it describes a generic developmental faithing process regardless of the object of one's faith. His description is as easily applicable to a Hindu as to a fundamentalist Christian and to all religious and/or quasi-religious faith. An atheist goes through similar stages of "faithing" as a Christian. What is different is the object of their commitment. When we apply Fowler's contributions on faith development to the Christian faith, we need to do so with insights from Scripture and a critical eye toward his stage descriptions. For Christians it is not just the development of faith that is important but also the development of faith in the triune God of Scripture. A mature faith in an incorrect or inappropriate object is ultimately worthless.

Christian Faith Development

Nevertheless, Fowler has provided great insight into stages of faith development. Using Fowler's contributions, we can view the stages of Christian faith development from within a Christian framework.

Stage One: Simple Faith. The basic characteristic of this stage is a childlike faith. This is the faith of a child or person who, like a child, places his or her trust in Christ and asks few if any questions. People may or may not grow out of this stage. They can be stunted or entrenched into a nonthinking adoption of whatever the authority (pastor, teacher, radio or TV preachers) says is the right thing to believe, accept and do. These persons are highly dependent on other persons' directions, instructions and the correct interpretation of the meaning of the Bible. These are bottle-fed, milk Christians always needing someone to nurture and care for them spiritually. These people go to church, Bible studies or conferences to be fed spiritual food. Unknowingly, sometimes, they snack on Christian fast foods and Christian junk food that appear good but are ultimately not going to nurture. They read their Bible because others tell them to do so. They learn because authorities teach them. Interpretation of the Bible, right and wrong behaviors, doctrines to believe, rituals to perform are received from others. They take no personal responsibility for their own spiritual growth and development. They apply teachings in a literal and rather mechanical, uncritical fashion. If the authority does not tell people at this stage what to do, then they will not make any changes in their behavior or thinking.

Stage Two: Identification and Beginnings of Internalization. These persons are still highly dependent on the input from external authorities. They receive Christian content and direction primarily from external sources. What distinguishes these people from stage one people is that they are beginning to filter their life's experiences and thoughts through their rudimentary personal faith. They begin to realize their own personal responsibility for their spiritual growth. Just like a child knows it is hungry and must eat, so these people realize the need to pursue spiritual nutrition. People begin to ask, "How does my faith interact with what I am being told?" They continue to go to others to find out how their faith is to function and interact with their experiences. Discipling and mentoring become important here because authorities are still considered models to copy. Categories of faith development and faith thinking are few and still immature (some are just plain shallow).

Stage Three: Internalization/Identification. Persons at this stage recognize their need for input from others, but they also recognize that they have a personal responsibility to grow up spiritually and not be so dependent on others. They still need and seek guidance and input from others, but they process this input in a new way. They do not uncritically accept and act because some respected authority says so. They take responsibility for their own spiritual decisions. Models and mentors are still important for these people because these serve to help them to search, feed and grow. Realizing that they are responsible for their own spiritual development, they maintain contact with their former primary authority source for general guidance rather than particular directions. Categories of faith are filled primarily by one's self with some additional input from others.

Stage Four: Internalization. People at this stage realize that they are ultimately responsible for their spiritual growth. They must feed themselves. They cannot be dependent on stimulation from other people. Nor do they want more Christian fast food from conferences. Models and mentors serve as external reminders of what they were becoming when dependent on others. Now the categories and content of their faith are filled almost exclusively by their own actions. Their lives are being changed because they themselves actively seek to have the Holy Spirit change them. Contact with others is important for community and mutual encouragement, not for spiritual milk.

Stage Five: Sustaining. People at this stage keep on keeping on. As Paul said, they are doing "everything to stand . . . firm" (Eph 6:13). They continually seek God in and for all aspects of their lives. Models and mentors are not necessary and are sometimes distractions. Categories and content of faith are filled, renewed, rearranged and revised as they read, study and meditate on Scripture and as the Holy Spirit interacts with their own hearts and minds. They walk in the Spirit. They realize that they must strive mightily to present themselves as mature in Christ (see Col 1:20-23). Their lives are being changed consistently because of their own constant seeking for spiritual renewal and development. They are "spiritually self-actualizing" Christians. The Christian community is a place for corporate worship* and ministry with the internal community and from which to minister to the world.

See also LIFE STAGES; SPIRITUAL FORMATION; SPIRITUAL GROWTH.

References and Resources
J. Astley and L. Astley, eds., *Christian Perspectives on Faith Development* (Grand Rapids: Eerdmans, 1992); C. Dykstra and S. Parks, *Faith Development and Fowler* (Birmingham, Ala.: Religious Education Press, 1986); J. W. Fowler, *Becoming Adult, Becoming Christian* (San Francisco: Harper & Row, 1984); J. W. Fowler, *Stages of Faith: The Psychology of Human Development and the Quest for Meaning* (San Francisco: Harper & Row, 1981); L. Kuhmerker, et al., *The Kohlberg Legacy for the Helping Profession* (Birmingham, Ala.: Religious Education Press, 1991).

John M. Dettoni

FAMILY

In the Western world *family* is a term applied to any group of people that claim to belong together, including same-sex couples. It is a freely contracted relationship between individual consenting adults. Traditional families (father, mother and children) are under attack not only from the option of many alternatives but also from an erosion of confidence within those families. Some argue that the nuclear family (mother, father, children) is dead except for the first two or three years of child rearing. In the light of this many Christians are appealing for a return to "family values"* and family goals* without realizing that *family* has no common, shared meaning.

Does Scripture point to a common core meaning of this basic and first human community? As we shall see, the "biblical family" looks much more like an African extended family than the stripped-down Western nuclear family. We will also consider why family life, even given its imperfections, is a location for faith formation and by its very nature a spiritual discipline.* A companion article explores the idea that for Christians the church* is their forever family (*see* Church-Family).

The Fragmented Family
Tremendous forces have conspired to reshape the family in the Western world.

The rise of wage labor and industrialization took work out of the household into the factory and office. The family changed from a unit of production to a unit of consumption. With the so-called invention of children, by which children came to be treated with new tenderness and removed from the family for education,* family roles were reduced once again. Political* changes have had their effect as well. The feudal system dealt with households, but later political forces tended to abstract the individual as a political unit. Indeed, the basic unit of society* in the Western world has become the individual*—a truly revolutionary change. Not surprisingly, family is understood in this cultural context as an arrangement between individuals rather than the way people experience a corporate identity.

Whereas the bourgeois family (composed of a master of a craft, his wife, children, other blood relatives, a fluctuating number of tradesmen, and apprentices all living together) functioned as a shared economic enterprise (Berger and Berger, pp. 87-104), the modern family is a stripped-down version with mother, father and children, moving from place to place, having few vocational roles other than the mutual meeting of emotional needs.* Many modern families are single-parent families. Blended families with children from various previous marriages* have convoluted and interlocking circles of belonging. Taking this trend to the logical extreme, the postmodern West, having shorn its roots with the Judeo-Christian faith, now wants to have family without risk. So what has emerged is no-fault divorce,* cohabiting* couples, both parents working outside the home, the demise of vocational homemaking,* and the professionalization* of parenting* in care centers and schools. All this is aided and abetted by the church, which has successfully moved Christian education* from the home* to the church. What Marx attempted by social revolution (the replacement of home education by state, and of families by collectives) the church has assisted by neglect.

The Changing Family

In spite of the popular misconception, the "nuclear Family" (a household consisting only of a married couple and their children) has a long history. Research has shown that in North America and Western Europe the nuclear family is not a modern invention arising from industrialization and urbanization but predates these trends by centuries, at least as far back as the High Middle Ages, though in Eastern Europe something closer to the extended family was more common (Berger and Berger, p. 87). Nuclear families in previous generations, however, did contain servants (now replaced by machines). Brigitte and Peter Berger argue that modernity did not produce the nuclear family; the nuclear family produced modernity through a closer relation between parents and children, greater parental influence and greater individuation (p. 91). All of this, however, is under serious attack and subject to bewildering forces of change.

People in other cultures are wrestling with their own changing family forms. The African family, once experienced as concentric circles of family, clan, tribe, often with polygamy at the center, experienced the disintegration of its nuclear core through colonization and urbanization (separating father and mother to gain remunerated employment) and a changed value of children (once a sign of wealth,* now a major cause of poverty*). In spite of all this, even first-generation city* dwellers retain profound ties to the family land. Asian families, characterized by hierarchy and power* structures, now face their own pressures of modernity and postmodernity.

In all cultures most of us belong to multiple families: our family of origin, the family created through marriage, the spouse's family we joined through marriage, and, in the case of multiple marriages, overlapping relationships with children and former spouses (because we cannot divorce family members). Add to this the Christian's experience of entering the family of God through faith in Jesus (see Church-Family), and we have one more family experience—this one less provisional, as it lasts forever! Notable in the Gospels is the record that Jesus lived with the complexity of competing loyalties to his "birth family" (Mary, Joseph and his siblings) and the family of Father, Son and Holy Spirit, as evidenced in the sensitive way he fulfilled his mother's request to work a miracle without betraying the Father's timing (Jn 2:1-11). At the cross he provided for his mother as a good son would (Jn 19:25-27). Apparently Jesus regarded family as an appropriate context in which to practice discipleship* (Mk 5:1-20) and even called siblings into his disciple community* (Mt 10:2-4).

All of this raises an important question. Is there a continuous core meaning to our nonchurch family that is not culturally crafted but divinely ordained?

Defining the Family Biblically

Family is a permanent human community that one enters by birth,* covenant (marriage) or adoption. The simplest and smallest family unit was the Adam and Eve covenant (dyad), through which persons not actually "next of kin" became closest relatives. This is the meaning of Adam's poetic and praise-full outburst "This is now bone of my bones and flesh of my flesh" (Gen 2:24). While Adam and Eve were commanded to "be fruitful and increase in number" (Gen 1:28), they were a God-imaging commu-

nity even before Eve brought forth a man "with the help of the LORD" (4:1). Even a childless couple is a core family, though they will continue to experience other levels of family life with their birth families, thus extending the family experience to other generations. So at the heart of the family experience are a man, a woman and child; this calls into serious question whether same-sex couples can ever be truly "family" in a divinely approved way (see Homosexuality). Cohumanity is central to the family experience.

Family is marked by covenant, that binding personal agreement by which a man and woman belong to each other "for better, for worse" (see Marriage). Covenant communicates the relational genius of family: each lives for the other and all live for the one. There is something like an unlimited liability toward one another in a family. This unconditional belonging extends to our parents even when we "leave" them to "cleave" to our spouse (Gen 2:24); the new core family is thus prioritized over the extended family. Even though we have left father and mother, however, we do not divorce our siblings and parents. We cannot! When we have children, we extend covenant belonging to them unilaterally, even before they can respond. But that covenant becomes bilateral when children are able to reciprocate. The covenant may, much later, become unilateral again as we become dependent parents needing care from our children (Balswick and Balswick, p. 21).

There are theological reasons for restricting the idea of family to the covenant community. First, in the Bible the first community on earth was the family, predating the church or the nation. Family is not a human invention but a divine creation, a matter of vocation or calling* rather than convenience and human choice.

Second, God is family. God exists communally as a triune God marked by covenant love (Jn 17:1) in which each person is for the other and all for the One. God is a family God. Thus every family in heaven and on earth derives its nature and dignity from God as family (Eph 3:14-15). A family God crafts family creatures. So the human family is a commentary on God, expounding something about the God whose image we reflect (Gen 1:26).

Third, Old Testament legislation dealt with family-plus-land units, as is graphically illustrated by the story of Ruth. These families were more like what we would call clans or extended families and constituted the basic social, kinship, legal and religious structures of the people of God. God ultimately owned the land but entrusted it to families, to whom it would be returned in the Jubilee (Lev 25:4-18). God deals with families under the Old Covenant.

Fourth, even under the New Covenant, where the people of God are not called to construct a holy nation, God continues to work through families. God's kingdom works through families as whole households (including servants and resident aliens) become Christians (Acts 16:32-33). Spouses are sanctified by their believing partner (1 Cor 7:14), and children grow up in the nurture and admonition of the Lord (Eph 6:1-4). Church leaders are expected to prove their ministry* first at home (1 Tim 3:4-5). So we may speak of the family as a domestic church, the basic ecclesial unit.

Family as Spiritual Discipline

The Second Vatican Council used the phrase "domestic church" to recapture the ancient idea that the family is a form of church and a place for evoking and applying faith. Families are the smallest possible units of congregational life and often the core of a local church. So we do not need to "bring the Lord into our homes" by a program of Christian education for the family, or even by family devotions, good as these are. God is already there, even if our family has problems. These reasons are important.

Issues that arise in family life set us up to find God freshly and to grow in discipleship. As already mentioned, family has covenant at its core. Covenant is a two-way lens that allows us to see something of the covenant love-life of God; at the same time, God's covenant with Israel and the church inspires our covenant life in marriage and family.

The warp and woof of family relational life both suggest godlikeness and invite us to seek God's help in living with relational integrity: forgiving* one another, welcoming one another, offering hospitality.* Parenting involves sustaining, guiding and relinquishing—all dimensions in which we learn from God as our ultimate parent. Childhood involves trusting, acknowledging and honoring—all fundamental to faith formation. Brothers and sisters learn to play* together and cooperate—both fundamental for living by grace through faith rather than by the performance of works. Grandparenting* involves enjoying (rather than using) and comforting; being grandchildren involves appreciating and, usually, mourning—again, all dimensions of the life of faith (Henley, pp. 33-105). What better school for Christian living could be contrived? What better laboratory for experimenting with faith?

Take the question of unconditional acceptance. As the older brother in the parable of the two prodigals discovered, one cannot experience the welcome of God while rejecting one's brother (Lk 15:11-32). Family life sets us up to experience the gospel—unconditional acceptance on the basis of relationship rather than performance. The elder brother in the parable prides himself on his impeccable behavior and hard work (15:29-30) but is really damned because grace and gratitude have not broken his hard heart. It is family life that invites him to live by faith and grace.

It is widely recognized that the family is the first environment in which we gain images of God as Father and the human paradigm for the feminine references to God in the Bible. Sometimes these images must be unlearned. Even in the best family we do not learn the fatherhood of God from our own parents; rather, we learn our fatherhood and motherhood from God. Nonetheless, our experience of parenting and being parented is evocative—a call to be converted to the fatherhood of God rather than to be convinced from our human parents. Child rearing turns out to be a moral and spiritual education for the parents. Children help parents grow up. We cannot give children affection, correction and a future with promise if we have not received these from God ourselves (see Blessing, Family). In the end, we need to ask not just how a family's children turned out but how the parents turned out!

The Jacob story in Genesis 25—35 demonstrates that God was determined to bless Jacob in the context of his actual family life, through his relations with parents, brother, wives and father-in-law, even though that family was riddled with favoritism, deceit, family secrets and multigenerational sin (see Family Problems). In the end, when Jacob was reconciled to his brother Esau, Jacob confessed that seeing his brother's face was "like seeing the face of God" (Gen 33:10). A perfect "Christian" family is not required for faith development*; the best place to meet God is right where we are. Even seriously troubled families can become arenas of spiritual formation* if the liabilities and difficulties are processed (sometimes the help of someone outside is needed for this).

To run away from our families is to run away from one place God wants to meet us. So we are invited to find God at the center of family life, in all of its relational dynamics and covenantal structure, rather than at the periphery through religious exercises.

See also CHURCH-FAMILY; FAMILY COMMUNICATION; FAMILY GOALS; FAMILY PROBLEMS; FAMILY VALUES.

References and Resources
R. S. Anderson and D. B. Guernsey, *On Being Family: A Social Theology of the Family* (Grand Rapids: Eerdmans, 1985); J. O. Balswick and J. K. Balswick, *The Family: A Christian Perspective on the Contemporary Home* (Grand Rapids: Baker, 1989); B. Berger and P. L. Berger, *The War over the Family* (Garden City, N.Y.: Doubleday, 1983); R. Clapp, *Families at the Crossroads: Beyond Traditional and Modern Options* (Downers Grove, Ill.: InterVarsity Press, 1993); M. Eastman, *Family, the Vital Factor: The Key to Society's Survival* (Melbourne: Collins Dove, 1989); J. A. Henley, *Accepting Life: The Ethics of Living in Families* (Melbourne: Joint Board of Christian Education, 1994); C. J. H. Wright, *God's People in God's Land: Family, Land and Property in the Old Testament* (Grand Rapids: Eerdmans, 1990).

R. Paul Stevens

FAMILY COMMUNICATION

"We can't communicate!" is the ever-common complaint to people-helpers from families that are not working well. A distraught parent says, "That rotten kid of ours just wants to go hang around McDonalds all night long. He never says anything to us without a sneer." A rejected wife suffering from urban cabin fever complains, "I have to phone my own husband's secretary to remind him about my birthday. And then when we go out for dinner, he talks more on his cell phone than to me!" Bad scenarios are numerous. Tragic examples are the content of books, cartoons, sermons, and late-night heartaches and tears.

However, family theorists have a different, less emotive, interpretation of broken communication. They argue that not communicating is a powerful expression of information as well as an editorial comment about the relationship. Not communicating is an effective expression of rejection that has the intended result—rebuffing the other member of the family. We cannot *not* communicate. In fact, all verbal and behavioral interaction is by definition some sort of powerful and purposeful communication.

All family communication is a message that is communication plus some evaluative comment on the quality of the family relationship (metacommunication). For example, a teenage boy with pitiable acne stutters to his library study partner, who is a Christie Brinkley look-alike, "I need to study for my math test a l-l-little bit l-l-longer. I'm going to come back after dinner. What about you?" She smiles and replies, "I guess I could do some more research on history." The facts are obvious: both are serious students! The metacommunication is also clear—another opportunity for being in psychosexual proximity has been achieved without rejection. Victory on all counts!

Levels of Communication

There are various message levels of communication. Not every transaction between communicants is intimate. At the least-intimate or most-superficial level of conversation, speaker and listener repeat worn-out but expected clichés. These may be anything from stereotypical greetings ("How ya doin'?") to preprogrammed discussion to avoid intimacy (for example, talking about the state of the economy or discussing the

sermon following a Sunday service). These are clichés because the communication is designed to avoid human contact rather than embrace intimacy. While superficial contact between people does occur, and this may have some value (acknowledging that you are there), these transactions are so predictable as to be exhausting, frustrating and depressing within families. Why? Because the emotional message is *You are not worth my commitment to really talking*. The *metacomment* (the comment about the comment) is greater than the comment.

The next level of interpersonal communication is what might be called *stranger communication* or *conversation*.* It is essentially the exchange of cognitive information (or reporting of facts) without much meaning or emotion.* This kind of reporting interchange is typical in business meetings. Families will occasionally choose to suffer with this kind of "facts transmission" rather than face the consequences of an emotional encounter—perhaps anger or blaming. In marriages and families that are lacking in respectful intimacy, much of the communication deteriorates to the level of reporting facts. Couples talk about the kids' schoolwork, the price of cabbages or the new neighbors down the block. This information might be true and important, but it does not build what is essential to family life. Many therapists, however, recommend that families who persistently fail at communication begin at this fairly inoffensive level. The injunction to "talk like strangers to each other" is good advice to those whose communication spirals down to blaming and hurt.

The next level of communication has to do with expressing one's values* and central emotional convictions. It is much deeper and more powerful than conversation. I remember well talking to my preadolescent daughter about her fears in starting at a new school the following day. In tears, she said, "But Daddy, what if they don't like me?" Her life was caught up in that brief explosion of worry and dread. Afraid of being left out when she had not yet had the chance of being accepted, she was expressing one of her central emotional convictions—"I need to be loved." Psychologists talk about the *teachable moment* in parenting. This is the time when the parent can communicate some essential virtue or value to the child. When a family member is expressing the central value of her life, much emotion is experienced. The communication is palpable. It is the same between husband and wife as well as between family generations. At this time the most effective communication may be active listening* and not talking at all. Attentive listening with a vector to the deep longings of the other is incredibly effective communication!

The deepest level of communication has to do with the personal and emotional commitment of your life to another. In wholesome marriages and families it is the joyful explosion of an unrequired "I love you!" The communion level of communication is also the experience of being accepted by the God who accepts us. No verbal communication goes on—it is more spirit to Spirit. And this communion fills both with joy! Also, the tentative glance of a single mother to her awkward teenager who is caught doing something right and the reluctant smiles that this produces speak of years of communication that can only mean that they have communed many miles together. Communication of this sort is often called *communion communication,* and it expresses belonging and acceptance.

Digital or Analogic?

Family communication is done in two modes: digital and analogic. *Digital communication* is verbal and conveys the content of the message. *Analogic communica-*

tion is nonverbal and carries most of the relational aspect of the message. For example, when I was a child, I often asked my father to bring me half an apple when I went to bed. I was not in need of the nourishment; I was not making excuses to stay up late. I was asking my dad, who couldn't seem to speak his warm emotions, to say what he thought of me. After walking up the nine stairs to my room, he would stand with the door open, silhouetted in the brightness, and place two corners of a green apple carefully into my sleepy hand. He was saying that he loved me, though he could never say it in words. In the morning there was often a bit of browned apple somewhere in my top bunk. Much later, as a married adult with little kids, expecting and anticipating a long drive home following a family get-together, Dad would come out and wipe the road dirt from my car lights. Analogic communication expresses without the use of words acceptance or rejection, hope or despair, confidence or worry and a future with grace or a future of failure.

Target the Heart

In the family and in the church* it is important to target our communication well. Blessings* and curses are powerful forms of communication. In 1 Corinthians 14:3 Paul says that "everyone who prophesies speaks to men for their strengthening, encouragement and comfort." In our family communication we need to be aware that we are constructing the future of our listeners, guaranteeing the outcome of our lives together. We can do this intentionally and effectively by targeting the heart. Communication is always more than the exposition of facts or the persuasive preaching of information. It needs in addition to be a declaration of our commitment and affection one to another. Effective families do more than have superficial conversations (though these, when they occur, are at least a conversation); such families express a wholesome blessing that calls for an imperative response.

For example, when my children were quite little, I would ask them vast existential questions such as "What are you going to be like when you grow up?" Of course, they would answer, "I don't know, Daddy." Then I would gaze down my outstretched arm to my pointing finger and say, "I think that I can see." Inevitably they would gaze off in the horizon of my imagination.* What was the vision that only their dad could know? And I would describe a life full of down-to-earth faith and practical romance with God. Theirs would be the pleasure of being fully alive. They would be a wholesome vector making a difference to the world. We would talk about the Holy Spirit sneaking into their lives with special gifts to give to others who needed what they had. I told them about the creativity that it takes to risk failing in the pursuit of God and that success* might occur too. I spoke into them that doing well in school was not very important but that doing well in life was really important.

In the family we target the things of the heart. But we also need this quality of communication in the fellowship* of the church family. With his church family in Thessalonica Paul says, "We loved you so much that we were delighted to share with you not only the gospel of God but our lives as well, because you had become so dear to us" (1 Thess 2:8). In both family and church we are conscripted to live emotionally and vulnerably and commitedly with one another, giving ourselves willingly.

Listening Hard and Speaking Hard

Jesus' last recorded exchange between Peter and Jesus (Jn 21) is a paradigm for wholesome family communication. Ex-pressiveness is difficult for many of us, and it certainly was for Peter. Peter and some of the other disciples had quit the family business to follow Jesus. Now they were defeated in this venture and returned to fishing. They were depressed and disheartened and felt like failures.* As they came to shore, dawn was breaking and they saw Jesus cooking over an open fire. Peter was beside himself with craziness that this dead Savior had come to life again! Clothed, he threw himself into the Sea of Galilee, swimming through his tiredness to be with Jesus. And Jesus asked him three times, "Do you love me?" After each query, Peter replied, "Yes, you know that I love you."

We are told that Peter was grieved to have had to repeat himself for something that seemed obvious to him. Jesus had a reason for such perseverance. In Matthew 4:4 Jesus said, "It is written: 'Man does not live on bread alone, but on every word that comes from the mouth of God.'" Peter had denied Jesus three times and now needed a word that came from the mouth of God. Jesus was giving Peter the opportunity to express his love three times, creating an opportunity for intimate communication. We have no way of knowing whether he asked Jesus for forgiveness. Perhaps, as in the case of the prodigal son, he did not ask for forgiveness because that expressive family affection was all he needed. Peter needed to say that he loved his Lord and to hear that this was sufficient. Because Jesus loved Peter, he created a perfect opportunity for Peter to say that he loved Jesus. With this experience Peter changed from an intimidated coward during Christ's crucifixion to a fearless witness after Jesus' ascension. In the same way Jack and Judith Balswick point to the power of family communication: "People struggling today to find intimacy in an impersonal society need to realize that they, too, can change by expressing love" (p. 210).

See also FAMILY; FAMILY PROBLEMS; FAMILY SYSTEMS; FAMILY VALUES; LISTENING.

References and Resources
R. Anderson and D. Guernsey, *On Being a Family: A Social Theology of the Family* (Grand Rapids: Eerdmans, 1985); J. O. Balswick and J. K. Balswick, *The Family: A Christian Perspective on the Contemporary Home* (Grand Rapids: Baker, 1989); W. M. Brody, *Family Dance: Building Positive Relationships Through Family Therapy* (Garden City, N.Y.: Anchor, 1977); E. H. Friedman, *Generation to Generation: Family Process in Church and Synagogue* (New York: Guilford, 1985); R. Richardson, *Family Ties That Bind* (Vancouver: Self-Counsel Press, 1984); V. Satir, *Conjoint Family Therapy* (Palo Alto, Calif.: Science & Behavior, 1967).

Paddy Ducklow

FAMILY GOALS

The old adage "If you don't know where you're going you'll never get there" is an important reason to establish family goals. Whether it is to envision new ways to relate to one another in family relations, to make plans about where to spend a family vacation* or to develop the spiritual lives of family members, setting goals is the way to make sure you will achieve what you want to have happen in your family life. A family* without a sense of direction wavers to and fro as external circumstances determine its future. A proactive family, in contrast, will make long- and short-term goals to turn their dreams into reality.

We invest ourselves in what we hold precious. For example, parents who value the spiritual growth* of their children will make principled efforts to attend church* and Sunday school.* In addition, they will find ways to incorporate devotional rituals within family life, to celebrate the traditions of their faith and to make special efforts to discuss current events in the context of their religious beliefs. Although these activities may not be written down anywhere as specific family goals, these behaviors emerge out of clearly formed values* in the hearts of the parents. But most families need more than a heart desire to convert their values into action. In fact, unless these values are specified in terms of goals and subgoals, they will most likely be left by the wayside.

A purposeful goal not only helps family members identify what is important but also helps them implement concrete ways of attaining their values. Good intentions are never enough! A family needs to agree on specific objectives that will help accomplish what its members hold dear. Family researchers (Delores Curran, Nick Stinnet) have discovered that families who work together toward common goals have a sense of meaning that enriches their common life. Whether it is making plans for a birthday* celebration, solving a family problem or accomplishing a specific task, a family reaches a deep sense of satisfaction when it joins together in this common effort. As each family member contributes to the family as a whole, they are appreciated for the unique part they play. The family that works together for common goals reaps the rewards of closeness and unity.

Goal-Setting Helps
How does a family go about setting family goals? Establishing a family council is a good place to start. This involves the family's setting aside a place and time for members to share their ideas about family needs, values and desires. Using the brainstorming approach, each member is encouraged to freely contribute any and all ideas that come to mind. The invitation to think "outside the lines" brings up many creative possibilities. One family member writes each idea down on a piece of paper until a long list

has been accumulated. There are no right or wrong ideas, and even the most outrageous suggestions are warmly received. Every member, from oldest to youngest, is taken seriously and treated honorably in this information-gathering process. This exercise assures that each family member is involved individually and corporately in the creation of family goals.

Next, the family chooses by consensus one particular goal from among the many ideas. Narrowing down the field can be difficult, but it is necessary to prioritize. Once the main goal is established, the family can begin to brainstorm about the specific behaviors that are needed to accomplish this goal. The family formulates subgoals (specific objectives) that will help them execute the greater goal. Subgoals need to be both realistic and "doable." Brainstorming, once again, is the best way to elicit a number of imaginative ideas. Once all of these are listed, each one must be evaluated in terms of whether it is reasonable and desirable for the whole family. In other words, it is a question of whether the family will be successful in following through.

Take the example of a family who wants to develop a deeper spiritual life. One subgoal may be to have devotions every night after supper at 5:30. Now it is time to evaluate. The teenagers may express objections because it interferes with their band or sports* activities after school. A younger child complains that it will be boring.* Mother says she wants the devotions to include creative activities, but Father prefers a simple Bible reading each night. As each member expresses their thoughts, feelings and ideas, the family becomes more realistic about what needs adjusting. Very often a compromise is made, such as having devotions at 5:30 on the three days a week that everyone is home.* The family decides to add variety by having everyone

take turns presenting the devotion. The bonus that emerges out of this compromise is that it extends the responsibility to each member. All these modifications serve to increase the likelihood of success. The family now has a plausible way of reaching its ultimate goal that works for it at this particular time in its life stage.*

An essential part of goal setting is for family members to make a commitment to keep part of the bargain. When the goal and subgoals have been evaluated together, it is relatively easy for individuals to cooperate. Clear, written objectives help everyone know exactly what is expected of them. Now it is time to clinch the deal.

Make a Contract*

Once the long-term goal and the short-term behavioral objectives are established, a covenant can be ratified or a contract can be signed to signify mutual commitment. This final step gives each family member a chance to promise, in front of others, that they will make every effort to do their part. This can be done by having a simple ceremonial handshake or by signing a written contract made up by the family at the end of the family council. The essential thing is that each person agrees to the conditions set forth and gives their word to keep the contract.

It is also vital to specify a time frame for this contract. Whether it is after one month or six months, it is best for the family to periodically review the progress made toward the goal. Meeting each week for family council is a good place to evaluate the effectiveness of the contract. The family asks itself, "How are we doing?" "Are the objectives helping us meet the metagoal?" and "Is there anything that needs to be changed?" These questions allow for needed correctives and innovative suggestions. An ongoing fresh perspective will continue to improve or reshape the subgoals.

When problems occur, the family must also agree to come back to the drawing board (family council) to renegotiate. This is not to be a time for blaming or defensiveness, but a chance to make things better. The thing to figure out is why a breakdown occurs. Recognizing barriers (were the goals too high?), considering various courses of action (what can we change?) or looking to alternatives (what haven't we tried?) helps the family figure out a new course of action. Since goals can be reached in a number of ways, changing immediate small steps is often the best way to assure achievement of the long-range goals. Minor setbacks are to be expected, and failure* is not viewed as a catastrophe; both are only opportunities to regroup and try again. Flexibility is the key! Listening* is the best path to ingenious solutions. It may be that encouragement, instruction or equipping* is needed. It is a time for family members to recommit themselves, to join hands and to take up the task once again.

Summary
Family goals are only as effective as its members' commitment to each other. Steps of action toward long- and short-range family goals require that everyone reach beyond individual goals. Family members must work together to be a family unit. As the apostle Paul explains, each unique part has something essential to offer the whole body and no one part can function effectively without the others. When we give of ourselves, set time apart, put forth effort and contribute our special giftedness, we serve the whole. Converting our values into goals requires a vision.* Family members must draw a landscape, plant the seeds, remove the obstacles and play their unique part in making their ultimate family dream a living reality.

See also FAMILY; FAMILY COMMUNICATION; PLANNING.

References and Resources
D. Curran, *Traits of a Healthy Family* (Minneapolis: Winston, 1983); D. Dinkmeyer and G. McKay, *Raising a Responsible Child* (New York: Simon and Schuster, 1973); R. Dreikurs and V. Soltz, *Children: The Challenge* (New York: Dutton, 1964); S. Simon, *Meeting Yourself Halfway: Thirty-one Values Clarification Strategies for Daily Living* (Niles, Ill.: Argus Communications, 1974).

Judith K. Balswick

FAMILY HISTORY
One of today's growing hobbies* is "doing your family history." What is it about this occupation that interests people? What keeps them at it year after year? Why are more people pursuing their family history now than in years gone by? What is the place for this, if any, in the Christian scheme of things?

People begin pursuing their family history for various reasons. Sometimes it is simply because they have retired (*see* Retirement) and want a hobby to give some structure to this period of transition in their lives. For others, friends got them involved, and they sensed the pleasure* and excitement their friends experienced as they delved deeper into the past. Others begin because they have developed a medical problem and want to see if it has its genesis in their family of origin. Sometimes it is the names inscribed in the front of a family Bible that start the search. My husband began because he was given a bundle of papers belonging to his recently deceased great-aunt and wanted to verify some of the information contained in them. I became interested because I was named after my great-grandmother and felt I would like to learn something about her.

The Value and Risk of Undertaking Family History

Viewed from one perspective, the Bible is a family history. It records the genealogies of many individual families (Gen 10:1—11:32), but it also records the story of the family of God through the ages. It contains not just Jesus' genealogy, with which the New Testament opens (Mt 1:1-17), but the social and religious history that fleshes that out. We cannot fully understand the impact of Jesus' birth, death and resurrection without understanding the overall scheme of God's relationship with Israel through the years. Precisely because the Bible contains the sagas of numerous families, there is much psychological, as well as spiritual, truth in it that speaks with deep insight to our own families today.

Just as an understanding of the Bible story gives us an appreciation of our spiritual roots, so an understanding of our family history can help us to understand who we are as families and individuals. With communities now so dispersed, and the family folklore no longer readily accessible through grandparents or other members of the older generation, we find ourselves digging into the past to discover our roots and link up with our heritage. The 1970 television series *Roots,* documenting the findings of Alex Haley's family history research, provoked an unprecedented desire on the part of many to trace their own family's origins.

This could all sound like selfish preoccupation, and for some it is. But those writing up their family history are also making a significant contribution to the wider culture,* especially local culture. Demographers have realized that family historians have a fund of knowledge to offer about members who moved from place to place, what occupations they pursued, and how often they relocated. Social historians, as well as medicos, also raid the findings of family historians to glean useful information for their own research.

One danger is that it can become addictive. It is easy to get consumed with the dead to the neglect of the living. Like a giant detective novel, there are many mysteries to be solved. Why did Grandmother leave Ireland when she did? Why did Great-grandfather leave his first wife and family in Germany when he emigrated? What happened to those other children listed on your great-grandmother's death certificate that you never heard of? Why does it say on this certificate that she was born in Canada when family folklore says she was born in New York?

We also must be ready for surprises. Sometimes those surprises are good ones, such as discovering we are related to some famous person; we may also discover skeletons in the family closet. Unraveling some of these puzzles can lead to a greater appreciation of why our family relates or makes the choices it does. This brings with it the possibility of healing memories buried deep in the family's past or of reestablishing relationships with estranged branches of the wider family. In many families there are secrets buried in the past that need to see the light of day so that forgiveness can take place and peace between family factions be restored. As Jesus said, "The truth will set you free" (Jn 8:32).

Ways of Researching Your Family History

How and where do you make a start on researching your family history? You begin with the most recent piece of accurate information that you have—perhaps the date of your grandfather's death. Armed with that, you can visit your local library and talk with the person who looks after the local history section. You can visit a bookstore and pick up something written on the topic, usually with "family history" or "genealogy" in the title. You can contact your local family history or genealogical society.

There is an amazing amount of information available now to assist you in your research. This includes birth,* death* and marriage* registers, shipping records, census results, military records, land sales registers, letters, journals, diaries, wills, ships' logs, government records, local histories and newspapers. Because of their particular interest in genealogy, the Mormons have established a remarkable collection of resources at their headquarters in Salt Lake City, Utah, as well as resource centers throughout America and overseas. Joining the nearest family history association or genealogical society is another positive step. There you will meet people keen to share what they have learned who will put you in touch with others who may be able to help.

It is also important before you begin to work out a way of organizing your research and its findings. Without this you will spend many fruitless hours trying to remember where you put something, what was the name of that book you read some fact in, or rereading records consulted five years earlier. There are many ways of doing this, but without doubt a computer is best and easiest, especially with materials stored on CD-ROM and on the Internet.

While most people want to research the history of their family of origin, others are keen to research the part of a different kind of "family" to which they belong, whether it be an organization* such as a bowling club* or a local church.* Not so many years ago congregations had annual "anniversaries"* where they celebrated their life together

and rehearsed various aspects of their history, often inviting a previous minister to preach at the focal event. These occasions probably ceased as they became a meaningless ritual, but they could have fulfilled an important function—providing an opportunity for the church to rehearse its story under God. Perhaps this kind of "family" history will help congregations to find fresh ways of celebrating their life together.

See also FAMILY; FAMILY PROBLEMS.

References and Resources
A. Eakle and J. Cerny, *The Source: A Guidebook to American Genealogy* (Salt Lake City: Ancestry, 1984).

Julie Banks

FAMILY PROBLEMS

All families* have problems! Living together through the thick and thin of everyday life, family members will encounter struggles and stressors all along the way. Whether it is a major problem like substance abuse, serious illness,* natural disaster or economic failure, or a minor difficulty like sibling rivalry, unhealthy coalitions in the family or personal conflicts between family members, it will take a toll on family relationships. Since the external problems are usually beyond the control of the family, this article will focus on relational problems that family members can change.

Four common problems that lead to internal family disharmony are conditional love,* shame, control and distance. If a family is to function effectively, members must first recognize and then learn to change these disruptive patterns. With that intention in mind, I will present each of these problems, highlighting their damaging impact on family relationships. Then I will offer four antithetical healing* principles that can bring harmony between family members. These healing principles are covenant (commitment and faithfulness), grace (acceptance and forgiveness), empowerment (competence and growth) and intimacy (closeness and communication). Knowing the difference between harmful and healing relationship dynamics will point families in the direction of health.* And, embracing these healing principles, family members will be able to combat the relational problems that cripple their functioning. Healing relationship principles will move family members toward well-being, whereas repeating the hurting patterns will move them toward further strife.

Loving That Is Conditional

Each member of a family needs to be loved for who they are! *Conditional* love, however, says a person is loved *if, because* or *when* he or she behaves a certain way. Love that depends on external behavior places an enormous burden on a family member to *earn* love rather than to *be* loved. In fact, conditional love becomes a leverage: love is withheld or withdrawn when a member's behavior is "unacceptable." This perpetuates the "try harder" compulsion to please others in order to feel acceptable. Family members who live under the dominating influence of conditional love begin to believe they have an internal flaw that makes them unworthy of being loved. Without the assurance that their family will "love them forever," even when they make mistakes, they become insecure. Conditional love leads to a pattern of distrust and untrustworthiness that spirals in a negative direction.

The exact opposite of conditional love is *unconditional* love. A compelling picture of God in the Bible is that of One who faithfully initiates and persistently pursues people through unconditional covenant love, even when they pull away and turn their back on him. Jehovah God of the Old Testament is the model parent who loves the children of Israel with a love that will not let go. A family that can keep on loving, even when members behave in unlovable ways, provides a basic trust and security for its members. Because it is inevitable that family members will disappoint and fail each other, it is absolutely essential that they experience the security of unconditional love. Trust is the foundation that makes connection and growth possible. Just as God's unconditional love is demonstrated through grace that accepts us "just as we are," so family life needs to be lived in an atmosphere of grace.

Shaming One Another

To forgive* and be forgiven is the hallmark of the Christian family. Unfortunately, families often live under the cloud of *shame* rather than grace. In shaming homes, family members set up a standard of perfection that is impossible to achieve. The strong focus on external behavior impedes that person's internal development. Members not only fear making mistakes but they believe they *are a mistake*, thinking they can never be good enough. In the innermost part of their being, they are ashamed of who they are. Totally discouraged by failing to live up to unreasonable standards, they give up! Though it may be their only defense, blaming themselves or others for their predicament leads only to further problems and irresponsible behavior.

The discouragement incurred in a shaming home defeats the hopeful message of God's *grace!* For God so loved and cherished each unique created person that he gave his only Son for them. The intent was to restore and reconcile. Likewise, a family of grace will embrace each member as a unique, cherished creation of God. While they acknowledge human failure, they also take hope in people's capacity to learn from mistakes and recover from imperfections. Repentance and forgiveness become the ways to reconciliation, hope and life. It is only when family members are loved, accepted and forgiven that they have the courage to begin anew.

Using Power to Control Others

Parents who *control* and coerce their children give the message that "might equals right." With this perspective, one inevitably tries to get more power* in order to lord it over others. This interpretation of power leads to serious problems of physical and emotional abuse.* Mostly it is the people who have very little power who resort to physical and mental punishment. In controlling families, members respond out of fear* rather than respect, cowering under the more powerful members. Dejected, they fail to develop an internal locus of control as they continually succumb to the demands of the controller. The question of what they do in the controller's absence ("out of sight is out of mind") is another serious problem. They may rebel and strike out in destructive ways. This "law and punishment" model keeps abusive systems perpetuating themselves from one generation to the next.

We can take a great deal of hope in the fact that Jesus radically redefined the notion of power. The model in the New Testament is one of *empowerment* or of using power *for* others. Just as the Holy Spirit empowers Christians to live out the life of faith, family members are called to nurture, equip, instruct, confront, encourage and assist one other in personal growth. Jesus announced that he came to serve and not to be served. The idea of laying down one's life for another family member is the extraordinary way of the cross. It is possible to turn the other cheek or go the second mile only if there is the strength of character to do it. When parents come alongside their children as moral and loving leaders who affirm* their children's strengths and build up their potential, they empower them to become responsible members of society.*

Keeping Emotional Distance

Families today are besieged by activities and conditions that keep them removed and *distanced* from each other. In a world that offers instant everything, it is difficult to take the time* that is required to develop close relationships. It is easier to hide behind fake masks rather than to reveal oneself in open, honest ways. If the family is a place where members experience rejection, the best way for family members to protect themselves from that kind of pain is to pretend they are okay when they are not. In addition, if members are loved only when they do acceptable things, or shamed when they make mistakes, or harshly punished when they fail, they will look for ways to anesthetize themselves from these condemnations. Addictive* behaviors, such as drinking, eating, overwork and so on, promise relief by taking one's mind off the self-defeating messages, but they only intensify the problem. These addictive substitutes are not only self-destructive but are destructive to relationships within the family. For when denial and cover-up become a way of life, they keep family members emotionally distanced from each other and are a barrier to intimacy, which is the healing force in family relationships.

In Genesis, Adam and Eve were described as being "naked and not ashamed" when they encountered each other. It would appear that they were completely open and vulnerable in their relationship. The psalms give a similar picture of *intimacy* when they express the psalmist's deepest thoughts and emotions of pain, joy, anguish, anger, victory and love to God in prayer. The scriptural truth that "there is no fear in love . . . perfect love drives out fear" (1 Jn 4:18) is a compelling reason to come before God, naked and not ashamed. There is safety in being loved unconditionally, being gracefully accepted and empowering others. In healing families, there is no need to hide or deny what one feels because all thoughts and feelings are honorable and listened to with compassion. When one is validated for being congruent (matching feelings and words), there is no need to cover up the truth, even when it is negative. In fact, conflicts offer us an exhilarating capacity for constructive growth when family members are able to hear and respond with appropriate understanding. Resolutions are sought in order to bring harmony and closeness between members. Intimacy is the fruit of vulnerable sharing and working through family problems together. It is the time a family spends together that deepens their level of interaction and emotional connection.

Finding Solutions

Once problems are recognized, the family has a great opportunity to deal effectively with them. The goal is to find a solution that can dissipate the negative energy that has piled up through past hurtful patterns of interaction. If your family is operating under the four disruptive relationship patterns, it is necessary to reverse these patterns. The family must *do something different* to break the old, hurting patterns and *add something new* in order to put the healing relationship principles in place. Here are some ideas for moving toward solutions.

First, one must declare the problem and commit to the solution. Admitting the inadequate past way and then indicating the desire to replace it with a more effective way is illustrated in the following statements: "I withhold my affection when you don't do what I say, and I scold and shame you when you do something I don't like, but I'd like to extend grace and acceptance instead!"; "I've been trying to force you into my way of doing things, but I know your way is equally good, and I will affirm you rather than criticize you"; "I realize I keep my distance by blaming you, and I will accept responsibility for my actions. It's important to me to find good ways to connect." The confession initiates the process. The vulnerable, "about-face" change of attitude opens others up in a way that will make a real difference. It is important to give some idea of what family relationships are when members are operating according to the four healing principles.

It is crucial to pay attention to the things family members already do that contribute to the four healing principles. You may want to ask all members to talk about the specific times when they have felt loved, accepted, empowered and emotionally close. Recognizing family strengths and particular activities that contribute to positive interaction provides specific behaviors to emulate. Discovering what the family is doing *right* is an important clue as to how the problem will be solved. By fostering positive behaviors, the family will be able to eliminate negative ones. The motto becomes: Keep doing those things that heal and quit doing the things that hurt!

Choosing to empower rather than to control, or deciding to accept rather than to shame, automatically reverses the negative trends. Eliminating unrealistic expectations means a person is free to discover what he or she can do well and to learn what's appropriate for their particular age and situation. Being vulnerable in relationships invites others to come toward us rather than pushes them away. Honest expression keeps one from hiding behind masks.

It is especially helpful for family members to make a list of *all* the behaviors they can think of that lead to the four healing principles. Then every member has the chance to make a conscious decision to incorporate these specific actions to get things rolling in the right direction. Repeating these patterns of positive relating becomes a way of life that continues to accentuate the positive.

An approach that focuses on solutions brings hope. Sometimes, however, a family cannot get to future solutions until they have paid sufficient attention to past hurts. In this case, repentance is a necessary part of the solution. Painful past events can continue to have a powerful negative influence unless members admit the wrongs so they can begin to reestablish trust. After reconciliation, they can put forth the remedial effort to make the desired changes.

A problem solved is a point of growth and celebration for the family. The solutions lead to a deeper level of intimacy in the family, which brings about more capacity for unconditional loving, acceptance and empowerment. Round and round it goes, one positive relationship principle contributing to another in an ongoing cycle of family unity.

See also FAMILY; FAMILY COMMUNICATION; FORGIVENESS; LOVE.

References and Resources
J. O. Balswick and J. K. Balswick, *The Family: A Christian Perspective on the Contemporary Home* (Grand Rapids: Baker, 1989); R. Campbell, *How to Really Love Your Child* (Wheaton, Ill.: Victor Books, 1978); R. Campbell, *How to Really Love Your Teenager* (Wheaton, Ill.: Victor Books, 1980); N. Stinnett et al., eds., *Family Strengths: Positive Models for Family Life* (Lincoln: University of Nebraska Press, 1979).

Judith K. Balswick

FAMILY SYSTEMS

Both of my parents grew up as only children. They often seemed baffled by the reality of their marriage* and their very-different-from-them children. Before bedtime they would sometimes tell us humorous family stories about their ineptitude in merging their expectations and dreams into their newly consecrated marriage, the merging of two family systems. As children, we laughed heartily at the thought of their mistakes, not aware that at the time those errors were for them major crises. Mom and Dad often tripped over "the way it should be." Both expected that the other would serve their unexamined personal and marital ambitions. They did not talk much—they missed being part of the communication generation that began in the 1950s. Both often seemed frustrated and exasperated, unsure of the rules. Drinking (and other distancing maneuvers) was the accepted way of coping with stress,* patterns they had learned from their growing-up years. As kids, we were often anxious within the overall atmosphere of uneasiness.

Many years later when I married into a well-connected, churchgoing family* with traditional rules and roles, I felt almost as excited about them as I did about my new wife. I felt as if I was finally at home. Life was planned and wonderfully predictable. Yet issues from my own family of origin often upset the balance of our new family dyad (my wife and myself), and I never felt completely accepted or understood in my extended family. They also felt that I never fully accepted their values* of what family life should be. When families of different kinds merge in marriage, there is the potential for change—this is what I call *good trouble!* My early marriage and family had lots of good trouble.

In this article family life is understood as a system, that is, as a whole composed of interconnected and interdependent members that are all the time influencing one another. No one lives entirely by himself or herself. This is true not only within the smallest family unit, sometimes called the *nuclear family*, but also between generations as family systems influence each other. The term *family of origin* refers to the family or families in which one is raised. Virginia Satir stressed the importance of the family of origin as "the main base against and around which most family blueprints are designed." She suggests that "it is easy to duplicate in your family the same things that happened in your growing up. This is true whether your family was a nurturing or a troubled one" (p. 124). This foundational insight, so often observed by psychiatrists and family counselors, was expressed centuries ago in the Bible where God says, "I, the LORD your God, am a jealous God, punishing the children for the sin of the fathers to the third and fourth generation of those who hate me, but showing love to a thousand generations of those who love me" (Deut 5:9-10). The promise of intergenerational grace in this last phrase is restated in Deuteronomy 5:29, which indicates that people are to live in harmony with God's ways "so that it might go well with them and their children forever." While family systems theory is less than fifty years old, it is essentially in harmony with the biblical revelation of how families, communities and the people of God function (Collins and Stevens, pp. 92-107).

Family of Origin

The problem with us as people is that we had parents, and of course so did they. While parents are sometimes a problem for us, it is a good thing that we had parents—and a good thing that they did as well. In our families we not only duplicate the lives from our families of origin, we sometimes potentiate (that is, increase the intensity of) the problems. To be a healthy member of a family, we need to practice forgiveness, which permits us to free our parents from the resentments we have accumulated about them. Forgiveness also frees us to determine our own way of living without the burden of the demands from our family of origin. This is a key to growth and maturity in thinking about the family as a system.

Through our family histories we can view the relationship dynamics and values transmitted through generations. Virtues and values can be embraced, and curses and criticisms can be challenged. This is the understanding of covenant making. Throughout our growing-up years, we learned how to make and keep covenants and the value of promises. We learned this from our parents, or we noticed the lack of this and promised to ourselves that we would be promise keepers. Through forgiveness, promise keeping and covenant making, we are empowered to bring health and grace to the next generation.

We did not choose our parents, nor did they choose us. Further, none of us had the opportunity to choose how to live in our families of origin. We adapted to pressing circumstances as best we could with the skills and experiences we had, just as they did. However, all of us can choose how we will live in our current families and interact within our various systems or communities. We do not need to replicate the unhealthy patterns of our families of origin, nor do we need to overadapt and do the opposite.

Wholeness

Virginia Satir uses the image of a mobile to explain how a system works. In the family mobile, every part of the family is understood in terms of the whole family and how individual parts affect the whole. Each part is considered to be interdependent, not autonomous. A movement or change in one part of the mobile affects the system throughout. Picture a mobile that hangs over an infant's crib as having people instead of animals or parts of the planetary system hanging from it. Envisioned in this way, events that initially touch one member of the family mobile cause other family members to reverberate in relationship to the change in the initial member. Thus, if a member of the family marries a distant cousin or a person from another race, graduates from medical school or contracts the AIDS virus, the surrounding family system is affected. The family mobile is altered, not just the individual member.

For example, Barry (a fourteen-year-old boy in a single-parent family from my counseling practice) stayed away from home for several weeks and made no contact with his understandably frantic mother. At a loss as to what to do, she became depressed, and the younger kids began to suffer as she drank from morning till night, ignoring their basic care. When Barry finally came home, he vowed to God that he would stay. His mother gave up drinking, and the family mood improved greatly. The siblings were delighted at this change and blessed their older brother for doing what was right in their eyes. As the mom became more functional and pleasant, Barry figured the family problem was solved and he could now live his own life again without the presumed obligation to be the "designated father." (Barry's father had divorced his mother and the children when Barry was just six years old.) Since life was now okay, Barry began to skip some school and stayed out late at night. Barry's mother then became upset and was soon as depressed as before, precipitating a crisis in the younger children, who began to display their own symptoms of depression.* Barry again saw the cost of his behaviors on the family and promised anew that he

would be a "good kid." The family resumed functioning as normal until the cycle repeated itself again. Barry's growing up affected both his mother and his siblings, and he felt trapped into being the absentee father that all people long to have and resent missing. His feeling of being trapped was felt by each of the other members of the system.

In the analogy of the family mobile, every time one part of the family changes position, the entire mobile shifts. All parts are unbalanced until the changed part returns to its original place. Barry feels impelled to "do good" for the good of the family. When Barry eventually moves out permanently from his family and creates his own independent life, the other parts of the family will adjust themselves to a new form of stability and security. Until then the family will require that he stay and function in ways that permit their stability and security. In family life each person is part of the whole. And the whole is more than the sum of the parts, as Aristotle said long ago. We are linked together invisibly in a relational, emotional and even a spiritual unity. But change within the system is not all bad.

Good Trouble

The Chinese word for *crisis* is composed of two pictorial characters, one meaning "danger" and the other "opportunity." Shifts in the family mobile can be considered family crises and are potentially *good trouble* through which positive change can come. Think of the crises that would be induced in the following examples: the middle son of a solid Orthodox Jewish family becomes a Christian; the workaholic father rolls the family minivan over a cliff and nearly dies; the ultrastable mother does not come home after work until 9 p.m. and looks a bit like a floozy; another child is conceived although the couple had agreed that "two

391

is enough"; two families blend, resulting in two fifteen-year-old stepsisters; a younger brother suffers a prolonged death from leukemia while the older sister does not feel understood; a middle-aged dad buys a sports car and begins wearing a jogging suit. All of the changes caused by these events can result in greater satisfaction and security. It would be a shame to waste such terrific crises.

Boundaries and Subsystems

Mother and father (wife and husband) together are a family subsystem. Their children are another family subsystem, as are the grandparents* and other extended relatives. In our family, our cocker spaniel and two cats are a significant, and too often an expensive, subsystem that precipitates some growth-producing tension between father and daughter! We would not be the same family without each competing system within our larger system we call with much affection "our family." Our family dinner table is a cacophony of information about other systems that are affecting our family: what happened at school, what craziness Tim did on *Home Improvements*, the CD sale at the mall and other families who are reported to be in greater crisis than ours. Some of this information enters into our family and affects us; some stays out or is kept out. This has to do with how our family is defined and the values and structure of our family unit. In systems thinking this is referred to as family *boundaries*, or the openness of the system to other systems.

The peer groups of both parents and children are systems that affect the experience of the family. Teenage kids may have friends who wear their caps carefully turned backward. Being their peers, they influence the kids and thus the family. The parents' peer group may be other middle-agers on the sideline of a soccer game or prayerful Christian adults in a church fellowship group. When these peer groups interact, there is a good chance of a crash at the intersection. Imagine the cap-wearing teen with his Bulls jacket coming to church one morning to meet a "suit" carrying a well-worn King James Bible who asks him to remove his hat out of respect. It should be said again that subsystem collision can result in growth for each subsystem. The issue of boundaries is whether we will permit what is outside of our understanding and experience to change us so as to help us grow.

Conclusions

This brief reflection on some of the basic dimensions of family systems shows that family life sets us up to know God and gain Christian maturity right at home. We were built for relationships, and family life helps us to see that isolated individuals simply do not exist. Further, we were built for covenant making and promise keeping—two graces we may experience in our lives whether our family experience has been good or bad. Even very hard experiences in family life can be experienced as God's good invitation to make changes for the better and to practice the grace of forgiveness. The influence of subsystems and other systems on our family system causes us continuously to define our family goals* and family values*—once more seeking God's mind in prayer and Scripture. Through it all the multigenerational impact of our behavior, whether bad or good, mentioned in Deuteronomy 5:9-10 is not just a curse but a blessing*: God's love extends "to a thousand generations."

See also BLESSING, FAMILY; FAMILY; FAMILY COMMUNICATION; FAMILY GOALS; FAMILY HISTORY; FAMILY PROBLEMS; FAMILY VALUES; PARENTING.

References and Resources

R. Anderson and D. Guernsey, *On Being a*

Family: A Social Theology of the Family (Grand Rapids: Eerdmans, 1985); J. O. Balswick and J. K. Balswick, *The Family: A Christian Perspective on the Contemporary Home* (Grand Rapids: Baker, 1989); W. M. Brody, *Family Dance: Building Positive Relationships Through Family Therapy* (Garden City, N.Y.: Anchor, 1977); P. Collins and R. P. Stevens, *The Equipping Pastor* (Washington, D.C.: Alban Institute, 1994); E. H. Friedman, *Generation to Generation: Family Process in Church and Synagogue* (New York: Guilford, 1985); R. Richardson, *Family Ties That Bind* (Vancouver: Self-Counsel Press, 1984); V. Satir, *Conjoint Family Ttherapy* (Palo Alto, Calif.: Science and Behavior Books, 1967).

Paddy Ducklow

FAMILY VALUES

I once approached a house that had a welcome sign on the left side of the front door and a keep-out sign on the right side. Such is the confusion of values in the Western world that simultaneously promotes family values such as togetherness, affirmation and forgiveness and antifamily values such as personal self-realization, psychic mobility (keeping all your options open), relational rentalism (only short-term commitments to others) and the right* to unlimited sexual expression. Nevertheless, even in this day of fractured families it is widely acknowledged that the family is the primary arena for forming spiritual understanding and moral values.

Largely through the work of humanistic psychologists such as Rollo May, Abraham Maslow, Fritz Perls, Erik Erikson, Carl Rogers and others, values* are back in the picture, even in the school system, where it is increasingly recognized that value-free education* is really impossible. Values continually brood in, over, around and within life. They are cherished behaviors, principles and attitudes. And the family is the first location, and undoubtedly the ultimate environment, for values formation. In a family context why are values important? What family values are biblically commended? How can family values be cultivated? (*See* Family; Family Communication; Family Goals.)

The Value of Values

Every family has a set of values, often unexpressed, that determines how decisions are made in the face of competing alternatives. Sometimes these are expressed in family mottoes, such as "Birthday parties always come before personal plans," "Dad is the head of this house," or "No secrets allowed in this family." More often values are subterranean, like an unseen aquifer that nourishes generation after generation without ever surfacing. These values express fundamental beliefs about what and who is important; how relationships should be fostered; what is the place of money, sex and power; who is entitled to make decisions and where God is in it all. Values determine behavior, give expression to beliefs and give meaning to everyday life. Values shape the culture of the family, the culture of the church as a family of families, and ultimately the culture of the nation.

Research on organizational culture* shows that every social organization can be pictured in three concentric circles. On the outside are the artifacts of the culture, enshrined in visible symbols (the welcome sign over the door, father sitting at the head of the table), rituals (we always start Christmas Day by singing carols) and codes (the last will* and testament). These symbols and artifacts express the reality that can be represented by a second, smaller concentric circle: family values, what the family cherishes. The values, in turn, express the family's beliefs (the smallest concentric circle—whether men and women are created equal, whether sex is a good gift of God, whether God has anything to do with everyday life). Together this family culture forms an all-embracing influence in child development. It is felt by anyone entering a family gathering, especially when one marries into a family and therefore really marries a family! One of the most significant areas of tension when two people get married is the marrying of two different sets of values (*see* Dating; Family Systems). Some people do not realize how deeply these values were formed within their family of origin until they are confronted in the transforming crucible of marriage.

Since values shape behavior and express beliefs, it is not surprising that Christians frequently find themselves caught between the claims of the kingdom and the sometimes idolatrous claims of their families (*see* Church-Family). That is what is behind the somewhat ambiguous words of Jesus about hating father and mother in order to follow him (Lk 14:26) and letting the dead bury the dead (Lk 9:60). Even when Christians live together in a family, it is likely that there will be some clash of values—a crisis that itself can become an arena for spiritual growth. Indeed, rather than seeing the family as an arena for spiritual disciplines* (such as daily Bible reading), we should see the family itself as a spiritual discipline. It is what Bruce Stevens calls "a theological nursery" (p. 14).

Commendable Values

As mentioned above, values are based on beliefs. The commendable values developed below are based on the following beliefs, here stated but not expounded: (1) the divine origin of family life as a covenant community and an expression of God's own family life in the Holy Trinity (Eph 3:15); (2) grace rather than perfection or excellence as the dominant motif of the Christian life; (3) the vocation of all God's people to be God's holy people and to do God's work in the world (*see* Calling; Laity); (4) the family as a domestic church, the smallest unit of church life (see R. P. Stevens, pp.

35-42); (5) the family as the primary unit of spiritual, relational and emotional formation, so that even parents grow up by having children; (6) the depoliticizing of the family by the grace of Christ so that Christians in families become a community of companionship, unity and mutual priesthood (Eph 5:21; 6:1-4); (7) the fact that Christ's work of redemption does not make people into angels or religious people but into full human beings to fulfill God's purposes in the world.

Based on these fundamental beliefs, almost all Christian values, from the Ten Commandments (Ex 20:1-17; Deut 5:6-21) to the sevenfold fruits of the Spirit (Gal 5:22-23), could be commended for persons living in families. Here we will examine biblically commended values in four categories that belong exclusively to family life (such as honoring parents), are especially suitable as family values (such as inheritance) or most likely to be cultivated in the warp and woof of everyday family life (such as contentment). Spiritual education does not begin with Sunday school* but with birth,* indeed with conception.* In each of the following categories we start with values that could properly be considered as part of the human vocation—whether or not persons are Christians—and end with values that are specific to persons of faith.

Relational values include (1) honoring parents, that is, respecting parents for one's whole life, though not subordinating oneself to them after leaving home and cleaving to husband or wife (Gen 2:24; Ex 20:12; 21:15; Lev 19:3; Deut 5:16; 21:18-21; Prov 19:26; 20:20; 28:24; Mt 10:36; 15:1-9; Eph 6:1-4; Col 3:20; *see* Grandparenting; Marriage; Parenting); (2) blessing or affirmation of one another (*see* Blessing), showing affectionate loyalty and building each other up with words and deeds (Gen 27; 48—49; Prov 31:28-31; Eph 4:29; Phil

4:8); and (3) forgiveness, letting the past be in the past and creating the possibility of a new future for another and even oneself (Ps 32:5; Prov 10:12; 19:11; Mk 11:25; Jn 8:11; Eph 4:32; Col 3:13; 1 Jn 1:9; 4:20; *see* Forgiveness; Hate; Love). In exalting these relational values, a family is showing that people are more important than things; a child's hurt feelings when a dish is dropped on the floor is more significant than some now-shattered pottery.

Social values include (1) procreation, bearing seed to create another generation in one's own image (Gen 5:3), for we are to experience salvation in the context of doing what we have been created for (Gen 1:28; 19:30-38; Ex 6:13-25; Deut 25:5-10; Judg 21; Ruth 4:18-22; Ps 127; 1 Tim 2:15; *see* Birth; Conception; Parenting); (2) togetherness without enmeshment, involving building a common life through interdependence, rather than independence or codependence, crafting a unity that is deeper and stronger because of the diversity of personalities and their gifts (Rom 12:15; Phil 2:4; *see* Family Systems), including prizing and respecting the other sex as complementary and necessary to fully image God (Gen 1:27); and (3) play, since the family that plays together is likely to stay together (Prov 8:30, *see* Leisure; Play; Sabbath; Vacations). In exalting these values, members of a family are called to live beyond themselves and to show love to their nearest and dearest neighbors. Family is a place to belong. In Robert Frost's poem "Death of a Hired Hand," the old farmer muses to his wife about the inconvenience of having the hired hand come back to the farm to die: "Home is the place where, when you have to go there, / They have to take you in." The farmer's wife has a better grasp of the matter when she replies, "I should have called it / Something you somehow haven't to deserve."

Vocational values include (1) service in the world through all the ways that humankind makes God's world work (Gen 2:15), ranging from public service through politics to giving food to the hungry (Mic 6:8; Mk 10:43; *see* Ministry; Service, Workplace; Work); (2) hospitality through which strangers and visitors are given a space where they are free to be themselves (Gen 18:1-15; Lev 19:33; 1 Tim 3:2; 5:10; Tit 1:8; Heb 13:2; 1 Pet 4:9; 3 Jn 8; *see* Hospitality) and through which those closest to us are allowed to develop in their own way in an environment of acceptance; and (3) mutual priesthood through which children bring God's message, presence and grace to parents (just as parents do to children; Eph 6:1-4) and through which husband and wives function not in a pre-Christian hierarchical way but in genuine partnership involving mutual submission and ministry (Eph 5:21-33; 1 Pet 2:5, 9). It is often noted that children growing up learn about God from their parents, even when their parents claim to have no faith or do not practice it. Just as infants see themselves mirrored in the eyes and facial expressions of their parents, they gain images of God, some of which require abandoning or transforming later in life. Children also learn whether becoming a pastor or a missionary is the ultimate vocation or whether all of God's people are called to the ministry (Eph 4:1; *see* Calling). In short, they can learn the truth of William Tyndale's statement: "There is no work better than another to please God; to pour water, to wash dishes, to be a souter [cobbler], or an apostle, all are one, as touching the deed, to please God" (p. 98).

Stewardship values include (1) treasuring a multigenerational inheritance involving the conservation of the land and the planet (*see* Ecology; Stewardship); (2) treasuring family assets for future generations—a matter that undergirded much of the Old Testament legislation, especially the returning of the land to families in the year of Jubilee (see Wright, pp. 119-28)—and saving up to provide for others, especially one's children (Ex 22:10-11; Lev 25:13, 23; Deut 20:19; 21:15-17; 1 Kings 21:3; Job 42:15; Prov 17:6; 19:4; 22:28; 2 Cor 12:14) and parents (Mk 7:11); (3) sharing, which involves lending, borrowing and almost unlimited liability within a family (Ex 22:25; Deut 15:1-11; 23:19; *see* Credit; Debt; Money), as well as generous more-than-a-tithe hilarious giving (2 Cor 9:7) to believers in need and to the Lord's work (Gen 14:20; Ex 34:26; Deut 14:22-24; 26:1-15; 1 Chron 29:2, 9; Prov 3:9; 11:24-25), willingness to work toward equality (2 Cor 8:13-15) between rich and poor Christians through gifts that empower rather than create dependence (Acts 2:44-47; 4:32-37; Rom 15:25-27; 1 Jn 3:17) and compassionate gifts and empowering help to the truly needy whether they have faith or not (Lev 19:9-10; Deut 23:24-25; 24:19-22; Prov 19:17; 22:9, 16, 22; 28:27; 31:8-9; Lk 4:18; Jas 1:27); and (4) contentment, which is living in continuous thanksgiving for what God has provided, whether much or little (Phil 4:12), and deciding not to yield to the siren advertisements* that say happiness is achieved by having yet another possession or experience (Deut 5:21; Josh 8:22-27; Prov 1:19; 15:16, 27; 16:8; Eccles 5:12; Mt 11:19-21; Lk 12:15; Rom 13:5; Eph 5:20; Phil 4:6). In most families the pocketbook (or bank book) is the last thing to get converted!

Conspicuously missing from the above list are the traditional Christian values of church attendance, family devotions and religious activities. The reason is significant: these are not values but rites and roles that support values (or discourage their formation). This raises the vital question of just how values are formed. Psychology has reminded us of the scriptural insight (Deut 5:9) that values—good and bad—get passed down generation to generation, even in dysfunctional families. (This is dramatically illustrated by the case of Jacob, who learned from his mother that the strategy needed to get your own way when you cannot trust those close to you or God is to use deceit. In Jacob's case deceit was passed along to his wives and children, showing up again even in the life of the much-loved Joseph.) But how can we foster the values mentioned above, and do so in such a way that does not relegate God to the religious periphery of family life fifteen minutes after the supper meal and a brief prayer before sleep?

Reinforcing Values

Thus far I have refrained from defining *family*, partly because the nuclear family, strained as it is to the breaking point, cannot bear the full load. Divorce and single parenting have taken their toll. They have also forced us to rethink *family* in the light of Scripture. *Family* in the Bible includes the idea of household, those joined by covenant, blood or adoption in a mutuality that includes not only the primal unit of mother, father and child but uncles and aunts, grandparents and cousins, friends and business partners and even "the alien within your gates" (Ex 20:10)—there not by right but by grace. Many a young person, struggling with her parents through adolescence (*see* Adolescence), has found profound acceptance and healing through a grandparent who really believed in her and prayed for her. So values are formed not merely by parental transmission but through family life in toto: who gets invited to dinner, how the stranger at the door is treated, when we speak of Uncle Frank the black sheep of the family, what we do when we have overspent our income, who makes the decisions about where a family vacation will be spent, whether Mom and Dad "still have sex" and view it prudishly or sacramentally (*see* Sexuality), how the church service is discussed over Sunday dinner, what is done when the daughter comes home with a boyfriend twenty years her senior.

Values clarification. Life is full of learning, most of it unconscious. So our first task in reinforcing values is to clarify the values we already hold. This can be done effectively through values-clarifying exercises outlined for families and church groups (Larson and Larson) or relating to work and vacation (Jones and Jones). Values can also be clarified through journaling, through family discussions and through taking each and every family crisis as a God-given opportunity to ask, "What are we presently cherishing that lead to this conflict or challenge?" It took Jacob twenty years to get hold of this truth and to admit to himself and God (Gen 32:27) that his name was Cheat/Jacob, though God had thrown up mirror after mirror in his life to bring him to himself—a prerequisite to his being blessed by God (see R. P. Stevens, pp. 43-53).

Values teaching. Parents do not often think of themselves as teachers; still less do children. But family life is a life-on-life environment for learning: the first school and the first theological college. The Bible advocates conversational teaching (*see* Conversation): "Impress them on your children. Talk about them when you sit at home and when you walk along the road, when you lie down and when you get up" (Deut 6:7). We teach all the time—over the supper table, when we walk or drive together, when we are making purchases in a store, as we say goodnight and pray by the bedside. Much of family life is sheer imitation of the same pattern as discipleship. The disciple (and the child) when he "is fully trained will be like his teacher" (or his parents; Lk 6:40). We are teaching even when we are not speaking. (One powerful memory during my teens is sneaking past my parents' open bedroom door late at night after a school dance or a date* and seeing my father or mother kneeling beside their bed, often together, undoubtedly including me in their intercession.)

Teaching is continuous, but there are teachable moments, such as when you are leaving for an important meeting and your daughter says, "Dad, what's so wrong about premarital sex?" These moments are to be prized, waited for, prayed over and seized as treasures hidden in the field. One of the most precious gifts children can give parents is their questions. Some questions arise spontaneously; others are evoked by patterns and habits (*see* Habits) of family life that at some point or other invite the question by a son or daughter (compare Josh 4:6: "What do these stones mean?").

Values embedded in traditions and rituals. It is important for families to celebrate Christmas, Easter and Thanksgiving (*see* Festivals); to read Scripture and good books as a daily ritual (*see* Reading); to tell stories, especially the stories of one's own family (*see* Storytelling); to keep the family genealogy, a family scrapbook or photo album as a treasury of values incarnated in experiences, relationships and events; to pray for one another and with one another; to worship* regularly with the people of God (*see* Church; Church in the Home; Fellowship; Membership, Church; Small Groups). Other rituals—not often considered—that communicate important values are unplugging the telephone during the family supper, watching television together (and so discussing the values implicit in mass media; *see* Mass Media; Television), taking an annual vacation,* keeping sabbath* and other customs unique to the family (such as going swimming in the ocean on New Year's Eve or taking a walk every Sunday afternoon).

One fundamental value to be treasured is the family itself, especially in this day when the family is out of favor. In a stunning article Michael Novak suggests there are two kinds of people in the world today: "individual people" and "family people." He reflects on how education and the media help children to become sophisticated in everything but the things most needful: "love, fidelity, childbearing, mutual help, care for parents and the elderly" (Novak, p. 44). Insightfully Novak notes that having children is no longer a welcome responsibility because "to have children is plainly, to cease being a child oneself" (p. 39). Children help parents to grow up, a maturation many resist in favor of perpetual adolescence without the burden of having a family. With equal insight Neil Postman in *The Disappearance of Childhood* laments the loss of childhood. He does not think we will forget that we need children. What he fears is that we are forgetting that children need childhood. Childhood is crucial to learning the discipline of delayed gratification, modesty in sexuality and self-restraint in manners and speech.

Not only are most of the values mentioned above countercultural, but valuing the carrier of these values, the family, is itself an act of resistance against the prevailing culture. To treasure family, to decide to live near one's extended family, to invest in family life as a holy ministry, to treat each family meal as the table of the Lord, is exactly the revolution so desperately needed today. Within the Jewish tradition mealtimes were especially viewed as holy occasions. This led to the practice in medieval Spain of burying the benevolent rich in coffins prepared from their table. Tables thus become rabbinic altars: "When two sit together and the words between them are of Torah, the divine presence is in their midst" (*'Abot* 3:3). God at home—this is the belief that undergirds biblical values formation in both content and method. In this way the ordinary becomes "crammed with heaven," as Elizabeth Barrett said.

See also CHURCH-FAMILY; FAMILY GOALS; FAMILY SYSTEMS; PARENTING; VALUES.

References and Resources

R. Frost, *Robert Frost, a Tribute to the Source,* with photographs by D. Jones and text by D. Bradley (New York: Holt, Rinehart and Winston, 1979); G. Jones and R. Jones, *Naturally Gifted: A Self-Discovery Workbook* (Downers Grove, Ill. : InterVarsity Press, 1993); R. S. Larson and D. E. Larson, *Values and Faith: Value-Clarifying Exercises for Family and Church Groups* (Minneapolis: Winston, 1976); M. Novak, "Family out of Favor," *Harper's,* 252 (April 1976) 37-46; N. Postman, *The Disappearance of Childhood* (New York: Vintage Books, 1994); E. H. Schein, *Organizational Culture and Leadership: A Dynamic View* (San Francisco: Jossey-Bass, 1991); B. Stevens, "Patterns of Eternity: Toward a Spirituality of Family," *Saint Mark's Review* 143 (Winter 1990) 13-17; R. P. Stevens, *Disciplines of the Hungry Heart: Christian Living Seven Days a Week* (Wheaton, Ill.: Harold Shaw, 1993); W. Tyndale, "A Parable of the Wicked Mammon" (1527), in *Doctrinal Treatises and Introductions to Different Portions of the Holy Scriptures by W. Tyndale,* ed. H. Walker (Cambridge: Parker Society/Cambridge University Press, 1848); C. Wright, *God's People in God's Land: Family, Land and Property in the Old Testament* (Grand Rapids: Eerdmans, 1990).

R. Paul Stevens

FAREWELL

Saying goodby is a grace to both the giver and the receiver. It is the mirror image of greeting.* It is also a daily experience as we leave home* for work* or school or bid coworkers farewell at the end of the workday. While we are never guaranteed to see again those we bid farewell, these daily rituals express our desire that they "fare well," and we confess there is no unfinished business between us. In other words, we are free to leave. On a deeper level we say goodby at significant transition points, when moving from one city to another, when leaving a job or a local church, when graduating from a school or college. Our final act of farewell is usually on our deathbed. Some people have great difficulty saying goodby; some avoid it altogether and leave people "dangling," wondering what they think of them and what is wrong. Sometimes the omission of farewells at significant transitions (such as leaving a job or church) is an indication of incomplete interior work in both the leaver and those being left (*see* Membership, Church). This happens most dramatically at the time of a wedding* when some are emotionally unable to leave father and mother in order to cleave to their spouse (*see* Marriage).

Farewells in the Bible

While the Bible does not use the word *farewell* or *goodby* frequently, it often describes people saying goodby to their children and grandchildren (sometimes with protracted partying*; Judg 19:4-10), parting from a friend (1 Sam 20:42), letting go of a dying loved one (*see* Grieving) or of one's own life (Judg 11:34-40; *see* Death), concluding public service (1 Sam 12) and leaving churches they love. Isaac said goodby as his death approached by blessing his sons (Gen 27:1-40), an act that should have communicated good will to his children but instead turned his sons against each other (Gen 27:41; *see* Blessing, Family).

Later, Laban, Jacob's father-in-law, complained that he was prevented from saying goodby to his children and grandchildren because they were stolen away secretly (Gen 31:28). The farewell that ensued when Laban caught up with the entourage is more like a warning than a blessing: "May the LORD keep watch between you and me when we are away from each other" (Gen 31:49) means the Lord must police this relationship because we will not be able to watch over each other! But even though the motives were mixed, this belated farewell brought closure and grace to a relational transition.

Two farewells, obviously crafted in parallel, are especially intriguing. When Elisha is called to follow and succeed Elijah as prophet, Elisha requests time "to kiss my father and mother good-by" (1 Kings 19:20), a permission that is granted. But when a would-be disciple of Jesus asks, "First let me go back and say good-by to my family" (Lk 9:61), Jesus expressly forbids it. In the first case the farewell was a healthy parting and included Elisha's sacrificing his farm equipment to "cut his ties" with his former occupation. In the second Jesus was dealing with self-styled volunteers who wanted simply to add discipleship to an already full life instead of being single-minded in the pursuit of God.

Paul, as an ecumenical traveler,* was always careful to say goodby (Acts 21:6; 2 Cor 2:13). Jesus used the Last Supper as a farewell meal and an opportunity to deal with unfinished business. The Fourth Gospel expands the spiritual meaning of this farewell in chapters 14—17. Most remarkable of all, Jesus served Communion to Judas at his farewell dinner.

Types of Farewells

This biblical study of farewells turns up a great variety of cultural expressions. Farewells today are also accompanied by handshakes, hugs, kisses, parties, long formal speeches, dramatic acts, deep bows, tips of the hat, passing the peace pipe, promises of prayer and letter writing (or E-mail messages), exchanges of business cards (often with great ceremony in Asia), an expensive meal in a restaurant (*see* Eating) or an exchange of gifts.* Especially in developing countries the failure to say goodby is a grievous wound, a statement that there is something obligatory and unfinished between the parties.

An illuminating example of saying goodby is Paul's final speech to the Ephesian elders (Acts 20:17-38). It includes many dimensions of a mature farewell. He rehearses his relationship to his friends (vv. 18-21), explains why he is leaving and will never see them again (vv. 22-25), declares that he has discharged his responsibilities fully (vv. 26-27) and exhorts them to remain faithful to Jesus (vv. 28-32). Finally Paul asserts that there is, to his knowledge, no indebtedness outstanding between them (vv. 33-37). Here is the grace of saying farewell at its best: each is empowered to carry on with life with no lingering obligations except to pray and love one another. A little farther along the way Paul had another farewell, this time with adults and children all saying goodby to Paul on the beach, with prayer and a walk together to the boat (Acts 21:5-6).

Once when I was completing a three-day seminar among rural church leaders in a village near the Uganda border, the senior elder stood up at the farewell dinner and, looking straight at me, said, "I forgive you of all the sins you have committed against us while you have been with us." Then he added, "And we trust you will, in the same way, forgive us." Once I got over the shock of wondering what terrible things I had done, I realized this was a gracious ministry: I was forgiven and free to leave; they were forgiven and free to let me go. Farewells should mostly be occasions for grace, not judgment, though we do have Jesus telling the itinerant disciples to "shake the dust off your feet" of the homes of those who refuse to take them or the gospel in (Mt 10:14)!

The Grace of Saying Goodby

Tragically, some people use a farewell as a time to get even, to express judgment, to deliver a curse, to lay burdens on people or to put others in a bind. When the leaver does not remain to deal with these or those being left refuse to do the relational work of letting go, there is a relational pollution that can affect generations in a family or church. A pastor, for example, who leaves a church "in a huff" often leaves decades of dis-ease in the church. To avoid dealing with reality, many people simply refrain from saying goodby and sneak away, as Jacob did from Laban. This too leaves hurt in the wake and reveals the state of the leaver's soul.*

Sometimes this grace is not expressed because of personal disorder. We can be addicted to a relationship, a job, a church relationship, a ministry assignment, a college community. Codependence rather than interdependence is one reason for this inability to say goodby. Even in a marriage* couples may not give each other freedom to have appropriate friends other than one's spouse or freedom to travel because they are merged, not married.

When a marriage breaks down and divorce* ensues, there is need for a deep goodby, something that rarely happens; instead most divorcing couples go through a lingering dying-but-never-dead-experience. The strangest marital goodby I have witnessed took place when a couple who had been separated for years had undertaken extensive marriage counseling but were never reconciled. The couple asked my wife and me to celebrate Communion* with them as their final goodby. It was a powerful statement that there was mutual forgiveness and they were still brother and sister in Christ even though they would not be husband and wife. Even under such desperate circumstances, saying farewell can be a means of grace.

Saying goodby calls us to trust God for those we love (or hate) since we cannot control the situation or the people ourselves. Bidding farewell is a profound reminder that we do not ultimately own anything in this life. It is a form of grieving.* As illustrated above, saying goodby invites us to make sure that we have forgiven and are forgiving,* two totally interdependent spiritual movements (Mt 6:12). At the same time it reveals the state of our own soul and invites a deeper journey inward (see Spiritual Disciplines). And if we have failed to say goodby or parted from a loved one with unfinished business and death now prevents our "making things right," we can rest in the grace of Christ to forgive us, to forgive ourselves and to heal even beyond the grave.

See also MEMBERSHIP, CHURCH; FELLOWSHIP; FORGIVENESS; GREETING; LETTER WRITING; MOBILITY.

R. Paul Stevens

FARMING

A biblical approach to farming may be described in three words: justice,* compassion and stewardship.* Justice requires freedom of access to resources in the context of responsibility (Amos 5:24). Compassion is a commitment to sharing and caring for the entire creation* (Ps 145). Justice and compassion together are a guide to ensure that all people are provided for. Stewardship is a recognition that the creation has inherent worth and therefore should be cared for, used responsibly and enhanced for future generations. Farmers employing the above are keepers of creation (Gen 1:28; 2:15). The ancient Scriptures still apply to the modern farmer awash in technological innovation.

Responsible Agriculture
National agricultural policies should reflect the prominence of food production as an essential sustainer of human survival, health* and enjoyment, and in doing so should encourage diverse food production and stewarding of the land.

Land distribution. When the people of Israel entered the Promised Land, God divided it equally among all their families* and required that the land revert to the original owning families every fifty years. The Creator established laws to maintain the egalitarian structure of society and to prevent the concentration of wealth* and power* (Lev 25:23-24). Those principles still hold. The family farm or community farm partnership is the central form of tenure enabling the most stewardly and just care of land and animals. Those doing the work should be actively involved in ownership* and management. Family farming instills in participants a high degree of motivation, initiative and personal responsibility.

Some farms are too big for these principles to apply consistently. Some retired farmers can be heard telling their children they have too much land. In other cases the transfer of ownership to the next generation is impossible because of the price of large farms. Such farms are ripe for takeover by large nonfarm corporations that do not generally come to farming with a compassionate attitude. The prophet Isaiah's words seem to have been written only yesterday: "Woe to you who add house to house and join field to field till no space is left and you live alone in the land" (Is 5:8). Abandoned farmsteads everywhere testify to this desolate picture.

Our nations would be blessed by more people farming. Rural communities* would be revitalized, enhancing family life and small business. More people would be in touch with creation.* Smaller farms can be more efficient in timing and application of operations. They are easier to shelter from eroding elements. Smaller farms also tend to have a mix of enterprises, including livestock, and so contribute naturally to soil fertility. Intensive livestock operations may not be large in acres but raise questions of stress on livestock and of collection and disposal of manure.

But smallness is no guarantee of good stewardship any more than bigness automatically means careless use of the creation. Large farms could bring people back to the land by decreasing mechanization and adding livestock. Rotating a variety of complementing crops and designing systems of farming that prevent soil erosion are also possible on a relatively large scale. Minimum till and no-till practices have been adopted on large farms with benefit to the soil.

Soil and cropping practices. The most valuable agricultural resource is soil. It is finite, fragile, disappearing and therefore in need of legislated protection (DeWitt, pp. 14, 16). Soil stewardship recognizes the inherent worth of creation and its potential for food production. Farmers have a responsibility to use cropping practices that build soil, produce high-quality food and fiber, and pose the least risk to the environment and human health (Jer 2:7; Goering, Norberg-Hodge and Page, pp. 10-22; Fairbairn, pp. 48-72).

To sustain soil fertility the nutrients removed with a crop must be replaced. Manures supply a broad range of nutrients with long-term residual effect. Manufactured or mined fertilizers, if used judiciously, can replace specific known depleted nutrients. Decisions on fertilizer use must take into account not only crop effect, but possible long-term effect on the soil. Blanket or routine fertilizer application is wasteful and can pollute.

Taking advantage of natural pest enemies and preventative measures should be the first line of defense against pests. Pesticides ought to be applied as a last resort and with regard to toxicity warnings. Prolonged use of the same pesticide on any given location will almost certainly develop resistant pest species. Some farmers are successful growing crops by using little or no pesticides.

Debt. The proverb "Neither a borrower nor a lender be" may seem impossible to a farmer. The bigger-is-better idea long promoted by farm suppliers and advisers, including government, is a trap of escalating costs and indebtedness. But where an individual may not survive alone, a community of small landholders working together may thrive. It is important that farmers own co-ops to preserve competition* in farm product supply and farm product sales where large private companies dominate.

Work and Technology*

Farm work is designed to be a joyful, purposeful response to God's call* to keep creation and till the earth (Gen 2:15). Agricultural work is to provide for the needs of food and fiber.

Humanity's God-given resourcefulness has resulted in the development of technology used in work (Ex 35:30-31). The impact of technology on agriculture has been particularly significant. Technology has liberated humanity from some drudgery and, through advances in medicine, transportation and communication, allowed us to appreciate creation more fully. Because of sin, however, technology has often been used to abuse the earth and its people. Many current ecological problems result from the unwise use of technology. To sustain farm production, the farmer must choose methods and applications that will grow useful crops without violating the creation (Brand, p. 136).

Four criteria derived from the Christian faith help us to evaluate and use technology responsibly. First, technology should help to build strong families and communities. Second, technology must affirm the dignity of persons as the image bearers of God and not as mere accessories to machines. Third, as God's stewards, we must use technology to preserve and enhance creation. Finally, we must endeavor to view technological advancements in their proper relation to God, ourselves and the creation. We should not allow them to become objects of worship or to seduce us away from dependence on God.

We must protect the quality and diversity of plant and animal species both inside and outside of agriculture. Natural environments maintain genetic diversity and serve as a source of beauty, inspiration and welfare. In the open environment and in the laboratory, we must preserve genetic continuity of plant and animal varieties. New products from laboratory recombination of genetic material, chemical fabrication and so on ought to pass strict testing and monitoring before they reach the farm. Developing and using technology that nurtures the land, crops, animals, workers and the community at large will be of service to God and of benefit to creation.

Marketing

Scripture is rich in references to the need for justice and compassion as our guideline for the distribution of goods, be they scarce or abundant. Crop failures and hunger grieve God, as scarcities cause human suffering. Yet no one necessarily deserves abundance. Rather, the harvested yield and finished livestock are to be received as blessings from our Creator. Their distribution must be equitable to both producer and consumer.

Within these guidelines producers should have the right to determine systems of marketing. Widespread ownership of farms and food processing and delivery businesses will decentralize power and prevent abuse. Consumers have the right to regular access to food at reasonable prices. Government must safeguard the public interest in the marketplace. Along with farmers and government, consumers have the responsibility to ensure that farmers receive prices enabling them to cover stewardly production costs and receive a responsible standard of living and to encourage maintenance of quality and safety in food processing and distribution.

Beyond the Farm Responsibility

People were created to function in community (1 Cor 12:12-31). The Bible teaches unity in diversity, not rugged individualism. Farmers on relatively small holdings can survive by sharing equipment and labor, building facilities together, pooling other expertise and perhaps setting up a credit pool, especially for new farmers.

In our small world, shrunk by telecommunication and exploitation of fossil fuel, it is increasingly obvious that the responsibilities of farming extend beyond the farm gate. Addressing off-farm as well as on-farm responsibilities requires some organization in the public arena. Christian influence may be possible to some extent in any general farm organization, but it is incumbent on Christian farmers to seek each other out and influence public policy. There is a great need for advocacy on behalf of the creation and for fulfilling the cultural mandate as recorded in Genesis 1:28.

Citizens must encourage and support the government in the proper execution of its task, as well as call it back to that task when it strays. Christians should work for governmental structures that serve biblical principles. Governments must ensure that communities and organizations* have the freedom to fulfill their God-given calling. Justice requires that governments pay special attention to the poor, that is, those persons, communities and countries that are deprived of the food, clothing and shelter needed for a responsible life toward God, others and creation.

Conclusion

The land and all that grows there are the Lord's (Ps 24; 50), and from it the Lord provides, involving the farmer as agent. Christian farmers, in awe of their assignment, must constantly reconform their lives to the truth (2 Chron 7:14). They have a responsibility to fill needs, reduce their burden of debt,* repopulate the countryside, restore the soil, reclaim the land, provide healthy food products for market, cooperate with neighbors* and serve them. It is a privilege to be part of the work of Christ in "making all things new" (Rev 21:5 NRSV).

See also COMMUNITY, RURAL; CREATION; ECOLOGY; SMALL TOWNS; STEWARDSHIP.

References and Resources

W. Berry, *A Continuous Harmony: Essays Cultural and Agricultural* (New York: Harcourt Brace, 1974); W. Berry, *The Gift of Good Land* (San Francisco: North Point Press, 1981); W. Berry, *Home Economics* (San Francisco: North Point Press, 1987); W. Berry, *The Unsettling of America* (San Francisco: Sierra Club, 1977); P. A. Brand, "A Handful of Mud," in *Tending the Garden,* ed. W. Granberg-Michaelson (Grand Rapids: Eerdmans, 1987) 136-50; C. B. DeWitt, *The Environment and the Christian* (Grand Rapids: Baker, 1991); G. L. Fairbairn, *Will the Bounty End?* (Saskatoon, Sask.: Western Producer Prairie Books, 1984); P. Goering, H. Norberg-Hodge and J. Page, *From the Ground Up* (London: Zed, 1993); W. Jackson, *Altars of Unknown Stone: Science and the Earth* (San Francisco: North Point Press, 1987); W. Jackson, *New Roots for Agriculture* (San Francisco: North Point Press, 1985); B. Kneen, *From Land to Mouth* (Toronto: NC Press, 1989); C. P. Lutz, *Farming the Lord's Land* (Minneapolis: Augsburg, 1980); National Research Council, *Alternative Agriculture* (Washington, D.C.: National Academy Press, 1989).

Verne M. Gleddie

FELLOWSHIP

If ever a word has been devalued, that word is *fellowship.* The fellowship hour after church* turns out to be ten minutes' worth of watery coffee, which most members of the congregation have skillfully evaded. "Where do you fellowship?" means "Where do you go for an occasional hour to hear the choir sing and the minister preach?" It all tends to be very superficial. However, it was not always thus in the Christian church, nor is it still in many parts of the Two-Thirds World, particularly in the great continent of Africa, where people would never dream of putting a strict time limit on relationships or settling for anything less than real interaction.

Of course, there were various expressions of fellowship in the ancient world. Athens in the fifth century B.C. with its *polis* and its democracy had almost invented fellowship. But disenchantment set in, as it did with Jewish institutions. The ordinary people were excluded from meaningful relationships and from any exercise of real power.* Therefore, if you were a Jew in the ancient world, you resorted increasingly to one of the *haburoth,* "brotherhoods," where you could enjoy some togetherness. If you were a Gentile, you would turn to one of the trade guilds or a partnership to prepare for your funeral: both were commonplace. Or you might turn to one of the mystery religions, through which you tried to make some sense of your life by participating in secret rituals of death and rebirth.

In one sense, therefore, Christian communities caused no surprise. They were part of a growing movement toward voluntary associations in the ancient world. Often these unofficial associations were called *koinōniai,* "fellowships," and the Romans were tolerant of them. But there was a qualitative difference in the fellowship of the Christians. Here were associations in which aristocrats and slaves, Roman citizens and provincials, Jews and Gentiles, rich and poor, men and women mixed without distinction and on equal terms. Here were societies possessing a quality of care and love* that amazed and attracted those who saw it. That is why, among other reasons, we find not only the New Testament writers but Ignatius, Clement and Tertullian in the second and third centuries laying such store on unity.

Harmony among Christians demonstrated something of the unity-in-diversity of the God they worshiped. Only a church that was manifestly united, where each member was free to share as the Holy Spirit moved him or her, could convince the visiting observer that God was among them. Many were convinced in this way. Tertullian, for example, notes the affection and purity that marked these Christian fellowship groups, fittingly called *brethren* (a nonsexist term in the first century) because of their common relationship to the heavenly Father. Worship,* fellowship and feasting were all carried out under the Father's eye. The lowly, the needy and the sick were shown particular consideration: "One in mind and soul, we do not hesitate to share our earthly goods with one another. All things are common among us except our wives." This very area, Tertullian unkindly pointed out, is where pagans were most willing to share. There was a great deal of love flowing in these Christian meetings, and it was sustained by "the sacred words with which we nourish faith, animate hope, make confidence assured, confirm good habits, and administer rebukes and censures" (Tertullian *Apology* 34).

What was the secret of this remarkable fellowship? There are a number of New Testament words that give us some insight into it— particularly *agapē* (love),

philadelphia (love and care for fellow members of God's family) and *koinōnia* (fellowship). *Koinōnia* basically means "joint participation in" and is not inherently a religious word. Like most important New Testament words it is scandalously and intentionally secular. *Koinōnia* is used of being partners in business (Lk 5:10) or sharing in an enterprise (Phil 4:15), and Paul uses it of his fellow workers (2 Cor 8:23). But, with explosive force, the first and main meaning of fellowship erupts from the pages of the New Testament.

Sharing in God

Fellowship as sharing in God is expressed in a number of ways in the New Testament (Rom 15:27; 1 Cor 1:9; 2 Cor 13:13; Phil 2:1; 1 Jn 1:3). The most breathtaking example is 2 Peter 1:4, where the recipients are saluted as being *koinōnoi,* "participants," in the very nature of God!

This fellowship with Jesus and his heavenly Father, in which the earliest Christians exulted, can be viewed in two ways. Fellowship can mean that we share our lives with Jesus: he is our friend, our brother with whom we can share our feelings and requests at any time of day or night. We can share our ordinary, humdrum lives with the Son of God! But there is a deeper sense in which this *koinōnia* can be construed. We share in his life. We share in his suffering (Phil 3:10; 1 Pet 4:13). We are raised with him (Eph 2:5-6). We will reign with him (2 Tim 2:12) and share his future glory (2 Thess 2:14). Not only does he share in our problems and difficulties, but we have a share even now in his own risen life, with touches of its power and traces of its glory: "When Christ, who is your life, appears, then you also will appear with him in glory" (Col 3:4).

Needless to say, fellowship with God is impaired by human wickedness and failure.* It is spoiled (1 Jn 1:16) but not abrogated. When we are conscious of wrongdoing in our lives, we need to confess it and ask for pardon (1 Jn 1:9; 2:1).

Sharing with Believers
Our fellowship is never from the alone to the Alone. It is jointly held with others, which makes the Christian faith so different from all self-improvement cults and faiths that seek fulfillment or enlightenment "for myself alone." The Christian faith is inescapably corporate (*see* Membership, Church). You cannot have fellowship with the triune God who *is* fellowship without that fellowship spilling over to others in the same family.

Paul referred to sharing with believers as "the right hand of fellowship" (Gal 2:9). He was referring to the reality behind the handshake. From the day of Pentecost onward the believers found themselves plunged into the apostles' fellowship (Acts 2:42). We do not choose our fellowship in the Christian family, for the choice has been made for us. After all, we cannot choose our brothers and sisters!

The Spirit teaches us to cry "Abba, Father," but never in isolation. The one to whom we cry is *our* Father! So fellowship in the New Testament means partnership both with God and with fellow Christians. And that double fellowship is perfectly expressed in the Lord's Supper,* where bread and wine are expressive of our relationship both with Jesus and with our fellow Christians (1 Cor 10:16-17).

Sharing Each Other's Situations
Fellowship also means sharing each other's joys and sorrows. First Corinthians 12:26 shows our intimate interdependence in the Christian body. So just as a family would rejoice when one member succeeds or grieve when one member fails, so it should be in the church.

Fellowship means sharing in each other's financial needs. In the very earli-est days the Jerusalem Christians shared their all (Acts 4:34-35). In Antioch the Christians showed their concern for the impending need of their brothers and sisters in Jerusalem (Acts 11:27-30). Gentile churches wanted to make a collection for the Jewish Christians through whom the Gentiles had learned the gospel (Rom 15:26). In all these instances the word used is *koinōnoi.* Its meaning of "fellowship" extended far beyond sympathy: it meant "sacrificial giving" (see also Rom 12:13; Gal 6:6; Phil 4:15). Christians did not see this as some unwelcome tax: they longed to give and to have a share in this sort of fellowship, even though it was beyond their means (2 Cor 8:4; compare 2 Cor 9:13). Christians gave to impoverished brothers and sisters out of obedience to the gospel: the recipients longed for them and prayed for them because of God's abundant generosity received through them. Thus joy and partnership abound, and it all springs from God's inexpressible generosity to them all (2 Cor 9:15).

Fellowship also means sharing in suffering and the consolation God gives. Suffering is an inescapable part of being human, and Christians are invited to be willing for a costly sharing. Paul suffered greatly. He expects his converts to suffer too. But just as he has known the comfort of Jesus, aided by their prayers (2 Cor 1:5, 7), Paul anticipates the same consolation for them. Peter gives us the same juxtaposition of suffering now and glory later (1 Pet 1:5). So too the author of Hebrews: "We shall sometimes be publicly exposed to abuse and affliction, and sometimes be *koinōnoi* with those so treated" (Heb 10:33, author trans. here and in Scriptures quoted below). But the writer urges them not to throw away their confidence, which awaits a great reward. After all, they follow a crucified yet risen Lord. Their destiny, in both respects, is to share in his.

Fellowship means sharing in an exclusive commitment, which sits ill with the happy-go-lucky Western world that is so prone to wanting to have its cake and eat it. But in Christianity is a black-and-white aspect that simply cannot be reduced to various shades of gray. The much misquoted 2 Corinthians 6:14-15 is stringent in this requirement: "Do not be mismated with unbelievers . . . what fellowship has light with darkness? . . . What has a believer in common with an unbeliever?" Paul is intransigent on the need to safeguard Christian purity and distinctiveness of life. So firm was he that he laid himself open to misinterpretation, as if he had been urging his followers to come out of the world altogether. He had to correct this impression: "But rather I wrote to you not to associate with anyone who bears the name of brother if he is guilty of immorality or greed, or is an idolater, reviler, drunkard or robber—not even to eat with such a one" (1 Cor 5:9-11; *see* Church Discipline).

Within the exclusive commitment of the church, fellowship means deep loving care for our brothers and sisters. *Philadelphia* (family affection) is second only to *agapē* (the undifferentiating, God-given love for all and sundry) in the ladder of virtues in 2 Peter 1:7. The difference between the two is simply this: *philadelphia* is the heaven-sent family love for other members of the family, while *agapē* is the outworking of God's unconditional love for the unlovely. Love like this is beautiful when it marks the life of any church. It is chilling when it is absent. This attractive mutual love, springing from the heart, is the fruit of reconciliation with the heavenly Lover (Rom 12:10; 1 Pet 1:22). New Testament writers take it almost for granted: it is, after all, taught and inspired by God himself (1 Thess 4:9). They are just concerned that it be constantly lived out in consistent Christian attitudes: "Let mutual love continue" (Heb 13:1 NRSV).

Sharing God's Work

Koinōnia is heavily tinged in the New Testament with the meaning of "joint partnership in the work of the Lord" (for example, 2 Cor 8:23; Phil 1:5; Heb 10:33). Paul's closest friends were those who shared the work with him, people like Titus, "my partner and fellow worker in your service" (2 Cor 8:23), and Aquila and Priscilla. There is a profound spiritual truth that deep fellowship is almost a byproduct of service.* Thus, fellowship is forged and bonded, not by studying it and discussing it, but by joining together in service for God.

Many churches are flaccid because their members want the joy of fellowship without the sweat of service. It is not to be had. For fellowship means sharing in the work of God and, in particular, evangelism.* Paul speaks very clearly about this in disclosing the flexibility and consistency, the courage and imagination,* the motivation and persistence with which he spreads the good news of Jesus to Jew and Gentile alike: "I have become all things to all men, that I might by all means save some. I do it all for the sake of the gospel, that I may share in its blessings" (1 Cor 9:22-23). Note *koinōnia*, "share," in the last verse. You really begin to taste the blessings of the gospel only when you set out to give it away.

Fellowship in the church of Jesus Christ is a many-splendored thing. It means sharing in the life of God. It means sharing with other believers. It means experiencing a wide range of the situations of other Christians. It means sharing in God's work.

Perhaps the best way of experiencing these four main aspects of Christian fellowship is in the house church* or small group* in the church. There the horizontal and the vertical axes of fellowship intersect. We have fellowship with the

407

Lord and with each other.

See also CHURCH; COMMUNITY; LOVE; MEMBERSHIP, CHURCH.

References and Resources
R. Banks, *Paul's Idea of Community: The Earliest Churches in Their Cultural Setting* (Peabody, Mass.: Hendrickson, 1994); A. R. George, *Communion with God in the New Testament* (London: Epworth, 1953); M. Green and R. P. Stevens, *New Testament Spirituality* (Guildford, U.K.: Eagle, 1994; portions of chapter 5 used with permission); E. Judge, *The Social Pattern of the Christian Groups in the First Century* (London: Tyndale, 1960); D. Prior, *Parish Renewal at the Grass Roots* (Grand Rapids: Asbury Press, 1987); E. Trueblood, *The Incendiary Fellowship* (New York: Harper & Row, 1969).

Michael Green

FEMININITY

Femininity has diverse meanings to women as well as men, depending on cultural, economic, political and religious factors. Western cultural notions of femininity have focused on outer body* image, femininity being something that one can even acquire through using various products. Even Scripture does not give a universal definition of femininity and masculinity, concentrating as it does on what it means to be a godly woman or a godly man. The biblical text does, however, give a clear and consistent picture of the notion of the feminine, particularly in relation to the intimate love of God. So this article will focus on the metaphorical language of feminine bodily imagery in the biblical text and its relevance in shaping our knowledge and experience of God. In Scripture God has feminine as well as masculine attributes. As God-imaging creatures, intricately woven by an incredible Creator, we have both masculine and feminine aspects within us, though as gendered human beings we respond differently to the movement of the Spirit in our lives. This biblical invitation to experience full personhood, female and male, in relation to God stands in stark contrast to the stereotypes of popular culture.

Cultural Notions of Femininity

Delicate features, soft voices, quiet hearts, slender bodies, smooth legs, demure tone, and light, frilly clothing are only a few of the characteristics that have been associated with the concept of femininity. Standard in many cultures is the emphasis on outer bodily qualities as the substantive foundation for femininity. This has been critiqued within academic, popular, secular and sacred circles. The heart of the criticism is the linking of the concept of femininity with a beau-ty image, a connection to which few whole-heartedly subscribe. This secular critique is congruent with the biblical notion that femininity is not an outward but an inward phenomenon—a state of being more than a state of doing.

Unfortunately femininity has been used to sell cars, toilet bowl cleaners and makeup and has been used to the detriment of women. Public discourse on this matter has revolved around the formation of femininity from patriarchal beauty norms rather than from values originating in women themselves. One scholar writes, "Patriarchal beauty norms, past and present, have been revealed as a carefully constructed narrative that creates artificial and hierarchical restrictions on the feminine appearance and other aspects of identity" (Callaghan, p. xiv). The feminine body image becomes a standardized size or shape, and women, not cherishing their whole body-soul, are relegated to lives of dieting, discouragement and eating disorders. One writer has compared the beauty myth to a religion: "The magazines transmit the beauty myth as the gospel of a new religion" (Wolf, p. 200). Beauty is obviously desirable but comes in many forms. It is a tragedy that a specific cultural definition of beauty has become the primary focus for definitions of femininity. Not surprisingly, there is a crisis in what it means to be feminine in this day and age.

Biblical Notion of the Feminine

There is no escaping the impact of what the media have fabricated and marketed as femininity. An unintended consequence of this is that "the cultural image of women, the public image, is distorted by patriarchy. We are more than victim or sexual plaything, and it is out of that 'more than' that we search for the face of God" (Proctor-Smith, p. 16). This search for a divine perspective on femininity and masculinity focuses more on who God is than who we are as feminine or masculine. To say that we are made in the image of God, male and female (Gen 1:27), is not to say God is like us; rather we are like God in ways we will now explore.

As mentioned before, there are many images and models in Scripture of what it means to be a godly woman or a godly man, but fewer statements about what it means to be feminine or masculine. For example, the woman of Proverbs 31 is both strong and gentle, wise and vigorous, compassionate and resourceful, creative and businesslike. Deborah, a vigorous woman leader in the book of Judges, exemplifies remarkable leadership skills. These godly qualities are visible in both men and women, and it is difficult to categorize them as only feminine or masculine. One thought worth exploring is that living fully in the image of God is living fully as feminine and masculine.

In stark contrast to equating femininity with bodily image, the biblical text gives a notion of the feminine that includes the body as a metaphor of God's love. Fundamental to this is the scriptural witness that God has masculine and feminine attributes. To say that God is a man or a woman is ultimately heretical. God is neither, but beyond all of our conceptions and categories of gender. The deepest understanding we can have of God is as the Trinity, a communion of love. Jesus is obviously male, yet both Jesus and God the Creator have feminine attributes. For example, Jesus refers to himself as a mother hen (Mt 23:37), and God is referred to as one giving birth (Is 42:13-14; 46:3), a midwife (Ps 22:9-10; Is 66:9-13) and an eagle in whom we take refuge (Deut 32:11-12; Ps 57:1).

Jesus includes both masculine and feminine examples when he teaches in parables, challenging the assumption of the male-centered world of New Testament times. When Jesus includes women in his parables, he reveals a down-to-earth God working through everyday life. The parables of the yeast (Lk 13:20), the woman and the lost coin (Lk 15:8-10) and the persistent widow (Lk 18: 1-8) speak of the mystery of God's breaking through the most ordinary moments of human life. Furthermore, the Hebrew word for *wisdom* is grammatically feminine. In the book of Proverbs *wisdom* expresses a feminine image of God, present from the creation and to be cherished now (Prov 8:11, 22-31). These verses are samples of many biblical passages that express the feminine and deserve our attention if we want to fully comprehend the nature of God.

Considering these aspects of femininity and masculinity gives us a clue to the relational aspect of living. This is summed up well by sociologist Annelies Knoppers in her work on gender relations when she says, "Femininity and masculinity are not aspects of femaleness and maleness existing independently of each other as static entities. Femininity and masculinity are constructed and reconstructed in a relational manner" (quoted in Van Leeuwen, p. 257). Texts in the Scriptures attributing feminine qualities to God show how God has an intimate, relational life with us. These metaphors, or word pictures, give visual and symbolical ways to grasp the text and invite the readers to experience the wide love of God bursting through their whole beings.

The cultural emphasis on the outward body as defining of femininity contributes to a dualistic understanding: body separated from heart, soul and mind. In contrast the biblical notion of the body affirms and even celebrates the person as an interconnected whole. The feminine bodily imagery embedded throughout the biblical text illuminates an image of God as identifying with the bodiliness of a woman and communicating love through bodily metaphors. This is in opposition to historical formulations of a woman's body or bodily functions as associated with sin and evil or, as articulated by Aquinas, the idea that "women are misbegotten males" (quoted in Clanton, p. 39).

Living Inside the Feminine Metaphors for God

As I reflect on the numerous metaphors of the feminine for God, I can personally share my own phenomenological understanding of them as a woman, particular to my experience. This does not mean that every woman may or should experience the bodily metaphors in the biblical text in this specific way, but I believe one person's lived experience can flesh out the universal experience more concretely. For women, our bodiliness is central to our being. We cannot escape the cycles of being women, whether we give birth or not. We are keenly aware of the cycles of menstruation,* hormonal fluxes, premenopause and menopause.* Change, birth,* death* and letting go are built into our bodies as females. This

pull to our bodies is one that organically gives us a *cyclical* understanding of the world rather than only a *linear* one. This, in turn, will affect a woman's perspective and the way she articulates the spiritual life, theology and ministry (see Carr; Fischer).

It is in bodily imagery that the feminine attributes of God are primarily visible in the biblical text. These bodily images do not focus exclusively on the mothering or nurturing qualities of God but impart a wider understanding of the spiritual life: intimacy with God, rhythms of life, waiting,* suffering, joy, receptivity and responsiveness. One of the words in the Old Testament used to convey God's immeasurable mercy and compassion for the Israelites has the same root that is used for womb: *raham*. This word conveys a deep love, akin to the natural bond of a child in the womb: "As a father [or mother] has compassion *[raham] on his [her] children, so the* LORD has compassion on those who fear him" (Ps 103:13). Womb love is God's love—a love that no force can break or alter, a strong, deep love that is woven with the threads of grace and mercy. This is echoed by the prophet Jeremiah when God says, "Before I formed you in the womb I knew you" (Jer 1:5). God knows us like that, providing womb love from a gentle and strong Creator. When we experience God's love for us as womb love, we profoundly enter the compassion of God and truly experience the scope of *raham*.

Another feminine metaphor in the biblical text that models for us something about the intimate relationship between God and ourselves is that of breast-feeding. The Old Testament exhorts the people to "nurse and be satisfied at her [Jerusalem's] comforting breasts" and to "drink deeply and delight in her overflowing abundance" (Is 66:11). Literally, the Hebrew expresses the passage with a more accurate reading: "For you will *suck* and be satisfied." As I breast-fed my children, I began to see the heart of God in this physical act of intimacy—flesh to flesh, skin to skin. Pondering this metaphor gives a glimpse of a God who is tenderly compassionate, intimately involved with life: breast-feeding at the heart of God. As I watched my babies sucking and delighting in being fed at my breasts, I was drawn to my Maker's presence in much the same way. This image meets me at my deepest point—a vulnerable one—and I am wooed to nurse at the breast of God's consolations.

Another potent feminine image in the biblical text is the eagle. The beautiful words in the Song of Moses remind us of this image combining strength and gentleness: "As an eagle stirs up its nest, and hovers over its young; as it spreads its wings, takes them up, and bears them aloft on its pinions" (Deut 32:11-12 NRSV). Bald eagles often soar the Pacific coastal skies of Canada and pull one into glory to see their grace and might. The image of the strong eagle soaring across the weather-beaten sky, protecting and nurturing her young, is liberating. As women, we need images of the feminine that also include strength. Through this image men and women can be strengthened by God's love as they both take refuge in God's wings and mount up with eagle's wings (Is 40:31).

While most of the passages I have cited relate to motherhood, femininity in the Bible is not limited to this. What these passages provide is an alternative concept of the feminine body to the one provided by the mass media.* The biblical text redefines the body as something wholesome and good that is even likened to the fierce love of God. God is One who suffers, gives birth, creates and continues to love us into existence and relationship. One learns more about who God *is* than what God *does* through the feminine di-

mension. This complements the masculine imagery of God, which focuses more on God's action in history. So through the feminine dimension of God, we are wooed back to the womb of God, to become God's beloved daughters and sons.

See also BODY; SEXUALITY.

References and Resources
K. A. Callaghan, ed., *Ideals of Feminine Beauty: Philosophical, Social and Cultural Dimensions* (Westport, Conn.: Greenwood, 1994); A. E. Carr, *Transforming Grace: Christian Tradition and Women's Experience* (San Francisco: Harper & Row, 1990); J. A. Clanton, *In Whose Image: God and Gender* (New York: Crossroad, 1990); K. Fischer, *Women at the Well: Feminist Perspectives on Spiritual Direction* (New York: Paulist, 1988); M. Proctor-Smith, "Out of the Silences: Feminist Resources for Knowing God," *Perspectives* 8, no. 3 (1993) 15-17; C. S. Schroeder, *In the Womb of God: Creative Nurturing for Your Soul* (Liguori, Mo.: Triumph/Liguori, 1995; portions quoted with permission); M. S. Van Leeuwen, ed., *After Eden: Facing the Challenge of Gender Reconciliation* (Grand Rapids: Eerdmans, 1993); N. Wolf, *The Beauty Myth: How Images of Beauty Are Used Against Women* (New York: Anchor/Doubleday, 1991).

Celeste Schroeder

FENCES

The word *fence* conjures up both negative and positive reactions. A popular song of the past that echoes a common turn of phrase, "Don't Fence Me In," reveals our preference for having plenty of space around us. We do not like to be hemmed in by restrictive boundaries. Though both the phrase and the song had their origins in life on the range in the American West, the sentiments they contain are shared by the majority of people in newer Western societies. Are fences a prerequisite for being good neighbors,* or do they destroy community?*

On the positive side, fences became necessary to protect animals and crops, even in the American West. People who live in towns* or cities* usually want to erect fences around their properties. There are interesting national differences here. For example, in the United States fences tend to be lower than elsewhere and are generally set up around the line of the house and back of the property, not along the sides of the front yard or between it and the street. This approach is now being imitated more frequently elsewhere.

All kinds of practical reasons are given for having fences. First, they keep children and pets within bounds. True, but if we had a more communal way of life, others could also keep an eye on children and animals. Second, fences also help prevent the wrong kind of intrusions upon our living arrangements by nosy neighbors. This is also understandable, but both intrusions and nosy neighbors might be partially handled in other ways, such as the design of the house. Third, fences enable us to develop our own particular landscape and gardens. Yes, but this can largely be done through the proper siting of trees, shrubs, beds and so on.

Often it is not the fact of a fence that is problematic; it is its size and extent. The basic difficulty is that our attitude toward fences betrays an inherent ambivalence. As much as the song mentioned above captures our desire for freedom,* our properties express our desire for privacy.* These apparently contradictory tendencies have a common root, namely, our desire for independence. We want to be free to go wherever we want and free from the demands of others. In the United States, at least, settling for fences around the back parts of people's homes may be a way of saying to others, "You can have some access to the public part of me, the part that I present to the world, but not to the private part of me hidden from sight." In other words, it is a sign of both openness and resistance to community.

The front yard is a form of transitional or semicommunal space: others are free to enter it, but there is no guarantee they will be welcomed into the private space of the house or at its rear. When a front yard is completely fenced off, the owners are sending a clear signal that this property has nothing to do with the wider community. If fences on any part of the property are too high for casual conversation,* the owners are indicating that they do not want much contact with neighbors. Some have experienced what happens when a fence between neighbors has to be torn down and replaced: for a time contact increases and a sense of community builds, but this ends abruptly the moment the new fence is up.

With respect to fences there are three main options before us. One is to look for properties that put them in their proper place, serving necessary physical functions without curtailing significant social ones. Another is to reduce the height and extent of fences on our existing property. A third is to go into a cooperative housing complex where there are open grounds between residences that can be used by all those who live around them and lend themselves to regular communal gatherings.

See also COMMUNITY; HOME; NEIGHBORHOOD.

References and Resources

J. Solomon, *The Signs of Our Time: Semiotics— The Hidden Messages of Environments, Objects and Cultural Images* (Los Angeles: Tarcher, 1988).

Robert Banks

FESTIVALS— CHRISTMAS

About two thousand years ago God gave his one and only son, Jesus, to the world.

He chose a young woman named Mary to bear this unblemished male child: "And she gave birth to a son" (Lk 2:6 NEB). The Redeemer was presented in the humble setting of a shepherd's cave and was laid in a manger, where animals went to be fed. It was the perfect place for the Savior to appear.

Everyone loves a new baby. This infant was no exception. With relatives in town for the census, many from the village of Bethlehem would have gone to see Jesus, but the Bible, for a significant purpose, mentions only two groups of visitors: humble shepherds and foreign kings. The prophecies concerning the Messiah focused on his dual mission, redeeming us from our sin and returning to reign in glory.

From the very moment Adam and Eve stepped out of perfection and walked into the darkness of the world, they needed to be redeemed. Israel lived with God's promise that he would send a savior. The period of waiting must have seemed endless. People of faith continued to assure the Israelites that one day the Messiah would come. Certainly there was enough evidence that God always keeps a promise!*

Advent

The word *Advent* is derived from a Latin root meaning "to come." Early Christian leaders recognized the need to set apart a special time to remember those long years of waiting and to provide time for people to prepare spiritually for the coming of Christmas. They acknowledged that getting ready for Jesus' coming has more than one meaning. Not only is it an annual celebration of an event that took place many years ago; it is a celebration of his coming to us each day as well as each year during the holy season. It is also a time to remember Jesus' promise to come again. True preparation for the coming of Christmas includes all of these elements.

The celebration is to begin on the fourth Sunday prior to Christmas Day, allowing four weeks for spiritual preparation. This decision was in keeping with Old Testament festivals, which often included a number of days of preparation prior to the holy day. In the tenth century the beginning of the Christian year was advanced to the first Sunday in Advent.

The Festival of Christmas

No one knows the exact day when Jesus was born. December 25, the date assigned to remember the birth, was introduced to counter the pagan feast of the sun god—the popular winter solstice festival held in Rome—the birthday of the Invincible Sun. This was a significant celebration in the cult of Mithras, the Persian god of light who was often identified with the sun. Long before the birth of Christ ancient people living in the Northern Hemisphere, observing the disappearance of the sun, expressed their fears in annual superstitious rituals.

The Christian celebration was intended to be a theological corrective. The season was chosen to recognize and proclaim that Christ was born into a dark world and that he is the true source of light. Christians wanted to mark the birth of the Son of God, who is the Light of the World, at a time when others were celebrating the mystery of the physical light coming back into the dark sky. The observance was intended to draw people away from superstition and myth and to help them focus on the deeper truth.

The theological corrective and observance of the birth of Jesus did not happen immediately after his life and death. For three hundred years after the ascension of Jesus to heaven, people remembered his death and resurrection. It was not until the early part of the fourth century that Christians felt a need to honor the birth of the Savior. In keeping

413

with Old Testament feasts and festivals, it was designated a feast day, called the Feast of the Nativity. The celebration featured a special mass in honor of the remembrance of his coming. It was thus called *Christ's Mass* and became known later as simply *Christmas*. This in itself is significant, for it was Christ who was being celebrated, not Christmas.

The Twelve Days of Christmas

Who celebrates a birth before the child arrives? What family stops celebrating the day after the birth? In the sixth century Christian leaders declared Christmas a twelve-day festival. December 25 to January 5 were designated feast days to remember the birth of Immanuel, which means "God is with us." The incarnation, God's becoming human in order to be at one with us, is a worthy reason to continue the celebration beyond December 25.

Epiphany

The focus of Christmas is on Jesus, the Lamb of God. Epiphany celebrates Christ the King! The word *Epiphany* comes from the Greek and means "appearance," "manifestation" or "showing forth." Epiphany, January 6, remembers the arrival of the kings who journeyed a long distance, guided by a special star, to honor the birth of the Christ Child. They said, "For we saw His star in the east, and have come to worship Him" (Mt 2:2 NASB). The adoration of the Magi represents the manifestation of Christ's glory to the Gentiles. The wise men clearly recognized who he was and worshiped him.

Celebrating Christmas

If you had never practiced any tradition in relation to Christmas, how might you celebrate the good news of the birth of the Savior? What might you do to show your appreciation for God's gift? An old Hebrew proverb is helpful as you con-

template your answer: "Put something where you can see it so your eye will remind your heart." The Christmas season is filled with myriad visual opportunities. Carefully choose the images you want your heart to remember.

See also FESTIVALS—EASTER; FESTIVALS—THANKSGIVING.

References and Resources

G. M. Nelson, *To Dance with God* (New York: Paulist, 1986) 59-126; R. E. Webber, ed., *The Services of the Christian Year,* vol. 5 of *The Complete Library of Christian Worship* (Nashville: Star Song, 1994) 157-222; M. Zimmerman, *Celebrating the Christian Year* (Minneapolis: Bethany House, 1993) 19-91.

Martha Zimmerman

FESTIVALS—EASTER

"The fact is that Christ did actually rise from the dead" (1 Cor 15:20 LB). Thanks be to God! What is Easter? Where did we get the Easter Bunny? What is Lent? The resurrection has been the central celebration of the church* from its beginning. For centuries people have gathered annually on hilltops, beaches and open meadows to greet the rising sun, a visual reminder of the risen Son of God. Easter is observed during the season of the Jewish Passover, within which Christ was crucified and rose again. Resurrection Day is the first Sunday following the first full moon on or after the first day of spring. If the full moon is on a Sunday, Resurrection Day is celebrated the following week.

History

The original Christian celebration was called *Pesach,* a name borrowed from the Hebrew word for "the Passover." For the first three centuries Christian believers reserved only one or two days for prayer in preparation for the celebration. The festival was not idolatrous, it was not called *Easter,* and it was not preceded by Lent.

The origin of Easter is found in Chaldean paganism. Astarte, or Ishtar, was a Babylonian goddess dedicated to a cult of fertility. The cult spread to Europe and was adopted by Teutonic people, who called this fertility goddess *Eostre* or *Oster*. Many pagan religions adored this consort of the god Baal, worshiping her with religious ceremonies. The festival was celebrated on the spring equinox with rabbits and brightly colored eggs. In ancient Egypt the rabbit was a popular fertility symbol because of its incredible reproductive record and was the obvious choice for a fertility festival.

The period for this pagan worship was called *Easter Month*. *Lent* comes from the word *Lencten,* which means "spring" and marks the lengthening of days in the spring. This was the dominant celebration devoted to the pagan worship of Astarte, or Eostre, and was marked by forty days of abstinence.

Christian leaders tried to change the emphasis by blending biblical themes with existing pagan practices. They established a forty-day fast to remember the forty days Jesus spent in the wilderness preparing for his earthly ministry (Mt 4:1-11) and the forty days Moses spent on Mount Sinai preparing to receive the Ten Commandments (Ex 34:28). The forty days of the pagan lent were stretched to forty-six days in the Christian calendar, with Sundays thus reserved for weekly celebrations of the resurrection.

Astarte worship was not easily suppressed by the new Christian Lent. A further attempt by church leaders in the sixth century to require the observance of the Christian season was met with resistance, violence and bloodshed. To secure the peace, a compromise transformed Pesach into Easter and gave the Chaldean goddess her subtle place in current cultural practices.

Shrove Tuesday

"Then I confessed my sins to you; . . . and you forgave all my sins" (Ps 32:5 TEV). The word *shrove,* or *shriving,* means "confession." Shrove, or Confession, Tuesday is the day before Ash Wednesday and the beginning of Lent. It was intended to be a time of relaxation in preparation for the long period of self-discipline, self-denial and self-sacrifice. Beginning in the fourth century Shrovetide turned into revelry and rioting; we know it better as Mardi Gras.

Lent required strict fasting, which meant indulgent foods such as eggs, butter and milk were not allowed. Pancakes became the main item on the menu because they used up those ingredients before the beginning of the fast. Here is a practical idea: Enjoy a pancake supper. Talk about the need for confession and consider fasting.

Ash Wednesday

"I turned to the Lord God and pleaded with him in prayer and petition, in fasting, and in sackcloth and ashes" (Dan 9:3).

Ash Wednesday opens the door to the season of Lent. Ashes symbolize humility and are a visual reminder of the vast difference between creatures and their Creator. They are a sign of sorrow and genuine regret. Historically the ashes used in Ash Wednesday ceremonies symbolize the need for repentance and a change of heart. The focus is on preparing oneself for the celebration of the resurrection. This is a time to repent and to prepare as a forgiven sinner to be received by the Lord. The words of the traditional liturgy warn: "Remember, O man, that you are dust. . . . Repent and believe the Good News." In Matthew 11:21 Jesus denounced the cities where many of his miracles had been performed because they did not repent "in sackcloth and ashes."

Here are some ways to celebrate Lent. (1) Begin by attending a worship service on Ash Wednesday. (2) For the next six and one-half weeks prepare for Resurrection Day. The extent to which it is effective in your life will depend on you. Jesus taught in Matthew 6 that we should fast, pray and give. Consider these important disciplines. (3) Lent provides a fresh opportunity for personal renewal. Think of ways to honor the Lord with your praise during these truly significant days. (4) Traditionally, ashes are made by burning palm branches used in the previous year's Palm Sunday celebration. If you do not participate in a congregation with this observance, consider writing the sins you wish to confess on a piece of paper. Gather and burn the papers with God's words of assurance that he "blots out your transgressions" and "remembers your sins no more" (Is 43:25).

Palm Sunday

"Blessed is He who comes in the name of the Lord; Hosanna in the highest!" (Mt 21:9 NASB). From the time of the giving of the law, sacrifice was ordained by God (Lev 1—7). Sin must be covered in order for us to be in the presence of a holy God.

The entry of Jesus into Jerusalem was the official presentation to Israel of the Messiah as King. The crowd was excited: shouting, waving palm branches and rejoicing. At last, the "Coming One" had arrived to deliver them. No one paid attention to the shepherds leading the sheep from Bethlehem into the city. It was the tenth day of the Hebrew month, Nisan, and they were "each one to take a lamb for themselves . . . an unblemished male" (Ex 12:3, 5 NASB). As the Lamb entered Jerusalem, the "Home of Israel," the paschal lambs were being led into the city in preparation for the Passover. Everyone knew that the way to be redeemed was to sacrifice a lamb, but they had forgotten.

Try this: Prop a little stuffed lamb on a bed of palm fronds in the center of the table where you eat. Read Exodus 12:1-6, John 1:29 and Matthew 21:1-10. Let these objects and texts help you remember the events as you prepare your heart for Good Friday.

Maundy Thursday/Passover

"A new command I give you: Love one another" (Jn 13:34). The name *Maundy* comes from the Latin words "it is commanded." This is in remembrance of the new commandment given by Jesus as he was celebrating his last Passover with the disciples. Here are some ways to celebrate Maundy Thursday: Celebrate the Passover Seder and Last Supper in your home with your family, or share cooking responsibilities with several families, a small group* or a house church. For a Christian Seder, recipes and instructions, see *Celebrate the Feasts* (Zimmerman). Then attend a Maundy Thursday service.

Good Friday

"Behold, the Lamb of God who takes away the sin of the world!" (Jn 1:29 NASB). Traditionally, Friday was the day of preparation for the sabbath. Clearly Jesus' death on the cross on this Friday prepared everything for us to be able to enjoy a permanent sabbath rest.* The day is called good because of the great benefit provided as a result of what took place.

Jesus died as the Passover Lamb, a picture from Exodus of God's rescuing the people from *physical* slavery in Egypt. The cross became the place of our deliverance, thus providing *spiritual* freedom. Jesus died wearing a crown. The sign over his head declared him to be King of the Jews.

Before celebrating Jesus' resurrection, remember his death: (1) On Friday morning cover the lights with pieces of black cloth. Be reminded that the "Light of the World" went out for three days. (2) Cover your dinner table with a black cloth. Along with the cutlery, set a nail at each place to remind everyone of personal responsibility in the crucifixion. Gather the family for breakfast. Read John 19:17-30 and Psalm 22. Pretend you are there. Share your feelings. (3) Attend a Good Friday service.

Holy Saturday

Leave everything in black. This is a quiet day of waiting. Read Matthew 27:62-66.

Resurrection Day

Mary announced, "I have seen the Lord!" (Jn 20:18 LB). Celebrate in some of the following ways: (1) Wake up early. With the words "Hallelujah, Christ is risen!" wake up each family member. (2) Spread your dinner table with a white cloth. Decorate with fresh flowers and lilies. Light white candles in safe places. All are reminders that Jesus is alive. (3) Go outside to a hill, mountain, river or park. Find a sunrise service or plan one yourself. Watch the sunrise and be reminded of God's Son; let him come alive in your heart. Read John 20:1-18 and Hebrews 11:25-26. Gather with family and friends, a small group or house-church group for breakfast. (4) Go to the church of your choice. Worship the risen Lord with joy!

See also FESTIVALS—CHRISTMAS; FESTIVALS—THANKSGIVING.

References and Resources

R. Foster, *Celebration of Discipline* (San Francisco: Harper & Row, 1978); R. E. Webber, ed., *The Services of the Christian Year,* vol. 5 of *The Complete Library of Christian Worship* (Nashville: Star Song, 1994) 373-426; M. Zimmerman, *Celebrate the Feasts* (Minneapolis: Bethany House, 1981); M. Zimmerman, *Celebrating the Christian Year* (Minneapolis: Bethany House, 1993).

Martha Zimmerman

FESTIVALS— THANKSGIVING

"Consider what great things he has done for you" (1 Sam 12:24). There is a remarkable scene near the beginning of the book *Never Cry Wolf.* The author is standing alone in the midst of the Alaskan wilderness as the plane that brought him fades into the distance. Overwhelmed by the rugged beauty, he finds a voice within him struggling to cry out for expression. "I wanted," he says, "I wanted to shout thanks to someone."

History

The first recorded celebration of Thanksgiving in North America was in Newfoundland in 1578. An English minister named Wolfall presided. There are records of another held in Maine in 1607.

In December 1619 thirty-eight men landed safely on the banks of the James River near Jamestown in Virginia. The English captain, John Woodleaf, read a directive from his charter declaring that the day of their arrival "shall be yearly and perpetually kept as a day of thanksgiving to God."

It was the Pilgrims' settlement at Plymouth, Massachusetts, that is most often remembered as the site of the first Thanksgiving. Governor Bradford ordered a three-day celebration in October 1621. In keeping with the biblical instructions in Leviticus 23:39 for the Feast of the Ingathering, its purpose was to give prayerful thanks to God for the blessing of the harvest. The Christian commitment and spiritual motivation of this little group of people are inspiring.

Importance

The desire of an individual to offer thanks to God goes back to the early chapters of Genesis: "Noah found favor in the eyes of the Lord" (Gen 6:8 NASB). And God said, "I will establish My covenant with you" (Gen 6:18 NASB). When Noah left the ark, having been saved by God, he "built an altar to the LORD . . . and offered burnt offerings on the altar. And the LORD smelled the soothing aroma" and promised, "While the earth remains, seedtime and harvest, and cold and heat, and summer and winter, and day and night shall not cease" (Gen 8:20-22 NASB). Noah modeled the importance of saying, "Thank you." And God blessed Noah and said, "Be fruitful and multiply, and fill the earth. . . . Every moving thing that is alive shall be food for you; I give all to you, as I gave the green plant" (Genesis 9:1, 3 NASB).

The experience of corporate thanksgiving finds expression in the annual harvest festival, that is, when Moses directed the people of Israel to observe a full week of thanksgiving after the ingathering of the harvest: "When you have gathered in the crops of the land, you shall celebrate the feast of the LORD for seven days" (Lev 23:39 NASB). David and Solomon continued the tradition, declaring special times of celebration and thanksgiving to God. After years of captivity the great leader Nehemiah called the people together to thank God, thereby reinstituting the instructions from Leviticus regarding the harvest festival. It is recorded that there was great rejoicing (Neh 8:17).

There are at least 140 passages of Scripture that deal with the subject of thanksgiving from a personal or corporate point of view. The word praise is used many more times. Praise means "to appreciate," "prize" and "consider precious and worthy of honor." Thanksgiving is a combination of words joined to express thanks to God. It is gratefulness followed by expressions of that gratitude. By far the most familiar passages of praise are found in the Psalms: "With my mouth I will give thanks abundantly to the LORD" (Ps 109:30 NASB); "Give thanks to the LORD, call on his name; make known among the nations what he has done" (105:1); "Enter his gate with thanksgiving" (100:4).

In the New Testament we read how Jesus constantly gave thanks to the Father and one year risked his life to celebrate the thanksgiving festival. Paul began nearly every one of his letters with an expression of thanks and urged us to give thanks in everything (1 Thess 5:18). In Romans 1:21 he describes those under the judgment of God as people who "though they knew God, they did not honor Him as God, or give thanks" (NASB). The writer of Hebrews in 13:15 tells us to "continually offer to God a sacrifice of praise—the fruit of lips that confess his name."

Celebrating

The Bible tells us to "rejoice always; pray without ceasing; in everything give thanks; for this is God's will for you in Christ Jesus" (1 Thess 5:16-18 NASB). There are many ways to give thanks; a number of ideas follow.

As a Hebrew proverb tells us, "Put something where you can see it so your eye will remind your heart."

Hang a cluster of Indian corn tied with an attractive bow on the front door. Remember the thankful spirit of the Pilgrims at Plymouth.

Lovingly assemble a harvest display with seasonal produce as your centerpiece.

Place a colorful leaf at each person's place at the holiday meal. On each leaf sprinkle several kernels of dried corn. Before the meal is served, take time to remember the hardships of the Pilgrims' first winter in the New World and how with God's help they overcame great difficulties. Take turns expressing your own gratitude for God's mercy.

Encourage children to make lists of

all the things for which they are thankful.

Through a food bank or Christian agency, discover local needs. Decide together how you will help. This is the season to share with others.

The real celebration of Thanksgiving is *thanksliving*. The best way to thank God for the gift of life is to live your life in a spirit of gratitude.

Deuteronomy 8:10 says, "When you have eaten and are satisfied, you shall bless the LORD your God for the good land which He has given you" (NASB). The chapter warns that when everything is going well, there is a tendency for your heart to become proud and thus forget the Lord. Take time to thank God for all of the good gifts that you enjoy. Live out the words of Deuteronomy 8:18, "But you shall remember the LORD your God" (NASB).

See also FESTIVALS—CHRISTMAS; FESTIVALS—EASTER; NATIONALISM.

References and Resources

G. Gaither and S. Dobson, *Let's Make a Memory* (Waco, Tex.: Word, 1983); J. Santino, *All Around the Year: Holidays and Celebrations in American Life* (Urbana: University of Illinois Press, 1994); S. W. Shenk, *Why Not Celebrate!* (Intercourse, Penn.: Good Books, 1987); D. Steindl-Rast, *Gratefulness: The Heart of Prayer* (New York: Paulist, 1984); M. Zimmerman, *Celebrate the Feasts* (Minneapolis: Bethany House, 1981); M. Zimmerman, *Celebrating the Christian Year* (Minneapolis: Bethany House, 1993).

Martha Zimmerman

FINANCIAL SUPPORT

The financial support of missionaries and people in professional Christian service has significant theological and spiritual implications. From the point of view of not-yet Christians, raising money to support Christian workers—sometimes in extravagant lifestyles—smacks of religious hucksterism and may "hin-der the gospel" (1 Cor 9:12). Some of those required by nondenominational* agencies to raise their own support feel they are forced to "sell themselves." On the other hand, Scripture solidly endorses the financial support of some Christian workers to fulfill their particular form of ministry.* The manner in which this is done can be either upbuilding or destructive for the person supported, the people whose support is enlisted and the watching world.

Paul's Teaching and Practice

More than any other part of the New Testament, the letters of Paul deal with financial support. In 1 Corinthians 9 Paul defends the right of apostles like himself (and by implication some other Christian workers) to be financially supported by Christians. His arguments are from the words of the Lord Jesus (1 Cor 9:14), the practice of Jews and Gentiles in supporting people who work in their temples (v. 13), the law (which provides for the ox that is treading out the grain; vv. 8-9) and the everyday principle that people should expect to be supported by their labor (v. 7). But then Paul explains why he refuses to exercise his rights as an apostle and chooses to serve as a tentmaker.* It has to do with two things: the advance of the gospel, which Paul believes is better served by being publicly free of personal greed or obligation to others, and Paul's own spiritual desire to preach the gospel free of charge as a love gift (compare Acts 18:1-3). We should remember that it was in Corinth that Paul had his most difficult time. He was accused and misunderstood because most traveling philosophers received patronage with all its attendant obligations—"he who pays the piper calls the tune." Paul's overall concern is for the gospel. This tentmaking approach, however, was not Paul's universal practice.

Paul did receive financial support

from the Philippian church, which is all the more remarkable because of its extreme poverty (2 Cor 8:2), though he did so reticently, as evidenced by what has been called his "thankless thank you" (Phil 4:14-19). There is no indication that Paul received their gifts while he was actually serving them or that he ever received support from other people while he was among them. In Ephesus Paul ministered for two years (Acts 19) supporting himself by the work* of his hands (20:13-38) in order to "help the weak" (20:35). Paul concluded that it is more "blessed to give [ministry free of charge] than to receive [the gifts of people]" (Acts 20:35). In Thessalonica he also toiled day and night so as not to be a burden (1 Thess 2:9) and as a model to those with poor attitudes toward work (2 Thess 3:8-10). We do not know what Paul did in Galatia, but at Philippi he taught the principle of mutual ministry (Gal 6:6)—which does not necessarily imply financial support, though this principle is mentioned in 1 Timothy 5:17-18.

Supporting Workers Today
What does all this mean for us today? First, we are dealing with grace, not with law. No one should press his or her rights to be supported. In the same way no church should require all of its workers to be tentmakers by refusing to support their elders, who are worth, in Paul's language, a "double honor" (1 Tim 5:17-18; the word used is the one used for the physician's honorarium).

Second, while being supported is an occasional privilege for Christian workers—perhaps one in one hundred—there is no mandate for people to go out seeking their own support; indeed, the spirit of the entire New Testament seems to point in the opposite direction, that is, doing all one can not to be a burden on others. It is the responsibility of the church to discern and call forth people to serve in a supported way. In other words, the call to be supported (unlike the call to ministry) does not come directly from God but comes from the people of God, who graciously free some to serve as supported workers.

Third, while there seems to be little justification for the almost universal practice today in parachurch agencies of sending people out to raise their own support, there is a strong case to be made for people raising the support for others, as Paul did by his teaching and his aggressive fundraising for the poor saints in Jerusalem (1 Cor 16:1-4; 2 Cor 8—9). One constructive approach to the contemporary dilemma is for people being led into a raise-your-own-support enterprise to prayerfully seek the counsel and help of the elders of their church and people known to them over a period of time. If these are unwilling or unable to raise their support for them, there is a clear biblical mandate as to what to do. They are not to send out begging prayer letters or crisscross the country with their hands out; they are to work (1 Thess 4:11-12; 2 Thess 3:6-13).

Fourth, Paul's practice and teaching suggest the need for flexibility from place to place and time to time during one's lifetime. In some situations the advance of the gospel is better served by refusing support and working as tentmakers; in other places it would be better served by being supported. The world will never be reached or fully served if we rely completely on supported Christian workers (*see* Tentmaking). Though it is the almost universal assumption of the seminary system, it is highly questionable whether one should ever make a lifelong career out of supported Christian ministry.

Varieties of Financial Support
While Paul's teaching and practice are central to this matter, the rest of the New

Testament is not silent on it. Indeed there are some seminal teachings and examples that point toward a rich diversity in financial support for our own day if we are willing to break free from the dominant model of the fully supported career worker. In the New Testament there are at least three kinds of support: (1) undertaking traveling expenses (Tit 3:12-14), (2) giving hospitality* (Mt 10:9-10; 3 Jn 6-8) and (3) providing living expenses, rather than a salary for work performed (Rom 16:2; 1 Cor 9; 1 Tim 5:17-18). Were these practiced today, as they occasionally are, there would be very constructive assistance to Christian workers, especially those who travel: providing a room and meals, buying someone's airfare, giving a lump sum for a tentmaking missionary relocating overseas, creating a suite in a home for a youth worker, including a single Christian worker in one's family, providing living expenses for a stated period of time. All these can be done by individuals willing to support others as part of their personal stewardship.* But what about the role of churches?

The New Testament offers several models of the way churches can be involved in giving and receiving support. First, one church can speed a worker on her way to another church by providing the means for making the journey or transition (Rom 15:23-24). Second, a church may support a worker in another church, as the Philippians supported Paul in Corinth and Thessalonica, at least until the church becomes established. Third, workers can be supported by the church they serve, a matter Paul defended but refused to practice himself. Fourth, a ministry team can support one another as Silas and Timothy appear to have supported Paul in Corinth (Acts 18:5) and as women disciples supported Jesus and his male disciples (Lk 8:3).

All of this suggests that the New Testament was much richer than the modern church and parachurch agencies in providing for flexible and appropriate options to support people: full time or part time, short-term or long-term, with pocket money or a full living, with full support or transition help to a tentmaking worker. Some doctors have formed team practices with the understanding that one in four will be released every few months for service in the Third World as a voluntary worker. Some seminary graduates have banded together in ministry teams with three people taking one remunerated position, embracing simple living and taking part-time employment* to assist with living expenses. Churches have been planted successfully by such arrangements. A few churches in the world have very large staffs with a very low budget by including people for periods of time in ministry teams, living together in community or boarded in homes of members, all associated with specific projects and partly as a combination of learning and serving.

The Discipline of Financial Support
Seeking financial support on the part of a Christian worker is also an opportunity for some deep interior work. Do I believe in this ministry sufficiently that I will engage in it by working with my hands or mind even if financial support is not forthcoming? Am I seeking work in the church because I believe deeply that there is nothing else in the world worth doing (a serious misunderstanding of work and ministry)? Am I willing to be accountable both in discerning the Lord's guidance* and in the exercise of ministry, or am I "independently" serving the Lord (a contradiction in terms)? Are there people around me who believe in what God is doing through me enough to raise my support if it is needed? Can I trust God for a living one way or another (either through being supported or in

finding work)?

For the church (or Christian community) there are equally important questions. Will supporting a worker help or hinder the gospel? Is the person to be supported sufficiently mature to qualify as an elder (1 Tim 3:1-13; Tit 1:6-9): well thought of by outsiders, proven family life, able to teach? What is the person's worldview*? Is ministry an escape? Will this person be helped or hindered by being supported? Does she have the maturity to survive the pressures of feeling she has to justify her salary and please the people who support her?

The recovery of integrity in financial support of Christian workers is critical to the advance of the gospel in the post-Christian West. When people are inoculated with mild forms of Christianity and are almost immune to the real thing, only a radical return to New Testament simplicity and authenticity has a chance of gaining a hearing and winning respect. Our situation is not very different from Corinth's, where religious hucksters and patronized teachers abounded. On a worldwide basis, only flexible and imaginative ways of supporting Christian workers can enable us to respond adequately to the challenge of the global mission of the people of God.

See also GIFT-GIVING; LEADERSHIP, CHURCH; MINISTRY; SIMPLER LIFESTYLE; STEWARDSHIP; TENTMAKING.

References and Resources

R. Allen, *Missionary Methods: St. Paul's or Ours?* (Grand Rapids: Eerdmans, 1992); J. M. Bassler, *God and Mammon: Asking for Money in the New Testament* (Nashville: Abingdon, 1991); J. M. Everts, "Financial Support," in *Dictionary of Paul and His Letters*, ed. G. F. Hawthorne, R. Martin and D. G. Reid (Downers Grove, Ill.: InterVarsity Press, 1993) 295-300; G. Georgi, *Remembering the Poor: The History of Paul's Collection for Jerusalem* (Nashville: Abingdon, 1992).

R. Paul Stevens

FIRING

In a culture in which one's identity* is usually defined by what one does, being fired is always a traumatic experience. If I no longer am a chemist, then who am I? If I no longer work for DuPont, then what am I? Losing one's job, for whatever reason, carries with it the stigma of failure.* It is considered one of the major causes of stress* that we humans can experience. Invariably the typical emotions* connected with grief* are experienced—shock, denial, loneliness, depression and, finally, anger.

Unjust and Just Reasons for Firing

The firings that are generally most easily understood by all parties are instances in which an employee knowingly violates the law* or an organization's written policy. Immediate dismissal without due process usually follows theft of the employer's property, physical violence against another employee, arson, the willful destruction of equipment and the operation of dangerous machinery while under the influence of alcohol or other drugs. In most cases where an employee willfully violates those rules established as cause for dismissal, the employee has no one to blame but himself or herself.

Other violations of written company policy may be less obvious, and due process should be granted. Habitual tardiness may be cause for dismissal. But is some consideration given for a public-transportation* system that is unreliable? The harassment of another employee, be it sexual, racial or based on age or some form of disability, is generally considered cause for dismissal. But in cases where harassment is not clearly defined, there must be due process, and the employee should be put on notice regarding any repetition of the wrongful act.

The matter of blame becomes more

cloudy when one is fired for poor performance. It has been said that almost every firing due to poor performance represents a failure of management.* This is certainly true for employees who truly want to do well, and most of us do. Did management fail at the point of hiring? Was the job description accurate? Were the performance standards reasonable? Was there a failure in the interviewing and selection process? Was the employee adequately trained? Were there any impediments to the employee's performance (poor equipment, distractions by others, too hot, too noisy, etc.)? Was good performance rewarded negatively? That is, is the best or fastest employee given the most assignments or asked to complete the work of a slower employee? Was there a periodic performance evaluation that was done honestly and professionally? Was the employee given realistic, measurable and attainable work goals on which to be evaluated? Was coaching provided to correct areas of substandard performance? Was there a system of warnings that alerted the next level of management of performance problems? Failures of any of the above are really failures of management.

In too many organizations supervisors and managers themselves are either poorly trained or incompetent. Time and time again managers and supervisors do not give employees honest evaluations of their completed work. Under such circumstances it should not be surprising that employees are shocked and angry when they are fired. They may not recognize the problem of poor management, but they do sense that something is unfair.

The Sacred Responsibility of Managers
Anyone who manages or supervises another has a sacred responsibility to his or her employees. When one considers the devastating effect firing has on most people, it should be apparent that the position of management carries with it a heavy responsibility. Top management should insist that all levels of supervisors be well trained and highly competent. If one is a manager who works for an organization where a high commitment to management excellence does not exist, each manager has the responsibility to educate oneself in the techniques of quality supervision. Just as we would expect a physician to have the highest professional commitment to the welfare of the patient, so also should we expect the supervisor/manager to have the highest professional commitment to the welfare of the worker.

Every employee is entitled to a periodic one-to-one sit-down evaluation of his or her performance by the immediate supervisor. Absolute honesty is crucial. Some Christians in management feel that they should be kind and forgiving in instances of unsatisfactory performance. They will, therefore, overrate the employee and avoid discussing unpleasant or difficult issues. Such a philosophy cheats an employee out of the help he or she is due and, in the long run, will hurt the employee's career.* Christian managers need to be as perceptive, fair and honest as possible. If an employee is not suited for the job, the sooner he or she learns about it, the sooner a job change can be made. It is unconscionable that some employers continue with poor performers for years and then, when the employees turn fifty, tell them they were unsuited for the work in the first place and must be let go.

A caring manager will give a poor performer an honest appraisal of the future of his or her career and then help the employee to find another position where the potential for success is greater. This process may take as long as a year or so, but it is the most caring way of firing someone. But before concluding that a marginal performer cannot improve, the supervisor/manager should provide personal coaching and additional training. The human-resource professional should be called in to help, and every effort should be made to help the employee succeed. If personal problems at home are involved, there should be a search for supportive resources, and if possible flexible working hours should be arranged. For those who argue that such special attention to marginal performers will cost the company money, there are two things to be said: the cost of hiring and training a replacement (with unknown future performance) costs money also, and an employee whose career has been saved and enhanced by management concern frequently turns out to be a highly productive and loyal employee.

"Innocent" Firings

While the preceding comments relate to employees who may have been fired for willfully disobeying the law or company rules or who have failed to perform up to standards, there are hundreds of thousands of people who have been fired through absolutely no fault of their own. These are the victims of corporate takeovers or of downsizing (or its more sanitized term *rightsizing*). For instance, company A merges with or purchases company B. There is a duplication of some departments (accounting, human resources, etc.), so entire departments in one company are abolished. In another case a company or organization may be losing money. In order to save the company from bankruptcy, and the probable loss of all jobs, it downsizes in one or more ways. Management might close one part of the organization that is a financial drag on the others, thereby leaving all employees in that entire unit without work. The company might dis-

continue certain functions previously carried out by employees (for example, food services, payroll or advertising) and contract out for these services, thus saving the costs of health care, pensions and other benefits. The organization might consolidate functions or locations, thus reducing the number of employees needed, and retain younger employees (at lower employment costs).

While being fired for poor performance should not come as a surprise, losing one's job due to corporate takeovers or downsizing can be unexpected and quite sudden. The general practice seems to be that employees are given virtually no advance notice: "Pack up your belongings and leave—now!" The fear is that if employees are given advance notice, they may destroy company equipment, steal company secrets or take other vindictive steps. The effect of all this on the employees who are fired is devastating. *Why me?* is the first question. It matters not that an employee has been a top-rated, extremely loyal and conscientious worker with a perfect attendance record. If the unit is abolished, the employee is out on the street. And, to top it off, there was no advance notice—even though top management had to know of the action weeks in advance. The final indignity sometimes is the appearance of hired security guards to prevent vengeance. Employees feel utterly betrayed.

Some businesses feel it is more compassionate to take the route of announcing publicly that in the next twelve months or so they will reduce the work force by a specified number. The effect of this procedure is that people wait for the ax to fall. The entire organization is on edge as rumors fly. The dismissals begin. Morale is terrible. Families are consumed by fear. Substance abuse and family violence are not uncommon.

The one redeeming belief in all this is that the downsizing is being done in order to make the organization profitable again and, thus, to save jobs. But what do we say about the profitable company that downsizes with the assertion that these steps are being taken to keep the company profitable? And what do we say about the profitable company that downsizes in order to reduce costs, improve profits and, thus, give its stock a good boost in price? Can workers take some solace in the knowledge that they were fired due to no fault of their own? Not usually. Once again we are back to the identity issue—no job, no identity, regardless of the reason. And whether or not you were responsible, society stigmatizes the unemployed.* The unemployed are failures.

The Effect of Firings

The effect of mass firings is not felt exclusively by those who have lost their jobs. While companies reduce the number of workers, they seldom reduce the amount of work.* Those who survive the firings are frequently burdened with more work. The pressures to perform are enormous. The employer has already demonstrated a propensity to reduce the work force. Who would risk being seen as uncooperative in such an environment? The byproduct of mass firings frequently is a fifty- to sixty-hour work week for those who have escaped. The impact on family life and personal health is great.

Some companies overshoot the mark in their mass firings. It becomes apparent in time that the survivors cannot handle all the work. So are some of the recently laid-off workers called back? Seldom. Instead temporary workers are secured from an agency. The "temps" are never on the corporate payroll and, therefore, do not get a pension, health care and other benefits. There have been instances in which a temp was secured to do the exact work he or she once did as

an employee. The move toward firing more employees and securing temporary workers is growing. It is estimated that by the year 2000 three out of every seven workers will be temps.

Another impact mass firings often have on the survivors is the sense of guilt. They were spared but their friends were fired. Psychologists say it is not unlike the feelings experienced by survivors of a fatal airplane crash or other catastrophe. It is called *survivor sickness*. Overwork, insecurity and sometimes guilt—these are the legacies of mass firings for those who have escaped the ax.

There is yet another group of workers hurt by downsizing: those who do the firing. As indicated earlier, some managers are reluctant to consider firing employees who are not performing well, for it is a painful task. How much more painful it is to fire good, loyal, competent workers whom top management has declared "redundant." Many might be close personal friends. How painful it must be to be told to reduce a department by an arbitrary 20 percent. Which ones go? On what basis do managers decide? How is it all explained to these fine people? For managers who have worked to develop an atmosphere of growth, expansion, hiring and training, the reduction of the work force runs counter to all their instincts. Increasingly, managers are electing to take a walk from their company rather than continue to be a part of a downsizing with which they disagree.

The Church's Response

Firing has become a commonplace event in America, but the shock, anger and pain do not lessen. As long as work and identity are so closely linked, the loss of work will continue to attack people's sense of identity and self-worth. Some Christian churches* have helped their unemployed members by providing support, paying for career counseling, establishing support groups and offering job-search programs. Typically, the job-search programs involve weekly meetings in which the unemployed gather to receive help from professionals in writing résumés, developing networks and having employment interviews.

There is one vital area in which the churches could do a better job: the Christian faith proclaims that a person's work does not define his or her worth in the eyes of God. The grace of God extends to all who live in a relationship with God. If the Christian church could somehow convince all believers that the loss of a job does not diminish one's worth in the eyes of God, perhaps firing could be less traumatic to all those involved. The question is, are the churches even trying?

See also ACCOUNTABILITY, WORKPLACE; INTEGRITY; LOYALTY, WORKPLACE; MANAGEMENT; WORK.

William E. Diehl

FORGIVENESS

Forgiveness is excruciatingly difficult. There are a hundred reasons why one cannot forgive and a thousand easier, more appealing alternatives. Many of these alternatives will accomplish something worthwhile. Some will enable us to forget the pain, others will help us to understand our feelings, and still others will enable us to transfer our hurt or anger onto something or someone else. But none of them will totally heal or restore the broken relationship.

Whether or not such healing or restoration is even necessary has been questioned by some. Why should a Jew forgive a Nazi or a woman her rapist? Do their enemies not deserve to die unforgiven? Would it make any difference to them if forgiveness were offered? Can the value or success of forgiveness be measured?

Are there not some cases where traveling the road of forgiveness simply raises more problems and opens more wounds than if the journey had never begun? Before examining the dynamics of forgiveness, it is important to establish what forgiveness is not.

Some Misconceptions

Understanding. To understand all is not to forgive all. Forgiveness is not dependent on our understanding everything about the person or the situation, nor is greater understanding a guarantee of forgiveness. We are being unrealistic if we expect to understand everything before we forgive. Situations and people are so complex and their depths are so unfathomable that we cannot afford the luxury of waiting until we understand before we forgive. On the other hand, people may understand all about a situation but still remain unforgiving. Greater understanding may facilitate forgiveness and may flow from forgiveness, but forgiveness is not dependent on it.

Forgetting. Similarly, forgiving is not forgetting—for three reasons. First, if hurts can be easily forgotten, no forgiveness is necessary. The hurts in question are no more than mere annoyances, here today, gone tomorrow. Second, forgetting may be no more than avoidance or suppression, a defense mechanism to avoid the demands of real forgiveness. Third, where true forgiveness is needed, and even after it has been achieved and experienced, forgetting does not happen automatically. We cannot forget on demand. Forgiving can still be sincere even if we remember. Forgetting must happen naturally as part of the longer forgiving process.

Avoidance. Forgiveness is not a way of avoidance. It is an alternative to revenge and retaliation, but it is not a way of opting out. On the contrary, because it gets to the root of the problem and refuses to exacerbate the hostility by multiplying the hurts, it is the only way of truly dealing with all aspects of the conflict situation.

Toleration. To forgive is not simply to accept or tolerate. Acceptance can be selective: it can be a way of looking at the good that is in each one of us, no matter how evil many of our actions may be, but it does not deal with the bad. It concentrates on the sober generosity of the drunkard, the family commitment of the terrorist or the conscientiousness of the adulterer. But it is the bad—the drunkenness, the murder, the adultery—which is unacceptable. That is what forgiveness tackles.

Getting Away with It. Finally, to forgive is not the same as saying that "it doesn't matter." Those who have wronged will still have to pay and bear the consequences of their actions—legally, socially or personally. A wrongdoer can be truly and completely forgiven, yet prosecuted. Forgiveness complements justice*; it does not replace it.

Forgiveness in Scripture
The Old Testament deals, in the main, with divine forgiveness. From the very beginning of salvation history God has been active in forgiveness. The promise* of Genesis 3:15, Noah's ark (Gen 6:13—9:17), the subsequent covenant (Gen 8:21-22) and the story of Abraham (Gen 12:1—25:10) are all early examples of God's determination to save and restore people into fellowship.* There is no single word for forgiveness in Hebrew, but rather a series of images. There is the image of paying a ransom price (*kipper;* Ex 30:15-16; Num 5:8; Is 6:7); taking away (*na';* Ex 32:32; Job 7:21; Mic 7:18); pardoning (*selach;* 1 Kings 8:30-39; Jer 31:34); and even passing over, overlooking (*'abar;* Mic 7:18; Prov 19:11). These are powerful and significant images. In-

itially, through the old covenant provisions of the scapegoat (Lev 16:20-22) and the general sacrificial system, God illustrated his willingness to overlook the sins of his people because they had been paid for, borne away, by someone or something else. God therefore has no call to remember their sins, for they are irrelevant (Ps 25:7; 103:9-12; Mic 7:19). Isaiah uses identical language as he looks forward to the ultimate scapegoat sacrifice who will bear the sins of the people (Is 53:8-12).

The New Testament makes it clear that this was Christ and that his sacrifice was sufficient for all time (Acts 8:32-33; Heb 10:10). It is in the light of Christ's sacrifice and our hope of eternal reconciliation with God that the New Testament writers employed the image of letting go *(aphiēmi)* to describe divine and therefore Christian forgiveness. As God has taken leave of our sins in Christ, so too we should let go of the sins committed against us (Mt 6:12; Eph 4:29-32). This is brought out most powerfully by the parable of the unforgiving servant (Mt 18:21-35), where an unforgiving spirit is portrayed starkly as nothing less than blasphemous. One of the reasons we find forgiveness so difficult is that we are offended by God's love,* which can forgive those who have so spitefully abused us. We are like the elder brother (Lk 15:28-32), resenting the grace of God and living unfree lives, bound by our own self-righteousness and prejudice. The key to forgiveness is to understand how much we ourselves have been forgiven by God. Like the woman in Luke 7:36-50, those who truly understand the depth of God's forgiveness are driven to love, not judgment (see also Mt 7:1-5).

Forgiving Oneself
Forgiveness is usually regarded as an interpersonal affair, but there is an in-

427

trapersonal aspect which is often overlooked. If we need to forgive ourselves and are unwilling to do so, this will hinder our forgiving others. Often the greater the sin, the less we are able to forgive ourselves: "Sin and self-forgiveness assume inverse proportions in our minds" (Stanley, p. 141). This is fundamentally a theological problem. We have not really understood or experienced the forgiveness of God, which is free, unmerited and unconditional. By refusing to forgive ourselves we betray a self-centered obsession that undermines the completeness of Christ's atoning work. We claim we don't forgive ourselves because we are unworthy, yet that is the whole point of the cross. Christ died because we were unworthy. We claim we have disappointed God, yet in reality it is only ourselves we have disappointed. How can God be disappointed when he knows us exactly as we are and yet forgives us?

Sometimes, as an alternative to self-forgiveness, we will engage in self-deprivation or penance in the mistaken belief that we know something bad about our sin that God does not already know. Alternatively, we will become compulsive activists, burying ourselves in good works in order to impress God and thereby "atone" for our wrongdoing.

The two main pillars of the early church had to learn what it was to forgive themselves. Peter, because of his denial of Christ, had possibly counted himself no longer a disciple (Mk 16:7; Jn 21:15-17), and Paul had to come to terms with atrocities he had personally inflicted on Christians before his conversion (1 Cor 15:9-10). Once we have grasped the extent and manner of God's forgiveness, we are without excuse in withholding forgiveness from anyone, and that includes ourselves.

Intercommunity Forgiveness
New factors are brought into the equa-

tion when one considers the area of intercommunity or international conflict. Often when peace is being negotiated it is asked: Can, or should, leaders ask for forgiveness on behalf of the whole nation for atrocities committed in their name? Is it possible for the wronged community* to grant that forgiveness on behalf of all of its citizens? If so, will the members of the "guilty" community feel the power of the forgiveness in any meaningful way? Such questions have recently been raised in relation to the Northern Ireland conflict, post-apartheid South Africa, the Middle East, Rwanda and Bosnia. Anniversaries* have also tended to raise these questions in terms of unresolved hurts from past conflicts. The five-hundredth anniversary of Columbus's arrival in North America (1992) sparked calls for apologies to be made to the native peoples, just as the fiftieth anniversary of the ending of the World War II in the Pacific (1995) prompted calls for Japanese apologies, and the one hundred and fiftieth anniversary of the Irish famine (1996) led to similar demands on the British.

The difficulty here is that in order to be effective, forgiveness requires the dynamics of human relationship. This presupposes a level of personal interaction. Forgiveness cannot take place by proxy or by means of words alone. It is virtually impossible for leaders to speak on behalf of all their citizens, much less on behalf of the citizens of previous centuries. It is similarly unrealistic, unhelpful, indeed prejudicial, of the citizens of a conquered nation to transfer their anger onto all the citizens of the conquering nation. Two things, however, can be done. First, where possible, individuals who have been wronged can begin the task of forgiving those individuals who have wronged them: the terrorist who planted the bomb, the soldier who fired the shot, the informer who pointed the finger or the witness who lied. Second, where the state has engaged in institutional injustice, it can ensure that those wrongs are righted and not allowed to recur. Land can be restored and protected, prisoners of conscience released and economic restitution made for the ravaging of property. Forgiveness is too serious and deep to be cheapened by pressurized apologies or cosmetic gestures that do nothing to ensure future justice and ongoing reconciliation (*see* Conflict Resolution).

Interpersonal Forgiveness

Lewis Smedes has correctly pointed out that while many things may hurt us—nature, circumstances, unjust systems—we can forgive only people (Smedes, 1984, pp. 5-6). Forgiveness is intensely relational and personal. So how does forgiveness actually work in the area of interpersonal relationships?

The main problem with forgiveness is that on the surface it appears to ignore or take lightly an incident of gross personal injustice. An injury has been inflicted, physically or emotionally, and someone has been hurt. The automatic human tendency is to hate and desire to get even. Forgiveness demands that we come to terms with such desires and gradually seek to be released from the power that the wound (and therefore the other person) has over us. Forgiveness is not about ignoring the injury. On the contrary, the forgiver acknowledges it and confronts it openly. Nor is the injury treated lightly. Rather, the forgiver treats it differently by freeing himself or herself from the endless consuming cycle of bitterness, hatred and retribution. The divine model is worth remembering here. God did not ignore our sin or treat it lightly. The death of Christ both dealt with the problem and made forgiveness possible.

Another problem with forgiveness is

that it may remain forever incomplete. The other party may not accept or experience the forgiveness because of circumstances such as death* or the continued hardness of their own heart. However, this does not mean that the forgiveness is any less real. As far as the forgiver is concerned, the act of forgiveness has achieved its purpose in freeing them from the hurt of the incident, even though full mutual reconciliation requires the cooperation of the other party. It is a temptation to shirk the task of forgiveness on the grounds that the other person does not wish to be forgiven. This is to misunderstand the purpose of forgiveness: forgiveness is not an offer and not dependent on another's repentance. While reconciliation consummates the act of forgiveness, the self-imposed alienation of the guilty party does not cheapen the release and joy of forgiveness any more than our continued rebellion against God undermines perfect divine forgiveness.

The Practice of Forgiveness

David Augsburger (1981) has highlighted the five stages of forgiveness: realizing the wrongdoing, reaffirming love, releasing the past, renewing repentance and rediscovering community. Smedes (1984) approaches the subject from the "inside," highlighting the four possible experiences of the forgiver: hurt, hatred,* healing* and reconciliation. Hurts must be differentiated from forgettable oversights, insensitivities or mere disappointments. Hurts penetrate deeply and involve betrayal, disloyalty or personal injury. "Hatred is a compliment" (Smedes, p. 24), for we are not treating the perpetrator as robotic or irredeemable but as a free, rational person who has behaved unacceptably. They should have known better. It is on the unacceptability of their actions that our hatred is focused. These, however, are stages we must pass through. We cannot hate forever, or it will consume us and forgiveness will never take place. Alongside these two approaches to the practice of forgiveness, I offer a third that deals with past, present and future.

1. *A new attitude.* This concerns how we deal with the past. We make a choice to deal with festering hurts and to embark on the journey of forgiveness. We decide neither to perpetuate the hostility nor to suppress the hurts and allow them to eat away inside us. A refusal to forgive binds us eternally to the past. Our personality becomes frozen, we cannot move on from the moment of the offense, and we are incapable of living fully in the present. As injured people, we too require soul* surgery. In some cases we need to admit our contribution to the breakdown in relationship. In other cases where we have been passive victims, we need to confess that we have allowed the event to hinder our spiritual growth* and that righteous anger has become self-righteous bitterness. By choosing the way of forgiveness we are prepared to change our attitude toward those who have hurt us. We are prepared to forget and to acknowledge that someday we may be able to love them. Loving Christians, if they are to model God, must keep no record of wrongs (1 Cor 13:5; Ps 103:3-4).

2. *A new perspective.* This concerns how we cope with the present. We begin by viewing people differently. We attempt to get outside the hurts and ragings of our present brokenness and see our enemy as God sees them (2 Cor 5:16). The temptation will be to view those who have injured us in a reductionist manner, seeing them totally in terms of their sin, when in reality they are normal people, a mixture of the image of God and sinful humanity. We are blinded to their true identity* because of the sin they have committed against us. Real forgiveness cannot take place unless we are prepared to see them as they truly are, and not as the demons we have perceived them to be in the midst of our hurt and anguish. A test of whether our anger is righteous and directed against the sin, or unrighteous and directed against the sinner, would be to ask ourselves whether we would find greater pleasure in the conversion or restoration of the sinner than in their destruction (ECONI, p. 10). Or can we imagine a situation where we would actively wish the person well (Smedes, 1984, p. 29)? This takes time, but a new perspective will enable us to work to that end.

3. *A new determination.* This deals with the possibilities of the future. Forgiveness opens the door to new possibilities in relationship which would have been unthought of at the start of the journey. That is why forgiveness must be unconditional. If we lay down conditions, it means we are choosing the future and seeking to manipulate the other person into satisfying our unrealistic demands. If our demands are truly just, then the God of justice* will see to it that they are met in the context of dialogue, growing trust and reconciliation. Reconciliation is not a return to old ways, a turning of the clock back to the exact moment of the offense. This is a new world. Circumstances have changed: the injured body* may be irreparably damaged, or the marriage* may be irretrievably lost because of new relationships. "We make our new beginnings, not where we used to be or where we wish we could be, but only where we are and with what we have at hand" (Smedes, p. 37). We can only forgive today with today's circumstances. "Forgiveness is letting what was, be gone; what will be, come; what is now, be" (Augsburger, 1981, p. 52).

Forgiveness naturally involves risks. We open the door not only to a bright new future but to the possibility of repeated injury. But where there is no risk, there is no need of forgiveness. Forgiveness does not deal with contracts* and guarantees but with covenant and trust. That is God's way with us, and it must be our way with each other (Deut 4:30-31).

The Power of Forgiveness

No one can force us to forgive, and all the pressures of personality and culture* are against it. Yet in spite of our culture's preoccupation with strength, machismo and getting even, to choose to forgive is to exhibit the greatest strength of all. Self-deception, avoidance and grudge-bearing are all easier options than loving confrontation, realism and forgiveness. When we forgive we are acting as free persons and treating others as such. The strength of the love that inspires forgiveness derives from respect and commitment. We see the other person as worth the respect and are prepared for the energy, time* and disappointment that may come. "Hate gives a temporary power for surviving today's brutality and it has a short-term power to move us into tough action for tomorrow. But hate lacks the staying-power to create a fairer future beyond revenge. . . . For long distance, forgiving is stronger than hate" (Smedes, 1984, p. 146). No greater example is needed than that of Christ himself, the embodiment of the kingdom of God, a kingdom of hope, forgiveness and reconciliation. It was he who, as he bore the physical agony of crucifixion, the emotional torture of the taunts and insults of passersby, and the spiritual weight of the sins of the world, found the strength to say: "Father, forgive them" (Lk 23:34).

See also CHURCH CONFLICT; CONFLICT RESOLUTION; HATRED; JUSTICE; LOVE.

References and Resources

D. Augsburger, *Caring Enough to Forgive* (Ventura, Calif.: Regal, 1981); D. Augsburger, *The Freedom of Forgiveness* (Chicago: Moody, 1988); Evangelical Contribution on Northern Ireland, *Forgiveness* (Belfast: ECONI, 1992); L. G. Jones, *Embodying Forgiveness: A Theological Analysis* (Grand Rapids, Mich.: Eerdmans, 1995); J. Patton, *Is Human Forgiveness Possible? A Pastoral Care Perspective* (Nashville: Abingdon, 1985); L. B. Smedes, *Caring and Commitment: Learning to Live the Love We Promise* (San Francisco: Harper & Row, 1988); L. B. Smedes, *Forgive and Forget: Healing the Hurts We Don't Deserve* (San Francisco: Harper & Row, 1984); C. Stanley, *Forgiveness* (Nashville: Thomas Nelson, 1987).

David J. Montgomery

FREEDOM

The quest for freedom is high on most people's agenda today, and it has also been one of the main threads of human history. We speak of freedom in many ways—personal freedom, freedom of speech and association, academic freedom, free trade, freedom of the press. We also talk about individual liberties, liberation theology and religious liberty. Other basic freedoms often discussed include freedom from want, fear or interference, and freedom of choice, conscience or opportunity. Common phrases that sum up many people's attitudes toward freedom include "doing your own thing," "going your own way," or "it's up to you (or me)." Recently, in one year alone more than one thousand books contained the word *freedom* in their titles. Yet the glowing way people in democracies spoke about their freedom a generation ago has given way to complaints that they are losing it as the hands of bureaucracies and big business extend into their private lives. Paradoxically, this is happening at the very time political freedom has come to totalitarian societies in many parts of the world.

The loss of freedom has been a recurring theme of many modern thinkers, especially those interested in the physical and social sciences. They have talked rather of the appearance of freedom and of our being conditioned and determined by biological, psychological and sociological conditions. Art* and literature have also struggled with the constraints on human freedom, as the writings of existentialists like Jean-Paul Sartre, pessimistic humanists like Somerset Maugham and Ernest Hemingway, and apocalyptists like H. G. Wells demonstrate. Similar themes are now appearing with greater frequency in popular film and music; this is especially interesting in view of their general tendency to promote individual and democratic freedom. The burgeoning of fantasy and science fiction has often been accompanied by dark visions of the future in which the human race is enslaved by an elite group, an oppressive ideology, a technological development or some combination of the three.

While Christians thinkers have often emphasized our lack of genuine freedom as a result of the Fall (Gen 3; Rom 5), apart from some writers influenced by Marxist thought they have generally held a positive view of the social and political freedoms available to people. There are occasional voices that speak in more reserved tones, such as lay theologian Jacques Ellul, who in his book *The Presence of the Kingdom* goes so far as to claim that in no other civilization have we been so constrained. Previously we may have been the slaves of hunger, natural circumstances or other people, but we have always managed to remain master of the greater part of our time and major use of our energies. The all-pervasive effects of our modern technologies* and bureaucracies actually render us less personally and socially free than people who lived in earlier times (Ellul, pp. 63-64). Even when we are personally free, we operate under certain constraints that are inherent in being creatures rather than the Creator, and in living in a fallen world.

An Early Christian View and Practice of Freedom

Freedom is generally regarded as *for* something, as giving people the opportunity of exercising choice in a range of areas. This is certainly one aspect of freedom. But the Bible sees it as involving far more. Already in Old Testament times, the freeing of God's people from Egypt was more than a liberation from the tyranny they were experiencing. It was a freedom to become a nation in their own land. From that point Israel's story is the struggle of God's attempts to preserve and deepen that freedom in the face of the people's willingness to yield it to alien gods, or for some among them to deprive others of it. Interestingly, it is on behalf of a deeper freedom that God for a time exiles the people from their own land and self-government. It is with the coming of Jesus that a fuller freedom becomes available (Jn 8:32). Among the New Testament writers it is Paul, who has rightly been called "the apostle of freedom," who gives most attention to this.

Paul's starting point is the common biblical belief that though human beings are made for God, each other and their world, they have lost their way in all three areas of life. As a result, they are enslaved and no longer free to properly know or pursue their real potential. This takes place in three main ways.

Humans find themselves under an inner compulsion to sin (Rom 6:17, 20; 7:14, 25). They put their confidence in their human endeavors ("works") or creaturely strength ("flesh"), and so are mostly preoccupied with their personal or group concerns and with their moral and religious heritage or accomplishments (Rom 2:17ff; 3:20; Phil 3:3ff).

Humans are unable to respond fully to the moral requirements of the law or the moral imperative written by God in their hearts (Rom 1:32; 3:23). So they drift into an immoral, or harden into a hypermoral, way of life through which they continue to express their self-centered natures (Rom 1:24ff; 10:1ff).

Humans are in bondage to physical or supernatural realities. Death (Rom 1:32; 6:5), various cosmic and social forces (Gal 4:3; Eph 6:12; Col 2:8), and Satan (2 Cor 4:4; Eph 2:2) blind their judgment, affect them adversely and ultimately destroy them (*see* Principalities and Powers).

The upshot of all this is that we are less free than we generally think and are all linked in a solidarity of sin (Rom 5:12ff). This does not mean that we altogether lack freedom. Up to a point we can understand God (Rom 1:19-21), do what is right (Rom 2:14) and develop a relatively well-functioning social and political way of life (Rom 13:1-7). But our capacities are severely limited and deeply flawed in each of these areas.

Only if we can see life differently, find release from these forces and receive power to change our patterns of behavior can we regain the freedom that was God's original intention for us (Gen 1—2). We can do these things because of his long-planned vision of a divine kingdom made possible by Christ's suffering for our bondage to sin, works and the flesh, and his conquest over supernatural powers, death* and Satan (2 Cor 5:21; Gal 3:13; Col 2:15). When Christ did this he became the representative and foundation of a new humanity (1 Cor 15:20ff; 2 Cor 4:6; 5:17; Eph 2:14-15). To live out this new freedom we have been granted, we need a new source of power,* and it is this that the Spirit provides. The Spirit grants us genuine freedom to choose a different way of life (Rom 5:5; 1 Cor 2:10-11), one that is based on truth and empowered by love.* We still experience the pull of the old life and sometimes yield to it, and only in the Last Day will we experience our full freedom in Christ (Rom 7:21-25). But we can live now in the knowledge that the issue has already been decided and that through the Spirit we are undergoing a profound transformation into the likeness of Christ (Rom 8:1-11; 2 Cor 3:16-18). This is why Paul can say, and say so confidently, "Where the Spirit of the Lord is, there is freedom" (2 Cor 3:17).

Some Dimensions and Expressions of Freedom

From a biblical point of view, then, there are three dimensions to freedom.

Freedom involves independence from *the physical and supernatural realities mentioned above.* These enslave and prevent us from becoming the people God wants us to be and doing the things God wants us to do. This dimension of freedom tends to be in view today only when people are experiencing some strong addiction or obsession. Then there is a clear recognition of what they need to be liberated from. Even when people constantly give in to various weaknesses or failings, they tend to think that this is because they do not know the full consequences of what they are doing or do not exert the inherent willpower they have to break free of these shortcomings. But sin is not basically due to ignorance, nor can it be overcome by an act of will. Twelve-step groups like Alcoholics Anonymous fully understand this, and it is why they are often effective instruments for change.

Freedom involves independence for *other things.* These include becoming a person full of the character of Christ (Gal 6:2) and virtues of the Spirit (Gal 5:22-23), undertaking new activities characterized by serving of God and others (Rom 7:17-18) and assisting in the ultimate liberation of the created order from its bondage to decay (Rom 8:18-23; 2 Cor 4:11-18). The majority of people do not understand this, and in fact tend to see religion as involving a loss of personal freedom. But it is in giving ourselves up to Christ that we discover true freedom.

All other forms of freedom are secondary compared to the life-changing freedom that springs from this, which, in any case, is not only internal but also external life, affecting a person's health, relationships and everyday behavior. Though other freedoms are important, without this at the core of a person's life they lack a proper center. For this reason, a genuine preaching of the gospel is the greatest and most political or revolutionary contribution anyone can make to human freedom in the world today.

Freedom involves interdependence with *others.* First of all we lean on God, with whom we now have the greatest intimacy and mutuality (Rom 8:15-18; Gal 4:1-7) and with whom we work freely and cooperatively (1 Cor 15:58). Second, we have an interdependence with others, which includes opening ourselves up to them (2 Cor 3:12; 6:11; 7:4; 8:2; 9:13) as well as loving and serving them (1 Cor 9:19; 1 Thess 2:8). Christians see a developing relationship and working partnership with God mostly as a consequence of our freedom through Christ. Indeed freedom in the truest sense is simply willing obedience to the One we most truly love— God, "whose service," as the Episcopal Book of Common Prayer beautifully puts it, "is perfect freedom." But little do we understand the vital connection between freedom and our relationship and partnership with others. We tend to think of freedom too much in individual, or even individualistic, terms. Yet, as Christ exhibited, true freedom issues not in self-service but in service of others (*see* Ministry). It also issues in deepening relationships, motivated and saturated by love, that open up even greater freedom for those involved and flow naturally into the lives of others in a liberating way. While marriage* and vocation are two expressions of this, so also are the church* and mission.*

These three dimensions of freedom have multiple levels of expression. Through them God encourages us to freely investigate every aspect of life— from examining the smallest particles of matter to studying the furthest reaches of space, from freeing people from personal constraints to liberating them from external forms of oppression, from inventing the simplest games* for children to exploring the most complex reaches of art and music,* from developing fresh ways of doing things unhindered by past traditions to formulating new forms of understanding institutional structures, from making one's contribution in neighborhood and civic life to engaging in wider social and political action on behalf of the greater freedom of others.

But as philosopher John Macmurray tirelessly pointed out, unless individual freedom finds expression in the freedom of community, other freedoms that we might desire are not built on a lasting foundation or are built in such a way that they become distorted and questionable. This is why one of the most significant contributions we can make to expanding political or democratic freedom is developing forms of Christian community inside and alongside our churches that can become the model, stimulus and support of our wider efforts.

We recognize that freedom is generally a developing phenomenon and that in some cases it exists long term under the most limited circumstances. For example, children progress to it gradually as parents reduce constraints on them; encourage them to criticize, judge and choose for themselves; and watch them voluntarily develop different views or embrace what they earlier believed on parental authority. Also, some people cannot escape living under all kinds of constraints—whether physical or psychological, religious or institutional, economic or political—over the long haul. Within these constraints they can still enjoy spiritual, mental and relational freedom and, as far as it is possible, they can still work toward greater freedom on all these fronts, knowing that not all depends on their efforts and that, whether they succeed or fail, ultimately there awaits them the full liberty of the kingdom of God. It is this anticipation that saves them from expecting too much or giving up in resignation. Meanwhile they are able to experience the multidimensional freedom of Christ that has come to them from God through the Spirit.

See also INDIVIDUAL; SPIRITUAL CONFLICT; SPIRITUAL GROWTH.

References and Resources

R. Banks, *Paul's Idea of Community* (Peabody, Mass.: Hendrickson, 1994); N. Berdyaev, *Freedom and the Spirit* (London: Bles, 1948); J. Ellul, *The Ethics of Freedom* (London: Mowbrays, 1976); J. Ellul, *The Presence of the Kingdom*, 2d ed. (Colorado Springs: Helmers and Howard, 1989); E. Fromm, *Escape from Freedom* (New York: Avon, 1941); Sidney Hook, ed., *Freedom and Experience* (Ithaca, N.Y.: Cornell University Press, 1947); R. N. Longenecker, *Paul: The Apostle of Liberty* (San Francisco: Harper & Row, 1966); M. Luther, *Christian Liberty* (Philadelphia: Fortress Press, 1957); J. Macmurray, *Conditions of Freedom* (Atlantic Light, N.J.: Humanities Press, 1993); J. Murphy-O'Connor, *Freedom and Love: The Guide for Christian Life* (Rome: St. Paul's Aldray, 1981); H. Thielicke, *The Freedom of the Christian Man: A Christian Confrontation with the Secular Gods* (New York: Harper & Row, 1963).

Robert Banks

FRIENDSHIP

The active promotion of the concept of friendship might lead us to the conclusion that it is widely experienced. We have friendly churches,* user-friendly machines and friendship evangelism.* Yet behind the rhetoric is a deep craving for what is seldom experienced—intimate, lifelong relationships in which persons are enjoyed simply for who they are

and not what they can do for us. Ironically, people who boast of "my friends" may be among the most lonely as they are encircled by acquaintances, business colleagues or others linked by obligations and benefits through an unwritten contract of the mutual meeting of needs. Friendship, in contrast, is not *for* anything except the friend, and therefore as a nonutilitarian relationship, friendship takes us to the center of Christian living. The history of a person's spiritual pilgrimage can usually be traced from the history of that person's friendships.

The Value of Friendship

In practical terms friendship is crucial to emotional and personal development. We learn to become fully human persons in part through our relational history. Some people get stuck in their development in a self-absorption stage and never move forward into give-and-take relationships that inevitably require some level of death to the self. Such people are not only friendless; in addition they usually have a diminished capacity to give and receive love of all kinds, including marital love. The marriage* relationship itself should not be required to meet all the friendship needs of each spouse and may be threatened by such unrealistic expectations. Nevertheless, it is commonly agreed that the basic recipe for a good marriage is friendship plus sex (McGinnis, p. 9). A truly biblical marriage is formed not only through friendship and sexual consummation but by the forging of a covenant. As we shall see, covenants are not exclusive to marriage and may strengthen the bond of same-sex or even other-sex friendships without the romantic or erotic dimension being present. If, as has been suggested, romantic/married love is two souls and one flesh, friendship is two bodies and one soul.

Friendship is good not only for our

personal development but also for our moral development. One reason is that friendship offers a second self with whom we share feelings, thoughts, moral judgments and criticism. Paul Wadell notes, "One reason we have friends is that there is a good we share with them, but the reason friendships grow and become such a delight is that we cannot be good without them, indeed, we cannot be good at all" (p. 6). Commenting on this, Stanley Hauerwas reflects that the preferential nature of friendship—through which we choose to relate intimately with a few people—has always seemed to contradict and oppose the Christian obligation to love everyone (cited in Wadell, p. x). But because friendship invites us to rejoice in the particularity, the specialness, of the other, we learn how to grow in love.* So particular friendships fit us better to love everyone. And mature friendships will admit, even seek, another friend.

Scripture occasionally uses *friendship* to describe the relationship of God with his people. Further, there is something like friendship in the Godhead since God is more "one" because of being three and not one in spite of being three. So true spirituality is essentially relational. Aelred of Rievaulx boldly paraphrased 1 John 4:16 as "God is friendship" (p. 65). Because "God is love" (1 John 4:8), to walk as children of God involves cultivating the relational life, including friendship. Far from being a diversion to the spiritual life, friendship is a path to God. But this view of friendship is something distinctive to the Christian faith.

The History of Friendship

In the Greek classics Aristotle and Cicero maintained that the good life cannot exist without friends living together and sharing in discussion and thought. In contrast, the Stoic Seneca believed the wise person can live perfectly well without friends. Where friendship existed in the Greek world, it was more of a sociopolitical relationship than the private and personal association sought today. Friends practiced together in the military academy, discussed politics* and joined together to promote a common public life (Allen, p. 36). In contrast, friendship today allows people to detach from the constraints of political, business and public life simply to enjoy a relationship. Friendship is more like play,* which is not useful though it is positively reinforcing. While the classical world ended with the isolation of friendship from community,* the eleventh-century rediscovery of friendship can be linked to renewed interest in the classical texts.

The twelfth-century Cistercian Christian Aelred of Rievaulx has left us a very substantial reflection on spiritual friendship in which he drew heavily on Cicero. Such monastic discussions of the place of friendship in the spiritual life are illustrative since they reflect the tension of living in and for the community first. These discussions raise the question of whether special friendships in a monastic community destroy community. This discussion continues today in Christian communities where it is feared that exclusive relationships will work against *koinōnia,* that is, "fellowship."* Brian McGuire catalogs the options evident in the history of spirituality, especially in the monastic tradition: (1) the way of solitude—God and the individual (desert fathers); (2) the way of asceticism—God and individuals banded together; (3) the way of harmony—God meets individuals through communal acts of discipline (Benedict); (4) the way of friendship—God meets the community through special friendship relationships that do not threaten the harmony of community life; and (5) the way of brotherhood—friendships do not have to be limited to the cloister (pp. 36-37).

A high point in the monastic tradition of friendship is the works of Aelred: *Mirror of Charity* (1140) and *Spiritual Friendship* (1160). Aelred's youth included habitual sexual sin with other men, either masturbation* or homosexual* acts. His victory over this led him both to condemn homosexual genital activity as an especially direct road to hell and, at the same time, to continue to believe in tenderness, affection, touching, being open and talking intimately about one's life. "Aelred's transference of sexual energy to spiritual fire came in the aftermath of the conversion to the monastic life at the age of twenty-four" (McGuire, p. 304). Unlike the more extreme desert fathers, Aelred dealt with the fear of sex in an all-male world by discarding passionlessness and insisting that warm love between friends of the same sex could be pure. This, however, did not come quickly or easily: "Jesus had become his love. As he made clear in *Mirror of Charity*, we must seek to concentrate on the flesh of Jesus the drives that otherwise would be directed towards the flesh of other men. One great passion took over and consumed all others, but instead of destroying his involvement in other men, the love of Jesus made human loves stable, permanent and part of the unity of the community" (McGuire, p. 329). Aelred underwent a lifelong process of conversion to this.

Aelred's Neo-Platonism envisioned a continuous movement from physical loves to pure love of God, from lower friendships to pure spiritual friendships that take us to the heart of God. So he categorized friendships as functional, receptive (director to disciple), reciprocal (pilgrims together) and finally the knitting of souls. Aelred's teaching is experiential: "He sought and found God in the impulses of his own heart and in the experience of men whom he knew through his reading and daily contacts" (McGuire, p. 322). Until recently Aelred's books were banned in some monasteries out of fear that special friendships would endanger the community. The problem is still with us.

The Western world today is organized in such a way that long and deep friendships are exceedingly difficult in spite of courses on winning friends and influencing people. Many of the "new values" of postmodern society militate against friendship, not to mention spiritual friendship. These so-called values include (1) *self-actualization,* meaning that the self should actualize its potential and transcend its limitations, which includes the duty to get out of an unfulfilling marriage; (2) *freedom to choose,* meaning that we must have control over our own bodies, even our own future; (3) *openness,* meaning that we must stay available to alternative experiences for psychic mobility and not get trapped in a relationship, a factor that partly explains commitment anxiety and fear of covenant relationships; (4) *regular sexual satisfaction as a human right,* meaning that all sexual choices are legitimate, that no judgment should be placed on whether a relationship is homosexual or heterosexual and that monogamy is a rude intrusion in the sexual paradise of this instant-gratification culture; (5) *intimacy,* meaning that part of the relief sought from anonymity and the lonely crowd will be found in satisfying the hunger for heightened and new stimuli in relationships, which usually involve sexual activity, to give us the best experience we can get; (6) *rentalism* (Alvin Toffler's word), meaning that we should be committed to transiency as a way of life so that the person gets lost in moving from one ad hoc experience to another, which involves treating people as commodities and allowing throwaway, commercial relationships to be used as sales prospects for insurance or for the gospel; (7) *professionalism*,* meaning that all relationships from pastoring to friendships can be reduced to a technology promoted by experts; (8) *revaluing of divorce*,* meaning that divorce is part of the growth sequence, a gateway to new values* and role experimentation. These new values of the postmodern society are held against the backdrop of the "old values," which are perceived as antivalues: lifelong fidelity and commitment, institutions and roles, responsibility for others, loyalty, closure and motherhood. While there is a hint of return to some of these old values in the postmodern consciousness, we must conclude that true friendship is largely countercultural. What many pursue, without knowing the difference, is pseudofriendship.

Signs of pseudofriendship are (1) *functional relationships* (we relate to people on the basis of what they do, what they can do for us, what they have done, rather than for who they are), (2) *promiscuous relationships* (we share ourselves inappropriately, not merely in the sexual sense, but by chattering away our lives indiscriminately and sharing intimately with strangers without the discipline of building trust and loyalty brick by brick), (3) *contractual relationships* (we agree to an exchange of goods and services in a conditional contract* that can be broken by either partner—even in the family of God, with church membership* often being based on an unspoken contract of the mutual meeting of needs) and (4) *addictive relationships* (we demand that others, even spouses, clients and parishioners, meet our neurotic needs). With considerable insight R. D. Laing comments on Western society in this way: "Can human beings be persons today? Can a man be his actual self with another man or woman? . . . We are effectively destroying ourselves by violence masquerading as love. . . . No wonder modern man is addicted to other persons and the more addicted, the less satisfied, the more lonely" (pp. 20, 50, 62). Tragically, even in the family of God there is a profound loneliness. People lack soul friends with whom they can share the pilgrimage of faith, and many with a deep need to be liked find themselves to be the object of a love-an-unlovely-person project. It is profoundly unsatisfying.

Biblical Friendship
The Bible addresses the subject of friendship from several angles: example, personal reflection and explicit theological reflection. After considering these, we will explore the direct teaching of Scripture on how to be friendly.

Biblical examples of friendship. An inspired example of soul friendship is found in Jonathan's friendship with David (1 Sam 18:1-4; 19:1-7; 20; 23:16-18; 2 Sam 1:17-27; 9:1-12). Characteristic of their model friendship is the disinterestedness of Jonathan's friendship with David: that relationship would make David and not Jonathan the successor to the throne. Such friendship was risky and costly because the two found themselves in a triangle of jealousy and love with Saul (Jonathan's father). The friendship was pure; at no time is there any hint of a homosexual element in it. Only once are we told about David's feelings toward Jonathan—in the lament over his death: "Your love to me was wonderful, passing the love of women. As a mother loves her only son, so I was loving you" (2 Sam 1:26 Vulgate). This same-sex friendship was secured by a covenant (1 Sam 18:3), a covenant which David honored long after his friend's death (2 Sam 9:1-13). God stood as a witness between the two (1 Sam 20:42). Most significant was the spirituality of the friendship: Jonathan sought to give David strength in the Lord, not in their relationship (1 Sam 23:16-18). In the

New Testament Paul's circle of friends provides another inspired example. Note his friendship with Barnabas and the list of friends in Romans 16.

Biblical reflection on friendship. An inspired reflection on friendship is found in Ecclesiastes 4:7-12, which includes beginning in verse 9 a discussion of the rewards of friendship ("Two are better than one, because they have a good reward for their work"). Such rewards are practical support when one falls down (v. 10), warmth (v. 11), protection (v. 12) and the hint of a spiritual presence (v. 12; "a cord of three strands is not easily broken").

The psalms offer the witness that even our friends will betray us (Ps 55:13-15) and that the search for a true friend will lead us to the existential conclusion that only God is our help. Nevertheless, the value and pleasure of the bond experienced between like-minded persons is exalted: "Behold, how good and pleasant it is when brothers dwell in unity" (Ps 133:1 RSV).

Biblical theology of friendship. The Bible puts human friendship into the context of the mystery of the relational life within God (Jn 17:21, 23, 26) and the gospel through which God makes friends out of his enemies. Friendship between God and humankind is the ultimate goal of God's grace and the spiritual journey, as modeled by Moses with whom God spoke on Sinai "face to face, as a man speaks with his friend" (Ex 33:11). Abraham was the friend of God (Is 41:8; Jas 2:23), and Job hungered for God's friendship more than he desired relief from his suffering: "Oh, for the days when I was in my prime, when God's intimate friendship blessed my house" (Job 29:4). Satan's question addressed the heart of Job's friendship with God: "Does Job fear God for nothing?" (Job 1:9). Friendship, even friendship with God, is not *for* anything. It has no utilitarian value. That is, our relationship to God should not be a commercial relationship in which we exchange piety for spiritual, even eternal, benefits.

In the Gospel of John Jesus said, "No longer do I call you servants, for the servant does not know what his master is doing; but I have called you friends" (Jn 15:15 RSV). But ordinary friendship is not an adequate metaphor for friendship with Jesus, for it involves obedience to his commands (Jn 15:14). Friendship with Jesus is inseparable from the truth about Jesus, for Jesus himself is truth. So it is more than mere sentimentality: to disobey his commands is to deny his friendship. Lewis Smedes underscores the truth that while most friendships either find or make equals, this friendship is different:

> We are not fellow travelers; he is leader and we are followers. We do not walk side by side; he is always before us. We are not equals; he is vastly superior. He is the sort of friend we could not long endure in ordinary life with ordinary people; few people can remain friends for long with someone who accepts them by grace, "in spite of what they are" . . . yet, in those invisible bonds of moral consistency, kept commitment, gracious forgiveness, untiring listening, and ultimate sacrifice, he is the best friend one can ever have. (Shuster and Muller, pp. 240-41)

While Jesus called for nonpreferential love for all (Mt 5:46; "If you love those who love you, what reward will you get?"), he obviously had preferential relationships himself: Lazarus, Mary and Martha (Jn 11:34-35), and the disciple whom he loved (Jn 13:23). Jesus demanded uncompromising loyalty to himself even if it meant severing deep human relationships (Lk 14:26), yet he accepted such special relationships and described his relationship with his followers as friendship. Jesus turns normal definitions inside out by calling us to make a brother out of our friend, a friend out of our neighbor and a neighbor out of our enemy.

The theological background for Jesus' view of friendship is the relational nature of the image of God (Gen 1:27) and the covenant "friendship" relationship within the personhood of God as Father, Son and Holy Spirit, a social relationship of love, mutual respect, common interest and relational joy: "Our fellowship is with the Father and with his Son, Jesus Christ" (1 Jn 1:3). Behind Aelred of Rievaulx's paraphrase of 1 John 4:16 ("God is friendship") is the implication that whoever lives in friendship lives in God. James adds to this the boundaries of God-inspired friendship by reflecting that friendship with the world is enmity with God: "Therefore whoever wishes to be a friend of the world makes himself an enemy of God" (Jas 4:4 RSV).

In a strangely provocative parable Jesus seems to argue for a certain expediency in friendships in view of the ultimate reward of living with friends eternally in heaven, for who would want to live in a friendless heaven? In Luke 16:9 Jesus said, "Use worldly wealth to gain friends for yourselves, so that when it is gone, you will be welcomed into eternal dwellings." His intent was not to encourage the commercialization of relationships (use you money to buy friendships), but to use your money to meet needs, and the relationships springing from this will last for eternity (the very thing the rich man in the parable in Lk 16:19-31 refused to do).

The last parable in Luke 16 invites the consideration of how to be friendly. In Luke 10:36 Jesus asked, "Which of these . . . was a neighbor . . . ?" in response to the question "Who is my neighbor?" in verse 29. In like manner, the question "How can I be a friend?" is more important than the frequently asked "Who is my friend?"

The Art of Friendship

Direct teaching on friendship is found in Proverbs, in which there is distilled wisdom on how to make and keep friends: being trustworthy and keeping secrets (Prov 11:12), being willing to forget offenses (17:9), renouncing conflict (25:8) and cultivating openness (27:6). In contrast, the book of Job pictures how *not* to be a friend through the negative example of the three "miserable comforters" (16:2) of Job: "In the book of Job friends are used as the audience for the man whom God has allowed to be deprived of everything. Eventually even the friends are gone. . . . The problem of Job is not whether or not to believe in friendship: it is whether to believe in one's friends" (McGuire, p. xix).

Job's friends started well: they had good intentions (to sympathize); they engaged in a joint effort (Job 2:11); they took a decisive step (set out from their homes); they responded genuinely (wept aloud; 2:12); they identified with him (sat on the ground for seven days; 2:13); they understood communion (no one said a word; 2:13). But when Job would not comply with their theological expectations, they stopped being friendly and became his enemies. In the depths of his loneliness, though surrounded by his friends, Job cries, "A despairing man should have the devotion of his friends, even though he forsakes the fear of the Almighty" (6:14), which is sometimes translated, "He who withholds kindness from a friend forsakes the fear of the Almighty. My brethren are treacherous as a torrent-bed" (6:14-15 RSV).

When Job's friends attacked, instead of inducing guilt they provoked Job to self-justification (which ironically seems to have moved him from his suicidal despair). Only later, when God's love was revealed, could Job repent on his own. Job's friends reacted rather than responded. They were threatened by a problem they could not solve, so they attacked the sufferer. Their theology was inadequate to cope with unjust suffering, but instead of talking to God about this, the way Job did and so was justified (Job 42:7), they tried to talk about God to Job. The negative example of Job's friends invites the consideration of what, positively, makes for friendship that is not only the mutual enjoyment of persons but also the mutual enrichment of spiritual life.

Spiritual Friendship

Soul friendship, as Aelred stated so succinctly, like friendship in general is nonutilitarian: "For spiritual friendship, which we call true, should be desired, not for consideration of any worldly advantage or for any extrinsic cause, but from the dignity of its own nature and the feelings of the human heart, so that its fruition and reward is nothing other than itself" (p. 60). David and Jonathan exemplify this in the Old Testament. Jesus' startling address of Judas, at the moment of his treachery, as "friend" (Mt 26:50) is the superlative New Testament example. But spiritual friendship is not merely the enjoyment of another. It is companionship and mutual encouragement along the path of discipleship*; it is friendship with Christ together. So Aelred says to his friend Ivo, "Here we are, you and I, and I hope a third, Christ, in our midst" (p. 51). Spiritual friendship is having "the same opinion, the same will, in matters human and divine, along with mutual benevolence and charity" (Aelred, p. 54).

People do not suddenly attain a deep level of soul friendship. Thus, Aelred analyzed the types and stages of spiritual friendships; they are *functional* (based on mutual interests), *receptive* (a person with strengths with a person with weaknesses), *reciprocal* (in which friends are pilgrims together, progressively taking off layers of masks) and the *knitting of souls* (through which, by an act of grace, two people are supernaturally joined and knit together). True friendship is mutual equality and intimacy reaching toward God. It is both a gift of grace and an accomplishment. True friendship is not playing God, not encouraging codependence, not advice giving, not controlling, not directing another, not counseling and not an alternative to counseling. It is listening* to the heart, getting in touch with the movement of God in another's life (1 Sam 3:8-21), prizing the unique spirituality of one's friend, exploring the full meaning of another's life in God, nurturing a friend's spiritual life and on occasion confronting a friend with hard issues (Acts 18:24-28). A spiritual friend is "someone to whom you dare to speak on terms of equality as to another self, one to whom you need have no fear to confess your failings; one to whom you can unblushingly make known what progress you have made in the spiritual life; one to whom you can entrust all the secrets of your heart and before whom you can place all your plans" (Aelred, p. 72). Telling an unedited version of our inner life is not something that can be reduced to a technique or an instant formula. Aelred wisely advised progressively disclosing oneself to a friend, testing and deepening the relationship and, when a friendship proves inappropriate, unstitching it stitch by stitch, the way it was formed.

So friendship is a way of understanding God. Friendship is a way of describing the Christian life. Friendship is an important addition to fellowship (*koinōnia*) in the church, for *koinōnia* includes all Christians and is based solely on grace, our common share in the saving work of Christ and our common family experience in God. But too often people in a Christian fellowship rely solely on the bond of grace and neglect the challenge of developing the skills of friendship, skills of loyalty, caring, listening, celebrating and discretion that can greatly deepen the life of the Christian community. But finally friendship is a way of describing spirituality, for we intuitively know that when we turn friendship into a technique or use it, we have debased something holy. James Houston says,

A true friend can never have a hidden motive for being a friend. He can have no hidden agenda. A friend is simply a friend, for the sake of friendship. In a much greater way, love for God is love for God's own sake. Bernard of Clairvaux wrote that our natural inclination is to love for our own sake. When we learn to love God, we still love him for our own sake. As we grow in friendship with God, we come to love him not just for ourselves alone, but also for God's sake. At last, we may reach a point where we love even ourselves for the sake of God. (pp. 195-96)

See also COMMUNITY; DISCIPLESHIP; FELLOWSHIP; LOVE; SPIRITUAL GROWTH.

References and Resources

Aelred of Rievaulx, *Spiritual Friendship*, trans. M. E. Laker (Kalamazoo, Mich.: Cistercian Publications, 1974); D. Allen, *Love: Christian Romance, Marriage, Friendship* (Cambridge, Mass.: Cowley Publications, 1987); J. Houston, *The Transforming Friendship: A Guide to Prayer* (Oxford: Lion Books, 1989); W. Hulme, *Dialogue in Despair: Pastoral Commentary on the Book of Job* (New York: Abingdon, 1968); W. P. Jones, "Friendship and Circles of Commitment," *Weavings* 7, no. 3 (1992) 36-40; M. Kelsey, *Companions on the Inner Way* (New York: Crossroad, 1983); R. D. Laing, *The Politics of Experience and the Bird of Paradise* (Harmondsworth, U.K.: Penguin, 1970); K. Leech, *Soul Friend: The Practice of Christian Spirituality* (San Francisco: Harper & Row, 1977); C. S. Lewis, *The Four Loves* (London: Collins, 1960); A. L. McGinnis, *The Friendship Factor* (Minneapolis: Augsburg, 1979); B. P. McGuire, *Friendship and Community: The Monastic Experience, 350-1250* (Kalamazoo, Mich.: Cistercian Publications, 1988); H. Nouwen, *Reaching Out* (Garden City, N.Y.: Doubleday, 1975); M. Shuster and R. A. Muller, *Perspectives on Christology: Essays in Honor of Paul K. Jewett (Grand Rapids: Zondervan, 1991); P. J. Wadell, *Friendship and the Moral Life* (Notre Dame, Ind.: University of Notre Dame Press, 1989).

R. Paul Stevens

G

GAMES

Games are like complex toys that people can play,* provided they know how and will obey the rules. Games can engage people fully. Each player at the checkerboard is there as a whole person, focused on playing. Games are bona fide, God-given invitations to be playful and therefore can open people to God.

God Enjoys Play

Whether the voice of Wisdom in Proverbs represents the Holy Spirit or Jesus Christ, it is striking that Wisdom was playing before God's face at the creation of the world, having fun (Prov 8:31; *mesha-heqeth* JB). God's wild beasts and Leviathan also frolic in creation (Job 40:20; Ps 104:24-26). Integral to the promise of the Lord's restoration of God's people as caretakers of creation on the new earth is that boys and girls shall be able to play in the streets without getting hurt (Is 11:6-9; Zech 8:1-8).

In the here and now joy is the primal gift of the Holy Spirit to those who receive the gift of salvation (Gal 5:22-23; 1 Thess 1:2-7). Thus sourpuss Christianity is certainly out of line with the God of the Bible and the communion of saints. Joy, however, is deeper than pleasure, for there is in jubilation a more outgoing, imaginative character than the satisfaction of merely being pleased. So joy, fun and glad exuberance are the normative traits of playing around and therefore form the clue to the meaning of games.

A Game Is Organized Play

Babies and children play in sandboxes or at the seashore, let mud ooze through their toes and laugh as the waves make them happy with God's slap of wetness. Grownups are often playful in a caress with their loved ones or indulge in wordplay, like puns. There is always an element of surprise in playing, such as the wonderful excitement experienced when riding a swing hung from the branch of a tree. This unpredictable element epitomizes play and other aspects of the ludic dimension of life. So playfulness explores the unexpected ambiguity that inheres all human activity and sometimes comes to the fore, especially in games.

More complex than simple play, games always have rules and usually demand a certain amount of skill from those who participate. Further, everything in the game happens in the realm of a make-believe reality. The players have to imagine somebody as "it" to play tag and must decide whether or not a player can tag back immediately upon becoming "it." Games thrive on uncertainty and usually involve some kind of guessing on what to do next. Should you aim for the wicket in your croquet shot or knock somebody else's ball into the rough? Every player strives to reach the end or goal of the game first, even though the elusive prize is imaginary. A great thing about games is that everyone, technically, begins evenly, and that evenness is recovered every time the game is restarted. So children can occasionally win over their parents, and the stronger may lose to the weaker thanks to the wonderful uncertainty that always goes with a real game, such as when the marble or bocce ball just happens to hit a piece of uneven ground. A game to its players is very close to what Wonderland was for Alice: During a player's turn in jumping rope, reciting limericks while jumping up and down, he or she can cheerfully have the illusion of being a prima donna. And children play the hunter and the hunted in kick the can with shivers of expectation and tables turned. Good games always carry the aura of adventure.

Do Games Have a Purpose?

Educators have long understood that children learn through playing games and that play is work for a nursery school child. So games serve a social purpose. Games that last are much more complex than any one person and have been shaped by societal milieux, historical circumstances and the faith perspective of cultural communities. Anthropologists have noted, for example, that Inuit children of the Canadian North played games of physical skill that fostered memory, rather than games of chance and strategy. Inuit childhood games were thus congruent with a harsh, subsistent life and world in which the young were nurtured to do their best but not at the expense of others. The games of the Iroquois in the New York area were more competitive athletic contests, tied to rites invoking rain or ceremonial dances for the blessing of fertility on the crops—matters outside human hands.

Naturalistic psychologist Karl Groos (1861-1946) interpreted games to be a kind of animal survival-kit practice that the young exercise to rehearse coping with adult activities. Pragmatist educator-theorist Jean Piaget (1896-1980) traced the development of games played by children (sensory-motor, then make-believe, finally symbolic games with rules) and found they geared very strictly to stages of a child's preverbal and postverbal accommodation and socialization toward external reality. Games for Piaget are indices of human maturation; full-grown, well-adjusted humans outgrow them. And many a Christian moralist has excused games only if they help Christians take themselves less seriously or help them work more efficiently afterward: Learn to relax and lose—it's good for you. Enjoy games as pleasant lessons in humility, perhaps even as a foretaste of a heaven free from drudgery.

A biblically directed conception of games will take us beyond the mere instrumental value of games. We should not miss the peculiar glory and blessing built into the play that God created us to enjoy, and we should not apologetically twist games into becoming a means for nonplayful ends. It is true that games generally help us discharge pent-up surplus energy, aggressive and otherwise, and games do prepare us to exercise competencies in nonthreatening situations—strength, agility, decisiveness or willingness not to be a poor loser. But games need to be reconceived as a diaconal service for mature people through which they thank God as the games invigorate the players' imagination.* Games are not something particularly childish or remedial, nor are they a middle-class luxury or a waste of time.* The refusal to play games or the indulgence in a life of constant game playing—each is an indication of an imbalanced and unhealthy spirituality.

The Rich Variety of Games in God's World

There are many, many games for children and adults to play. Within the rough taxonomy that follows the games appear in order of their complexity, with the most elementary appearing first:

□ basic movement and control (kite flying, roller-skating, swimming, bicycling, skiing, gymnastics)

□ testing physical properties (making mud pies, molding clay, sawing wood)

□ chase and capture and lost and found (hide-and-seek, blindman's buff, fishing, hunting)

□ display (dressing up, participating in parades)

□ skill competence (catching a ball, spinning tops, shooting marbles, horseshoes, quoits, darts, group juggling, spelling bees)

□ guessing (Who am I? charades, Pictionary)

□ puzzles (fitting shapes in holes, jigsaw pictures, crosswords, anagrams, Scrabble)

□ get-acquainted (passing grapefruit from neck to neck, forming group tableaux)

□ chance (dominoes, card games, board games with dice, mahjong)

□ combative strategy (checkers, chess, tennis, squash, pickup team sports)

□ trust-relationships (blind fall and catch, Balderdash)

□ sheer pretense (masquerade party)

One can turn almost any fascination or activity that has flair into a game so long as there is an obstacle to overcome or something whimsical that eludes straightforward calculation and implementation. There is much to be said for inventing our own games. Games that are no longer homemade but are standardized and manufactured, as with board games, remove to arm's length the congealed play of a homespun game. Boxed games are like secondary sources, and one needs to be wary of the imported spirit hidden in the prefabricated game. Is the game inherently ruthless (the Darwinian Monopoly)? fact-ridden (Trivial Pursuit)? ingenuous (Authors)? fantastically extravagant (Dungeons and Dragons)? During the 1960s there was a rise in noncompetitive group games, such as "mixers" made up for occasional social gatherings (see *The New Games Book* and *More New Games*), which were wholesomely critical of the overly intense, win-at-all-costs mentality that followed World War II and hurts genuine play. Computer games* also are a mixed blessing, as they teach us to interact with a machine in a socially isolated context.

Games of chance, such as card games or games with dice, have often been stigmatized by Christians as evil pastimes (or been co-opted by the church for charitable purposes—for example, bingo). Rather than approach games of chance as a violation of belief in God's providence, or suppose that the element of chance is playing loosely with God's will, we should view hidden cards in bridge and unpredictable dice as simply a handy way to bring the play in reality to the fore. Picking up six vowels and only one consonant during a turn in Scrabble or throwing a double six so you land on a penalty square in a board game is "accidental," but the chance draw or throw calls upon all your human ingenuity to achieve more with less—precisely the imaginative challenge amid the laughable surprises of any game. And God sees the ludic crux of games and says, "It is good!"

When Games Go Bad

Game theorist Roger Caillois (1913-1978) puts his analytic finger correctly on what corrupts games: when the very real boundary of imagination that defines their terrain and structure is violated, the play of players and games is ruined (Caillois, pp. 43-55). Godless indulgence in sportive amusement that is licentious and idolatrous is clearly wrong

(Ex 32:1-6; 1 Cor 10:6-13). Further, games themselves can be denatured. To cheat at hopscotch or even to play marbles for keeps is to end the playfulness. Gambling is always the murder of a game, because gambling violates the allusive play of the God-created game world and enslaves fun in the straitjacket of mammon. Lotteries are an illicit turn to games even if they be legal tender.

Video games are mechanized, with a built-in drive for speed and power, which augurs poorly for leisure and harbors an imaginative, consumerized violence that is the antithesis of personal relaxation. A dubious quality of computerized virtual-reality* games is their conjuring of decorporealized illusions that appear more real than ordinary imaginative reality, in which one enjoys throwing Frisbees or boomerangs and knows the laughter of touching bony backs in a game of leapfrog. To call professional sports* a game is a misnomer. The gladiatorial contests of professional sports worldwide bank on the thrill of God's ludic gift and honed acrobatic human skill, but in our days, so close in temper to those of Noah (Mt 24:36-44), professional sports have corporately adulterated the game element into an abnormal, fascinating play-for-pay spectacle, as beautiful as an expensive cancer.

Redeeming the Time by Playing Games

Game opportunities bear a redemptive slant when they awaken and stretch the players' imagination to rejoice in the miraculous surprises God has created for us to experience together. The best games may not be those one can become ever more skilled at, sharpening the competitive edge, but those that most generously spread around communal good humor and a refreshing playfulness based on feeling at home in God's world despite the secularized brutalization of all things bright and beautiful.

Games that lean toward bonding younger and older generations in good fun, that tickle smiles to the faces of those who have been abused or wasted, that cement friendship* because the playing time, you remember afterward, was as holy as good prayer—such games, many still to be invented by the saints, carry a coefficient of the Lord God's grace and offset both an obsession with pleasure and a workaholic* mania. When Christ returns, one could do worse than be found with an orphan visiting a zoo of God's fantastic animals or playing checkers with a lonely widow or widower in a deserted convalescent home, letting them be imaginatively useful and take initiative in joyfully jumping your king. There will be no games in hell, only ennui.

See also IMAGINATION; LEISURE; PLAY; RECREATION; SABBATH.

References and Resources

J. Byl, "Coming to Terms with Play, Game, Sport and Athletics," in *Christianity and Leisure: Issues in a Pluralistic Society,* ed. P. Heintzman, G. Van Andel and T. Visker (Sioux Center, Iowa: Dordt College Press, 1994); R. Caillois, *Man, Play and Games,* trans. M. Barash (New York: Schocken, 1979); A. Fluegelman, *More New Games* (Garden City, N.Y.: Doubleday, 1981); A. Fluegelman, *The New Games Book* (Garden City, N.Y.: Doubleday, 1976); B. Frey, W. Ingram, T. McWhortor and W. D. Romanowski, *At Work and Play, Biblical Insight to Daily Obedience* (Jordan Station, Ont.: Paideia Press, 1986); J. Piaget, pt. 2 of "Play," in *Play, Dreams and Imitation in Childhood,* trans. C. Gattegno and F. M. Hodgson (New York: Norton, 1962); H. B. Schwartzman, *Play and Culture,* vol. 4 of the proceedings of the annual meeting of the Association for the Anthropological Study of Play (West Point, N.Y.: Leisure Press, 1980); T. Visker, "Play, Game and Sport in a Reformed Biblical Worldview," in *Christianity and Leisure: Issues in a Pluralistic Society,* ed. P. Heintzman, G. Van Andel and T. Visker (Sioux Center, Iowa: Dordt College Press, 1994).

Calvin Seerveld

GARDENING

For many people gardening is a favorite pastime. It is not confined to those who have open space around their family homes. Apartment dwellers with small enclosed areas of ground or room for window boxes and indoor plants can also take gardening seriously. Tending other people's gardens, whether attached to a home, an institution, a shopping mall,* a public building or a park, may offer employment. Market gardening often takes the form of a family business. For some people, growing vegetables in the yard is primarily a way of providing food for themselves and their dependents. Others are more interested in growing flowers, shrubs and trees. For some people, as, for example, head gardeners, landscape gardeners and supervisors of botanic gardens, gardening becomes a master trade* or profession.*

Gardening is an activity that tends to generate passionate commitment. While this is true of any hobby,* especially those that are also trades, because of its setting and character gardening gives rise to the kinds of feelings a farmer has for the land. This is not surprising, for gardening is a form of farming* in miniature. As such, it is one of the chief ways we in the city* have managed to retain continuity between the modern and premodern world. Yet gardening has also given rise to a wide range of clubs,* exhibitions, magazines, books, classes and programs that are very much part of contemporary life.

Gardens and Gardening in the Bible

References to gardens go back at least to the second millennium before Christ. In the ancient Near East, cultivation of gardens was widely practiced. Royal families often established large tree-covered parks and nurtured vegetable gardens for the special use of the royal cooks.

Even small landholders had their plots and orchards for herbs and fruit trees. Some gardens were famous well beyond their country's borders, as, for example, the hanging gardens in Babylon.

In the second chapter of the Bible we come across the Garden of Eden. This garden was planted by God: it is God who is described as the one responsible for the trees and their produce (Gen 2:9-10). And the garden was intended not only for the first man and woman but for God's own use and pleasure: God is portrayed as "walking in the garden in the cool of the day" (Gen 3:8). The description of Eden suggests that it was a kind of arboretum, with various species of trees (Ezek 31:8) bearing fruit for animals as well as humans (Gen 1:30) and carrying seed for their future multiplication (Gen 1:12). There was also a stream watering the Garden (Gen 2:10). It was the responsibility of the first human pair to "till it and keep it" and to "freely eat" of it (Gen 2:15, 16 NRSV). In other words, the Garden not only ensured their physical survival and provided natural beauty* but was a context for fulfilling their vocation. It was also a place that exhibited the mutual dependence of human beings and the divine creation on one another. It was a complete divine-human-material ecosystem.

References to gardens occur elsewhere in the Bible. Sometimes these belong to ordinary people (Deut 11:10; 1 Kings 21:1; Lk 13:19), but mostly it is royal gardens or vineyards that are in view (2 Kings 25:4; Neh 3:15; Eccles 2:4-6; Jer 39:4; 52:7). These were mainly kitchen gardens and grew melons, cucumbers, onions, leeks, garlics and an array of herbs and aromatic plants. Sometimes sumptuous meals took place in garden settings (Esther 7:7-8), and on occasion young people courted one another there (Song 6:1-3, 11-12). Less well-off people who nevertheless owned some property would have planted less exotic vegetables and trees, such as beans and lentils or fig and almond trees. Even in exile the Israelites were encouraged "to plant gardens and eat what they produce" (Jer 29:5).

Significant events in God's purposes sometimes happen in gardens, beginning with the fall of the first human pair (Gen 3:1-7). Idol worship often took place in a garden, perhaps surrounding a shrine (Is 1:29; 66:17), and consequently sometimes the prophets pass judgment on the gardens themselves (Amos 4:9). Jesus' final prayers and arrest took place in a garden (Mt 26:36-56). In view of what happened in the first garden, many theologians have commented on the divine symmetry involved in the prayers in Gethsemane. Gardens and their produce are also used metaphorically to speak of many other things, for example, of the beauty of a loved one (Song 4:12—5:1), of the coming divine ruler and his kingdom (Is 4:2; 11:1-2; Lk 13:18-19), of the integration of the Gentiles into the chosen people, under the new covenant (Rom 11:17-24), and of the Christian's growth to maturity (Mt 7:17-20; Jn 15:2-8; Gal 5:22; *see* Spiritual Growth). The coming and character of the kingdom of God is also depicted in terms of a garden (Is 55:12-13; Amos 9:14), sometimes as restoring the Garden of Eden (Is 51:3; Joel 2:3; 3:18; Ezek 36:33-6; 47:1-2) with God standing within it (Zech 14:4, 8). This picture of a celestial "garden city" is most beautifully brought before us in the book of Revelation (Rev 22:1-2).

Gardening as a Parable of God's Kingdom

The Bible begins and ends with humankind—and God—in a garden. In the beginning, God comes down to be with the first man and woman, whom he has placed in the Garden of Eden to tend it. In the last chapter of Revelation, the celestial city that God has prepared as an eternal dwelling place of humankind with himself is likened to a garden. In between these two the judgment of God against sin, and the way for the eternal dwelling of man with God, also finds its critical point of resolution in a garden. In the Garden of Gethsemane Jesus, the divine Son come to earth, says yes to the Father's way of salvation, opening a way of life for all who believe in the Son.

Beyond these critical points in salvation history, we have already seen how the garden functions—metaphorically and otherwise—throughout Scripture. The Christian person can hardly be involved in gardening, whether as a casual pastime or as an intense pursuit, without experiencing gardening as a metaphor, parable or allegory of the kingdom of God and of Christian life in the kingdom of God. In the context of the parable of the sower in the Gospels, we encounter these words of Jesus: "Let anyone with ears to hear listen" (Mk 4:9 NRSV). There is a comparable imperative for a gardener in the present time, arising as the Spirit of God illumines our contemporary experience of the garden: let anyone with eyes see the ways of God with humankind in the whole range of gardening experiences. Some of the more significant experiences in gardening invite our attention.

First, however, it is worthwhile to pass in review elements of the gardening experience. Gardening is an art, and every art has its disciplines, its imperative steps or categories. In light of the fact that the range of "gardens" may vary from African violets in a sunny kitchen window to an extensive garden covering many acres, it is clear that the categories will differ for each gardener. Some important moments in gardening include the decision to have a garden, location of garden, choice of garden type or style (according to personal taste and capability), building the soil foundation with nutrients suited to the plant, choosing from literally thousands of seeds and plants, tilling (deeply!) the soil for young plants, watering, weeding, protecting plants against outer and inner enemies such as birds and parasites, thinning, pruning, harvesting—and celebrating the harvest! Some of these categories have many subheadings. Most categories are featured in the Bible as well as in our contemporary experience of gardening. We choose only eight for brief comment; those that have eyes to see will understand how each of them may be a pointer to the ways of God with and in humankind.

Soil. Although there are exceptions, most gardens flourish and offer the best growth and fruit only when planted in "good" soil. To be sure, the definition of "good" soil varies according to the plant. Although some plants grow in sand and rock and others in clay, they are the exceptions that prove the rule. It is very frustrating to begin the whole gardening process with the wrong soil, soil to which the plant is a stranger, soil which does not support good growth. As a result, the plant will not mature according to its kind. Only when the seed or plant is placed in good soil does it flourish according to its kind. In the parable of the sower, *we,* the hearers of the Word of God, are likened to the seedbed—whether it be a hardened pathway, rocky ground or good soil (Mk 4:8, 20). The tragedy all about us and in us is that there is such a scarcity of good soil for the planting of God's seed. "Let anyone with ears to hear listen!"

Planting. After the gardener has chosen the right soil, prepared the seedbed for planting and chosen the right seeds or plants, the all-important work of planting itself begins. This is also an art. One just doesn't "stick" a plant in the ground (like a stick!) or throw some seed at the seedbed. Planting has to take place at the right time and in the right way. Sometimes there is only a very narrow "window" for planting time. When the time is right, as when frost is past and the warmth of the sun is at hand, seed has to be planted at the correct depth, with the right spacing, and covered carefully and correctly. Then the ground has to be firmed up and watered to hasten the sprouting of the seed and the rooting and establishment of the young plant. Young seedlings have to be tenderly placed in a hole of the right depth and size and firmly set in the soil so that they can quickly root in the good soil. The common expression "tender loving care" has to come into its own in the planting of a garden if there is to be a garden worthy of the name. We who so carefully tend our earthly gardens are called to account again and again in respect to the way we plant the gardens of our lives and the lives of others for whom we are responsible. Paul, the missionary pastor, appears as a forerunner in this respect (1 Cor 3:6).

Water. No sooner is a seed or plant bedded in the good soil than there is a cry for water. Without water the young plant will wither and die. Watering is again an art. When to water, how to water, and how much to water are all major decisions in sustaining and nurturing the life of a sprouting seed and a growing plant. There must be enough water to penetrate the soil and saturate it with moisture. Care must be taken in applying water to some plants lest they mildew or suffer sunburn. The lack of timely watering in the beginning can be determinative for the whole future life of a plant, resulting in stunted growth and lesser harvests. Strangely enough too much water can also damage, even destroy, a tender young plant or rot a seed. If Paul could present himself as a planter, Apollos was presented as one who watered the Corinthian planting (1 Cor 3:6).

Whether we are planters or waterers of God's garden, whatever form that may take, we are called to be disciplined artists in our work.

Protection. The tender plant, and the mature plant as well, needs protection. From the moment it leaves the gardener's hand, the seed or plant is fragile and vulnerable. Whether or not the danger is a bird swooping down, as in the parable of Jesus (Mk 4:4, 15), the seed and the plant are subject to an unending series of inner and outer enemies. The attacks may come in the form of birds, animal intruders, insects, winds, scorching sun, hail, frost and blight—as well as through ourselves. For a dedicated gardener, mistakenly stepping on a tender plant is always an unhappy moment. Some of the enemies attack from without, while others do their evil work within the plant. Stronger and more mature plants fare better before some of these enemies, but all are vulnerable. The Bible is filled with admonitions and warnings to those tending God's gardens about enemies without and within.

Weeding. Weeding is critical to gardening. Weeds are here understood as intruders in the garden—and weeding is a way of ridding the garden of the intruder. Weeds steal water, light and nutrients from the soil, nourishing themselves and leaving the good planting dwarfed, if not worthless. It seems that weeds never stop coming. In the parable of the sower Jesus uses graphic language to describe the impact of weeds: "the thorns grew up and choked it" (Mk 4:7, 18-19 NRSV). Every gardener understands just how apt the word *choked* is here! Thus, wherever possible, the imperative is always "weed now." If weeds are given freedom to flourish, later on one may well destroy a plant as the weed is pulled out (Mt 13:29). Oddly enough, it seems that there are always new weed enemies to battle in modern gardens.

More dangerous are the intruders which intrude into our everyday lives and into our world.

Thinning. Less familiar and less dramatic than planting, watering and weeding, thinning is no less essential for the health of plants and garden as a whole. If, in planting, too many seeds fall in more or less the same spot and all sprout, the net effect can be as fateful as an invasion of weeds. Thus the gardener must, however reluctantly, pluck out the surplus seedlings. If this is not done early, the plants contesting for nutrients, light, water and air will fall short of the standards, becoming stunted and ultimately worthless. Thinning offers a particularly significant parable for modern times, wherein so many lesser things, perhaps good in themselves, vie for our attention, distracting us from the central claim of God on our lives.

Pruning. When Jesus likened himself to a vine and his Father to the vinegrower (Jn 15:1-12), he placed the urgency of pruning before the church* for all time. If thinning is an action in which the gardener needs a certain boldness, then pruning makes even greater demands. It is not easy to put the pruning shear or saw to a vine or tree to which one has long given tender loving care, but holding back can be fatal. Dead wood not only is worthless but can also harbor disease. Old wood needs to be removed to allow expansion room for new branches that will bear fruit (Jn 15:2). In the grapevine, the goal is to produce grapes, not grapevines—hence the necessity of the pruning knife. The sharpened blade is not nice, but it is necessary.

Harvesting. Some gardens are purely ornamental and do not offer a harvest as such. Here the delight of the gardener is in the resultant color, shape, texture, contrast and natural beauty of a planting. In a fruit or vegetable garden, vineyard or orchard, all the movements of gardening lead up to the harvest—not just the mature, even lovely plant, vine or tree. The good gardener knows what kind of harvest to expect, and when the fruit is ready for picking and eating. The good gardener who has long since planted, nurtured and patiently waited, celebrates the harvest. Every good gardener knows the joy of cutting and presenting a large bouquet of flowers or a basketful of colorful and fragrant fruit. Here the gardener's forerunner is Jesus, who expresses delight in the lily blossom: "Consider the lilies of the field, how they grow; they neither toil nor spin, yet I tell you, even Solomon in all his glory was not clothed like one of these" (Mt 6:28-29 NRSV). Those are the words of a person who knew how to gratefully celebrate the harvest. Good gardeners know what they are working for, and they know how to celebrate the results of their labor.

The gardener who has labored and waited, and waited and labored, knows how much of the life and growth of the garden lie outside human hands. The sprouting of the seed, the weather, external conditions, the growing of the tender plant to maturity, blossoming and bearing fruit—these things and much else lie beyond the work and will of the gardener. At the end of the day, gardening is a mystery.

Gardens and Gardening Today

Though the development of tenements in expanding cities from the end of the eighteenth century separated many people from the land, the growth of suburbia* from the end of the nineteenth century gave many an opportunity to reconnect with the land in the form of working the small plots around their homes or in public areas. For many such people, the old adage "you can take a person out of a farm but you can't take the farm out of a person" proved true. Though farming became increasingly restricted to a smaller percentage of the population, suburbia led to the democratizing of gardening, which till then had been a pastime more for the elite than for the ordinary person. In North America the form gardens took was influenced less by the small vegetable plots and orchards around the house typical of farms, or the mixed vegetable and flower beds and shrubs characteristic of the English cottage garden, than by the influence of transcendental naturalists like Henry David Thoreau, with their preference for wide-open spaces and trees. This, and the domination of nature writing by ideas of wilderness* rather than cultivation, explains why gardens do not appear much in the poetry and fiction of North American writers, and why nature writings and anthologies do not generally include articles on gardening.

See also FARMING; HOBBIES; LEISURE.

References and Resource

R. Banks, *God the Worker: Journeys into the Mind, Heart and Imagination of God* (Valley Forge, Penn.: Judson, 1994); H. Crabtree, *The Christian Life: Traditional Metaphors and Contemporary Theologies* (Cambridge, Mass.: Harvard University Press, 1991); M. Francis and R. T. Hester, eds., *The Meaning of Gardens: Idea, Place and Action* (Cambridge: MIT Press, 1990); E. Hymans, *A History of Gardens and Gardening* (London: Dent, 1970); S. C. Juengst, *Like a Garden: A Biblical Spirituality of Growth* (St. Louis: Westminster/John Knox, 1996); P. Keller, *A Gardener Looks at the Fruit of the Spirit* (Irving, Tex.: Word, 1986); B. Marranca, ed., *American Garden Writing: Gleanings from Garden Lives Then and Now* (New York: Penguin, 1988); E. Perenyi, *Green Thoughts: A Writer in the Garden* (New York: Vintage, 1981).

Robert Banks and Robert P. Meye

GIFT-GIVING

Gift-giving is a thermometer of the soul. It reveals what we think we possess, and whether we can love.* Ironically, the very rich are sometimes less generous because their gifts often come with strings attached as a form of control. The very poor, with apparently little to give away, may give their last loaf of bread, like the widow who gave all she had to the temple (Lk 21:1-4). My wife and I still sleep nightly under one of the most generous gifts of all, a red blanket given to us almost thirty years ago by an ex-prostitute then on welfare.

Gift-receiving is also a thermometer of the soul. It is "more blessed to give than to receive," as Jesus says (Acts 20:35), but receiving is usually harder. Sometimes the reluctance or refusal to receive a gift indicates the absolute need for independence and the fear of being under obligation to perform some duty in return. In the case of the dependent poor, gift-receiving often means enduring the demeaning experience of being the object of someone else's patronage. Charity is not always love. The refusal of the receivers to say thank you—so distressing to some givers—may be a symptom of this internal struggle or a silent statement that the relatively rich benefactor really "owes" this support. In other words, it is not a gift but a duty.

Both giving and receiving gifts are not only thermometers of generosity and love; they are also barometers that indicate which way the soul is changing—like the weather.* Over a lifetime, our experience of gifts indicates whether our soul is shriveling into hard-heartedness or heading toward the eternally generous environment of heaven. Some people are perpetually "giving" because they are hungry for relationships and addicted to people, but there is less true generosity in this than is immediately apparent. So gift-giving is both a spiritual discipline and an arena requiring spiritual discernment, especially when we consider the great range and meanings of gifts.

A Lifetime of Giving and Receiving

Usually our first gifts are received before we are old enough to say thank you. The first gift is a name, an act that establishes a child's identity and, in the process, reveals the parents as well (Kass and Kass, pp. 15, 18). Then follows a host of other gifts, such as a baby outfit, then birthday* gifts, Christmas* gifts, goodwill gifts from relatives, rewards (really "pay") for performance at school. Infants and children sometimes give gifts during this period, often to the delight of their parents—a smile, a kiss and laughter—but these are given unconsciously. Perhaps this very unconsciousness, so natural to a child, is the very thing most needed to be cultivated in adult life so we can give without our left hand knowing what our right is doing (Mt 6:3; compare Mt 25:38).

At an early age many children learn that gifts may be used as a form of manipulation or "guilt money" for a sin committed. This occurs in a most tragic way when there is sexual abuse.* In some families children never receive gifts without strings attached; all gifts received are implied obligations or explicit rewards rather than sacraments of love and appreciation. They learn too quickly that Christmas trees are surrounded by exchanges of mutual obligations (carefully balanced to the dollar), that "favors" by a boss or employee are messages to perform, that politicians can be influenced by gifts and that flowers are a way of saying "I'm sorry I hurt you." The final gift of our parents, expressed in their last will* and testament, may turn out to be no gift at all but rather a posthumous form of control. We receive very few gifts in this life. Probably we give few as well.

Gift-giving comes only with a struggle, even to the youngest child who presumably has not yet been enculturated to a me-first culture. It starts in the sandbox, sharing a toy with a neighbor, or in the home when we use our precious savings as a child to buy Mom a birthday present. Giving does not come easily and does not seem to come spontaneously. Jesus was able to descriptively note, "You then, though you are evil, know how to give good gifts to your children" (Lk 11:13), but he was commenting on the basic goodwill parents feel toward children, something which Paul referred to much later (2 Cor 12:14). Part of the Christian education of the family is learning how to give and receive, but this starts with the parents' ability to model this.

Cultures vary on this matter, and we learn very quickly "what is expected," such as a small gift when you arrive at the door to have dinner in someone's home, a large gift in advance of making a business deal with favorable terms to your own company (is this a bribe?), a present to the parents of the woman you intend to marry or a "gift" (sometimes euphemistically called a "user fee") expected by border guards or officials in government offices in many developing countries. But learning what is expected is not learning how to give.

Gifts and Nongifts

Some "gifts" are simply *commercial transactions* or *fulfilled contracts*. These are simply negotiated exchanges of valuable items (money or things) according to a written or unwritten contract. Much that passes for Christmas* "giving" is really a series of carefully managed mutual exchanges, often with goodwill and generosity but, nevertheless, under obligation. It is a social shame to receive a gift at Christmas from someone to whom you have not given. Real Christmas gifts, like the gifts presented by the Magi (Mt 2:11), are not expected and are sacraments of appreciation.

Other gifts are *instruments of manipulation*. A donor contributes a large sum to a Christian organization knowing that his or her votes on the board will carry more weight than those of lesser givers. Sometimes, when the donor's will is thwarted, financial support is reduced or withdrawn, a barometer reading of what is happening in their soul-life. Proverbs notes (without commenting on the morality of the matter) that "a gift opens the way for the giver" (18:16). Jacob's psychologically contrived gift to his estranged brother is a stunning example of this (Gen 32:13-21). Bribes openly state the intention to influence and control even when they are given secretly. In the parallelism of Proverbs "a gift given in secret" is the same thing as "a bribe concealed in the cloak" that "pacifies great wrath" (21:14). Sometimes the control factor is not so much a direct appeal for power* as it is a matter of manipulating opinion—a form of personal advertising.* Ananias and Sapphira pretended to have given more than they did to the church, thus lying to God (Acts 5:4). They did this because they wanted status in the Christian community. Both the book of Proverbs (25:14) and Jesus (Mt 6:2) warn against trumpeting our giving.

In their purest form gifts are *sacraments of goodwill*. They are relatively free of the desire for personal gain, either in a material sense or in public approval. Such gifts see a need and give from the heart, not expecting anything in return, not even thanks. They say to another, "You are a special person." They are love incarnate. The three wise men expressed their worship of Christ through their gifts, as did the widow with her two last coins (Lk 21:1-4). The Antiochian Christians, hearing of the famine in Judea, sent gifts to the Christians there by the hands of Barnabas and Saul (Acts 11:29-30). Later Paul expanded on this generous gift by raising funds throughout the Gentile churches in aid of the poor Jewish Christians in Judea as a sacramental expression of love, equality and mutual ministry between Jews and Gentiles in

Christ (2 Cor 8:12, 20; 9:5). Especially commendable (from God's perspective) was the generosity of the Gentile Cornelius before becoming a Christian. The angels told him, "Your prayers and gifts to the poor have come up as a memorial offering before God" (Acts 10:4).

The greatest gift of all is the *gift of salvation in Jesus Christ* (Eph 2:8). This gift above all others is undeserved, unexpected and comes with no strings attached. It is an expression of God's unconditional love for humankind (Jn 3:16) and can never be repaid. It is precisely because of the poverty of our souls in giving and receiving that we have trouble receiving forgiveness, atonement, access to God, membership in God's family and eternal life as free gifts. We feel we must earn it either before or after receiving the gift. We misinterpret the gift as an exchange in which God gives salvation *because of* our good works (Rom 4:4) or as a contract in which we *owe* God a lifetime of sacrificial service. In fact there is nothing we can do to make God love us or to make God stop loving us. It is precisely the offense this gift causes to human pride that makes so many people unwilling to enter into the joy of salvation.

Spiritual gifts* bear the character of the ultimate gift (Eph 4:8, 11). They are *charisms* of God's love expressed through human beings not because of our worthiness in character or training but as a pure present. As with all gifts, the ultimate gift and the penultimate spiritual gifts can neither be deserved nor revoked (Rom 11:29). They should stimulate the fundamental posture of gratitude rather than pride, love-inspired service rather than dutiful performance, spontaneous giving (Rom 12:8) rather than carefully orchestrated bribes. The reason for such giving and receiving is deeply theological.

The Theology of Giving and Receiving

Everything we have, everything we receive and everything we give ultimately belongs to God. So giving and receiving must be considered as part of stewardship.* We are trustees of God's possessions, never absolute owners (*see* Ownership). That should make giving easier, more thoughtful and more generous. But there is something even deeper in this ministry of giving and receiving.

God is the ultimate giver and the ultimate receiver. Within God's triune life Father, Son and Holy Spirit continuously and eternally give and receive from each other. It is the nature of love to do both, and God is love (1 Jn 4:16). Some of Jesus' words are sacred inspired windows on the generosity in the heart of God. The Father gives the Son into the world (Jn 3:16) but not without giving him his power, authority, glory (Jn 8:54), people (Jn 6:37) and love (Jn 17:24). The Son gives praise (Lk 10:21) and glory (Jn 17:4) to the Father. Jesus is the perfect model of selfless impoverishment to enrich others (2 Cor 8:9). The Spirit is given into the world (Acts 1:4) but also gives deference, love and glory to the Father and the Son (Jn 16:13-15). God not only continually gives within the loving communion of the Godhead but also continuously receives. When Paul says, "God loves a cheerful [literally a 'hilarious'] giver" (2 Cor 9:7), one who gives in an uncalculating and spontaneously generous way, he is saying that we are most godlike when our giving is least calculated, reciprocal, contractual or laced with ulterior motive. So both giving and receiving are spiritual disciplines.

The Spirituality of Giving and Receiving

Giving and receiving are both delightful and dangerous. Offering a gift to the Lord's servant, as Naaman did when he was healed by God through Elisha (2 Kings 5:15), is a holy act communicating gratitude and praise to God. Refusing the gift, as Elisha wisely did (2 Kings 5:16), communicated something essential: this ministry was God's ministry and could not be hired or remunerated. In contrast, Elisha's servant, Gehazi, went after the gift and destroyed his own soul (2 Kings 5:19-27). Chasing after gifts is the special temptation of public servants of God who earn their living by ministry* (Is 1:23). Paul steadfastly refused to do this (Phil 4:17), primarily so he could offer ministry as a free gift and not hinder the gospel (1 Cor 9:12). He quoted the words of Jesus, "It is more blessed to give than to receive" (Acts 20:35) in the context of giving ministry without obligation (see Financial Support).

Giving to God is also dangerous. Jesus says we should make sure we are right with our brothers and sisters first, leaving our gift-giving incomplete "at the altar" until relationships are straightened out (Mt 5:23-24). God is not impressed with vertical generosity that is not expressed horizontally. Nor is God impressed with generous giving to the church at the expense of family* (Mt 15:5-6). Paradoxically, giving to our neighbor turns out to be giving to God, as the parable of Jesus indicates (Mt 25:40). But one form of giving is not approved anywhere in the Bible—displayed giving. Those who give so that all may see already have their desired reward—to be seen by people. Instead, says Jesus, let "your giving . . . be in secret. Then your Father, who sees what is done in secret, will reward you" (Mt 6:3-4). The delight of giving is the pleasure it brings God.

If giving is a spiritual discipline, so is receiving. It invites gratitude to God, receiving what we are given as from God himself. This frees us from an unhealthy sense of obligation to the donor and makes each gift, as it was for Paul, something that gives praise to God (Phil 4:18). Refusal to receive anything from others is both a negative spiritual symptom (we insist on being autonomous) and a spiritual invitation (to grow in healthy interdependence). Giving and receiving are thermometers and barometers of the soul.

The Practice of Giving and Receiving

Many practical matters emerge from this discussion. First, holy gift-giving and receiving begins, as it did for the apostle Paul, with giving ourselves to God (2 Cor 8:5) and then to others. Generosity starts with the self-sacrifice that, paradoxically, leads to being rich in the things that matter. This is the source of all other giving and receiving. Second, offering ministry free of charge is especially commendable. Christian service is essentially a volunteer and amateur matter, in the original sense of the word amateur—one who works for love. The temptation of greed is especially serious in matters dealing publicly with God and the gospel. Third, giving to the poor and needy requires special sensitivity on the parts of both giver and receiver. Anonymous giving is one way, but not the only way, of avoiding patronage and dependency. A better way is to allow for mutual giving, as Paul encouraged between the Jewish and Gentile Christians, though with a difference in kind (Rom 15:27). Fourth, we can be creative in gift-giving. Time* is one of the most valuable gifts. Handmade gifts, thoughtfully crafted to suit the intended receiver, can communicate the message intended: you are special and I appreciate you. Fifth, we can prayerfully cultivate hilarious giving and spontaneity, even when the cultural context requires giving as a social obligation. Finally, we can turn receiving—usually harder than giving—into prayer for gratitude to God and the joy of giving. In the end our giving and receiving tells as much about our spirituality as our prayer life; indeed they are each a reflection of the other.

See also FESTIVALS—CHRISTMAS; FESTIVALS—THANKSGIVING; FINANCIAL SUPPORT; STEWARDSHIP .

References and Resources

C. Brown, "Gift, Pledge, Corban," in *New International Dictionary of New Testament Theology*, ed. C. Brown (Grand Rapids: Zondervan, 1989) 2:39-44; A. A. Kass and L. R. Kass, "What's Your Name?" *First Things*, November 1995, 14-25; R. Titmuss, *The Gift Relationship* (London: Allen and Unwin, 1970).

R. Paul Stevens

GLOBAL VILLAGE

The generations living today are the first to experience earth as a planet. Pictures taken from a spacecraft of this immensely beautiful, but surprisingly fragile, planet have had a profound effect on our worldview.* But even before these first pictures flashed back from space, in 1962 the Canadian Marshall McLuhan had already coined the phrase *global village* to express the effect of technological advances in electronics on our consciousness: "The human family now exists under conditions of a 'global village.' We live in a single constricted space resonant with tribal drums" (p. 31). We feel the world has shrunk to a single town* in which everyone knows each other's business. Everyday life is now a global matter. We eat, play, think, work and pray globally, even when we are not conscious of it. Martin Luther King Jr. said, "Before you finish eating breakfast this morning, you've depended on more than half the world" (quoted in "Who Are Our Suppliers?").

Understanding Globalization

Globalize (as an active verb) is "to make worldwide in scope and application." This definition hints that human beings have a part in creating a global consciousness, that we are world makers—something which the Bible affirms. In this article *globalization* will refer to consciousness of one earth, one world and one church and our response to that in living as responsible stewards of one earth and one world and as members of one church. There are several dimensions of this global-village experience (Snyder, pp. 24-25).

First, the environment is a global issue. Toxic chemicals used on a grand scale in North America can affect the quality of the shield around the earth that protects all human beings from harmful radiation. Second, transfer of technology* from country to country and global cooperation in major projects, such as space travel and medical research projects, have led to one world of scientific expertise. Third, communication is globalized. The information superhighway* allows us to access information from computers worldwide. Fourth, we are moving toward a global culture. Popular music, dress styles, soft drinks, equal roles for women and more egalitarian social relationships are becoming increasingly "the same" worldwide. Fifth, the economies of all nations are linked in one giant system. A *Time* article noted, "The world's financial markets are so intertwined that when one itches, the others scratch" ("They're All Connected"). Sixth, the whole world is viewed as a single market with a global business culture. Seventh, politics is being globalized in the worldwide trend toward democracy, though this trend lacks a unified ideological or philosophical basis. We are witnessing the relativizing of everything, including values,* morals and faith. Eight, travel* is not merely the means of getting somewhere to do business or experience leisure.* It is a way of life, a global lifestyle. Ninth, urbanization is a global phenomenon with people moving from rural areas to cities. But there is a sameness in all cities, especially their slums. These nine trends seem to be irresistible directions, but they are not welcomed by everyone and are possibly not as omnipotent as is sometimes claimed.

Paradoxically, on the edge of realizing one-earth and one-world consciousness, we are finding the village breaking down into warring neighborhoods, cliques, ghettos and clans—possibly out of the need for survival culturally and economically. When you belong to everyone, you belong to no one. And you do not know who you are. Tribalism is on the rise, as is ethnic consciousness. There is a resurgence of religious fundamentalism, especially in Islam. Smaller political units, based on race, language or clan, are emerging in the struggle to find identity in one world culture, as evidenced in Canada and the Balkans. Poverty,* far from being eradicated, is on the increase with threatening possibilities. Tad Homer-Dixon says,

> Think of a stretch limo in the pot-holed streets of New York City, where homeless beggars live. Inside the limo are the air-conditioned post-industrial regions of North America, Europe, the emerging Pacific Rim, and a few other isolated places, with their trade summitry and computer-information highways. Outside is the rest of mankind, going in a completely different direction. (quoted in Kaplan, p. 60)

Is it really true, as Ted Turner stated in a CNN (Cable News Network) memo to his staff, that "there are no foreigners in a global world"?

Thinking Christianly and Globally

Biblically, we have global work to do. Our basic human vocation in Genesis 1—2 is a threefold call to commune with God, to build community on earth and to be cocreators with God as we take care of God's world. This involves not only creating a global consciousness but developing the earth and the world as respons-

ible stewards. The computer technician's work is as holy as the ministry* of the pioneer cross-cultural church-planter.

We also have a global mission. Fundamental to the idea of *mission* is "to be sent" or "to be on the go." The earth cannot be "filled" (Gen 1:28) without moving. The Great Commission (the "go" of the gospel) does not replace or even subordinate the cultural commission; it rather creates the context for its fulfillment and, by reconciling us to God, empowers people to become fully human and to humanize the world as world makers. Much of the Christian mission in the first century was undertaken in the context of movement: Lydia, a textile merchant from Thyatira whom Paul met at Philippi; the planting of churches along the trade routes in Asia, such as Colosse; through the conversion of people in the Hall of Tyrannus during Paul's two-year marketplace mission in Ephesus. Today we should expect international travelers, people on overseas assignment, people doing business with multinationals, to be frontline people in God's mission of both humanizing the world and sharing the gospel.

We are also called to develop a global unity. The command to "fill the earth," as we have already noted, required movement, the scattering of people. Genesis 11 then must be understood as both judgment and fulfillment. The people of Babel refused to scatter under God to populate and develop the world. Instead they attempted to solidify their autonomous life apart from God by building a tower that symbolized their identity, forging a "community" that was uniform and homogenous. This bland sameness is not unlike much of what is happening today in the globalization of culture and spirituality. But God judged this experiment in unity and forced the Babelites to scatter. Not until Pentecost do we see what God is really after: a richly diverse community* of people who are more one, rather than less one, because of their diversities, but united in their love of God and each other.

Global unity is not, however, a "mashed potato unity" in which peoples lose their identity, culture, spiritual gift and personality in one merged communalism. Rather it is the rich social complex for which Jesus prayed (Jn 17: 18, 21-22), resembling community in the triune God. In this richly diverse unity there is a need for nations* (Acts 17:26) and for cultural diversity. Neither monoculturalism (the celebration of unity without diversity) nor multiculturalism* as commonly promoted (the celebration of diversity without unity) fulfills God's intent.

In this matter the church of Jesus Christ is positioned to do a most exemplary thing: to demonstrate how believers in the developing world and in the developed world, believers from different races and cultures, can be truly one in a way that celebrates, rather than blurs, the differences. Paul's great missionary passion was not simply to win converts but to build a great interdependent, international and transcultural church of Jews and Gentiles, one new humanity (Eph 2:15), in which there would be both unity and equality (2 Cor 8:14). It is only "together with all the saints" (Eph 3:18) that we can know Christ fully or even be fully human. So what can we do to realize this vision?

Acting Christianly and Globally

It has been said that we should think globally but act locally. That comment can be questioned both descriptively (our neighbors are now global neighbors) and theologically (God's mission is both local and global). Much can be done both locally and globally to be world makers in a fully Christian sense.

First, we can become consciously aware of our global interdependence every time we eat a meal or go shopping.* We should find out where things came from, express our gratitude to God for the gift of international labor (perhaps during a grace) and do what we can to exercise Christian justice when we make purchases.

Second, we can learn from the global experience in microcosm in the diversity we experience in our schools, colleges, businesses, churches and neighborhoods. To do this, we must address our own ethnocentrism,* confront our prejudices and learn to prize the contribution of people who are different from us. We need to go and listen before we go and tell.

Third, we can educate ourselves on the systemic nature of globalization: how political, economic and social structures and systems are so interdependent that all the elements in the world "mobile" are interconnected. This will keep us from assuming that our unemployed neighbor is simply lazy. It will also help us pray for, vote for and lobby* for global justice and peace. To deal with one world today, one must understand the complexity of the principalities and powers.*

Fourth, we should seek opportunities to experience other cultures, preferably in situations that take us beyond our own comfort zones. Better than roaring through Cairo on an air-conditioned tour bus is returning to the same village or business enterprise annually to build relationships and learn interpersonally. Local churches in the West can be linked with local churches overseas. Both will be transformed by the connection.

Fifth, we can find ways to express stewardship* on a global basis. What would it mean, for example, (heeding Paul's request in 2 Cor 8:13) to achieve equality between the poorer churches of the developing world and the richer churches of the developed world? What spiritual growth would come to a family that engaged in practical sharing to alleviate world poverty, including alms giving, development and confronting the powers?

Sixth, some Christian people can serve globally without becoming traditional missionaries. They can gain a marketable skill and be tentmakers, supporting themselves in a short-term or long-term mission cross-culturally.*

Seventh, we should regard global business (largely through multinationals), global education (with the great learning exchanges), global technology and global travel as opportunities to engage in mission that is equally important to the traditional church-planting missionary. People doing this should be prayerfully supported in their local churches and treated as tentmaking missionaries. The world will never be reached or humanized by traditional missionaries that are fully supported financially.

Eighth, we must confront our own religious imperialism and colonialism. An African once commented that most church-growth specialists come from the part of the world where the church is not growing! Western theological education, church technology and spirituality should not be marketed globally with colonizing intent but shared in a true dialogue in which all are enriched. The center of the Christian world has undoubtedly shifted from Europe to North America and now to Africa and Asia. Will Singapore, or in a few years Bejing, become the new Antioch?

However threatening or exciting we take globalization to be, the new consciousness and the practical opportunities afforded by the global village offer Christian people an unparalleled opportunity to know God better and fulfill God's mission on earth. If the church does not take up its global mission, perhaps God will raise up business to do it.

Cynthia Barnum's challenge to businesspeople is worth repeating to Christians: "Are you ready, able and willing to do what you do anytime, anywhere, with anyone?" (p. 144).

See also ETHNOCENTRISM; MISSION; MISSIONS; MULTICULTURALISM; STEWARDSHIP; TRAVELING.

References and Resources
C. F. Barnum, "Effective Membership in the Global Business Community," in *New Traditions in Business,* ed. J. Renesch (San Francisco: Berrett-Koehler, 1992) 141-56; R. D. Kaplan, "The Coming Anarchy," *Atlantic Monthly,* February 1994, 44-76; M. McLuhan, *The Gutenberg Galaxy* (Toronto: University of Toronto Press, 1962); B. Nicholls, *Contextualization: A Theology of Gospel and Culture* (Downers Grove, Ill.: InterVarsity Press, 1979); H. A. Snyder, *Earth Currents: The Struggle for the World's Soul* (Nashville: Abingdon, 1995); M. L. Stackhouse, *Apologia: Contextualization, Globalization and Mission in Theological Education* (Grand Rapids: Eerdmans, 1988); R. P. Stevens, "Marketing the Faith: A Reflection on the Importing and Exporting of Western Theological Education," *Crux* 28, no. 2 (1992) 6-18; "They're All Connected," *Time* 140, no. 5 (3 August 1992) 25; "Who Are Our Suppliers?" *Marketplace,* March/April 1991, 11; L. Wilkinson, "One Earth, One World, One Church," *Crux* 28, no. 1 (1992) 28-36.

R. Paul Stevens

GODPARENTING

Godparents are adult Christians who act as sponsors at the baptism* of an infant or small child, answering the questions addressed to the child by speaking the church's* statement of faith on the child's behalf. In theory, this is understood to be the beginning of a lifelong calling* for the godparent, who takes on a responsibility, along with the parents, for the spiritual nurture of the child. In practice, there tends to be little significance attached to godparenting as a spiritual calling. Why do we have godparents in the first place? What does it mean to be a godparent? How might one live out that role as the child grows up? These questions are rarely addressed, with the result that godparenting tends to become a purely ceremonial role, like that of a bridesmaid or groomsman. Yet the concept carries great potential. This potential is being fulfilled by members of ethnic traditions that emphasize godparenting and by individuals who find their own ways to connect with their godchild in an enduring relationship with a spiritual focus.

How Did the Role of the Godparent Develop?

In the earliest centuries, babies or small children were usually brought to the baptismal font by a parent, who answered the creedal questions for the child. Both Hippolytus and Augustine assume this practice, though Augustine allows that persons other than parents may sponsor a child when necessary (e.g., a master bringing a slave child, a dedicated virgin bringing a once-exposed infant she rescued and is rearing). By the sixth century there is evidence from both the East (Pseudo-Dionysius) and the West (Caesarius) that persons other than the parent are "receiving the child from the font."

We do not know exactly why this shift in practice away from parent sponsors occurred. It seems to have been a grassroots phenomenon. There is no record of any official church pronouncement urging nonparental sponsors. Only centuries after the custom was established would there be a rule to that effect. It seems to have been the choice of the parents themselves to involve another adult in their child's life in this way, thereby ensuring that adult's interest in the child's welfare. Just think, a sacramental role in the Christian tradition created by and for the people! When theologians first mention it, it is already an established custom, and the role of

the sponsor is understood to be one of moral guidance and teaching, especially teaching the child to pray.

In the Middle Ages godparenting became tremendously important as a social institution in Western Europe, a nonbiological extension to the kinship structure. By asking someone to sponsor your child, you formed a quasi-familial bond between that person and your family, a bond that had important social and economic, as well as spiritual, aspects. The godparent was bound to the child in a reciprocal relation of duties and responsibilities. The godparent was expected to give gifts and throw the baptismal party and to provide protection for the child. In return, the godchild owed the godparent a special kind of lifelong respect.

Protestant Reformers who supported infant baptism maintained the role of godparent, though with varying degrees of enthusiasm. Luther, while noting that sponsorship was a human addition to the sacrament, commended it as an ancient and pious custom. Calvin downplayed the godparental role in order to place the emphasis on the parents' own responsibility.

Since the sixteenth century, godparenthood as a social institution has gradually decreased in importance in western European societies, especially in northern Europe. It survived somewhat better in southern and eastern Europe, and from Spain spread to Latin America and the Philippines, where it developed into a crucial aspect of the kinship structure. Today in the United States, the practice of godparenting is continued in Presbyterian, Lutheran, Episcopal, African Methodist Episcopal, Roman Catholic, Eastern Orthodox and some United Church of Christ and United Methodist churches, as well as in some Baptist churches, where the godparents are involved in the dedication service. The social significance and definition of that role varies according to ethnic and regional background more than denominationally. Some Latino and African-American godparents have a clear sense of the nature of their continuing obligation to the godchild (which can include financial support and rearing the child if the parents die), while many people of northern European extraction have little social guidance as to the nature of the godparent's role.

Why Should We Care About the Godparental Role Today?

Bringing a child up in the faith is the responsibility of the whole Christian community.* The parents (see Parenting) have the primary responsibility, but they cannot do it alone. This communal responsibility is taken on by Sunday-school teachers, pastors, confirmation mentors, youth leaders, "church grandparents" (in programs that pair children with elderly persons within a congregation), house churches, (see Church in the Home), godparents and others who take a personal interest in children and their spiritual nurture. Of all such relationships, that between godparent and godchild has the distinction of not being locality-dependent, so that it can last throughout a child's growing up.

The need of children for concerned adults in their lives in addition to their parents is harder than ever to meet in our cultural setting. Mobility,* the isolation of the nuclear family,* the decline of community ties in neighborhoods* and the increase in single-parent families are all factors that make this need more acute and more difficult to fill. Any custom that can create closer adult-child bonds deserves cultivating.

In the self-consciously liturgical churches, the liturgical movement has brought a greatly increased focus on the lifelong centrality of baptism to Christian identity. Baptism is not just an entry

rite, and certainly not just a life-cycle rite for Christian babies. Baptism is seen as incorporation into the death of Jesus and, through the cross, into the promise of the resurrection. Churches that practice infant baptism teach that in baptism the child is adopted into God's covenant people and called into ministry* for the sake of the world, an identity and a mission that are (at least!) lifelong. Helping godparents understand and live out their calling is one way to raise awareness of baptism as the enduring core of Christian identity. If godparents can come to see their role as one of remembering with the child that she or he is baptized, the institution of godparenthood can be a key part of baptismally focused renewal.

Churches that do not have godparents as part of their tradition might consider adopting the practice, even if it would not have a baptismal focus. Some churches that do not practice infant baptism have adapted the godparental role to their situation, letting parents choose godparents who participate in the service of dedication, agreeing to share with the parents the responsibility for the child's spiritual nurture. The task of bringing a child up in the faith is much the same regardless of when the child comes to be baptized. All children could use an extra adult or two to connect with them in a long-term, person-to-person way and feel a special concern for their spiritual development.

How Can Godparents Live Out Their Calling?

The calling of a godparent is to help the parents raise the child in the faith. This means finding ways to share with the child about God, faith and values.* Few people in our cultural setting are comfortable talking about matters of faith, and even fewer have any idea of how to do that with a child. What should I do—

461

ask him if he likes church? give her a doll that says prayers? If the only "religious" things I can think of to do feel uncomfortably preachy or pious, I will never explicitly address the spiritual side of life at all.

One of the responsibilities of the Christian community is to teach adults how to listen to children and share the faith with them. For centuries godparents have been told, "Be an example to the child, and pray for him"—advice which did little to help them form a relationship with the child where the faith might be nurtured. Godparents need much more concrete advice about ways to dialogue with children about the things that matter, ways to form a long-distance relationship with a child, ways to remind a child that she is baptized and explore with her what that means.

Here are some of the things that godparents might do as ways to share the faith with their godchildren: Draw pictures together about Bible stories, baptism, Christmas* or Easter.* Mark the child's baptismal anniversary,* rather than the birthday.* Give presents that recall baptism symbolically, like bath or pool toys. Let the child designate some of your charitable giving. Play games* that allow for discussion of feelings and values (e.g., the Ungame, LifeStories, Choices). Make a bedtime tape where you sing a Christian lullaby. Talk together about what to pray for. Make a personalized Advent calendar. Go together to a synagogue's sabbath* service, or to a Greek Orthodox Easter midnight service. Give (or read on tape) well-written children's books that address religious issues: the nature of God, the problem of evil and suffering. (There is no more appropriate godparental present than *The Lion, the Witch and the Wardrobe*—dedicated by C. S. Lewis to his goddaughter, Lucy!)

It is important to note that many of these things can be done by long-distance godparents. One of the main things the church needs to get across to people in our mobile society is that it is possible for an adult to form and maintain a significant relationship with a child who is far away. Many people do not believe this is possible, particularly with a small child, and even if they think it can be done, they probably need to be taught how to do it. Long-distance godparents could find helpful ideas on relationship-forming in how-to books written for long-distance grandparents or noncustodial parents.

Godparents who faithfully live out their calling cannot help but grow in faith themselves. There is no better spiritual discipline* than learning to listen respectfully to a child; after all, Jesus said we should look to a child as a model of faith and should become like children ourselves. There is no better way to have the stories and images of the faith come alive in a new way than to hear them in a child's telling, to see them in a child's drawing. The adolescent's driving demand for honesty can challenge us to face up to theology's unanswerable questions, to admit our limits and our compromises. These opportunities for growth in faith should not be restricted to parents alone. As children need other caring adults in their lives besides parents, so adults need the chance to become a soul friend to a child.

See also CHURCH-FAMILY; PARENTING.

References and Resources
J. G. Fitzpatrick, *Something More: Nurturing Your Child's Spiritual Growth* (New York: Penguin, 1991); J. M. Hull, *God-Talk with Young Children* (Philadelphia: Trinity, 1991); J. H. Lynch, *Godparents and Kinship in Early Medieval Europe* (Princeton, N.J.: Princeton University Press, 1986); E. Ramshaw, *The Godparent Book* (Chicago: Liturgy Training Publications, 1993).

Elaine J. Ramshaw

GOSSIP

The word *gossip* comes from the Anglo-Saxon words for *God* and *sibling* and originally meant "akin to God," thus referring to someone who was spiritually linked with another by giving a name to the other as a sponsor at his or her baptism.* Then *gossip* came to denote "talking about another who belonged to the same community." Gradually it began to have a pejorative meaning. Now it means "taking an unwarranted interest in people's affairs," often by passing on unfavorable information about them.

Good and Bad Gossip

There is a proper place for talking about other people in their absence in a constructive way, whether positively or negatively, even if the line between these two is not always easy to discern. There is also room for talking about others playfully, indeed as a form of play.* This is just one form of talking about "nothing in particular," of talk for talking's sake, without any further intention.

So far as we can judge, gossip in the pejorative sense has always been a part of human life. There are many references to it in the Old Testament, especially in Proverbs. The gossip is one who betrays a secret or confidence and therefore cannot be trusted (Prov 11:13). The person who listens to gossip finds it hard to resist because it is so tasty (Prov 18:8; 26:22). It is a destructive activity, for it inflames quarrels (Prov 26:20) and breaks friendships* (Prov 16:28). Gossips are also referred to negatively in the New Testament (2 Cor 12:20; 1 Tim 5:13).

Later times contain many examples of the way gossip based on untruths or half-truths has ostracized or destroyed a person in a small community (such as the condemnations of witchcraft in seventeenth-century Salem, Massachusetts) or in a particular institution (as in Lillian Hellman's variously titled play and film *These Three* and *The Loudest Whisper*). Today gossip in general has become a full-time industry. The rise of the mass media,* beginning with newspapers* and culminating in television,* has broadened the number of people who can eavesdrop helpfully or unhelpfully on the doings of others. The local gossip has given way to the gossip columnist, whose sole profession is to relay news about people that others do not strictly need to know. While all societies have taken an interest in the doings of elite or disreputable groups within them, the focus on celebrities and criminals in modern societies has exponentially increased. Much of what passes for news today is simply a form of gossip, some defensible or harmless but much of it a form of public voyeurism in which we too readily become accomplices.

At the everyday level, gossip continues to be a fact of life in all kinds of groups. With the growth of large cities and breakdown of local neighborhoods, this is now concentrated more in the workplace and in voluntary organizations like the church* or school, though it can still appear anywhere. In some cases talking about others at work* or at church is simply an informal way of keeping in step with what is going on and who is involved. It is a kind of human bulletin board or information exchange. In others it is simply a form of playful interaction, which is not designed to put anyone down or advance ourselves. Unless we are careful, however, this already contains some dangers and can easily spill over into something that is actually or potentially damaging.

We all have experience of the way in which one person or a small group* can start unfounded or half-true rumors about others that soon become common property and are assumed to be basically true. Sometimes this is done unthink-

463

ingly, sometimes deliberately. Either way, even if the objects of gossip get a chance to privately or publicly respond, they find it difficult to clear themselves absolutely. Gossip has a way of sticking, partly because it throws its target on the defensive and into a self-justifying mode (the "Have you stopped beating your wife?" syndrome) and partly because our fallen human hearts secretly enjoy hearing about other's failings (in order to bolster ourselves). In such settings, even within the family circle, we need to remember the New Testament warnings that we will be judged for every idle word that we utter (Mt 12:36) and that a small spark can begin a raging forest fire, one that eventually consumes ourselves as well as others (Jas 3:5-6).

How Can Gossip Be Sanctified?

We should recognize that some forms of talking about others, even behind their backs, is a natural human activity. We belong to a wider society, and there are certain matters affecting its well-being, or our common interest, that it is not improper to hear or tell others about. We also belong to primary or more extended communities within which there is a legitimate place for talking about each other's concerns. For example, when a member of the community* in difficulty shares the trouble, others are enabled to respond helpfully. Furthermore, good gossip is a way of maintaining communal awareness and communal identity and of reminding ourselves of our bonds with and obligations to others. As the poet-essayist Kathleen Norris explains, gossip can provide comic relief for people who are living under tension and can be a way of praising or thanking others who have done individuals or the community a good turn (p. 76). Gossip is often the way small groups, institutions and places express their solidarity.

We should recognize that some forms of talking about others are illegitimate. For example, we should not generally share information about others that they would not share themselves, especially when this would injure their reputation or embarrass them in any significant way. If in doubt, we should first seek their permission to do so. We should also keep people's secrets and confidences when these have been entrusted to us. This has to do directly with faith, for by this means we "keep faith" with, or remain faithful to, those who have trusted us with some private information. To breach this faith is to act in an ungospel-like way. It is also a form of theft: people's experiences are basically their property, and they have a right to share them with others. In such cases we must allow them the privilege of telling their own story.

We should recognize the necessity of avoiding the company of those who take an unwarranted interest in others' affairs and who are overly talkative about this (Prov 20:19). People often engage in this as a response to some weakness, failure,* need* or longing within themselves. The Bible suggests that when people have too little to do, or are too much on their own, they have a tendency to gossip (2 Thess 3:11; 1 Tim 5:13). We should exercise care ourselves when we find ourselves personally in such a situation and should help others we encounter at such a time to avoid the temptation to "say what they ought not." We should also help those who have too little to do to find a more constructive outlet for their energies and those who are too much alone to find a community within which their need to share with others will find a more legitimate expression.

Despite these clarifications and strategies, it is still sometimes difficult to tell the difference between harmful gossip and appropriate conversation.* How can we discern this? We can do so through examining our motives and asking God for wisdom before we say anything; through checking with someone we trust who is also in possession of the information; through asking whether we would, if necessary, be willing to say to others face to face what we are willing to say behind their backs; through learning from the experience of being the objects of gossip ourselves. If we are wise, we also learn from our mistakes, that is, through trial and error.

As Kathleen Norris reminds us, however, at its best gossip can be

> morally instructive, illustrating the ways ordinary people survive the worst that happens to them; or, conversely, the ways in which self-pity, anger, and despair can overwhelm or destroy them. Gossip is theology translated into experience. In it we hear great stories of conversion . . . as well as stories of failure. We can see that pride does really go before a fall, and that hope is essential. Especially as through it we keep track of those who are undergoing some major lifechange, or who are suffering some major loss, if we are really aware when we gossip we are also praying, not only for them but for ourselves. (p. 76)

See also CONVERSATION; LISTENING; SPEAKING.

References and Resources

K. Norris, *Dakota: A Spiritual Biography* (New York: Ticknor & Fields, 1993).

Robert Banks

GRANDPARENTING

Grandparents do not come in the same package in which they used to arrive. In some ethnic and racial groups the grandparent, usually the grandfather, is still the authoritarian patriarch, whereas in many Western countries the grandparent is seen in very different, more senti-

mental or marginal, terms. Attitudes toward them and expressed by them vary enormously with striking differences.

The Changing Face of Grandparenting
Age and the attitude toward age are certainly one difference in grandparenting today. Another is style—from the grandparent who acts like a teenager to the grandparent who appears never to have enjoyed life. Marital status is a further factor. One set of grandparents may have retained an intact marriage,* while others have had more than one partner. Likewise the grandchild may possess either no acknowledged grandparents or several, depending on the definition of marriage and family* and how the stresses have been processed.

Values* and convictions of grandparents vary considerably. The grandparents may be people of faith. That faith may nourish them and those who belong to them. On the other hand, for whatever reason, it may repel all who are affected by them. They may be grandparents whose lives are consumed by their own self-absorbed lifestyle; they care only about themselves. Many popular and technical books on aging,* for example, do not even mention grandparenting. The attitudes with which grandparents approach life also differ enormously. Some grandparents embrace life, deal constructively with their losses and maintain a sense of optimism and hope. Others become negative, are critical of the oncoming generation and cover life, family and community with a blanket of darkness.

Changes in family and society are obviously affecting the experience of grandparenting, especially the amount and nature of support and the degree to which it is reciprocal. Robert O. Hanson (p. 13) points out factors that affect the ability of a family to support grandparents. These include the reality that multigenerational families are becoming more common, partly because of the declining birth rate and increased longevity. There is a much greater generation span, and there is a lack of siblings in the younger generation to share the burden of support. Longevity means that adult caregivers are likely to spend more years caring for their parents than providing support for their own children.

All the other problems that arise from how family is constituted today complicate the issues. These include the increase in divorce,* blended and single-parent families, the large number of women entering the work force, and geographical mobility. These factors, added to improved health care, mean that age-related disabilities happen much later in life. Family caregivers are assuming that role later in their own lives, at a time when they may themselves be vulnerable both physically and financially.

The role of grandparenting and attitudes toward particular grandparents are caught up in a rapidly changing society, and the rate of change is difficult to keep up with. Nevertheless, grandparents can and often do play a highly significant role in family life today.

What's the Good of Grandparenting?

Margaret Mead believed that it takes three generations to rear a child. At the same time she reacted against the view that the grandparent is "to be a resource and yet not an interference, to keep themselves out of the picture—not to interfere, not to spoil, not to insist, not to intrude" (quoted in Carter and McGoldrick, p. 318). Mead also made the acute observation "From grandparents children learn to understand something about the reality of the world not only before they were born, but also before their parents were born. . . . Experiences of the past gives them means of enjoying the future" (quoted in Fowler and McCutcheon, p. 201). How can they do this if they are constantly "out of the picture"?

Grandparents are a significant influence on the future generation, for both intact and broken families: "Grandparent access visits can be a vital factor in the well being and development of children of divorced parents—often essential role models for absent or missing mothers or fathers" (Wells, p. 35). But if grandparents are good for children, the reverse is also true. Rosemary Wells lists what it means to have a grandchild: (1) your family will live on into the future; (2) you are given a second chance to be a better parent; (3) you can enjoy helping the children (with schoolwork and at playtime); (4) your grandchild may achieve things you or your child did not (p. 35). This may seem a modest list, but in a world where both parents work, an available grandparent can make a huge difference even with a modest investment of time.

Grandparenting does other things for the grandparent as well. Because losses are common and cumulative at this point in life, depression* and self-absorption can very quickly devour the grandparent. So can self-indulgence. Caring for one's grandchildren without making favorites is one way of escaping the domination of one's moods and feelings. Finding a support system in the local church and in one's relationship to God will further enable the grandparent to cope better with these challenges. In extreme cases where the grandparent takes over the parenting role, a support system within the local church will be absolutely essential.

The Pitfalls of Grandparenting

In normal circumstances grandparents do best when they have healthy and clear boundaries, keep out of destructive triangles and do not engage in "cutoffs," to use the language of family systems. Good boundaries means that they are "up front" about what they will do for the family members, are generous and loving in their support but do not allow unreasonable demands to be made on them. This does not refer simply to gross demands that come close to elder abuse. Grandparents must respect their own persons and legitimate needs* and find a balance between their own needs and those of others, including their grandchildren. Expectations that are clear and negotiated without emotional blackmail are healthy for all the parties.

Grandparents can very easily get "triangled" in a way that is tough on the actual parent. For example, very few adolescents think highly of their parents! Being a gentle advocate for the parents may be necessary and even occasionally desirable. Being a coconspirator is not. Some families are conflict-ridden. They are quick to quarrel and slow to reconcile. People get cut off. Grandparents can make a large contribution to the family by refusing to engage in cutting off people from their emotional support system. They can listen, reflect, refuse to be judge and jury, and keep doors open. They must never undercut parents.

Indeed, grandparents can and should learn not to volunteer advice unless it is requested. The less initiative they demonstrate here, the more likely they are to be asked and the advice heeded. Some grandparents may end up as surrogate parents for all kinds of reasons, but the grandchildren do not need to be the pawns in any family disputes.

The Contribution Grandparents Make

Grandparents can model what long-term commitments produce. Even if a marriage falls apart, they can still demonstrate that malice, revenge, hatred,* guilt and shame also need not dominate. Grandparents can demonstrate respect for others. This should be shown in attitudes to the opposite gender and to minorities of all kinds. As the keeper of family history, grandparents also need to be careful not to overindulge in anecdotage. As grandchildren get older, they will want to know more about their family story. Family secrets may need to be handled carefully but not buried.

The most important contribution a grandparent can make is in terms of imparting and modeling faith. For the Christian, finding creative and life-affirming ways of doing this is the greatest challenge of grandparenting. No other responsibility comes close to this; when it is effective, no other joy exceeds it. Of course, it includes praying for grandchildren; it must also involve a lifestyle that affirms anything that is said. It means taking advantage of teachable moments, which should be natural, not contrived, and joyful, not legalistic.

Grandchildren need grandparents. Grandparents need relationships with their children and grandchildren. There comes a day when it changes from giving support to receiving it. The capacity to do both with grace is not always easy. But when it is done with grace, the rewards for everyone are exceptional. To be an active, godly grandparent is more satisfying than being a self-absorbed successful senior citizen grasping for rewards that never come to the people who cannot think and act beyond themselves. If a person's chief aim is to glorify God and enjoy God forever, grandparenting offers a significant role in fulfilling this objective.

See also FAMILY; FAMILY COMMUNICATION; FAMILY SYSTEMS; PARENTING

References and Resources
B. Carter and M. McGoldrick, eds., *The Changing Family Life Cycle* (2nd ed.; Boston: Allyn & Bacon, 1989); M. Fowler and P. McCutcheon, eds., *Songs of Experience* (New York: Ballantine, 1991); R. O. Hanson, *Relationships in Old Age*

(New York: Guilford, 1994); R. Wells, *Your Grandchild and You* (Oxford, U.K.: Sheldon Press, 1990).

R. D. Bell

GREETING

Each culture has its own customs of greeting. These typically involve the exchange of standard questions and responses, the expression of emotion and the performance of distinctive gestures—shaking hands, hugging, kissing, bowing, kneeling, clapping, patting one's chest and so on. Often the specific words and actions are defined by the relative social position of the two parties meeting: thus, we greet our friends differently than we would a king.

Purpose of Greeting

The purpose of greeting is to establish relationship. It is the first thing communicated in any meeting and can have several positive effects.

First, a greeting serves to recognize other people. In a world where people are often together but not in relationship, the act of greeting recognizes individuals as being worthy of relationship. It says, "You are significant to me." It may also say, "You are so significant to me that I remember you." This is the first step in offering hospitality* and leads naturally to a welcome, that is, to an invitation for people to be at home where we are. This is what the world did not offer Jesus when he came to us (Jn 1:11) but what Jesus offers people who come to him (Jn 1:37-39).

Second, a greeting can affirm others. The image we have of ourselves is partially dependent on how others respond to us. Thus, greeting can be a way of strengthening another person's self-image. It says, "I think you are a valuable and gifted person."

Third, a greeting can invoke a blessing.* As with a salutation, the greeter expresses a wish of peace or well-being over the other person. Even something as simple as "Good morning" can be a means of bringing goodness into another's day. For the Christian the greeting can be a prayer: "Lord, bless this morning with your goodness."

Problems with Greeting

Unfortunately, greetings may degenerate into routine performances of outward displays of fellowship* that lack depth. When words are spoken merely to maintain appearances, they become lies—conveyers of nonreality. Recognition, affirmation and blessing may express the appearance of relationship, but in fact it is only a façade. Not only can greetings be given falsely, but they can be received falsely for merely selfish reasons. Jesus criticized the Pharisees for this: "You love . . . to be greeted with respect in the marketplaces" (Lk 11:43 NRSV).

In contrast, Jesus challenged his followers not to wait to be greeted but to take the initiative themselves, to greet rather than to be greeted. Furthermore, he challenged them to greet those outside their familiar circle of friends (Lk 14:12-14). By this first step in loving their enemies, Jesus' followers would be known (Mt 5:43-48).

Christian Greetings

"Peace," *shalom* in Hebrew, was the standard Jewish greeting in Jesus' day. It expressed in a nutshell the Jews' hope for God's rule in the age to come—a life characterized by security, welfare and relational harmony. No doubt the twelve disciples heard Jesus use it many times and never thought much of it. But on resurrection Sunday when Jesus suddenly appeared before them and greeted them, "Peace be with you" (Jn 20:19), they could hardly have failed to appreciate the profundity of his words. Those who feared for their lives received peace.

In his letters Paul transformed the traditional greeting to reflect the new experience of the gospel. The standard Greek greeting was *chairein;* Paul changed it to *charis* ("grace")—a slight change in spelling but a profound change in meaning. Combining this with the Hebrew tradition, he typically greeted people in his letters with "Grace and peace to you." However, he would often make the significance explicit by adding "from God our Father and the Lord Jesus Christ." He thereby set the stage for explaining the reality of the gospel: peace (that is, the hope of the Jews) and grace (that is, the means by which God has made peace possible).

Paul's letters were far from formal, impersonal theological documents; they were living letters seasoned with personal greetings, especially Romans 16. Paul's greetings in his letters found their counterpart in the mutual greetings of the earliest Christian congregations, who customarily met each other with the kiss of peace (1 Cor 16:20; 2 Cor 13:12) or sent greetings to one another by letter or through traveling Christians (Col 4:14). These descriptive and prescriptive examples in the New Testament show that greeting is a way of deepening the family experience of the people of God. The Lord's Supper* and reading the Scriptures should not be neglected, but neither should we neglect greeting one another.

Perhaps the most astounding greeting in the Bible is that of the father in the parable of the prodigal son (Lk 15:11-24). After becoming destitute, the wayward son realizes his only hope is in returning home. He rehearses his own greeting by which he hopes to regain favor with his father, but his father surprises him. The father runs to meet him on the road, greets him first with hugs and kisses, and welcomes him home with a feast fit for an honored guest. Such open acceptance would shock the typical Palestinian man, who would say the father has lowered himself too far. And yet this is how God treats those who return to him after wandering away!

See also BLESSING; CONVERSATION; FAREWELL.

References and Resources
G. L. Sittser, *Loving Across Our Differences* (Downers Grove, Ill.: InterVarsity Press, 1994).

Gerry Schoberg

GRIEVING

Grief is an emotion* of intense sadness resulting from loss. It is a response to pain, injury, tragedy or deprivation in the person's world, not a sadness from largely internal causes such as depression.* *Grief,* the noun form, designates the emotion; *grieving,* the verb, form, the process. We shall use the verb, since grieving is a progressive emotional process that in its normal form is time-limited, purposive, goal-directed and restoratively healing.* We shall explore its stages, tasks and meaning.

The Stages of Grief
John Bowlby, an English psychiatrist who studied children separated from their mothers during wartime, observed three primary stages of loss—protest, disorganization, reorganization. These have been paraphrased and elaborated by many others, for example, "shock, suffering, recovery" or "shock, numbness, struggle between fantasy and reality, breakthrough or mourning, selective recollection connected with stabbing pain, and finally, acceptance of loss and the reaffirmation of life itself" (Oates, pp. 36-50). We shall use the three stages of shock, regression and adaptation.

Shock. The immediate impact of a major loss—death,* divorce,* accident or illness—is a state of numbness, distancing, disbelief, emotional outcry, then curiosity. One wants to know what has actually happened. With a death, the three questions are "What was the cause?" "How deep was the suffering?" and "Could it have been avoided?" During shock, the concern of friends, the rituals of community and the public memorials for the person lost assist the bereaved in maintaining balance. The grieving feel a loss of reality, a degree of depersonalization and often an increase in exhaustion, irritability, suspicion or anxiety.*

Regression. With the loss of someone and the severing of relationship with the person lost or dead, the grieving person is thrown back upon the self, on its defenses and coping skills. *Regression* is a return to the basic core of the self to find resources for healing within. It is an adaptive regression in service of the ego (the acronym is ARISE), which occurs on three levels: (1) return to childhood feelings of abandonment, helplessness and crying; (2) return to a childhood frame of reference of marked withdrawal, self-centeredness and self-absorption; (3) return to a childhood fear with magical thinking, superstition, primitive fears of punishment and matching fantasies of omnipotence ("I could have averted the tragedy if I had only . . ."). Anger, guilt, blame, scapegoating, paranoid fears, doubts, loss of faith, primitive religiosity, either/or judgments, obsessive preoccupations, deification or demonization of the one lost, anxiety and self-devaluation all flood the grieving person in cycles, which gradually spiral forward. The backward movement is necessary for the task of forging ahead through the loss. Regression is crouching in order to leap forward in gradual adaptation.

Adaptation. Step by step, the grieving person gives up the regressive forms and substitutes adaptive behaviors. As the loss is owned, the person lets go—of the other, the loss, the pain—and steps into the future. The broken internal world is healed; the broken person begins to feel whole, like a person again. Coping with grief does not take a continuous course. Rather, there are days of coping followed by days of unreality.

The Tasks of Grieving

The work that must be done in grieving is progressive, yet cyclical. One must (1) rehearse the sadness to set the frozen grief in motion; (2) express the unacceptable feelings in order to own the injury and open it to the light; (3) sort out the life agenda by working through the emotional chaos, the ambivalent feelings and the conflicting thoughts and attitudes; (4) come to terms with reality—the reality of the loss, the reality of the new situation and its possibilities; and (5) choose life by facing the future, reframing the loss, internalizing the learnings and recovering hope. In fulfilling these tasks, one accepts the reality of the loss, experiences the pain, adjusts to a radically changed environment and reinvests one's life energy.

The Meaning of Grieving

According to Dorothy Soelle, "We must view with suspicion all theology that is prepain" (from a public address, New York, 1986). The experience of grieving challenges the comfortable theologies of safety and security in the protecting hands of a Divine Parent who protects us from all grief and loss. Several key learnings will gradually surface. First, suffering is not only the result of evil and sin; it is also part of creation. Life is composed of both joy and pain, gift and grief, gain and loss, birth* and death. There is gladness and sadness throughout all creation. Second, God is our help, not our escape. God walks with us through pain rather than waltzes us out of it. The God of our Lord Jesus Christ is the God whom Christ revealed to us. This is a God who is nailed to a cross in radical identification with both creatures and creation and is vulnerable to suffering in an apparent weakness that confronts violence with righteousness, suffering with sacrificial love. Third, our grief, our suffering, our pain, matters to God, matters to those who are Christ's presence (his body), matters before our own inner judge, who seeks integrity within. Our pain is significant, is meaningful, is a part of the redemptive acceptance of life and its struggles, is a means of experiencing grace in our everyday existence.

See also DEATH; EMOTIONS.

References and Resources
K. Mitchell and H. Anderson, *All Our Losses, All Our Griefs* (Philadelphia: Westminster, 1982); R. Neale, *The Art of Dying* (New York: Harper & Row, 1974); W. E. Oates, *Pastoral Care and Counseling in Grief and Separation* (Philadelphia: Fortress, 1976); G. Westberg, *Good Grief* (Philadelphia: Fortress, 1962).

David Augsburger

GUIDANCE

All Christians need and desire guidance. It is implicit in the existence of a personal God who cares, leads and enters into personal relationships with his creatures so they will accomplish his purpose on earth. With such a God Christians should be among the most decisive people on earth. In reality Christians are often the most indecisive, partly because of some mistaken ideas about guidance (*see* Vocational Guidance). In this article we will explore the myths about guidance, scriptural images of the guide and the guided, and some steps for doing the will of God. The outcome can be well expressed in the prayer in Psalm 143:8-10: "Show me the way I should go. . . . Teach me to do

your will, for you are my God; may your good Spirit lead me on level ground."

Myths and Misunderstandings
There are at least eight obstacles to gaining a truly biblical approach to discovering and doing the will of God.

God's wonderful plan. It is a myth and misunderstanding that God has a wonderful plan for your life; God has something better—a wonderful purpose (Eph 1:9). God's purpose is that you should live to the praise of his glory (Eph 1:12, 14) and participate in his grand purpose of renewing everything under the headship of Jesus Christ (Eph 1:10). The difference between a plan and a purpose is like the difference between a blueprint and a stream that carries people along even though they may make adjustments along the way.

Your decisions and God. It is a myth and misunderstanding that God wants to make the decisions for you. Sometimes people cry out, "God, please take control of my life." In reality God does not want to make robots out of us and normally does not answer such prayers positively. The Bible does not sanctify passivity, that is, always waiting and wanting to be acted upon.

God's one way. It is a myth and misunderstanding that there is only one way to do the will of God. Sometimes this is called the "center of his will" syndrome. It is promoted by popular Christianity but is not found in Scripture. There are many ways of doing God's will within his purpose.

Knowing God's will. It is a myth and misunderstanding that God's will is difficult to discover. The pagan world says this, and pagan religions therefore make much of guidance and seeking guidance through priestly divination. Occult and magic practices follow the same path. People look for signs and portents. But followers of Jesus are given in the Bible both wisdom and the Spirit of God to guide (Ps 25:9; 48:14; Prov 3:5-6; Jn 16:13).

Signs and wonders. It is a myth and misunderstanding that God's guidance is normally associated with supernatural signs and messages through prophecies, "fleeces" and extraordinary phenomena. In the book of Acts and the Epistles we see Christians constantly using their redeemed judgment (Acts 6:3; 15:36; 20:16; Rom 1:10-13; 1 Cor 16:4-9; 2 Cor 1:5—2:4). All cases of supernatural leading were unsought. Sometimes people wait for supernatural phenomena when they should be practicing what they already know of God's will.

Open doors. It is a myth and misunderstanding that God normally calls through "open" doors. Believers are encouraged not only to go through open doors of opportunity (1 Cor 16:9) but to break down closed doors for God (Acts 4:19-20). Sometimes relying on open doors amounts to being guided by circumstances.

Not natural. It is a myth and misunderstanding that what is natural for you—including the way you are made and what you think in your own mind—is probably not the will of God. Just the reverse: God has written his will into the very fibers of our personality and spiritual gifts.* We fulfill God's will by doing what he created us to do. Our best thoughts are from God. In Christ we have a renewed mind (Rom 12:2; 1 Cor 2:16; 2 Cor 5:17).

Beginning again. It is a myth and misunderstanding that when you make a mistake, you have to go back and start again—if you can! Grace means the exact opposite. God's grace enables us to live fully in the present, free from the past, anticipating a glorious future. In God's sovereignty, our mistakes—and the mistakes others have committed against us (Gen 50:20)—are incorporated into God's great purpose for our lives and for creation.

Having debunked these myths, we turn now to the Scripture to find three empowering visions of the Guide and the guided.

Images of the Guide and the Guided

Remarkably, the Bible has no definitive word for *guidance*. What the Bible presents is three relational metaphors of God and the chosen people. The message is sublimely simple: it is more important to be in relationship to the Guide than to have an experience of guidance. It is more important to be shown God's ways (Ps 25:4) than to find out the perfect way for ourselves. Be in relationship with the Guide and one will be guided; seek guidance and one may miss the best thing of all!

The sheep and shepherd. This universal image in John 10 gives us a powerful paradigm. The shepherd "calls" and "leads," and the sheep "listen to his voice," "know his voice" and "follow him" (Jn 10:3-4).

Father/mother and son/daughter. Parents move from close supervision with detailed instructions to growing freedom for their children, including their assuming responsibility and deciding from internal motivation rather than external constraint (*see* Parenting). God the Father sends the Spirit into our hearts giving us the freedom, motivation and privileges of being sons or daughters of the divine family (Gal 4:1-11). The goal is maturity—the master concept of the Christian life (Eph 4:13; Col 1:28).

Friend with friend. The ultimate exposition of this learning relationship between Jesus and his followers is found in John 15:13-16. As a friend, Jesus tells us his Father's business and plan. As the friends of Jesus—and not merely his servants—we make our own decisions, doing what he commands based on the revealed mind of the Father (*see* Friendship).

Practical Steps

With these three images before us, we can indicate some positive, practical steps in discovering and doing the will of God.

Know and obey the Scriptures. The primary way we gain the mind of God is by exposing ourselves daily to reading and ingesting God's Word (*see* Spiritual Disciplines; Spiritual Growth). The Bible shows us (1) God's sovereign will (the mystery that is revealed: that God wants to restore the whole of creation in Christ), (2) God's moral will (so one does not need to ask whether premarital sex or gossiping* is right or wrong) and (3) God's individual will (each of us is called to live for the praise of God's glory; Eph 1:12).

Pray. The most important fruit of prayer is not so much the guidance obtained but a deeper relationship with the Guide. Persons who live lives of unceasing prayer* will normally find making decisions within God's will easy. Such persons *become* God's will.

Cultivate a renewed mind. When God's law is written within your heart (Ps 40:8), your own biases, prejudices and fleshly stubbornness are dealt with day in and day out. What is needed is sound judgment (Acts 15:28), to think of ourselves "with sober judgment" (Rom 12:3). What we gain by seeking God in the midst of life is encouraged by a large section of the Old Testament and the book of James—wisdom.

Seek godly counsel (Prov 11:14). God leads us in the context of a community,* as is amply illustrated by Paul's consultation with his companions after receiving a personal vision of a Macedonian man calling for help (Acts 16:9-10). Our primary Christian community, especially in a small group* or house church, is the normal context for us to experience the leading of God. One caution, however, is this: sometimes people claiming to have a word from the Lord for us can be wrong, as Paul concluded in Acts 21:4.

Do the thing at hand for God's glory. Your present obedience will predispose you to be guided in the future. It is much easier to steer a moving car than a stalled one!

Be open to supernatural confirmation. But be focused on seeking the Lord, not signs from the Lord.

When you have made a decision, do not keep looking back. Trust God's sovereignty in your life. Doing God's will requires walking by faith, not by sight. We find our acceptance and approval in our relationship with God, not in reading favorable circumstances. You will probably not find out that you actually did God's will until long after, possibly until long, long after.

See also SPIRITUAL DISCIPLINES; VISION; VOCATIONAL GUIDANCE; WAITING.

R. Paul Stevens

H

HABITS

A habit is primarily an action, an acquired pattern of behavior, that is done often and therefore easily. Some so-called bad habits are hard to break because they are so well rehearsed that they appear to be automatic. Thought patterns and self-talk can also take on the nature of a habit due to the amount of repetition of the same thought that an individual entertains. Popular books such as *The Seven Habits of Highly Effective People* and *Habits of the Heart* show that life patterns can work for good or ill in individuals and society as a whole.

A Way of Life

Though the Bible seldom makes use of the word *habit*, it does have a great deal to say about one's "way of life," what one "believes and practices." Certainly the Scriptures encourage acquired patterns of behavior that are godly and so well rehearsed and done so often as to come easily. For example, Job regularly practiced being a priest-father so that his children would walk regularly in forgiveness (Job 1:5). Jesus was known to have two habits (noted as "customs" in the NIV): regularly attending the synagogue (Lk 4:16) and teaching when a crowd gathered (Mk 10:1). The apostle Paul similarly had the ministry habit of going to the synagogues to reason with the Jews from the Scriptures that Jesus was the Christ (Acts 17:2). Near the end of his life Paul could say to young Timothy about Paul's habits: "You, however, know all about my teaching, my way of life, my purpose, faith, patience, love, endurance, persecution, sufferings" (2 Tim 3:10).

The Bible also shows that people can develop negative and ungodly habits. Jeremiah speaks the Lord's mind about Jehoiakim by saying that his way of life from his youth was not to listen or to obey God (Jer 22:21). Behind the false teaching in Ephesus is the widows' habit of gossiping* from house to house (1 Tim 5:13). The author to the Hebrews tells the believers he writes because they have gotten out of the habit of meeting together and encouraging one another to love and good works and therefore have gotten into a habit of not persevering in the faith (Heb 10:24-25).

Becoming What You Do

By developing habits one becomes what one does. This is readily apparent in the proverbs of Solomon. The stated purpose of this collection of wise sayings is "for acquiring a disciplined and prudent life" (Prov 1:3). A cursory reading of Proverbs 11—14 shows the acquired speech habits of the wise and the foolish. The wise have learned how to guard their tongue, keep secrets, and use kind and true words (11:13; 12:17, 22-23, 25; 13:3), while the foolish have practiced gossip, mockery, and reckless and rash words (11:9, 13; 12:17-18, 22; 13:1, 3;

14:6). The New Testament encourages the believer to become who he or she is in Christ by the habitual practice of putting off the flesh and putting on Christ (compare Col 3 and Eph 4—5), of walking in the Spirit (Rom 8; Gal 5) and setting the mind on the things of the Spirit (Rom 8). What one repeatedly practices does become an automatic part of one's behavior.

Unlearning Habits

Difficulties in developing godly habits stem primarily from three arenas: (1) learned and acted-out behaviors, whether poor, neutral or sinful, that are left unexamined; (2) negative patterns of thinking or belief that are not challenged and unlearned; and (3) unrealistically high expectations that lead to continued self-defeating minimal goal achievement. Classic behavioral psychology suggests that when pleasure* accompanies behavior, the behavior is likely to repeat. Bad habits usually have some form of pleasurable payoff, which reinforces the continued behavior. Changing the cues that precede the undesirable behavior helps break the automatic behavior. The Christian who is serious about breaking ungodly habits will seek both prayer and counseling wisdom in order to ensure that there are not hidden reinforcers to the undesirable behavior.

What You See Is What You Do

Establishing new and godly habits assumes that one has experienced the new nature in Christ and the accompanying promptings of the Spirit to pursue the ways of God. Building on this foundation, you can help yourself with several practical steps. First, observe and imitate the behavior you want to develop. You can imitate the behavior of Jesus or the apostle Paul (1 Cor 4:16; 1 Thess 1:6; 2 Thess 3:7) or another person who demonstrates a positive attitude or behavior. Interacting with a model is a powerful force for change. Second, examine your life to see where you are already doing even a little bit of the behavior. Understand what you are doing right—what thoughts, motives, pleasures and so on accompany the behavior, regardless of how occasional it is—and do more of it. Third, positively reinforce the new behaviors you are seeking to establish as habits. Built-in reinforcers are a plus, but don't depend on these. Finally, give yourself some time. If you have lived out a habit for years, then it will take more than a week to change.

A Promise

As you go about establishing godly habits, remember the promises of Solomon's wisdom for those who find a way of life, who acquire a pattern of behavior consistent with the fear of God: prolonged life, favor and a good name in the sight of God and others (Prov 3:2-3).

See also DISCIPLESHIP; FAMILY VALUES; SPIRITUAL DISCIPLINES; SPIRITUAL FORMATION; SPIRITUAL GROWTH; VALUES; VIRTUES.

References and Resources

R. Bellah et al., *Habits of the Heart: Individualism and Commitment in American Life* (Berkeley: University of California Press, 1985); D. G. Benner, *Baker Encyclopedia of Psychology* (Grand Rapids: Baker, 1985); S. R. Covey, *The Seven Habits of Highly Effective People* (New York: Fireside/Simon & Schuster, 1989); L. Ezell, *Private Obsessions* (Dallas: Word, 1991); D. M. L. Jones, *Spiritual Depression—Its Causes and Cure* (London: Pickering and Inglis, 1965).

Michael Nichols

HATE

Some say the world will end in fire,
Some say in ice.
From what I've tasted of desire
I hold with those who favor fire.
But if it had to perish twice,

I think I know enough of hate
To say that for destruction ice
Is also great
And would suffice. (Robert Frost,
    "Fire and Ice")

Frost's experience is that of humankind, for all people have come into contact with hate. One dictionary defines *hate* as "to have strong dislike or ill will for; loathe; despise." This same attitude was well known in Scripture, mostly in a negative sense and closely related to anger. We will examine these powerful personal dispositions.

The Bible and Emotions

In the Bible neither hate nor anger is an emotion.* We use the term *anger* to describe what we feel when someone injures us. Given a threat or injury (emotional or physical), our body pours adrenaline into the bloodstream, and we get ready to fight or flee. We also have some automatic angry thoughts, which flash into our minds in a fraction of a second. The Bible does not condemn this automatic response, for it is given by God to protect us. But as soon as the automatic response flashes by, we have a choice, even if we at first are not aware of it. We can choose to act out our inner feelings of anger (often a once-and-done action); we can choose to let our anger settle into a disposition of hatred toward the other person or object (which is acted out later as vengeance); or we can choose to resolve our anger (and its resulting hatred) in another way.

What One Should Hate

The Bible does not have much good to say about human anger (2 Cor 12:20; Gal 5:20; Eph 4:31; Col 3:8; 1 Tim 2:8; Jas 1:19-20), for it is too uncontrollable and does not produce God's type of righteousness. But there are some things that godly people should hate (that is, loathe or despise). These include bribes (Ex 18:21; Prov 15:27), evildoers (Ps 5:5; 26:5; 45:7; 119:113), idolaters (Ps 31:6), evil ways (Ps 97:10; 101:3; Amos 5:15; Rom 12:9; Rev 2:6), falsehood (Ps 119:163; Prov 13:5), proud, arrogant or perverted speech (Prov 8:13), bloodshed and violence (Ezek 35:6; Mal 2:16) and divorce* (Mal 2:16). When it comes to the evildoers, it is especially important to note that hatred is not anger but a disposition that finds what they do distasteful and thus does not in any way admire them.

What God tells us to hate is in tension with our culture,* which parades such things before our eyes in movies, television* and print, often trying to get us to admire what God says to despise. More difficult for us are the sayings of Jesus that call us to hate our parents (Lk 14:26) or lives (Jn 12:25). In these cases *hate* is used in contrast with our love of Christ. That is, when parents (to whom in an ancient culture one was to show lifelong respect and obedience) or even the drive to preserve our own lives gets in the way of loyalty to Christ, we should firmly reject them, even with a shudder at what destruction such temptation could do to us. Thus Scripture teaches there is "a time to hate" (Eccles 3:8).

Psychology also teaches us that there is a time to hate. If one does not hate (in the sense of dislike and reject) evil, then that person is some form of a sociopath. Such people, because they do not experience evil as distasteful, may not only tolerate others' doing it but may also enjoy being spectators of evil (such as people who have observes a rape or murder without intervening in any way) or even perpetrators. One of the difficult problems in victim-offender reconciliation is getting the offender to experience what he or she did as evil.

While many of the behaviors God tells us to hate are objectionable to society and the lack of sensitivity to them is defined as a personality disorder, the Scripture argues that society as a whole has become desensitized to evil. Desensitization implies that acts of violence and other forms of evil that today are considered bad by society may in time come to be viewed as normal. While this is obvious in the human tolerance of rebellion against God, texts such as Genesis 4:23-24; 6:5-6, 11; and Romans 1:18-32 show that the same process of desensitization takes place in the areas of violence, sexuality* and the like. Unfortunately, Christians have tended to reflect societal values more than Scripture's, as one sees in the extreme case of the sociopathic society of the Third Reich, in which most evangelical Christians did nothing to protest against the evil creeping into German society.

What One Should Not Hate

The Scripture also clearly says there are some things we should not hate. The chief of these is God (Ex 20:5), followed by our brother or sister (or member of our faith community; Lev 19:17; 1 Jn 3:15; 4:20). Here we notice the difference between hate and anger, for we may be disappointed, frustrated and angry when God does not do what we expect, but we should not let this settle into a disposition of loathing or rejection. Job, for example, expresses his hurt and anger to God but refuses to turn away from him. Finally, we should not hate discipline (Ps 50:17; Prov 12:1; Amos 5:10). While we do not want to hear rebuke, Scripture tells us to embrace it, for it is good for us. The list of what not to hate is short, for Scripture usually talks about its opposite—love.* Thus love of God and fellow community members (and even enemies) is emphasized throughout Scripture.

Psychology likewise teaches us that nursed anger or hatred is unhealthy, even if through denial we push it so deep within that we are not aware of it ourselves. On the one hand, the hatred often crops up in dysfunctional ways in other relationships (for example, hatred of a parent may be quite destructive in one's own marriage). On the other hand, psychosomatic medicine links hatred of people to all sorts of diseases: ulcers, heart problems, cancer and arthritis, to name only a few. Ignoring what the Bible says about hatred can be literally self-destructive.

Dealing with Hate and Anger

If individuals find themselves hating things we should love or not hating what we should hate, Scripture calls for repentance. However, the temptation is to fall into anger (a sharp and hard attack) rather than hatred (a despising or loathing), even toward those things we are taught to hate, and then hate our brother or sister, whom we should not hate. Rather than rationalizing this sin ("It is really righteous indignation" or "They are not part of my church or denomination"), Scripture suggests a solution. Even if the person is truly an enemy, we should love him or her, which does not mean having a positive emotional response but doing concrete deeds of kindness (Lk 6:22, 27). This love does not include accepting the evil of the enemy, for while we are told to love the enemy, we are never told to love his or her evil. In fact, part of this love is forgiveness (for example, Mt 6:12, 14-15; 18:21-22, 35), which means a recognition that evil has been done to us, followed by a choice to release the "debt" and suffer the evil rather than to seek vengeance or repayment. By doing this, we are able to recognize, rather than deny or rationalize, anger and also deal with it so it does not "give the devil a foothold" (Eph 4:26-27).

See also CONFLICT RESOLUTION; EMOTIONS; LOVE.

References and Resources
D. Augsburger, *Caring Enough to Confront* (Glendale, Calif.: Regal Books, 1981); R. Frost, D. Jones and D. Bradley, *Robert Frost, a Tribute to the Source* (New York: Holt, Rinehart and Winston, 1979); B. Ghezzi and M. Kinzer, *Emotions as Resources* (Ann Arbor, Mich.: Servant, 1983).

Peter Davids

HEALING

Healing involves a process of bringing or restoring wholeness and sound functioning to every aspect of human life, which includes bodily integrity, emotional balance, mental well-being and spiritual aliveness. The English word *health** literally means "wholeness," and so *to heal* means "to make whole." This broad-based definition sometimes includes what is popularly known as "inner healing," where the focus is more specifically on psychological and emotional wounds and their repair. For some, the metaphor of healing has been extended to include the process of reconciliation of broken interpersonal relationships at the level of the community,* society, races and nations, a process that includes the development of a just and benevolent social and political order, as well as a responsible policy on ecology,* which reflects stewardship* of the earth. Here, we are primarily concerned with the healing of individual human lives in all its various dimensions.

Healing as Curing and Caring

Unfortunately, healing in modern Western culture has been restricted to scientifically accurate diagnosis and treatment and tends to focus on the sick person's disease, not illness (where "disease" and "illness" are, respectively, the objective and subjective aspects of one's sickness). Admittedly, the sophistication and success of Western medical technology have contributed much to establish this model of healing. But in the last two decades a number of writers have seen that healing encompasses a broader domain and have challenged the narrower assumptions of the healing profession.* For example, Edmund Pellegrino insists that healing requires not only competence in curing disease but also compassion in sharing in the suffering of the patient, the latter requiring vulnerability on the healer's part. Eric Cassell notes the importance of the healer's role in caring for, not just curing, the sick. This involves communicating scientific knowledge that will help patients to "own" and to "work on" the illness, as well as connecting the feelings between healer and patient. Prior to both of these the Christian doctor and psychologist Paul Tournier initiated a movement and wrote consistently about a medicine for the whole person. Curing and caring, communicating and connecting are integral parts of the healing function.

Unless the healing profession exercises this dual function, the sick may be cured of the disease but remain unhealed. Conversely, when patients' feeling and suffering are shared by their healers in facing the sickness, thereby freeing them from their isolation and alienation from self and community due to the disease, they may experience a real sense of being healed, even though the disease may remained uncured. As Howard Brody notes, to be compassionate in sharing the patient's suffering is itself a powerful form of healing that scientific curative skills do not provide. Therefore, compassion as a virtue* for the healing profession must be cultivated, and this can be achieved only if the healer's character is formed and nurtured by a compassionate community. At the present state of affairs, the medical profession does not live up to this expectation and requirement. Thus the healing profession is in great need of cultivating virtuous characters in addition to providing technical skills in order for it to claim to be a true healing profession.

Biblical Perspectives on Healing

In the Bible health is first and foremost a divine gift. When sickness occurs, the sick turn to God, the Physician of his people, for healing. God and God alone is the ultimate source of all healing. "I am the LORD, who heals you" (Ex 15:26), says the Lord to Israel. In the New Testament we see that healing is a crucial and integral part of Jesus' earthly ministry. It is estimated that one-fifth to one-third of the Gospel record is related to healings. As Matthew says, "Jesus went throughout Galilee, teaching in their synagogues, preaching the good news of the kingdom, and healing every disease and sickness among the people" (Mt 4:23). And because the biblical view of health is holistic, biblical healing includes the entire person. Thus in Jesus' healing ministry, he was concerned not only with restoration of physical health but also, indeed primarily, with restoration of relationships with God and others. Because Jesus also believed that sickness and disease may result from an evil agency or demon possession, his healing through exorcism indicates the presence and the power of the kingdom of God (*see* Principalities and Powers; Spiritual Conflict). In this new order people are set free from the power and bondage of evil in all its forms and restored to personal wholeness in all its dimensions—physical, mental, relational. Thus, biblical concepts of healing and salvation are integrally related.

Healing Through Medicine

To acknowledge that God is the ultimate healer does not mean that healings are exclusively spiritual. The art of medicine was employed in both Old and New Testaments for healing purposes (Gen 50:2; 2 Chron 16:12; Job 13:4; Jer 8:22). Isaiah's prescription of a fig poultice to heal King Hezekiah (2 Kings 20:7; Is 38:21) shows that God heals through medical means, utilizing materials that are part of the creation. Christ considered it normal for people to consult physicians (Mt 9:12). Oil as a medicine was frequently employed by Jesus' disciples (Mk 6:13; Lk 10:34). James, the brother of Jesus, specifically mentions the use of oil as part of his recommended healing process. The oil specified was apparently olive oil, which in first-century Palestine was the treatment of choice for many acute and chronic illnesses. The directive to "anoint" (or to "apply)" with oil (Jas 5:14) suggests that the oil is meant to be used medicinally rather than ritually or sacramentally. These examples show that the Bible is not opposed to the use of medicines and medical arts for our healing. God works through medicine as well as direct intervention, and our faith is not so much in medicine per se as in the Creator of medicine.

Faith and Healing

In the New Testament, and especially in the healing ministry of Christ, faith is a dominant human factor. In many instances the faith of the sick or someone else's faith on his behalf appears to be almost a prerequisite for healing (for example, Mt 8:13; 9:2, 22, 29; 15:28). There is also indication either that Jesus cannot heal or that his healing is delayed due to people's lack of faith (Mt 13:58; 17:20; Mk 6:5-6). Not surprisingly some people today are very preoccupied with the role of faith in healing.

A careful analysis shows that out of the twenty-six healing accounts in the Gospels, faith is mentioned in only twelve. In a number of cases the sick person was not even present when Jesus was asked to heal him or her. Rather than say Jesus heals where there is faith, we should say that his healing ministry provides an opportunity for human faith to express itself as an indication of the sufferer's desire to be healed. This is different from saying that Jesus' healing power requires the cooperation of human faith or is subjected to human manipulation through faith or the lack of it. God heals primarily out of mercy (Mt 14:14; 20:34; Mk 1:41; Lk 7:13), out of compassion in response to a cry for help (Mt 15:22; 17:15; Mk 9:22, 27; Lk 17:13), as a manifestation of divine glory (Jn 4:54; 9:2; 11:4) and on a few occasions as a fulfillment of Scripture (Mt 8:16-17; 11:2-6; 12:15-21; Lk 7:18-23). It would be a grave mistake to ask ourselves whether or not we have enough faith for a certain healing to take place. This is to base healing on our faith and not on God. One's faith is not in a healing taking place but in God's faithfulness, goodness, power and mercy. Our task as healers is to commend the sick to the Lord, trusting in his loving goodness; our task is not to predict what the Lord will specifically do.

Miraculous Healing

Miraculous healing is a special case of divine providence when the natural order of things is set aside for a particular purpose. In this regard, Christian attitudes are much divided. There are those who believe that miraculous healings belong exclusively to the apostolic age and cannot be expected to take place today. If there are miracles to be worked, it is human beings who must work them. At the other extreme are those who believe that healing, including miraculous healing, will always take place if there is faith. In this view Christ has already won these blessings for us through the cross, and all we have to do is to apply the fruits of the redemption to our lives (Mt 8:16-17; 1 Pet 2:24; compare Is 53:4-5). Christ's atonement is effective in overcoming both sin and sickness, and healing is therefore a birthright of all Christians. The healing ministries of Jesus and his apostles are extendable to our present time through the ministry of the Holy Spirit in the church. In this most extreme form of triumphalism, the relationship between prayer and healing is absolutely unqualified, with human faith as the only limiting factor.

In between these two poles are those who take the middle of the road, acknowledging the loving goodness and sovereignty of God in healing. This position does not see miracles as impossible— God can and will perform miracles when he sees fit to do so. But there is doubt as to God's desire and intention to perform such healing as a matter of course. The kingdom of God has come and is yet to be consummated, but we have been assured of the final victory over all our diseases and sickness in the final bodily resurrection (1 Cor 15:50-57). At times God heals dramatically, as in the case of Lazarus, but at other times God does not heal at all, as in the case of Paul's thorn of the flesh. The general will of God is that humankind should be made whole. But this wholeness may include the shaping of character and spiritual advancement though the occasion of sickness and suffering.

Healing and Redemption

Especially in the New Testament, physical healing is not considered to be a complete restoration of human well-being. Complete healing must take place on the basis of redemption, which brings forgiveness of sins, reconciliation with God and renewal of relationships with others. Jesus undertook his healing ministry in the context of his preaching and teaching because he did not come primarily to heal physically, but to redeem people wholly. This observation is further reinforced by the fact that in the early church there are four recorded cases in which the sick were not healed: Paul (2 Cor 12:7), Epaphroditus (Phil 2:25-30), Timothy (1 Tim 5:23) and Trophimus (2 Tim 4:20). These incidences also suggest that healing concerns the whole person, body and soul. Physical healing is not always the only answer to illness.

We may also gain some insights into the biblical holistic approach to healing through word usage. The word *iaomai*, which means exclusively "physical healing," is not the most common word to represent healing. *Therapeuō*, from which we get our words *therapy* and *therapeutic*, is the most frequently used word in the New Testament for "healing." It carries a special emphasis on the personal relationship between the healer and the healed and denotes the completeness of personal restoration. Another word, *sōzō*, is perhaps the most significant word for understanding the New Testament concept of healing. Originally the word carried a strong connotation of deliverance from danger. In the New Testament, where it is used twenty times, it suggests deliverance from danger, disease and death of the whole person, both physical and spiritual In the healings of Jesus *sōzō* refers not to a part of the body but to the whole person. It is the word *sōzō* that unites the biblical notion of healing and salvation.

The most interesting case studies of the comprehensive concept of healing in the Gospels is the healing of the woman with the flow of blood (Mt 9:21-22; Mk 5:26-34; Lk 8:43-48). While Mark uses the word *iaomai* and Luke uses *therapeuō* to describe the failure of the medical treatment provided by physicians, all three writers—Matthew, Mark and Luke—use *sōzō* to describe Jesus' healing, which restores the woman to a state of "peace" (*eirēnē*), which is equivalent to the Hebrew word *shalom*, meaning "wholeness."

Only when she has peace does Jesus pronounce that the woman is freed or delivered from the bondage of her sufferings. In a similar manner James uses the word *sōzō* in his epistle (5:15) to indicate that in response to the prayer of faith, the sick person will be made well. This is accompanied by the promise that he or she will be raised by the Lord and will be forgiven of the sins he or she may have committed. To be *raised up* means a full restoration to one's former state of vitality and strength, and to have one's sin forgiven—clearly the spiritual realm of the sick person—completes the healing of the whole person. This then is the holistic concept of healing in the Bible.

See also BODY; HEALTH; SICKNESS; SPIRITUAL GIFTS; WAITING.

References and Resources
H. Brody, *The Healer's Power* (New Haven, Conn.: Yale University Press, 1992); E. J. Cassell, *The Healer's Art: A New Approach to the Doctor-Patient Relationship* (New York: Penguin, 1976); F. MacNutt, *Healing* (Notre Dame, Ind.: Ave Maria, 1974); B. Palmer, ed., *Medicine and the Bible*, (Carlisle, U.K.: Paternoster Press, 1986); E. D. Pellegrino, "Being Ill and Being Healed: Some Reflections on the Grounding of Medical Morality," in *The Humanity of the Ill: Phenomenological Perspectives*, ed. V. Kestenbaum (Knoxville: University of Tennessee Press, 1982) 157-66; P. Tournier, *The Healing of Persons* (San Francisco: Harper & Row, 1983); B. B. Warfield, *Miracles: Yesterday and Today, True and False* (Grand Rapids: Eerdmans, 1965); J. Wilkinson, *Health and Healing* (Edinburgh: T & T Clark, 1980).

Edwin Hui

HEALTH

All agree that health is one of the most precious assets a person can possess, yet there is no consensus as to what health is. Some want to restrict the meaning of health to "a state of physical well-being without significant impairment of function." But modern psychosomatic theories, which relate our physical well-being to a whole host of psychosocial factors, render this narrow definition of health inadequate. If we accept humankind as essentially a multidimensional unity consisting of mechanical, chemical, biological, psychological, spiritual and historical dimensions, then any attempt to define health in terms of physical well-being is to reduce it to one dimension, or to dissociate one's body from one's unified self—something both illogical and impossible to do.

Health as Wholeness

We take a more holistic perspective of humankind. Each person is "one," uniting within himself or herself all dimensions of life so that in health as well as in sickness there is a "mutual within-each-otherness" of the dimensions. That is, whenever one dimension is affected, all the other dimensions are involved. This implies that health is ultimately wholeness, an idea embodied in the ideal of the *savior* (*sōtēr*), which precisely means the "healer" who makes people healthy and whole. The ideal healer* is the one universal healer, the Savior, Jesus Christ, who has come to bring in God's kingdom in which we are restored to wholeness. The World Health Organization seems to have captured part of this holistic conception of health when it defines health as "a state of complete physical, mental and social well-being and not merely the absence of disease or infirmity." From a Christian perspective the social dimension would include a relationship with the Creator and not just with fellow created human beings.

Health and the Image of God

The biblical creation accounts (Genesis 1—2) support this notion of health. Genesis 2:7 tells us, "The LORD God formed the man from the dust of the ground and breathed into his nostrils the breath of life, and the man become

a living being." In creating human beings out of the dust of the earth (material) and breathing into us the breath of life (immaterial), God has explicitly created a psychosomatic unity (*nephesh*)—a living being. Hebrew does not have a parallel for our word *body*.* The reason is they never regarded it as a separate entity with a reality of its own. In contrast to the Greek mind, which tends to dichotomize body and soul* and holds that the body is inferior to the soul, the Hebrew mind sees us as an ensouled body or an embodied soul rather than a soul possessing a body. Because of this, Old Testament writers do not present health in physical terms, and Jesus did not see his healing role as primarily physical. For both, health relates to the whole person.

The Genesis creation account also emphasizes the relational or social dimension of human beings:

> Then God said, "Let us make man in our image, in our likeness, and let them rule over the fish of the sea and the birds of the air, over the livestock, over all the earth, and over all the creatures that move along the ground." So God created man in his own image, in the image of God he created him; male and female he created them. (Gen 1:26-27)

Note the plural "us." Also note the pronouncement that "it is not good for the man to be alone" (Gen 2:18). These words emphasize the social nature of human beings as a reflection of the social character of God. This text also indicates that the social dimension includes human beings' relationship to the rest of the creation.* They are to exercise dominion over nature, which, if properly understood, is meant to be loving nurture and responsible stewardship,* not the abuse and exploitation that modern people believe they are authorized to do.

Only when we maintain the harmony of person-person and person-nature relationships will we fulfill God's intention and purpose of creating us in the divine image. If God is love (1 Jn 4:8), then our image bearing is first and foremost constituted by loving relations: with nature, fellow human beings and ultimately with God—a state of physical, mental, social and spiritual well-being. We are then truly integrated, authentic and fulfilled. In this view health is a divine gift, pure grace. To maintain health is to remain within the bounds of grace in obedience to God's word and purposes, loving God, fellow human beings and the created world. As such, to be healthy is to image God.

Health as Shalom

The Hebrew word *shalom* is translated as "peace" 172 times out of 250 times in the Old Testament. But *peace* in this case means much more than the absence of strife. It is used in various contexts to express the idea of totality, completeness, soundness, welfare, well-being, prosperity, wholeness and harmony. It refers to every area of life: personal, mental, physical, corporate and national. In this sense, *shalom* is probably the closest word in the Old Testament to *health.* Implicit in the word *shalom* and its verb form *shalom* is the idea of unimpaired relationships with God, self, others and nature. *Shalom,* therefore, incorporates and integrates the concepts of holiness and righteousness. In practice it means living a covenanted life, set apart for a morally committed existence in relationships accountable to God, self and others. To be healthy then includes being holy and righteous.

Shalom also strongly implies the idea of fulfillment. In almost two-thirds of its usage in the Bible, it describes the state of fulfillment, specifically the fulfillment of God's covenant of peace with humankind. This kind of fulfillment has its source in God and is the result of God's

gracious activity in the covenant. *Shalom* is God's presence. God is the one who speaks *shalom* to his people (Ps 85:8), and in the so-called Aaronic benediction (Num 6:24-26), the one to whom God has given *shalom* is identified as the one who is blessed,* guarded and treated graciously by Yahweh. *Shalom* is fulfillment through divine presence, specifically through the Messiah, Emmanuel, the Prince of Peace (*sar shalom*), who will bring fulfillment and righteousness (Is 32:17). Paul identifies Christ as our peace (Eph 2:14), the messianic prince who through self-sacrifice brings redemption, righteousness, fulfillment and wholeness to humankind. It is for this reason that the meaning of health in the New Testament, as in the Old Testament, includes themes such as blessedness, wholeness, maturity and holiness. This blessedness—*makarios*—which can be translated as "good health," is taught in the beatitudes (Mt 5:1-12) and is received through a transformation of the whole person oriented to the principles and values of the kingdom of heaven.

Health as Good

Understanding health in this way provides a different perspective on well-being. While physical health is good, it is not necessarily the only good and certainly not the ultimate good. We do not deny that our physical infirmities are real or should be removed, but in some special circumstances they may actually make a contribution to our flourishing. It is interesting to note that some secular medical social scientists have also developed a health-within-illness perspective, which sees illness as an event that can accelerate human growth (Jones and Meleis). Indeed, a healthy life includes an ability to cope with disease, suffering and death* and to integrate them as part of one's life. It is for this reason that Paul thinks that his lack of physical well-being is more than compensated by his participation in the suffering of Christ (2 Cor 12:7-16). Many biblical figures and believers throughout church history have considered that their physical health could be sacrificed at times for the sake of God's cause in the world.

Health and Responsibility

This multidimensional context for understanding health also suggests that we have a larger share of responsibility for our health than we often assume. When we think of health in a strictly physical and biomedical model, we tend to conceive ill health as an intrusion of a foreign agent (bacteria, virus) that breaks down part of the system (heart, liver) or as a result of some accident, matters over which we have no control. When we become ill, we adopt the sick role that largely exempts us from some or all of our responsibilities. A holistic concept of health reminds us that we are not that innocent. If we are determined to assault our bodies with tobacco, alcohol or a high-fat diet, are we really innocent when we suffer from bronchitis, cirrhosis and coronary artery disease? Paul teaches that our body is God's temple (1 Cor 3:16; 6:19; 2 Cor 6:16), holding us responsible for some of its maintenance. In this regard social scientists have also highlighted personal responsibility by defining health as a personal virtue and a task that each person cultivates through self-awareness and self-discipline (Illich).

Two points of caution should be noted. First, personal responsibility does not mean that we must pursue health and well-being to the point of obsession. Contemporary society has become addicted* to health. So to idolize health is to confuse God with his temple. Second, personal responsibility includes accountability not only to oneself but also to other people. An interpersonal and social understanding of health insists that we assume some responsibility for other people's sickness. We all contribute to the social conditions in which we live. The gap between the rich and the poor, sexual permissiveness, media violence, consumer* culture and environmental pollutions have adversely affected our public health. The line between personal and public health is not well demarcated. As a spiritual community, Christians must take to heart our share of social responsibility in health as an expression of our loving our neighbors.

See also BODY; HEALING, SICKNESS; SOUL.

References and Resources

I. Illich, *Medical Nemesis* (New York: Pantheon, 1976); P. Jones and A. I. Meleis, "Health as Empowerment," *Advances in Nursing Science* 15, no. 3 (1993) 1-14; S. E. Lammers and A. Verkey, eds., *Moral Medicine* (Grand Rapids: Eerdmans, 1987) 150-72.

Edwin Huis

HOBBIES AND CRAFTS

Hobbies are leisure or free-time activities that do not need to have a value to anyone other than to the person who engages in them, activities such as stamp collecting or raising tropical fish. Most hobbies fall into one of two categories: collecting or creating. Some hobbyists belong to hobby clubs,* many of which are national in scope. *Crafts,* which overlap with hobbies but can be distinguished from them, are activities in which one makes something personally or with simple tools, not in a mass-produced way and usually as a solitary activity. In contrast to machine-made clothes, precooked foods and plastic toys, in pursuit of a craft we build, stitch, weave, carve and print with our own hands. In this article crafts and hobbies will be considered together because many hobbies involve the regular pursuit of a particular craft (*see* Quilting). Exceptions to this exist, such as gardening* and cycling, which are not crafts but can be hobbies (*see* Recreation; Sports).

One obvious difference between crafts and hobbies is that some people pursue a craft as their major occupation, while in the nature of things a hobby is always something a person does alongside his or her primary occupation. Indeed, as Witold Rybczynski points out, hobbies allow people to compensate for the drudgery of their daily occupation by gaining competence and skills that make work more meaningful (p. 224). The person who spends all day doing data entry on a computer* finds great joy in spending his or her evenings in the workshop restoring old pianos. It is tempting to speak of hobbies as "avocational" (and therefore more interesting), but, as we will see, hobbies are part of and caught up in our vocation or calling. In "Two Tramps in Mud Time" Robert Frost beautifully expressed this integration of leisure with work as seeing one thing with two eyes. So the fact that some people are able to sell the work they have made as hobbyists is incidental. Not to be missed, though, is the special value hobbies play in developing good work habits in children and helping people discover the kind of work* they most enjoy. For many, pursuing hobbies is an experiential form of vocational guidance.*

While there are some extrinsic values in hobbies, people begin them mainly for the sheer joy of doing them. Their value is intrinsic. Making money or supplying family needs is generally not the issue. Apart from the hobbyists' lack of concern about profit, what further distinguishes hobbies is the exceptional passion devoted to them beyond what the activity itself deserves (Rybczynski, p. 198), not unlike the passion that people devote to recreation. My son and I climbed Mount Kenya in Africa. We stayed the night before the ascent in a tiny hotel at the start of the trail. The manager grilled us on what we were doing: "You white people come to climb the mountain. You usually get mountain sickness from the altitude. You come back six days later exhausted. You do not make any money doing it. In fact you spend money. Why do you do it?" G. K. Chesterton describes leisure* as essentially a matter of freedom: not only freedom from work, but freedom to do *something* (to take up one's chosen hobby), freedom to do *anything* (to climb a mountain just because it is there) and, best of all, freedom to do *nothing* (a kind of civilized loafing, to borrow H. A. Overstreet's term). Hobbies and crafts fall into the first two categories of freedoms.

The History of Hobbies and Crafts

Rybczynski notes that the English word *hobby* has a curious history (p. 195). The medieval root *hobbin* was the affectionate name given to cart horses. So the original meaning of hobby was "a small horse or pony," clearly associated with play rather than work. Figures of horse heads attached to sticks were used in pantomimes, and the Morris dancers attached figures of horses to their waists while they danced. Hobbyhorses were toy horses given to children. "Riding one's hobbyhorse" became something adults did when they indulged in trivial pastimes—which is exactly what we do when we engage in hobbies. They serve no adequate purpose to justify the expenditure of time and money. They are a form of adult toy.

The list of hobbies (many of which are also crafts) enumerated in Reader's Digest Crafts & Hobbies is overwhelming, though not exhaustive: leatherwork, macramé, decoupage, candlemaking, papermaking, basketry, spinning and dyeing, weaving, batik and tie-dyeing, stained

485

glass, string art, origami, pottery, quilting, modeling, casting sculptures, drawing, painting, printmaking, printing on fabric, stenciling, collage, wood sculpture, metalworking, drying and preserving flowers, mosaics, lapidary, jewelry, woodworking, picture framing, preserving fruit, bread baking, winemaking, restoring furniture and bookbinding.

Each hobby has a history. For example, collecting old things seems to have emerged in the Western world during the nineteenth century—thence the emergence of the museum as a Victorian passion. Wealthy people amassed collections of Japanese porcelain, prints and Asian exotica, while people of lesser means collected pressed flowers, matchboxes and stamps. The first written reference to stamp collecting occurs in 1842 (*Reader's Digest,* p. 197). Today people collect bottles, matches from hotels, seashells, hockey and baseball cards, coffee mugs and, in my own case, oil lamps from as many centuries and countries as I can. Why? Why turn yet one more wooden bowl on a lathe, weave another mat, make another stained-glass lamp or purchase yet another model railroad magazine to read on the subway? Why climb a mountain? The question raised by the motel manager at the base of Mount Kenya issued from a survival culture*; my son and I live in an identity culture.

As a relatively recent invention in human history, hobbies emerged along with affluence and have little place in survival cultures except among the few who are wealthy. Like everything else in the Western world, they have been commercialized. Industries that support them, however, are by and large a blessing; they do not take away from the essential experience of doing something for fun rather than profit. When a hobby turns into a business, it ceases to be a hobby. With crafts it is different. Through-

out history crafts have been essentially occupational, though, as we will see, not exclusively so. Crafts can be done for profit or pleasure or both.

Crafts have a long history, as long as the human race. While we have no indication that Adam took up stone masonry or painting, making things by hand is implicit in the original mandate to "have dominion" over everything (Gen 1:26 NRSV) and to "work [the world] and take care of it" (Gen 2:15). Adam and Eve were world makers, culture makers and therefore the first craftspeople. They were commissioned to shape as well as use and appreciate the created order. They were the first landscape gardeners, the first builders and the very first collectors. They were the first persons to note that things are good in themselves and worth having for the simple enjoyment they provide.

The creation account notes that "the gold of that land [the land of Havilah, watered by the Eden river system] is good; aromatic resin and onyx are also there" (Gen 2:12). Was Eve (or her descendant) the first jeweler, the first collector of beautiful ornaments, the first inventor of perfume, the first metalworker? It is difficult to imagine that everything in the garden was provided just for humankind to make a living. Occupations did soon begin to develop, including crafts (in the more formal sense): "Jabal . . . was the father of those who live in tents and raise livestock [signaling the transition from nomadic life to sedentary, with its attendant need for barter and trade]. His brother's name was Jubal; he was the father of all who play the harp and flute. . . . Tubal-Cain . . . forged all kinds of tools out of bronze and iron" (Gen 4:20-22). But crafts served the dual function of assisting in the business of living and allowing human beings to enjoy themselves and God's creation.

The list of crafts noted in the Bible is impressive, as the old volume *Occupations in the Bible* amply shows. Even more impressive is the way the Bible shows that God is a craftsperson. In *God the Worker* Robert Banks expounds many of the metaphors for God in the Bible that are drawn from human activities, such as weaver, knitter, potter, musician, gardener, builder and metalworker, just to mention a few. Godlike people do godlike things. God works and enjoys making beautiful things and says, "It is good." God, as Karl Barth said so profoundly, "is beautiful." This craftwork is both holy work and holy play.*

Inside Trivial Pursuits

The only person in the Old Testament specifically said to be filled with the Holy Spirit was a craftsperson: "I [God] have filled him [Bezalel] with the Spirit of God, with skill, ability and knowledge in all kinds of crafts—to make artistic designs for work in gold, silver and bronze, to cut and set stones, to work in wood, and to engage in all kinds of craftsmanship" (Ex 31:3-5). Craftsmanship,* whether for embellishing the tabernacle of God (as in the case of Bezalel) or embellishing one's home (as I have seen in the simplest mud homes in Africa), is potentially a holy ministry.

We now concern ourselves with the place of hobbies and crafts in a theology and spirituality of everyday life (for a consideration of a theology and spirituality of crafts as a primary occupation, *see* Craftsmanship; Work). Can they be justified? Need they be? Can they be sanctified and become, as they were for Bezalel, holy ministries? To whom is the ministry? Can a ministry to oneself—the sheer pleasure of doing something enjoyable or making something beautiful—be a ministry? The answer must be approached along several lines.

First, personal creativity is implicit in the dignity of being a human being made in the image of God. As coworkers with God, we have a limited capacity for cocreativity. While we do not, as God does, create from nothing in the strict sense, we share godlikeness in creating things that are truly new. When I decided to make my own photographic enlarger out of an abandoned bellows camera, the end result was not as good as commercial enlargers, but I had designed it myself and made it with my own hands. Quite apart from whether anyone else notices and copies what we have made, which in this case actually happened, there is something profoundly satisfying in carrying out such a project. In an essay on art Dorothy Sayers maintains that the distinctive contribution of Christianity to the field of aesthetics is actually this move from art (and therefore crafts) as representing something that already exists to art* as creating something new, something that had never existed before. It is godlike so to do and godlike to look at one's finished craft and say, "It is good." When such crafts are used as gifts to others, which is one good use to which they may be put, others may share this holy joy.

Second, the Christian life is essentially an amateur affair. In recent times we have witnessed the professionalizing of almost everything (see Professions/ Professionalism), including housecleaning, pest control and, tragically, ministry (*see* Clergy; Laity). But the Christian person has an essentially amateur status, not in the common meaning of "second-class" and "untrained," but in the original sense of the Latin word *amator* (lover). An amateur is someone who does something for love or simply because he or she loves to do it. The sum of our obligations to God, our neighbors, God's creation and ourselves is simply to love. Loveless work, like loveless ministry, is a stench to God and dehumanizing for others. One service rendered by the so-called craft revolution and the passion people who invest in their hobbies is the recovery of love as the primary motive for doing anything worthwhile in this life or the next. Some Christians may find it a bitter pill indeed to swallow on the day of judgment when they hear that one person's loving needlepoint was more pleasing to God than another's dutiful but loveless committee work in the church (compare Lk 17:10).

Third, hobbies and crafts can be personally restorative, a valid form of recreation. Just as bird watching and gardening can restore the soul,* so tumbling rocks in a grinder, working leather or poring over one's pictures in an album can bring rest* and renewal. It is sometimes argued that any human work that could be replaced by a machine was essentially dehumanizing anyway. There is some truth in this observation, especially when one thinks of the debilitating effect of routine, repetitive work on punch presses and assembly lines. I spent one whole summer making rivets by hand, the most uninspiring activity of my life. Such labor (for it is hard to call it work) can be somewhat redeemed by technology* and robotics. On the other hand, many of these same "dehumanizing" jobs can and should be done by people as hobbies. This changes the character of the activity entirely—offering a chance to bring one's own creativity to bear on it and to experience the satisfaction of putting a personal stamp on one's work. My wife and I built a country cabin without power tools, without skill saw, power hammer, crane, cement mixer or bulldozer. There is a level of personal renewal that comes from such activities that would be lost if one had to mass-produce cabins for a living.

But like all other aspects of everyday life, hobbies and crafts contain implicit temptations. As noted above, one distin-

guishing mark of a hobby is simply that people invest in it a passion that is out of proportion to its apparent value. "Riding one's hobbyhorse" involves indulging in trivial pastimes in a way that is quite out of proportion. At times this can verge on idolatry. Idolatry is simply making something One's ultimate concern other than the one who is ultimate. Rybczynski notes that while we have the word *workaholism* (*see* Drivenness), we have no parallel word for someone who is possessed by play (p. 17). It is one thing to liberate recreation, hobbies and leisure from the paralysis of sheer duty (for example, playing golf because of the social obligation). It is quite another to liberate a person from living for her hobby, living for the weekend, living for the workroom. As with all other forms of work, leisure, sports and recreation, hobbies and crafts need to be purged by a more compelling passion, a transforming love for God above all other loves.

See also CLUBS; CRAFTSMANSHIP; GARDENING; LEISURE; PLAY; QUILTING; RECREATION.

References and Resources
R. Banks, *God the Worker: Journeys into the Mind, Heart and Imagination of God* (Valley Forge, Penn.: Judson, 1994); R. F. Capon, *An Offering of Uncles: The Priesthood of Adam and the Shape of the World* (New York: Crossroad, 1982); W. Duckat, *Beggar to King: All the Occupations of Biblical Times* (Garden City, N.Y.: Doubleday, 1968); L. Hardy, *The Fabric of This World* (Grand Rapids: Eerdmans, 1990); *Reader's Digest Crafts & Hobbies* (Pleasantville, N.Y.: Reader's Digest Association, 1989); W. Rybczynski, *Waiting for the Weekend* (New York: Viking Penguin, 1991); D. L. Sayers, *Christian Letters to a Post-Christian World* (Grand Rapids: Eerdmans, 1969).

R. Paul Stevens

HOME

The word *home* has a broad range of meanings. On a personal level, it can refer to our immediate and physical place of residence; this may be a house, an apartment or condominium, a studio, boarding house, trailer park, retirement community, college dormitory or even a street corner. Home can also be descriptive of our "roots"; the place in which we grew up; our town, city, state or country of origin. Quite apart from a sense of place, home can describe the welcome and embrace of close friends* or family* members with whom we have a shared history. Or it can be descriptive of something for which we long; either that which we once had and desire to re-create or that which we have never experienced but ardently dream of.

Whatever definitions we use, our experiences of home, both past and present, are deeply formative. For some, *home* conjures up warm and secure mem-ories of the past or is representative of all that is good and wholesome in the present. For others, to speak of home is to resurrect past, painful experiences, a reminder of what one never had or does not have. As we face the ever-present realities of family dysfunction and breakdown, economic struggle and the increasing pressures of urban life, we are confronted with the fact that our experiences of homes, both positive and negative, shape who we are. We are products of our homes.

Also, regardless of culture,* we cannot avoid the vitality of the home as the expression of what it means to be human. Home gathers up so many of our deepest physical, emotional and spiritual needs and gives flesh to our longings and hopes for the future. In the United States homeownership, a privilege out of reach for many, is still central to the "American dream," for it stands as a monument to our drive for independence and our cravings for security and belonging.

The Home in the New Testament
In line with the Old Testament emphasis on the home as a place of protection, for raising a family, for rest,* prayer and hospitality,* and as part of one's legacy to one's children, the home in the New Testament plays a prominent role in the ministry* and mission* of Jesus, and in the unfolding story of the early church.*

A Place of Spiritual Encounter. Though it is true that Jesus ministered and proclaimed in synagogue and temple, his favored place of ministry was the home. There was nothing that Jesus did in the name of the Father that he was not prepared to do in the home. His choice of home as a primary place of interaction is consistent with his incarnational mission; no longer was the presence of God confined to the temple, mediated by priests, but it was now the immediate and daily experience of all those who respond in faith. And that presence was encountered in the most ordinary settings, the home included.

Spiritual encounters take many forms. In the New Testament God was encountered and responded to through healing* and deliverance (Mt 8:14-17; Mk 2:1; 5:35-43; Lk 14:1-4), worship* and prayer (Mt 2:1; 26:6-13, 30; Lk 1:39-55; Jn 12:1-8; Acts 2:1-4; 12:12), and through hearing and receiving from God (Mt 1:20; 2:13; Lk 2:6-38; Jn 19:19-23; Acts 2:1-4; 9:11). All these happened in the home.

A Place of Community. As community* is vital to the Christian church, so in the New Testament the home is vital to the nurture of community. Jesus spent a substantial amount of time in homes building relationships. One of his favorite activities was eating* and drinking in the homes of his friends (Mt 8:15; Lk 10:38-42; Jn 12:2). The Passover meal he shared with his disciples in a home prior to his crucifixion (Lk 22:7-38) signified the beginning of a tradition that is still today the mark of community in the Christian church.

As we examine the life of the early

church, it is apparent that the home played host more than any other venue to the development of community (Acts 2:42-47). The early church was almost exclusively a network of house churches (Rom 16:3-5; Col 4:15; Philem 2). Without the house as a meeting place for teaching,* fellowship,* worship and mission, it is hard to imagine how the early church would have found its feet.

A Place of Ministry. As well as playing host to the initial process of cohesion among the earliest believers, the home was the place where the open invitation into God's kingdom was extended to all who would hear. Jesus chose to do much of his teaching and preaching in homes, most often while reclining at a meal table (*see* Eating), sharing his time with "tax collectors and 'sinners' " (Lk 5:30; 15:1-2; 19:5-7). He visited and ate with Samaritans and saw many become his followers (Jn 4:39). He confronted the Pharisees in their homes (Lk 11:37-38; 14:1-6) and he welcomed into the home prostitutes, the demon-possessed and the sick (Mt 8:16-17; 26:6-13; Mk 2:1). The home was the place where Jesus took his disciples aside to explain and instruct (Mt 13:36-52; 17:25; 18:35). The home was where Nicodemus came seeking truth (Jn 3:1-21), and it was where the crowds gathered to hear Jesus preach (Mk 2:1; 3:19-21).

The home played host to the beginnings of the church (Acts 2:14). Early and rapid growth was centered in the home (Acts 2:46). As the persecution of the church moved from "house to house" (Acts 8:3), so the preaching of the good news happened "house to house" as well (Acts 5:42; 20:20). The opening of the church to the Gentiles sprang from events in the home (Acts 10:25-48), and Paul's subsequent mission to the Gentile world could not have happened without the network of households that extended hospitality to him

during his journeys (Acts 17:5; 18:2-3; 20:7-12; 21:8, 16).

A Place of Expectation. As we examine the role of the home in the New Testament, two realities emerge. Jesus existed very much in the present. He was the presence of God in physical form, to be touched, seen and heard. Wherever he went, he embodied the immediate concern of the kingdom for the here and now. Just as God in flesh was not a mere convenience but a vital theological reality, so Jesus present in the house was not an irrelevant aside but a tangible expression of God in their midst. All the concerns, duties and relationships embodied in the house were gathered up into the concerns of the kingdom. This is obvious from the number of stories of household duties and objects Jesus told to explain the nature of the kingdom of God (Mt 7:2-24; 25:31-46; Mk 10:29; Lk 11:5-10; 14:7-14; 15:8-10). The concerns of the earthly home were not cast aside by Jesus in favor of gazing off into the future. Rather, the kingdom was understood as present and immediate, even in the home.

On the other hand we have Jesus' promise that he goes to prepare a place for those who believe, a home with many rooms (Jn 14:2). This is part of the kingdom yet to be. It is with this sense of the kingdom now and not yet, the present reality of the home and the home yet to be, which validates the tensions felt by those endeavoring to live fully in the present and yet fully anticipating. Author Wendy Wright describes the human longing for stability and caring—the longing for home and the longing for meaning and ultimacy—the longing for homecoming. It is somewhere in between these two realities that believers are called to live.

Contemporary Attitudes Toward the Home

While for a majority of people in newer

Western societies owning a home, especially a house, is part of their "dream," fewer and fewer are able to afford this. In the United States the number is less than 60 percent. Where homes can be purchased, mortgages now take up an average of around 40 percent of income, up 15 percent from a generation ago (*see* Debt). This is partly due to inflation in house and apartment prices and partly to the increased size of houses and apartments today. Mortgages often tie up people's income for a large portion of their working life, with the result that most people are in debt over accommodation requirements for most of their lives.

Despite people's longing for "a home of their own," as in the past but even more so in the present, they tend to view where they live as a temporary resting place. Because of high mobility,* most people pass through many dwelling places during their lifetime. The phenomenon of the "mobile" home is simply the latest expression of this. In many cases, both marriage* partners are now working outside the home. Domestic space is therefore generally empty during the day and often on weekends, though the appearance of telecommuting is having a small effect on this.

Yet the idea of home remains strong. Most people see having a home as essential for their contentment or fulfillment, as a basis for security and stability, and as a fortress of privacy or "haven in a heartless world" (Lasch). They also tend to view their home as a status symbol, as an extension of their personality or as an opportunity to have a taste of nature on their doorstep. For some it is primarily an investment. Our homes, therefore, are significant to us in a variety of ways. That explains why they occupy so much of our attention and mean so much to us.

We are now living in a time when suburbia,* the main context for the places people live, is undergoing change

and reconsideration. It is not simply a case of fewer people being able to live there, or the urbanizing of many suburban settings, but the way suburbia has strengthened the gap between private and public life.

Architects and sociologists are voicing their common concern that the way we have been planning and building urban neighborhoods has disregarded the balance necessary to a well-functioning society between the home as private space and the home as a place of community. In his book *A Better Place to Live: Reshaping the American Suburb,* Philip Langdon argues that since the end of World War II, the front porch as the place of community interaction and the focus of family activity has been overtaken by the secluded back yard, complete with pool and barbecue area. Take a drive through any new housing development and you will find the front façades of the houses dominated by two- and three-car garages, with the main entrance to the home hidden off to the side. In many cases sidewalks no longer exist, and public gathering places are a secondary concern. According to Langdon and others, personal convenience and privacy now determine the architecture of our homes. Neighborhood considerations are of lesser concern. The proponents of New Urbanism contend that the way we build our homes must reflect to a greater extent the fact that we are community and public beings.

A Christian Response

The question must be asked: As those seeking to integrate our Christian faith with all of life, how do we interpret God's purposes for the home, and how do we nurture our homes of today and tomorrow as places of God's presence? Apart from our recognition of our thankfulness for God's providential provision of "a roof over our heads," we should consider the following dimensions of the homes in which we live.

A Sacred Place. When one considers, as we have, the range of significant events to which the home played host—the incarnation, the commissioning of the disciples, the last supper, the resurrection appearances, Pentecost, the opening of the church to the Gentiles, the blossoming of the early church—it is hard to deny the home its role as a place of God's gracious and transforming presence. God's presence through the Holy Spirit can form, nurture, refresh, heal and call us, and it is ours to be experienced in the home. The Roman Catholic Church's post-Vatican II declaration of the family as "domestic church" reminds us of the sacredness of place and interaction in the home. Unfortunately, we do not often appreciate the very immediate, divine presence that surrounds us there. It is our challenge to find ways to recognize and respond to the presence and call of God, and to experience in the solitude and relationship of the home the immediacy of "God with us."

A Place of Relationship. The traditional bonds of community are a fragile thing in today's world. This is certainly true in the home. As our lives become more fragmented, finding time together as households is increasingly difficult. Shared mealtimes are often sacrificed in the interests of individual agendas. More often than not, the television* is the gathering point in the home, an object that discourages rather than nurtures communication. If we are serious about the home as a place of interaction, then careful thought should be given to some practical matters of priority. Creating common schedules that prioritize time together is essential. Consideration could be given to the arrangement of furniture in common areas. Too often the television set is the organizing point in our living rooms. Placing it elsewhere

and intentionally creating spaces that invite interaction through the simple rearrangement of chairs and lighting can make a substantial difference.

A Place of Refuge. While in the majority of instances recorded in the New Testament the focus of home ministry and interaction is on the open door, there are also significant instances of the house as a place to close the door on outside demands (Mt 6:6; 8:14; Mk 5:38-43; Lk 1:24, 56). There will be times in the life of every household when it is more appropriate to focus on the healing and well-being of those within than to extend a welcome to outsiders. The various seasons of life each come with their unique challenges and demands. Our homes must serve as places of refuge, withdrawal, healing, comfort and solitude to varying degrees throughout our occupancy. Sensitivity to the changing needs of our household members must always be seen as a valid expression of our response to God's call. It is interesting to note the occasions in which Jesus directed one of those he healed to "go home" (Mk 5:19; 8:22-26; Lk 5:25). He did not direct them to go and do, go and proclaim, or go into all the world: he simply commanded them to return to their homes.

A Place of Mission. In a society that values independence and privacy, it is perhaps our greatest challenge to stand apart, to model the welcome and embrace of the gospel where we live. The call to mission is a call to friendship.* Such a call requires an open door, inviting conversation and redemptive relationship. The church is often rebuked for being more a fortress that guards the faith than an open table to which all are welcomed and where faith is shared. The home is ideally suited to model the latter. An integrated Christian faith is a key issue here too. Our place of worship and fellowship is most often separate from our place of living. In today's urban world the two can be not only in different buildings but in two completely separate parts of the city. Many today are rediscovering the New Testament house-church model (*see* Church in the Home), which helped tremendously in reintegrating these separate worlds and in re-centering the home as a primary place of mission in the world. Where possible, we can also use our homes as places for exercising hospitality to those who are traveling or on vacation, those who are engaged in itinerant ministry or home from overseas mission, and those who are temporarily homeless. While not everyone is able to have a guest room available to any who may need it, those who can afford to do so can provide one as a tangible sign of their welcoming attitude to others.

A Place of Recreation. The home is a place where we can relax, be ourselves, rest and enjoy leisure.* It provides opportunities for play* with our families, and for creativity in the way we decorate and furnish—not necessarily an expensive affair, as the simple but beautiful and peaceful homes of many Mennonites and rural folk attest. The home is a context in which many people pursue their hobbies* and crafts,* extending and enriching themselves in satisfying ways that may also be beneficial to others. The uncertainty or chaos of the world outside is sometimes compensated for by the stability and order of the home. Meanwhile, the space around the house allows people to re-create the earth through sowing and planting flowers, shrubs and trees (*see* Gardening). In some cases the front and back yards of a home become a miniature Garden of Eden that signals to us our longing for the coming Heavenly Garden City (Rev 22:1-5).

Conclusion

In light of these considerations, we should consider carefully not just where we should live but where *God* wants us to live. First of all, this requires understanding our calling,* for this will have much to say about where we should reside. In deciding this we need to take into account our location with respect to our work,* schools, parks, the needy and public transport.*

Second, we should think through what kind of home we need rather than what kind of home we want, which is often not much different from what most others desire. How much should we be governed by the principles of simplicity (*see* Simpler Lifestyle), of stewardship* of God's creation,* and, if we are able to build a home, of its compatibility with other dwellings, integrity in terms of style, and quality in terms of craftsmanship?

Third, we should give thought to having and arranging spaces inside the home so that they serve their proper function and are an expression of our values* and priorities. Do we want our home to be a showcase to impress outsiders, or do we want it to be a place that nurtures relationships and provides security for those who live there? Do we want our home to be a perfect example of orderliness and tidiness, or do we want it to be a place of welcome, embrace and peace for the visitor? Do we want it to open up to the creation around it and the street on which it is placed, or seal us from these?

Instead of assuming that the single-family home or individual apartment is the embodiment of our personal desires and needs, we should also consider the benefits of cooperative housing or shared living arrangements, such as friends buying or renting adjoining houses, or living with others in a Christian community. Congregations can also give thought to helping young families put a deposit on their first home, developing a street community where members live near one another and intentionally minister to their neighborhood, or providing low-cost housing for seniors.

In summary, the home is indeed, potentially at least, a sacred place in which the presence and purposes of God can be discovered and responded to. As a people who long for the fulfillment of God's promise of an eternal home to which we are welcomed with open arms, we have the opportunity in the present moment to experience and to be "the household of God" (1 Tim 3:15 NRSV). Our homes can be gathered up in that experience.

See also CHURCH IN THE HOME; HOSPITALITY; SUBURBIA.

References and Resources
C. Alexander, *A Timeless Way of Building* (New York: Oxford University Press, 1979); R. J. Banks, *Paul's Idea of Community* (Peabody, Mass.: Hendrickson, 1994); T. Howard, *Hallowed Be This House* (San Francisco: Ignatius, 1976); T. Kidder, *House* (New York: Houghton Mifflin, 1985); P. Kratz, *The New Urbanism: Toward an Architecture of Community* (New York: McGraw-Hill, 1994); P. Langdon, *A Better Place to Live: Reshaping the American Suburb* (Amherst: University of Massachusetts, 1994); C. Lasch, *Haven in a Heartless World* (New York: Basic Books, 1977); C. C. Marcus and Sarkissian, *Housing As If People Mattered* (Los Angeles: UCLA Press, 1986); W. Rybczynski, *Home: A Short History of an Idea* (New York: Viking, 1986); J. Solomon, *The Signs of Our Time* (Los Angeles: J. P. Tarcher, 1988); J. F. C. Turner, *Housing by People: Towards Autonomy in Building Environments* (New York: Pantheon, 1976); J. A. Walter, *The Human Home: The Myth of the Sacred Environment* (Tring, U. K.: Lion, 1982); W. M. Wright, *Sacred Dwelling: A Spirituality of Family Life* (New York: Crossroad, 1990).

Simon Holt and Robert Banks

HOME VIDEO

Perhaps no new medium has been adopted more rapidly around the world than video. Portable video cameras and especially the ubiquitous videocassette recorder (VCR) spread around the globe during the late 1980s and early 1990s, affecting everything from news coverage to international politics and family life.

The Home-Video Theater
The most significant uses of video occur in the home. Indeed, video transformed many homes into private movie* theaters, where family members could view at their own discretion commercially produced videotapes of tens of thousands of feature films, educational products, exercise programs, pornographic materials, political propaganda made by special-interest groups, and their own family-made productions. Initially teenagers were the principal consumers of videocassettes, and viewing adult-oriented movies with friends became a rite of passage, especially for North American adolescents. By the mid-1990s, however, home viewing of movie videos was a massive industry that surpassed movie box-office revenues and encompassed practically all sectors of society.

In one sense, home video is merely an expansion of television. Many movies available on videotape are also available on broadcast or cable television. Also, VCRs are sometimes used to record cable or broadcast programming for repeated viewing or for viewing at a different time.

Technological improvements in home-video imaging and audio helped to make home video a medium distinct from television. Larger and less expensive television sets encourage families to establish video viewing areas or even entire video rooms in their homes. Moreover, hi-fi sound systems enable viewers at home to emulate the aural impact of the movie-theater screening room. As a result, home viewing of movies is more formal, collective and planned than regular television watching, although not necessarily any more reflective or discerning.

Most people prefer to rent or purchase newly released video movies. Even classic movies are now widely rented at video shops. In Third World countries there is an enormous market in illegal copies of recent films, especially action-oriented Hollywood films starring high-profile actors. The video industry caters to this appetite for new films, a strategy that does not always serve well the more discerning video user who seeks older, high-quality movies.

Video Gaming

Video games are part of a large high-tech industry designed primarily to fulfill one human want: the desire to overcome personal boredom* in the home. A few games purport to be educational, or to enhance small-motor skills, but the vast majority of them is almost purely for personal entertainment.* Not surprisingly, children with the greatest leisure time are the prime market for these games. These children have the most time to spend and the least inhibitions about computer* technologies.

For all of their high-tech wizardry, video games are a poor substitute for more traditional board games* and yard games. Most video games depend on a market of lone players, whereas other games depend on small groups searching for relational activities. Even when groups play video games, the play is directed at the monitor, not at players. While most other gaming fosters interpersonal communication among players, video gaming usually eclipses it.

Video games also have addictive* qualities for players. Foremost among them is the sheer rush of adrenaline that players feel during the peak moments of action-oriented video games. Nearly as important is the competitive determination to beat the game, if not the other players. Rewards are immediate, even if the game has to be restarted for the player to try to advance to the next level. Finally, home-video games temporarily satisfy compulsive personalities, which need to be doing something as quickly and as frequently as possible.

Video games are not all bad, but they are clearly inferior and addictive substitutes for relational forms of recreation.* The best video games are not time-bound, superenergy visual extravaganzas but multiplayer inducements to communicate about the subject matter of the game. Unfortunately, males do not feel the need for intimacy as strongly as females, so the video industry matches its male-oriented product development and marketing to these nonrelational players. Video games are largely the province of bored males who satisfy some of their cravings for power by blasting away the enemies, time and time again.

Home Video as Family History and Parable

Low-cost equipment is a boon to amateur video production, especially in the home. A growing number of families are using video photography to preserve memorable events. This kind of family video history alters both the way family life is conducted and how families relate to their pasts. In the best uses, video can help families enjoy and learn from their own personal stories of life.

Video, even more than film and still photography,* leads families to emphasize the preservation of events rather than actual events themselves. In other words, family life is increasingly staged for the camera and thereby for the memorable record the video provides. Sometimes the change is not exceedingly important (for example, when the wedding party must stand during the service or when graduates march during commencement). In other cases, however, the sheer availability of the video camera redirects the action (for example, the videographer instructs children during a visit to the beach to build a sandcastle or to go swimming or directs a toddler on Christmas morning to frolic in the pile of discarded wrapping paper and bows—all the drama for "the camera").

One positive aspect of this video-mindedness is the way it can instill a familial sense of the value of special occasions. Video encourages families to find more value in their time together, to see such family times as out of the ordinary (Eccles 3:1). The medium can even foster greater preparation for family events in the hope of maximizing their video potential. This is true of vacation* planning, which typically includes some options that are more "videogenic" than others.

However, video can easily rob family life of its spontaneous joy and irreproducible memories. When the video camera is present, families tend to swap their unplanned antics for staged behavior. Suddenly the normal spontaneity of life disappears, even the spontaneity left in ritualized ceremonies such as baptisms and graduations. In addition, video focuses a family's collective memory only on the events that can be recorded. Unless a family consciously tries to keep alive the oral stories of nonrecorded events, the video memories will eclipse the recollection of them.

The Future of Video

Video technology complements the computer and has a bright future. Although videotape will eventually be replaced by CD-ROMs or other forms of digital storage, video movies and games will likely take up even more leisure time. Three important trends will shape the future of video and will influence the users of this technology.*

First, video will become an increasingly interactive medium. A new genre of movies, for example, will become something like video games, with the viewer choosing plot directions. Meanwhile, the interactivity of video games will be enhanced by faster action and a greater array of play choices. In its own way home-video production will share this increased interactivity in the form of greater user control over the production process, including the home use of graphics, editors, sound enhancements and special effects. Interactivity will increase the creative options of users.

Second, video will emerge as an essential technology. Like radio* and television* before it, video will shift from a luxury item to a foundational home medium. In fact, video will subsume television, if not the computer, in many homes. Along the way video will take on all kinds of new uses based on the CD-ROM and other storage devices. These may include such things as home reference work, educational programs, video telephones and home shopping.*

Third, video will shape domestic life, just as its predecessor, television, has for decades. Families will continue to dedicate more of their leisure* time to video, seduced by the medium's specialized fare for all ages, lifestyles and ideologies. Domestic architecture and furniture will be influenced by the desires of video viewers, perhaps even more than by the need for strong family life and interpersonal relations generally.

See also COMPUTER GAMES; ENTERTAINMENT; GAMES; LEISURE; PHOTOGRAPHY; TELEVISION.

Quentin J. Schultze

HOMEMAKING

Homemaking as a vocation has had very bad publicity in recent years. The popular media delight in caricaturing homemakers. She—such a person is usually, but certainly not always, female—is pictured as having no intellectual awareness; she makes no contribution to the family income; she has no glamour, status or productivity.

For Christians, the story of Mary and Martha (Lk 10:38-41) seems to confirm what the pundits of the media are saying: homemaking, at least the kind practiced by Martha, is second best. Many a good homemaker has had a sneaking sympathy for Martha. After all, somebody had to prepare the food and do the dishes! Yet implicit in Jesus' approval of Mary is a condemnation of Martha's busyness.

It is not surprising that full-time homemakers make up an increasingly small percentage of the population. Is homemaking a profession that is still necessary or valid? Is an intelligent and competent person wasting God-given talents* when deciding to stay at home* to care for the family*? What do homemakers need from others to save them from extinction? To answer these questions, we need to clarify what homemaking is and see what Christians can bring to it, following the examples of the biblical role models we have been given.

What Is Homemaking?

Perhaps the most dreaded question a homemaker faces is "So, what do you do?" When we meet strangers in social situations, this is often the conversation* opener. The answer "I am a homemaker" often terminates the conversation abruptly, and the questioner moves off to network* more profitably elsewhere. If there is a further question, often it is "So, what do you do all day?" uttered in a tone of incredulity if the homemaker does not also have a job outside the home. The problem is that the answer seems so mundane: "I care for my family; I clean and tidy and organize the house; I plan and cook and serve meals; I wel-

come and provide for our guests." It is hard to express the intangibles: being there for others, creating a warm and sheltering place, teaching basic values,* modeling the attitudes and ways of God.

Homemaking, if practiced lovingly and conscientiously, ranges far beyond the physical tasks that make up the day-to-day routine. It can be defined as that which develops and nurtures the family at its central core—its traditions, beliefs, values and strengths and the unique character of the family. Homemakers care for the physical surroundings and physical needs, not as ends in themselves, but as part of the overall fostering of the family's well-being (see Adornment; Eating; Sleeping; Walking).

In Jesus' ministry we see how physical acts can have both practical application and spiritual significance. He washed his disciples' feet because they were hot and dirty, thus making his companions feel welcome and comfortable (Jn 13:5). Yet it was also an opportunity for him to describe the cleansing of forgiveness. Creating and caring for a physical environment bring into being an atmosphere in which people are loved, cherished and nurtured in their whole being.

Homemaking is an act of human creativity. The attitude and personality of homemakers, the spirit with which they approach their task, shape and define the homes they make. In the original act of creation God brought order out of chaos. Establishing a home exercises a similar kind of creativity. Homemaking is also an expression of providence. It maintains and enhances order within and around the family, much as God maintains and orders the universe. An obvious point of difference, as any homemaker would be quick to acknowledge, is that God's cosmic order has lasted rather longer than the order created in a home! The finished product—the home, which is much more than a house—is as unique as are the creatures that God made.

Christian Homemaking

While every home is a personal piece of art,* homes that are fashioned by Christians will share certain characteristics because of their common striving to be obedient to God. Just as an artist's work, however individual, may still be representative of a particular school or style, so the Christian's home will show evidence of the work of the Holy Spirit. It will be marked by the presence of (or the seeking after) the fruit of the Spirit: "love, joy, peace, patience, kindness, goodness, faithfulness, gentleness and self-control" (Gal 5:22-23). The homemaker, because of the nature of her work at the very heart of the home, is able to influence those in her care and affect the atmosphere in the home.

If love,* the first-mentioned fruit of the Spirit, is present in a home, how will it show itself? Christian love, as distinct from the secular version, is defined by God's love for us. In sending Jesus to live his love before us, God proved in the flesh the value of unconditional love. In sending the Spirit to indwell us, God showed us love intimately involved with the everyday life of the believer. This is not love from afar; this is love close up. A homemaker has an unusual opportunity to exemplify incarnational love because so much of her—or his—work must be done in the details of daily life, and her presence is as important as anything that she does. Love then will not be merely intellectual or emotional but gloriously practical and down-to-earth, that is, truly incarnational.

Similarly, peacefulness is a goal of the Christian homemaker. This does not mean the absence of noise, debate or argument. A home may have occasional or even frequent discord, as well as constant happy noise, and still be a place of peace. Here conflicts are resolved in an atmosphere of love, forgiveness and mutual submission to God's will. Peace is an intangible phenomenon. A home may be superficially peaceful yet, underneath the veneer of calm, full of hatred* and disunity. True peace ultimately can only come from God because forgiveness is its most important ingredient. Those who live in peace with God and themselves are more able to generate and promote peacefulness in the home. Alongside incarnational character, then, there is in homemaking a redemptive dimension as well.

The best homemakers manage to create a place where people matter more than material things. This often marks the difference between a housekeeper and a homemaker, as shown in the story of Martha and Mary. Martha was "worried and upset about things" (Lk 10:41). Her concentration was primarily on the pots and pans and food; she seemed to see them as an end in themselves. Mary chose to sit near Jesus and listen to him. In so doing she demonstrated her priority: her friendship* with Jesus. Mary may have seen the things that Martha did as one way to express love and hospitality.* But the way Mary chose, the homemaking rather than the housekeeping way, was clearly acceptable to Jesus.

Homemakers' Contribution

The commitment of homemakers to care for the home and family clearly benefits those around them. Less obvious, perhaps, is their enormous contribution to the whole of society. They have much to give the neighborhoods* in which they live. They are often at the forefront of the army of volunteers* whose hard work adds so much to the general good. They can give the gift of time, and their focus on caring for others makes them natural resources for churches and community organizations. At a time when the disintegration of the traditional family is contributing to serious societal ills, they proclaim by their career choice that family means more than the status, money* and job satisfaction offered by a career* outside the home. In fact they are actually making a significant contribution to the welfare and renewal of society!

Traditionally homemaking has included the care and nurture of children. (Of course, there are many examples of wonderful homemakers who did not combine these two roles.) The decline of homemakers has brought about a crisis in our society: who will care for the children? In the confusing debate over what constitutes the best environment for child rearing, some truths are clear: children thrive in an atmosphere that is stable, loving and consistent, where they are respected as unique individuals and given both guidance and freedom appropriate to their age and ability. There are a number of good reasons, besides historical precedence, for the family's homemaker to care for its children. Homemakers have the time flexibility that allows for adaptation to children's changing needs as they grow. Being cared for in their own home enhances their sense of security and emotional stability. The homemaker's commitment to putting people first makes her an ideal caregiver.

What Homemakers Need

If little value is placed on their skills, homemakers are vulnerable to low self-esteem.* They need strong encouragement and affirmation* from family and friends. Low self-esteem can also result from a lack of a sense of identity, because identity is closely associated in our society with what job we do. Like all other Christians, homemakers need to find their primary source of identity in their relationship with God. It is not what we do but who we are—children of God—that gives our lives worth and purpose.

In a profession* that offers little in the way of status, homemakers need positive role models. They are unlikely to find them in the popular mass media,* where intelligent women run corporations and homemakers have traded their brains for dishcloths. Even the male homemaker in a well-known comic* strip is depicted as overwhelmed by chaos, sunk in lethargy and lacking in decisiveness. One picture of the ideal homemaker is found in Proverbs 31. Here is a woman who is industrious, loving, honorable; she has status in her community, the love of her husband, the respect of her children. It is a compelling picture and one that has strengthened homemakers for many generations. Another glimpse is provided in Romans 16:3-5. Priscilla was a homemaker and was involved in the family business; she also cohosted with her husband a church in her home and extended hospitality to itinerant Christian workers.

The Example of Jesus

We must not overlook the best biblical role model—Jesus. At first glance this may seem either absurd (he did not even have a home) or obvious (all Christians are called to walk in his footsteps and live as he lived). Looking closely at Jesus' interaction with various people, we see a man with a homemaker's heart. He too worked at physical tasks that were important but also imbued with spiritual significance. He had neither a home nor a nuclear family, yet he was the quintessential homemaker.

Jesus was concerned about the physical well-being of those he met. He healed people because he cared about them, not just to demonstrate his miraculous power or to authenticate his claims. He urged his disciples to feed the hungry crowds. Commentators have discussed the feeding of the multitude in terms of Jesus' challenge to his disciples: he wanted to stretch their faith, to encourage them to trust him even as they took on a greater leadership role. Yet it is equally true to say that he wanted to feed them because they were hungry; he felt compassion for both their spiritual (Mk 6:34) and physical (Mt 15:32) need.

A similar incident occurred on the shore of the Sea of Tiberias after Jesus' resurrection (Jn 21). When the disciples returned to the shore after a night of fishing, they found Jesus barbecuing fish for their breakfast. Maybe, as some have suggested, he wanted to prove by eating* that his resurrected body was a real one, not a ghostly apparition. Yet he also must have known how hungry they would have been after a night of fishing. By preparing their breakfast, he was reminding them of his deep abiding love. He wanted them to experience the warmth of the fire in the chill of the morning. The reality of his presence must have brought all the joy of a homecoming. On that shore he made a home for them where the meeting of their physical needs coincided with the meeting of their emotional and spiritual needs. He did it because he loved them. Here is the essence of homemaking.

As Jesus spoke with his disciples about his ascension, he gave an intriguing glimpse into his occupation until they would be reunited with him for eternity. "I go and prepare a place for you," he told them, "that where I am you may be also" (Jn 14:3 RSV). The image is a profoundly moving one: Jesus, who knows us intimately and loves us boundlessly, is preparing a home for us in which to spend eternity. An occupation so honored by the Lord Jesus is surely one that any of his followers can be proud to pursue.

See also FAMILY TRADITIONS; HOBBIES AND CRAFTS; HOSPITALITY; LOVE; MAR-RIAGE; NEIGHBORHOOD; VOLUNTEER WORK.

References and Resources
R. Andre, *Homemakers: The Forgotten Workers* (Chicago: University of Chicago Press, 1981); W. Droel, *Homemakers* (Chicago: ACTA, 1990).

Susan Norman

HOMEWORK

Homework is ubiquitous at every level of schooling today because parents, teachers and students all believe that it increases academic achievement. Unfortunately, when teachers assign work for home, individual differences among students are all too often ignored, inappropriate reading assignments are included, there is little scope for creative thinking, and finished assignments are rarely corrected, graded and returned to students (Rickards, p. 831). These are inadequacies that stem from such traditional schooling techniques as rote learning and teacher domination.

These traditional techniques prevailed until relatively recently. In the synagogues of ancient Israel, for example, teachers required their students to memorize portions of the Old Testament (Deut 6:7-9). In short, homework represented the main part of education.* Teachers devoted the major portion of class time to checking up on the previous night's assignments. At the end of class, teachers outlined the information that students next had to master and memorize at home. Students were expected to demonstrate their competence on return to class. The whole process lacked the variety of activities that characterize education today.

In many countries today the traditional style of education survives. Japanese students, for instance, devote more time to homework than they spend in school. Education's purpose in Japan is to permit access to the best universities through success in rote examinations. Many North Americans also regard factual recall as the main purpose of education and hence support systems in which homework demands only memorization. There are, however, better ways of studying at home.

Successful Homework

It is well known that the ideal formula for academic achievement and maintenance of stable values is found when parent, teacher and child work voluntarily as a single team (Comer, p. 34). Research established the worth of this formula only recently. Good homework approximates the ideal because all key actors share a common task. Few homes, however, provide the cultural setting necessary for parental involvement. On the average in North America only one in six homes has the literary tradition and social stability for significant parental support. While a parent need not be competent in the subject matter, there must be an intelligent interest in what is going on if the trio is to function successfully.

As a result, the students who benefit most from homework come from homes in which parents are literate and in which social conditions ensure a quiet and supportive environment. It is just here that the opportunities are greatest for Christian parents to assist in the educational process. Emphases on honesty and excellence are values that they can bring (Eph 6:4). Their contributions will be greatest when homework is a logical extension of classroom studies, is geared to the needs of students and is assessed by teachers before further study is undertaken. Students from nonliterate homes experience very different problems with their homework.

Supervised Study

One writer notes that one-third of parents in North America are functionally illiterate, while another third are uncomfortable with literary pursuits and rarely read (Dixon, p. 215). The ability of these parents to support homework, let alone participate in students' studies, is virtually nil. The only answer for these students is either supervised study after hours at school or private tutoring. A high degree of student interest is essential for success in these cases. Here again, volunteer Christian parents who can serve as role models are invaluable mentors for those who lack this kind of support at home.

The social pressures that militate against any infringement on after-school activities, however, make this kind of provision extremely unpopular. Young people value games,* hanging out with friends, watching television,* other leisure* interests and part-time employment. These pursuits are also vital components of general education (Cremin, p. viii). Furthermore, children who come from culturally deprived homes place exceptional value on these social aspects of life.

See also DRIVENNESS; EDUCATION; READING; WORK.

References and Resources

J. P. Comer, "Is 'Parenting' Essential to Good Teaching?" *NEA Today,* January 6, 1988, 34-40; L. A. Cremin, *Popular Education and Its Discontents* (New York: Harper & Row, 1990); R. G. Des Dixon, *Future Schools and How to Get There from Here: A Primer for Evolutionaries* (Toronto: ECW Press, 1992); J. P. Rickards, "Homework," in *Encyclopedia of Educational Research,* ed. H. E. Mitzel, 5th ed. (New York: Free Press, 1982) 2:831-34.

Angus Gunn

HOMOSEXUALITY

Although the term *homosexuality* has emerged from the shadows into everyday conversation and is widely understood as referring to sexual attraction between members of the same sex, it remains a confusing term with multiple nuances. Some even prefer to refer to *homosexualities* to avoid the impression that it is one phenomenon and that it takes only one form.

A Recent Term

Sexual activities with persons of the same sex have been known throughout history and across all cultures, though much more is written about the activities of men than of women. The term *homosexuality* was coined only in 1892, while the activist terms *lesbian* and *gay* are still more recent (1970s and 1950s, respectively). These latter terms are not synonymous with homosexuality but were coined to express affirmation and to replace earlier terms (including *buggery* and *sodomy,* from biblical and legal language) that had become pejorative. Such changes mean that there is not only a change in the interpretation of same-sex behavior and attitudes but also ambiguity, when referring to earlier references, whether the same concept is being described. Many contemporary writers seek to interpret the biblical references as relating to temple prostitution and culturally endorsed practices rather than the homosexual acts of today. Hence cultural meaning is often advanced as a way of reinterpreting the morality of homosexual activity.

A Long Story

Homosexual acts have been recorded throughout history. Sociologists and anthropologists have identified many different expressions associated with rituals, initiation rites and use of power. These do not assume a lifetime orientation or even a predominant attraction to the same sex. No society in history has endorsed adult homosexual relationships of the kind advocated today. Evidence of exclusive homosexuality has

been sketchy, probably due to its rarity. Much of the evidence relates to the enforced isolation of monasticism, denying heterosexual outlet.

Seemingly higher prevalence only received significant attention after the Kinsey reports (1948 and 1953) mistakenly suggested 4 percent of adult men are exclusively homosexual and 10 percent are predominantly homosexual (and fewer women). This apparently scientific work brought confusion both to science and to morality, since it made false claims yet appeared to challenge traditional morality. Kinsey's study combined information about sexual attraction with reports of actual sexual behavior. Thus the traditional Jewish and Christian distinctions became blurred. A full, sensitive response requires a distinction between the person with a homoerotic attraction and the one who engages in homosexual behavior. This difference has profound implications for our response personally, pastorally, theologically and politically.

While earlier societies have often institutionalized homosexual behavior, either giving it limited sanction or developing strong taboos against it, homosexual behavior has never been incorporated as a "normal" or "natural" expression. Claims that the normality of homosexual behavior can be sustained by the observation of animal behavior do not hold up since this is never a sustained pattern, but rather an occasional variant where it occurs. The current ideology of the gay movement is to bring homosexuality into the mainstream of sexuality* as one among several preferences of equal legitimacy. This is a radical alternative to traditional thinking and gains strength in the Western world not only from its appeal to civil rights claims but also from maintaining orientation and behavior as inseparable. By contrast the large number of nonpracticing homosexuals provide evidence that orientation does not necessarily demand a behavioralresponse.

Many Viewpoints

A fast-growing literature provides different and conflicting interpretations that arise from their varied starting assumptions. Represented in this literature are
☐ personal biographies of Christians and others advocating the endorsement of the gay lifestyle as largely predetermined, something to be accepted, not fought;
☐ personal biographies of those (especially Christians) who have experienced a reorientation away from their homosexuality and proclaim release is possible;
☐ accounts of therapy by clinicians, some arguing change is never real or lasting and others citing a growing body of evidence that real change can and does occur;
☐ moral and theological discussions regarding homosexual behavior with varying conclusions depending on the adoption of a conservative or liberal interpretation of the Scriptures;
☐ evidence from the biological sciences suggesting some fundamental difference (genetic or hormonal) that might indicate a built-in predisposition to becoming homosexual (with a clear political agenda of legitimizing the gay movement, this rush of studies has been shown repeatedly to be misleading and inadequate);
☐ evidence from the social sciences suggesting links with early relationships, parenting* patterns and/or significant seduction experiences (these arguments take many forms, and their variety indicates that no one theory is sufficient for all presentations of homosexual inclination).

The absence of a single compelling explanation points to the complexity of the phenomenon and suggests at least that there are many possible precursors to becoming homosexual, as well as various forms of expression. Nature and nurture appear to contribute to differing degrees for any given man or woman, and stereotyping should be avoided.

Biblical Sources

There is wide disagreement about the meaning of biblical texts regarding homosexuality. Proof texting needs to be avoided. Such material as appears in the Old and New Testaments should be understood in the wider framework of teaching about creation and the purpose of sexuality. There is no support for the judgmental view that the Scriptures condemn the homosexual (as many activists assert), but there is clear teaching about involvement in homosexual practices. Hence the traditional distinction between orientation and behavior (or the sinner and the sin), which has been blurred by science since Kinsey, deserves to be reemphasized.

Homosexual practices do receive mention in both the Old and New Testaments, but such references are few. The conservative interpretation of passages such as Genesis 19:5-9; Leviticus 18:22; 20:13; Judges 19:22-28; Romans 1:26-32; 1 Corinthians 6:9-10; and 1 Timothy 1:8-11 is that there is a clear condemnation of homosexual behavior that goes beyond the commands to Israel and has binding significance for Christians today. This interpretation comes from setting such specific injunctions into the broader context of sexuality generally, especially the creation principle of male and female.

A great deal hinges on the interpretation of the term *natural* as used in Romans 1. Confusion arises when *natural* is used to indicate "according to nature," as a naturally occurring phenomenon, since there are many things, good and bad, that occur naturally. That something occurs naturally does not automatically vindicate it. However, Paul's use of the term is undoubtedly in a moral sense—that is, *natural* as something in accordance with God's purposes for creation and over against that which is *unnatural,* or morally wrong. Making such distinctions, we can assert that homosexual behavior is natural in the first sense (it occurs in nature) but unnatural in the second sense as used by Paul.

Such a position nonetheless needs to be balanced by the limited attention given in the Bible to this matter, suggesting that its significance should not be exaggerated. Homosexual behavior appears in the New Testament among catalogs of sins without any indication that it is more heinous than lying or greediness. Further, though we recognize homosexuality to be both male and female, there is almost no reference to lesbianism (except Rom 1:26-27). We should not automatically equate the lesbian and the gay experience, and current research suggests there are significant psychological differences between them.

Practical Responses

It helps to distinguish the *individual* experiencing homosexual attraction from the gay *movement*, which insists that this is entirely normal and morally neutral. Long-standing moral principles that have shaped cultures* over centuries need not be abandoned because scientific findings appear to be generating new insights. In this area science is tentative, exploratory, biased and frequently shown to be wrong. Klaus Bockmuehl has cautioned against responding too hurriedly to the latest opinions:

> The church of Jesus Christ has to resist the trend that would ironically make *it* the agent for abolition of its own ethical norms, and abolition for

which neither the Old nor the New Testament offers the slightest justification. The biblical norms are relevant precisely because they deal with homosexual behavior, which is exactly the problem today. (pp. 12-18)

What About Change?

While the gay movement insists change is not possible and should not be attempted, such simple stereotyping should be resisted. There are wide varieties of expression and experience. While activists publicly clamor for acceptance, others quietly suffer and long to be different. Change, if sought, is achieved successfully by some, but for others the pattern is, humanly speaking, unchangeable. Acceptance of a celibate lifestyle is one legitimate option for those in that situation.

Defining what constitutes change is difficult. In the past a shift toward heterosexual interest and then marriage were claimed as adequate evidence for successful change, but some now argue that such changes are secondary to a more fundamental change. Some follow the argument advanced by E. Moberly (1983) that the underlying problem is not a problem with the opposite sex but with the same sex. Developmental theorists argue that a poor relationship with the same-sex parent produces a woundedness that can be healed only through development of strong, positive same-sex relationships. The issue, then, is not primarily one of sexual needs at all but one of unmet developmental needs. Hence successful change arises first in the establishment of good (nonsexual) same-sex bonding, out of which heterosexual relationships may flow.

A good deal of successful therapy has been reported following these assumptions for those, both men and women, who seek change. This developmental learning model stands over against the many efforts to demonstrate a biological basis for homosexuality. Without denying that some biological linkages may one day get beyond conjecture and speculative reports, it is most helpful to understand the biological contribution as one predisposing factor among many. The individual's later life experiences combine with significant choices to determine the outcome. The gay movement strongly resists the possibility of choice these days (though it is not long since the term *sexual preference* came into fashion). Nonetheless, those who do change claim that choice is possible. And the research data clearly suggest that many with homosexual tendencies choose not to be active.

Hence we may conclude that change is possible for some, and the Christian gospel offers hope rather than condemnation. It is also clear that in our present state of knowledge, not all who wish to change can do so. A major theme when change does occur is a move away from the sexual focus to growth into personal wholeness and strong relationships. The Christian homosexual who seeks to live according to God's purposes commonly experiences loneliness, frustration, alienation and depression* but can be offered friendship* and support without fear when the stereotypes are challenged. Within the churches there is need for clear teaching about sexuality and its expression in all its forms, combined with a strong pastoral response to those who have emotional, interpersonal and spiritual as well as sexual needs.

See also FEMININITY; SEXUALITY; SINGLENESS.

References and Resources

K. Bockmuehl, "Homosexuality in Biblical Perspective," *Christianity Today*, 16 February 1973, 12-18; A. C. Kinsey, W. B. Pomeroy and C. E. Martin, *Sexual Behavior in the Human Male* (Philadelphia: Saunders, 1948); A. C. Kinsey et al., *Sexual Behavior in the Human Female* (Philadelphia: Saunders, 1953); E. Moberly, *Homosexuality: A New Christian Ethic* (Cambridge: James Clarke, 1983); T. Schmidt, *Straight and Narrow? Compassion and Clarity in the Homosexuality Debate* (Downers Grove, Ill.: InterVarsity Press, 1995).

John Court

HOSPITALITY

Hospitality is "the act or practice of being hospitable; the reception and entertainment of guests, visitors, or strangers with liberality and good will" (*New Shorter Oxford English Dictionary*). The Latin root of the word *hospitality* is *hospes,* which refers to a guest, visitor, host or stranger. In opposition we find *hostis:* stranger, foreigner or enemy. Our word *hospital* is derived from the first term, and the word *hostility* from the latter. The contrast sheds a first light on what lies at the heart of hospitality.

Hospitality is often confused with entertaining.* Although we also speak of entertaining a guest, this word is more descriptive of the act of diverting or of amusing. Entertainment could represent a superficial hospitality, but it is possible to entertain without being hospitable.

A Definition of Christian Hospitality

Scripture is the testimonial of God's relentless hospitality toward his creatures. The Old Testament and New Testament contain abundant evidence of the importance of hospitality as a social and religious expectation. The God who made and sustains us wishes to welcome everyone into his household through Jesus Christ. Therefore, Christian hospitality can be defined as the reality of divine hospitality experienced and expressed in the life of God's children. In other words, Christian hospitality is the reflection of God's character in the life of each Christian and of the church. It is a lifestyle, a visible portrayal of the first commandment to love God and neighbor. It is being ready and available as food, drink, comfort and welcome for people. It is stretching our hearts and resources for the welfare of others and to the glory of God. Consequently, hospitality goes far beyond the act of entertaining to become an all-encompassing approach to Christian life in general and to relationships in particular. When we practice hospitality, this realization should make us all the more dependent on the Holy Spirit.

Hospitality in the Old Testament

As we read through the Old Testament, we find that ancient Israelite hospitality was more than mere entertainment. In an age when there were no inns or hostels, it was a necessity of life. Hospitality was a matter of survival for the traveler, the merchant, the itinerant prophet, the landless Levite, the relative on his way to visit kin, the needy and the foreigner. Hospitality ensures that the guest, whether Israelite or an alien, could expect food, lodging and protection. The well-being of a guest was the host's moral and religious obligation.

Although hospitality in the Old Testament had various expressions, at its core were its religious and social dimensions: to love* God was to love human beings, to be hospitable was a response to Yahweh's own kindness toward Israel. From a religious point of view, the manner in which a householder received a guest (such as by providing fresh water for the traveler's dusty feet) and the kind of meal served were interpreted as evidence of the host's character and commitment to honor Yahweh. Hospitality or the lack of it would, therefore, augment or damage the host's reputation. From a social perspective, through hospitality God created a net and network of human interdependence designed to se-

cure the basic necessities of those who were at some kind of disadvantage, especially the poor and landless.

Despite the lack in Hebrew of a technical word for hospitality, in a number of Old Testament passages it is either clearly implied or directly prescribed, as when God commanded Israel to care for the widow, the orphan and the stranger (Deut 10:17-19; 24:17-22; Prov 14:31; Amos 5:11-12). In some narratives hospitality is indirectly portrayed and serves as the backdrop for a biblical episode or theophany (Gen 24:10-60). In prophetic books hospitality is related to true justice expressed in terms of respecting the rights of kin, the orphan, the widow, the poor and the stranger (Zech 7:8-14). In the person of Boaz the book of Ruth offers one of the richest examples of this kind of hospitality. Even a religious act such as fasting lost its value when separated from concrete expressions of social righteousness such as hospitality (Is 58:6-7, 10). In the wisdom literature Wisdom is presented as extending her hospitality to any person lacking understanding (Prov 9:1-6, 13-18). And in the book of Job Eliphaz interprets Job's misfortune as God's judgment on the latter due to his absence of hospitality (Job 22:6-11).

These and other Old Testament passages express the socioreligious importance attributed to the practice of hospitality, which surpassed the mere act of entertaining. God's people were to "remember that you were slaves in Egypt and the LORD your God redeemed you from there. That is why I command you to do this [to care for the needy]" (Deut 24:18). At the root of this lies a deep care by God for his creatures. In an age when there were no civil and human rights committees and no unemployment insurance,* God established a community* in which religious devotion and social concern were a part of daily living. Therefore, God's laws were not just fingerprints but divine footprints. The Israelites were to follow them and thus provide a tangible picture of what a genuine human society should be like. In this light, hospitality was nothing less than Israel's response to divine love as well as to human need.

Hospitality in the New Testament

The basic guidelines presented by God to Israel in the Old Testament carried over into the New Testament. However, in the latter there is a new message, the gospel, as well as a new community, the church,* which together reaffirm and dramatically increase the role of hospitality in furthering God's kingdom. If the Old Testament injunctions on hospitality were specific to Israel, in the New Testament the call* to practice hospitality extends to everyone who accepts Christ as Lord (Eph 2:1-8). As Jesus had reached out to humankind, so the early Christians were to provide material and spiritual assistance to any needy person and to the saints in particular (Eph 4:28; 1 Jn 3:16-18). The driving force behind the hospitality of the early Christians was the awareness that because God in Christ had loved them first, they were to love their neighbor (1 Jn 4:10-12, 9-21). Far from dwelling on this as a mere theological ideal, they lived it out to the extent of their abilities and resources in relationship to one another and the world. Christ had called his followers to be on the giving end (Jn 15:12), and their hospitality was a response to this *vocatio* (Latin for "calling").

The New Testament abounds with evidence of hospitality. There are numerous accounts of Jesus in the role of the host or that of a guest. As a host he fed crowds who had not made provision for themselves (Mk 6:30-44; 8:1-11; Jn 6:5-15). Before his crucifixion Jesus hosted his farewell dinner with his disciples. That night the bread and the wine became the symbols of the sacrificial nature of divine hospitality (Lk 22:7-19). After the resurrection he walked to Emmaus with two distraught disciples, who only recognized him when he broke bread and offered it to them at the dinner table (Lk 24:13-35). Around that time he also prepared breakfast on the beach for some disciples returning from a miraculous catch of fish in the Sea of Galilee (Jn 21:1-14).

As a guest Jesus would often teach his table companions and even confront his adversaries, so carrying on his Father's business over a meal (Lk 14:1-14; 19:11-26). He repeatedly enjoyed the hospitality of his friends Mary, Martha and Lazarus in Bethany and on one occasion told his overwhelmed hostess that spending time with the divine guest was more important than flawless entertaining (Lk 10:39-42). While in Jericho, much to the displeasure of his detractors, he invited himself into a tax collector's home (Lk 19:1-10).

Two of Christ's most powerful teachings on hospitality appear in Luke 14:12-14 and Matthew 25:31-46. The first upholds the unconditional openhandedness with which we are to treat the economically dependent and the outcasts. The second tacitly assumes hospitality in the actions of feeding, giving a drink, providing lodging, providing clothing, caring for the sick and visiting those in prison. These became the common practices of the early church, the visible witnesses of kingdom come.

The place of hospitality is also reinforced in Christ's parables that involve food and drink, meals or banquets (Lk 14:15-24; 15:22-31; 16:19-21; 17:7-10). These stories gain in richness and relevance as we see them through the eyes of hospitality. Furthermore, they challenge the audience to look at the spiritual implications of commonplace situations: a kind foreigner, a neighbor's midnight request for bread, a beggar at the rich man's door.

The Lord's Supper (*see* Communion) is the supreme example of God's hospitality. It reassures us of God's relentless care and his unwavering goodwill toward his creatures: his own Son is the host and the sacrifice, the Bread of Life and the Cup of Salvation. God invites us to take refuge under his protective eye, to satiate our souls on divine love, to quench our thirst with life-giving divine truths and to sit and converse in the divine. And then God bids us to look sideways and share this good gift (*eu-charis* in Greek) with others in the assurance of the future supper of the Lamb.

The early church also offers a prime example of Christian hospitality in action as they devoted themselves to alms giving, love feasts, the support of teachers and church leaders, the care of widows, orphans, the sick, the infirm, the poor, the disabled, slaves and prisoners, the burial of the poor, succor to victims of calamities, provision of employment and hospitality to visiting missionaries (Acts 4:32-35; Rom 16:23; Gal 3:26; Heb 13:1-3; 1 Pet 4:9; 1 Jn 3:16-18; 3 Jn 5-8). This kind of liberality was characteristic of house churches as well as Christian households (*see* Home). Third John presents the contrast between two church leaders: one named Gaius, who used hospitality to assist the work of missionaries and evangelists, and the other named Diotrephes, who opposed the apostle Paul by precluding hospitality. However, despite external threats from a society antagonistic to Christianity and internal disagreements, the early church carried on with God's tradition of hospitality.

Hospitality Today

We live in a society saturated with messages. There is music in shopping centers, ads at bus stops and railway stations and inside and outside buses and trains. Many cars have stereos, people carry Walkmans, and in most homes television* sets function several hours a day. Hospitality can provide us with a haven. A simple, thoughtful meal is a sanctuary that must not be desecrated. It is an intimate time not to be sacrificed to the vociferous media gods that seem to have taken over our society. As Christ "eagerly desired" to share the last supper with his disciples (Lk 22:15), so we must convey the same message to family, friends and friends-to-be. A healthy homemade dinner, candles, flowers in a vase and a fresh tablecloth are ways of sacramentalizing the ordinary. These touches say, "I care. I treasure our time together." Hospitality guards intimacy, which lies not in closed doors but in dismissing the pervasive intermissions and distractions that rob us from togetherness. Hospitality offers a way to reach out to a society suffering the effects of disintegrated families, loneliness and alienation.

Hospitality as a reflection of God's character will stem from a transformed life, a heart touched by the love of God and the awareness that all we own is his. We are stewards* of the material possessions (whatever these might be), knowledge, talents,* abilities and time entrusted to us. There are many ways of extending hospitality, some of them were already practiced by the Israelites and by the early church and Christ himself. In particular, there are three gifts the contemporary Christian host can offer, namely, prayer, time and acceptance.

Hospitality and prayer go hand in hand. Through prayer God opens our eyes to people's needs that can be met through us. Prayer also prepares our hearts for whatever the encounter with the recipient of our hospitality might bring. While, humanly speaking, we can control certain aspects of the entertaining process, true Christian hospitality demands that we entrust our guest and ourselves to God. We are completely dependent on God if we wish to give emotional, spiritual and material refreshment. Prayer, as attentiveness to God, is as necessary in the church as it is in the home in the context of hospitality. Whether we reach out corporately or individually, prayer will create the ambience for the work of the Trinity.

"I do not have time to have people over!" is one of the common excuses for the lack of hospitality. The book of Proverbs encourages us to count our days so that we will become wiser. When we look at Christ, we get a good picture of where and how he invested his time. He spent most of it with people and among people. People were his passion, the reason for him to interrupt eternity and come into human history. At the appointed time, people were the reason his life was cut short on the cross. People were the object of his redemptive sacrifice. His time was subject to divine purpose. Often his followers seem to work in the opposite direction: we submit divine purpose to the availability of our personal time. Hospitality helps us counter this tendency because when we receive a guest in the name of Christ, we create a parenthesis in the midst of all our other activities. In it God can meet host and guest. Through acts of hospitality, we offer our time as a living sacrifice to the God who did not abandon us to random fate and who has called us to invest our days as his Son did.

Acceptance is an expression of our heartfelt hospitality, as it reflects a welcoming attitude. Acceptance is the room we give people to be who they are. It is the opposite of putting them "in a box." Acceptance, the "room with a view" to the other person, is created in our minds and hearts and finds expression in acts of hospitality. Acceptance is the key to hospitality, as it portrays the welcoming attitude of our God who in so doing never compromised his character. That

is why acceptance must not be confused with political correctness. The first has its basis in the experience of God's immutable grace and holiness; the latter is an ever-shifting societal code of expected attitudes. Perhaps there are few other gifts as costly as honest acceptance. But who can measure its impact on someone searching for a solid foundation in life or a proof that God still cares or a place of refuge and restoration? Through hospitality we extend God's acceptance and welcome and acknowledge our own needs to become more gracious and Christlike in our dealings with people.

Hospitality as an Act of Worship

There are many ways in which we can express our gratitude to God for the gift of eternal life, for the material and spiritual provisions we receive during our pilgrimage on earth. We can sing, pray, speak, dance or write. We can also stand in silent awe. We can cry in worship.* It is in times like these that we become aware of the fact that all we are and have comes from God.

Christian hospitality is also a form of worship—whether as a private act or a corporate effort—when it is a heartfelt response to God, the imitation of his welcoming character, the reflection of a restored *imago Dei,* the mark of kingdom values* and priorities. As we offer hospitality, we echo the original voice, "Come and sup with me." To welcome, to feed, to comfort or to assist someone in God's name is a way of affirming our devotion and allegiance to the Giver of all good gifts. As hospitality points to God, it becomes a way of honoring God.

It is not possible to express the immeasurable privilege of being made co-workers in God's kingdom, sowers of seeds of hope through acts of hospitality. We have a cloud of witnesses from the Old and New Testaments and beyond that attest to the blessings* that come to those who live hospitable lives. With the nourishment of the Bread of Eternal Life broken for us, we are called to carry on with God's tradition of hospitality: issue the invitation, extend the table, receive the guests, wash their feet, bring out the spread, tell them that God has been good to us. In the mundane we celebrate the sacredness of life in Christ. We toast in anticipation of the kingdom banquet. We affirm that hospitality is not merely a nice metaphor of what God has offered us but a spontaneous and genuine act of worship to the God who withheld nothing to bring us back into relationship with himself and with one another. Christians and churches that embrace hospitality reflect God's character and enhance God's glory. Having been welcomed into God's household, as debtors to grace we reach out to friend and stranger to the praise of God's name.

See also EATING; FELLOWSHIP; GREETING; LOVE; TIME; WORSHIP.

References and Resources

R. Banks, *Going to Church in the First Century* (Chipping Norton, N.S.W.: Hexagon Press, 1980); R. Banks and J. Banks, *The Home Church* (Sutherland, N.S.W.: Albatross, 1986); R. F. Capon, *The Supper of the Lamb* (Garden City, N.Y.: Doubleday, 1969); R. Duck, "Toward an Understanding of Hospitality in the Old Testament," M. C. S. thesis, Regent College, Vancouver, B.C., 1980; A. Harnack, *The Mission and Expansion of Christianity in the First Three Centuries* (New York: Harper & Row, 1962); A. Heron, *Table and Tradition* (Philadelphia: Westminster, 1983); T. Howard, *Splendor in the Ordinary* (Wheaton, Ill.: Tyndale, 1976); R. P. Hromas, *Celebrate the Feast* (Torrance, Calif.: Ark Productions, 1982); J. Koenig, *New Testament Hospitality* (Philadelphia: Fortress, 1980); K. B. Mains, *Open Heart, Open Home* (Elgin, Ill.: David C. Cook, 1976); *New Shorter Oxford English Dictionary* (Oxford: Clarendon, 1993) 1:1266; B. Rowlinson, *Creative Hospitality* (Campbell, Calif.: Green Leaf, 1981); E. Schaeffer, *Hidden Art* (London: Norfolk Press, 1971); J. Vanier, *Community and Growth* (Toronto: Griffin House, 1993).

Patricia Kerr

HUMOR

Humor is the ability to perceive and enjoy the absurdities and incongruities of life. Someone with a good sense of humor has a keen awareness of disproportion, which takes many forms, including parody and impersonation, satire, understatement, hyperbole, irony, wit, slapstick and practical jokes. Not all humor, however, is edifying. Good humor pokes fun at things people can change, such as prejudice, pickiness or cliquishness. Satirist Jonathan Swift was a master at this form of humor. Bad humor lampoons things people cannot change, such as gender, race or physical handicaps, and, as such, is not edifying but is tasteless, inappropriate and humiliating. Comedians Andrew Dice Clay and the late Sam Kinison became famous for their misogyny and use of four-letter words, but the laughter they provoked from their audiences was at the expense of others.

How Does Humor Work?

Actor Rowan Atkinson (*Black Adder, Mr. Bean*) claims that humor depends on giving sudden shocks that undermine the basic principles of our everyday existence. He maintains that comedy is based on fear—the momentary fright that occurs when we think these basic principles have been undermined—followed by our immense relief that they have not but only appear to have been through trickery. It is this quick tension-and-release that triggers our laughter. Consider the musician-comedian Victor Borge, seated at the Bosendorfer grand piano, about to accompany a buxom soprano standing near him. He begins to play; she opens her mouth with a high A and bowls him over. Borge stops playing, gets up and raises the lid of the piano bench. The audience holds its breath. Does he have a gag in there? Or worse, a gun? No! He retrieves a seat belt with which to fasten himself securely to the bench to prevent further injury during the aria! The audience roars with laughter and relief.

The Power of Humor

Clever humor can be subversive when it aims to bring down the high and mighty. Humor reminds us of our fragility and is threatening to the proud and those who take themselves too seriously. Consider Monty Python's parody of British governmental profligacy in their "Ministry of Silly Walks" sketch, which supposes that people can receive grants to fund research on crazy ways to walk down the street. In some countries comedians would be imprisoned for this kind of impudence! The Marx Brothers understood the power of humor joined to anarchy: each of their best films sets up a rigid social structure and then smashes it.

As complex social structures staffed by fallible human beings, churches* and parachurch organizations* often deserve to be the targets of humor, for when the "sacred veil" of religion hides pompous behavior, corruption and needless bureaucracy, humor is necessary to pull back the veil and reveal the truth. Individual Christians also need to be reminded of the necessity to be humble: "The common mistake of 'born again' Christians rises out of their conscious efforts to look redeemed. . . . When the 'born again' act like they have got it as nobody else does, . . . the Truth stands ready to spotlight that incongruity, trigger the humor, close the gap and set them straight with their experience" (Parrott, p. 45).

The power of humor is disarming and threatening. Allowing someone to disarm you with humor implies trust and a willingness to let down your guard. But the power of humor can be used for the wrong reasons. Actor-director Penny Marshall notes that humor can be used as a defense mechanism by the paranoid, self-deprecating person, who quickly makes fun of herself before anyone else can. Actor Gene Wilder remarks that humor can be a manipulative tool to get attention and love. Author Eugene Peterson observes that our society is so bereft of joy that instead of exploring the reasons for our unhappiness, we pay entertainers to make us laugh so that we can forget our troubles (p. 92). Perhaps this is why sitcoms are among the most popular and enduring forms of television entertainment.*

Humor as Catharsis

Humor can help us understand pain and suffering. In Woody Allen's film *Crimes and Misdemeanors* a character states, "Humor equals tragedy plus time." Actor W. C. Fields once noted, "I never saw anything funny that wasn't terrible" (Parrott, p. 17). The union of tragic events and parody usually results in so-called black humor, which is not appreciated by everyone. War is a popular theme, as in the musical number "Springtime for Hitler" from Mel Brooks's film *The Producers*. The highly acclaimed television series *M*A*S*H*, set during the Korean War, was based on black humor. In these instances it is not the tragic event that is being lampooned, but irrational human behavior.

Humor also allows us to cope with the dullness of daily routine. This is the domain of standup comics, who provoke laughter with their treatment of such topics as dating* and going to the dentist. Comedian George Carlin asks his audience if they have ever noticed how the handrail on an escalator moves just a little bit faster than the stairs. Comic Steve Wright announces straight-facedly that since his doctor told him he needs contact lenses only for reading, he got "flip-ups." Humor is democratic—it has the power to unite a roomful of people who can share a laugh over a common experience.

Humor and Creation

"God must have a sense of humor. After all, he created you, didn't he?" goes the wisecrack. God does have a sense of humor, which can be discerned by examining how he uses his power in seemingly irrational and whimsical ways. For example, he chose Moses, an ineloquent speaker, to lead his chosen people (Ex 4:10-11). He asked Gideon to go up against ten thousand armed warriors with three hundred soldiers carrying clay pots, torches and horns (Judg 7). He arranged for old Sarah to give birth to baby Isaac (Gen 21:1-7). He ordained that the Savior of the world should be born in a stable to a poor woman who was not married (Lk 1:26-38; 2:1-7). And he created humans, who are unique among the animals in that they have a sense of humor. Humorist Strickland Gilliland puts it this way: "We have a very adroit God who, having put the element of adversity into his creation of man, balanced it with humor in his nature so that he might endure it" (Parrott, p. viii).

Good humor engages us in playful creativity, often by combining two things that ordinarily would not occur together. Consider Monty Python's sketch in which mountain climbers scaling Mount Everest are concerned not so much with safely reaching each station of the climb but with the hair salons that are supposedly located there and how they will have their hair done once they reach them! Some playful humor is simply silly, as in the Peter Cook and Dudley Moore sketch about the restaurant called The Frog and Peach, so named because its menu boasts two items: Frog à la Pêche and Pêche a la Frog.

Humor and Redemption

A good laugh reestablishes a sense of perspective about ourselves and our inability to justify ourselves. As Bob Parrott puts it, "Some of a person's most comic incongruities arise from one's efforts to justify one's actions. . . . This humor helps us see the futility of all efforts of self-justification and urges us to look to another source for justification. That source is God's grace" (p. 25). Effective humor can be redemptive when we laugh at our efforts to determine what is (our estranged sinful selves) and what ought to be (the image of Christ). It is for this reason that comedian John Cleese (Monty Python, *Fawlty Towers*) states in an interview with Melvin Bragg that the seven deadly sins provide some of the funniest comic material. Consider Monsieur Creosote from the Monty Python movie *The Meaning of Life.* He weighs at least four hundred pounds, and when the waiter brings him the menu, he curtly says, "I'll have the lot!" He proceeds to gorge to his satisfaction. But when the waiter brings him an after-dinner mint, he turns it down. The waiter then convinces him to eat it by telling him that "it's wafer thin," whereupon Creosote gobbles it up and then proceeds to regurgitate all his food. The scene concludes with Creosote exploding all over the restaurant. Hyperbole? Yes! A critique of gluttony? Absolutely!

Jesus Had a Sense of Humor

It stands to reason that if God created humans with a sense of humor and if Jesus was fully human in addition to being divine, then Jesus must have had a sense of humor. While the Gospel writers recorded instances when Jesus wept (Lk 19:41, Jn 11:35), they did not feel it important to chronicle his laughter. But it is impossible to think that Jesus did not love to laugh—after all, he loved children, who laugh easily. Also, Jesus must have had a personality that people found attractive. Joseph Soria states, "Christians confess Jesus Christ to be 'true God and true Man' at one and the same time. That is why I maintain that he was not only habitually in good spirits, but had a marvelous sense of humor. To deny this would imply either rejecting his human nature, or placing his divinity in doubt" (p. 55).

Jesus was what we would call today a *lateral thinker,* meaning that his creativity would allow him to respond to people in unorthodox, and therefore unsettling, ways. He had a fine sense of hyperbole, claiming that "it is easier for a camel to go through the eye of a needle than for a rich man to enter the kingdom of God" (Mt 19:24). He accused the Pharisees of being blind guides who "strain out a gnat but swallow a camel" (Mt 23:24). He was also adept at using biting irony, as when he rebuked the Pharisees for inventing their own petty laws and placing them above God's teachings, saying, "You have a fine way of setting aside the commands of God in order to observe your own traditions!" (Mk 7:9). Jesus was a master of witty repartee, as in the case when a man in the crowd shouted, "Teacher, tell my brother to divide the inheritance with me." Without skipping a beat, Jesus retorted, "Man, who appointed me a judge or an arbiter between you?" (Lk 12:13-14). Jesus had an attractive personality and a powerful charisma that people found either so hard to resist that they had to follow him around or so threatening that they clamored for his death. Parrott notes that "Jesus used humor freely, thus permitting in his own humanity the greatness to prevail over the potentially tragic" (p. 17).

It is no accident that Jesus was Jewish, inheriting a folklore tradition filled with wit and irony. Nathan Ausubel states, "Jews have received their tempering from an unflinching realism learned for a high fee in the school of life; they have always felt the need of fortifying their spirits with the armor of laughter against the barbs of the world" (Ausubel, p. ix). The tradition continues to this day: among famous comedians of the twentieth century, Jews are represented in numbers disproportionate to their population. Consider Jack Benny, Danny Kaye, Charlie Chaplin, Gilda Radner, Marty Feldman, Mel Brooks, Shelley Berman, Allan Sherman, Billy Crystal, Rodney Dangerfield, Stan Frieberg, Robert Klein and many others.

Humor Provides a Glimpse of Heaven
At its best a good belly laugh can give us a tiny taste of the joys awaiting us in heaven. Parrott states, "That step beyond humor that leads to joy comes when one realizes what one has going for one, when one accepts that the Truth that exposes the incongruity also accepts one who remains a mixture of ambiguities" (p. 48). When humor reveals the frailties of humanity, it makes us marvel that God can love us as much as he does—so much so that he allowed his precious Son to live as one of us. As Soria puts it, "Good humor can be a physiological condition. And it can be achieved even though one is not feeling very well, perhaps through human maturity. But, when this happens in an habitual and heroic way, it is assuredly a sign of Christian sanctity. For then it is a surrendered and joyful acceptance of the will of God" (p. 56).

See also ENTERTAINMENT; LAUGHTER; LEISURE.

References and Resources
R. Atkinson, "Visual Comedy," *Funny Business* (a Showtime and Tiger Television coproduction in association with the BBC and Devillier Donegan Enterprises, 1992); N. Ausubel, ed., *A Treasury of Jewish Folklore* (New York: Crown, 1948); J. Cleese, interview by M. Bragg, shown on the Arts & Entertainment television channel; B. W. Parrott, *Ontology of Humor* (New York: Philosophical Library, 1982); E. Peterson, *A Long Obedience in the Same Direction* (Downers Grove, Ill.: InterVarsity Press, 1980); J. L. Soria, "The Good Humor of Saints," *The Idler,* no. 37 (September-October 1992) 55-56.

Kathryn Lockhart

I

IMAGINATION

All of us know the parable of the rich man and Lazarus in Luke 16:19-31. Many sermons interpret the story as referring only to how people will respond to Jesus' death and resurrection. But all good stories have layers or levels of meaning, and this one is no exception. For instance, the story of Lazarus concerns justice, welfare, community, responsibility, the proper distribution of wealth and a host of other issues that reverberate with social and political implications. But here is another interpretation. The story of Lazarus is a story that defines imagination by its opposite: imagination failed, unexercised, atrophied.

Imagination: The Organ of Meaning

The rich man could not imagine a life that included homeless people or people to whom he owed compassion or help. He could not envision an eternity of fire and thirst and anguish. Then, when he was finally in the middle of his eternal bad situation and wanted to help his brothers, he could not imagine failure. But Abraham knew that the five brothers each had an imagination no more active than the one the rich man had. They lacked, as C. S. Lewis would say, the "organ of meaning" (p. 265). They could not hear, see, touch, taste, smell or even *think* with their imagination. Not that they were born without an imagination; no one is. But they lacked practice in using imagination.

In *Through the Looking Glass* Lewis Carroll gives us a different take on the story of Lazarus. The White Queen is speaking to Alice.

"I can't believe that," said Alice.

"Can't you?" the Queen said, in a pitying tone. "Try again: draw a long breath and shut your eyes."

Alice laughed. "There's no use trying," she said: "one *can't* believe impossible things."

"I daresay you haven't had much practice," said the Queen. "When I was your age, I always did it for half-an-hour a day. Why, sometimes I've believed as many as six impossible things before breakfast." (Carroll, p. 251)

There are a lot of Alices in the Bible and a lot today. I have often been one myself. Alice-types have no ears, to use Jesus' term. They refuse to exercise the organ they were born with. And imagination is as important, as essential, an organ as the heart, the lungs, the liver. I might even go so far as to make an extravagant claim and say that imagination is even more important, because without it there is no point in the heart's pumping and the lungs' bellowing. To live we need more than the basic physiological requirements. We need meaning and the means to find meaning. Enter imagination.

Let me repeat what C. S. Lewis says about imagination in "Bluspels and Flalansferes." He claims that "reason is the natural organ of truth; imagination

514

is the natural organ of meaning" (p. 265). He makes these two statements equal, syntactically as well as semantically. It is not enough, Lewis is claiming, to have reason; we also need imagination, for without it we do not have a clue as to what truth means.

Lewis's claim is deceptively simple and, like all deceptively simple statements, hard to explain. One thing is certain. It is not enough in life for us to have facts, data, information—the stuff we are inundated with in our culture. We need to know purpose, intention, implication, possible consequences, multiple perspectives. We need to live imaginatively.

How do we do this? How do we understand imagination? We do so with imagination itself, with imagination in action. But to understand something using the very thing you are trying to understand presents great difficulties. In that way imagination is rather like language, which is intimately related to defining and using imagination. Or imagination is like the Incarnation. As that great rhetorician and theologian Saint Augustine said about Jesus, he is both the destination and the road to the destination. So with imagination—it is the object we study and the tool we use in order to study it. For the moment, though, it is enough to say that imagination provides ways of seeing, and so living, life.

Imagination and Metaphor

With all that in mind—in imagination, if you will—I would like to quote the Bible, specifically Psalms, though I could use some of Jesus' parables or Paul's letters.

> He is like a tree planted by streams of
> water,
> which yields its fruit in season
> and whose leaf does not wither. (Ps 1:3)

> They are like chaff
> that the wind blows away. (Ps 1:4)

> You are a shield around me, O LORD.
> (Ps 3:3)

> Strike all my enemies on the jaw;
> break the teeth of the wicked.
> (Ps 3:7)

> He who is pregnant with evil
> and conceives trouble gives birth
> to disillusionment. (Ps 7:14)

> The heavens declare the glory of God;
> the skies proclaim the work of his
> hands.
> Day after day they pour forth speech;
> night after night they display knowl-
> edge. (Ps 19:1-2)

A pattern begins to emerge—a pattern of imagination and a central, indeed a fundamental, function of imagination. We could call it image-making or metaphor making. We could call it part of rhetoric, that ancient art which Augus-tine so ably defended in *On Christian Doctrine*.

In metaphor we use one object to understand another—even if the two objects appear to have nothing in common. That is the tricky part of metaphor, which is like an unexpected and unpredictable equation, an odd, quirky $a = b$. To understand a, so the metaphor maker claims, we need to figure out b, and vice versa. We need to think about the characteristics of each object. Then we need to ask what the two objects *might* possibly have in common. For instance, what do the heavens have to do with a garrulous group of people? Or what does the Christian community have to do with vines and branches? But first ask, how do vines and branches grow? What are the roots like? What about the branches? What happens when a vine wants or needs to climb? What does it look for? Once we have answered such questions, then we can begin to understand what the metaphor tells us about the characteristics of a Christian's relationship to Jesus or how Christians should relate to one another. One object or idea is described in comparison to or with something else.

In the psalms we find such nature metaphors: good people compared to fruitful trees (Ps 1:3), wicked people to chaff (Ps 1:4). Most of us know what a ripe tree looks and smells like, and some of us, at least, know what chaff feels like—its stiff, cutting edges, its lack of weight. Strip the wheat and what remains has no meaning—no function, no use. So the psalmist is saying that though wicked people may cut or injure, ultimately they are impotent. In other words, they are not human.

On the other hand, imagine this from Psalm 7:14: evil people are pregnant, giving birth to disillusionment—a feminine metaphor as well as a genetic one. John Milton must have known this passage well, for he uses a similar idea in his great epic, *Paradise Lost.* When I read this psalm, I picture the character Disillusionment roaming the cities, wandering around the country, spreading a malaise, an angst, a depression that the citizenry cannot seem to fight—this sounds a lot like our own time.

We are all familiar with the metaphors of God as shield, warrior, fortress and so forth. The Old Testament, in particular, is filled with masculine, military metaphors. In the passage where God breaks the teeth of the wicked (Ps 3:7), the metaphor provides a specific picture—God as boxer or foot soldier. He has personally taken on that pregnant enemy. Metaphors, then— or imagination—make *concrete* what might only be an abstract idea. To say God will protect you, as true as that might be, is not nearly as strong as saying God is going to hand your enemy the one-two punch. No one could ever accuse the psalmist of lacking imagination.

So far I have claimed that imagination is biblical—as we see from Jesus' storytelling and the psalms. I have claimed that we are born with at least the possibility of imagination, if only metaphorically speaking. Although I have not used the Latin phrase *imago Dei,* it has been lurking beneath my words all along. *Imagination* is the image of God in us. As J. R. R. Tolkien, among others, has said, we make because God makes. I have also said that imagination and language go hand in hand. And finally I have claimed that without imagination we understand nothing.

The Biology of Imagination
These claims come from philosophical, theological and aesthetic perspectives. Now I want to turn to the physiological or neurological level. It appears from the latest research into how the brain functions that imagination is an essential part of our neurological makeup. We are, quite literally, *hard-wired* in the image of God. Just as language is inevitable, given normal circumstances, so is imagination. And even when things go astray—say with autism or frontal lobe damage— people still appear to have an imagination, albeit of a different kind, even when they do not have much else, even language. None of us can fully function— can actually consider ourselves *human*— without imagination. We find evidence for this in several places: in studies of memory, in the way cells grow, in the biological nature of play and joy.

First, let us consider memory. Without imagination we could not remember. And if we could not remember, then what? How would we form relationships with people or communities? How would we be able to grieve, laugh, cry, tell stories, participate in all the small and great rituals and celebrations that mark a life? Think, if you will, of a graduation, a wedding, a funeral. Had you no memory, what meaning would a graduation have? Would it matter that your son or daughter, your sister or brother—or even you yourself—was leaving high school for college or college for a career? What difference would it make to attend the wedding of the daughter or son of an old friend? Would you even have an old friend to begin with? No, because you would not have any concept of *old* at all. And without a concept of old—or *of before*—you would not have any concept of *new*—or *after.* We know people whose memory is not much; we probably know people whose memory has begun to fail or fade. Think of the terror of Alzheim-er's—terror for the person who knows at first that he or she will soon have no memory—but the greater anguish is that of the people who still do remember, the friends and relatives of the Alzheimer's victim.

Of course, without memory many other normal human experiences would be denied us—learning, reading, watching films, even worship. What would Easter or Christmas mean? Pentecost? or Sundays? Oliver Sacks in *An Anthropologist on Mars: Seven Paradoxical Tales* quotes Eva Brann, the philosopher, as calling memory "the storehouse of the imagination" (p. 176). Notice the metaphor—storehouse, a place where farmers put grain, food. So Brann is saying that memory *feeds* imagination. She encourages us, in Sacks's words, to "see memories as imaginative, as creative, from the start," for

> Imaginative memory not only stores for us the passing moments of perception; it also transfigures, distances, vivifies, defangs—reshapes formed impressions, turns oppressive immediacies into wide vistas . . . loosens the rigid grip of an acute desire and transforms it into a fertile design. (Sacks, p. 176)

Brann's description sounds like the work of the healing, life-giving, life-transforming God for whom there are no mistakes, castoffs or leftovers among people, as the stories Sacks tells remind us. And each of Brann's verbs is a metaphor, reinforcing

the view that we cannot know or explain our knowing without imagination.

Just as we need imagination, then, for a full, healthy exercise of our memory, how we remember indicates the inborn nature of imagination. Cellular biologists provide another piece of evidence for the physiological understanding of imagination. One of the characteristics of imagination, imitation or mimicry appears to be built into the way life begins. In *The Beauty of the Beastly* science writer Nancy Angier explains Hox genes by noting that "the embryo is constructed as a whole series of repetitious segments: the new section of the body grows out as a mimic of the portion preceding it, and variations are subsequently added to each section to lend the final body its complexity of parts" (p. 85). Her description is reminiscent of a composition with theme and variation or with Tolkien's notion that we are subcreators with God as the original Creator. There is a marvelous elegance of design in the biology of imagination.

Angier also explores the biological base for laughter* and joy. Play, for instance, appears to help the brain grow, thus providing a reason children need to play,* why imagination is crucial for full development. In addition, for reasons still unclear to biologists, joy—unadulterated happiness—helps the body heal or even prevent illness: "[Researchers] suspect . . . that sensations like optimism, curiosity and rapture—the giddy, goofy desire to throw the arms wide and serenade the sweetness of spring—not only make life worth living but make life last longer" (p. 194). Although she calls optimism, curiosity and rapture "sensations," clearly these are characteristics of imagination, particularly curiosity.

If imagination is part of our immune system, part of our cellular structure, part of the structure of the brain itself, then it is fundamental to life. We do indeed need imagination. But what else does imagination affect? We need it for many if not all of our sensory perceptions—color, smell, touch, shape, visual perception, hearing. When the man born blind and healed by Jesus says that he saw men as trees, walking, two things are going on. First, the man uses a simile—metaphoric language, the work of imagination. Second, he is telling us that his visual perceptions, his visual imagination, needs some practice. We *learn* to see, and we learn it early. We can also forget how to see. And those born blind have never learned. To the man born blind, a man appeared like a tree; he had not yet learned what a man *looked* like. Not that he knew what a tree looked like either; rather, he was speculating, conjecturing, imagining, based on what he had been told, that men were like trees—upright, had limbs, could bend and so forth (for a further discussion of how the blind use visual metaphors, see Dennett, p. 55). So blindness is not simply physiological but imaginative and cognitive.

Sometimes we cannot see the forest for the trees, the whole for the confusing parts. For the newly sighted—or the newly hearing—this is overwhelmingly true. When Isaiah promises that the ears of the deaf will open, the tongues of the dumb loosen up and the eyes of the blind see, he is making a physiological, neurological and imaginative promise. The miracles of God, then, are far richer than we imagine and far more imaginative as well.

We could not get through a day, much less a lifetime, without using imagination. We could not sit in a chair, lift a fork, light a candle or kneel to pray. Although painters, writers, architects, city planners or psychiatrists may be more conscious of imagination than we are, we cannot function at even the most basic level without imagination.

Living Imaginatively

Why should we settle for uninformed, unaware or automatic imaginative living? Why should we not practice our imagination as fully as we are able? There is much we can do, though we may not always realize it.

To begin, we can read as a way to stimulate curiosity (*see* Reading). We can also relearn how to see, just as the man born blind had to relearn visual perceptions. Let me quote again from Sacks, writing about a man who after a cataract operation was seeing for the first time since he was quite young: "As Virgil explored the rooms of his house, investigating, so to speak, the visual constru;tion of the world, I was reminded of an infant moving his hand to and fro before his eyes, waggling his head, turning it this way and that, in his primal construction of the world" (p. 127). As all parents know, every normal baby does this, every one. Sacks continues:

> Most of us have no sense of the immensity of this construction, for we perform it seamlessly, unconsciously, thousands of times every day, at a glance. But this is not so for a baby, it was not so for Virgil, and it is not so for, say, an artist who wants to experience his elemental perceptions afresh and anew. (p. 127)

That last phrase is crucial—"an artist who wants to experience his elemental perceptions afresh and anew." Part of daily imaginative living could well involve practicing what visual artists do.

Occasionally, when one of my writing classes is dragging, I will ask students to go outside or stare out the window and notice every tiny thing they can. "What do you see?" I ask. At first they tell me obvious things—a brick wall, a plant, sky, clouds, people. And with each answer I ask, "And what else?" Usually we stop long before we should, for I do not recall any student getting to things like cones, triangles, squares, a hypotenuse—and yet we are surrounded by geometry. Few students notice the multiple shades of green, blue, white or tan or the various textures from rough to smooth and everything in between. Paul Cézanne once wrote, "The same subject seen from a different angle gives a subject for study of the highest interest and so varied that I think I could be occupied for months without changing my place, simply bending more to the right or left" (quoted in Sacks, p. 128). What if we did this with some object—a refrigerator, a tennis racquet, a pair of shoes? Or what if we did this with a person? an idea? a too-favorite Bible passage?

People who live imaginative lives are "what if" people. They respond to ideas and events with a "what if" attitude. They behave in "what if" ways. "What if" is a big idea, as big as God, for it is the practice of God. God thinks: What if I gave this guy named Mozart musical ability? Or what if I gave this Dutchman a passion for paint, for light and shadow? Or this woman a love of fabric or yarn or test tubes? What if that person over there had a fondness for order and pattern? What if you loved numbers—or flour and yeast? What if you would like to smell dirt on your hands or crushed herbs, peonies or lilacs? Or machine oil?

These, however, as good as they are, are "what if" ideas that center on the self. Imaginative living—true Christ-bearing, imaginative living—means going beyond the self. For instance, I know a professor at a Christian college who volunteers hours a week to spend with AIDS patients. Others read to the blind, become friends with lonely old people whose families ignore them, work in co-ops or in adult literacy programs, help organic farmers, resist developers. All these people are practicing "what if" living by using their imagination in empathic ways.

Every time we say "what if" or act in a "what if" way, we respond as creatures made in the image of the Creator—from the great imagination to our own.

See also ART; BEAUTY.

References and Resources

N. Angier, *The Beauty of the Beastly: New Views of the Nature of Life* (Boston: Houghton Mifflin, 1995); L. Carroll, *The Annotated Alice: Alice's Adventure in Wonderland and Through the Looking Glass,* with introduction and notes by M. Gardner (New York: Wings Books, 1960); D. C. Dennett, *Consciousness Explained* (Boston: Little, Brown, 1991); C. Forbes, *Imagination: Embracing a Theology of Wonder* (Portland, Ore.: Multnomah, 1986); C. A. Huttar, ed., *Imagination and the Spirit: Essays in Literature and the Christian Faith Presented to Clyde S. Kilby* (Grand Rapids: Eerdmans, 1971); C. S. Lewis, "Bluspels and Flalansferes," in *Selected Literary Essays,* ed. W. Hooper (Oxford: Oxford University Press, 1969); O. Sacks, *An Anthropologist on Mars: Seven Paradoxical Tales* (New York: Knopf, 1995).

Cheryl Forbes

IMMIGRATION

An old adage says "Distant fields look greener." Perhaps that is the principal reason humans have migrated for as long as we have lived on this earth. Uncounted multitudes have fled homelands due to war, persecution, rejection, disease, famine and other natural disasters. That is migration from necessity. Today we call such people *refugees* and reserve the terms *emigrant* and *immigrant* for those who choose voluntarily to uproot themselves and make a new beginning in a foreign land.

Patterns of Immigration

It is not always a greener field, usually an economic one, that motivates the emigrant. It may be plain old human curiosity. What is on the other side of the mountain or plain? Today that curiosity has taken us into space, although it has yet to make us immigrants there. Perhaps that will occur in the twenty-first century.

Curiosity involves risk. We test ourselves against formidable barriers in order to prove to others—and to ourselves—that we can do it! The reasons for emigration are seemingly exhaustless. We are looking for new resources for our talents* or interests; we have a new political allegiance, a new faith or a marriage (compare Ruth 1:16-17 RSV). For the earliest men and women it would seem that migration was an ongoing way of life. Perhaps "wandering" would be a better term (Fairchild, pp. 1-4). They were nomads. No place was home.*

The first emigration recorded in the Bible was not voluntary. Adam and Eve left their true home because they were no longer worthy of it. Perhaps humans ever since have been on a search for home—certainly God's ancient people have been. At least in part the "wandering" Jews have preserved their identity because God had called a *time** holy long before a *place* was called holy. In all their exiles they preserved that holy day—the sabbath*—and it preserved them.

Significant migrations in history came about because of a spiritual vision. People wanted space in which they would be free to develop a community life consistent with their deepest convictions. To a degree that was the origin of the American colonies and the basis of many later migrations to America. The "emptiness" of the New World was a vacuum that sucked out the restless and oppressed of the crowded Old World. Today the exploding populations of the Third World still see the United States, Canada and Australia as open space, opportunity and freedom.

At the center of the biblical story is the specific call to Abram to journey toward a land where he would be free to worship God and to father a new nation through whom the whole earth would be blessed. When Abram set out, he did not know the land to which he was being drawn. He simply knew God's call and

obeyed (Gen 12:1-4; Heb 11:8). A later form of such a spiritual vision stemmed from the call to share the gospel, beginning with Paul, continuing through the years and flowering in the great missionary movement of recent centuries. Thousands upon thousands of Christians have left home and security for an unknown future because of their love of the one who emigrated from heaven to earth out of love for us. None of our emigrations can compare with his. He gave up all that we might have all (2 Cor 8:9; Phil 2:5-8).

Problems Created by Immigration

Though humans have been emigrating since they first left Eden, there are significant differences and new problems today. In past history immigrants rarely had a clear picture of the world to which they were moving. Reaching it involved a perilous and uncertain journey that might take months or years. In today's global village* with its bewildering cafeteria of information—movies,* radio,* television,* newspapers, journals, libraries—people often have a very detailed picture of the place of their new dreams. Increasingly, they are even able to purchase a home, secure a business and arrange schooling before they leave for their new home. Getting there has also changed to a matter of hours, even from the other side of the globe. But these possibilities create new problems. The immigrant's picture of the new homeland may be too dependent on distorted images presented in movies and TV.

Perhaps more importantly, the very swiftness of the journey produces a severe culture shock and an inability to adjust to new circumstances. The former long journey with its hardships weaned emigrants from the old land and prepared them for the difficulties of the new. How important were the long, hard days in the wilderness to the preparation of the Israelites for their new land (Num

11:1-6; 13:25-33; 14:1-3)?

The sheer numbers involved in modern immigrations are now posing cultural, ideological and economic crises for the accepting countries. This is precipitated not only by the extraordinary floods of refugees but also by people choosing a new country when they might have remained in their homeland. France, with its deep-seated desire to preserve the French "fact" in language, social concept, government and the secular state, is now struggling with increasing numbers of Muslims, who do not separate religion and politics. Similarly in the Canadian province of British Columbia, which eagerly seized the influx of Asiatic money coming in with wealthy immigrants from the East, now finds the Asiatic "tail" wagging the old Canadian "dog"—and the clock cannot be turned back. In the United States, newer states like California, which was partly built on immigrant labor, now feel overwhelmed by the alleged drain on public money and institutions by the influx of people from south of the border.

These problems are multiplied many times over if immigrants of necessity are added to immigrants of choice. Countries bordering on nations shaken by civil war and anarchy find themselves inundated by waves of desperate refugees with no desire to be immigrants and few resources to establish a new life. Threatening the economic stability of the host countries creates deep resentments, feeds racism and fosters social instability.

Issues for Christians

Immigration raises distressing and profound issues for Christians, especially those who serve in government and must often help make decisions seemingly contradictory to their deepest spiritual instincts and convictions. What does the good Samaritan do in these circumstances? How many immigrants and refugees should a nation attempt to absorb? Should the measure applied be the ability to preserve the lifestyle of the average citizen in the host country? But what if the desperate conditions in the country from which the immigrants are coming have been created in part by the greed, racism, political interference and economic imperialism that have made possible the host country's lifestyle? In a world of such enormous disparities in health, safety and economic well-being, how can true Christians refuse to extend a welcome even if it means their own hurt? While there is no simple answer, there is a call to deep soul searching.

The example of Israel is a rebuke to other Western countries. In the years 1990 to 1994 Israel absorbed 550,000 new immigrants, equivalent to one and a half million in Ohio or Ontario. It is true that their immigration was and is largely an ethnic and religious movement without parallel. Nevertheless, the problems of absorption are if anything far more acute than in the established economies and cultures of the West. Further, the welcome was extended to Muslims trapped in a war-torn Bosnia. Resolving this issue, while not easy, depends on the values held by the host nation.

In addition to immigrants by choice and refugees by necessity, there have always been immigrants without choice—slaves and deportees. America was in part founded by the former, Australia by the latter. In the case of America the social sore of slavery was seriously aggravated by the prejudices of racist laws after emancipation (Bennett, pp. 192, 225-26). It has resulted in a seemingly unending tragedy that not only is an enormous burden on the United States but also saps its moral influence as a superpower in the eyes of the world (Brzezinski, p. 101). Forced immigration followed by unaccepted emancipation casts its shadow over succeeding generations. Christians whose contemporary privileges are rooted in such a past cannot simply dismiss the shadow of today as not of their making. Their privileges were bought at the price of those past prejudices.

Again, when immigrants come in such numbers that they begin to form a sizable minority in the host country, can their demands for recognition of their traditions and their religion be denied? Should Muslim girls be allowed to wear hijabs (head coverings) in the public school? Should the public school system recognize the sacred holidays of Jews, Muslims or Sikhs? Should Christmas carols be banned in schools for fear of offense to those of other faiths? In Canada a storm broke out over the permission given to Sikhs joining the Royal Canadian Mounted Police to wear their turbans rather than the image-laden, broad-brimmed Stetsons. Instead should an attempt be made to have the immigrants accept the traditions and convictions of the host country?

Impact on Countries with Christian Traditions

Eventually a country experiencing such immigration begins to redefine itself. A country rooted in Judeo-Christian origins with strong Christian traditions and a tacit recognition of the Christian faith finds it profoundly disturbing to ask if it can any longer be considered, even nominally, a "Christian" country. This problem is even more acute in those countries where there is still a state church.

On the other hand, if a country relinquishes its links to the Christian faith in its public traditions, such as the oath of citizenship and the public role of the churches on formal occasions, does that deliver people to a religious and moral relativism that privatizes faith? Will its new secularism be a religion antagonistic to all transcendental values and to any conviction of ultimate truths?

This is not the problem of the Christian minority in a secular state such as France or in a Muslim state such as Pakistan, where, like the early Christians, it must learn how to fit in yet still graciously and appropriately challenge the received ideology and values. This is a post-Christian problem. This is the problem of a country whose public values have to a considerable degree been shaped by the Christian faith even though they have often been overridden by the values of imperialism and the marketplace. Is the tide of immigration leading us to a more honest recognition of a truth that has always been—that such societies are not Christian countries? If so, what does it mean to give Christian leadership in such a society, which is now pluralist but has a historic Christian tradition?

So far the influx into our Western countries of great numbers of people of different ethnic backgrounds, including visible minorities and foreign faiths, is largely the experience of our metropolitan areas. For the most part small towns* and rural areas remain less disturbed. That in itself creates new tensions between the increasingly liberal cities and the generally conservative nonurban areas. But the writing is on the wall for them too as immigrants settle, find their political voices and secure economic clout. In the United States, California most possibly typifies the future of this trend.

Christians as Spiritual Immigrants

The man or woman of faith has always been called, like our Savior, to live in a world largely indifferent or antagonistic to a true life of spiritual pilgrimage and vision. This call has often been obscured by our attempts to establish a culture influenced by Judeo-Christian values. Perhaps the tragedy of Christendom (echoed in the later social gospel) was that we were deceived into thinking that we could create a Christian state and culture.* But Christendom has collapsed. Perhaps now with the ebb and flow of immigration around the global village mixing old and new, the familiar and the strange, we are also seeing the collapse of that which in part flowed from it—Western civilization.

One of the results of the globalization of our countries through immigration may be the realization that Christians have always to a degree been immigrants, even in their own countries. Ever since Eden men and women of faith, like Abraham of old, have looked for "the city which has *foundations,* whose builder and maker is God" (Heb 11:10 RSV, emphasis added). The book of Revelation gives us a vision of a city* let down out of heaven by whose light the nations shall walk and into which the kings of the earth will bring their glory and the honor of their nations (Rev 21:2, 22-26). But we must never forget that the city is not of our making. No, we are immigrants always looking for the promise, looking for home.

But the sureness and nature of the vision may both sustain and guide us as we realize that we are called now to being immigrants in a special way: not to leave for another land or culture where we think we may be able to create a Christian society but to understand that we are on a spiritual journey that will never really be accepted by our society wherever we may be. At the same time, like the Israelites in exile in Babylon, we are called to work* for the well-being of the city where we live and to influence it for God as far as we have opportunity (Jer 29:7).

Such influence for a Christian must surely deeply involve the ministry of reconciliation and justice.* It is those who truly know in the depths of their spirits that they are forgiven who are able both to forgive and to open the doorway for others to forgive (Mt 18:23-35). As immigration accelerates and both old prejudices and new and uncomfortable changes in society increase frictions, surely Christians should be able to exercise a healing* ministry in the name of Christ the reconciler. At the same time we, who know that the Spirit is not bound by time and space, may be able to recognize and honor the work of the Spirit wherever we find it (Jn 3:8; compare Mal 1:10-11; Acts 10—11). It is the Spirit who reconciles us and frees us to live wholeheartedly within our times even while we look beyond our times.

Being such an immigrant may give us a new relationship with our new immigrant-citizens, "strangers and afraid in a world they have not made" (Housman, 12:111). We have much to learn from them and much to share. Being such an immigrant is at the very heart of our faith. Being a Christian is being an immigrant in the steps of our incarnate, crucified and risen Lord and looking for his return.

See also CITIZENSHIP; CULTURE; ETHNOCENTRISM; GLOBAL VILLAGE; MULTICULTURALISM; NATIONALISM; RACISM; TRAVELING.

References and Resources
L. Bennett Jr., *Before the Mayflower: A History of Black America* (Chicago: Johnson Publishing, 1969); R. W. Bibby, *Mosaic Madness* (Toronto: Stoddard Publishing, 1943); L. F. Bouvier, *Peaceful Invasions: Immigration and Changing America* (Lanham, Md.: University Press of America, 1992); Z. Brzezinski, *Out of Control: Global Turmoil on the Eve of the 21st Century* (New York: Scribner, 1993); H. Butterfield, *Christianity and History* (London: Fontana Books, 1957); *The Changing Course of International Migration* (Paris: Organization for Economic Cooperation and Development, 1993); J. Dawson, *Healing America's Wounds* (Ventura, Calif.: Regal, 1994); H. P. Fairchild, *Immigration: A World Movement and Its American Significance* (rev. ed.; New York: Macmillan, 1925); A. E. Housman, *Complete Poems: Last Poems* (New York: Henry Holt, 1959); A. Meier, *The Making of Black America* (New York: Atheneum, 1969); C. H.

Pinnock, *A Wideness in God's Mercy* (Grand Rapids: Zondervan, 1992).

Wilber Sutherland

INDIVIDUAL

Being or becoming an individual is a goal to which most people aspire. It means that we are not like everyone else, that we are different from the mass. Children are raised to be individuals in their own right. Advertisers* lure us by their reference to some product containing an individual flavor, being the choice of discerning individuals or marking us out as being more individual. We prize the democratic system for the way it places such a high value on the individual, and criticize totalitarian systems such as fascism and communism for the way they subject individuals to the dictates of the state. When others try to make us conform to some viewpoint, standard or expectation, we complain about the danger of losing our individuality. As President Bill Clinton said in one of his national addresses: "In America to be an individual is our highest value."

Yet for some time now our most acute social critics have been telling us that an overemphasis on the individual lies at the heart of what is wrong with American society. This is the main burden of the influential book by the well-known sociologist Robert Bellah and his associates, *Habits of the Heart,* which traces the effect of this on weakening levels of commitment in both private and public life. They chart the degree to which marriage,* family* and other personal relationships, including therapeutic ones, are subverted by this trend. It even affects local politics,* civic volunteerism, citizenship* and the wider implications of religion. According to Bellah and his group, though we often talk the language of community* and are mindful of the welfare of others, we are primarily preoccupied with our individual selves. This is eating away at what little is left of community in our countries today.

Social commentators in other newer Western countries, such as Reginald Bibby in Canada (1987), find this analysis to be equally true, in even some respects more true, for their own societies. With their less communal and republican origins, there is even less sense of community to erode, making the effects of individualism on the public arena more noticeably destructive. Throughout the West our undue stress on the individual is fragmenting family life, diminishing our sense of friendship,* isolating neighbors* from one another, making the workplace* increasingly competitive, involving us in court cases more often, reducing our involvement in civic affairs, diminishing our interest in politics and making religion a private matter. Unless we do something about this, they argue, our whole way of life is in danger of falling apart.

Origins
Where did this emphasis on the individual originate? The word *individuum,* from which our word *individual* and related terms comes, was coined by the Roman moralist Cicero in the first century B.C. to translate the Greek word *atomen,* meaning "the smallest building block of reality." Over the course of many centuries the word came to focus on the basic personal, instead of material, unit. The term *individualism* first appeared in the writings of Alexis de Tocqueville in his seminal analysis of American society in the early 1800s. If it was documented this early in our history, where did our modern understanding of the sacredness of the individual and right to think, judge and decide for ourselves come from?

First, our emphasis on the individual has roots in the Bible, with the dignity it accords to every person through their creation in the image of God and personal responsibility toward God and one another. In biblical communities, however, the individual is embedded in and accountable to the wider community. In Old Testament times this was the family, locality, tribe and nation; today it is the family, church* and city.* This understanding was reaffirmed and extended during the Reformation, among the Puritans and in Anabaptist circles.

A second basis for our modern individualism is the civic republicanism that emerged in the city-states of the Renaissance and was further developed in the early days of the American colonies. This highlighted the role and contribution of the individual citizen, but always in the context of wider moral, religious and political responsibilities.

A third source lies in the eighteenth-century Enlightenment and nineteenth-century utilitarianism. These movements focused more strongly on the individual apart from personal relationships and public responsibilities and encouraged each person to work for whatever would maximize the good for the majority of people. Through the influence of nineteenth-century romanticism and twentieth-century secularism, there was a move toward an expressive individualism which valued above all each person's assertion of his or her identity and aspirations. It is this third source that now dominates, and without our being aware of it, colors the way many Christians think and operate.

Two Misleading Oppositions

We are in a Catch-22 situation: valuing the individual yet doing so in a way that results in the individual becoming an endangered species. We can understand this problem by looking at the way most people use the word and by considering what people define individual over against.

Individual Versus Society. When asked what is the opposite of individual, most people will say something like society.* Any attack on the individual is generally regarded as making a case for a collective approach to life that squeezes out individuality, as if these are the only alternatives. This, it is argued, was the problem with fascism, communism and now a resurgent Islam. Many would add that it is the problem with even a democratic socialist approach to government.* But individual and society should not be set over against one another as antitheses: the choice between them is not an either-or. Setting them up this way is like insisting that there is a polar opposition between people and their natural environment. While some have lived as if these two were at odds with one another, either loathing the created world or abusing it, in fact none of us can survive physically without it. The natural environment provides the air we breathe, the ground we walk on, the sun that warms us, the food we eat (*see* Ecology). It is similar with society. Though some people have a negative view of it or seek to isolate themselves from it, none of us can become persons without it. It provides the language we use, the conventions we operate by, the supply lines we depend on, the structures that employ us and so on. Diminish any of these and we diminish ourselves. They are essential to our development and well-being.

Individual Versus Institution. In ordinary speech individuals are also often set over against institutions. The two are often spoken about as if they were inherently in tension. The more individual you are, the less likely you are to fit into an institution; the more you are identified with an institution, the less individual you become. Again we are in the presence of a false polarization. As with the relationship between the individual and society, in reality there is no such thing as an individual apart from institutions. Even a Robinson Crusoe or hermit still feels the effects of whatever institutional associations they had beforehand. From the moment of birth individuals are set in a web of relationships and structures.* This begins with the family, which is itself a system or small institution (*see* Family System), the school, sports and leisure* clubs,* the church, work* or profession,* health-care and insurance systems, local and national bureaucracies.*

These organizations* help shape who we are as a person, in enabling as well as disabling ways. Whatever their weaknesses or even destructive tendencies, most people can point to specific education,* benefits, challenges and opportunities that belonging to these institutions provided. So individual and institution can be partners: individual and institutional growth occur most powerfully when each is assisting the other. Belonging to a church should have convinced us that this is the case, for most churches are institutions or contain small organizations within them. Voluntary associations have also often provided great benefits for their members and provided an impetus for their personal growth. The mutual benefit for both individual and institution is also demonstrated in the most exemplary and highly regarded businesses today.

Two Unfortunate Confusions

Individual and Individualism. It should be clear that a proper understanding of being an individual is not antithetical to relating connection with a wider group or involvement in an institution. Behind these misleading oppositions lies a confusion in our understanding of individual and individualism. In my experience most people cannot tell the difference between the two. Any criticism of individualism is taken to be an attack on

being an individual. It is as if a critique of consumerism*—a way of life in which shopping* is a mentality rather than an activity, so that everything, including relationships and religion, is shopped around for—were understood as an attack on doing any shopping at all! Individualism is a view of self that divorces us from others except where involvement with them is instrumental to our own advancement or growth. This itself is not identical with the ideal of the so-called rugged individual, for, as the sociologist Robert Wuthnow has pointed out, part of the latter involves a degree of concern for others and altruistic actions, or at least does not regard these two as in contradiction. The younger generation, who tend to describe themselves as individualists, to some extent also view themselves in webs of relationships, especially with family and peers.

It is a more self-centered, at times narcissistic, form of individual preoccupation that is growing like a cancer in modern societies. We see this between spouses as marriages become more contractual in nature, with children who are increasingly viewed as an impediment to adult fulfillment, among friends when they see the relationship in terms of its usefulness rather than just being-ness, in small groups which are valued so long as they provide therapeutic benefits for their members. In all these ways, individualistic attitudes destroy from within the relationships and institutions individuals need in order to develop and flourish. The individualist does not understand the difference between self-centered behavior, which is present even when one is focused on the best part of oneself, and the self-regarding behavior in which everyone needs to be engaged as part of their proper self-care—physically, emotionally, relationally, intellectually, culturally and spiritually. The latter is compatible with and nourished in the company of others and in well-functioning institutions; the former is not.

Individual and Community. The possibility of an individual and a network of significant others, or community, belonging together has already been raised. One example of this is the loving bond between a man and a woman in marriage where this is understood covenantally rather than contractually. Genuine love* between two people, involving mutual giving and receiving, does not diminish the individuals concerned but enhances them. For love is not a scarce resource to be divided such that if one gets more the other gets less. What happens is that the more two people give to one another the more love is generated and the more each gets in return. There is a paradox here. The more two people give themselves to each other and interpenetrate each other's lives, the more individual they become. It is a considerable tragedy at present that the search for individual actualization by two people in marriage is leading not only to a greater incidence of separation and divorce* but to a lessening sense of selfhood and fulfillment in the partners themselves. From this example we can see other possibilities for community between people that enlarges rather than contracts them and also creates a vital corporate force that has its own value and impact on those who come in contact with it.

This is the missing third alternative to the two choices available—the individualist and collectivist approaches to life. While this third alternative is not totally lacking in societies uninfluenced by the Judeo-Christian worldview,* it is more in the background and less influential there. Pre- and non-Western societies tend to subsume the individual too much at the expense of the group; secular Western societies tend to devalue the group in favor of an emphasis on the individual. But individual and community really belong together: you cannot have one without the other. It is precisely through relationships, with God and others, that our identity* is chiefly formed. The higher the quality of their relationships, the more of a unique individual we tend to become.

A good example of this is the early Christian view of the church. The family of God or body of Christ is at one and the same time a model of the individual-in-the-community and of community-in-the-individual (*see* Church-Family). One aspect of this is beautifully captured in Alexandre Dumas's motto for the Three Musketeers: "All for one and one for all." Another is enshrined in the way God is conceived as sharing aspects of divine truth and love with various people in the church so that only as they come together and share these does everyone understand God fully. As individual Christians we should also be involved in bringing the spirit of community into the institutions of our society, and in doing this our churches should play a supportive and modeling role. One form this takes today is the growth of a communitarian approach to social life. This too is the way the Spirit ministers to people, transforming them into the likeness of Christ and equipping them for God's purposes.

Other aspects of this subject including individual rights* and privacy* are explored in separate articles. In conclusion, it is well to remember the biblical portrait of both the original creation* as well as the final re-creation. It is man and woman as a unit who are made in the image of God, not two separate individuals. It was God's intention that they should live together as "one flesh," in communion with God and in harmony with the world God had made. In the last day it is a transfigured and resurrected community, not just a collection of individuals, that appears before God to worship together and enjoy a common life in God. In the church at present we do not seem to be preparing ourselves too well for that prospect. What is happening in our wider society is even more questionable. A genuinely Christian understanding of the individual, as a communally formed and communally oriented person, would help us deal with these situations.

See also CHURCH; CHURCH-FAMILY; COMMUNITY; PRIVACY; RIGHTS; SOCIETY.

References and Resources
Y. Arieli, *Individualism and Nationalism in American Ideology* (Cambridge, Mass.: Harvard University Press, 1964); R. N. Bellah et al., *Habits of the Heart: Individualism and Commitment in American Life* (San Francisco: Harper & Row, 1986); R. W. Bibby, *Fragmented Gods* (Toronto: Irwin, 1987); P. E. Hammond, *Religion and Personal Autonomy: The Third Disestablishment in America* (Columbia: University of South Carolina Press, 1982); C. N. Kraus, *The Authentic Witness: Credibility and Authority* (Grand Rapids: Eerdmans, 1979); C. Lasch, *The Culture of Narcissism: American Life in an Age of Diminishing Expectations* (New York: W. W. Norton, 1978); P. Leinberger and B. Tucker, *The New Individualists: The Generation After the Organization Man* (New York: Harper, 1991); A. MacIntyre, *After Virtue*, 2d ed. (Notre Dame, Ind.: University of Notre Dame Press, 1984); B. A. Shain, *The Myth of American Individualism: The Protestant Origins of American Political Thought* (Princeton: Princeton University Press, 1994); C. Taylor, *The Sources of the Self: The Making of the Modern Identity* (Cambridge, Mass.: Harvard University Press, 1989).

Robert Banks

INFORMATION SUPERHIGHWAY

For the half-century that digital computers* have been available, they have nearly always been seen as stand-alone devices. If a person had a computing problem, he or she would somehow connect to a computer, transmit the problem to it and receive the solution back. The sophistication of the input devices and the problems to be solved have changed substantially as computers have evolved. The basic model of input, compute and output, however, has remained relatively static. Computers have been simply the middle member for a pair of binary interactions with human beings.

Recently this model has been expanded by an entirely new vision of the appropriate flow of information between human beings and computers. The closed circle of input, compute and output is replaced by a web. In the new model, computers and humans are part of a complex network of communication that may flow from human to machine to human (as in the old model) but also from human to human or machine to machine. This arbitrary flow of information across an ill-defined web of computers is popularly called the Information Superhighway.

So far the Information Superhighway is more dream than reality. But that dream is taking form in quite concrete political* and technological* choices that we are currently making. The essence of the dream is accessing information on computers around the world without regard to physical location. All our information—commercial transactions, descriptions of skills and capabilities, credit histories, and even personal communications—can be retrieved, transferred and edited remotely, regardless of what computer they actually reside on.

Evolving the Highway System
While the Information Superhighway is mostly a matter of political vision and planning, a number of current realities give us an insight into the ways it would transform our lives. These capabilities will be enhanced as our current information network (which is still a kind of "Information Oregon Trail") evolves

into a secure medium with tools that can support access to its information treasures.

Over the past few decades, the United States Department of Defense (mostly through its Advanced Research Projects Agency, ARPA) and several large European agencies have independently explored the significance of allowing computer systems to network with each other. Research along these lines marked a dramatic change in thinking about the way computers could serve human needs.

Much of the evolution of computer systems involved making them faster and more powerful so that individual machines could be used to solve increasingly complex problems. Networking machines together did not help them solve more complex problems at all, because the control integration required to martial networked resources against a single computational problem was lacking. But networking did create and solve an entirely different set of problems.

Although computers, when networked, cannot solve more complex problems, they can exchange information more easily and widely. This information exchange turns out to be profoundly important because it makes use of computers for what they have come to do most: remember our information. When computers are networked, they have the potential to share the information they maintain for us with other people and other computers. In the end, this entire web of the Information Superhighway will allow information to travel along arbitrary paths to its destination.

When compared against this vision, today's tools are quite primitive. But they provide access to *some* information across *some* paths to *some* destinations on the network. People today access information networks in two basic, and basically different, ways.

On-line Access Vehicles

Commercial On-line Services. A number of providers such as CompuServe, America Online and Prodigy offer their subscribers electronic messaging and discussion services as well as a set of resources provided by the content industry. Messaging in on-line services is usually easiest and most transparent with other members of the same service. Messaging outside the on-line service is now often possible but may be more convoluted.

Another service provided by on-line services is discussion. "Chat" groups and other topical discussion groups are a major draw of the on-line services. These groups may be for users of particular computer software, or for shared interests like rock climbing, or "just" for company. Some can be conducted in real time while others have built-in delays.

On-line services also provide a vehicle for content providers to distribute their goods. News services such as Dow Jones News Retrieval, magazines like *Consumer Reports* and *Worth,* and encyclopedia vendors all use on-line services as distribution channels for their content.

On-line services are for the most part self-contained islands of information. If yours has a good encyclopedia available, all is well, but if it is available only on another service, you are out of luck. Connections outside the on-line services are becoming more common and easier to navigate all the time, but they are still exceptional. Most subscribers stay on their original on-line island.

The Internet. If the on-line services are like isolated neighborhoods of users, the Internet is like a complex urban megalopolis. The Internet, a direct outgrowth of ARPA's experiments in computer networking, is a loose confederation of thousands of computers that offer various kinds of information services to each other and the users who have accounts on member machines.

Many of the services provided by Internet computers are very similar to those of the on-line services. Messaging, discussion groups and file archives are all part of the Internet's diffuse resources. Some content providers also allow basic Internet access to their resources, but this is less developed than in the on-line services.

In general, people gain access to the Internet through their work or school. Private access is relatively more expensive than group access to the on-line services, so Internet access tends to be organizationally mediated. The Internet also tends to be more arcane and cryptic than the on-line services. This is because it originated in a culture of computer professionals who had learned to have no problem with such a lack of user-friendliness. This aspect of the Internet is slowly changing, but the power* lying behind the Internet's rather brutal veneer keeps people coming to it in spite of the learning curve it requires.

Current Pathways

Whether people access the on-line world of information through an on-line service or over the Internet itself, they do so to obtain a variety of services not easily available elsewhere. Even where similar services are available outside the on-line world, the on-line versions are distinctive.

Electronic Mail. The most transparent example of this distinctiveness is electronic mail. From one point of view, electronic mail (e-mail) is just another form of instant communication like the telephone or fax. But for several reasons electronic mail turns out to be extremely convenient for a variety of communications.

E-mail uses the same tools for responding as for receiving. By contrast, a conventional letter requires a letter opener to receive but a pen, paper, envelope and stamp to respond. This difference in reception and response tools adds a substantial overhead to the communication, and busy people will not complete it unless it is very important. One can, however, dash off an e-mail reply with very little overhead and no tools other than the ones used to receive the mail.

People can receive e-mail quickly and respond to it at their leisure. As it happens, many communications need to reach their destination quickly but do not require quick response. Electronic mail is ideal for these communications.

E-mail mail leaves a "paper trail" automatically. Many business communications need to leave documentation behind them. Telephone* calls, while personal, are not self-documenting and so require an additional activity to create an audit trail. Electronic mail is often just as personal and quick as a telephone call but documents itself in the communication process.

Discussion Groups. At their most puerile, these discussion groups are mere college "bull sessions" without even the grace required by face-to-face communication. In some cases, however, the discussion can be extremely helpful. The most common helpful discussions currently focus on using various pieces of computer hardware and software. People are more than happy to share their success and failure stories and can be quite helpful to others in the discussion group (*see* Discussion).

Discussion groups in the on-line services can be called *chat sessions* or *bulletin boards.* On the Internet, they are referred to as *Usenet groups.* Information tends to flow quite freely in these groups, and all advice is offered in a "let the buyer beware" mode. This tends to give on-line discussion groups a frontier air about them. Good information is out there, but finding and using it requires determination and discernment.

In general, the signal-to-noise ratio in on-line discussions is extremely low. So little useful information is provided by some groups that readers routinely use automatic means (filters, robots and "kill files") to sort out the potentially interesting from the useless. Other groups have spawned "mediated" counterparts where postings to the group are passed through a judging process before being distributed. One example of this is the mediated counterpart of the rec.humor Usenet group, appropriately called rec.humor.funny to distinguish it from its unmediated cousin.

Information Files. The traditional content industries (publishing, education* and entertainment) and other information providers now also have offerings on the Information Superhighway. Information files may be computer software or encyclopedia articles or technical specifications. They are usually provided in relatively portable file formats so they can be downloaded and adapted or printed on the user's computer.

The information provided on-line has managed to raise anew the problems with traditional copyright laws that the photocopy machine hinted at. For centuries, content providers have charged for their information by charging for the medium which carried it. Book publishers were really selling information, but they made their money by restricting the supply of the medium that carried that information, the printed page. Electronic media, in contrast, are virtually free, and as a result information carried electronically can be duplicated again and again at marginal cost. This aspect of the on-line world is causing serious heartburn for the traditional information providers because their ability to restrict information by restricting the supply of the distribution medium is disappearing.

The World Wide Web. The Web, or WWW, is a distributed ad hoc system of information, sound, graphics and other media files. It originated at CERN, the European nuclear research facility in Switzerland, and now has linked nodes all over the world.

The Web works by giving Internet-connected computers the ability to serve "Web pages," documents composed in HTML (HyperText Markup Language). HTML allows authors to provide platform independent content that refers to Web pages on other Internet computers using hyperlinks. These hyperlinks refer to files on computers anywhere in the world using a Universal Resource Locator (URL).

Using software called a Web browser, these hyperlinked URLs can be traversed without the user even knowing where the resource resides. Several browsers (especially Mosaic and Netscape) have made the Web popular and have fed the explosion of Internet resources as well as provided access to them.

The Future of the Superhighway

The World Wide Web and the browsers that exploit it are our most important glimmer of the power available to us over a future Information Superhighway. Vast amounts of information navigated using arbitrary hyperlinks sounds like a set of services useful to business, educational and commercial concerns.

One important piece of the Information Superhighway that has yet to be constructed is the ability to send secure information over the network. Credit card* orders and bank transfers cannot currently be accommodated on the Internet because the security of the transactions cannot be guaranteed.

Even in the absence of these security systems, commerce on the Internet has grown substantially in the last few years. Today it is a remarkable advertising* medium, especially for that dimension of advertising which is essentially informative. As pioneering organizations like Commercenet and their descendants chart the course of business over the network, we can expect it to have a profound impact on many forms of commercial life, such as mail-order catalogs (which can be distributed far more cheaply and widely in soft copy over a network) and service negotiation.

Eventually we can expect service, delivery, education and even government to be conducted substantially over the Information Superhighway. On-line "town meetings" and public discussions have already occurred in the United States and elsewhere. And government entities are providing Web pages and other information sources for constituents and other interested parties. Participation in democracies around the world has another important vehicle with the Internet, for it is certainly easier to drop your senator e-mail than to write and send a traditional letter.

Challenges for Christians
The Information Superhighway offers many benefits, but with these come several challenges.

As with all advances in technology this one is a mixed blessing, facilitating our communication and exchange and at the same time extending some present imbalances. On one hand, the Information Superhighway opens up possibilities of improving access to a wide range of sources and democratizing discussion of them. This is a real advantage, one that is in many respects similar to what happened when the telephone was first introduced. On the other hand, it may reinforce the dominance of data and information over interpretation and wisdom, increase information overload and induce people to spend more time on their computers than with people. It

could have further implications as well.

On the Social Level. Although the cost of computers continues to decrease, it still costs money to obtain equipment and use a provider to get on the Information Superhighway. Thus poorer and more marginal groups in society may still to some extent miss out and become further disadvantaged. Also, people with poor relational skills may be tempted to feel that they are achieving intimacy through electronics when there is no technical fix for these. While using the Net may help some to grow in confidence in their ability to communicate, relationships mainly grow through speaking* and listening* to actual others, preferably when eye contact can be made and feelings "read."

On the Moral Level. Parts of the Net are in danger of being co-opted by advertisers looking for fresh ways to get customers. It is also already being used to solicit a wider audience for pornography. There is a need for users of the Net to monitor both their own and their children's use of it. In some cases technical devices can be used to block children from gaining access to certain services. While legislated regulation of suppliers is one course of action here, unlike television,* Net providers are more information exchanges than prepackaged senders. As with other technologies, all dimensions of grappling with the principalities and powers* are involved in using, developing and harnessing this new tool.

On the Spiritual Level. All power-based technologies offer an implicit temptation to idolatry. This is part of the "technological illusion" (Ellul). Many people spend too much time on the Net and direct their major energies to exploiting its potential. Computer addiction* is a serious alternative focus for daily life. It is important to keep the Information Superhighway in its place, as a servant.

One way of doing this is to "fast" or take a "sabbath"* from its use on a regular basis, so as to keep it in proper perspective. Another is to maintain something akin to old-fashioned leisurely letter writing* where this is the more appropriate form of communication.

At the same time, the Information Superhighway allows for some level of communication—consider it "small talk" if you like—between members of family and colleagues separated geographically. Small talk is not to be despised, especially if the new technology allows generations to communicate (grandparents and grandchildren, for example). Relationships are partly built on regular small talk, and the latter can also lead to big talk, the full sharing of personhood in community*, family,* church-family* and in spiritual friendships.* And anything that makes it possible for people to keep in touch with one another at minimal expense over long distances can be welcomed by Christians.

As private citizens, churches, businesses, government and banks increasingly turn to the Information Superhighway, there will undoubtedly be an ever-deepening hunger for the personal and for warm human relationships. Since persons are always at the center of the kingdom of God, God's people face an unparalleled opportunity to humanize the world for God's glory.

See also COMPUTER; COMPUTER GAMES.

Hal Miller

INNER CITY

Widely used and rarely defined, the term *inner city* seems to have come into common usage in the 1960s. Although in the past *inner city* was sometimes interchangeable with *central city,* the two terms now have quite different connotations. Both refer to the geographic core of a city,* with *inner city* connoting not only geography but dense population, physical deterioration of buildings, poverty* and poor access to services.

More recently, *inner city* has become a label for any area of a city with certain types of social ills, including high crime rates, poor schools and high dropout rates, drug* sales and drug use, and so on. In Los Angeles, the south-central area is referred to as inner city; it is a residential area and not near the core or central city, yet the fact that it is inner city would not be questioned. Thus an inner-city area may not even be near the city center. Rather than expressing location, the term now connotes characteristics related to certain social problems regardless of location. Even smaller towns in rural areas that exhibit high crime rates, gangs and so on are said to be developing "inner-city problems."

These strong connotations developed through usage have led to the term being used as a symbol of some of the social ills and evils feared by society as a whole. "Inner city" as a symbol is laden with fear. The function of the symbol is to distance a person from these fears. After the Rodney King disturbances in Los Angeles in 1992, the deepest fears were not among those who lived in the inner city where the fires had burned but among those who lived in surrounding areas. The fear stemmed from the possibility that the problems usually contained in certain areas might be spreading to "safer" areas. In reality the different parts of a city are not separate from each other. They are interrelated parts of an organic system, much like the human body.* One part may show an illness, but the whole body is affected. In fact the cause of the illness may lie elsewhere.

The discussion of inner city is tied to a related discussion within the discipline of urban sociology regarding the definition of *urban*. Historically *urban* referred to a place. However, it is becoming increasingly clear that urban is not so much a place as it is social processes rooted in but not contained within a city.

To be understood, these processes must be seen in their global* context. The situation of increasing deterioration of many American inner cities is related to a strong antiurban bias that favors the American dream of a house in the suburbs* over life in the city. At one time referred to as "white flight," this flight crosses racial and ethnic lines and, in fact, is the fleeing of those with economic means, thus leaving inner-city areas stripped of resources. This antiurban bias is not found in many cities of the majority world, where the cities are seen as a place of hope and opportunity. There the poor are most often found in squatter settlements that surround the edges of large cities.

See also CITY; SUBURBIA.

References and Resources
W. G. Flanagan, *Contemporary Urban Sociology* (Cambridge: Cambridge University Press, 1993); J. J. Palen, *The Urban World* (New York: McGraw-Hill, 1981).

Jude Tiesam

INSURANCE
Insurance is a means by which individuals,* families,* businesses and other organizations reduce or eliminate financial uncertainties in areas of life where there are predictable possibilities of financial loss. People exchange a small but predictable amount of money, their premium, for a larger, uncertain loss. Because the insurer can predict average losses over a large population, the risk is evened out and shared. The fortunate many who escape major loss help the unfortunate few who experience it. Kinds of insurance normally purchased by individuals include life, fire, theft or damage to personal property, legal liability, disability, unemployment, health and travel insurance.

The Insuring of Almost Everything and Everyone
Individuals, of course, buy some of these types of insurance for personal protection. Groups like businesses or corporations buy insurance for their employees; business partners may buy it to provide the means of buying out a partner's share in business upon his or her death.* In Canada and other countries with a social welfare philosophy, the government or state agencies buy insurance by means of taxes.* Insurance provided by the state in this way is compulsory rather than voluntary.

Insurance, however, protects not only individuals (and by extension their families) but also corporations, nonprofit agencies and governments. They may insure to cover the safe transfer of goods, the reliability of monies deposited in banks, the nonpayment of loans and the loss or destruction of major assets. Of course, though it may not be obvious to the person or organizations purchasing insurance, many significant risks cannot be reduced through insurance: war and insurrection, nuclear holocaust, ecological disaster (acts of humankind widely and over time) and natural disasters of colossal proportion (commonly called "acts of God").

In the Western world many individuals use a significant percentage of their income to pay for various forms of insurance, in excess of 10 percent in many cases if compulsory insurance provided by taxation is also considered. Some people complain of being "insurance poor"—spending so much to cover potential losses in the future that they have not enough to live properly today. Others are underinsured and may face a future without either personal assets or social network to cover major losses or reverses. In most developing countries individual insurance is the privilege of the rich and powerful; the poor and middle class rely on the age-old securities of family and church.* Significantly, before there was a major insurance industry, the church pioneered in establishing burial societies during times of plague and mutual aid societies (especially for widows, orphans and the destitute), providing hospitality* and asylum to fugitives, travelers and shipwrecked seamen; and setting up the first hospitals for the sick—a stunning and little-told story (Oliver, p. 116).

Is insurance merely a modern invention to satisfy an artificially induced need in the consumer society? Is there a biblical foundation for buying and selling insurance? When does protecting against risk become a refusal to trust God?

The History of Insurance

While widespread provision of insurance is a relatively modern affair, the idea of insurance has a long history, dating to ancient Babylon many centuries before Christ. Marine insurance was the first. It covered potential losses by traders and merchants who had to borrow funds (using their ships as collateral) to finance their trade. According to contract, if the merchant was robbed of his goods, suppliers agreed to cancel the loan in exchange for a premium paid. This was formalized in the Code of Hammurabi. The Greeks, Hindus and Romans borrowed some of these codified arrangements and adapted them.

Life and health insurance had beginnings in ancient Greece (600 B.C.) and became part of the benefits of belonging to guilds and trade associations, the precursors of modern unions.* The first insurance contract was signed in Genoa in 1347, and the first life insurance with "insurable interest" (A.D. 1430) concerned the lives of pregnant wives and slaves. England developed "Friendly Societies" to insure industrial workers, and the Great Fire of London (1666) propelled the fire insurance industry forward. Lacking solid actuarial research and administrative know-how, many fledgling attempts to provide insurance folded, including some early attempts to establish insurance companies in the North American colonies. The first permanent life insurance company was formed in the U.S. in 1759; then followed health insurance (1847), automobile (1898) and group hospitalization (1936). Some of these companies were and are mutually owned by the insured; others operate as corporations with shareholders. Major factors in the evolution of multifaceted and near-universal insurance in the Western world are industrialization (with its hazards for injury and loss), urbanization* (with its attendant risk of theft), mobility* (with the loss of a stable family support group and land that can be worked) and privatization (with the reduction of society* to the autonomous individual [see Individual]).

Thinking About Risk

At first glance the Bible seems to advise us not to think about future risks. The birds and lilies do not worry. "Yet your heavenly Father feeds them" (Mt 6:26). It is the unbelieving Gentiles who run after all these things (food and clothing). But Jesus is not condemning us for planning for the future so much as warning us not to be anxious about it: "Do not worry about tomorrow, for tomorrow will worry about itself" (Mt 6:34). We cannot add a day to our life by worrying; probably we will do the reverse. Indeed the way we respond to risk is a significant thermometer of our faith and spirituality.

Insurance does not deal with all risks, and perhaps not even the most important risks, such as losing friendships,* personal worth, love,* hope or faith. No one through buying insurance can guarantee long life, good health,* satisfying work,* personal contentment, a happy marriage,* good neighbors, intimate friendships and children that bring joy to the heart. On a grand scale we cannot insure against the breakdown of a whole society or the ecosystem (though there is much we can do to prevent these). There is no insurance that can be purchased against marriage failure, loss of meaning, personal suffering or, most crucial of all, our eternal salvation.

We cope with risk in several ways: by ignoring it, assuming (or retaining) it, eliminating the possibility of loss, transferring the loss to someone else, or anticipating the loss and planning toward it.

On the first two options, it is folly to ignore risk, a game of let's pretend that is bound to catch up disastrously with reality someday. We must assume or retain the most important risks and the most crucial potential losses. For the Christian this means trusting in God's providential care, believing that even temporary reverses will be transformed into general good, as exemplified by the victory of the cross of Jesus. By retaining or assuming these noninsurable risks, we are called not only to trust God but to exercise faithful stewardship* of our life, marriage, home, driving, possessions and ultimately the environment. God is the ultimate owner* of everything; what we render is stewardship or regency. So the proper management of our lives is intended to reduce risk. Keeping an automobile in good repair, for example, is assuming the risk and managing it by good stewardship.

In most cases the third option, eliminating the possibility of loss, can be done only by refusing to accept the adventure of life. Driving a car, traveling,* investing our talents in a community, getting married, having children and even joining a church are risky enterprises. Tragically, some people are like the one-talent man in Jesus' parable (Mt 25:24-25), protecting themselves against any possible loss and so losing what they thought they had. People who refuse to invest themselves in order to eliminate all possible losses end up losing something more precious than what they protected—the joy of life.

Transferring risk to someone else, the fourth option, is not something we can normally do with risks that we must personally undertake. But this is an acceptable way of coping with some potential financial losses that could ruin one's business in a single stroke. For example, a surety bond guaranteeing the completion of a building according to written specifications transfers the risk from the person building the structure to the insurer. Such ways of managing risk are called for in a society that is composed not merely of a collection of individual farmers or tradespeople but of corporations and powerful structures.*

The most common way to manage risk is to share it through buying insurance. Most insurance is simply a form of neighbor love expressed impersonally without knowing who our neighbors are. The insurance company becomes our symbolic neighbor. Through knowledge of past experience, careful prediction of future possibilities and accumulation of funds over a wide population base, insurance companies are able to cover the enormous losses of a few and the minor losses of the many, and have enough left over to cover their operating costs and make a legitimate profit for the shareholders.

Prayerful Insurance

Here are a few guidelines for Christians to consider when thinking about insurance.

Plan wisely for your family's future. In many cases it is unloving *not* to buy insurance, since it may force your family to embrace involuntary poverty* to care for you in a time of extreme need. Wisely insuring is a form of neighbor love and part of our stewardship. But one must be careful that the companies trusted with funds are reliable since there are many cases of bankruptcy. Companies like Standard & Spoors and Moody's, and a new index called TRAC rate insurance companies for their strength, liquidity and solvency. Advertised reliability is not a sufficient guide.

Keep insurance in perspective; don't overvalue it. Our eyes can all too easily be diverted from the uninsurable risks that are much more deserving of our stewardship and prayerful attention: marriages, self-esteem* of children, friendships and the joy of our salvation.

Never let buying insurance be an alternative to trusting God. An advertisement* for an insurance company boasted, "A promise I'm forever watching out for you." Only God can do that. As Jesus said, our heavenly Father knows what we need and cares for us. Even more, we have an exuberant, risk-taking God who wants his creatures to experience life as an adventure. Significantly, the problem of the fearful investor in the parable of the talents (Mt 25:24) was not his analysis of a potential loss but his conception of his master (representing God) as one who could not be trusted with his mistakes and reverses.

Beware of overinsuring. It is just as foolish to become "insurance poor" as to ignore insurable risks. We are meant to enjoy life and to thrive, not live cramped little lives. Often, insurance can be reduced or not even purchased (as in the case of collision insurance on a car) if one has put aside savings that can be used in the eventuality of a sustainable loss. Very valuable possessions (like inherited items) may be too expensive to insure, and wise management, combined with the attitude of "holding things lightly," is more prudent than covering every eventuality. Simpler living* is a matter of perspective and not just net worth. A wise philosophy is to self-insure for small problems and use an insurance company's money for large ones. When looking at disability insurance, for example, we should choose a longer waiting period (90 to 120 days) so that in the event of disability we can use our own resources for the short term, thereby reducing the cost. Some people recommend as a rule of thumb purchasing ten times one's income in life insurance.

Help family members sustain their losses. It is lamentable that the basic unit of Western society has become the isolated individual covering all his or her potential losses rather than the family looking after one another. Insuring everything possible may inadvertently assist in the dissolution of the one organic community, besides the church, that can provide care and support during times of crisis and loss. Families can agree together what risks they will undertake mutually, including care of people when they are sick or old. Jesus roundly condemned the Pharisees for neglecting their responsibilities to their parents, a form of "honoring" them (Ex 20:12) by dedicating their assets to the Lord's work, a system called corban (Mt 15:3-6). Paul says that if we do not care for our own families we are worse than unbelievers (1 Tim 5:8).

Lend aid to others in the body of Christ who need it. The church has an important role to play as the equalizer of risk. In the earliest church in Jerusalem, people sold their surplus goods to provide for anyone in need (Acts 2:44-45; 4:32-37). Later came other forms of economic sharing, such as famine relief (11:27-30), occupational sharing (Aquila and Priscilla with Paul in making tents) and mutual aid gift-giving* (the great love gift from the Gentile church—1 Cor 16:2; 2 Cor 8—9). It is all too easy to claim it would never work in our urbanized, mobile society where most people move every four or five years. But a commitment to a house church or an intentional community not to move (see Mobility), while countercultural, may be a concrete step toward true community (see Fellowship). We have something to learn from churches in the developing world on this matter. When someone dies in Kenya, the church gathers to make gifts to the family —not just the grieving spouse—to provide a living and a future for the survivors.

Remember those in society who are uninsured (the disadvantaged and destitute), and act on their behalf. In our modern times risk and loss are systemic problems, not merely matters of personal character and integrity. The Scriptures warning against idleness assume that unemployed* people are lazy, whereas today the unemployed are often victimized by systemic problems, sometimes through economies halfway around the world. So in coping with risk today, we must exercise cultural and organizational as well as personal stewardship (see Principalities and Powers). We must fight against the abuse of unemployment and health insurance schemes if they are government-funded and abused. We need to lobby* for legislative change to care for disadvantaged and marginalized people in our society.

Conclusion

Like most advances in the Western world, the growth of the insurance industry is a mixed blessing. With careful man-

agement, reaffirmation of the providence of God and wise stewardship of our lives, buying some insurance is an act of neighbor love and personal responsibility, doing what we can so we won't be a burden on others (1 Thess 4:12; 2 Thess 3:8). In reality, we can never eliminate that possibility fully. And where true family and church community exist, mutual caring is not a burden but part of the unlimited liability of family love. The temptation of too much insurance, or a wrong attitude, can lead to an illusory feeling that we can control our own futures and live autonomously without God. Like many facets of everyday life, this one calls us to a life of prayer, spiritual discernment and loving action.

References and Resources
J. L. Athearn, *Risk and Insurance* (St. Paul: West, 1981); K. Black Jr., "Insurance," in *The Encyclopedia Americana* (Danbury, Conn.: Grolier, 1989)15:233-39; K. Black Jr. and S. S. Huebner, *Life Insurance* (Englewood Cliffs, N.J.: Prentice-Hall, 1982); E. H. Oliver, *The Social Achievements of the Christian Church* (Toronto: United Church of Canada, 1930); N. A. Williams, *Insurance* (Cincinnati: South-Western Publications, 1984).

R. Paul Stevens

INTEGRITY

"Teacher," they said, "we know you are a man of integrity and that you teach the way of God in accordance with the truth" (Mt 22:16). Teaching in accordance with truth: his hearers saw in Jesus a person whose words and actions came together with the ring of credibility.

A Character Issue
Integrity is about character. Character encompasses more than beliefs and opinions. It denotes the core values* and commitments that define a person and ultimately shape the person's life. We live out of our character regardless of the

stated beliefs, opinions or values that we proclaim. Character flows from the soul* of the person. *Integrity* refers to the consistency of character that matches words and actions, vision and choices, values and behaviors. It is life lived with consistency. *Character* refers to those internal core values that shape all that a person does.

A life lived with integrity is one in which all aspects of a person are fully integrated; it is a holistic life. In mathematics an integer is a whole number that cannot be divided into parts which are themselves whole numbers. Integrity is like that. It is that coherence of character that presents a single face to the world: "What you see is what you get."

In his marvelous book *Leadership Jazz,* Max DePree talks about voice and touch. Integrity keeps voice and touch together, being sure that what you say is matched by what you do—external consistency— living what you believe, communicating the same truth in your words and your living. DePree's comments focus on the second level of integrity—internal consistency. At its core integrity is living with words and actions that reflect the internal values of your soul.

Integrity is about truth and honesty. It means saying what you mean and meaning what you say, letting "your 'Yes' be yes, and your 'No,' no" (Jas 5:12). Integrity assumes a correlation between what you say is true and what is actually true. This is difficult in a world in which truth is increasingly seen to be relative, but for the Christian that means correspondence with truth as it has been revealed by God.

Being Trustworthy
Internal and external consistency produce credibility and trust, which we might call *integrity of relationship.* Personal relationships are built on trust; they require that persons be credible, believable, trustworthy. Trust is both earned and given. Relational integrity assumes that the person who presents himself or herself to you in relationship is in fact a true expression of that person—the assumed consistency of word and action, the assumed correlation between character and presentation.

Just as trustworthiness between people is based on consistency in character, so in organizations* there should be coherence between the culture or values of the organization and the actual policies, processes and behaviors of the organization. In *Organizational Culture and Leadership,* Edgar Schein argues clearly that every organization has its own culture, that is, an underlying set of assumptions, beliefs and values that control the way it lives out its organizational life. The actions of an organization over time always reflect this organizational character or culture.* Many organizations these days also are attempting to express their corporate values in creeds or other publicly stated value commitments. In this case integrity refers to the consistency between the stated values of the organization and the actual actions of the organization that flow from its culture. Where there is consistency, there is integrity. Where there is no consistency, there is organizational dissonance, and people get caught in the middle and trust is lost.

Integrity is about consistency of living that allows the character of one's soul to find expression in the living of one's life—in word and deed. Organizationally integrity means the culture of an organization finds congruent expression in the policies, procedures and stated values of the corporate community. Integrity is about truth, honesty, trust and consistency; it is a matter of character.

See also LOYALTY, WORKPLACE; ORGANIZATIONAL CULTURE AND CHANGE; ORGANIZATIONAL VALUES; PROMISING.

References and Resources
J. P. Hess, *Integrity: Let Your Yea Be Yea* (Scottdale, Penn.: Herald, 1978); W. L. Sullivan, *Work and Integrity: The Crisis and Promise of Professionalism in America Today* (San Francisco: Harper, 1995).

Walter Wright

INVESTMENT

Investment is the employment of assets (money or otherwise) into a scheme that is potentially profitable in the foreseeable future. This simple definition contains four assumptions: (1) assets should be put to work; (2) they should be profitable and fruitful (that is, you should get more than you put in); (3) the future rather than the immediate present is in view; and (4) there is managed risk of loss or failure. In this article we will consider these assumptions, reflect on them theologically and offer some general guidelines, leaving specific investment advice to qualified professionals. In addition we will consider the Christian life as a form of investment in which both monetary and nonmonetary investments may accumulate what Jesus called "treasure in heaven."

The Confusing Array of Investment Opportunities
Investment takes several forms: savings accounts, ownership of one's home,* pension plans, putting money into one's own business, purchasing government bonds or bank-guaranteed investment certificates, owning a fraction of a corporation (stock) and gaining a promissory certificate from a corporation with specified amount of interest (debenture). The option of hiding money in a mattress or burying it in the back yard is always present, but besides the obvious risk of theft there is inflation, which means that one hundred dollars tucked into a mattress in 1945 had only fifty dollars' purchasing power in 1970. Hence, not investing means reducing the value of your capital.

Most people recognize the importance of putting aside some of their disposable income into a *savings account* to be kept for emergencies or a rainy day. This form of investment has the advantage of permitting the money to be withdrawn anytime but the disadvantage that it earns a small rate of interest (a percentage of the total) while it is "working" for the bank or credit union. Usually the interest paid on savings accounts is less than inflation—the increasing price level of a basket of defined consumer goods, usually measured as the annualized increase in the Consumer Price Index. In some Third World countries the inflation rate is so high (upward to 100 percent a year) that investing in savings accounts appears counterproductive. One usually finds the wealthy minority investing in foreign so-called hard currency countries, draining the home country of desperately needed capital.

Another common investment worldwide is one's own *farm* or *home*. This is generally a double-duty investment: first, property like this meets a family need for housing, and, in the case of a farm, income; and second, it is a hedge against inflation since the value of a home normally increases through time. In Canada and the United States it remains one of the few legitimate investments that do not attract taxation for the profit earned. (The other tax-exempt gain is proceeds from life insurance and, for Canada only, the winnings of a lottery or other "windfall" venture.) Indebtedness associated with home ownership usually is in the long run wise (*see* Debt; Home). Real estate, however, is not a "liquid" (easily converted to money) asset, may take months to sell and is susceptible to cyclical market trends.

In urbanized, industrialized or information societies a *pension plan* is usually an important investment because it is likely that we will be forced to retire* from remunerated employment before we die, and it is unlikely (though desirable) that family,* community* and church* will be able to care for us in our extended declining years. In older societies and in some Third World countries the family farm provided free housing and food, and one's children cared for the aging until they died. But even in these countries rapid urbanization and industrialization is breaking down the family pension-plan system. In most Western countries pensions are wisely built up over one's working years through participation in a government plan, and wisely augmented through one's own workplace and/or a voluntary program such as a registered retired savings plan (RRSP or IRA). Most corporation or voluntary pension plans involve a wide selection of investment vehicles (stocks, bonds, mutual funds, mortgages and real estate) that are calculated to grow continuously with only a reasonable managed risk of loss, since the risk is diversified into many different investments. The expected return should be rationalized to the managed risk to the capital: the more risky the venture, the greater the "cost" expected for the capital loaned.

In addition to the above investments, many citizens are able to invest in private businesses (through personal loans), the government (through bonds), banks (through investment certificates) and public corporations (through purchasing stocks and convertible debentures). Principles that are important to consider in making such investments are safety and preservation of the invested capital; diversification (not having "all one's eggs in one basket"); liquidity (how easily the principal sum could be recovered); expected income and the previous perform-

ance of the investment; and tax* consequences. For example, an RRSP or IRA allows investors to defer taxes on the principal amount invested until the pension is actually used. Through the magic of compound interest (interest earned on the capital increased by the interest), with time and prudent investing one could have a sizable nest egg in this tax-deferred program for retirement.

Toward a Theology of Investment

Some Christians think it is wrong to plan for the future. After all, have you ever seen a worried bird (Mt 6:26)? What if Jesus comes tonight? Isn't it wrong to think about making money—a form of greed? The only safe investment is in the Lord's work: "Only one life, 'twill soon be past, only what's done for Jesus will last."

Return to our original assumptions about investing. First, we said that money or assets should be put to work. This is in effect what God said to Adam and Eve in the Garden of Eden: put it all to work (Gen 1:26-29; 2:15). Second, we said that it should be profitable or fruitful. God's creation mandate to the first couple was to be fruitful, to fill the earth and to flourish. Seeds are not meant to be kept in bottles or bins forever. That way they can never bear fruit. Rather they should be sown into the soil and produce a hundredfold—a rather good return on the original investment (Mt 13:23).

Third, the future rather than the immediate present or the past is in view. Some African and Asian cultures are oriented backward as the spirits of ancestors keep "catching up" to the present generation. We would then be like people standing on a bridge over a fast-flowing river watching the water come toward us. But the Christian perspective is to turn around and watch where the river is going. We are future-oriented. Heaven calls us. The Second Coming of Christ beckons us toward the new heaven and the new earth. We are, as Jürgen Moltmann so accurately says, living not at sunset but at the dawning of a new day. Christ might come today—we should be ready. But he may not come for a thousand years—we should be ready for even a long wait like the wise virgins in Jesus' parable (Mt 25:1-13). It is precisely this balanced Christian view—longing for Christ to come soon but building for the long haul—that is the eschatological perspective provided by the New Testament. Martin Luther once said that if he knew Christ was coming tomorrow he would still plant a little tree today. Investment in the future is exactly what Christians should do, no matter how black the sky may seem according to a secular analysis.

Then take the fourth assumption— that risk must be assumed. Most people think that investment risk is simply the potential to lose money. But there are at least four kinds of risk to be considered: *business risk* (that the business or corporation will go out of business and not be able to meet its financial obligations); *liquidity risk* (that there may not be a buyer if you want to sell an investment quickly); *market risk* (that the fluctuating financial market may render your investment of less value); *purchasing power risk* (that the investment will not be able to exceed inflation by a satisfactory margin). All four kinds spell the potential for some kind of loss or failure. The more immediate issues are to consider whether the process is in place for continuously monitoring the risk and whether the expected return is proportional to the monitored risk. But it is impossible to invest without some risk. And failure* might even become one of the most important learning moments. Wisdom comes more from failure than from success.*

We explored a theology of risk briefly in the article on insurance.* Risk theorists note that there are several ways of coping with risk: ignoring it, assuming (or retaining) it, eliminating the possibility of loss, transferring the loss to someone else, and anticipating the loss and planning toward it. On the first, it is folly to ignore risk, a game of let's pretend that is bound to catch up disastrously with reality someday. On the most important possibilities and uncertainties, we must assume or retain the risk. By retaining or assuming these noninsurable risks we are called not only to trust God but to exercise faithful stewardship* of our lives to reduce risk. In making investments this means diversifying, seeking wise counsel and not taking unnecessary risks to make big money quickly, the latter falling into the category of speculation or gambling. The proverbs counsel rejecting get-rich-quick schemes in favor of making small regular gains over a period of time, so accumulating wealth through wisdom and patience. "Dishonest money dwindles away, but he who gathers money little by little makes it grow" (Prov. 13:11). In all cases eliminating the possibility of loss totally is possible only by refusing to accept the adventure of life, for there is the dwindling of our purchasing power through inflation.

What would make us accept the risks attendant on making investments? One thing would be a God who takes risks! God took an enormous risk in making a creature with free will, in committing to the family of Abraham, in slipping into the human family as a vulnerable child. But the lamb was slain from the foundation of the earth. For the Christian this means trusting in God's providential care of us and of God's world, and believing that even temporary reverses will be transformed into general good, as exemplified by the victory of the cross of Jesus.

God Loves Investment

Although not addressing the issue of financial assets, the parable of the talents in Matthew (25:14-30) and the parable of the ten minas in Luke (19:11-27) are suggestive with regard to a theology of investment. There are three things we can do with what God has entrusted to us. First we can *squander* it, wasting it as the younger prodigal did in the far county, as humankind has largely done with the created earth. Some people think they are undertaking Christian stewardship* when they give away large amounts of money without any regard to the effect it has. They feel good, but the recipient feels obligated, patronized or disempowered. In reality it is squandering—disinvestment.

Second we can *hoard* it, like the one-talent man who, with his wrong view of his God (Mt 25:24-25; compare Lk 19:21), wrapped up what he had in a handkerchief because he was afraid to lose it. He did not realize that he could keep this only by giving it away! What motivated the one-talent man was fear. Most people would commend him for his prudence and find the judgment of the master unbelievably severe. After all, did not the one-talent man return what was trusted, all in one piece with nothing lost? Did he not treasure what was entrusted to his stewardship? Yet the master condemns him. The reason for the fear of loss and failure is the one-talent man's inadequate view of his master: "I knew that you are a hard man, harvesting where you have not sown and gathering where you have not scattered seed." With that kind of God, who would want to take a risk?

In many of his parables Jesus presents an apparently ridiculous view of God—though one often held subconsciously—to shock people into converting to the real God, who is not immovable and harsh but wonderfully personal. Though Jesus does not actually say this, he expects us to think, "Believe in a God who will squeeze everything he can out of you, who will never forgive a mistake, who will swat you down to hell if you mess things up even once, and this is what you get: a pinched, unimaginative, no-risk-taking and utterly deadly life. Believe in the God and Father of the Lord Jesus, and you will be inspired to try things out, to experiment, to take risks and to flourish." So instead of squandering or hoarding with such a God, we are invited to *invest*, risky as it is. *Investment* is another word for *stewardship*, which is simply another word for Christian service. But there is more to investment than putting our money into a mutual fund.

Investing in Heaven

Giving directly to church, Christian missions* and our families can be one form of investment even though the returns are not gained personally and one's personal capital is reduced (*see* Gift-Giving; Stewardship). Further, not all investments are monetary and this-worldly. Jesus' words are haunting: "Do not store up for yourselves treasures on earth, where moth and rust destroy, and where thieves break in and steal. But store up for yourselves treasures in heaven, where moth and rust do not destroy, and where thieves do not break in and steal. For where your treasure is, there your heart will be also" (Mt 6:19-21). What does it mean to invest in heaven? How is it possible that this investment has guarantees of a "return" which can never be given for investments "on earth"?

First, we are to invest in heaven through our everyday life, work* and homemaking* by doing even the simplest chores* with faith, hope and love.* According to Paul in 1 Corinthians 3:10-15, it is not the religious character of the work (Bible studies, witnessing,* charitable work) that makes work last forever but Christ: this is a call to do our work with faith, hope and love. In some way beyond our imagination even simple work is actually a ministry to Jesus (Mt 25:31-46); that is what faith points to. Love makes chores and quilt-making* last forever (1 Cor 13:8-13). And hope? There is a wonderful correspondence to work we do in this life and work in the next. Our ultimate future is not to be free-floating spirits in heaven but fully resurrected persons in a new earth and a new heaven (Rev 21—22)—working, playing and worshiping in one glorious eternal sabbath.* Just as the resurrected body of Jesus had scars, though now glorified, so this material world, scarred and worked over by humankind, will one day be transfigured into a new world in which even the glories of the nations will be brought into the New Jerusalem (Rev 21:24; Stevens, p. 31). So our first eternal investment is simply to do everything in everyday life for God (Col 3:22-24). It is literally true that "only what's done for Christ will last," though this does not require going into a Christian service career or spending one's time in church work, as is commonly thought.

Second, we are to invest primarily in people, especially the poor. The only treasure we can take from this life to the next is the relationships we have made through Jesus. The teaching of Jesus leaves us with the unmistakable challenge to have a hands-on relationship with the poor and to accept some form of voluntary impoverishment. We must do this for the sake of the poor and for the sake of our own souls. A newspaper article asks, "Why should we care about the Third World?" and answers, "Because our economic, environmental and political future is inextricably linked with it." But there is a deeper reason. The rich cannot be saved without the poor.

There is no doubt in my mind that in telling two parables about money and friendship (the shrewd manager and the rich man and Lazarus—Lk 16) and by placing them in juxtaposition, Jesus and Luke intend to motivate us to make friends with the poor. With outrageous freedom Jesus tells about a shrewd manager who used money to make friends by reducing the loans owed to his master so when he would lose his job these friends would look after him forever (Lk 16:1-9). The magnetic center of this parable is a shocking exhortation from the lips of Jesus: "I tell you, use worldly wealth to gain friends for yourselves, so that when it is gone, you will be welcomed into eternal dwellings" (16:9). The second parable, Lazarus and the rich man, gives an empowering negative example of a person who did not use his wealth to make friends of the poor and thus was not welcomed by them into an eternal home. Sandwiched in between these two parables is a section about the Law and the Prophets, which uniformly teach mercy to the poor (16:16-18).

The thrust of Luke 16 is the call to use our money to make friends with the poor, the sick, the powerless, the stranger and the refugee. The unconverted heart believes that there is nothing the poor can do for us. They are not worth being the object of our investment. They will not advance our cause or increase our security. But these two parables make the daring claim that what we gain through befriending the poor is love. Often the poor are richer than the rich in the treasures that really matter— in relationships. "He who is kind to the poor lends to the LORD, and he will reward him for what he has done" (Prov 19:17). Genuinely disempowered people cannot pay back loans, and therefore we should regard such giving as lending to the Lord. Paradoxically we gain it back with interest (22:9)!

Most of this article has focused on the return we are looking for in our own investments. But there is another way of considering the matter of investment.

God is looking for a return on his investment in us (Mt 25:19). What we do with assets and money entrusted to us is like a foreshadowing of the last judgment; our use declares what we really think about God. The gambler has no faith in God but hopes for good luck. The hoarder believes in a vengeful, demanding God. The investor declares that God can be trusted, that God gives what is required and that all investments made with faith, hope and love will bear a return, if not in this life then in the next.

See also CREDIT; DEBT; MONEY; POVERTY; POWER; PRINCIPALITIES AND POWERS; STEWARDSHIP.

References and Resources

F. Amling, *Investments,* 5th ed. (Englewood Cliffs, N.J.: Prentice-Hall, 1984); J. Chrysostom, *On Wealth and Poverty,* trans. Catherine P. Roth (Crestwood, N.Y.: St. Vladimir's Seminary Press, 1984); J. Ellul, *Money and Power,* trans. L. Neff (Downers Grove, Ill.: InterVarsity Press, 1984); R. Foster, *Money, Sex and Power* (San Francisco: Harper & Row, 1985); E. B. Gup, *The Basics of Investing* (New York: Wiley, 1986); R. P. Stevens, *Disciplines of the Hungry Heart* (Wheaton, Ill: Harold Shaw, 1993).

R. Paul Stevens

J

JUSTICE

"With liberty and justice for all," concludes the Pledge of Allegiance many of us Americans learned as little children. This pride in "justice" is at the core of our conception of government but seems as well a deep inner sense of obligation. We instinctively decry injustices, morally offended at the breach they create. Whether a member of a revolutionary force seeking the overthrow of tyrannical government, or merely an armchair critic of some local court decision, we feel passionately about the issue of justice.

What does justice require? Conflicting answers to that question form the foundation of disputes ranging from international geopolitical issues to local tax* policy. The universality of the term, and the desire of any "cause" to claim it, illustrate the richness of the concept and its ambiguity. Everyone claims their view is just. The fact that legal systems, philosophers and citizens all sense the need to claim that "justice" is on their side suggests the innate power of the concept.

What Is Justice?

While philosophers have long debated what constitutes justice, the essential meaning is at least partially clear. The images of the goddesses of justice in Greek mythology suggest some of the basic themes. The goddess stands sometimes blindfolded—a symbol of *impartiality*. Other times the goddess holds up the balance scales—a common symbol today of law.* The scales reflect the weighing to find what is *true* and *fair,* testing the true value of what is weighed. These attributes are the basis for the *judgment* the goddess executes as symbolized by the sword often carried in her hand. In these images we have much of our common notions of justice—impartiality, truth and fairness.

These classic cultural images of goddesses of justice testify also to the transcendent character and transcultural commitment to the principle of justice. Our Western philosophic and legal tradition is rich in the search for justice. For Greek thinkers, justice was one of the four cardinal virtues.* Plato gave justice a central role in the moral life of man and society,* as the virtue which binds the common life. Aristotle devoted one book in his *Nicomachean Ethics* to justice.

While Greeks contributed the philosophic dimensions of justice, Rome focused more on law and administration. Romans sought to develop a legal system that embodied their conception of justice; their special contribution to the quest for justice was the systematic way they established and effectively administrated laws.

The Biblical Contribution

If Greeks and Romans dealt with law at the level of philosophy and politics,* it was the "people of the book," the Hebrews, not only with philosophy and bureaucracy but also with their concrete relational principles, who provided much of the moral and ethical dimension to justice that we inherited. Our very emotional commitment to justice owes much to our spiritual heritage from Israel. The Scriptures make strong statements about the concept of justice.

Justice is a dimension of God's character. For the Jews, justice was not merely a human quest in the context of a world ruled by fickle gods, as among the Greeks, but rooted directly in the character of God. Thus the biblical witness about justice begins with the fact that Yahweh was a God of "justice," and it is from this that the richness of biblical justice expands (Ps 72:1-4, 99:4). Justice was found through divine revelation and not through human searching. There was an inherent and revealed justice which God, and to a limited extent nature itself, revealed. All nations are subject to this justice (Amos 1—2; Romans 1).

Justice is an ethical, moral category. The moral dimension of justice is demonstrated by the fact that the very word for justice in the Scriptures is often translated as "righteousness." Justice is not simply a matter of structures,* and certainly not abstractions, but is intimately connected with right living. In the New Testament we are encouraged to "seek first his kingdom and his righteousness" (Mt 6:33). There is an integral relationship in Scripture between the concepts of righteousness and justice. To do justice is to act rightly. Thus justice is not so much a political or legal theory as a moral and spiritual call.

Justice is the duty of humanity under God. That justice is the demand of God for all nations, and the special duty of Israel, the covenant people, is made clear from the prophetic calls and denunciations. Injustice is condemned. Amos declares,

"Let justice roll on like a river" (Amos 5:24), and the judgment of God falls on Israel for institutional and personal injustice. Doing justice is not a tangential or merely consequential aspect of God's people—it is at the core of the obligation of a covenant people. So central is this duty that God rejects the worship of people who allow or participate in injustice around them (Amos 5:21-24).

Justice is chiefly action, not philosophy. For the Old Testament, justice was not a mere philosophic virtue. Indeed, little time is spent with the nuances of "justice." The emphasis is on doing justice—on action. The prophets insisted on justice "at the gate"—the local court where the elders ruled. It was a justice that required fair dealing in business transactions, credit arrangements, buying and selling of goods, the administration of justice generally. Its enemies were privilege, bribery and unfair advantages (Amos 5:11-15; 8:4ff).

Justice is concern for the weak against power and privilege. The Old Testament evidences a special concern for justice for the poor and oppressed. If there were any place where injustice might be observed, it was with the poor, widows and orphans who lacked the knowledge or power* to assure justice and were often victims of "sharp" traders and corrupt politicians. Some have turned this biblical concern into a Marxist view of an oppressed class embodying truth and a liberation theology. It is, however, more properly seen simply as a recognition that these are the persons who are typically the victims (see Amos 2:7; 4:1; 5:11-12; 8:4ff). This moves the biblical view of justice beyond a mere concern for impartiality; it involves particularity toward those who are most vulnerable, for otherwise they will not receive a fair deal.

Justice and Objective Truth

In the biblical tradition one key element

emerges about justice. We noted that justice is often seen chiefly in procedural or generalized terms, a question of fairness and equality for the law. Much of our modern sense of justice is also loaded with these procedural commitments: public trials, due process, equal protection and so on. But often the question is, What is fair? Unless there is some universal guide, a truth to which we turn, the debate is simply one of rhetoric with all claiming they represent justice. What is the actual content or substance of justice? Unless justice is merely procedure, then justice must also relate to what is "right."

The biblical tradition is clear. Justice is not just *impartiality* of judgment, it is judgment in accord with *right* and *truth*—with *righteousness*. It is judgment in accord with an objective standard. It is *fair* because not everyone gets the same reward or punishment; the reward or punishment is deserved. Biblical thought was not alone in emphasizing the necessity of assessing one's duties and rights in order to really "do justice." The idea of *right,* giving people their due, is also part of Greco-Roman thought. According to Justinian, justice was "to render to each on his right." Socrates saw it as "giving to each man what is proper or due to him." Even the utilitarian J. S. Mill said justice was what another has a right to claim from us, and hence not mere generosity.

Thus one cannot really define justice or measure its achievement, or have some confidence in a permanent standard, without an inquiry into what is right inherently. Societies which establish justice without a reference to eternal standards typically degenerate into tyranny, as the communist experience so clearly evidences. Thus the issue of justice is ultimately linked to questions of theology, belief and so-called natural law.

Contemporary Confusion

The Divorce of Justice from Norms. "Jurisprudence is deserted," declared one student of philosophy. Sadly the great historic relationship between justice and right that we have noted has largely disappeared. Little is left of the concept of justice but political advocacy. The collapse of a worldview* has affected the study of justice as much as any discipline.

In today's pluralistic and positivistic culture, justice loses authority and potency. There is no longer a consensus on what is "right" or "true." Where this objective standard is absent, justice becomes an illusive quality without any defining limits. *Justice* has largely lost any real objective meaning and simply becomes a political slogan. The radical Marxist speaks of "revolutionary" justice while killing his opponents; the political activist might speak of "radical" justice or "gender" justice. Justice means only their personal view. We are left with a jurisprudence much like the biblical condemnation that "everyone did what was right in his own eyes" (Judg 21:25 NKJV). Compare this with Proverbs, where the discovery of what is "right and just and fair" begins "with the fear of the LORD" (Prov 1:3-7).

Justice as Mere Process and Skill. In today's value-confusion, *justice* as the term used in political and social life is almost totally process matters—means, not ends. Justice is due process, hearings, public trials and democratic processes. This leads to justice becoming merely formal or instrumental. When it comes to ends and goals there is only silence or confusion. Parallel to this is a shift in philosophy and culture* to see justice as the work of courts, lawyers and government. It has become a sort of skill or special interest of a segment of the community.*

Most citizens do not see justice as an aspect of their own duty. This shrinking of the vitality of the principle of justice robs it of its social, political and spiritual meaning. Combined with its loss of moral content, it becomes less relevant. Thus the story of the friend of a supreme court justice who, on dropping him off at the court one day, bid him farewell with the advice "Do justice," to which the justice was said to reply, "That is not my job. I do law."

Christians and Justice

Teaching Justice. Christians, inheritors of biblical tradition, must be lovers and do-ers of justice. Yet too often justice has been a rare topic of teaching. Faithfulness to Scripture and to the character of God requires Christians to "let justice roll on like a river."

Rooting Out Structural Injustice. We have sensitive radars that quickly detect personal injustices—disparity in criminal sentencing, unfair enforcement of the law, police brutality. Biblical justice is to be evident in every relationship—for example, fairness in business practices. However, justice involves not just individuals,* but systems* and structures* as well. In Greek thought and in biblical traditions justice was not only an attribute of individual relations, but also a governing principle for society as a whole. Biblical thought compels the recognition that whole institutions and nations may embody evil and act unjustly. Indeed, often institutionalized injustice is the most difficult to root out because it is intractably settled into, and hidden within, the culture.* Institutions such as slavery were long defended by people who were personally committed to justice but failed to see the structural injustice involved.

American evangelical Christianity has often ignored social and public justice. We have forgotten not only the biblical heritage, but also that of the Wesleyan revivals where the recovery of vital faith affected the public institutions of society. The antislavery movement is part of that heritage. Today issues of justice demand a prophetic and biblical voice. Areas such as protection of human life, genetic engineering, race relations, economic systems and criminal justice systems ought to call for the clearest Christian thinking.

*Carrying Out Justice as a Calling.** Perhaps the most critical need is to change our concept of justice. Justice doesn't just merely reside in courts and books as we so often think; justice actively works in us when we are faithful to our calling and to our God. The church ought to be a community uniquely recognized for its vital commitment to justice. By so doing we might return the concept to its holy place—before the throne of God.

See also LAWS; SOCIAL ACTION.

References and Resources

J. Dengerink, *The Idea of Justice in Christian Perspective* (Toronto: Wedge, 1978); K. L. Oresti and M. Brouch, "Righteousness, Righteousness of God," in *Dictionary of Paul and His Letters,* ed. G. F. Hawthorne, R. P. Martin and D. G. Reid (Downers Grove, Ill.: InterVarsity Press, 1993) 827-37; N. Snaith, *The Distinctive Ideas of the Old Testament* (New York: Schocken Books, 1964); M. Walzer, *Spheres of Justice: A Defense of Pluralism and Equity* (New York: Basic Books, 1983).

Lynn Buzzard

L

LAITY

George Bernard Shaw once said that every profession* is a conspiracy against the laity. But there is a problem with this cynical remark when it is applied to the church.* It is pointless to launch a conspiracy against something that no longer exists. The New Testament does not reveal two peoples: the professional clergy* (those who are superior, gifted and powerful) and the laity (those who are inferior, untrained and powerless). Rather there is one people: the laity (in Greek *laos*), which includes the leaders. Moreover the leaders, like the led, are first and foremost members of the laity and share the exquisite honor of the people of God (1 Pet 2:9-10). Indeed the cultivation of professionalism by leaders of the church is incongruous with the essentially amateur nature of all Christian ministry.* It is the work of love* (as the root meaning of *amateur* indicates). To recover a biblical perspective on the people of God, we may need to abolish the words *laity* and *clergy*. We may also need to reinvent a way of expressing the dignity and duty of the ordinary Christian. In preparation for this we must first examine the biblical data, then reflect theologically on the identity and vocation of the people of God and finally consider what this all means.

Biblical Data

New Testament authors rejected two disparaging "laity" words available to them when describing the people of God under the newly reconstituted covenant in Christ: *laikos* and *idiōtēs*. The word *laikos* (belonging to the common people) is not used at all in the New Testament. It was first used for Christians by Clement of Rome at the end of the first century to describe the place of laity in worship when the presbyters were being deprived of their functions. The other word, *idiōtēs*, root of the English word *idiot*, means "layperson in contrast to an expert or specialist." This pejorative word is much closer to Bernard Shaw's use of the term *laity*, but it is never used as a self-description by Christians! In Acts 4:13 members of the Jewish Sanhedrin expressed their amazement that these "unschooled, ordinary men" (in this case the *idiōtai* were Peter and John) could preach with eloquent power. The word is also used in 1 Corinthians 14:23 to describe the outsider who wanders into a Christian meeting and cannot understand what is going on.

Instead of *laikos* and *idiōtēs* New Testament writers use two other words. The Greek word *laos* originally meant "the people or the crowd." It was eventually employed in the Greek translation of the Old Testament (LXX) as the universal designation for "the people of God" translating the Hebrew *am*. This word may be properly translated "laity," but to do so we would need to reinterpret its meaning. It does not mean "untrained" or "ordinary"; rather it means "the people of God" (Acts 15:14; Rom 9:25; 1 Pet 2:9)—a truly extraordinary people—and includes rather than excludes those who were priests. While in the church today we have two classes of people separated by education,* ordination and intonation—the laity (who receive the ministry) and the clergy (who give the ministry)—in the New Testament there is only one ministering people with leaders, also members of the *laos,* serving them to equip* the people for the work of the ministry (Eph 4:11-12).

Remarkably, the second word used to describe the whole people of God is the Greek word *klēros,* the word from which our English *clergy* is derived. The word means "assigned by lot or inheritance" and is used for the privileges and appointment of all the people of God (Gal 3:29; Eph 1:11; Col 1:12). With the exception of Ignatius of Antioch (who used *klēros* to describe the martyr), the term was not used for "clergy" until the third century. It is only at that time that the term *laity* reappears. As Alexandre Faivre shows, laypersons can exist only when they have an opposite against which they can define themselves, and until the second century there simply was no such opposite (p. 23)!

The church in the New Testament has no laypeople in the usual sense of that word and is full of clergy in the true sense of that word. A biblical theology of the laity must communicate this.

A People Without Laity or Clergy

When we step into the church of the New Testament, we meet a single people (*laos*) marked by universal Spirit-giftedness, priesthood, empowerment, calling and ministry. The church as a whole is the true ministerium, a community of prophets, teachers, priests and princes/princesses serving God through Jesus in the power of the Spirit seven days a week.

All are clergy in the sense of being appointed by God to service* and dignified as God's inheritance. All are laity in the sense of having their identity rooted in the people of God. All exercise ministry. All receive ministry. That is the constitution of the church.

But when we step into the modern church, we see something quite different. Deeply ingrained there is the belief that the full-time ministry is the highest human vocation. From the perspective of the New Testament, however, a part-time option has never been available! It is only when a person feels he or she is not able to go into the ministry that the second-best alternative is to spend discretionary time in church-related activities. Instead of the pastor's becoming an assistant to the people for their ministry in the church and world, equipping thus gets reduced to making paraclergy out of the rest of the members of the church in order to assist the minister.

Not surprisingly, few businesspeople think of themselves as full-time ministers in the marketplace. Fewer still are encouraged in this by their churches. Hardly anyone gets commissioned to service in the world. Christians in the first century would have found such a state of affairs anachronistic—a throwback to the situation before Christ came when only a few in Israel knew the Lord, when only one tribe was named as priests and when only a select few heard the call of God on their lives. Nothing but a Copernican revolution of the mind and heart can change this heretical state of affairs.

Toward a Trinitarian Theology of the Laity

To accomplish this transformation, a theology *of* the laity that is also a theology *by* the laity must be written, articulated and embodied. But this theology must not merely explore the identity and vocation of the nonclergy portion of the people. This would be a compensatory theology attempting to overcome seventeen centuries of clericalism. Reactionary theology is neither life-giving nor peaceable, and it is the recovery of the unity of God's people that is at stake. The apostle Paul was faced in his own day with something roughly parallel to clericalism, namely, performance of the law as a means of gaining righteousness and defining membership. Paul's approach to the problem gives us an important clue. He went behind discussions of the law to rediscover something that preceded the law and gave it meaning—namely, the promise (Gal 3:15-18). In a biblical theology of the laity we must get behind the clergy-lay problem that has plagued the church since the third century and find out what God originally intended for his people. To do this we must explore, first, what kind of God we are encountering and, second, what it means to be a people like God.

A fully trinitarian approach is needed, since the identity and ministry of the *laos* are shaped by the God whose people we are. God has called out "a *laos* for himself" (Acts 15:14) or as the King James Version puts it, "a people for his name." If the identity of the *laos* comes from the Trinity, the vocation of the *laos* also comes from the triune God. In this way both the being and the doing, both the identity and the vocation, of the *laos* will be considered.

Trinitarian Ministry

The ministry of the *laos* is not generated exclusively by the people, whether from duty or gratitude. All ministry is God's ministry. God's ministry continues through his people. This ministry begins not when we join the church to help do God's work but when we join God (Jn 1:12) and have "fellowship . . . with the Father and with his Son" (1 Jn 1:3). *Laos* ministry is participation in the ingoing ministry of God (Father, Son and Spirit) and simultaneously participation in the outgoing (sending) ministry of God. "As you sent me into the world," said Jesus, "I have sent them into the world" (Jn 17:18). On the first (the ingoing), God is "lover, the beloved and the love itself," as Jürgen Moltmann puts it (p. 32). On the second, God is sender, sent and the sending.

So there were ministry and mission* within God before there was a world taking place (Jn 17:5, 24). This precreation ministry was neither curative nor redemptive. There was nothing broken or fallen to restore, even though "the Lamb . . . slain from the creation of the world" (Rev 13:8) is an evocative hint of God's redemptive willingness. God's ministry is creative and unitive (Rev 17:21-23) as well as curative and redemptive; thus, we find a broader definition of service than is normally ascribed to the term *ministry*. The same is true of the ministry of the people of God—thus challenging the common evangelical preoccupation with the Great Commission (Mt 28:19-20) as the exclusive definition of ministry, as important as that mandate is.

Trinitarian Peoplehood

To this rich understanding of peoplehood and ministry each of the three persons of the Godhead contributes. The Father creates, providentially sustains and forms a covenantal framework for all existence. The Son incarnates, transfigures and redeems. The Spirit empowers and fills with God's own presence. But each shares—coinheres interpenetrates, cooperates—in the others so that it is theologically inappropriate to stereotype the ministry of any one. But that is exactly what happens.

Christians tend to "play favorites" when it comes to describing peoplehood and ministry. For order, providence and sustaining the structures of society we appeal to the Father. The Son is associated with redemption and winning the lost. The Holy Spirit is the focus of those seeking renewal, empowering charisms and direct religious experience. Churches and denominations* tend to form around one of the three: Father denominations emphasize reverent worship* and stewardship.* Son denominations stress discipleship* and evangelism,* thus furthering the work of the kingdom of God. Spirit denominations promote spiritual gifts* and graces. The implications of this specialist approach for peoplehood, vocation and church leadership* can be expressed in the following table:

	PEOPLE-HOOD	VOCATION	LEADER-SHIP
FATHER	Covenant community	Creational stewardship	Hierarchical
SON	Kingdom community	Christocratic service	Servant
SPIRIT	Charismatic community	Exercising gifts; empowerment	Charismatic

A rich and full doctrine of the Trinity avoids such stereotyping. God is more than the sum of the Three. God is not God apart from the way the Father, Son and Holy Spirit give and receive from each other what they essentially are. "One God"—the primary confession of Islam—is ironically the Christian's deepest praise. We affirm that God is more One because God is Three. The *laos* too does not have a "mashed potato" unity, as is sometimes alleged, but a rich social unity in which each member becomes more himself or herself through experiencing an out-of-oneself *(ek-static)* community life. Unity is not the means to the end—a practical necessity to get the church's work done. Unity is the end, the goal, the ministry itself (Jn 17:22; Eph 1:10; 4:13). To be *laos* then is not merely to be a bouquet of Christians or a cluster of saints. To be *laos* means to be simultaneously communal and personal. In the long history of trinitarian reflection, this supreme idea of the personal and interpersonal within God forms the true basis for the identity and vocation of the God-imaging people.

Implications for Laypeople

The implications of this for peoplehood are substantial. Being *laos* means that members of Christ coinhere, interanimate and pour life into one another without coalescence or merger. The Greek church fathers spoke of this as *perichōrēsis*, mutual indwelling within God as a model for mutuality in the people of God. It means belonging communally without being communistic or being a collective. Moreover, and pertinent to the clergy-lay dilemma, being a perichoretic people means being a community without hierarchy. The community of Father, Son and Spirit finds its earthly reflection "not in the autocracy of a single ruler but in the democratic community of free people, not in the lordship of man over the woman but in their equal mutuality, not in an ecclesiastical hierarchy but in a fellowship church" (Moltmann, p. viii). Such a community can have leadership and diversity without hierarchy; it can be a community without superiors and subordinates; it can be a church without laity or clergy—in the usual sense of these terms. Three conclusions may be drawn from this.

First, there is no such thing as an individual layperson. If, as I have proposed above, we live out the Christian life interdependently, the individual Christian is an oxymoron. Consistent with the Old Testament, the saints in Paul's letters are really a unit. The saints are the church, which is the body of Christ. Believers are held together in what can be conceived as a corporate, inclusive personality. It is biblically inconceivable for a person to be a believer in Christ and not be a member of this community. John Wesley once observed that the Bible knows nothing of solitary religion. The believer's identity is corporate as well as individual. In Christ we can say, "I am us!" Whereas the basic unit of the church is the individual member, for Paul the basic uniqueness of the individual arises from his or her membership in the church.

Second, there is no hierarchy of ministries. In his seminal work on the theology of the laity Hendrik Kraemer says, "All members of the *ecclesia* have in principle the same calling, responsibility and dignity, have their part in the apostolic and ministerial nature and calling of the church" (p. 160). Incarnating our loving submission to Christ's lordship in every arena of life precludes saying that certain tasks are in themselves holy and others are sacred. *Laos* theology is concerned not only about the work of the ministry but also about the ministry of work. William Tyndale, the English Reformer, was considered heretical and executed for teaching, among other things, that "there is no work better than another to please God; to pour water, to wash dishes, to be a souter [cobbler], or an apostle, all are one, as touching the deed, to please God" (p. 98).

Third, supported Christian ministry is not the vocation of vocations but merely one way of responding to the single call that comes to all (Eph 4:1). Most expositions about ministry are magnetically attracted to the supreme place of the ordained professional as the minister-par-excellence. It is small wonder that laypersons aspiring to ministry attempt to become amateur clergypersons or paraclergy. There is some reason for this. Work in the church is strategic because the church is the prototype community* and the outcropping of the kingdom of God, but work in the church is important only in view of what its members will be and do in society. Church leadership* must be evaluated not in terms of its priestly character but by whether the saints are equipped for the work of the ministry seven days a week (Eph 4:11-12).

The Recovery of the Amateur Vocation
Meditating on the triune God takes us inevitably to the profound revelation of John 17. In that chapter Christ reflects on the love the Father had for him even before the creation of the world (Jn 17:24) and prays that the Father's love may be in the disciples (17:26) while disciples and Master, disciple and disciple, and Son and Father all mutually indwell one another (17:22-23, 26). This gives new and deeper meaning to the well-worn text "God is love" (1 Jn 4:16). Love is not merely an attribute of God, but love is who God is and what God does. That is what Moltmann meant when he reflected on a line by Augustine that God is "lover, the beloved and the love itself" (p. 58). This was also expressed by the trinitarian theologian John Duns Scotus (c. 1265-1308) when he affirmed that creation and redemption flow out of the love that is within God. The world was made by love, runs on love and will end with a glorious eternal love-in. In the same way love is the being and the doing of the *laos*.

The laity does not get its ministry from doing good works on earth to please God but from participating in the love life of God the lover, beloved and love. In the same way the laity gets its mission by participating in the mission of God. The Father sent the Son; the Son sends the *laos* "as the Father has sent me"

(Jn 20:21; compare 17:18). Lay mission derives from the outgoing serving heart of God, who is missionary, missionized and mission all at once. To be true to our dignity, duty and destiny as the people of God, we do not "do" ministry or "have" a mission. We are ministry and are mission insofar as we truly are the people of God.

"Only a layperson" is a phrase that must never be found on our lips. It is irreverent and demeaning. It denies that God has adopted, called, empowered and gifted us to receive the incredible privilege of being colovers of God, lovers of one another and those who share God's love for the world. This is our identity—a molecular social identity. The duke of Windsor, recalling his upbringing in the royal house of King George V, claimed that every day his father would say, "Never forget who you are." Better yet is never to forget whose we are. We are not *laikoi* or *idiōtēs*. We are *laos* and *klēros*. Laity in the popular sense no longer exists in Christ. It is useless to mount a conspiracy against it by promoting professionalism in ministry. It is equally ludicrous to liberate such a laity. Why try to liberate what is no longer alive? That people—segmented into higher and lower, subject and object of ministry, ministers and "their" people—no longer exists except as a tragic anachronism. Instead, there is the *laos* of the triune God. We get our identity and our vocation from being the people of the triune God. And the ministry of that people is to love and be loved. It is so sublimely simple that we could miss its reverent beauty and its life-giving potential.

See also CLERGY; EQUIPPING; MINISTRY.

References and Resources
E. Best, *One Body in Christ: A Study in the Relationship of the Church to Christ in the Epistles of the Apostle Paul* (London: SPCK, 1955); A. Faivre, *The Emergence of the Laity in the Early Church* (New York: Paulist, 1990); C. Gunton, *The One, the Three and the Many: God, Creation and the Culture of Modernity* (Cambridge: Cambridge University Press, 1993); J. Houston, "Trinity and the Christian Life," lecture at Regent College, Vancouver, B.C., 1994; E. Hui, "Trinity and Creation," lecture at Regent College, Vancouver, B.C., 1994; H. Kraemer, *A Theology of the Laity* (Philadelphia: Westminster, 1958); J. Moltmann, *The Trinity and the Kingdom*, trans. M. Kohl (San Francisco: Harper & Row, 1991); G. Ogden, *The New Reformation: Returning the Ministry to the People of God* (Grand Rapids: Zondervan, 1990); R. P. Stevens, *Liberating the Laity* (Downers Grove, Ill.: InterVarsity Press, 1985); W. Tyndale, "A Parable of the Wicked Mammon" (1527), in *Doctrinal Treatises and Introductions to Different Portions of the Holy Scriptures by W. Tyndale*, ed. H. Walker (Cambridge: Parker Society/Cambridge University Press, 1848).

R. Paul Stevens

LAUGHTER

Laughter is a convulsive physiological response to psychological stimuli, such as humorous material, or physical stimuli, such as tickling. The sudden release of tension during laughter causes a decrease in skeletal muscle tone, literally rendering the body "weak with laughter." The diaphragm contracts and relaxes rapidly, often leading to hiccups or coughing. Some people double over and shake uncontrollably as though they were having seizures ("a fit of laughter").

The Best Medicine?
Laughter has long been propounded as medicine—even in the Bible: "A cheerful heart is good medicine, but a crushed spirit dries up the bones" (Prov 17:22). A hearty laugh is a form of "internal jogging" that exercises the lungs and stimulates the circulatory system. Physicians have noted that laughter acts as an anesthetic by distracting the patient's attention from pain—by reducing tension, by changing the patient's expectations and by increasing the patient's production of

endorphins, which are natural painkillers (Peter and Dana, pp. 7-9). Psychologists note that clowns and their regressive form of humor* can coax people out of a state of withdrawal (Moody, pp. 27, 111-15).

Kinds of Laughter

What makes us laugh? Comedian John Cleese (Monty Python, *Fawlty Towers*) claims that laughter is a socially sanctioned way to express disapproval, especially of egotism. In the Bible there are many references to scornful laughter, usually directed at one's enemies: "[Jesus] said, 'Go away. The girl is not dead but asleep.' But they laughed at him" (Mt 9:24). Such laughter does not stem from joy but from pride. The psalmist, in his limited understanding of the divine nature, ascribes to God human characteristics, making God appear callous: "The wicked plot against the righteous . . . but the Lord laughs at the wicked, for he knows their day is coming" (Ps 37:12-13). Nevertheless, God, being omnipotent, will have "the last laugh."

There is a lot of laughter on television,* some of it phony, like the laugh tracks added to a sitcom. Because we do not know where to find true joy, this empty laughter symbolizes our culture's pursuit of happiness through superficial means. We laugh because everyone else is laughing or because we are drinking alcohol, which removes our inhibitions, or because the material is so embarrassing we do not know what else to do. Taken out of the context of a relationship with God, "laughter is foolish," as the teacher in Ecclesiastes points out (2:2). Laughter provides only a temporary relief from our troubles and is not a reliable anesthetic: "Even in laughter the heart may ache, and joy may end in grief" (Prov 14:13). Eugene Peterson points out that we cannot make ourselves happy—only God can: "Joy is not a re-

quirement of Christian discipleship, it is a consequence" (Peterson, p. 92).

The purest laughter comes from the purest joy, which only God can provide: "Laughter is the delight that things are working together for good to them that love God" (Peterson, p. 96). Take, for example, the birth* of Isaac to Abraham and Sarah (Gen 18—21). Initially Sarah laughs sardonically at God and his promise to send her a son in her old age. Then, when God fulfills his promise, Abraham names their son Isaac (meaning "he laughs"), and Sarah laughs joyfully with God, saying, "God has brought me laughter, and everyone who hears about this will laugh with me" (Gen 21:6).

Laughter and Tears

We might think that laughing and crying are opposites, but they are very closely connected because they both help release tension. Furthermore, one can lead to another, as when we belly laugh so hard that our eyes water or when tears of frustration and anger turn to chuckles when we realize how silly we are acting. For Christians and non-Christians alike, laughter is inevitably balanced with tears. As the Teacher notes, there is "a time to weep and a time to laugh" (Eccles 3:4). The difference for Christians is that laughter ultimately triumphs: "One of the most interesting and remarkable things that Christians learn is that laughter does not exclude weeping. Christian joy is not an escape from sorrow. Pain and hardship still come, but they are unable to drive out the happiness of the redeemed" (Peterson, p. 96).

The Laughter of Children

Parents eagerly anticipate their baby's first smiles and chuckles, which are major milestones in early childhood development. Such behavior reassures the parents that their child is fully human. Laughter comes easily to children—note that parents must teach their children when *not* to laugh. When Jesus calls us to be childlike (Mt 18:1-10; 19:13-15), he is commanding us not only to be innocent, teachable and loving but to express our joy by laughing easily. But he is also asking us to laugh as children do, without ceasing to be serious. As J. I. Packer puts it, "Unsmiling seriousness is really no virtue" (p. 15).

Jesus Laughed

Jesus loved children; therefore, he must have loved to hear them laugh. Jesus himself had a wry sense of humor and must have made his followers laugh often. Since Jesus was divine, he would have the capacity to be infinitely happy, but his temporary humanity would mask the depth of his joy. Being sinless, Jesus could not laugh at his own defects, nor could he, being all-merciful, poke fun at the physical shortcomings of others. But Jesus had a well-developed sense of wit, irony and hyperbole that he readily used to criticize bad behavior, such as greed and pride.

Laughter as a Glimpse of Heaven

The joy experienced by those who walk with the Lord has both a past and a future (Peterson, p. 93). The past is the history of God's great miracles. The future is the anticipation that God will continue to perform miracles and the promise that in heaven we will experience pure joy. The psalmist writes, "Those who sow in tears will reap with songs of joy" (Ps 126:5). Luke quotes Jesus promising, "Blessed are you who weep now, for you will laugh" (Lk 6:21). That sense of freedom and release that we feel when we have a really good knee-slapping laugh is just a glimpse of the joy we will experience in heaven.

See also HUMOR; PLEASURE.

References and Resources

C. Hyers, *And God Created Laughter: The Bible as*

Divine Comedy (Atlanta: John Knox, 1987); R. A. Moody Jr., *Laugh After Laugh: The Healing Power of Humor* (Jacksonville, Fla.: Headwaters Press, 1978); J. I. Packer, "Humor Is a Funny Thing," *Christianity Today,* 22 October 1990, 15; L. J. Peter and B. Dana, *The Laughter Prescription* (New York: Ballantine, 1982); E. Peterson, *A Long Obedience in the Same Direction* (Downers Grove, Ill.: InterVarsity Press, 1980); C. Samra, *The Joyful Christ: The Healing Power of Humor* (San Francisco: Harper & Row, 1985); B. Sanders, *Sudden Glory: Laughter as Subversive History* (Boston: Beacon, 1995).

Kathryn E. Lockhart

LAW

"There oughta be a law." "Here comes the law." "We are saved by grace and not by law." These common phrases reflect the enormous variety of the uses of the term *law,* which indeed means many things.

For a student of the Old Testament, *law* may mean the Torah, the five books of the Law, which are the formative body of Scripture to which the Jew looks for the essence of their faith history. For the New Testament scholar studying Paul, *law* refers to the whole body of the righteous demands of God—a righteousness that we cannot possibly fulfill and, therefore, cannot be the basis for our salvation. We are saved, not by law, but by the unmerited favor of God—his grace. For the legislator, *law* means the established and acknowledged rules that create rights* and impose duties in society. For the political scientist, the *law* may mean a way of government, as, for example, in "a rule of law, and not of men." *Law* reflects a commitment to established, open processes of governance, rather than the caprice or partiality of chance or privilege. For the philosopher, *law* may even mean those principles that are natural or inherent—natural law— which binds all persons everywhere, as, for example, the view that animated the Declaration of Independence that there are certain "inalienable rights" because we were "endowed by a Creator" with them. For the citizen, the *law* may simply mean the police, as in the "strong arm of the law" or "Have you called the law?"

While all these usages are common in daily language, *law* more properly and historically refers to those rules, obligations and duties that bind us in some manner and are expressions of some authority. The elements are rule, authority and obligation.

What Is Law?

While philosophic debates about the nature and sources of law may seem to have little relevance, the debate today about law is quite critical. Historically, Western law was built on some fundamental assumptions. These assumptions included the core concept that while human law was a product of kings, courts or legislatures, nevertheless, there was a "higher law" to which human law was accountable and should reflect. Thus, human law was subservient to God's law, which could be discerned through nature and revelation. Many theologians and jurists insisted that any human law that was contrary to this higher law, or divine law, was not really law at all. For them, the very term *law* was reserved for laws not inconsistent with God's laws.

Religion and Law: Historic Partners Now Estranged

This basic philosophy of law and a higher law shaped much of the English common law and the early American legal experience. William Blackstone, the famous English lawyer who so influenced American law, represented this tradition, and his writings embedded it deeply in American legal thought. As correlates of that view of law, other principles emerged: that law was a rational, orderly process; that it invited obedience because it was "right"; that it reflected moral truth.

This natural-law jurisprudence is a reflection of a much longer relationship between law and religion. The earliest origins of law were all closely intertwined with religion itself, as is evident in the Old Testament law. In primitive cultures the law was seen as an expression of the gods. Human beings did not "make" law; they "discovered" it. In medieval and Reformation Europe, law and religion were not estranged as they are today but were intimately related. Theologians studied law, and lawyers theology. Law and theology were almost twins—both concerned with matters of duty and authority. They were the pillars of culture* and order. Today, with the "crisis of authority" (as Hannah Arendt has characterized our age) our culture faces, both culture and order seem at times in disarray—neither capturing the imagination or allegiance of much of the public.

Shifting Theories and the Rise of Positivism

The natural-law theory dominated America for generations of lawyers, legislators and theorists. Today this has largely been replaced with a view of law that does not regard it as a principled, much less divine, process. Reflecting the larger skepticism and positivism of the intellectual trends, this view sees God as either nonexistent or irrelevant to human processes. The law is viewed simply as a social process—the product of competing social interests and goals. Some, reflecting Marxist notions, see law as a reflection of economics. In perhaps what is the dominant school of thought, law is in fact nothing but an expression of power. That law is "whoever has the guns" suggests this view.

Oliver Wendell Holmes, an American jurist, reflected this shift away from ultimate sources of law to an exclusive humanistic endeavor when he insisted that "law is not a brooding omnipresence in the sky." For him law was basically just experience. Roscoe Pound, another legal scholar, hailed this new jurisprudence as a victory for pragmatism with the "human factor" now in its proper central place.

The most recent fashionable legal-philosophic trend is often referred to as *deconstructionist*. Its core roots again reject any ultimate validity to law. For the deconstructionist, law is simply a sociopolitical process, and we need to take away its transcendent mask. By getting behind the law, we can see, for example, that it is all about racism* or sexism, or—you fill in the blank.

Losing the Reference Point

The rejection of law's roots in any higher law has substantial implications. As Jacques Ellul noted in his *Theological Foundation of Law*, when law loses its connection with any ultimate principles, it becomes simply a social or political tool or, even worse, simply a means of exercising state power. Rather than a check on the power of the state, it becomes the principal vehicle of expansive state authority. Law as mere power knows no principled limits.

Modern critics of this positivism have warned of the consequences of such a view. When stripped of its ultimate reference point is justice not left to the whims and vagaries of human will? Gustav Radbruch, a modern critic, suggested that Nazi Germany was simply legal positivism running its natural course. Emil Brunner, the theologian, said, "The totalitarian state is solely legal positivism in political practice" (p. 15).

Indeed, modern American law reflects many of these philosophic changes. The radical shifts in the law in regard to homosexuality* and abortion* illustrate this. Whereas once lawmakers might have sought historic moral principles as guides for law, and judges not uncommonly looked to history and even the Bible for guidance on interpreting and applying it, now the question is simply, What do those now in charge think? References to spiritual authority or some conception of God's law would find only contempt today.

It is no wonder that this philosophy has led to a loss of respect for law, growing lawlessness and a dissonance between what the law may say and what moral and religious commitments may demand. This may account for the fact that while law is a growth industry—more laws and more lawyers than ever—we are in fact probably less lawful than ever. As one writer has suggested, "A nation's lawfulness is inversely proportional to the number of its laws." When people have lost their basic moorings that result in lawful, right conduct, then the state tends to adopt more and more laws to regulate life and tell people what to do. As another noted, when a nation loses its respect for law, it does not get anarchy; it gets little laws.

For all these reasons many have suggested there is a crisis in law today. Harold Berman, who has watched this develop over his years as a professor at Harvard and then at Emory, has written of the "massive loss of confidence" in law and declared, "The historical soil of the western legal tradition is being washed away."

Alexis de Tocqueville once suggested that if there were an American aristocracy, it "occupies the judicial bench and bar." The observation does reflect America's almost preoccupation with law. The "rule of law" has been our pride, and we have successfully exported it. Even where it is honored in the breach, nations feel obliged to at least pretend they operate under law. This is why the modern collapse of principled law is such a threat.

The tragedy of the loss of an essentially moral tone to law is compounded by the fact that the great affirmations of law seem inevitably moral in character. Even Holmes said the law was "the witness and external deposit of our moral life." Talk of human rights, equal protection and due process invites us to think we are talking, not just about statutes, but about something more fundamental, inherent—the essence of our humanity and common life. But where do these principles come from?

Christian Engagement with Law

For most of American history, Christians had little to do with the law. The legal profession was often not seen as a worthy calling,* and serious believers shunned legal matters. The avoidance of law and politics more generally reflected, most believe, a confused theology that saw Christian faith as exclusively a private matter with little relevance for public affairs or government. The rural character of much of American evangelicalism and a revivalist and pietist tradition reinforced this separation of faith from engagement with law.

More recently, recovering a theology that emphasized not only personal salvation but the lordship of Christ over all of life and disturbed at the moral crisis of the nation* and the direction of law, many Christians have reengaged with the law. The Christian Legal Society (CLS) took the lead in seeking to equip Christian students to see law as a calling in which they could live consistently with their Christian faith. CLS and other groups have taken a more proactive engagement with court cases affecting religious liberties and moral issues. Other groups encouraged Christians to become involved in local, state and national office and reclaim their heritage.

Today the law and especially Christians as they engage the law face a wide range of complex issues, many of which have no simple answers but all of which demand the most careful examination. Among the urgent ones faced today are the following.

Law and morality. What is the relationship between law and morality? This is a perennial problem, difficult but unavoidable. It is far too simplistic to say, You can't legislate morality. The law constantly legislates morality—it presumably requires equal protection, not on a whim, but because it believes it is right. It proscribes theft because it believes it is wrong. Moral rules and principles are built into the fabric of a society, and this fabric produces and is sustained by law. But what are the limits? The modern sexual revolution, abortion debates, the emerging technology* of genetic engineering (*see* Conception), all require us to carefully consider the relationship of law to moral principles and the maintenance of cultural values. There are undoubtedly areas in which legislating moral conduct would be ineffective, too costly for freedom* or destructive of the value of the conduct itself. On the other hand, the notion that moral truth is irrelevant in shaping the law is a cultural disaster. We need to maximize the principled debates about law, not minimize them.

Law and freedom. Another perennial issue is the balance between freedom and law. The recent American experience is a confusing mix of massively expanding law in some spheres and the abandonment of law in others. Never have we had such economic or environmental or civil rights legislation, but laws relating to other moral issues—for example, abortion, homosexuality, indecency, pornography—all seem to have shrunk under a wave of individualism.* Is there a principled basis for these contrasting approaches? What does a Christian understanding of human nature suggest in this regard? How does Paul's emphasis on the law as a restrainer of evil help?

Can a culture survive without normative content, and how does law relate to that?

Civil disobedience. Civil disobedience* is as American as apple pie. American history from the Revolution to antislavery, civil rights and antiwar efforts has produced a legion of civil disobedients, many of whom grounded their disobedience on a higher law. From Moses, through Daniel and into the New Testament, there has always been a biblical affirmation, "We must obey God rather than men." The principle that God must be honored when there is a clear clash between duties to government and duties to God has been consistently recognized in biblical and theological writings and set forth as a guiding principle by classic thinkers such as Augustine and Aquinas. But more than philosophy, the principle has been the practice of believers throughout history. Foxe's *Book of Martyrs* was, for an earlier generation, a witness to this principle. In modern times the church in the Soviet Union, China and other places of oppression has had to live out this principle—often painfully.

As our law becomes more secular, as there is increasing hostility to Christian values* and norms of conduct, as the state becomes more intrusive in the internal affairs of churches and families, law avoidance and disobedience are options that may arise with increased frequency, even as they do today for believers in other parts of the world. How do we balance the biblical teachings of submission to authority? What are the limits of our duty to law or to government? When may we, and when must we, as faithful Christians say no to government?

Conclusion

The theologian Markus Barth wrote glowingly, "The law remains one of the greatest and richest gifts of God. It is

incomparable. It is a holy, righteous and good thing." In contrast, Mr. Bumble in Dickens's *Oliver Twist* declared, "The law is an ass—an idiot." The law is probably both of these things. The task of citizen and believer is to discern where the law today reflects the values that nurture life and where the law, as an aspect of fallen human nature, no longer serves life but reflects the corruption of evil. Certainly in a democratic state with substantial freedoms of expression, the challenge to believers is to call for a law that has an ultimate source of authority. As one writer urged, "Let there be a new day, a day when law will receive a gift of a soul."

See also CIVIL DISOBEDIENCE; INDIVIDUAL; JUSTICE; LAW ENFORCEMENT; SOCIAL ACTION.

References and Resources
J. Allegretti, *The Lawyer's Calling: Christian Faith and Legal Practice* (New York: Paulist, 1996); H. J. Berman, *The Interaction of Law and Religion* (Nashville: Abingdon, 1974); Emil Brunner, *Justice and the Social Order* (New York: Harper & Row, 1945); Jacques Ellul, *The Theological Foundation of Law* (New York: Seabury, 1969).

Lynn Buzzard

LAW ENFORCEMENT

In an article some years ago, a police officer posed the following problem: If Christians are to love their fellows, suffer on their behalf, submit to the assaults of evil, pray without ceasing and set their minds on higher things, then how can one be a police officer and serve God, and how can one see police work as Christian service? There is, the author concluded, a deep moral ambiguity in policing that needs to be recognized, not only by those who engage in it, but also by all of us who rely on it ("In This World," p. 253). Yet even if we grant this troubled conclusion, we are not left to reflect on such paradoxes without assistance. The following discussion seeks to indicate some directions that Christian reflection might take.

Background

Human frailty has made it necessary that our communal life be directed not only by our personal and congregational lights (whether Christian or otherwise) but also through various institutional mechanisms that promulgate rules, regulations and directives. This much seems to be implicit in the concession of kingship (1 Sam 8), the exilic concern for the welfare of Babylon (Jer 29:7) and the Pauline recognition that even secular authorities may be ministers of God's justice for the common good (Rom 13:1-7; 1 Tim 2:1-2). In the awareness of this John Locke, a seventeenth-century writer, argued that humankind has a need for three governmental institutions: a legislature to determine shared rules, a judiciary to interpret and apply them and an executive to give them effect.

It is to the last of these, the executive, that law enforcement belongs. Initially a communal responsibility (Phillips, pp. 17-32; Ascoli, chap. 1), law enforcement has tended to become increasingly professionalized as communities have grown in size and complexity. Nowadays such enforcement generally falls to police, though policing as we know it has been around for less than two hundred years, and the work of law enforcement today is shared among many agencies, both private and public—private security agents, corrections officers, IRS agents, postal inspectors and so on. For simplicity, our focus will be on the police.

Neither the biblical witness nor contemporary reality would limit police work to law enforcement. Indeed, if we look to the larger picture of biblical and contemporary concerns, it is preferable to see in policing a dominant concern with social peacekeeping, that is, the fostering and maintenance of a social environment in which individuals, families and groups can pursue their legitimate goals. For a Christian that will include the preservation of a social order that allows people access to and freedom to express the life of God's kingdom. It does not imply the imposition of Christian values.* In relation to a police officer's conduct of his or her work, there are two or three biblical passages that may have fairly direct relevance to the work of a Christian police officer.

When John the Baptist is asked by soldiers *(strateuomenoi)* what is required of them, he tells them that they must not engage in blackmail or extortion (as characteristic abuses of their authority) and that they should be content with their pay (Lk 3:14). It is not clear whether the lack of satisfaction with their pay is what leads such officers into corruption, though such an understanding helps to explain why that issue was mentioned. What is clear, however, and is still true, is the significant temptation to corruption that is inherent in police work. Note, however, that it is not simply the self-servingness of corruption on which John the Baptist focuses but the abuse of authority that is involved. Such too is the concern of Jesus.

Jesus contrasts the authority of earthly rulers with the authority to which his disciples are to aspire: true greatness is to be found not in lording it over others but rather in service (Mk 10:42-45; Lk 22:25-26). Although police do have an earthly authority to exercise, a Christian officer will be inclined to recognize its conditional and limited character. As the Son of Man came to transform the world via an eschewal of earthly power (Mt 4:1-11; 26:52-54), so too must his servants not seek to change it by means of that power.

Contemporary Issues

Although the biblical material is sparse,

there are several problematic dimensions of contemporary police work on which Christian reflection is appropriate. The three issues considered here involve force, deception and loyalty.*

Use of force. As the film *Witness* amply illustrated, Christian pacifists will be reluctant to countenance even the police use of force. And certainly there is a scriptural aversion to seeking to achieve significant spiritual ends by recourse to force (Mt 26:52-54). Yet the biblical writers do not seem to support a total rejection of all force, at least in the mundane pursuit of social order.

The real problem concerns limits. Although some police officers have felt that what is necessitated by their work cannot be sanctioned by faith ("In This World," pp. 249-53), the more general concern is the need to avoid excess because of the recognition that those with whom one must sometimes deal were created in God's image, have before them the possibility of redemption and must therefore not be denigrated and depersonalized. Any force used must be appropriate and reasonable, guided by the legitimate law enforcement ends that need to be achieved, that is, in the case of police, by the needs of apprehension rather than those of punishment.

Use of deceptive practices. With the decline of the third degree, police have needed to find alternative ways of acquiring evidence necessary to meet the high expectations of the criminal justice system (proof beyond a reasonable doubt). And so there has been an increase in the use of deceptive tactics—from the use of informants and ruses, to wiretapping and bugging. Can such deception be justified?

Once again the problem is one of limits. Truthfulness is an important value, but not the only one. Just as the Hebrew midwives lied to Pharaoh and were blessed for it (Ex 1:15-21), so one may sometimes promote a greater good by engaging in some form of deception. Police, therefore, in order to secure or restore a just order, may sanction the use of deceptive practices. The danger with this is that such practices—just because of the secretiveness involved—will be misused and will avoid the scrutiny to which such deviations from a norm of truthfulness should have. It is no accident that Satan is said to be the source of lies (Jn 8:44; compare Gen 3) and that lying is generally condemned (Prov 12:22; 13:5). But not everyone has an entitlement to full truthfulness (2 Kings 6:12-20). In their investigative and interrogatory practices, police may seek to elicit the truth by means of deception, but such activity will need to be constrained by a recognition that those who are being deceived must not be degraded. Furthermore, deception is not justified at all in the courtroom, for not only is the officer there sworn to tell the truth, but a lack of truthfulness in that context will undermine the integrity of the very forum within which other deceptive practices can be appropriately scrutinized.

Loyalty to fellow officers. Police culture is marked by deep loyalties. This has been one of policing's great strengths, for in the face of perceived danger, it has enabled officers to rise above the limitations of self-interest to serve a collective purpose. Yet much of the criticism that is associated with police work has centered on another facet of that loyalty—the so-called blue wall of silence—that has often served to shield officers from public accountability.* The blue wall, though born of loyalty, is also reinforced by fear and cynicism and ultimately perverts the very value that it seeks to manifest.

At the heart of loyalty lies the need to transcend our private and self-interested pursuits and to risk ourselves for the sake of some greater value, whether it is the good of another or some cause. Jesus' observation that there is no greater love to be shown than that displayed when a person lays down his life for his friends (Jn 15:13) captures the essence of loyal love. Yet, as with other values, loyalty needs to be moderated by integrity. The loyalty of scoundrels is not more to be valued than the honor among thieves. Or, to put it somewhat differently, the loyalty that police officers owe to each other needs to engage with the loyalty that they owe to the community they serve, the loyalty they owe to the ideals that underpin their work and, in the case of Christian officers, the ultimate loyalty they owe to their Lord and his ways.

See also CIVIL DISOBEDIENCE; JUSTICE; LAW; PRINCIPALITIES AND POWERS; STRUCTURES.

References and Resources

D. Ascoli, *The Queen's Peace: The Origins and Development of the Metropolitan Police, 1829-1979* (London: W. Hamilton, 1979); G. Forster, *"To Live Good": The Police and the Community* (Bramcote, Notts, U.K.: Grove Books, 1982); S. Holdaway, "Policing and Consent," *Modern Churchman* 25, no. 3 (1983) 30-39; "In This World: By a Policeman," *Student World* 56, no. 3 (1963) 247-53; J. Kleinig, *The Ethics of Policing* (Cambridge: Cambridge University Press, 1995); E. A. Malloy, *The Ethics of Law Enforcement and Criminal Punishment* (Washington, D.C.: University Press of America, 1982); A. Phillips, *Ancient Israel's Criminal Law: A New Approach to the Decalogue* (New York: Schocken, 1970); T. L. Winright, "The Perpetrator as Person: Theological Reflections on the Just War Tradition and the Use of Force by Police," *Criminal Justice Ethics* 14, no. 2 (1995) 37-56.

John Kleinig

LEADERSHIP

Where have all the leaders gone? Why is it so difficult to recognize displays of leadership today? Are we in a leadership vacuum? Is failed leadership behind the failure of moral and ethical patterns of service?

The answers would seem to be yes if we consider the nature of the criticism that appears in the press and is expressed by frustrated workers and volunteers in very troubled organizations.* The church,* academy and marketplace declare major unresolved conflicts and challenges with their identity and viability to be a result of failed leadership.

Leadership literature has expanded significantly in the last ten years. Books are coming to the bookstores each month attempting to explain this concept and give us instruction on how to lead. Unfortunately, leadership is still not easily understood, and its practice is in short supply.

The basic question is: What is leadership? Do we have an adequate understanding? Is there a Christian view of leadership that could make a difference in these difficult times?

Most of us define leadership as decisive, appropriate and timely action on the part of a person who holds a position of authority. When we say there is no leadership, we usually mean that we feel like nothing is happening to deal with growing problems within our context. We want "strong" leadership to deal with the problems we see or dilemmas we face. Is this common understanding of a leader's role an adequate description of leadership?

The answer to this question is an emphatic no. It is not sufficient even though it holds some truth. Leaders are in short supply in the church, academy and marketplace as a result of misconceptions of leadership and its secularization. A Christian theology of leadership has the most potential to respond to this problem. With a biblical understanding of spirituality, character and community, a Christian approach provides a powerful and effective model for leadership practice and transformation.

A Secular Perspective on Leadership

The standard model for leadership evolves and takes its shape from the predominant worldview.* It places a high value on independence and self-sufficiency. The leader depends on learned skills, experiences and decision-making ability. These are regarded as the key attributes of leadership. The emphasis is on doing—accomplishing tasks, achieving goals—and little attention is given to relationships. When it exists, the relationship can be termed transactional (contractual). The model is focused on the uses of power,* authority and position. With this secular approach leadership skills are focused on management,* "bottom-line" outcomes and quantifiable models. The model has given us the independent "tough-minded" leader and suggests that leadership is essentially a masculine enterprise.

This view of leadership has emphasized a reverse service* model in that "followers" provide service to the person in authority. Service flows up rather than down. An organization exists to facilitate the leader in accomplishing his or her goals. Within this model, relationships between leaders and others are merely a means to the end. There is a low appreciation of community but a strong emphasis on the needs of the organization. Persons are valued to the extent that they add value in reaching organizational goals. An influential model for this type of leadership comes from the military and gives us lines of authority with a very heavy emphasis on competing and winning.

The model also stresses the importance of personality or "persona" over against character. Moral or ethical strategies might be employed to solve problems but are considered secondary.

Vision comes from the leader or the needs of the organization as defined by the leader. The potential of the leader and organization is virtually unlimited, given enough skill and knowledge. There is no room for God or the spiritual dimension. The model does not recognize evil or sin as a part of culture; nor does it see God's active involvement in history and our daily lives.

An Evolving Secular Model

New voices have been heard within the marketplace that are reshaping the accepted view of leadership. A movement is developing around a growing criticism of graduate education,* clarifying distinctions between management* and leadership, the influence of cultural modeling from Japan, the idea of servant leadership, inclusion of women and the introduction of the transformational leadership standard. Character, spirituality, community and relational leadership have found new adherents. The standard model of the marketplace is evolving into an understanding of leadership as an art with a focus on character and the quality of community.*

This model has been developing over the last ten years and is expressed in many recent popular leadership books: *The Web of Inclusion, Leadership Is an Art, Mind of a Manager, Soul of a Leader, Love and Profit: The Art of Caring Leadership, Leading with Soul: An Uncommon Journey of Spirit, The Female Advantage: Women's Ways of Leadership* and *Spirit at Work: Discovering the Spirituality in Leadership*. These writings and the new movement are a response to failed leadership and an attempt to find meaning in work.* While this is reforming the secular model, it still lacks a developed philosophy and a recognition of where these "new" ideas originate.

A Christian Perspective on Leadership

Christian theology contemplates the model of a triune God. From this comes the powerful image of relationships and being in community. Christian leadership is about spirituality, character and community.

The idea of the presence of God's Spirit gives us a very strong notion of our inclusion in and empowerment for the community of God. Spirituality is the center, heart and beginning point for Christian leadership. This spiritual position determines everything, from the character formation of the leader, to the interpretation of the leaders' vision, to the understanding that most issues of leadership can be resolved only at the spiritual (not merely at the moral) level. Developing a Christian theology of leadership accents the centrality of a radical discipleship to Christ.

Character is the conduit for producing Christian service and leadership. We lead out of who we are in Christ. Our relationship with Christ forms and shapes our person. This is a lifelong process and relies on the bumps and bruises of life to make markings that define who we are when no one is watching. We cannot separate our service and leadership from this composite picture of our values,* beliefs and godly nature. Self-insight and a learning and growing disposition ensure a maturing character and a more responsive leadership style. Courage is the character trait that provides a catalysis for Christian leadership. This is a byproduct of our relationship with Christ and a fully explored self.

The Christian leader's obedience to Christ produces service. Both the horizontal and the vertical relationship define and provide direction for leadership through service, close partnership with God and a strong concern for community. We are drawn to God's vision of eternal life, and we know that bringing God's kingdom to life on earth is a primary goal of leadership. This is our highest calling, our driving vision. We also know that the primary focus in this process is making disciples of Christ and bringing them into fellowship with God and God's community. But also central is extending justice and compassion in and through every arena of life and every place where we work. God is a partner in this process and shares with us divine "power" to help us accomplish this goal. The presence of God is actively engaged in this kingdom-making process. Building community might be the most sacred of leadership pursuits, for leaders are attempting to bring their communities into full service to each other and God.

The Christian framework understands sin and the nature of evil. Therefore it is able to define reality and cultural context more clearly. It also takes a very different position when it comes to the notion of self-sufficiency. Dependence on and obedience to God is the highest and best use of a Christian leader's time and energy. The nature of relationships in this model is covenantal and transformational.

A Definition of Christian Leadership

Christian leadership is an art form of worshiping Christ, a teaching and serving process that envisions, influences, shapes and enhances so that both leaders and followers realize God's goals for change within their community. This definition has several important key words and concepts.

☐ *Art form*—not necessarily an exact science, but rather a creative process that comes from the expression of an individual. There is no formula for leadership behavior or personality, as it comes in many sizes and shapes.

☐ *Worship*—the process holds up something higher than itself. Christian leadership from beginning to end is done sacrificially to God.

☐ *Teaching*—the primary process of leadership. Christian leaders are "teachers" and influence by bringing others along in the learning/shaping development process.

☐ *Service*—the vehicle of the leader is the needs of others. Service flows out of obedience to a master, in this case God, who directs our leadership into service to others within our community.

☐ *Envisioning*—we measure our leaders by their ability to interpret God's vision. Without a vision people perish, and this vision is the discovery of God's best for us.

☐ *Shapes and enhances*—leadership is a sculpturing exercise that creates and builds in positive ways.

☐ *Leaders*—leadership is not a solo event. It involves a team, and its goal is empowerment of other leaders.

☐ *Followers*—they are an integral and potent force in the leadership process. We judge leaders by the quality of the community formed in the exercise of leadership.

☐ *God's Goals*—we are obedient to God's call, both individually and corporately. We seek divine direction and wisdom for our community.

☐ *Change*—the end of leadership is metamorphosis within the needs of community. This is a transformation that brings God's kingdom to light and its practice into the world.

☐ *Community*—everything is done within the confines of relationship. Leadership accountability, service and effectiveness are measured within the standards of the community.

The Practice of Christian Leadership
The Christian leader places himself or herself into the hands of God and becomes a living sacrifice to Christ. This is expressed as a call to service. God provides the context, and the community adds the confirmation. From this spiritual relationship, accountability* to God and community is exercised. To be a Christian leader is to be countercultural,

to be about the process of change. The leader is a radical follower of Christ and servant to others who is marked by several key practices.

1. *Serves God faithfully and obediently.* Our attention and focus is on God. We lead out of this spiritual relationship to God as servant and friend. This requires a very special attentiveness to hearing God through Scripture, community and prayer. Our goal is to serve God faithfully.

2. *Discerns God's vision.* Leadership is about vision. The translation of this vision into specific contexts is the role of leadership. God's vision is in tension with current "reality," and leadership is the process of dealing with this dissonance.

3. *Develops the leadership team.* Leadership is about relationships and working together for a common purpose. Solo leadership is not consistent with God, nor is it a particularly effective leadership style. We need to build a team for leadership to become effective. Spouse, family and significant others represent the informal dimensions of this, while staff and selected position holders provide the formal component.

4. *Communicates, prays and teaches.* Leaders need skills to function effectively. The teaching dimension serves as the primary stimulus and tool of leadership. Through it communication flows and prayer becomes an intervening variable. People of prayer are given greater access to God. This produces change, which is the goal of leadership. Effective leaders are communicators that keep the vision alive.

5. *Builds God's community.* The most significant leadership task is to build community. Community is a representation of God's kingdom on earth. It is culture,* purpose, identity and God's love.* We judge effective leadership in terms of the "tone of the body" that they build up rooted in God.

567

6. *Inculcates God's values.* Values (*see* Organizational Values) are a representation of culture (*see* Organizational Culture) and set the context for leadership teaching. Storytelling,* word pictures and modeling are the leader's tools in embedding values in the community.

7. *Disciples and empowers God's people.* In the Christian model, power is dispersed. It is given away to those who would lead and serve. People in community are being prepared to have their gifts used for the vision and purpose of the community.

8. *Stewards God's resources.* Management is important to effective leadership. Planning, budgeting, allocating and controlling are aspects that require attention from leaders. Stewardship* builds discipline and provides a view of resources as being on loan from God.

9. *Shepherds God's people.* Caring for others is the centerpost of leadership service. Knowing those who have been entrusted to us and responding to their needs is a critical leadership issue.

10. *Renews God's organization.* The process of change is about renewal (*see* Organizational Culture and Change). Leaders guide organizations and communities to higher levels through transformation and renewal. Renewal begins with the individual and moves to the edges of the community.

11. *Develops future leaders.* The preparation of leaders for the community is a primary task of leadership. The successful accomplishment of this activity results in effective leadership. This is also leadership development and succession. Emerging leaders ensure the vitality of community and renewal of the organization.

Where have all the leaders gone? They are led to misconceptions about leadership. Most are content with management practices that focus on making things work. Many follow a secular model that does not produce and mentor leaders. While some are attracted to ethical decision-making, spirituality that comes from the power within and principle-centered leadership, unfortunately these strategies fall short. They explore only the fringe of what represents the most powerful potential to deal with failed leadership in our generation. We must rediscover the biblical model of Christian leadership that transforms our character, community and organizations and produces love and service to others.

See also CHURCH LEADERSHIP; MANAGEMENT.

References and Resources

J. Autry, *Love and Profit: The Art of Caring Leadership* (New York: Avon, 1991); W. Bennis and B. Nanus, *Leaders: The Strategies for Taking Charge* (New York: Harper & Row, 1985); L. Bolman and T. Deal, *Leading with Soul: An Uncommon Journey of Spirit* (San Francisco: Jossey-Bass, 1995); J. M. Burns, *Leadership* (New York: Harper & Row, 1978); J. Conger et al., *Spirit at Work: Discovering the Spirituality in Leadership* (San Francisco: Jossey-Bass, 1994); S. Covey, *The Seven Habits of Highly Effective People* (New York: Simon & Schuster, 1989); M. De Pree, *Leadership Is an Art* (New York: Doubleday, 1989); J. Gardner, *On Leadership* (New York, Free Press, 1990); R. Greenleaf, *Servant Leadership* (Mahweh, N.J.: Paulist, 1977); S. Hel-gesen, *The Female Advantage: Women's Ways of Leadership* (New York: Doubleday, 1990); S. Helgesen, *The Web of Inclusion* (New York: Currency, 1995); J. Kouzes and B. Posner, *The Leadership Challenge* (San Francisco: Jossey-Bass, 1987); H. Nouwen, *In the Name of Jesus: Reflections on Christian Leadership* (New York: Crossroad, 1991).

Patrick Lattore

LEADERSHIP, CHURCH

Attitudes toward leadership and the practices of leaders in the church* are rarely informed by theological truth or spiritual perspective. On the one hand, people in the church regard leadership as a necessary evil, something which we must have in order to moderate the competing self-interests of members who, left to their own devices, would plunge the church into self-destructing chaos. Good leadership keeps bad leadership from emerging! On the other hand, leadership is sometimes invested with a quasi-divine authority, often with a focus on preaching,* administering the sacraments* or exercising charismatic ministry, so that some members feel one must not touch or criticize the Lord's anointed. The pastor is like Moses to the people.

On the first extreme, the Old Testament contains a disturbing allegory (Jotham's parable of the thornbush, Judg 9:7-15) which suggests that leadership is something seized by those who have nothing constructive to give! This negativity about office and leadership roles seems reinforced by two other Old Testament examples: Gideon's rejection of the invitation to be king because he knew the Lord was King of Israel (Judg 8:22-23) and Saul's appointment as the first king, which appears to have been a divine, though ultimately providential, concession to human faithlessness (1 Sam 8:6-9). On the other extreme is Diotrephes, "who loves to be first" (3 Jn 9) in the church, matched by thoughtless believers who idolize and idealize their pastors as mouthpieces for God. Writing in the context of Hitler's rise, Dietrich Bonhoeffer expounded this pathology by noting that when leader becomes Leader, the person in front cannot let people see his face; they can only see from behind. In between these extremes are millions of voluntary and remunerated leaders who serve the church either reluctantly or wholeheartedly, often with little recognition or sense of doing this as a ministry.*

The Ministry of Leadership

Sometimes a leader is defined simply as anyone who obtains followers. But in the church it is different. Church leaders are not merely people who get followers for themselves; they are people who get followers for Jesus. Their service helps people themselves to get directly in touch with the Head of the church. They are not intermediaries, as were the priests, prophets and some of the kings under the Old Testament. Now that Christ has come and the Spirit has been poured out, all the people know the Lord, from the least to the greatest (Jer 31:34). Pastor-teachers and other designated leaders of the church do not run the church. Their job is to teach, administer, manage, shepherd and equip people so that the people grow into maturity, into the measure of the stature of the fullness of Christ (Eph 4:13), so the body of Christ, the church, is built up and people are equipped* for ministry in the church and world.

In a sense all believers are leaders in that they have a sphere of influence in which they can encourage people in a Godward direction and assist in drawing out the spiritual gifts* and service in others. This means that the real task of leaders is to unleash and develop the leader that is in every person. But in a special sense, leaders who influence the whole of the congregation are gifts of God and therefore noted among the gift lists of the New Testament.

Prophets, priests and princes. One common way to approach church leadership is to explore the three major patterns of leadership in the Old Testament: prophets (like Isaiah), priests (like Aaron) and princes (like David). Prophets spoke for God using the typical phrase "Thus says the Lord." They verbalized the obligations of Israel's covenantal relationship with the living God. Priests expressed covenantal life in terms of the holiness of God. They were bridge builders who blessed God on behalf of the world and people and blessed the people and the world on behalf of God. Kings were a visible link between God and the people, expressing the rule of God through a visible monarch, much as Adam and Eve were mandated to be God's visible representatives on earth. Kings were tested by covenant fidelity and would lose their leadership, as Saul did, when they lost their relationship with God.

While these three forms of Old Testament leadership are often viewed as analogies for church leadership, this is a tragic anachronism. Christ has come and embodied completely the ministry of prophet, priest and prince in his own person, so that the newly reconstituted people of God as a whole now enters into Christ's leadership. That is why we may speak truly of the prophethood of all believers (Acts 2:17), the priesthood of all believers (1 Pet 2:5, 9; Rev 1:6) and the royal rule of all believers (1 Pet 2:9; Rev 5:10) as we share the life of Christ's kingdom. These leadership roles are now whole-people or laity* roles. No single priest can represent God to the church. Church leadership will encompass these three offices but empower the whole people of God to exercise them in the church and in the world.

Charismatic and official leadership. There is another Old Testament analogy for which greater continuity in the New Testament can be found. The tension between charismatic leaders, such as the judges and prophets like Amos, and official leaders, such as David and Solomon, yields a fascinating and useful study. Much of church life today is influenced by a lopsided emphasis on either unappointed charismatic leadership or top-down leadership through elders and ordained pastors. Each has its value: charismatic leadership can guarantee the right job for the right person, encourages innovation and inspires confidence, while official leadership can encourage ongoing stable structures, continuity and accountability. Both were needed under the old covenant, an insight Moses expressed when he approved the nonordained charismatic ministry of Eldad and Medad (Num 11:24-30). And both are needed in the church today.

But all too often charismatic leadership is suppressed in the name of stability, and official leadership is snubbed for fear of quenching the Spirit. Tragically, some churches try to institutionalize charismatic leadership by appointing a person with prophetic gifts as senior pastor (an action that is frustrating to both the church and the pastor) or by insisting that all official leaders, such as elders, give evidence of innovative charismatic ministry (which could lead these elders into perpetual frustration with the demands of office). This same tension is apparent in the New Testament, where it appears the Corinthian church so prioritized the charismatic leaders that they rejected even the apostle Paul!

Diversity of leaders and leadership. The rich diversity of leadership words in the New Testament suggests that there are many ways to function as a leader in the body of Christ. In Romans 12:8 the word for leadership is a verb, not a noun, *proistēmi* (the one who goes before); in 1 Corinthians 12:28 leadership is a function, not a position, *kybernēsis* (administrators); in Philippians 1:1 the word for leadership is a term for a minor responsibility, *episkopoi* (overseers; see also Acts 20:28; 1 Tim 3:1); in 1 Timothy 3:8 the word represents a position of lower status, *diakonos* (servant); in Titus 1:5 the word for leadership is a descriptive term, *presbyteroi* (elders, or older, wiser people); and in Ephesians 4:11 the word is a metaphor, not a title, *poimenes* (pastors or shepherds). Obviously some are offices, some are not. But all are ministries. One thing that stands out in all these passages is that leadership is a group or corporate, not a solo or individual, affair.

Contrary to what is sometimes alleged, Scripture does not give us a single biblical pattern of church leadership except what is suggested by the paradoxical term *servant-leader* (Mt 20:25-28; Jn 13:1-17; Eph 5:21). All three major patterns of church government—presbyterian (rule by plural elders), episcopal (rule by bishops) and congregational (rule by the people)—are claimed to be the biblical pattern, but no single model of church order is mandated. There is a theological reason for this: under the old covenant God was the ultimate leader of the people of Israel (which was therefore a true theocracy, with human servant-leaders facilitating God's purposes with his people), and under the new covenant Christ is the head of the church (Eph 1:22-23; 5:23) and its true leader. No human leader in the New Testament is ever called the head of the church. So, not surprisingly, Scripture provides multiple models of leadership for the people of God, each suited to the occasion and context, including elders, presbyters, bishops/overseers, deacons, deaconesses, evangelists, apostles, prophets and pastor-teachers.

Some leaders in the New Testament just emerged; some were nominated by the people (Acts 6:1-7); some were appointed by apostles. The Seven took care of the widows. James led the Jerusalem Council. Many gifted women gave leadership to the churches (see Rom 16). The common factors are appropriateness and spiritual integrity.* The particular form leadership takes is secondary to its theological purpose and practical character. Ironically, the purpose of church leadership is not to lead the church but to equip people to relate to its true Leader. Jesus himself said that we should not allow anyone else to call us "leader" or "master" because we have one leader, Jesus (Mt 23:8-12). This text in Matthew should cause us to be cautious about using leadership language for anyone but Christ, and it should also haunt all of us who aspire to leadership or who are dragged, kicking and screaming against our wills, into leadership posts. The theological purpose of equipping others to relate to Jesus must inform our practice and attitudes.

Toward a Theology of Leadership

A cursed blessing. Leadership is a blessing and gift of God. Humankind was originally mandated by God to give leadership to the rest of the created order as a loving stewardship* in order to take care of creation (Gen 1:28-30; 2:15) in grateful humility before God. This original leadership was perverted by human sin into autonomous and arrogant exploitation of the earth and all human relationships. Even the most delicate and immediate context of human life, the relationship between man and woman, was changed from a side-by-side relationship of companionship (Gen 2:24) to "rule" (Gen 3:16) by the male and "revolt" by the female—for that is what the Hebrew word for "desire" (3:16) actually means. This is not what God intended or wants; it is what God has allowed humankind to bring upon itself to experience the results of sin. By the grace of Christ the curse is substantially reversed in this life, permitting mutual submission (Eph 5:21), which depoliticizes the marriage relationship.

The marriage relationship finds its spiritual counterpart in church leadership. Church leaders do not rule in an ultimate sense, since the church has one head, Christ. When they rule outside of the rule of Christ, they will often incite revolt or pathological compliance. Compliance is a psychological adaptation to pain; it is less painful to go along with the ruler than to speak up or resist. But there is always a sliver of resentment in the compliant person, a sliver that will manifest itself in either depression or revolt—both being spiritually unhealthy. So leadership is a cursed blessing: even with the substantial redemption accomplished by Christ in the here and now, leaders and followers will continue to wrestle with control and compliance. But there is more to leadership than disciplining and compensating for the flesh—what human nature (and the world) has become because of sin.

Natural and supernatural leadership. Leadership is something God gives widely and generously to the human family. The various New Testament words for leadership in the church do not preclude the use of natural leadership gifts or talents.* But Scripture points to an extra element that concerns motive and style. For example, in the gift passage in Romans 12:6-8 the extra element appears in the process of doing something for God: "If it is leadership, let him govern diligently." The extra element is the diligence.

So-called secular management* skills have their place in the church, especially if this extra element is in place. Put differently, leadership in the church is not mere leadership but is something that takes place in God. It is a refraction of the continuing ministry of Jesus through his own people. These ministries may be expressed in offices, but they may also be expressed situationally, even temporarily by people who have not been officially appointed but are informal leaders in the church. They, however, are subject to the ordering and shepherding of the official leaders, just as the official leaders need to be responsible to the prophetic challenge of charismatic leaders.

Official leadership. So what is the distinctive ministry of church leaders? Most important of all is the modeling role. They exemplify Christian character and demonstrate in their handling of people the ways of God. Together the official leadership of the church (here envisioned as a group of elders, a church council or a pastoral team) have three further responsibilities: doctrine, that is, shaping, monitoring and leading in public teaching so that the people of God become mature, not being blown here and there by every wind of doctrine (Eph 4:14); discipline, that is, dealing with difficult pastoral and moral situations as well as discerning gifting and qualifications for leadership, missionary service and public roles; and direction, that is, discerning and communicating the vision of this particular congregation and orchestrating the priorities in terms of finances and human resources to accomplish these priorities.

Strictly speaking, the administration and implementation of doctrine, discipline and direction are management roles, but in local church leadership, particularly in smaller churches, the same people manage as lead. In a larger church the voluntary, part-time leaders must assume a role closer to an advisory one, with remunerated staff doing the implementing. This latter situation has peculiar hazards to pastors if they are relegated to the role of gofers and do not share in the formation of policy or, conversely, if they treat their elders or council as a mere board of reference without empowering laypeople for real leadership. Needless to say, there are many problems associated with church leadership, many of which are not considered directly in the Bible.

Problems of Leadership

One obvious problem occurs when someone is placed in an office or role for which God has not apparently equipped him or her. Sometimes a church outgrows its leadership. Someone who was a fine pastor or elder for a small church* may become incapacitated when the church grows larger. There are many advantages of the small church, not least of which is the fact that more people, comparatively speaking, may enter into the service of leadership, whereas very few people are endowed by God with both the natural and supernatural charisma to lead a megachurch* of five thousand. This is a matter not directly considered by Scripture, though the New Testament assumes the church is a size that facilitates true community and face-to-face relationships.

Leadership style. Another matter not considered in the Bible is leadership style. A pastor with a directive style serving a highly educated congregation accustomed to participating in decision—making is almost certain to run into opposition and may be discharged. A collegial, consultative style may run afoul in a blue-collar church where people want a union boss. Further, cultural factors are at work. In an anti-authority culture, leaders will find themselves without followers and questioned at every turn. In crisis times people will expect too much of leaders and will blame most of the problems on their poor performance.

It is seldom realized that to a large extent a local congregation gets the leadership it deserves. Leaders are for the most part created by followers. As Bonhoeffer once said, the group is the womb of the leader. Since each local church will be, like each individual family, a unique system (Collins and Stevens), leadership exercised in one context may not be transferable to another, a matter which should be considered by both volunteers and remunerated church staff when they change churches. Much frustration experienced by leaders has more to do with failing to discern the context than with lack of gifting in the leader. In the same way, churches that are dissatisfied with their leaders need to ask what kind of leaders they are producing and why.

Leadership power. Power,* however, turns out to be one of the most vexed problems for leaders. Of the many ways of regarding power, the many forms in which power is manifested (information, referral, position, coercion, persuasion, etc.) and the many ways of using power (power brokering, power sharing, overpowering), the most biblical approach is empowering: giving resources, information, opportunity and encouragement to others so they can fulfill God's ministry through them in the church and the world. This is the essence of equipping. Simply stated, the primary purpose of church leaders is not to do the ministry of the church themselves but to empower every individual member and the congregation as a whole to fulfill God's purpose for them in service, mainly in the world. Voluntary and paid church leaders need to be held accountable to this biblical purpose (Eph 4:11-12) and evaluated on the basis not of how well they have performed but how well they have helped others serve!

Questions that arise for leaders in actual service include these: Do I have a need to lead? Am I gaining my identity from a position in the church, or is that based in who I am before God? Does my leadership serve my own interests or those of God's people? Do I have a need to control? Am I too sensitive to criticism and in need of continual approval? Do I love and serve God's people as they are rather than demand they accept what I want to give them? Why do Christian leaders fail morally? Is there dependence or addiction in my or the church's approach to leadership?

For the people there are related questions. Do we have a need *not* to be led? Do we pray for leaders even more than we criticize them? What does our church do to its leaders and why? Do we accept leadership as a gift from God, or do we devalue it? Do we bring the best out of our leaders, equipping them just as they are called of God to equip us? Do we expect leaders to do for us what the Lord intends to do?

The Discipline of Leading

These questions suggest that both leading and following—the absolute necessity for effective church leadership—are spiritual disciplines that direct us to God and invite us to live a life of faith. For leaders this yields important practical applications. The primary qualification for leadership in the church is not the presence of discernible spiritual gifts but *maturity of character*, namely, fidelity in marriage, self-control, being hospitable, not addicted, not a lover of money and not quarrelsome (1 Tim 3:1-7). The cultivation of these qualities in the context of everyday life is the most important theological education for church leadership and is normally neglected by the seminary system. The *standards for leadership* in the New Testament are higher than the standards for membership.* An elder must be "above reproach" (1 Tim 3:2). Leaders have a symbolic role, a modeling function. Therefore moral, relational, financial and sexual sins by members would be dealt with by church discipline* leading to full and immediate restoration, but those same sins by leaders will lead to the loss of leadership, at least for an extended period of time, because the confidence and respect of the people have been violated.

Since no single person in the body of Christ, even a gifted, experienced pastor, fully has the mind of Christ, and since Christ dwells fully not in the individual believer but in the body (Eph 1:23), *plural leadership* is the norm (compare Acts 13:1; 1 Tim 4:14). This leads to more thoughtful and balanced decisions that will be implemented more easily because of the extended process of consultation.

It allows for the mutual ministry of other leaders—discerning, encouraging, exhorting, correcting—and releases the solo leader from an impossible burden. Such plural leadership may take various forms: a staff team, a college of leaders including a mix of voluntary elders and remunerated staff, or a group of lay leaders sharing the leadership role together.

Exercising leadership requires spiritual discernment and often engages one in *spiritual warfare*. William Stringfellow observed that "the most poignant victim of the demonic in America today is the so-called leader" (p. 89). Complex principalities and powers* (Eph 6:12), which though part of God's good creation are manipulable by the evil one, victimize even the best intentions of leaders. Stringfellow observes, "They are left with titles, but without effectual authority; with the trappings of power but without control over the institutions they lead; in nominal command, but bereft of dominion" (p. 88). Church leadership is not exempt from such systemic struggles.

Since the enduring force of leadership in the church comes not from the force of one's personality or the unassailability of one's position but rather from *one's real life in God,* the strength of Christian leadership is humility, that powerful meekness. Servant-leaders in the church are not first of all servants of the people, for this is the path to premature burnout. They are primarily servants of God—seeking God's interests and priorities in the life of the church—and therefore are freed to serve the deepest needs of the people.

Since all church leadership is time-bound and contextual, *continual accountability and discernment* are needed. The ultimate test of maturity in leadership is the willingness not to step up but to step down to make room for others. Speaking to this, an Indian brother advises that we lead from the end, not the front, of the line. P. T. Chandapilla says that "those committed to the vocation of servanthood . . . will remain there to see the line move (the line is determined by the human factor in any situation). They are happy to see others get ahead of them." There is a lot of time for prayer and meditation at the end of the line.

The Discipline of Following

Thus leaders are also followers, followers of Christ, and willing to accept the leadership of others. This turns out to be the harder discipline. Almost all aspire to be leaders; few aspire to be followers. Following involves the recognition that we must operate not as a cluster of independent individuals but as the body of Christ. God has designed the body for interdependence, not codependence or independence. On a deeper level, following requires personal humility and the crucifixion of pride. Too rarely do leaders say, "I am laying all my professional skills, abilities, and economic resources at your disposal. Take them and use them as you see fit." We are too proud to give our lives away to people who are not perfect.

Accepting the leadership ministry of others is also a call to faith. We must entrust both the leaders and the process to God's sovereignty. Leaders will make mistakes. But God is more than able to make all things—even mistakes—work together for good (Rom 8:28). Following also requires discernment. As stated earlier, control and compliance are the structures of pseudoleadership and pseudofollowing. Discerning leaders call forth participation, discussion and even opposition; they are not satisfied with either control or compliance. Better yet is to cultivate decision-making processes that lead to true mutual submission. Discerning followers also can read their own compliant responses, or the controlling tendencies of leaders, name these un-

worthy strategies and insist on a process of mutual submission.

So there is something in the Bible better than a prescription for the ideal leadership structure in the local church. There is a theology and spirituality of leadership that makes the experience of giving and receiving leadership—something we all must do at some level—an incentive for spiritual growth.* In the end, Jesus must have had this in mind when he forbade the disciples to seek leadership positions (Mk 10:35-45) and reminded them that he was their only leader. Only when leadership is for God and focused on helping everyone depend on God, rather than on the pastor or elder, is it safe and productive to be a leader, for then one's identity is first of all to be a follower.

See also AUTHORITY, CHURCH; EQUIPPING; INTEGRITY; MINISTRY; ORGANIZATIONAL CULTURE AND CHANGE; ORGANIZATIONAL VALUES; POWER; VISION.

References and Resources
R. S. Anderson, *Minding God's Business* (Grand Rapids: Eerdmans, 1986); R. Banks, *Paul's Idea of Community* (Grand Rapids: Eerdmans, 1980); D. Bonhoeffer, *No Rusty Swords* (San Francisco: Harper & Row, 1965); P. Collins and R. P. Stevens, *The Equipping Pastor* (Washington, D.C.: Alban Institute, 1994); M. DePree, *Leadership Is an Art* (New York: Doubleday, 1992); E. H. Friedman, *Generation to Generation: Family Process in Church and Synagogue* (New York: Guilford, 1985); R. K. Greenleaf, *Servant Leadership* (New York: Paulist, 1977); E. B. Habecker, *The Other Side of Leadership: Coming to Terms with the Responsibilities That Accompany God-Given Authority* (Wheaton, Ill.: Victor, 1989); T. W. Manson, *Ministry and Priesthood: Christ's and Ours* (London: Epworth Press, 1958); H. Nouwen, *In the Name of Jesus: Reflections on Christian Leadership* (New York: Crossroad, 1993); A. W. Schaef and D. Fassel, *The Addictive Organization* (San Francisco: Harper & Row, 1988); W. Stringfellow, *An Ethic for Christians and Other Aliens in a Strange Land* (Waco, Tex.: Word, 1973).

R. Paul Stevens

LEISURE

Leisure was not a problem to me until I became sixteen. At that age my father confronted me with "the negative spiritual implications" of my serious pursuit of leisure. I had my own photographic darkroom, a stamp collection, a home-built hi-fi system, a record collection of jazz and Bach, and a workroom where I made water skis, boats and wooden furniture. I worked hard at school (my occupation in those days); I also played hard, but I hardly ever did nothing—such as lounging on the sofa or soaking up the sun. "But it's all for number one [meaning me]," complained my father.

Thus began my lifelong fascination with and fear of leisure. This was heightened when I became a Christian. The equation of godliness with religious busyness runs deep in the Christian soul. We have a work ethic* but no equivalent leisure ethic. Work is seen as dignified, meaningful, purposeful, and even as a ministry. But what about leisure? Can it be holy? Are some leisure activities (or inactivities) holy and others not?

The Many Faces of Nonwork

Leisure is normally defined in terms of "freedom from," principally freedom from the demands of work.* But a more rounded definition includes the idea of "freedom for" something. Nonetheless, as G. K. Chesterton pointed out, this freedom is complex because it includes freedom to do something, freedom to do anything and freedom to do nothing (Rybczynski, p. 15). For example, freedom to do something is the leisure of taking a canoe trip in the wilderness, something I could not have done during the university student year. Even the freedom to get away to the country can have a work dimension, as I soon learned when our family acquired a summer cottage and we snaked our way weekend after weekend in a line of cars "to get

away from it all." Leisure, further, may be freedom to do anything, such as waking up on Labor Day with no set plans, free to choose between going for a bike ride, reading a good book, listening to Brahms or going to a movie—or all four! What makes it leisureful is the fact there is no compulsion, no obligation and no premeditation. But for Chesterton, himself a workaholic, the purest form of leisure is the freedom to do nothing, the very thing many Christians—because they lack a good theology—are unable to do without guilt (*see* Vacations).

Freedom to do something. Recreation* seems to fit Chesterton's first definition best. It is leisure that is action-filled and result-oriented, a form of employment. It is planned leisure, like the weekly tennis match or the morning jog. While it is a form of freedom, it is intimately related to what we do the rest of the week. This could be called *useful leisure* since it provides a diversion from our normal activities. But what about *useless leisure*?

Hobbies* are leisure activities that have no value to anyone other than the person who engages in them, whether it is stamp collecting or raising tropical fish. So many things can be included in Chesterton's first category: crafts (*see* Quilting), playing a musical instrument (*see* Music; Music, Christian), taking photos (*see* Photography) or making home movies, traveling,* experimenting with gourmet cooking (*see* Eating; Meal Preparation) and walking.* All of these, while potentially restorative, may be chosen intentionally, thoughtfully and regularly. But what of the leisure of not even having a plan?

Freedom to do anything. It is precisely to gain the freedom to do anything that many city dwellers aspire to have a weekend country retreat. Witold Rybczynski analyzes this trend to get away from it all from the time of Pliny to the present (pp. 162-85) to show that the rustic cottage is not rural life itself (*see* Farming; Community, Rural) but a mirror image of the city.* This form of leisure has been thoroughly commercialized through the promotion of leisure parks, leisure homes and leisure toys such as the ATV (all-terrain vehicle) and the jet boat. Indeed the automobile* was first of all a plaything, an instrument of leisure, allowing as it did the owners to go wherever they wanted, whenever they wanted without relying on the scheduling of public transportation (*see* Commuting; Mobility).

The most common form of leisure chosen by North Americans is television,* which is too often a passive activity, though it does not necessarily have to be. Virtual reality* ratchets the level of near-total engagement a notch further. In contrast reading,* now that it is mainly a private solitary activity rather than a shared group one, allows one to become engaged on a voluntary basis, filling in the blanks with one's imagination. Entertainment* in all of its forms is easily accessed by going to a movie,* attending a concert (*see* Culture) or getting a video to watch for the evening. Leisure and culture* in all of its forms are intimately related. We are making, and not merely expressing, culture by what we choose when we can do anything. The root word for leisure in the Latin is *licere*, which means "to be permitted." Leisure is really a state of the mind, a habit* or *habitus* of the soul. But some choices do more to nurture our souls than others.

The leisures noted above all spring from the freedom to do anything and offer the opportunity to cultivate one's own particular pleasure.* But what about Chesterton's purest form of leisure—the freedom to do nothing? Christians especially fear this kind of leisure because of the many scriptural prohibitions against idleness and sloth, sloth being one of the seven deadly sins.

Leisure as sloth. Several New York advertising agencies were commissioned, tongue in cheek, to promote the seven deadly sins. It was an ironical assignment, since most advertising* actually cultivates these very temptations. The ad for sloth was especially insightful. It showed Adam and Eve in the pristine beauty of the Garden experiencing exquisite pleasure. "If the original sin had been sloth," opined the copywriter, "we would still be in Paradise." The ad contains a half-truth: ambition* turned bad (the opposite of sloth) led to the expulsion from the Garden. It also contains a half-error: a slothful person would never enjoy the Garden, let alone cultivate it! Sloth and idleness are usually regarded as identical, but this is not necessarily the case.

Hardly anyone has more eloquently expounded the sin of sloth than the seventeenth-century Puritan Richard Baxter. In his comprehensive guide to everyday life, sloth and idleness are carefully distinguished: "Sloth signifieth chiefly the indisposition of the mind and body; and idleness signifieth the actual neglect or omission of our duties. Sloth is an averseness to labor, through a carnal love of ease, or indulgence to the flesh" (part 1, x, p. 378). Sloth is easily identified: when the very thought of labor is troublesome, when ease seems sweet, when the easy part of some duty is culled out, when you work with a constant weariness of mind, when you consistently offer excuses or delays and when little impediments stop you.

The best of the Puritans actually had a positive understanding of leisure. One of the earliest, Richard Rogers, advocated a daily schedule made up of eight hours of work, eight hours of sleep and eight hours of relaxation with friends, books or the creation. The original Puritan attitude toward the sabbath was not of a day full of restrictions on what people could or could not do, but a day free from the burden of work that could be given to all kinds of playful activities, for example, playing games, enjoying company or leisurely reading. Baxter's searing judgment, mentioned earlier, must be understood in the context of the Puritan doctrine of work and calling*: "Suffer not your fancies to run after sensual, vain delights; for these will make you weary of your callings" (p. 382). Every person, not just ministers and missionaries, has the call of God on his or her life, a call to serve God for the common good (commonweal). Sloth is a vocational sin, living as though one had not been summoned by God to a holy purpose (Eph 4:1).

The good of doing nothing. Leisure as doing nothing need not be sloth if it arises, as Luther would say, from the Word of God and prayer (that is, meaning it is an actual sign that you believe God is running the world and you can therefore take some rest). But when doing nothing is separated from an all-embracing vocation of living to the glory of God (Eph 1:12), leisure may be sloth. In the Western world retirement* often plunges a person into a life of socialized and institutionalized sloth, though it need not do so (*see* Volunteer Work). In many Third World countries older people still work and rest, having meaningful roles in their families, farms and villages. We have much to learn about leisure from so-called underdeveloped societies.

In summary, doing nothing, as well as doing something and anything, may be useful in the deepest sense, though not in a utilitarian way. At its simplest level leisure is a diversion providing the opportunity to set aside our normal employment so that we can break out of our routines and experience a needed release. At a deeper level leisure provides relaxation and rest,* refreshing us for all of life. Slothful people, as well as worka-

holics, are bored or boring.* Still deeper leisure is restorative, providing opportunity for creative thoughts, cultivating memories and gaining perspective. But at its deepest level leisure is transformative, contributing to our continual conversion into childlike people who enjoy God and delight in God's creation. To understand and experience leisure fully, and to resist trivializing it or turning it into a purely consumer activity as much popular culture tempts us to do, we must think biblically.

Called to Leisure

There are three great biblical themes that will help us develop a theology and spirituality of leisure. Taken together, these themes show that leisure is not avocational (something we do as an alternative to our calling) but truly part of our vocation.

The mandate to enjoy God's creation. Unfortunately, theologians have concentrated on the "dominion" or "rule" aspect of the so-called creation mandate (Gen 1:28) and have neglected the implications of God's joy over creation (Gen 1:31). God's will is that humankind flourish. It takes more than work to fulfill this God-given vocation; it also takes enjoyment, luxuriating in God's bounty, experiencing pure delight and real leisure. Adam and Eve were placed as kings and queens in a pleasure garden that was, at the same time, a sanctuary garden for meeting with God. Life was meant to be fun and holy at the same time.

Two Old Testament books expound God's good gift of enjoyment. The book of Ecclesiastes contains a dim view of the pursuit of pleasure that is the result of human striving and ingenuity, but strongly affirms that God has given us power to enjoy life (Eccles 3:13; 5:19). The Song of Songs expounds the meaning of Adam's exclamation of praise to God at finding and enjoying a partner suitable for him (Gen 2:23). Sex* play in the right context can be holy play (Stevens, pp. 60-64). Indeed, play* can link us with God as much as work does. So one mark of the presence of the Holy Spirit in our lives is the ability to live exuberantly. Leisure is a subset of joy, and joy is what Jesus came to bring (Jn 15:11). Being bored is an insult to God (*see* Boredom). So is living compulsively as though we could fulfill ourselves.

The theology of grace. Humankind, now fallen in sin and twisted in nature, is accepted by God solely and simply by God's undeserved kindness expressed in the death and resurrection of Christ and appropriated by faith. People who do not trust God's grace will either work or play themselves to death trying to find salvation by their own efforts. To do nothing leaves them feeling guilty. In contrast, people with confidence in the gospel are free to do nothing. The Old Testament sign of this was sabbath,* which was the weekly statement that Israel could trust God to care and provide. People who cannot "afford" (in the nonmonetary sense) to experience leisure as part of the daily round are taking themselves too seriously and not taking God seriously enough. Both leisure and sabbath are playful, restorative and nonutilitarian. But sabbath is contemplative—directed toward God; leisure is more hedonistic—directed toward ourselves. Sabbath is a divine requirement; leisure is a divine permission. Sabbath is a boon to society, to culture and even the earth, aiming at the threefold harmony of God, humankind and creation; leisure is essentially a personal freedom and pleasure. In other words, sabbath is more central to our vocation as God-imaging men and women than is leisure.

The theology of time. In the Western world time* is a commodity, a resource to be managed, rather than a gift of God. Often people think they can organize quality time with their spouse, children, friends or even themselves by scheduling time. Compulsive personalities bring to the planning of their vacations all the tendencies of scheduling they use in business. But quality time with God, self and others cannot be organized. One enters expectantly into more free-floating time, all the while making quantity time available by "wasting" it "unproductively."

Often the most memorable moments on a vacation are those completely unplanned, the true surprises—the flat tire on the car that resulted in your seeking help at a nearby farm, where a calf was being born; being stormbound on a canoe trip and telling your life story to a companion; the "chance" discovery while traveling of ancient fresco on the ceiling of a hermit's cave. Surprise links us with our most surprising God, who alone in the universe has the leisure to do "whatever pleases him" (Ps 115:3). So a theology of time will help us to waste time in a holy way and to welcome surprise. Leisure is part of what makes life a holy adventure. The adventure, however, is not without temptation. Just as work is fraught with temptations (chiefly to establish our identity by what we do), so leisure is a testing ground.

The Temptations of Leisure

Whether, like Jesus, one is "led by the Spirit into the desert" (Mt 4:1) or merely goes into the wilderness (or a first-class hotel) in search of a change or a rest, leisure may entail wrestling with subtle diversions. Earlier we explored the besetting sin of sloth. Here we will attempt to get inside sloth by exploring the three temptations of Adam and Eve in the Garden of Eden (with which one may compare the three temptations set out in 1 Jn 2:16).

The first was the temptation to experience godless sensuality. Eve saw that the forbidden fruit was "good for food" (Gen 3:6). Scripture does not suggest anything negative about the goodness of the fruit's taste, nor does it prohibit sensual enjoyment. All of the delights of the body—taste, sight, smell, touch and sexual pleasure—in their place are part of a genuinely human existence. Too much of the church's tradition has been influenced by Neo-Platonic dualism; it has tried to make angels out of Christians and exalted the monastic life as the epitome of discipleship.

The issue, however, is between godly and godless sensuality. The first involves obedience and glorifying God. Enjoying food, wine and sensual pleasure can and should lead to increased gratitude to God and exuberance in daily life. But it can also separate us from God. The difference between gluttony (one of the seven deadly sins) and holy feasting is spirituality (*see* Eating). The glutton lives to eat and, therefore, never gets enough and eventually becomes bored through satiation. The Christian lives for God and, therefore, enjoys a good meal as an act of worship and does this with thanksgiving (Rom 14:6).

The second temptation was to cultivate a godless aesthetic. Eve observed that the fruit was "pleasing to the eye" (Gen 3:6). Typically leisure experiences involve things that are visually satisfying: exquisite photography in a movie, a wild storm pounding a frail campsite, mountains clothed in layers of shaded blue and a piece of art. But the aesthetic experience has its own temptation. Thomas Jefferson once described his experience of seeing a large Drouais canvas: "I lost all idea of time, even the consciousness of my own existence." This is similar to the experience of the rock climber who said, "One tends to get immersed in what's going on around him . . . so involved that he might lose consciousness of his own identity and melt into the

rock" (Csikszentmihalyi, p. vii). The aesthetic experience engages people so deeply that they feel released from concerns about past and future, losing self-consciousness in what is an intrinsically satisfying experience. In this respect it is much like play. And like play, if divorced from the rest of our vocation or from relationship with God, the aesthetic experience tempts us to think we have gained human transcendence—a contradiction in terms.

The issue is not *what* one sees but *how*. The difference is between *looking* as a mere physical activity and *seeing*, which like hearing and listening* involves the whole person and calls for insight, judgment and spiritual discernment. Leisure can offer the opportunity to slow down and to concentrate, to see and not just to look, and by seeing to discover "the world in a grain of sand . . . eternity in an hour" (William Blake), thus equipping us to return to the rest of our life with open eyes and a heart that leaps up to God.

The third and most subtle temptation was the seduction of godless experience. Eve noted that the forbidden fruit was "desired to make one wise" (Gen 3:6 NRSV). The devil had suggested that if Adam and Eve acted independently from God, they could become "like God, knowing good and evil" (Gen 3:5), "knowing" not just in the intellectual sense but in the Hebrew sense of full intercourse with the object of knowing. Here is the nub of the matter. Adam and Eve were tempted to transcend their creatureliness, to have the experience of both good and evil without reference to God—in other words, to become divine themselves. To do this they had to become practical atheists, living as though there were no other god. The heart of sin is simply failing to live in perpetual gratitude (*see* Festivals—Thanksgiving) and reverence of God (Rom 1:21). This is the issue behind the most inward of the Ten Commandments—the exhortation not to covet (Ex 20:17). Do we love God enough to be content? If not, we must always crave some new experience, which, though it has the appearance of leisure like any addiction,* is subject to the law of diminishing returns.

The antidote to all this, as Richard Baxter reminds us, is passion for God, zeal for the church and the people of God, a deep, intelligent and willful hunger to know God. This passion takes a constant resolution of the soul to do God's will that is more like natural heat than a fever. It involves repenting of sin and embracing God's Word as a way of life: "Zeal and diligence are the victorious enemies of sin and Satan. . . . Zeal burneth up lust, and covetousness, and pride and sensuality" (Baxter, p. 384).

Contrary to what many may think, however, this passion for God does not lead to the religionizing of leisure, such as establishing Christian leisure parks and spiritual cruises and producing Christian music albums (see Music, Christian). On the contrary, it is precisely in the ordinary that we are to find God. So, rather than cataloging approved "Christian" leisure activities (or inactivities), we now briefly consider some practical guidelines that will deepen our experience of leisure as a ministry to ourselves (!) that pleases God.

How to Live Playfully

Read your own present leisure style. If you feel guilty when you do nothing and always choose leisure activities that allow you to play hard just as you work hard, you may be bringing into your leisure life the same compulsiveness that infects your daily work (see Drivenness).

Choose free time over extra pay. Get out of the rat race of working longer and harder (or taking extra jobs) in order to consume more goods (see Simpler Life-

style; Stewardship). By and large people today are working longer hours than people did prior to the Industrial Revolution. People have opted for the luxury items and take extra work or a part-time job to afford them. Instead of joining the conspicuous consumers, Christians should demonstrate their freedom to rest and to enjoy things in life that cost little or nothing.

Embrace both leisure and sabbath. Do not expect leisure to do for you what sabbath can. Unlike leisure, sabbath is celebrated weekly (as a day of refreshing worship and rest), daily (as a conscious entering into God's own refreshment; Ex 31:17) and eternally (as a way of describing salvation in Christ). Leisure and sabbath overlap—worship refreshes and transforms. Some leisure leads to contemplation, but leisure and sabbath are not coextensive. We often think we need more leisure when what we need is to enter more deeply into Christ's sabbath rest (Mt 11:28).

Choose edifying leisure, not debilitating "pleasures." We would do well to rethink the Puritan advice on this matter. Many forms of entertainment, some sports, some popular and high culture, wound the soul, divert from God and feed a godless sensuality or a godless aesthetic. Put positively, we should cultivate a taste for the best in leisure (Ryken, p. 22).

Choose leisure that expresses family values* and makes them a matter of family education (see Family Goals). The saying "The family that plays together stays together" may be as true as "The family that prays together stays together." Leisure is socially bonding and becomes an important arena of self-disclosure. It allows us to put aside our need to produce and simply to enjoy one another. This is also true of friendships,* marriages* and church fellowships.

Discover solitary leisure activities (or

inactivities) that are personally restorative. Self-denial is not the only command of Christ. The cultivation of oneself—gifts, talents,* interests and capacities—is also part and parcel of Christian growth. Not everything must be useful, sensible and balanced. Neither Paul nor Jesus lived a balanced life. Occasional extravagance (Mk 14:6) and taking holy risks (Mt 25:24-27) reflect living for and loving a God of plenty, joy, generosity and exuberance.

The Christian life is fun. It is not always fun—contrary to the argument of the "Christian" hedonists. But it is certainly not boring—not if it is life lived in harmony with the God who creates, works, rests and says, even of God's own leisure life as he wants to say of ours, "It is good." Part of learning to enjoy God forever is to learn to enjoy ourselves.

See also DRIVENNESS; ENTERTAINMENT; HOBBIES AND CRAFTS; RECREATION; REST; SABBATH; TIME; WORK ETHIC, PROTESTANT; WALKING.

References and Resources
R. Banks, *The Tyranny of Time: When 24 Hours Is Not Enough* (Downers Grove, Ill.: InterVarsity Press, 1983); R. Baxter, *The Practical Works of Richard Baxter,* vol. 1 (Ligonier, Penn.: Soli Deo Gloria Publications, 1990); G. K. Chesterton, *Selected Essays* (London: Collins, 1966) 212-16; M. Csikszentmihalyi, *Art of Seeing: An Interpretation of the Aesthetic Encounter* (Malibu, Calif.: J. Paul Getty Trust, 1990); C. Cummings, *The Mystery of the Ordinary* (San Francisco: Harper & Row, 1982); E. A. Dryer, *Earth Crammed with Heaven: A Spirituality of Everyday Life* (New York: Paulist, 1994); P. A. Heintzman, *A Christian Perspective on the Philosophy of Leisure* (Ottawa: National Library of Canada, 1985); J. H. Huizinga, *Homo Ludens: A Study of the Play-Element in Culture* (London: Paladin, 1949); R. K. Johnston, *The Christian at Play* (Grand Rapids: Eerdmans, 1983); S. B. Linder, *The Harried Leisure Class* (New York: Columbia University Press, 1971); J. Oswald, *The Leisure Crisis: A Biblical Perspective on Guilt-Free Leisure* (Wheaton, Ill.: Victor Books, 1987); J. Pieper, *Leisure: The Basis of Culture,* trans. A. Dru (London: Collins, 1965); W. Rybczynski,

Waiting for the Weekend (New York: Viking Penguin, 1991); L. Ryken, *Work and Leisure in Christian Perspective* (Portland, Ore.: Multnomah, 1987); R. P. Stevens, *Marriage Spirituality* (Downers Grove, Ill.: InterVarsity Press, 1989).

R. Paul Stevens

LETTER WRITING

Down through the centuries, letter writing has played an important role in the lives of individuals, families, friends, colleagues, advisers and officials. One of the best-known examples is the celebrated exchange of letters during the Middle Ages between Abelard and Heloise, who, though heads of religious orders, wrestled with the nature of love* and friendship.* Other examples include the vigorous pastoral letters of the converted slave trader John Newman and the deeply personal and theological letters written from prison by Dietrich Bonhoeffer before his death at the hands of the Gestapo.

The Disappearing Art of Letter Writing
In the nineteenth century letter writing became a popular activity. This was particularly the case among women, and they produced some fine examples and collections of letter writing. The early decades of this century saw an enormous increase in the numbers of letters, mainly of a business or official nature. With the advent of the telephone,* personal notes and cards began to replace letters, and custom-length aerograms replaced the regular, leisurely lengthed letters that friends and families used to exchange. With the introduction of faxes and now e-mail and lower international telephone costs, there has been a marked reduction in traditional letter writing. In 1977 household-to-household missives accounted for 6 percent of the U.S. mail; fifteen years later that fig-

ure dropped to 4.4 percent. For all the increase in public educational facilities, there also seems to be a deterioration in the quality of letters, as Ken Burns's television series on the Civil War so eloquently reminded us. It is also probably the case that people read letters more quickly and reread them less often. Since phone messages are not preserved, fax paper has questionable life span, and e-mail communications are rarely saved, it will be more difficult in the future to reconstruct people's thoughts and lives from what they have written.

Letter Writing in Earlier Times

Communicating through letters could be as old as writing itself. Originally messages were sent on leaves, bark or stone, and later on leather, linen and wax. The earliest form of paper was made from papyrus reeds several centuries before the coming of Christ. From the time of Israel's kings onward, the Bible contains many references to, and examples of, letters. Most of these are official documents. Sometimes their full text is reproduced (see Ezra 4:8-23; 5:6-17; Neh 6:5-8; Jer 19:1-13). The use of papyrus, which was so light and easy to carry, opened up the possibility of ordinary people writing letters. Since not everyone was literate, scribes could be hired to do this, which became a regular part- or full-time occupation. Those who were literate often used secretaries for lengthier letters if their eyesight was poor (as was probably the case with Paul; Gal 6:11).

Due to the durability of paper under dry conditions, many thousands of these letters have survived. Most of them are brief, formal and fairly stereotyped. Their contents deal with personal, familial or business matters, and many are designed for maintaining friendship. Letters were regarded as equivalent to or simply another form of the personal presence of their authors. They were generally carried by people known to those who wrote them, often slaves or subordinates, who would also bring back replies, though mail services had existed in large organized societies for some centuries (for example, Esther 3:13; 8:10). From the third century A.D. onward, letters containing money* or sensitive information were often entrusted to Christians, since they could be depended on not to steal or divulge their contents.

Examples of longer, more didactic or public letters also survive from this period. Some of the early philosophers, for example, Plato, Aristotle and Epicurus, occasionally used letters for teaching purposes. But it was the publication of 931 letters by the Roman moralist Cicero, after his death, that opened the way for letters to be taken seriously as a public educational device. Many other collections followed thereafter. Some of these, as with Seneca and Epicurus, verged on being epistolary treatises rather than genuine letters. There were also books or manuals on letter-writing style. These discussed different types of letters—for example, of introduction, apology, gratitude, accusation, praise, criticism, consolation, friendship.

The apostolic letters in the New Testament, including the seven letters to the churches in Revelation, fall midway between the two categories of personal and public letters. Some, like 2 and 3 John or the letter to Philemon, are relatively informal. Others, such as the letter to the Hebrews or to the Romans, are semiformal in character and contain lengthier theological and ethical discussions. Even so, they are more personal in tone and more concrete in character than letters by contemporary philosophers. As well as dealing with matters of religious belief and church life, they touch on such everyday issues as whether to buy meat in the marketplace, how to order your time,* how to behave at certain kinds of dinner parties,* whether to get married or remain single, when husband and wife should or should not have sex* and what is the best way of resolving legal disputes between Christians.

See also FRIENDSHIP; GOSSIP; TELEPHONE; TIME.

References and Resources
W. G. Doty, *Letters in Primitive Christianity* (Philadelphia, Penn.: Fortress, 1973). Donna E. Schaper, *Why Write Letters: Ten Ways to Simplify—and Enjoy—Your Life* (New York: Pilgrim, 1995).

Robert Banks

LIFE STAGES

With a proper understanding of life stages, we who teach, preach, parent, counsel or just befriend can communicate more effectively the truth of the Word of God. If we understand life stages, then we do not delude ourselves into thinking that just because we said something profound it was understood. There are some things too deep for less mature people to understand. We know the futility of attempting to explain the concept of the Trinity to a five-year-old. Yet in many other ways we attempt to teach something just as complex to immature people. Both Hebrews 4 and 1 Co-rinthians 3 show that all teachers need to be aware of the developmental life stages of the learners. If we are not aware, we can actually communicate the wrong thing.

Development from less to more mature stages throughout life always carries with it some struggles and pain. Children learn to walk, but they fall down many times, injuring at least their pride and sometimes their bodies. But they continue to learn to walk until they can do so without falling. So it is with all development. The discomfort of current ways of dealing with life spurs us on to seek more adequate ways to handle it. The search causes pain because it means letting go of less mature ways of dealing with ideas, events and people and the development of new ways we cannot fully know until after we have completed our development in that area.

The Domains of Life Stages
From conception* until death,* all people go through normal human life stages. These stages have six major domains: the physical (the most easily observed and measured, which can be used as an example of how growth and development occur in the other five domains); cognitive (or mental); social; affective (or emotional, psychological); moral; and spiritual (or faith). Some potential for development occurs in each period of life within each of the six domains.

In some domains, there is an expansion of what is already there. For example, once children learn how to multiply, they can multiply not just 2×2 but large, more complex numbers. For true growth to occur, however, there must be a change in how persons structure their reality. There must be a shift in their perception. This shift is called a change in development or a change in construction of responses to their experiences with their environment. Children learn arithmetic early in their life. But it is probably impossible to teach people to think algebraically until they have developed new mental constructs for handling abstract ideas. So it is in all of the domains of life and throughout all of human life: there are times of expanding what is already developed and there are times to fashion new ways of dealing with the world. Expansion of existing ways of thinking allows for more detailed handling of our environment and our responses to it. Construction of new modes of development allows for new ways of dealing with our environment. Just as arithmetic allows for a certain amount of handling of our experience with numbers, so mathematics allows for a new way of handling mathematical experiences that arithmetic itself could never provide.

The Main Features of Life Stages

Life stages in all these domains are predictable, descriptive and in some sense prescriptive. They are predictable because each stage of life has a relatively universal timetable that most normal people follow. For example, children do not walk by themselves until they can crawl, and even then they begin to walk by holding on to things. The age they begin to walk by themselves varies from child to child and from culture to culture. But all normal children learn to walk by first holding on to things, and they do so according to their own timetable. All the many other life stages are patterned in similar ways to walking. Earlier, less mature stages are necessary for, though not the only cause of, development into later and more mature stages.

These life stages are descriptive because scientific observations have been and continue to be made of people at all ages of their lives. Characteristics common to each stage have been assembled into descriptions of behaviors and thinking that are common to each life stage. These descriptions are generalizations that apply to all human beings across cultures. To be sure, there are some cultural variations, but the basic characteristics are similar across cultures.

Finally, these life stages are prescriptive in that all people must go through each of these stages in order to become more mature. We could say that the rolling-over, sitting-up and walking stages of human physical development are necessary for the ability to run. Likewise, all

the less mature stages are prescriptive for later, more mature stages. Because the stages are predictable and descriptive, they are also prescriptive. People must go through these and no other stages. Of course, one must always, in the realm of behavioral science, be open to new descriptions of stages and the discovery of stages heretofore unmeasured. But, once these stages have been observed, they in turn become prescriptive. There are many who argue that description and predictability do not equate with prescription. Yet it is difficult to think of predictable stages that are necessary for growth without their becoming prescriptive.

Textbooks that deal with human development give specifics of all six of the domains and all of the life stages. Three developmental domains, however, are of high concern for Christians, namely cognitive, moral and spiritual. These three areas are the ones that human beings use to understand and apply Scripture. They are the primary ones that define our relationships with our own selves, our fellow human beings and our God. Since the last of these is treated elsewhere (*see* Faith Development), here we will focus on the first two.

Cognitive Life Stages

The cognitive domain deals with the mental processing of our experiences and thoughts. The pioneer of cognitive development is Swiss researcher Jean Piaget. Piaget identified four stages of mental or cognitive development.

Stage one is called the Sensory-Motor stage. This begins at birth and goes through the second year of life. At first infants have only reflexive actions without intentionality. From these primitive reflexes they develop into intentional actions but ones that usually involve much mental reflection. Much of this stage's actions are solving problems: learning and interacting with their environment through the use of the five senses, and motor or muscular activities. Language begins here, but much of it is copying the words of those who teach them to speak.

Stage two is called Preoperational and usually begins sometime during the second year and continues till about the seventh year of life. Thinking at this stage is concerned with what is perceived through their senses. Children's thought is usually limited to their own circumscribed world. Though their thinking is limited in this way, children often ask questions about things that they cannot perceive, such as "What does God look like?"

Stage three is called Concrete Operations. Children often enter this stage around age seven or eight, sometimes a year or so younger. True intellectual activities occur here. But at this stage logic is limited to concrete problems. Abstract reasoning, theological ideas and philosophical thinking are not part of this stage's repertoire of reasoning. At least 50 percent of the adult population of the United States are reported to have halted at this stage of development. This means that unless they undergo some significant experiential change, a large percentage of those in churches* as well as in the marketplace cannot understand abstract ideas about God, salvation and other theological concepts. The implications of this for Christian ministry,* evangelism* and Christian growth are substantial.

Stage four is called Formal Operations. In this stage people are able to think abstractly. Usually this stage begins, if it ever does, around age twelve. Many people are not well settled into this until the latter part of adolescence* or even adulthood. A sizable portion of the adult American population never achieves this level of cognitive maturity. This stage is necessary for understanding much of Scripture, especially the Old Testament prophets, the New Testament epistles and much of Jesus' teaching.

Moral Development
The second major domain considers the rationale for making moral judgments, that is, how we go about deciding whether something is good or bad, right or wrong, moral or immoral. Lawrence Kohlberg has been the pioneer in this area. He identified three levels of moral development with two stages in each level, giving six stages of moral development. For our purposes, we will look only at Kohlberg's three levels, not the stages. We will also look at a fourth level that can be identified.

Level one is called the Preconventional Level. This level focuses on issues of right and wrong being dependent on the results to the person making the judgments. People at this level consider the consequences to themselves. If the consequences are good, then the judgment is that a certain action is good, moral and right. If the consequences are negative to those making the judgment, then they decide that their judgments and actions were wrong. The major focus for making these decisions is an egocentric approach to justice.* Justice is what is good for the person him- or herself. What happens to others is not a major issue.

People at this level understand God's offer of salvation as just because by simply believing and receiving Jesus a person escapes hell and gets the good life in heaven. Not a bad deal, according to level-one thinkers. Level one is the marketplace morality: "What's in it for me?" and "If I do something for you, what will I get in return?" Issues of noble justice or self-sacrificing love do not cloud people's thinking at this level.

Level two is called the Conventional Level. At this level people make moral judgments and moral acts based on what they think are the expectations of significant others or the law* of the land. Their concern is to do what is expected of them. Peers, family,* parents* and other significant people play a major role in helping people do what is right. For these people, laws of right and wrong are maintained either by their significant others or by the laws of society.* In either case, they have moved from being egocentric in their judgments to being concerned with an external moral perspective. This is the major level of most people. Concepts of justice as a principle to be applied in fairness to all others or selfless love are not major issues for people at this level.

Persons at level two respond to the gospel either because a significant other person has introduced Jesus to them or because they understand the biblical law of God that sin must be punished and God himself is willing to forgive those who receive his reconciling gift through Jesus Christ. It is not the consequences of sin or the anticipation of heavenly rewards that make the difference here. It is, rather, that God wants to befriend them forever.

Level three is called the Postconventional or Principled Level. At this level people are concerned that laws and conventions are just in and of themselves. Justice is measured by impartiality and fairness, not by relationships. The picture or statue of blindfolded Justice holding the balance of law in her hand is the model here. Everyone is treated equally. This is not the same measurement that a level-one person would want to exact. Rather it is that all be given a fair chance.

People at this level respond to the good news through the universal demonstration of God's justice and forbearance. By becoming reconciled to God, they realize that they will be participants with God's plans for the universe. They

will be indwelt by the Spirit of God.

There is a level four that Kohlberg suggests but rejects as not being a true stage. I accept it and call it the Agapic Level. On this level people do not look at the consequences for themselves, nor do they consider what others think or even what the law says, nor are they concerned with equal justice for all. They make their decisions on the law of love as found especially in the life and death of Jesus and in the moral teaching of the apostles in Romans and 1 John. Agapic love asks not what is required nor what the circumstances are; it asks what the other person needs and how such love can be best expressed. This is the love that God demonstrated to us, thereby showing his justice (Rom 3:23-26; 5:8). People at level four are not enamored by being privy to the mind of God but by the beauty* of beholding God. Like Moses, they have seen One who is invisible (Heb 11:27) and are willing to live radically altered lives of selfless love for the world that God so loved.

In summary, moral development stages approach God from four different perspectives. Level-one people love God because God gives them rewards, especially eternal life. Level-two people love God because God is their friend. Level-three people love God because God has given them insight into his character and actions. Level-four people love like God loves.

Because life can be understood as progressing from less to more mature stages, we can more effectively communicate the Word of God to others as we take this into account. Understanding the basic questions that people face on their life journeys and the developmental issues that each stage sets forth, we can construct more meaningful learning experiences. Understanding life stages also can help us be empathetic toward those who are going through the difficult times of moving from less to more mature stages. Knowing that the movement is God-ordained and therefore normal results in a certain relaxation on our part. We can recognize that God is at work within ourselves and others. We are not complete but imperfect people who are developing continually into the fullness and likeness of Jesus Christ.

See also ADOLESCENCE; CHRISTIAN GROWTH; EDUCATION; FAITH DEVELOPMENT; MENOPAUSE.

References and Resources

D. Aleshire, *Faithcare: Ministry to All God's People Through the Ages of Life* (Philadelphia: Westminster, 1990); A. Brodzinsky, *Life Span Human Development* (Austin, Tex.: Holt, Rinehart & Winston, 1979); D. Levinson et al., *The Seasons of a Man's Life* (New York: Knopf, 1978); L. L. Steele, *On the Way: A Practical Theology of Christian Formation* (Grand Rapids: Baker, 1990).

John M. Dettoni

LISTENING

Our basic anatomy of two ears and one mouth is highly suggestive. We probably should do twice as much listening as speaking. If speaking* is a spiritual discipline, refraining from speech to listen to the words of others or to God's word is equally crucial to living Christianly. The control factor, however, is more subtle and more demanding in the case of listening. Marshall McLuhan makes the rather obvious suggestion that nature has not equipped us with ear-lids. So we compensate for what he calls "nature's oversight" by selective listening (McLuhan and Fiere, p. 111). Rather than consider this internal control as an oversight, we could regard it as a divinely planned opportunity for spiritual growth. So Jesus says, "Consider carefully how you listen" (Lk 8:18), not only because all will be revealed eventually (v. 17), but because if you listen well, you will gain even

more to hear. So listening is a key to the inner treasures of the soul.

Listening and Self-Discipline

James says, "Everyone should be quick to listen, slow to speak" (Jas 1:19). The context refers to both listening to others and listening to the Word of God (Jas 1:21), two facets of listening that are inextricably interrelated. Instead of finishing another's sentence, we should listen to the soul expressed in the words. She who holds her tongue in check is in control of her whole person (Jas 3:2-4). Dietrich Bonhoeffer in his classic *Life Together* says, "Thus it must be a decisive rule of every Christian fellowship that each individual is prohibited from saying much that occurs to him" (p. 92). So both speaking and listening involve discernment. Speaking metaphorically, Job says, "Does not the ear test words as the tongue tastes food?" (Job 12:11), a point with which the young man Elihu fully concurs (34:3-4) as he invites Job along with the three unfriendly "comforters" to "learn together what is good."

So the self-discipline involved in the ministry of listening is not just *how* we listen but *to what*. While we are inundated by a thousand advertisements and siren appeals to the flesh every day, we should heed Solomon's advice of "turning your ear to wisdom and applying your heart to understanding" (Prov 2:2; compare 23:12), whether it is a life-giving rebuke (15:31), the law (28:9) or the cry of the poor (21:13). Listening not only *is* selective; it *should be*. We must systematically reduce certain influences in order to attend to those that make us truly wise.

Listening as a Relational Gift

The apostle Paul expounded the metaphor of the body suggesting that some people are like the ears (1 Cor 12:17). He was, however, promoting interdependence rather than delegation of listening ministry to certain specially endowed members. James exhorts all believers to be "quick to listen" (Jas 1:19), which he links in the same verse to "slow to become angry." We are less likely to feel thwarted and, therefore, get angry if we know what is going on inside another person. Further, if we listen deeply to the soul of another, we will more likely be confronted with our own shortcomings (Jas 1:21), more willing to listen to ourselves and less likely either to provoke to anger or to be so provoked. By listening, we renounce control over the one who is speaking and communicate worth.

Listening is a relational compliment. This is true not only for fellow human beings but of God himself. By opening our hearts to hear God's word, we worship God and pay the greatest compliment possible. The reverse is also gloriously true: that God speaks "with his ears." By patiently attending to our cry (Ps 17:6; 31:2; 34:15; Is 59:1), God communicates his love as eloquently as in his articulated speech. His silence is both revelatory and evocative. In the same way, our willingness to cultivate the discipline of solitude is a profound statement of the esteem with which we hold God and our availability to his speech. Richard Foster says, "One reason we can hardly bear to remain silent is that it makes us feel so helpless. We are so accustomed to relying upon words to manage and control others. . . . One of the fruits of silence is the freedom to let our justification rest entirely with God. We don't need to straighten others out" (p. 88).

How to Listen

It is widely recognized that the starting point in all counseling relationships is listening. The same is manifestly true for friendships* and in deepening a marriage* relationship. By listening we convey our desire to understand, to take seriously the viewpoint of another. When we listen, we refrain from giving advice, preaching* or even expressing an opinion until we have first taken the person seriously and gained trust (Collins, p. 290). Adapting the advice given by the psychiatrist Armand Nicholi, we can summarize the following dimensions of listening: (1) having enough awareness of one's own conflicts to avoid reacting in a way that interferes with the person's free expression of thoughts and feelings; (2) avoiding subtle verbal or nonverbal expressions of negative judgment; (3) waiting through periods of silence or tears until the person summons up the courage to say more; (4) hearing not only what the person says but what he or she is trying to say; (5) using both ears and eyes to detect messages that come from tone of voice, posture and other nonverbal cues; (6) avoiding looking away while a person is speaking; (7) limiting the number of mental excursions into one's own fantasies while another is speaking; (8) practicing the full acceptance of the person no matter what is said (Collins, pp. 26-27).

The last point deserves more comment. To accomplish acceptance through listening without condoning or condemning is spiritually demanding. To do this without condemnation, one must have experienced deep forgiveness in one's own life, since we condemn or condone what is still unresolved in our own past. And to show acceptance of a fellow sinner without excusing sin cannot be done without compassion, that quality that links us so closely with the heart of God. So listening, like speaking, reveals the person, casts us on God for his grace and invites us to move forward in the life of discipleship.

Listening as a Spiritual Discipline

Just as speech reveals the person, so the quality of listening reveals the soul within. Stopped-up ears come from hearts "as hard as flint" (Zech 7:11-12). Open ears reveal a tender and responsive soul. This is true whether one listens to God or to another person. By learning to attend to the thoughts, feelings and values of others, we are positioning ourselves to attend to God. Of course, the reverse is equally true. Bonhoeffer puts it negatively: "But he who can no longer listen to his brother will soon be no longer listening to God either; he will be doing nothing but prattle in the presence of God" (p. 98). That prattle leads to the famine prophesied by Amos, not of food or water but "of hearing the words of the LORD" (Amos 8:10-12). Good speakers are good listeners. They have the "instructed tongue" of those who have learned from God in their own lives and therefore are able to sustain the weary with their own words (Is 50:4). God opens the mouth of his servant by wakening the ears of that servant, just as Jesus opened the mouth of the mute person by opening his ears (Mk 7:33), a sign that the day of salvation had truly arrived (Is 35:5-6).

Those unready to obey what they hear from God are called "dull of hearing" (Mt 13:15 KJV), implying that they have their internal ear-lids down (Mk 8:18; Rev 2:7, 11, 17, 29). Sometimes this willful stoppage is accomplished by externally plugging the ears (Acts 7:57), but more commonly it is an internal predisposition *not* to hear because they are unwilling to obey, something that the apostles of Jesus called "uncircumcised in heart and ears" (Acts 7:51 NRSV). The ear as an organ of reception has not yet heard the full joy and beauty of heavenly sound (1 Cor 2:9). Heaven will be the ultimate listening experience, as the book of Revelation shows (Rev 4—5), and we live with true heavenly mindedness by practicing the disciplines of faithful (that is, faith-full) listening to Scripture, to the hearts of others and to the voice of God speaking to us in our life experiences.

See also COUNSELING, LAY; SPEAKING; TEACHING.

References and Resources

D. Bonhoeffer, *Life Together,* trans. J. W. Doberstein (New York: Harper & Row, 1954); G. R. Collins, *Christian Counseling: A Comprehensive Guide* (Waco, Tex.: Word, 1980); R. Foster, *Celebration of Discipline* (New York: Harper & Row, 1978); M. McLuhan and Q. Fiere, *The Medium Is the Message* (New York: Bantam, 1967); J. Pedersen, *Israel: Its Life and Culture,* 4 vols. (London: Oxford University Press, 1963); H. W. Wolff, *Anthropology of the Old Testament,* trans. M. Kohl (Philadelphia: Fortress, 1964).

R. Paul Stevens

LOBBYING

In political language the noun *lobby* refers to a room or hallway near a legislative chamber, a place where lawmakers can meet constituents and other guests. As a political activity, lobbying is the attempt, at times actually carried out in a lobby, by individuals advocating their own or a group's interests to influence decision-makers. While many ordinary citizens try to influence public officials, lobbyists are usually paid professionals, often associated with a law or public relations firm, and very knowledgeable about power relationships and effective intervention in the governmental process.

A Biblical Perspective

Because the Bible was not written in democratic times, we have no discussion in Scripture of the propriety of lobbying or of any attendant difficulties or pitfalls. We do, however, have numerous biblical accounts of lobbying, many with successful results. Joseph lobbied Egyptian authorities on several matters relating to the people of Israel (for example, Gen 47:1-12). Moses and his associates lobbied hard in the attempt to convince Pharaoh that the Egyptian government should let his people go. Daniel and his friends lobbied Babylonian officials concerning special privileges relating to diet and lifestyle (Dan 1:5-21). Esther lobbied King Xerxes to the point of risking her life to bring relief to her people (Esther 5:1-8). Haman, of course, lobbied hard and with ulterior motives to bring about changes in the legislation governing religious practices (Esther 3:1-12). Many prophets in the Old Testament lobbied kings and emperors for an array of causes, usually involving issues of public justice or private lifestyle.

In the New Testament we read that a crowd lobbied persistently for the release of Barabbas and the crucifixion of Jesus (Mt 27:15-26). The mother of James and John lobbied the King of kings about positions of privilege for her sons (Mt 20:20-23). Subsequently they also lobbied for themselves (Mk 10:35-40). Gamaliel lobbied with others in the Sanhedrin about being very careful how they treated Peter and the other apostles (Acts 5:33-42). Paul lobbied the authorities for fair and reasonable treatment after they had mistreated him (Acts 16:35-39). Certain Jewish leaders lobbied Festus to have Paul transferred to Jerusalem (Acts 25:1-5). One could even say that John the Baptist lobbied King Herod about his marital misbehavior (Jn 14:1-12).

In addition to the aforementioned biblical examples of lobbying, there are passages in the New Testament that clearly mandate lobbying as a legitimate part of the political process (Mt 17:24-27; 22:15-22; Rom 13:1-7; 1 Tim 2:1-4; Tit 3:1-2; 1 Pet 2:13-17). Since the institution of government is strongly affirmed, we need to ascertain why lobbying should be included in the biblically affirmed political system.

Lobbying as Part of the Governmental Process

Governing has become an extremely complex and difficult task. Those who govern need to get as much informed input as possible into their decision-making. Lobbyists, by advancing arguments, provide important input. In the United States hundreds of interest groups, such as the American Civil Liberties Union, the American Medical Association and the National Rifle Association, provide extensive input into the legislative, administrative and even the judicial branches of government.

In Canada the number of lobbying groups is somewhat less, but even so, scores of nationally important organizations, such as the Canadian Labour Congress, the Canadian Teachers Federation and the Royal Canadian Legion, play a significant lobbying role in the development and implementation of public policies relating to their interests. In these two countries and in other democracies, governments and bureaucrats rely extensively on lobbyists for accurate and up-to-date facts and very useful, although perhaps self-serving, analyses. Lobbyists can generally be trusted because they know that if they do not present accurate and honest information, they quickly lose all credibility.

In free societies such as the United States and Canada, lobbyists exercising their constituted right of free speech look for opportunities to advance their cause. Some lobbyists focus on single issues, such as abortion* or pornography; others, for example, Greenpeace, the Sierra Club and some feminist groups, work to advance a more generalized ideological perspective. In the United States, with its weak party discipline and separation of powers, lobbyists find many access points. In a cabinet-dominated parliamentary system such as Canada's, strict party discipline means that lobbyists tend to focus mainly on the cabinet, regulatory agencies and bureaucrats. With the entrenchment of the Charter of Rights and Freedoms in 1982, the Canadian situation is becoming more like the American. While in Canada lobbying is less pervasive than in the United States, in both countries it constitutes a vital feedback mechanism.

The Negative Connotations of Lobbying
Many people consider lobbying to be suspect. Some critics point out that lobbyists often relay selfish and narrow views, thus giving reinforcement to particular, rather than general, interests. The general good, it is alleged, thus suffers. Others speak about well-financed lobbyists acquiring additional benefits for those who are already powerful and privileged. Unorganized and marginalized groups fall even further back. Still others point to questionable practices or even outright bribery and blackmail.

Some wrongdoing clearly exists, but evil is probably no more prevalent among lobbyists than in fallen society generally. In any event, lobbying has acquired a negative connotation for many, but the evil lies not in its intrinsic nature but in the extent of abuse by some practitioners.

The Positive Aspects of Lobbying
Many elected and other public officials have come to rely heavily on the continuing input of lobbyists. Such officials are grateful for the extensive and factually accurate information that is provided quickly and at no direct cost. They know that a democracy functions best when there is extensive citizen feedback. They also know that most citizens are apathetic and neglect to convey their views. Officials realize that when lobbyists communicate their expertise, concerns and wishes, they are, in fact, compensating for widespread inaction on the part of individual citizens. In fact, while individual lobbyists tend to provide incomplete and partial responses, collectively they help public decision-makers to discern the public interest.

Lobbying also contributes to the achievement of a better political and social situation by helping to keep governments in check, by providing safety valves for public or group anger, by the lobbyists monitoring one another and by informing the media and the public. In sum, group input and lobbying are not only legitimate in the God-mandated political system but may well be essential for the efficient functioning of a mature democracy. In a sin-plagued world we cannot eliminate self-interest, but we can regulate it and, up to a point, actually use it to advance the common good.

Lobbying as Christian Witness
Many Christians, perhaps most, belong to at least one interest group that lobbies to enhance that group's economic well-being or set of values. As other-oriented citizens, Christians can help to shape a more enlightened stance on the part of such generally non-Christian groups than would otherwise be the case.

As members of specifically Christian groups, such as The Lord's Day Alliance, Citizens for Public Justice, Christians for Public Decency, the Evangelical Fellowship of Canada and the National Association of Evangelicals, Christians can do even more. Christians can make a unique and significant contribution in supporting people who lobby for more fairness, greater respect for human dignity, better stewardship* of the Lord's creation* and the adoption of more enlightened and more moral policies generally. Even small groups that have done their homework can be surprisingly influential in their lobbying endeavors, especially if they come with a non-self-serving agenda.

Christians, when true to the calling* to love one's neighbors, stress in their lobbying the well-being of others and not only themselves. Followers of Christ desire procedural fairness, identify with the marginalized and the exploited, and seek to be positive and constructive. Naturally, Christians associated with lobbying should avoid all use of undue pressure; they need to be scrupulously honest, and they must never adopt means that undermine Christian goals.

In the area of lobbying many Christians have been guilty of duplicity. Generally they have not hesitated to pressure governments for their own advantage but have often been reluctant to speak up for others because they have deemed such speaking up to be too political. In fact, it is more Christlike to speak up for someone else's cause than to press for one's own advantage.

In the give-and-take of everyday politics* Christians have missed many opportunities. Many seem to have forgotten that if they remain silent and uninvolved, the extensive and persuasive input of vast numbers of non-Christian lobbyists will prevail. Government policies in general continue to become more wide-ranging and pervasive. Pressure groups—labor, business, welfare, agricultural, educational, professional, ecological and many more—continue to play a major role, largely by lobbying, in shaping these policies. Will Christians vacate the public square, or will Christians see lobbying as a challenge and an opportunity to bear witness* for what is right and true and good?

See also CITIZENSHIP; POLITICS; POWER; PRINCIPALITIES AND POWERS; VOTING.

References and Resources

J. M. Berry, *Lobbying for the People: The Political Behavior of Public Interest Groups* (Princeton, N.J.: Princeton University Press, 1977); D. L. Bon, *Lobbying: A Right? A Necessity? A Danger?* (Ottawa: Conference Board of Canada, 1981); P. Malvern, *Persuaders: Lobbying, Influence Peddling and Political Corruption in Canada* (Toronto: Methuen, 1985); N. J. Ornstein and S. Elder, *Interest Groups, Lobbying and Policy-Making* (Washington, D.C.: Congressional Quarterly Press, 1978); J. H. Redekop, *Religious Pressure Groups in the Canadian Political System*, Research Paper Series 8470 (Waterloo, Ont.: Wilfrid Laurier University, 1991).

John H. Redekop

LOVE

Love, a word much overused and underdefined today, is employed promiscuously of everything from cars to diapers to dog food and is largely equated with feelings. Love, the most crucial and central concept in Christian theology and ethics, is also one of the most theologically, ethically, psychologically and culturally ambiguous concepts, with diverse interpretations and contradictory definitions. Love, to have a clear referent, requires not only a theological base and a philosophical framework but also a psychological dynamic and ethical content and context. This will be the outline for our exploration of the forms and types of love.

Theological Base of Love

Love is considered one of the three primary theological virtues* along with faith and hope. Throughout the centuries of theological writing, the analysis of love has centered on love as self-giving *agapē*. The nature of *agapē* has moved through a progression of emphases. As (1) *benevolence,* that is to love the unlovely and the unlovable, *agapē* is the generous, altruistic, compassionate love that values the neighbor* self-forgetfully, in a self-disinterested concern for his or her welfare. It is in no way dependent on the recipient's merit or worth, but only on the lover's generosity. As (2) *obedience* that acts to love the other because of role, command or moral imperative, *agapē* is the faithful, willing obedience to the moral imperative to act for the good of the neighbor in fulfillment of the command of Christ. As (3) *self-sacrifice* that seeks to love the other at the lover's expense—the other's need comes first—*agapē* is self-sacrificial service to the neighbor, which puts the other's needs above one's own, even at great cost to the self. As (4) *equal regard* that perceives the other as equally worthful, even as one knows the self to be precious and of irreducible worth *agapē* is thus both an act of the will—to exercise compassion toward the other without reservation—and an act of the heart—to value self and other unconditionally. Such love regards the neighbor as loved even when enmity exists, that is, when the other is the enemy.

The first view, benevolence, has been the dominant interpretation of love in Christian history. Most modern and postmodern theologians critique it for its paternalistic element. The fourth view, equal regard, is now more frequently pursued since it is capable of embracing the other three, that is, benevolence, obedience and self-sacrifice, in a way that takes wholeness, justice and well-being seriously for all humankind, including enemies.

Agapē has frequently been defined as "disinterested love," which allows, even supports, an atomistic individualism, a curious insularity. When it is seen as a total, unselfish form of love that utterly disregards any response, this unilateral love becomes entirely a matter of what I unilaterally offer to do for someone out there or down there in benevolent generosity. But *agapē* cannot be individualized in such a manner; it is at heart a sharing of experience, a recognition of our underlying kinship in the kin-dom of God. It is an equal regard grounded in our common existence as creatures from the hand of the Creator, who loves all equally.

We have often been trapped or limited by etymological analyses of words, such as the terms for *love* in the Scripture. Our understanding of Christian love ought not to hinge on the root meanings of classical Greek verbs, nor on particular usages, but on the decisive test of the central understanding of love in the overall meaning of the New Testament witness to love, of the incarnation's demonstration of love, of the full impact of the life, teaching, death, resurrection and presence of the loving Christ. The past, present and future reality of the people of God—the church*—as the community* of love is the body of Christ.

In the biblical world there were at least five words used to designate forms of love, although only three of these appear in the New Testament: (1) *eros,* the search for an object in aesthetic, passionate or spiritual love; (2) *philia,* the preferential bond of affection, friendship* and social solidarity; (3) *storgē,* the caregiving love of compassion; (4) *agapē,* the nonpreferential, self-giving love of equal respect; and (5) *koinōnia,* which is love in the mutuality of community, in the sharing of the common life in covenant and commitment (*see* Fellowship). The fifth love is more than a search for an object (*eros*) or altruistic self-giving (*agapē*); it is an expression of mutuality in which giving and receiving are united (*koinōnia*). This is the authentic word for Christian love, the end of the trajectory of the multiple words (*eros, philia, storgē, agapē, koinōnia*). The word *koinōnia,* from *koinos* "in common," expresses the fellowship-creating drive toward mutuality, the fellowship-fulfilling goal of equality, the fellowship-celebrating joy of community, the fellowship discipline of impartiality: "May the *grace* of the Lord Jesus Christ, and the *love* of God, and the *fellowship* of the Holy Spirit be with you all" (2 Cor 13:14, emphasis added).

A Philosophical Framework

Each type of love has received philosophical analysis, but *eros, philia* and *agapē* have been the primary foci. Here we shall selectively draw only on the notion of *agapē. Agapē* is a profound concern for the welfare of another, to be understanding and to understand the other without any desire to control the other, to be thanked by the other or to enjoy the process. *Agapē* is a decisive distributing of benefit to self and others. We may view it as a continuum from other-forgetfulness to self-forgetfulness with intermediary steps of preferring self, equal parity and preferring other. *Forgetting the other* allows the person to choose a course of action with no concern for the other's welfare. *Preferring self* may take into account the other's good but gives more value to one's own need* or advantage. *Equal parity* offers equal weight to both self and other in a mathematics of truly equal division of good and bad. *Preferring the other* demands that a person, while taking self-needs seriously, should always give preference to the other. *Self-forgetting* suggests that the person prizes the other so highly that thoughts of the self occur only in relation to the other's needs of fulfillment.

When *agapē* is tempered with justice,* equal parity becomes a criterion for evaluating what is creative for the other, for the relations and also for the self. The balance point between a just concern for both parties and their needs may vary with the context, the circumstances, the special situations of either. Yet *agapē*, accepting the human need as a necessary point of preferring the other, works toward the parity of equality.

Gene Outka has sought to isolate a basic normative content to Christian love, a virtue that it possesses irrespective of the circumstances. Does love have a normative status comparable to utilitarianism or the Kantian categorical imperative? The three fundamental features of *agapē* he sees as being most systematic and recurrent are these: (1) an "equal regard for the neighbor that in crucial respects is independent and unalterable" (p. 9); (2) self-sacrifice, "the inevitable historical manifestation of *agapē* insofar as *agapē* was not accommodated to self-interest" (p. 24); (3) mutuality, characteristic of those actions "which establish or enhance some sort of exchange between the parties, developing a sense of community and perhaps friendship" (p. 36). These three definitions—equal regard, self-sacrifice and mutuality—all suggest that the love defined is being or has been mediated by justice and balances an unstable equilibrium.

The Psychological Dynamic

In his analysis of love as unifying power, Paul Tillich wrote, "Love is the tension between union and separation" (p. 25). Love is the moving power of life that seeks the unity of the separated. The individual needs to find unity with other selves but without sacrificing its own or violating the other's identity. This retains the centeredness of each person without absorption or abandonment by the other. These polarities—absorption or abandonment, engulfment or ignoring, union or separation—express the basic fears as well as the essential needs for balanced personhood. According to Fritz Perls, the Gestalt theorist, "To love another is to move as close as possible without either violating the other or losing oneself," as Erik Erickson affirms (Perls et al., p. 419). More than a balance point, love is an active process of mutuality. Mature love seeks the mutuality that expresses the reciprocity of give and take in a relationship. But the practice of a love that seeks mutuality can be pursued by one person whether the other reciprocates or not. Unconditional positive regard can be given whether the other responds or returns such valuing, as Carl Rogers has taught.

Many psychological theorists assume the principle of *psychological hedonism,* which holds that all human beings are driven to seek pleasure* for themselves and to avoid pain. An outstanding exponent of this view is Sigmund Freud, who formulated the *pleasure principle* as the basic expression of human motivation. The contrasting view is that of *psychological altruism,* which supports the human capacity of self-love as distinct from pleasure for the self, which is selfishness. Love of self and love of other are complementary. A true concern for one's own welfare cannot be divided from concern for the welfare of significant others, and true self-love motivates one to see others with equal respect. Eric Fromm has articulated this perspective and points toward the possibilities of humans' coming to value self and other as a means of reducing the alienation of human society* and of increasing the possibilities of persons' valuing giving above getting, valuing being above having or doing. This vision of an innate harmony between egoism and altruism has become a basic assumption for human potential, existential and the many varieties of popular psychology, in contrast to the analytic and object relations theorists, who see the two in eternal tension.

Ethical Content

If the concept is to have any meaning, love requires an ethical community. Ethical practice does not occur in human isolation or in individual decision. It arises within community and directly by the commitments of the person. It is in a particular community that the practice of love takes form, receives content, finds direction, achieves fulfillment. The ethic that has emerged from the tradi-tion of Immanuel Kant places central emphasis on reason to the belittlement of feeling. He grounds ethics on a foundation of laws that are universal (in that all rational beings would need to subscribe to them). Thus, he held that the universal principle of respect for all rational beings as ends in themselves and never as mere means constitutes the measure of genuine love. The Aristotelian perspective, in contrast, views love not as a universal law but as a virtue that is central to the formulation and sustaining of human community.

Christian theology is grounded in the passionate, eternal, self-giving, unconditional love of God. The presence of God in the birth, life, teaching and death of Christ presents divine love in human experience and community. The incarnation, crucifixion and resurrection are not as much the infusion of supernatural love as the transformation of the natural human experience, the restoration of created human possibilities, the gift of grace that restores the courage to love, the commitment to care even for the enemy, the participation in the power of the Spirit, which enables us to go beyond the common human capacity to love to an uncommon experience of *agapē* in relationships and community.

See also EMOTIONS; FELLOWSHIP; GIFT-GIVING.

References and Resources

E. Erikson, *Insight and Responsibility* (New York: Norton, 1964); E. Fromm, *The Art of Loving* (New York: Harper, 1956); C. S. Lewis, *The Four Loves* (New York: Harcourt Brace Jovanovich, 1960); G. Outka, *Agape: An Ethical Analysis* (New Haven, Conn.: Yale University Press, 1972); F. Perls et al., *Gestalt Therapy* (New York: Dell, 1951); C. Rogers, *On Becoming a Person* (Boston: Houghton Mifflin, 1961); P. Tillich, *Love, Power and Justice* (New York: Oxford University Press, 1954).

David Augsburger

LOYALTY, WORKPLACE

A generation ago organizations* expected their employees to make a commitment to the company and its mission. In return for that commitment the employee could expect the organization to provide employment and growth opportunities. It was a covenant of reciprocal expectations. Both the employee and the company expected and received a degree of loyalty. This reciprocal loyalty reached its extreme in the paternalism of the Pullman company during the development of the railroad. In today's marketplace loyalty no longer works that way.

The Erosion of Loyalty in the Workplace
Peter Block in his book *The Empowered Manager* reminds us that companies are not in business to take care of their employees. Ultimately only God will take care of you. While organizations still want their employees to make a commitment to the mission and the good of the company and while employees still want organizations who will take care of them and guarantee employment, both sides recognize that the constraints of the modern marketplace make these expectations unrealistic.

Max DePree, former chairman of the Herman Miller Company—a Fortune 500 company often listed among the best places to work in the United States—regularly notes that workers today are essentially volunteers. He is talking about volunteers not in the sense that they are unpaid but in the sense that they understand they have something to offer and expect a return on the investment* of their time and energy. They choose to work* where they work because of the exchange that the company offers. It is not a matter of loyalty. They are mobile and understand that they can choose to leave as easily as they choose to stay, taking their time,* energy and knowledge with them to a new company where the exchange is better.

Another factor is also at work today. Global competitiveness and the changing marketplace are forcing companies to drastically reduce the work force, restructuring and reengineering themselves to be leaner and more competitive. The loyalty covenant is no longer shaping their attitudes toward employees. In his recent book *The End of Work,* Jeremy Rifkin argues that the rapid progress of technology* and information systems has created a rising technological unemployment, with millions of jobs being eliminated every year. Corporations are still loyal to their mission, to their investors, to their suppliers and indeed to those employees who remain, while they remain. The fact that they may eventually be replaced, however, severely limits the scope and depth of that loyalty.

On the one hand, we have workers who understand that their jobs can be eliminated and thus are looking out for themselves. In the organizations they serve, remaining competitive and providing a satisfactory return to their investors are necessary for survival and thus take precedence over loyalty to specific individuals. On the other hand, the rapid increase in unemployment* following the progress in technology will eventually make it so difficult for workers to find other positions that the "volunteer's" choice may, in fact, be removed. These two views both support the current attitudes toward loyalty and at the same time are at odds with one another. So what role does loyalty play in today's workplace?

Loyalty in the Workplace Today
Loyalty is still an appropriate concept with regard to mission, to organizational values,* to personal growth and relationships, and to God.

Loyalty to the mission. Every organization is formed around a mission,* a specific purpose that defines each person's contribution within the organizational community.* While the unquestioning loyalty to the company of earlier decades is no longer appropriate, it is appropriate for an organization to expect its people to be committed to the mission of the community in which they choose to work. That commitment should draw employees into continually improving the contributions they make to the organization so that the mission can be achieved. It is the mission that brings them into relationship with the organization, and as long as they work in that context, the mission deserves their loyalty and the investment of their talents.*

Loyalty to the values. Similarly, every organization operates with an organizational culture,* a set of assumptions and beliefs that, if the organization is operating with integrity,* will be expressed in the values by which it lives its corporate life. Organizations have the right to expect employees who choose to work in that community to exhibit a loyalty to the organizational values. It is these values that define the relationships of the people within the organization and the environment in which they work.

Loyalty to personal growth, yours and others'. As Peter Block has noted, while the organization should be expected to provide a responsible return on the investment of its employees, the company cannot be counted on to guarantee employment or future employability. It is incumbent upon employees to accept responsibility for their own growth, both in their ability to make a significant contribution to the organization and in their development for future employment in that company or another. Personal growth is the responsibility of the individual, and it may or may not be assisted by the organization. At the same time, employees in most cases work in relationships. It is appropriate that the loyalty we bring as individuals to our own growth and development be extended to those with whom we work. When the Christian concept of community is brought to the organization, it is a necessary corollary that individuals make a commitment of loyalty to one another in their relationships.

Loyalty to God. In the final analysis this is where loyalty is lodged. For example, Paul wrote to the Colossian congregation a letter that was to be read at the same time they were to accept Onesimus, the runaway slave, back into their midst as a Christian brother. He said, "Whatever you do, work at it with all your heart, as working for the Lord, not for men, since you know that you will receive an inheritance from the Lord as a reward. It is the Lord Christ you are serving" (Col 3:23-24).

Christians in the marketplace work with full loyalty to God, a loyalty that manifests itself in commitment to the mission—the work to be done. This loyalty is also expressed in a commitment to the values of the community in which they choose to work, a commitment to grow both in their knowledge of God and in their ability to make a contribution to the organization and a commitment to the growth and well-being of those around them.

See also CALLING; CAREER; LEADERSHIP; MANAGEMENT; ORGANIZATION; ORGANIZATIONAL CULTURE AND CHANGE; ORGANIZATIONAL VALUES; WORK.

References and Resources

H. Blamires, *The Christian Mind* (London: SPCK, 1963); B. A. Grosman, *Corporate Loyalty: A Trust Betrayed* (Toronto: Penguin, 1988).

Walter Wright Jr.

M

MANAGEMENT

Management is a relationship between a leader and followers that focuses on a specific set of tasks within an organization,* business, church* or voluntary society. Both management and leadership* have become hot topics, with volumes written to define them and to differentiate between them. Within the organizational context, they are closely linked. Both focus on getting something done, but there is a difference. Peter Drucker says that *management* focuses on doing things right, while *leadership* focuses on doing the right thing.

The Interdependence of Management and Leadership

Both management and leadership are concerned with results, with getting something done by involving others. Both assume three essential components: leaders/managers, followers and mission* or objective. Both refer to the relationship between the leader and the follower in which the leader seeks to influence the behavior, values* or vision of the follower for the purpose of accomplishing a mission shared by both leader and follower. The mission gives purpose to the relationship. So does the follower. Without followers there is no leadership, no management.

Go back to Drucker's distinction. Management tends to focus internally within the organization on the task at hand, working for stability and efficiency; leadership tends to focus beyond the immediate task, seeking change and renewal. In every organization both are necessary and complementary. Here again, the follower has something to say. Leadership and management are always determined by the followers and the expectations they have of managers and leaders. They expect from their managers coordination, feedback, plans, order or organization, the provision of resources and information, and access to the decision-making processes of the organization. They expect from the leaders of the organization vision, renewal and motivation for change. No one can lead or manage until a follower chooses to accept that influence and follow.

Management is a relationship between a leader and followers that focuses on a specific set of tasks within the organizational mission. Leadership is a relationship that involves the followers in a process that leads to the results intended by the mission.

Management Styles

There is a wide variation in leadership styles that determines what the involvement of the follower in the management process means. The relationship between leader and follower can be dominated by the leader or by the follower. Volumes have been written arguing for a variety of leadership styles, ranging from autocratic to democratic. At one end of

599

the scale, an autocratic manager makes all decisions and announces his or her decisions to the followers, giving specific direction to their behaviors. At the other extreme, a fully democratic manager gives the decisions to the group and participates as one of the group. In between those extremes are a variety of consultative stages, in which the manager might seek feedback from the followers but still retain the decision, or might allow the followers to decide subject to his or her approval.

The general consensus today recognizes that the appropriate mode of follower involvement varies from day to day, from person to person and from task to task. There is no one right style of participation. Sometimes it is more effective for a leader to give direction, sometimes to consult and sometimes to take direction. This is called contingency theory or situational leadership. It operates on two basic assumptions. First, the style of leadership becomes more participative as the follower becomes more competent and confident in carrying out the assignment. Second, the goal of the leadership relationship is to develop the competence and confidence of the follower to such a level that the follower can lead on his or her own.

This approach to leadership is very follower-oriented. It seeks to develop the follower and adapts the management relationship accordingly. This flexibility, however, carries some risk. Leaders who prefer a particular style of leadership may choose to stay within their comfort zone rather than adapt for the growth of the follower. This is particularly a problem for leaders who like a more controlling autocratic approach. The contingency model allows them to declare that the follower is not competent enough, and thus they must be more directive in their leadership. As an alternative James O'Toole calls for a values-based approach to leadership that begins with a respect for persons and places follower growth ahead of leader preference. Follower participation is critical to the management process as leader and follower participate in a process that leads to the achievement of the mission objectives.

Management Process

Over the years writers have identified four to seven components of the management process. In the 1960s Alex MacKenzie published "The Management Wheel" in the *Harvard Business Review,* identifying five sequential and two continuous components that make up the management process: planning, organizing, staffing, leading, controlling, deciding and communicating. In the last decade this was revised and updated by *HBR,* but the same key elements were retained. Other writers have developed variations on these components, most often combining them into planning, organizing, leading and controlling or evaluating.

Planning refers to the management process of identifying the mission and the values of the organization and developing strategies for their implementation. It involves discovering and defining the purpose that brings the organization into being as well as the culture or character that defines how things are done (*see* Organizational Culture; Organizational Values). It asks: Do we still believe the mission and follow it? Are we controlled by the mission and values? Planning involves an audit of organizational activities. It asks: What are we doing now? Does it move us toward our mission? What else could we be doing? What can we stop doing? Planning involves the development of organizational strategies—the goals, objectives and actions of the organization. It determines the specific, attainable, measurable results that the organization wants to accomplish within a determined time frame. Planning involves the allocation of organizational resources. It determines the human, physical and financial support necessary to attain the objectives and how they must be distributed. Planning involves the delegation of organizational responsibility. It determines the actions, the individual tasks that must be performed by a given date, by a specific person, to implement the plan. The management process is responsible to see that an effective plan for implementation is in place, detailing who will do what, and when, and how it will be reported and evaluated.

Organizing refers to the management process of providing the structure and resources to implement the organization's plan. This is an important part of the coordinating and stabilizing function of management. Organizing involves identifying and grouping the tasks to be completed and the assignment of each task to a specific person or group of persons. This is the point of *delegation,* where responsibility to lead is given from the leader to the follower, at least for this specific task. Organizing also involves the acquisition, distribution and control of the human, physical and financial resources needed to assure the effective attainment of mission objectives. The management function of organizing brings the organization into existence and equips it for effective operation. It provides the structure for accountability* that forms the linkage between the planning and the staffing functions.

Staffing refers to the management process of providing the human resources—the gifts and skills needed to implement the plan. Traditionally staffing involves six functions: human resource planning, the identification of the organization's needs for people to carry out its activities; personnel policy development, the setting up of proce-

dures for the care and nurture of the organization's people; employment, the recruitment, selection and orientation of the people who will form the organization; performance review, the evaluation of the people within the organization to enable them to grow in their work performance and in their lives; career* development, the support and training of persons to enhance their personal and vocational development; and compensation administration, the provision of wages and benefits to the people in the organization in return for their work and commitment.

Leading refers to the management process of providing direction and involvement in every area of the organization's development. The staffing function identifies and selects the people who will form the organization. The leading function provides them with a support system to ensure their success.* Leaders are always there for the staff, not the staff for the leaders. Leading involves vision*—the understanding and articulation of the mission and culture* of the organization in a way that empowers the people. Leading involves delegation—the assignment of responsibility and authority to persons so that they might lead within the organization. Leading involves motivation and coaching—the inspiration and encouragement of people to accomplish their assignment. Leading involves coordination. It maintains a network of relationships among the people of the organization. Leading involves service. Leaders make a commitment to the well-being of the organization, the achievement of its mission, the development of its people and the impact it has on the community in which it serves. It is important to note that power* and authority are given by the organization (by its people) to be given to the people to enable them to carry out their assignment. The leader is there to serve the follower. It is not unusual to hear the question "Who reports to you?" A much better question is "For whose success are you responsible?" Leading is the management function of taking responsibility for the success of the people within the organization to ensure that the mission will be achieved.

Controlling refers to assessing and monitoring the progress and completion of organizational objectives. How are we doing? Are we making progress toward our mission? Controlling involves the development of standards for performance. What will a good job look like? What is quality work in this situation? What do we expect from our organization? Controlling involves measurement of performance and results. It asks how we *know* how well we are doing. Controlling also involves the appraisal of performance against standards: how well we *are* doing. Controlling involves the correction of performance deviation: if I am not doing my job well, how do I improve? Controlling involves the reinforcement of performance that is up to standard: if I am doing well, tell me!

The most common control system in most organizations is the budget. The operating budget attempts to quantify the organization's plan in measurable format that allows periodic feedback and opportunity for adjustment. The information from the controlling function of the management process provides the information that fuels the planning function, and the sequential management process continues through another cycle: planning, organizing, staffing, leading, controlling.

Along with these five sequential components of the management process, MacKenzie identified two continuous functions: deciding and communicating.

Deciding is a continuous management function that occurs in each of the sequential components of the process. It includes defining the problems that make a decision necessary—opportunity, lack, choice. It identifies the decision objectives—what we are seeking to accomplish. It develops alternatives—what the options are. It takes the risk of choosing an alternative—selecting the best option. It includes the implementation of the decision—putting the decision to work. Decision-making is one of the most critical functions of leadership within the management process. Some would argue that it is the most critical function because it involves the risk of the unknown. It does not require leadership to decide between two unequal alternatives when one is clearly the better choice. Leadership is required when both options are equal and it is not clear which is the better choice. Leadership risks when making a decision when the alternatives are equal, a decision that frees the people up to get on with their work.

Communicating is another continuous function of the management process. It is the function that links all of the areas of the organization's development. Communicating is the vital link that relates people and processes to the purpose and task of the organization. Information is friendly. A major part of the management process is ensuring that the people within the organization have the information they need to make the best decisions and carry out their assignments effectively for the achievement of the mission.

In addition to all these dimensions of management, which are shared equally by Christians and those without faith, there is another vital and powerful continuous component of the management process for the Christian manager.

Prayer is an acknowledgment of dependence on God. It is a way to seek wisdom, to see things from God's perspective, to look at one's work through the eyes of Jesus. We pray not so much with the expectation that God will make the decision for us as to express weakness and dependence. Praying brings us into the mind of God so that we may understand what is important, what is at stake and what are the values that must be preserved. Praying often draws on different thinking or brain patterns and allows insights that do not always emerge from rational thinking and discussion. One of the deepest prayers of Christian managers is that we will do no harm. We pray, however, in the final confidence that we cannot frustrate the sovereign will of God.

Management is a relationship between leader and follower that involves both in planning, organizing, staffing, leading, controlling, deciding, communicating and praying for the accomplishment of the shared mission objectives that brings them into relationship with the organization.

See also LEADERSHIP.

References and Resources
P. Block, *The Empowered Manager* (San Francisco: Jossey-Bass, 1993); M. De Pree, *Leadership Is an Art* (New York: Doubleday, 1989); M. De Pree, *Leadership Jazz* (New York: Doubleday, 1992); P. Drucker, *Effective Executive* (New York: HarperCollins, 1993); J. M. Kouzes and B. Z. Posner, *Credibility* (San Francisco: Jossey-Bass, 1993); J. O'Toole, *Leading Change: Overcoming the Ideology of Comfort and Tyranny of Custom* (San Francisco: Jossey-Bass, 1995); G. Tucker, *The Faith-Work Connection* (Toronto: Anglican Books Centre, 1987).

Walter Wright

MARRIAGE

Brenda was a pert twenty-four-year-old who worked behind the counter in a photofinishing store. I often brought my film there for developing. One day I noticed a tiny diamond ring on her engagement finger. She told me that just last night she had become engaged to the man she was living with. I bragged about how I had been well married for over twenty years. Her face whitened. "I have never met anyone married that long!" she said. I asked her if she would remain married throughout her life, and she answered, "I don't think so. I don't know anyone who has been married for twenty years." Both she and I were amazed by the encounter.

Faithful Attraction
A pastor visiting a fourth-grade Sunday-school class asked the class, "What does God say about marriage?" Immediately one boy replied, "Father, forgive them, for they know not what they do!" Many marrying couples do not know what they are doing. But the statisticians say they are still doing it successfully.

The good news for most married couples is very good indeed. There is a resurgence in faith about marital faithfulness, which researchers are calling *faithful attraction*. Andrew Greeley reports, on the basis of four surveys of couples, that 90 percent of American spouses have been faithful since they were married. Also, more than 60 percent say their marriage is very happy, 75 percent say their spouse is their best friend, and over 80 percent say they would marry the same person again if they had to do it over. *Faith Alive* magazine (July 1994) asked their Canadian readers (mostly church attendees) to rate their marriages, and on average they rated their marriages with a B+. Over 95 percent of women and men had not had an extramarital relationship, though about 12 percent of men reported that they had been tempted. Of those who rated their marriages with an A+, the most common thread was "seeking God's kingdom first."

The marrying couple may well not know what they are doing, but they know what they want. Willard Harley in his book *His Needs, Her Needs* points out what he has discovered as the priorities of the sexes in the order of importance. A man desires sexual fulfillment, recreational companionship, an attractive spouse, domestic support and, finally, admiration from his wife. Harley's research indicates that a woman desires affection, conversation,* honesty and openness, financial support and family commitment. With such different expectations, it is little wonder that the process of becoming one is so fraught with challenges and opportunities.

The Bible speaks often about marriage, but nowhere so eloquently as in the creation story in Genesis 2:18-25. The section begins with this striking announcement by God: "It is not good for the man to be alone. I will make a helper suitable for him" (Gen 2:18). Adam is alone, and that state is "not good"—the only thing in creation that God judges to be not good. As the man began to function as God had intended him (naming the animals that God brought to him), he became profoundly aware that all the beasts had "equal others," but he did not. He became lonely. Being alone is always a negative concept in biblical history, for the full life is found in community with all of God's people (see Eccles 4:9-12; Jer 16:1-9).

The Need for a Helpmate

Christian marriage is particularly unpalatable to some because of the sacrifice or submission implied, so it is thought, in the phrase "helper suitable" (translated in the KJV as "help meet"). God, however, does not think of this term as a pejorative one. He takes this word *helper* upon himself in several passages in Scripture, for example, "Who is like you, a people saved by the LORD? He is your shield and helper and your glorious sword" (Deut 33:29). The word *helper* essentially describes one who provides

what is lacking in the other. The woman by relative difference but essential equality would be the man's fitting complement. What he lacked, she supplied. And it is equally true that what she lacked, he would supply. The man was thus created in such a way that he needs the help of a partner. Human beings cannot fulfill their destiny without such mutual assistance. What the Bible does not do is spell this out in terms of specific roles.

Several years ago there was a teaching in the church that it was the husband's responsibility to do the home finances as an expression of his God-ordained leadership. This might work well with businessmen or accountants, but with me the teaching was disastrous. Now having control of our modest income, I quickly gave much of it away to those needier, and I spent the rest on books that I was sure I would need one day (many of the books are still unread!). Eventually I came to my senses and returned the responsibility to the member of our family who had the requisite gifting. My wife made up for my lack (and financial deficit) when she used her gifting for our benefit. This is what it is to be a helper. What the man lacks, the woman supplies. So Scripture explains the need for a companion; it also explores the process of becoming married.

Marriage as a Three-Stage Process

Mike Mason, author of *The Mystery of Marriage,* comments that "a marriage is not a joining of two worlds but an abandoning of two worlds in order that one new one might be formed" (p. 91). This was not in Brenda's mind (nor probably her fiancé's) as they began to think about marriage. For her the idea of merging two worlds into one is a dusty virtue for antiquated Christians. But the concept of offering up your own life for the blessing of another is both biblical and profoundly psychological. Marriage is a continual three-stage process that involves leaving, being united and becoming one: "For this reason a man will leave his father and mother and be united to his wife, and they will become one flesh. The man and his wife were both naked, and they felt no shame" (Gen 2:24-25). Each of these three dimensions is needed for a complete marriage.

Marital leaving. The process of leaving means disengaging from one's family of origin (the family that you were born into and where you formed your initial preadult values and view of the world). It has to do with ending the dependency on the original family and becoming "jointly autonomous" with your mate. It may also mean giving up adolescent* expectations of sexual intimacy so that the marriage can be free to enjoy the pleasures and disciplines of marital love* or relinquishing the fantasies of being forever nurtured and adored. Whatever kind of leaving is required, the leaving will be ongoing. It is not a "been there, done that" phenomenon. There is a continual leaving of the old to engage the new, even after many years of marriage (*see* Family Systems).

Many couples in marriage counseling find they must work through this issue of leaving. When the first or second child comes around and needs extra care, they begin to parent as they were parented. The problem is that both parents were parented differently and conflicts arise. Both will need to rethink their ideas of what parenting* is about. This is the process of leaving. It is a continual process and is provoked by the inevitable conflicts of living in marital proximity.

Marital union. The idea of being united with one's wife or husband as found in Genesis 2:24 raises the question, How do spouses become intimate? This too is a continual process in which none of us is an expert. To be continually united involves many everyday skills of friendship.* This is why good friendships so often lead to secure and satisfying marriages. Being united involves mutual affection and mutual appreciation. There is no one who can live in the intimacy that marriage requires without the affirmation* of one's partner. Also, it is impossible to become close friends without the glue of emotions* and their effective communication. These emotions may be unpleasant ones (for example, anger or resentment) or the more pleasant emotions of marital arousal and love. Further, becoming united requires simple acceptance of the other and the skills of conflict resolution* and anger reduction. No one masters all of these skills on his or her wedding day. Husband and wife are continually becoming more united, more unified, more intimate with each other.

Obviously, intimacy is hard work. Many couples, however, think that marital intimacy is a hormonal gift that bubbles them into ecstasy. It is easy for them to fall into despair when they are disillusioned by the necessary work (by the way, it is great to give up illusions that are untrue). But when a couple gets over the disappointment that intimacy is work, they can galvanize their resources to be a missionary to each other's intimacy needs. This is what it means to be united.

Young people grow up looking for the "right one." When our teenagers talk this way, I interrupt them with the terribly parental judgment, "How are you becoming the perfect person for your future mate?" They need to be converted from the idea that their future marital bliss is caught up in finding the perfect one. Rather, marital intimacy is the mutual commitment of being the right one for the other.

Marital sexuality. Sexual intimacy, and not just spiritual and emotional intimacy, is also hard work—though perhaps it was not for Adam. I can envision Adam running across plains and through rivers, brushing aside giraffes and pelicans in pursuit of his equal other, Eve. Along the way he utters the first hymn of praise in the Bible ("here at last"; Gen 2:23 NRSV) and the first poem ("bone of my bones"; Gen 2:23). Having seen all of creation designed for a partner, he discovered his own, and he did not need a course in sexual education to know what to do. Adam and Eve had no books, no illustrated dictionaries, no specially priced videocassettes. They enjoyed a naive integrity, absolutely without the experience or knowledge of sin, as the motif of nakedness suggests. They experienced no shame and felt no fear of rejection.

This is the hope of all young adults who decide to live together (*see* Cohabiting). They are desperately trying to get back to Eden. They want the simplicity and naiveté of the Adam and Eve who knew no sin. But unlike the Eden couple, they are cheating and lying to themselves. They have had imperfect parents, who have transmitted generations of fear, unhappiness and twistedness (along with much good) to them. They have developed conflictual personalities that make them suitable to be bachelors and spinsters but never to be husbands and wives. They have developed competing ambitions* that place them at loggerheads with each other. They have laughed at Bart Simpson too long and sung Madonna's lyrics too long and shopped in malls with perfectly bodied mannequins for too long. In short, they are not naive at all. They know too much. And their experience of sexual union is something less than full communion.

The idea of becoming one flesh expresses the complete personal community of one man and one woman as spiritual-physical-sexual-family unity. How do two become one? It is difficult, say the psychologists. It is impossible, say

the realists. It is a miracle, say the religionists. And it is all three. I call it the "mystery of transfiguration." When Jesus was on the mountain with his friends, he was transfigured in their view (Mt 17:2-3). He acted the same, talked the same, but he was now seen in right relationship with all of eternity. A similar transfiguration occurs when a man becomes a husband and a woman becomes a wife. These are not role changes; this is the beginning of the process of becoming the other's *other*. Two are becoming one in view of each other.

The Vows of Mystery

The wedding vows express the process of transfiguration. The wedding vows not only describe the commitments of marriage, but they obligate one to another. They are not merely descriptive; they carry the weight of the word spoken (*see* Promising). Just as God created life out of the spoken word, the vows powerfully implement the process of transfiguration. Carelessly spoken vows carry such carelessness throughout the duration of the marriage. Vows taken as if God sustains the covenant carry the sacredness throughout the couple's journey. The marriage vows from *The Book of Alternative Services of the Anglican Church of Canada* illustrate the mystery well.

"I take you . . ." suggests the activity of a freely disposed individual who entrusts himself or herself to another. It is the most profound ontology: to choose and to be chosen. Marital "taking" has great power. It is the power of acceptance. It is one of the needs of all human beings—to be accepted as we are. In marital taking we accept our spouse without the anticipation of changing. Too many spouses endeavor to create the spouse over into their own image. It takes many couples years to discover that a copy is a cheap imitation.

"To be . . ." speaks of the transition

from one state of being into another. Marriage is not so much a role change as a profound transfiguration into being a husband or wife, not a mere man or woman. The marital transfiguration usually leads to parental transfiguration—the becoming of a father or a mother (*see* Parenting). These transfigurations are a continual process and therefore involve continual change. So the process of mutual acceptance is never a once-and-for-all event.

"My lawfully wedded wife/husband..." speaks of the community aspect of marriage. It is accepted and affirmed as good for society and is the covenental hope of the community for the future. Marriage always has this beyond-ourselves dimension. In the marriage ceremony the pastor may address to all present, "Will you do all in your power to support and uphold this marriage?" As the community answers in faith, "We will," they echo the covenant of the couple to each other. Sometimes when a couple is remarrying, they quote the passage from Ecclesiastes 4:12: "Though one may be overpowered, two can defend themselves. A cord of three strands is not quickly broken." Their confession is that they were not together on their first try. Their hope is that with God empowering their marriage and with faith making it alive, their covenant will not be ruined. It is with great confidence that a minister marries a couple who depend fully on God. But there is another dependence: the believing community, who will be "God with skin on" when their marriage is straining.

"To have..." speaks of the delight and pleasure of the marital covenant. *To have* is to be thrilled with the discovery that now the spouse has what he or she has waited for. It is a my-beloved-is-mine experience. *Having* also includes tragedies as well as joys. Problems and challenges are not interruptions in the marriage.

Embracing the complexities, disappointments and genuine hurts is as much a part of marital having as relishing the excitements.

"And to hold from this day forward ..." speaks of the permanence of the *having. Holding* your spouse speaks of sustaining the power of the vows throughout the marriage. How do you hold your spouse? Ask yourself these questions: How do you talk about your mate when he or she is not there to hear? Do you hold him to be valuable to your children or when jesting with friends? Is it your plan every day to discover more of her giftedness, to empower and not to limit your spouse? A couple in conflict described their problems: "I try to hold her back. She gets so emotional. I just wish that I had married someone who would not be so demanding." Are you trying to hold her back out of fear? Or are you holding to empower her? The Bible frees me from the responsibility of controlling my spouse, whom I can now hold with open hands.

"For better, for worse; for richer for poorer; in sickness and in health ..." is a reality statement. There will be many highs and lows, and the covenant is sufficient for all of them. If a couple has not significantly suffered, it is probably because they are still young in their marital journey. James tells us to "consider it pure joy ... whenever you face trials of many kinds" (Jas 1:2). There is an inevitability about these trials—they will come—but they can be appropriated for the good of the marriage and for the blessing of the couple. Some couples do not think that trials produce a good marital crop. When struggles inevitably materialize, they think that they have married the wrong one. Challenges are reminders to become the right one.

"To love ..." emphasizes the emotion (*eros*) and the motivation (*agapē*) of the covenant. This kind of love is both vertical (from ecstasy to sadness) and horizontal (from now to eternity). Much is said in popular marriage books about the various kinds of love. There is friendship love, erotic love, steadfast love and dependency love. The list is quite exhaustive. At different times of the couple's journey, different loves are required. The love of middle-aged spouses is quite different from the love of aged grandparents* preparing to move into a retirement village, where their grandchildren can come for lunch on Sundays. Newlywed love is unique and quite unrepeatable (thankfully). Marital permanence and satisfaction have to do with reading the stages of your marriage as to the kind of love that is best.

"And to cherish . . ." speaks of the attitude of prizing the chosen other. *Cherishing* is to put the right value on the marriage and the one loved. Cherishing is the penicillin to the sickness of coveting, coveting another or another's marriage. Coveting was Eden's first sin. Adam and Eve disbelieved that God would provide what was necessary for them to live life to the full. They thought they needed something more than God had provided. They did not love God enough to be content—so searing the first marriage. The remedy for coveting—in relation to both God and one's spouse—is cherishing: receiving and valuing fully what has been given. This is the everyday plea of marital therapy clients the world around: "Cherish me. Value me. Love me."

"Until death do us part . . ." is also a reality statement of marriage. In the midst of the teary happiness of the wedding vows, reality enters in. This covenant will be broken by death. In the birth of marriage intimacies, the *d* word is spoken not so much as an interruption but as a reminder of reality. This aspect of the vow reminds the couple of the permanence of the covenant. As Mason writes,

> One thing very important to know in marriage is that there is always a way out. And the way out is not divorce! No, the way out in marriage (no matter how bad things may get) is simply to put everything we have back on the line, our whole hearts and lives, just as we did the moment we took our vows. We must return to an attitude of total abandonment, of throwing all of our natural cautiousness and defensiveness to the winds and putting ourselves entirely in the hands of love by an act of the will. Instead of falling in love, we may now have to march into it. (p. 125)

"According to God's holy ordinance . . ." speaks of the One who enacts and empowers the covenant. It is God's ordinance because it is God who "holds the paper." While the registrations of our marriages are filed in the appropriate governmental offices, God holds and sustains the covenant that is the marriage itself. It God who transfigures man to husband and woman to wife. It is God who empowers this union. What vows! But what a God! And what a mystery marriage is!

A Picture of Christian Marriage

Richard Selzer in his book *Mortal Lessons* wonderfully pictures what marriage is.

> I stand by the bed where a young woman lies, her face postoperative, her mouth twisted in palsy, clownish. A tiny twig of the facial nerve, the one to the muscles of her mouth, has been severed. The surgeon had followed with religious fervor the curve of her flesh; I promise you that. Nevertheless, to remove the tumor in her cheek, I had cut the little nerve. Her young husband is in the room. He stands on the opposite side of the bed, and together they seem to dwell

in the evening lamplight, isolated from me, private. Who are they, I ask myself, he and this wrymouth I have made, who gaze at and touch each other so generously, greedily? The young woman speaks. "Will my mouth always be like this?" she asks. "Yes," I say, "it will. It is because the nerve was cut." She nods, and is silent. But the young man smiles. "I like it," he says. "It is kind of cute." All at once I know who he is. I understand, and I lower my gaze. One is not bold in an encounter with a god. Unmindful, he bends to kiss her crooked mouth, and I am so close I can see how he twists his own lips to accommodate to hers, to show her that their kiss still works. (pp. 45-46)

See also CONFLICT RESOLUTION; DIVORCE; LOVE; SEXUALITY.

References and Resources
H. Clinebell and C. Clinebell, *The Intimate Marriage* (New York: Harper & Row, 1970); B. Farrel et al., *Pure Pleasure: Making Your Marriage a Great Affair* (Downers Grove, Ill.: InterVarsity Press, 1994); M. Mason, *The Mystery of Marriage* (Portland, Ore.: Multnomah, 1985); J. H. Olthius, *I Pledge You My Troth: A Christian View of Marriage, Family, Friendship* (New York: Harper & Row, 1975); R. Selzer, *Mortal Lessons: Notes on the Art of Surgery* (New York: Simon & Schuster, 1976); R. P. Stevens, *Married for Good* (Downers Grove, Ill.: InterVarsity Press, 1986); R. P. Stevens, *Marriage Spirituality* (Downers Grove, Ill.: InterVarsity Press, 1989); E. Wheat, *Love Life* (Grand Rapids: Zondervan, 1980); N. Wright, *Communication: Key to Your Marriage* (Glendale, Calif.: Gospel Light, 1979).

Paddy Ducklow

MASS MEDIA

The mass media can be traced to Gutenberg's printing presses, which copied vernacular Bibles in German and helped launch the Protestant Reformation. Today the media include not only books but radio,* television,* movies,* periodicals such as comic books, newspapers and magazines, recording media such as videotapes, audiotapes and disks, and the increasingly popular CD-ROM. Regardless of the technology* employed, all mass media share one major characteristic: they enable a relatively small number of individuals to communicate with a large, more or less impersonal, audience.

The Functions of Mass Media
Overt. The overt functions of the mass media are quite obvious. Most of these media purport to entertain audiences with interesting stories or enticing aural or visual presentations. Other media, such as newspapers, many magazines and nonfiction books, provide information about the world. In addition are media of persuasion, such as advertising* and, in totalitarian societies, political propaganda.

Priestly. It is helpful, however, to look deeper than the overt functions of the mass media. Perhaps the most significant covert role of the media is a kind of priestly function that helps the masses articulate their basic values* and beliefs. This is especially true in a market system, where the economic goal of media is to maximize audiences for advertisers. In this context the media try to create messages that resonate with general consumer tastes and interests, as well as with fundamental values and beliefs. The major purpose of such media is not to alter audiences' perceptions as much as to tell audiences what they want to hear, to show them what they want to see and generally to confirm existing beliefs regardless of their validity or veracity.

This priestly function exists across the spectrum of informative, persuasive and entertaining media. News stories, for instance, implicitly take the viewpoint that evil results from the wicked actions of evil people, not from any human defect that would implicate the entire human race.

Such a popular theology confirms the common precepts that audiences wish to believe, namely, that evil can be eliminated by removing evil people from society. Similarly, television commercials, billboards and magazine advertisements reinforce the public hope that various products and services can make anyone happy, beautiful or popular. Even the entertainment media join in this prophetic role by confirming a myth such as individualism through various narrative formulas. From a priestly perspective, the media accept the world the way it is and make it even more that way.

Prophetic. Media also function as prophets by purporting to bring truth to the people. We see this not just in news media (for example, newspaper columnists and TV-news anchors) but also in political talk-radio (thus saith the host), literature (novels that "reveal" aspects of life and the human condition) and cinema (the filmmaker's vision of the human condition). Media offer this type of prophetic word or image whenever they claim a new insight, privileged information or prescient knowledge.

Of course it is often difficult to determine the line between prophetic and priestly media without both critical discernment and a standard of truth external to the media. A popular political talk-show host and an established highbrow novelist may seem to have little in common when in fact each one panders his or her prophetic insights to a particular audience predisposed to such beliefs.

Mass Media and the Culture Wars

In many parts of the world, the mass media have a growing cultural influence over all areas of life. Most importantly they compete for authority with local nurturing institutions, including the family,* schools and churches.* This tension creates waves of antagonisms between media elites and the leaders of local groups who feel that their ways of life are threatened by the media. Many of the battles over sex, violence and profanity in the media, for example, are rooted in conflicting moral standards represented by Hollywood (or the Western world) on the one hand and particular religious, ethnic or nationalistic identities on the other.

While some groups merely criticize the media, others take the more positive approach of establishing their own, alternative media. The trend toward mass media is always challenged by this countervailing force of media that serve distinct cultural, even religious, groups. Christians, for example, have their own publishing houses, periodicals, radio and television stations and networks, and recording industry. Ironically, evangelicals often view these specialized media as evangelism* when, in fact, distinctly Christian media rarely appeal to the broader culture.*

Newer electronic media also promise to give religious groups an opportunity to organize in opposition to mainstream media. Fax machines, satellites and especially electronic mail (computer-to-computer communication) are important challenges to traditional broadcasting and publishing. It remains to be seen, however, whether new media will eventually become merely a part of the existing media empires, commercial or ideological.

The Media-Savvy Christian

It is increasingly apparent that the church needs media-savvy believers. Among the greatest needs are (1) well-informed, discerning critics of the mainstream mass media, (2) gifted writers and producers who can work in both Christian and mainstream media, (3) talented engineers and technicians who can help connect the church to the new world of electronic media, (4) articulate

Christians who can help establish public policies ensuring that the media do not become the exclusive domain of self-interested business or ideological groups and (5) motivated teachers who will educate future generations of Christian media professionals and critics.

See also CULTURE; LEISURE; RECREATION; TELEVISION.

References and Resources
J. Ellul, *Propaganda: The Formation of Men's Attitudes* (New York: Knopf, 1971); J. D. Hunter, *Culture Wars: The Struggle to Define America* (New York: BasicBooks, 1991); M. McLuhan, *Gutenberg Galaxy: The Making of Typographic Man* (Toronto: University of Toronto Press, 1965); M. McLuhan, *The Medium Is the Message* (New York: Bantam, 1967); Q. J. Schultze, ed., *American Evangelicals and the Mass Media: Perspectives on the Relationship Between American Evangelicals and the Mass Media* (Grand Rapids: Zondervan/Academie Books, 1990).

Quentin J. Schultze

MASTURBATION

Masturbation, or self-stimulation that produces erotic arousal, is nearly universally practiced (more frequently by men then women) from infancy through old age. The practice is subject to varying interpretations that range from being a gift of God to always being a sin. Before you jump to a quick conclusion, consider the following discussion.

God's Original Intention
God created man and woman as sexual beings with desires and passionate longings. These passions and desires are part of God's good creation. Therefore, infants desire nurture, children desire responsiveness, preadolescents desire close friends, teens desire loving friends, and adults desire companionship and sexual intimacy. God created us with sexual desires in order to create and nurture the bond between husband and wife

(Gen 2:24; 1 Cor 7:3-5), to provide intimate pleasure (Prov 5:18-19) and to sustain creation through offspring (Mal 2:15). Since God created the male and female bodies for one another, for intimacy and relationship, masturbation by its very nature falls short of the full expression of sexuality* God intended. Yet it is interesting that there are only two forms of sexual expression not prohibited in the Bible: sex within the marriage* relationship (by the Bible's overt affirmation) and masturbation (by the Bible's silence on the subject). Solomon says of these passions that God has placed within us, and of love in particular, that "love is as strong as death. . . . It burns like blazing fire, like a mighty flame" (Song 8:6). The discovery, acceptance, appreciation and nurture of this blazing fire within is a good and godly pilgrimage.

As with all pilgrimages, on this one there are detours and obstacles along the way. Because we are fallen creatures, our passions can lead us away from God and healthy sexuality. According to the New Testament, especially Paul, to be driven by the passions of fallen human nature is to be enslaved to sin. This affects the whole person, including the mind and the will (Rom 1:26). A person's desires can lead to ungodly acts (Eph 4:22), to gratification apart from good (Gal 5:16), to the breakup of marriage (compare Mt 5:28), to distance from God (Eph 2:3). Even prayer can be misused (Jas 4:1-3).

The solution to fallen flesh in the New Testament is to receive God's love and Holy Spirit and to follow after the prompting of the Spirit (Rom 8:9-11; Gal 5:16-18). With regard to sexuality, as one walks after the Spirit, one realizes that both by the purchase accomplished by Christ on the cross and by the indwelling of the Holy Spirit one's body belongs to the Lord, not to sexual immorality (1 Cor 6:9-29). Further, self-control is one of the fruits of the Spirit. Self-control is the grace-enacted restraining or moderating of one's desires or having power over oneself rather than being mastered by anything (1 Cor 7:5, 9; 9:25; Gal 5:23). Redeemed sexuality, then, could include the following: accepting sexual desire and sensuality as God's good creation; repenting from the cultural sexual ethic toward God's purposes for sexuality; developing the ability to accept nurturing from others, including God, and to nurture self, that is, to know and express desires, wants and areas of discomfort; developing warm and caring friendships* that are not erotic or genital with the same and opposite sex; and seeking a special mutual intimacy in marriage in which each person willingly abandons the self to the other sexually in a temporary surrender of ego and control that grows and matures over time.

Understanding Masturbation

How does all this apply to the issue of masturbation? First we look at masturbation as an expression of the passion of fallen human nature. In children masturbatory behaviors can become a negative behavior pattern leading to extreme withdrawal when children do not have enough interaction with people or activities, are severely punished for playing with their genitals or are inappropriately sexually stimulated by others. In adolescence* and beyond, fantasy generally accompanies masturbation. We know from behavioral psychology that pleasure,* more than pain, shapes behavior. What gives pleasure is likely to be repeated.

When an individual repeatedly masturbates to an unhealthy fantasy (that is, one involving power, manipulation, coercion, or one-sided, nonconsenting same-sex or multiple-partner relationships), the pleasure experience imprints the fantasy's sexual misbeliefs ("What feels good is good"; "What feels good

must be right"; "I must be gay"; "I am so horny I can't control myself") and increases the proclivity to act out the fantasy. Counselors repeatedly see unhealthy masturbatory fantasies as part of inappropriate and illegal compulsive sexual behaviors. The personal cost of an unhealthy masturbatory fantasy/behavior is an increase in isolation and loneliness, the creation of unrealistic expectations and imprinting that may lead to destructive behaviors. In marriage an unhealthy masturbatory fantasy/behavior may weaken the marital and emotional bond, increasing the distance between spouses. In these situations the person is mastered by his or her passions and is out of control and in need of God's grace as well as clinical wisdom in order to follow after the Spirit, to regain self-control and to honor the Lord with his or her body.

Second, we look at masturbation as an expression of redeemed sexuality. To experience and accept one's body* as a gift from God means that looking, touching and experiencing pleasure is a normal, developmental part of healthy sexuality. Further, a healthy masturbatory fantasy/behavior (that is, one that anticipates or images a monogamous, mutual, heterosexual marriage relationship) can assist a person in developing sexual awareness and sensitivity, in learning about genital arousal and orgasm, in anticipating or focusing on appropriate future marital relationships rather than being promiscuous, and in easing the transition into shared intimacies in marriage. There are often times in marriage when one's spouse is not available for sexual intimacy; masturbation with a fantasy imaging mutual positive experiences with one's spouse is an acceptable alternative if it increases openness and closeness rather than distance. On the other hand, not all arousal needs to be pursued. Arousal can be allowed to subside with no impediment to the self or the relationship.

Practical Strategies
In making decisions about masturbation and fantasy you may find the following points and questions helpful.

Thank God for your sexual feelings and for the Spirit, who redeems our passions and leads us in self-control (whether present or still to come).

Know that you can control your fantasy and that you are responsible for your behavior. God has created you in Christ for this maturity.

If you feel stuck in a negative pattern, resist despising yourself; resist focusing too much on this one area of your life. Seek competent counsel, and remember that God welcomes you and will not cast you off.

When you sense yourself becoming aroused, engage your mind and ask yourself a few questions before you decide to masturbate. By being in touch with your emotional experiences and open before God, you can decide whether to continue or to allow the arousal to dissipate and deal with the feelings and thoughts accompanying the arousal. Ask yourself what has triggered this arousal: positive desire? delight in passions? anger? sadness? frustration? If the emotions* are negative, deal with these. Masturbation will be inappropriate. Also ask yourself what consequences you will experience in relationship to God, to significant others and to yourself: appreciation? positive anticipation? coolness? distance? regret? guilt? Make your decision in light of your answers.

See also IMAGINATION; PLEASURE; SEXUALITY.

References and Resources
D. G. Benner, *Baker Encyclopedia of Psychology* (Grand Rapids: Baker, 1985); G. R. Collins, *Christian Counseling: A Comprehensive Guide*

(Waco, Tex.: Word, 1980); J. R. Johnson, "Toward a Biblical Approach to Masturbation," *Journal of Psychology and Theology* 10, no. 2 (1982) 137-46; C. Penner and J. Penner, *Counseling for Sexual Disorders* (Dallas: Word Publications, 1990); C. Penner and J. Penner, *Sexual Facts for the Family* (Dallas: Word Publications, 1992); J. White, *Eros Defiled* (Downers Grove, Ill.: InterVarsity Press, 1977).

Mike Nichols

MEAL PREPARATION
Meal preparation can be a delight; but for most of us, most of the time, it is more like drudgery. This conflict between drudgery and delight lies at the heart of the Mary-Martha story (Lk 10:38-42). Martha's preparations for Jesus' visit weren't the real problem—a look at the wording is revealing: "Martha was *distracted* by *all* the preparations that *had* to be made" (emphasis added). It is clear that Martha opened her home to Jesus with the *strength* of frenetic, hard work—but not with her heart, soul* and mind as did her sister, Mary, who listened. Thus her necessary preparations were all drudgery and no delight.

The Meaning of the Mundane
In the busyness of preparing our meals, we need to see the meaning in the mundane, the delight beyond the drudgery. We do not merely prepare *feedings* (as if for animals). The simplest meal, even when we are alone, can be a communion with God through his creation*—which is why we say grace before we eat. To gather foods from garden or orchard is to be reminded of the richness and diversity of creation; God said, "Everything that lives and moves will be food for you" (Gen 9:3). Likewise the peeling, chopping and slicing of vegetables, the testing and tasting of sauces, the kneading and shaping of breads are both labor and a means of loving. Meals can sustain both body* and soul, and can with care be

celebrations of all that it means to be a human being made in the image of God. This transformation, through loving preparation, of "feeding" into a *meal* becomes a way to love God with all our heart, soul, mind and strength.

Jesus himself not only affirmed the meaning of meals but was concerned with their preparation. His first miracle was "preparing" extra wine for a wedding. One time he broke bread and fish for four thousand people—another time for five thousand (and he saved the leftovers too). On his last evening with the disciples before his death,* Jesus arranged the details and broke the bread for the Passover meal. And one of his last recorded acts after the resurrection was making a simple seaside meal of roasted fish and some bread: "Come and have breakfast," he said to his friends, after their hard night's work (Jn 21:12). Thus our meal preparations are hallowed by Jesus' example.

The Ministry of Hospitality*

But in North America, according to recent studies, we increasingly avoid the whole bother of meal preparation by "eating out." More and more we rely on restaurants for "special" meals not only for ourselves but also for a relief from the pressure of home hospitality. Sometimes this substitute is a necessary means of coping with a busy schedule. But we should look with critical eyes at the busyness in our lives that keeps us from preparing meals for family* and friends. We would do well to remember Jesus' example and the biblical maxim to "practice hospitality" (Rom 12:13). Preparing meals is part of a larger pattern of opening our home* life to others. Giving up meal preparation can be a danger signal of Martha-living versus Mary-listening.

Part of the problem may be that we've so increased our expectations of how the house ought to look and what we ought to serve and how very perfect everything—including ourselves—should be that we've lost sight of the whole point of preparing a meal. A way back is to remember the beautiful phrase from Psalm 23: "You prepare a table before me." God creates a place for us always—no matter what is going on or who is around ("in the presence of my enemies").

We can learn much about this ability to "prepare a table" from other traditions. A young German woman, when asked if she doesn't feel tired and left out when she spends long hours in the kitchen preparing a traditional German Christmas dinner, replies, "I've been taught that preparing a beautiful meal for friends is a way of loving them; I think about them and their joy in my meal while I cook." A Jewish mother *as a matter of tradition* prays for the members of her family, kneading love* into the loaves as she makes her sabbath* challah bread. The Mennonite cookbook *Extending the Table* abounds with stories of meals from all over the world—meal preparations that begin automatically, whenever a guest arrives. Such preparations ring with the thoroughness of celebration over the prodigal son in Jesus' story. Whether strangers or strayed sons, all who come to our home should be welcomed with some token of the fatted calf—exuberance with which that father welcomed his son.

Despite these principles of hospitality—which we would all affirm—sometimes it's hard to rationalize the time it takes to make meals over and over, day in, day out. At such times we might find it helpful to take a slightly different approach to help us recover the joy of preparing and serving meals in the midst of all the work. Here are a few suggestions:

Make food from scratch. It's usually better that way, and has more of your own love in it. But a good meal from basic ingredients need not be a complicated, multicourse extravagance. Soup and warm bread or biscuits can be deeply satisfying and mean only two preparations, a simple place setting and a minimum of up-and-down from the table after serving. Such a meal focuses attention on the daily bread of sustenance and on the enjoyment of the meal together.

Cook from ingredients obtained directly from their source. The plants and animals which produce our food are God's creations, not just raw material. Whether the ingredients be from our own garden or a farmer's market, knowing where our food comes from helps us to appreciate both those other creations and the kind of husbandry that brings them to our table. Our urban culture* often traps us as unknowing participants in patterns of agriculture that we would deplore if we knew about them. Checking out the sources of our food and buying from farmers who care about the creatures they grow for us can shift us, and our whole society,* toward patterns of life that are more responsible to creation and Creator.

Serve with creativity. Any meal—even toast and tea—gains elegance and a great deal of spiritual and emotional flavor from the way it is served. A tablecloth and folded cloth napkins, wood or pottery serving bowls (or even shells for jam or a sauce), candles—any one of these can transform a simple meal into a statement: "We love you; we care for you; we want this meal to be a special time for you."

Prepare a meal with friends. If the prospect of making a complicated meal seems overwhelming, one wonderful solution is to cook it together with our guests. When we work alongside friends to accomplish a goal—such as making a casserole or a pie—often the getting-to-know-each-other part of the meal is made easy. When our hands and bodies

are busy, our souls can relax from the social pressure to say the right bright thing.

Celebrate the Lord's Supper in the context of a real meal. All meals have been hallowed by the meal of bread and wine that Jesus gave to his disciples as a pattern of remembering for all believers. Usually our Communion meal is a pale wafer-and-sip substitute for the richly meaningful complete meal, the Seder supper, that is the ancient Hebrew origin of the Christian Eucharist. Placing Communion in the midst of that meal—or any meal—is a way of restoring community to Christian Communion.

In 2 Kings, a war was averted when the king of Israel, at Elisha's command, prepared a great feast and served it to the raiding bands from Aran. Our meals may not stop wars, but they may be one of the best ways to bring family members, friends and churches* together.

See also EATING; HOMEMAKING; HOSPITALITY.

References and Resources
R. F. Capon, *Supper of the Lamb* (New York: Harvest Books/Harcourt Brace Jovanovich, 1969); A. Schmemann, *For the Life of the World* (Crestwood, N.Y.: St. Vladimir's Seminary Press, 1982); J. Handrich Schlabach, *Extending the Table* (Scottdale, Penn.: Herald Press, 1991); M. Zimmerman, *Celebrate the Feasts* (Minneapolis: Bethany House, 1981).

Mary Ruth Wilkinson

MEGACHURCH
Large congregations are not a new phenomenon. They have existed at certain times across all the main branches of Christendom. One only has to look at the size of medieval Catholic cathedrals, attend the services of some Orthodox churches or visit meeting places associated with great Protestant preachers like Charles Spurgeon or D. L. Moody to realize this. What is new is the number of

very large churches that have appeared during the last generation.

The emergence of so many megachurches is a notable feature of recent church life. Yet even medium-sized congregations of around five hundred or more members are still comparatively rare. For example, only 1 in every 24 Presbyterian Church (U.S.A.) congregations, 1 in every 36 American Baptist, 1 in every 47 United Methodist and 1 in every 87 United Church of Christ (UCC) have such numbers. Episcopalians and Southern Baptists do even better than Presbyterians; the Christian Church (Disciples of Christ) and Church of God have fewer than the UCC.

A growing number of churches have several thousand members, and some more than ten thousand. Some churches overseas are immense. At latest count David (Yonggi) Cho's Presbyterian church in Seoul had around 750,000 members, though these can only be accommodated in a series of services over the weekend and by decentralizing other services around the city. According to the original meaning of the word *church** as "a gathering" or "an assembly," this is not a single congregation but rather multiple congregations bound together under a single leadership (*see* Leadership, Church).

The most recent estimates suggest that only around 6 percent of churches in the United States can be called large or megachurches, and these represent about 14 percent, or one-seventh, of the churchgoing population. While this is a significant phenomenon, to put it in perspective, we should compare it with the rise of the charismatic house-church movement in England, which also attracts around 15 percent of the churchgoing population, primarily in small or medium-sized congregations. (*see* Church in the Home).

Strengths

The strengths of megachurches are their openness to change, their emphasis on the importance of the local church, their cultural sensitivity to what will interest outsiders and their recognition of the value of the behavioral and communication sciences. In a sense they are the religious counterpart to the large shopping malls* that have grown up on the edge of suburban cities and major metropolises. Like them they are strong on innovation, are set in a centralized location easily accessible by car, offer a full range of attractive facilities and programs from which to choose, and make use of the latest data and technology* to target their activities.

The leadership of megachurches is generally constructed along the best corporate lines, revolving around a charismatic counterpart of the chief executive officer. Megachurches engage in skillful, and often tasteful, marketing to targeted constituencies of what they have to offer. All this is often symbolized in functional and expressive contemporary buildings in a spacious parklike campus or mall-like setting. Most of them contain eating* areas and places for socializing, services of various kinds for those in need, and a festive atmosphere and experience with lots of other people. The latest version of the megachurch phenomenon, the so-called metachurch model, anticipates increased growth beyond the capabilities of any one meeting place or parking area by advocating the decentralization of many activities to a range of locations with only occasional full-scale gatherings for celebration, perhaps in a convention center, amphitheater or even stadium.

Megachurches differ in emphasis. Most, those more traditional in character, frame their main gatherings primarily for their regular attenders, though they generally do so in a way that is culturally attuned to their members' as well as to outsiders' needs* and longings. An increasing number orient their main meetings, *seeker services* as they call them, primarily to outsiders who are open to or have begun a spiritual journey. Such services avoid all that is unfamiliar to a non-Christian audience and so omit religious jargon, creedal affirmations, Scripture reading and expository preaching.* Some megachurches, on the analogy of the newer "power stores," are more specialized in approach, targeting a particular subculture, such as the "baby busters" (the under-thirties generation), and orienting their music, preaching and dramatic presentations to that age group.

Megachurches will often hold services of a more conventional kind for their core members at some other time during the week. They will also generally provide a substantial Christian education* program for their members, highly segmented according to interest, concern or need. Here and there a few are developing their own programs in theological education. Many of them also have a number of ministries and services to their wider community, as well as a commitment to mission in other parts of the world. A number of them have become show-and-tell centers for pastors and lay leaders from across the country and overseas. Increasingly megachurches are networking with each other, assisted by parachurch groups like the Leadership Foundation that are committed to enhancing them and increasing their number.

Weaknesses and Responses to Them

Critics of megachurches argue that they have several serious weaknesses. Some attack their tendency to rely on human strategies, borrowed from the advertising* and marketing world, rather than on the Holy Spirit. This, it is said, opens them up to purveying values* more closely associated with modernity than with Christianity, such as a reliance on numbers, techniques and success,* and so softening the hard edges of the gospel of sacrifice and suffering. Others point to the class and racial homogeneity that is found in many megachurches. Critics also attack the temptation in the megachurches to focus on the personal, spiritual and moral at the expense of social issues and structures.* Still others point to their tendency to drain people away from smaller churches that cannot compete with the range and quality of groups and other services, let alone physical surroundings or corporate worship,* that megachurches provide.

Defenders of megachurches reply that they are not adapting or assimilating Christianity to the modern world but opening up and drawing in the modern world to Christianity. Contemporary communication methods and technologies are neutral; it all depends on what you use them for (a position that others are quick to challenge, as does Os Guinness). They also argue that churches among any people group develop most quickly on the homogeneous church growth principle (though in an increasingly pluralistic society this tends to have less force). Many megachurches are also engaged in charitable aid and mission programs (but do not tend to be in the vanguard for structural or institutional change). They also tend to have a planned approach to gradually introducing attenders to the full dimensions of discipleship* and giving them multiple opportunities for service (generally still focused on the church, however, and not always as far-reaching as what we find among the early Christians).

There is something to learn from the megachurch about cultural awareness, the use of jargon-free communication, sensitivity to people's needs and longings, and developing hands-on training and homegrown leadership. But we should also consider whether vital things are lost, such as making love of God and neighbor* the center and criterion of church life, moving away from a needs-based consumer approach to God in favor of one more focused on gratitude and service,* and relying more on organic rather than organized ways of training and growing leaders. Another troubling factor is that up to 80 percent of megachurch attendance comes from transfer membership rather than the unchurched.

Current Trends

In any case it is interesting to see signs of a move away from megachurches. The growing interest in living and working in a given region in a city is turning people away from metropolitan to more local churches, and the desire for community* is tending to attract people to congregations where they feel less overwhelmed by numbers. This is where the metachurch idea and the necessity of a strong cell-group life in a large church become imperative (*see* Church in the Home; Small Groups). Also, a recent comprehensive study by a major denomination in the United States revealed that in general the larger the church people attended, the less commitment and giving they were likely to exhibit; the smaller the church, the more they tended to be involved in, felt responsible for and contributed to it. As a result, some are now beginning to turn away from encouraging ever bigger churches to planting smaller churches instead.

These trends do not rule out an ongoing function for a number of very large churches. There is room for some to act as mission churches, reaching out to seekers and outsiders, and as feeder institutions to the other churches in their region, perhaps partly supported by such churches in their wide-ranging evangelistic work. There is also room for others to develop into what might be termed *cathedral churches,* offering a range of educational, organizational, networking* and training services to smaller and medium-sized churches in their region. Such churches would be helped by a stronger theological understanding of, and distinction between, church and mission* and of ordinary Christians' vocation in the world as well as the church.

See also CHURCH BUILDINGS; CHURCH, SMALL; CONSUMERISM; EVANGELISM; WORSHIP.

References and Resources
L. Anderson, *A Church for the Twenty-first Century* (Minneapolis: Bethany House, 1992); P. Y. Cho with R. W. Manzano, *More Than Numbers* (Waco, Tex.: Word, 1984); C. George, *Prepare Your Church to Meet the Future* (New York: Revell, 1991); O. Guinness, *Dining with the Devil: The Megachurch Movement Flirts with Modernity* (Grand Rapids: Baker, 1993); R. H. Schuller, *Your Church Has a Fantastic Future* (Ventura, Calif.: Regal, 1986); D. A. Womack, *The Pyramid Principle of Church Growth* (Minneapolis: Bethany Fellowship, 1977).

Robert Banks

MEMBERSHIP, CHURCH

For most Christians choosing a church home is one of the most difficult decisions they feel called upon to make. Do you go where you are needed or where your needs will be met? Do you choose a church that will be best for your children even though it is less stimulating for the parents? Do you go to the church nearest to your home or nearest your work? Should you choose a church in the home—with its intimacy and life-centeredness—or a large church with programs and groups for all ages and interests? Is loyalty to a denomination important, so that moving from one city to another means getting connected with the "branch" store in the new location? Are there specific dangers in joining a nondenominational* community church with no external links or systems of accountability beyond itself? This dilemma is made worse by the lowered expectations of church membership in the Western world compared to the biblical understanding.

Pseudomembership

In a society characterized by "throwaway" relationships, membership is something "tried on," exchanged or not practiced at all. This is deeply tragic because the experience of peoplehood is central to Christianity. Several problems militate against church membership that has a for-better-or-for-worse quality.

Church shopping. In the Western world church is treated as a commodity. Many people shop around for the "best" church and when they find it, join it, remaining only as long as the church maintains the excellence of its product—contemporary worship,* good music,* great preaching* and a womb-to-tomb program. For their part, church leaders conform to the culture and adapt their product to gain a larger share of the market.

Church dating. Further, membership in the church today is much like the common-law marriage euphemistically called "living together." Cohabitation* is an unwritten emotional contract in which a man and a woman agree to live together so long as they both shall love and their mutual needs are met. It is noncovenantal. Indeed, to get married is to change the dynamics of the relationship so profoundly that it could spell the end! In the same way many people associate with a local church, possibly with their names on the church roll, but have not made a covenant to belong. When

the first sign of trouble comes or another church down the road seduces them, they are gone.

Church hopping. Polygamy has a parallel in church membership. God originally intended that a man and woman would belong in a two-shall-become-one marriage* involving leaving, cleaving and one flesh (Gen 2:24). In the same way, we cannot make concrete our membership in the people of God by belonging to all the local congregations in the world, or even two or three, a rapidly growing trend. Membership needs to be made concrete in a specific fellowship* where we can be known, loved, rebuked, exhorted, disciplined and equipped* for service.

Church swapping. There is a further parallel to the polygamous marriage. In our society rampant divorce* leads to serial polygamy, one spouse after another, though still in some ways belonging to former spouses. In the same way some people move from church to church. Often this happens in the context of relocating in another city. The average Canadian and American moves every four to five years, thus militating against the long-term relationships that make church membership both challenging and maturing. This mobility* can be resisted. But when it is not, people often fail to leave the former church emotionally. Again, using marriage language, we say they cannot "cleave" (Gen 2:24 KJV) because they have not "left." They have not gone through a process of grieving* that would have enabled this to take place.

Rethinking Membership

Throughout church history, membership has taken many forms. In the early church becoming a Christian meant joining a despised and persecuted sect in an all-or-nothing way—often with considerable risks involved. When Christianity became the official religion of the Roman Empire, being a citizen* began to be identified with belonging to the church. This situation prompted the monks to flee to the desert to form voluntary and high-commitment Christian communities as a protest against an increasingly worldly church. For several centuries this two-level membership existed and still does in most of the Christian world today. Following the Protestant Reformation, however, people were left with a choice between state churches (where, again, citizenship was equivalent to church membership) and so-called free churches involving voluntary membership often at great cost.

Roman and Orthodox churches made use of the parish concept that both assumes membership (if you live in an area) and invites participation at a more-than-nominal level. There are some parts of the world in which there is such a high percentage of Christians—in some African countries, for example—that we have technically something close to Christendom—a Christian society, though tragically we must note that nominalism is rampant and there seems to be little connection between faith and everyday morality. But for most of the world Christendom is past, and we must reinvent church membership by returning to our source document, the New Testament.

Belonging to God. In the Bible we are invited, first of all, not to join the church but to join God! The nuptial invitation of Jesus is simply to belong to him forever. We then become a child of God in God's family (the family of Father, Son and Holy Spirit; Jn 1:12); we call God *Abba;* we dwell in the love of God, which is the love eternally expressed between Father, Son and Holy Spirit. Becoming a Christian is simply getting "into" God. Once joining God, we are automatically members of the people of God. Formal-

izing that membership in terms of belonging to a specific local congregation is important for Christian growth, but it is meaningless unless we have joined God. Decide for Christ and you have already decided for membership in the church. We cannot have Jesus without his people; he is married to his bride, even if that bride, as the English poet Swinburne once sneered, is "leprous."

Belonging to God's people. It is impossible to experience all the "togethers" in Paul's letters without have specific people to whom you are joined. Paul crafted new words by joining the Greek word *syn,* "together with," to nouns and verbs to communicate that it is impossible to be in Christ alone. We are members together, joined together, heirs together, embodied together, growing together, being built together and held together. In addition there are all the "one anothers" in the New Testament. Belong to one another (Rom 12:10); carry one another's burdens (Gal 6:2); forgive one another (Col 3:13); love one another (Jn 13:34); and speak the truth to one another (Eph 4:25). The individual Christian—in the Western sense of an isolated person—does not exist. Join God and you have joined God's family. "Sir, you wish to serve God and go to heaven?" asked a "serious young man" in response to a question from John Wesley. "Remember that you cannot serve him alone. You must therefore find companions or make them; the Bible knows nothing of solitary religion."

In reality this is a great boon. The local church is a place to belong, serve, grow and know God together. We belong together not because of our appearance, expertise, usefulness, race or performance but because of *whose* we are—an identity formed through being and becoming rather than doing and achieving. We serve together because ministry* is not a number of solo efforts by religious entrepreneurs but the synergism of spiritual gifts* combined in dynamic partnership. We grow together because the church context is a life context that nurtures maturity as we continuously rub shoulders with (and sometimes rub the wrong way) our brothers and sisters in Christ (*see* Church-Family). We know God together because each person's experience, gift and personality enlarge ours; it is "together with all the saints" (Eph 3:18) that we can know the width, height and depth of the love of God.

There is nothing like the church on earth. God's church is a collection of ordinary people who have nothing in common except their love for Jesus but who call each other brothers and sisters and would risk their lives for each other. Jews and Gentiles, black and white, rich and poor, educated and uneducated, extrovert and introvert, experience a miraculous equality that is, nevertheless, not a bland sameness: "All for one, and one for all."

Belonging to sinners. But here is the rub: the church is a community of sinners in process of being saved. When people join a church, they have what Dietrich Bonhoeffer once called a "wishdream" (p. 26) of the perfect community. Some spend a lifetime looking for the perfect church. Not finding it, some try to start their own. The reason is very deep: they are not prepared to commit themselves to sinners. So, like Judas, they make only a partial commitment to the people of God as they find it. As an astute African once said, like Judas they find their identity in rebellion against their brothers and sisters. God hates such visionary dreaming. God wants us to love real people, not ideal people, just as God does. There is a profound spiritual issue involved in this. If we refuse to associate with sinners, we are implicitly forgetting that Jesus has associated with us.

Belonging to sinners covenantally. There

must be something like "for better or for worse" involved. When trouble comes, when a leader fails, when there is a budget crunch, when there is fighting, it is tempting to leave and find another church where we can experience, at least for a few months, a religious equivalent of infatuation. Some people move from one church infatuation to another because they are in love with the idea of being spiritually stimulated. They want romance rather than covenant marriage, but by running on a romantic high, they short-circuit spiritual growth* and have only superficial relationships. Almost all of the exhortations in the New Testament (such as "be filled with the Holy Spirit"; Eph 5:18) and most of the promises of the New Testament (such as the fruit of the Spirit; Gal 5:22-23) are *community* messages. They come through belonging, not flirting. So joining the church is a covenant issue.

Choosing a Church Home

People go about choosing a church in different ways.

Choosing unconsciously. Many people choose churches that unconsciously fit their personality or spirituality types. If they are given to emotional expressiveness, they choose a charismatic church. If they love structure,* they go for a liturgical community. If they have recently received the gift of tongues, they choose a church that maximizes spiritual gifts rather than one that takes social justice* seriously. If they love classical music, they go to a church with a pipe organ rather than one that composes new songs. Yet we grow most when we are challenged in a diverse community (*see* Spiritual Formation; Spiritual Growth). The habituated, structured person may profit from immersion in a spontaneous fellowship; the person who loves the unpredictability of a Spirit-filled fellowship often needs more structure and depth.

621

We may grow more, and contribute more, in a fellowship that does not merely reinforce our "strengths," which often are weaknesses in disguise. Yet all of this assumes we have a choice—something that is alien to the New Testament.

Choosing geographically. The New Testament situation finds its closest contemporary counterpart in small towns in rural areas where there is only one church. Where there are several churches in a town, one for each denomination, the situation is usually settled by remaining in the tradition of your family. Moving from one to another becomes a matter of small-town gossip,* though this is not a good reason to refrain from making a change. Choosing a church home in larger cities that serve a mobile society is like trying to choose a product as we wander through a supermarket: often we end up relying on advertising* to tell us what to do. Most people opt for trying out a number of churches by attending Sunday services. Usually this involves taking the spiritual temperature of the people by assessing the quality of worship and the friendliness of the people and by "tasting" the sermon. This method of discernment is just as illusory as assessing the prospects for a life partner by attending a series of high-school dances. Worship is much more than worship services. It is not even intended primarily for *our* benefit and pleasure. And real fellowship is experienced not in a handshake at the door and a hug during the service (*see* Sugar, Sugary) but in sharing all the dimensions of everyday life with other believers. Sermons are meant to evoke faith, not to entertain.

Choosing discerningly. A better way is to find out what various churches believe, their mission statement, whether they believe and practice every-member ministry. Interview some of the members as well as some of the leaders. Ask to meet

with people in their homes rather than in the church building.* This gives you insight into the translation of faith into everyday life.

If you pray continuously and keep a journal, choosing a church can become a spiritual discipline.* It will raise all kinds of questions that can be turned into contemplation: How has God made you? How should you resolve the competing agendas of self and family*? Have you dealt with hurts you experienced in previous fellowships? What are your own longings for service and ministry? Why do you feel most comfortable in some situations but more challenged in others? Do you still have passion for God? Do you love God's people as they are? In short, there may be no better way to overcome the ubiquitous pressure to treat membership as a commodity than to go deeper with yourself, your God and your closest neighbors in life—usually spouse and family. But how do you join?

The Lost Art of Joining

Systems thinking helps us understand and respond to the complexity of joining a church. In systems thinking the whole is more than the sum of the parts: the body is not just a collection of individual believers but a living whole with a life of its own. Each local church is a unique system. Further, except in large churches (*see* Megachurch), every member is related to every other like elements in a mobile; move one element and every other element must adjust. The relationship of members in a healthy system is characterized as interdependence—that lovely balance of the twin needs to be "me" and to be "we" (Friedman). Persons are not merged into one homogenous sect as in the "melting pot church" or loosely connected as in the "bouquet of Christians" church (Collins and Stevens, p. 21) without mutual ministry and belonging. The first church tends to codependence, the second church to independence. While sometimes we are called upon to join such churches and gradually help challenge and even change these systems, a different image of the church emerges in the early Christian writings.

The body, family or covenant church —all New Testament metaphors (see Collins and Stevens, pp. 92-107)—has interdependent members, coordinated together, enriching one another through their diversity. The body is more one *because* of the many.

Joining a new system. Understanding the local church as a system is most helpful in joining a church. First, one cannot really join if one belongs to another church and has not left. Leaving precedes cleaving, though it is usually a process rather than a single event. Further, each local church is a unique system, and in a sense, membership is not transferable. You must join this unique community for what it is. Comparisons are both unwise and counterproductive.

The joiner and the joined. Joining involves not only the joiner but those being joined. Some new members are frozen out because the system is stuck—frozen for fear of getting bigger or unwilling to have "our cozy fellowship" changed by the addition of new people. So joining the church is a spiritual discipline not only for the joiner but also for the rest of the church. Old members must keep joining, since the church keeps changing as members leave and join. Why are we so unwilling to change? What is it about this new member that threatens us? Do we want to grow, not so much in numbers as in faith and life?

Joining the past. It does not take long to discover that there are unresolved problems in most local congregations. Some of them go back to the pathology of the founding pastor or to major families whose power was thwarted at some point. Usually a small incident in the present provokes a turmoil in the fellowship far beyond its importance because of problems passed from one generation to the next. But these crises are great opportunities to identify unresolved systemic problems and deal with them. To do this, we must ask a lot of questions to find out the history of the fellowship, to discover why certain people quit and left and why others quit and stayed. New members are often able to retain a measure of emotional detachment in such crises, ask pertinent questions, help identify problems and so equip the church to grow in unity, love and health.

If joining the church is an art that must be recovered, so must the art of welcoming new members. Often this determines the way the member will relate to and understand the church in future years (Crabtree, p. 12).

The Lost Art of Welcoming

Here are some steps churches can take to evoke deeper membership at the point of entry, ways that are consistent with both systems theory and biblical truth.

Give the new member time to join. Davida Crabtree advises not rushing people into formal membership and, when people are ready for it, requiring participation in several membership class sessions. Many churches treat membership as a marriage without engagement, without premarital counseling and without much forethought. No wonder there are so many church membership divorces! Such hasty marriages may be stimulated by anxiety. Trust will allow people to take their time.

Explain the systemic dimensions of membership. Crabtree touched on four themes in premembership classes: (1) the church's way of working, (2) gifts identification, not only for in-church ministry but for all of life, (3) introduction to the ministry of the laity and (4) frank talk about faith and money, including the tradition, denominational relationships and setting in Christian history (pp. 13-14). Since true covenantal membership is mutual and bilateral, the process of receiving a new member is also an opportunity to expound the implications for the other members.

Make joining concrete and covenantal. Symbols are important in any organizational culture.* For example, the offering of "the right hand of fellowship," as it is called in some churches, or a similar ritual has a powerfully evocative impact on both the new member and the church (really the "new" church), just as the vows "for better, for worse" in a wedding service can hardly be witnessed without tears. If new members are welcomed officially by several representatives of the church, the act symbolizes joining the church, not joining the pastor.

Make joining a continuous process. The church you join tomorrow will not be the church you joined yesterday. A systemic approach to church membership will involve more than passing on information gained in a membership class. Members who have been leaders in other churches and some who have not yet been leaders will have to find a new leadership role in this new church just as pastors do. Church leaders will need to care for and support people through a process that may take months, possibly even years, as people find their own place in a new church. Remaining a member means participating in a continuous process of renegotiating one's place in the system.

Be aware of the dangers of joining. Some people are all too ready to join—indeed to become addicted to the church. Some churches are addictive organizations (*see* Organizational Culture and Change) requiring a total commitment that should never be demanded. With unhealthy people their emotional health and the

church's well-being are inseparably tied. Their expectations of the church are the sum of what a healthy person should expect from family, church, neighborhood, school, extended family, friends, self and God. Tragically, we must confess that some churches love members like this because they "do all the work."

In summary, church membership needs to be reinvented today. It starts with joining God and continues with joining God's people. It continues through a process of continuous joining as the system we join alters and is altered even by ourselves. This turns out to be a profound spiritual discipline, since it raises important questions about ourselves and our relationship with the gospel. Often, as in a marriage, the moment when we feel like leaving a church can be the most important moment of spiritual growth.

See also ACCOUNTABILITY, RELATIONAL; BAPTISM; CHURCH DISCIPLINE, DISCIPLESHIP; EQUIPPING; MINISTRY; SERVICE.

References and Resources

D. Bonhoeffer, *Life Together* (New York: Harper & Row, 1954); M. Bowen and M. Kerr, *Family Evaluation: An Approach Based on Bowen Theory* (New York: Norton, 1988); P. Collins and R. P. Stevens, *The Equipping Pastor: A Systems Approach to Empowering the People of God* (Washington, D.C.: Alban Institute, 1993), portions quoted with permission; D. F. Crabtree, *The Empowering Church: How One Congregation Supports Lay People's Ministries in the World* (Washington, D.C.: Alban Institute, 1989); E. H. Friedman, *Generation to Generation: Family Process in Church and Synagogue* (New York: Guilford, 1985); G. L. Sittser, *Loving Across Our Differences* (Downers Grove, Ill.: InterVarsity Press, 1994).

R. Paul Stevens

MENOPAUSE AND MALE CLIMACTERIC

The term *climacteric* can be applied to both men and women since the word suggests consummation or completion, in this case of one facet of reproductive life. The term *menopause* can properly be used only of females, since it means the end, or "pause," of the menses. The popular term *male menopause* is really an oxymoron. Menopause for a woman is the cessation of monthly menstruation, but it is much more: it is also a life transition that invites a woman to find meaning in life on the basis of something other than her fertility and the monthly patterns that have provided an internal structure (*see* Menstruation). The male climacteric is a more gentle transition, though it is sometimes associated with marker events such as buying a first sports car or giving up playing football. For the male the period is characterized by the biologic waning of his sexual desire and capacity. Usually the desire exceeds the capacity, and this may lead to painful and destructive attempts to recover sexual prowess with "someone else," usually younger and more attractive. So the male experience also has both physiological and spiritual implications for the person and his marriage.

Mutual Ministry in Life Transitions
A theology and spirituality of life transitions can equip men and women to assist each other through this significant passage. That is why we have written about these experiences as a husband and wife partnership.

The physical changes associated with pre-, pere- (during) and postmenopause lead women to experience many related psychological dimensions. Married women are afraid they will no longer be attractive to their husbands. Single women, perhaps still hoping until now that they might bear children, receive a profound signal from their bodies that they will not be able to do so. Men are afraid of losing their prowess. In a sexually oriented society in which a woman

must look young, thin and beautiful and a man must be macho and virile, both men and women will struggle with their self-image and identity as they approach this midlife transition and enter into maturity. This is especially exacerbated by a society that idolizes youth and physical beauty* as projected in the icons of the mass media* and advertising.* Tragically unlike older, and a few rural, societies, Western society does not normally treasure the wisdom and integrated maturity that can be the special asset of this period in the aging* process. In tribal cultures not only men but women gain status as they grow older and are regarded as sexual persons throughout their whole life (Bourgeois-Law, p. 11).

In the Western world the transition for both men and women is surrounded with myths. For the woman there is the myth that since she has lost her ovarian hormones, she is no longer interested in sexual intimacy. But the lack of estrogen does not tell the whole story. Gisèle Bourgeois-Law notes that "adrenal, thyroid and growth hormones are also believed to influence human sexual behavior" (p. 11). The head (brain) is still the major sexual organ! Human sexuality* is too complex a matter to be explained by any single physiological factor. Many women enjoy intimate sexual expression even more than in former days, for it allows them and their husbands to express the unitive, and not only the procreative, aspects of sexual love. Sometimes sexual dysfunction in a marriage at this point is blamed on menopause when the actual cause is a psychological dissatisfaction with the marriage relationship as a whole.

For the man passage into middle and late adulthood is a less distinct experience unmarked by a dramatic change in his body or obvious emotional symptoms. With increasing age it takes him longer, and he requires more help to achieve an erection. He may desire or attempt fewer occasions of sexual intercourse—perhaps less than once a week. But this decline, contrary to popular thought, may have social and psychological causes and not merely physical ones (Aitken and Sobrero, p. 262). Some men blame their sexual withering on their physiological "running down" when it may be influenced profoundly by such factors as the loss of work-related identity through retirement.* Contrary to what is thought, many men are able to enjoy their marriage relationship more as a whole as they grow older in a way that includes sexual intimacy because of the quality, rather than quantity, of such encounters. Indeed, the occasions for intercourse, while possibly less frequent, may have deeper meaning and beauty because of the investment of the husband's and wife's years together. Just as an understanding husband can care for his wife through her more dramatic change of life, so an understanding wife can enhance rather than diminish her husband's expression of covenant love in their mature years, especially if they talk about it.

Understanding Menopause

Both female menopause and the male climacteric can be thought of as puberty in reverse. In the teens we contend with oily skin, genital moisture and hair growth. In maturity we find ourselves coping with dryness, brittleness, sagginess and hair loss! In the female symptoms can last from as short a time as a few weeks to as long as four years. Some women have no symptoms other than the stopping of their monthly periods. The hypothalamus in the brain has a considerable responsibility for the changes that actually occur. It sends messages to the ovaries to make more estrogen and, at the same time, stimulates the temperature center. This is believed to

be the cause of the common hot flashes and night sweats. With the slowing down and eventual cessation of estrogen being produced in the ovaries, some or all of the following symptoms may occur: headaches, sleep disturbance, labile (flat) moods, mental fogging, weight gain, shorter menstrual cycles, spotting and vaginal dryness, this last making intercourse without supplemental lubrication uncomfortable.

The major dilemma is whether to look at menopause as a natural process to be left to take its course or as a disease to be treated by alleviating troublesome symptoms. The question of what is normal or abnormal is therefore raised for each woman, and this turns out to be not merely a medical question but a theological one. Calling a natural process a disease can be problematic when one wants a healthy attitude to growing old graciously. But there is also a sociological factor in this matter for women today. We are living longer than previous generations. Many women in developing countries do not live beyond menopause. But where they live this long, the desire to stay young is almost universal.

Today estrogen replacement is the elixir of youth to make this somewhat turbulent period more comfortable and to slow down the aging process. But there are risks. Estrogen is powerful stuff. Receptors from the brain to the bones and liver are affected by its presence, not just the reproductive organs. It poses as a wonder drug, but taking what doctors call *hormone replacement therapy* (HRT) is a complicated matter. When our thyroid gland is deficient, we take thyroxin. When our pancreas is deficient in producing insulin, as in the case of diabetes, we take additional insulin without question. Why not take a replacement when our ovaries stop producing estrogen? Each woman, in consultation with physicians, must decide for herself whether the advantages outweigh the risks. Significantly, of the 22 million women in North America who have been given a prescription for estrogen, as few as 20 to 30 percent get the prescription filled, and only 10 percent continue past a year to receive the long-term benefits.

On the pro side of taking HRT are the following. First, there is the relief of menopausal symptoms: hot flashes, night sweats and vaginal dryness. Second, heart disease is prevented by making the blood vessels pliable, thereby lessening the chances of blockages and improving the ratio of good cholesterol (HDL) over bad cholesterol (LDL). Third, estrogen prevents osteoporosis through retarding the thinning of bones, which make postmenopausal women vulnerable to fractures. Fourth, it reduces the risk of colon cancer, some studies suggesting by as much as 55 percent. Fifth, it slows mental deterioration and improves the memory, reducing the onset of Alzheimer's disease in around 30 to 60 percent of people (Elias). Finally, hormone replacement preserves skin elasticity and helps maintain collagen, which keeps tissues moist and plump.

On the con side is the increase in the possibility of cancer of the female reproductive organs: breast, ovaries and uterus. Dosages, however, are now greatly reduced compared with twenty years ago, and the risks are less onerous. Women who have had hysterectomies (uterus removal) and their ovaries removed are at much less risk. In general it is worth bearing in mind that eight times as many women die of heart attacks as die of breast cancer (Wallis, p. 34). Other less-serious side effects experienced by a small percentage of women are monthly bleeding even until age sixty, abnormal blood clots, benign fibroid tumors, gallstones and increased weight, especially in the thighs.

Given how recently this option has been available and how many questions remain unanswered, it is not surprising that some women feel they are like guinea pigs when it comes to HRT. There are natural alternatives: eating a diet rich in calcium and low in fat, consuming foods containing estrogen (soybeans, Mexican yams and tofu), using multivitamins including vitamin E supplements, exercising (both aerobics for heart and weight-bearing exercises for osteoporosis) and stopping smoking. But many women are thankful to be able to take estrogen. I am one of them, inasmuch as I have had an hysterectomy with ovaries removed, have a family history of heart disease, have no history of breast cancer and have the possibility of developing osteoporosis.

The psychological dimensions of menopause are related to both the physiological changes noted above and expectations generated by society. Like puberty, it is a time of emotional turmoil. Most women experience an emotional relinquishment of fertility, especially singles who have never born a child. At the same time many women desire sexual intimacy more and wonder if their desire is normal, especially if their husband appears to be winding down. The fear of aging and a degradation of self-image are undoubtedly influenced by society in which, as in the West, a postmenopausal woman feels she has lost status. There is, however, an interesting contrast in Japanese society, in which women age with the anticipation of being venerated as they pass through menopause and become respected elders (Hall, p. 11; Lock, p. 1270). All of this suggests that there is more than a clinical disease involved here. Bourgeois-Law concludes in this way: "When dysfunction and dissatisfaction are identified, an approach including empathy, respect and encouragement can restore what has been lost" (p. 14).

Understanding the Passages in a Man's Life

As mentioned above, the male experience of the climacteric may be a more gradual transition. One of the most significant transitions occurs between 40 and 45, when early adulthood is terminated and middle adulthood is entered. Much good work can be done during this 40 to 45 transition (what Jung called the "noon" of life) and the transition that follows later between 60 and 65 (the "afternoon and evening"): developing a greater capacity for intimacy, getting in touch with our feminine side and becoming more of a mentor than a doer. At the same time men are experiencing the loss of youthful energies and are confronted with the certainty of their own inevitable death.* As Daniel Levinson notes, "To experience the dangers and the possibilities of this period is, however, to open a Pandora's box of unconscious fantasies and anxieties" (p. 26). Thus many men, trying to recycle the missed opportunities of an earlier stage and becoming disoriented by their fantasies, abruptly change careers. They buy sports cars and a new wardrobe. And tragically some, like the menopausal priests in Malachi's day, divorce* the wife of their youth for someone who can "turn them on" (Mal 2:14-16).

Add to this the physiological changes in a man's body, and you have a recipe for self-inflicted trauma. Alternatively, you have also an invitation to a deeper spirituality and reevaluation of the meaning of a man's life. While the male climacteric is progressive and diffuse, it is characterized by the need for more prolonged and direct stimulation to achieve an erection and ejaculation. Sometimes men unkindly blame this on their aging wives when it is within the sphere of their own biology. Some commonly used medications, such as antihypertensives and antidepressants, may reduce sexual interest and capacity. In this, as with the woman's experience, it is all too easy to epitomize what is "normal" when each person is unique. Once again communication with one's spouse and friends, empathy and appropriate help can make this time of transition one of the most fruitful periods of a man's life relationally and spiritually.

Theological Reflection

So how are we to think Christianly about this matter? When I (Paul) first read Levinson's book on this, I realized that I was a textbook case with all the right marker events, but then I realized that this scheme does not explain my life at all! My life is ultimately explained by the initiative, providence and acceptance of God. In the same way I (Gail) cannot explain my life by consulting a medical text. We are both mysteries, uniquely fashioned by God and brought together as husband and wife to support and love each other through all of life's transitions, especially when there is not complete synchronism of our experiences. As one author said, "We need withering and senescence lest we deceive ourselves into imagining that everything we desire could be given through more of the same kind of life. . . . We need withering if we are to cultivate within ourselves the deepest rhythm of love—the mystery of self-giving and self-sacrifice that is God's love" (Meilaender, pp. 18-19).

Each season has its own challenge, sometimes more for one partner than the other. If, early in one's marriage, the male was more ready for sexual intimacy, especially during pregnancies and menstrual periods—a difference that invited personal and spiritual growth, understanding and true love—we are entering into a period when these differences may be somewhat reversed. Love listens, understands, waits and supplies what is needed. We testify together that this is the richest time of our married life.

We cannot believe that a sequence of changes programmed in our bodies by our gracious Creator is wrong or evil. Scripture does not deal directly with female menopause and the male climacteric, but it does provide a redemptive perspective. It proposes that God is with us always at each stage of life and that he is with us for good. It offers, as the Puritans understood so well, a way to live fully now by preparing to die and be resurrected—a heavenly mindedness that allows us to flourish now without idolizing, for example, youth. Further, Scripture tells the stories of people who found God in these moments of their lives: Sarah, who knew again "pleasure" (Gen 18:12) in her old age; Anna, the widow praying night and day in the temple; Simeon, the righteous old man—these last two finding in the Christ child the true climax of their lives (Lk 2:25-38).

Living our lives under the initiative, providential care and acceptance of God equips us to see these life transitions as privileged moments. In these moments we can reaffirm the centrality of love* as the mark of true personal maturity; we can recover our identities on the basis of who we love rather than what we are able to do; we can prepare ourselves to die and be resurrected by relinquishing our youth and middle age. As with all crises, this one is both danger and opportunity. Scripture invites us to seize the latter and in doing so to be found contented in God himself.

See also AGING; BODY; DEATH; MARRIAGE; MENSTRUATION; PARENTING; RETIREMENT; SEXUALITY.

References and Resources
G. S. Aitken and A. J. Sobrero, *Dr. Hannah and Abraham Stone's "A Marriage Manual,"* 7th ed. (New York: Simon & Schuster, 1965); J. Balswick, *Men at the Crossroads: Beyond Traditional Roles and Modern Options* (Downers Grove, Ill.: InterVarsity Press, 1992); G. Bour-geois-Law, "Menopause and Sexuality," *Contemporary OB/GYN,* August 1995, 10-14; M. Elias, in *USA Today,* 20 November 1995, Life sec., 1D; D. P. H. Hall, "Dodging Time," *Contemporary Ob/Gyn,* June 1995, 8-16; D. J. Levinson, *The Seasons of a Man's Life* (New York: Knopf, 1978); M. Lock, "Medicine and Culture: Contested Meanings of the Menopause," *Lancet* 337 (1991) 1270; G. Meilaender, "Mortality: The Measure of Our Days," *First Things* 10 (February 1991) 14-21; C. Wallis, "The Estrogen Dilemma," *Time,* 26 June 1995, 32-39.

Gail C. and R. Paul Stevens

MENSTRUATION

I became a woman and a child in the same year. I experienced menarche at the age of thirteen; two months later I offered my life to the Father in response to his great love in Jesus, with which he had been wooing me all my life. I doubt that in my naiveté I had any grasp at all of what it would come to mean—either to live in the world as a woman or to live as a child of God, the joys or the sorrows. This article reflects on the relationship between the two journeys: being a woman and being a child of God.

My menstrual cycle has always been a source of frustration, anxiety* and pain. Not only is my cycle highly irregular, but I suffer from a more extreme type of dysmenorrhea. There are limited medical solutions for these. I have accepted some treatments and chosen to reject others. Most women experience only mild symptoms, but I am one of the unfortunate few, a statistic in medical journals. Though I often dialogue with God on these matters, my end of the conversation usually consists of fragmented thoughts: *Oh God, please don't let me get my period today—I've got so much to do! Oh, why didn't you make me like my friends who barely notice their cycle? Why does this have to interfere with my life? Oh, make this pain go away . . . please!* But with recent inspiration I have been engaging in a new stream of reflection. It is nothing so grand as a theology of menstruation; it is rather a more personal inquiry into the relationship between my spiritual formation and my rather unique monthly rhythms.

The Spirituality of Every Month Life

If God is forming me spiritually in my everyday life, is he doing the same in my "every month" life? For me this is the quintessential test of the idea that God is present in all aspects of life. If he is involved in the very dimension of routine that causes me such frustration and anxiety, then surely he is present in every other aspect of my life. If he can work through my menstrual cycle to form me into all he knows me to be, then he can work through every other "nonspiritual" part of my life.

The physiological event and the rhythms of menstruation are not only biological processes. Psychological research has attested to the fact that these are an integral part of women's emotional lives (*see* Femininity). And if this is so, then any discussion of spirituality for women cannot afford to ignore them. The type of gnostic dualism that divorces the spiritual from the body* may have done far more harm to Christian women throughout history than to Christian men.

In her reflection on family spirituality, Wendy Wright discusses the importance of setting this dualism aright:

In contradistinction to our Christian heritage that has been shaped by men's perceptions and has drunk deep of philosophical springs that often make a sharp distinction between body and spirit, the experience of woman in family cannot separate the two. Woman's attention is given much of the time, at least subliminally, to the experience of being held and entered, to the cyclical wetness and dryness of fertility and infertility, to the flow and cessation of menstruation, to the profound body-changes of pregnancy, to the fluids of lactation, to the carrying, washing, feeding, and caressing of bodies, to the physical sensations of menopause. To pray a woman's prayer is to celebrate . . . and grieve out of the miracle of the female body. It is to pray the whole person, body and spirit entwined. It is to pray with the rhythms of all created life. (pp. 113-14)

For a woman to set out to learn to pray with the rhythms of her created life is to embark on a lifelong journey. And this is what I hope to do.

The menstrual cycle itself is a fruitful concept for spiritual reflection. One can consider its link with the miracle of life and reproduction or images of the womb in Scripture (Ps 139). It involves the flow of blood, which is a rich symbol in the Christian faith, related to our very salvation. The changes from one stage of the month to another are reminders of all the cycles of life—the change of the hours, the seasons, the monumental shifts in our life cycles, even the ups and downs of our spiritual pilgrimage. The changes are also a comforting monument to the constancy of God, whose character, unlike ours, is the same yesterday, today and forever.

Beyond these, there are two streams of thought that have been especially meaningful to me. The first is that the distress and pain my body suffers cause me to consistently affirm that I am integrally connected with the "groaning as in the pains of childbirth" (Rom 8:22) in which the whole creation engages as it is subjected to frustration. I join with the entire world in groaning as I wait eagerly for the redemption of my body. For who hopes for what she already has (Rom 8:24)?

The second is menstruation's reminder of how sin has affected women.

Menstrual disorders are linked to child-bearing pain, the first result of sin mentioned in Genesis 3:16. Both the groaning and the curse lead me to consider the other result—patriarchy. Though as a woman I live in an unjust world which oppresses women, I am sustained by a God who, through incarnation as the Word, displayed once and for all that he is not a patriarchal tyrant. On the contrary, Jesus came to set me free from the law of sin and death, and he inaugurated the kingdom within which the effects of the curse begin to dissipate. I feel especially comforted by his act of healing a bleeding woman, which is found in all three of the Synoptic Gospels (Mt 9:20-22; Mk 5:25-34; Lk 8:43-48). Although through the centuries misreadings of Old Testament regulations for women such as Leviticus 15:19-31 have "canonized the view that something natural to women . . . was especially unsuitable for intimacy with God" (Carmody, p. 20), Jesus clearly demonstrated a profound distinction under the new covenant by drawing public attention to his willingness to become "unclean" by touching and healing this woman. The good news for women is one of liberation. So my menstruation is to me a reminder of both the kingdom to come and the kingdom come.

Reflection has also led me to see that the structure of my experience month after tedious month shapes my spiritual life. It does this by providing built-in gifts that I would never be drawn to seek voluntarily but are gifts nevertheless.

Rhythms of Grace

First, and most obvious, my cycle ensures that I am given weeks of peak performance. I tackle my tasks with strong determination, efficiency and abundant energy. I sleep peacefully, love courageously and laugh at life. It is not difficult to see the gift of God here, although it must be acknowledged that these weeks would not seem so precious were it not for the others. After ovulation I experience a time in which my emotions are tender and I am prone to gentle tears. I have tended to label this as just an emotional shift caused by fluctuating hormones, but I am beginning to see that it is more. Through the shift God often miraculously grants me a deeper awareness of his loving heart, as well as a softening of my heart toward family and friends.

The part of my cycle that causes me the most consternation is the week or more in which I invariably experience many symptoms of what is commonly called premenstrual syndrome. Symptoms may include water retention (causing tenderness, bloatedness, weight gain, backaches), altered blood sugar levels (causing hostility, headaches, food cravings), and sodium and potassium imbalance (causing fatigue, tension, depression; Wilson, pp. 21-30). I use the term *premenstrual syndrome* (PMS) for simplicity's sake and with caution, fully realizing that there exists a current and unwarranted fascination with PMS.

Most studies of premenstrual syndrome have been based on poor research methods, but due to a propensity —by both men and women—to attribute women's behavior to their biology, PMS has grown in popularity, sprouting its own myths. The term has been mindlessly applied to all women even though evidence suggests that only a small percentage of women suffer from the syndrome. Most women merely experience normal premenstrual changes.

During this time I feel extremely jittery, experiencing elevated levels of unrest, irritability, anxiety and tension. This change invariably drives me back to God, for it is then that I become aware of my deep need for the power of the Holy Spirit to live a holy life. At other times I rely heavily on my habits of courtesy and deference in my relationships and forget to love with his strength. But during PMS days the illusion of niceness is shattered. I come face to face with the awful humiliation of knowing that without his love I am nothing. Without a continual prayer for his love to overcome my irritability, I am completely capable of treating those closest to me with angry injustice. Without God's intervention the potential for discord and heated conflict lurks in my very cells.

This experience is a matter for both a theological and an experiential understanding of sanctification. How do I walk the balance between being compassionate with myself during a vexing temptation and simultaneously taking responsibility for my own actions, refusing to slough off any sin committed by blaming it on "that time of the month"? This is the time when I am especially conscious of the war of sin within me.

I have known victories, celebrated with God, but I have also been forced to confess that in anger and anxiety I have sinned. This repentance has a uniquely bitter taste to my pride, for it is unlike other times when my sins may be to me less glaring and I can still shy from the label "sinner saved by grace." Here, I have no choice but to acknowledge my actions as wrong. It would be impossible to do otherwise. God does not bring this temptation to test me (Jas 1:13-14); he has always proved faithful and just, readily forgiving and purifying me (1 Jn 1:9). Even more humbling, though, is asking forgiveness of those close to me. Because any irritation or hostility is always directed toward people, I need to exercise the discipline of asking to be forgiven for my sharpness and unfairness. Here is where I reluctantly learn that "our successes and our glories are not the stuff of community, but our sins and failures

are" (Palmer, p. 31).

The most disheartening part of my monthly life is the actual onset of menstruation. This is due to the extreme nature of my dysmenorrhea—debilitating cramping that causes pain to shoot outward from my uterus to my entire body. I feel the pain from the tips of my fingers to the tips of my toes. If I fail to take medication at the first awareness of cramping, I will invariably spend an hour or two huddled on the floor in agony. After this, medication and the administration of heat dull the pain to a tiring ache that puts me out of commission for a day and leaves me in need of extra rest for another.

There are many reasons why this is a discouraging time. Because my cycle is highly irregular, I cannot accurately predict the exact day I should expect my period. My body can spend days sending me false alarms in the form of cramping; this has often led me to refuse to act, quite certain my period will interfere. Often it does not. So it is with resolve that I have recently begun to change my perspective and be as engaged in life as I can, until the moment the real pain strikes. This shift to active waiting, to participating fully in plans and forming commitments, knowing they may be abruptly canceled, is a metaphor of the life of the church as we await the return of Jesus. While we live and act in anticipation, we are not to "stand here looking into the sky" (Acts 1:11). The unpredictability of such a disrupting event gives me twelve times each year to decide to accept God's timing or resent it and chafe at it.

Accepting the timing is no easy task, for menstruation often comes in what I judge to be extremely poor timing—in the midst of a crucial assignment or just before a long-anticipated celebration. I do not control my cycle, but I can choose my response. This means twelve opportunities a year to practice submission and acceptance. Hannah Hurnard speaks of this very process in the introduction to her allegory *Hinds' Feet on High Places:*

> The High Places of . . . union with Christ cannot be reached by any mental reckoning of self to be dead to sin, or by seeking to devise some way or discipline by which the will can be crucified. The only way is by learning to accept, day by day, the actual conditions . . . permitted by God, by a continually repeated laying down of our own will and acceptance of his as it is presented to us in the form of . . . the things which happen to us. Every acceptance of his will becomes an altar of sacrifice, and every such surrender and abandonment of ourselves to his will is a means of furthering us on the way to the High Places which he desires to bring every child of his while they are still living on earth. (pp. 11-12)

The recurring encounter with physical pain is also part of my discipleship.* Although the pain is to a certain extent controllable, is always alleviated each month and is from a known cause, I monthly share in the fellowship* of suffering with those who suffer chronic pain. I wonder what level of patience I would be able to maintain with others' physical ills in the absence of this always-ready-to-return experience. Through sharpness of pain God sharpens my compassion, as Tilden Edwards also observes: "Though I hate aching, I recognize that tinge of grace in it that brings me closer to the suffering side of everyone, and opens up a little more compassion" (Edwards, p. 208). My own experience with pain means that I join the many, identifying with and learning from their insights. As Christians we are called neither to masochistically enjoy pain nor to focus much attention on the cause of suffering. Rather we are to take concern for our own reactions to it. The result God

often appears to be concerned with is our spiritual formation (Rom 5:3-5; Heb 12:10-11; Jas 1:2-4; 1 Pet 1:6-7). If this is so, then my own responses to bodily aching each month need redemption so that I may become more like Christ.

So the question becomes, How can I give God my trust, believing that he will bring something of value from the inevitable down days in my life's rhythm? And if this commitment is the decision to rejoice, then I am led to an even more difficult question: How can I rejoice in the midst of what, on the surface, would seem to be an entirely unredeemable part of my everyday life? The answer may lie primarily in an openness to the truth that God is present and wants to bless me with that presence—not only in the structure of my cycle but also in the days of suffering themselves. It is through a new awareness of that presence that I will be able to rejoice at *all* times of the month (Phil 4:4-5).

God is present in my menstrual period, not through any conjuring of my own, but through his grace, a concept I experience yet hardly comprehend. Tim Hansel, who himself experiences chronic physical pain, calls grace "the central invitation to life . . . a glimpse, not just of what life can be, but of what life really is" (pp. 107-8). He maintains that our limitations can "become the very invitation to discover fully the dimensions of grace, the improbable path to God's otherwise hidden blessing" (Hansel, pp. 108-9). Through the limitations imposed by my menstrual period, God issues an invitation to experience his gracious presence in ways that are otherwise foreign to my daily life.

Menstrual Sabbath

The most prevalent obstacle to entering this "invitation to life" is my propensity for what Susan Muto and Adrian van Kaam call *functionalism*. Functionalism takes over our lives when we "feel pushed and pulled to perform efficiently and effectively, no matter what suffers . . . [thinking that] to do is vastly more important than to be" (Muto and van Kaam, p. 146). Christians are not exempt from functionalism, for we come to value service as the meaning and measure of Christian commitment. If we relax, the guilt we exhale shakes the unvoiced conviction that the only meaning of life is to be useful to God. The fruits of functionalism are incompatible with grace. How better to come face to face with grace than through a humdrum time when "my relationship with the world is one of giving in and giving up, surrendering, yielding, and letting go," when I must "renounce temporarily all agent and manipulative purposes" (Cummings, p. 71)? How better to let grace heal my overrefined conscience, which convinces me that to see a need is to incur an obligation to meet that need? How better to let grace set me free from the "cramping legalism of time" (McConnell, p. 69)? How better to renounce self-justification and grasp the significance of the gospel I so often betray with my functionalistic lifestyle—that it is through Christ's work alone that I find worth, acceptance and justification?

Precisely because it is a useless and unproductive time, my monthly menstruation is one of the means that God, in his grace, has given me for dealing with the principalities and powers (Eph 6:12) that exploit my weakness in this area. Parker Palmer believes there is a vast conspiracy against such times. So it is vital to pay attention to those unintentional moments that come "whether or not we seek them, are ready for them, or know what to do when they arrive" (Palmer, p. 26). I have no control over the limitation of painful, exhausting menstruation. But it is possible for me to more consciously pay attention to God's grace in the quiet, contemplative moments that come unbidden during each monthly downtime. A helpful way to do this is to view this time as a type of sabbath.*

There are a striking number of sabbath elements present in my time of menstruation. Marva Dawn describes four elements of sabbath: ceasing, resting, embracing, feasting. With the exception of the last, all are possible within these two days each month. Ceasing is the most naturally embedded in my experience precisely because my body is too exhausted to allow any other response. In my debilitated state I cease not only from work but also from anxiety, from my "incessant need to produce and accomplish" (Dawn, p. 29) and from my self-sufficient striving to be god of my life. This stems not from a noble heart but from a weary heart that has no choice but to let go. I become acutely aware of my poverty.

There is more intentionality involved in resting.* I can choose to go beyond physical repose to spiritual rest. I recall times when I have received spiritual rest in the midst of the aching, the moments when God has had my exclusive attention and we have had meandering conversations. But I am now interested in how I might set aside this recovery time as an intentional sabbath, embracing sabbath values. I can choose to deliberately fulfill the spirit of the command to keep the sabbath by cultivating an attitude of "rejoicing in God's care, trusting dependence . . . renewed dedication to him . . . remembrance of his saving deeds" (Cummings, p. 73). Is this possible in the midst of physical pain? After the first few hours of sharp pain are gone, it is.

Wasting Time with God

My menstrual period can make space in my life for what Richard Foster calls the *sabbath prayer* or the *prayer of rest.* I am in no shape for long bouts of intercessory or authoritative prayer. But I can choose to renounce both manipulative control over God and my world and "listless passivity," in favor of leaning into cultivation of solitude, silence and recollection. After abstaining from normal patterns of activity and interaction in order to discover that my strength comes from God alone, I need to go further and renounce all the "agitated creaturely activity" of grasping control, which hinders God's work in me (Foster, p. 101). This is an active choice, for without it my menstrual period can easily degenerate into an impatient time of frittering away the aching hours with television or novels or demanding my husband's company in my misery. But if I cannot engage in this type of prayer during a day characterized by the grace of limitations, how do I expect to do it on any other day?

Foster encourages me to radically alter my expectation of menstruation, to look forward to the recovery hours as a lovers' tryst with God: "Our Eternal Lover lures us back regularly into his presence with anticipation and delight. . . . We are glad to waste time with God, for we are pleased with the company" (Foster, p. 77). And as I know from my walk with him, "the hour of discomfort and anxiety is totally forgotten. What we remember forever is the hour of love" (Saunders, as quoted in L'Engle, p. 33). To engage in sabbath prayer is to encounter God not only in that moment but in all of everyday life. It is also to bow to the truth that God's purposes for my life (unlike my own) do not need to be revised to adjust to limitations embedded in any part of my menstrual cycle. Rather, the rhythms of my life move according to his original plan. My call is to be alert to the realization that these rhythms find true life within the larger rhythms of God's amazing grace.

See also BODY; FEMININITY; SABBATH; SEXUALITY.

References and Resources
D. L. Carmody, *Biblical Women* (New York: Crossroad, 1988); C. Cummings, *The Mystery of the Ordinary* (San Francisco: Harper & Row, 1982); M. J. Dawn, *Keeping the Sabbath Wholly* (Grand Rapids: Eerdmans, 1989); T. Edwards, *Living Simply Through the Day* (New York: Paulist, 1977); M. J. Evans, *Woman in the Bible* (Downers Grove, Ill.: InterVarsity Press, 1983); R. Foster, *Prayer* (San Francisco: Harper & Row, 1992); T. Hansel, *You Gotta Keep Dancin'* (Elgin, Ill.: David C. Cook, 1985); H. Hurnard, *Hinds' Feet on High Places* (Wheaton, Ill.: Tyndale, 1977); M. L'Engle, *And It Was Good* (Wheaton, Ill.: Harold Shaw, 1983); W. T. McConnell, *The Gift of Time* (Downers Grove, Ill.: InterVarsity Press, 1983); S. Muto and A. van Kaam, *Commitment: Key to Christian Maturity* (New York: Paulist, Press, 1989); P. J. Palmer, *The Active Life* (New York: HarperCollins, 1990); R. Wilson, *Controlling Pre-Menstrual Syndrome* (Markham, Ont.: Fitzhenry & Whiteside, 1988); W. M. Wright, *Sacred Dwelling* (New York: Crossroad, 1990).

Valerie Pyke Parks

MINISTRY

The word *ministry* is derived in both Greek and Hebrew from a word that simply means "service." A Christian servant is someone who puts himself or herself at God's disposal for the benefit of others and for the stewardship* of God's world. Christian service*—commonly called *ministry*—accords with God's purposes for people and the world and has the touch of God, often unknown to the servant. Christian service makes no distinction between the sacred and the secular. Washing dishes, designing a computer program, preaching a sermon and healing the sick are all one, as William Tyndale said so long ago, "as touching the deed to please God." How far this is from contemporary thinking about ministry!

Contemporary Definitions
Ministry is an "accordion" word that has

come to mean whatever we put into it! Sometimes ministry is defined by *place* (work* done in the temple or church), *function* (tasks done for the sake of the whole, such as leading), *need* (meeting spiritual needs) and *titles* or *designations* (Reverend). Ministry is normally associated with what the minister does—preaching,* pastoral care,* evangelism,* sacramental ministry, touching and handling the things of God. What really lasts, so it is thought, is service associated with church activities. All the rest is temporal, of passing or minor significance. Such clerically defined service is usually associated with a secret call to ministry that comes to a few people alongside the general calling to Christ experienced by all believers. Yet careful analysis of the New Testament does not support the idea of a secret call to the professional* ministry.

In the New Testament service lasts and has significance to God not because of its religious character but because it is done in faith, hope and love* (1 Cor 3:9-15; 13:13; 1 Thess 1:3). Sermons may dissolve in the fire of the final judgment because they were preached for vainglory, while a sweater knitted in love may be a ministry to Jesus (Mt 25:40). "Only one life, 'twill soon be past; only what's done for Christ will last" has a deeper meaning than commonly taken by those who think they must leave a so-called secular job and enter professional ministry in order to do lasting ministry.

Biblical Definitions

In the Hebrew Scriptures two words are normally used for *service* and *ministry:* (1) *sharat,* which is personal service rendered to an important personage, such as a ruler (Gen 39:4), and the ministry of worship on the part of those who stand in a special relationship to God, such as priests (Ex 28:35) and (2) *abad,* which combines the meaning of "to work or to make" and "to worship." In Genesis 2 Adam and Eve are depicted as kings-priests offering their work and worship simultaneously to God in the sanctuary-garden, which is the center of the world.

Ministry words in the New Testament do not yield anything like a clergy-lay distinction: *hypēretēs* (helmsman), *doulos* (slave), *therapeuō* (attend, care for, treat, heal), *latreuō* (serve, worship, but never in a sacerdotal or sanctuary sense) and *diakonia* (any service rendered in love). Equally significant is the fact that several words meaning "rule," "control," "priest" and "official" are not used to describe ministry. Instead the New Testament writers use a term generally associated with those who are in another's employ and have a dependent status. The most common word for the service of love—*diakonia,* which originally referred to "waiting at table" but came to designate any action on behalf of others, small or important—takes on a new dignity in the Christian context.

So in the light of both Old and New Testament precedents, the following definition is proposed: *Ministry* (service) is any activity for which God is able to say, "It is good" (Gen 1:31), and potentially involves a two-directional priestly service: touching people and places for God and touching God for people and places (whether or not it is known to the servant that God is ministered to by his or her action; Mt 25:31-46). I use the word *priestly* here not in the sacerdotal sense but to suggest that ministry involves mediating God's presence and purpose to the entire creation and offering that creation to God in stewardship, thanksgiving and intercession. To this matter the Old Testament makes a stunning contribution.

Old Testament Contributions

In terms of Old Testament examples, this definition would embrace the ministry of Adam and Eve, the Levites, parents with their children, rulers and politicians, craftspeople, artists and musicians, those acting on behalf of the poor or exercising social justice, persons engaging in reflection and sharing wisdom, and prophets bringing God's word to people and situations. Today this means that ministry includes the work of homemaking,* neighbor* love, accounting, town planning, social work, the professions* and various forms of public Christian service in churches and society.* The Old Testament offers several enriching perspectives on the ministry of God's people, including covenant (doing arising from belonging), peoplehood (with a corporate solidarity) and sabbath.* But one of the most striking is the royal priesthood.

Royal priesthood. Israel was founded to become "a kingdom of priests and a holy nation" (Ex 19:6). This appears to be "the priesthood of all believers" before Christ, something never fully apprehended within Old Testament times. It may be argued that Israel's vocation to the nations always assumes the priesthood of the people as the primary priesthood, with the establishment of the special Aaronic and Levitic priesthood as instrumental and functional—equipping* the people to distinguish between the sacred and the profane (Ex 19:22) so that the people could fulfill their priestly role to the nations and the creation. The vision was not abandoned. In Isaiah 61:6 the prophet envisions the whole nation serving God as priests, including even the Gentiles (Is 56:6-9). This dream was fulfilled in Christ in a manner beyond, but not in opposition to, the revelation of the Old Testament (Rom 9—11; Eph 2:11-22).

In the Old Testament ministry is not a solitary, individual activity. Ministry is people service. The idea that each person can be his or her own priest is not supported either by New Testament

teaching or by its Old Testament antecedents. Under the old covenant the priesthood within the people was given for the realization of the missionary priesthood of the people as a whole, a vocation signaled in the promise to Abraham (Gen 12:3), reinforced by the prophetic comedy of Jonah's reluctant missionary excursion, the winsome prophecy of Zechariah (Zech 8:23), the vision of universal prophecy in Joel 2:28-32 and finally the enigmatic suffering of the Servant (Is 49:6; 52:13—53:12). In continuity with the former Israel, the Israel of God in Christ (Gal 6:16), now reconstituted with believing Jews and Gentiles, exists for the glory of God and for mission* in the world. It must never become a self-serving institution. Mission is not an occasional activity for those so inclined but is part of the very being of the people of God. That transforms our vision of lay ministry, as does the next Old Testament perspective.

The servant and service. We have already explored the double-edged meaning of *abad:* service and worship. What is easily overlooked is that the servant is a servant *of God.* It is difficult to appreciate how foreign this is to contemporary views of ministry, which boil down to serving people for God's sake rather than serving God's interests in people and in creation. The servant passages in Isaiah make this point explicitly: the servant is God's servant, pure and simple. In the last twenty-seven chapters of Isaiah, the term occurs twenty times in the singular (chaps. 39—53) and eleven times in the plural (chaps. 54—66). Most commonly the plural use refers to the nation Israel. But there are passages in which the servant is differentiated from Israel and possesses a mission to Israel (Is 41:1-7; 49:1-9; 50:4-10; 52:13—53:12). So a single individual was envisioned, an individual who would gather up all the service expected of Israel in his own person and undertake a mission not only to Israel but through it to the world. Paradoxically, because this servant is also divine, God becomes his own servant in this individual.

That service was fulfilled in Christ the Messiah-Servant, not merely the prophets, priests and kings. New Testament apostles, prophets, evangelists and pastor-teachers are not the culmination of their Old Testament counterparts. That is the fatal equation that leads to exclusively male pastors and priests. All Old Testament leadership* and service is fulfilled in Jesus, not in New Testament elders and church leaders. In Christ the people as a whole become the servant of the Lord. Here leaders are merely people whose service to other servants is their leadership. Clericalism is thus effectively eliminated.

Ironically, this Old Testament perspective can save us from a hierarchy of ministries. Incarnating our loving submission to Christ's lordship in every arena of life precludes saying that certain tasks are in themselves holy and others are sacred. Hendrik Kraemer puts it this way: "All members of the *ecclesia* have in principle the same calling, responsibility and dignity, have their part in the apostolic and ministerial nature and calling of the church" (p. 160). Ministry is work and work is ministry for the Christian. Luther never tired of pressing this truth:

> The idea that the service to God should have only to do with a church altar, singing, reading, sacrifice, and the like is without doubt but the worst trick of the devil. How could the devil have led us more effectively astray than by the narrow conception that service to God takes place only in church and by works done therein. . . . The whole world could abound with services to the Lord—not only in churches but also in the home,

kitchen, workshop, field. (quoted in Feuchts, p. 80)

It is true that the church was hampered in the third and following centuries by adopting anachronistic Old Testament priestly models to justify the exclusive practice of Christian sacramental officiants. Today it is professionalized models of ministry that strengthen their understanding. But perhaps more crucial for the challenge of transcending clericalism in the church today is to rediscover the comprehensive, empowering vision of the ministry of the people of God in the Old Testament! Yet the New Testament takes us a step further.

New Testament Contributions

In the New Testament we are introduced to a church that is ministerium (a ministering community), to flexible and changing leadership forms adapted to the situation, to a community in which men and women serve together in full partnership, to a people in which all are called (Eph 4:1), to a community in which ordination as a rite or ceremony that confers power or office does not exist, to a community in which leadership equips all the people to fulfill their calling in the church and world. The theological reasons for this every-member ministry are set as follows.

First, all the people of God have experienced the inbreaking of the reign and kingdom of God. There are no first- and second-class citizens (those who follow the evangelical/gospel counsels and those who are "just" Christians).

Second, all the people of God are called to service. The nonreligious word *diakoneō* is used by Jesus to describe the thing that makes a person a disciple (Lk 22:27; Acts 19:22). Paul also takes the secular word *diakonia* and fills it with Christian meaning. Any service in love is ministry!

Third, all the people of God are empowered and endowed with spiritual gifts.* Gifts and graces of God are not limited to a particular group. They are given to all members of the people of God.

Fourth, all the people of God are invited into the royal priesthood. Apart from describing Christ's high priesthood (Heb 4:14-5:10; 7:1—10:18) the word *hiereus* (priest) is not used for individual servants and leaders in the New Testament (except for the Jewish priests). Now that Christ has fulfilled the priesthood, the whole believing community becomes the "priesthood of believers" (1 Pet 2:9-11; Rev 1:6; 5:10). This priesthood is community-based (arising from the corporate life of the believing community), God-oriented (blessing* God through worship,* mission and work) and world-directed (blessing the world by declaring his glory to the nations).

Sacred and Secular Service

Most discussions of the church's ministry and mission revolve around the two great mandates in the Bible: the cultural mandate (Gen 1:27-30) and the Great Commission (Mt 28:19-20). The first seems to invite secular service (earth keeping, politics, science and social justice), and the second sacred service (preaching, evangelism and witness). Reformed churches stress the cultural mandate and the importance for Christians to take care of the earth, to become involved in salting politics, education and culture and so to transform God's world. Most evangelicals line up behind the Great Commission as the constituting mandate for the people of God, believing that saving an eternal soul cannot be compared with the passing value of designing a human city or enacting just legislation.

Separating these two mandates has been tragic. Where the gospel ministry and our creational stewardship are separated, Christianity becomes privatized.

Mission is separated from life and becomes a discretionary-time activity. Social action and evangelism become separated and competitive. As Charles Sweazie once said, social action without evangelism is like sowing grains of sand in the soil; evangelism without social action quickly heads toward superstition. In contrast to the dichotomized Christianity of the modern West, Christians of the first two centuries—and to some extent in developing countries today—shared the gospel of Jesus *and* did what they could to deal with plagues, abortion, the rights of women and the needs of travelers for hospitality. The record of this is truly inspiring (Oliver).

Christ's purpose in saving us is partly to restore our true humanity. And the "one new humanity" (Eph 2:15 NRSV) we have become in Christ is not religious but fully human. The last Adam, Christ—Adam at last!—restores the potential of the first Adam and Eve. But this more than fulfills the creation mandate. Returning to the foundational texts in Genesis gives us a liberating perspective on what God purposed for his creatures. In fact Adam and Eve had three full-time jobs, not one.

Full-time communion with God. As we have already seen, Adam and Eve dwelt in continuous awareness of God in a garden-sanctuary. Communion with God was a full-time job. A pregnant hint of this is found in Genesis 3:8 with the references to the garden pair walking and talking with God in the cool of the day. While the evening conversation was a highlight of the day, communion—living, moving, and having their being in God—was a twenty-four-hour-a-day occupation, as it should be with us. This challenge to dwell with God, repeated explicitly in the visions of Ezekiel and Revelation, is something that continuously occupies the one new humanity in Christ. It can never be reduced to a quiet-time devotional or be delegated to an evangelist or spiritual director. It is everyone's full-time job.

Full-time community building. Community building is the second full-time job. Humankind was created male and female in the image of God (Gen 1:27), signifying that the first pair were called to live in grateful awareness of their cohumanity and joint reflection of the image of God (Gen 1:26-28); only together they were a mysterious expression of God's own dignity (Eph 5:32). As designed by God, male and female are equal partners and heirs of the grace of life, complementary rather than hierarchical. The image of God is therefore relational or communal.

One practical dimension of this is the call to reproduce (Gen 1:28) and to build a family, a prototype of the church. So all community building can potentially be a ministry about which God can say, "It is good." It is, however, a full-time job and can never be reduced to a diversion, even if one should make one's living by counseling or town planning.

Full-time cocreativity. We are called to make God's world work and to enhance it. Work encompasses the full range of human tasks from farming to genetic engineering, from needlepoint to accounting. Humankind must never be unemployed, even if remunerated employment is not available or needed. Cocreativity too is a full-time job. The renewal of all creation in Christ is envisaged by the gospel, not merely the saving of individual souls. The lay vocation involves sharing with Christ his complete work of redemption and renewal. The purpose of fulfilling the missionary mandate (Mt 28:16-20) is to make not saints or angels but fully human beings who will be the vanguard of Christ's new creation of people and the world, anticipating the consummation of the kingdom (Gen 1:26-30; Is 65:17—66:24; 2 Cor 5:17-21;

Eph 2:15; 3:10; Col 1:20; Heb 2:5-17; Rev 21:5).

This is not to reduce the Great Commission to making disciples of Jesus so that they will fulfill the original creation and cultural mandate of Genesis 1:27-29. There is more to being Christians and more to being fully human than being merely stewards of God's resources and developing human culture. Evangelicals, having correctly insisted on more, have also generally neglected crucial dimensions in God's declared intentions for his creatures. Communion, community building and cocreativity, therefore, combine the tasks of evangelism, pastoral care, earth keeping, creative work and social justice.

Trinitarian Ministry

All human ministry is derivative, not delegated. All ministry is God's ministry. There was ministry in God before there was a world, before there was sin, before there was the need for redemption. Therefore ministry is not imitating God (as holiness is not the imitation of Christ) but being incorporated and conformed to God's ministry. In reality, this means being incorporated into the love of God. This brings a deeper understanding and practice to the three dimensions developed above.

Communion—colovers of God. Coloving means that we are drawn into the love life within the heart of God. It is the heart of what "loving" God means. As we commune with God, are known by God and practice God's daily presence, we are actually giving and receiving ministry. The purpose of creation is the glorification of God, and the purpose of God-imaging creatures is to have communion with God.

Community building—loving one another. Human beings are by nature relational and are designed not merely to respond to God but to resemble God through sharing themselves and self-giving. The new creation restores this capacity. It invites us to participate in one another's lives; to love neighbor, family and friend and be loved; to celebrate cohumanity and celebrate sexuality. Many do not think of this as ministry, service or priesthood, but it is. Indeed, a theology of the laity* must inform us of the theology and spirituality of our relational life in everyday circumstances.

Cocreativity—loving the world. Creation is expressive of God's character, an overflow of the love within God. The world was created to be ultimately transfigured and glorified. Incarnation and resurrection are the highest expression of nature and not only what God did to redeem the world. So a truly evangelical theology of the laity is not only a rescue effort but accords with God's purposes for the world. What is truly astounding is that humankind has, through the Spirit's irruption in our lives, the privilege of participating in the creative and the re-creative work of God. But it is also incarnational and resurrectional. As Kraemer so profoundly shows, Christian ministry is not merely a call to ethical living but to participation in a divinely created order of existence that is undergoing change as a result of the Spirit's transforming power.

Christian service is making ourselves available to God's love so that we can love people and God's world for God's own glory. What we will discover one day, to our immense surprise, is that quite ordinary services we rendered on earth brought blessing to the Lord (Mt 25:31-46).

See also CLERGY; EQUIPPING; LAITY; LEADERSHIP, CHURCH; SERVICE, WORKPLACE.

References and Resources

R. Banks, *Paul's Idea of Community* (Peabody, Mass.: Hendrickson, 1994); O. Cullmann, *The Christology of the New Testament* (London: SCM, 1977); A. Faivre, *The Emergence of the Laity in the Early Church* (New York: Paulist, 1990); D. J. Falk, "A New Testament Theology of Calling with Reference to the 'Call to the Ministry,' " MCS thesis, Regent College, Vancouver, B.C., May 1990; O. E. Feucht, *Everyone a Minister* (St. Louis: Concordia, 1958); J. Houston, "Trinity and the Christian Life," lecture at Regent College, Vancouver, B.C., 1994; H. Kraemer, *A Theology of the Laity* (Philadelphia: Westminster, 1958); H. R. Niebuhr, *The Purpose of the Church and Its Ministry* (New York: Harper & Brothers, 1956); G. Ogden, *The New Reformation: Returning the Ministry to the People of God* (Grand Rapids: Zondervan, 1990); E. H. Oliver, *The Social Achievements of the Christian Church* (Toronto: United Church of Canada, 1930); W. J. Rademacher, *Lay Ministry: A Theological, Spiritual and Pastoral Handbook* (New York: Crossroad, 1991); C. A. Voltz, *Pastoral Life and Practice in the Early Church* (Minneapolis: Augsburg, 1990); M. Warkentin, *Ordination: A Biblical-Historical View* (Grand Rapids: Eerdmans, 1982); J. H. Yoder, *The Fullness of Christ: Paul's Vision of Universal Ministry* (Elgin, Ill.: Brethren Press, 1987).

R. Paul Stevens

MISCARRIAGE

Early perinatal loss or miscarriage is increasingly being given its full significance as not only the loss of a pregnancy* but the untimely death* of an individual person who has to some extent been part of a family* (*see* Conception). In the eyes of society* miscarriage often occurs unnoticed. The lost child is unseen, unnamed and unacknowledged through an obituary. There are often no physical remains to bury with the rituals that usually afford comfort to a grieving* family. It can be a lonely vigil described by a spectrum of evolving emotions*—shock, ambivalence, guilt and anger. Unfortunately, it can also be a time of alienation, rejection and shame. The premature death of these unbeheld children confronts us with our own mortality and provokes us to wrestle with the meaning of human suffering.

Multifaceted Loss

Kowalski notes that "perinatal death encompasses each type of loss—loss of a significant person, loss of some aspect of the self (reproductive health), loss of external objects, loss of a stage of life, loss of a dream inherent in the parents' desire to have a child and loss of creation" (cited in Ney, p. 1193). Fortunately, there is a growing trend to encourage couples to realize the full extent of their loss by, if they so choose, holding, naming, blessing* and saying farewell* to their stillborn children and by keeping mementos: footprints, a hair lock, photographs or ultrasound images.

Parents' involvement in a memorial service when there is no body* may be helpful for the completion of mourning even if only "two or three come together" and informally share their feelings (Mt 18:20). The value of rituals cannot be underestimated. They represent "a rope bridge of knotted symbols strung across an abyss" (Grimes in Van Biema, p. 8). We use them to navigate the passages of birth,* initiation, marriage* and death. Live children are blessed and welcomed after birth by passing through water (in many Christian traditions) or being held up through smoke or sunlight (Native American). A stillborn child can by ceremony be recognized to be a person, now deceased, but with a soul* properly commended to God, making the grieving completable.

In the case of early pregnancy loss, the "unfinished baby" more likely than not has been completed and claimed by the mother even if there is no body to weep over. Because the fetus or embryo who dies early in pregnancy through spontaneous miscarriage, ectopic pregnancy or even elective termination (see Abortion) may not have been seen and known, the death may not be considered worthy of recognition and mourning. "Such ignorance of the significance of the loss on the part of society, friends, and even the woman herself impedes the bereavement process and may interfere with bonding to future children" (Ney, p. 1193).

Although each person responds individually, medical research has delineated stages as described by women who experienced recovery from a miscarriage. These dovetail with accepted patterns and tasks of grieving. Initially uncertainty progresses to shock and denial. Parents may express anger outwardly as injustice or inwardly as guilt as they actualize and accept the reality of the loss. During the stage of searching and yearning they identify and release their distress, sorrow and pain. Disorganization occurs as they are adjusting to life without the thoughts and plans for the new baby. Confronting or avoiding painful reminders of the miscarriage occurs when having to tell others the news, seeing the nursery, pregnant women or other babies, marking the first menstrual period, sexual intercourse, the baby's due date and the anniversary* of the loss. During the stage of reorientation parents successfully withdraw emotional energy from the loss and reinvest it in other activities and plans for the future.

The degree of prenatal bonding and grief may vary considerably. Each woman's experience is uniquely influenced by what the pregnancy meant to her and her family. Some factors that influence the perceived value of the pregnancy include the ease of becoming pregnant, the perceived age of the mother and pressure to conceive, and whether the pregnancy was planned. An experienced mother may have a deeper sense of loss, having endowed the unborn child with specific characteristics and perhaps even a name. Alternatively they may sense some relief if the pregnancy had come sooner than planned. Women who have not successfully carried a child to term may feel more profound doubt of their reproductive health. If an ultrasound examination has been done, the images add to the reality of the fetal existence, as do hearing fetal heartbeats and perceiving movements internally or even externally that may have been shared with a spouse and other children. Also, the duration of the anticipatory time during the warning symptoms of bleeding and cramping can influence how deeply she may have begun to attach herself.

Adding to the complexity of the recovery and contributing to the distress, a D&C (surgical dilation and curettage) may be required to remove remaining placental and decaying fetal tissue that has not passed spontaneously, preventing ongoing bleeding and infection. The operation itself may be perceived as a possible threat to the mother's health, and despite ultrasound confirmation of the fetal death, in periods of uncertainty or denial she may feel that they are taking her baby. In later stages of gestational death, when a D&C is not possible, induction of labor after a brief but agonizing waiting period is often recommended for the protection of the mother's health. A marathon of labor and birth ensues with no reward of a child's cry (see Birth). During this delicate interfacing between patient and caregivers, the quality of the support greatly alters the woman's experience, for better or worse.

Unfortunately, physicians may be vulnerable to frustration when they cannot cure. They may be paternalistic, indifferent, impatient and unfamiliar with grief. Physicians and hospital staff need to treat the patient compassionately as a person hurting and not a "body bleeding." Giving permission to express a range of feelings, providing explanations and information, checking back for understanding, giving specific directions about what to expect and do during recovery, adequate pain control and compassionate listening* are all valuable ways to assist a woman through this difficult time. Specific reassurances include the fact that miscarriages are common and represent an inevitable process that often cannot be prevented or arrested by maternal or medical efforts. It is nature taking its course.

Specific concerns may arise about the cause of death, requiring many follow-up visits to unravel all the nagging questions and worries. It is particularly valuable to address and appease unnecessary guilt for causing or failing to prevent the loss. Scientific evidence suggests that physical activity, vomiting, sexual intercourse, stress and ambivalent feelings toward the pregnancy do *not* cause miscarriage. There may be more involved questions concerning the contributions of possible maternal infections or disease, exposure to medications and toxins, smoking and alcohol. These are rarely implicated in early pregnancy loss. As science unravels the mystery of conception,* evidence points to a staggering degree of naturally occurring loss from perhaps half of all fertilized ova failing to implant to many pregnancies that are lost during late menstrual flow before their presence is even surmised. A significant number of examined embryos and fetuses that have spontaneously miscarried have microscopically evident chromosomal abnormalities. It remains to be fully demonstrated that genetic errors detectable on a molecular level and immunologic rejection will likely account for the balance. Although this may provide reassurance that the pregnancy "wasn't meant to be," many families feel the additional blow of failure and guilt that an abnormality has occurred and ambivalence toward losing something "less than what was intended." Disappointment in

God's lack of intervention on behalf of their child can be difficult to express.

Response of the Family

Partners grieve but often express themselves in different ways from their wives. A man may keep his sorrow to himself so that his wife will not know his grief and thus double her own. Paradoxically, his silence adds to the apparent silence of God. The range, intensity, duration and progression of responses are not usually synchronous between partners. A delicate balance alternating between intense communication and the guarding of each other's solitude is necessary for couples to respect and support one another at this time. The pregnancy may have meant more to one of the parents. Faith and hope may ebb and flow unpredictably. The loss of a lifetime of plans, dreams and aspirations leaves a void that may be filled by a small glimpse of eternity. Couples who share intimately can enlighten each other's darkness and carry faith for one another at a time when hope seems lost. We must, however, ultimately trust that God himself will answer us in places of deepest questioning and doubt, strengthening the mortar of our faith through adversity.

Siblings are not to be forgotten. A young child can perceive his parents' grief but is incapable of fully understanding or relieving it. Excluding children by withholding news of what has occurred or failing to share feelings does not reduce pain. In the absence of age-appropriate explanations children are prone to fantasy and a correspondingly greater degree of distress. "Magical thinking," whereby children imagine they have caused the death of a sibling, is common and needs to be addressed, especially with later gestational loss. Children who are born after a pregnancy loss can become "replacement children" and may experience increased parental expectations and confusion of their identity. Ideally, the deceased sibling is neither forgotten nor replaced, and the parents in healing* and health* can embrace the new child fully and uniquely.

Response of Friends and Encouragement from Scripture

Family and friends who are not sure what to say but attempt to be supportive should not underestimate their significance. Phone calls, cards, flowers, meals, quiet visits and prayers are palpable expressions of love* that buoys and balances a family in the midst of deep waters.

Kathleen Nielson, as a grieving mother, describes the refuge she found in her faith. "At a time when I felt a terrible emptiness inside, I inhaled the breath of God by taking Scripture into myself. At a time when I did not know what to say to God, through his Word I was able to open myself to Christ, who in the beginning was the Word" (pp. 10-11). "I knew God had preserved my baby in His way that is higher than mine. In His priceless, unfailing love" (Ps 36:6-9) he had taken her son to himself and would preserve him pure and holy forever. Her child was "in the shadow of God's wings," "feasting on the abundance of God's house" and "drinking from his river of delights." "Knowing my baby would be cared for and delighted by God himself comforted me immensely as I wept over a child I held but would never feed."

From Despair to Hope

It is little wonder that in many cultures and previous generations pregnancy was kept secret until it was no longer concealable. Technology* can now provide confirmation at earlier stages, chemically and visually, of the presence of this new individual. There are Scriptures that affirm our belonging and intrinsic value even in the womb (Job 10:8-11; Ps 22:9-10; 139:13-16), and it is clear that pregnancy loss was mourned even in biblical times. A progression can be traced from Old Testament to New Testament that is analogous to the grieving process itself, leading us from despair to hope.

Jeremiah in profound depression* cursed himself and the man who told his father of his birth (Jer 20:14-18). Job cried, "Why then did you bring me out of the womb? I wish I had died before any eye saw me" (Job 10:18). "Why was I not hidden in the ground like a stillborn child, like an infant who never saw the light of day?" (Job 3:16). Scripture does not euphemize, gloss over or glorify death.

In David's grief for the loss of his son conceived after adultery and murder we see premature death as an unalterable state associated with guilt. "Can I bring him back again? I will go to him, but he will not return to me" (2 Sam 12:23). Premature death sometimes counts as death incurred through sin (1 Sam 2:3; Job 22:15; 36:14). However, a careful look at Genesis 2 reveals that there is a distinction made between death that is deserved and threatened and death that belongs to the natural state of the creature. Death when it finally occurs is explained in reminiscence of man's creation: "until you return to the ground, since from it you were taken; for dust you are and to dust you will return" (Gen 3:19). Ultimately, one fate comes to all, to the righteous and the wicked, and to the clean and the unclean.

The psalmist gives us the new message that God's hand reaches into the world of the dead (Ps 139:8). The first heralding of the resurrection occurs in Isaiah 26:19: "Your dead will live; their bodies will rise." The author of Revelation assures us that "God himself will be with them and be their God. He will wipe every tear from their eyes. There will be

no more death or mourning or crying or pain" (Rev 21:3-4). God's promise is that this time of anguish will pass, making way for the hope of ultimate healing and reconciliation. In contemplating the earthly tragedy of the Pietà—Mary cradling her dead son—we find ourselves full circle from the stable and relinquished is the hope shared by all parents that *they* will be the ones cradled in old age by their surviving children. The miscarried or stillborn child is a person whose development is interrupted by natural defects, an extinguished flame who awaits final consummation when they, with us, will be fully restored in the likeness of Christ himself.

See also BIRTH; CONCEPTION; DEATH; GRIEVING; PREGNANCY.

References and Resources
E. C. Hui, *Questions of Right and Wrong* (Vancouver: Regent College, 1994); D. Manca, "Women's Experience of Miscarriage," *Canadian Family Physician* 37 (September 1991) 1871-77; G. García Márquez, *The Circle of Life: Rituals from the Human Family Album* (San Francisco: Harper, 1991); P. Ney, "The Effects of Pregnancy Loss on Children's Health," *Social Science Medicine* 38, no. 9 (1994) 1193-1200; K. B. Nielson, "The Day the Heart Beat Stopped," *Focus on the Family*, March 1993, 10-11; R. Smolan, *The Power to Heal* (New York: Prentice-Hall, 1990); R. W. Swanson, "Parents Experiencing Perinatal Loss: The Physician's Role," *Canadian Family Physician* 32 (March 1986) 599-602; D. van Biema, "The Journey of Our Lives," *Life*, October 1991; H. W. Wolff, *Anthropology of the Old Testament* (Philadelphia: Fortress, 1974).

Carol Anderson

MISSION

Mission means, most basically, a sending forth. In popular speech it has come to mean almost the same thing as *purpose*. Thus many businesses and organizations* have "mission statements" that define the purpose for their existence.

This secular use of *mission* derives,

however, from the Christian usage. *Mission,* in its English usage, is fundamentally a Christian word. As God sent Jesus Christ into the world, so the church,* the body* of Christ, is sent into the world to continue Christ's mission. This is the basic meaning of *mission.*

Christians often talk about the *mission* of the church, and of Christian *missions.* Here we discuss mission; see also the accompanying article on missions.*

Mission Begins with God

The New Testament affirms the grounding of mission in God. In Jesus' last words to his apostles he said: "As the Father has sent me, I am sending you" (Jn 20:21). Earlier Jesus had told them, "Whoever wants to become great among you must be your servant, and whoever wants to be first must be your slave—just as the Son of Man did not come to be served, but to serve, and to give his life as a ransom for many" (Mt 20:26-28). The basic impulse of Christian mission is found here, in the example and teaching of Jesus. When Jesus washed the apostles' feet he said, "I have set you an example that you should do as I have done for you" (Jn 13:15). One of those apostles, Peter, later said that if we suffer, this is a part of our calling—because "Christ suffered for you, leaving you an example, that you should follow in his steps" (1 Pet 2:21, see also Phil 2:5-13).

Mission, then, is based in Jesus Christ—in his example and his commission. Jesus formed a community of disciples who were to live the kind of life he lived, empowered by the Spirit. And he made it plain that he was giving his followers a world mission: "Go into all the world and preach the good news to all creation" (Mk 16:15). He instructed his first apostles to "go and make disciples of all nations" (Mt 28:19). He said he would give them the Holy Spirit for this task: "You will receive power when the Holy Spirit

comes on you; and you will be my witnesses . . . to the ends of the earth" (Acts 1:8). Clearly Jesus intended a sending forth of his disciples into all the world, "just as" the Father sent him into the world. So mission is grounded in Jesus.

More fundamentally, mission is grounded in the nature and character of the Three-in-One God, the Trinity. God is an everliving communion or community of holy love,* a constant love-flow among Father, Son and Holy Spirit. Mission begins as the "overflow" of God's love in creating, sustaining and renewing the universe. Thus the power of the mutual love shared among Father, Son and Holy Spirit is the source of Jesus' own mission. A God of such love certainly will be a God with a mission to share this loving trinitarian passion with the whole world. As God the Father sent Jesus Christ into the world in the power of the Holy Spirit, so God sends the church into the world powered by the Spirit to make the love and truth of Jesus Christ known everywhere.

There are many hints of God's concern with mission throughout Scripture. After the sin of Adam and Eve, God himself went "on a mission," looking for the guilty pair in the Garden. Later he sent Abraham and Sarah to begin a new people, Israel, who would be God's missionaries to the world. When God called Abraham he told him, "All peoples on earth will be blessed through you" (Gen 12:3). Through Israel would come, in turn, the Messiah. Over the long course of Old Testament history God raised up prophets and prophetesses, sending them to call the people back to faithfulness. Occasionally we get glimpses of a broader mission to the nations, as when God sent Jonah to Nineveh.

In the call and the covenant with Israel, we see the character of God. God desires to share truth and love with the nations, and Israel is chosen to play a key part. It is a double calling: They must first be faithful, honoring and worshiping God alone, so they don't betray the mission. And they must be God's visible demonstration to the nations, "a kingdom of priests and a holy nation," a "treasured possession" chosen "out of all nations" (Ex 19:4-6).

The fountain of mission, then, is none other than God, who seeks to share and demonstrate his truth and love throughout the whole created world.

Mission Is Global Good News

The mission of the church is good news to the world. It is good news first because of who Jesus is and of what God has done and is doing through him. Yet the Christian mission is not only about Jesus as a person. It includes God's purpose to bring reconciliation or *shalom* to all creation* through him. Scripture expresses this broad sense of mission in various ways. In both Testaments God's overarching purpose is frequently called "the kingdom of God." This theme is expressed most profoundly in Ephesians 1:10 and Colossians 1:15-20: God is carrying out a plan, an "economy," "to bring all things in heaven and on earth together under one head, even Christ" (Eph 1:10). "For God was pleased to have all his fullness dwell in [Jesus Christ], and through him to reconcile to himself all things, whether things on earth or things in heaven, by making peace through his blood, shed on the cross" (Col 1:20).

The Christian mission is good news about personal, social, ecological and cosmic healing and reconciliation. It proclaims good news to people, to tribes, nations and ethnic enclaves, to culture* and to nature itself. It is good news for time* and for eternity, salvation for the universe in all its dimensions. The Christian mission is thus vastly comprehensive, even as it is specific and local for

each believer and congregation. It is addressed to the whole creation, in four senses:

1. The mission is directed to the individual human person, "calling for the conversion of heart and mind" (Lesslie Newbigin) so that life is lived after the pattern of Jesus Christ. While mission is addressed to all people everywhere, it is particularly a mission to the poor, the masses, the underclasses of the world. Though it excludes none who come to God with a "humble and contrite" heart (Ps 51:17; Is 57:15), its energy is directed primarily toward the poor.

2. The Christian mission is addressed to society,* to social life, "the structures of public life, calling for the righting of wrong and the liberation of the oppressed" (Lesslie Newbigin). It is good news to the social order.

3. The church's mission is addressed also to the underlying patterns and presuppositions of culture, the "root paradigms" that form worldviews* and govern definitions of truth and reality. It calls for their transformation away from partial or ideological truths to a comprehensive worldview in which each particle and particular has its proper place.

4. Mission is addressed also to the whole cosmos—"the rocks and the mountains," the earth and the planets. God speaks through God's Word to the whole created order. In Scripture, the Word of God is at times directed to the material environment itself: "O land, land, land, hear the word of the LORD!" (Jer 22:29). God tells Ezekiel, "Say to the southern forest: 'Hear the word of the LORD' " (Ezek 20:47). "Prophesy to the mountains of Israel, . . . 'You . . . will produce branches and fruit for my people Israel, for they will soon come home. I am concerned for you and will look on you with favor' " (Ezek 36:1, 8-9).

In other words, the Christian mission proclaims *healing** or reconciliation in the four ways people are alienated in our world: from God, from themselves, from other people and from the natural created order, the total environment. Yet the Christian mission may at times appear to be bad news, for it challenges the world's idolatries, exposing the false gods of ideology, nation, religion, technology,* power, the self and nature.

This broad view of mission raises some questions, however. What is the actual mission the church is called to carry out? Who is responsible for the mission? And can the church really fulfill its mission?

What Is the Church's Mission?
Mission means continuing Jesus' work in the world. What did Jesus do? He gave this summary: "The blind receive sight, the lame walk, those who have leprosy are cured, the deaf hear, the dead are raised, and the good news is preached to the poor" (Lk 7:22). Jesus said his disciples would continue his work and would "do even greater things than these, because [he was] going to the Father" (Jn 14:12). "Greater" presumably means not more dramatic or more powerful, but the extension of Jesus' ministry into all the world through the church. The reason Jesus' disciples would do greater works was that Jesus was going to the Father and would send the Holy Spirit (Jn 15:26-27; 16:7).

The Christian mission, then, is to faithfully fulfill the work of Jesus Christ. God calls the church into mission. It is not just our idea. Mission is our responsibility in thankful obedience to God's call (see Calling).

There are many dimensions to this mission, but for simplicity we describe it as *building Christian community,* *serving people* at their point of hurt or need (see Ministry), *sharing the good news of Jesus Christ* (see Evangelism; Witness) so people may come to experience new life in

him, and *building a just society* (see Social Action).

Building Christian Community. While the church is not an end in itself, redemptive mission requires a visible Christian community that really functions as the body of Christ. This is why the New Testament so frequently speaks of the importance of *being* the community that embodies mission. Mission is not just something we do; it is who we are. In this sense the saying is true: The church does not have a mission; the mission has a church. This is why Scripture instructs us, "Let the word of Christ dwell in you richly as you teach and admonish one another with all wisdom, and as you sing psalms, hymns and spiritual songs with gratitude in your hearts to God" (Col 3:16). "Let us not give up meeting together, . . . but let us encourage one another" and "consider how we may spur one another on toward love and good deeds" (Heb 10:24-25; see Church).

Serving People in Need. Since authentic mission is grounded in the outreaching love of God in Jesus Christ, Christians feel love-compelled to respond to human need wherever they find it. Jesus illustrated this in his parable of the good Samaritan. The love of Christ overwhelms the barriers of race, prejudice and culture, impelling believers to meet human need as Jesus did.

Sharing the Good News of Jesus Christ. The church tells others about Christ so that they too may come to experience new life in him. The church is called to proclaim the good news of salvation in Jesus Christ throughout the world, making disciples and building faithful Christian communities. Two of the most characteristic words in Acts are *martyreō,* "to bear witness"* (from which comes the English word *martyr*), and *euanggelizō,* "to proclaim good news" (from which comes the English word *evangelize*). Both these words occur over twenty times in Acts. The passion of the early church was to tell the good news about Jesus and the resurrection, bearing witness to what had been seen and heard. Those who experience Jesus Christ as Savior know the meaning of Paul's words "a new creation; the old has gone, the new has come!" (2 Cor 5:17).

Building a Just Society. Since God gives the church a creation-wide mission, Christians are responsible to show God's reconciliation in every area. The Bible often expresses this as a concern for justice and righteousness. Jesus said his disciples should "seek first [God's] kingdom and his righteousness" (Mt 6:33). The close linking of justice* and righteousness throughout the Old Testament requires taking Matthew 6:33 to mean "Seek to manifest the just rule of God," or "Seek the justice of God's kingdom," not simply personal, private righteousness. Jesus calls the church to seek God's righteousness/justice in the world. Christians want to see God's will done *on earth* as it is in heaven (Mt 6:10). The mission of the church is to pray and work so that this may be true in every area of society, with particular concern for the poor and oppressed.

Who Are the Missionaries?

Who is responsible for the Christian mission? According to the Bible, the whole people of God. First Peter 2:9 states this most clearly: "But you are a chosen people, a royal priesthood, a holy nation, a people belonging to God, that you may declare the praises of him who called you out of darkness into his wonderful light." This passage describes the church, all Christian believers. The church is a "priesthood," a people commissioned to serve God in the world. It is "a people." Here the Greek text uses the word *laos,* from which we get the term "laity."* The Bible says all the "laity" (the whole church) is called to mission. In the New

Testament there is no distinction between "clergy"* and "laity," because "laity" includes everyone (including pastors), and all the "laity" are ministers. The New Testament distinguishes between different kinds of ministries (not all are called to be pastors or teachers), but not between "ministers" and "laymen." Although Christians may have different ministries according to their spiritual gifts,* the whole church is called to mission.

This means that the Christian mission is *in the world* even more than it is in the church. The Christian mission is to be carried out in every area of culture,* among all the peoples of the earth, in every dimension of human life, from the hearth and kitchen to global politics and economics. At all life's intersections Christians are to carry out "the ministry of reconciliation" (2 Cor 5:18; *see* Ministry; Tentmaking; Work).

A primary function of the local church is to help believers find and fulfill their ministry in the world, both individually and together in the shared ministry of church and family.

Can the Church Really Fulfill Its Mission?

Christians often talk in lofty terms about the Christian mission. But is this realistic? Frequently the church has no sense of mission or carries out mission in the wrong spirit or in hurtful ways. How can we talk about mission with proper humility and yet affirm what Christ has told us? The answer is twofold.

First, the mission is God's mission, and God will fulfill his purpose. God promises us that the time is coming when "at the name of Jesus every knee should bow, in heaven and on earth and under the earth, and every tongue confess that Jesus Christ is Lord, to the glory of God the Father" (Phil 2:10-11). Jesus promised, "I will build my church, and the gates of Hades will not overcome it" (Mt 16:18). Our confidence is in God's faithfulness and power, not in our own efforts.

Second, God has given us his Holy Spirit, and by his Spirit he empowers and repeatedly renews the church down through history. Whenever we are tempted to despair of the church's mission—whether because of the external challenges or the church's own betrayal of the gospel—we can turn again in repentance, faith and hope to God and the renewing work of the Spirit.

Mission in My Life

Every Christian has been given a mission from God. Since we each find our mission in the larger life of the church, we may think of living our mission in three dimensions: our mission to God, to other believers and to the world.

Our Mission to God. Our mission to the world is grounded in our relationship to God. Worship and faithful service is our Godward mission. This is the essential vertical dimension of mission. We are called to offer "spiritual sacrifices acceptable to God through Jesus Christ" (1 Pet 2:5), to "continually offer to God a sacrifice of praise" (Heb 13:15).

Our Mission to Each Other. Since we are called not just individually but primarily as the body of Christ in the world, we also have a mission to each other. Our mission is to help the church be in mission. The New Testament addresses this repeatedly when it says we are to love each other, encourage each other, teach and reprove each other, and bear one another's burdens (*see* Fellowship). As noted earlier, Paul writes to the Colossians, "Let the word of Christ dwell in you richly as you teach and admonish one another with all wisdom" (Col 3:16). As Christians we are to "encourage one another daily" so that none of us becomes "hardened by sin's deceitfulness" (Heb 3:13). These teachings are more than

advice for our own spiritual growth.* They are our mission to the body.

Our Mission to the World. God has given the church the mission to "declare the praises of him who called [us] out of darkness into his wonderful light" (1 Pet 2:9). Each one of us fits in some way into the church's mission to point to Jesus Christ and to continue his work. But this happens in very different ways. Some people's mission to the world is primarily through their home* and family life (*see* Family). Others fulfill their mission mainly through jobs and careers. Various kinds of creative expression, whether or not a part of one's job, may be the main avenue of mission. Some are prophets and evangelists; others are artists and homemakers.* The important thing is that our life genuinely be mission—living for God's purposes—not merely doing our own thing. And here we each need the discerning guidance of the larger community of believers. In this way we find our place in the body, discover our spiritual gifts and help carry out the mission of God.

See also CALLING; CHURCH; CHURCH-FAMILY; DISCIPLESHIP; EVANGELISM; HEALING; JUSTICE; LAITY; MISSIONS; POVERTY; SOCIAL ACTION; WITNESS; WORSHIP.

References and Resources
D. Bosch, *Transforming Mission* (Maryknoll, N.Y.: Orbis, 1991); E. S. Jones, *Christ's Alternative to Communism* (New York: Abingdon, 1935); H. A. Snyder, *Liberating the Church: The Ecology of Church and Kingdom* (Downers Grove, Ill.: InterVarsity Press, 1983); J. Stott, *Christian Mission in the Modern World* (Downers Grove, Ill.: InterVarsity Press, 1975); R. D. Winter and S. C. Hawthorne, eds., *Perspectives on the World Christian Movement*, rev. ed. (Pasadena, Calif.: William Carey Library, 1992).

Howard A. Snyder

MISSIONS

In popular usage, *missions* means Christian witness* in other lands. This use derives mainly from the modern Protestant missionary movement of the past two centuries and indirectly from earlier Roman Catholic precedents. But in recent decades the term has taken on additional nuances. Today some people insist that the term *missions* should be replaced by *mission*,* in part because of the historical connection between missions and Western colonialism. This article reviews the story of Christian missions, then summarizes the status of Christian missions at the end of the twentieth century.

An Overview of Christian Missions

Jesus commissioned his disciples to be "witnesses in Jerusalem, and in all Judea and Samaria, and to the ends of the earth" (Acts 1:8). He also said the key was love: "This is how everyone will recognize that you are my disciples—when they see the love you have for each other" (Jn 13:35, The Message). With remarkable energy the early church did what Jesus said. But it was not primarily the apostles who carried the message to new areas. Rather, as "persecution broke out against the church at Jerusalem" (Acts 8:1), the believers were scattered, and they shared the good news wherever they went. Most witnessed only to fellow Jews, but some Greek-speaking Jewish believers "began to speak to Greeks also, telling them the good news about the Lord Jesus" (Acts 11:20). Thus the dynamic, multicultural church in Antioch was born and soon became the launching pad of the missionary work of Paul, Barnabas, Silas, Mark and probably others.

Four things impelled the early church into missionary outreach: the commission of Jesus, the pouring out of the Holy Spirit, the church's intense, mutually supportive community life and persecution. God used all of these. The church became a many-celled, increasingly diverse extension of the original little community of men and women who were Jesus' most intimate disciples. Their love and care gave them something to share, but it also brought opposition and conflict—just as Jesus had predicted. Jesus was still with them through the Holy Spirit, and the Spirit sent many of them out into the world. Yet we should remember that most Christians stayed in their own towns and neighborhoods, raising their families and living "peaceful and quiet lives in all godliness and holiness" (1 Tim 2:2), witnessing to Christ by their deeds and lives. They became the spiritual and material support base for those whom God commissioned to carry the good news to other peoples. This was their mission, and it was a key part of the broader missionary outreach of the Christian community.

From that crucial Day of Pentecost, about A.D. 33, until the present, the drama Jesus initiated and predicted in Acts 1:8 has been unfolding. The gospel has gone forth "to the ends of the earth," especially in the nineteenth and twentieth centuries. Missiologists estimate that there are some twelve thousand distinct ethnolinguistic "people groups" in the world, and that by 1995 about nine thousand of them had living, functioning Christian churches within them. The global church is more diverse than ever in history. How did this happen?

To All the Earth

The church spread north, south, east and west from Palestine. Because the New Testament gives special prominence to Paul's missionary activity, and because European Christianity has had such a global impact, many people assume that the main direction of church growth has been from east to west (from the Middle East to Europe and the Americas). So in many places Christianity has been seen as a Western religion.

But this is only part of the story.

Not only did Paul go west; the apostle Thomas went east. Other Christian missionaries spread south into Africa and north into the Slavic lands. By the sixth century, Christians were found as far east as India and throughout North Africa. Christians in India of the Saint Thomas (Mar Thoma) Church believe their church was founded by the apostle Thomas, and the claim now seems historically plausible.

There was also a strong church in Syria for several centuries. Christian missionaries later carried the gospel to China and Japan, though nearly all traces of their work prior to the modern era eventually disappeared. These missionaries faced many difficulties. The great Jesuit missionary to Asia, Francis Xavier (1506-1552), complained that "Christian" merchants from Europe discredited the gospel by their lifestyles and business practices.

Europe was evangelized during the first half of the Middle Ages. Many tribes and kingdoms turned to Christianity. Though sometimes the reasons were partly political and conversions were shallow, the Middle Ages offer striking examples of authentic Christian missions and movements of renewal. The most effective missionary activity was carried out by Christian "orders," communities of men (and sometimes women) dedicated to poverty, celibacy and spreading the gospel among unreached peoples. The Irish Celtic missionary Columban (550-615) and his monastic brothers evangelized parts of France. The British missionary Boniface (680-754), commissioned by Pope Gregory II to convert the German people, was so successful that historian Christopher Dawson said Boniface "had a deeper influence on the history of Europe than any Englishman who ever lived." Boniface was ably assisted by a number of missionary nuns, including his godly cousin Lioba. This was pioneer missionary work.

Opposition and Extension

The spread of Islam from the seventh to the fifteenth centuries dramatically changed the face of Christian missions. This religious-military-political crusade largely supplanted Christianity throughout the Middle East and North Africa and reached into Europe as far as Bosnia and northern Spain, where it was checked by European armies. Its spread east was even more dramatic, as evidenced today by large Muslim populations from Afghanistan and Iran to Indonesia and Malaysia. The medieval Christian Crusades, in a tragic distortion of Christian mission, fought to win back the Holy Land from Islam. Although ultimately unsuccessful, the Crusades left a heritage of bitterness between Islam and Christianity that still survives.

At the beginning of the modern era the Jesuits carried out successful missionary work in South America and elsewhere. But as often happens when mission is allied with empire, Christian witness was compromised by political intrigue and economic greed. The great age of Protestant missions, beginning in the early 1700s, saw an unprecedented spread of the gospel worldwide that still continues. Most Protestant churches today outside the North Atlantic region trace their origin to missionary outreach between 1800 and 1914, the period historian Kenneth Latourette called "the Great Century." Since this missionary advance often coincided with the colonial expansion of the Western powers, especially in Africa and Asia, it was sometimes shallow and patronizing. Missionaries often assumed that European "Christian" culture* was a part of the gospel. Yet Christianity took deep root, especially in many parts of Africa—ongoing testimony to the power of the gospel.

Global Christianity has changed dramatically since 1900. David Barrett writes in *The World Christian Encyclopedia,*

> Christianity has become the most extensive and universal religion in history. There are today Christians and organized Christian churches in every inhabited country on earth. . . . For the first time in history, [the church is now] ecumenical in the literal meaning of the word: its boundaries are coextensive with the *oikumene,* "the whole inhabited world."

Christian Missions Today

The church has always had a world mission. But the emergence of Christianity as universal in a numerical and geographic sense is historically new. In the nineteen centuries following Jesus' resurrection, Christianity grew to include one-third of all humanity; yet more than 80 percent of these were whites. In the twentieth century Christianity has declined or lost its vibrancy in Europe and North America but has grown dramatically elsewhere. Today Christians number more than half the population in two-thirds of the world's 225 nations and still constitute one-third of humanity (though many of these are nominal or "cultural" Christians). About 60 percent of all Christians are urbanized, as compared with a little over 40 percent of the world population. Most significantly, from being predominantly white, Christianity is now an amalgam of the races and peoples of the world, with whites numbering 40 percent or less.

Today missions have become a highly complex global, international enterprise. Korean churches send missionaries to Russia, China, the United States and other lands. Brazilian missionaries serve in dozens of countries. Mission organizations like Youth with a Mission and the International Fellowship of Evangelical Students send teams of mixed nationalities and races. Many missionaries today are "tentmakers"*—teachers, engineers, architects and other professionals. Like Priscilla and Aquila, they travel to other countries or peoples, hold jobs there and witness through work, informal contacts and daily life experiences. Many other Christians find their mission field among college and university students studying abroad.

Today most missionaries come from the vigorous Christian churches in Asia, Africa and Latin America. The church's center of gravity has shifted from Europe and North America to the South and East, from traditionally Christian lands to the whole world.

As Christianity enters the twenty-first century, missions face four major challenges:

☐ massive urbanization, with hundreds of huge megacities around the globe, many of them crowded with the poor;

☐ relationship with the other great world religions, particularly Islam, Buddhism and Hinduism;

☐ how to cope with a materialistic, high-tech culture in economically dynamic regions like the Pacific Rim;

☐ an emerging global* society, increasingly interconnected but also torn by ethnic, cultural and economic tensions.

Thus faithful Christian mission in coming decades will require effective urban witness, faithful interreligious mission and dialogue, discipleship* that challenges technological materialism and a compelling vision for global society.

Your Place in World Missions

Since all Christians are to be Jesus' disciples and to help make disciples, all should be involved in missions at some level. Some of the most common ways are

☐ serving short-term among a different people group as a means of sharing the gospel. Some do this as a part of their work* or profession.* Others are sent by various Christian sponsoring agencies.

☐ participating in a house church or other small group* that "adopts" a particular unreached people or a church in another culture and serves them through prayer, information sharing and financial support. Contact can be by mail, video, short trips and e-mail.

☐ supporting career missionaries in their work, whether through individual giving or through a house church, congregation or denominational program.

☐ prayer. Increasingly useful resources for helping to extend Christian missions through prayer are available. All Christians can be involved in missions through prayer, both individually and in their Christian fellowships.

See also EVANGELISM; GLOBAL VILLAGE; MISSION; MULTICULTURALISM; PLURALISM; SOCIAL ACTION; TENTMAKING; WITNESS.

References and Resources
D. B. Barrett, ed., *World Christian Encyclopedia* (Nairobi, Kenya: Oxford University Press, 1982); P. Johnstone, *Operation World: The Day-by-Day Guide to Praying for the World*, 5th ed. (Grand Rapids: Zondervan, 1993); R. Keeley, ed., *Christianity: A World Faith* (Herts., U.K.: Lion, 1985); K. S. Latourette, *History of the Expansion of Christianity*, 7 vols. (Grand Rapids: Zondervan, 1978); S. H. Moffett, *A History of Christianity in Asia*, vol. 1, *Beginnings to 1500* (New York: Harper, 1992); S. Neill, *A History of Christian Missions*, rev. ed. (New York: Penguin, 1986), R. A. Tucker, *From Jerusalem to Irian Jaya: A Biographical History of Christian Missions* (Grand Rapids: Zondervan, 1983).

Howard A. Snyder

MOBILITY

Mobility is a way of life in all modern societies, especially in newer ones like the United States, Canada and Australia. In these countries approximately one person in five moves each year. Some people, and persons in some parts of these countries, are more mobile than others. For example, young couples without children in southern California move on average every two or three years, while singles in Silicon Valley, south of San Francisco, move on average more than once a year, often around the valley itself. But overall during a five-year period between 50 percent and 60 percent of the population moves, and over a decade this rises to around 75 percent.

People move not only within countries but also between them. Indeed, in the twentieth century we have probably witnessed the largest ever movements of people from one country to another. In some cases, such as the northward drift to the United States from various parts of Latin America, this is motivated by the dream of a better life. Within a generation Hispanics will number more than 50 percent of the population of cities like Los Angeles. In other cases people are driven from their own country or feel compelled to leave it because of persecution, oppression or even genocide. On a different level altogether, travel* and tourism have become big business, resulting in increasing numbers of people moving intensively and extensively around various parts of the world as well as around their own countries.

Though they reside in one location, most people frequently move around cities or regions over long distances on a daily or weekly basis. Some work is mainly mobile. This is true for drivers, salespeople, journalists, deliverers, realtors, seasonal workers, cowboys, sailors and pilots. In some cases previously fixed workplaces* are becoming mobile, especially as cars develop into complete mobile office systems with cellular phone, fax machine, word processor, printer and even perhaps two-way radio. Employees are also moving more frequently from workplace to workplace or from one line of work to another. Virtually gone are the days of the lifetime company employee: the average worker now holds down five or more different types of job during the course of a lifetime.

Overall it has been estimated that people today cover around thirty to thirty-five times the distance traveled by their grandparents. These high rates and varied kinds of mobility raise a number of important questions. Why are we so mobile? What are the personal and communal effects of mobility? Where is mobility talked about in the Bible, and does this throw light on our culturally different situation? When and where should we move or not move, and what criteria should govern our decision? How can we better manage the moves we feel are right to make?

Why Are We So Mobile?

The roots of mobility in newer Western societies lie primarily in their mobile beginnings. These countries were entered by people who chose or were forced to move to them. Once there, many immigrants did not stay in one place but continued to move across the countryside. It was Frederick Jackson Turner who, toward the end of the last century, first argued that the experience of successive frontiers in the United States significantly shaped individual character and democratic institutions in America. The frontier mentality was characterized by repeated hopes for improvement, by struggles with primitive conditions, by an emphasis on expediency and acquisitiveness, by restless energy and optimism, by individualism and materialism. Though the outcome was somewhat different in Canada and Australia, where the wilderness was not won but itself won against the intruders, the expansion of people into open spaces and their movement between them still had a marked effect.

Somewhere in the midst of this ongoing mobility a subtle but decisive change took place, particularly in the United States. The immigrants' belief that their hopes would be fulfilled if they could find the right place in which to settle down turned into the belief that the very process of continually moving was itself the way to experience fulfillment. In his influential book Wendell Berry calls this the *unsettling*, rather than the *settling*, of America, for people tended to exploit, rather than care for, the land on which they settled and, when they realized this, left it behind for greener pastures. This exploiting and leaving was the beginning of the disposable society, which eventually transformed itself into the phenomenon of the disposable individual, one who successively leaves a worn-out or failed version of the self behind and by moving on again and again hopes to remake or reinvent his or her selfhood.

What Are the Effects of Mobility?

Mobility can have a number of positive effects. These include freedom from persecution or a restrictive context and the opportunity to begin again especially after making a mistake, to move to a healthier or simply more pleasant environment, to get closer to family or leave behind an abusive family situation, to increase educational or cultural possibilities, to find a better job and commute* fewer hours, to develop a lifestyle more consistent with basic values* or last, but not least for many Christians, to fulfill a sense of vocation or mission.*

There can also be negative effects. Among these are the loss of a sense of roots and place, leaving behind extended family and friends, difficulties in readjusting and higher levels of restlessness, a diminished desire and capacity to become committed to people and contexts the more one moves, and a tendency toward greater relativism in beliefs and values. Though few people are aware of it, the increase in mobility during the last century has also increased the degree of bureaucratic* control and regulation of people moving or traveling.

A significant effect of mobility that people do not take sufficiently into account is an increase in levels of personal stress.* The well-known Social Readjustment Rating Scale helps people determine how much stress they are likely to encounter as they undergo various experiences. As well as a change in residence (20 points), a move generally involves a change in schools (26 points), a different line of work (36 points) or work responsibilities (29 points), a spouse's having to stop or begin work (26 points), and a change in church (19 points) and social activities (18 points). Sometimes a move involves increased marital arguments (35 points), separation from a member of the immediate family (29 points), or a change in living conditions (25 points) or in recreational habits (19 points). When we add the energy expended on adapting to a different climate and to unfamiliar locations, these points often add up to a fair degree of stress: once they reach 300, there is a 90 percent probability of people's experiencing acute insomnia and developing an illness.

Finally, mobility involves a change in churches, which not only involves an additional 20 or more points on the scale but deprives the congregation left behind of the ongoing presence and contribution of those who are moving. One of the most serious unrecognized factors militating against developing community* in local churches today is that roughly 20 percent of their members are turning over each year, among them some of their most committed people. How do you build deep community in such a transient setting?

What Does the Bible Say About Mobility?
The Bible presents us with a complex picture of people moving around and staying put. God's question to the heavenly court, "Whom shall I send? And who will go for us?" (Is 6:8), is probably the passage that first comes to mind in thinking about mobility. Note, however, that this sending and going dealt mostly with a vocational rather than geographical change for the prophet. But other significant figures within the nation of Israel and among the early Christians—from Abraham through Jonah to Paul—were highly mobile. This was largely true of Jesus himself. The lives of others, such as Moses and Peter, were a blend of mobility and stability. In contrast, others—like Solomon and James—had a largely settled existence. The nation of Israel itself went through long stretches of stability in Egypt and Canaan, intermixed with wanderings through the desert and a time of exile. In a deeper sense, as the writer to the Hebrews puts it, all these people were "longing for a better country—a heavenly one" (Heb 11:16), but this is not to say that their earthly existence was made up of continual pilgrimage.

Most of the aforementioned biblical figures, even the chosen people as a whole, were called to a rather unusual work* and therefore should not be treated as exact role models for all Christians with respect to mobility. But the criteria by which they decided to stay put or move on, how short or long a time to remain or travel around, and how to cope with an unsettled life when it came their way have something to say.

Paul is an interesting example with regard to mobility, for we have more evidence concerning his movements than we have for most biblical figures. The apostle worked out the geographical boundaries within which he would move around and beyond which he would not go (Rom 15:19-20). Moreover, Paul did not equate the need or opportunity to do something with the call of God to attend to it—sometimes another factor also had to be present (2 Cor 2:12-13). He viewed his work as completed in a particular area once he had established it in an influential center from which it would spread elsewhere of its own accord (Rom 15:21-23). Except when Paul was forced out, he did not leave a place until he had completed what he had set out to do and had done so in a quality way (1 Cor 3:10-15). Furthermore, the apostle limited how much he attempted within these boundaries to the divine gifts and instructions he had been given, allowing others to look after the rest (Rom 12:3, 6). For all the difficulties and anxieties Paul encountered (2 Cor 11:26-27), overall he learned to be content in whatever circumstances he found himself (Phil 4:11-13).

What Are Our Criteria for Moving?

Building on the criteria found in Scripture, and assuming there is no overriding decisive argument for moving such as the radical state of a person's health or absolute lack of work, we ask what concrete guidance can be given to those contemplating a move.

First, make a list of all the stakeholders in the move, that is, all those affected by the decision. This would normally include family* and relatives but should also cover friends,* fellow churchgoers, colleagues and neighbors, as well as other people and institutions who have been part of your life and who will lose something by your leaving. This same list will help you assess how much you will lose through being physically separated from these people. Too often a decision to move is based purely on whether it will improve a person's job prospects or provide higher pay* or whether relocation will be to a "nicer" area with a better climate. I know of more than one couple who decided that what they and their

children were gaining from and giving to their church at the time was more important than a higher salary and status. In all this it is important to count the hidden costs and gains, internal as well as external, that are often overlooked in making a decision.

Second, if you do not have it already, develop a clear sense of your own values and priorities. What is most important to you in your life, and what priority would you give to those items at the top of the list? What would you most miss if all of a sudden you were deprived of it? What stage of life are you in or moving into with respect to family, work, Christian ministry* and spiritual growth*? If you have a spouse, what does he or she most require over the next few years, and what can you most give to or gain from the one closest to you? All too often decisions about staying or moving are made without springing from or taking into account the basic values around which our lives as Christians should revolve.

Third, work out where the authority lies for making the decision. Does it lie, as is sometimes the case, with the person who will be most advantaged by the move, often the male in the household? When a couple and/or children are involved, does the decision depend on both spouses' coming to agreement or on the whole family, at least including children of a reasonable age, reaching a decision? When people belong to a small group,* how much involvement should this primary Christian community have through asking questions, contributing wisdom, engaging in prayer and seeking a word of knowledge from God? What role do nearby friends have in this process, since they will be seriously affected by the outcome? In other words, how is God's will best discerned in such a corporate situation as opposed to a matter that is purely individual or familial? Should a discernment group made of several confidants and key stakeholders be called together to help work through the issue?

Further Considerations

Two clarifications are in order. Sometimes the answer to the question about moving is neither yes nor no but *not yet*. Not all moves have to be made immediately: often a delay enables some factors that are hindering to dissolve or some of the reservations people are experiencing to dissipate. So waiting,* which most people find difficult, is a genuine option. Also, deciding to stay rather than move is just as much a choice in its own right. Occasionally such a process unearths stronger grounds for staying than those considering a move had beforehand. Given the rate of mobility today, and its detrimental effects on community generally, the question that God may be asking of many people is not "Who will go for us?" but rather "Who will stay for us?" How else will community be revitalized and deepened in our churches, neighborhoods and cities today?

To whatever extent we are or are not mobile, most of us would benefit from knowing how to handle mobility better. It is helpful here to begin by identifying those aspects of the move that are most threatening or that promise the quickest rewards. Also, work out with family members concrete strategies for minimizing problems and maximizing satisfactions. Consider whatever plans you make as a commitment to those who find the move most difficult and put them into practice as soon as possible. Involve any who are willing to help in the move so that the burden is shared more widely. Try to find one person in your new location who can answer questions you might have, act as an interpreter of local customs and direct you to any services that may be helpful. Give yourselves a buffer zone of at least one or two weeks to prepare for the

move and to settle in and recover from it.

See also CALLING/VOCATION; GUIDANCE; TRAVELING.

References and Resources

W. Berry, *The Unsettling of America: Culture and Agriculture* (New York: Avon, 1972); M. B. Emerson and C. Cameron, *Moving: The Challenge of Change* (Nashville: Abingdon, 1988); J. McInnes, *The New Pilgrims* (Sydney: Sutherland, 1980); J. Naisbitt, *Megatrends* (New York: Warner, 1982); W. Stegner, *The American West as Living Space* (Ann Arbor: University of Michigan Press, 1987); F. J. Turner, *The Frontier in American History* (New York: Henry Holt, 1920); J. A. Walter, *The Human Home: The Myth of the Sacred Environment* (Tring, Herts, U.K.: Lion, 1982).

Robert Banks

MONEY

Money matters. It seems that money, like sex, is at the core of everything that we human beings do. The life-giving power of money in modern society is godlike. Easy it is for the moral scold to declaim that it should not be so. But the simple fact is, like it or not, that money has nearly omnipotent control over the human race. Its powers range over life and death and everything in between. In its hand is authority to bestow food, shelter and facilities that are basic to lives of human dignity. In abundance money gives us an almost royal freedom to do whatever we please—to travel, to enjoy fine things, to educate our children, to grow old in good health and security. And an excess of money quite literally gives us the power of life and death over others. Even our paltry pocket money placed monthly in the right envelope can literally save people from hunger, disease and worse. Money matters so very much because if we have it, we live and if we have a lot of it, we flourish, we ascend to Olympian heights of freedom and power, and we (and perhaps others too) live long and prosper. But without money, we perish, or if we have only a precious little of it, we (as much of the earth does) wallow in a squalor of mere subsistence. It does seem that money—mammon—rules the earth.

Money is, therefore, also a matter for the religions. It is a kind of challenger to their position in the world. Karl Marx and Thomas Jefferson, two men as different from each other in their economic beliefs as they could be, had in common a deep skepticism toward religion. They were skeptical because they observed how religions often distract people from the present material conditions of life. The spiritual strategy of religions, they believed, was to evade our ancient enemy—poverty—rather than bravely to face and slay it in honest and mortal combat.

Indeed, throughout the groaning world today no matter is more urgent to the religions than the matter of what to do about money. The great powers of poverty, sickness, illiteracy, AIDS, malnutrition and starvation rage on a global scale as never before. In the pitiful, blank faces of sallow-cheeked children (who enter our homes routinely on cable television), we truly see the dark angel of death.* And his darkness soars on wings made of otherworldly spiritualism; the want of money makes him strong. Money, it seems, is our only hope, the only power on earth that can fell him. Yet according to Jesus, "You cannot serve both God and Money" (Mt 6:24). What can this mean? In what way ought money matter to the Christian? In what way ought it not to matter?

Money Matters in Christian History

In its history Christianity, unlike a good many of the world's faiths, never was purely spiritual in its vision. That is mainly because Christianity erected its entire worldview upon a strong doctrine of creation.* As the first article of the Apostles' Creed implies, to the Christian the material world is something much greater than a mere physical presence or a transitory stage on which more deeply spiritual stories will play out. The material world is God's creation, and it is thus good. The material world is not indifferent, illusory or evil, as it is in many religious visions (consider the great faiths of Hinduism and Buddhism). It is itself something real, essential, good and, we dare say, even sacred.

In the Christian tradition material wealth is directly associated with God's good creation and thus with God's will and vision for human beings on earth. Upon opening the Old and New Testaments, we see in a very short time that this is so. There is something about material wealth* and poverty* in almost every section of the Bible from Genesis to Revelation. In the Bible it matters that we are rich or poor. The whole story connects money with the story of God and God's people. It is not too strong to say that money (or at least material life) is at the root of all that God is said to have done in history, and it is at the root of all that counts as good or evil among the people of God. No subject was addressed by Christ more often than this one, and there really is no Christian doctrine we can think about very long before we come up against questions about economic life—especially if we are relatively rich in the context of a world that is generally poor. To the Christian, then, money not only matters in a transitory way; it is somehow connected with the redemption and eternal destinies of human beings.

Christians realized from the beginning that the matter of wealth was a matter of great theological and spiritual urgency (Gonzalez, pp. x-xvi). Early Christian thinkers all knew that spiritualism or dualism would not do. From sacred tradition, especially the prophets and Jesus, they knew that how we live as economic persons reveals, even exposes, who we are as spiritual persons. The economic life, they reasoned, is a kind of incarnation of the spiritual life. It is a sequence of actions that speak our hearts more loudly than pious words can do. To the extent that our works cannot be disjoined from faith, the ancients rightly judged that the matter of money (or wealth generally) was a matter that had the mark of eternity about it.

As there are now, there were arguments, debates, disagreements and plain old muddles over the problem. Should we have personal possessions at all? If yes (as most agreed we must), then in what quantity and form? How much was too much or too little? The answers of the early Christians tended toward the ascetic (Gonzalez, pp. 71-214). Most looked upon an excess of wealth as spiritually dangerous and morally evil. Throughout the Middle Ages to the Protestant Reformation, the most brilliant thinkers were disposed to denigrate the pursuit of material prosperity. Their model was mainly Jesus, whom they interpreted to have lived a life of poverty and to have enjoined such a life upon his followers.

There is a tendency in today's consumer* society for certain Christians to lionize these historic figures as models of spirituality. But before romanticism sets in, we ought to keep in mind that the moral contest of gaining and having money in their day was very different from that of our own time. Not always but generally in ancient times, it was the rule that one person's gain was another person's loss. Only a very small and powerful elite had material wealth in excess, while the vast majority lived in conditions that we would find beneath the dignity of any human being. To such a world—the world of Augustine, Aquinas and Calvin —Jesus' words about mammon were unambiguous. It was difficult to go out and acquire great fortune without doing things that amounted morally to theft from weaker brothers and sisters. But even as great men spoke old words to an old time, a new economic world was being born. It would require new words.

Like its thinking about science, philosophy, music, art and much else, Christian thinking about economic life stood well until the modern revolutions struck. Then it seemed that nothing stood very well anymore. In the centuries before, life seemed an unbroken, nearly changeless and endless rule by monarchs and a condition of poverty for the vast majority (who as the poor, it was just presumed, would always be with us). The centuries after brought one destabilizing shock after another to the older order. The social order that had stood for more than a thousand years fell like some great old tree. A new world grew up in its place at such dazzling speed that we have not caught up with it yet. All the systems of civilization were reordered, and this was made possible in large measure by the astonishing success of the new economic system that had emerged.

For the first time in human history a people began seriously to think that poverty (just as tyranny) might be erased from the face of the earth (Lay Commission, pp. 10-17). In a new land, under a new political and intellectual order, a new people began to flourish in a new way. Ordinary men and women became wealthy as only nobility had done in ages gone. But they had not attained their good fortunes through the genetic line of heredity, nor had they gained by exploiting weaker folk. They had attained it through the honest labor of their hands, even by providing needed services to others in a cycle of prosperity. Their gain had, in effect, been gain for their fellows. In a remarkably brief span of time, this new middle class of people became the majority of the population. The poor became a minority, yet even they had hope of one day being set free from poverty. They knew that we cannot serve both God and mammon, but it seemed that God had served them with it and that he had called them to serve him in prosperity. New words were needed for this new time, and they are needed still.

Money Matters to the Christian Today

Today debates rage among Christians over money and the material goods of this world. What should be done with the great fortune we have amassed? How should we live? What would God have us think and do? The trouble is that we are at sail in a sea of delights while most of the world and some of us at home are intolerably poor. Socialism was the hue and cry of some, but its glory has faded. Defenders of the free market—capitalism—have won the war of ideas, or so it seems. But that does not solve the spiritual problem of economic identity. How ought we to live our economic lives in such a world? When does our respect for money become worship of the god mammon? How much may we freely enjoy? How much ought we in justice to give? For most, the various questions boil down to one: how are we to view the realm of the superfluous, that which exceeds the mere "necessaries of life," as Charles Wesley called them?

Some rail against the having and enjoying of superfluous wealth while others in the world hunger and thirst. In their view any countenance of the superfluous is immoral. Our lives and national systems must be rebuilt upon the principle of meeting only our real needs and then the needs of others (Sider). Their appeal is primarily to the biblical prophets and Jesus who, they say, stood against the rich and for the poor.

Others disagree. They argue that the economics of necessity spell global depression of our consumption-driven systems. The outcome would hardly be liberation of the poor from poverty, but instead poverty for almost everyone. They also point to many passages of Scripture that give God's blessing on the enjoyment of extravagant and superfluous things (Griffiths). What are we to think and do about money, about the superfluous?

The Two Voices of Scripture on Money

We are forced by the nature of the debate to return to our first principles. We must go to Scripture and seek to hear the Word of God in a new way. But when we turn to the Bible for help, we are soon daunted by discovering (if we do not know it already) that the text seems to speak with two voices that are, distressingly, in conflict. The one voice says that to be rich is to have received a blessing from God. It says that material riches are a means by which God expresses redemptive love for his people and makes them flourish. Material riches bring to pass the very vision of delight that our good God had for us.

The other voice is dark with warnings about money. It says that money is a curse, that the rich are accursed, that riches are the wages of sin and unrighteousness, especially toward the poor, with whom God takes his stand against the rich. Many would say that this second voice is essentially the voice of Jesus and that it does not speak good news to those who have more than enough money. Can we hear the two voices of Scripture as one harmonious word from God? Or are we doomed forever to a dialect of dissonance and paradox? The harmony is difficult to hear, but with care it can be done.

Delight and Compassion Embrace

If we listen to the deepest levels of each

voice—the one that blesses and the other that curses the rich—we learn that delight and compassion are not alien to each other. Since the one entails the other, in their truest shapes they embrace. Of course, they may become alien to each other—there is a delight that turns hard, into self-indulgent and unjust hedonism, and there is a compassion that turns cold, into righteous, pitiless and joyless moralism. But they need not do so. Indeed, in Scripture, we never really have delight in its truest and fullest sense without compassion, nor do we have compassionate justice, shalom in the truest and fullest sense, without delight.

Let us briefly consider four representative biblical narratives: the creation, the exodus, the exile and the ministry of Christ. For in these narratives, God has given us the elemental structures of a worldview.

In its lyrical, almost liturgical way, Genesis 1 (and Gen 2—3) pictures God's making a material world that is, as we said before, good and even sacred. Here the spiritual and physical worlds are as one. More so, God breathed into the lump of earth that was to become a human being. Human beings are pictured as spiritually endowed physical beings that God designed to inhabit a physical world. And it was "good," as God wished it to be. Even more so, the physical realm is characterized as a pleasure garden that humans are to till and keep as well as enjoy, except that they must not touch the wicked fruit of the knowledge of good and evil. So the most basic vision of human existence as God intended it to be is one of luxurious delight in physicality within a world of moral limits and obligations. This goes to the core of life itself as the ancient Hebrews thought of it (Schneider, pp. 43-64).

The story of the exodus carries on the same double-tinged theme. God rescues the Hebrew people from physical bondage in Egypt and consummates their liberation by giving them a land flowing with milk and honey. It is God, not themselves, who makes them rich and powerful in the land. Because they represent God, they must be especially concerned with those in their midst who have no wealth or power—with the widow, the orphan, the sojourner, the poor. As the people of this God, they must also empower the powerless, enrich those without riches. In their delight they must seek justice, wherein justice means not allowing that any fellow Israelite be poor. Theirs must be a land shining on a hill to the nations, where delight and compassion embrace in a sacred and plainly political way. The whole of the law thus weds delight with compassion, compassion with delight (Limburg, pp. 25-38).

The same double-edged theme shapes the narrative of the exile. The reason God sends his people back into captivity is that the ruling rich have gorged themselves without grieving for the poor. They are not God's people in the most profound spiritual sense of that concept. The exodus is thus reversed physically, just as it had already been turned back spiritually. The prophets thunder, not against the sacred delight that God blessed, but against the dark hedonism that God warned about in the first place. We cannot elaborate how these themes unfold throughout the so-called wisdom literature—Job, Ecclesiastes, Proverbs, even the Song of Songs—but indeed they do (Van Leeuwen, pp. 36-39).

If there is a place in biblical history where we might think delight is sacrificed on the altar of compassion, it would be in the story of Jesus—the story that ends at Golgotha. But delight in the physicality of the world does not die in the heart of Jesus; in him it is reborn and set free again on its way to true shalom for this earth. It is true that in his vision of it we hunger and thirst for the day, for it is not yet. But if we inspect things a little more closely, it is here, as it was already in him.

Moral theology has awakened us in earnest to the "radical Jesus," the Jesus who, in stark contrast to the Sunday-school cliché, stood like a stern prophet against the powers of his time. He did not fear them. Without reserve Jesus used his tongue like a whip against those who were rich, and indeed he blessed the poor, who would inherit the earth (Wolterstorff, p. 73). Many have drawn from this that Jesus was himself literally poor and that material poverty went with his life of self-denial and suffering (Sider, p. 61). But this image of Jesus simplifies things too much.

Today's moral theologians have written precious little about another Jesus whose identity emerges in the Gospels. They neglect the "Christ of delight," who bewildered his religious peers by eating and drinking, rather than fasting. He was the suffering servant, but since he came eating and drinking, pious ones who knew better labeled him a drunkard and a glutton. They, like Judas, could not fathom the freedom he had for wasteful celebration. When he, at his good pleasure, permitted the woman of ill repute to pour the jar of pure nard over his head, that was worth a year's income at a good job and could have been sold and given to the poor. Jesus broke the seal of the vessel that bottled up the forces of darkness that would betray and crucify him.

Christian economic life should flow naturally from a Christian identity that is, if possible, at one, in perfect harmony, with both delight and compassion. We should be in our bodies little Israels, miniature versions of Jesus in our circumstances, those who know the difference between the blessedness of delight and the accursedness of debauchery. Of course, it is not always possible to be so blessed and faithful at the same time. At times we may have to be poorer than we would like to be in order to keep our souls from harm. But there is no ideal to be found in this, any more than it ought to be our ideal to keep the poor around us from flourishing in true shalom. If possible, let our lives be written epistles of wonder at the blessings that God lavishes upon us so that we, as God's people, might go forth and do likewise among those who hunger and thirst in poverty for the coming kingdom of God.

There is much more to say. But these biblical narratives offer us a valuable guide for mapping out the details of economic life. How much to enjoy, to invest, to spend on family; how much to give to church, charities, individuals in need—these are matters for a lifetime. What really matters, however, is that our economic lives spring forth from souls neither too withered for delight nor too hard for compassion. In that harmony we seek the right rhythm for seeking first the kingdom of God.

See also CREDIT; CREDIT CARD; DEBT; FINANCIAL SUPPORT; INVESTMENT; POWER; PRINCIPALITIES AND POWERS; SIMPLER LIFESTYLE; STEWARDSHIP; WEALTH.

References and Resources

J. Ellul, *Money and Power* (Downers Grove, Ill.: InterVarsity Press, 1984); J. L. Gonzalez, *Faith and Wealth: A History of the Origin, Significance and Use of Money* (San Francisco: Harper & Row, 1990); B. Griffiths, *The Creation of Wealth: A Christian's Case for Capitalism* (Downers Grove, Ill.: InterVarsity Press, 1984); Lay Commission on Catholic Social Teaching and the U.S. Economy, *Toward the Future: Catholic Thought and the U.S. Economy* (North Tarrytown, N.Y.: Author, 1984); J. Limburg, *The Prophets and the Powerless* (Atlanta: John Knox, 1977); J. Schneider, *Godly Materialism: Rethinking Money and Possessions* (Downers Grove, Ill.: InterVarsity Press, 1994); R. Sider, *Rich Christians in an Age of Hunger* (3rd ed.; Dallas: Word, 1990); R. Van Leeuwen, "Enjoying Creation—

Within Limits," in *The Midas Trap* (Wheaton, Ill.: Scripture Press/Victor Books, 1990); N. Wolterstorff, *Until Justice and Peace Embrace* (Grand Rapids: Eerdmans, 1983).

J. Schreider

MOVIES

Movies are a form of mass media* that can also be called an art* form. They can inform and enlighten as well as entertain.* The majority of Americans go to movies, and the international audience for movies continues to grow. Moving pictures have undeniably had a great impact on Western culture.* But has that influence been good or bad? Is movie viewing a good or bad thing for Christians? There are many ways to evaluate these questions.

Movies as a Way to Read the Culture
In a culture that is fast becoming postliterate as well as post-Christian, movies are primary definers of American culture—both shaping and reflecting current values.* In fact, movies may express the dominant American belief system more accurately than any organized religion. Going to the movies can become a quasi-religious ritual. Theologian John Wiley Nelson comments: "The set of beliefs and values offered by American culture are not beliefs and values to which we are converted. We grow up believing that they are true."

For Nelson, the cinematic paradigm is the Western, which he calls the "classic ritual form, the 'High Mass' of the predominant American belief system." Although the classic Western is not as much in favor now as it was in the seventies when Nelson came up with this thesis, he broadly defines the Western form to include gangster and detective movies.

Nelson's description of the classic Western formula as one in which no character participates in both good and evil and which inevitably ends with a violent resolution applies to many recent "action" films. It also applies to the mythic, immensely popular *Star Wars* series.

To theologian Robert Jewett, *Star Wars,* a film that some people saw dozens of times, involves a "ritualistic reenactment of a story of salvation comparable to the function of religious rituals studied by anthropologists and theologians." *Star Wars* provides a good case study on different ways a movie can be reviewed. Many (probably most) saw it simply as fast-paced entertainment or, as director George Lucas put it, as a modern fairy tale.* Some Christians, disturbed by the magic and references to "the force" in a context that was not specifically Christian, worried that the movie had a New Age slant and viewed it very negatively. Others (like myself) saw in *Star Wars* a mythology about the cosmic struggle between the powers of good and evil (with good ultimately triumphing), which, although not specifically Christian, contained resonances of truth about the human condition.

Jewett argues that *Star Wars* contains an alternative gospel. He describes "the force" in *Star Wars,* given only to an elite few, as tending toward "fascism" and compares it unfavorably to the power of the gospel, which is described by Paul as available to all who believe. Through the dialogue he sets up between Paul and a variety of current movies, Jewett not only compares the gospel of modern culture to the gospel of Jesus Christ but also exegetes Paul for our age.

Moral Criteria for Viewing Movies
Traditionally the two main areas of moral concern about movies have centered on the issues of sex and violence. These are appropriate areas for concern.

Evidence indicates that violence in

the media does lead to violence in our society. Overexposure to media violence can also desensitize people to the pain and suffering of others, making them less likely to respond to need. In movies sexual acts can be much more explicit than on network TV.* (Explicit sex was one way movie studios fought back against TV.) But even when explicit sexuality is not portrayed, attitudes and values are being conveyed. Studies have shown that most sex portrayed (or alluded to) in movies or on TV is between unmarried partners.

As we know, sex and violence are part of the human condition and are dealt with in the Bible and in other great literature (*see* Sexuality). So we need to evaluate the way these issues are handled. Is the sex gratuitous? (One leading American filmmaker says that the studio made him add an explicit sex scene to his first feature film before they would distribute it.) Is the violence real? Does it convey the pain and horror of taking a life? Or is it fake—are bodies flying around with no sense of loss or of the value of the lives taken?

The areas of sex and violence are of general concern; this is how movies are given ratings. But there are other issues.

Goodness, Truth and Beauty

Biblically we are called to think about things that are "true, just, pure, lovely and good" (Phil 4:8). For some those criteria will cut down drastically on the number of movies viewed. Others may feel that movies are a barometer of current values and concerns, helping them learn how to be "salt" in their culture. They may want to understand the wider culture, even if it involves viewing movies that are expressions of despair and alienation.

One way of evaluating a film is to ask, "Is it true?" Yet almost all movies made today have a lie at their core; they have

created a world where God does not exist. Even inoffensive Disney movies usually portray a universe where there is no sense of transcendence and there are no believers. This does not mean that none of these films have value, but it makes films that at least wrestle with the question of God's existence (whether or not they come to a conclusion) all the more noteworthy. A related lie is that Christians, if they do appear, are portrayed as ridiculous or psychotic. Commercially produced films rarely treat believers seriously—as normal human beings.

This is not to say that films should be evaluated only in terms of their messages. A film may be of value because of the beauty* of its cinematography, musical score or the power of a performance. However, artistic beauty is not always linked with truth or goodness. There is no disputing the genius of Leni Riefensthal's work, but she put her filmmaking abilities at the service of the Third Reich, so that her beautiful images manipulate you toward sympathy with an ugly philosophy.

Explicit and Implicit Values

Some films are intentionally didactic. For example, the film *Gandhi* educated filmgoers about the Indian independence movement and may have caused some viewers to think seriously about nonviolent conflict resolution.* The film *The Last Emperor* examined an interesting and, for many Westerners, obscure period of Chinese history. These films taught us something about history, deliberately.

Other movies may not be *about* history, but they have become part of an archive that unintentionally reveals something about our changing social mores. For example, the changing roles of women in movies from the 1920s to the 1990s tell us a lot about our social history. War movies, and the ways our enemies are portrayed, also tell volumes about the national mood at certain points in history. During World War II movies overtly extolled values such as patriotism and heroism. But movies may also convey values unintentionally. Director Federico Fellini has described how much his attitudes as a boy were influenced by American movies. Growing up under the constrictions of Fascist Italy, Fellini greatly admired the openness and freedom portrayed in American films.

Unfortunately, movies can also represent American values at their worst. Violent action films like the *Rambo* series have been some of our most popular international exports. So many movies portray glamorous, affluent lifestyles that people for whom those lifestyles are not even remotely obtainable can feel that they are missing out on the good things in life. (In contrast, the biblical message is that the really good things in life are not those that we can buy with a credit card.*)

Movies can also make it possible for us to gain insight into worlds very different from our own. A movie like Vittorio De Sica's classic *The Bicycle Thief,* for example, can lead to a more sympathetic understanding of what it is like to be poor,* teaching us gratitude for what we may otherwise take for granted. Some movies, like *The Gods Must Be Crazy,* deal directly with the clash of values between cultures and help us examine some of our basic assumptions.

Can Movies Be Used Redemptively?

According to the social critic Jacques Ellul, "No image is able to convey any truth at all. This explains in part why all 'spiritual' films are failures." Malcolm Muggeridge argued that any image is a "graven image" and should be avoided. (At the same time Muggeridge himself made an excellent series of documentary films about heroes of the faith called

A Third Testament.) It is true that many films made by Christian film companies are well-intentioned examples of badly made, simplistic propaganda. But there are exceptions. The Billy Graham film *The Hiding Place,* which tells the story of a Christian who hid Jews during the Nazi occupation of the Netherlands, is a powerful witness,* as is the film *Romero,* which tells the story of the martyred Salvadoran archbishop. One reason these films are so good is that in telling the stories of real people the Christian message is not overly simplified.

Another biographical film, *Chariots of Fire,* also offers a positive witness, even though the film was not made by Christians. It tells the story of the Olympic runner Eric Liddell and shows Liddell as a complex person of integrity.*

But the concerns of commentators like Muggeridge and Ellul go beyond content. They raise questions about the inherent nature of the media that needs to be considered.

Movies on the Big and Small Screen

Movies can have a powerful impact. The large screen, complete darkness and lack of commercial distractions can create a dreamlike sensation, making the movie's message more seductive. It is interesting that movie palaces came into their prime in Western culture at the same time, in the 1920s and 1930s, that church* attendance began to fall. Movie theaters might be seen as temples to secular popular culture. Television generally, including movies on TV, produces less of a sense of awe, is less of a communal experience and has less visceral impact.

As a medium, videos* inhabit a middle ground. There is more control of what is watched and when it is watched than with either TV or theatergoing. Parents find that allowing children access to an approved video library as an alternative to TV allows them much more control. With video it is possible to approach film-viewing much more purposefully; viewers can browse through a director's entire body of work, as they would the work of a favorite author. Commentators have written about VCRs' contribution to "cocooning." It will be interesting to see what kind of long-range cultural effect videos will have.

The Dream World Versus Reality

Marshal McLuhan has said that the filmmaker transfers the viewer from one world to another created by film. "That is so obvious and happens so completely, that those undergoing the experience accept it subliminally and without critical awareness."

We are now encountering a generation of younger filmmakers who make films that are not inspired by their own life experiences or events in history but by movies they viewed while growing up; this is what shaped them. Steven Spielberg has said that his *Indiana Jones* series was inspired by Saturday matinees he watched as a boy. Director Quentin Tarantino's filmmaking is also largely based on old movies and television shows. It is usual for one generation of artists to pay homage to a previous one. But this is different; it is a substitution of realities.

We may be moving away from an art form based on real experience and deeper into what McLuhan refers to as our collective unconscious dream. Entering into a director's dream world is not necessarily bad (some directors, like Fellini, create delightful worlds), but we do not want to be robbed of our own dreams* and imaginations.*

Resisting Seduction: Thinking Critically

To resist the kind of passivity media consumption can produce, we need to maintain an alert and critical attitude. Reading* books is a good antidote, as they engage our intellect rather than our senses. Critic Nicola Chiaromonte says: "The cinema derives its power from its ability to arouse an emotional reaction that is both immediate and certain. Whereas a poem or a novel cannot come alive without the reader's elaboration." This raises the question of what movie watching does to the development of a healthy imagination.

It might be helpful to reflect on how a film has affected you. How do you feel as you leave the theater? Are you demoralized, angry and depressed? Or has the film given you some insight into life or human nature? Has it left you feeling more attuned to the feelings and needs of the people around you, or less so? What do you know about the worldview* of the writer or director?

Discussing the values and intent of a film with friends can help; discussing them with Christian friends can help define mutual values that counter those of the popular culture. Writing about a film in your journal may help you express clearly what may have only been a sense of vague unease while you were watching it. Reading several reviews from different perspectives can also help.

For those of us who are Christians and love movies, developing a critical perspective is imperative. As Marshall McLuhan has warned, "Without the mirror of the mind, nobody can live a human life in the face of our present mechanized dream."

See also CULTURE; ENTERTAINMENT; IMAGINATION; LEISURE; MASS MEDIA; READING; TELEVISION; THEATER, LIVE.

References and Resources

J. Ellul, *The Humiliation of the Word* (Grand Rapids: Eerdmans, 1985); L. Jacobs, ed., *The Movies as Medium* (New York: Farrar, Straus and Giroux, 1970); R. Jewett, *Saint Paul at the Movies: The Apostle's Dialogue with American Culture* (Louisville: Westminster/John Knox Press, 1993); A. MacDonald, *Movies in Close-Up:*

Getting the Most from Film and Video (Downers Grove, Ill.: InterVarsity Press, 1992); M. McLuhan, *Understanding Media: The Extensions of Man* (New York: Signet, 1964); M. Muggeridge, *Christ and the Media* (Grand Rapids: Eerdmans, 1977); J. W. Nelson, *Your God Is Alive and Well and Appearing in Popular Culture* (Philadelphia: Westminster, 1976).

Sharon Gallagher

MULTICULTURALISM

Most newer Western societies, and increasingly some older ones, are made up of people from many ethnic, national, religious, linguistic and geographical regions of the world. These people came, and still come, carrying with them the culture* in which they were raised. The meeting of these cultures in new social settings results in the process known as multiculturalism.

Our human identity is shaped dialogically, through our relationships with others. If we learn about and from each other, especially those who are different from us, we will be more tolerant and accepting. Multiculturalism is people from varied ethnic and cultural origins living together in harmony.

The Emergence of Multiculturalism

In the past the term *cultural pluralism* expressed the dominant "melting pot" image that symbolized the assimilation of immigrants* into the USA, an assimilation requiring both linguistic and cultural adjustments. Pluralism* is covered in a separate article. *Multiculturalism* was coined in the early 1960s to define the official government policy of the Canadian "mosaic," which encouraged immigrants to retain their cultural and ethnic diversity as a mark of identity. Such immigrants had to choose between French and English, but more recently other cultural heritages have been encouraged through government policy. The definition of multiculturalism has changed

somewhat over the years and is now used wherever there is an egalitarian recognition of ethnic or racial difference. This is often embodied in such terms as *African-American, Asian-American, French-Canadian and Chinese-Canadian*.

As an ideology, multiculturalism represents the institutionalization of distinctiveness, answering the need for personal cultural recognition. It assumes mutual tolerance and coexistence between ethnic groups and presupposes a low degree of prejudice and discrimination. Multiculturalism strives for "difference-blindness" and at the same time assumes relativism—every approach to values* and culture is equally valid. Critics of multicultural policy suggest that it is not in fact antiracist and fails to address racism* by accentuating the peripheral aspects of a culture such as the arts, festivals, food and clothing. Vertical racism, that gives privileges to some and discriminates against others on the basis of arbitrary racial factors, is especially unaddressed by this ideology.

As a process, multiculturalism assumes movement along some continuum from a monocultural understanding (including ethnocentrism*) through biculturalism to a more complex social reality. To achieve this people must learn communication skills and form crosscultural relationships. Supporters of multicultural education* submit that people need to feel comfortable in settings where cultures other than their own are represented (Pusch, p. 21), in classrooms, community meetings, churches* and business settings. This process involves not only an individual but a communal adjustment. Supporters of multiculturalism suggest that changes in educational content will help students discover the value of other ethnic traditions and cultures through exposure at an early age to varieties of ethnic food, dress, festivals, literature, music and art.*

It is still being debated whether multiculturalism truly counteracts racism.

The Liberal Democratic Roots

Multiculturalism has at its roots the basic premise of a liberal democracy, that people are all free, equal and able to determine their own good. Building on this, multiculturalism adds that ethnic and cultural differences should be respected and sustained. Such democracies are then forced to balance two different political policies: the position of political neutrality on such matters as the total separation of state and church, and the institutionalization of different, perhaps opposing cultures. The basic assumption that all people are free and equal, now being challenged as a Western point of view, is not shared by all nations or religions.

Supporters of multiculturalism suggest that voluntary maintenance of ethnic and cultural ties has several advantages for the immigrant (Alladin). It provides a place to belong when the newcomer is first in the country, provides strong economic possibilities based on ethnic connections and opens up an easier access to political voice. Multiculturalism provides a way of reducing disharmony between diverse ethnic groups as well as providing a place for those groups who do not assimilate. It also challenges the rigid and close-minded to become more open.

By its very definition multicultural society encompasses a range of moral disagreements on a variety of issues, including the value of different cultures. Paradoxically, supporting cultural diversity can result in encouraging opposition to the basic tolerance on which that recognition rests. Cultural institutions can develop that may oppose the liberal democracy that allows their existence. Resolution of such disagreements requires the educational effort of state, schools, churches and community* groups.

Opponents of multiculturalism suggest that the process creates ethnic divisions and enclaves that fight against the collective national efforts. Critics ask what it means to be a hyphenated citizen and what happens to loyalties when the nation calls for support. They argue that ethnic groups become exclusivist and promote homogeneity for the purpose of securing political power. Multiculturalism also fails to address the differences within an ethnic group. There can be substantial class differences between immigrants, particularly if government selection of immigrants gives preferential entry to the highly educated or financial elite and, at the other end of the spectrum, refugees. How are we to think of this?

Multiculturalism in Christian Perspective

As early as historic records have been kept, humans have been faced with the relocation of people and the occupation of homelands by stronger tribal or national groups. This is demonstrated by the records of Egyptian and Babylonian expansion, the exploits of Alexander the Great and the growth of the Roman Empire. Some of the struggles associated with this are reflected in the Bible. For example, when the Israelites were exiled to Babylon, the prophet Jeremiah encouraged them to work and live there, adapting to their new situation but still preserving their religious faith as they continued to pray for their deliverance and return to their own land. The Old Testament law, however, instructs the Jews to strictly enforce the Jewish religious regulations even for foreigners living in their land (Ex 12:19, 48; 20:10). And the Jews struggled to maintain their Jewish distinctiveness in a foreign land.

Paul's suggested method for reaching

people with the gospel was remarkably different. He tried to understand the customs and practices of those he hoped to influence, becoming like the people he wanted to reach. "I have become all things to all men so that by all possible means I might save some" (1 Cor 9:22). Paul went to them—the essence of the idea of mission*—but today the multicultural climate has brought the ethnic and cultural mix to us. Differing forms of worship,* ritual practices, rites of passage and even religious attire are no longer the stories of foreign lands and mission fields; they are part of the multicultural community. To apply Paul's principle today, we must learn as much as possible about the culture of our neighbors in order to live alongside them and present the gospel. Debate rages today about how to do this without falling into relativism on the one hand or exclusivism on the other. The values, the worldview* and the religious belief of my neighbor may include ways to salvation outside of Christ.

Where do we go from here? The school and the church need to promote teaching which helps to reduce tensions between ethnic groups, supporting antiracism and combating discrimination. To develop intercultural competence we need to understand our own worldview and how our ethnocentrism can be reshaped. We need an increased global* awareness of how our actions, decisions and lifestyles affect other people. Multiculturalism, instead of rendering mission work obsolete, provides an opportunity for the church to fulfill its missionary task. The stakes are high at the global level. We can strive for harmony, or we can return to isolationism and suspicion and all that comes from them.

See also COMMUNITY; ETHNOCENTRISM; GLOBAL VILLAGE; INFORMATION SUPERHIGHWAY; PLURALISM; RACISM.

References and Resources

M. I. Alladin, ed., *Multiculturalism in the 1990s: Policies, Practices and Implications* (Edmonton: EISA Publishers, 1993); F. Anthias, "Connecting 'Race' and Ethnic Phenomena," *Sociology* 26, no. 3 (August 1992); N. Bissoondath, *Selling Illusions: The Cult of Multiculturalism in Canada* (Toronto: Penguin, 1994); A. Schlesinger, *The Disuniting of America* (New York: Norton, 1992); C. E. Sleeter, ed., *Empowerment Through Multicultural Education* (Albany: State University of New York Press, 1991); C. Taylor, *Multiculturalism: Examining the Politics of Recognition* (Princeton: Princeton University Press, 1994); R. Todd, *Education in a Multicultural Society* (London: Cassell, 1991).

Brian F. Stelck

MUSIC

Music is an irrepressible expression of our being. We have, after all, been created with our very own musical instrument—the voice. To sing is a fundamental musical reflex and something that God obviously wants us to enjoy. For most people it seems to come naturally. Small children sing when they are playing happily; at the other end of life the elderly love to hear songs they remember from their earlier days—the former driven by contentment and hopefulness, the latter by nostalgia and personal memories. From birth* to death,* music is intertwined around many of life's activities. We seem to enter the world with a predilection for music, and when we leave it, we know that it is going to be an ongoing activity in heaven (Is 51:11).

The Universal Gift

Music, whether instrumental or vocal, is an enriching adjunct to rejoicing and celebration. It also has healing and comforting properties: Saul experienced this under David's musical ministrations (1 Sam 16:23), as do many who today find burdened hearts lifted up by music that touches their needs. Research in recent years suggests that music has an important role to play in mental therapy. There are even claims that students preparing for exams perform better having studied against a background of Mozart's music! Whether this can be proven convincingly is another question, but at a less sensational level it is clear that music is a uniquely divine gift with powerful potential, without which the world would be a distinctly sadder place.

Nearly all cultures* have their own musical tradition, be it Inuit throat singing, Balinese gamelan, the European symphony orchestra or Scottish bagpipes. Instrumental music, song and dance have been wedded from the earliest times and remain a vital form of emotional expression around the world, whether soloistic or communal, formal or informal. Music celebrates marriage* and ministers to the grieving*; it helps to rally political protest and strengthens the resolve of the oppressed. Paul and Silas sang in prison (Acts 16:25), as Christ and the disciples did before taking those irrevocable steps into the Garden of Gethsemane (Mt 26:30). Come what may, music has emerged and reemerged resiliently from the debris of a fallen world.

As a part of God's general providence, music helps divert a disturbed world from despair and, much like food, is intended to be universally enjoyed. All cultures enjoy a distinct musical language; many non-European societies enjoy the unifying effect of an integrated heritage of music passed from one generation to the next with minimal alteration to its character. By contrast, Western music has been marked by a restless urge to experiment and change. As the centuries have passed, this has accelerated and reached a point where today a vast variety of styles and a sharp division between formal and popular music have brought about fragmentation rather than unity. Many people welcome today's fragmentation as a rich opportunity for individ-

ual expression and personal choice, but there is no denying that it also speaks to some extent of the loss of cohesion in our society.

Music can be designed specifically to glorify God (*see* Music, Christian). In Western culture some of its greatest music has emerged in the attempt; unfortunately, so has some of its worst. The best (George Frederick Handel's *Messiah* being an obvious example) emerged from the centuries during which the focus of European music was the church,* from plainchant and medieval polyphony to the baroque riches of Johann Sebastian Bach (1685-1750). Society was more integrated up to that point, and faith gave it cohesiveness. With the Enlightenment and the loss of that unity, secular and spiritual music pursued separate and wildly different paths. All significant musical experiment and progress now passed to the secular world; Protestant and evangelical music became trivialized and simplistic, eventually ending up under the umbrella of the entertainment* industry. We are still greatly affected by that split, and to determine what music—sacred or secular—we listen to, espouse and pass on to future generations, we need to exercise discernment.

Discernment
As with all such gifts, we require discernment in our approach to music because it operates within a fallen world. Music is subject to exploitation, misapplication and distortion and can become highly manipulative in certain situations. One healthy approach is to challenge received wisdom about what is "popular," "cool," "neat," "relevant" and "superior." The labeling of music in this way has brought about a musical "apartheid" that sets up artificial barriers. It encourages uncritical loyalty to tastes tightly controlled by commercial interests and fosters prejudice against anything out of the

ordinary or requiring a little more concentration.

One myth worth challenging is the widely held notion that some kinds of music are in and of themselves boring,* snobbish or evil. These epithets are no more true of music than it was of the food discussed in Paul's first letter to the Corinthians (1 Cor 8:4-13). Food is part of God's general providence and like the rain comes to the just and the unjust (Mt 5:45). Similarly, the ingredients that go into making music are created by God: acoustics, resonance, timbre, pitch and rhythm. What matters is how skillfully these ingredients are handled by the musicians and, most importantly, to what ultimate purpose the product is dedicated.

Some music has clearly become associated with messages of great darkness. Heavy metal, rap and some other forms of rock frequently promote values and behavior that Christians can only condemn. Extremely high noise levels, the persistent repetition of motifs, a relentlessly heavy beat and aggressive body language can convey a menacing tone. In some instances classical music has been used to similar ends: in Carl Orff's choral work *Carmina Burana* (1935-36) and Richard Strauss's opera *Salome* (1905), music has been used to heighten topics of sensuality and cruelty. In most cases, however, discernment should be focused on the lyrics, the culture and personalities behind the product rather than the music itself, though in rock culture this separation can be difficult. Generally speaking, music is a neutral force, which can be devoted to glorifying the Lord God or can simply convey everyday human thoughts and emotions,* good or bad.

Our discernment might be clouded by popular myths about certain types of music, myths that are simply imaginary or redundant. Jazz comes to mind—one of the most creative and skillful musical forms of our day. Like rock, its roots can be traced back to earthy and often sexual expression. But jazz today is not primarily perceived in those terms; of far more interest to its enthusiasts are its opportunities for improvisatory skill and instrumental virtuosity. In a different way classical music is perceived in many minds to be boring, snobbish, elitist and in the hands of performers who are all well over fifty. Even if these epithets were vaguely true in the past, they are certainly not today. The concert hall has long ceased to be the exclusive domain of the well-heeled, and on stage brilliant young musicians are in the vanguard. And young people are increasingly listening to them, having apparently developed a broader range of taste than their predecessors.

Today discernment is necessary in music not only to warn us of what some of its more controversial output is saying—especially for the sake of the young—but also to cultivate informed taste and discover riches other than those prepackaged for us. To suggest this is not a criticism of the pop industry; it is simply wise consumer practice in a society largely shaped by mass marketing. We need to be watchful without being naive. We must apply discernment, recognizing, however, that our conclusions may not coincide with those of other people.

Music and Others

The music we support and listen to is often heard by others—in the dorm, at home,* in the car, at work,* or leaking from Walkman headphones on the bus. It is, however unconsciously, a form of communication as well as a statement about us. It may drive people away or attract them. Some relationships have parted over music, while many friendships* have started out with a common delight in music. Not everyone may like what we like, but we do have an influence on life around us, even in such a private matter. The dismaying intrusion of "elevator music" into our society should remind us that we have no right to subject everyone to our musical preferences. By cranking up the radio at the beach or by playing an unrelenting diet of background music in the workplace,* we violate the right of others to their personal choice and their right to silence.

Music as Adventure

We can gain new perceptions and understanding if we refuse to settle for the ordinary and explore new territory. We do not always have to have a Christian text set by a Christian composer to enjoy the exciting gift of music. We can catch glimpses of God's glory through music that is spiritually neutral: a Brahms symphony, a jazz improvisation, a performance by a brass quintet or the sound of a children's choir. This realization will open up a wealth of styles and instrumental and vocal combinations including revisited and newly explored areas such as Renaissance, Celtic, international and electroacoustic music.

If you are really an intrepid explorer, dissonant and atonal music can prove fascinating. It has been dismissed by many—in and out of the church—as an unwelcome reflection of the confusion and disorder of the twentieth century (although such music is typically very tightly organized). Nevertheless, dissonance and atonality (music with no identifiable key) has been at the center of important twentieth-century compositional experiments. Many are certainly not easy listening,* but they convey hard truths about life that cannot be reflected convincingly in comfortable harmonies and conventional forms, either in the popular or the classical vein.

The enormity of the issues of human suffering and death has driven modern composers like Olivier Messiaen (1908-1992) and Poland's Krzysztof Penderecki (b. 1933)—both Christians, as it happens—to exploit the extremes of tonality and instrumentation. The music of Igor Stravinsky (1882-1971) reflects some of the earlier radical stylistic changes of his century, from the densely scored *Rite of Spring* (1911-1913) to the neoclassical *Pulcinella* (1919-1920) and the *Mass* (1944-1948). Music by current composers such as Arvo Part (listen to his wonderful Te Deum) and John Tavener represents the postmodernist school; some of their latest work is delightfully transparent, reflective and accessible. Listeners may come away stimulated or disturbed, but then honest statements tend to have these effects.

Exploration is the key to a fuller enjoyment of music. It is the opposite of a passive acceptance of that which we can so effortlessly access through our radios, television* sets and video players, especially that driven by the commercial media. Exploration will open up fields not of the obvious and predictable but of the intriguing and the delightful.

Listening to Music

State-of-the-art digital technology* has made personal music listening an exciting experience. Headphone listening in dorms and apartments can be very pleasing for you and a great relief for your neighbors! Concertgoers are often disappointed that live auditorium sound is not as dramatic and as detailed as compact disk (CD) reproduction. A live performance will inevitably seem more distant, but the ear quickly adjusts, and in any case the communal experience, the ambience and the visual aspect of a real concert more than compensate. Before or after the concert is also a good forum for socializing, which the solitude of the headset cannot offer.

Participating in Music

Joining with others in making music is perhaps the most rewarding of musical experiences for those who, at either an amateur or a semiprofessional level, can play an instrument or sing in a choir. The beneficial effects are amazing: participants frequently speak of coming to a rehearsal weary after a day's work only to find that they are refreshed and uplifted. For Christians of all levels of musical attainment, there is the unique opportunity to sing in communal worship,* where the critical ingredient is the attitude of the heart. There is an interesting metaphor for the church in group music making: working together under leadership to achieve a common goal of harmony and unity.

God can speak to us individually and collectively through music; the music may be by a Christian, and spiritual words may be involved—or not. Because music is a gift that falls on the just and the unjust, we owe it to ourselves to enjoy it to the full while having our discerning wits about us.

See also MUSIC, CHRISTIAN; PLEASURE; WORSHIP.

References and Resources

J. Buckley, ed., *Classical Music on CD—The Rough Guide: An A to Z of Composers and Recordings* (London: Rough Guides, 1994); A. Copland, *What to Listen for in Music* (New York: Mentor, 1953); M. Wold and E. Cykler, *An Introduction to Music and Art in the Western World* (Dubuque, Iowa: William C. Brown, 1991).

Ed Norman

MUSIC, CHRISTIAN

God delights in music*; Scripture repeatedly endorses it. The Old Testament abounds with indirect as well as detailed references to its use. The song of Miriam recorded in Exodus 15:21 and the account of the ceremonial inauguration of Solomon's newly built temple in 2 Chron-

icles 5:12-13 are just two glimpses of different uses of music as a response to, and worship of, God. As well as encouragement to break into song as a private response to God, we are given a rich deposit of psalms, which have nourished and served God's people through the ages.

By contrast, the New Testament has very little to say about the subject. Other than a few indirect references—such as the trumpet sounding at the resurrection of the dead (1 Cor 15:52)—Paul's injunction to "speak to one another with psalms, hymns and spiritual songs" (Eph 5:19) is as specific as it gets, and this passage is open to a variety of interpretations. Nevertheless, it is clear that music is a universal gift from God without which our world, as well as our worship,* would be greatly impoverished.

One could argue that there is no such thing as Christian music any more than there is Christian air or Christian food. The musical practices we read of in the Old Testament employed idioms and instruments held in common with the pagan civilizations around them. Yet when we dedicate universal gifts like this solely to God's glory, the transforming power of the Holy Spirit turns them into something unique, ministering to individuals and congregations at a profoundly spiritual level. We do have a vital role in this process, and the extent of the transformation, if history is a reliable judge, depends very much on how much thought, effort and integrity we ourselves bring to the music we are offering.

World Music and Western Music

Today's non-European cultures nearly all seem to enjoy a common language of music, which is woven into the fabric of life, just as it was an integrated part of Jewish society. In non-Western and African-American cultures, singers, dancers and drummers carry from one generation to another a commonly understood musical language that seems able to adapt to every mood, from celebration to mourning. Christians in these cultures are increasingly grafting indigenous music into their worship. In a different vein, churches* of the Eastern Orthodox tradition, notably the Greek and Russian branches, make a sharp distinction between secular and sacred, preserving a distinctive and rich musical tradition for worship. In these systems music takes its designated place naturally—it knows when to pipe up and when to keep silent.

For better or worse, this kind of stability is not a characteristic of Western music. Through the centuries its progress has been increasingly restless and subject to rapid development and, more recently, fragmentation. It has also become commercially marketed and has grown to a point where today we face an overwhelming smorgasbord of classical and popular styles, not unlike a multichannel cable system. One consequence of this postmodern diversity is that Christians are unable to agree upon a unified musical language—a situation that could be seen as healthy diversity but that more typically encourages uncritical standards and reinforces division.

We can understand better how we reached this point by looking at how Christian music developed; there may even be clues in it for molding a distinct, unified music for the future. The story of music from the early church up to the present day acts as a kind of mirror. Much like an archaeological site, it reveals how music was used and shaped at different periods. It reveals successes and failures. Like all history, it keeps us humble by reminding us that the latest is not always the best. Indeed, there have been times of remarkable wisdom and holiness in the church* that we will always do well to reflect upon.

Looking at the Time Line

Any serious textbook dealing with the history of European music reads at first (often for several chapters) like a history of church music. All that we take for granted in music—our tonal system, rhythmic conventions, the means by which we write down music—was cradled and nourished within the church. Despite the growth of humanism and the expansion of secular music in the Renaissance, the church remained a vital focus of musical activity until the middle of the eighteenth century. We can trace this in the style of music that prevailed until roughly 1750: plainchant, motets, anthems, liturgical settings, organ music, cantatas, oratorios and so on, alongside a smaller, but growing, body of secular song and instrumental music.

As we examine this archaeological dig of musical history, we can sense a historic tension between artists and church authority.* There is a recurring concern about the sensual lure of music—its ability to dominate worship and obscure, rather than illuminate, the Word. Augustine, sundry popes and bishops, Martin Luther, John Calvin, the Puritans, modern evangelicals, charismatic leaders and Vatican II have all expressed this concern in one way or another.

In its concern for purity of worship, Calvinism legislated musical austerity in church worship. Only the psalms were permitted, sung in unison without accompaniment. The Puritans applied the same tradition in England and brought it to the New World. Instruments were out of the question, and even the pipe organ was a problem. On the Continent the Calvinists discouraged or forbade it; in England organs were sometimes physically destroyed. Yet despite the severity of this approach, there can be great beauty in simple, plain music, and this ascetic musical tradition is still greatly valued in certain branches of the

Presbyterian Church.

In contrast to the Calvinist tradition, Martin Luther's affirmative view of music fostered one of the richest musical movements in Protestant culture. Here we discover music designed to glorify God and incorporate all people, not just a select few. It is centered on the Lutheran chorale, which draws from a wide range of sacred and secular melodies and is the basis of our modern congregational hymnody. The movement arising from Luther became the framework for exciting new music by Protestant composers who dedicated their work to the church: Jan Sweelinck, Heinrich Schutz, Johann Pachelbel and Dietrich Buxtehude, to name just a few. At the height of this era one figure stands out supremely—Johann Sebastian Bach (1685-1750).

A combination of superlative skill, extraordinary energy and evident Christian commitment gives Bach's music an unusual degree of integrity and attractiveness. His nearly two hundred cantatas for the church, his moving settings of Christ's passion (from St. Matthew and St. John), the great B Minor Mass and his organ chorale preludes reveal not only a vibrant personal faith but also a thorough understanding of theology as well as consummate skill. In the society in which Bach lived, rigorous, disciplined training was a prerequisite to musical leadership,* particularly in the church; good ideas were not enough.

Music really does reveal a lot, but the poetry set to it perhaps reveals even more: early Latin hymn texts stressing God's holiness and majesty; sixteenth-century texts focusing on our unworthiness, the hymns of Charles Wesley and Isaac Watts full of assurance and the prospect of eternal life. An unquestioned trinitarian belief and a clear view of the human condition shine through the words and music of these periods leading up to the turbulent nineteenth century. It is fascinating to see what happened next.

Bach died in 1750, and Handel—also a profoundly Christian musician—died shortly thereafter. Observing what followed, we can see how the character of Christian music was unlikely to be the same again. The influence that the church had for so long exerted upon the course of music and art* dropped away. The character of music changed abruptly as the focus moved from the church to the concert hall and the opera house. Music could not consider itself primarily Christian any longer, because all of its exciting new developments were taking place outside the church's sphere of influence.

We can trace how the church retreated from an increasingly hostile secular world to create its own in-house art and music: typically a sentimental, otherworldly type of expression, which has held sway in the churches up to the present day. Looking at a chorus collection of the later nineteenth century, such as Ira D. Sankey's *Sacred Songs and Solos,* we see the impact of mass production on Christian music. It became a widely disseminated, prepackaged, functional and pietistic product. Of course, there are even within these stylistic confines some attractive and effective compositions that have rightly survived the test of time, but the overall quality of music during this period reflects a general decline in the fortunes of spiritual music.

Today and the Future

What will future generations make of our present-day music? There will be those compositions whose distinctive content and careful crafting will have secured them a permanent place in the Christian repertoire. But on a broader scale, future generations will probably observe that whereas the church once shaped secular culture,* our contemporary worship music has been largely shaped by the commercial world. They might well lament the absence of a more authentic and durable kind of music that might have been passed from generation to generation with some pride. They will wonder— as we should—why original, creative, thoughtful options tended to be ignored in favor of commercially and technologically driven products. But there are more profound issues that go to the heart of the matter.

In its more distinguished periods Christian music has been marked by a confluence of excellence and humility. Excellence is human endeavor at its best, regardless of the simplicity or complexity of the task. Humility involves a servant-like attitude, a realization that there is always room for improvement and that history has much to teach us. The two should be held together by an acknowledgment that none of it will bear fruit without God's grace and blessing.* This is not to imply that humility is wholly absent today or that there is no genuinely creative work by individual Christian musicians working in the popular genre. The challenge, however, for all Christians working in the musical domain is how to keep ego out of the equation, for it will do its best to emerge somehow.

In so-called formal music the dangers lie in using specialized training and aesthetic judgment to adopt a position of superiority within the fellowship.* Nothing alienates people more effectively, and the discouragement of fine music in our churches has undoubtedly come about largely because of this tendency. Different dangers, ones much closer to the surface, lurk in the commercially influenced popular idioms. Here the music from the outset has been designed to draw upon easily tapped and easily manipulated emotions*; the power placed in the hands of leaders and composers working in this genre thus requires extremely thoughtful control if a manipulative and sometimes sensual dynamic is not to be confused with the workings of the Holy Spirit.

When music is transformed by God's grace, it becomes distinctive and ministers to individuals and congregations at a profoundly spiritual level going far beyond mere entertainment.* It can reinforce truth and fellowship and even offer brief glimpses of an eternal glory that we will one day share in the presence of the Lord God himself. Our part is to ensure that we bring—like the sacrificial offerings of old—only the very best for God to bless.

See also CULTURE; MUSIC; WORSHIP.

References and Resources

H. M. Best, *Music Through the Eyes of Faith* (San Francisco: Harper, 1993); D. P. Hustad, *Jubilate II—Church Music in Worship and Renewal* (Carol Stream, Ill.: Hope Publishing, 1993); A. Wilson-Dickson, *The Story of Christian Music* (Batavia, Ill.: Lion, 1992).

Edward Norman

N

NATIONALISM

What is nationalism? Where does it come from? How does it differ from patriotism? What are its benefits and drawbacks?

The Nature of Nationalism

Nationalism is the belief that the major source of human identity, perhaps even the ultimate source of human identity, is membership in a cultural grouping called a *nation*. Often the defining cultural parameter is language, but this is by no means always the case. Territory, political* arrangements, purported common ancestry, common history in war and other cultural characteristics can be important. Sometimes the parameter is religion, which always plays some role as a shaper of other facets of human culture.*

By themselves cultural characteristics are never enough to mark out a nation. Some people with common characteristics see themselves as a nation; others do not. Consequently many suggest that a nation is simply a group of people that *thinks* it is a nation. In this sense nationalism is simply a view we take of ourselves and who we are. This is one reason most nationalists point to shared important events in their history—usually of battle, either lamenting an unjust defeat that the nation lives to rectify or celebrating a victory that marks the worth of the nation. War itself is often a great boost to nationalism. When people share powerful experiences, they develop a shared identity.

A common, though not universal, feature of nationalism is that proponents want to see their peoplehood embodied in a political structure.* This reflects the belief that the best political structure is somehow the expression of a particular nation. At other times political leaders try to shape the people in their territory *into* a nation by trying to overcome differences between members of the population based on tribe or religion or language. Both of these are efforts to produce a *nation-state*. All too often the terms *country*, *state* and *nation* are used interchangeably.

Nationalism (the love of a people) is, however, not the same as patriotism (the love of a country). Attachment to a particular country may stem from its beauty, belief in its peaceful history, admiration for its political institutions or any of a thousand reasons that have little to do with nationalism. Nationalism, including political nationalism, is an attachment to a people themselves.

The Origins of Nationalism

There is an ongoing dispute as to whether nationalism is an ancient or modern phenomenon. Clearly there have always been peoples, and peoples have always had an attachment to particular lands and to those who live there. People have always distinguished themselves from others and have marked off distinct territories: biblical (and modern) Israel is an example of this. But Israel's identity did not spring from being a people but from following the Lord, the one true God. Peoplehood was a manifestation of something else, which was much more important and which could even challenge peoplehood itself.

In the ancient world this produced transnational empires, such as Babylon or Rome, that were the embodiment of a religious idea or of the will of a king. In the medieval period the idea of Christendom was in principle more important than any local cultural grouping or political order. Marriage* and education* were demarcated not by a local political authority but by a transnational church,* which even used its own distinct languages. Language did not represent a people but the more universal ideals of Latin or Greek Christianity. Islam has followed the same pattern with its emphasis on the Umma, the peoplehood of Islam, and with Arabic as the language of divine revelation.

In the modern age the identity provided by the traditional religions has been severely weakened, and political ideologies such as communism and fascism have filled the gap. The most potent of these new ideologies is nationalism, which has certainly appeared in a much more developed form since the nineteenth century, especially in Europe after the 1789 French Revolution's glorification of the "people." From there it has spread to Eastern Europe and Latin America, and as a result of twentieth-century decolonization, to the rest of the world. In the era of the United Nations, with its doctrine of "the right of self-determination of peoples," nationalism has since become the major political organizing force in the world.

The Dangers of Nationalism

Any state will and should be a reflection of the particular people or peoples who live in its territory. Nevertheless, the notion that political boundaries should coincide with nations should be resisted strenuously. There is no state anywhere in the world that contains only one people of one nation. Consequently any nation-state necessarily has within its borders people who would then be regarded as not of the nation and so as second-class citizens.

Since modern states exert so much power* over economic, social and cultural life, the idea that political life is the expression of a people will have negative consequences both inside and outside the state. Inside it means that attachment to the cultural or political unit overwhelms other attachments. This can happen in dramatic ways, such as in persecution of or discrimination against strangers or noncitizens (*see* Immigration). It can also be more subtle, involving the common assumption that the key parameter of social welfare, trade, language or church organization should be national or state boundaries. In marked contrast to the example of earlier Christians, most denominations* have their own borders drawn along the boundaries of the state. Most of us simply take it for granted that our worship* should be in the language of our people, such as English, rather than seeing language as the expression of a religious peoplehood, such as Latin in Catholicism or Arabic in Islam. The common habit of placing national flags in churches betrays the same mindset.

Outside, it creates conflicts with other states, since there will always be members of one nation inside the boundaries of another nation-state. Consequently there is a huge incentive to expand the state to incorporate members of one's own nation in the state next door or to exert pressure on neighboring states to protect them or to eject one's own "foreigners" and create refugees (a process now becoming known as *ethnic cleansing*). At the same time, if national self-interest is accepted normatively as the highest good, then there are fewer reasons of principle to restrain the nation-state's actions in pursuit of its goals. In this sense nationalism is the chief cause of war in the modern world.

Nationalism and Religion

The settlements concerning religion after the Reformation illustrate some of the dangers of nationalism and religion. The European religious wars of the sixteenth and seventeenth centuries contained a complex of competing goals and powers. Apart from struggles between Catholics and Protestants and among Protestants themselves (such as Lutherans, Calvinists and Anabaptists), there were struggles between and within the rising political powers. European rulers wished to control, and defend themselves from, each other and also to consolidate their control in their own territories. This involved not only subjugating other political forces but gaining control over the other influential and powerful institution in society—the church. The result was a struggle between church and church, between state and church, and between state and state.

The dominant formula for peace coming out of this poisonous stew was one that divided the church along national and political boundaries. The treaties of Augsburg and Westphalia adopted the formula *cuius regio, eius religio* (whoever is the ruler, that will be the religion), though they did not use the saying per se. Those of a different religion were given the option of conforming or moving to live in a different territory, one where their own religious persuasion held sway. (While this clearly creates problems, we should at least note that it is a step up from simply killing or imprisoning religious dissenters.)

While this was a formula relating church forms to political power rather than nations per se, it reinforced the tendency to see political, religious and cultural boundaries as the same thing. Consequently religion and religious freedom became hostage to the growing nation-states.

The same patterns continue in the modern age: religion is often treated as if it were a national or state possession. This is often a problem within Christianity, especially Orthodoxy. The Orthodox churches gave cohesion and identity to many eastern nations when they suffered under centuries of Islamic occupation. The church was almost the heart of the nation. But this brave stance means that Orthodoxy too often identifies itself with the nation, and the nation with it. Other religious bodies are castigated as foreign interlopers.

For example, Serbs view conversions to Catholicism as "surreptitious movements toward Croatization." Even Lutherans are regarded as "Croats." In Armenia those outside the Armenian Apostolic Church are increasingly being described as "foreign." In Bulgaria the head of the Baptist Union says those in the Orthodox Church "believe evangelicals . . . are destroying their culture." The Cretan Orthodox Bishops have claimed that "there is no bigger gift . . . to . . . our nation than safeguarding this national treasure [the Orthodox faith] at any cost against all efforts of adulteration. This has a direct relation to our culture and identity" (*Network News International*, Sept. 1994).

Regional or national religions, such as Hinduism and Shintoism, argue that religions are tied to particular regions and peoples. Some Indians and Nepalese argue that their country is *Hindu* (which means "the religion of the Indus Valley"); hence other religions are foreign and imperialist. State assistance is denied to those who convert to non-Hindu religions.

The identification of religion with nation and nation with religion is something Christians should avoid at all costs. It is a direct violation of the growth of a body in which there is "neither Jew nor Greek" (Gal 3:28).

Sensitivity to Nationalism

While we need to be suspicious of nationalism, we need to recognize that its root is often not a desire to dominate but rather a desire to resist a history of discrimination, persecution or defeat. Nationalism thrives when its supporters feel that their freedom as a people is under threat. All nationalisms contain within themselves the spark that, for example, ignites Jews remembering the Holocaust to vow, "Never again." As Michael Ignatieff has said in conversation, "For a people who have known genocide, there is only one thing that will do: a nation-state of their own." This fear continues as a fear of what one's neighbors* will do if the state collapses. For those who live in the tortured areas of the world such as central Africa, the Balkans or the Caucasus, this fear is amply justified and illustrated. In this sense antinationalism is too often simply the view held by those who can take a stable political order for granted. We need to be careful of uniformly condemning the actions of those who live in chaotic areas. They know that unless they have something of strategic significance like oil, neither the United Nations nor any other world power will defend them. So they are prepared to do it themselves.

Ambiguities of Nationalism

Distinct peoples are very real entities and need to be properly acknowledged. Their national identities must never be taken as ultimate and will be given a varying weight depending on whether they are in the United States, South Africa, Israel or Belgium. The Bible itself shows this tension. On one hand, it places great stress on the common origin and peoplehood of humankind (Gen 1; 1 Pet 2:9-10). It was God's will to fill the earth through the scattering of the descendants of Noah (Gen 9:9; 10), a divine intention that preceded the fall (Gen 1:28). The sin of Babel (Gen 11) was not the scattering of the peoples but the seeking of a homogeneous unity in revolt against God. So, on the other hand, the origin of distinct peoples is depicted at Babel as a means to divide humankind to limit the effect of its sinful pride (Gen 11:1-9). In this sense nations are seen as a manifestation not of creation but of human sin. They are also described subsequently, however, as bearers of human historical responsibility. Cultures and nations also have a place in the end times (Is 60; Rev 21—22). As so often happens, God takes the results of sin and turns them to blessing.

Consequently, although nationalism as an ideology should be rejected, we need to be aware that it can also be a type of survival mechanism. This means that we should have some sympathy with its gentler forms, especially when people are under threat or are attempting to shake off the control of a colonial power.

We must avoid and fight idolatrous forms of nationalism and even many of its gentler, but equally seductive, elements in more peaceful lands. We need to forsake the paraphernalia of nationalism within our church structures, and when we consider matters of war, trade, language and immigration,* to do so in dialogue not only with our nation-state but also in conversation with fellow believers around the world. Christians should not easily fight against one another at the behest of national leaders.

See also CIVIL DISOBEDIENCE; ETHNO-

CENTRISM; MULTICULTURALISM; PLURAL-
ISM; RACISM.

References and Resources
Boston Review 19 (October-November 1994)
2-34 (special issue on "Patriotism or Cos-
mopolitanism?"); E. Hobsbawm, *Nations and
Nationalism Since 1780: Programme, Myth, Reality* (Cambridge: Cambridge University Press,
1990); M. Ignatieff, *Blood and Belonging: Journeys into the New Nationalism* (New York: Farrar,
Straus & Giroux, 1993); O. R. Johnston, *Nationhood: Toward a Christian Perspective* (Oxford:
Oxford University Press, 1980); H. Kohn, *The
Idea of Nationalism: A Study of Its Origin and
Background* (New York: Macmillan, 1967);
News Network International, January 1994, Sep-
tember 1994 and September 1995.

Paul M. Marshall

NEED

The human being is widely seen today as
a bundle of needs. It is good to have
needs, and meeting needs is considered
the ultimate good—a very different view
from that espoused by Buddhism and
Christianity. Needs may result from progress or from manipulation by advertisers,
but this does not explain the popularity
in everyday language of needs talk,
which is better seen as a modern secular
ethic.

The Modern Language of Need
It is often asserted that ours is a society
that values hedonism, pleasure* and personal autonomy. What is rarely noticed,
however, is how often people justify actions not in terms of pleasure or choice
or wants but in terms of need. Advertisements* are as likely to say, "You need
Vim!" as "Choose Vim!" or "Vim is fun!"
In everyday language people say the car
needs washing, the housework needs doing or a holiday is needed in order to
make their choices and preferences
carry more weight. In pressure-group
politics, you advance your cause more by
saying you *need* X than by saying you

merely *want* X.

At the level of pop psychology, needs
talk is very common. People are said to
need work,* love* and affirmation*;
child rearing is seen not as teaching children values* but as meeting their needs
for love, security, praise, play* and new
experiences. Marriage* is seen as a mutual meeting of needs, and when either
or both partners cannot meet the other's
psychological needs, divorce* is deemed
justifiable. Abraham Maslow's theory of
a hierarchy of needs (life, safety/secu-
rity, belonging/affection, respect/self-
respect, self-actualization) has been
particularly influential. In his view, only
as lower-order needs are met can higher-
order needs be attended to.

In previous centuries the word *need*
was used primarily as a verb in circumstances such as "I need the hammer. Can
you pass it to me please?" In the twentieth century its use as an abstract noun
proliferated: the *need* for affection, the
need to be needed, the *need* for affirmation, health-care *needs,* special educational *needs,* basic human *needs* and so on.
Such language removes each need from
its specific purpose and portrays it as
existing in itself within the human race
or within a particular population or individual. The human being is seen as a
bundle of needs, and life the project of
meeting needs.

Much needs talk is only rhetoric: we
do not need everything that advertisers,
therapists, governments,* parents and
spouses tell us we need. It is curious that
a fun-loving, choice-loving population
persists in using a language that portrays
itself as dominated by necessity. At the
same time, many needs *are* real, and
needs are expanding. With the decline
of mass transportation, people need cars
to get to work and to the shops. With
dwellings now built without basements
or verandas, people need air conditioning in order to keep cool. Psychological

needs for identity and affirmation may well be on the increase. As society becomes more affluent and welfare services more widespread, needs increase.

Other Approaches

Other cultures and philosophies have seen need in very different ways. In Buddhism needs or wants are minimized as they cause suffering. Favorinus, one of the ancient Greek school of Cynics, likewise noted that "great needs . . . spring from great wealth; and often the best way of getting what we want is to get rid of what we have." This idea that wealth* does not meet but creates need was taken up by the eighteenth-century philosopher Jean-Jacques Rousseau and more recently by various advocates of simple living.

The Old Testament acknowledges that as a result of the Fall, scarcity and toil have entered the human condition. Meeting needs has indeed become the human project, but it is a curse, not something to be gloried in. The Judaic hope is of a society whose members are motivated not by their own need but in response to an ever-loving God. This hope is embodied in the jubilee legislation that aimed to ensure that each family* would always have access to the goodness of the land (Lev 25). And it is elaborated in the New Testament's discussion of God's unmerited grace.

Jesus did not have many of today's basic human needs met in his own life. By present standards he was materially poor, his sexual needs were not met in marriage, and he gave up his job in order to become an itinerant, unpaid preacher and healer. Far from basing life on the needs of the self, he taught we should take up our cross and deny our self. Yet people criticized Jesus not for being an ascetic but for enjoying life. Christians therefore see the perfect human being, Jesus, as one who was unconcerned with

his own needs and lived instead in response to God's grace. Paul wrote of conflict between the spirit and the flesh, indicating that we should master some things that claim to be needs, not give in to them (Gal 5:16-26).

Explaining Need

There are two common explanations of the modern proliferation of needs. Both are deficient, and I will propose a third explanation.

First, needs are seen as progress. In this view, as the economy and civilization advance, new needs become apparent and may be attended to. In Maslow's view personal as well as economic growth reveals new needs; indeed, this is vital to the very process of growth. It is difficult, however, to believe that all needs represent progress, such as the need for nuclear weapons to defend ourselves. Nor is it certain that all needs need to be met: a man's sexual needs do not excuse his raping a woman. In fact, any need that is not self-evidently good demonstrates that what makes a need good is not that it is necessary but that it is underlain by good values and purposes. Needs do indeed proliferate, but that does not mean they should all be met or represent progress.

Second, needs are seen as ideology. Some critics have proposed that needs are manufactured by big business, psychiatrists, doctors and social workers in order to keep themselves in business. Other critics have argued that rather than subject ourselves to expert definitions of material, medical, social or other *need*, we should instead assert our self-defined *wants*, possibly in relation to communally agreed-upon *rights*. From the 1960s, this critique was articulated by socialists such as Herbert Marcuse and Ivan Illich, but from the late 1970s it become central to the New Right's critique of the welfare state and of centralized government planning.

This critical explanation entails many dubious assumptions, for example, that advertisers are able to manipulate us at will and also that we could ever independently of experts define our own wants. It fails also to explain the currency of the language of need in everyday life, removed from the worlds of advertising or welfare.

Third, I propose viewing need as a secular ethic. I argue that the key to understanding *need* in all its forms is the word's implied imperative that purports to be about facts. The needs of human beings, of women, of children, of workers—whether for love, education,* employment, security or whatever—are portrayed as facts. But unlike most facts, needs imply action: if you have a need, it must be met. This combination of factuality and necessity provides a powerful motive. It is especially powerful in the modern secular world, in which motives based on revelation, duty or tradition are out of fashion. In a society that pays lip service to science and to facts, need provides a motive that smuggles ethics and morality back in without anyone's noticing. People must justify their actions to self and others, and need provides a strong justification. Need is the most common form today of an ethic based not on revelation but on nature.

Many needs, especially those derived from humanistic psychology, are believed to reside within the individual self. They therefore provide an apparently objective way of talking about an otherwise very subjective self. The language of need resolves the modern tension between the objective language of science and the subjective language of feeling and desire.

Logically, however, needs have imperative force because of implied values.* "This starving man needs food" means that he needs food and that we should give him food, not only because of his objective state of starvation but also because the speaker values human life. Because the underlying values are unstated, a popular pseudoscientific ethical language has been developed without its user realizing it.

See also JUSTICE; POVERTY; SIMPLER LIFE-STYLE; SOCIAL ACTION.

References and Resources
A. Maslow, *Motivation and Personality* (New York: Harper & Row, 1968); P. Springborg, *The Problem of Human Needs and the Critique of Civilization* (London: Allen & Unwin, 1981); T. Walter, *Need: The New Religion* (Downers Grove, Ill.: InterVarsity Press, 1985).

Tony Walter

NEGOTIATING

Negotiating is part of our daily lives as Christians. Parents are constantly negotiating with their children about when to go to bed, when they can watch television, what time they, as teenagers, need to be home and so on. We negotiate the purchase of a new home or a new automobile. When we travel, we sometimes encounter cultures in which virtually everything one buys has to be negotiated.

The Universality of Negotiating
In the world of business, negotiation is a frequent occurrence. For example, the construction industry is a fertile bed of negotiations. The developer of a proposed condominium project may negotiate with an architect to do a design not to exceed a certain budgeted figure. The developer then takes bids from general contractors and negotiates with the lowest bidders to secure the best possible deal. The successful general contractor thereupon negotiates with a multitude of material suppliers who have bid on the project. Again, the general contractor

seeks to get the lowest price possible from a reliable subcontractor or material supplier. From top to bottom, there are negotiations, and more often than not they involve deception and untruths.

Negotiations also appear in the Bible. Perhaps the best-known account occurs when Abraham negotiates with God, who has determined to sweep away the evil of Sodom and Gomorrah (Gen 18:16-33). Abraham pleaded that a just God would not destroy the entire city if there were fifty righteous people therein. God agreed. Then Abraham asked if the city could be spared if the righteous numbered forty-five. Again, God agreed. Abraham negotiated for forty, then thirty, then twenty and finally ten. God agreed not to destroy the city if within it were ten righteous people. Abraham had to be pleased with his negotiations. God, who held all the cards, must also have been content with the outcome, or else God would not have given in.

Jesus refused to negotiate with the devil during his forty-day fast in the wilderness (Mt 4:1-11; Mk 1:12-13; Lk 4:1-13), but he did give in to his mother's plea at the wedding at Cana (Jn 2:1-11). The Canaanite woman successfully negotiated with Jesus to heal her daughter, who was tormented by demons. He denied her request at first, but her reply that "even the dogs eat the crumbs that fall from their masters' table" caused him to relent (Mt 15:27). Jesus must have been content with the outcome, or else he would not have yielded.

In the case of God with Abraham and Jesus with the Canaanite woman, the power was all on the side of the ones being persuaded. We call that "holding all the cards." Neither Abraham nor the Canaanite woman had any power to compel God or Jesus to change his mind. There are times in life when we hold all the cards and can be persuaded to change a position by the appeal of another. We give in to the persistence of a child or to the plea of a beggar. As long as we are in control, negotiating is easy.

When Negotiating Is Hard

But in most of everyday life we do not hold all the cards. Then negotiating can become stressful. I want to buy a certain model car, and the salesperson wants to sell it. I want to get the lowest possible price out of the deal; the salesperson wants to get the highest possible price. I hold the money; the salesperson holds the car. Arriving at an agreeable price can be a stressful experience.

Negotiating in the workplace can also be very stressful because of the high stakes involved. Most notable is the area of labor-management negotiations. When a labor contract is due for renewal, labor representatives initially come to the table with greater demands than they can possibly attain. In turn, the management representative offers less than they know they are ultimately willing to grant. Negotiations begin. Each side usually makes token concessions as a show of good faith. They remain firm, however, on their major positions. The union's ultimate weapon is a strike, but both sides can be hurt by a long strike. And both sides know that. As negotiations continue, each side makes "final" offers to the other, yet each side suspects that it can get an even better final offer. Thus, labor and management negotiators are forced to be untruthful and deceptive by the very nature of the process. Given this reality, can one be a labor or management negotiator and still be a Christian?

When Negotiating Is Questionable

Responses to that question generally take one of three forms. The first is a simple no. Where deception and untruth are the required job skills, a Christian has no place in the work. The second answer is yes because there is no connection between what goes on in church* on Sunday and what one does during the rest of the week. The third response is more interesting. Here again the position is yes; one can be a Christian labor negotiator. The reason given is that all involved know the negotiations are a "game*" in which both sides realize they are the victims of deception and untruth. A Christian negotiator asks, "Am I really telling a lie when my adversary expects that I will try to deceive?" It is an appropriate question for Christian ethicists. Can a labor or management negotiator, who is absolutely truthful in all parts of his or her private life, be excused for telling lies at the negotiating table because everyone knows it is part of the negotiating game? Is this really telling lies, or should such behavior be described and viewed under some other category as it would be in a game?

In areas that directly affect the public, such as government services and transportation, third-party intervention in the negotiating process is common. Arbitration by a neutral third party offers a way out of the game of untruth and deception. Arbitrators seek to find a solution in which both sides get something of what they wanted. "Win-win" settlements are the objective, but neither party wins everything it sought. But even here a game is played. To suggest arbitration, particularly binding arbitration, implies that your adversary is in a stronger negotiating position than you are. That being the case, your adversary will be reluctant to go along with the arbitration on the assumption that you are conceding that you have a weaker position.

Negotiating is frequently the required path to obtaining many business and government contracts. The federal government, including the military, negotiates many of its contracts, even though sealed bids are initially sought for specific plans and specifications. Suppliers may differ with respect to terms and conditions, delivery times or other features of a bid. The purchaser must negotiate these aspects of a bid in order to ensure that the contract is awarded to the best supplier. But when each side struggles to better the other, lies and deceit are common. Here, again, it is seen as a game, but sometimes as a game involving victory at all costs.

Christian Negotiation

From a Christian standpoint, negotiations are best carried out when each person places himself or herself in the shoes of the other. When there is a good understanding of the needs and desires of the other person, each side should strive to meet those needs. Negotiating should not be a contest in which each party strives to get the maximum from the other. Rather, it should be a cooperative effort to meet the basic needs and some desires of each other. *Win-win* is indeed the solution sought. In doing so, the Christian who negotiates on behalf of some group will be criticized for not being more aggressive. At this point the Christian negotiator will have to explain the justice of meeting mutual needs or, having failed to do so, decide to either forget about justice or quit the job.

See also BUSINESS ETHICS; COMPETITION; COMPROMISE; CONFLICT RESOLUTION; INTEGRITY; JUSTICE; UNIONS.

William E. Diehl

NEIGHBORHOOD

The word *neighborhood* can be defined in two related ways. Physically it can refer to a place, generally residential, whose boundaries are recognizable in some way, whether through its overall design, road system or some natural feature. Socially it can refer to a set of ties established by people within a specified territory, sometimes because of their homogeneity or the existence of local institutions—such as a shopping center, schools or churches—that draw them together. Though the second meaning has been highlighted more in recent research, people's residential setting—especially the block-length section of the street on which they live—continues to play a part in developing relationships.

In general the word refers to a piece of territory in which persons residing had some sense of common identity and some acquaintance with or knowledge of each other. Sometimes neighborhoods had long histories or traditions, with many of the same families or occupations continuing over several generations or even centuries. Although the industrial and then technological revolutions led to a weakening of this (even as they have opened up new ways of experiencing what a neighborhood provided), in advanced postindustrial societies neighborhoods in the traditional sense survive. This is still the case in some inner-city* areas—one thinks of the African-American use of the word *hood* or Hispanic *barrio*. Women working at home and working-class people generally still have a stronger sense of neighborhood and more strongly developed relationships with neighbors than others. So do some places which have a predominantly homogeneous lifestyle, such as Greenwich Village or Venice Beach. Catholic congregations have also tended to continue regarding their neighborhoods as an extension of the parish. Occasionally a relatively stable part of a suburb* or town* has a similar character.

Neighborhoods come in many sizes and forms, but similarities between them appear in many parts of a country. In his book *The Clustering of America* Michael Jones provides a vivid portrait of as many as forty different neighborhood types that can be identified throughout the United States, each with its own distinctive values, lifestyles and eccentricities. Among the types he documents are what he calls blue-blood estates, money and brains, young influentials, God's country, blue-chip blues, bohemian mix, gray power, black enterprise, new homesteaders, rank and file, towns and gowns, new melting pot, middle America, shotguns and pickups, coaltown and cornburg, agribusiness, emergent minorities, single-city blues, back country folks, grain belt, heavy industry, Hispanic mix, and public assistance. This list reminds us how varied neighborhoods can be, even more so when we realize that many of the above are in transition and that over a long period of time all tend to undergo significant change.

The Changing Nature of Neighborhood
Many factors have changed the nature of neighborhoods. Greater mobility* means that families do not stay as long in a given area, breaking relationships and weakening stability. Also contributing to this is the severing of the link between where people live and where they work.* The breakup of families through divorce* also disrupts some members' connections with their locality. Inventions such as the telephone* and automobile* have increased the distances people can travel and reduced the time spent in their localities. Meanwhile radio* and especially television* keep people inside their homes more. The growing use of computers* and the coming of the Information Superhighway* means that people do not even have to leave their homes, let alone talk to their neighbors, to communicate with others. Even the use of fences* and the grid system of streets plays a part in shaping the nature of the neighborhood.

In the light of all these changes, it is

not surprising that laments for the loss of neighborhood are many and deeply felt. But some changes have resulted in a mutation of neighborhood rather than its disappearance. This takes many forms, but I give just two examples.

First, it has generally been believed that the flight from the inner city to the suburbs led to people's becoming less neighborly than they were in their more impoverished urban settings. Studies suggest, however, that this is not usually the case. The move, even in working-class suburbs, generally led to people spending as much, if not more, time with their new neighbors as with their old ones. It could be argued that this was at the expense of the neighborhoods that they left, but this is not entirely true. Sometimes many people left around the same time for nearby suburbs and continued some of their former links. Also neighborhoods go through cycles when by natural attrition ties get weakened or broken, and in many cases inner-city neighborhoods have been undergoing renovation as others move in and establish new neighborhood patterns. Nor should we forget that part of what encouraged traditional neighborhoods was people working in close proximity to one another: the close social relations people often develop in their workplaces separate from their homes is not so much a new form of neighborhood as simply the part of the old form relocated. Some evidence for this comes from the fact that women who work outside the home do not develop stronger links with neighbors than men who do so, though they may have more focused ones.

Second, the extending of lines of communication through the telephone, automobile and now personal computer have also created new links between people, or strengthened existing ones. This expands people's sense of neighborhood but does not necessarily mean that they spend more time making contact with such people than they would in previous times walking from one house or farm to another. It does not necessarily mean that they see the people they are mainly in contact with any less frequently or for shorter periods of time. Nor does it mean that the relationships they develop are any less intense. It may mean one or all of these things but not always or necessarily. However, because of the increasing busyness* (see Time) in modern society and what appears to be growing individualism (see Community; Individual), people do need to be more intentional about maintaining and deepening their neighborly links or relationships. This extended sense of neighborhood should not be alien to Christians, who prize highly Jesus' story of the good Samaritan with its challenging definition of neighbor (Lk 10:25-37).

Neighbor in Bible and Theology

The parable of the good Samaritan is far from the only injunction in Scripture about our responsibilities in this area. In the Old Testament the word *neighbor* refers almost exclusively to a fellow Israelite. Neighbor relationships assume certain moral obligations based on the command "Love your neighbor as yourself" (Lev 19:18) and play a significant role in the detail of the Old Testament Law. In the Ten Commandments we are forbidden to "give false witness against [our] neighbor" or "covet [our] neighbor's house" (Ex 20:16-17). We are to respect our neighbor's property (Ex 22:14) and show mercy to our neighbor (Ex 22:26-27). In other law codes we are warned against cheating our neighbor or endangering our neighbor's life, and required to confront rather than take revenge on a neighbor who has wronged us (Lev 19:13-18). We are to show charity to our neighbor (Deut 15:11) and have a concern for one another's welfare

(Deut 22:1-4). Elsewhere in the Old Testament we are advised not to hurt our neighbor but to strengthen the relationship of trust between us, and not fend our neighbor off but share with a neighbor when requested to do so (Prov 3:27-29). Where justice and compassion are absent in a neighborhood, God's judgment is severe. It is directed against anyone who would slander (Ps 101:5), cheat (Jer 22:13) or defile (Hab 2:15) a neighbor, as well as against anyone who would kill (Ex 21:14).

In the New Testament, Jesus reiterates the need to "to love your neighbor as yourself" (Mt 19:19). As already mentioned, in his teaching he redefines the term *neighbor* to reflect the inclusive nature of the kingdom he had come to establish (Lk 10:29-30). Much of his earthly ministry was neighborhood-centered as he wandered from village to village and ministered in houses and streets (Mt 8:14-17; Lk 7:12). Many of his parables were drawn from aspects of neighborhood life, illustrating the presence and challenge of God "in our own back yard" (Lk 6:46-49; 11:5-10; 15). Elsewhere in the New Testament the command to "love your neighbor as yourself" is restated no less than nine times. Paul describes this injunction as a summary of "the entire law" (Rom 13:9; Gal 5:14), and James as the "royal law" (Jam 2:8).

These injunctions should color all proximate relationships, whether with those at some distance or those who are close by. Among theologians it is probably Karl Barth who has highlighted the importance of neighbor as a criterion for our behavior. He argues that our responsibility to our neighbor is the concrete form that the Word of God, especially concerning reconciliation, takes in our daily life. This concern and compassion for our neighbors takes us beyond our inherent capacity for self-interest, leads us to repentance since we so often fail those around us, challenges us to do what is lawful and right for us to do, and allows us to see our neighbor as a witness, messenger, reminder and confirmation of our Lord. The centrality of the neighbor is also a constant reminder to us that issues of morality have a personal face.

Tending the Residential Neighborhood
Although the meaning of neighborhood is being extended or redefined in many ways, we should not abandon all responsibility to the physical neighborhood in which we live. In the first place this is counterproductive. Unless there is some sense of local identity and pride, neighborhoods tend to lose important services. Unless local parks are used, they often become centers for drug handling or undesirable, even threatening, behavior. It is precisely because so many neighborhoods are empty during the day or at certain times in the year that crime* increases within them. When crises happen at home, neighbors are often the only ones close enough to call for help, and if we do not know them this is more difficult to do. In more general ways neighborhoods are also an underappreciated source of community. The importance of the mosaic of small encounters they make possible—greeting one another over the back fence or in the street, assisting each other in small ways when some difficulty arises, fraternizing and sometimes cooperating when everyone is affected by the same difficult conditions, borrowing or loaning some household or garden item, keeping an eye on each other's property when people are away—should not be underestimated.

For these and other reasons there has actually been a reviving commitment to local areas at the grassroots level (in the form of neighborhood watches, residents' associations, neighborhood councils and neighborhood coalitions), at the intermediate-level community (advisory

689

committees, district councils or priority boards) and at the highest level (departments of neighborhoods, citizens advisory boards, divisions of neighborhood affairs and offices of neighborhood associations). While people's involvement in these is sometimes primarily self-regarding—they are concerned about their own safety or property values—in other cases it is also or mainly other-regarding, motivated by concern for those who are less fortunate than themselves or for the welfare of the neighborhood as a whole.

As individuals and families we can do several things to encourage or enhance our local area: sit out in our front yard or on our porch so we have more contact with neighbors; invite neighbors for a drink, barbecue or meal from time to time; go for walks regularly around the neighborhood, especially at times when people are more likely to be home, so we will encounter neighbors and begin to develop an acquaintance with them; welcome new neighbors, and arrange farewells for departing ones; hold annual block parties, encourage Halloween visits or organize neighborhood caroling at Christmas, drawing in some neighbors to plan these events; offer our home as the local polling booth if we have the opportunity; support local shops, services, schools and churches to build up stronger neighborhood connections; establish neighborhood hobby groups or exhibitions for those who have common interests; and develop voluntary associations for raising local issues or helping needy neighbors.

As members of churches we could not only endorse these kinds of activities but make a special effort to become part of our immediate neighborhood by these additional means: hold some meetings in members' homes rather than concentrating them all on the church grounds; encourage some members to live near one another so that they can engage in joint ministry to those around them; become involved as a congregation in addressing justice issues and social needs in the neighborhood; put before some members a vision for taking up civic responsibilities; make our buildings available for community meetings and activities as well as for congregational use; set up on the church property a small neighborhood park, drop-in center, counseling service, preschool, or Christian bookstore and coffeehouse; and visit the neighborhood and ask in what ways the church could be of practical service to the people in it.

These are only some of the possibilities open to us that can lead the way to more Christlike attitudes and actions toward our neighbors.

See also CITY; COMMUNITY; SMALL TOWNS.

References and Resources

C. S. Fischer, *To Dwell Among Friends: Personal Networks in Towns and City* (Chicago: University of Chicago Press, 1982); C. S. Fischer, *The Urban Experience* (New York: Harcourt Brace Jovanovich, 1984); F. M. Lappe and P. M. Du Bois, *The Quickening of America: Rebuilding Our Nation, Remaking Our Lives* (San Francisco: Jossey-Bass, 1994); M. Slattery and M. Droel, *Christians in Their Neighborhood* (Chicago: Southwest Catholic Cluster, n.d.); M. J. Weiss, *The Clustering of America* (New York: Harper & Row, 1988).

Robert Banks

NETWORKING

The importance of networking in everyday working life is dramatized in the film *Wall Street,* Oliver Stone's showcasing of the fascinating world of financial investment. The main character is Gordon Gecko (Michael Douglas), who reigns over an empire of impressive money market monopolies. The stable of people he knows, privileged information he accesses and continuous communication he engages in add up to a networking superstar. Bud (Charlie Sheen) attempts to emulate Gecko both in his competence as a power broker and in the networking skills necessary to guarantee domination in that world.

Networking as a Feature of Contemporary Life

In its exposé of stock market realities *Wall Street* demonstrates the inescapability of networking as a fixed feature of contemporary working life. Indeed, networking is most frequently associated with job and career* environments. But it has evolved as a dimension of everyday life beyond the confines of the workplace. In the busy and segmented urban life of most North Americans, networking is required to find friends and to establish a community of connections. With our nostalgic and idealized notions of relationships, we are apt to suspect networking as too formal and utilitarian for our romantic aspirations. But in the reality of city* life, networking becomes the necessary bridge to identify and nurture meaningful relationships. Whether practiced consciously or accidentally, networking is a relational habit for many people.

Networks require a measure of intentionality and civility.* Networkers are influential precisely because they know what they want and initiate processes to attain their desires and aspirations. People, called *players,* who vigorously pursue strategic positioning recognize that in a competitive social setting, civility* and a measure of concern for others in networking are crucial for any short-term or long-term gains. Because of the pervasiveness of networking, a moral imagination* should be employed to appreciate and assess its contribution to contemporary daily life.

Networking in Organizational Life

The twentieth century has seen the astro-

nomical growth of large institutions. With this organizational trend has come a dramatic increase in professionals to manage and operate these bureaucratic enterprises. Concurrent with these developments has been the globalization of institutional relations in government, business* and ecclesiastical sectors (*see* Global Village). All of these new realities mandate leadership* styles that mobilize networking capacities. *Networking* is the process of creating and maintaining a pattern of informal linkages among individuals and institutions. In a swiftly changing social environment, new and flexible interconnections become necessary. Leaders must be highly skilled in constructing or re-creating the linkages necessary to function effectively (Gardner, p. 62).

The recent proliferation of publications dissecting organizational culture* and submitting prescriptions for successful leadership of diverse institutions frequently includes discussions of networking. The near-totalitarian presence of organizational life is the catalyst for this saturation of printed resources to assist leaders and players to operate with confidence. In today's entrepreneurial and innovative climate, internal networking emerges as a primary ingredient in being productive. The constant moving around of people and processes means that humans rather than formal mechanisms become the principal carriers of information and integrative links between different departments within an organization. Mobility* is a key factor as a network-forming vehicle and thus becomes an admission ticket to the power centers. An organization's opportunity structure*—movement to privileged and prestigious positions—is directly related to the power* structure (Kanter, p. 164). Networking has become one of the preferred competencies to contribute to a healthy company and to procure advancement possibilities. The wise executive or manager carefully place in strategic positions individuals who are networkers by inclination. This inclusion of networkers enables the establishment of informal cross-boundary working groups that energize the entire corporate culture (Gardner, p. 163).

External networking is also a work of innovative trends in institutional development currently in fashion. The best companies relate even to their competitors (see Competition). Building alliances enhances communication and mutuality. In a cutthroat approach to organizational relations there tend to be losers all the way around. Healthy alliance building produces mutual benefits for each partner and for society as a whole. Leaders must nurture outside networks of allies in the many other segments of society whose cooperation is desired for a significant result (Gardner, p. 104).

Networking and the Spirituality of Daily Life

Networking is an individual and institutional activity. The movement of structures suggests the inevitability of involvement in networks. The globalization and urbanization of contemporary life also mean that institutions are interdependent and are necessarily interfacing as their respective missions and operations pull them into a marketplace of connections. Organizational life is an extension of the created world—part of what is often called the *cultural mandate*.

God, who is a Trinity, created the world in a relational manner and wired it to be a communicative network. These relational and communicative processes have been distorted and demented as they moved east of Eden. The life, death and resurrection of Jesus Christ has brought the possibility of a more complete reconciliation into these processes.

It is now possible to network in a manner that is reconciling in its intent and expression.

Networking is one essential dimension of the ministry of reconciliation the apostle Paul speaks of so intently (2 Cor 5:19). The several implications of the ministry of reconciliation for networking are exemplified in Jesus, mandated by the Creator and empowered by the Spirit. The primary implication is the deliberate communication to the neighbor (see Neighborhood), including the stranger. The love* of neighbor and stranger that Jesus demands becomes the starting point for the networking activity associated with our job and civic life. Networking is that public part of our daily life in which we recognize our oneness, our unity, our interdependence on one another. Indeed, we are strangers and likely will remain as such, but we inhabit common space, share resources, convene around mutual opportunities and generally must learn to live and work together. The public drama in which we all are participants reveals a life in which strangers inevitably come into daily contact with others and learn to solve problems together and enrich and enlarge each other's perspectives. We are all part of a web, linked in a network (Palmer, pp. 19-20).

The church is to be a communion of communions. Jesus has called people together from disparate multicultural* environments to be witnesses of the kingdom of God. Networking is a spiritual discipline* of the ecumenical church to celebrate our unity in the gospel and affirm the different ministries in the world of the public. Jesus' vision of a unified and commissioned church mandates a spirituality that includes networking as part of its habit of ecumenism and mission* in the world (Marty, p. 79). A spirituality of daily life recognizes the vitality of networking in the discipleship* of the Christian and in the public vocation of the church.

See also FELLOWSHIP; FRIENDSHIP; ORGANIZATION.

References and Resources
W. Baker, *Networking Smart* (New York: McGraw-Hill, 1994); J. W. Gardner, *On Leadership* (New York: Free Press, 1990); R. S. Kanter, *The Change Masters* (New York: Simon & Schuster, 1983); M. Marty, *The Public Church* (New York: Crossroad, 1981); P. Palmer, *The Company of Strangers* (New York: Crossroad, 1981).

Scott Young

NEW REPRODUCTIVE TECHNOLOGY

Formerly a mysterious, elusive event that occurred only in the secret and dark places of a woman's body,* conception* is now subjected to the blinding light of the laboratory and the scrutiny and manipulation of medical technology.* Beneath the dazzling miracle of healthy children born to long-suffering infertile couples lies a shadowy moral twilight. The same technology affords contemplation of the possibility of "designer children" through prenatal diagnosis, sex selection, abortion,* and, ultimately, cloning and genetic engineering. The advent of surrogacy and egg and sperm donation is the logical extension of separating the procreative and unitive acts that began with the widespread use of contraception.* Placed outside the temple of a covenantal relationship, modern conception is often complicated by consumerist* influences of a marketplace that needs purging, just as Jesus cleansed the synagogue (Jn 2:13-16).

Reproductive Miracles
The bitter agony of barrenness is well recognized biblically, and God's faithfulness to his promises is exemplified in reproductive miracles (Elizabeth in Lk 1:13, Sarah in Gen 18:10 and Hannah in 1 Sam 1:10). It is no less prodigious for those couples whose infertility, be it blocked fallopian tubes or low sperm count, can be overcome by the *in vitro* (literally, "in glass") uniting of their own sperm and ovum. In vitro fertilization (IVF) is accomplished outside the mother's body when sperm and ovum spontaneously meet in a laboratory dish or by microinjection of disabled sperm directly into the ovum. Successful embryos that begin dividing are placed in the womb, where they may or may not implant and result in a pregnancy. The ownership, freezing, storage and use of unplaced embryos are fraught with controversy. Some couples claim them and feel responsible to give each embryo an opportunity for womb placement. Others sell their embryos (along with sperm or harvested eggs) to finance these expensive treatments with their variable success rates and odds that at times resemble gambling. Successful pregnancies are often complicated by multiple gestations, forcing selective abortion of some implanted embryos to ensure that a smaller number (twins or triplets) will reach viability. There are higher rates of prematurity and complications for which society* ultimately bears responsibility in the care of the disabled and vulnerable. Many people feel public funding would be better spent in prevention of infertility (usually a result of sexually transmissible diseases) and in the encouragement and support of women who wish to carry a baby to term instead of having an abortion with the intent to give an inestimable gift to an adopting couple.

Once conception can occur outside the relational context of human sexuality, reproductive capabilities are imparted to single people, homosexual couples and postmenopausal women. Among those polled, fewest people object to nonanonymous arrangements occurring between family members (e.g., a woman donating eggs or carrying a child for her sister). But what are the rights of the child? To whom do they belong: to the genetic, gestational (birthing) or social parents? Theologian Gino Concetti said that "a couple does not have the right to have a child at any cost, but a child does have a right to be created in a natural way" ("Talk of the Streets"). The complex ramifications of parenting non-biologic children are akin to the established practice of adoption. Questions of responsibility and rights are raised when more then one set of parents have claims on a child, who may ultimately become torn apart in a court lacking Solomon's wisdom.

Another facet of NRTs is *prenatal diagnosis*. Under the guise of providing reassurance of normalcy or preparation for defects, the thorny issue is raised whether parents can justly subject both society and an abnormal child to "wrongful birth." Does a child have a right to have intrauterine euthanasia* to prevent inevitable "indignities" and suffering as predicted by prenatal tests should the pregnancy* continue and birth* occur? Prenatal diagnosis is the first of many potential steps in altering the type of children that society will admit. At the present time it involves sampling of fetal cells from the placenta at an early stage in pregnancy (chorionic villus sampling) or from amniotic fluid closer to the time to quickening (amniocentesis). In the case of IVF, early cells can be removed from the multicellular embryo prior to being placed in the womb. In research settings these cells have also been successfully duplicated or cloned (artificial twinning). In the future, fetal cells that appear in the maternal circulation may be sampled, providing information without potential harm to the fetus.

As with most genetic diagnoses, a positive result represents a "fate" without

hope of a cure at this stage of technology. The alternatives include termination of a pregnancy or, with IVF, a decision not to implant that particular embryo. Gene therapy and rare intrauterine interventions are as of yet experimental but represent distinct possibilities for the future.

With the advent of DNA manipulation and reconstruction through virus vectors, the power to correct critical genetically coded errors becomes a possibility. The DNA molecule takes on a new identity as a pharmacologic agent for curing perhaps even such commonly fatal ailments as heart disease and cancers. We are taking evolution into our own hands when we consider gene therapy. We need to recall that the seducing power unleashed from the splitting of the atom was wielded in a destructive fashion on Hiroshima. In the blinding excitement of the genetic revolution we too easily forget the responsibilities inherent in the biting of this apple core—as we seek knowledge of the "good and evil" inherent in our genes, navigating with fewer ethical absolutes than ever before.

Ethical Considerations

While the full exploration of the ethical ramifications of genetic engineering and NRTs exceeds the scope of this article, the following two concerns are foremost: the commercialization of reproduction and the redefinition of human dignity in narrower terms.

Commercialization of Reproduction. Desperate infertile couples are at the mercy of a profit-driven reproductive industry and are prone to exploitation in research settings. The selling of human tissue, eggs, sperm and embryos contravenes human dignity. Disadvantaged women may sell their reproductive capacities by entering into surrogacy arrangements where they may carry a genetically related or unrelated child to term and relinquish their rights to the child (if healthy), all for a sum of money that is usually less than what the legal brokers receive who represent the commissioning couple renting her womb. The transfer of funds is never enough to occupy the void and compensate her grief,* let alone the dehumanization she suffers. Remunerated surrogacy is ominously reminiscent of slavery. Children begin to be viewed as technological accomplishments, commodities and luxury accessories that enhance social status. Identically cloned embryos may one day be frozen and banked for future use as organ donors or replacement children. Even aborted female fetuses can provide eggs, making it possible to be a genetic parent without having been born. The media captures our attention for commercial purposes by focusing on the marginal and the maudlin. In the process our sensibilities are flattened and theater obscures the truth.

Is Human Dignity Most Threatened by the Disease or the Cure? What are the motives we bring to the reconstruction of the human race through NRTs? What values will be paramount in shaping the chosen characteristics of the future generations? Challenging responsible stewardship,* NRTs give human pride and rebellion every possibility for expression. Will we be motivated by vanity, perfectionism and elitism in choosing cosmetically appealing physical or superior intellectual characteristics? By sex selection (accomplished by preferential sperm treatment, selective implantation or abortion), will we produce "ideal" families with offspring of both sexes or offspring representative of the more valued sex (usually male)? In some areas of China where ultrasound imaging and abortion are readily available, the number of boys born is significantly greater than the number of live-born girls, fueled by strict incentives imposed by the government to limit families to one child. Even the seemingly altruistic desire to prevent suffering and promote health is worn thin by the means by which it is achieved —intrauterine euthanasia and embryo experimentation.

The understated message is that we no longer value and are unwilling to protect the vulnerable, the diseased and the deformed in society. The unspoken corollary of the option for prenatal testing is that no one should *knowingly* permit a less than perfect baby to be born. We wrongly sense a moral obligation to dispatch ourselves before we are violated by nature. What is being lost is the essential fact that human beings do not lose their dignity by virtue of an inability to control what cannot be controlled, such as birth defects, disability, illness,* aging* and death.* "It is the equivalent of saying that to possess human dignity with any degree of certainty one must be forever free of adversity" (Stolberg, p. 146). We are reminded that Christ on the cross maintained his human dignity in the face of suffering and slander.

Recovering Reproductive Reverence
In contemplating incarnation, Mary, by gentle persuasion, conceives miraculously within the confines of a betrothed covenantal relationship. However, she is given no clear indication as to whether Jesus is genetically her child conceived of the Holy Spirit. Joseph also is visited by angels and told of the child's coming. In the mysterious incarnation of "God-in-utero," one wonders whether the genetic material that Jesus Christ possessed was contributed miraculously by one or both of his earthly parents. Did he enter into the human family pervasively and integrally, sharing his father's dexterity for carpentry and his mother's gentility? Did Mary act as a willing surrogate for the transplantation of perfected DNA, somehow unencumbered with the scourges of

humanity, making Jesus a transcendent physicality from the moment of conception? Or did the transforming power of the Holy Spirit preclude the necessity for Jesus to have had anything more than the expected human complement of genetic material?

Ultimately, the hope we have for the future *is not eugenics but Jesus.* Children represent expressions of our trust in God's intent that "the world should go on," but they are not the means to ultimate sanctification, permanence and perfection. It is unlikely we will ever splice out all the genes that contribute to our brokenness and separation from God. The severing of procreation from sexual activity within the confines of marital fidelity is the harbinger of the disintegration we experience when we threaten our dignity by attempting to separate soul* and body. Doubt is the shadow cast by faith. As we plunge into the genetic age may the transcendent presence of God's justice and beneficence guide us in the complex decisions that await our ethical scrutiny.

See also BIRTH; CONCEPTION; EUTHANASIA; MISCARRIAGE; PREGNANCY.

References and Resources

P. Baird, *Proceed with Care: Final Report of the Royal Commission on New Reproductive Technologies* (Minister of Government Services, Canada, 1993); P. Teilhard de Chardin, *The Appearance of Man* (New York: Harper, 1965); E. C. Hui, *Questions of Right and Wrong* (Vancouver: Regent College, 1994); S. D. Stolberg, "Human Dignity and Disease, Disability, Suffering," *Humane Medicine* 1, no. 4 (1995) 144-47; "Talk of the Streets," *Time,* January 23, 1995, 10.

Carol Anderson

NEWSPAPERS

Throughout most of history, governments have controlled the flow of public information. Ancient Rome produced written public announcements, and eighth-century Beijing published a daily *News of the Palace.* Later, great nobles in Europe employed writers to record their personal events. However, any news that came out of the palace was crafted to cast leaders in the best possible light. It was not until Johann Gutenberg's invention of movable type in 1450 that ordinary citizens had the means to publish reports and opinions. Early broadsheets recorded Columbus's discovery of the New World in 1492 and the English defeat of the Spanish Armada in 1588. The number of private newspapers grew to about twenty in England by the mid-1600s. But as newspapers exercised more freedom to report and comment on issues, government leaders began to crack down. Parliament enacted laws prohibiting criticism of the government. The first newspaper in the American colonies, *Public Occurrences in Boston,* was shut down after its first edition criticized the government's handling of the war with France. In a landmark case that laid a foundation for the freedom of the press, a jury in 1735 found a New York printer named John Peter Zenger not guilty of libeling the governor of the province. The jury decided that a person could not claim damages if the information, even if objectionable, was true. Newspapers grew in number and influence as America moved from a colony to a world power.

A hundred years ago, newspapers had a virtual monopoly on news and information. That is no longer the case. Today newspapers compete with network television,* cable television, radio,* "want-ad" flyers and on-line computer* services for consumers (*see* Information Superhighway) and advertising* dollars. However, the greatest threat to the newspaper industry is not competition with other media but rather competition for people's time.*

What Is a Newspaper?

A newspaper is a business. Some newspapers are privately owned; many belong to newspaper chains. Unlike radio and television, where advertising and marketing have tight control over station programming, newspapers have a long tradition of keeping editorial decisions free from the influence of advertising and marketing. As a business, newspapers must be responsive to two major customers: advertisers and readers. If an advertiser does not see results (e.g., customers spending more money at its store), the business will stop advertising in the newspaper. In the same way, if readers do not find what they like or like what they find, they will stop buying the newspaper.

A newspaper is an institution. The larger the paper, the more defined its editorial position will be. Newspapers with a national circulation, such as the *New York Times, Wall Street Journal* and *USA Today,* will have a clear editorial position on issues (liberal, conservative, moderate, etc.). In community newspapers (suburban dailies and weeklies), the editorial position may vary according to whoever is in charge at any given time.

A newspaper is a human enterprise. Hollywood often portrays reporters and editors as unethical cutthroats who will spare nothing—including the truth—to smear someone's reputation all over the front page. Fortunately, the vast majority of journalists care deeply about being accurate, objective and fair. The First Amendment may guarantee freedom of the press, but libel laws hold journalists accountable: the information published must be true, and, if not, the errors must have been made without malice and after making every reasonable effort to confirm the information. Journalists are also restrained by their own consciences. Many journalists live in the communities their newspaper covers; they own homes, send their children to public schools,

coach in the Little League and so on.

In summary, a newspaper is a human institution that is in the business of providing reliable information to other people.

How to Read a Newspaper

No one has the time to read every article and every advertisement in a newspaper, nor should they. Not everything in the paper is relevant to them, and some information may be harmful (1 Cor 10:23).

Most newspapers today are designed for "scanning." Charts, graphics and listings make it easy to find the weather report, stock prices, scores of games and TV schedules. The rest of the newspaper can be scanned by simply glancing at the headlines and the first one or two paragraphs of each story.

Scanning helps keep state, national and world news in perspective. It is possible to give too much time and energy to developments that are far away while ignoring the needs in our own communities. Henry David Thoreau noted how people were so fascinated with the idea of constructing a telegraph from Maine to Texas and laying a cable from America to Europe. "But Maine and Texas, it may be, have nothing important to communicate," he wrote, and "perchance the first news that will leak through into the broad flapping American ear will be that Princess Adelaide has the whooping cough" (*Walden,* quoted in Postman, p. 65). In the same way today, much of the news, though fascinating, is irrelevant.

There is no single way to read a newspaper article. It depends to a large degree on the type of material: news, feature, opinion, entertainment and sports.

News. The six basic questions of a reporter are who, what, where, when, how and why. But the reader should expect to find answers to several hidden questions as well: "Who or what is the source of information?" Every news story has a source, and the reporter usually reveals whether the information comes from a government official, a witness, a police officer, a public meeting, a court document and so on. While the practice of using information from unnamed sources is controversial and sometimes wrongly employed, it has proven to be the only means of exposing the truth in some cases, particularly in stories about graft and corruption.

"How reliable is this information?" A newspaper is only as good as its information. If the paper consistently prints erroneous information, it will lose its credibility and eventually its readers. Recognizing this, most journalists make sure they have a document (a report, minutes of a meeting, court docket, etc.) and confirmation of information from a second person.

"Is the story fair?" Gathering and reporting news is a highly selective process. The reporter chooses which facts he or she has collected to include in the article and which information to emphasize. The editor decides how and where the story should run in the paper, thus assigning a value to it in comparison with other news in the paper that day. The reporter is not merely a "scribe"; rather, he or she is expected to interpret the significance of words and actions. There is a fine line between interpretation and opinion, and articles may reflect a bias. Often a reporter will not even be conscious of this bias (Bozell and Baker, p. 3).

Opinion. Newspapers offer opportunity on the opinion page for people to comment on issues. There are five formats for opinion: *editorial,* the official opinion of the newspaper; *column,* the opinion of an individual writer; *political cartoon,* the opinion of the cartoonist; *guest column,* the view of a responsible spokesperson; and *letter to the editor,* the opinion of any reader.

Entertainment and Sports. These are the playgrounds of a newspaper. Nothing in them is essential to daily living. Rather, they offer escape and fun. However, the articles in these sections often go to one of two extremes: they either make people into idols or they destroy the same human beings. Not knowing these people personally does not exempt us from the Bible's warnings about slander and gossip: "The words of a gossip are like choice morsels; they go down to a man's inmost parts" (Prov 18:8). The key is to focus on what takes place on the field, stage or screen.

Features. Many articles in a newspaper focus not on *what* happened yesterday but rather on what is *happening* these days. These feature articles may run throughout the paper or in separate sections called Living, Lifestyle, Health, Business, Religion, Education and so on. Many provide information (about an unusual disease, selecting a college, deciding whether to refinance a home, etc.) that could help the reader or someone the reader knows. The articles generally reflect human-centered solutions to problems, which may not address the root causes and may even contradict Christian teachings.

How to Respond to Newspapers

☐ Keep newspapers in proper perspective. Newspapers have their shortcomings. They are often superficial in their coverage, arrogant in their opinions and focused on problems instead of solutions (though the same might also be said of many people outside of newspapers!). At worst, they are "unconsciously" part of what the late BBC commentator Malcolm Muggeridge called "a mighty brainwashing operation, whereby all traditional standards and values are being denigrated to the point of disappearing" (Muggeridge, p. 60).

Sociologist Neil Postman is equally

pessimistic about the influence of the media, but his criticism is focused primarily on television. The invention of television was no less revolutionary than the invention of the printing press, he says, because TV "changes the structure of public discourse" and is "creating new forms of truth-telling." The image has become more important than the idea. As a result, he says, "the seriousness, clarity and above all, value of public discourse dangerously declines" (p. 29).

☐ Take part in the "public forum." Newspapers, for all of their shortcomings, offer one of the few remaining forums for public discourse. In fact, the growing "public forum" movement among many newspapers aims to involve all segments of a community. Many papers set up "focus groups" to discuss issues and to hear feedback from readers. Many also are actively seeking more letters and guest columns from readers. Both provide opportunities for Christians to become involved in public discourse.

☐ Reflect on the world portrayed in the newspaper. Evil is obvious. It is evident in stories about tragedy, crime and injustice. But newspapers are also full of signs of hope: the birth of a child; a wedding* announcement; a fiftieth anniversary* celebration; a courageous battle to overcome illness; a dedicated teacher's commitment; a church's response to the poor and hungry. A newspaper may give a distorted view of the balance of good and evil, but that does not excuse us from our call to focus on "whatever is true, . . . noble, . . . right, . . . pure, . . . lovely, . . . admirable, . . . excellent or praiseworthy" (Phil 4:8).

☐ Respond in some way to something you read. If "knowledge puffs up," as the apostle Paul says (1 Cor 8:1), Christians today should beware of an all-out "information explosion." The daily news can place an oppressive weight on the hu-

man heart. But God does not intend for us to bear that weight on our own. It is Christ's burden (Mt 11:28-30). Though we shoulder one end of his yoke, our end is "easy" and "light." The key is to shift the weight over to Christ in prayer, and only then, in Christ, to turn knowledge into an act of love.* It can be as simple as cutting out a photograph of a friend's child and sending it to them with a note sending a card to a neighbor graduating from high school, alerting a church member of an article about a medical condition he or she has just been diagnosed as having, or as involved as sending a check to help total strangers rebuild their home after a fire or writing a letter of encouragement to a social worker or police officer who works in the trenches of society's most difficult and heart-wrenching conditions.

Newspapers are not perfect. Their view of reality is often distorted. And Christianity is seldom the defining viewpoint of an editorial board. But within each newspaper are stories of real people trying to make it through life the best they can. Some stories are inspiring; others are heartbreaking. To a heart that is willing to be broken and a will that is yielded to Christ, one newspaper contains enough opportunities for service and food for prayer to last most people a lifetime.

See also CITIZENSHIP; COMICS; COMMUNITY; GLOBAL VILLAGE; INFORMATION SUPERHIGHWAY; MASS MEDIA; READING.

References and Resources

L. B. Bozell III and B. Baker, eds., *And That's The Way It Isn't: A Reference Guide to Media Bias* (Alexandria, Va.: Media Research Center, 1990); M. Muggeridge, *Christ and the Media* (Grand Rapids: Eerdmans, 1977); W. G. Pippert, *An Ethics of News: A Reporter's Search for Truth* (Washington, D.C.: Georgetown University Press, 1989); N. Postman, *Amusing Ourselves to Death: Public Discourse in the Age of Show Business* (New York: Penguin Books, 1985).

Stephen Crowe

NOISE

We live surrounded by almost constant noise. Some of it comes to us from the highly mechanized way of life that we have invented. The city* never sleeps: even in the early hours of the morning there are cars on the freeway, dogs barking vociferously, and sirens wailing in the distance. Some of the noise comes from our entertainment* technologies*—radios* blare, ghetto-blasters vibrate and televisions* echo from open windows.

Some time ago I went into the countryside to do some filming in a quiet, pastoral setting. Although I was nearly fifty miles from a city, noisy modern inventions constantly intruded on my efforts. Tractors on distant farms and aircraft passing overhead provided little opportunity for capturing natural scenes and sounds. Even in quite different settings, such as a regular church* service, it is remarkable how few people are able to wait or meditate in silence before corporate worship* begins.

Sometimes it seems as if we have succeeded in abolishing silence in our modern world. The teenager whose constant companion is a Walkman, the shopping mall* with its never-ending Muzak and the time of Holy Communion* with its piano accompaniment show how little we can live without sound, even when we are focusing directly on God. We have become addicted to noise, hooked on it and unable to function without having continual fixes of artificial sound. Unfortunately, noise-peddlers are on every side, only too willing to feed our habit. It is no wonder that our age has been called "the Age of Noise" (Aldous Huxley).

The Role of Silence

The word *noise* comes to us from medieval French and is possibly connected to the Latin word for nausea. We use it mainly in two ways, to refer to the aural effect of vibrations we pick up or to sounds that stand out from their background. In the first case it is virtually equivalent to *sound*, especially intrusive sounds that we would prefer not to hear.

The Bible provides us with instances of unwanted noise. For example, God finds the noise of the people's "songs" (Amos 5:23) and cries (Is 17:12) distasteful. The prophets also call at times for "silence" before the Lord (Hab 2:20), and the wisdom writings encourage the prudent person to "keep silence" (Amos 5:13). Through the psalm writer we are enjoined "to be still, and know that I am God" (Ps 46:10). God encounters Elijah in the desert not through wind, earthquake or fire but in a still, small voice or "a quiet, gentle sound" (1 Kings 19:11-12 NCV). Though the universe will finally pass away with a "loud noise" (2 Pet 3:10), heaven itself, though full of praise to God, has its moments of quiet (Rev 8:1).

Other religious writings also seek to put unwanted noise in its place. In pre-biblical versions of the flood story, it is the noise rather than the immorality of human beings that sets one of the god's teeth on edge. Zen Buddhism has always had a central place for silence, as for example in the encouragement to meditate on the sound of "one hand clapping." A rabbi quoted in the Jewish Mishnah observed, "All my days I have grown up among the sages, and I have found nothing better than silence."

The necessity of silence for listening and relating to God, for gaining self-awareness and insight into others, and for appreciation of the world around us and of life generally has been a regular theme in Christian teaching. Among Christian thinkers, Blaise Pascal declared that we avoid quiet because we are not willing to contemplate our actual state or the divine grandeur around us. T. S. Eliot wrote that in time it is difficult to hear the Word because there is not enough silence for us to discern it. Karl Barth commends the model of the one quiet person who in our distracted and pressured age can help a whole roomful of people to begin finding peace and rhythm in their lives.

The Divine Place of Sound

Yet in the Bible, silence or quiet is never portrayed as an absolute. Some Christian mystics have held that all sound is harmful and that God is essentially silent. Among the earliest proponents of this view, Saint Isaac the Syrian regarded silence as the language of the kingdom of heaven, and Syriac Menander believed that there is nothing better than silence. In early modern times John of the Cross wrote that the Son of God, the Word, existed in "everlasting silence," and a hymn by the Quaker John Greenleaf Whittier speaks of "the silence of eternity interpreted by love."

Yet the creation* is full of what we call "natural sounds," from the simplest and gentlest to the sharpest and most violent. Think of the rustling of leaves, the running of water over rocks, the chirping of a cricket and a sudden clap of thunder. It is not true, as some have said, that unlike humanly engendered noise such sounds are merely punctuation marks, not sentences. The forest and ocean may sometimes be deathly quiet, but generally they hum or sigh with a mosaic of minor noises. God has also given us the capacity to make interesting, satisfying and sometimes ravishing noises. Music* of all kinds, from the popular to the classical, has at its best exhibited these qualities. The sound of laughter* is also generally a delight and, as the psalms frequently remind us, even crying and sobbing have their proper place in the divine scheme of things.

Of course we cannot forget the central place the Bible gives to the Word as the main vehicle of God's revelation.

Though God may hide at times and wear the cloak of silence, speech is integral to the way God relates to us. This is not the repetitive, endless chatter of those who think they are heard for their many words or admired for their rhetorical gifts (*see* Preaching; Speaking). There is nothing mindless, distracting or superfluous in God's communication, only what is thoughtful, centered and appropriate. It has a rhythm of sound and silence, for it is out of silence that wisdom and the timely word are born. As the wisdom writings insist, there is a time to speak and a time to remain silent (Eccles 3:7). But sometimes it is impossible for God's messenger to keep quiet (Jer 4:19), and sometimes God's victory can be announced only with a shout (Josh 6:10).

God is also intensely musical and is depicted in the Bible as the source, author and even performer of music (see Banks). Music played a significant part in the life of Israel and the early church. Some of this was noisy, like the triumphant procession of the ark up to Jerusalem (1 Chron 15:28). In the temple the people were to praise God not just with harps and lyres but with "loud" and "crashing" cymbals (Ps 150:5), not just quietly but with "shouts" of joy (Ps 98:4) and praise (Ps 149:6).

Putting Noise in Its Place

It is true that our tolerance levels vary and even change over the years so far as noise is concerned. Some people appear to be relatively indifferent to noise, some are extremely sensitive to it, and others fall somewhere in between. This can lead to conflicts over the amount and type of noise in the common spaces they occupy. There are also the significantly deaf who can scarcely get enough of whatever noise is available to them. There are no formulas for specifying how much or how little noise is desirable.

But there are certain physiological boundaries we should not cross. Beyond a certain limit, duration and intensity, noise can increase blood pressure and heart rate, slow breathing, change the electrical resistance of the skin, increase skeletomuscular tension and affect the stomach and intestines. Those who listen regularly to music at 120 decibels will only deafen themselves and lose much of their God-given capacity to hear. There is objective evidence that loud industrial, traffic and aircraft noise is harmful and sometimes physically and psychologically injurious.

The solution to this lies partly in our own hands. Sometimes it is good to fast from certain kinds of noise for a while all the better to hear other sounds that we often miss, above all the sound of God's voice. From time to time this is something the whole family* can engage in. But the solution also lies partly in the hands of others. Those with responsibility for the environment of our workplaces* and cities should ensure that levels are compatible with employees' capacities. Sometimes a collective response can reduce the amount of noise in a street or neighborhood, office or factory. Most of us have a need for periods of withdrawal into an informal or formal retreat setting to balance the amount of noise we have to cope with most of the time. Yet we should also seek to see God's imprint and hear God's voice in and through the range of sounds that fill our days: in most cases God is not completely absent from them and may even be saying something through them.

When all is said and done, there is too much noise in the world today—in our cities, in our homes,* in our meetings and in our prayers—even in our churches and Christian organizations. Holding noise at bay or finding a place of quiet helps clear space to hear God and others more clearly and respond to both more deeply. Sometimes there is nothing more eloquent and communicative than a husband and wife sitting or walking in silence, experiencing harmony with one another and their surroundings. At such times "silence is golden," as the proverb runs, a kind of "holy uselessness" that is resonant with the most wonderful benefits. As John Climacus wrote in *The Ladder of Divine Ascent:* "Intelligent silence is the mother of prayer, freedom from bondage, custodian of zeal, a guard on our thoughts . . . the opponent of dogmatism, a growth of knowledge, hidden progress, the secret journey upward" (quoted in Allison).

See also SPIRITUAL DISCIPLINES.

References and Resources

D. C. Allison Jr., *The Silence of Angels* (Valley Forge, Penn.: Trinity Press International, 1995); R. Banks, *God the Worker: Journeys into the Mind, Will and Imagination of God* (Valley Forge, Penn.: Judson, 1994); K. D. Kryter, *The Effects of Noise on Man* (New York: Academic, 1970).

Robert Banks

NONDENOMINATIONAL

The idea of nondenominationalism appeals to rugged individualism, the "I can do anything by myself" mentality that pushes settlers, explorers and entrepreneurs. Indeed, nondenominationalism in its purest form seems to appeal to the entrepreneur and the independent person who do not appreciate the confines of seemingly less-than-dynamic denominational bureaucracy, thinking and control.

The Meaning of Nondenominational

Nondenominational is a label that can be attached to both churches* and parachurch organizations.* Both these types of ecclesiastical organizations can be unaffiliated with any larger formal expression of their particular organization's purpose, values and mission. Thus, such well-known parachurch organizations as Young Life, Youth for Christ, Youth with a Mission, Campus Crusade for Christ, InterVarsity Christian Fellowship and others are not attached to any denomination. They serve interdenominationally and cross-denominationally. There are a number of Christian elementary and secondary schools, colleges, Bible colleges and theological seminaries that have the same unaffiliated character. Schools like Wheaton College, Gordon College, Westmont College, Moody Bible Institute and seminaries such as Yale Divinity School, Harvard Divinity School, Gordon-Conwell Theological Seminary, Dallas Theological Seminary and Fuller Theological Seminary all are intentionally nondenominational. The usual preference in many of these organizations is to call themselves multidenominational or interdenominational. Regent College in Vancouver, British Columbia, has adopted the term *transdenominational.* One must note that many so-called denominational colleges and seminaries owe their financial existence to the fact that a great number of their students come from outside of the sponsoring denomination.

Many presidents of schools and seminaries like to downplay their independence. They will cite the number of denominations represented in their school and the number of graduates serving in denominational settings. The truth, however, is that no matter how many of their students come from denominational backgrounds, the schools themselves do not answer to any of those external ecclesiastical authorities. They are quite independent of any denominational hierarchy. To be sure, each school has its own internal hierarchy, but that is the extent of such a hierarchy. Except as required by law and accrediting agencies, they answer to no one outside of the school's formal structures.

Local churches are also found in the nondenominational camp. This means that they are unaffiliated with any sort of denomination. They are often called *independent* or *unaligned* or *unaffiliated.* Whatever the adjective, the fact remains that these churches, like their nondenominational schools, are unattached to any other ecclesiastical authority. They are independent of all external ecclesiastical law and regulations, and, more importantly, they are laws and regulations to themselves alone. Each church is its own hierarchy: pastor and/or official board and church congregation. These churches report to no one outside of their own local structure, although some churches do belong to more or less loosely organized fellowships of likeminded churches and parachurch organizations.

Some Valued Characteristics

Nondenominationalists have several shared characteristics. First, they are independent and unaffiliated with external, controlling, governing bodies. They value the independence that such an unaligned relationship provides. They like the idea that their own official board sets policies, governs and administers without interference from some office at central headquarters. They also like the idea that whatever funds they raise will all go to the individual organization; no assessment is paid to the central office. They value highly their independence.

Second, their independence can allow for faster decision-making and changes when these are called for. Reports do not have to be sent to headquarters to be studied, analyzed and questioned by people who are far removed from the nitty-gritty of the local situation. Thus, there is freedom to move and act as Spirit-directed people and not be hedged in by the countless committees,* chairpeople, books of order, rules and regulations that a denomination often imposes upon its members. This freedom to act quickly is relished by nondenominational people.

Third, nondenominational pastors and leaders can move from one church or parachurch organization and even, on certain occasions, into and out of denominational organizations without the hassle of bureaucratic hurdles. Nondenominational leaders are free to be led by the Spirit rather than depend on the machinations of organizational leadership and the entangled webs of their bureaucracies.

Therefore, the major characteristic of nondenominationalism is freedom: freedom from external organizational restraints and perceived impediments to desired goals and program developments.

Some Common Difficulties
There are also some major difficulties with nondenominationalism. One is that the very independence that is so welcomed can lead to isolation from fellowship.* Leaders, including pastors, churches and parachurch organizations, can exist in a state of more or less isolation, separated from many of their Christian brothers and sisters outside of their particular organization. Before one decides to become a committed nondenominationalist, one must count the cost of being more or less alone through much of one's life of ministry.

Second, nondenominationalism can produce a mentality that is closed to further input that differs from one's own preconceived ideas. Nondenominationalists can fall into the trap that they alone have truth and know how best to minister. This mentality cuts off fellowship and critical interaction with those who differ

even a little from them and makes nondenominationalists interact only with themselves. The richness of the body of Christ is neglected because of the isolation from the broader contacts that a denomination can provide. Nondenominationalists need to be aware of and take steps to avoid being closed-minded and isolated.

Third, paid leaders—for example, pastors, presidents of organizations and other staff—are often neglected when it comes to salary, health benefits, vacation time, study leave, outside speaking engagements, retirement and other such financial matters. Denominations usually have at least minimum criteria regarding these business items. Nondenominational organizations do what is right in their own eyes. All the problems, and the blessings, of the book of Judges come to the forefront here. Some nondenominational organizations take very good care of their employed staff. Other organizations seek to maximize the work and minimize the remuneration. Sometimes difficult questions have to be asked to ascertain how a nondenominational organization views its paid leaders and staff.

Fourth, nondenominational organizations usually are lax in defining how to terminate a person from the paid staff (*see* Firing). Sometimes a pastor will find that he or she has been fired with just a few weeks' or sometimes just a few minutes' notice! Protection from the vicissitudes of the assembled corporation is necessary before a person becomes a member of such an organization.

With these four caveats in mind, the independent, entrepreneurial, freedom-loving person can join a nondenominational organization and make a major impact for Christ and his kingdom.

See also DENOMINATIONS; NETWORKING; ORGANIZATION; STRUCTURES, CHURCH.

John M. Dettoni

O

OFFICE POLITICS

The term *office politics* generally is seen as derogatory. Yet within any organization where numbers of people interact daily, there are degrees of office politics ranging from the simple and accommodating to the complex and highly destructive.

Levels of Office Politics
Office politics in its simplest form is politic, that is, prudent or expedient, to "fit" in with one's organization. It makes sense for a person to follow, without any objective of advancement, the customs and mores of the organization as long as his or her personal conscience is not subverted. For example, if a person's coworkers dress modestly, maintain a neat workplace and respect the privacy of others, it is not politic to wear loud clothes, be a slob at one's desk and constantly interrupt the work of others with small talk (*see* Dress Code, Workplace). If the coworkers maintain a voluntary fund in order to buy flowers for those who are sick or have lost loved ones, it is not politic to refuse to contribute. More than likely a worker can fulfill his or her job responsibilities and receive no adverse performance reviews without fitting in with the prevailing office mores. But everyday operations seem to go better in the workplace if everyone accepts the local customs.

As a worker contemplates advancement within the organization, however, the level of office politics is raised, for he or she must go beyond just fitting in. For example, if my goal were to advance, I would consider the person responsible for recommending my raises or my promotion, for I would need to be politic with that person. Furthermore, in simple innocence, I would make certain my supervisor is aware of my work product. I would turn to that person for help when I have a problem because I need to have him or her care about the quality of my work. At this political level, I am not trying to gain any special favors at the expense of others, but I would just want to make certain my work is recognized at least as fully as my coworkers.

I move to the next level of office politics when I strive to be known and recognized beyond the level of my immediate supervisor. How does upper management dress? That's the way I would dress. What seems to be the favorite sport of higher management? If it is golf, I would learn golf. If it is tennis, that would be for me. Which of the next higher managers is the boss of my immediate supervisor? Does he or she have a favorite charity? I would work for it. Does he or she belong to a church? I would join there and hope we could serve on the same committee. Does he or she regularly go to a certain sporting event or theater or orchestra? I would be there too. If I played my cards right, my supervisor's boss would comment on what a fine, up-and-coming employee I seem to be, and in turn my supervisor would take more interest in me, giving me special attention.

Have I reached the derogatory level of office politics yet? Perhaps, but what is wrong with what I have done? Consider an example from the Bible. A bit of office politics crops up in the New Testament when the mother of James and John asked Jesus to declare that one of her sons would sit on his right hand and one on his left in his kingdom (Mt 20:20-21). The request had nothing to do with superior performance or ability. It was purely a request for special treatment. Jesus chided the brothers and said such a request was not his to grant. The other ten disciples became angry with James and John. So Jesus called them together and told them that "whoever wants to become great among you must be your servant" (Mk 10:43).

As a worker advances into management in an organization, he or she begins to develop networks or alliances of supportive people in other departments or locations. The network is helpful in passing along information that relates to further opportunities for career advancement. The alliances are helpful in advancing the worker's projects or assignments. At this point office politics comes into full bloom. A helpful way of approaching and assessing this level of office politics is to consider an example.

A Focal Case

Let's assume that you, as a department manager, have come up with an idea for a new product line that you are convinced will be highly profitable to the company. Or, if you are in a human-service agency, let's assume you have an idea for expansion into a new field of services that you are convinced will vastly expand the importance of your agency in the community. Or, if you are in a hospital or university or financial services organiza-

tion, let's assume you have a plan for a new and highly sophisticated information system that will increase efficiency and reduce costs dramatically. You take your idea to your senior vice president, and he is immediately sold on it. He wants to back it because he is convinced it will benefit the organization just as you envision and because he sees another benefit—a personal one. If the idea succeeds, he will get the credit for sponsoring it, and that may put him in line for the president's job in two years. He is in competition with other senior vice presidents, and this project may label him as the clear choice. So he gives you his full support.

As you develop the plan, you talk to others in your network and enlist their support. You have close contacts in marketing, treasury, human resources, production, legal, public relations and other departments. Some of the department heads like your idea and can see possible benefits to them or their careers if it succeeds. There is one complication: your project will tax the full financial resources of the organization. If the project fails, the organization will be in serious trouble. Meanwhile other ideas will get little attention because of the limited resources.

Another senior vice president hears of the plan and is convinced it is a bad one. She is also aware that your boss may use the plan as a vehicle to becoming president. Through her own network and alliances, she mounts a campaign to stop your plan. She, too, has contacts in all the departments you do, and so the political battle begins. Each side moves ahead with its plan to sell the board of directors on its viewpoint. The board must decide. Your senior vice president and others he has enlisted lobby the chief executive officer (CEO). The other side does the same. Meanwhile the networks are working. Members of the board are contacted discreetly. Casual contacts at country clubs or community events provide an opportunity for more discreet campaigning. Secretaries are enlisted to learn what they can from secretaries on the opposing side. You learn of some of the arguments of the opposing side and draw up ways to refute them. Both sides seem perfectly willing to discredit individuals on the opposing side who have made mistakes in the past. All this and the CEO has not even been formally presented with the plan.

The day comes, and your side is there with all the guns it can muster. A team makes an outstanding case for your idea. The chair of the board, who appears very impressed and praises everyone highly, wants to hear from those opposing the idea and indicates the board will need a few days to decide. You are disappointed, but what can you do?

Three days later the CEO calls a meeting of the senior staff. You are also invited. You are on cloud nine as everyone gathers in the boardroom. He quickly gets to the point and gives three reasons why the board has reluctantly decided to turn down your proposal. The vote was seven to six. You are stunned. So is your boss. As you leave the meeting, everyone is convinced that the other side did a better job of political maneuvering. Only one more board member voting for your side would have made the difference.

The fallout of the battle is felt for years after. Workers are angry and from time to time try to get even. Was the decision based on the merits and appropriate pressing of the idea, or was it simply a case of vicious office politics? It depends on whom you ask. Sometimes an innocent, good-willed initiative becomes polluted by the self-interest of others. The proposal in this example got into trouble when people let the idea of how to help the company take second place to the fight for personal political power.

Remember Jesus' admonition that "whoever wants to become great among you must be your servant" (Mk 10:43).

Office politics can be innocent and harmless and can even accomplish very good things for an organization as long as people put the welfare of others ahead of their own. We call such actions *statesmanship*. Statesmanship is the high road of working within an organization. Office power struggles are the low road.

See also GOSSIP; MANAGEMENT; NETWORKING; POLITICS; PROMOTION.

William E. Diehl

ORGANIZATION

Everyday life is bound up in organizational life. We work* for business corporations, belong to clubs,* become members* of churches,* sit on committees,* link with political parties, experience citizenship,* struggle with bureaucracy, submit to government, attend colleges and schools, participate in unions,* join professional* societies and get health care through complex systems.* Most of our waking hours are spent in an organizational context.

God, it is often thought, is interested only in people, not in organizations. In contrast, the Bible reveals a God who deals with nations and people groups, who created and upholds a structured, ordered context in which humankind can thrive (Gen 1—2; Col 1:15-17). God has a purpose for the largest corporations, such as General Motors, and the smallest club. In this article we will develop a theology of institutional life, which will consider how organizations function, the problems we encounter (organizational sickness and sin) and some directions for seeking organizational holiness (for specific challenges, *see* Organizational Culture and Change; Organizational Values).

Can Anything Good Come from an Organization?

An *organization* is a collection of people or entities formed into a whole composed of interdependent parts to accomplish a purpose. Organizations are characterized by regularized ways of operating (rules), repetitiveness in procedures (traditions), permanence (institutionalization), a distinctive milieu (culture*), patterns of influence (power*) and a governance structure (authority). No good idea in history has made a substantial impact on society* without becoming incarnated in institutions and organizations. Even Francis of Assisi would have been an isolated saint with a limited influence had he not founded the Franciscan order.

Organizations are essentially created for our good. They serve to coordinate people and resources to accomplish a mission, and they often provide a context for meaningful work that cannot be done by individuals or informed groups. Organizations can be healing, energizing and life-giving. They can also be hurtful, draining and destructive. The process of becoming organized does have risks; institutions are by nature intractable and resistant to change. In the worst of cases organizations can become demonic and idolatrous. This downside of organizational life has a theological explanation: organizations, including the organizational life of the church, participate in the fallenness of all structures in this world.

It is often said that the church is an organism and *not* an organization. In fact, it is both. As an organism the church is a living entity, pulsating with the life of God's Spirit; it is the body of Christ, the family of God, the covenant community. But the church is also an organization—ordered in a structured life with office-holders, patterns of accountability and decision-making, traditions, power structures and an implicit or explicit organizational mission. In the short run the church can be the most influential organization in society, and in some countries it has been or still is. In the long run the church will outlast all other organizations and be consummated in the heavenly Jerusalem—a city-church-state-environment—though this can only be seen with the eye of faith.

The most apparently influential organization in the modern world is the business corporation. Since it is so adaptive, many thinkers today regard business as potentially the most creative force on earth for dealing with global issues: "The churches, governments, and our learning institutions . . . have become too cumbersome for today's modern pace, where constant change is the norm" (Renesch, p 11). Edward Simon, president of Herman Miller, says that "business is the only institution that has a chance, as far as I can see, to fundamentally improve the injustice that exists in the world" (quoted in Senge, p. 5). In a prophetic book edited by John Renesch, twelve leading thinkers explain what business is becoming. (1) The company is a community, not merely a corporation; it is a system for being, not merely a system for production and profit. (2) The new image of the manager is that of a spiritual elder caring for the souls of the employees. (3) Employees are members of the body working interdependently for the common good. (4) While mission statements, vision, goals and values will continue to *push* a company, a "higher purpose" (parallel to the "Higher Power" made popular by Alcoholics Anonymous) will *pull* a company forward. (5) The corporation is an equipping* (learning) organization that provides an environment for every-member service (ministry*) so that each person will become more human, more creative and more integrated with the higher purpose. Many firms have already progressed in these directions.

Critical to this thinking is the increased awareness of the connectedness and wholeness of everything, in other words, a systems worldview.* Instead of dog-eat-dog competition,* people are cultivating interdependence and cooperation: "Although we may compete, we are nevertheless each part of a unity, so that no one 'wins' unless we all do" (Harman, quoted in Renesch, p. 15). The model system is the body of Christ, in which "the eye cannot say to the hand, 'I don't need you!'" (1 Cor 12:21). But the theoretical development of systems thinking came first from observing other living organisms.

Understanding Organizations as Systems

As early as the mid-1920s Ludwig von Bertalanffy, a practicing biologist, began to understand living organisms in a systems way (p. 12). He recognized that biological organisms could not be adequately understood by the classical Newtonian method, which regarded each object as a collection of distinct and disconnected parts. Instead of seeing the whole as the sum of the parts, he said we should see the whole as more than its parts (Bertalanffy, p. 31). This means that unity in an organism is a complex whole, an idea promoted centuries before by Aristotle.

Other concepts implicit in systems thinking are homeostasis (the tendency of any organization to return to the tried and true, like the keel of a sailboat), isomorphism (the structural similarity of fields or systems that may be intrinsically different but behave the same way) and synergy (the mutual reinforcement that comes by the total effect of two or more elements in a system or organization). Family systems* theory, developed in the 1950s, works with such concepts as fusion and differentiation (the need to be both

"we" and "me") and intergenerational transmission (the way problems and blessings* are handed down generation after generation in both families and churches). As I show elsewhere (Collins and Stevens, chap. 6), there is substantial biblical congruency with this way of thinking, though one needs to be critically aware of the presuppositions of some of the more radical systems thinkers (Collins and Stevens, epilogue).

As a new way of thinking about reality, systems theory has recently been applied to a host of other fields, including transportation systems, national financial planning, outer space exploration, leadership, management and large complex organizations. Ministers of finance are now painfully aware that the economic health of their country cannot be achieved by tinkering with only one factor, such as the prime lending rate for banks, but is the result of many complex factors, most of which cannot be controlled. Along with its applications to family therapy and family ministry, systems theory has recently been applied to pastoral care* and leadership* in the church (Friedman; Pattison). So systems thinking helps us understand how organizations work; it also helps us grasp what goes wrong with organizations.

The Sick Organization

Symptoms of disease in an organization are similar to those observed in unhealthy individuals. Organizations can be directionless, weak, manipulative and addictive. Some organizations "eat people up," consuming their vitality rather than energizing them. When leaders in an organization burn out, it is often a systemic problem: an overfunctioning leader is in a codependent relationship with underfunctioning members who are adapting to his or her "all-competence." While all might complain about the status quo, they have usually contracted (often unconsciously) to keep it that way.

Some businesses, corporations and organizations can become all-consuming alternatives to family,* church and neighborhood.* Taken to an extreme, an organization can become demonic, turning people away from the love of God and leading to paralyzing and deadening lifestyles. The organization has become an alternative to the kingdom of God, that yeast that leavens everything in everyday life.

The addictive organization is an extreme example of what can go wrong. While we become increasingly aware of the addictions in our society—sex, money, chemical substances, power and romance—we should also be willing to ask hard questions about the addictive functioning of organizations. The first level of addiction occurs when an addict is in a key position. If the president or pastor is addicted to work or power, the members will never be able to do enough to please him or her, but they will keep trying (*see* Drivenness). The second level of addiction occurs when the organization supports addicts—perhaps alcoholics or workaholics—in their addictive functioning as an *enabler*. Anne Wilson Schaef gives an all-too-common example of a church that had an alcoholic in a key position: the church spent an inordinate amount of energy trying not to notice that the person was doing a poor job on an important committee (Schaef, p. 118). The same thing happens among old-boy networks in clubs and businesses. The third level is organizational addiction—when the organization itself provides the fix. People who look to the organization to be the family they never had are setting themselves up for disillusionment. Some people working for high-tech, high-demand firms feel they are not working for a corporation but more for a religious order. In such cases

the mission of the organization (even if it is the church) has become too important. The fourth level of organizational addiction is when the organization itself functions as an addict. "In these cases," notes Schaef, "there is an incongruity between what the organization says its mission is and what it actually does" in personnel practices, emphasis on control and how it interprets and works with power (p. 18).

The Sinful Organization

Are the organizations described above sick or sinful? Can we speak of organizational sin and repentance, organizational conversion? The analogy between individuals and organizations applies once again. Organizational illness predisposes to sin; organizational sin makes the organization and its members sick.

A theology of organizational life includes two complementary ingredients. First, God created a structured organized life as a context for human beings to thrive. Second, God gave humankind the capacity and mandate to craft organizations as part of the cultural mandate (Gen 1:26-28). Simply put, organizations were intended to exist to serve God and God's purposes in the world in the three ways human beings were to express their calling*: (1) building communion with God, (2) building community with people and (3) developing their earth's potential through cocreativity with God (*see* Laity; Ministry). The service to be rendered by the human enterprise was symbolized in the Old Testament by what is sometimes called the threefold office of prophets, priests and princes. The prophets discerned and brought justice; the priests taught and brought peace; the princes governed and brought service* to the world.

Tragically all organizations have fallen, both the God-ordained institutions of state, church, family and marriage* and the humanly made organizations of clubs, workplaces* and all kinds of human enterprises. Individual sin in Genesis 3 leads to systemic evil, a complex of negativity that resists God's purposes in the world. Organizations have become part of the principalities and powers,* which were created good but have now become tyrannical, colonized by Satan and intractable. The organization of the tower of Babel (Gen 11) is a case in point. It is the inversion of the three God-given purposes for an organization: building a name for themselves instead of cultivating communion with God; forging a homogeneous unity of people instead of building a richly diverse community; resisting God's creative and cultural mandate by putting their energies into a single enterprise glorifying human beings and skills.

Sinful organizations are autonomous, inflexible to God's leading and self-serving. Separated from God, organizations and their memberships tend to become arrogant and take on a life of their own. This is a danger in many major corporations and governments and even in churches. Is redemption possible? Does conversion apply to organizations and not just to people? What would a redeemed organization look like? (To explore the extent to which redemption of the visible and invisible structures of life has been accomplished by Christ, *see* Principalities and Powers. To consider the ways of encountering fallen structures, *see* Structures.)

The Virtuous Organization

A virtuous organization is not merely a collection of Christians working for the same business, not-for-profit society or church. It is much more. Holiness has to do with values, the way people are treated, relationships, the way power is used organizationally and the ultimate purpose of the organization. Ironically, a group of Christians may craft an unholy organization that is self-serving and destructive to people, while a group of nonbelievers may form an organization that, unknown to them, accords with God's purposes. The following are ways in which holiness is expressed organizationally, all of them based on a biblical theology.

Trusteeship. The organization has a purpose that is larger than its own self-interest and fulfills some aspect of God's threefold call in the human vocation: communion with God, community building and cocreativity. Prophetic business thinkers today speak of this as a higher purpose that *pulls* the organization rather than as a mission statement that *pushes* or *drives* it. The virtuous organization has a sacred trust handed to it, often through the vision of its founder though ultimately from God, again usually unknown to the people working for it. Critical to this way of thinking is developing trusteeship—being stewards of a vision—rather than gaining ownership (*see* Ownership). Richard Broholm has expressed the difference this way: ownership appeals to self-interest and captures an organization for the agendas of the members ("This is *my* mission") while trusteeship appeals to a sense of calling* or vocation ("This is our mission, which we have been given").

Community. The virtuous organization is concerned to build, to cultivate a rich, healthy interdependency of all the people involved: administrators and workers, employees and customers, shareholders and staff, students and faculty, caregivers and clients. All levels of personnel in the organization from the sweepers to the CEO are treated with equal dignity. People are not considered as human resources to be manipulated and used but as God-imaging creatures with inestimable value. Difference is not feared but welcomed as contributing to a rich social unity of personalities, gifts and talents. In theological terms the goal is Pentecost (the rich, interdependent unity of many peoples) rather than Babel (a bland, homogenous uniformity).

Service. The ultimate goal of the organization is to serve. Service takes us to the heart of ministry in the world, as attested by the four servant songs in Isaiah (Is 42:1-9; 49:1-6; 50:4-9; 52:13—53:12) and the words of Jesus (Mt 20:26-27). If it is a business, the purpose is not primarily making a financial profit but adding value to the customers, though it is value for which customers will normally pay a fee. The organization serves, and so do its members. Since the Greek word for *service* is the same as that for *ministry,* Christians in the organization may regard themselves as those in full-time Christian ministry.

Equipping and learning. Every human interaction and every contact with the structures of the organization are regarded as an opportunity for equipping (Eph 4:11-12)—bringing the best out of people, drawing out gifts and talents* and assisting people to become mature. The CEO and those beside her regard themselves as primarily equippers rather than do-it-yourself leaders. They equip people and the culture in their time allocation, attitudes to control and power, focus of time investment, commitment to team building and willingness to work with people developmentally. In line with this, the challenges and problems of the organization are addressed primarily in a conceptual and theological manner rather than with programmatic, expedient answers. It is, as Peter Senge expounds, a learning organization.

Values. The organizational values* foundational to the company are shaped by biblical and theological realities: faith, hope and love. This frequently repeated triad of virtues (1 Cor 13:13; 1 Thess 1:3) can be translated into values for both persons and structures. (1) *Faith* is seeing and trusting the invisible as well as the visible potential of each and every human being and every organizational situation. (2) *Hope* is responding to the gains and losses of the present in the confidence of a future worth laboring towards—confidence and courage in relationships and organizationally. (3) *Love** is relating unconditionally to people to meet their real needs, caring unconditionally for imperfect people, communicating their worth and value independently of their performance. Love also means showing caring loyalty to the culture, structures and values of the organizational system.

Soul. The employees or members are gently nudged in the direction of living and working by ultimate sources—through inspiration that renews, rather than by principles that function as laws to direct and restrain. The organization invites and evokes faith. Those on a spiritual journey are invited to consider discipleship* to Jesus not only by sensitive and appropriate verbal witness of those who are believers but by the aroma of Christ in the structures and organizational culture.*

As noted before, many Christian organizations are not really Christian in terms of trusteeship, community, service, equipping, values and soul. Some secular organizations seem closer to this goal. The challenge of making organizational change in these directions is a matter for separate consideration (*see* Organizational Culture and Change). What should be apparent is that organizational life itself is a spiritual discipline.* Spirituality is not something imposed on an organization through religious practices or language; it is implicit in the challenge of working together for the commonwealth (the common good). Organizational life invites faith, appeals to the soul. It also reveals systemic sin, and it cries out for systemic redemption. The issues of competition, creativity, cooperation and cocreativity invite people in organizations to engage in a process of transformation that moves from the person to the organization and eventually from the transformation of organizations to the transformation of the world. As with all other human enterprises, organizational life will experience only partial redemption in this life and must wait for the inauguration of the new heaven and new earth.

See also ORGANIZATIONAL CULTURE AND CHANGE; ORGANIZATIONAL VALUES; POWER; POWER, WORKPLACE; PRINCIPALITIES AND POWERS; STRUCTURES; SYSTEM.

References and Resources
R. Anderson, *Minding God's Business* (Grand Rapids: Eerdmans, 1986); L. von Bertalanffy, *Perspectives on General System Theory: Scientific-Philosophical Studies* (New York: Braziller, 1975); M. Bowen and M. Kerr, *Family Evaluation: An Approach Based on Bowen Theory* (New York: Norton, 1988); P. Collins and R. P. Stevens, *The Equipping Pastor: A Systems Approach to Empowering the People of God* (Washington, D.C.: Alban Institute, 1993); E. H. Friedman, *Generation to Generation: Family Process in Church and Synagogue* (New York: Guilford, 1985); M. E. Pattison, *Pastor and People—A Systems Approach* (Philadelphia: Fortress, 1977); J. Renesch, ed., *New Traditions in Business: Spirit and Leadership in the Twenty-first Century* (San Francisco: Berrett-Koehler, 1992); A. W. Schaef, "Is the Church an Addictive Organization?" *Christian Century* 107, no. 1 (1990) 18-21; A. W. Schaef and D. Fassel, *The Addictive Organization* (San Francisco: Harper & Row, 1988); P. M. Senge, *The Fifth Discipline: The Art and Practice of the Learning Organization* (New York: Doubleday, 1990).

R. Paul Stevens

ORGANIZATIONAL CULTURE AND CHANGE

Culture* is a dimension not only in the life of countries and ethnic groups but also in organizations.* Every organization has a corporate "feeling" or environment that communicates to new and old members what is important and what is permitted. This is true of businesses, small groups,* clubs,* churches,* nonprofit and parachurch organizations.* The minute a person walks into the meeting room, the store, the office or the sanctuary, he or she picks up a nonverbal message that is more powerful than such mottoes as "The customer is number one"; "We exist to give extraordinary service"; "This is a friendly, family church." Culture turns out to be profoundly influential in determining behavior, expressing values* and enabling or preventing change.

Understanding Organizational Culture
People are sometimes frustrated, without understanding why, in trying to bring about change in an organization. Try to introduce women into an all-male kayaking club, and one encounters almost irresistible forces, none of which is rationally expressed or constitutionally codified. Further, some successful changes get reversed in a few months because they were not congruent with the culture of the organization; other changes are made easily for reasons that are not apparent unless one understands the invisible but all-pervasive impact of organizational environment. To change the culture itself is possibly the most substantial change that can be made. It has a multiple impact on everything else. A man in a museum looking at the colossal skeleton of a dinosaur that once triumphantly roamed the earth turned to the woman beside him and asked, "What happened? Why did they die out?" She said, "The climate changed."

Motivation is primarily related to the culture. We draw motivation out of people in a healthy, life-giving organization. It is inspired, not compelled. Motivation is a result of a process in a group or system and is not just generated exclusively from within the individual. So motivation is only marginally increased by trying to get *people* motivated through incentives or threats. It needs to be considered culturally and systemically (*see* System).

The classic study on organizational culture is Edgar H. Schein's *Organizational Culture and Leadership.* His central thesis is that much of what is mysterious about leadership becomes clearer "if we . . . link leadership specifically to creating and changing culture" (Schein, p. xi). According to Schein, culture includes each of the following but is deeper than any one of them: (1) the observed behavioral regularities in a group (for example, really good employees show up for work fifteen minutes early); (2) the dominant values of the group (for example, church attendance is the ultimate expression of spirituality in a local church); (3) the rules or "ropes" of the group (for example, the usual way to climb the hierarchy is to engage in leisure-time diversions with your superior); and (4) the feeling or climate that is conveyed (for example, while not prohibited, it is also not acceptable to bring forward negative comments in staff meetings). Schein says that culture concerns the underlying assumptions and beliefs that are shared by members of the organization and often operate unconsciously (p. 6).

The factors at work in an organizational culture can be pictured as three concentric circles. On the outside are the symbols, artifacts and visible signs of the culture, which are often incarnated in logos, mottoes, the appearance of a building, the way people dress and the titles by which people are addressed. The middle circle represents the values that underlie the more visible processes (*see* comments on faith, hope and love in Organizational Values). Values are simply what is cherished by the organization. Often these are unexpressed and unconscious. Sometimes the stated values are incongruent with the real values that inform the culture. For example, a business may claim that it cherishes strong family life for its employees but actually requires the sacrifice of family for the corporation. The smallest circle (and the least visible) represents the beliefs that inform the values. For example, a church may believe that women should be under men in a hierarchical arrangement. That belief will fundamentally affect the values and visible "artifacts" of the congregation. Beliefs are expressed in values, and values are expressed in symbols, cues and visible patterns of behavior.

Forming the Organizational Culture
In most organizations, culture is not formed overnight but through a long process. In the church, culture often originates with the founding pastor, who projects his or her own vision of what is right and valued and how people are to be treated. In a business it is often the founding president. In a college it is the founding principal. One element of the mysterious quality of leadership* called *charisma* is how it enables a leader to embed his or her fundamental assumptions into the organization or group. This is done by whom the leader pays attention to, how the leader reacts to critical situations, whether the leader intentionally coaches other leaders, what criteria the leader uses for praising and rewarding others and on what basis the leader recruits or rejects other leaders.

Years before I understood anything about culture, I observed that each organization has something like a genetic code embedded at the time of conception that determines most of what it will become. The future of a person is in large measure the unraveling of his or her genetic code. In organizations the founding moment, person and principles are likewise exceedingly important. An organization that starts with certain assumptions about the nature of the community, its style of leadership and mission in society will find it very difficult, though not impossible, to change its culture later.

As the group evolves, members take on the founder's assumptions, usually unconsciously. Some groups never allow their founder to die or leave, no matter how many successors have come and gone. Cultures tend to incarnate not only the strengths of founders but also their weaknesses. An organization would be helped if it could have a once-and-for-all funeral service for its founder! But whoever suggests this will often be resisted by the culture. In fact, the opposite approach is usually more fruitful: finding out everything we can about the contribution our predecessors have made and appreciating their gifts to the organization. One thing is certain: founders are influential. Schein's work is extremely helpful in elaborating what happens at various stages in a group's history (p. 191) and the importance of stories (about the "good old days") in transmitting the culture of a group (p. 241).

Reflecting Theologically on Culture
Whether in a church or a business, the leader of an organization is in some sense the "minister of culture." Another way of expressing this is to think of being an environmental engineer—a person who cultivates an organization's culture so that the people in the organization will thrive. This task is implicit in the broad vocation of being human beings through which we are called to be culture and world makers (Gen 1:26-28). God created the first culture* in fashioning the sanctuary-garden for Adam and Eve, a garden with boundaries, structures, limits, challenges, work to do and

pleasures to enjoy. The first human culture was a sabbath* culture. There was a threefold harmony of God, humankind and creation. But once human beings sinned, they created cultures that would not bring rest to people or the earth.

The men and women of Babel (Gen 11:1-11) wanted to create a monolithic, homogenous culture, and God judged that. Imagine what would have happened if that arrogant, self-serving and total-uniformity culture had dominated the human enterprise for thousands of years! In place of Babel God crafted a colorful, pluralistic* culture at Pentecost through which those from many languages and peoples heard the wonderful works of God in their own languages (Acts 2:8). What God wants on earth is a rich social unity that thrives on diversity.

In passing, we may note that the Old Testament gives us a few hints of God's grace in secular or pagan organizations. The culture of the Egyptian prison equipped Joseph to emerge as its leader (Gen 39:20-23). As cupbearer to the pagan king Artaxerxes, Nehemiah was able to express his concern over the state of Jerusalem and be empowered to return to rebuild the walls (Neh 2). God was at work in both. Daniel was skilled in the culture of the Persians and in that context was able to play a seminal role in the destiny of his people (Dan 1—6).

In the New Testament Paul was continually engineering culture. His great lifelong vision was to create under God a church culture that embraced Jews and Gentiles as equal heirs, members and partners in Christ. His grasp of the gospel meant that Jews did not become Gentiles in Christ, nor did Gentiles become Jews. Rather both were incorporated into a "new humanity" (Eph 2:15 NRSV) that transcended these profound distinctions without obliterating the differences. The same was true of men and women, slave and free. Central to Paul's

715

ministry was a passion inspired by the gospel: God's community on earth must be richly diverse but, at the same time, must treat all members as equal (2 Cor 8:14). We can only speculate to what extent this carried over into his tentmaking business in which he was essentially self-employed, though often working side by side with that marvelous tentmaking* couple Aquila and Priscilla.

The final cultural image in the Bible is the most empowering. In the new heaven and the new earth (Rev 21—22) every person's contribution is evoked in the fulfillment of the priesthood of all believers (Rev 1:6). Every nation, tongue and tribe is preserved rather than merged into one homogenous uniformity. Our future in Christ is to become not angels but full human beings in our resurrection bodies as we work and play in this fulfilled sabbath—the threefold harmony of God, humankind and creation. Even the kings of the earth bring their wealth and gifts into the holy city (Rev 21:24). All human creativity finds perfect fulfillment, and every tear of frustration is wiped away (Rev 7:17). What a response this should evoke! Keeping heaven in view turns out to be the most practical thing on earth.

Making Organizational Change

We are not in heaven yet. Indeed, all human organizations are approximations. Human organizations have fallen and have been captivated by the principalities and powers.* These powers have been unmasked and disarmed by Christ (Col 2:15), but the best we can hope for in this life is substantial, not complete, redemption. Gaining that—and it is as part of our public discipleship—involves organizational change. Organizational change involves culture. And changing the culture is difficult. How difficult change is!

A cultural approach to change. Chang-

ing the artifacts—to use Schein's phrase—might involve moving the Sunday service to the church hall, where the chairs can be arranged in circles to increase participation, or having a staff meeting every Monday to improve communication. But unless the fundamental assumptions of the organization are understood, cultivated and gradually changed, such equipping* initiatives may be as effective as rearranging the deck chairs on the *Titanic* when the ship is going down. When the leader and the culture collide, the culture will probably win!

Schein's research shows, however, that culture-change mechanisms are at work in every stage of a group's history—birth, midlife and maturity (which he calls maturity and/or stagnation, decline and/or rebirth; p. 270). He also shows that change becomes increasingly more difficult as a group becomes more established. While all change is motivated and does not happen randomly, "many changes do not go in the direction that the motivated persons wanted them to go" (Schein, pp. 300-301) because they were unaware of other forces in the culture that were simultaneously acting. So being the leader of this process is complex indeed.

Several strategies are useful here. First, understand the culture before you try to change anything. Give the culture its due. It influences everything. Second, recognize that the culture cannot be manipulated. While you can manage and control many parts of the environment of an organization (the president keeps her office door open all the time), the culture itself with its taken-for-granted underlying assumptions cannot be manipulated. Third, good leadership articulates and reinforces the culture, especially those parts consistent with the vision of the organization. If this is not done, people are unlikely to accept any serious change. During a time of changing culture, leaders have to bear some of the pain and anxiety felt in the group at the same time that they seek to make the members feel secure. Fourth, sometimes direct change in a culture can be promoted by introducing new people in leadership, by promoting maverick individuals from within and, more especially, people from outside who hold slightly different assumptions. The appointment of a new pastor, a new assistant, a new board chairperson, a new president is an opportunity for cultural change. Finally, change takes time (Schein, pp. 297-327).

A systemic approach to change. A systems* approach treats an organization as a whole that is more than the sum of the parts, in which each member and each subsystem is influenced by and influences the others. It can be easily pictured as a mobile: movement in one element requires adjustment in all the others. Edwin Friedman, a family systems* therapist, has some additional insights on how a leader can bring change to a system. He uses the concept of *homeostasis,* that marvelous capacity of human bodies and social systems to regain their balance after a trauma. Every system has a natural tendency to maintain the status quo (homeostasis), just as a keel keeps the sailboat upright. The system does this when new response patterns are required through a threat, tragedy or positive change. Thus the system returns to the tried and tested rather than shifts to operate on a revised and improved basis (morphogenesis). A negative biblical example of homeostasis is the return of converted Jews in the first few years to a less-than-full expression of Christian unity with Gentile believers, a hypocrisy that Paul fervently challenged (Gal 2:11-21). A positive example of morphogenesis is the extraordinary resolution of the council of Jerusalem (Acts 15:1-29) in which the church changed the terms upon which Jews and Gentiles could have fellowship together.

To bring about systemic change, leaders must first join the system, becoming an integral part of the whole and negotiating their place within it. The director, pastor or president must lead the way in this. In fact this involves many stages of negotiation as the leader finds his or her place in the organization (Pattison). Then the leader might take an initiative that has a ripple effect throughout the system. Usually a problem will surface without provocation. But if a problem does not surface, something as inconsequential as changing the location of the water cooler or removing it altogether will do. How he or she responds to the ripple is crucial because the response of the system will be a reflection of all the systemic factors that make it stable, including the multigenerational influences. The provoked or unprovoked crisis is an opportunity to explain what is going on and to appeal, as Barnabas, Paul and Peter did in the Jerusalem council (Acts 15:1-35), to systemic values that can be expressed in a more constructive way. The Chinese word for *crisis* is composed of two characters, one of which means "danger" and the other "opportunity." The systemic leader welcomes the opportunity of every crisis and sometimes will provoke one.

Using family systems theory, Friedman says we bring greatest change in a system by concentrating not on the dissenting or sick member but on the person or persons in the group who have the greatest capacity to bring change (p. 22). The equipping leader must always remember that the only person open to definite and immediate change is herself or himself! A systems view encourages us to see that changing ourselves can make a difference to the those with whom we are interdependent.

In the context of counseling families,

Virginia Satir makes a remarkable statement about systems leadership that applies to all kinds of organizations. She says, "I consider myself the leader of the process in the interview but not the leader of the people." This, she continues, "is based on the fact that I am the one who knows what the process I am trying to produce is all about. I want to help people to become their own designers of their own choice-making" (Satir, pp. 251-52).

So organizational leadership is not simply leading individual people in an organization. Leaders must work with the whole—culture and systems included. Process leadership asks questions, clarifies goals, orients people to their mission, maintains and explains the culture and helps people and subsystems take responsibility for their own systemic life. In the end leaders are charged with the awesome task of creating an environment in which people change themselves.

See also EQUIPPING; LEADERSHIP; MANAGEMENT; POWER; ORGANIZATION; ORGANIZATIONAL VALUES; STRUCTURE.

References and Resources

P. Collins and R. P. Stevens, *The Equipping Pastor: A Systems Approach to Empowering the People of God* (Washington, D.C.: Alban Institute, 1993; portions quoted with permission); M. DePree, *Leadership Is an Art* (New York: Doubleday, 1992); E. H. Friedman, *Generation to Generation: Family Process in Church and Synagogue* (New York: Guilford, 1985); R. K. Greenleaf, *Servant Leadership: A Journey into the Nature of Legitimate Power and Greatness* (New York: Paulist, 1977); M. E. Pattison, *Pastor and People—A Systems Approach* (Philadelphia: Fortress, 1977); J. Renesch, ed., *New Traditions in Business* (San Francisco: Berrett-Koehler, 1992); V. Satir, *Conjoint Family Therapy*, rev. ed. (Palo Alto, Calif.: Science and Behavior, 1983); E. H. Schein, *Organizational Culture and Leadership: A Dynamic View* (San Francisco: Jossey-Bass, 1991).

R. Paul Stevens

ORGANIZATIONAL VALUES

In organizational life, values determine what is cherished and important and how an organization is shaped and managed. The human body operates on blood; an organization operates on values, whether good or bad. Ideally these values are thoughtfully conceived and clearly stated in a document that can be read by members of the organization and recipients of the organization's service. Sometimes the real functioning values of an organization are in conflict with the advertised ones. So the process of getting people to clarify what values are actually operating and what values should be foundational is one of the most important exercises that can be undertaken in organizational life.

The Virtuous Organization

Values should cover the full range of organizational life: how people are treated, especially when being hired or fired,* how mistakes are dealt with, how resources are used, how people relate, how decisions are made, how power* is handled, how purposes are clarified and how work* is performed. A virtuous organization would be shaped by three foundational organizational values from the Bible: faith, hope and love* (*see* Organization). These values can be applied to both persons and structures in organizations that are not overtly Christian but where people in positions of influence can shape the values of the organization. Obviously in a church or parachurch organization* faith, hope and love can be applied directly (though they often are not!). But in a secular organization these revealed values must be translated, with loss of some of the original meaning.

Faith is seeing and acting in harmony with God's will. It is seeing and trusting the invisible as well as the visible potential of every person, situation and structure (compare Heb 11:1). *Hope* is expressing courage and confidence in relational and organizational contexts. It is responding to the gains and losses of the present (with both people and structures) in the confidence of a future worth laboring for and embracing. *Love* is caring loyalty for people, cultures, structures and values. It is relating unconditionally to people in order to meet their real needs, communicating their worth and value independently of their performance. Love must also be directed to the structures* as part of the world that God loves.

These three values are founded on *truth* about people, situations and ultimate reality. Truth is not abstract but concrete, holistically experienced (mind, body and spirit) in a way that is reliable and stable. We will now develop these values in both personal and organizational terms.

Faith in an Organizational Context

Faith is the response of the whole person to the full revelation of God's person (Rom 10:14-17) and intentions for the created order (Heb 11:3). Faith is a revolt against living on the basis of appearances. It is not merely a belief system but a total life orientation involving trust and action in all kinds of life situations (Heb 11:4-16). Faith is better considered as a verb than as a noun. Faith is based on the Word of God, the persuasion of the Spirit and the paradigm of Jesus, but it leads to concrete action. How does this apply in a secular organization?

Personal faith. Faith requires seeing people and situations the way God does and acting in relation to them in view of the potential for change, integration and wholeness that God holds before each person and every human enterprise. While full communion with God is a possibility reserved for those who become children of God through faith (Jn 1:12), persons of faith working in organizations of various kinds are invited to translate their own communion with God into a form of communion with their neighbors in the workplace.* This is not so much possibility thinking or a search for human transcendence as for divine possibilities and capacities for transcendence that God makes available.

Organizational faith. In the same way a person of faith sees and acts upon structures and organizational culture.* Normally this results in openness to the possibility of substantial, though limited, change and transformation of an organization. Faith will inspire creative action to make the structures (as well as the people in them) reflect divine values and purposes in a way that is attractive to others.

Hope in an Organizational Context

Hope is resting in the revealed and certain conclusion of the created order to shape our response to the present gains and losses. It involves understanding and living in the present in view of the future, allowing the vision of God's kingdom to inspire our confidence in the future. Hope equips us with courage to hold essential values in uncertain times and to take appropriate steps to plan for tomorrow. The person who has been "saved by hope" can incorporate hope relationally and structurally in the life of an organization. While there is some loss of meaning in this process, incorporating hope in an organization plants a pregnant hint that there is something more and invites people to move towards it. Of the three virtues, the one most urgently needed today is probably hope, for it is the one that gives people the confidence that the other two are possible.

Personal hope. Hope means never giving up on people (confidence) and helping people deal with the reality of their lives (courage), in terms of both their need for change and the positive fruits that can be appropriated through a re-alignment of their lives.

Organizational hope. Hope means never giving up on situations (confidence) and empowering the structures, values and culture of an organization (courage) to live in harmony with king-dom values and realities, even if in the short haul we appear to be engaging in fruitless activity or experiencing re-verses. Hope inspires people in business to see their work as "playing heaven" (as children "play house" as a way of growing up) and "speeding" the day of the Lord (2 Pet 3:12) by bringing our business and organizational ventures into greater cor-respondence with what will be charac-teristic of the new heaven and the new earth. In some way beyond our imagina-tion, hope points toward the transfigura-tion, not the obliteration, of our work and enterprises in this world.

Love in an Organizational Context

In the Old Testament covenant love (*he-sed*) is love plus loyalty or affectionate loyalty. It also includes *ahabah,* the love that reaches out to incorporate the out-sider. Covenant love is more concerned with relationships than commodities. It is not merely a sentiment but involves active caring and creative loyalty. In the New Testament *agapē* illuminates and extends this further through the sacrifi-cial ministry of Jesus and the generous pouring out of the Spirit that encom-passes not only people but the creation itself. This means that material realities and ordered structures in this world are the objects of God's love and should, therefore, be the object of ours. How does this get translated into organiza-tional life?

Personal love. Though we love in a more limited way than God, our love should reflect that love as we show caring loyalty* to employees, members, clients, peers and customers. This involves meet-ing true needs, going the extra mile in relationships, understanding empatheti-cally the other person's situation, sup-porting another's integrity,* remaining faithful to the published values of the organization. Love makes us stay with people even when we find them unpleas-ant, when they "push our buttons" or when they do not meet our expectations for development. Love means we do not jump to conclusions about the motives of our customers. And even when we must deal with negative reality, we will communicate worth and create an op-portunity for people to change and have a second chance.

Organizational love. Love inspires car-ing loyalty to the structures and values of the organizational system—loving the company systemically, structurally and culturally. As God loved the world, we are called to lay down our selves, not only for people, but for organizations and com-munities so that they will be humanized and transformed. In the process hope-fully some people will embrace Christ as their Lord. A being-redeemed-commu-nity can express God's kindness and so lead people to repentance for sin (Rom 2:4). Gratitude is a good enough reason to return to the seeking Father, and a loving organization should evoke grati-tude.

The Value of Values

Several assumptions in this reflection in-vite further study and discussion: (1) that Christian values* are good for every-body; (2) that Christian values are rele-vant not only to individual persons but to the structural and cultural contexts in which those persons live and work; (3) that people on a spiritual journey may embrace and live at least partly by Chris-tian values—to their benefit and the benefit of their neighbors; (4) that God shows grace even to people who do not ask for it; (5) that values may serve as the law did prior to the coming of Christ—a good gift that may unfortunately become a trap through pointing to impossibly high standards—but nevertheless point us to Christ (Gal 3:24); (6) that translating Christian values in a secular context means that Christians in the marketplace have a ministry* as valuable as pastoral or missionary service; (7) that rediscovering kingdom values in the marketplace may create a learning context for Christians—a theological school in the marketplace. In the end organizational life can become for believers one more context for worship,* in spite of all the difficulties.

A ministry to structures desires, but is not dependent on, the hope that other people will become believers. This ministry is worthwhile in itself—a faithful, hopeful and loving ministry of lining ourselves up with the kingdom of God. Our service* is goal oriented, but the goal is beyond this life. In biblical revelation the future determines the present. All our life and work in human organizations are a dress rehearsal for the final performance in the new heaven and the new earth, which will be inaugurated when Christ comes again. The end of the human story will involve renewed structures in a new heaven and earth. In the new Jerusalem faith will be realized in sight, hope in fulfillment, but love will be the continuous plot line and experience of life in the heavenly city.

See also ORGANIZATION; ORGANIZATIONAL CULTURE AND CHANGE; SERVICE, WORKPLACE; VALUES.

References and Resources

R. Benne, *Ordinary Saints: An Introduction to the Christian Life* (Philadelphia: Fortress, 1988); P. Block, *The Empowered Manager* (San Francisco: Jossey-Bass, 1987); M. De Pree, *Leadership Is an Art* (New York: Doubleday, 1992); J. Renesch, ed., *New Traditions in Business* (San Francisco: New Leaders, 1991); E. H. Schein, *Organizational Culture and Leadership: A Dynamic View* (San Francisco: Jossey-Bass, 1991); G. Tucker, *The Faith-Work Connection* (Toronto: Anglican Book Centre, 1987).

R. Paul Stevens

OWNERSHIP, PRIVATE

The issue of ownership is a large one. At the public level it raises profound questions that have preoccupied philosophers, economists, legal thinkers and political scientists, as well as creating many national and international conflicts. It has also raised complex decisions involving politicians, civil servants, lawyers and corporate managers, leading to wide-ranging antitrust laws, court battles and family* quarrels. Historically, ideas of possession took root more tenaciously in North American soil than elsewhere, perhaps because so many people who came to the New World were have-nots. As the information society grows and the Information Superhighway* becomes more extensive, ownership issues are becoming increasingly problematic in areas relating to copyright and privacy.*

The topic raises several pertinent questions for us. What does private ownership mean? How much should we own? What is involved in saying "this is mine" or "that is yours"? When should ownership be an individual and when a joint affair? How does private ownership—of property, vehicles, possessions—appear and work within the economy of God, not just human economy?

The Nature of Private Ownership Today

In our society* ownership involves primarily our right to acquire, use, enjoy and dispose of our assets—whether land, wealth,* home,* animal, goods or copyrights, trademarks, policies or professional rights of tenure—in whatever way we choose, subject to legal provisions.

The foundation of ownership is possession, but this is not enough when someone else has a stronger claim. We can own things individually or in partnership with someone else, such as a spouse or family, or with strangers, such as a time-share arrangement in a condominium. We can own something permanently or temporarily (for example, until someone comes of age). We can own things in the absolute sense or in a derivative but de facto absolute, such as holding a ninety-nine-year housing lease from a government agency. But ownership involves not only the claim *this is mine* but in some sense *this is me.* For in some measure what we own tends to reflect who we are. It is a symbolic expression or concrete extension of ourselves. In other words, it has to do with being as well as having.

Ownership can be established in many ways, in some cases simply by holding possession or by shaking hands, in others only after finalizing protracted agreements. People may also exercise their ownership in a wide variety of ways—well or badly according to their care for what they own, selfishly or generously depending on how little or much they share with others, ostentatiously or modestly according to whether they flaunt their possessions, carefully or casually according to whether or not they give forethought to the fate of what they own when they die (*see* Will, Last).

Christian Attitudes Toward Ownership
In Christian tradition, the moral dimensions of private ownership have been often addressed. Thomas Aquinas taught that private property was not a right in natural law but only in human law, and that its use must not reflect avarice or waste but temperance, generosity, benefaction and almsgiving. The Puritans also tended to encourage modesty in the area of possessions, thrift with respect to money, and generosity with respect to giving. Apart from occasional documents, such as the *Pastoral Constitution on the Modern World* or certain World Council of Churches reports, in recent times the church* has done little to question widespread possessive attitudes toward ownership or the social obligations attached to it. This is no doubt partly because church congregations themselves often own large holdings.

What happens when we view ownership from God's point of view? For many Christians this changes little. They may view what they own as coming from God's hand and as a sign of God's blessing,* but that is the extent of the issue. This is the position of some conservative believers who regard the right to private ownership as an integral part of the Christian message. They may see this right as an indispensable element of being an individual.* "Without property, without something that really belongs to a person and characterizes him, it is difficult to be more than a cipher or a cog" (Harold Brown in Chewning, 2:127).

In other cases, looking at ownership from God's perspective has led Christians to the view that they should own things only in common, not privately. This is the position of some branches of the Christian community* movement. These people often regard the practice of common ownership as indispensable to being a disciple of Christ. As with monks and nuns in the older Catholic tradition, unless a person yields up their private property, or future right to it, they have not reached a mature level of Christian obedience.

Ownership in Biblical Perspective
The Old Testament concern to grant each Israelite a portion in the land suggests that having some property is an important part of belonging to God's people (Num 26:52-56; Josh 13—19). There were laws against moving land-

marks and therefore stealing another's property (Deut 19:14; Prov 22:28), and injunctions against stealing others' property (Ex 20:15; Prov 11:1; 16:11). Property may be acquired on the basis of a gift (Deut 1:8) or inheritance (Deut 21:16; Prov 19:14). Its use by the owner is guaranteed even when someone else is using the goods involved (Ex 22:7-8). It is the inalienability of land that lies behind the provision that every fiftieth year, the year of Jubilee, lands and houses that someone had been forced to sell to another for the sake of survival were to resort to the original owner (Lev 25:8-34; 27:17-24). For though people might sell their land, it must always be possible for the family to get it back (Lev 25:25). In this respect the old covenant is unapologetically materialistic.

On the other hand, there is a continuing emphasis on God being the ultimate owner of the land: "The land must not be sold permanently, because the land is mine and you are but aliens and my tenants" (Lev 25:23). The highest possible use of property is also to honor God with any increase that it brings (Prov 3:9). Apart from land, houses and possessions, there were other objects a person could own that exceed what we are accustomed to today: in the case of a man they included his wife and daughters as well as slaves (Ex 20:17). Though some people owned a great deal, exemplary servants of God rate other things as more important than material wealth (Gen 13:8-12). An excessive view of owning, which tends to trust in riches, love of luxury and oppression of the poor, is consistently condemned by the prophets (Is 3:16-23; 10:1-2; Ezek 7:19-21; Amos 6:1, 4; Mic 2:1-2).

In light of the full teaching of the New Testament—which does not insist on common property for all Christians but on the generous, sacrificial sharing of one's resources (see 1 Cor 16:1-4; 2 Cor 8:1-9)—a place for what we call private property appears again, though, for reasons I shall indicate in a moment, this is not the best way of describing it. On the other hand, the practice of Jesus and his disciples suggests an abandoning of ownership for those involved in a common mission (Lk 5:11, 28; 14:25-33; 18:18-23, 28-30). There was financial sharing among the disciples as well as among Paul and his coworkers, though the apostle certainly earned wages for distributing to others (Jn 12:4-6; 13:27-29; Acts 20:34). Though the example of the early church in Jerusalem is often cited in support of this practice, a closer reading of the text shows that it was surplus property that was sold and distributed to those who had need (Acts 2:44-45; 4:32; Rom 12:13). In the early churches this practice may not have been as exceptional as many think, nor mainly a product of intense apocalyptic expectation. Certainly Paul regards one of the purposes of possessions as the possibility they provide of giving to others (Eph 4:28). There is evidence of Christians sharing some of their possessions throughout at least the next five centuries (Grant).

Underlying both approaches is something more fundamental that does not always come to the surface. What we call ownership, whether individual or joint, would be better termed trusteeship or stewardship.* In a profound sense there is only one Owner. Everything comes from and belongs to God (Ps 24:1-2; 95:4-5). What we have is, strictly speaking, not given to us to own in any absolute sense. It is rather entrusted to us: we are made trustees of what comes our way and are accountable for how well we use it to serve God and to serve others. We do not have a right to any of our possessions; they are given from God, who could take from us at any time. It is our responsibility to view what we "own" through the lens of our calling* to reflect God's character and ways, to fulfill the ministry* and vocation God has given us, and to share with others in the church or who are in genuine need.

Some Principles of Responsible Ownership

The first time I encountered an attitude toward ownership based on trusteeship rather than possessiveness was in the form of a churchgoer who offered me the use of his automobile on Sundays whenever I needed it. I thanked him profusely for his generosity, but he replied, "There is nothing generous about it. This car is not mine but God's. God has entrusted it to me for my own use and for my family, as well as any of God's people who would benefit from it. I am simply trying to put it to the use for which it was intended."

This is how we should regard all that we own. By no means does this require us to be undiscerning about who we entrust what God has entrusted to us to. Some people will demand that we share; of these we should beware. Others will accept our open-handed offers but not handle what we share with them carefully, as we would handle it ourselves or as they would want us to handle something of theirs. Some will even abuse or exploit what comes their way, or only receive but never reciprocate, even when they could do so. Precisely because we are trustees of what we have, we must learn how to balance our own and our dependents' or Christian community's needs with those of other needy people with whom we come in contact. We also need to ensure as far as we can that what we share with others is kept in the best possible condition so that it can continue to be of benefit to people. Sometimes this will mean saying no to otherwise appropriate people.

We should also consider carefully how much we need to own as individuals or as a family, or how much we could own

certain things in common with others. The danger of wanting to possess too much was strongly criticized by Jesus (Lk 12:15). Our households—inside and out—are full of possessions which we use only once a week or less. When we live close to others whom we know, we could share or jointly own many tools and implements and even appliances. Under some circumstances, within the family, this can even be arranged with cars or homes. This raises larger questions about owning property and how much we should own. This need will vary from person to person, and will depend on a whole variety of factors, such as our income level, dependents, vocation and setting. There is no uniform answer, except perhaps to say that among middle- or upper-class believers, generally much less could be owned than is generally the case. But this raises the issue of a home ownership (see Home) and simpler lifestyle,* on which more is written elsewhere in this book.

Beyond such questions is the deeper issue of sorting out how much we own what we have or how much it owns us! It is one thing for what we own to be an expression or extension of ourselves. It is altogether another if it defines us and our life revolves too much around it. This basic issue is a matter for serious reflection, for at stake is nothing less than idolatry (Eph 5:5; Col 3:5). But then the sharing of what we own also calls for much prayer, advice, discernment and learning from experience. It is a risky adventure of faith in which we will sometimes make poor judgment calls and at other times entertain angels unawares. Though they sound as if they are polar opposites, we should always remember that owning and giving are actually closely related, just as are individual* and community. This is certainly the case with God, and increasingly we see the connection between the two. We live constantly within and through that tension as we gradually reflect more of God's own nonpossessive nature and large-hearted view of ownership.

See also COMMUNITY; INVESTMENT; MONEY; STEWARDSHIP.

References and Resources

W. Brueggemann, *The Land* (Philadelphia: Fortress, 1977); R. C. Chewning, *Biblical Principles and Economics: The Foundations* (Colorado Springs: NavPress, 1989); E. Fromm, *To Have or to Be?* (New York: Harper & Row, 1976); R. M. Grant, *Early Christianity and Society* (San Francisco: Harper & Row, 1977); D. J. Hall, *The Steward: A Biblical Symbol Come of Age* (Grand Rapids: Eerdmans, 1990); M. Hengel, *Property and Riches in the Early Church* (Philadelphia: Fortress, 1974); L. T. Johnson, *Sharing Possessions: Mandate and Symbol of Faith* (Philadelphia: Fortress, 1981); C. B. MacPherson, *The Political Theory of Possessive Individualism* (New York: Oxford University Press, 1964); G. Marcel, *Creative Fidelity* (New York: Farrar, Straus, 1964).

Robert Banks

P

PARACHURCH ORGANIZATIONS

Para means "beside" or "alongside." Thus parachurch organizations are usually understood as Christian ministry*organizations* that function "alongside" Christian congregations and denominations.* InterVarsity Christian Fellowship and Promise Keepers, for example, are not denominations or congregations but exist to serve the church.*

Parachurch organizations have often been controversial in the larger life of the church. This is because they raise basic questions about the nature of the church and its mission.*

The three main characteristics of parachurch organizations as usually understood are (1) they are not congregations or denominational structures, (2) they exist to serve the larger church, and (3) they function interdenominationally. As we will see, however, this is not an adequate definition. Similar organizations that function within one denomination only and with some formal link to the denomination are generally seen as "auxiliaries" within the denomination rather than as parachurch organizations. A women's missionary society within a specific denomination would not usually be seen as a parachurch organization. Yet its aim, structure and function might be much like those of a parachurch organization.

Well-known examples of parachurch organizations include the Billy Graham Evangelistic Association, World Vision International, Campus Crusade for Christ, the American Bible Society and Youth With a Mission (YWAM). Christian colleges and seminaries might also be placed in this category, though the term is less often used of them. Many parachurch organizations operate internationally or globally, and those that function primarily in one country often have counterparts in other countries.

Dynamics of Parachurch Structures

Parachurch organizations may be grouped in two categories: renewal structures and outreach structures. Renewal structures endeavor to help Christians or churches become more spiritually vital and are usually mainly concerned with the internal life of the church. Outreach structures exist to help the church fulfill its mission in the world, whether in evangelism,* compassionate service or social justice.* Examples of renewal structures today include Renovaré, which works "for the renewal of the church in all her multifaceted expressions," Walk Through the Bible, the Cursillo Movement and various charismatic renewal networks. Well-known outreach structures include the U.S. Center for World Mission, the Navigators and Jews for Jesus. Some parachurch organizations bridge these two categories, though their main focus is usually in one or the other.

Parachurch organizations are essentially entrepreneurial, with all the strengths and weaknesses that accompany such enterprises. Initially they tend to be dynamic, visionary, flexible and successful. They also tend to be autocratic in structure, independent of accountable supervision and competitive —and often undergo a crisis of organization and vision when the original founder passes from the scene.

A criticism often raised of parachurch organizations concerns accountability.* Legally and structurally these organizations are usually accountable to no one but themselves, which can lead to abuses. Well-publicized scandals involving some U.S. televangelists in the 1980s are a case in point. Most credible parachurch organizations counter this danger by forming controlling oversight boards of respected Christian leaders and by following approved business practices. In the United States many such organizations are now members of the Evangelical Council for Financial Accountability (itself a parachurch organization) and follow its guidelines for ethical conduct.

Parachurch Organizations and Voluntary Societies

Parachurch organizations are a type of voluntary society. Voluntary societies flourished in England, continental Europe and the United States over the past three centuries as society became more democratic and fluid. In late eighteenth-century and early nineteenth-century England, for instance, hundreds of societies, such as the Society for the Reformation of Manners and the Society for Bettering the Condition of the Poor, were formed by concerned Christian leaders. Some five hundred such societies sprang up in England between 1800 and 1850, mostly through the initiative of evangelicals. In the established church environment of England many of these were seen as broadly Anglican, but

most in fact came to be what today are called parachurch organizations.

Why have parachurch structures arisen over the course of church history? The most basic reason is a sense of vision* and calling,* often linked to frustration with existing church institutions. This is true of all parachurch groups (as defined more inclusively below), not just paradenominational structures. But three other factors have historically contributed to the proliferation of such groups.

1. Church-state issues. Where there was a state church, as in England, voluntary or parachurch societies might be formed by those who felt the church should not be allied with the state or to meet a need the state church was not meeting. In some cases such groups were declared illegal by the government because they were outside the control of the state-sponsored church. Conversely, in contexts of official state and church separation (such as the United States), parachurch groups proliferated in part because of the freedom to do so.

2. Democracy. In pluralistic democratic societies, parachurch organizations have flourished because the society itself was voluntaristic and encouraged independent, entrepreneurial endeavors. Some observers suggest that in the United States this was compounded further by the "frontier spirit," especially in the nineteenth century. In such democratic contexts parachurch groups often have many secular and philanthropic parallels. In the United States, secular parallels would include the American Red Cross, the American Legion, various lodges and service clubs such as Kiwanis and Rotary.

3. Intradenominational battles. Doctrinal disagreements and struggles, often compounded by political and financial issues, have also spawned many parachurch groups. Some were formed to

promote a particular cause within the denomination, others to carry out a task being neglected by the denomination. Thousands of such organizations exist. Some examples are Presbyterians United for Biblical Concerns, the Mission Society for United Methodists and various charismatic renewal committees.

Underlying all these dynamics is the theological and sociological fact that Christians live in particular cultural contexts where they must necessarily create structures or "wineskins" for shared life and mission.

There are tens of thousands of parachurch organizations throughout the world. Recent decades have seen a flowering of new organizations of this type in places like Hong Kong, Brazil and Korea as church membership* and mission consciousness have grown dramatically in the nineteenth and early twentieth centuries.

Is "Parachurch" Still "Church"?

Fundamentally, parachurch organizations testify to the energy and vitality of the gospel and the church. They spring up because Christians want to renew and extend the church's witness. They are, and have been, a fact of the church's life.

Missiologist Ralph Winter argues that parachurch organizations have always existed in church history. Winter uses the term *sodality* (common in Roman Catholicism), meaning a mission structure that does not claim to be a congregation but that exists for a specific and limited mission. A congregation or denomination Winter calls a *modality*. The apostle Paul's missionary network and the various orders within the Roman Catholic Church would be examples of sodalities. Much of the missionary work of the church has been carried out by such structures,* whether Catholic orders or the more or less independent

Protestant missionary societies that have proliferated from the nineteenth century till today, especially in areas where the church has been growing rapidly.

Yet there is a continuing debate about these organizations. Do they really have a proper place in Christianity? Are they theologically and biblically valid? Denominational and other church leaders have sometimes accused parachurch organizations of competing with the church and, like parasites, drawing off leadership and financial resources. Parachurch leaders respond that their organizations exist solely to serve the church and its mission, often adding that they are doing work the church has failed to do.

This discussion actually raises more basic questions of church and church structure. What is the church? If the church is the body* of Christ, the community of God's people, then what shall we say about all the diverse institutions, organizations, denominations and architectural structures that we commonly include under the umbrella "church"? What really is "church" and what is "parachurch"? If the church is in fact the whole Christian community, living and serving in a wide variety of organizational structures, we may view parachurch organizations as all those secondary but important structures that God uses to extend his kingdom throughout the earth.

Historically the debate over parachurch structures has involved two opposing tendencies. One sees recognized ecclesiastical structures as part of the essence of the church. This tendency "sacralizes" these structures; that is, it considers them sacred (since they are part of the church) and thus not essentially to be questioned. The opposite tendency takes a thoroughgoing anti-institutional stance, saying that all such structures are unbiblical and invalid, and must be scrapped. Both, really, are extreme views with no clear biblical basis.

The Church and Its Structures

A better option is to see all human-made structures, including denominational ones, as pragmatic parachurch structures, not part of the essence of the church itself. All these structures—church buildings and denominational bureaucracies, as well as organizations like World Vision or Campus Crusade for Christ—are really parachurch structures, because as *structures* they exist alongside and parallel to the living, breathing community of God's people. They assist the church (if they function faithfully) but are not themselves the body of Christ. These structures are useful to the extent that they aid the church in its mission. But they are human inventions and are culturally determined. A denominational structure is as much a human invention as is a missionary society. Both were created by Christians to help believers faithfully fulfill their Christian calling as they understood it. Neither the structure of the United Presbyterian Church nor that of Youth With a Mission, for instance, is prescribed in the Bible. But both seek to help Christians be faithful to what Scripture tells us.

Whereas the church itself is part of the "new wine" of the gospel, all parachurch structures are "wineskins"—useful, at times indispensable, but also subject to wear and decay. Biblically, the church is the body of Christ, the family of God, the community of God's people. If it is faithful to Scripture, the church can be nothing other than this. Institutional structures, then, are best seen as something different from the church—potentially useful aids to the church's life and ministry, but never a part of the essence of the church. But Christians themselves, living and serving in many subcommunities within these structures, are the church.

Generally, parachurch structures have been thought of as extradenominational or interdenominational organizations such as the Billy Graham Evangelistic Association or perhaps a council or association of churches. Denominations themselves are not usually thought of as parachurch structures. But since biblically the church is always people and can only be people, any institutional structure—a denomination, mission agency, Christian college, evangelical publishing house or evangelistic association—is a parachurch structure. In other words, biblically speaking, both an evangelistic association and a denominational organization are parachurch structures, while the communities of believers within these structures are the church. Parachurch structures, including denominations, may be legitimate and necessary but are not themselves the church.

Does this mean that all church structures are really parachurch structures? That no structures are themselves part of the essence of the church? When we look at the New Testament, we find no specific denominational or organizational structures prescribed, though we do find the beginnings of organization (for example, elders and deacons). Just for this reason, Christians down through history have developed different understandings as to what are the best or most biblically faithful models of organization. In the case of denominational structures, for example, three main traditions have developed: episcopal (based on the centrality of bishops [*episkopoi* in the Greek New Testament]), presbyterian (based on having "presbyters" or "elders" in each church) and congregational (based on the shared life and decision-making of each congregation).

Biblically speaking, all these human-made structures, denominational or otherwise, are best seen as parachurch. This distinction between the church (as the community of God's people) and parachurch structures helps us practically in three ways.

First, that which is always crossculturally relevant (the biblically understood church) is distinguished from that which is culturally bound and determined (human structures). Thus we are free to see the church as culturally relevant and involved and yet not as culturally bound.

Second, we are free to modify these parachurch structures as culture* changes, for they are not themselves the church and are largely culturally rather than biblically determined.

Third, this distinction makes it possible to see a wide range of legitimacy in denominational confessions and structures. We do not need to think other Christians are wrong if they hold to a different denominational or organizational tradition. Since these structures are not themselves the church and are culturally determined, whole volumes of controversy and polemic lose their urgency. They become merely secondary. Widely varying confessions are freed (at least potentially) to concentrate on that which unites them: being the people of God and carrying out their kingdom tasks. Thus structural differences and questions can be relegated to the plane of functionality and historical relativity. The crucial consideration for structure, then, becomes not biblical legitimacy but functional relevancy. The important question becomes not the theological validity of our structures but whether our structures help us fulfill God's mission.

Three Practical Lessons

Viewing parachurch structures and their relationship to the body of Christ in this light, we may draw some practical conclusions for church and structure today.

1. From a biblical standpoint, the key missionary structure is the church as the community of God's people—not the particular organizational forms it uses. Any faithful group of Christians engaged in mission can be a legitimate embodiment of the church, provided the structures they use are not incompatible with the church itself. This is true of foreign missionaries as well as of Christians in their own neighborhoods. Wherever faithful Christians are, there is the church; and these believers are responsible to demonstrate the visible reality of Christian community. The real point of distinction therefore is between the church as the community of God's people and all institutional expressions of the church. If Christ is really in them, Christian believers can never go to another culture and leave the church behind. But they can, and often should, leave behind or modify the parachurch forms peculiar to their own culture.

2. Parachurch structures for the church's mission of evangelism, service and justice* may be created wherever necessary to get the job done. While the church is God's agent for cosmic reconciliation, dynamic parachurch structures can be effective human agents of reconciliation. God uses them to spread his kingdom more rapidly and effectively. Denominational groups can freely collaborate with other parachurch structures that do work they themselves cannot do or that help them carry on their own witness. Such organizations, however, should always be directed ultimately toward the formation and edification of the church (though in widely different ways) or the extension of the church's ministry in the world, not allowing themselves to be confused with the church or to become ends in themselves.

3. Since they are human and culturally determined, all parachurch structures should be subjected to continuous,

rigorous sociological and theological evaluation to monitor their fidelity to the church and their effectiveness as instruments of God's mission. Today many parachurch structures welcome this kind of evaluation and even provide for it themselves.

Christian leaders should not hesitate to make the most exacting sociological studies of mission agencies, evangelistic movements, denominational structures and so forth. Some parachurch structures should be devoted exclusively to this task, serving as "think tanks" and research centers (as a number of structures are in fact today). History teaches us that with time ecclesiastical structures often succumb to institutionalism, hindering rather than helping the church. The fact that God has raised up a movement is no warranty against eventual infidelity or self-centeredness. If we remember that these structures are not themselves the church but are parachurch, we can freely ask whether they are really serving God's mission—and change or abolish them if they are not.

An institution, it is said, is the lengthened shadow of a pioneering leader. History bears this out. If we think of the Franciscan Order, we think of Saint Francis; if we think of the Lutheran Church, we think of Martin Luther; if we think of the Overseas Missionary Fellowship (formerly China Inland Mission), we think of Hudson Taylor. Anthropologist Anthony Wallace says all organized religions, in fact, are "relics of old revitalization movements." While this may be going too far, it does underscore the fact that most parachurch organizations within orthodox Christianity trace back to people and movements that God apparently used to revitalize the church.

What has been true in the past will probably continue into the future. God will continue to raise up leaders and movements, but because of human weakness none of these will be perfect and all will make mistakes. New forms of parachurch organizations may develop as the Internet and other electronic networking become more common. Christians everywhere will continue to face the challenge of creating and using structures that are redemptive and effective, not merely self-serving—structures that are both biblically faithful and culturally relevant.

See also DENOMINATIONS; MISSION; MISSIONS; STRUCTURES.

References and Resources
C. J. Mellis, *Committed Communities: Fresh Streams for World Missions* (South Pasadena, Calif.: William Carey Library, 1976); B. L. Shelley, "Parachurch Groups," in *Dictionary of Christianity in America,* ed. D. G. Reid et al. (Downers Grove, Ill.: InterVarsity Press, 1990) 863-65; H. A. Snyder, *The Community of the King* (Downers Grove, Ill.: InterVarsity Press, 1977); H. A. Snyder, *The Problem of Wineskins* (Downers Grove, Ill.: InterVarsity Press, 1975); R. D. Winter, "The Two Structures of God's Redemptive Mission," in *Perspectives on the World Christian Movement,* ed. R. D. Winter and S. C. Hawthorne, rev. ed. (Pasadena, Calif.: William Carey Library, 1992).

Howard A. Snyder

PARENTING
Parenting is an interactive family process in which adults undertake a primary role in forming children in body* (through conception* and care), soul* (through personality development and love*), and spirit (through nurturing hunger for God). Ironically, this relationship forms not only children but parents. Children, without knowing it, help their parents "grow up." So it is entirely appropriate to ask not only how the children ended up but also how the parents turned out!

Parenting today is a threatened calling* from both the outside and the inside. From the outside there is the professionalization of parenting (letting the experts do it for us) and preoccupation with the technology* of parenting. On the inside there is an erosion of confidence that ordinary people can parent well, and that it is worth doing at all. It has not always been this way.

Paradoxically, in earlier survival cultures and even some developing countries today, children were prized as wealth* and parenting was passionately desired even though people inevitably experienced failures. In the identity culture of the West—where people are bent on finding and actualizing themselves—parenting is frequently viewed as an unwelcome and troubling distraction from one's primary vocation outside the home.* This is especially tragic when the parent, like Eli in the Bible (1 Sam 2:12-36), is in religious or public service and refuses to regard parenting with the same vocational importance as preaching,* counseling or public leadership.* The intention of this article is not to focus on the question of how to parent, important as that is, but to explore the underlying theological and spiritual questions of why we should parent at all and why parenting has such spiritual significance.

Parenting as Vocation

What is lacking in the Western world is a rationale for having and raising children. In older cultures becoming a parent was assumed of those who married. In modern cultures, however, marriage* and conception are not necessarily linked, the influence of Roman Catholic teaching on this matter notwithstanding. As we approach an almost perfectly efficient contraceptive* society, it is now possible to delay having children indefinitely while one pursues buying a house, establishing a career and gaining personal happiness. The urgency of this question—Why have babies?—is raised a

notch further by the new reproductive technologies,* which call into question the church's traditional teaching that it is copulation that produces (and ought to produce) offspring. Childless couples who want children and are unable or unwilling to adopt may now resort to in vitro fertilization or even surrogate parenthood. A contemporary Catholic ethicist notes that where Augustine "found it necessary to remind Jerome that it is not marriage that produces babies but sex, it may be necessary to point out in an age of new reproductive technologies that it need not be sex but can still be love" (Henley 1990, p. 18). Never before has it been so urgent to lift parenting above a simple biological urge and elevate it to a holy calling.

A vocation or calling* is a life direction and service that is embraced not merely by one's will or through social constraint, but as a response to a divine summons and for purposes beyond our own personal fulfilment. When we experience calling we say such things as "I was born for this." We find joy in our calling even when we experience failures*—as we inevitably will as parents—because our vocation is bound up in the promises of God, who is determined to bring the whole story to a worthy end. And, in the end, our vocational service is meaningful because we are accountable to God (and not just to ourselves) for walking worthy of our vocation (Eph 4:1). Vocation means our life matters to God. So parenting is a vocation because it is divinely constituted (Gen 1:27-28), is accomplished in partnership with God, invites a life of faith and stewardship and is implicitly spiritual—a Godlike thing. Parenting is a path to God, not a diversion from spiritual life. It is not merely a setting in which spiritual disciplines* take place—around the family meal, for example—it is a spiritual discipline itself.

Parenting is something we accomplish with God, even if we are unaware of the divine partner in the process. When we procreate we are creating "before" (pro) God and cooperating with God, without whom the creation of a new person would be impossible (Gen 4:1). Theological attempts to unpack this mystery are woefully inadequate, including the traditional explanation by Aquinas that human parents provide the embryonic material while God provides the "sensitive" soul, an approach now being challenged by a more thoroughly unified biblical understanding of human personhood. Inadequate as it is, this traditional theological understanding reinforces the truth that parenting is a divine-human partnership, not an exclusively human achievement.

Parenting invites us Godward. For all, and especially for those who have difficulty conceiving, bearing and raising a children is a matter of "waiting on the Lord," a waiting* that may lead to taking other initiatives to become parents, or even to other expressions of vocation such as serving the children of others. Even after a child is conceived or adopted we must wait on the Lord for the outcome of his or her life—something we can neither predict nor control, try as we may. Implicit in this is the idea of stewardship.* We are entrusted with children; we do not own them.

Parenting as Stewardship

Children are gifts from God to us, gifts which we never "own" but of which we are stewards, in a way so deeply understood by Hannah in the Old Testament (1 Sam 1:28). This same idea is communicated by the concept of hospitality:* we create a welcoming space for children where they can be free to be themselves, neither smothered nor "dumped." Both stewardship and hospitality suggest that parents have more responsibilities than rights. Stanley Hauerwas suggests that a

child is always in this sense adopted, since the child belongs to the parents in a provisional and limited way (Henley, 1990, p. 21). This is reinforced in the actual experience of parenting when parents discover that they do not have dominion over the child. They cannot determine that their child will replicate them in the world. A child will not, no matter how hard we try, fulfill our unfulfilled ambitions for this life, or give us a status we have not found in being a child of God.

One practical expression of parental stewardship is the simple truth that no one chooses his or her parents; but in like manner we do not choose in a detailed way our children, even should we adopt them. So this vocation of parenthood is distributed among people of various talents, a phenomenon which may lie behind the commandment to "honor" one's parents (Ex 20:12) even if one has little reason to be grateful to them (Henley 1990, p. 20). But there is more to this than a divine randomness. Grace can be discovered even through very negative family experiences if these are processed.

Parenting as Ministering the Gospel

The family as predicament and blessing reflects the gospel in daily life, and pleads it, as poignantly revealed in the parable of the prodigal son (Lk 15:11-32). Robert Frost crafted a statement by a farmer whose old hired hand came home to die: "Home is the place where, when you have to go there, they have to take you in." The farmer resented the intrusion. But the farmer's wife had a deeper insight. She said, "I should have called it something you somehow haven't to deserve." More than obligation is built into the structure of the human family. There is the possibility of grace, belongingness, belovedness, undeserved kindness. One does not need to go farther than one's own front porch to be faced with gospel issues and to be found by God. So it was entirely appropriate that the Second Vatican Council used the phrase "domestic church" to recapture the ancient idea that the family is a form of church and not just the reverse. We do not need to bring the Lord "into" our homes by a program of Christian education,* or even family devotions, good as these are. God is already "where two or three are gathered," whether the family is "good" or "not so good." There are no perfect families, but there is no better family for us to be formed into personal and Christian maturity than the one into which we were born, adopted or entered by the marriage covenant. Thus parenting is truly vocational in its origin; but it is a ministry in its effect on people—both parents and children.

Parents too are under the "nurture and admonition of the Lord" (Eph 6:1-4 KJV; see Blessing, Family). In all families the parenting experience "sets us up" to give and receive ministry from God and others through the issues of everyday life in family, including such things as the need for unconditional acceptance and self-worth, the challenge of "leaving father and mother," the images of God as Father as well as feminine images of God, and issues of who is in control. The Greek word for "ministry"* is simply the same word as "service." So we can consider parenting as a form of family service in which people are touched for God and by God in the normal everyday transactions and relationships of family life. One way of describing this two-way ministry (God to people and people to God) is the biblical concept of priesthood.

Parenting as Priesthood

In a family where some or all the members are Christians, the priesthood of all believers (1 Pet 2:9) means that the father is not *the* priest of the family but rather one of them! So the challenge of parenting is not only to raise godly children but to become godly parents. This comes about through a communal ministry in the home. Each believer is priest to the others. Often the children are priests to the parents—declaring through their innocent wisdom the direct accessibility and trustworthiness of God. In this way children demonstrate the childlikeness which parents themselves are called to emulate. Put differently, every member of the family has the potential to be a spiritual director to the other members, and the family as a whole acts as a corporate priesthood for one another. We do this by praying, by playing, by raising questions, in affirming where and how God is at work in our midst and by directing one another to find our ultimate security and hope in God not in their family.

Prayer is an important part of this priestly ministry since it brings people and situations to God and invites God to touch people and situations. The Bible does not specifically require that a family pray out loud together—though it can be a good thing to do—but it strongly advocates prayer *for* one another. The prayers of Paul in Ephesians 1:16-23 and 3:14-19 are great patterns for priestly intercessory prayer for other members of the family. As children approach adulthood, discerning parents will pray more and say less. By the time they become grandparents* parents learn that prayer is probably their most important continuing ministry to their children and grandchildren.

Unlike Job's friends, who talked too much *about* God, and more like Job, who talked *to* God about all that was happening, parents are invited to increasingly become people who learn about God by wrestling in prayer, especially prayer for their family. Luther once said that "living, or rather dying and being damned make a theologian, not understanding, reading or speculating." He could have added "parenting" to the first part of his sentence. Some parents, too anxious to have their children declare faith at the earliest possible age, stuff them with Christian information so they arrive at the teens "knowing it all" and immune to discovering something personal, instead of hungering for God and wanting more. Another way of expressing this developmental approach to parenting is through the biblical concept of discipling.

Parenting as Discipling

The connection between the words *discipline* and *discipleship* (both stemming from the Latin *discipulus,* meaning "learner") is a complicated one (Lee, pp. 268-71) and has led some to advocate parental discipline by punishment and others to reject punishment completely in favor of noncoercive education. In fact, the Bible includes the element of punishment in its idea of discipline but always in the context of something greater: the covenant love which encourages growth and not simply to control.

Discipleship,* so perfectly exemplified in the relation of Jesus and his disciples, is a helpful model of parenting for several reasons: (1) the context is not the classroom but life-on-life relationships; (2) learning is continuous and unscheduled; (3) the learning relationship is primarily one of imitation rather than the transmission of information (Lk 6:40); and (4) the primary motivation of discipline is not the need to control but the desire to encourage self-control and other fruits of the Spirit.

Obviously this cannot happen without the parent's being self-reflective. This is especially needed because a family is constantly changing like a mobile with elements moving and influencing all the other elements. Systems theory is

one contemporary way of understanding this; congruent with this is the biblical idea of family as covenant.

Parenting as Ministers of the Covenant

The covenant is a binding personal agreement to belong, involving mutuality, love and loyalty. Systems theory, in line with the biblical ideas of family and church, helps us understand the simultaneous need to be "we" (an identity formed in community) and "me" (a differentiated individual). A healthy family is a covenant community in which we are more one because of our diversity, rather than being unified by blurring the differences and merging members into a homogenous unit. The process of building such a community involves constant change for all the members of the family.

The development of a child should start with bonding, attaching to at least one significant adult who is really "crazy" about him or her. Without this bonding a child will grow up looking for the bonding he or she missed and, according to Bowlby's attachment theory, will more likely become a driven* person, possibly even addicted.*

But this early dependence must progress toward interdependence. The covenant actually starts in a unilateral way by the parents' action in claiming the child as their own, at a stage when the child cannot reciprocate. But the covenant becomes bilateral as the growing child affirms a family identity while becoming differentiated from parents. In one sense parents are continuously preparing their children "to leave home" from the very first months, and the failure to do this (assuming healthy initial attachment) leads to enmeshed families where the children cannot "leave father and mother" (Gen 2:24) even when they marry, and the parents are unable to "let go." In their covenant ministry parents encourage belonging and differentiation *at the same time,* giving them both roots and wings. Ultimately in a mature covenant, when the parents are old and infirm the circle is completed as children care for their parents when their parents can no longer care for themselves (Balswick and Balswick, 1987, pp. 41-42).

Throughout this process of development within the family, parents are powerfully teaching their children the meaning of covenant and therefore suggesting the fundamental basis of our relationship with God—one of belonging rather than performing. In addition, parents are preparing their children to be capable of forming their own family covenant through marriage, if God should so lead. Indeed, even a dysfunctional family experience, if properly processed, can be an asset in preparing for marriage.* Understanding intergenerational sin (problems passed on from generation to generation until they are broken) and, more significantly, intergenerational grace (Ex 20:5-6) is crucial to being free to leave home and to form another family.

So an important ministry of parents is the forming, keeping and developing of a covenant community in which through all the changing life stages* people simultaneously belong unconditionally and are encouraged to change and develop uniquely. This view of family ministry profoundly challenges both the Western family (as a collection of individuals) and the Eastern (as a merged unit). It also challenges parents to be constantly adapting to their changing ministry. During the developmental stages of children various parenting styles will commend themselves: more authoritarian (directive) in the earliest months, more authoritative (high control with positive encouragement) during the growing years, and more permissive (nondemanding and warmly accepting) when children reach adulthood (Atkinson and Wilson, p. 61).

There are several practical implications that arise from a theology and spirituality of parenting. First, recognize parenting as a vocation more important than service outside the home because it is the most tangible expression of God as parent. Second, give up ownership of your child to God; your child is a trusted gift and a precious guest. Third, hear the gospel and live it through living graciously at home, not giving everyone what they deserve. Fourth, pray for your children and encourage them to pray for you. Fifth, put discipline in the context of discipleship. Sixth, build community that balances the need to be "we" with the need to be "me." Finally, enjoy your children.

Can Christian parents guarantee that their children will become believers? No, not even by "doing it right" in all spheres of parenting. Indeed, some research suggests that inward and authentic faith in young people is found just as much in families where parents were authoritarian as among those who were permissive at the wrong stage (Atkinson and Wilson, pp. 51-62). Good parenting can facilitate a child's growing up to become whole and open to God but cannot guarantee faith. That is the result of a miraculous and mysterious cooperation of human and divine wills. When a child raised in a healthy, affirming home does not embrace faith, at least in the present, it is not a sign of bad parenting. The story is not yet finished, as we learn when the curtain comes down in the story of the two prodigal sons, one at home but in the far country in his heart, the other at home in body and soul.

Parenting does not have guarantees, except the growth of the parents. Parenting is not really *for* anything: not for the certain transmission of faith to another generation, not for the pleasure of having children rise up and call us blessed, not for the satisfaction of producing high achievers. Parenting as a spiritual discipline is for God, who in the end is the only one who can say "Well done." And God approves of our parenting, as Luther so clearly proclaimed, not because of the merits of our performance but because we did our parenting for God. "God with all his angels and creatures is smiling," said Luther, "not because that father is washing diapers, but because he is doing so in Christian faith." Everyone who has reflected deeply on this ministry and vocation attests that parenting is an act of faith. But faith is not a leap in the dark but a hearty trust in the God who has made himself known in Christ and will one day show us what we really did in parenting our children.

See also BIRTH; CONCEPTION; FAMILY; FAMILY BLESSING; FAMILY COMMUNICATION; FAMILY PROBLEMS; FAMILY SYSTEMS; FAMILY TRADITIONS; FAMILY VALUES; HOMEMAKING; SEXUALITY.

References and Resources
H. T. Atkinson and F. R. Wilson, "The Relationship Between Parenting Style and the Spiritual Well-Being and Religiosity of College Students," *Christian Education Journal* 11 (Winter 1991) 51-62; J. O. Balswick and J. K. Balswick, *The Family: A Christian Perspective on the Contemporary Home* (Grand Rapids: Baker, 1989); J. O. Balswick and J. K. Balswick, "A Theological Basis for Family Relationships," *Journal of Psychology and Christianity* 6, no. 3 (Fall 1987) 37-49; E. Boyer, *Finding God at Home: Family Life as a Spiritual Discipline* (San Francisco: Harper & Row, 1991); R. Clapp, *Families at the Crossroads: Beyond Traditional and Modern Options* (Downers Grove, Ill.: InterVarsity Press, 1993); V. Hearn, ed., *What They Did Right: Reflections on Parents by Their Children* (Wheaton, Ill.: Tyndale, 1974); J. Henley, "The Vocation of Parenting—with Surrogates," *St. Mark's Review,* Winter 1990, 16-25; J. Henley, *Accepting Life: The Ethics of Living in Families* (Melbourne: Joint Board of Christian Education, 1994); C. Lee, "Parenting as Discipleship: A Contextual Motif for Christian Parent Education," *Journal of Psychology and Theology* 19, no. 3 (1991) 268-77; B. Narramore, *Help! I'm a Parent* (Grand Rapids: Zondervan, 1972); M. Novak, "Family out of Favor," *Harper's,* April 1976; C. M. Sell, *Family Ministry: The Enrichment of Family Life Through the Church* (Grand Rapids: Zondervan, 1981); G. Smalley and J. T. Trent, *The Blessing* (Nashville: Thomas Nelson, 1986); R. P. Stevens, "A Day with the Family," in *Disciplines of the Hungry Heart* (Wheaton, Ill.: Harold Shaw, 1993) 35-64; J. Taylor, *Innocent Wisdom: Children as Spiritual Guides* (Cleveland: Pilgrim Press, 1989).

R. Paul Stevens

PART-TIME EMPLOYMENT

We tend to regard part-time employment as the exception rather than the rule. Historically this was not the case. While some people have always performed the equivalent of what we call "a full-day's work" for pay, in many respects the Industrial Revolution was the creator of the full-time salaried job. It also increased working hours by a half or more over what people had traditionally known. For most of human history the majority of people have engaged in several activities in several locations in the course of a week, often without monetary payment, rather than a single task in one setting (*see* Volunteer Work). In the winter months most people worked less than a full day's labor, adjusting their hours according to the number of daylight hours and the dictates of the weather. Work responsibilities were also spread more evenly through the extended family rather than concentrated on one, now often two, members of a nuclear family.

The Growing Incidence of Part-Time Employment

Even in recent times, part-time employment has been the norm rather than the exception for certain kinds of people. Women have frequently held part-time or less-than-average full-time positions, and after a period of decline this older pattern is now returning. Large numbers of immigrants, even those who have been in a country for some time, also have part-time or occasional work. Many rural workers are involved in seasonal work. So too are many students in schools, colleges and universities, though increasingly these continue to hold down part-time positions alongside their studies. Overall, part-time employment has been steadily growing during the last decade and looks set to continue doing so well into the future.

There are various reasons for the trend: (1) the downsizing of many workplaces and contracting out of responsibilities to other people, (2) a lower outlay on salaries, insurance and health schemes, (3) the greater flexibility required by many new kinds of work, (4) the growing desire for self-employed or multisided work, (5) the search on the part of some baby boomers and many baby busters for a more balanced life and (6) the call of God upon some to launch out into freelance or tentmaking* Christian service.

Some social commentators believe that we are in the midst of a paradigm shift with respect to work. The traditional job is dying. For example, the number of people who are part- or full-time telecommuters doubled in a two-year period, and the number of traditional or traditional-looking jobs even in a country like Great Britain is about 25 percent of the total work force. In years to come, increasing numbers of people will find themselves "dejobbed." We are moving toward a workplace without jobs as we have known them. The bulk of jobs are on the way to becoming temporary rather than permanent. Guaranteed employment and tenured positions will be a thing of the past. The existence of the much-written-about organization man or woman, who is wedded to a firm or company for much of his or her life, or the career path of rising

through a sequence of jobs that increased in salary, responsibility and complexity will be rare (*see* Career).

In the entertainment* and communications industries, traditional job structures ultimately became too inflexible to cope with the constantly changing nature of the work. This will prove to be the case in other kinds of workplaces. Individuals called in to perform a particular function, telecommuters working for several firms at the same time, teams or even whole firms hired for a particular project, these are the wave of the future. The result will be an ever larger number of what the freelance consultant William Bridges calls *vendor workers*, who sell their services to a variety of clients and tend to work on projects on a short-term basis. While such a development opens up the possibility of further exploitation by employers, as has often been the case with part-time employment, this will be offset by the competitiveness of certain work situations, the high quality of the people being employed and the beginning of protective structures or regulations for part-time workers.

A Survival Guide to Part-Time Employment

A greater challenge may well be the psychological, social and economic adjustments workers will have to make to manage and benefit from these changes. Those already in part-time work have always had to cope with the sense of inferiority associated with not having a full-time job. Workers who in some industries have already shifted from a five- to a four-day working week have had difficulty adjusting to not being able to socialize during their time off with their friends in traditional jobs. If, as is likely, some part-time work takes on the pattern of shiftwork* or working at different hours, the long-observed problems of physical, psychological and marital problems experienced by such people will spread. Since economies—from benefit provisions to tax collection—are still largely built around traditional employment arrangements, there is still little recognition or support from the government for the emerging part-time employment economy. On the other hand, some businesses are taking responsibility to develop new financial practices and packages for the new kind of worker.

What can part-time workers themselves do to make a satisfactory transition from traditional employment into this new situation? First, it requires a more inner-directed and self-motivated attitude than a traditional job. This is not always easy in an increasingly outer-directed and peer-motivated culture. Giving additional time to prayer and meditation, especially to journaling one's daily life, strengthens one's inner life with God and develops a greater capacity for one to stand on one's own. If selling oneself is also awkward, focusing on what could be contributed to specific projects, rather than what one has to offer generally, may help overcome the difficulty.

It is also important to establish contact with others who are working part time. People can then meet regularly to talk about common concerns arising from their nonstandard working practice. Congregations and some parachurch organizations could help develop such groups. In addition, belonging to a support group or home church within a congregation creates a place where people can talk and pray about their work and provides a weekly anchor and reference point.

Since part-time work does not always have the regular rhythms of a traditional job (for example, working intensively one day or one week with little to do the next), it is important to learn and live with flexibility. This is not necessarily easy, and individuals will differ in their attempts and ability to deal with it. For most it is important to establish "islands of order" (Bridges), routines that hold fast even in the most demanding work schedules but especially during spells when there is less to do. These may include reflection and prayer times (*see* Spiritual Disciplines), hobbies,* exercise or sports,* ongoing commitments to others, a project or a cause. While these may expand or contract according to circumstances, they will be a consistent feature of one's day or week.

Since part-time workers, especially those who are self-employed, are often among the lowest paid, and even if well paid sometimes have highly fluctuating incomes, it is imperative for them to have a broader financial support system. This could take different forms, and I offer two from my own experience. Those in the same work position could agree to help each other out or have a common fund from which any can draw when necessary but must repay as soon as his or her position stabilizes. A church-based support or communal group could also commit itself to helping one or more of its members during the transition into part-time employment or during other difficult times.

The wider challenge of part-time work, especially if it becomes more entrenched in our society, presents considerable challenges to Christians, though no more so than those already faced by members of some industries and those involved in freelance work. It is helpful to remember that the tradition of part-time work has some significant Christian precedents. We often forget that the apostle Paul was mostly a part-time, not full-time, missionary, who made tents to support himself and his associates (Acts 18:3; 20:33-34; 2 Thess 3:6-10). The secret to living this way, he said, lies in learning "to be content whatever the circumstances," knowing "what it is to be in need" and "what it is to have plenty," doing "everything through him who gives strength" (Phil 4:11-13).

See also CALLING; SELF-ESTEEM; SHIFT-WORK; WORK.

References and Resources
W. Bridges, *Jobshift: How to Prosper in a Workplace Without Jobs* (London: Nicholas Brealey, 1995); C. Handy, *The Age of Unreason* (Boston: Harvard Business School, 1989); J. B. Schor, *The Overworked American: The Unexpected Decline of Leisure* (New York: Basic Books, 1991).

Robert Banks

PARTYING

Do people of faith have any joy and fun, or is that privilege only enjoyed by unbelievers or experienced totally separate from faith? Definitely not!

Both the Hebrew and Christian Scriptures tell us that we are a people with absolute and eternal reasons to celebrate. The sabbath* was established in the beginning as a way to break from work, reflect on its outcomes and celebrate that we are much more than our work (*see* Leisure; Recreation; Rest). We are creatures made in the image and likeness of God (Gen 1:31—2:3; Deut 5:12-15)! The early Christians moved this celebration to Sunday to commemorate the resurrection and the provision of new life through faith (Mt 12:1-14; Rev 1:10). The Hebrew people had excellent musicians, who created celebrations and led them. Some of the leading ones include Jubal (Gen 4:21), Miriam (Ex 15:20-21), David (1 Sam 16:23; 1 Chron 16:42; 23:5; 25:1-8), Elisha's minstrel (2 Kings 3:15) and Asaph (1 Chron 16:5; Ps 73—83). Jesus launched his ministry of reconciliation at a wedding* party. John says, "Jesus did this, the first of his signs, in Cana of Galilee, and revealed his glory; and his disciples believed in him"

(Jn 2:11 NRSV). God's glory brings great joy, and it is to be acknowledged and shared (*see* Blessing). Jesus also attended a dinner party to celebrate the conversion and beginning of the new life of a despised tax collector, once again demonstrating what true joy is all about (Lk 5:27-39).

However, our cultural understanding of *partying* is different. It is associated with reveling. A *party pooper* is one who refuses to join in the fun and go along with everyone else. Here we see a very human view of enjoyment that only has group and individual pleasure* as its end. Our culture's view of partying is illustrated in events like the end of the workday *happy hour,* when friends unwind, connect and review their work and lives. At other times gatherings turn into wild and mindless binges of drinking and other pleasure-seeking activities. These tend to be a temporary escape from reality rather than a celebration of it. Increasingly this has become the fate of special ceremonies like Christmas and New Year's or transitional events like anniversaries,* marriages,* job promotions or birthdays.*

Although the word *party* is only used in Scripture to denote a political group, there are many reports of parties as well as warnings about misuse and exhortations to celebrate. The abuse of alcohol is candidly and painfully described through several stories of bad parties. Noah abused one of his three sons after a drinking bout that left him naked and unconscious (Gen 9:20-25). Daughters desperate to conceive and continue the family line got their father drunk and then lay with him (Gen 19:30-38). David attempted to use alcohol to trick the husband of a woman he had seduced so the husband might appear to be the source of her pregnancy (2 Sam 11:2-13). The king of Persia, Ahasuerus, demanded that his wife display her beauty for his drinking guests during a seven-day party: she refused and he retaliated by replacing her (Esther 1:4-22). When Aaron was appointed by the people to take over in Moses' absence, there was a raucous celebration that Moses strongly condemned upon his return (Ex 32:1-26).

Another interesting type of incident is the good celebration that is misunderstood. Jesus' disciples were among the thousands of Jews gathered in Jerusalem for Pentecost, but they were so animated and excited that observers thought they must be drunk. Actually, they were overwhelmed with joy at the fullness of the Holy Spirit of God, as promised by the Hebrew prophet Joel (Acts 2:1-13; compare Joel 2:28-32). Those who observed this could not understand it but could only judge it by their own experiences and values.* This is still to be expected in the ongoing tension between Christian community and the culture* in which it resides. People of faith will be regularly misunderstood. For instance, as the early church began to celebrate Communion,* or the Lord's Supper, rumors spread throughout the Roman Empire that they were cannibals. People of faith are also directed to celebrate wholesome love,* commitment and sexuality* with weddings and courtship. The most sublime description of this in Scripture is found in the Song of Solomon, as two lovers give voice to their passion and dedication for one another.

People of faith are beckoned to bring their best to celebrations of faith and life. Jesus provided fine wine (Jn 2:1-12). David employed musicians to help Israel worship* (1 Sam 18:6-7). James charged the early church to sing with each other (Jas 5:13). Poetry, dance and drama are all to be employed to assist people of faith in worship and celebration of our Lord and his kingdom (Ex 15:1-21; Judg 5; 1 Sam 2:1-10; Lk 1:46-55). And finally

we learn that heaven will be a celebratory banquet acknowledging the removal of all pain and sorrow (Rev 19:1-10).

Party on, believers. We have much to celebrate in thanksgiving to God and as a witness to the watching world.

See also ANNIVERSARIES; BIRTHDAYS; EATING; PLEASURE; WEDDINGS.

References and Resources
E. Otto and T. Schramm, *Festival and Joy* (Nashville: Abingdon, 1977).

Pete Hammond

PASTORAL CARE

Pastoral care is the help Christians offer to people in need, whether the need is physical, emotional, mental or spiritual. The person in need may be a Christian, a seeker or a person currently committed to another faith. One does not earn pastoral care. A gracious God moves and empowers Christians to offer care to persons in need.

Jesus as a Model for Pastoral Care
The Gospels indicate that Jesus intended to model pastoral care in his own ministry.* He charged the Twelve on their mission, "Heal the sick, raise the dead, cleanse those who have leprosy, drive out demons. Freely you have received, freely give" (Mt 10:8). They were to carry out the same caring ministries they had seen in him.

In John 3 Jesus meets Nicodemus, who holds a position of great power in the Judaism of his day, and demonstrates how confrontation can be an appropriate act of caring love. In John 4 Jesus encounters a woman who has no inherent claim on Jesus because she represents an alien people, the Samaritans. She fails to meet the moral expectations of her day or ours, having been divorced five times and in a current live-in relationship. Jesus models a care that accurately perceives the needs and attitudes of this woman, demonstrating the power of acceptance for those who have known only rejection. In John 5 Jesus selects the one man at the pool of Bethesda who had been sick for so long that he had given up any hope of ever getting well. Jesus forces him to explore his feelings and values on his way to wholeness. John 8:1-11 centers on a woman caught in the act of adultery who was being used as a test case to entrap Jesus. Jesus restores her personhood and worth as a human being as he models accurate empathy. In John 9 Jesus is at the center of a conflict with the Pharisees about a man born blind. The Pharisees cannot celebrate the restoration of his sight. Instead they intensify the conflict by excommunication. In this encounter Jesus models the positive use of conflict to achieve a just end. These representative examples show Jesus as a model of pastoral care, meeting each person at the point of a specific need, respecting the dignity and worth of every person, honoring each person's individuality and tailoring a specific response to the needs of the person before him. He intended that all Christians would follow his example and become caregivers, a matter explored in the New Testament letters.

Pastoral Care in the Epistles

Most of the letters of the New Testament were addressed to churches, not solely to church leaders. Even a casual reading reveals that all Christians were responsible for pastoral care.

All Christians were to "love one another deeply, from the heart" (1 Pet 1:22), "bear with each other and forgive" (Col 3:13) and "serve one another in love" (Gal 5:13). All Christians receive the comfort of God "in all our troubles, so that we can comfort those in any trouble with the comfort we ourselves have received from God" (2 Cor 1:4).

While acts of healing* seem to be attributed primarily to apostles, it is clear that all Christians have a specific responsibility to offer care to people in need. The apostolic church could not draw any distinction between the care offered by all Christians and the care that was the distinct responsibility of those holding a pastoral office.

The Beginnings of Pastoral Offices

The newly forming church* discovered a need for a fair and just distribution of food and appointed the Seven to this specific task. The earliest church planters formed the first believers in any city into a church under the care of appointed elders (Acts 14:23). By the end of their ministries the apostles had recognized the need for the emerging pastoral offices of bishop or overseer, elder, deacon and widow. The care that was exercised by all Christians in discerning and meeting human needs became a designated responsibility of these emerging servant leaders.

This movement to concentrate pastoral care in the hands of those holding pastoral offices, discernible in the Pastoral Epistles, becomes the dominant understanding of ministry in the second and third centuries. What had been the expectation and responsibility of every Christian in the apostolic church became the focused responsibility of pastoral leaders within a century.

Two factors accelerated this trajectory: the abuse of power by some and the requirement for an ordered approach to ministry to exercise church discipline. Thomas Oden documents this transfer of responsibility in the *Constitutions of the Holy Apostles,* Cyprian, Origen, Ignatius of Antioch and John Chrysostom (Oden, pp. 41-53). By the fourth century pastoral care had become the specific responsibility of those holding pastoral offices, to the exclusion of the ministry of the whole people of God. The development of the church in both its Eastern and Western divisions reinforced the principle that pastoral care was the responsibility and ministry of those holding pastoral or priestly office. At no point in the history of the church prior to the sixteenth century was there any significant movement to broaden pastoral care to include all Christians as caregivers.

The Unfulfilled Promise of the Reformation

The three central themes of the Reformation in the writings of Martin Luther were faith alone as the basis for salvation, Scripture alone as the supreme authority for faith and practice, and the priesthood of all believers. For one shining moment in history it appeared that all Christians would, once again, be recognized as caregivers. All Christians were encouraged to exercise their priestly ministries. Unfortunately, in the most radical expressions of the Reformation, chaos reigned in this experimental church without orders. By 1526 Luther had restored the offices of priest and pastor (Oden, pp. 85-86). In 1530 he wrote,

> It does not help their case to say that all Christians are priests. It is true that all Christians are priests, but not all are pastors. For to be a pastor one not only must be a Christian and a priest but must have an office and a field of work committed to him. This call and command make pastors and preachers. (Oden, p. 95)

Calvin divided the work of ministry into three orders: minister, elder and deacon. All were set apart by ordination, but the latter two were designated lay offices. Elements of pastoral care were assigned to all three offices. The effect of this broadening of ministry to include some laypersons was to exclude all others from the ministry of caregiving.

The Radical Reformation of the Anabaptists presented a perfect opportunity to extend the caregiving ministries to the whole people of God. Nevertheless, Menno Simons strongly resisted the extension of the ministry of admonition beyond those ordained: "No one is to undertake of himself to preach or admonish from church to church unless he be sent or ordained thereto by the congregation or the elders" (Oden, p. 86).

By the time Richard Baxter codified pastoral expectations, the caregiving ministry had been limited to pastors only. He admonishes,

> Flocks must ordinarily be no greater than we are capable of overseeing. . . . If the pastoral office consists in overseeing all the flock, then surely the number of souls under the care of each pastor must not be greater than he is able to take such heed to as is here required. (Oden, p. 88)

As the Protestant churches entered the twentieth century, pastoral care was assigned almost exclusively to pastors. While the Reformed Churches ordained laypersons to the offices of elder and deacon, in practice their duties were limited and primary care became a pastoral expectation.

The Professionalization of Ministry in the Twentieth Century

Parallel to the movement to raise standards in all of the professions, pastoral ministry succumbed to the pressure to "professionalize" early in the century. Theological seminaries, once the precinct for seasoned pastors to pass on rich experiences in ministry to a new generation, became graduate schools of religion, especially university divinity schools, yearning for a legitimate credentialing process and controlled by the academe and the quest for the Ph.D. Pastoral care became an area of specialization under the influence of Anton Boisen (1876-

1965), founder of the "Chicago School," and his disciple, Seward Hiltner, who shaped two generations of ministers in mainline churches. Another of Boisen's students, Wayne Oates, carried this "professionalization" approach into the Southern Baptist seminaries and churches. Pastoral care became a specialty that required several quarters of highly structured clinical pastoral education (CPE) before one could be certified as professionally qualified. The net result of this movement was to remove the ministry of caregiving even further away for the ordinary Christian. Pastoral care became the province of a very few credentialed specialists.

Recovering Pastoral Care for the Whole People of God

At this point in history Hendrik Kraemer and J. C. Hoekendijk began to tell the broader church about the discoveries of the Dutch during World War II, when pastors were forcibly removed from their churches and the people of God were required to rediscover the truth that all ministry belongs to the whole church. In the recognition that God would never leave the church without essential ministries empowered by the Spirit, the Dutch recovered a more biblical view of ministry. Once the laity were liberated, the church discovered how limiting was every definition of pastoral care that confined this essential ministry solely to pastors. This liberation is a process that has not yet been completed.

Only in recent years could pastoral care have been defined as the care Christians offer to people in need. Simultaneous with this theological recovery was the development of the small group* movement throughout the North American churches. As groups multiplied, the equipping* of lay leaders became essential. Pastors began to see themselves not as the primary deliverers of pastoral care but as equippers of lay leaders, who became the primary caregivers. In thousands of churches organized around some form of the small group model, primary care is the responsibility of the members of the small group as they care for each other, their families and the people in their primary circles. The responsibility for the quality and continuity of this care is vested in the small group leader, who is designated the primary caregiver. Baptism* has been reinstated as the ordination to this ministry. Effective care throughout the whole church has been multiplied exponentially.

See also EQUIPPING; LAITY; MINISTRY; SPIRITUAL FORMATION.

References and Resources
R. Baxter, *The Reformed Pastor* (Portland, Ore.: Multnomah, 1982); G. Bernados, *The Diary of a Country Priest,* trans. P. Morris (London: Fontana, 1956); T. C. Oden, *Classical Pastoral Care,* vol. 1, *Becoming a Minister* (Grand Rapids: Baker, 1987); M. J. Steinbron, *Can the Pastor Do It Alone? A Model for Preparing Lay People for Lay Pastoring* (Ventura, Calif.: Regal, 1987); R. P. Stevens, *The Equipper's Guide to Every-Member Ministry* (Downers Grove, Ill.: InterVarsity Press, 1992); H. W. Stone, *The Caring Church: A Guide for Lay Pastoral Care* (San Francisco: Harper & Row, 1983).

John C. Zimmerman

PETS

It seems that dogs were the first animals to be become pets, probably in Paleolithic times. Evidence from paintings and carvings in ancient tombs of Mesopotamia and Egypt suggests this. These dogs also assisted in the hunting of food. At a later date, c. 2000-1600 B.C., horses and cats became domesticated, the former for riding, the latter to keep the rat population under control. Being domesticated does not necessarily mean that these immediately became pets. Human beings, however, seem to have developed an affection for the animals with whom they worked.

Some animals, such as the seeing-eye dog, continue to have these dual roles today. On farms all over the world the distinction between pet and worker is often blurred, with dogs being used to herd sheep and cattle, sheep to "mow" the grass, and chickens and ducks to produce eggs. All these animals develop personalities that demand relationship. It is only recently that animals have become pets in the sense in which we use that word today, with their purpose being solely for the comfort and companionship of human beings. Though dogs, cats and horses remain favorites as pets, many other species make up the inventory of a modern pet store—rabbits, guinea pigs, hamsters, gerbils, birds, fish, turtles and even reptiles. There is now also the phenomenon of breeding animals to produce more aesthetically pleasing varieties of pets. Some people will pay a high price to own a pet that comes with a piece of paper proving its pedigree.

For centuries humans have celebrated their relationship with animals in art,* music* and literature. From the earliest times dogs were depicted in caves and on tombs. The crypts in European cathedrals are full of casks topped with effigies in brass or stone of the master or mistress with a whippet at their feet. Stories such as "Puss in Boots" and "Dick Whittington's Cat" have been standard fare with children for a couple of centuries. In recent times, as a visit to most bookstores proves, there has been a proliferation of stories about pets by such well-known authors as James Herriot, Paul Gallico, May Sarton and others. Pets have also been the inspiration for such comic-strip humor as Snoopy, Garfield, and Tom and Jerry (*see* Comics). Over the years a slew of movies* have paid homage to a variety of pets, some of whom have become household names—

Lassie Come Home (featuring a dog), *Black Beauty* (a horse), *The Yearling* (a deer), *Flipper* (a dolphin), *Homeward Bound* (two dogs and a cat), and *Babe* (a pig), to name a few. Pets get a poorer showing in music, but as Andrew Lloyd Webber's *Cats* demonstrates, they are not totally absent.

To see how humans have come to value their pets you only have to consider the number of advertisements* on television* or stocks on display in supermarkets for pet food, the array of books and manuals about pets available in shops and libraries, the range of pet shows and ornaments in the shape of pets, or the amount of money* that we spend annually on our pets (*see* Stewardship). In some circles the latter is a cause for concern, for it is interpreted as an indication that our pets have become too important in our lives. It is definitely time to pause and think when we learn that in the West most people spend more money on their pets than they give to people less fortunate than themselves, whether to charities in their own country or aid programs overseas!

Indeed we are no longer content to provide our pets with the basics of life. We want to supply them with luxuries, either as an occasional treat or as the staple of life. Once upon a time pets were fed scraps supplemented by as little deliberately bought food as possible; now we feed them scientifically balanced formulas for whatever stage of life they are at. Once we treated their sicknesses* ourselves; now we not only take them to the vet when they are sick but also give them annual checkups with vaccinations and teeth-cleaning. Some animals are on long-term costly treatments for heart disease, arthritis and other complaints in much the same way as their human counterparts. There is even a growing business in funerals and cemeteries for pets, as well as in pet psychology and counseling.

A Proper Perspective on Pets

Though the Bible has plenty to say about the welfare of animals and portrays God's concern for those that live among humans (Jon 4:11) as well as in the wild (Ps 104:10-18), it has nothing to say about pets in our sense of the word. While its general interest in animals—extending to their resting on the sabbath* as humans do (Ex 20:8-11)—encourages us to care for those with whom we develop a special relationship, it also counsels us against giving too much attention to any living being or material object. Have not we crossed the line here and gone from caring for our pets to giving them too big a priority in our lives, making idols of our pets? Some would argue, like Judas in the Gospels, that the money spent on pets would be better given to the poor. However, the poor, as Jesus said, are always with us (Mt 26:11), and we need to balance our commitment to the poor with the enjoyment of God's gifts, including pets.

Pets add much richness to our lives. They bring companionship, affection and a listening ear. For this reason it is not hard to understand why dogs and cats are by far the most popular choices as pets. They are there to greet us when we arrive home, they offer us unconditional love, asking only a modicum of attention in return, they sense our moods and know when we are in need of comfort and affection, and they are willing to listen to us without interrupting. The warmth of their bodies as we stroke them or their nestling on our knees brings great psychological and physical comfort as well.

Those in the health professions are slowly realizing what wonderful allies they have in pets. As a result pets are beginning to be provided to people in hospitals and in seniors' homes. Even those involved in caring for emotionally disturbed youngsters are realizing that pets have an important role to play in their rehabilitation. Animal therapy, as it is called, is a growing phenomenon.

Parents have long appreciated how much their children have to learn from having a pet in the home. Through having to look after a pet, children learn that animals have to be cared for, helping develop responsibility. A pet has to be fed regularly, provided with hygienic conditions to live in and given regular affection. Without these the pet will not thrive, and neither will children or any other animal deprived of such care. While it is true that animals cannot talk, anyone watching a child with a loved pet knows that communication takes place. As children develop a relationship with a pet, they begin to read the pet's body language. The children start to know when the pet wants something to eat or drink, needs to go outside or just wants attention. They even learn when the animal is pleased or displeased. These are good skills to learn. They have wonderful crossover value in the child's relationships with other humans. Where there is more than one species of pet in a home, such as a dog and a cat, children have the opportunity to learn that animals who are natural enemies can live in peace when they are loved by the same person.

Pets can also be a means of spiritual grace and understanding. Just as animals are referred to throughout the Bible to portray divine things (Is 53:7; Mt 3:16), so too God makes himself known to people through their pets. I have heard people claim that they first understood God's unconditional love through the love their pet extended to them. I have often watched my own cat, seemingly fast asleep but instantly alert at the slightest noise, and reflected on the example of what it means to rest in the Lord.

Someone asked C. S. Lewis whether he thought his dog would go to heaven. Lewis replied that as Scripture was silent on the matter, he could not be sure. However, since the kingdom of God is portrayed metaphorically as embracing animals, and since his dog was so much a part of him, he was inclined to hope that this would be the case.

See also CHORES; FAMILY; GREETING.

Resources and References
J. Sobosan, *Bless the Beasts* (New York: Crossroad, 1991).

Julie Banks

PHOTOGRAPHY

Eastman Kodak's motto, "You press the button, we do the rest," marked the introduction of mass photography. With easy-to-operate cameras and flexible roll films invented by George Eastman in 1888, snapshots could be taken by everyone almost everywhere, not just by professionals lugging heavy glass plates, tripods and processing equipment into the field to expose their plates for minutes and sometimes hours. Photography is the "production of visible images by the action of light" (*Encyclopedia Americana*, 1989, 22:1). Until recently this exclusively involved a camera and a light-sensitive film, but the development of digital photography with electronic imaging, compact disks and computer enhancement now offers both the amateur and the professional new opportunities for interpreting what they see with the naked eye.

Cameras have many uses today. They are *weapons,* as suggested by the intrusive words we use to describe "capturing" something for propaganda or advertising*; they are *memory-makers* used to preserve selected experiences as souvenirs; they are an *art medium* for aesthetic expression. These three uses of the camera have altered our way of perceiving. On one hand, art photographers see penetratively and intensively and can help others to do so; on the other hand, casual photographers armed with their so-called idiot-proof cameras snapping everything in sight in order to get it and take it home (which they cannot do), trampling on sacred sites without reverence or patience, are not really seeing at all. Sometimes they would be better off not taking pictures but simply looking at and being present to the scene. Making home movies (a series of still pictures that give the illusion of motion) and videotaping can extend this complicated process of seeing and not seeing even further (*see* Home Video). All this has happened in just under two centuries, but the idea behind photography has a long history and a rich theological foundation.

Humankind as Image-Maker
Replicating what one sees, interpreting its meaning and expressing one's own feelings about it through some medium, so making something genuinely new, are part of the cultural mandate given by God (Gen 1:28-30). Such creativity is evidenced in the earliest cave drawings and is the heart of true art.* As with all aspects of the human vocation, making images comes with a temptation. It is all too easy to attribute ultimate meaning to the image one has created, to idolize it (Ex 20:4; Rom 1:23) and to invest the devotion of one's heart in a human creation rather than in God. The prohibition against making images of God and worshiping them is particularly illustrative of the problem; the image of God crafted by human beings (whether through graphic or theological expression) will always be something less than a personal God who is full of surprises and cannot be reduced to human dimensions. Idols "have ears, but cannot hear" (Ps 115:6), in contrast to the living God, who "does whatever pleases him" (Ps 115:3). This warning notwithstanding, making im-

ages is not only worth the risk; it is mandated. We were created to be cocreators, artistically designed to become artists, imagined into life by God (Gen 1:26) to become imagining creatures.

Cultures influenced by the strongly anti-image bias of Islam tend to be antiphotographic. It is sometimes thought that photographing a person tampers with the essence of that person. In contrast, Christianity, founded on the miracle of the incarnation (Jn 1:14), has affirmed that images expressed in down-to-earth matter (paint or silver salts) can communicate truth in ways complementary to spoken or written words. Words can appeal to our spirit; art enters the soul* through another door than intellect. In the Greek and Russian Orthodox churches a long tradition of iconography has flourished precisely because the Eastern church believed so strongly that the grace of God should be expressed through visual media (Baggley, p. 9). Making images is implicit in the holy materialism of the faith and its founder.

Photography is art and can be Christian art, precisely because it is not mere replication but a creative interpretation of reality, an externalizing of truth, an enfleshment, and not just an illustration of truth. It can be revelation. So photography, along with all other visual arts, is a way of knowing. It is a way of knowing with a long history.

Image-Maker as Shutterbug

The theory behind taking photographs was first enunciated by Aristotle, who described how light waves behave when projected through a small aperture (*Encyclopedia Americana*, 1989, 2:9). Building on this idea led to the development of the *camera obscura* in the Middle Ages. The camera obscura was a darkened room with an opening in the wall that created images (reversed and upside down). This was reduced in size to a box,

thus permitting artists and architects to use the device to trace images, and with the development of light-sensitive materials using silver salts, semipermanent images could be obtained. The development of photography was spurred further by the Renaissance interest in reproducing nature and the increasing public demand for realistic portraits.

Eventually in 1830 this led to the *daguerreotype* (a silver-covered copper plate), which revolutionized portraiture and opened up expeditionary photography for travelers.* With the development of paper *prints* from negatives in 1940, family albums and, equally important, illustrations for books and periodicals became possible. Further developments into the twentieth century included gelatin-based papers, user-friendly cameras, color film, flash powder and flash bulbs. Two new cameras, the Leica and Ermanox, predecessors of the 35mm camera, allowed people to take cameras almost anywhere, even to political conferences, inspiring the term *candid camera* (*Encyclopedia Americana*, 1989, 22:20). Eventually electronic flash, instant cameras, fully automated cameras, throwaway cameras and the digitalized camera have been developed and popularized. But to what end?

Over the decades cameras have been used as a tool for reproducing nature (the first real subject), for producing realistic portraits, for providing pictures of places and peoples seen by travelers and international ambassadors, for making social statements about the plight of minorities and oppressed peoples, for journalistic reports of wars and political events, for propaganda (during World War II), for advertising and fashion promotion and for artistic expression. Today art photographers try to express a meaningful slice of life, "the humorous, the bizarre, the typical, and the surreal associations of everyday life" (*Encyclope-*

dia Americana, 1989, 22:23). Undoubtedly the pervasive effect of photography has altered our expectations and our ways of learning. Since the picture-journals *Life* and *Look* started in the 1930s, we have come to expect pictures in magazines, newspapers and textbooks. But is one picture worth a thousand words? What does all this picture taking mean?

Shutterbug as Artist

An advertisement for a 35mm camera reads, "We take pictures to record our personal vision of the world." As photographer Bob Llewellyn says, "Every photograph you make is a self-portrait" (quoted in Doeffinger, p. 10). *Photographic realism* is really an oxymoron because there is always a wonderful subjectivity in what the photographer sees through the lens of the camera. So along with the camera as weapon, aid to memory and art medium, we must add *mirror.* But the mirror is not used simply to know ourselves.

First, photography is for *newscasting*—showing to others a happening or unusual event that will arouse interest and stimulate reflection. The subject could be the positive delight of a child in turning on an outside tap and sprinkling herself with water or the awesome power of a tropical storm tearing up the concrete deck of a wharf. There is more than simple recording involved in this. The sacraments,* festivals* and memorials of the Old and New Testaments assist us to relive the past and interpret the meaning of the present in the light of something that has happened—a lived and relived history. In the same way photographs create living history, though not in the arrogant way claimed by some film advertisements that our picture creates an image that will last forever.

Second, photography is for *communication* in which the language "spoken" is not a string of intelligible words but the linkage of texture, line, shape, form and color into a fluent message that may "praise, carp, clarify, or obscure" (Doeffinger, p. 37). We cannot speak fluently in the language of photography until we know our subject well enough. The trouble often is that we have only a nodding acquaintance with what we photograph. We have looked but not seen. So our preconceptions take over, preventing reflection on the meaning of the subject and true expression of our feelings about it (Doeffinger, p. 37).

Third, photography is for *celebration.* A camera licenses us "to observe and delight in the world" (Doeffinger, p. 57). Just as Adam delighted in his wife (Gen 2:24), so humankind is meant to turn the observation of creation and people into worship of God. We can do this in photographing the most common, everyday things, thus making, as photographer Edward Weston says, "the commonplace unusual" (quoted in Doeffinger, p. 22). Pictures of a meal set on a table, wrinkled skin, a bathtub, curtains in a window, a corn broom resting in the corner of a room, all help us revise our thinking about everyday life evoking feelings and spirituality.

What makes a good photograph is surprise (by showing an unusual perspective or an unusual subject), feeling (by creating a mood), relationality (by exploring the connections of life), wholeness (by expressing a viewpoint through composition) and simplicity (by "saying" only one thing clearly). There is so much more to photography than pressing the button and letting the processor do the rest. The camera sees indiscriminately, nonselectively, sweeping everything into its rectangular view. In fact the camera does not see at all. It simply records light. The human eye and brain, in contrast, focus on sensations that interest us because of our wants, preconceptions and feelings. We see what is in our heart, just as we speak* what is within us. So to take a good photograph people must, paradoxically, train themselves to see as the camera does (nonselectively) and then compose the picture to express what they actually see (selectively). This is why most of the millions of pictures taken annually are snap*shots* (bullets fired at an object) rather than doors of perception.

Like all achievements of technology,* mass photography is a mixed blessing. If the development of a universal photographic culture has become a way of knowing, it has also become a way of unknowing, a way of missing reality. If we vacuously snap everything in sight, we have allowed picture taking to usurp seeing; we express an unimaginative view of a world not worth celebrating and a God not delightful to worship. Probably all photographers can profit by becoming more contemplative, reflecting on their own feelings and preconceptions, their own beliefs and unbeliefs. Have we seen or merely looked? Do we know our subject well enough to respect it? Do we reverence life enough, as God-imaging and God-worshiping creatures, to revel in what we have seen? Can we savor it even if the picture does not turn out or we forget to take the camera along?

See also ART; HOBBIES AND CRAFTS; MOVIES.

References and Resources
The Art of Photography (Alexandria, Va.: Time-Life, 1971); J. Baggley, *Doors of Perception: Icons and Their Spiritual Significance* (Crestwood, N.Y.: St. Vladimir's Seminary Press, 1988); D. Doeffinger, *The Art of Seeing* (Rochester, N.Y.: Eastman Kodak, 1992).

R. Paul Stevens

PLANNING

Thomas Carlyle said, "Nothing is more terrible than activity without insight."

With even greater wisdom Proverbs notes, "Many are the plans in a man's heart, but it is the LORD's purpose that prevails" (Prov 19:21).

Planning is something everyone does, says they do or would like to do. It is remarkable how much personal planning happens in the course of one day: choosing clothes to wear, getting the trash and recycling out on time, planning the fastest route to the job according to morning traffic flows, scheduling errands and taxiing children to their activities, deciding how much money to withdraw from the ATM (automated teller machine), filling out the form to join the CD (compact disk) club, ensuring meal ingredients are available and cooked at approximately the same time, programming the VCR (videocassette recorder), choosing a clock alarm setting in order to maximize sleep and minimize panic the next morning. Given all of this, we have not begun to touch the planning required at work,* through school and in community involvements.

Much of this planning is conscious, deliberate and efficient. When things go wrong, we resolve to plan better. Perhaps we think about buying a book or attending a workshop on the topic of planning. But the basic questions are, How do we know (before the results) what a good approach to planning might be? How do we evaluate the approaches to planning that are constantly being suggested in this accelerated, acronymic age in which we live? What is the difference between personal planning and planning as a group? Finally, if we can figure out what planning is, does a distinctively Christian view of it exist?

The Nature and Variety of Planning
There are as many definitions of planning as there are definitions of leadership.* Standard dictionaries suggest two basic approaches: *planning* as arranging

the parts of or designing something and *planning* as devising or projecting the achievement of something. Unless we are in a design profession such as architecture,* the latter is more what we have in mind when we think of planning. That is not to say that planning to fulfill an aim is an uncreative process: once a purpose has been identified, assessing and marshaling resources, selecting structures* and activities, and evaluating results related to the purpose all involve a lot of creativity. Sometimes the planning process seems unconscious or instantaneous, but by definition some kind of intentionality and mental work must be involved with planning. Very brief analyses of options for their efficiency (minimum resources), elegance (simple structures) and effectiveness (maximum results) are going on all the time in our daily lives, even if we are not very aware of the process.

For example, you want to go out for an evening and therefore begin to contact baby sitters on your list (assuming you are fortunate enough to have a list). Your first choice to phone may seem random or instinctual, but it is really the product of a rapid planning process. You have made assessments of the choices and decided on the option that is most (1) efficient (who is most likely ready and willing), (2) elegant (who comes with no strings attached, for example, with no need to negotiate with a teen's parents or to return the favor, in the case of baby-sitting exchanges) and (3) effective (who is most reliable based on reputation and experience). Or perhaps you just maximized the particular value that is most important to you at this time. No wonder these simple tasks tire us out.

In more formal group processes, such as we encounter in work settings and organizations, there are layers of planning to consider. First is identifying the purpose driving the plan (some people call this the *mission* or *vision**). Next is assessing or assembling resources (for example, money*) and structures (that is, the right groupings of people, lines of communication and policies). Then there are the selection and sequencing of activities that will contribute to the purpose. I have just described various nuances of planning: planning as intention (we plan to . . .), planning as preparation (planning for a trip), planning as a program of choices (the first step in the plan is . . .) and planning as implementation (who will do what by when). Finally, there is evaluating how it all worked out. This last stage, often neglected and sometimes painful, is actually vital. A group of successful executives was once asked how they had come to make such good decisions. Their answer was "Experience." They were then asked how they got experience. The answer they immediately gave was "Bad decisions." Evaluated experience is a key raw ingredient of good planning.

There is an additional layer of the formal planning process we must note, that is, how exactly people are supposed to approach the various decisions just described. This is sometimes called *planning the planning*. This preliminary planning requires a process of its own; it too is a stage that is often neglected, for people launch into formulating a plan without thinking about how to do the planning and what kind of plan is desired. The fact is that there are many different ways to do planning or make decisions, especially in a group. Will voting or a consensus approach be used? Can closure on the discussion be invoked? Who will chair, and what will be the chair's duties and powers? What planning model will be followed? (See "How to Plan Anything," below, for one approach.)

There are also many different types of plans: long- or short-range, strategic (focused on key purposes) or action, comprehensive or single-issue. Finally, there are different approaches to the components of planning, for example, cost-benefit analysis, pros and cons, computer simulation and brainstorming. In modern technological* society, planning has been reduced to a technique, thus presenting further ambiguities for followers of One who appeared not to plan, at least not in the modern technological manner (see Cadbury, *The Peril of Modernizing Jesus*). Are all these approaches equally valid for the Christian? Even more profoundly, is planning itself valid for the believer? The negative warning of James 4:13-17 is at least a prohibition against boasting in our plans as though we were gods, which is a form of practical atheism.

Divine Planning and Ours

Few would disagree that we are to be guided by plans. The main debate in Christian circles concerns how the plans originate: through a human process or as a revelation from God. There are instances when God's instructions to individuals are very specific (for example, Abram's being directed to leave his homeland for Canaan in Gen 12:1) and detailed (for example, the plans given to Moses for the tabernacle in Ex 26:30; compare Ezek 43:10). We see Jesus following a plan, for example, as he generally restricts himself to a Jewish rather than Gentile ministry, as he tries to manage the public relations around his miracles and as he sets his face toward Jerusalem. However, it is difficult in the case of Jesus to distinguish between revelation and methodical planning—in fact, we are not given much insight into the latter at all. When he selected the twelve apostles, it was after an all-night prayer session. Was there any "human" planning going on in that case, or is the planning of the faithful supposed to be

merely a matter of getting in touch with God's intentions? One textbook on social planning offered this definition of its topic: "Planning is the guidance of future actions" (Forester, p. 3). But surely guidance* is to be left to God.

It is true that God is Planner. The Scriptures are full of testimony to this notion. The Lord declares through the prophecy in Isaiah 14:24, "Surely, as I have planned, so it will be, and as I have purposed, so it will stand." Paul echoes the sentiment in Ephesians 1:11: "In him we were also chosen, having been predestined according to the plan of him who works out everything in conformity with the purpose of his will" (see also 2 Kings 19:25; Ps 33:11; 40:5; Is 23:8-9; 25:1; 37:26; Jer 29:11; Heb 11:40). It is clear that whereas God's plans cannot be thwarted (Job 42:2; Prov 21:30), God is quite capable of thwarting the plans of his creatures and is especially willing to do so when those plans are evil (Job 5:12; Ps 64:5-8; Is 8:10). One of the most famous case studies of such thwarting is the attempted construction of the tower of Babel in Genesis 11. Sometimes less-than-perfect human plans are woven into God's overall plan, as Joseph testified to his brothers in Genesis 50:20: "You intended to harm me, but God intended it for good to accomplish what is now being done, the saving of many lives." The same idea emerges in David's plan to build a temple: he is prevented, but the task is transferred by God to Solomon (1 Chron 28). The concept of God's redeeming our plans is most powerfully seen in God's superintending the conspiracy surrounding the execution of his own Son (Acts 2:23).

The question that remains after observing this strong theology of divine planning is whether or not any room exists for appropriate human planning. Concerns about the dangers inherent in human planning have also been raised in other spheres (for example, Jacques Ellul's critique of technicized economic planning). God's word in the middle of the Babel story seems to echo these concerns: "If as one people speaking the same language they have begun to do this, then nothing they plan to do will be impossible for them" (Gen 11:6). However, other biblical evidence seems to allow a role for human planning processes. The aforementioned story of Joseph is one case: though one knows he is in Egypt by God's design and God does reveal details about the upcoming famine in that land, Joseph also seems to play a role, based on gifting* and wisdom, in coming up with the plan to save the nation (Gen 41:33-40). Such a picture fits well with the strand in the New Testament that describes believers as God's fellow workers (1 Cor 3:5-9; 2 Cor 6:1; 1 Thess 3:2). This is both a humbling and an exciting concept. A last bit of evidence is the tacit support given to planning in Proverbs. It is true that many cautions and limitations are put on planning in this book (Prov 19:21), but all of this assumes first that planning is a human activity that God expects and endorses (for example, Prov 14:22; compare Is 32:8).

Personality and a Theology of Planning
Some, because of how they are shaped as people, would like to believe that planning as a human process can or should be avoided or at least severely curtailed. Resistance to planning within Christian organizations may be especially exhibited by members who are weary of planning in the rest of their lives and who, for example, come to church services for a break. But the resistance may run even deeper. Antiplanners may claim that their personality does not suit planning. They are free spirits, letting each minute, hour and day unfold as a series of spontaneous events and choices. However, as

soon as they admit the notion of choice, they have admitted the reality of planning as well. To select one thing over another requires a plan, even if it is established and implemented in an instant. Moreover, even if the semblance of a Thoreau-like spontaneous life were sustainable, the decision to operate in this fashion itself represents a plan!

Further, those weak on planning may buttress personality with spirituality: they say they are guided by the Holy Spirit, making plans unnecessary. There are two problems with this approach. It confuses process and product, and it is bad theology. Whether or not the Spirit is involved with the choices that make up a plan does nothing to invalidate planning; the Spirit may very well guide you in the details of a plan, but a plan nevertheless results. Why would the Spirit be unable to influence a human planning process that is submitted to him? To believe otherwise is to be overprotective of the Spirit. Furthermore, the decision to be prayerful, or to adopt a waiting, listening attitude, involves planning, specifically planning how to plan. The bad theology of what might be called overdependence on the Spirit's leading is that it ignores God's awesome creativity in actually giving his creatures free will. Whatever the input of the Spirit, in God's economy there still are real human choices with real consequences. Without trying to solve all of the philosophical issues of determinism and free will, let it suffice to say that the notion of human freedom prevents planning from being cast aside out of some kind of respect for God's sovereignty.

Finally, action-oriented persons, though accepting the general defense of planning, may want to short-circuit the process, moving quickly to tasks rather than getting bogged down in interminable planning processes. Again, though there is wisdom in being reminded about efficient processes and the importance of implementation, the solution for frustrated activists is to leave the earlier parts of the planning process to others and come in only at the end. As Jesus himself suggested in a couple of brief parables on counting the cost, there is reason for taking time and care in planning (Lk 14:28-32).

The above discussion does suggest that a distinction can be drawn between personal planning and that done within organizations. When it comes to planning in your individual life, perhaps cautions against being overly technical are in order. We must be honest enough to admit that the idea of consciously selecting a purpose and being rigorously guided by it may be more of a modern concept than a reflection of the life of Jesus. Consider how one writer has described the Lord's approach:

> Whatever he said and did was not brought by him into accord with some external criterion; it sprang from an inner coordination of life. In such cases logical consistency is not always present and is not intended; but a moral consistency may be there, an habitual reaction. . . . Perhaps some day in the future historical students of the gospels will realize that there is more profit in inquiring into these hidden habits of his soul than in attempting to fit the anecdotes and sayings of Jesus into a program of his life. (Cadbury, pp. 148-49)

To apply these sentiments too quickly to organizational planning, however, may be misguided.

The fact must be faced that some of the reasons for avoiding planning in groups involve the flesh more than the soul.* Planning is hard work, not meant for the lazy or undisciplined; planning permits evaluation, not meant for the insecure; planning builds teamwork, not meant for the antisocial. With this having

been said, it is important to recognize legitimate differences in the way believers approach planning. The key is to see that all planning is not automatically labeled as being unspiritual and all spirituality as being unplanned: "Such attitudes prejudge all planning as being carnal and ignore the validity of a third option: Spirit-guided planning. Let each be fully persuaded in his own mind, but let the spiritual nonplanner be careful lest he judge the planner as being necessarily carnal" (Alexander, p. 19).

How to Plan Anything

So what might Spirit-guided planning look like? There are many patterns that may be followed in planning for organizations. Here is one that seeks to honor God and, when used in a group, to honor God's people as your colleagues.

Commit your planning to God. Always begin with a commitment to God, not to have him bless your plans, but to have your plans caught up in his (Prov 16:3). This requires an understanding of God's purposes as revealed in his Word and a sober interpretation of current reality (read Is 22). You cannot stop too often in a planning process to ask for God's direction and correction.

Define the planning task or the purpose. What exactly are you trying to achieve? Many wasted hours will be avoided if you can answer this question as clearly as possible (Acts 15:6).

Identify personal goals and motives that you bring to the planning process. This is especially important in planning with a group. For example, some may be interested in building teamwork through consensus approaches to planning and combined efforts in implementation; others may want to get the meetings over as quickly as possible so that they can get into action by themselves. One can imagine the different agendas that Paul and Barnabas brought to planning the second missionary journey (Act 15:36-41). Sometimes motives need to be submitted to God and reconciled before planning can proceed (Prov 16:2).

Establish the facts or context. This can include a list of external constraints, an inventory of resources and an analysis of current structures (groups and policies). It also includes understanding the history of a project (Acts 15:7-18).

Generate action ideas. What could be done to fulfill the task? The more ideas, the better. If you are engaged in a personal planning process, this is the step (along with the next two) in which the biblical value of multiple advisers comes into play (Prov 11:14; 15:22; 20:18; 24:6). The value of group planning processes is, of course, that "many heads" are built right in. The Spirit works through the plurality and gifting in a group context, and the implementation is partially done if the group is involved in the process (*see* Leadership, Church; Management).

Package the ideas into major options. Such packaging makes evaluating the options easier, for there are only so many things that can be considered at once. Do not give in to a sense of urgency and take shortcuts through the process. This logical linking of options is a distinct step in planning. As with the whole process, take time on it (Prov 21:5); it will make the next step easier.

Assess the option packages. Which one best serves the task or purpose? Use any tools that make sense, for example, a list of pros and cons for each option. Get input from everyone in the group (or from everyone in your group of advisers). Pray for wisdom and insight (1 Kings 3:9-10; Jas 1:5).

Draw a conclusion. In some ways this is easier when the final authority falls on the chair (Acts 15:19) or when you are dealing with a personal decision (though going against advice can be painful; for example, see Acts 20:12-14). However,

there is power in a consensus decision, as many people will be behind it emotionally and practically.

Implement your plan with holy boldness. (Note that implementation may require another planning process.) We are saved by grace, not by works, including the works of planning. We step out knowing that God goes before us, will forgive us and will work all things together for good (Rom 8:28). He has already paid the price for our imperfection; he requires only faithfulness from us as planners.

Be prepared for course corrections. Paul did plan the itineraries for his missionary journeys (2 Cor 1:15-17), but he also knew that plans had to be changed sometimes (Rom 1:13) and himself encountered course corrections (for example, Acts 16:6-10). We must hold all plans lightly before the Lord (Prov 16:1, 9; 19:21) and before changing circumstances.

Although not a guarantee of good results, this sort of careful process can lead to an agreement between God's Spirit and God's people that brings him glory (Acts 15:28).

The Benefits of Planning

Christians can benefit from good planning in many spheres. For Christians as individuals, these spheres are career* choice and attainment, marriage,* budgeting, personal mission statements and family goals.* For Christians as church members, these spheres are small group* contracting, management and eldership decisions. For Christians as neighbors, there are increasing opportunities and needs for public participation in urban planning. Finally, for Christians as global* citizens, there is a place for involvement in national and international planning issues.

There are several ways that planning can help in any of these spheres. First, there is a basis for evaluation and redirection based on a clear purpose and activities meant to serve that purpose. Second, there is a basis for saying no, for avoiding lower priorities and weaker ideas that distract from the main purpose. Time is the ultimate limited resource that must be protected in good planning: "I can do only one thing at a time, but I can avoid doing many things simultaneously" (Ashleigh Brilliant). Third, good planning means that personal and group resources can be released most powerfully: "Within most Christian groups is an enormous amount of creativity. Let us encourage and stimulate this potential in every possible way. Let us urge people to think creatively on every aspect of our purposes, to be bold to experiment with new objectives, fresh strategies . . . and tactics . . . and to innovate wherever desirable so that we can more effectively fulfill our purposes" (Alexander, p. 21).

See also GUIDANCE; TIME; VOCATIONAL GUIDANCE.

References and Resources

J. W. Alexander, *Managing Our Work* (Downers Grove, Ill.: InterVarsity Press, 1975); R. S. Anderson, *Minding God's Business* (Grand Rapids: Eerdmans, 1986); H. J. Cadbury, *The Peril of Modernizing Jesus* (London: SPCK, 1962); K. L. Callahan, *Twelve Keys to an Effective Church* (San Francisco: Harper & Row, 1983); J. Ellul, *The Technological Society* (New York: Vintage Books, 1964); J. Forester, *Planning in the Face of Power* (Berkeley: University of California Press, 1989).

Dan Williams

PLAY

Christians know they are to work* (Gen 1:28; Jn 9:4; Col 3:23-24; 2 Thess 3:10-13). They are not so sure they should play. As workers, Christians are God's coworkers involved in redeeming the creation.* This preoccupation with work is reinforced by our Western culture.* As Wayne Oates humorously, but pointedly, summarized over two decades ago, "The workaholic's way of life is considered in America to be at one and the same time a religious virtue, a form of patriotism, the way to win friends and influence people and the way to be healthy, wealthy, and wise" (p. 12).

The Problem of Play

Given this "blessing" from both church and culture, it is not surprising that North Americans are continuing to work longer hours and that their culture is leisure oriented. Since World War II there has been an increase in purchasing power, paid vacations,* life expectancy and recreational* activity. Nevertheless, upwards of two-thirds of workers express discontentment and dissatisfaction with their working lives and continue to work long hours and to define their meaning primarily in terms of the workplace.

In the United States since 1980 the percentage of those working more than 50 hours a week has consistently increased, and the number of leisure hours for adults has continued to drop (from 26.2 hours in 1973 to 16.6 hours in 1987). Americans are both playing and enjoying their work less. This problem with play is compounded by four factors: (1) the difficulty for those in poverty* to have the freedom of spirit to play, (2) the trend of women working both in the workplace and disproportionately to men in the home,* (3) the effect of consumerism* in producing hectic and frenetic lives and (4) a twisted understanding of play as escapism, passivity, hedonism or narcissism. No wonder Christians especially struggle with play. Yet when humans play authentically, they immediately sense its value.

When Is "Play" Play?

As with love* or art,* the definition of *play* is elusive. It is, however, possible to describe some of the central features of play. Johan Huizinga does this well. He says play is

> a free activity standing quite consciously outside "ordinary" life as being "not serious," but at the same time absorbing the player intensely and utterly. It is an activity connected with no material interest, and no profit can be gained by it. It proceeds within its own proper boundaries of time and space according to fixed rules and in an orderly manner. It promotes the formation of social groupings. (Huizinga, p. 13)

Child psychologist Jean Piaget adds helpfully that play is always done "for the pleasure of the activity" (pp. 92-93). We can best understand the essence of play by looking at four pairs of descriptors.

Playtimes and playgrounds. Play always carries with it a new time and a new space that function as "parentheses" in the life of the participant. Everyday life comes to a standstill for the duration of the experience (for example, the ballgame, the concert, the solitaire game), and the boundaries of one's world are forged anew (for example, one does not ask if the movie *The Lion King* is true or good, or to the degree that one does, he or she is no longer playing).

Individual freedom and loving community. People voluntarily choose to play; it cannot be coerced. Yet players also sense that they have been invited into play by a potential coplayer and/or a play object. Thus, while at play they must treat other players and "playthings" as personal, creating with them a community (compare the child talking to the baseball as it is thrown against the concrete building or the lovers who participate in a mutual process of give and take). It has been said, "Freedom does not die in love; it is born there" (Sadler, p. 243).

Spontaneity and design. Regardless of prior preparation, which is often quite rigorous (compare the dancer or the concert pianist), there is spontaneity at the heart of play. As we jump, sing or skip, our spirits soar. But such abandon is never at the expense of play's orderliness. Every game of cricket is an occasion for new possibility, but without the rules "it's not cricket." Music* is the occasion for the spirit to wonder, but only through the strict appropriation of certain rules of tone, harmony and timing.

Nonutilitarian, yet productive. Play cannot be entered into with continuing outside interest if it is to become play. Although the insurance agent might play golf with a client to get a contract,* it is only when business can be suspended that the game of golf ceases to be a form of work. Yet although play can have no ulterior motive or material interest (compare worshiping God as an act of *play*), it is not without fruitful consequence. In play one is able to do four things: (1) to create strong bonds with others and the world, (2) to emancipate one's spirit, (3) to rediscover life in its entirety as the player becomes involved in the wholeness of her or his being and (4) to experience joy and delight that lingers. In these ways the player finds perspective for reengagement in the workaday world.

There are, of course, many examples of the trivialization of play. One need only think of the strikes in professional baseball and hockey when the game has become sheer business at the expense of the fans. It is possible for play to be exploitive, as the goose-stepping parades of Nazi Germany remind us. One of my favorite quotations comes from Eric Gill who said, "It is a sin to eat inferior ice cream" (quoted in Kerr, p. 277). Such a statement has nothing to do with calories or with human perversity but with the recognition that to eat ice cream that tastes bad is to act in a self-contradictory manner.

Although play can be corrupted, all of us have experienced its fullness and value. Why is it that I care about what happens to the Chicago Bears or that I look forward to next year's ballet season? Because I have a longing for play.

Biblical Paradigms and Models

Throughout its pages the Bible recognizes the importance of play, though we have failed to see it. Ecclesiastes advises us to enjoy our food and drink and the person we love. The Song of Songs is devoted exclusively to the playfulness of human sexuality.* The sabbath* has as its most basic definition a time of "nonwork." Throughout the Old Testament we encounter the festivals* and dances of God's people. The practice of hospitality* was an occasion for work to stop and a wholeness in life to be regained. Similarly in the New Testament Jesus' own life exhibited a healthy rhythm of work and play. His times alone and his friendship* with those like Mary, Martha and Lazarus show us that play was important to him.

Yet, we have systematically ignored or misinterpreted these texts. Christians have wondered how Ecclesiastes ever made it into the canon and have misinterpreted the author as writing only about life "under the sun" (that is, secular existence; Eccles 1:14). For centuries the church has attempted to reinterpret the Song of Songs as an allegory about God's love for them. Many of us grew up in a context that interpreted the sabbath ordinance as applying primarily to our worship.* We have failed to understand that Old Testament practices concerning hospitality have aesthetic as well as ethical dimensions—they were occasions for a party.* Were the instances of friendship in the life of Jesus simply another way of proclaiming his messiahship, or were they also expressions of his own humanity? In ways such as these,

Christians have failed to let Scripture teach us concerning a God-intended rhythm of work and play, play and work. Like our wider culture, we have adopted an undialectical commitment to work as our basic ideology.

Basic to a biblical understanding of play is a recognition that Scripture's concerns include creation as well as redemption. There are multiple theological emphases within its chapters. In Genesis 1 and 2, for example, God is portrayed as working and resting. His rest* included enjoyment of creation and fellowship with humankind. Here is the basic paradigm for us: created in the image of God, we are to be creatures who both work and play.

This creational perspective is picked up in the call for a fundamental rhythm within human existence, the sabbath (for example, Ex 34:21-22). For the Hebrew the sabbath was not chiefly a time for worship but an occasion for relativizing one's work (compare Ex 16:22-30). It was not by the efforts of those who gathered up manna, but only through the gracious provision of God, that the Israelites found life and safety. Although the restatement of the Ten Commandments in Deuteronomy 5 justifies the sabbath practice in terms of being God's coworkers, in the prior account in Exodus 20 the rationale for the sabbath is referenced to God alone. Through the sabbath we are invited to "remember" that life is a gift as well as a task.

This creational perspective is continued in the wisdom literature of the Old Testament as well as in those books such as the Song of Songs and Psalms in which theological argument is based on God's acts in creation. The Song of Songs opens a window into the beauty and wholeness of human love, which can instruct us as to our own sexual relationships. Psalm 23 sings a song of trust in the Lord by using two analogies that include work and play—shepherding and hospitality. Psalm 104 celebrates the fact that as God's creatures we are to cultivate the earth both to provide bread for our needs, wine to make our heart glad and oil to make our faces shine (Ps 104:14-15). Ecclesiastes mounts a frontal assault on workaholism, which would foolishly try to find meaning in life independent of the God who has created us, and instead finds in Genesis 1—11 sufficient insight to portray our lot in life as enjoying our work and our play (Eccles 9:7-10).

The Christian at Play

The evidence for play in the Bible is extensive, particularly in those discussions that are rooted in creation theology. But even in the books of the Law and the Prophets, as in the New Testament, we find culturally specific examples of Israel at play. In festival and feast, in dance and friendship, play's strong motifs surface. A God-intended human lifestyle of work and play finds its basis in creation and its full possibility in Jesus' re-creation (compare Heb 4).

Films such as *Chariots of Fire* and *The Shawshank Redemption* portray the importance of play within human existence. So, too, have writers as diverse as C. S. Lewis, Peter Berger and Dietrich Bonhoeffer. In *Surprised by Joy* Lewis describes those moments of play—reading Beatrix Potter or George MacDonald, smelling a currant bush or listening to Wagner—when he felt himself ushered into a reality that was illuminating for all existence. In his book *A Rumor of Angels* Peter Berger finds "signals of transcendence" when our living toward death is bracketed and we experience "eternity" in play (p. 52). And in *Letters and Papers from Prison* (p. 193) Dietrich Bonhoeffer, writing out of his cell as he faced death because of his opposition to Hitler during World War II, commented on the general shape of human life:

> I wonder whether it is possible . . . to regain the idea of the Church as providing an understanding of the area of freedom (art, education, friendship, play). . . . Who is there, for instance, in our times, who can devote himself with an easy mind to music, friendship, games, or happiness? Surely not the "ethical" man, but only the Christian (January 23, 1944).

See also ART; BOREDOM; DRIVENNESS; LEISURE; RECREATION; SABBATH; SPORTS; VACATIONS; WORK; WORK ETHIC, PROTESTANT.

References and Resources

P. Berger, *A Rumor of Angels* (Garden City, N.Y.: Doubleday/Anchor, 1970); D. Bonhoeffer, *Letters and Papers from Prison,* ed. E. Bethge, rev. ed., (New York: Macmillan, 1967); P. Heintz-man, G. Van Andel and T. Visker, *Christianity and Leisure* (Sioux City, Iowa: Dordt College Press, 1994); J. Huizinga, *Homo Ludens* (Boston: Beacon Press, 1955); R. K. Johnston, *The Christian at Play* (Grand Rapids: Eerdmans, 1983); W. Kerr, *The Decline of Pleasure* (New York: Simon & Schuster, 1962); C. S. Lewis, *Surprised by Joy* (New York: Harcourt, Brace & World/Harvest Books, 1955); Wayne Oates, *Confessions of a Workaholic* (New York: World, 1971); J. Piaget, *Play, Dreams and Imitation in Childhood,* trans. C. Gattegno and F.M. Hodgson (New York: Norton, 1962); W. Sadler Jr., "Play: A Basic Human Structure Involving Love and Freedom," *Review of Existential Psychology and Psychiatry* 6 (Fall 1966) 237-45..

Robert K. Johnston

PLEASURE

Why are some foods enjoyable? Or certain movies*? Or the completing of a particular project? Why does a sunset bring pleasure? A relationship? An enemy's being foiled? Is the "pleasure" in each case the same pleasure? Or is the pleasure specific to the object/event? And why in each of these examples can pleasure sometimes be absent? It is difficult to pin down the elusive character of pleasure.

Some have held that pleasure comes

from freely engaging in an act (e.g., hiking, working). But sometimes pleasure surprises you. Others have seen pleasure as more a matter of the will, when one attains a desired object (e.g., a team's winning the Superbowl). But what of a sunset? Still others believe pleasure to derive from moving from potentially to actually knowing something (e.g., meeting your daughter after a prolonged absence). Pleasure is all this and more. It is the natural accompaniment of one's well-being and has usually been understood as central to any understanding of human motivation and values.*

Webster defines *pleasure* as "the gratification of the senses or of the mind; agreeable sensations or emotions; the feeling produced by enjoyment or the expectation of good." Pleasure's exact character remains ambiguous. It can be a matter of the intellect, or an emotion,* or a sensation, for it has to do with the whole person. It is related to "enjoyment," "contentment," "happiness" and "blessedness."

Such pleasure is central to God's intention for humankind. It was characteristic of life in the Garden and is again made central in the biblical portrayal of our future life with God: "They will hunger no more, and thirst no more . . . for the Lamb at the center of the throne will be their shepherd, and he will guide them to springs of the water of life, and God will wipe away every tear from their eyes" (Rev 7:16-17 NRSV).

Pleasure and Pain

In the biblical text quoted above, pleasure is linked closely with pain—with hunger and thirst and tears. Yet many in Western society seek today to shield themselves from all pain. By stressing affluence and overindulgence, and by papering over all that is unpleasant, however, the culture of the West has found pleasure strangely hollow. Paul Brand has argued, based on his work with lepers, that the inability to sense pain also destroys opportunities for pleasure. This would seem metaphorically to be the case.

Brand quotes the Chinese philosopher Lin Yutang, who summarizes an ancient Chinese formula for happiness. Among the thirty supreme pleasures in life are such mixtures of pain and pleasure as (1) finally being able to scratch a private part when alone (!) and (2) feeling rain on dry skin after being thirsty in a dry and dusty land. As Augustine noted, "Everywhere a greater joy is preceded by a greater suffering." It is not pain's absence but its secession that is significant.

Two Misunderstandings of Pleasure

Hedonism. This term has been used rather broadly to cover any philosophy of life that elevates pleasure. Although there have been advocates of hedonism throughout the ages, it has more often been critiqued. One recalls the ancient Greek king Tantalus, who, having stolen ambrosia from the gods, is condemned to thirst for water that is always receding as he stoops to drink and to hunger for a fruit that swings out of reach as he seeks to pick it. Pleasure, when it is stolen or fixed upon, soon becomes tantalizingly out of reach.

The writer of Ecclesiastes discusses this problem regarding pleasure's apotheosis. "Come now, I will make a test of pleasure; enjoy yourself" (Eccles 2:1 NRSV). The Preacher gives himself to all forms of enjoyment—wine, houses, gardens, pools, possessions, treasures, singers, concubines—only to find his life vain: "I said . . . of pleasure, 'What use is it?' " (Eccles 2:2 NRSV). To devote oneself to pleasure paradoxically produces despair. "Whoever loves pleasure will suffer want" (Prov 21:17 NRSV; cf. Prov 14:12-13; Lk 8:14; 2 Tim 3:4).

Christians have rightly counseled against all forms of promiscuous pleasure—being consumed by sex, food or materialism—for such activity proves hollow. In this way the Christian church has echoed the sage advice of Ecclesiastes. When pleasure becomes a compulsion, even an addiction,* it ceases to be pleasurable without increasingly strong "fixes." Rather than create satisfaction, such overindulgence in pleasure produces low self-esteem, a sense of alienation, a difficulty in handling stress* and an increased level of anxiety.* Hedonistic pleasure is a perversion of true pleasure.

But although few Christians would advocate in the abstract such hedonism, many Christians, particularly in the West, are living a modified hedonistic lifestyle. The title of Neil Postman's critique of television,* *Amusing Ourselves to Death*, captures the essence of pleasure's contemporary misuse. "Eat, drink and be merry, for tomorrow we die" is more characteristic of the life patterns of many Christians than we would care to admit. In his apocalyptic novel *Brave New World*, Aldous Huxley provides a similarly dark vision of a people controlled by too much pleasure. He portrays people as overcome by the technologies* they adore. Reduced to egoism and passivity, they lose all capacity to think. Truth becomes irrelevant in this trivial culture. Here again is an updated hedonism all too close to the reality of Western culture.*

Asceticism. If hedonism is characterized by an overindulgence in pleasure, asceticism is characterized by its underindulgence. Christians have found it easy to critique a fixation on pleasure (even if they are sometimes inconsistent in practice), but they have found it more difficult to recognize pleasure's wrongful denial. Asceticism teaches that one ought out of principle and devotion to deny one's desires, to absent oneself from authentic good and/or to inflict pain on oneself. Such action is not seen by ascetics as an end in itself but is carried out (1) to free the soul* for pursuit of higher knowledge, (2) to avoid the world, which is thought to be evil, or (3) to imitate the cross of Jesus. It is thought that by repressing pleasure one can test one's devotion to God and attain to a special knowledge of the divine. Out of such beliefs arose some forms of the monastic life.

Augustine, writing in *De doctrina Christiana* (A.D. 427), sought to distinguish between things that are for enjoyment and things that are for use. To take "pleasure for its own sake" in anything other than God would be sinful. Thus Augustine counseled it to be wrong to enjoy eating* or sex or other natural "pleasures." Instead, these activities should be viewed instrumentally as a means whereby we can better enjoy God. We should not take pleasure in the temporal, thought Augustine, but only in the eternal.

Such a disparagement of everyday life has led Christians throughout the ages to undervalue the pleasure of God's creation. In Victorian England "worldly" amusements were avoided—theaters, novel-reading, dancing, alcohol, card-playing. Even the playing of charades was to be limited to children. A similar suspicion of life's commonplace joys leads some Christians today to question their "right" to have pleasure. Behind this continuing legacy is an incipient dualism, a pitting of body* against soul. In this way created life is misunderstood. Rather than reduce or deny pleasurable activity, perception and emotion, Christians need (1) to discover a wider range of pleasure in the whole of God's creation* and (2) to root that pleasure in its ultimate source—God the Creator and Re-creator of life.

Pleasure: Its Divine Possibility

Pleasure can be holy or profane, licit or illicit. If it turns one from God, the Creator of all pleasure, it is sinful (cf. Lk 8:14; 1 Tim 5:6; 2 Tim 3:4; Tit 3:3; Jas 4:3-4; 2 Pet 2:13). But the same pleasure can also turn one toward God, the giver of all life (cf. Ps 104:10-15; Eccles 2:24-25; 5:19; 9:7; Acts 14:17; Phil 2:13; 1 Tim 6:17; Jas 1:17).

Nowhere is life's dual possibility better highlighted than in the book of Ecclesiastes. We have seen above how the Preacher finds hedonistic pleasure to be vain. But this wisdom writer also interrupts his otherwise frontal assault on humankind's misguided attempt to independently find meaning in life to advise readers to enjoy life from God as a gift. We are to accept our lot with pleasure and enjoy the days of our lives that are granted us by God (cf. 2:24-26; 3:12-13, 22; 5:18-19; 8:15; 11:8, 9). The Preacher exhorts:

> Go, eat your bread with enjoyment, and drink your wine with a merry heart; for God has long ago approved what you do. Let your garments always be white; do not let oil be lacking on your head. Enjoy life with the wife whom you love. . . . Whatever your hand finds to do, do with your might. (Eccles 9:7-10 NRSV)

Despite his inability to discover any ultimate or overarching purpose for life, and despite the pervasive reality of death,* the writer of Ecclesiastes finds in the blessings of life given by the Creator to his creatures a sure cause to rejoice.

Pleasure: A Potential Path to God

The experience of pleasure needs no outside validation. It is a natural consequence of the gift of life from God the Creator and Sustainer (1 Tim 4:1-4). Yet the experience of pleasure can lead to a belief in God. G. K. Chesterton in *Orthodoxy* remembered his conversion and linked it to his reflection on the sense of delight and wonder that at times marked his world. So too did C. S. Lewis, who in his spiritual autobiography, *Surprised by Joy,* understood Joy as a voice speaking at his side—"something too near to see, too plain to be understood, on this side of knowledge" (Lewis, p. 180). This Joy he experienced as he listened to Wagner, gazed at a flowering currant bush and read George MacDonald. Through experiences such as these, both Chesterton and Lewis concluded that the world could not explain itself, nor the "magic" in it. If this magic, or Joy, was to have meaning, which it was perceived to have, it must have, in Chesterton's words, "someone to mean it." In this way, pleasure was the indirect means by which both of these writers came to Christianity.

References and Resources

P. Brand with P. Yancey, *Pain: The Gift Nobody Wants* (Grand Rapids: Zondervan, 1994); G. K. Chesterton, *Orthodoxy* (New York: Lane, 1909); A. Huxley, *Brave New World* (New York: Harper, 1989); R. K. Johnston, "'Confessions of a Workaholic': A Reappraisal of Qoheleth," in *Reflecting with Solomon,* ed. R. B. Zuck (Grand Rapids: Baker, 1994) 133-48; W. Kerr, *The Decline of Pleasure* (New York: Simon & Schuster, 1962); C. S. Lewis, *Surprised by Joy* (New York: Harcourt Brace & World/Harvest Books, 1955); J. I. Packer, *Hot Tub Religion* (Wheaton, Ill.: Tyndale, 1987); J. Piper, *Desiring God: Meditations of a Christian Hedonist* (Portland, Ore.: Multnomah, 1986); N. Postman, *Amusing Ourselves to Death* (New York: Penguin Books, 1985); P. Yancey, "The Problem of Pleasure," *Christianity Today* 32, no. 9 (1988) 80.

Robert K. Johnston

PLURALISM

In the words of *Webster's Ninth New Collegiate Dictionary, pluralism* refers to "a state of society in which members of diverse ethnic, racial, religious, or social groups maintain an autonomous participation in and development of their traditional culture* or special interest within the confines of a common civilization." *Religious pluralism* refers to a society* in which at least two religions have a significant number of followers. Ethnic, racial and cultural pluralism describe a society in which at least two distinct groups, according to these criteria, coexist. Such a society—as found in Canada, the United States, India, Russia and other nations—is often termed multicultural.*

According to these categories, Christianity can aptly be described as multicultural in its teaching, its appeal and its following. Christianity cannot, however, be accurately described as multireligious. While Christianity often functions in a religiously plural setting and affirms the propriety of such a situation, it is religiously specific, not eclectic or open-ended, in its teaching.

Cultural Pluralism

Increased mobility and migration have made cultural pluralism a reality in most countries. This situation is widely applauded by many secular observers. Increasing diversity is seen as an enriching development. Christians, too, affirm the propriety of cultural and racial diversity (*see* Racism). After all, the Christian church is transnational, multiethnic, multicultural and multilingual. In Acts 10:34, 35 we read that "God does not show favoritism but accepts [people] from every nation who fear him and do what is right." We read, even more explicitly, that "there is no difference between Jew and Gentile—the same Lord is Lord of all and richly blesses all who call on him" (Rom 10:12). And again, "There is neither Jew nor Greek, slave nor free, male nor female, for you are all one in Christ Jesus" (Gal 3:28).

When true to their calling, Christians are in the forefront in accepting people of other backgrounds, races and cultures. One would expect them to be stronger on this point than anyone else. Christianity, after all, teaches not only broad toleration but, in its emphasis on the universal brotherhood and sisterhood of all people, also strong affirmation of diversity. Its intolerance of intolerance helps to break down all social barriers. This effect was confirmed early; the first Pentecost service was a great multicultural celebration (Acts 2:5-12). If Christians are not true to their creed concerning cultural pluralism, they will lack credibility when they assert the uniqueness of Christianity in a religiously plural world.

Religious Pluralism

In recent decades many countries, including Canada and the United States, have become increasingly pluralistic in terms of religious beliefs. New religions have been established and have spread. This trend will likely continue.

Many non-Christians and many Christians applaud this religious diversification. At the very least they see it as no threat to their beliefs, and at the most they see it as an enrichment of the social fabric. Many such observers react in this manner because they see religious beliefs as part of a person's cultural identity, not as an overarching framework that encompasses and shapes all of a person's life. This blurring of the distinction between cultural pluralism and religious pluralism marginalizes religion and relegates faith to the private realm. When orthodox Christians, for whom faith is paramount and transcultural, reject such a cultural definition of religion and disagree with the assertion that like cultures all religions are of equal value, they are often accused of being intolerant and bigoted.

These opposing views are at the heart of the present "culture war." If all religions are equally valid, and if none is expected to make a claim other than to be accepted as one of many equal faiths, then by what logic should one religion ever be accepted as dominant or even as preferred? And why, even where Christianity is still numerically dominant, should the Christian ethic be given any preferential treatment? Indeed, in a religiously plural society, why should society nurture any value system whatsoever?

Response to Religious Pluralism

How should orthodox Christians react to the increasing religious pluralism in their society, and how should they respond to these assessments and accusations? Should they press for societal approval of and support for traditional biblical Christianity?

In this connection some fundamental truths need to be clarified. The true Christian church can function very well in both minority and majority situations. Further, we must acknowledge that the normal situation is for Christians to function as a minority in a non-Christian society. Also, unless a positive response to the Christian gospel is voluntary, it is meaningless. Therefore, even while Christians vigorously promote the desirability of accepting "God's truth," they also acknowledge the option of rejecting it. God has given them that option; they must give it to others. Accordingly, Christians ought never to use the arm of the law in an attempt to coerce belief or to proselytize captive audiences.

In all societies Christians utilize the private sector to propagate the gospel. In doing so they do not hesitate to underscore the following truths. First, no society or educational system can be fully neutral or value-free. No society is "religionless," if by *religion* we mean "a cause, principle, or system of beliefs held to with ardor and faith" (Webster's). Significantly, the United States Supreme Court stated in its 1960 *Torcaso* decision that "secular humanism" functions as a "non-theistic religion."

Second, given the fundamental Christian emphasis on human dignity and freedom for all—an emphasis rooted deeply in Christian theology—it is not surprising to discover that a free society thrives best in a Christian milieu. John Warwick Montgomery has asserted that "Christianity is the one faith that can make a stand on human rights that is more than an extension of a particular prejudice." In similar vein the late Reinhold Niebuhr once observed that "democracy is that child of which Christianity need never be ashamed."

Third, in a mature democratic polity, laws* on difficult moral issues often remain as proximate or interim solutions to controversial dilemmas. Groups with sharply differing views must compromise.* If any preference is to be given to a particular view in a religiously plural society, it should logically be given to the position advanced by the majority religious persuasion, whether that be the Jewish community in Israel, the Islamic community in Iran or the Christian community in Canada and the United States.

Fourth, throughout history, dominant religions have enjoyed some privileges. For example, in any country the religious holidays of one religion, or at most two, are officially celebrated. Without such an arrangement the situation could become chaotic.

The standard Christian response to the question of rights* and privileges also includes the notion that in a society in which Christianity is the dominant religion, minority religions must always benefit. They must be treated fairly and with profound respect. This must be done even though true believers in any faith, and especially if they are dominant, find it difficult to support full rights for a perspective they believe to be fundamentally in error. Both democracy and Christianity, however, require such a stance. Conversely, a Christian or any other religious minority should not demand that the public ethos must fully incorporate minority values.* Religious minorities do, of course, have a right to demand freedom* as well as fair and reasonable treatment.

Although Christians, whether in a religiously plural society or not, insist on broad religious freedom for all, such an insistence does not mean that they deem all religions to be equal. That is a different matter. And the reasons are sound. Not only do the various religions make mutually exclusive claims, but Jesus specifically made claims that do not allow Christians to grant other religions equal validity. This assertion of a unique status for Christianity should, however, go hand in hand with the affirmation of whatever is praiseworthy—and there is much—in other faiths.

At all times, but especially in a milieu of religious pluralism, Christians should not be ignorant about or reject people of other faiths. Equally important, they should not be intimidated or angered by religious pluralism, nor withdraw.

Affirming Christianity in a World of Religious Pluralism

Whether in a religiously plural situation or not, faithful Christians do not hesitate to proclaim their conviction that "salvation is found in no one else, for there is no other name under heaven . . . by which we must be saved" (Acts 4:12). Such proclamation is done with boldness but also with tact and sensitivity. The profound truth is announced joyfully but humbly.

At no time is the existence of religious pluralism denounced. After all, given the fact of God's gift of free will to all of humanity, the existence of such a situation should be expected. Beyond that, Christians see a religiously plural society as an arena of opportunity. Since it is deemed good to spend much time, effort and money to send missionaries abroad to place them in such settings, should it not also be deemed equally good when the sending congregations find themselves in similar situations? It is therefore not surprising that many Christians view such a situation not as a lamentable problem but as an auspicious challenge—one for which they thank God.

See also MISSION; MULTICULTURALISM; RACISM.

References and Resources

A. Bloom, *The Closing of the American Mind* (New York: Simon & Schuster, 1987); A. Fernando, *The Christian's Attitude Toward World Religions* (Wheaton, Ill.: Tyndale, 1987); J. Newman, *Foundations of Religious Tolerance* (Toronto: University of Toronto Press, 1982); D. C. Posterski, *Reinventing Evangelism* (Downers Grove, Ill.: InterVarsity Press, 1989); J. Stott, *Christian Mission in the Modern World* (Downers Grove, Ill.: InterVarsity Press, 1975); J. Stott, *Involvement: Being a Responsible Christian in a Non-Christian Society*, vol. 1 (Old Tappan, N.J.: Revell, 1984).

John H. Redekop

POLITICAL PARTIES, JOINING

Should Christians in a democratic society join political parties? In recent decades this question has become increasingly important as governments legislate policies in a growing list of moral areas and often make decisions running counter to traditional Christian values. Many believers wonder whether they should try to influence party stances. In developing a response we need to keep several basic truths in mind.

Three Basic Truths

First, government was established by God; it is not part of the realm of darkness. Paul wrote, "Everyone must submit himself to the governing authorities, for there is no authority except that which God has established. The authorities that exist have been established by God" (Rom 13:1). Jesus expressed similar sentiments when, concerning the payment of taxes, he instructed his disciples and the Pharisees to give to Caesar what is Caesar's and to God what is God's (Mt 22:21). Paul urged that "requests, prayers, intercession and thanksgiving be made for everyone—for kings and all those in authority" (1 Tim 2:1-2). Similarly, we read that believers should "fear God, honor the king" (1 Pet 2:17). We need to keep these biblical affirmations of government in mind. Political activity, including partisan involvement, is not inherently suspect.

Of course, given the primacy of the kingdom of God over all political realms, any political involvement, including party affiliation, must be conditional and secondary. Early in their public ministry the apostles found themselves having to choose between obeying the civic authorities in Jerusalem and obeying Jesus' specific instructions. Twice they specifically disobeyed civic authorities (Acts 4:18-20; 5:27-29). All partisan and other political activity by Christians must reflect that same priority.

Second, since in many countries the scope of governmental activity in modern times has become enormous, with almost half of the entire gross domestic product flowing through government hands at one level or another, we cannot exercise inclusive stewardship* without focusing on that part of the economy. In a democracy we have extensive opportunity to influence governmental and bureaucratic decisions. Individually and collectively believers have the ability to provide consequential input. For individuals, party membership provides a key access point. And that brings us to a cardinal truth in Christian ethics: opportunity plus ability equals accountability.

To a significant degree, membership in a political party can be seen as an opportunity to advance the greater good. That such membership can also be used for less praiseworthy purposes goes without saying—but that is a different matter. Political parties, especially in mature democracies, tend to be rather loose and amorphous entities and open to many ideas. Members usually take note of carefully articulated viewpoints. Christians can use this fact to spell out their concerns and their values.* While one should not expect that the large parties, seeking to win broad electoral approval, will readily adopt specifically Christian policies, they will usually take them into consideration in developing their stances. At the very least parties want to garner Christian votes.

Third, political parties, especially the pragmatic parties that dominate Canadian and American politics, constantly need the leaven Christians can provide. The need is particularly great at a time of seriously declining public and political morality and at a time when politics has become extremely important. After all, to a large extent government and the political realm have now replaced the church* as the most important structure shaping society.* If believers do not express God's call for public righteousness and work to achieve it in the party organizations that shape many policies and select many decision-makers, then who will?

Throughout history Christians have constituted a major voice in society championing justice,* compassion, procedural integrity and freedom.* Parties in political office and in opposition need to hear such exhortation—they need to hear it often, clearly and loudly. What better way can one imagine to communicate such values to political leaders than from within the party apparatus?

At least since the time of William Wilberforce (1759-1833) and his relentless—and ultimately successful—partisan campaign to abolish the slave trade in the British Empire, an array of party members, both elected and nonelected, has demonstrated in various countries that dedicated Christians can utilize party structures to do much good. Though their voices are usually in the minority and their calls for righteousness have often been shunted aside, this is no reason for discouragement. The ultimate test in the kingdom is not success but faithfulness, and as Edmund Burke observed more than two centuries ago, "All that is essential for the triumph of evil is that good men do nothing."

Three Queries

At this juncture we need to address some basic queries. First, does not joining a political party run the risk of bringing disunity to the body of Christ? If the Christian community involved contemplates the matter carefully and prayerfully and the political activist is prudent, it almost assuredly will not do so. While the church, as a body, should not be affiliated with any political party, it must remain free to speak with credibility to all parties and to all leaders.

Individuals, for a variety of reasons ranging from particular expertise to political conviction, should be given liberty, even encouragement, to join a political party. Individuals must not, however, claim to speak on behalf of their faith group. They must never compromise the autonomy of their congregation or its leaders. They may enjoy broad support for their views, but they speak as individuals and should say so. Other Christians in the family of believers may, for good reason, choose to express Christian views in the structures of a different party. On the other hand, if a group of Christians on their own form an organization to influence or even penetrate a political party, it is their democratic and God-given right to do so.

Second, have Christians anything distinctive to contribute to political parties? Yes, not only do they by their presence represent a significant and concerned sector of society, but they also have the opportunity to ask questions that no one else is asking, articulate values that go beyond their own self-interest and uphold the common good. At all times they are prepared to remind their fellow party members that governments at all levels have a divine mandate to be "God's servant" both as an encouragement to those who live justly and as a deterrent to those who engage in wrongdoing.

Christian party members have an exceptionally great opportunity to influence party orientations and policies when they can point to offender reconciliation activity, ministry to prison inmates, overseas volunteer assistance, appropriate distribution of agricultural surpluses, efforts to improve race relations, good farming practices, enlightened employer-employee relations and daycare and preschool programs. Political parties need to hear what Christians are doing. Christian party members can perform an important educative role.

Third, should Christians be more inclined to join one kind of party than another? No general rule can be established. At various times, however, certain parties seem to have greater openness to Christian input than do others. It can also be argued, of course, that those parties least sympathetic to a Christian perspective are the ones in greatest need of hearing it.

Conclusion

Membership in a political party, as also membership in a labor union,* a professional association or a farmers' organization, should not be undertaken lightly. All of these entities can be arenas of witness* and service.* They all need a strong Christian presence. They are part of "all the world" into which Jesus sent us (Mk 16:15). Those believers with the ability and opportunity to be a presence in these places should not hesitate to rise to the challenge. They should do so conscientiously and gladly. They should seek counsel and should be given a blessing, at least by their small fellowship* groups but ideally by the congregations to which they belong. As they maintain their priorities and practice discerning involvement, they then enter into their party's activities to the extent that Christian servanthood permits.

See also CITIZENSHIP; PRINCIPALITIES AND POWERS; SOCIAL ACTION; VOTING.

John H. Redekop

POLITICS

The term *politics* is often used to refer to all situations in which power* is important. Hence we speak of office politics,* sexual politics, church politics, and so on. Occasionally we are told that everything is *political*, which might be true in a trivial way but is not very enlightening, since it means the same as saying that nothing is political. If war and cooking are both essentially politics, then the word cannot mean very much. This is like saying that everything is educational or everything is sexual. *Politics* is also used to refer to manipulation, lust for power, double-dealing and outright graft. This is well captured in Ambrose Bierce's *The Devil's Dictionary:* "POLITICS, n. A strife of interests masquerading as a contest of principles. The conduct of public affairs for private advantage." While this activity is widespread, it is clearly one we should avoid and repress.

This article will focus on two other meanings of politics. The first refers to the activity of governments and rulers and our activity in relation to them. The second is politics as electioneering, winning votes, lobbying,* gathering public support and legislative horse trading (*see* Voting). Both of these important aspects of life merit our attention and support.

The Place of Politics
C. S. Lewis remarked that Christians make two equal and opposite mistakes about evil spirits. Either we ignore them, or else we become obsessed with them and treat them as the key to everything else. The same habits of heart and mind occur in Christian responses to politics. Some Christians, often evangelicals and fundamentalists, still reject politics as worldly. Others, increasingly including evangelicals and fundamentalists, tend to act as though the gospel had a particularly political focus. Neither view is biblical.

Politics is not the center of existence. The Bible stresses the importance of the individual, the family* and the church* as well as government. Government is not the ultimate or final authority in society; it is only one institution alongside others. At the same time it is equally wrong to try to separate the gospel from politics. The Bible focuses not only on the church but also on political authorities as those charged by God with exercising a ministry of justice. In fact, the Old Testament pays far more attention to the doings of judges, kings and lawgivers than it does to priests. In general the tenor of our proper response is well captured in the title of H. M. Kuitert's *Everything Is Politics, but Politics Is Not Everything.*

The Bible and Politics
The ministry of government began when God gave to Noah and to humankind generally the authority to judge evil, up to and including murder (Gen 9:6). This authority is delegated from God. Jesus declared that "all power in heaven and

on earth" is his (Mt 28:18). When Paul proclaimed that Jesus created, upholds and redeems every aspect of the world, he emphasized that this included political things: "thrones or dominions or principalities or authorities—all things were created through him and for him" (Col 1:16 RSV). Hence politics is, or can be, the service of God, a ministry.* Indeed John Calvin remarked, doubtless with some exaggeration, that "civil authority is a calling not only holy and lawful before God, but also the most sacred and by far the most honorable of all callings in the whole life of mortal men" (*Institutes* 4.20.4 [Battles translation]).

The diversity of government. The Scriptures do not present us with one model of politics. Abraham was a type of tribal chief: he was a father and priest of his tribe as well as its head. This stage of Israel's life was a literal patriarchy. Moses was a priest and ruler and lawgiver, though no longer the father of the people. Later God appointed priests and then judges, so that the priestly and political tasks became distinct. Still later God reluctantly appointed kings to rule the nation (1 Sam 8:6-9). The roles of kings and priests were kept clearly distinct. In fact, two kings, Jeroboam and Uzziah, were severely punished (one by death from leprosy) for taking over the role of the priests and offering sacrifices, even though their motives were not bad ones (1 Kings 12:25-13:6; 2 Chron 26:16-23). In this sense the so-called separation of church and state is not an American invention but has roots in the Old Testament.

Guidelines for politics. While there is no one type of political order commended in the Scriptures, there are consistent guidelines for what the political authorities are to do as servants of God. Political authority is related to justice,* that is, with protecting everyone's rightful place

in God's world (Ps 45:4-8; 72:1-4). The apostles express this as rightly rewarding good and judiciously condemning evil (Rom 13:1-8; 1 Pet 2:13-14). A major element of doing justice is defending and succoring the poor, the widow and the orphan (Ex 22:21-24; Deut 10:7, 18; Ps 72). The Scriptures also stress that government should be impartial. Judges are to be like God, not least in the sense that they are not respecters of persons. God declared his love for the foreigner and the sojourner in Israel (*see* Immigration) and called judges to be impartial in conflicts between Israelites and strangers (Ex 23:12; Deut 10:17-19; Jer 23:3). This implies that the people of God should not expect any undue favors from a godly ruler if they are in the wrong. A Christian ruler gives no special privilege to Christians.

Political rulers and jurisdictions are also limited. They cannot claim the total or final allegiance of human beings; otherwise, they have ceased being servants and have become idols, taking over God's place and authority. While Paul affirms that the powers that be are God's ministers (Rom 13:1-8), Peter tells us that "we must obey God rather than men" (Acts 5:29; see also 4:19 and 1 Pet 2:13-14). These emphases are combined in Jesus' admonition to give to God the things that are God's and to Caesar the things that are Caesar's (Mk 12:13-17). We are all responsible to God in distinct ways (Eph 5:21—6:9; 1 Tim 3). Neither a president nor a legislature nor a court nor a constitution nor a people (or bishop or boss or teacher or parent) can claim to be the final authority.

The limits of politics. The biblical directives of justice, impartiality and limits mean, among other things, that we should not think of governments as the solvers of all social problems nor be surprised when we discover that they cannot deal with everything. After all, the major sin, the root of all sin, is failing to love God, and no government power can overcome this. The fact that something is properly condemned or properly advocated by the church does not mean that the government has to rectify it. Our politics should not be merely a listing of human ills coupled with a demand for political action. Rather we need to discern what type of actions properly fall within the government's ministry, ability and jurisdiction. Consequently we cannot just develop our list of problems—which might include divorce,* pornography, homosexuality,* environmental degradation, sexual inequality and low wages—and expect political solutions to our hopes, desires and wishes. Instead we must try to understand the Christian task of government as we seek to follow biblical directives in diverse, and often post-Christian, societies.

Accepting the limits of politics does not mean that we are simply accepting sin; rather it means that we are careful about our means of combating sin. The Scriptures emphasize God's patience in addition to God's judgment. God will judge, but this will mainly take place in the future. So now we need to endure. Jesus told the parable of a man who sowed good seed on his field and whose enemies planted weeds among the seeds at night. When asked whether the weeds should be uprooted, Jesus replied, "No, because while you are pulling the weeds, you may root up the wheat with them. Let both grow together until the harvest" and then separate them (Mt 13:29-30). Jesus went on to explain the meaning of the day of judgment when God would separate out evildoers (Mt 13:36-43). If God is patient even with those who do evil, how much more should we be willing to live alongside others in peace. We do not have to believe that all other ways of life are good, that it does not matter what anyone believes or that all moral

views are equal. We simply need to acknowledge that politics is not the means of resolving fundamental religious matters. Politics rather provides just conditions for people, whatever their differing beliefs. The question is not whether people are doing the right thing; it is whether or not it is the government's job to stop them.

In fact, the Scriptures go beyond patient acceptance, showing not only that God allows people to live even in disobedience but also that God still cares for them even as they do so. Jesus told us to love not only our friends but also our enemies, just like God, who "makes his sun rise on the evil and on the good, and sends rain on the just and on the unjust" (Mt 5:45 RSV). God doesn't just tolerate those who oppose him; he actively cares for and loves them. Given God's reluctant (and temporary) acceptance of some human sins, we should exercise discernment and focus our political attention on those matters we can most clearly discern as the government's responsibility. This would involve, for example, the destruction of human life in abortion* or the plight of the poor (*see* Poverty). Similarly, any conflict between other bodies in society will require the government's judicial function. Other matters, such as the decline of the family, are perhaps much more the responsibility of the church and of families* themselves. Of course, political decisions should protect family life and not discriminate against families, but this is not to be identified with asking political leaders to enforce a Christian standard of marriage.*

Coercion. Since one of government's tasks is punishing people, and people usually do not want to be punished, it is accepted throughout the Bible from Noah onward that political authorities may have to compel people to follow their dictates and that this can require the use of force. Such coercion is not so much taught in the Bible as it seems to be assumed as a necessary fact of life. While particular instances of political force are condemned, the practice in general is not. It seems to be an assumption, in the context of sin, that if the government cannot use force to carry out its duties, it would not be able to carry out those duties at all and so would cease to exist (*see* Crime; Law Enforcement).

Politics and sin. Especially because of the association between politics and coercion, some theologians argue that politics arises only because of sin. Almost nobody thinks that violence and coercion are God's intention from the beginning and, therefore, a necessary feature of the created reality of the world. But there is still the issue of whether God intended human life to be lived without politics and allowed political structures to arise only to minimize the effects of human sin or whether some form of (noncoercive) political arrangement was intended from the beginning, an arrangement that, because of sin, took a particular coercive form.

Two questions hinge on the issue of God's intention. First, to what degree can Christians participate in political activity that involves or depends on coercion? Second, does government have only the negative task of restraining sin and correcting its consequences, or does it also have a positive task of promoting justice that will continue in the new earth? If we accept the latter view, we are likely to want a more active governmental role. The book of Revelation says that kings will bring the glory and honor of the nations into the New Jerusalem, which suggests that the political enterprise has merit even apart from sin (Rev 21:24-26). Moreover, this conception of the political appears to be implicit in the statement in Colossians 1:16 that thrones and rulers—both invisible and visible—were created by Christ and for Christ (*see* Principalities and Powers; Structures).

Theocracy and Democracy
Many people think that the Bible does not really contain politics but only a theocracy, wherein God ruled directly. However, the term *theocracy*, literally meaning "rule by God," is not found in the Bible but was coined by Josephus, a first-century Jewish historian, to emphasize God's direct involvement in Israelite affairs as distinct from divine involvement in the monarchies of other lands. However, Josephus also described Moses as Israel's lawgiver and could not make up his mind whether God is only the ultimate source of authority or also directly wields that authority.

This confusion between God as source and God as direct actor has plagued the term *theocracy* ever since its coinage. If the term is used to mean belief in God's direct acting, then it would seem to require something like God's continual appearance, a type of oracle or else a human being claiming to give unmediated divine guidance. Examples of the first can perhaps be found in the Old Testament before the time of Noah (ending perhaps at Gen 9:6). Examples of the third might be the claims of Pharaonic Egypt, imperial Rome or imperial Japan. Since Jesus is really human and divine, the church could perhaps be said to have been a genuine theocracy while Jesus was on earth. This could also be the case when the Holy Spirit leads directly. But few people, even including charismatics, believe that this is the only form of rule, and most accept the need for some official mediation of the divine will for the political order (*see* Leadership, Church). If theocracy is used in this narrow sense, there is nothing in the Christian faith that should lead Christians to be theocrats in the present age.

Societies in which the source of political authority is held to be God or God's law include many more than those usually described as theocratic. God's sovereignty can be mediated or exercised by priests and kings, and also by judges, prime ministers, elected legislators and the population itself. Many theories of democracy maintain that the people exercise political authority, but they also believe that such authority is in turn given to the people by God and so is derived from God's ownership of their lives. This is also the source of many influential theories of human rights.* Similarly, many Western constitutional democracies maintain that their laws reflect a higher divine or natural law. The American Declaration of Independence speaks of political authority ("rights") as being given by "Nature's God." The Canadian constitution speaks of itself as founded on principles that recognize the "supremacy of God." Hence it is quite possible to be at one and the same time both a representative democracy and a so-called theocracy. Believing, as Christians should, that God is the source of political authority can be quite compatible with what is generally, if somewhat loosely, called "democracy."

The Bible does not advocate democracy or, indeed, any other form of government. It is much more interested that the governing powers act justly. Nevertheless, there are grounds for believing that democracy (or, better, government that is representative of the people) better reflects God's will for political arrangements than other types of government. Monarchy entered Israel's life only reluctantly and with dire warning from God about its negative consequences (1 Sam 8:11-18). After the exodus the Israelites saw themselves as God's free slaves, subject to him alone (Judg 8:23). The Bible is consistent in viewing any form of authority as a form of servanthood (Mt 20:8; Mk 9:25), and it also stresses the themes of office, responsibility and covenant. For example, elders (variously described as "princes," "foremen," "heads" and "leaders"; see Ex 5:6, 15, 19; 19:7; Num 1:16; 11:16; 26:9) derived their authority from God and were often appointed by such people as Moses or Samuel. But at the same time they are described as being chosen by the people of Israel (Num 1:16; 11:16; 26:9; Deut 19). The people of Israel were called to agree to the laws and to commit themselves to God's commands (Ex 19:7). When Saul was chosen as king by God, he was also elected from among the people by lot (1 Sam 8—10). The people shared in the responsibility of political office by helping to choose their leaders and committing themselves to honor and obey them.

The notion of *covenant* is central to an understanding of politics. A covenant was not simply a deal, a quid pro quo: it was a commitment of mutual promise and responsibility, a relation that set the pattern for life (1 Kings 9:4-5; Ps 132). Israel's political life was marked by covenants between the kings, the elders, the people and God, wherein Israel took on a corporate responsibility to uphold the law of God (Deut 27; 2 Sam 5:3). Hence leaders and people are responsible to one another and mutually responsible to God. Political authority is not a theocracy but an act of self-government. This is the root of a biblical notion of democracy, or representative government.

Politics as Winning Public Opinion

A biblical view of politics requires being both responsible to do God's will and also responsible to the population at large in deciding what that will is. Hence politics involves the need to do what is right and also the responsibility to win popular support for what is right. If either of these is lacking, we will degenerate into pragmatism or authoritarianism, respectively. Since a Christian view of politics necessarily has these "democratic" elements and since the people are usually divided in their views, we must be open to the whole jumble of the other meaning of politics: the attempt to persuade people of what it is right to do and to gather popular support for a course of action. Since this takes place in an arena of hundreds of thousands, or millions, of people, it requires a principled attempt to make deals, build coalitions, share power, trade off, give everyone a place and get half a loaf rather than none.

Christians are often uncomfortable with politics in this sense, for it seems unprincipled. They would much prefer some direct official implementation of a true principle. Yet the alternative to politics as vote grubbing and opinion shaping is authoritarianism or totalitarianism. Typically elections and political life are messy. If we take the divine responsibility of all human beings to be doers of justice and stewards of political power seriously, we must take politics seriously. Often the compromising nature of politics is summarized in the apt cliché that "politics is the art of the possible." A useful expansion of this was given by French president Jacques Chirac: "Politics is not the art of the possible, but the art of making possible what is necessary." Perhaps we could even expand this to say that politics is the art of gaining support and making possible that which is right.

The Manner of Our Politics

One of our greatest needs is for political discernment. Most political matters cannot be related to only a few biblical texts; hence, we need to work with an overall view of the political task. We also need to be careful of the manner of our work. Too often Christian political efforts are imagined and described as crusades: the word itself is even used. This has several drawbacks. One is that it suffuses politics with military and warlike metaphors. Sometimes this might be necessary, but often it merely poisons the atmosphere, demonizes opponents and does more harm than good. It also implies a campaign with a single end and one soon to be achieved. But this ends up reducing politics to a set of issues instead of the ongoing and never-ending task of running the public life of a people (which, of course, always has issues within it). It also drains energy in a short-term effort, so that when the "crusade" is finished, whether in success or failure, the effort, and often much future effort, is abandoned.

As Jim Skillen has pointed out, we must realize that "politics is not something done in a moment of passion with a simple moral zealousness. Politics is more like raising a family, or running a business, or stewarding a farm. It requires lifelong commitment, patience, steadiness, and great attention to detail day after day." It is a difficult and necessary ministry, and we need to take it up.

See also NEGOTIATING; NETWORKING; POWER; PRINCIPALITIES AND POWERS; STRUCTURES; SYSTEM; VOTING.

References and Resources

J. Calvin, *Institutes of the Christian Religion*, ed. J. T. McNeill, trans. F. L. Battles (Philadelphia: Westminster Press, 1960); B. Crick, *In Defense of Politics* (Chicago: University of Chicago Press, 1973); H. M. Kuitert, *Everything Is Politics, but Politics Is Not Everything* (Grand Rapids: Eerdmans, 1986); P. Marshall, *Thine Is the Kingdom* (Grand Rapids: Eerdmans, 1986); J. W. Skillen, *The Scattered Voice: Christians at Odds in the Public Square* (Grand Rapids: Zondervan, 1990).

Paul Marshall

POLLUTION

Pollution is an old word for "uncleanness" that has taken on grim new meanings in the modern world. The word occurs frequently in the Old Testament to translate words for ritual or moral defilement, often associated with idolatry. In modern usage the word rarely refers to explicit moral failing but almost always to the defilement of the natural world—air, water, soil—through the careless disposal of wastes from human civilization. This is the meaning of *pollution* with which we are most concerned here. But ultimately the moral and environmental dimensions of pollution must be considered together.

Natural Waste

To understand environmental pollution, it is helpful to consider the way created life on earth normally disposes of "waste products." All living things produce wastes: plants give off oxygen; animals, carbon dioxide; feces, urine and dead bodies are likewise waste and in some cases, in the wrong places, "pollution." But the created world is organized in such a way that one creature's waste is another creature's necessity (*see* Ecology). "Pollution" exists temporarily only on a small scale. When considered as a whole, the totality of living and nonliving processes "recycles" individual waste products so there is no real pollution. A compost pile is a small example of the recycling capabilities of the whole planet. Lines from an eloquent poem by Walt Whitman called "This Compost" express very well the way the earth normally deals with "pollution." Asking "how can it be that the ground itself does not sicken?" since it is "work'd over and over with sour dead," Whitman concludes:

> Now I am terrified at the Earth, it is that calm and patient,
> It grows such sweet things out of such corruptions,
> It turns harmless and stainless on its axis, with such endless successions of diseas'd corpses,

> It distills such exquisite winds out of such infused fetor,
> It renews with such unwitting looks its prodigal, annual, sumptuous crops,
> It gives such divine materials to men, and accepts such leavings from them at last.

On the planetary level, in the earth God created and recognized as "very good," there is no real pollution. Pollution as we know it today is a uniquely human, and modern, problem. It has come about because of our ability to create materials that the earth cannot accept and recycle through the processes built into the creation. Unlike the rest of the created world, we human beings, especially in the last half-century, have developed an economy and a technology* that do not depend on natural cycles but that regard the earth as an inexhaustible stockpile of resources and an unfillable sink for our waste. Since the earth is neither inexhaustible nor unfillable, pollution has become more and more of a reality.

Unnatural Waste

On one level, therefore, pollution is a symptom of a much larger problem: the tendency of our increasingly technologized and urban civilization to ignore the constraints placed on us by our creatureliness. We throw things "away"—in landfills, oceans, rivers and the air—as though we could ignore the limits of the planet. Pollution is not simply a matter of garbage or litter: it is a symptom of a fundamental flaw in the nature of modern societies. The long-range consequences of forgetting our creatureliness are rapidly becoming more evident.

Specifically, we have created over seventy thousand new chemical combinations with which living things are unable to cope. The vast majority of these have not been tested for their effects on life. (The rule for new chemicals seems to be "innocent until proven guilty.") Increases in cancer among humans and rapid decline in the numbers and vitality of many other living things are probably associated with this sudden increase in materials that cannot naturally be "recycled"—though, as manufacturers are quick to point out, absolute proof of damaging effects is hard to come by.

Perhaps more serious are the ways in which various forms of pollution seem to be affecting the operation of the whole planet. There is little doubt by now that our release into the atmosphere of a number of chlorine-based compounds is resulting in the destruction of the ozone layer, a marvelous provision of the Creator for protecting the earth's surface from harmful radiation. In the same way, the rapid release of carbon dioxide into the atmosphere, from the burning of fossil fuels and the destruction of forests, is almost certain to bring about global warming and other major climatic changes at a rate far faster than living systems can easily adapt to.

Christian Stewardship*

What ought a Christian's response be to this polluted, and polluting, civilization? We can respond on two levels. Most obviously, and immediately, we need to do all we can on the personal level to bring our use of materials into line with created cycles. As creatures in God's image, with a unique responsibility to the Creator for creation,* we need to stop treating creation as though it were a great dump for our garbage, and the way to begin is to minimize what we ourselves throw "away." The popular formula "reduce/reuse/recycle" is good advice. But important as recycling is, it should always be a last resort. It is far better to *not use* (or reuse) polluting materials at all. So perhaps the formula ought to be preceded by another imperative: *refuse.* We need to refuse, whenever possible, to buy things that cannot be gracefully, harmlessly taken up and reused in the cycles of creation. Every Christian's goal ought to be the elimination of "throwaway" garbage.

But it is very difficult to refuse such things when the whole society assumes "throw away" policies. So just as important as these individual changes of habit is the hard work of bringing our whole culture* to a place where pollution is unacceptable. Is such a thing possible? Or is an unpolluted world only an eschatological dream? If it is possible, it will be through individuals bringing righteousness to bear on such vast forces as the free market and the nature of our technology.

See also CREATION; ECOLOGY; NEED; STEWARDSHIP; TECHNOLOGY.

References and Resources

L. Brown, *State of the World* (New York: Norton, 1984); Earthworks Group, *Fifty Simple Things You Can Do to Save the Earth* (New York: Andrews and McNeel, 1991); P. Hawken, *The Ecology of Commerce: A Declaration of Sustainability* (New York: Harper, 1993); L. Wilkinson and M. R. Wilkinson, *Caring for Creation in Your Own Backyard* (Ann Arbor, Mich.: Vine Books, 1992).

Loren Wilkinson

POVERTY

Our global village* has a population of about 5.5 billion people in 190 countries. Poverty is without doubt one of the most persistent and universal tragedies of our post-World War II world order. We need to ask ourselves, though, why poverty is such a major problem in two-thirds of our world and a minor (yet growing) problem in the one-third of the world we call the First, or developed (overdeveloped), part of the world. The food and technology* do exist to provide the basic needs for the ever-growing population on this fragile earth, our island home, yet the problem of organization and distribution continues to plague us.

A Global Problem

More than 1 billion people live in a state of absolute poverty—the situation in which people stumble from moment to moment searching for adequate food, nutrition, shelter and clothing. Another billion live in a state of relative poverty—in which basic human needs are inadequately met and a subsistence standard of living is rarely realized. Almost 40 percent of the people on this planet live in a constant state of absolute or relative poverty. This is increasingly becoming a nagging problem in the First World also.

Forty thousand children a day die of hunger-related causes, and many others linger on, barely meeting minimal standards for physical growth and development. More hard facts could be used to highlight the immense inequities and disparities in our world order, but a merely descriptive overview of the reality of the dilemma does not deal with the deeper question of why poverty exists in such ominous dimensions. Jacques Attali points to this question when he says, "Above all, the marginalization and misery of 3 billion men, women, and children in Africa, Latin America, and much of Asia, especially India and China, hangs heavily over the promise of sustained prosperity and freedom in the privileged North" (p. 13).

The "privileged North" is also facing the grim reality of growing poverty as the distant Third World is making itself felt in the First World. Studies on the growing emergence of poverty in the First World highlight how a hard-core Third World is moving from the outskirts, across the boundary and into the center of the First World. Poverty in the United States is certainly on the rise. Zbigniew Brzezinski in his fine book *Out of Control* describes this reality:

> with the shameful total of 32.7 percent of all black Americans living below the poverty line—one of every three!—but with also 11.3 percent of white Americans similarly afflicted, combining for a total of 35.7 million Americans (including several million helplessly homeless) living in conditions unworthy of the peerless global power. (p. 105)

As a human problem and not merely a Third World dilemma, the poverty question urgently bids us to respond. But our response will probably turn on how we interpret the reasons or causes of poverty. There historically have been three distinct, yet overlapping, means of dealing with poverty.

Approaching the Problem

The first response to poverty or human suffering is the emergency "deal with the symptoms" mentality. Huge amounts of food and other supplies are poured into a disaster-stricken area, and those giving believe this Band-Aid approach will, temporarily, deal with the problem. We must not minimize the importance of this approach to dealing with the plight of the poor. It is positively supported by many scriptural exhortations (Prov 19:7; Mt 25:37-40). But we must be careful we do not allow this to become the permanent way of counteracting the problem. Philanthropy, works of mercy and charity have their important place, but if we do not ask why the poor are poor, we might, in the long run, further contribute to the problem. Ironically, charity may hinder a long-term solution to the problem of poverty in any Third World country by destroying local initiatives or local agriculture. It also may cause a chronic dependency on foreign aid that will not easily be broken.

The second, and more insightful, approach to dealing with poverty is the notion of development. But *development* is a sort of protean word that needs constantly to be brought before the dock. Much significant damage has been done in the name of development. Megaprojects employing inappropriate technology might give the First World a sense of being compassionate, but the consequences have often been disastrous in the Third World. There are complex reasons for this, but we must always be wary of the language of development. At the same time we must recognize there are good development projects that build solid and sustainable infrastructures within a community. At its best the idea of development builds on the notion that aid might enable the starving to eat, but if you teach people how to fish rather than giving them the fish, they will, in the long run, be quite capable of being self-sufficient. This is neighbor love (Mt 22:39) at its best.

The third approach to the question of poverty raises the issue of justice,* which also is a scriptural mandate (Ps 82:3; Mic 6:8). But this approach calls into question the limitation of aid and development. The First World tends to pride itself on its aid and development packages, but probing deeper, we might discover that while this "comfortable compassion" eases some guilt, it increases the plight of the wretched of the earth. In the long run the world order we inhabit is dominated by powerful interest groups and states, and even though we might patiently teach the poor how to be more efficient with the newest fishing techniques, all the best development theory and projects will come to nil if the water is polluted or the rich want the land. This raises for us, in a rather stark and compelling way, the justice-power question and forces us to see that we cannot sidestep the issue of politics* when we deal with poverty.

The Politics of Hunger
The politics of hunger—how and why the other half dies in our world order—exposes the politics of our world order,

issues such as war and the way we select, screen and censor information. The 1991 Gulf War is a classic case in point. Because Saudi Arabia, Iraq, Kuwait, Iran and the United Arab Emirates have 60 percent of the world's known oil reserves, the issue of the control of oil is an essential one. The Secretary of Defense at the time of the war, Richard Cheney, said, "The USA and our major partners cannot afford to have those resources controlled by someone who is fundamentally hostile to our interests" (O'Brien, p. 144).

The peerless global power dispatched 500,000 troops, spent $50 billion within weeks, left an estimated 200,000 Iraqis dead and destroyed the infrastructure of Iraq. At the present time, more than 1 million Iraqi children are seriously malnourished and more than 100,000 are seriously ill; many of them may die. Why were we so concerned and why did we act so quickly after Iraq invaded Kuwait when we said nothing when Turkey brutalized the Kurds (the largest people group in the world without a homeland), the Chinese slaughtered the Tibetans, the Indonesians liquidated the East Timorese, Acheh and other ethnic people, and the Guatemalans reduced the Mayans to servile status?

The language of liberation and human rights means little if it is selectively applied to serve our imperial interests. Kuwait had a highly questionable human rights record before the Gulf War. The First World cared little about how Kuwait treated the Palestinians or other migrant workers in Kuwait as long as the flow of oil remained safe and secure. I have raised the question of the Gulf War because it brings into focus the limitations of aid and development when major issues of power* are at stake. Oil is a substantive power nexus; hence when power and justice collide, the sword is quick to assault justice and silence the pen. The poor are the predictable victims of power that is not hedged in by love and justice. And it is these poor who cry, How long, oh Lord, how long?

"I looked, and there before me was a pale horse! Its rider was named Death, and Hades was following close behind him. They were given power over a fourth of the earth to kill by sword, famine and plague, and by the wild beasts of the earth" (Rev 6:8). There is little doubt that the pale horse whose name is death rides across large parts of the landscape of the earth. More than a fourth of the world is covered by this horse and its First-World riders. Poverty is the desperate child that pleads before this ravenous warlord. Aid promises some temporary relief; development, in a limited way, keeps the rider at a distance for some. Justice insists we challenge the pale horse and the sickle the rider carries. Blessed are those who hunger and thirst after justice. Those who long for justice realize that the dysfunctional relationship between power and poverty is at the center of our dilemma, and power, by its very nature, resists in subtle and implicit ways being removed from its sable throne.

Facing Poverty

Conor Cruise O'Brien observes that it is natural for people in the advanced world not to face poverty at all: "Yet when flinching from reality becomes habitual in the life of an individual, he is found to be insane" (p. 141). Expounding this habitual flinching, O'Brien continues:

> The advanced world may well be like, and feel like, a closed and guarded palace, in a city gripped by the plague. . . . The traditional ethic will require larger and larger doses of its traditional built-in antidotes—the forces of hypocrisy and cultivated inattention combined with a certain minimum of alms. (p. 141)

O'Brien has identified some of the major issues in the First World as we face the poverty question. Our hypocrisy allows us to blame the poor for their poverty while we play a significant role in creating and maintaining the poverty. Our hypocrisy regarding the Gulf War is a classic case. We studiously cultivate a mindset of inattention when it comes to asking the deeper questions of why poverty exists while indulgently cultivating a lifestyle of inflated wants and conspicuous consumption. We do not like to be seen as a callous people, so we comfortably assuage our guilt (if and when it is a problem) by helping in ways that do not help.

Poverty is a real and pressing reality for many in our feudal world order. We need to ask ourselves why the poor are poor and attempt to work on solutions to this problem. Aid, development and justice approaches, if combined, offer a means to deal with the poverty dilemma. At the same time the First World needs to face some built-in defense mechanisms and means of denial. We need to ask ourselves how and why we, as individuals and as a people, flinch from suffering and poverty. We must examine how we use hypocrisy, "cultivated inattention" and "a certain minimum of alms" to avoid facing the tougher and more rigorous questions that the poor would ask of us and that we, before God, must ask of ourselves. Otherwise we short-circuit the full liberation inaugurated by Jesus of Nazareth, who said,

> The Spirit of the Lord is on me,
> because he has anointed me
> to preach good news to the poor.
> He has sent me to proclaim freedom
> for the prisoners
> and recovery of sight for the blind,
> to release the oppressed,
> to proclaim the year of the Lord's
> favor. (Lk 4:18-19)

See also CONSUMERISM; JUSTICE; POLITICS;

POWER; PRINCIPALITIES AND POWERS; SIM-
PLER LIFESTYLE; STEWARDSHIP; WEALTH.

References and Resources

J. Attali, *Millennium: Winners and Losers in the Coming World Order* (New York: Times Books, 1991); Z. Brzezinski, *Out of Control: Global Turmoil on the Eve of the 21st Century* (New York: Scribner's, 1993); C. Elliott, *Comfortable Compassion: Poverty, Power and the Church* (London: Hodder & Stoughton, 1987); P. Harrison, *Inside the Third World* (London: Penguin, 1990); F. M. Lappé and J. Collins, *Food First: Beyond the Myth of Scarcity* (Boston: Houghton Mifflin, 1977); C. C. O'Brien, *On the Eve of the Millennium* (Toronto: Anansi, 1994).

Ron Dart

POWER

Power is troubling for many Christians. We are suspicious that its exercise violates the ethos of the Sermon on the Mount with its call for meekness and willingness to be last. Power is also easily corrupted. In Lord Acton's well-known words, "Power tends to corrupt; absolute power corrupts absolutely." The more power we have, the more evil we can do, and the more likely is the devil to seek to waylay us.

The Ambiguities of Power

Power is frequently used to oppress and exploit others (Mic 2:1-2; Jas 5:1-6). Many contemporary feminists call for the abolition of the power model of society and organizations and brand its attendant hierarchical structure as a remnant of discredited patriarchal and unchristian ways. In its place they call for an ethic of sharing and collegiality. Anabaptist and other circles that stress nonviolence warn of the seductions of power politics* and instead urge us to take up the role of servants who simply and humbly follow Jesus' commands.

At the same time many Christians see no particular virtue in refusing to exercise power while the world and the church engage in oppression and injustice. We also tend to appreciate good leaders. Anyone who has sat through an unstructured meeting or a small group with ostensibly no one in charge or when no one will make a suggestion for fear of upsetting someone else knows the yearning for proper structure and authority. Christians are especially divided about whether we should ever exercise the forms of power we usually call *coercion* and *violence*. Those who do accept them insist that they can only be used as a last resort. The division roughly parallels the distinction between those who are committed exclusively to nonviolence and those who accept just war views.

Usually we end up exercising power. Some do so with sneaking guilt. Others just accept power and its consequence uncritically, whether it is the coercion that lies behind most political power, the marginalizing of others produced by intellectual power or the dehumanizing that may come from applying business models to church or vice versa. This ambiguity is reflected in the "theology of the powers," which is associated especially with Walter Wink. This view says that power formations were originally a good gift of God, but now that they have fallen, we must work with them but maintain a continuing aloofness to their seductions.

Types of Power

There are many forms of power, including wealth,* appointed office, intelligence, access to information, charisma, skill, physical strength and military means. Power can include control of things, like cars or word processors, as well as control of people. It exists not only in large-scale settings, for we can speak of a powerful argument, a powerful computer or a powerful sermon. Anything that can accomplish an end is a form of power.

Biblically, all power comes from God

and belongs to God (Mt 26:64; Jn 19:11). The New Testament draws explicit attention to Jesus' power: his power over all things is a manifestation of his kingdom (Mk 4:14; 5:17; 11:20-22). God's power is delegated to human agents in the form of authority or office (Gen 1:26-28; Ps 8:5-8). This includes those within the church structures, such as elders or apostles, and also those in other positions, such as kings or teachers.

The Right Use of Power

We cannot reject power as such. It is a pervasive and inescapable fact of our lives as God's creatures. While it may be true that power corrupts, it is also true that an unwillingness to use legitimate power can also corrupt. We must be cautious with power, even suspicious of it, and we must carefully judge the forms of power and the ends of power, but we can never escape the God-given responsibility to exercise power. Jesus continually stressed the right use of power and the right types of power. He emphasized that the key to power is that it is a means of servanthood, thus reversing the common understanding (Mk 10:42-45; Jn 10:17-18). Paul also emphasized that "the governing authorities" are "God's servant for your good" (Rom 13:1-4 NRSV). This might sound trite to us, accustomed as we are to the language of public servants, but these were radical words when applied to Roman emperors and their subjects. To put it mildly, in the ancient world servanthood was not usually taken to be an attribute of imperial power.

It may also help us to use the common distinction between *power* (generally understood as the mere ability to achieve something) and *authority* (understood as legitimate power), which is close to the New Testament's distinction between *dynamis* (2 Cor 8:3; Eph 3:16) and *exousia* (Mt 21:23-27). The late Jewish philosopher Hannah Arendt even went so far as to treat these two as opposites: that is, people are reduced to exercising power when authority is not possible. We do not need to polarize these so sharply in order to benefit from the distinction. The existence of legitimate authority highlights the fact that even authority over people need not be exercised contrary to the will of those subject to it. Many forms of authority stem from leadership* that wins people over gladly, something that Jesus, along with any good preacher or political leader, exemplifies. Even a great general commands not merely by military discipline and threat but by inspiring those who are commanded. A willingness to risk death comes from inspiration as well as fear.

Authority and Gift

The form of power called *authority* is clearly something we should exercise. The exercise of such authority is in turn tied to the gifts we have been given by God. When we have a particular gift— whether healing, administration, preaching* or auto maintenance—we already have a factual authority in that area because we have an insight, and therefore an ability. We should follow good administrators in organizations, follow good medical advice in areas of health and learn wise ways from wise elders. In each case we are thereby recognizing an authority, a power, and at the same time we are conferring an authority and submitting to legitimate power. The key to using power well is not trying to avoid it in a desperate search for a world in which no one is ever subject to another but rather knowing its strengths and temptations. It means recognizing and submitting to giftedness as a blessing from God.

See also ORGANIZATION; POLITICS; POWER, WORKPLACE; PRINCIPALITIES AND POWERS; STRUCTURES; SYSTEM.

References and Resources
K. Rahner, "The Theology of Power," in *Theological Investigations* (Baltimore: Helicon, 1966) 4:391-409; P. Schouls, *Insight, Authority and Power* (Toronto: Wedge, 1972); W. Wink, *Engaging the Powers* (Philadelphia: Fortress, 1992); W. Wink, *Naming the Powers* (Philadelphia: Fortress, 1984); W. Wink, *Unmasking the Powers* (Philadelphia: Fortress, 1986).

Paul Marshall

POWER, WORKPLACE

Power* is the ability or capacity to act. It refers to strength, influence and control. In the workplace power of different sorts is required to perform the services or create the products intended by the business or institution. Industrial power, for example, is a composite of natural resources, energy supplies, good ideas and design, capable management and productive workers. The power of a community or political organization depends on its financial and human resources, ideas, programs, leadership and constituency of workers and supporters.

Our interest in power in the workplace is focused primarily on how policy and direction are set, how plans are made and carried out, how influence is distributed among the people. Employees, including middle managers, are often frustrated by what seems to be their lack of real power. It often seems that responsibilities are not commensurate with authority or power; there is not enough of the latter to fulfill the former.

In this article we are considering *power* not in general but in the workplace. How can we better understand power and then respond as thoughtful Christians? What are the purposes of this work for which power is sought? What kind of power is to be sought by the people of God? How can Christians relate to power in the workplace as it is configured in our world?

Personal Power

First, our personal power in the workplace is dependent primarily on our competence,* skill and fitness for the tasks we are assigned. Our motivation as Christians to competence and excellence is based not on the potential for rewards from our employers but on our desire to please and honor God: "Whatever you do, in word or deed, do everything in the name of the Lord Jesus, giving thanks to God the Father through him" (Col 3:17 NRSV). This applies even to the work of a slave: "Whatever your task, put yourselves into it, as done for the Lord and not for your masters, since you know that from the Lord you will receive the inheritance as your reward; you serve the Lord Christ" (Col 3:23-24). To be persecuted, or disempowered, in the workplace because of our failure to perform well is not praiseworthy. On occasion, despite our good performance, we may suffer unfairly. Ordinarily, however, we will be rewarded not only by God but by our employers if we carry out our tasks with godly excellence.

Second, power in the workplace is often dependent on our relational skills. It is a matter of whom you know and how you treat others. The tempting and cynical approach is to use and manipulate others for selfish purposes, but Christians reject this as the power of darkness. As the children of light, Christians model their relationships on those of their Lord. Thus we reach out in concern to the low as well as the great, to those who need us as well as those we need. Christ teaches us to relate to others always as unique persons made in God's image and likeness. We care for others as God cares for us. Our basic stance is that of servants of God, freely and graciously giving knowledge, assistance and care. Our competitiveness* is directed against the true enemies of human well-being—poverty,* loneliness, pain and meaninglessness—not against our fellow beings. Such relational servanthood will on occasion be misunderstood, demeaned or exploited by others. In the worst case we may need to seek other employment or simply commit our cause to God. However, such servanthood will more often result in the appreciation and approval of our colleagues. The servant of all may become the leader with moral and personal power if not with institutionally recognized position (Lk 22:24-27).

Third, power in the workplace depends on our communication. The cynical approach might include a quest for power through deception and falsehood. Résumés and reports might be falsified; flattery or intimidation might be communicated in a quest for advantage. But for Christians power through communication is based on "speaking the truth in love" (Eph 4:15; compare vv. 25, 29). God's truthful word created the world; the Word of God became flesh and lived among us (Jn 1). The truth of Jesus Christ sets us free. These themes govern our workplace communications, be they internal to the company or external representations of our products and services. Though there may be short-term power payoffs through deception or gossip,* over the longer haul the truth will win out. One who habitually communicates the truth in love acquires long-term personal power in the workplace.

Finally, power in the workplace, as elsewhere, is partly a function of our character. Our specific actions are always important, but our character is our ongoing constellation of traits, attributes, dispositions, habits* and capacities. Our character is "who we are," not just "what we do" in this or that circumstance. Our reputation may not do justice to our real character at times, but over the long haul a Christian character that is shaped by faith, hope and love,* by the Beatitudes, will experience and display the power of God as we are progressively being re-formed toward the image of Jesus Christ.

Structural Power

Power is never merely a personal issue. It is also a function of corporate structures* and processes and of role definition and distribution (*see* System). People of great skill, relational and communicational excellence, and admirable character are sometimes disempowered by forces and structures larger than themselves. To the extent we are able, we need to understand and improve this corporate and structural context. Our reform efforts may be motivated by a desire to be better able to flourish in our own work. But we also must be mindful of others in our workplace who suffer from such injustice. Christians with managerial and administrative roles will be motivated to justice and fairness knowing that they, in turn, are accountable to a Master in heaven, who is invariably just, fair, liberating and loving (Eph 5:1).

In order to have empowered people in the workplace, employees must be given authority commensurate with their responsibility. Employees need to be assisted in the acquisition and improvement of their personal skills and placed in work roles that allow their expression. The opportunity for helpful, meaningful relationships among employees must be maintained. Communication, both speaking* and listening,* needs to be free and should be encouraged. The development of the whole person, that is, character and relationships, needs to be valued.

Christians, following their Lord, will exhibit special care for those with little power and weak voice, personally or culturally. Cultural habits and prejudices based on race, gender, age and other such nonwork distinctions have too often meant that some voices were unheard, some abilities untapped, some deserving promotions overlooked. Christians must not allow their practices and attitudes to be shaped by such worldly patterns (Rom 12:1-2). Our goal is to see and recognize all our colleagues with the eyes of Christ, honor each of them in the dignity bestowed by their Creator and empower them with the strength of God.

In addition to those cultural habits and prejudices that make up a large part of the organizational culture* of the workplace, the official structures defining the workplace, that is, the systems and policies, should be the focus of Christian scrutiny. An empowering corporate culture will demonstrate fairness in hiring, promotion,* compensation, discipline and dismissal processes (see Firing). If hiring, compensation, communication, decision-making and other policies are preserving a disempowering organizational structure, then these policies may need to be examined and reformed.

The Power of God and the Powers of the World

In the workplace, where many of us spend most of our lives, we desire that we and others be set free and empowered to flourish to the best of our God-given abilities. We find, however, that the powerful weight of tradition and habit, of money* and production demands, of policies, laws* and regulations often severely constrain our possibilities. Struggling against more than a particular organization or oppressive boss, we often experience the spiritual dominance of what the Bible calls "principalities and powers."* We find ourselves in a spiritual battle, not just a personal or organizational conflict. Many of us have come home from work, even from presumably Christian workplaces, bowed down, discouraged, powerless and feeling defeated.

While the "microresponses" suggested above are important, it is essential to recall and accept the "macroperspective" on our situation. If our struggle is ultimately a spiritual battle, albeit with identifiable human elements, then our point of departure must be spiritual. Here we reconnect with the gospel of Jesus, which, while appearing weak, is truly the "power of God" (Rom 1:16; 1 Cor 2:5). As individuals we believe that despite our weakness, we "can do all things through him [Christ] who strengthens" us (Phil 4:13 NRSV). Moreover, we are not alone but are part of the church, which received the promise "You will receive power when the Holy Spirit has come upon you" (Acts 1:8 NRSV).

For Christians, then, power in the workplace is not just a function of personal excellence, relational skill, communication ability and solid character. Nor is gaining power simply the result of structural reforms and improved corporate character. It is fundamentally dependent on our drawing on the powerful strength of God, his Spirit and his people. We draw on these sources as we worship, as we pray, as we share our common life and struggle together on behalf of the kingdom of God.

See also ORGANIZATION; ORGANIZATIONAL CULTURE AND CHANGE; POWER; PRINCIPALITIES AND POWERS; STRUCTURES; SYSTEM.

References and Resources
H. Berkhof, Christ and the Powers, trans. J. H. Yoder (Scottdale, Penn.: Herald, 1962); W. Diehl, Thank God It's Monday (Philadelphia: Fortress, 1976); H. Schleir, Principalities and Powers in the New Testament (New York: Herder & Herder, 1964); W. Wink, Naming the Powers: The Language of Power in the New Testament (Philadelphia: Fortress, 1984); W. Wink, Unmasking the Powers: The Invisible Forces That Determine Human Existence (Philadelphia: Fortress, 1986).

David W. Gill

PRAYER, CORPORATE

Prayer is one of the most self-revealing acts of a human being. It is simply communion with God. Perhaps that is one reason why almost all books on prayer and spiritual disciplines* focus mainly on individual prayer. How can we share what is most intimate except with God alone? Even congregational liturgical prayers, as valuable as they are in congregational worship,* may serve to protect individuals from sharing their inmost selves through a form recited in unison. These can all too easily become a collection of standardized requests and confessions rather than praying together as one people with each contributing to the whole.

Our reluctance to pray corporately is incorrectly strengthened by the apparent preference of Jesus for prayer "in the closet." Jesus condemned the hypocrites for their love of praying publicly in the synagogue and on street corners "to be seen of men" (Mt 6:5). "When you pray," exhorts Jesus, "go into your room, close the door and pray to your Father . . . who sees what is done in secret" (6:6). Is there a place for corporate prayer? What is the theology and spirituality of such prayer? When is it appropriate? How is it hindered?

Corporate Prayer in the Bible

The story of salvation starts with the people's desperate cry for help. Deuteronomy says it was *because* of that corporate prayer that God delivered the people "with a mighty hand and an outstretched arm" (Deut 26:7-8). Eventually God directed that a temple should be built for corporate prayer, "a house of prayer for all nations" (Is 56:7). At its dedication God promised: "If my people . . . will humble themselves and pray and seek my face and turn from their wicked ways, then I will hear from heaven and forgive their sin and will heal their land" (2 Chron 7:14). The epitome of corporate prayer under the old covenant was the gathering of the people in the temple for sacrifices, festivals, sabbath* worship and times of national crisis.

In the New Testament, the people as a whole become the house of prayer for all nations. The laity* is the temple of the Spirit (1 Cor 3:16). Individual and corporate prayer takes place all week long wherever the people are—gathered to break bread, read Scripture, worship and edify one another, and dispersed for their priesthood in the world. As Elton Trueblood said so aptly, you cannot "go" to church*; you "are" the church wherever you go. So the people (*see* Laity) are a portable sanctuary of communion with God. When believers are dispersed, they are praying priests in the world. When they are together, they are a fellowship of prayer. In the New Testament we see this fellowship of prayer in the upper room (Acts 2:1), from home to home (2:42), in Mary's house (12:12) and in numerous house churches (*see* Church in the Home) throughout the Roman world—and as believing Jews in the temple together (2:46).

The last book of the Bible envisions our permanent sanctuary—the new heaven and new earth. Our ultimate future in Christ is continuous corporate prayer as elders, living creatures, angels, martyrs and all peoples join in worship of the Lamb. Heaven is silent for a half-hour to hear the prayers of the saints and then responds with thunder (Rev 8:1-5). Something happens when God's people pray. Pascal once said that through prayer God gives humankind the dignity of limited causality. Even in heaven God hears the cries of his people and responds.

Patterns of Corporate Prayer

One of the most remarkable corporate

prayers is found in Acts 4:23-31, where, upon the release of Peter and John from custody, "they raised their voices together in prayer to God." What follows is a prayer rich in scriptural allusion and apparently offered *together*. We do not know exactly how this happened; probably the text contains the essence of various prayers wonderfully harmonized by the Spirit. While we cannot definitely answer this question, we can identify various ways in which people can pray together today.

Some corporate prayers are *a collection of multiple individual prayers,* as when people gather silently in a church building to pray, gaining mutual visible support from others in their personal prayers. *Liturgical prayers,* such as those found in prayer books, and *prayers led by a worship leader* go a step further by inviting people to offer the same prayer, though there is no guarantee that they are together. The so-called Lord's Prayer (Mt 6:9-13), really the disciples' prayer, is an especially good model of this, though Jesus said, "This is *how* you should pray," not "This is *what* you should pray." Often such praying is collectivized individual prayers—creating uniformity rather than expounding the rich unity of the body of Christ that is enhanced by a variety of giftedness.

Some churches practice group prayer in a way that invites everyone to pray individually out loud, possibly using a prayer language if so gifted. At its worst this is merely a collection of people "doing their own things" in a public cacophony; at its best there is often a Spirit-led harmony in such utterances that is wonderfully edifying. In prayer meetings, especially in a small group* or house church, spontaneous prayers offered out loud by various individuals can become a *symphony of prayer,* each prayer building on, and adding to, the previous to make a harmonious whole. Sometimes this is

called *conversational prayer.* But the term is misleading. It suggests that the conversation is strictly on the horizontal level, whereas symphonic prayer is a conversation with God in which each person, like an instrument in an orchestra, contributes a distinctive sound to the whole. The point of corporate prayer is not uniformity but unity in communion with God.

Threats to Corporate Prayer

Obviously, this unity is threatened by showy prayers delivered to impress others. This, and not corporateness, was the concern of Jesus in Matthew 6:1-4. It is also threatened by unspiritual feelings of inferiority which quench the contribution of new or struggling believers. Just as each and every spiritual gift, including those we think "less honorable" (1 Cor 12:23), is needed to build the body of Christ in unity, so every heart cry makes an authentic contribution to people prayer. There are no bad prayers if they are prayers to God (rather than addresses to people). It is spiritual tyranny to insist, as some church leaders do, that people must pray in a certain way. And it is spiritual pride and abuse* to judge the quality of another prayer.

Paul deals with a further threat in 1 Timothy 2. Corporate prayer is a reflection of our relational life. If we are competitive or have broken relationships, it will be contaminated, if offered at all. Paul says he wants men "to lift up holy hands in prayer, *without anger and disputing*" (1 Tim 2:8) and women to pray dressed "modestly, with decency and propriety" (2:9). There is reason to think that the women in Ephesus were dominating the men (2:12), just as in other places and times (more commonly, in fact) men have dominated women in the church. Politics and power plays prohibit corporate prayer and "attaining" the unity of the Son of God (Eph 4:13). Some churches insist on men praying only with men and women with women, short-changing the rich unity and mutual contributions of male and female together in Christ.

Why Pray Together?

Here are several reasons we pray together:

God hears and responds to the cries of people when they come together for that purpose. Corporate wrestling with God in prayer is valued by him. We can think of the many instances of personal prayers—Paul pleading to have his thorn removed, Abraham haggling over Sodom, Jacob wrestling with the angel and Jesus struggling in the garden. And now under the new covenant, we are to be a people passionately seeking God in prayer together. "Cast yourself into his arms" is an exhortation to those who pray both individually and corporately, "not to be caressed but to wrestle with Him. He loves that holy war" (Forsyth, p. 92).

When we pray together, we join Jesus in his prayer for the people of God. We build on the communion and communication that is already taking place within the triune God. P. T. Forsyth says this brilliantly: "The real power of prayer in history is not a fusillade of praying units of whom Christ is the chief, but it is the corporate action of a Saviour-Intercessor and his community, a volume and energy of prayer organized in a Holy Spirit and in the Church the Spirit creates" (quoted in Peterson, p. 87).

Prayer is the most direct way to know God. Forsyth says that "prayer is to the religious life what original research is to science—by it we get direct contact with reality" (p. 78). Knowing God is not merely an individual quest; first and foremost it is a people desire (Eph 1:15-23). And corporate prayer is fundamental to both our individual and communal growing into the knowledge of the Son of God. It is only "together with all the saints" (Eph 3:18) that we can know the height and depth and can dwell in the trinitarian love of God.

When we pray together we help one another to pray better. Often the voice of another gives expression to a hidden longing or heartache. In the same way we become a symphony of praise and gratitude in corporate prayer, rather than an orchestra composed of only one instrument. Synergy is the dynamic impact of two chemicals taken as medicines together and having a multiple effect. In the same way corporate prayer contributes to a growing unity like that found in Father, Son and Holy Spirit (Eph 4:3-6).

Corporate prayer is a way of ministering to one another. It is a part of the mutual priesthood of all believers. If Spirit-filling is essentially a corporate experience (Eph 5:18), if spiritual growth* takes place mainly in the company of believers, if God can only be known together, then corporate prayer is one way we can love and serve one another.

Nonetheless, corporate prayer is a "useless" activity. Basically we pray together not to get better results from our prayer—a kind of unionized bargaining process—but simply to delight in God together. Too often we allow a utilitarian dimension to creep into prayer, praying for what we get out of it. What God did for Job can happen to us in our prayers. God did not "answer" his prayers or heal his sickness but did something better. God revealed himself and lifted Job into contemplation (Job 38—41). Faith, and the prayer that is expressed through it, is not "for" anything (Job 1:9), as the devil would have it. South American theologian Gustavo Gutiérrez has said, "Prayer is an experience of gratuity. This 'pointless' act, this 'squandered' time, reminds us that the Lord is beyond being categorized as useful or useless" (p. 206). In the end, the point of corporate prayer, whether in a small group or a cathedral, is simply to be able to say with Job, not "Now I see it all" but "Now my eyes have seen you" (Job 42:5).

See also FELLOWSHIP; SPIRITUAL DISCIPLINES; SPIRITUAL GROWTH.

References and Resources

P. T. Forsyth, *The Soul of Prayer,* 3rd ed. (London: Independent, 1954); R. Foster, *Celebration of Discipline* (San Francisco: Harper & Row, 1978); G. Gutiérrez, *On Job: God-Talk and the Suffering of the Innocent,* trans. M. J. O'Connell (Maryknoll, N.Y.: Orbis Books, 1987); R. P. Martin, *Worship in the Early Church* (Grand Rapids: Eerdmans, 1974); E. Peterson, "The Last Word on Prayer," in *Reversed Thunder: The Revelation of John and the Praying Imagination* (San Francisco: Harper & Row, 1988).

R. Paul Stevens

PREACHING

Preaching is hard work; listening to sermons is harder still. The reasons are not difficult to diagnose: the ubiquitous influence of high-tech advertising,* the loss of oratory in contemporary culture,* word-weariness as an effect of being overdosed with information and the fragmenting or dulling effect of visual media.* Jaded listeners today are like the people who listened to, but did not hear, the prophet Ezekiel. "My people come to you, as they usually do, and sit before you to listen to your words, but they do not put them into practice. . . . To them you are nothing more than one who sings love songs with a beautiful voice and plays an instrument well, for they hear your words but do not put them into practice" (Ezek 33:31-32). In fact it has never been easy to hear or to deliver sermons. In 1857 Anthony Trollope wrote in *Barchester Towers:* "There is, perhaps, no greater hardships at present inflicted on mankind in civilized and free countries, than the necessity of listening to sermons" (quoted in Nouwen, p. 23). The low estimate of preaching in the world today is in sharp contrast to the high estimate of preaching in Scripture and among the converted.

What Is Preaching?

Preaching is "making present and appropriate to the hearers the revelation of God" (Craddock, p. 51). A sermon is meant to be the real presence of Christ. Preaching is bringing the living Word (Christ) through the written Word (Bible) by means of the spoken word (preaching). The New Testament has a far richer vocabulary than modern Christians to describe the many ways of doing this: prophesying (speaking with immediacy and directness), teaching,* proclaiming, dialoging, debating, exhorting, persuading, correcting, evangelizing,* conversing,* admonishing and encouraging. Preaching sermons is part but not all there is to preaching.

The sermon, in the sense of a twenty-five-minute message constructed in a formal way for maximum persuasive effect, is an art form that arose in the Christian West from a combination of Hebrew prophecy, Greek rhetoric, Jewish synagogue preaching and the impact of the Christian gospel (Dargon 1:14). Originally the Latin word *sermo* meant "dialogue" because early Christian instruction involved interaction with hearers (*see* Teaching). This art form is a means of communication through which almost any spiritual gift* can be expressed —teaching, exhorting, showing mercy, discerning, leading or even administering. In this sense it is like writing, singing or making movies.* Preaching itself is not a gift but a vehicle for gifts.

While preaching is more than the presentation of prepared messages from the pulpit, one indication of the vitality of the church* since the fourth century (when church buildings as we know them developed) has always been the quality of pulpit preaching. It is not an overstatement when surveying church history to conclude that "whenever preaching has declined Christianity has become stagnant" (Wiersbe and Perry, p. 9). After a thousand years of being relegated to secondary status, there was a genuine revival in preaching in the Protestant Reformation. There is need of a revival of biblical preaching today.

Even though formal sermonic preaching has been important for centuries, much of the influential preaching throughout history has been done by lay people untrained in rabbinic preaching or Greek rhetoric. Most of these were volunteers rather than paid ministers: the apostles, ordinary tradespeople, women in Caesar's household, Origen, slaves, the lay preachers of renewal movements like the Salvation Army and the thousands of lay preachers in house churches in China (see Tentmaking).

Why Preaching?

In some parts of the Third World, the church is growing like a beneficent forest fire. I can stand in a marketplace of rural Africa and quickly get a crowd to hear my message. Many will respond. This situation may continue for a little longer. But in the Western post-Christian world, and increasingly as we experience the global village,* preaching gets harder. The cardinal communication rule is "Don't preach at me!" It is tempting to give it up altogether and settle for talk shows, interviews and "warm, fuzzy" conversations.* Or we could use the Information Superhighway* or television* set to hook up electronically with one of the few "great preachers" left in the world. Why listen to an ordinary preacher? Why preach at all?

The reasons to preach and to listen to preaching are deeply theological. First, we have a preaching God who speaks to and through human beings. Second, the central document of the Christian faith—the Bible—is itself a sermon, taking the revelation of God and "bringing it home" through human personalities to multiple cultures and contexts. Third, God continues to call and empower people to speak on God's behalf as spokespersons. Fourth, the spoken word will always have a winsome power because speaking* communicates truth strained through personality and is inescapably personal—the very thing postmodern men and women crave. Socrates once said, "I would rather write upon the hearts of living men than upon the skins of sheep" (quoted in Pattison, p. 2). Fifth, the basic human condition has not changed: we need good news. The heart of preaching is the proclamation of news especially to the outsider even more than the edification of believers.

The apostle Paul asks, "And how will they hear without someone preaching to them?" (Rom 10:14). Behind that preaching, Paul argues, is the sending God. Preaching originates in the initiative of God and is sustained by it. Preaching is designed by God to reach even the people who resist the news they so desperately need. There is some truth in the observation that the world is producing a type of person to whom it is impossible to preach the gospel. But as P. T. Forsyth said, the preacher is "there not simply to speak what people care to hear but also to make them care for what you must speak" (p. 94). This brings up an important question.

Who Should Preach?

Possibly everyone! Now that the Holy Spirit has been poured out on the people of God beginning with the day of Pentecost, there is universal potential for prophecy—inspired speech from God. "Your sons and daughters will prophesy," proclaimed Peter, quoting Joel's prophecy (Acts 2:17). In contrast to the Old Testament there is a thrilling assumption throughout the New: the prophethood of all believers. This means that every Christian is capable of delivering God's Word. What was formerly the sacred responsibility of a few special leaders—prophets, priests and princes—is now universalized in the laity,* the people of God as a whole. Each believer should be able to "give an answer to everyone who asks you to give the reason for the hope that you have" (1 Pet 3:15). Paul expected prophecy (immediate and direct words to build up others) to be regularly expressed by ordinary members of the church (1 Cor 14:1-3; Col 3:16). Witness* is every Christian's vocation, whether it happens "in season," in contexts where this is expected, or "out of season," as a serendipity (2 Tim 4:2).

Most of the preaching in the history of the church has been done by ordinary Christians who are unremembered. Foster describes the situation ably for the first few decades:

> Much of the preaching would doubtless be to small groups, often an incidental opportunity which left little chance for preparation. One needed to be always ready. Perhaps it would be a casual group in the marketplace gathering round as a conversation or an argument is overheard, and turns into open-air preaching. Or it might be a family where one member is an inquirer, and on visiting him or her one finds, as Peter did in the home of Cornelius (and many a missionary nowadays), the whole company gathered, parents and children and slaves. (Foster, p. 51)

So the first task of the pastor-preachers in the church is to prepare the whole church to become articulate. P. T. Forsyth states this brilliantly: "The one great preacher in history, I contend, is the church. And the first business of the individual preacher is to enable the church to preach" (p. 53). Church leaders do

this by equipping* other people to share the pulpit—thus enlarging the scope and depth of the preaching ministry. But more especially preachers do this by equipping all the people to know God, to be able to make God known and to be able to open God's Word for themselves. It is a widespread church tragedy, and a travesty of biblical preaching, that people can listen to two sermons a Sunday for their whole lives and not know how to open the Bible for themselves. Discussing the text and the sermon in small groups* before or after the message will do much to equip both the church and the preacher. Restoring a conversational dimension to preaching, so fundamental to the early church, allows for mutual learning and life application.

The solution, however, is not to give everyone "a turn in the pulpit," making Sunday services into the world's greatest amateur hour. Martin Luther—a firm believer that every Christian should bear the Word of God—was careful to distinguish the in-house preaching ministry in *ecclesia* from the ministry of believers in *diaspora* Monday to Saturday, what someone has called "on-the-street guerrilla preaching."

> When [the Christian] is in a place where there are no Christians, he needs no other call than the fact that he is a Christian, inwardly called and anointed by God; he is bound by the duty of brotherly love to preach to the erring heathens or non-Christians and to teach them the Gospel, even though no one call him to this work. . . . When the Christian is in a place where there are Christians, who have the same power and right as he, he should not thrust himself forward, but should rather let himself be called and drawn forth to preach and teach in the stead and by the commission of the rest. (Luther, p. 80).

Preaching by ordinary members of the

church in both pulpit and parlor often has extraordinary winsomeness, laced as it is with story and illustration from everyday life.

What to Preach
There is almost no greater revolt in Christendom today than the universal revolt against bad preaching. Far too often today the fare being offered is baptized psychology, stream of consciousness, dialogues without any transcendent point of reference, and commentaries on "the scene." The problem is deeper than mere technique. Preachers are commissioned to bring messages that are not their own—messages from Scripture.

Biblical preaching is crucial for four reasons: (1) preachers have no authority in themselves; (2) God's Word has the power of its own fulfillment and can generate new life; (3) only the Bible in its "full counsel" can correct the tendency for preachers to ride a favorite hobbyhorse; and (4) the Bible is the supreme preacher to the preacher, as Forsyth says, "the sacrament of God to the soul" (p. 12).

All preaching then should be expository in that it finds its content and manner of delivery from the Bible. The preacher does this not merely by explaining the text verse by verse—a good thing to do—but by elliptically going round and round the two foci of the ancient Word and the Spirit-informed application to the situations of the day. In this way the walls between the first century and the present fall down. Moses, Jesus or Paul speaks, and the person today hears.

How to Preach
Much has been written about the art of preparing a sermon. Methodologies include the homiletical plot (Eugene Lowry), saying one thing (Stott), using the narrative form (Buechner) or the expository form (Robinson), and creating a context in which hearers convince themselves of the truth (Buttrick). These are all ways to go beyond the "three points and a poem" of the traditional sermon (a structure that generally delivers three sermons rather than one). All preaching starts with an introduction, a development and a conclusion, with application to life along the way, preferably not being left to the conclusion.

But there is something more important than the technology of sermon preparation. The genius of effective preaching through the centuries is expressed by John Stott: "The preparation of the preacher is more important than the preparation of the sermon." Does the preacher have passion for his subject? Has the preacher applied this message to himself? Does the preacher love me? Does the preacher respect me? How does the preacher live? When we analyze what people mean when they say "Don't preach at me," we may discover that this is a natural and justifiable revulsion about being talked "at," or "talked down to," by someone who does not really care or who has not taken the trouble to find out who we are. Implicit in the complaint is a call for incarnational preaching, the very thing biblical preaching demands.

The biblical understanding of speaking is that the message and the messenger are one. The person comes right out of the mouth (Mt 12:34; 15:18). Someone who had heard many sermons once summarized what he looked for in the preacher: (1) evidence of a deep relationship with the Bible, (2) willingness to spend time with people, (3) a prophetic stance—not someone who reads the newspaper and believes it, and (4) an obvious deep relationship with words. On this last point Buechner points out that the gospel is closer to fairy tale* than newscast—it is too good not to be true

(p. 81). So what is desperately needed today is not only good messages but preachable persons—deep people through whom God speaks.

Fundamental to anointed preaching is dependence on God, prayerful expectation that God will speak, humility before the truth of God's Word, a heart purged of selfish ambition* and a hunger in the preacher to *live* the truth. God may choose to anoint the ministry of a hypocrite from time to time, but sooner or later that person's words, unlike those of Samuel (1 Sam 3:19), will "fall to the ground" resultless and dead. It is a simple fact of life: you cannot give bread if you do not have bread. Forsyth names the problem:

> Churches and preachers are choked with a crowd of paltry things kept in place by no sure authority, and dignified by no governing power. Both ministers and churches have as much of a struggle to get time for spiritual culture as if it were none of their business. . . . And religion becomes an ambulance, not a pioneer. (pp. 116-17)

But the spirituality of preaching is not only the cultivation of inner authenticity in the preacher; it is dependence on the Spirit. Spirituality is *Spirit*uality.

The Holy Spirit takes ordinary human speech and transforms it, often without the preacher's knowing, into a word that addresses the human heart. Because of this, oratory and manipulative technique are both inappropriate and irreverent (1 Cor 2:1-5; 1 Thess 1:5). The Spirit does the persuading and does so in a way that profoundly respects the personality of the listener. The anointing of God's Spirit—so fundamental to effective preaching—may happen in the preparation of study, in the act of delivery, in the hearing, or in any combination of these. Depending on the Spirit, however, is not an excuse for shoddy preparation, nor does it guarantee "an anointed message." There is a mystery to preaching. It a fool's task. So is listening.*

How to Listen to Sermons

In the article on listening I noted that we are not fitted anatomically with ear lids. So the decision to hear is more subtle, intuitive and inward. If only the preacher could guarantee continuous hearing! But that can be done only by the listener, and even then through a spiritual discipline. John Stott's summary of predisposing factors (here paraphrased) for the preacher to be available to the Holy Spirit apply equally to the hearer: (1) conscious dependence on God (to hear God speak—a miracle of communication), (2) meekness (to submit to the written Word of God), (3) godly ambition* (to desire a genuine encounter with Christ), and (4) faith (to rely on the Spirit's power rather than our own analytic skills).

There is work for the listener to do before, during and after a sermon. Beforehand, it helps to read and meditate on the passage. Some churches follow lectionaries which facilitate multiple learning contexts. Discussion before, during or after the message will restore the normal corporate context for hearing the Word of God. During the sermon we should have the Bible open and follow the sermon in the text, praying all the while both for the preacher and for ourselves. What is he or she really trying to say? What is the burden of this message? Is the sermon a faithful expression of the passage being expounded? Afterward we should ask: What is there to obey in this sermon, what promise to lay hold of, what issue in my life to be adjusted, what sin to be repented of, what good news to be appropriated? These are dimensions of the response of believers to preaching.

In 1 Corinthians 14:24-25 Paul gives a stunning description of the unbeliever's response to true preaching: "He will be convinced by all that he is a sinner and will be judged by all, and the secrets of his heart will be laid bare. So he will fall down and worship God, exclaiming, 'God is really among you!' " No less should happen when a sermon is preached to believers. The Scriptures are written, Jesus said to the Pharisees, not so that people will find life in the Scriptures, but so they will "come to [Jesus] to have life" (Jn 5:40). Preaching should be the Christ-event, the written Word expressed through the spoken word so that people will encounter the living Word.

See also CONVERSATION; EVANGELISM; TEACHING; WITNESS.

Resources and References

F. Buechner, *Telling the Truth: The Gospel as Tragedy, Comedy and Fairy Tale* (San Francisco: Harper & Row, 1977); D. Buttrick, *Homiletic: Moves and Structures* (Philadelphia: Fortress Press, 1987); F. Craddock, *Preaching* (Nashville: Abingdon Press, 1985); E. Dargan, *A History of Preaching*, 2 vols. (New York: George H. Doran, 1905); P. T. Forsyth, *Positive Preaching and the Modern Mind* (London: Independent Press, 1907); J. Foster, *After the Apostles* (London: SCM Press, 1951); E. Lowry, *The Homiletical Plot: The Sermon as Narrative Art Form* (Philadelphia: John Knox Press, 1975); M. Luther, "The Right and Power of a Congregation or Community to Judge All Teaching and to Call, Appoint and Dismiss Teachers, Established and Proved from Scripture," in *Works of Martin Luther*, vol. 4, trans. A. T. W. Steinhaeuser (Philadelphia: Castle Press, 1931); Henry Mitchell, *The Recovery of Preaching* (San Francisco: Harper & Row, 1977); H. Nouwen, *Creative Ministry* (Garden City, N.Y.: Image Books/Doubleday, 1971); T. H. Pattison, *The History of Christian Preaching* (Philadelphia: American Baptist Publication Society, 1903); H. W. Robinson, *Biblical Preaching: The Development and Delivery of Expository Sermons* (Grand Rapids: Baker, 1980); J. R. W. Stott, *Between Two Worlds: The Art of Preaching in the Twentieth Century* (Grand Rapids: Eerdmans, 1982); W. W. Wiersbe and L. M. Perry, *The Wycliffe Handbook of Preaching and Preachers* (Chicago: Moody Press, 1984).

R. Paul Stevens

PREGNANCY

Once conception* has occurred, a human life miraculously unfolds in the nurturing womb, inspiring the scriptural metaphor of pregnancy as "fruitful waiting." The mother's experiences are as diverse as seasonal changes as she marks time in contemplation, preparation, prayer and hope. Intrauterine life is celebrated in Psalm 139 and Ecclesiastes 11:5, confirming God's faithful presence as we are "fearfully and wonderfully made." It is a mysterious journey, marked by growth and development not only for mother and child but for the entire family, as love* expands to embrace a new member.

A Mother's Seasonal Expectations

Invested with an inner garden,* a pregnant woman becomes the object of processes beyond her control in a way not unlike the seasonal changes a gardener observes. Scripture reassures us of God's plan, purpose and hope for the future (Ps 104:19; Jer 29:11; Is 43:1-2). The child's presence is signaled by detectable hormonal and physical changes from the very start of the pregnancy. In autumn the excitement of the news is heralded by a brilliant arboreal display of colors and meteors that fall earthward—fireworks from heaven. As light lessens and the fog rolls in off the sea, there may be a seasonal clouding of volition and certainty held just weeks before. Perhaps even the wisdom of the decision to become pregnant may be doubted as nausea and fatigue obscure joy, calling into question the energy and ability to become a responsible and loving parent. Tearfulness mists or rains in torrential bursts of emotion. Concentration is fragmented by anxiety,* and distraction makes everyday tasks more burdensome. Nausea and hypersensitive taste and smell confer vigilance in avoiding exposing the vulnerable embryo to possible toxins. As trees release their leaves, so is relinquishing essential for this season of preparation. The woman yields the constancy of her body shape to metamorphosis and surrenders her independence as she considers how her activities and decisions will affect the child she carries within. If it is a first pregnancy, forever altered is the exclusivity of being "just us two." This is a time to plant bulbs of hope deep beyond the reach of the threat of frost's fingers (*see* Miscarriage).

The clear winter days afford a heightened scrutiny of people that before had escaped her notice—pregnant and nursing mothers, children in fathers' arms. Anticipating new responsibilities, values* and priorities, and changes in identity* demands tremendous effort and time.* Burying herself in quiet seclusion, the woman nourishes roots, reconnecting with her concept of family by reliving childhood memories. She may retreat to reading and inner places of imagining and prayer (Rom 12:12). The days are short and the nights are long. This hibernation is essential for many creatures in winter, who conserve their resources by resting until spring's awakening.

Midway through pregnancy subtlety and secrecy give way to the visibly expanding cradle of the womb. Now undeniable, the pregnancy becomes publicly anticipated. Anchored no longer in her monthly menstrual cycle (*see* Menstruation), she finds new identity as a mother-to-be. She is the object of others' encouragement and advice, sometimes conflicting and excessive (Mary and Elizabeth share their pregnancies in Lk 1). How often do strangers smile and with overly eager hands stretch out reflexively to sense this new life! Like spring stirring beneath the ground, the baby's movements become distinguishable from internal intestinal sensations. The tangible relationship of a mother and child begins when she no-

tices her baby's pattern of activity and responses to her changing positions and shared sounds of music and voices. Fathers and siblings finally become participants, appreciating the baby's vitality by touch or sharing the visual images of the ultrasound that delineates the fetus' form and movement.

Summer ripens in a plethora of glow and sweat. With heavy abundance she is a tree laden with fruit and swollen breasts. She chronicles long days and short nights with insomnia arising from mild discomforts or the sheer elation of the imminent harvest. This change is more bearable when considered a conditioning preparation for the sleep deprivation and altered rhythms that inevitably accompany the birth of baby. "I actually remember feeling delight at 2:00 in the morning when the baby woke for his feed, because I so longed to have another look at him" (Margaret Drabble, in Ward, p. 13).

The Fetal Dance

Complete at conception,* within the fertilized ovum are the DNA designs whose secrets will be elaborated in this mysterious "becoming" that persists well beyond birth*—in fact until death.* A genetically unique individual, the human embryo passes through sequential transformations, beginning as a single primordial cell that reenacts the evolutionary story of the entire species. Cells divide, migrate, polarize and specialize, becoming organs, cartilage and bone. Only two weeks after the first missed menstrual period, a primitive tubal heart is already beating in an embryo the size of a small bean. Common to fish eggs and the mammalian embryo is a yoke sac, a source of nourishment; in the human embryo it provides blood cells until bone marrow forms and it is no longer needed. Also vestigial, the embryo's tail disappears.

As the fetal brain cells develop, we are reminded of God's prompting to evolve life towards greater and greater awareness of self and Maker. The Creator pushed beyond the probability of statistics to place consciousness on this cooling crust of earth. "He has set eternity in the hearts of men; yet they cannot fathom what God has done from beginning to end" (Eccles 3:11). By birth, *all* of the 100 billion brain cells of adult life are present, although the labyrinthine connections are woven throughout early life and are influenced by experience and inhibited by alcohol. This loom's complexity is elaborated by the fact that each cell may ultimately communicate with between one thousand and ten thousand other cells through sixty different chemical messengers (neurotransmitters). The total number of possible interactions exceeds the number of particles in the universe. The human brain is the most highly organized structure known! There is no lack of stimulation in the womb and the hard wiring begins long before birth.

Consider the evolving awareness of the fetus swimming in a warm intrauterine sea. Our blood is the sea continued in our veins—we are the fruits of the ocean born to walk on the land. As surf pounds rhythmically against the shore, so the earliest perception of sounds from the fourth month in pregnancy is the primitive drum of our mother's heart. Unlike a swimmer who dives down from the surface, trapping a muffling air cushion in the auditory canal, the fetus experiences amplified sounds when transmitted uninterrupted through water to the eardrum. The womb is anything but quiet. Externally we share the sound world, and internally the fetus hears profound bowel gurgling and the rhythmic surging of placental blood to its own quicker-paced heartbeat superimposed on the slower maternal base beat.

From a hand-clapping, feet-marching rhythm echoed in our earliest perceptions comes the primal response of *dance.* Children sing before they speak and sway before they walk, interpreting and synchronizing themselves with the rhythms of human pulsations. Dance has been historically the earliest outlet for emotion, at the dawn of rituals and the arts, giving the inarticulate a voice as a personal form of prayer ("a time to dance," Eccles 3:4). John the Baptist "leaped for joy" in the womb at Mary's arrival (Lk 1:44). The lively movements of the fetus are visible on ultrasound as early as ten weeks from the last missed period—months before they are perceptible by the mother or an outside hand. Consider the modern wonder of the ultrasound images that elaborate a beating heart, a delicate profile, a thumb being sucked and the Doppler-amplified heart sounds that reverberate through the doctor's examining room. These are among the technological changes that have enhanced bonding and allayed anxiety.

The sensuous world of the fetus consists of the tactile embrace of the womb, the response of the mother's pat to the place of a kick, positional changes in the inner ear as tiny stones falling with gravity stimulate hair cells in one of three directional canals translating "up," "down" and "side to side." There is uniformity in the protective amniotic bath, with constant satiety, warmth and darkness or a reddish glow. It is a safe, sterile and buoyant place to practice the primal skills of sucking, grasping, clinging and dancing. It is this focused, rhythmic environment of our prememory existence that we try as adults to re-create through meditation, chants or even jogging. Medicine increasingly acknowledges that the relaxation response appears essential for health and coping with illnesses,* pain or stress.* By imagining her child's intrauterine experience, the expectant mother practices relaxation and rhythmic, controlled breathing, so preparing herself for the trials of labor (*see* Birth).

Cocreators with Each Other and God

As creation unfolds within the expectant mother at the instigation of the awaiting father, they acknowledge that the child is not formed by their own concepts. They have worked but cannot take credit, they are creating but not possessing. Pregnancy's task is to begin to relinquish our hold on the individual within, whose love, respect and obedience are engendered beyond parental control. Our child's destiny, although of utmost concern, is not entirely in our hands. We stand parallel, shoulder to shoulder before our Maker, neither slave nor master, king nor pawn.

As the child begins so near to the heart of the mother, it is understandable that in contemplating birth she anticipates a rending that is lifelong, a vulnerability to hurt and be hurt. We are inevitably imperfect parents in the forgiving arms of our heavenly Father. Even into the womb we glimpse our humanity. Amniotic fluid is the brine of sweat and tears, secreted around the developing fetus, welling up from the deepest recesses of joy, sorrow and toil, a salient harbinger of the inherent suffering that our connectedness entails as being parent and child. The baptismal tides of confession and forgiveness* can cleanse and preserve the vitality of unconditional love within the family and our identity and hope as children of God, sowing in tears and reaping with shouts of joy (see Ps 126:5). We are all pregnantly awaiting ultimate healing* and reconciliation in the new heaven and the new earth; each season is weathered in faith and trust that God will be faithful to his promises.

See also CONCEPTION; BIRTH; BREAST-FEEDING.

References and Resources
F. G. Bushe, "When in This State: The Relaxation Response," *Wellness* 2, no. 5 (November/December 1992) 28-33; C. DeMarco, *Take Charge of Your Body* (Winlaw, B.C.: The Well Woman, 1994); L. Nilsson, *A Child Is Born* (New York: Dell, 1993); C. J. Shatze, "The Developing Brain," *Scientific American*, September 19, 1992, 60-67; J. M. Ward, *Motherhood, a Gift of Love* (Hong Kong: Running Press, 1991).

Carol Anderson

PRINCIPALITIES AND POWERS

Life in this world is not easy. Your child watches television* in a neighbor's home, and you discover later that some of the material was pornographic. Your church* is denied the right to expand its building because of a residents' lobby in the neighborhood. Your boss requires you to do graphic art for a business with dubious connections. The school system* teaches a godless approach to all subjects including the creation of the world. Your money* seems to purchase less and less because of global economic factors over which you have no power.*

The reason for the complexity of life is not simply the perversity and sin of individual human beings or even the cumulative effect of all the sinners in the world, but something more systemic, something all-embracing. For every visible foreground to a person's life—embracing family,* work,* community service,* leisure,* citizenship* and church —there is an invisible background that is profoundly influential. We want to do good, to serve God and our neighbor, to do an honest day's work, but we find ourselves confronted with "the system"— with frozen tradition, with intractable institutions, with deeply engrained social patterns that resist us, and, finally, with the world of spiritual beings and forces. What makes life difficult is systemic evil.

In this article we will look at the biblical evidence for an invisible world that affects us both positively and negatively, consider how people interpret and experience this world and suggest some approaches to living victoriously in the battle of life.

Identifying the Powers

The trouble we experience in the world is multifaceted and comes to us through unjust or unloving structures, systems of business and finance, principles of conformity, language and social patterns, customs and traditions that marginalize the life of faith or positively oppose it, and the ever-present influence of the mass media.* In addition there is the world of the spirits. All these are interdependently, systemically resistant to God's purposes in the world and dog the steps of believers. The Bible says relatively little about the ultimate source of evil. Rather it concentrates on describing the complexity of our life in this world and, most important of all, God's ultimate supremacy over all the powers. Scripture describes the realities encountered by people in their life in this world by means of various names, among them *the world, the flesh, demons, Satan, angels* and *the divine council*. This includes a variety of evil personages and forces unified under a single head, Satan, who is totally opposed to God and God's purposes in this world. The Bible also talks about *principalities and powers*.

Naming the Powers

Paul deals with the trouble of living in this world through a cluster of terms that include *power(s), thrones, authorities, virtues, dominions, names* and *thrones* (Rom 8:38; 1 Cor 15:24; Eph 1:21; 3:10; 6:12; Col 1:16; 2:10, 15). We will explore them under the general title *principalities and powers*. Each term must be understood in the immediate context of its use and in the larger context of the Bible as a whole. *Rulers* (*archai;* Rom 8:38; 1 Cor 15:24; Eph 1:21; 6:12; Col 1:16) refers to those in charge. The whole of this present world is under rulers who crucified Christ (1 Cor 2:8) and who are on their way to destruction. Satan is the ruler of the kingdom of the air (Eph 2:2). The *authorities* (*exousiai;* Rom 13:1; 1 Cor 15:24; Eph 1:21; 6:12; Col 1:16; 2:15) are those who have the right to decide on behalf of others, generally through the entitlements of an office, administrative as well as political, local as well as imperial, as in the case of the Roman governor (Rom 13:1).

In contrast, Paul uses some phrases that appear to deal not with earthly rulers but with heavenly realms: "the powers of this dark world" (Eph 6:12), "the spiritual forces of evil in the heavenly realms" (Eph 6:12) and "the basic principles of the world" (*stoicheia;* Gal 4:3, 8-10). *Thrones* (*thronoi;* Col 1:16) may allude, according to intertestamental literature, to thrones occupied by angels who were created and redeemed by Christ (see Col 1:15-20). *Powers* (*dynameis;* Rom 8:38; 1 Cor 15:24; Eph 1:21) may refer to spiritual beings and the angelic armies of God, since the term is used in the Greek version of Daniel and in *1 Enoch*. *Dominions* and *lordships* (*kyriotētes;* Eph 1:21; Col 1:16) may suggest "spheres of influence formerly understood to be ruled by the gods of the nations" (Reid, pp. 746-52) or the influence of idols (1 Cor 8:5).

The interpretation of these terms has generally followed one of three lines. First, these powers are a mythic projection of the human dis-ease onto the cosmos. Second, these powers describe structures of earthly existence: tradition, morality, justice and order. Third, these powers are sociopolitical and spiritual forces, both the outer and the inner structures of life, both the earthly and the heavenly. It is this last view that seems most persuasive.

A stunning example of how the inner and outer realities of a power are intertwined and inseparable is the case of money. Mammon is an alternative god; the name *Mammon* in Aramaic comes from the word *Amen,* which means firmness or stability. It is not surprising that a common English phrase is "the almighty dollar." As Jacques Ellul (pp. 76-77, 81, 93) shows, wealth has some of the pretended claims of deity: (1) it is capable of moving other things and claims a certain autonomy; (2) it is invested with spiritual power that can enslave us, replacing single-minded love for God and neighbor with commercial relationships in which even the soul is bought (Rev 18:11-13); (3) it is more or less personal. So money, "unrighteous mammon" (Lk 16:9 RSV), is a form or appearance of another power (Eph 1:21).

So we encounter both supernatural and earthly forces in the world. These make their appeal and persuade us to give them their loyalty, sometimes appropriately as good servants of God (such as government and social structures like marriage) but usually as intransigent and unruly alternatives to the kingdom of God. It is critical to understand these powers in the light of our current social situation.

Experiencing the Powers

Fallen social structures. Many authors, some of whom are cited, understand our experience of resistance as primarily the structures of earthly life, structures that hold society together but have gone wild. These powers can best be described by anthropology, psychology and sociology. We experience these as political, financial and juridical forces (Barth); traditions, doctrines and practices that regulate religion and life (Barth); dominant images and cultural icons like Marilyn Monroe (Stringfellow); corporate institutions like GM or IBM (Stringfellow); ideologies like communism, capitalism and democracy (Stringfellow); the power of money or mammon (Ellul); and the inner aspect of all the outer manifestations of power in society (Wink). Most people writing about these are concerned with the hermeneutical question of how to identify powers in society today rather than the metaphysical question of the nature of their existence. We do not have an adequate explanation of why structures so frequently become tyrannical. But if there are inadequacies in locating the powers exclusively in the human realm of structure and tradition, there are dangers as well in locating them exclusively in the angelic and demonic.

Personal spiritual beings. This approach assumes that the heart of our experience of multilevel resistance is the presence of personal spiritual beings that are capable of purposeful activity. Representative of this approach is the following quotation of Heinrich Schleir:

> Satan and his hordes, those manifold developments and effusions of the spirit of wickedness with their combination of intelligence and lust for power, exist by influencing the world and mankind in every sector and at all levels, and by making them instruments and bearers of their powers. There is nothing on earth which is absolutely immune from their power. They can occupy the human body, the human spirit, what we call "nature," and even the forms, bearers and situations of history. Even religions, including the Christian teaching, can become tools of their activity. Their spirit penetrates and overwhelms everything. (pp. 28-29)

A number of popular novels and treatments of spiritual warfare, notably the works of Frank Peretti and David Watson, take this approach. Its strength is that without these powers we lack an adequate explanation of why structures so regularly become tyrannical. Its weakness is that too often it focuses energy only on prayer and spiritual warfare instead of also working to change structures, traditions and images in a concrete way.

Western society has largely rejected the spiritual interpretation of life. Even the church has frequently turned to social analysis to find out what is going on and left out the spiritual realities behind and within the visible and present. The influence of such people as Charles Darwin in science, Sigmund Freud in psychology and Karl Marx in politics has certainly contributed to this one-dimensional view of reality. But the Christian in the world must deal with both the seen and the unseen. And Scripture witnesses to the complexity of systemic evil: structures, spiritual hosts, angels and demons, the devil and the last enemy, death (1 Cor 15:24-27)—all arenas for Christian resistance.

Systemic evil. The approach taken here is sometimes called "the double reference" interpretation because it regards the visible human rulers and authorities as political vehicles for cosmic, invisible powers. A truly biblical theology of the powers must include the Gospels, wherein Jesus is clearly depicted as encountering evil spiritual beings (Lk 9:1) as well as structures. So in reality many of the seemingly autonomous powers are being influenced by Satan himself. And in some cases the alien power (Satan) has home rule.

The complex vision of the last book of the Bible reveals multiple (and systemically interdependent) levels of difficulty, which can be pictured as concentric circles of influence: the red dragon (Satan; Rev 12) at the center of it all, the two beasts (Rev 13) representing diabolical authority and super-naturalism, the harlot (Rev 17) representing the sum total of pagan culture and Babylon (Rev 18) as the world system. This elaborate picture shows that the Christian in the world encounters not only a multifaceted opposition but one in which there are interdependently connected dimensions. This elaborate vision in Revelation shows us that the political power of Romans 13 (then the good servant of God) has become in Revelation 13 the instrument of Satan (in this case the same government but more colonized and corrupted)—thus showing the way in which supernatural forces and personages may influence and corrupt human institutions, structures, and patterns of cultural and social life. What we encounter in public discipleship is systemic evil, interconnected realms of dissent that do not operate in isolation from one another.

Understanding the Powers

Good theology can help us make sense of our life in this world and equip us to live victoriously. Scripture shows that God has both visible and invisible servants. All were created good. All have been corrupted. All have been substantially redeemed by Christ's saving work. All are personally ambiguous in the work they do. All will be finally and fully redeemed in the last day when Christ comes again and transfers the kingdoms of this world to the Father.

The good powers. Far from being the result of the Fall and a necessary evil to protect us from ourselves, these powers are part of God's *good* creation. They are not innately evil. They are made by Christ and for Christ! Paul claims that through Christ "all things were created: things in heaven and on earth, visible and invisible, whether thrones or powers or rulers or authorities; all things were created by him and for him" (Col 1:16). This, as Hendrik Berkhof brilliantly describes it, is the invisible background of creation, "the dikes with which God encircles His good creation, to keep it in His fellowship and protect it from chaos" (p. 28). They were intended to form a framework in which we live out our lives for God's glory. Four such frameworks are marriage,* family, nation and law,* each ordained by God for our good. For example, without marriage and family, relationships would become meaningless; children would grow without the shelter of marriage.

The fallen and colonized powers. Along with some supernatural beings (2 Pet 2:4; Jude 6:2), these same structures have become broken, hostile and resistant to God's rule. Ephesians 6 claims we should resist these fallen powers as part of our daily existence. There will be no cessation of this spiritual conflict until Christ comes again or until we depart to be with Christ, whichever comes first. Some of these powers have taken on a life of their own, making idolatrous claims on human beings: government, religion, culture, various "isms" symbolized in the names and titles that dominate the news (Gal 4:8-9; Eph 1:21). In Ephesians 6 Paul suggests these powers have been "colonized" (though the term is not used) by Satan himself.

The overpowered powers. No Old Testament passage is quoted as frequently in the New Testament as Psalm 110:1, which declares that all the powers have been subjugated by the Messiah-Christ. Throughout the Gospels Jesus is seen as supreme over the evil spirits. He casts out demons by the finger of God (Lk 11:20); he destroys the power of Satan (Mt 12:26; Mk 3:23-26; Lk 11:18); he enters the strong man's house and plunders his goods (Mk 3:27). This extraordinary power of Jesus to overpower the powers is delegated to his followers (Mt 10:1; Mk 3:14-15; 6:7; Lk 9:1-2; 10:1). Paul's further development of this elaborates the extensiveness of Christ's work now that he has died and been resurrected.

Paul variously describes how the hostile powers have been subjugated: they have been abrogated, stripped, led in triumphal procession or into captivity, made to genuflect, pacified or reconciled (1 Cor 15:24-26; Eph 1:22; 4:8-10; Phil 2:10; Col 1:20; 2:15). Drawing on the three phrases of Colossians 2:15, Berkhof points out three things Christ did to the powers. First, Christ made a public example of them. What once were considered to be fundamental realities are not seen as rivals and adversaries of God (Berkhof, p. 38). As divine irony, the title "King of the Jews" was placed over the cross in the three languages representing the powers that crucified Jesus: Hebrew (the language of religion), Latin (the language of government) and Greek (the language of culture). By volunteering to be victimized by the powers through his death and thus using the powers to accomplish a mighty saving act, Jesus put them in their place as instruments of God rather than autonomous regents, showing how illusionary are their pretended claims. Second, Christ triumphed over them, the resurrection being proof that Jesus is stronger than the powers, including the power of death (1 Cor 15:26; Heb 2:15). Third, Christ disarmed the powers, stripping them of the power and authority by which they deceived the world, namely, the illusion that they are godlike and all-powerful and that devotion to them is the ultimate goal of life.

Oscar Cullman compares the powers to chained beasts kicking themselves to death. Between the resurrection of Jesus and the Second Coming they are tied to a rope, still free to evince their demonic character but nevertheless bound. Cullman used a helpful analogy to explain the tension. D-Day was the day during World War II when the beaches of Normandy were invaded and the battle was turned. One could say the war was "won" that day even though there were months of battling ahead and many lives still to be lost. V-Day was the day of final victory. Christ's coming and death represent D-Day, but we must still live in the overlap of the ages as we wait for the final consummation of the kingdom at the Second Coming of Christ (Cullman, p. 84).

Grappling with the Powers

There are four historic approaches to the powers, all of which have their place in Christian mission*: (1) exorcism and intercession, (2) suffering powerlessness, (3) creative participation and (4) just revolution (*see* Structures). The church, however, must engage in a full-orbed approach, which includes discernment among other approaches.

Discernment. The Prayer Book of the Anglican and the Episcopal Church provides a handy summary of our multifaceted problem: "the world, the flesh and the devil." Each must be fought differently. We deal with the spirit of the world through nonconformity with it and conformity with the will of God (Rom 12:2). We deal with our lower nature by mortification (identifying with Christ's crucifixion) and aspiration (breathing in the Spirit). We deal with the devil by resisting and fleeing (Jas 4:7; Rev 12:11). It is a multifronted battle. And our Lord meets us at each of these fronts: *transfiguring us* from within (Rom 12:2) so we can transform, rather than be conformed by, the world as we penetrate it in our work and mission; *bearing Spirit fruit* through us (Gal 5:22, 25) as we determine to walk in the Spirit and regard the flesh as crucified; and *overcoming the evil one,* the devil (Rev 12:10), as we put on Christ's armor through all kinds of prayer (Eph 6:13-18).

Prayer. Karl Barth once said that "to clasp the hands in prayer is the beginning of an uprising against the disorder of the world" (quoted in Leech, p. 68; see Jas 4:7; Rev 12:10-11). Paul uses an elaborate metaphor for arming ourselves in Ephesians 6:10-18 by referring to the armor worn by a Roman soldier. The belt of truth means living with integrity. The breastplate of righteousness involves having right relations with God and living righteously. The "go" of the gospel implies that we are ready and "on the way" to share the gospel—there is more than defense here! The shield of faith deflects the enemy's attacks, and the helmet of salvation brings assurance to our minds that we belong to a God who will never divorce us. The sword of the Spirit is the Word of God, read, obeyed and spoken. All these are ways of "putting on Christ": Christ's righteousness, Christ's message, Christ's faith, Christ's finished work on the cross and Christ's Word. All of these are put on by prayer: prayer on all occasions and all kinds of prayer (Eph 6:18).

Preaching the gospel. The first and most effective strategy against the false claims of the powers is preaching* the gospel. Our duty is not to bring the powers to *our* knees: this is Christ's task. Our duty is to arm ourselves with Christ (Eph 6:10-18) and to preach his cross. However much we attempt to "Christianize" the powers, we must not bypass preaching the gospel and calling people to embrace the reign of Christ through repentance and faith. Some of these powers deserve the loyal submission of Christians (Rom 13:1). Some of them should be Christianized by the involvement of Christians and the church in creational and re-creational tasks: directing the resources of the world in education, politics and culture to serve human beings as defined by God's intention. Some powers will be unmasked by the martyrdom of faithful believers (Rev 12:11).

Public discipleship. Christ's complete victory over the principalities and powers, over Satan, sin and death, assures us that there is nowhere in the universe so demonic that a Christian might not be called to serve there. We fight a war that is already won. Therefore as far as is now possible, Christians should Christianize the powers, pacify the powers through involvement in education, government and social action, all the while knowing that the task of subjugating them is reserved for Christ alone (Eph 1:10; Phil 2:10-11). We work on the problems of pollution, food distribution, injustice, genetic engineering and the proliferation of violence and weaponry, knowing that this work is ministry and holy. In the short run our contribution may seem unsuccessful, but in the long run it will be gloriously successful because we are cooperating with what Christ wants to do in renewing all creation.

Living with practical heavenly-mindedness. Jürgen Moltmann spoke of eschatology, or the "end times," as the most pastoral of all theological disciplines because it shows us that we are living at the dawning of a new day rather than at the sunset of human history (p. 31). Keeping the end times in view is critical to grappling victoriously with the powers: it shows us that work done in this world is not resultless but, in some way beyond our imagination, contributes to a world without end. Eschatology also liberates us from a messianic complex (or inappropriate egoism), since the future is ultimately in God's hands. The kingdom will come to consummation in God's own way and time. Lesslie Newbigin comments on this with great depth:

> We can commit ourselves without reserve to all the secular work our shared humanity requires of us, knowing that nothing we do in itself is good enough to form part of that city's building, knowing that everything—from our most secret prayers to our most public political acts—is part of that sin-stained human nature

that must go down into the valley of death and judgment, and yet knowing that as we offer it up to the Father in the name of Christ and in the power of the Spirit, it is safe with him and—purged in fire—it will find its place in the holy city at the end. (p. 136)

See also ORGANIZATION; ORGANIZATIONAL CULTURE AND CHANGE; ORGANIZATIONAL VALUES; POLITICS; POWER; POWER, WORKPLACE; SPIRITUAL CONFLICT; STRUCTURES; STRUCTURES, CHURCH; SYSTEM.

References and Resources

M. Barth, *Ephesians*, 2 vols., Anchor Bible (Garden City, N.Y.: Doubleday, 1974); P. L. Berger, *The Sacred Canopy: Elements of a Sociological Theory of Religion* (Garden City, N.Y.: Doubleday, 1967); H. Berkhof, *Christ and the Powers*, trans. J. H. Yoder (Scottdale, Penn.: Herald, 1962); G. B. Caird, *Principalities and Powers: A Study in Pauline Theology* (Oxford: Clarendon, 1956); O. Cullman, *Christ and Time: The Primitive Christian Conception of Time and History*, trans. F. V. Filson (London: SCM, 1951); J. Ellul, *Money and Power*, trans. L. Neff (Downers Grove, Ill.: InterVarsity Press, 1984); J. Moltmann, *Theology of Hope*, trans. J. W. Leitch (New York: Harper & Row, 1967); K. Leech, *True Prayer: An Invitation to Christian Spirituality* (San Francisco: Harper & Row, 1980); R. Mouw, *Politics and Biblical Drama* (Grand Rapids: Eerdmans, 1976); L. Newbigin, *Honest Religion for Secular Man* (Philadelphia: Fortress, 1966); D. G. Reid, "Principalities and Powers," in *Dictionary of Paul and His Letters*, ed. G. F. Hawthorne, R. Martin and D. G. Reid (Downers Grove, Ill.: InterVarsity Press, 1993) 746-52; H. Schleir, *Principalities and Powers in the New Testament* (New York: Herder & Herder, 1964); J. S. Stewart, *A Faith to Proclaim* (London: Hodder & Stoughton, 1953); W. Stringfellow, *An Ethic for Christians and Other Aliens in a Strange Land* (Waco, Tex.: Word, 1973); W. Stringfellow, *Free in Obedience* (New York: Seabury, 1964); W. Wink, *Engaging the Powers: Discernment and Resistance in a World of Domination* (Minneapolis: Fortress, 1992); W. Wink, *Naming the Powers: The Language of Power in the New Testament* (Philadelphia: Fortress, 1984); W. Wink, *Unmasking the Powers: The Invisible Forces That Determine Human Existence* (Philadelphia: Fortress, 1986); J. H. Yoder, *The Politics of Jesus* (Grand Rapids: Eerdmans, 1972).

R. Paul Stevens

PRIVACY

Privacy is one of the most highly prized values.* We regard having time and space to ourselves as both a need and, increasingly, a right. This includes freedom from any outside force that would deny or diminish our rightful privacy. Although privacy is not as basic as the need for air to breathe, food to eat and opportunity to sleep,* we want the freedom, at least temporarily, to avoid contact with other human beings and to be secure from coercion by those who wish to falsely impose on us. Privacy is related to solitude, as well as to secrecy, integrity and identity, but is not identical with these. There are four particular ways in which privacy can be invaded in other than physical ways, namely, intrusion into a person's private activities or affairs, public disclosure of embarrassing facts, publicity that places a person in a false light, and appropriation of someone's name or likeness for another's advantage.

Why do we have such a concern for privacy? Negatively we may be wishing to escape from the demanding or oppressive presence of others, whether this takes place informally or in more public ways. Positively we may wish to be on our own to care for ourselves, to engage in various interests, to meditate or to keep company with God. In an age of increasing institutional, political and electronic intrusion in our lives, the issue of privacy has become more central, and there is considerable discussion about ways in which it can be protected and legislated. The degree to which it is possible is dependent on a number of variables. These include the group and population density, residential patterns and housing size, rates of interaction and the nature of relationships, division of labor and separation of roles. It is also affected by such factors as the scheduling and pace of life, amount of noise and movement, intrusion of technology (such as the telephone*) and bureaucracy.

How and Where Did a Concern for Privacy Arise?

Many anthropologists have sought to determine how important privacy was in preindustrial societies. The answer is clear. Although in such societies most things were done in groups and relationships were highly valued, people sometimes felt trapped in or overwhelmed by the company of others and felt the need to withdraw for a while. They reached a point at which they just did not wish to keep on talking, perform a particular task or share a secret. The bottom line is a fear of unwanted intrusion or of offensive exposure and the desire to escape from this. In such societies, however, privacy was less of an issue than in our societies today: since a public sector hardly existed, there was no thought of private rights over against public authorities. Even in more developed preindustrial societies, in which there was a recognition of both private and public spheres, such rights did not formally exist.

These kinds of rights began to emerge in classical Greece, where the social elite sought immunity from the obligations and punishments imposed on their slaves, and there were partial attempts at providing a political shield for weaker individuals requiring protection from the harsher consequences of the prevailing order. In the Old Testament responsibility for this was given a stronger religious and moral base and was increasingly viewed as an individual as well as a corporate affair. The prophetic insistence on the individual's as well as the group's relationship with God, despite the mediating role of the priests in connection with sacrifices, highlighted a realm of private behavior on which even the ruler and administrators could not intrude.

The Reformation's rejection of the confessional in favor of direct communion between the individual and God and the Anabaptists' creation of voluntary-based rather than state-dependent churches led to the broadening of individual and corporate privacy. This was also helped by the gradual extension of property rights in various European countries. Ultimately these led to the development of both social acknowledgment of the importance of privacy and legal protection against its invasion. A general right to privacy was not legislated in the United States by the Supreme Court until 1965. During the last two centuries the growth of individualism, a concern for personal rights and the power of new technology to gather data on people or increase surveillance over them have increased the demand and need for privacy.

How Do We Distinguish Between Proper and Improper Privacy?

For the reasons mentioned above, it is important to have regular time and space to ourselves and to be protected from coercive invasions of these. This is the case in the family, in schools, in the workplace* and in Christian communities. Children and teenagers need privacy as much as adults. Certain activities, such as engaging in sex or relating to God, require privacy. Even in a jail this must be permitted. Consider the freedom the anti-Nazi theologian and activist Dietrich Bonhoeffer exercised in a cell a few feet square and within the constraints of a prison schedule: the private reflections and prayers that came out of that situation have challenged and stimulated two generations of readers.

Fortunately no set of conditions, however constraining, can fully determine privacy. There is also an opposite problem today. We live in a world in which many people are either afraid of being alone or think that people spending time on their own are simply wasting it. Many parents feel anxious when their children are doing nothing, even though it is highly important for them to be on their own from time to time and simply sit free from activities and responsibilities. Often in families and groups, including some Christian communities, there is a failure to recognize the importance of private times and inner space. This includes the freedom to keep some secrets and the necessity of maintaining confidences. Overt or covert attempts to pry them out of people or share them inappropriately with others are inexcusable. So too is the intrusion of the press upon private celebrations or tragedies in the name of public interest.

But how do we know when we have crossed the line into behavior that is overly privatized or protective, in which privacy becomes pathological rather than healthy? This takes place when behavior is premised on an individualistic definition of human nature rather than on the biblical idea of the individual in community. Allowing each individual to decide what is public without any reference to others is as great a mistake as allowing the state* to determine what is or is not permissible in private. For example, allowing children a bed of their own may be a wise thing to do (even if it is a only recent child-rearing practice), but does every child need his or her own room or, as in the majority of American homes now, personal television* set and, increasingly, telephone and computer? Can it be right to design rooms and houses, as is so often done now, to provide maximum privacy at the expense of encouraging shared living: doors are hung to screen most of the room entered through them, and exteriors of houses are built so that all one can see is several blank garage doors and a living room used only on formal occasions? Is it in accord with a biblical understanding of community* that many Christians in small groups* hold back from sharing the most pressing tensions, challenges and decisions they are facing? How long can we tolerate the growing tendency for people to opt out of concern for or involvement in public life in favor of pursuing their private ends?

When it comes to providing protection for privacy, however, the problem is increasingly the reverse. As a result of computerized technology, workplace scrutiny, insurance monitoring and sales documentation, private information has increasingly become more public, outstripping legal and institutional efforts to keep these in balance with basic personal and group freedoms. There is also the problem of unapproved sharing of data banks and of credit and census information. This is particularly worrisome when marketing specialists integrate data from magazine subscriptions, credit-card operations and arts supporters into superlists or market files such as People Finder or catalogues like the Direct Marketing List Source. This is also troubling when government agencies synthesize personal data through information gathered by health, welfare, taxation and other sources. Electronic surveillance, both audio and video, has become increasingly sophisticated, all the way from simply registering how often people use the phone or how long they are on it to installing phone taps and observing actions through a camera.

When other basic human freedoms are placed in jeopardy by too narrow a focus on protecting ourselves, invasions of privacy occur at other levels. For example, it is now possible for someone to

be under surveillance—though not by anyone organization—throughout most of the day. There are cameras to catch speeders on freeways as they travel to work, camcorders in many parking garages keeping an eye on security, computers monitoring the speed of transactions in workplaces, store and credit-card receipts from lunchtime purchases or discount club memberships itemizing everything a person buys and digital machines recording every phone call at home. Once ZIP codes have their promised extra four numbers, marketers and agencies will be able to zero in on the particular side of the street on which we live, on selected floors on high-rise apartments, on many of the habits of small groups and even individuals.

How Do We Strike a Balance Between Privacy and Society?

In the Bible we read of Jesus withdrawing for times alone (Lk 5:16; 9:28)—generally after an exhausting occasion (Mk 6:46) or before an important decision (Lk 6:12-16). But we also see him taking part in community with his disciples (Mt 15:16-17; Mk 4:10). He commends private prayer by individuals (Mt 6:6); yet at times the disciples drew aside privately as a group (Lk 9:18). Privacy can be a communal as well as individual experience. There are guidelines in Jesus' practice here that we can profitably emulate, both in our individual lives and in our intentional small groups and house churches. At the outset we see that a concern for privacy should always be balanced by a concern for community. We should have an equal concern for the quality of both. As Henri Nouwen points out in his book *Reaching Out*, what we learn from solitude gives us the personal and spiritual resources for extending hospitality* to one another in our Christian communities and to the stranger in our neighborhoods,* cities* and wider civic realm. The reverse is also true, for what we gain through our experience of community and through our involvement in public affairs enhances the depth of our privacy.

Ironically, if we do not strike the right balance between privacy and the rest of life, we become more isolated from one another, resulting in greater social fragmentation. This, in turn, calls for a greater degree of social organization and personal intrusion to enable a society* to function. In other words, too much of a stress on privacy ultimately tends to subvert rather than enhance it. The end result is not very different from what happens when we become too dependent on another person or institution: their privacy tends to be invaded, or they just surrender it. Only a delicate balance between the private and public realms—in families* and friendships,* in clubs* and congregations, in neighborhoods and cities—provides the basis for a proper development of both individuals and their communities, both smaller and larger.

See also ARCHITECTURE, URBAN; COMMUNITY; HOME; INDIVIDUAL; RIGHTS; SECRETS.

References and Resources

D. A. Marchand, *The Politics of Privacy, Computers, and Criminal Justice Records: Controlling the Social Costs of Technological Change* (Arlington, Va.: Vanamere Press, 1980); J. McInnes, *The New Pilgrims* (Sydney: Albatross, 1980); B. Moore Jr., *Privacy: Studies in Social and Cultural History* (Armonk, N.Y.: M. E. Sharpe, 1984); "Privacy," in *International Encyclopedia of the Social Sciences* (New York: Macmillan, 1968) 12:480-87; J. Smith, *Managing Privacy: Information Technology and Corporate America* (Chapel Hill: University of North Carolina Press, 1994).

Robert Banks

PROFESSIONS/ PROFESSIONALISM

The professionalization of work,* one of the characteristics of modern society, is a matter about which Christians can profitably reflect. Sociologists speak of the professionalization of everyone (Wilensky, pp. 137-58) and everything from housecleaning to car repairs. But can everyone and everything be professionalized? The word *professional* is difficult to define. The idea has Christian roots, and Christians, both professional and nonprofessional, have reason not only to reflect on this occupational trend but to respond with appropriate Christian action. This article will explore the Christian roots of professions, the difficulty of defining professionalism in modern life, the dangers of professionalism and a Christian response.

Christian Roots

Prior to A.D. 500 the generic term *profession* (*pro-fateri;* to confess, own, acknowledge) was understood only in a religious sense. Both office bearers in the church and ordinary members profess their allegiance to Christ, to the gospel and to service in God's kingdom. Though such "professions" were predated by the oath of Hippocrates and the claims of shamans to understand the mysteries of life and death, it is substantially true that "the mother of all the learned professions is the church" (Reader, p. 11). In the New Testament we read about professing godliness (1 Tim 2:10) and professing the gospel (1 Tim 6:12). A professional is therefore someone who makes a public declaration of service to God. In a special sense the medieval church used *profession* for the vow of poverty,* chastity and obedience made by those entering the religious life, thus creating a religious professional elite. Reacting to this, Luther recovered the biblical universality of calling,* insisting that all, and not just priests, nuns and monks, were called of God.

The modern world has secularized this idea of a holy calling from something with a divine source outside oneself to an occupation with a special status and special responsibilities. To be a professional is the opposite of an amateur. Instead of professing to serve God, the modern professional claims a unique role that brings him or her deep fulfillment. In answer to the question of what is professed, E. C. Hughes says, "They profess to know better than others the nature of certain matters, to know better than their clients what ails them or their affairs" (p. 1). George Bernard Shaw made one of his characters say that every profession is a conspiracy against the laity.* It is vitally important to consider whether this is true.

Defining Professions and Professionalism

A broad outline of the traits of a profession include the following: (1) it is a full-time occupation (amateurs might do the same thing as an avocation); (2) it is viewed loosely as a *calling*, that is, an occupation that places behavioral and ethical demands on the person who engages in it; (3) it is based on special, often esoteric, knowledge that usually involves training of exceptional duration; (4) it is regulated by a credentialing process usually administered by a peer organization and thus excludes those not so trained; (5) it is dedicated to the service of the community* and is not intrinsically self-serving; (6) it allows professionals considerable autonomy as they exercise their own judgment and authority. In practice this leads to an elitist occupation.

Wilbert E. Moore says, "The bond established by shared mysteries, exemplified in technical language and common styles of work and even common attire, bespeaks a consciousness of being set apart" (p. 9). Thus, in the modern world, not only doctors (who in England were long denied professional status because of the manual skills involved in surgery) and lawyers but engineers, accountants, the clergy* and (increasingly) managers are accorded a professional status. Further, in a technological* society tradespeople* with esoteric skills in repairing computers, for example, have become professionalized.

The sixfold "trait" definition of a profession has been attacked by those who question the service* role of professions and single out other distinguishing marks. One is wealth.* While the original idea is that a professional does not work for pay but rather is paid to work, the high level of remuneration is now viewed commonly as a distinguishing mark and a motivating reason for entrance into a profession. Another mark is education*; the professional is first and foremost an educated human being. To this Alfred North Whitehead said that "the term profession means an avocation whose activities are subjected to theoretical analysis, and are modified by theoretical conclusions derived from that analysis" (quoted in Hoitenga, p. 302). Since the 1960s, however, a third mark has been highlighted—power.*

Professional help, it is claimed, leads to dependence on the part of clients and therefore disables rather than enables them (De Vries, p. 153). The emotional neutrality so widely promoted by professionals leads to less care than that given by those who simply love,* that is, amateurs (those who work for love, as the original meaning implies). Ivan Illich calls for the abolition of occupational expertise not, as Adam Smith and Karl Marx do, because of its effect on the workers but because of what it does to the consumers (Freidson, p. 13). So added to the difficulty of defining what occupations may be called professions is this further confusion of whether professions and professionalization are good things.

Advantages

After considering the question of whether professions are necessary, Eliot Freidson makes a case for expertise, credentials and the institutionalizing of professional standards. There is simply not enough time* in life to learn every form of expertise. Professions are based on a division of labor, so fundamental to a developed society. Such a division expresses a functional difference and not necessarily a difference in value and worth. Further, since ideas and skills cannot be advanced without becoming institutionalized, some form of credentialing is needed to protect society's members from the disaster of ill-informed choices (Freidson, pp. 22-23).

Still, the dangers of professionalization are all too apparent. Professional life can corrupt the soul* of the very Christians who take up the challenge of serving God's redeeming purpose in the world, not just in the church.

Dangers

The autonomy of professional life, based as it is on advanced knowledge, all too easily leads to smug self-reliance, pride of place and position. Among God's covenant people even a king must "not consider himself better than his brothers" (Deut 17:20) nor "accumulate large amounts of silver and gold" (Deut 17:17).

The structure* of professional life rewards success* and all too easily leads to a meritocracy in which service gives way to a psychology of entitlement. Success blinds professionals to the reality that grace is Christ's gift to the broken, the needy, the blind and the wretched. Human achievement gets scant mention in the Bible. Scripture offers a theology of response to God's achievements rather than to human expertise, of wisdom rather than success, of service rather than power. Without love, excellence all too easily becomes an idol. Technique may be safely learned only when one has determined in the heart that love is the most essential thing.

Because of the sacrifices they have undertaken in their long educational preparation, professionals all too often come to believe they deserve a special status and higher income (Hatch, p. 97). Frequently professionals find their identity in their work and measure their worth by what they do, rather than by who (or more important, whose) they are.

We require a deeper analysis of what is wrong with the professions. Christians diagnosing the problems of the world usually concentrate on hunger, poverty and war. But systemic evil is more complex and comprehensive. The principalities and powers (Eph 6:12-13) that Christians daily battle range from fallen social structures to the demonic. The very structure of professionalism in our society reflects not only the fallen human nature of those who have polluted the original vision of people professing Christ in their work, but systemic disorder. The result is that the very institutions established to serve others now serve themselves. Christians take their places in the world with hope but not easily. The hope involves living as a Christian amateur even while serving within a profession. This is especially difficult for those who are called to the professional ministry.*

Christian Amateurs

The term *professional Christian* makes no theological sense at all. At heart Christians are amateurs who serve for the love of God, the love of serving and the love of those they serve. Three things militate against the professionalization of Christian service: one cannot be a Christian for a living; one cannot be a part-time follower of Christ; one cannot base one's discipleship on peer review. *Professional ministry* itself is an oxymoron. *Ministry* is service to God and others marked by faith, hope and love. No one can be a specialist with God, though four basic models of ministry in history offer patterns of presumed specialization: (1) the sacramental model based on credentialing through ordination, (2) the cloistered religious model of monasticism, (3) the learned pastor model that has arisen since the Renaissance and (4) the organizational model of contemporary management* culture. Each model offers a criterion for excellence and elitism. But it is questionable whether pastoral, missionary or parachurch service should be regarded as a professional career* to be pursued for life (*see* Financial Support).

The professionalization of ministry may have some benefits (Noyce, pp. 975-76), but it normally contributes to the tragic and unscriptural dualism of laity and clergy, unless of course we return to the original meaning of professional as one who professes faith, hope, love and justice. At the heart of Christian leadership is the idea of giving away everything one has in order to equip all the saints for the work of ministry (Eph 4:11-12; *see* Equipping). Further, Christian ministry is never a one-way delivery system undertaken by highly trained experts but a mutual enrichment and empowerment (Rom 1:12). The recovery of a true amateur motivation is essential to the recovery of integrity in Christian ministry. But this is not the only way Christians may respond to the crisis of professionalism.

Recovering True Professionalism

One contribution the church can make is the humanization of professional edu-cation. John Stuart Mill once said,

> Men are men before they are lawyers, or physicians, or merchants, or manufacturers. . . . What professional men should carry away with them from the University, is not professional knowledge, but that which should direct the use of other professional knowledge, and bring the light of general culture to illuminate the technicalities of a special pursuit. (quoted in Hoitenga, p. 303)

Having lost the Christian (and therefore humanizing, though not humanist) foundation, the modern university has become a multiversity. Christians have the prophetic task of proclaiming a worldview* for professional life that is fully integrated and includes moral education, the development of character and personal mentoring, all facets of professional education that preceded the present technical career preparation. The professional must be a person, a whole person.

Traditional professions were rooted in a special brotherhood of people who regarded their service as a special calling and *therefore* were worthy of trust by clients, patients and parishioners. The order of priority has been reversed in modern life. Professionals are expected to provide excellence in service as measured by standards, thus resulting in trust. The shift from interpersonal trust based on personal integrity* to technical competence guaranteed by credentials is signaled by the widespread use of advertising* to identify professional services and assure confidence in their use. Even if it were desirable, it is unrealistic to attempt to turn the clock back and eliminate the need for professional stan-dards. Nevertheless, developing persons of integrity remains the greatest challenge in professional education and life. The Christian faith, with its emphasis on maturity as the master educational concept (Eph 4:13), is eminently relevant.

One of the hallmarks of professional life is excellence. The Christian serving in professional life in a so-called secular career will strive for the best. But excellence is not the goal or even the measure of Christian service, whether in church leadership* or business management. Love is that goal: "If I . . . surrender my body to the flames, but have not love, I gain nothing" (1 Cor 13:3). Emotional neutrality and professional impassivity will lead to a lower quality of care than that given in love. Love empowers and serves even when there is no immediate financial reward or even the reward of visible results. Indeed, the results of our lives are not seen in this life. So the Christian professional, who is simultaneously an amateur, lives by faith, hope and love. In doing so, Christians can recover the original meaning of *professionals* as people who profess a holy calling.

See also CALLING; CAREER; INTEGRITY; ORGANIZATION; POWER; SERVICE; TRADES; WORK.

References and Resources

J. W. Carroll, "The Professional Model of Ministry—Is It Worth Saving?" *Theological Education* (Spring 1985) 7-48; A. M. Carr-Saunders and P. M. Wilson, *The Professions* (New York: Oxford University Press, 1933); R. G. De Vries, "Christian Responsibility in Professional Society: A Reply to Hoitenga," *Christian Scholar's Review* 13, no. 2 (1984) 151-57; E. Freidson, "Are Professions Necessary?" in *The Authority of Experts,* ed. T. L. Haskell (Bloomington: Indiana University Press, 1984) 1-14; N. O. Hatch, "The Perils of Being a Professional," *Christianity Today* 35, no. 13 (1991) 96-97; D. J. Hoitenga, "Christianity and the Professions," *Christian Scholars Review* 10, no. 4 (1981) 296-309; E. C. Hughes, "Professions," in *The Professions in America,* ed. K. S. Lynn (Boston: Beacon Press, 1965); I. Illich, "Useful Unemployment and Its Professional Enemies," in *Toward a Theology of Needs* (New York: Bantam New Age Books, 1980); D. B. Kraybill and P. P. Good, eds., *Perils of Professionalism* (Scottdale, Penn.: Herald, 1982); W. E. Moore, *The Professions: Roles and Rules* (New York: Russell Sage, 1970); G. Noyce, "The Pastor Is (Also) a Professional," *Christian Century* 105, no. 21 (1988) 975-76; W. J. Reader, *Professional Men: The Rise of the Professional Classes in Nineteenth Century England* (New York: Basic Books, 1966); H. L. Wilensky, "The Professionalization of Everyone?" *American Journal of Sociology* 70, no. 2 (1964/1965) 137-58.

R. Paul Stevens

PROFIT

Profit, as defined by the accounting profession, is the excess of a business's total revenues over total costs. Economists define *pure profit* as the amount of money* remaining after making all payments for productive services and raw materials after the going rate of payments for the capital invested has been deducted. Profit is the estimated claim on wealth* that can be used as capital for new efforts to create wealth. A Christian perspective on profit requires a correct understanding of what profit actually is, how it is created, who has a just claim on it and what role it plays in a business, all in the context of a biblical understanding of human nature, stewardship,* justice* and community.*

Understanding Profit

Profit in an organization* must be understood in the context of the productivity of capital. In the long term, the return on invested capital must exceed the cost of capital to the organization. If the firm fails to do this, it is technically a destroyer of all kinds of wealth in society—finances, intellect and humanity.

The corporation does not exist for its own survival. Business organizations are organized as stewards of resources to meet needs* and aspirations in society. Every organization has a vocation, a specific reason for existence (*see* Calling). The primary vocation of business is the production of goods and services to sustain and enhance the human experience, thus contributing to the fulfillment of the cultural mandate given to us in creation* (Gen 1:28-30). The measure of the organization's fidelity to that vocation is the value it creates in society. As a member of an interlocking system of associations, business organizations exist for the common good and ultimately will be judged by the degree to which they cooperate with God in implementing his purposes for creation.

If an organization produces a product or service that does not fulfill a need or aspiration, it loses its legitimate reason for existence. Companies exist only as they continue to benefit customers. When they no longer create goods or services that are valued, they will be unable to create profit and will cease to exist. For example, the makers of buggies ceased to exist when customers no longer chose the horse as the primary means of transportation.

Profit and the Purpose of Business

Fundamentally, the purpose of business is to create a customer, not to make a profit. But when they are properly functioning, organizations will make a profit. This differentiation between purpose and function is critical for Christians who are trying to reflect on how they are called to express their faith in the workplace. Function focuses on economic criteria while purpose asks, Profit for what reason?

Profit is perhaps best understood analogously: profit to a business is like blood to a person. Just as persons cannot live without blood, organizations cannot live without profit. Just as healthy persons do not live *for* their blood, organizations do not live *for* profit. They cannot live without it, but do not live for it. In the same way, we eat to live rather than live to eat. Organizations must have profit to guarantee their survival. Never-

theless, any discussion of profit must first be placed in the philosophical framework of the mission or purpose of the organization. We need additional criteria besides profit for measuring a company's performance.

How Profit Is Created

The creation of profit begins with the production of goods and services that fulfil human needs. Taken from the user's perspective, the customer is the ultimate definer of value. In a market economy, customers exchange money for the value created by the goods or services.

Creating value for the customer, however, is not the same thing as creating profit for the organization. Profit from the firm's perspective is the incremental value that exceeds the cost of creating that value. So how do companies create a profit? The first determinant of this is how they create revenue. In a market economy, customers are free to purchase what they value. In the short run, the greatest influence on what price they pay is demand. The availability of the particular good in the context of its demand will determine the transaction price. But over the long term in a competitive market economy with access to information, the cost of production is the major driver of the transaction price. Taken together, demand and cost of production seem to establish the transaction price as simply "what the market will bear."

Although economists generally affirm that a just price is what the market will bear, Christians are required to reflect on this in light of the biblical message. Is there such a thing as an unethical amount of profit on a transaction?

Profit and Justice

Underlying the transaction by which the customer exchanges money for goods or services is the issue of justice, specifically commutative justice, which prohibits doing harm. Justice is a primary expression of vocation for all Christians in the marketplace. For an exchange to be just, both the seller and the buyer must receive an equivalence of exchange. To accomplish this, both must be empowered with equal competence. The price must not be established because the buyer is ignorant and uninformed about the product or service. This is the purpose of advertising.* Assuming a noncoercive environment, a free exchange should take place. The seller offers a value that fulfills a need in the customer for which the customer willingly pays. In the coercive world of advertising this free exchange is usually compromised.

The biblical framework for this evaluation is covenant and justice in the context of community.* Covenant implies a relationship that exists to serve the well-being of all parties to it, including the communities in which the organizations serve. They serve their neighbor with the exchange of goods and the promise that the customer will receive the goods they were promised. As Karl Marx insisted, justice in the business covenant concerns fair play not only with the customer but also with the producer. He argued that companies do so by purchasing the one commodity that can create a value greater than its own—labor power. Marx tried to dispel the illusion that laborers were well paid for their work. Labor creates value, and when it is not remunerated it is being exploited. What Marx failed to discern is that capital is never produced by labor alone, but rather reproduces itself. The amount of profit is determined not only by the price the customer pays but also by the value of the labor and the productivity of capital. So we must think deeply about not only just compensation for labor but also the stewardship of resources, especially the capital entrusted to the corporation.

Business as Stewardship

In economics, the ultimate cost of any product is the nonuse of resources for some other end. This principle is known as "alternative cost" analysis. If a firm fails to create a return in excess of its cost of capital, in the long run it is destroying the wealth that was entrusted to it. Consequently, it is the responsibility of the board of directors and stockholders of the organization—as stewards of the previously existing capital—to ensure that the resources are being deployed so that the capital reproduces itself for future sustenance. This responsibility is not just for the stockholders but also for employees, customers, suppliers and the communities in which they live and work. In the long run, all of these "stakeholders" are harmed if the organization fails to deploy its capital effectively.

The other justice and stewardship issue is the cost of labor. In the short run, as in the case of prices, the relationship of supply and demand determines the cost of labor to the firm. The *minimum subsistence level theory* (what was later referred to as the "iron law of wages") was developed by Anne Robert Jacques Turgot in 1766. This theory held that competition* among workers lowers the wage to the minimum subsistence level. Wages are determined by what is required for the support of the laborer in the short run. Over the longer term, it has been argued that wages are determined by a "standard of living" which reflects the laborers' psychological requirement for sustaining family life. If wages fall below that level, the rate of growth of the working population would be negative, and decline in the labor supply would over time raise wages.

While this helps clarify how wages move over time, economic justice requires that we consider our responsibility to the whole person. Work* that engages the whole person should enable the worker to provide for his or her family. Additionally, work has value beyond financial remuneration. Our calling to be coworkers with God in the world means that we have been imbued with authority and decision-making capacity. Therefore, we will consider not only the instrumental value of work to the worker and the company—wages and productive service—but also the intrinsic value of the work in the development of the whole person.

A further theological issue is what to do with profit. When the firm creates profit in excess of its cost-of-capital, to whom should the surplus go and what criteria should be used to distribute it?

Distributing Profit

The potential recipients of this "pure profit" are the stakeholders referred to above: stockholders, employees, customers, suppliers and communities. We must distribute "surplus profit" in a way congruent with the biblical witness that balances responsibilities, risk and return.

Stockholders entrust their capital to an organization. By doing so, they should be compensated for the opportunities foreclosed by trusting their savings to one organization over another (see Investment). Any profit less than "pure profit" belongs to the stockholders, who are not being justly compensated for their investment until the "profit" level equals the rate of return captured in the cost of capital.

To determine what responsibilities the company has to distribute surplus profit to the stockholders, the following issues must be considered: First, what is the level of risk in the industry? Second, did the stockholders forgo any return during a start-up period? Have all the aggregate requirements for return on capital been realized? (Capital is continuous as opposed to a sunk cost, so no static period for defining value can ever

be absolute.) Third, what is the relationship among the stakeholders for creating value? Is an ongoing access to capital the primary sustainer of competitive advantage? Is the business a capital-intensive business as opposed to a labor-intensive business? (If so, it is equitable for those who are the providers of capital to be rewarded and to receive the highest return, as they are the most responsible for its success and have taken the greatest risk.)

Now we must consider whether employees should share in the profit. Profit sharing for employees is growing in popularity for utilitarian purposes; that is, it seems to work. But there is a more important reason. From the perspective of justice and community, profit sharing links performance to the community. Each member is independent and contributes to the communal well-being. Consequently, each person feels some measure of accountability for results. Because we were created as relational people, being accountable and responsible for the effort of the community as a whole correctly aligns the individual and the community in a consistent way. We were created to live and work in this way—for the common good.

How much profit relative to other stakeholders should go to employees is dependent on the following issues: First, is the business a labor-intensive business? Is the primary value related to the efforts of the employees, or is the business an extremely capital-intensive business? And second, what is the level of risk associated for the employee—physical, psychological and in terms of time or lost opportunities for the future? (Employees also have a "cost-of-capital" in that their labor value is at risk when they join a firm. They forgo future opportunities for developing their skills and knowledge when they commit themselves to an organization. Employees should be justly rewarded for that commitment when it creates exceptional profit.)

Suppliers are part of the independent community of the organization and therefore have a stake in the performance of a firm. Relationships with suppliers should be structured to reward them for the value they bring to the company. If the work of a particular supplier is a major strategic advantage, then their compensation should include access in some way to the profit they help create. This clearly enhances the relationship between the two organizations and creates the sense of common unity.

The communities where an organization conducts business are also responsible for the success of the organization. School systems,* social services and arts programs all play a role in shaping the capacities and character of the employees. Additionally, they all have a stake in the ongoing success of the firm.

Customers also have a stake in the firm because they depend on it to meet their needs. Therefore, the firm has a responsibility to reinvest future funds to ensure its ability to continue to service the needs of customers. In these ways all stakeholders should share in the profits of a business.

Conclusion

Some have argued that business has no social responsibility other than making a profit ethically. This fails to understand the systemic nature of the economy and human community. A business does not operate in a vacuum but is the recipient of shared cultural and intellectual wealth and is accountable to the community. As a major influence on life in today's society, business has a responsibility to reflect on what that means. It is strategically positioned in society to express justice, covenant community and stewardship. In so doing, business can fulfill its calling and serve God's purposes on earth for the good of humankind and creation.

See also ADVERTISING; COMPETITION; INVESTMENT; JUSTICE; ORGANIZATIONS; WEALTH; WORK.

Donald E. Flow

PROMISING

A young man and young woman stand before friends and relatives and promise to be faithful to each other so long as they both shall live—an awesome moment. In a brief but dignified service a father and mother promise their child to the Lord. A business promises satisfaction or your money back. A young, dying widow in her last hours asks her brother, already married with two children, to promise to raise her child as his own. What is the good of making promises? Are there levels of promising, with levels of moral obligation? How are we to distinguish promising from vow making? How does promising affect our relation with God and others? Is it ever right, perhaps even holy, to break a promise? What happens when we do?

Promises, Vows and Oaths

Promises are voluntary obligations made in a social context to person or group who can anticipate some benefit or blessing.* A promise is more than a mere expression of intention (for example, "I would like to marry you"); it is a commitment, a self-imposed investment of one's person and/or resources. Although the promisee has a right to expect some performance, he or she can waive the option and release the promiser from the commitment.

The words or signs of a promise are charged with the full force of our personalities. This is a uniquely human attribute (neither dogs nor dolphins make promises)—as is acknowledged both by those who hold faith in God and by those who do not (compare Nietzsche, p.38).

Vows and oaths are both similar to and different from promises; it is not surprising that the two are often confused. As in the case of promises, these are an investment of the person with awesome consequences. An oath is similar to a vow except that in making an oath, one usually appeals to something, such as the Bible, to verify the utter determination with which one speaks. In the play *A Man for All Seasons* the chancellor of England Thomas More, tempted to break his vow and oath to the church and Christ by approving the divorce of the queen, says to his daughter, "When a man takes an oath, Meg, he's holding his own self in his own hands. Like water. And if he opens his fingers *then*—he needn't hope to find himself again" (emphasis mine).

We do not break vows (with or without oaths) so much as we break ourselves against them. But while similar to promises in expressing personal decision, vows and oaths need not be made in a social context or to another person. A childless woman might vow to give her child back to God if she is able to conceive (for example, Hannah in 1 Sam 1:11). With a vow there may be no one (except God) to overhear the commitment, and there may be no one else who can release you from having made it, even if the vow is overheard by witnesses. A vow is a "self-imposed commitment to do something, which creates a right on the part of nobody" (Robins, p. 85).

Significantly, the traditional marriage service contains both promises and vows, though most weddings* ignore the distinction. The promises are usually drawn out with questions: "Do you take this man/woman . . . to love and to cherish, so long as you both shall live?" The answer, "I do," is an agreement to a promise between the bride and groom that gives each an expectation of performance and, technically, the right to release the other for nonperformance. In other words, the promise is both mutual and conditional; the failure to be faithful—breaking the promise—could lead to being released from the promise by the injured party.

The vows, which usually follow the questions, go further. Here the bride and groom each say, "I take you to be my wedded wife/husband." It is not a performance contract that can be easily broken by noncompliance with the terms. Nor is it merely an exchange of promises made to each other. These are irrevocable vows made in the presence of God. Each hears the other's vow but does not respond with anything like "I accept the terms of your commitment." They are expressions of what this person gives in the relationship, regardless of what he or she gets, with no conditions, certainly not the unwritten ones that are present in most weddings today: "so long as we both shall love" or "so long as you meet my emotional and sexual needs." The other party can release me from my promise but not my vow. In *The Mystery of Marriage* Mike Mason wisely observes that we make vows because we know we cannot keep the promises! So in a deep sense we do not keep the vows; they keep us. They keep us focused on promise keeping.

Other examples of vows that are distinct from promises include the vow sometimes made on a sickbed (for example, "If I am healed, I will go into the ministry") or the one of a less-favored member in a family (again made privately and unconditionally) to prove his or her superiority over a favored sibling. Negative vows are made, for example, to avenge an enemy, or to never be like one's mother, which almost always leads to a disturbing measure of replication.

Vows are dangerous. Many family problems* originate in a secret vow that wreaks havoc generation after generation. Some vows have consequences far beyond what was intended. In the Bible Jephthah, the charismatic leader of Israel, vowed in battle to offer to God whatever came through the door of his house to greet him if the Ammonites were given into his hands—not knowing he would be welcomed by his virgin daughter (Judg 11:29-40).

Why Make Promises?

Promises can be short-term or long-term, lighthearted or solemn, unilateral or mutual. Promises can be made between individuals, between groups and between an individual and a group (as is the case with political and business promises). Promises can be formalized in written contracts or made simply by speaking.* Cultures differ in this matter. In parts of Asia one's word and a handshake will confirm a million-dollar business promise, whereas in North America the deal must be formalized in writing and notarized, perhaps because a person's word cannot be taken at face value. Promises can be extracted under duress (a deathbed promise), offered unwisely when intoxicated (with liquor or infatuation) or made thoughtfully and soberly "in the fear of God" (as the old marriage service puts it). Attitudes toward promise keeping range from the cynical quip "Promises are made to be broken" to the reverent fidelity of a man who, when asked why he continues to visit his ailing wife in the hospital, though she barely recognizes him, replies, "I made a promise."

Promises are critical to living with faith, hope and love.* These three Christian virtues* are not merely good for Christians; they are fundamental to living a genuinely human existence. Faith means trust; hope means having a future prospect; love means living communally for others. These virtues are as basic to running an organization (*see* Organizational Values) as to maintaining relationships.

Promising is needed for relational trust. We have no basis for relying on another person apart from knowing his or her intention through promising. There can be no collaboration of human beings without it. Lewis Smedes says, "The future of the human family rides on the fragile fibers of a promise spoken" (p. 17). Without promising we could only perceive an instance of a person's behavior and would have no foundation for making plans that require reliability and predictability. Imagine living in a family in which you never knew from day to day whether others were for or against you. A political party that makes no promises because it has no intentions is surely less trustworthy than one that makes promises that will be hard to keep. Just as we have faith in God because of God's promises, so we have trust in others—and hope.

Promising is critical to having a future with hope. According to Smedes, paraphrasing Hannah Arendt, "The only way to overcome the unpredictability of your future is the power of promising. If forgiving is the only remedy for a painful past, promising is the only remedy for your uncertain future" (p. 16). Without promises we would live instantaneous lives, inventing meaning day by day because we cannot forecast the future. In a truly awesome way the Creator has permitted us to determine our futures, albeit in a limited way, by making promises. G. K. Chesterton says the person who makes a vow "makes an appointment with himself at some distant time or place" (quoted in Smedes, p. 18). This is the paradox of promising: we must give up freedom (to keep all our options open) to gain the freedom of determining to be present to another in the future.

Promising is needed for full expression of

love. Promising defines corporate and social life. Without it we have to invent community instant by instant. For example, cohabiting* is togetherness without promises and therefore is a fragile, temporary community* that is less than true love. "If you love me, you will marry me" is an ancient heart cry founded on wisdom; love makes promises. Since couples keep changing over the years, promises can keep them growing in love.

Promises are also the invisible warp and woof of family life, holding people together through the inevitable transitions from infancy to empty nesting, but always belonging. The implicit promise of family life is that we will be there for each other whether we deserve it or not. Likewise social, business and political life can thrive only on promise making and promise keeping. Without promising the social fabric would disintegrate. Human transactions would be only as reliable as the intention of the moment. It is critical that we understand and recover the disappearing art of making promises.Extensive psychological, philosophical and sociological study has been undertaken to understand how we go about making I-promise expressions (Vitek; Robins). What is needed in addition to this is a theology of promising.

Holy Promises

Promising takes us to the heart of God and, not surprisingly, reveals the extent to which we are God-imaging creatures. We are less than human when we stop promising, more like God when we engage in promising.

We have a promise-making God. In the Old Testament promise preceded the law. Before God instructed his people on how to live (the Ten Commandments), God addressed them with a promise— the covenant—that brought dignity, identity and hope. The promise given to Abraham determined the whole future of Israel and those who become children of Abraham through faith in Jesus Christ. In general, the promise of God has three parts: a presence, a people and a place. God promises to be with us, to bless us with the dignity of being God's people and to give us a place to belong. The promise of a presence is expressed in statements like "My Presence will go with you" (Ex 33:14) and "I am with you" (Gen 28:15). The promise of a people came first with the miracle family given to Abraham, a family that would become a people belonging to God through which even the Gentiles would be blessed (Gen 15:5; 22:18). The promise of a place to belong is found first in the gift of the land (Gen 15:18), a promise conditional on obedience. But the covenant itself (the relationship) and the promise (the intention behind it) were unconditional. No matter what Israel did, God would keep his promise.

God keeps his promises. To keep the basic promise given to Abraham (Gen 12:1-3; 15:1, 4-5; 17:1-16) and the people of God, God rescued the Hebrew slaves from Egypt, returned his exiles from Babylon and sent his own Son into the world (Gal 3:14). The promise of God's presence is fulfilled in the first coming of Jesus, through the gift of the Holy Spirit, who is called "what my Father has promised" (Lk 24:49; compare Acts 1:4; 2:33), and in the Second Coming of Jesus—the visible, glorious and universal revelation of Jesus at the end of human history. God kept his promise of a people by forming something greater than national Israel: the new international, interracial fellowship created by Jesus (Eph 2:15). In the New Testament the ultimate place to belong is not a piece of land but the city of God in the new heaven and the new earth (Heb 11:13-16). All of God's promises are " 'Yes' in Christ" (2 Cor 1:20).

Godlike people make promises and keep

them. Because we are made in the image of God, our speaking expresses the intent of our souls* through words fraught with unavoidable consequences. When an Israelite pronounced a blessing (one form of promising), he or she did not merely offer good wishes for the future. Rather, the soul was offered and something happened (Gen 48:15; Pedersen, 1:200). Isaac could not recall the blessing he gave to Jacob, even though it was accomplished by deception, because Isaac had put himself into it. To withdraw his blessing would be to destroy himself; further, he intuitively understood the hand of God in it all. By his blessing Isaac made Jacob lord over Esau (Gen 27:37). Such speech is not only powerful; it is deeply revealing of the person who speaks. When we speak, the person comes out of the mouth.

Promises, vows and oaths reveal one's integrity. When words become trivialized—as has happened in the Western world—we think we must convince people that we really mean it by making oaths in the strength of something outside of ourselves, such as a sacred object. To this Jesus says simply, "Let your 'Yes' be 'Yes,' and your 'No,' 'No'" (Mt 5:37). While this may not mean we should refuse to sign a contract or swear on the Bible in court if required, it does mean we should become the kind of people who do not need these devices because our words are utterly reliable—because we are.

Breaking Promises

Can and should promises be broken? Are there promises that should never have been made, and others that should not be kept?

First, a promise implies intent and knowing the intent of one's heart. Therefore a promise made under the influence of alcohol or romantic infatuation is something less than a full-hearted prom-

ise. We cannot be absolved of responsibility, however, for giving our consciousness away to a chemical substance or to the chemistry of a relationship. Especially in the case of marriage made "under the influence," one should, in the words of the English Puritan William Perkins, "repent of that his bad entrance [to that calling] and to do the duties of his calling with diligence and good conscience, waiting after this for further approbation from God, and also from men: which when he has in any measure obtained, he may with good conscience proceed in his calling" (Perkins, p. 762). A child's promise, while important, cannot be treated the same as an adult promise. It would be tragic for children to be held to vows from which they can never recover, even though they were not old enough to know what they were doing.

Second, a promise made under duress, such as a deathbed promise extracted under the emotions of impending grief,* violates the voluntary aspect of such an obligation. Being forced or manipulated into a shotgun wedding, agreeing to raise someone's children or avenge someone's enemy, or keeping an unhealthy family secret denies the essential voluntary nature of promise making. In the case of a deathbed promise, the promisee is not in a position (after death) to waive the rights she or he presumably has been given by the promiser.

Third, a promise that is simply wrong and requires an immoral act for its fulfillment may, indeed must, be broken, albeit with sorrow and repentance, for to break one's word is to damage trust, hope and community and to sin against our own persons. Only when faith, hope and love are better served by confessing one's bad promise should such desperate action be taken. A significant biblical example of breaking a promise for a higher morality is the refusal of the Israelites to kill Jonathan for eating honey even though King Saul had bound them under oath to curse anyone who ate before evening (1 Sam 14:24-30).

All of these examples reinforce that promises are godlike things not to be rattled off in a newspaper advertisement to get customers by deception, mumbled in front of a justice of the peace to fulfill a duty, gushed in a romantic relationship in order to have sex or extracted from another human being under emotional pressure to secure care for your children. Promising is dealing with souls, yours and others, promisers and promisees. One of the real indications of true godliness is the promises we make and keep. As Smedes says, "Promise keeping is a powerful means of grace in a time when people hardly depend on each other to remember and live by their word" (p. 16).

See also CONTRACTS; FRIENDSHIP; MARRIAGE; SPEAKING.

Resources and References

M. Baker, ed., *The Family: Changing Trends in Canada* (Toronto: McGraw-Hill Ryerson, 1984); M. Mason, *The Mystery of Marriage* (Portland, Ore.: Multnomah, 1985); F. Nietzsche, *On the Genealogy of Morality*, ed. K. Ansell-Pearson, trans. C. Diethe (New York: Cambridge University Press, 1994); J. Pedersen, *Israel: Its Life and Culture*, 4 vols. (London: Oxford University Press, 1963); W. Perkins, "A Treatise of the Vocations or Callings of Men, with the Sorts and Kinds of Them, and the Right Use Thereof," in *The Works of That Famous and Worthy Minister of Christ in the University of Cambridge* (London: John Legatt, 1626) 748-79; M. H. Robins, *Promising, Intending and Moral Autonomy* (Cambridge: Cambridge University Press, 1984); L. B. Smedes, "The Power of Promising," *Christianity Today* 27 (21 January 1983) 16-19; W. Vitek, *Promising* (Philadelphia: Temple University Press, 1993); H. W. Wolff, *Anthropology of the Old Testament*, trans. M. Kohl (Philadelphia: Fortress, 1964).

R. Paul Stevens

PROMOTION

Many employees have the ambition* to advance into positions of greater responsibility within their organization. As organizations grow and senior employees retire, positions open up in the organization into which employees can be promoted. If the number of openings match the aspirations of eager employees, everyone is happy. The problem is that this seldom happens. Advancement in an organization seldom comes as soon or as rapidly as aspiring employees wish. Nor do the needs of the organization always fit the skills and experience of these eager employees. In both cases frustration may result.

Advantages and Disadvantages of Promotion

Promotion has some positive dimensions and advantages. First, the opportunity to advance is a high motivator; as a consequence, the organization benefits by the work of zealous workers. Second, the organization benefits by the infusion of new ideas and enthusiasm as younger employees work their way up the organizational chart. Third, a promotion is a clear indication of the worth of an employee and an affirmation of his or her good performance. It gives an employee the opportunity to grow and use his or her talents to the greater benefit of all. Fourth, promotions bring with them increased earnings at a time when younger families have growing financial needs.

Promotion also has negative dimensions and disadvantages. First, as some employees are passed over in promotions, motivation fades and negativism or indifference may develop to the detriment of the organization. Second, while promotions bring youthful thinking and enthusiasm into the organization, there may be a loss of experience as senior employees leave. Third, the self-esteem of those who are not promoted may fall, and this may spill over into other parts of their lives. Failure to win a promotion may be seen by the employee, the family and others as failure in life. Fourth, some promotions require transfer to another location. If the employee has a working spouse, the decision to accept the promotion will certainly be influenced by the spouse's ability to move also. If children are involved, the move can be traumatic for them. In some organizations, to turn down a promotion for family reasons eliminates the employee from ever again being offered a promotion. Finally, the principle of earning a promotion as a result of hard work is contrary to the theological principle of God's assurance that we are accepted (saved) by our Creator without any merit of our own. The assurance of the grace of God is difficult to accept in a workplace where good performance is the key to promotions.

Unwise or Unfair Promotions

Up to this point, the premise has been that promotions come as the result of good performance. But what if that's not the case? What if I am a member of a union where the contract with management clearly states that promotions will be based on seniority? A poor performer in my work group will be promoted ahead of me, even though she knows nothing about the job, simply because of seniority. To add insult to injury, I may be assigned to train this person. Is this fair?

Apart from union situations, my superior performance may be overlooked in favor of a less qualified worker whom my supervisor happens to like. Sometimes outside pressure is put on my supervisor to promote a poorer performer (see Office Politics). Or perhaps I am passed over in favor of a female, minority or handicapped person in order to correct the organization's past discriminatory practices against such persons. In order to reduce costs, some companies promote junior, lower-paid employees at the expense of more senior, higher-paid workers. This practice can result in age discrimination suits brought by disgruntled employees who have been passed over. Not to receive a promotion for any of the reasons above, when one knows that one's performance has been outstanding, can be dispiriting.

There are other realities at work that can be even more dispiriting. As organizations "downsize" (see Firing) or "right size" in order to reduce costs, entire departments may be abolished. Not only is the job into which I had hoped to be promoted gone, but my present job is gone. I am given the opportunity to accept a demotion into another part of the company or accept a special separation package and leave. A similar situation can result from mergers or acquisitions. The reality of life is that for many workers high performance and good experience do not result in a promotion.

Managing Promotions

Some managers, in an effort to get greater productivity, intentionally set up competition* between two contenders for a promotion. It is quite commonly done at the top levels of business corporations. But regardless of the level in the organization, such competition can become destructive. The competitors can put all their time and energy into their work at the expense of family life and their own health. Such competition can even spill over into the defamation of the other's character and competence.* It can become so vicious that when the winner receives his/her sought-for promotion, the loser feels obliged to leave the company.

The Peter Principle says that people are promoted to their level of incompetency. There is a great deal of truth to this statement, but the fault lies much more with those who did the promoting than those who were promoted. Management* can make a number of errors in the process of deciding upon a promotion.

First, it is difficult *not* to reward a star employee with a promotion into the first level of management. But it may be a mistake. The example most frequently cited is the promotion of a star salesperson into a terrible sales manager. While selling and managing both require people skills, managers help others to work effectively while salespersons do the work themselves. The same problem can arise in promoting research scientists, computer analysts, teachers, doctors, social service providers and many others into management positions. Management should not assume that the star performers will become star managers. Perhaps a mediocre salesperson can become a top-notch sales manager.

A second fault of top management is in not providing enough training for the job into which someone is promoted. Doing computer analysis is much different from managing computer analysts. In making such a transition, it is not only wise but a matter of justice to give the employee professional help in how to be a manager. It is interesting to note that the higher one goes in an organization, the less training one gets in a promotion. It is assumed that the senior vice president in the law department will know how to be an effective president. Sometimes this is true, sometimes not.

Persons moving into their first management position encounter the problem of how to deal with their former peers. As one among equals in their work group, these new managers used to socialize freely with certain members of the group. Some were very good friends; perhaps one was the new manager's very best friend. In the new role the manager cannot have personal favorites. Will the group accept and respect the new role their former coworker has been given? And what about the best friend? Can the new manager frankly and openly address the best friend's performance weaknesses? Will the new manager try to maintain the best-friend relationship off the job but lay it aside on the job? Will it work?

Refusing Promotions

Up to this point we have assumed that all workers want and will accept a promotion. Such is not always the case. As indicated earlier, if a promotion involves a move to a new location and the interests of a spouse and/or children must be considered, an employee may elect not to accept the promotion. At times this may happen in favor of retaining links with the local church to which one is strongly committed or from which one is presently gaining some greater benefit. More and more organizations are trying to reduce the problem by helping locate a job for the spouse at the new location. But depending on where children are in school, the decision may still be negative. While some companies blacklist an employee for refusing to move, wiser organizations recognize that talent is talent and what is "no" to a move today may be "yes" to a move in five years.

Some employees may reject a promotion because they are perfectly happy ding what they are doing. They like the 9-to-5 ritual where everything is fairly predictable and change comes slowly. They do their jobs very well and will continue to do so. Why spoil a good situation? is their reasoning. Some employees turn down a promotion because the new job would subject them to stressful situations. They do not want to be held responsible for the work of a group of people. They rebel at the thought of having to evaluate another person's performance, of recommending pay raises and, perhaps, of firing* someone.

Reflecting on Promotions

The Bible contains numerous accounts

of good performance resulting in promotions. Genesis records the remarkable story of Joseph, who advanced from being a prisoner in Egypt to the second-in-command under Pharaoh as a result of his good work. Jesus' well-known parable of the talents (Mt 25:14-30; Lk 19:12-27) has the master promoting the slaves who performed the best in increasing the talents* with which they were entrusted. The slave who did not perform well was cast out. At the same time, the Bible also clearly reminds us of the grace of God, a grace that is freely given, without any merit of our own.

For the Christian who is dedicated to a life of service, promotions provide the opportunity to use one's God-given talents to greater good in the workplace. At the same time, the heavy influence of performance in the awarding of promotions can easily change one's focus from what God has done for us to what we have done for ourselves.

See also AMBITION; COMPETITION; DRIVENNESS; OFFICE POLITICS.

References and Resources

J. A. Berbaum and S. M. Steer, *Why Work? Careers and Employment in Biblical Perspective* (Grand Rapids: Baker, 1986); D. Braybrooke, "The Right to Be Hired, Promoted, Retained," in *Ethics in the World of Business* (Totowa, N.J.: Rowman & Allanheld, 1983) 145-76; W. Diehl, *Thank God It's Monday* (Philadelphia: Fortress, 1982); R. Mattson and A. Miller, *Finding a Job You Can Love* (Nashville: Thomas Nelson, 1982); L. T. Peter and R. Hull, *The Peter Principle* (New York: William Morrow, 1969); R. E. Slocum, *Ordinary Christians in a High-Tech World* (Waco, Tex.: Word, 1986); G. Tucker, *The Faith-Work Connection: A Practical Application of Christian Values in the Marketplace* (Toronto: Anglican Book Centre, 1987).

William E. Diehl

PUBLIC SPACES

A public space is a space open to people's informal and varied use. It is a space ready to be filled by whatever human content we give it. Public spaces come in many forms and are crucial to our building community* in neighborhoods, towns* and cities.* The three most important types of public space are pavements (or sidewalks), parks (or playgrounds) and plazas (or squares). Why do we need such places? What makes some attractive to people and some not, and turns some into little-used or even unsafe areas? How should we use or reclaim these spaces?

Sidewalks and Pavements

In ancient times people made shorter trips on foot along gradually developed tracks or through cleared open spaces. As proper roads were built and vehicles increased, especially in and around cities, the amount and movement of traffic was regulated so that people could walk around safely or gather freely together. In ancient Rome, for example, commercial vehicles were able to enter the city only at night, after people's daily rounds and public responsibilities were finished.

With the growth of the middle class and increase in horse-drawn carriages, and then the arrival of automobiles,* walking* and socializing were increasingly confined to sidewalks. But sometimes, as with boardwalks and promenades, these were quite expansive. In varying degrees all these enabled people to do errands and gather informally, children to play* and observe life, and adults sometimes to sit and socialize on benches or in sidewalk cafés. In densely packed urban areas, with terraced houses and narrow streets, a large part of people's social life occurred in such spaces. It was here that the sense and experience of a neighborhood* were largely developed.

With the mass production of automobiles, traffic quickly increased in both amount and speed. As many streets were broadened to accommodate cars, sidewalks tended to narrow. In many new housing developments sidewalks do not exist at all, while private ownership of many lake- and beachfronts has prevented promenades and cliff walks from being built. Where crime has increased, large parts of inner-city areas have become unsafe at night and even during the day for some people. The density of traffic flow and creation of thoroughfares on many urban and suburban streets have seriously reduced or virtually destroyed contact between people who live along them, especially those who are on opposite sides of the road. Empirical studies can now predict how quickly this will happen and what defensive actions people will take. Overall there is an increasing tendency for the social life of both adults and children to move from the street to the backyard and from the steps (or porch) to the front rooms, and back rooms, of the house.

In her perceptive and prophetic account of American cities, Jane Jacobs speaks of sidewalks as being the heart of urban social life. They have, or should have, a more significant role than either parks or plazas. City life depends on how open sidewalks are to use and how widely they can be used by individuals and groups for spontaneous and organized, creative and routine, purposes. If sidewalks are to be really effective, housing along them should not be too far apart, the sidewalks themselves should be broad enough for children to play games* and gather spontaneously, and traffic speed and flow should be regulated so that contact can be maintained across streets. Public activities, whether voluntary or official, should grow out of the informal public life of a street rather than be artificially organized. Safety should be a normal community function arising simply from more eyes looking at

the street and more people using it. There is, therefore, less need for something as organized as a "neighborhood watch."

If we are serious about renewing community in densely populated neighborhoods, then agitating for suitable sidewalks is actually more important than pressing for more parks and playgrounds, where there are generally fewer people present and less adult company or supervision. Of course, simply creating more space of this kind will not of itself alter much. It must be accompanied by other changes in people's lifestyle—for example, spending more time around and outside apartments or small businesses, relying less on the automobile and exercise machines and more on walking, showing more interest in one's neighbors and recognizing the multilayered value of common activities. In particular, at least one person on a street needs to emerge as a public character in frequent contact with a wide circle of people. This might be a local neighborhood-watch organizer (a modern version of the town crier), a people person or a street pastor. There is a wonderful vocation here for Christians in particular.

Urban planners, architects and developers involved in creating new urban spaces should give more thought to what made older neighborhoods more sociable and safer places in which to live, as well as to a proper mix of public, commercial, social and private spaces. This should also be part of building new or renovating old suburbs, for thinning out residences tends to lead to less, not more, community and to more, not less, danger. More attention should also be given to the pattern and use of streets, replacing the blocklike grid with one developed more like the spokes on a wheel. In all these ways there is a strong vocational contribution to be made by such people.

Parks and Playgrounds

Parks have a long history. The description of the Garden of Eden in Genesis 2 is reminiscent of a park, and in ancient times many imperial capitals had parklike areas. A well-known example is the Hanging Gardens of Babylon. A central feature of medieval towns and villages, especially in England, was the commons, a piece of undeveloped public land that could be used for socializing, grazing or festivals. From the time of the Enlightenment, parks began to take on a more ordered shape. In line with the basic position given to mathematics and the new emphasis on human order and control, the planning of parks gained in importance. New kinds of parks came into existence, such as botanical gardens, though the Romantic movement later gave impetus to more natural arrangements. Through the influence of figures such as Frederick Remington in the mid-nineteenth century, a movement grew in North America to preserve and develop public spaces into parks on a wide scale. Later still more specialized playgrounds came into being, sometimes based within parks, sometimes separate from them.

Today parks and playgrounds can be found in most places where people live, including suburbs and even smaller rural settlements. Some are extremely large and carefully developed, such as Central Park in New York City, offering multifarious uses. Others, such as Griffith Park in Los Angeles, contain an interesting mixture of planned and relatively natural space. Parks attract people who want to relax or meditate, socialize and eat with others, exercise or play games, hold communal events or public celebrations.

Unfortunately in some locations parks have also become places where people may be mugged or attacked, where drugs are readily available and used, where street people sleep and even reside, and where gangs gather or mark out turf. In other locations parks have become largely empty, being used only occasionally by the people around them. There are various reasons why parks meet these unfortunate fates: (1) people are too busy with work and other leisure activities to use parks regularly; (2) the community has broken down, resulting in inadequate neighborhood supervision of parks and children's playgrounds; (3) some parks and playgrounds are inconveniently sited or designed in ways that are not user-friendly; (4) the community's unemployed or marginal residents lack job opportunities or available space where they can gather; (5) gangs and street people sometimes claim and fight over such public territory.

Since parks are the breathing places of the city, opening them up more for public use requires a range of strategies. Individual Christians, churches* and other religious organizations can make a significant contribution to these. Those who live within range of a park can find ways—as individuals, families, friends, neighbors, home churches and congregations—to make regular use of it for any or all of the purposes mentioned. Those who work near city parks and who use lunch breaks to work or shop rather than relax, meditate, socialize or play could spend more time in parks for any of these purposes, overcoming the proven resistance people have to walking to any place that is more than two hundred yards away. And, where necessary, neighborhood watches could expand their responsibilities to protect parks and playgrounds in the vicinity from antisocial or criminal behavior.

There are other actions that can be taken. Congregations that have a reasonably sized property could turn some of the space into a small park or playground for the use of nearby residents. Congregations and residents could also put pressure on city officials to upgrade and multiply facilities in parks so that they can have the widest range of uses. Urban planners and developers could do more to site playgrounds and parks where it is easiest for people to gather and to construct them in such a way that they are inviting and safe. (It is seldom recognized, for example, that the amount of public use of a park depends to a large extent on whether people can see easily into it. That is, if a park is more than four or five steps up from the pavement or is ringed by hedges or non-see-through fences, its use decreases exponentially.)

Plazas and Squares

A plaza is a form of public space that has a long and respected history. Though it predates western European civilization, it is best known to us through many fine examples in Mediterranean countries, especially in Spain and Italy. The Spanish word *plaza* means simply "place," and the related Italian term *piazza* means "broad way" or "street." Originally these were not planned: the typical broad, open square developed organically out of the need for large-scale public marketplaces. Probably the best known and admired example today is the Piazza San Marco in Venice. From the Renaissance onward, planning of such spaces became more common, with special attention being paid to the visual and architectural, more than commercial and social, aspect. In English-speaking cultures, the term *square* was more commonly used.

Outside western Europe, cultures affected by Spanish influence built cities containing fine plazas, and there were imitations elsewhere. With the advent of the car, many plazas and squares were broken up by roads. The generously sized King's Square in Copenhagen, for example, was divided into forty-eight pedestrian islands separated by roads. Over the last two or three decades, there has been a move to close densely used roads in the center of some cities and allow only pedestrian or service traffic. In some places this leads to a re-creation of the pedestrian mall, but where there are broad roads or boulevards, there is a partial restoration of the plaza. Here and there older plazas and squares have been returned to their original condition.

The advantages of the classical plaza or square were many. It invited people to gather in large numbers, not only for the purposes of buying and selling but also for the purpose of socializing more generally. The classical plaza generated what the urban designer Jan Geyl calls "life between buildings" as compared to life squeezed out by buildings (or roads). The plaza was large enough, and the activities within it comprehensive enough, to represent some sense of the whole city. Surrounded as it was by many of the city's most important buildings, which were also built on a scale that did not dwarf their inhabitants, the plaza gave people a feeling for the unity of the city.

In any town of reasonable size, there is a great need for such public spaces. Since they provide a meeting place for all interested citizens, they are a kind of public living room where people can gather in large or small groups, socialize, advocate various causes, buy and sell, refresh themselves, engage in civic and political activities, dance and hold festivals. The plazas or squares need to be an appropriate size for the city or town of which they are a part. They should also contain plenty of places to sit, whether publicly provided benches or seats in open-air cafés, and seating needs to be flexible, facing onto the square as well as around tables.

In recent times the word *plaza* has been appropriated by shopping centers, but these are restricted spaces compared with the free and varied uses people can make of genuine plazas. Shopping malls* are private, not public, spaces, whose activities are controlled by their owners, not by the people in general. The siting of such centers on the edge of suburbs or cities also fragments the population, making it more difficult to reinvent the plaza in any effective way.

But wherever public plazas and squares exist, we should seek to enjoy them and invite others to them. As well as using them for a range of informal purposes, groups and congregations should look for ways to develop appropriate pockets of activity around the edges of the square. These could be artistic, dramatic or evangelistic in character and should spring from a desire to "seek the welfare of the city" (Jer 29:7 NRSV), not merely use it as a means to our own ends.

Conclusion

In general, what turns available public spaces into interactive public places is a shift in the public attitude toward life; that is, life is as much about being and relating as about doing and achieving. Once life is viewed in this way, communities can provide places that are conducive to our becoming aware of other people and being addressed by them, to the opportunity to engage in play and in spontaneous or informal celebrations, to ease of interaction with the natural or humanly created environment, to the presence of a sense of adventure, mystery or new possibilities, to an ethos that connects us with the past and therefore helps shape identity and multiple lines of connection to lived reality.

See also ARCHITECTURE, URBAN; COMMUNITY; SHOPPING MALLS.

References and Resources

C. Alexander, S. Ishikawa and M. Silverstein, *A Pattern Language: Towns, Buildings, Construc-tion* (New York: Oxford University Press, 1977); D. Engwicht, *Reclaiming Our Cities and Towns: Better Living with Less Traffic* (Philadelphia: New Society, 1993); J. Geyl, *Life Between Buildings: Using Public Space* (New York: Van Nostrand Reinhold, 1987); J. Jacobs, *The Death and Life of Great American Cities* (New York: Vintage Books, 1961).

Robert Banks

PUBLIC TRANSPORTATION

There are many complaints about public transport. In most cities it has been in decline for decades. In advanced Western societies the heyday of mass transit by train, bus, tram and ferry was in the earlier part of the twentieth century. Only in former communist countries like Russia, or smaller overpopulated countries like Japan, are the bulk of the people moved around every day by public transport. In the West some countries and cities maintain excellent public transport systems; the more densely settled and highly efficient parts of Europe have an integrated rail system, Zurich has its trams, and Paris the Metro. Elsewhere a city is sometimes graced by a particular form of public transport facility that functions well, but rarely do all parts of the system work together to provide an integrated transportation service.

People (mostly those who hardly use public transport) often blame government cutbacks for the deterioration of such transportation services. The main cause, however, was the introduction of the automobile,* and the major culprit the average person. Los Angeles is a perfect example. It is little known that until the 1920s Los Angeles had the largest and most efficient public transport systems in the world, with over 10,000 miles of tramlines. But as automobiles became less expensive, people chose to buy and use them instead. People's demand for better and faster roads soon began to take money away from public transport, and in time even tram routes were paved over to form the huge freeways that are synonymous with the city. Auto owners now argue that public transport is not as important as the betterment of the road system.

Other arguments against public transport have been its lack of convenience in some areas and problems with safety in larger cities. The first stems in part from the original cutbacks but also from the complex character of cities that developed with the automobile. The second is a byproduct of other difficulties, in part, the middle-class flight from the city center.

Even with less money spent on it in a cost-saving period, the expense of public transport has led some politicians to argue that it should pay for itself and not be a drain on the public purse. This is extremely short-sighted and unjust. The fact is that by moving around enormous numbers of people in the most economical way, public transport supports the whole infrastructure of a city's economy and contributes significantly to its productivity. Think of the public cost and chaos involved in turning most of this over to the automobile, even if everyone could afford to own one. Such a policy is also unjust because it places a further financial burden on those who are least able to carry it—disadvantaged groups who most depend on public transport. They are already subsidizing the even greater cost of providing freeways and improving roads for better-off members of society. On the contrary, it is to a city's advantage to invest heavily in the very best public transport system where it can be most effective. There are movements and groups in the city which can be served better by private transport, and it is important to know the proper benefits and limits of both.

The coming of the automobile brought many advantages, especially greater convenience, flexibility and privacy. But this was at a heavy price: the toll of deaths and injuries, escalating pollution* and disrupted neighborhoods.* The automobile also marginalized groups who were too poor, young, infirm or old to purchase one. Those who relied on public transport—the needy and unemployed, many ethnic groups, young mothers and children, the elderly and incapacitated—became more and more disadvantaged. In time, public transport covered fewer areas, took longer to reach destinations, became less comfortable and, as mentioned, grew increasingly unsafe. On the whole, the vote for the automobile was a vote by the better off against the worse off, and Christians were involved in this as much as others. Scarcely any of those who owned a car thought or cared about its impact on these people or on the quality of city life. As local governments ask for more money to improve public transport services, it is often car owners who vote these down in favor of improved roads.

The Positive Future for Public Transport

In the last decade or two public transport has begun to make a comeback or has undergone redevelopment. Around and between many large cities, new rail and tram lines are under construction. Very fast trains are being introduced, and articulated trams carry more people and move around more quickly. There are also more regular and accessible commuter air flights. On waterways, hovercraft and aqua jet ferries have improved the efficiency of ferry services.

With car travel becoming more frustrating due to gridlock on freeways and longer travel times, over the last ten years use of public transport has increased for the first time in decades. The numbers may not as yet be large, but they continue to grow. It is news indeed when the fastest-growing commuter train service in America is right in the heart of Los Angeles, the city most identified with, and shaped by, the automobile commuter.

Other interesting experiments in public transport are presently under construction. The introduction of very fast trains on high-density routes has already been mentioned. In several cities door-to-door shuttle or minibus services, once only for the handicapped and elderly, have now become computer coordinated and available to everyone: this is an attempt to combine the advantages of taxis and buses at a reasonable cost. In some places, like Hamburg in northern Germany, "smart" traffic systems regulate signals and road use by means of a central video and computer headquarters to improve traffic flow and advise on the quickest routes. In developing economies, like Russia, where there are not enough cabs to go around, anyone is permitted to use their car as a taxi.

What can we, as Christians, do to improve public transport? Depending on the position we are in, there are a number of steps we can take:

☐ Use public instead of private transport where appropriate, thus supporting the system and also becoming acquainted with the kinds of people who use it, many of whom we have little contact with under normal circumstances.

☐ Raise people's awareness of the importance of public transport in our congregations, and encourage members to use it where practicable or possible.

☐ Be prepared to vote in favor of initiatives which will improve public transport, especially for more disadvantaged groups, even if it takes funds away from road-building in one's own area.

☐ Seek ways individually or corporately of advocating for an equitable distribution of transport possibilities for all groups in society, especially where these are eroded by private transport.

☐ Be willing to pay the true costs of private transport so that more money will be available to improve the public transport from which so much money* has been diverted.

At root we need to undergo a basic repentance on this matter. We require a new frame of mind about public transport, seeing it as an essential part of life in the city which we have a responsibility to help maintain, whether or not we use it much ourselves. Public transport makes a vital contribution to the efficiency, productivity and quality of life of a city. Supporting it is one of the ways in which "we seek the welfare of the city," as we have been instructed to do (Jer 29:7 RSV). Public transport also has a vital contribution to make to the life of marginal people in the city. This means that supporting it is one of the most significant acts of social justice we can perform. We do not generally think of public transport in that light, but it is time we began to do so.

See also AUTOMOBILE; CITY; COMMUTING; MOBILITY; POLLUTION; WAITING.

References and Resources

T. Bendixson, *Instead of Cars* (London: Temple Smith, 1974); D. Engwicht, *Reclaiming Our Cities and Towns: Better Living with Less Traffic* (Philadelphia: New Society, 1993); J. Lengenfelter, "Public Transport and Urban Witness," *Urban Mission* 5, no. 4 (1988) 5-10; S. Plowden, *Taming Traffic* (London: Andre Deutsch, 1980); T. R. Stone, *Beyond the Automobile* (New York: Prentice-Hall, 1971).

Robert Banks

Q

QUILTING

"She selects wool and flax and works with eager hands. . . . She makes coverings for her bed" (Prov 31:13, 22). If quilters (who are usually women but occasionally men) ever required encouragement to make quilts, they need go no further than these two verses describing activities of the wife of noble character. But the whole business of quilting goes much further and encompasses many of the things that God desires to see bound up in the activity of our lives. When one ponders the act of making and giving a quilt, the love* expressed is real—the desire to keep another warm, to comfort and nurture, to spend time on behalf of another, to give a gift* of beauty. A quilt may be a token of celebration, commemoration or thanksgiving. And furthermore, the gathering of quilters develops community* while encouraging the expression of creativity.

Anatomy of a Quilt

So let us look at the concept of quilting as an expression of our spirituality, beginning with the quilt itself. The quilt top is usually made up of many different fabrics—some beautiful, some interesting, some dark and murky and some bright and glowing. These can readily be translated into the experiences of our lives as we consider our beautiful thoughts, words and deeds that are prayers to God in their own right; the

interesting times such as travel* and education* that have played a part in molding our lives; the ugly experiences that cause us shame and need to be cleansed through confession and forgiveness;* and the bright glow of our Lord and Savior as his influence shines through our actions.

The quilt backing, which must be strong and serviceable, is like our desire to withstand worldly ways and our determination to seek the narrow road: "For wide is the gate and broad is the road that leads to destruction, and many enter through it. But small is the gate and narrow the road that leads to life, and only a few find it" (Mt 7:13-14).

The soft batting between these layers suggests to me the grace of God. And the quilting stitches, which cover every square inch, decorate, strengthen, invade every layer and influence the life of the quilt, as does the work of the Holy Spirit in our lives. The only remaining component is the binding around the edges, without which the quilt is not usable, attractive, or durable, as batting strays from between unfinished layers. The binding is our regular prayer and study time when we communicate with God and God with us. It is the strong, vital finishing touch.

So when we consider ourselves as a quilt, the concept of quilts as art*—to be hung on a cold and oblivious wall—is most unappealing. Rather, a quilt is to keep someone you love warm; and whether it is a blue-ribbon masterpiece or a humble scrap quilt, its prime purpose is to nurture. Thus the making of a quilt becomes a true expression of love.

Comfort

At times the giving of a quilt can also be a tangible expression of comfort. Since a quilt by its very nature keeps a person warm, it is the logical thing to offer a person who may be hurting physically or emotionally. God intended the work of his hands to be used, and the makers of quilts do too: "He who fashioned and made the earth, he founded it; he did not create it to be empty, but formed it to be inhabited" (Is 45:18). A quilter also makes a quilt to be inhabited, and with the exception of quilts as art, very rarely are they solely intended to be kept at arm's length.

In the days of the homesteaders, who suffered constant and often tragic privations, neighboring women would routinely show up with an armful of quilts as practical and loving comfort. In a book of recollections one homesteader remembers: "They took all the pretty quilts to the Baptist Church. They was [sic] for the poor people and the missions. And sometimes if somebody lost their house to a fire or a twister, the women would all go with a stack of quilts and say, 'These is a gift from the ladies of The First Baptist Church'" (Cooper and Buferd, p. 29).

Not only are quilts a comfort in times of trial, but the very act of quilting can be a means of dealing with grief* or anxiety.* A homesteader recalls, "After my boy Razzie died when he was fourteen, I began to quilt in earnest, all day sometimes. . . . I lost my spirit for housework for a long time but quiltin' was a comfort" (Cooper and Buferd, p. 107). I have used the making of a quilt to relieve almost unbearable anxiety. During the Gulf War, when so many lives were at stake, including some who were very

dear to me, I found myself wondering whether the world would ever be the same again and despaired over the tremendous loss of life that was taking place. Looking back, I am not surprised that during those days I made the Coalition Quilt, a design that required fabrics of very different patterns to mesh closely with one another. It reminded me of all the troops from different countries, with their diverse cultures and methods, that were able to mesh together to make a successful, cohesive effort. The very act of expressing my despair and prayers of deliverance in a quilt had a calming effect on my soul.

So whether we are being comforted by the warmth of a quilt made as an expression of love for us or are making a quilt as a means of gaining comfort ourselves, we can see the parallel to the loving arms of the Father that enfold us so warmly in times of need.

Product or Process?

In terms of motivation, quilters generally fall into one of two main categories. There are those for whom the goal to produce a particular quilt for a particular purpose is the key. These people are governed by the do-or-die, success-or-failure philosophy as described in *The Active Life:* "Instrumental action is governed by the logic of success or failure; [it] traps us in a system of praise or blame, credit or shame, a system that gives primacy to goals and external evaluations" (Palmer, p. 23). Admittedly these people may be more productive in a worldly sense, and depending on their circumstances, it may be of vital importance to have a product to show for time spent. Today's women are busy; sadly, it is almost socially unacceptable not to be busy.

For women working inside or outside the home, and particularly for working moms, life is a parade of constant activity with often little tangible evidence to show for it. Few jobs result in a recognizable monument, unless you happen to be an architect or sculptor. Meals get eaten, laundry is dirtied, and car pools flow on forever. Embarking on a project that results in a quilt becomes a way of capturing in a useful object at least a portion of a woman's expenditure of energy. But how much more fortunate are those who are able to enjoy the process as an expression of a God-given gift: "An expressive act is one taken because if I did not take it I would be denying my own insight, gift, nature. By taking an expressive act, an act not obsessed with outcomes, I come closer to making the contribution that is mine to make in the scheme of things" (Palmer, p. 24). Expressing ourselves, enjoying and learning from the process regardless of the outcome, becomes an exploration of our giftedness. We can delight in the blessing* and learn and grow as we work,* rather than be so compelled to produce that the experience is no more than a grind.

Creativity

Certainly the making of a quilt is usually an act of inspiration and creativity.* It gives us an opportunity to understand the pleasure God experienced as he went about creating the earth and all that is in it. We begin with the gift of our eyes and hands, both needed for the process of selecting pattern, color scheme and fabrics and for the actual making of a quilt. These are very tangible and vital tools, but they do not begin to encompass the essence of creativity.

Creativity goes far beyond the mere production of an item and is most vividly illustrated in Chuang Tzu's poem "The Woodcarver." This poem describes the process by which a master woodcarver divests himself of all extraneous thoughts and concerns through contem-

plation upon the marriage of his spirit with the project at hand. The result is a bell stand of extraordinary beauty, a testimony to true creativity. But not everyone can be a master artist, and the degree of creativity with which we are blessed is a gift from God that is measured differently for each of us. Thus by accepting the uniqueness of our gift and expressing it sincerely in our actions, we are glorifying God. So whether it is through our daily work, the carving of a beautiful bell stand or the making of a cozy quilt, we express our spirituality through the work of our hands.

Beauty

God has given us the gift of beauty, an appreciation of it and the ability to create beautiful things. Although it is necessary to make useful items, Robert Banks expresses God's desire for something more:

God is interested in more than an object's use value: God is not just a utilitarian. The aesthetic dimension of life is also important. God is interested in creating a pleasing impression upon the senses. The eyes and all the senses do not only exist for practical purposes. They exist to gaze on and delight in what has been created. . . . Beauty comes in various guises and God is interested in surrounding us with many varieties of it. (p. 172)

Beautiful quilts invariably honor principles of good design, such as rhythmical lines, variety of shapes, delightful color combinations and interesting textures. And where can we better gain our inspiration than in the beauty of nature that surrounds us? We can learn a great deal by examining God's use of these principles in the perfection of his creation. Such inspiration is usually readily accessible to us, but for those who are deprived of beauty, there develops a bleakness of spirit that can exacerbate an already depressed or lonely feeling. A homesteader on the plains of west Texas poignantly remembers, "There was an emptiness as far as the eye could see. How could a human endure? . . . The color was dull yellow and brown . . . the houses was built underground and called dugouts. . . . Mama's best quilts were her dugout quilts because that was when she really needed something pretty" (Cooper and Buferd, pp. 22, 24).

This hunger for beauty is a reality in our lives, and those who are obliged to deny beauty, such as Amish women dressed in their dark clothing and living in homes devoid of decoration, nevertheless seek to express themselves in elaborate quilting designs and magnificent flower gardens. Beauty delights the senses and brings joy into our lives, so let us recognize the hand of God and give thanks for every beautiful thing we see.

Thanksgiving

Never has the essence of the spirituality of quilt making been more eloquently expressed than in T. Davis Bunn's book The Quilt. The story describes the closing months of a godly woman's life and her determination to obey God's desire for her to make one last quilt. Despite hands that are crippled with arthritis, this old lady inspires a group of young relatives and friends to aid her in making the quilt and lovingly instructs them that the quilt is to be a prayer of thanksgiving: "We're going to sit here and thank Him for all these wonders. Every cut, every stitch, every piece we lay down, each one's going to have its own little prayer to help set it in place" (Bunn, p. 56). She felt that the world was speeding up so fast that you get "busy standing still" (p. 80) and that the truly important things were rapidly being forgotten:

Paul says just plain as the nose on your face that this is one of the most basic responsibilities we have. We must glo-

rify God and we must give thanks to Him. . . . Doesn't matter a whit, that quilt being finished. What's important is those ladies in there remembering what it's like to be really and truly grateful to the Lord. (Bunn, pp. 80, 82)

An elderly man, whose assistance had facilitated a life-changing move for me as a young woman, was diagnosed with pancreatic cancer and given only five weeks to live. Although I knew he would never live long enough to enjoy it, I was determined to make a quilt for him to express my thanksgiving. Every minute spent making the quilt gave me an opportunity to dwell on the generosity of this man and the depth of my gratitude. It was truly a memorial to a person I loved and respected. As it happened, he died the day the quilt was ready to take to him, and he did not receive it. But time has shown me that God provided this soothing activity to get me through a tough time, and I was left with a reminder of my benefactor to cherish in the future.

Community

One of the most familiar aspects of quilting is the quilting bee—a gathering of women of all ages and stages around a quilting frame. In days gone by, this was a multifaceted time when younger women were taught the finer points of technique by the older women, food and recipes were shared and camaraderie was developed. Joys and sorrows were aired, and advice and consolation offered. The quilting bee could be a regular occurrence, a casual drop-in or a special event, such as an accompaniment to a barn raising.

Sometimes a quilting bee might be made up of just a few members of the immediate family: "The art was controlled and handed down by women, usually mother, grandmother, or aunt. The best elements of teaching were often combined over the construction of a quilt: early and often loving instruction, tradition, discipline, planning and completing a task, moral reinforcement. Quilting was a virtue" (Cooper and Buferd, p. 17). Whether the bee quilters were a few family members or a convivial group of neighbors, the bottom line was, as it is today, the development of community.* It is touching to hear the confidences that quilters today feel comfortable enough to share as they gather with heads bowed over their work. There is a sense of timelessness when this happens, and a feeling of sisterhood envelops the group. One would pray that God's presence in the spirit of love and trust that develops in the room would beckon to those who do not already belong to him.

In homesteading days this feeling of community was a lifeline for hardworking, isolated and lonely women. The security sensed in this woman's words as she likens the community to a quilt sums up the feeling:

Oh yes, then the community came next. Roots reaching out from one ranch to the next, from one house to the next . . . a whole network, a grid of support. A quilt. In our imagination we rose over the house and looked down on the patches of land spread flat out like a good quilt as far as the eye could see. (Cooper and Buferd, p. 25)

God created us to be loving, caring and sharing people, and the whole process of quilt making encompasses these attributes in an everyday activity. May you be fortunate enough to receive the beautiful gift of a quilt or, even better, to become a quilt maker yourself!

See also ART; BEAUTY; CRAFTSMANSHIP; HOBBIES AND CRAFTS; HOMEMAKING; LEISURE.

References and Resources

R. Banks, *God the Worker* (Valley Forge, Penn.: Judson, 1994); T. D. Bunn, *The Quilt* (Minneapolis: Bethany House, 1993); P. Cooper and N. B. Buferd, *The Quilters* (Garden City, N.Y.: Anchor/Doubleday, 1978); P. Palmer, *The Active Life* (San Francisco: Harper & Row, 1994).

Jenny McDermid

R

RACISM

For several years Los Angeles has been the center of the world's interest in the sensational. It began with the on-camera bludgeoning of a African-American motorist at the hands of white police officers. When the resultant trial of those officers ended in an acquittal, parts of the black and Hispanic communities erupted in the worst urban uprising in U.S. history. This trauma was followed one year later by a devastating series of fires that blackened thousands of choice acreage in the Los Angeles basin. The fires were the handiwork of arsonists. Then came a severe earthquake and the loss of lives and destruction of properties, and the disruption of the flow of commerce for months. A few months later the ex-wife of one of America's famed athletes was murdered along with a family friend. The athlete-celebrity was charged with the murder, and there followed court proceedings that prompted some members of the fourth estate to dub it "the trial of the century."

It wasn't the trial of the century. In the 1990s there were still some Americans who could recall the Lindbergh kidnapping and trial; the case of Julius and Ethel Rosenberg, the husband-and-wife team accused of espionage and later executed, the first Americans thus sentenced by an American civil court; war crime trials from Nuremberg to Tokyo; the trial of the infamous Lieutenant Colonel Adolf Eichmann, archiect of the extermination of six million Jews; the sensational trial of Francis Gary Powers, whose clandestine U-2 flight over Russia was terminated when he was blown out of the sky by a well-aimed missile; the landmark *Brown v. Board of Education* decision of the U.S. Supreme Court. No, the trial of O. J. Simpson was by no means the trial of the century. Why then did it become, and why has it remained, such a traumatic experience for most Americans?

The Simpson trial once again raised the specter of racism in American life—racism at the core of a major urban police department, racism as an underlying reality that haunts an America already deeply divided over a wide variety of issues ranging from the economy to the political viability of the two-party system, racism as an integral part of the very process of justice* in an American courtroom. But this issue of racism and the courts was dragged out in the open long before O. J. graduated from junior high. For many black Americans and certainly for the white press, the "trial of the century" took place in 1955, just one year after the *Brown* decision, in a sweltering courtroom in Sumner, Mississippi, the county of Tallahatchie.

Roy Bryant and J. W. Milam, two white men, had been arrested and charged with the brutal murder of a black teenager. Emmit Till was visiting relatives in Money, Mississippi, and while there apparently committed the unpardonable crime of making some flirtatious remarks to a white woman, the wife of Bryant. Bryant and Milam, half-brothers by birth and unified in their hatred of blacks, found young Till and decided, as Milam said, to "make an example of you—just so everybody can know how me and my folks stand." They dragged him to the banks of the Tallahatchie River, shot him in the head with a .45, wired him to a cotton-gin fan and dumped his body into the water. The trial lasted five days even though the outcome had already been determined. The all-white jury deliberated exactly sixty-seven minutes, and Bryant and Milam were set free. The trial was over, but the coverage accorded it in the national press was a turning point in the handling of high-profile law cases that touched on the civil rights of black Americans. Until the Till trial the press—really the Northern press—had ignored murders and maimings of blacks. After all, such things happened in the South, which was considered backward, poor and without significant clout in Washington. The exposure of Southern justice in a Sumner courtroom changed all that.

The Till case also cast another layer of doubt across the consciousness of black people in the American system of justice. To be sure, in 1954 the Supreme Court of the land had decided in favor of blacks by ending the system of segregation in public schools. Yet when the Simpson case ended in the summer of 1995, for most Americans, black and white, the issue wasn't over. The decision for acquittal released a toxic cloud over the nation, an acid rain of latent feelings about race that simply won't go away.

Of course the America of the 1990s is not the America of the 1950s. For one thing, white America cannot, and does not, look on black America in the same way as it did in the fifties. *Brown v. Board*

of Education changed all that. Prejudice and discrimination still exists, but it can no longer be sanctioned by law to the extent it had been before 1954. The struggle had taken nearly four hundred years, but the dream had now been extended to all Americans by law.

Education* is one thing; justice in a courtroom where blacks were not always permitted to serve on juries was quite another. In short, black participation in the justice system is a recent advance in human relations. It is still haunted by this dark specter of racism. The Simpson trial was viewed by many Americans as something of a parable of race relations, and, unfortunately, the protagonists or the players in the drama tended always to be black and white. But the Los Angeles of 1995 is made up of multiple ethnicities ranging from Asian to Samoan, Pakistani to Somali, and is actually a mosaic of the world's Third World peoples. The trial itself was an apt picture of the racial complexity of the area, with an Asian-American judge; African-American, Hispanic-American and Anglo-American jury; an African-American defendant; and teams of lawyers representing a mix of blacks and whites. This was truly an all-American courtroom. This was not Grandfather's courtroom. But before it was over, it was Grandfather's emotional nightmare.

But if L.A. was exposed as a microcosm of a society not yet free of its historical obsession, the rest of the onlookers in the world community could scarcely breathe easily in the wake of their own problems in human relations. The Middle East is still a smoldering powder keg as Arabs eye Jews with suspicion and scorn, while many Jews view any attempt at peace as a sellout by their leaders. The murder of Israel's prime minister, Yitzak Rabin, in November of 1995 by a Jewish student served notice on the world community that hatred can mask itself as political ideology sanctioned by religious fundamentalism. No one looking on as Serbs and Croats slaughter each other could fail to recognize ancient tribalism at work, attitudes which if expressed in South Africa would have been labeled racist. Indeed, racism has stained human relations throughout Europe as skinheads and neo-Nazis have emerged to challenge the notion that Europe had purged itself of the grisly racism of Eichmann and Hitler.

Racism's Development as an Ideology

But what is racism? As an idea or concept, it seems to have emerged among Europeans caught in the turbulence of social and political change during the mid-nineteenth century. These changes included the creation of the nation-state and the rise of a new class of people, the middle class or the bourgeoisie. New ideas in the sciences and radical thinking about the very nature of everyday life were changing the way people saw themselves and their destinies. The grip of the church was being loosened, and reason had come to play the central role in explaining everything. Accompanying these crucial intellectual movements were important breakthroughs in industry and rapid expansion in colonial acquisitions. Of signal importance was the colonial exploits of Europeans in "the scramble for Africa." This was the era of men like Cecil Rhodes, who, in his famous remark revealing the passion of his life, exclaimed, "I would annex the planets if I could."

During this turbulent era, from the third quarter of the nineteenth century through the first quarter of the twentieth, race thinking, which had surfaced in the eighteenth century as one of the many opinions that intellectuals debated, began to develop as an ideology among Europeans. It was the development of race thinking as an ideology that gave racism its strength later on. For an ideology carries with it the ability to offer its adherents a rationale, a focal point, for their cultural apparatus. When racism, for example, became an ideology in Germany, it formed the basis for Hitler's elaborate rationale for the extermination of Jews. By then racism was simply the ideology of white, Aryan superiority.

With the rise of colonialism came unprecedented wealth.* This taste of wealth led to the need for further expansion and greater wealth. In the process the emerging bourgeoisie in Europe were exposed to peoples of other cultures and vastly different lifestyles, and the establishment of foreign policy became necessary. These people possessed vast riches whose attraction to Europeans proved to be irresistible. In the process of securing these colonial empires, and subjugating millions of these people, all of whom were people of color, there arose a need for some rationale by which such conquests could be validated. One such device was to develop theories of superiority based on "race."

Early attempts to define a people *as a people* were tied more to matters of nationhood than to physical characteristics. Nevertheless, theories of nationhood can easily devolve into ideologies of nationalism, and nationalism takes on an almost mystical quality, a quasi-religious character, usually associated with the notion of "chosenness." At the vicious end of that movement are some of the most heinous atrocities in history, perpetrated by peoples who have felt themselves to be chosen to national superiority over others. It should come as no surprise that this notion of chosenness was usually baptized by religious holy water.

Viewed more romantically, on the surface at least, the term is related to the idea that all of humankind is gathered in "races" and that while all races are created equal, some are more equal than others. Scientists have argued for some time now that the term *race* has lost all meaning, especially among lay men and women. The problem with the term, say these scientists, is that it is usually loaded with the private meanings of those persons who use it. Thus it is devoid of approved scientific meanings and becomes something more like an obsession, a bias, a dilemma. Other scientists argue instead that not only does the term have meaning but it alone explains why such enormous gaps exist between people of different racial groups. This debate rages currently in the United States because of the conservative tilt in national politics as it affects social policy.

Education. The issue of race has figured prominently in crucial matters related to education. In 1923 Carl Campbell Bringham authored a book entitled *A Study in American Intelligence* in which he decried what he called the taint of racial admixture in America, a threat that would place the country in a jeopardy far worse than any other European or American nation. To reinforce his assertions, Bringham used the findings of other scientists to categorize American society into four groups, with Nordic, blue-eyed people at the top and people of African origin at the bottom. Variations of this cataloging had occurred before within the scientific community, and all such efforts had been banished under the weight of more enlightened investigations. But in 1925 Bringham became a director of testing for the College Board and became the architect of the Scholastic Aptitude Test (SAT), which ever since has been the sole instrument in the hands of the educational establishment to measure student abilities judged suitable for admission in the nation's colleges. The question this authorship raises even at this late date is whether the test was intended to meas-

ure "merit" or whether it was an artful dodge perpetrated by a racist, by which cultural advantage was the real criterion on which "aptitude" was based.

Affirmative Action. Affirmative action developed in the United States to offset tendencies toward discrimination in the workplace—discrimination that was aimed particularly at black males. As a federal policy, affirmative action began to take shape during the administration of President Richard Nixon. It was one of the first coherent plans aimed at ensuring that blacks would be hired in federal contracting jobs. Nixon's plan, called the Philadelphia Plan of 1969, was an attempt to provide jobs for blacks. But Nixon, always the shrewd politician, had his own motives. The plan was also an attempt to undercut the influence of the Democratic Party among white union workers. The argument was that if white workers could be persuaded that their jobs were being taken by blacks, they would become open to switching their allegiance from the Democrats to the Republicans. The plan began to work, and in the years that followed there emerged a distinct segment of the work force identified by the 1980s as "Reagan Democrats."

In recent years, as the political climate of the country moved further to the right, the ever-present attack on affirmative action intensified. The emotional language most often expressed was that whites were now the targets of "reverse discrimination." This became the new code phrase with which to attack nearly all the rights minorities had gained during the late sixties and early seventies. The feeling was, and it was more feeling than fact, that minority gains were made almost entirely at the expense of white Americans; nonwhites had secured preferential treatment in every field from college entrance to jobs in construction.

It can be seen that from the beginning, affirmative action has been an element of political strategy used by all parties and that race has been a major tool in such political maneuvers. By now most people in the black and minority communities—those most affected by the Supreme Court decision outlawing affirmative action—have concluded that attempts to eradicate affirmative action had been motivated by racist attitudes all along. They feel that even though the words employed to either defend or defeat affirmative action had been selected so as to include such important considerations as gender, religion or national origin, just beneath the surface, in the collective gut of most white Americans, the issue was always about race: "The niggers are gettin' all the breaks. They're takin' over the country."

Social Science. The crusade against affirmative action became important because it enabled some social scientists to emerge with research which seemed to prove the intellectual inferiority of minorities, especially blacks. Such publications have been around for years in both America and Europe and, in light of the history of racialist writings, sound like the material stemming from the days of slavery. But this new research is far more sophisticated, and while most educators and politicians disclaim any belief in its findings, the material has had a powerful impact on those who claim to have a contract with America. The gist of research by such scholars as Arthur Jensen of the University of California and Charles Murray and Richard J. Herrnstein is that on the basis of class or genetics, black people are inferior intellectually to whites and Asians. The implications of this research have added scientific support to emotion-laden issues ranging from immigration* to SAT scores to affirmative action. The intellectual conflict over intelligence has also helped expose the reality of race relations in the country—black people and white people share in a common obsession, and seem to be linked inextricably by this specter.

Why does such research focus on black people of African descent? After all, the United States has always been a hyphenated society, an immigrant haven. Are black people really so inferior to all other immigrants that special scientific research is needed to demonstrate it? Or is there a bias among some scientists?

It has been noted that scientists who delve into matters of genetics are usually conservative. Dinesh D'Souza, a provocateur of the far right, released a seven-hundred-word tome in September 1995 which joined the battle of eugenics and race thinking. "Poverty and deprivation are not the cause," he says, "but the result of low intelligence" (quoted in Fish, p. 132). D'Souza, an immigrant from Bombay, is the darling of the American Enterprise Institute, funded by the ultraconservative Olin Foundation. His argument was so offensive that several African-American conservatives who had been associated with anti-affirmative-action legislation for years resigned in protest from the institute. On the other hand, scholars who tend to criticize conservative findings in the name of environmental causality tend to be more liberal in their leanings. So it seems that scholars arrive at the laboratory with ideological agendas. They are looking for something to prove, and so proceed to prove it.

White Racism

Race relations in the United States have been and continue to be a family affair between white Americans and their fellow African-American citizens. This has been true since Thomas Jefferson expressed the wish that people of African descent could be proven as human as persons of European background. He clearly had his doubts—this after he had declared that all men were created equal. To be sure there have always been other "racial groups" on the scene, and by now more are coming into the country by the planeload. They don't have a clue about what they're getting into as far as human relations are concerned. But when Americans talk about race relations, they usually mean black-white relations. And this affair between blacks and whites is not always, or even usually, a study in logic or rationality. It is about perceptions and emotions. Gayle Pemberton, an American educator writing about the difficult task of teaching minority students, put it succinctly: "Existing simultaneously in American culture are two competing emotions: the first is that minority people are just like white people; the second is that they are not. And individuals are rarely conscious of how they select the line where the first ends and the second begins." The key here is the idea that white people are the standard by which all other nonwhites are to be measured. It is this idea that lies at the heart of any definition of racism.

Racism as an idea is inextricably linked with Europeans and their American cousins. To be sure, there are all sorts of attitudes and horrific behaviors among all peoples of the earth. Getting along has never been easy. But if you ask nonwhite people who have been exposed to white people for any length of time, they will identify racism as a peculiar "white problem." This was the finding of the Kerner Report after the devastating riots that enveloped several of America's largest cities in the late sixties. After acknowledging that an understanding of these riots was "a massive tangle of issues and circumstances," the commission concluded that "certain fundamental matters are clear. Of these, the most fundamental is the racial attitude and behavior of white Americans toward black Americans. White racism is essentially responsible for the explosive mixture which has been accumulating in our cites since the end of World War 2" (Report, p. 203).

The problem seems to be an attitude, and it can be so intrinsic to one's self-definition as to be unrecognized. It is an internalized ideology of an assumed superiority over anyone who is nonwhite. Technically, it is called the ideology of white supremacy. But surely this view of racism that places the blame solely at the feet of white persons is patently false. Racism exists in all parts of the world, and among or between all peoples. Hannah Arendt argued years ago that two ideologies had managed to survive in the tough arena of historical debate—the one having to do with the economic struggle of classes and the other with the struggle of races. That Americans could still be impressed with the latter after all the country has been through testifies to the virility of this ideology. The ideology of white supremacy has become a given, the starting point in the assessment of nonwhite persons whether they are applying for a job at Joe's pizza joint or running for president of the United States.

Conclusion

What the matter of racism comes down to, at the popular level, is far more simple than studies in genetics or environmental factors. The matter comes down to color. American society is still a "pigmentocracy" in spite of all the so-called progress the country has made in race relations. Persons are judged by the color of their skin by people who have never heard of Bringham or D'Souza. When this judgment has the clout of institutional power, institutional racism is the result. Most white Americans rarely consider the impact of this dimension of the problem because they have never suffered through the experience. White Americans do not suffer discrimination because of ideas that nonwhite persons have of them. One suspects that to avoid the possibility of this, white Americans have rejected social legislation that would level the playing field.

Here, as always, the issue is not the progress of a democratic society toward equality. The issue is power.* Racism, finally, is just another notion in the heads of people who play at being deity—until it is married to power. So at the end of the century we are faced with a dilemma which has embarrassed the nation since its very beginning, the struggle, as one black ethicist put it, between "powerless conscience and conscienceless power." Put that way, the resolutions may not lie in the direction of politics,* or science. The issue is, as it has always been, a spiritual one. And the solution lies in the willingness of people—whatever their skin color—to yield to the God who looks not on the outward appearance but on the heart.

See also ETHNOCENTRISM; MULTICULTURALISM; NEIGHBORHOOD; PLURALISM; SOCIAL ACTION.

References and Resources
Dinesh D'Souza, *The End of Racism* (New York: Simon & Schuster, 1995); D. D'Souza, *Illiberal Education* (New York: Ashland, 1992); S. Fish, "How the Pot Got to Call the Kettle Black," *The Atlantic Monthly,* November 1993; A. Hacker, *Two Nations: Black and White, Separate, Hostile, Unequal* (New York: Scribner's, 1992); R. J. Herrnstein and C. Murray, *The Bell Curve* (New York: Simon & Schuster, 1995); W. Pannell, *The Coming Race Wars: A Cry for Reconciliation* (Grand Rapids: Zondervan, 1993); G. Pemberton, *On Teaching the Minority Student* (booklet; Brunswick, Maine: Bowdoin College, 1988); T. Powell, *The Persistence of Racism in America* (Lanham, Md.: Littlefield Adams, 1995); *Report of the National Advisory Commission on Civil Disorders* (New York: Bantam, 1968); S. Terkel, *Race: How Blacks and Whites Think About the American Obsession* (New York: New York Press, 1992); C. West, *Race Matters* (Boston: Beacon, 1993).

William Pannell

RADIO LISTENING

The first radio broadcast had auspicious beginnings. On Christmas Eve 1906 the first wireless voice transmission broadcast readings from the Scripture. From this radio has evolved internationally into a full spectrum of human voices that reflect and reinforce various subcultures and lifestyles as well as latent and dramatic revolutions. The pervasiveness of radio can be illustrated through an adaptation of Deuteronomy 6:7-9:

> Let your children listen to it at all times. Listen to it at home, at work. Listen to it when you get up and when you lie down. Bind it on your head. Listen to it while you walk and while you jog. Listen to it in every room of your house, in your car and in your office.

The Company We Keep

In essence, radio is a company of strangers to whom we show hospitality.* Those we walk with or stand beside or sit next to may be the wicked or sinners or scoffers (Ps 1). They are guests we invite into the private rooms of our heart and mind, sometimes to receive advice from, sometimes to share our moods with, sometimes to escape through. While at first it is they who entertain* us, we soon find ourselves entertaining them, singing their praises to acquaintances or lamenting when we lose them outside our cities. Since the company we keep reflects and influences whom (or what) we love,* as people in Christ we must examine carefully the radio company we keep to monitor if such friends are nurturing our love of God (Deut 6:4-6; 1 Cor 15:33).

Radio brings about and reinforces groupings in society* through each individual station's choice of a market position. A station's radio presentation results from its mixture of four kinds of communication: songs, talk, news and commercials. Among stations in a culture,* the ratio of music to information at any given time may reflect the nature and stability of the society. Within nations in distress, more information may dominate the radio; with greater leisure,* more music* may be heard.

The sum of the parts is a radio station's *format.* The radio station's persona attracts a group of like-minded people. Radio stations can become leaders in articulating the perspectives and language of various subcultures. To understand the power and authority in the heavenlies (Eph 1:21; 3:10; 6:12) exercised through radio stations (especially with non-Christian formats), we must analyze each of the four elements.

Radio Songs: Stories in Lyrics Among Peers

Individuals exercise personal tastes when they play their favorite song or music video. In listening to a radio station, however, an individual listens to songs that have been recommended for airplay by record promoters in the business of shaping profitable "star" franchises and selected for broadcast by program directors trying to attract the largest audience.

An individual also listens to the radio as part of a community emotionally drawn into the world presented through the accumulated stories in the lyrics. The impact from listening to such suggesting, beguiling stories can be considerable, since identification with people in stories is an element in the shaping of personal character (as through imitation of persons in the stories of the Bible). Indeed, the power of songs on a radio station is its persistent solicitation and nurture of a peer group of listeners who are evolving similar attitudes toward love. Most radio songs are about relationships, especially the waxing and waning of love. Even nonvocal music frequently harks back to originals with love lyrics (excepting certain rock, classical and alternative music).

Certain musical genres may tend toward a masculine (country) or feminine (adult contemporary) perspective or toward a youthful (rock) or intellectual (jazz, classical) bent. Whether male or female, young or old, cerebral or emotive, the person in Christ should critically examine the stories being sung in light of the grand cosmic story of Christ's love for the church (Eph 5:22-33) and in comparison to the shape of a life obeying the command to love neighbor* and enemy. For the person in Christ, the normal descriptions of musical styles (country, pop, rock and so on) are not as important as being alert to the conduct being presented as acceptable between men and women in the cumulative story line of the radio station's canonical lyrics. The songs' stories of reconciliation or separation between humans is, of course, incomplete (and misleading) without the story of reconciliation to the Father through the Son's faithfulness and without the experience of spiritual blessings in Christ here and in the heavenlies (Eph 1:3; 2:6).

Radio Talk: Drama, Announcing and Dialogue

Before other electronic media existed (for example, television,* video home system (VHS), computer*), the storytelling* function of radio songs was much enlarged by the storytelling in dramatic presentation. Early American radio is remembered for its radio theater (for example, the "War of the Worlds" broadcast) and its radio crime* stories, which elicited protests about the effects of such violence upon children. With few exceptions, such as *Prairie Home Companion*'s tales of Lake Wobegon, stories on the big and small screens have replaced stories from the radio theater.

Sometimes called *deejays* or *disc jockeys,* announcers (air personalities) serve the important function of stitching together the music fabric in such a way that the listener recognizes and identifies with a certain style. Fashions do change, but the popular announcers, whose characteristic pitch and timbre remain, promote loyal listenerships. Their interpretive comments on song or weather or events are not unimportant; they weave a web of norms that over time can raise or lower the listener's embarrassment quotient, that is, the ability to blush and feel shame.

Without television's visual images to seduce, distract or possibly misdirect, *talk radio* is sometimes considered as a better medium for argument and dialogue about ideas. But the person in Christ must understand this electronic Areopagus for what it is: a forum for entertaining and often sensational topics that the radio host controls. Not only must believers evaluate how the topics relate to kingdom concerns (Mt 5—7), they must resist sitting with radio babblers, Christian or not, who are false prophets or scoffers.

Radio News: Selection, Entertainment and Immediacy

Talk radio reacts to the news of the day. The human ear has an itch for news, even though there is nothing new under the sun in human behavior. Since what is heard in radio newscasts frequently becomes the subject of conversation at mealtime, the person in Christ must discriminate what things in the news are really worthy of consideration (Phil 4:8).

Music stations in particular most frequently take the news they report from newspapers. What is written in the wire service is, of course, not just any news or all the news, and certainly not the most significant news. What is "fit to print" reflects the hearing and biases of the reporter and editor and is filtered again through the radio announcer, who excerpts or rewrites and reads. Time to digest and gain perspective is unavailable.

Music stations also report as many news stories as possible as briefly as possible. Despite radio's immediacy, through its collapse of spatial distance the listener rarely has adequate social connections to the events or the places, much less to the witnesses. The listener must scramble to evaluate what is true and what is significant. Hearing of political intrigue or threats from nations or communities or individuals, the person in Christ—remembering that God sits in the heavens laughing at the pretensions of nations and rulers (Ps 2)—is steadied in prayer that the Father's will be done and kingdom come.

Radio news is chosen with an ear to what is most interesting and entertaining to the station's particular listenership. From a steady diet of such radio news, table talk can easily become preoccupied with issues from the domain of the flesh (Rom 8:5; Gal 5:19-21). Daily attentiveness to the ways of the righteous (Ps 1) and the kingdom of God (Ps 2) in the book of Psalms can provide salutary correctives to the predisposed topics suggested by radio news.

Radio Commercials: Desire, Need and Preference

The interest of companies in advertising* on the radio testifies to radio's reach into target markets and to the power of repetition. The marketability of radio advertising has led to the viability of private ownership (licensing) of radio stations rather than sole government control.

All advertising attempts to either change desire into need* or impartiality into preference. A Christian's stewardship* can be either aided or misdirected through radio advertisements. To the person in Christ the desire for and use of possessions are fundamental barometers of faithful obedience and disclosures of what is loved and served (Mt 6:24-34; Acts 3—6; 2 Cor 8—9). A thankful heart to the Father, who richly provides everything for our enjoyment, can promote habits of generosity and protection from overreaching (1 Tim 6:17-19), no matter the level of enticement in the commercial.

Listening to the Radio in Faith, Love and Hope

Faith comes by hearing and hearing through the word of Christ (Rom 10:17). The word of Christ is gospel, as *news* and as *story*. For the one who listens to the radio, leisure and escape are mediated through the news it reports and the stories it sings. At times, the good news (Rom 1:16) and the story of fulfilled events (Lk 1:1), that is, the gospel, contradict and challenge the news and stories on radio. At other times, the news and stories on radio illustrate the conviction that God has imprisoned all in disobedience in order to be merciful to all (Rom 11:32; compare Rom 1—3).

The refrains of radio love songs are influential tutors. The attractions and desires between a man and woman are powerful and naturally find expression in poetic songs, as even in Scripture (Song of Songs). The understanding of Christ's love for the church* does, however, set an encompassing perspective on God's way of achieving unity and reconciliation while issuing challenges to competing recommendations about relationships. Since the defining struggle is not really against flesh and blood (contra most stories on radio) but against the spiritual forces of evil in the heavenlies (Eph 6:12), the presence of Christ at God's right hand raises the confidence that indeed loving one another and maintaining unity will effect God's eternal peace plan.

Radio can and does offer oases in wilderness wanderings. Our eating and drinking and working (Eccles 2:24) can be enhanced through listening to the radio. Its pleasures are, as pleasures are, immediate and gone with the wind. As with any ephemeral or short-lived diversion, hope for the longer journey may go begging. Yet hearing about tragedies and dilemmas in far-flung places need not intensify frustration and helplessness in the heart of the believer. Hope is manifest and expressed in prayer, even while the Spirit's anticipations and delights make this creation's decay all the more clear (Rom 8:18-27).

Radio whispers, sometimes shouts, various messages in our ears. The person in Christ walks, stands and sits with this companion. Some friends are better than others.

See also ADVERTISING; ENTERTAINMENT; LEISURE; MASS MEDIA; MUSIC; RECREATION; STORYTELLING.

References and Resources

R. Banks, *God the Worker* (Valley Forge, Penn.: Judson, 1994); W. Brueggemann, *Israel's Praise: Doxology Against Idolatry and Ideology* (Philadelphia: Fortress, 1988); C. Cook, *All That Glitters* (Chicago: Moody, 1992); D. Harned, "Visual and Aural Worlds," in *Images for Self-Recognition* (New York: Seabury, 1977); M. Keith, *The Radio Station*, 3d ed. (Boston: Focal Press, 1993); J. Meyrowitz, *No Sense of Place: The Impact of Electronic Media on Social Behavior* (New York: Oxford, 1985); M. Olasky, *Prodigal Press: The Anti-Christian Bias of the American News Media* (Wheaton, Ill.: Crossway, 1988); V. S. Owens, "The Radio and the Psalms," in *The Total Image* (Grand Rapids: Eerdmans, 1980) 1-12; N. Postman, *Amusing Ourselves to Death: Public Discourse in the Age of Show Business* (New York: Viking, 1985); R. Snow, "Radio: The Companion Medium," in *Creating Media Culture* (Beverly Hills, Calif.: Sage, 1983) 99-124; S. Starker, *Evil Influences: Crusades Against the Mass Media* (New Brunswick, N.J.: Transaction Books, 1989).

David Worley

READING

Reading is the process by which we arrive at meaning in response to the stimulus of print. But confined to this definition, we may miss the wonder of reading, which is, quite simply, the miracle of mind meeting mind in a conversation that transcends time. Reading can be a lifelong source of information, instruction and delight.

Reading and Literacy

Because the Christian faith is grounded in and sustained by a body of sacred literature in the form of the Old and New Testaments, literacy has been linked to the proclamation of the good news concerning Jesus. In England literacy was the great gift of the Reformation and the printing press. William Tyndale's wish that the Bible would be available to every plowboy and milkmaid in England became increasingly realized throughout the late sixteenth and early seventeenth centuries, so that by the mid-seventeenth century even a poor man's son like John Bunyan could read the Scriptures and write his response to them for an eager audience of readers from the same social class. Reading historian Harvey J. Graff says, "Puritan strongholds were among the most education-conscious and literate centers in England. In their intense piety and concern about individual access to the Word, Puritans expected their adherents to learn to read" (p. 162). This emphasis on education* for literacy helped form a word-centered society, which existed for several centuries before being challenged by the visual media.

The many kinds of reading we do may be roughly categorized under three headings. The first, reading to learn, is the approach we take to informative texts. In this kind of reading we usually preview the material, formulating questions that will guide our reading; we then read, review the material in terms of recalling answers to the questions we had shaped and reread where necessary to complete our understanding. The second, reading to function, is the approach we take to utilitarian materials like labels and manuals and do-it-yourself instructions. In this kind of reading we test our understanding by action. The third, reading to satisfy personal interests, is the approach we take to literary works. Reading to satisfy our hunger to hear God's voice and know God personally is a special aspect of this last category of reading and sustains our spiritual life.

Reading the Bible

Since the Bible is a compendium of different kinds of literature, we might at various times take any of a number of approaches to it. We might read Leviticus, for example, to learn the nature of Jewish ritual law, to arrive at general guidelines for responsible moral choices in view of accountability to a holy God or to understand the nature of Hebrew legal literature. Or we might read the Pauline epistles for information about the early church* and its attitudes, to learn how to function as God's people living in the period between Jesus' incarnation and return, to examine the literary form of informal letters* or to satisfy our inner hunger to hear and know God's voice. As literature the Bible can be read as many particular stories describing encounters with God or as one great story that demonstrates God's gracious interaction with humankind (Frye). But the Bible is far more than a literary experience. When illumined by the Spirit of God, the "holy Scriptures . . . are able to make [us] wise for salvation through faith in Christ Jesus" (2 Tim 3:15).

The Bible can be read by believers individually with an openness to hearing the Word of God; this is the practice of many in their quiet time or private devotions (Bockmuehl). But the Bible needs also to be read corporately by small groups* of Christians in community* and as they gather in larger groups for worship,* for remembrance of Christ's death* and for the preaching* of the Word. It needs also to be read corporately in an ongoing discussion between theologians, scholars, pastors and the laity,* as the church searches for an ever fuller understanding of the Bible to guide its beliefs, doctrines and practice.

In modern literary criticism there is an increasing awareness that every reading act comprises an interaction of what the reader brings to the text and what the text brings to the reader. Attention is being paid to the way in which we reconfigure what is configured in the text (to use the terminology of hermeneutist Paul Ricoeur), taking into account the personal and cultural lenses through which we view textual materials.

But there is something more involved in the process of reading than reader interaction. The Holy Spirit is present when believers read the Scripture and will continue to be present in the church until the end of the age. Because of the Spirit's guiding presence within the Christian community, we can have confidence that the Scriptures will continue to instruct and challenge the church in its faith and practice, with new light breaking forth (for historical examples of this process, see Swartley).

Reading Other Works

While the Bible will form the core of the Christian's understanding of God and of life, there is a wide domain of good books beyond the Bible to enjoy and be nurtured by. Christians are sometimes afraid to encounter ideas that do not reinforce their own or are taught to think of time spent reading fiction as frivolous. But we should explore our ideas and others' ideas through reading and thoughtfully weighing them against the Scriptures. One purpose of doing this is to have our own vision* of life enlarged or challenged by the visions conveyed by excellent writers of fiction and drama. Guides to good literature might be used to begin such a pilgrimage into literature; the Great Books approach will lead the reader into the basic texts of Western civilization; more simply and flexibly, course descriptions from university or college courses can be used to guide explorations of specific fields or areas of interest.

Literature can be approached in a number of ways: by time period (you might want to read medieval poetry and prose or novels of the eighteenth century), by author or by theme. As an example of theme, one might consider death and dying from the point of view of the yearnings expressed in ancient literature (*The Epic of Gilgamesh;* the biblical books of Job and Ecclesiastes); in descriptions in classic and contemporary literature (Chaucer's *Book of the Duchess;* Bunyan's conclusions in both parts of *The Pilgrim's Progress;* William Faulkner's *As I Lay Dying;* Rudy Wiebe's *My Lovely Enemy*); in discussions in contemporary psychotherapy (Ernest Becker's *The Denial of Death* and Elisabeth Kübler-Ross's *On Death and Dying*); in readings from Christian experience (David Watson's *Fear No Evil*); in resources for Christian pastoral care* (David K. Switzer's *The Dynamics of Grief*); and finally in the riches of Christian theology (Jürgen Moltmann's *The Crucified God;* John R. W. Stott's *The Cross of Christ*). Accompanied by meditation on such biblical passages as Psalm 23, Psalm 90, the passion and resurrection narratives in the Gospels, their expositions in Acts and Pauline passages like 1 Corinthians 15 and Philippians 1, such an exploration through reading would open up a wide perspective and equip one to think clearly and Christianly about the "unthinkable"— that is, death.

Making a practice of always reading one or more books is probably the best way to keep reading. Many people enjoy being part of a readers' circle, in which members of the group take turns suggesting a book to read and the group meets to discuss the books as they are read. Regular reading of book-review sections in several respected magazines will keep you alert to new publications.

Encouraging Young Readers

With the visual media taking over many hours of children's lives, Christian parents should be serious and intentional about helping their children form the habit of reading. Reading encourages a use of the mind and imagination* that is not required in television* viewing. Reading also extends the period of "charm, malleability, innocence and curiosity of children" which the visual media transform into "pseudo-adulthood," according to Neil Postman (p. xiii). Habits* of lifelong reading are most likely to be developed in a home in which the adults read for enjoyment, information and personal growth themselves. If books are present in the home and read and discussed in the view and hearing of the children, reading will be seen as a natural part of everyday life. Good reading habits begin with an association between books, reading and loving care; the child snuggled into a parental lap, enjoying the total experience of love* and story, pictures and voice, is a child on the way to becoming a reader.

Parents are often highly anxious about their children's learning to read and try to promote it by means of phonics workbooks and other aids. Most reading experts agree that putting pressure on children in this way is more likely to

turn off developing readers than to help them (on this, see Elkind). Since reading requires an array of skills and experiences, the home* that provides rich visual and tactile learning experiences and creates opportunities for storytelling* and conversation* lays the foundation on which more formal instruction can be based.

In a television-dominated age is it possible to instill a love for the Scriptures? Certainly it is, but it is not easy. Some form of regular Bible reading with children, kept short and made an integral part of mealtime or bedtime rituals, provides the best basis for a lifetime love for and knowledge of the Scriptures. Families could begin with simplified, sequential Bible stories and move on to participatory shared readings at levels appropriate to children's abilities. Or, very simply, families could include a brief reading of a few verses of Scripture as part of the blessing at the beginning or conclusion of a meal. Still, the best pattern of instruction is the one laid out in Deuteronomy: "Fix these words of mine in your hearts and minds. . . . Teach them to your children, talking about them when you sit at home and when you walk along the road, when you lie down and when you get up" (Deut 11:18-19). The Scriptures wholly integrated into life and thought will be passed on lovingly from one generation to another.

Conclusion

Reading is of great importance throughout the Bible. Christians, like Jews, are people of the Book. The writing of the New Testament documents presupposes that many among those who were first called Christians were literate and that others would listen to the oral readings of the stories of Jesus' life, death and resurrection. Although Jesus himself left no written records, his many citations from the Old Testament show his deep biblical literacy. He opened his earthly ministry with a reading of the Hebrew Bible within the congregation at Nazareth. In this scene all the elements of reading sacred text are delineated: a congregation or body of people who hold the text to be sacred and the public reading and discussion of that text, in which the current readers take their place in succession with previous generations who have read and commented on the text. It is in the context of these elements that Jesus offers a radical rereading of the text, declaring, "Today this scripture is fulfilled in your hearing" (Lk 4:21).

One of the early conversion narratives, the story of the Ethiopian official, is the story of an evangelist's offering a rereading of an Old Testament text so that the reader can see Jesus in it (Acts 8:26-40). And the book of Revelation not only sees future events as written on a sealed scroll (chap. 5) but is itself self-consciously a book that is to be read by the church until the return of Christ (1:3; 22:7-21). We would do well to cultivate ourselves as readers as we whisper or cry, with the readers of all ages, "Come, Lord Jesus."

See also FAMILY GOALS; PARENTING; SPIRITUAL DISCIPLINES; SPIRITUAL GROWTH.

References and Resources

M. J. Adler and C. Van Doren, *How to Read a Book: The Classic Guide to Intelligent Reading* (New York: Simon & Schuster, 1972); K. Bockmuehl, *Listening to the God Who Speaks* (Colorado Springs: Helmers & Howard, 1990); D. Elkind, *The Hurried Child* (Reading, Mass.: Addison-Wesley, 1981); N. Frye, *The Great Code: The Bible and Literature* (New York: Harcourt Brace Jovanovich, 1982); H. J. Graff, *The Legacies of Literacy* (Bloomington: Indiana University Press, 1987); J. Lindskoog and K. Lindskoog, *How to Grow a Young Reader* (Wheaton, Ill.: Harold Shaw, 1989); N. Postman, *The Disappearance of Childhood* (New York: Dell, 1982); J. W. Sire, *How to Read Slowly: Reading for Comprehension* (Wheaton, Ill.: Harold Shaw, 1989) W. Swartley, S*lavery, Sabbath, War and Women: Case Studies in Biblical Interpretation* (Scottdale, Penn.: Herald, 1983).

Maxine Hancock

REASONING

"Be ready always to give an answer to every man that asketh you a reason of the hope that is in you with meekness and fear (1 Pet 3:15 KJV).

Reasoning is an activity through which humans acquire, organize and justify their knowledge and plan and evaluate courses of action. A narrower term than *thinking, reasoning* has the sense of thought that is organized into some sort of connected structure or network. This structure is usually only immanent in our thinking, but it is displayed explicitly when we are in the act of communicating our knowledge in the form of an argument or in the act of reflecting upon it.

Neither reasoning, pure and simple, nor correct reasoning is the province of intellectuals alone. We all engage in it in almost all human activities that involve communication or planning.* Our common verbs to judge, to argue, to persuade, to claim, to show, to prove, to evaluate and others all describe activities that employ reasoning to a greater or lesser degree. We constantly make arguments and evaluate arguments put forward by others. Consider the following examples:

☐ This car led all others in sales last year. It's just what you're looking for!

☐ Candidate X supports welfare cuts, so we should vote for him.

☐ The disciples knew that by publicly claiming that Jesus was alive, they were facing persecution, perhaps to the point of death. Only the explanation that Jesus was indeed raised from the dead explains this boldness.

☐ Since Jesus commands his disciples to turn the other cheek, we ought to refrain from self-defense.

We deal with arguments of these kinds every day. Making and evaluating arguments are activities more like conversation,* work* or recreation* than a quality or characteristic such as intelligence, health* or strength. The question is not whether we will reason but whether we will do so well or poorly.

Kinds of Reasoning

We use the term *argument* to describe the basic structure of reasoning. Arguments must have at least two parts. The position or point for which one argues is called the *claim* or the *conclusion*. If we liken reasoning to a plant, what we usually see is the stem and leaves—not the roots. The "point" of the plant, if one can speak of a plant as having a point, is the part that is above ground. Yet without the roots, there would be no plant. In a similar way, the usual form in which we encounter reasoning is as a claim. Such claims can be controversial: "Jesus was truly raised from the dead!" "Abortion is murder." Claims can also be quite pedestrian: "The Bible is an authoritative book for Christians"; "Murder is wrong"; "Turkey is the best meat for dinner tonight."

When asked for support for our claim, we offer *premises* or *grounds*. We say something to the effect, "These are the relevant facts that lead us to say what we say" or "Such passages as Matthew 28:6-9 and 1 Corinthians 15:3-8 clearly state that Jesus rose from the dead." We can label these verses as the grounds for the claim that Jesus is truly raised from the dead. Are these the only grounds we could employ? No. Is this the only claim that might use these passages as grounds? No again. Perhaps the person making the claim is a new convert giving his testimony. Lacking biblical knowledge, he would be at a loss to offer any particular scriptural reference. In its place he might, when questioned, simply reply, "Mary, my youth pastor, told me so." This kind of answer is just as much a provision of grounds as is the citing of Scripture. Of course, the effectiveness of these two types of answer varies from situation to situation.

So the second of the two most basic parts of an argument is the grounds, or premises, that are put forward to support the claim. Grounds for arguments can vary widely; sometimes we call them the *facts* or *reasons* or *data* or *supporting evidence*. Often when we are asked to support a claim, this kind of answer is enough. Thus, the most basic form of an argument can be represented as follows: Grounds, therefore Claim (G C). Note the arrow pointing from the grounds to the claim. This symbol is highly significant, for it suggests that an argument must go somewhere. The arrow means that the statements are not merely an assertion but are an invitation to the reader or listener to move from one position (acceptance of the grounds) to another (acceptance of the claim).

But what if a person responds, "How do you get from a Bible verse to such a claim?" This kind of question asks for a different kind of premise, which we call a *warrant*. A warrant is a rule that bridges the gap between the grounds and the claim. Constructing the whole chain of reasoning thus far, we might have the claim "Jesus was truly raised from the dead!" grounded on the statement in 1 Corinthians 15. A possible warrant for moving from these grounds to this claim might be "Every statement of the Bible that so represents itself is factual." On the other hand, if our grounds are the fact of Mary's testimony, we might offer as warrant "Mary is a credible witness."

Notice that both of the warrants are more general than either the grounds or the claim. The first one speaks not just of this one Bible verse but of many. Mary's being a credible witness means that she is always or usually reliable. Notice, also, that one argument often leads to another. If challenged, we could treat our warrant "Mary is a credible witness" as a claim. We might ground this claim with statements like "Mary is a sober, intelligent person" and "Mary always tells the truth." So as we begin to give reasons for claims we make, we find that our knowledge is connected together as a network of arguments.

Philosophers and logicians have classified types of reasoning or forms of arguments. A *deductive argument* is one such that if the premises are true, the conclusion must be true. The Greek philosopher Aristotle (384-322 B.C.) contributed a great deal to our understanding of deductive arguments. He was interested in forms of arguments called *syllogisms*. The following is an example (no account of reasoning would be complete without this tired old example!):

All men are mortal.

Socrates is a man.

Therefore Socrates is mortal.

An interesting question is, Why do deductive arguments work? How do they manage to convey certitude regarding their claims? The usual way of answering this question (since the development of modern logic, at least) is to say that the claim is already contained (implicitly) in the premises. So, for example, the knowledge that all men are mortal includes the knowledge that the man Socrates is mortal. We may become aware of something new, psychologically speaking, by means of deductive argument, but we never actually expand or increase our knowledge.

This raises another question: If deductive reasoning cannot lead to genuinely new knowledge, where do we get new knowledge? Whence come the general statements that are the stock in trade of deductive arguments? A common answer to these two interrelated questions is *induction*. If deduction (as it is said) reasons from the general (all men) to the particular (Socrates), then induction is its converse—reasoning from a collection of particulars to a general state-

ment: My mother has red hair, and she has a hot temper. My sister has red hair, and she has a hot temper. My brother has red hair, and he has a hot temper. Therefore, all redheads have hot tempers. This is induction at its simplest. And just as there are deductive arguments more complex than a syllogism, so there are inductive arguments more complex than this one. What all inductive arguments have in common is that their claims enlarge upon, go beyond, the evidence. So inductive reasoning is essential for expanding our knowledge. Its drawback is that it does so at the expense of the comforting certitude of deductive reasoning—we can never be sure that the next redhead will not be different.

Our most valuable intellectual tool for protecting against rash inductive generalizations is *statistics*. Statisticians have intriguing formulas for calculating the probability that a generalization is accurate based on the size of the sample observed and on a few other assumptions. They have formulated precisely the intuitive recognition that if I have only observed a few redheaded people, I am on very shaky ground concluding that all (or most) redheads have hot tempers.

Inductive reasoning is a powerful tool in science and in everyday reasoning as well. Nonetheless, it does not provide an adequate account of how knowledge grows. If scientific reasoning were limited to induction, we would have a collection of natural laws based on observed regularities, but we would have no theoretical knowledge. And it is the theoretical knowledge that explains the regularities. So we must have a form of reasoning that gives us a different kind of knowledge. This is just what we find with *hypothetical reasoning*.

Consider this example: You come home from work and find the front door ajar and muddy tracks leading into the kitchen. These are the facts or observations. You form a hypothesis: The kids are home. You have not seen them, but you infer that they are there because their presence provides the best explanation of the facts you have observed.

Note the difference between hypothetical reasoning and induction. The latter would allow you to conclude something like the following: I see muddy tracks in the hall; I see muddy tracks in the kitchen. Probably there are muddy tracks in all the other rooms as well. Hypothetical reasoning is not aimed at knowledge of more tracks but at the cause of the tracks—the explanation of how they got there. So we can see why this kind of reasoning is called *hypothetical*. We extend our knowledge by inventing hypotheses that, if true, would explain the observed facts.

We can never be certain of a conclusion based on hypothetical reasoning. This is because we can never be sure that there is no better explanation of the data than the one(s) we have considered. In the example above, it may turn out that the open door and muddy tracks were instead left by a prowler.

It is important in reasoning to recognize the different strengths of our arguments. Deductive arguments are the strongest; inductive and hypothetical arguments are weaker, depending on how much evidence we have and other factors. We indicate the strength of our arguments by using qualifiers: *probably, certainly, necessarily* and *possibly* are some of the more common ones. It might appear at first glance that using these qualifiers would weaken the argument. Instead, by explicitly limiting the scope of the argument, we strengthen our position. Another way to improve the persuasive force of an argument is to recognize possible rebuttals or conditions under which the argument might fail.

Reason, Reasoning and Faith

Philosophers reason. We need only notice the vast number of books on logic and reasoning to know this. Logic, mathematics and some theoretical parts of science are the fields in which we find deductive arguments. Scientists reason. They make inductive generalizations, which we call *laws of nature,* and then formulate hypotheses to explain the regularities. Lawyers reason in the courtroom. Business managers make judgments about the best policies to follow. If we were to stop here, we might get the idea that only those who are intellectually well trained engage in reasoning, but the examples used above show that ordinary people reason all the time. In recognition of this fact, the ancients defined humans as "rational animals." Thus, they identified rationality as the quality that set humans apart from animals. Christians in the past have adopted this view and combined it with an understanding that it was this rationality that constituted the image of God in humans. Whenever the Greek philosophical inheritance has been in the ascendancy—even as it is in so many ways in the modern period—humans are judged to be at their best when reason dominates and the passions or emotions are in subjugation to reason. More recently, though, this preference for reason over emotion* has been called into question. Many claim that we mischaracterize and oversimplify when we see reason as simply in competition with the other aspects of personality and denigrate feeling or emotion.

In the past few centuries Western thought has increasingly valued rationality. We speak of the Enlightenment as the Age of Reason. Christians have felt the burden of this cultural valuation and have, in some spheres, been preoccupied with the relation between reason and faith. However, the reason that is often opposed to faith is a narrower conception than we are dealing with here. In this sense, *reason* is being used to designate a body of knowledge known by means of human inquiry alone, without the aid of revelation. It is valuable to distinguish this sense of reason from reasoning as a human activity. When we see reasoning as a human activity, the conflict or competition between faith and reason disappears. In fact, faith, when it becomes articulate, will always involve some reasoning.

Christian Uses of Reason

As Christians, there are many areas in which we reason. It will be helpful to show some examples from a few of these areas.

Apologetics. First Peter 3:15 tells believers to be prepared to give a reason for their hope when asked. In our terminology we might say that our interlocutor is asking for the grounds for a Christian claim. Although the claim in question may well be an articulation of our faith, it is just as likely that the claim is an implicit one evidenced in our lives. One may ask us, for example, in the context of the death* of a loved one, "How can you be so peaceful with all that you are going through?" In such a case we have said nothing about a hope, yet our actions presuppose the ability to make such a claim.

Biblical interpretation. Bible readers are constantly faced with questions about the meaning of texts and how to apply them today. For example, what does Paul mean in saying that women should have their heads covered in worship "because of the angels" (1 Cor 11:10)? Sunday-school* teachers, pastors and biblical scholars will all make claims about the meaning of such a passage and will draw further conclusions about what it means for church life today.

Ethics. Christians constantly engage in ethical reasoning. For example, does the commandment not to kill ground the claim that Christians must stay out of the army? What does Jesus' love* command imply for our decision about how to care for Grandmother?

Preaching. Sermons generally have as grounds some scriptural text. As claims, sermons teach doctrine; they provide guidance* for the life of the church; they interpret the world. Church members often reason about the quality of the sermon in the car on the way home.

Christian education. Education* is sometimes narrowly conceived as packing information into the brains of students. Given the account of reasoning in this article, a much broader and more helpful understanding can be attained. True education seeks to link these pieces of information with other pieces in a structure that makes sense. When a lesson makes sense to a student, it is often structured so that some of the information is seen as grounds and some as claims, linked in a chain by various warrants that are themselves other bits of information. Thus, we can conceive of Christian education* as giving students the tools with which to think critically about their faith, to see connections between disparate facts and to justify their beliefs when called upon to do so.

See also CHRISTIAN EDUCATION; CONVERSATION; EDUCATION; SPEAKING; TEACHING.

References and Resources

N. Murphy, *Reasoning and Rhetoric in Religion* (Valley Forge, Penn.:Trinity Press, 1994); S. Toulmin, *The Uses of Argument* (Cambridge: Cambridge University Press, 1958).

Richard Heyduck and Nancey Murphy

RECREATION

As the word implies, *recreation* is re-creation. That is, something has become out of kilter and needs to be restored to what it was: a healthy body a balanced, tranquil disposition, or a stable, expressive emotional life. Recreation is one means, though not the only one, of restoring body, mind and soul, thereby bringing rest.* Recreation is also one dimension of leisure.*

Recreation as Useful Leisure

The 1988 *New Lexicon* dictionary defines recreation as a "leisure-time activity engaged in for the sake of refreshment or entertainment." As useful leisure, recreation may take many forms, usually chosen for reasons of personality or social pressure. Such dutiful recreations include self-improvement disciplines such as reading and bicycling, competitive sports* such as golf and hockey, and skill-testing pastimes such as canoeing and sailing. These may be taken up for a variety of reasons: improved performance at work,* the desire to vent competitive energies in a safe arena, the need to prove oneself or to belong to a school. In the Western world almost all recreations have professionalized, and the huge leisure industry promotes correct costumes, proper equipment and professional training. The picture of my brother and me wearing our winter school clothes and simple wooden skis strapped to our boots on our way to Rosedale Golf Course is laughable today when one needs a skintight aerodynamic ski suit and state-of-the-art equipment because, in part, of how one will "be seen" on the ski tow.

Not only is the choice of recreations affected by our social situation and personality (I tend to avoid competitive sports and choose activities like canoeing or walking), they are also affected by our life situation. Carpentry was a recreation for me while I was a pastor. When I became a tentmaking* church-planter and earned my living by carpentry, I found no refreshment in crafting things from wood. When my wife and I live in rural Africa, we take a long walk each evening before sundown. Our neighbors always ask, "Where to?" When we reply, "Just for a walk," they stare in disbelief because walking for them is a means of transportation to the market, not a means of recreation. It is easy to assume from this that people living in rural areas or in less-developed countries do not need recreation. But they do, and they choose what fits their culture: spending half a day in the village on market day, having an extended tea with friends and, in the case of children, inventing their own sports and games.

Robert Bolles in *The Three Boxes of Life* expounds our imbalanced life span: education for the first twenty years of life, work for the next forty until retirement,* to be followed by an orgy of leisure until we die. What is needed, he argues, is a better balance between all three throughout life, including meaningful, though perhaps unpaid, work in retirement. Even recreation can become boring* if there is nothing else in life. Still recreation is part of the complete life for Christians as well as others.

What Makes Recreation Christian?

Some might think that belonging to a church baseball team makes that form of play "spiritual." Anyone who has ever played on such a team knows that the flesh-Spirit conflict rages just as fiercely in a Christian team, though usually with a little less swearing! Others seek recreation by going on a Christian cruise or by playing shuffleboard in a Christian leisure park. But what makes recreation Christian is not the religious character or context, both of which are the husks of the matter. The heart has to do with the character of action and the intent of the person.

On the first point, we are drawn back to God's threefold mandate to humankind in the opening chapters of Genesis: (1) to live in communion with God, (2) to build community (cohumanity, family, church, nation; Gen 1:26) and (3) to express cocreativity in making God's world work and to develop its potential (2:15; see Laity; Service). Recreation that erodes our communion with God, like playing games* that toy with the demonic or that encourage predatory competition* (such as some boxing or wrestling matches), or that is destructive of God's creation (such as some forms of backcountry driving on ecologically sensitive terrain) is out of sync with God's threefold call to us (see Ecology; Stewardship). In contrast, recreations that encourage playfulness in the presence of God (such as golf), build teamwork and deepen relationships (such as playing football or Scrabble) or encourage stewardship of the earth (such as sailing or backpacking) are to be preferred. Becoming Christians does not make us angels but full human beings. Recreation should express the dignity of being human, neither dehumanizing the players nor dehumanizing the earth. A recreation becomes Christian not because of its religious label or the fact that we enjoy it with other Christians but because it lines up with God's purpose for humankind, a purpose to which Christ restores us. But there is more.

On the second point (the intent of the person), recreation becomes Christian in virtue of being born of gospel reality. This means, quite simply, playing by grace instead of works (for a more complete theological foundation for recreation, see Leisure). Failing to take time for recreation because "there is so much to do" or "I am so busy at work" is usually an indication that the doctrine of justification by grace through faith (we are accepted by God not in virtue of our performance but solely by trusting Christ) has not yet penetrated our lei-

sure life. Paradoxically, as Leland Ryken points out, "Many of the people who feel guilty about taking time for leisure also feel guilty because they work too much" (p. 20). Martin Luther was brilliantly eloquent on this matter. In his "Treatise on Good Works" Luther uses a powerful analogy:

> When a husband and wife really love each other, have pleasure in each other, and thoroughly believe in their love, who teaches them how they are to behave one to another, what they are to do or not to do, say or not to say, what they are to think? Confidence alone teaches them all this, and even more than is necessary. For such a man there is no distinction in works. He does the great and the important as gladly as the small and the unimportant, and vice versa. Thus a Christian person who lives in this confidence toward God knows all things, can do all things, ventures everything that needs to be done, and does everything gladly and willingly, not that she or he may gain merits and good works, but because it is a pleasure to please God in doing these things. They simply serve God with no thought of reward, content that their service pleases God. On the other hand, he who is not at one with God, or is in a state of doubt, worries and starts looking for ways and means to do enough and to influence God with his many good works. (pp. 26-27)

Recreation, paradoxically, is one of those little "works" we do that don't try to prove anything to God or even ourselves. We have been proven, more accurately approved, by Christ. Therefore we are free to play* wholeheartedly. We can really get into it. The gospel frees us to rest because God's achievements are what count in the end. We are free to enjoy recreation not with a heavy heart (wishing we were out doing really "Christian" work) but exuberantly because we have gospel confidence.

Recreation is creational—lining up with God's purposes for the created order. It is evocative of the gospel, inviting us to relax in the grace of God rather than our own achievements. But finally it has an eschatological dimension, pointing to God's final re-creation of the universe. Therefore it is a foretaste of life in the kingdom.

Luther also said that it is "living, or rather dying and being damned that makes a theologian, not understanding, reading or speculating" (quoted in McGrath, p. 152). Could it not also be that it is by playing—one dimension of living—that we become practical theologians enfleshing our real belief about the goodness, grace and final purpose of God?

See also BOREDOM; HOBBIES AND CRAFTS; LEISURE; QUILTING; REST; SABBATH; VACATIONS.

References and Resources
R. Bolles, *The Three Boxes of Life* (Berkeley, Calif.: Ten Speed Press, 1993); R. K. Johnston, *The Christian at Play* (Grand Rapids: Eerdmans, 1983); M. Luther, "Treatise on Good Works," in *Luther's Works,* trans. W. A. Lambert, ed. J. Atkinson (Philadelphia: Fortress, 1966) 44:15-114; A. E. McGrath, *Luther's Theology of the Cross: Martin Luther's Theological Breakthrough* (Oxford: Basil Blackwell, 1985); W. Rybcznski, *Waiting for the Weekend* (New York: Viking Penguin, 1991); L. Ryken, "Teach Us to Play, Lord," *Christianity Today* 35, no. 16 (1991) 20-22.

R. Paul Stevens

REST

Rest is a central concept in the Christian life embracing, on the personal level, sleep, serenity, sabbath and salvation. On a creational level, rest is the goal of creation and the result of salvation. As we will see, resting has theological and spiritual overtones: our rest patterns express our real beliefs about God and life. Restless people have not found peace with God or with themselves. Restless societies are out of sync with God's purposes. Rest is a discipleship issue and a matter of Christian growth for the individual. From a more comprehensive perspective we should see rest as the goal of creation as the threefold rest of God, humankind and creation, which is best expressed in the concept of sabbath. This involves social rest (instead of social instability), economic rest (instead of economic slavery), creational rest (instead of environmental rape).

On the personal level, rest in sleep* is a temporary cessation of activity in order to refresh body and soul, sometimes through dreaming.* Of course one can oversleep. Oversleep, like overwork, is moral sloth and a spiritual disease. But for most people sleep, like other forms of rest, is a problem. Indeed, insomnia is probably the number one physical problem in Western societies today. Many do not bless themselves and God with a good night's sleep. Some cannot. One cannot sleep if one bears the world's problems on one's shoulders, in other words, if one is playing God. "He grants sleep to those he loves" interprets the first part of the verse in Psalm 127:2: "In vain you rise early and stay up late, toiling for food to eat." It also explains verse 1: if you work at night to get things done, it is not the Lord who is building the house but just your own efforts. Justification by grace through faith leads to justification expressed in sleep: resting in Christ's finished work, resting in God's sovereignty, resting in the Spirit's ongoing creative ministry. Failure to sleep may have physiological causes, but more often than not, insomnia has roots in one's theology and spirituality. The gospel of Jesus literally puts a person to sleep.

Serenity, another form of rest, comes largely through leisure and play. In this case *rest* means "repose," "refreshment" and "restoring equilibrium to one's body and person." It is not merely taking a "pause that refreshes" (in order to get back to work as soon as possible), as Robert Johnston once characterized the Protestant view of play. Rest is good simply for its own sake. We should avoid trying to buy this rest.

Leisure is defined negatively as "time free from alienating and oppressive work" and positively as "time liberated for creativity, social interaction, self-realization, fantasy and play." But in the Western world a tragic exchange is made. People work for money and try to buy rest: a media experience, a gourmet meal or an expensive vacation in an exotic getaway. The problem is that when we get "there," we bring our work with us. Many people say they have to get back to work to feel rested again! "Leisure," Gordon Dahl says, "has come to mean little more than an ever more furious orgy of consumption. . . . This 'virtuous materialism'. . . . offers men the choice of either working themselves to death or consuming themselves to death—or both" (Johnston, p. 11). The day of rest has become another day of work (*see* Consumerism).

We need both leisure and sabbath.* But we need sabbath more than we need leisure. Sabbath—daily (as we live contemplatively) and weekly (keeping a day for recreating worship and play)—is both a divine principle and a gracious gift. In a sense we do not keep sabbath; sabbath keeps us—keeps us focused on the really real, keeps us centered on meaning and purpose, keeps our priorities right. Sabbath is not only a day but a lifestyle lived in harmony with God's purpose for everything there is: the threefold harmony of God, humankind and creation.

Death* is the final rest in this life. Often described as "sleeping," death is not the annihilation of life but true rest. It is relinquishing this life's burdens, restoring full bodily life in the resurrection of the body and renewing life in the new heaven and the new earth (Rev 21—22) in the presence of God forever.

Not surprisingly, Jesus chose the word *rest* to describe salvation. Gathering up biblical concepts that encompass serenity, sabbath and salvation, Jesus gave his gospel invitation: "Come to me . . . and I will give you rest" (Mt 11:28). In a translation of an Aramaic version of this verse the sabbath allusion is more apparent: "Come to me and I will rest [sabbath] you; you will find sabbath for your souls." Rest encompasses both creation's purpose and salvation's goal. The author of the letter to the Hebrews invites us paradoxically to "make every effort to enter that rest" (Heb 4:11). Rest is what we are saved for; rest is the way we are saved. People who cannot retire, who cannot relinquish anything in this life, who cannot stop working, who cannot put down a task, who cannot let someone else take over, who have never done enough to feel prepared to enter that rest or, in the words of the psalmist, cannot let the Lord "build the house" (Ps 127:1), do not know the meaning of rest. Augustine's much-quoted line is apt: "You [God] have made us for yourself, and our hearts find no rest until they rest in You." This great insight applies not only to eternal but also to temporal rest.

See also CREATION; ECOLOGY; LEISURE; PLAY; RECREATION; SABBATH; SLEEPING.

References and Resources

R. Banks, *The Tyranny of Time: When 24 Hours Is Not Enough* (Downers Grove, Ill.: InterVarsity Press, 1983); P. A. Heintzman, *A Christian Perspective on the Philosophy of Leisure* (Ottawa: National Library of Canada, 1985); R. K. Johnston, *The Christian at Play* (Grand Rapids: Eerdmans, 1983); J. Oswald, *The Leisure Crisis: A Biblical Perspective on Guilt-Free Leisure* (Wheaton, Ill.: Victor Books, 1987); L. Ryken, *Work and Leisure in Christian Perspective* (Portland, Ore.: Multnomah, 1987).

R. Paul Stevens

RETIREMENT

It is helpful to think of retirement as a time of transition when the grind of the workplace* is finally exchanged for a less-stressful and more-leisured lifestyle. Retirement is, therefore, to be welcomed rather than dreaded. Nevertheless, retirement may involve some pain: reduced income (although occupational pensions are becoming more common), loss of status (particularly if there have been prestigious trappings associated with one's job) and being cut off from the camaraderie of the workplace. But if retirement involves loss, it also has its rewards. In earlier times, comfortable retirement was only possible for a select few: today, thanks to social security and retirement benefits, it is within the reach of all. Society has come to recognize that men and women who have reached a certain age are entitled to the privileges of retirement. Life has its rhythms: "For everything there is a season, and a time for every matter under heaven: a time to be born, and a time to die" (Eccles 3:1-2 NRSV). It was a beneficent and merciful Creator who ordained that we should work only six days in the week and rest on the seventh. Retirement is to be welcomed as an opportunity for the enjoyment of life.

Traumatic Retirement

Unhappily, there are some who unexpectedly find themselves retrenched and faced with involuntary and premature retirement. It is not surprising that for them the term *retirement* has sinister overtones, for it is associated with "getting the sack." In the bad old days, that was an ever-present reality. In military parlance the word *retirement* still has negative associations. In warfare it is a synonym for "withdrawal" and was often a prelude to defeat. The editors of the fifth and final volume of *A History of Private Life* argue

that retirement, however camouflaged, is a tragic misfortune: "To expel a man from social life at age sixty, when he is still able and eager to work, is an act that must be shrouded in honorable rhetoric so as to hide its ignominious character." But that is an extreme view. Involuntary retirement consequent upon retrenchment or ill health is however a special problem. Of course, the pace of retired life is so different from that of working life that the abrupt change can be wrenching and, for those not ready to retire, disastrous.

Planning for Positive Retirement

Retirement, if associated with reasonable financial security, is a richly rewarding experience, opening the door to a wealth of creative and fulfilling activities. Retirement should be approached positively. It is emphatically not a sentence of death.* In our modern world most people are able to look forward to twenty or thirty or more years of retirement during which they can pursue other purposes and other goals. Nicolas Coni, William Davison and Stephen Webster, in their authoritative book *Ageing*, argue that planning for retirement cannot start too soon. Even children, they suggest, should receive instruction about retirement. Interests explored in youth can in retirement be developed and enjoyed to the full. Therefore, they argue, as retirement approaches, it is important to consider what interests you have previously enjoyed and can now revert to.

The goal must be self-fulfillment, not self-indulgence. Jesus spelled out some of the dangers. He told a parable about a man who, having accumulated ample goods, decides that this is the time to take his ease and to eat, drink and be merry. He glibly assumes that he has many years ahead of him as well as ample goods. But death taps him on the shoulder and says, "You have forgotten me, my friend." Jesus comments, "This is how it will be with anyone who stores up things for himself but is not rich toward God" (Lk 12:21). Dean Inge, the acerbic dean of Saint Paul's Cathedral in London, warns that men of fifty need to beware of a sort of fatty degeneration of the conscience* when they are not much inclined to fight against anything, least of all against their sins. Retirees need to take note.

When to Retire

People are living longer and retiring earlier. At least a quarter and possibly a third of all the human beings who have ever lived beyond the age of sixty are alive today. Fortunately most people can now look forward to decades of active social life before the onset of the physical and mental handicaps that reduce individual autonomy and define old age. Those who are able to do so are, therefore, likely to retire before "the doors on the street are shut, and the sound of the grinding is low . . . when one is afraid of heights, and terrors are in the road . . . and desire fails" (Eccles 12:4-5 NRSV). The time of retirement will depend on a variety of personal and financial considerations.

The advantages of early retirement are many: the opportunity to take up other interests, to adopt a different style and pace of living, to engage in part-time employment,* to undertake charitable and volunteer work,* to participate more fully and practically in the work of the church* and, perhaps belatedly, to spend more time with one's spouse and family.

The disadvantages of early retirement are living on a reduced income, the difficulty of finding activities and interests that are worthwhile and fulfilling, and the tendency of allowing oneself to vegetate and go to seed. The worst scenario is being reduced to the desperate expedient of killing time.* Financial consid-

erations weigh heavily with most people. Median incomes for retirees are markedly lower than those for people in their middle years, even when adjustments are made for family size. Most retired people are dependent on social security and retirement benefits apart from savings and investments.* Early retirement may mean these are diminished or postponed. Nevertheless, demographers point out that on the average older people, with their years of asset accumulation behind them, own more and owe less than younger people. Further, the majority of older married people own their own homes.* Allowance needs to be made for the certainty of increasing medical expenses in future years. Whereas older people spend less than younger people on budgetary items (including leisure items), they spend more on items relating to health, particularly when there is no comprehensive program for medical insurance available.

The mandatory age for retirement is becoming progressively lower. This makes the transition difficult for those who believe they are still in full possession of all their powers and who enjoy their work. Politicians are exceedingly reluctant to admit that they ought to retire at the age of sixty-five. Ronald Reagan in the United States, Winston Churchill in England and Konrad Adenauer in Germany were all in office in their seventies; Churchill and Adenauer remained into their eighties. Pope John XXIII, who inaugurated far-reaching changes within the Roman Catholic Church, was not elected pope until he was seventy-eight. In other walks of life there is, however, widespread support for a mandatory age of retirement.

Retirement should be embraced positively as a well-earned reward. If it can be seized early, so much the better. Those who retire early by choice have happier and longer retirements than those who resent retirement and are bitter about it. Those who have enjoyed variety in life are more likely to do so in retirement than those who have not. Once the decision to retire has been made (or made for one), there are some urgent practical problems to be faced.

Where to Live?

The obvious options are to continue to live in one's own home, to purchase a condo, to lease an apartment, to move into a retirement village. The decision is a highly personal one. Some are jealous of their independence and prefer to be alone; others enjoy community living. Some prefer the country; others prefer the city. These personal factors will dictate one's choice. There are also the factors such as access to transportation and health services.

There are public as well as private factors involved in the choice of location. A characteristic of contemporary life is community planning, with its impact on the physical and social environment and its influence on day-to-day activities and human contacts. This includes proximity to one's church. Retirees do not as a rule avail themselves of freedom from occupational commitments to move away from their former homes. Rates of moving are higher among younger age groups. When older people move, they are more likely to move within the confines of their immediate locale than to change their community setting. Ties to one's place of residence become stronger as one grows older. Those who own their own home, or have strong social connections with their neighborhood, are least willing to move.

In Western society the ideal today is the nuclear family.* Once the ideal was several generations together in one home—grandparents, unmarried uncles and aunts, parents and their children, all as one extended family—but that ideal does not hold today. Joy Davidman, in her little classic on the Ten Commandments entitled *Smoke on the Mountain,* cleverly adapts one of Grimms' fairy tales and satirizes the way in which the old are, in modern households, made to feel an embarrassing encumbrance. Once they were lovingly cared for; the modern "serpent's-tooth" method, she accuses, is to lead Grandpa gently but firmly to the local asylum, there to tuck him out of sight and out of mind as a case of senile dementia (p. 58).

Patterns of living in today's society have changed dramatically, so much so that instead of the extended family, what we have is subdivision into two or even three generations of distinct nuclear families: the young people with their dependent children, the middle-aged parents and the aged generation of grandparents. Many family units today are single-parent families, thus complicating the picture further. As life expectancy has increased, husbands and wives are more likely to survive together, living independently. The ability to do so presupposes continued health, when in fact aging is accompanied by ills such as rheumatism, arthritis, heart disease and high blood pressure. Further, there will be increasing visits to the doctor, periodic hospitalizations, restricted activity and days spent in bed. In the United States four out of five persons over the age of sixty-five have at least one chronic condition.

If, on balance, the decision is made to relocate, one must consider a variety of practical matters: the advantage of single rather than multiple levels, sufficient space for one's possessions and visitors, ease of maintenance, heating and air conditioning, convenient access and security. Retirement villages have become increasingly popular, particularly complexes that cater to a variety of needs. The usual pattern is separate houses or self-servicing individual units within a larger complex, residential accommodation with servicing as well as meals provided, and nursing homes together with a hospital annex. The whole complex is under the supervision of an administrator. Specialized staff are employed as well as that typical twentieth-century innovation—diversionary therapists who are responsible for community activities.

Complexes that provide a full range of accommodation, from totally independent units for those who require no assistance through sheltered accommodation to full nursing care, have a very great appeal. It is necessary to buy into these schemes, and the price is high. But once in, there is the guarantee of being provided for at whatever the level of need. Churches have moved extensively into this field and provide highly professional services in a Christian context. Through the death of a spouse, many elderly people find themselves left living alone. Many married women end their lives as widows. For such people, some form of communal living is often the answer.

What to Do?

Those who have enjoyed variety in life are more likely to do so in retirement than those who have not. A full, broad education* is also likely to stand one in good stead. Those who have found happiness and job fulfillment are the ones who are most likely to find satisfaction and fulfillment in active retirement. Those who approach retirement happily and expectantly are those likely to use retirement well. Of course, retirement is less likely to be happy when it occurs without warning, due to either sudden retrenchment or ill health, but even then retirement opens up new possibilities.

It is foolish to adopt the view that you can't teach old dogs new tricks. This has been clearly demonstrated when younger students and more mature stu-

dents are enrolled in the same courses. The older students usually do better because of their higher motivation and their increased self-knowledge. Retirement opens the door to the pursuit of new intellectual and cultural interests. This can be immensely rewarding. The nature of the subject does not matter, provided it gives pleasure. One can learn, or relearn, a foreign language to assist with travel* plans or reading.* There are also adult-education courses available in most cities. For those remote from the cities there are long-distance teaching techniques (see Information Superhighway). Using one's mind and keeping it agile and nimble are believed to offer some protection from dementia.

Physical activity as well as cultural is important. Retirement is an opportunity to take up new sports* and to improve one's skills in the sports one already enjoys. It has been said that fitness is a luxury for the young but is essential for the old! The fitter you are, the less likely you are to become ill, and the more quickly you are likely to make a full recovery should your health break down. It is the elderly who are most likely to suffer from illness in Western society, and their illnesses are probably due to degenerative changes in their bodies. It pays to invest time and energy in staying fit. Physical fitness can be regained during retirement, and muscles that have wasted due to lack of use during a sedentary life can be redeveloped. It is not necessary to indulge in dangerous or macho sports to ensure fitness; activities such as walking* or swimming or cultivating a garden* help.

Taking up sports and vigorous exercise in later life need not be dangerous. The secret to any new activity is starting gently and gradually working up to a peak. Whether it takes weeks or years does not matter, so long as one finds pleasure in it and practices regularly. Exertion can cause even the young to sweat, get breathless and have palpitations! The goal of *mens sana in corpore sana* (a sound mind in a sound body) is to be sought, not only for one's own sake, but for the sake of others.

Retirement can degenerate into a life of appalling selfishness, narcissism and self-indulgence, but retirement can also make possible a life of loving thoughtfulness and service. Humanitarian and charitable organizations need help; such regular volunteer work also helps the retiree. Authorities note that a common reason for seeking early retirement is the craving to be freed from the rigid routine and the exacting demands of a full-time job, but for most people, structure in one's life pattern is important and continues to be important after retirement. Retirement is an opportunity to restructure one's routine and to adopt a pattern that is less rigid and tightly packed. Demands on one's time will multiply. The ideal is balance—balance between one's physical and mental activities, one's volunteer work and one's family. Structure and routine should therefore be used to maximize the pleasure and the joy of retirement.

See also AGING; DEATH; MENOPAUSE AND MALE CLIMACTERIC.

References and Resources

P. Ariès and G. Duby, eds., *A History of Private Life* (Cambridge, Mass.: Belknap/Harvard University Press, 1987-1991); J. E. Birren, ed., *Handbook of the Aging and the Individual: Psychological and Biological Aspects* (Chicago: University of Chicago Press, 1959); N. Coni, W. Davison and S. Webster, *Ageing: The Facts* (Oxford: Oxford University Press, 1992); J. Davidman, *Smoke on the Mountain* (London: Hodder & Stoughton); H. Humisett, *Retirement Guide: An Overall Plan for a Comfortable Future* (Vancouver, B.C.: Self Council Press, 1990); H. D. Shelton, *Older Population in the United States* (New York: Wiley, 1958); C. Tibbetts, ed., *Handbook of Social Gerontology* (Chicago: University of Chicago Press, 1960).

Stuart Barton Babbage

RIGHTS

As currently discussed, rights are a product of the Enlightenment. The Scriptures speak so little about rights that it would scarcely be an exaggeration to say that "rights" are not a scriptural concept. What the Scriptures speak of are duties and justice:* "He has shown you, O man, what is good. And what does the LORD require of you? To act justly and to love mercy and to walk humbly with your God" (Mic 6:8).

Justice, as one of the cardinal virtues,* relates to giving and is due to others and to God. Rights, as they are most frequently spoken of today, are things viewed as *owed* to us. The scriptural uses of *rights* are generally confined to matters that relate to property and inheritance (Deut 21:16; 1 Chron 5:1-2).

Rights in Tradition

It is impossible to say definitely where the first writings on rights come from. The Greek and Roman writers of the fourth and fifth centuries B.C. emphasized the importance of conscience* and stated that there was no duty to obey unjust laws.* The idea of human rights developed slowly and did not become defined the way we know them now until much later.

In 1215 King John of England signed the Magna Carta. This document set out principles such as the freedom of the church* and no imprisonment "except by lawful judgment." Such matters were later incorporated into international documents such as the Universal Declaration of Human Rights (December 10, 1948). Now a host of local laws (human rights legislation and constitutional documents such as the American Bill of Rights or the Canadian Charter of Rights and Freedoms) set out the rights we are familiar with today (rights to security of the person, freedom, of expression, freedom of religion and of the press, equality, etc.). Yet rights must be kept clear over time. While these rights constitute the core of what may be termed "traditional" rights, there are still disagreements about what should be considered rights. The Canadian Charter does not protect the "right to property" that is recognized in many other countries and has deleted references to the "rights of the family" found in the early Canadian Bill of Rights. There have also been a host of international legal documents that deal with human rights. Recent U.N. conferences in Cairo (1994) and Beijing (1995) show that the contents of United Nations documents will be hotly contested on the basis of ideological positions that may be in stark variance from earlier conceptions of "rights" and the human person.

As John Hittinger has written (citing Stanley Hauerwas):

> The rights discourse carries with it many assumptions about human nature and the moral order that run contrary to the very things to be protected; assumptions involving unbounded freedom or an individualist conception of political order. (Hittenger, p. 247)

A catalog of rights is set out at the end of the Jacques Maritain book and in Paul Marshall's article. What can be said of modern conceptions of rights is that they focus on liberty without any belief in mastery of the self or moral responsibility. Without a working understanding of virtue (containing both of these missing aspects of the person), it is questionable whether there can be any valid understanding of "rights" at all: we seem to be cast adrift in the featureless sea of "values."*

Rights in Everyday Life

An important set of observations has been made surrounding rights and contemporary society by the English writer Lesslie Newbigin. He notes that there are two main difficulties with the concept of rights. First, when society* has accepted no public doctrine about the purpose for which all things and all persons exist, there is no basis for adjudicating between needs and wants. Disputes about wants and needs* are inevitable but without consensus as to purpose—unresolvable except by power.*

Second, both parties rely on the concept of the rights of the individual.* Though set out in legislation, rights are void of meaning unless there are parties who acknowledge the responsibility to meet the claim of right. Since there is no corresponding public doctrine about human responsibility, the multiple and contrary claims to right can only destroy society.

"Rights" can be viewed in a similar way to "values" or "virtues." The lack of articulated purposes in relation to techniques in contemporary society means that we have the greatest difficulty determining how competing rights claims are to be adjudicated or whether a particular right exists in a certain situation (i.e. whether there is a "right" to homosexual marriages or to euthanasia*). It can be seen that without a sense of the substantive principles as well as processes that must be the basis of a civilized order, there can be no convincing way to determine the content and application of rights in a particular case.

Skepticism about the basis of rights has led to frequent debates between those calling themselves communitarians and various types of liberals. Communitarians see liberals as fragmenting the state and furthering alienation. Generally, they wish to affirm that people have obligations in community* as well as rights. The theoretical grounding of both communitarian and current liberal positions do not suggest that the debates about the current meaning of rights will (or can) be settled.

See also COMMUNITY; FREEDOM; INDIVID- UAL; OWNERSHIP, PRIVATE; SOCIETY; VAL- UES; VIRTUES.

References and Resources
M. A. Glendon, *Rights Talk: The Impoverishment of Political Discourse* (New York: Free Press, 1993); M. A. Glendon and D. Blankenhorn, eds., *Seedbeds of Virtue* (Lanham, Md.: Madi- son Books, 1995); J. P. Lapp and J. P. Hittinger, "Rights," in *In Search of a National Morality,* ed. W. B. Ball (Grand Rapids: Baker; San Fran- cisco: Ignatius, 1992); A. McIntyre, *After Virtue* (Notre Dame, Ind.: Notre Dame University Press, 1984); P. Marshall, "Rights, Human," in *The New Dictionary of Christian Ethics and Pas- toral Theology,* ed. D. Atkinson, D. Field, A. Holmes, O. Donovan (Downers Grove, Ill.: InterVarsity Press, 1995) 747-50; L. Newbigin, *Truth to Tell* (Grand Rapids: Eerdmans, 1991); C. Taylor, "Cross-Purposes: The Liberal-Com- munitarian Debate," in *Philosophical Arguments* (Cambridge, Mass.: Harvard University Press, 1995).

Iain T. Benson

S

SABBATH

Sabbath is what our leisure-hungry and work-addicted culture* desperately needs. But the very word brings to most minds negation, absence and all the restrictions well-meaning Christians have over the years placed on Sunday. This article will explore the biblical meaning of rest,* the theological meaning of sabbath, and sabbath as a life-giving discipline. In the end we will see that we do not keep sabbath so much as sabbath keeps us!

The Ultimate Rest

The negative view of sabbath has some foundation. The Hebrew word *shabath* means "to stop," "to desist," "to cease from doing." The first formalized reference to sabbath in the Ten Commandments clearly requires desisting from labor one day a week, though it does not legislate six days of labor: "Remember the Sabbath day by keeping it holy. Six days you shall labor and do all your work, but the seventh day is a Sabbath to the LORD your God. On it you shall not do any work" (Ex 20:8-11). As Witold Rybczynski notes, viewing the weekend as a day or two in which one is not required to work* and viewing it as a period in which one is required *not* to work are not the same thing (p. 60). Sabbath, however, is more, but not less, than a twenty-four-hour day of enforced rest. A weekly experience of rest is fundamental to our regaining perspective and entering the rest that is essential to personal, social and creational survival. Of all the Ten Commandments, being negligent of this one has resulted in more deaths than even the prohibition against murder. Heart disease and other stress-related ailments have taken their toll. Especially in the postmodern Western world, we are killing ourselves by neglecting sabbath.

But sabbath rest is more than keeping one day a week. Rest is not merely cessation but appropriation. There is a positive meaning to sabbath that takes us beyond the simple etymology of the word. Israel was commanded to enjoy the day—to enjoy rest! Rest is a state of body, mind and soul* that is essential for health,* both physical and spiritual. It involves restoring balance, rejuvenating energies, regaining perspective, allowing our emotional energies to recover, being in harmony with our own bodies and, especially, enjoying God. Rest is a multifaceted blessing that includes sleep,* dreaming,* recreation,* vacations,* play* and leisure.* But sabbath is rest in its purest and most complete form, probably because it involves gaining the threefold harmony of God, humankind and creation.

Harmony with God means that we have peace with God, enter God's own rest and enjoy God. Tragically, some people do not even like God, let alone enjoy God! Harmony with humankind means that our own persons are rejuvenated and given perspective. Unlike leisure, which is concerned primarily with cultivating oneself, sabbath ministers to the self indirectly by recovering our focus on God, renewal being a byproduct. Harmony with creation suggests that God's desire is not only that people have rest but even animals and the land, every seven years as well as one day a week (Ex 20:10; Deut 15:1-12). This threefold harmony can also be expressed in the terms of prayer* (God-humankind harmony), play (harmony with oneself) and peacemaking (humankind-creation/social harmony): enjoying God, enjoying ourselves and celebrating creation.

To show how fundamental sabbath is to the life of faith, Scripture describes the creation of Adam and Eve on the sixth day as the penultimate creation, the climax coming the next day, the sabbath. Nothing is closer to God's mind and heart than the creation of sabbath. Adam woke up from his unconscious sleep not to start his work of caring for God's world but to experience rest. Adam and Eve's first vocational experience was to waste time for good and for God. Only if we do the same can we understand why we are to take care of God's world, build community and pray.

No Trivial Pursuit
There is a theology of leisure in the Bible, but it is secondary to the great and extensive material on sabbath. What we find from Genesis to Revelation is not the cultivation of a perfect balance of work and leisure but of work and sabbath. There are deep theological reasons for this.

Sabbath reveals the heart of God. God rested on the seventh day (Gen 2:2), but this was not mere cessation; it was refreshment (Ex 31:17). God literally put aside the work of creation both to enjoy rest ("It was very good"; Gen 1:31) and to put creation in its place (it is good but

not God). So the people that were first called to bear God's image on earth—Israel—were given two archetypal images of salvation to proclaim good news to others and to be refreshed in their own faith: the exodus (symbolized in the festival of Passover) and the sabbath (their weekly reminder that God is in charge; Moltmann, p. 287). Both exodus (a dramatic rescue accomplished by the mighty hand of God) and sabbath (a period that implies trusting in God's provision enough to set aside one's work) are tangible signs of having faith in a God of grace. The kind of God we actually worship is revealed by whether or not we keep sabbath.

Sabbath was not to be an experience of multiple restrictions; Israel was to "call the Sabbath a delight" (Is 58:13). This delight was not eliminated by the coming of Christ but rather was intensified as we wait for full manifestation of Christ and the kingdom, when full rest will be attained. Jesus claimed to be Lord of the sabbath (Mk 2:27-28) and declared that he fulfilled rather than annulled it. Being sabbath's lord did not mean Jesus could break it at will; rather, it means that the Lord fulfilled sabbath's meaning and intent. Therefore Jesus healed and gleaned in the fields (as a poor man) on Saturday, the Jewish sabbath. More importantly he embodied sabbath by restoring people to God through forgiveness of sins, healing the sick and bringing unmitigated joy, the first stage of the threefold harmony of God, creation and humankind that will receive its final fulfillment when Christ comes again. In the New Jerusalem (Rev 21—22) the Lamb is everywhere (we enjoy God in uninterrupted communion), creation is renewed (not only the new heavens but even a new material earth!), and people are released for permanent creativity and exquisite joy. So there is a rich sabbath overtone in the invitation of

Jesus: "Come to me, all you who are weary and burdened, and I will give you rest" (Mt 11:28-30).

Sabbath reveals God's intentions for the world. It is the celebration of creation. Jürgen Moltmann speaks of this as the "feast of creation." Put differently, sabbath involves the redemption of both space and time,* the reharmonizing of God, humankind and creation in both spatial (and material) as well as temporal terms.

Regarding the redemption of space, sabbath brings both the enjoyment and stewardship of creation. This positive delight is witnessed in God's own word of praise, "It was very good" (Gen 1:31), and echoed in Adam's first burst of praise at the creation of Eve, "At last!" (Gen 2:23 RSV). This celebration of creation is also found in the book of Job, which contains an African safari for the purpose of viewing two really untamable animals (probably the hippopotamus and the crocodile) and a voyage in a weather satellite to show Job that God really enjoys influencing the climate, much of which is not for our benefit or even experienced by human beings. In this profound contemplation God reveals that he enjoys being God! In the light of this Job and the rest of humankind can join God as coworkers and cocreators, "playing God" with God by making things. That is part of the joy of hobbies and crafts.* We are recovering sabbath when we are creative, a matter that illuminates the edifying effect of healthy recreation. But it is not only space that gets rejuvenated by sabbath.

First and foremost sabbath is the redemption of time. To the unreflective and the religiously dutiful, sabbath might appear to be a waste of time. Nothing is accomplished, or so it seems. But in reality something indispensable to rest is taking place: time is being recovered as a gift from God rather than a resource to be managed.

The first mention of holiness in the Bible refers to time: "And God blessed the seventh day and made it holy" (Gen 2:3). In contrast, humankind seems preoccupied with making holy places. In his brilliant exposition of sabbath, Abraham Heschel observes that all pantheistic religions are religions of space and sacred places, in contrast to the faith of Israel, which is concerned with the redemption of time (pp. 4-6). The prophets maintained that the day of the Lord was more important than the house of the Lord. Not only religion but also technology* have been concerned primarily with the conquest of space. In the process we have forfeited experiencing holiness in time. Heschel says, "There is a realm of time where the goal is not to have but to be, not to own but to give, not to control but to share, not to subdue but to be in accord" (p. 3). The great cathedrals, he maintains, are cathedrals in time. And sabbath is the holy architecture of time. The meaning of sabbath is precisely this:

> Six days a week we live under the tyranny of things in space; on the Sabbath we try to become attuned to *holiness in time.* It is a day on which we are called upon to share what is eternal in time, to turn from the results of creation to the mystery of creation; from the world of creation to the creation of the world. (Heschel, p. 10)

Surprisingly God's work in creating the world is presented in Scripture as play. Wisdom describes herself as "the craftsman at [God's] side. . . . filled with delight day after day, rejoicing always in his presence, rejoicing in the whole world and delighting in mankind" (Prov 8:30-31). Sabbath and play have much in common.

Sabbath reveals the playfulness of God. Sabbath for humankind is playing heaven. The best way to learn to work is to play at it! Children do this naturally before the dreadful process of growing up drives a wedge between work and play. They play house and so fit themselves for being grownups in their own homes. When we "play" heaven—by cocreating with God, by delighting in creation, by making things fit a heavenly model and by worshiping—we are anticipating the joys of being fully "grown-up" men and women in Christ in heaven (where we truly become children again!). Once again Heschel is eloquent on this subject: "Sabbath is an example of the world to come" (p. 73). He further explains:

> Judaism tries to foster the vision of life as a pilgrimage to the seventh day; the longing for the Sabbath all the days of the week which is a form of longing for the eternal Sabbath all the days of our lives. It seeks to displace the coveting of things in space for coveting the things in time, teaching man to covet the seventh day all days of the week. . . . It is as if the command: *Do not covet things in space,* were correlated with the unspoken word: *Do covet things in time.* (Heschel, pp. 90-91)

The Jewish answer to the problem of civilization, maintains Heschel, quoting Rabbi Simeon ben Yohai, "is not to flee from the realm of space; [it is] to work with things of space, but to be in love with eternity" (p. 117). It turns out that heavenly-minded people are, as C. S. Lewis once said, those who are also of most earthly use (p. 51).

Having the Time of Our Lives

We have been exploring sabbath as a lifestyle, something that informs and transforms all the facets of everyday life: work, leisure, family life, vacations and even sleep. We have good scriptural warrant for universalizing sabbath in a way that makes it an everyday reality rather than a one-day-a-week affair. The apostle Paul said, "One man considers one day more sacred than another; another con-

siders every day alike. Each one should be fully convinced in his own mind" (Rom 14:5). Sabbath is *optional,* which opens up the possibility of every day being regarded as such: "He who regards one day as special, does so to the Lord. . . . For none of us lives to himself alone" (Rom 14:6-7).

Sabbath lifestyle. Paul was not original in expressing this idea but was merely expounding the words and deeds of Jesus. In Jesus' day many had reduced sabbath observance to a task, a work to be performed. The religious people of his day were hedging the day with a myriad of prohibitions either to make it happen or to protect it from impiety. So the day came to be served both for its own sake and for the merit people obtained in doing it just right. In contrast, Jesus viewed sabbath as something given by God for people's benefit, not bondage: "The Sabbath was made for man, not man for the Sabbath" (Mk 2:27). Jesus regarded himself as Lord even of the sabbath. He enjoyed the day by doing what his Father loves to do on the sabbath: creating and recreating, resting and bringing rest to others.

It is difficult to resist the conclusion, given the number of miracles Jesus worked on the sabbath, that Jesus deliberately chose to do most of his healings on Saturday! He had a point to make: sabbath is not the absence of work but experiencing the joy of God and entering into God's work. The author of the letter to the Hebrews had this same thought when he called us to "make every effort to enter that rest" (Heb 4:11), "for anyone who enters God's rest also rests from his own work, just as God did from his" (Heb 4:10). This author hints that entering sabbath is, ironically, hard work for us because we are so driven to make sabbath a personal performance, a thing we make happen, rather than a delicious relaxation in God. So sabbath becomes the model of salvation.

Mini-sabbaths. Most Christians find that whether or not they have kept a special day, they need a time dedicated to God every day, generally in the morning. Women with small children may find another time of day more profitable, and husbands can care for children during this time to give a "sabbath gift" to their spouse. But it is important to explore the reason for a daily quiet time. Spiritual disciplines* are not ways of finding God or of attaining sanctification but of chasing away obstacles that keep us from being continuously found by God. It is a mighty work on our part to make ourselves truly available to God. The farmer cannot make the seeds grow, but he must work hard in cultivating the soil. That is what daily sabbath involves.

There is a further reason. Our society* continuously inundates us with messages to buy, to consume* and to experience. It is impossible to be unaffected by the ubiquitous appeal of the advertising* world to the flesh. That is reason enough to spend time each day in a mini-sabbath. But the purpose is not merely to bank good thoughts before we are besieged by greed, pride, sex and violence in the world out there. The purpose is to shape how we are to live. It seems imperative to me that persons committed to making every day sabbath must learn how to reduce the stimulation they receive from society. They will see fewer movies,* watch less television* and monitor more carefully what they read. According to the gastronomic world, we are what we eat, and in the realm of the soul, we are what we see and hear. We want to live each hour for God, experiencing God's presence and pleasure.

I am actually making an unpopular proposal, for adopting a sabbath lifestyle will result in less need for leisure activities and diversions. The world offers work and leisure (without sabbath). The Bible offers work and sabbath (with leisure). Leisure and sabbath are not necessarily the same thing. Sabbath involves the threefold harmony of God, ourselves and creation. Prayer and Bible reading are part of this, but so may be digging a garden, making a model boat, trying a new recipe, visiting the lonely and liberating the oppressed (Is 58:6). For a full experience of sabbath we will contemplate creation, redemption and our complete consummation in heaven. Sabbath is contemplative; it directs us toward God and informs us of the meaning of life. But it also leads to an active lifestyle in line with the Old Testament Jubilee year: the sabbath of sabbaths (Lev 25; Lk 4:18-19). Leisure, which is so much less than this, can become a diversion from sabbath and an unsatisfying one at that.

Part of sabbath living is to see that we get a good night's sleep every night, as far as it is possible. Most people in North America are constantly tired—and no wonder, given the frantic work and leisure schedule. God literally refreshes his beloved daily in sleep (Ps 4:8; 127:1-2). Refreshed in sleep and renewed by our exposure to the life-giving power of Scripture and prayer, we can face the demands of work.

Sunday sabbath. Having considered the universalization of sabbath in a lifestyle, we must now address the question of sabbath as one day a week. The emergence of the Jewish sabbath in the context of societies that did not have a seven-day week is a fascinating study in itself. The further emergence of the Christian Sunday in relation to the Jewish sabbath is a complicated matter. Obviously early Jewish Christians celebrated both the sabbath (sundown Friday to sundown Saturday) and the Lord's Supper on Resurrection Day (Sunday) before returning to work on Sunday. In time, sabbath observance diminished, normally without having the Christian Sunday take on all the characteristics of Jewish sabbath (Rybczynski, p. 66). But the Christianization of the Roman Empire had its effect on Sunday. Formal law relating to Sunday observance was first enacted in 321 by Emperor Constantine, who forbade people to work on "the venerable day of the Sun." But it was not until the twelfth century that the term *Christian sabbath* was used, marking as it does the grafting of the sabbath tradition, especially in its negative restrictions, on to the Lord's Day (Rybczynski, pp. 70-71). Needless to say, in North America the Lord's Day is almost gone, though some businesses still observe a weekly holiday on Sunday.

Some form of weekly or regular sabbath is not an optional extra for the New Testament Christian. It is fundamental to spiritual health and even to emotional health, as some medical studies have shown. But keeping one day as a special day of reflection on the meaning of the other six is increasingly difficult in a secularized society that now exploits Sunday as the ultimate day for shopping* and leisure activities. For pastors Sunday is a workday, and I recommend that they keep a Jewish sabbath: Friday sundown to Saturday sundown. Each person will find a pattern that fits, at least for a while. Different occupational experiences and changes in family responsibilities will cause us to adjust our pattern from time to time. A friend of mine spends every Thursday in the lounge of a nearby first-class hotel reading his Bible and Christian classics. Personally I find two complete days every two or three weeks are most suitable for me. I take these days away from the telephone and the workplace and spend them any way I wish. Sometimes I walk or watch a sunset. Sometimes I like to build something.

Often these special-day sabbaths are splendid opportunities to follow one of the many spiritual disciplines that have enriched the spirituality of the church over the centuries: Bible meditation, confession, waiting prayer, intercession for others. An excellent guide for this is *Celebration of Discipline* by Richard Foster. A whole book of the Bible can be read at one sitting, or a single verse can become the subject of meditation for several hours. Time can be spent reflecting on parables or waiting* for new ones to come through God's creation.* Sabbath is also an ideal time for the journey inward, exploring what Thoreau called "the Atlantic and Pacific of one's own being alone." Very active people need to stop long enough to let their soul catch up to their body. An old Arab saying is that a person's soul can travel as fast as a camel. If that is true, then some of us need to stop still for a long time to get connected. *Religion,* in the true meaning of the word, is that which binds together, so making us whole. When we create space and time to be real with God, important questions often surface, questions that can lead to more connectedness.

I have, until now, been exploring an individual use of sabbath as a special day. I have done so deliberately because I am convinced that one can only afford to be in Christian community if one has learned how to be alone with God. Otherwise we tend to feed parasitically on the corporate life of the church. But now I must offer a word about sabbath in regard to the church. I have come to believe that worship* in the context of fellowship* is the most important thing we do in the gathered life of the church. If sabbath is being liberated from the tyranny of performance to rediscover our identities through love,* then worship is an obvious way to keep the sabbath. We do not worship for what we get out of it. That would bring our utilitarian work ethic into worship. Ironically, praise "works" precisely because it lifts us above our compulsion to make everything useful. It is mere enjoyment of God, nothing more, nothing less. All our worship on earth is like a grand rehearsal, worth doing for its own sake, but intended to prepare for a grander occasion. Sabbath days help us to "play heaven." May we not also view sabbath as a way of "playing" with God, celebrating the mutual delight God and we his covenant partners have in each other and the work we do together?

In the deepest sense we do not keep sabbath; the sabbath keeps us. On our own we are not capable of sustaining our orientation toward God and our heavenly direction. That leaves us with a biblical paradox: we must labor to enter that rest (Heb 4:11). Sabbath keeps us focused on the heart of God, the intentions of God for the world, the playfulness of God. Sabbath keeps us heaven-bound. Moltmann says,

> The celebration of the sabbath leads to an intensified capacity for perceiving the loveliness of everything— food, clothing, the body, the soul—because existence itself is glorious. Questions about the possibility of "producing" something, or about utility, are forgotten in the face of the beauty of all created things, which have their meaning simply in their very selves. (p. 286)

Undoubtedly we would do a better job of looking after the earth if we spent the time of our lives playing heaven, at least one day a week.

Ultimate sabbath. In reality Sunday for the Christian is not simply the Jewish sabbath moved a day later. As Moltmann points out, Sunday is the messianic extension of Israel's sabbath and a witness to the new creation brought by Christ. It seems pointless to debate whether sabbath should be kept on Saturday or Sunday when the New Testament points to a greater experience than simply "keeping the sabbath." Sabbath cannot be contained in the practice of "keeping one day." Therefore a curious phrase appears in the second century in the *Epistle of Barnabas:* "the eighth day." In this primitive Christian document, Barnabas looks forward to an ultimate fulfillment of sabbath when the Son of Man comes. Speaking for God, Barnabas says,

> The present sabbaths are not acceptable to me, but that which I have made, in which I will give rest to all things and make the beginning of an eighth day, that is the beginning of another world. Wherefore we also celebrate with gladness (on Sunday and the rest of the week) the eighth day in which Jesus also rose from the dead and was made manifest and ascended into Heaven. (*Barn.* 15:8-9)

So it is with good reason that the Russian theologian Nikolai Berdyaev spoke of the event of Easter as the eighth day of creation. What was created at the beginning, all that we are and have and all the days of the week, enter at Easter into the beginning of the glorification of everything, a glorification in which the gulf between toil and rest is closed.

Because the eighth day has begun, we live simultaneously both *in* this world and *for* the coming world. The transfiguration of everything has begun. So the purpose of keeping one day a week, keeping one hour a day and living every day sabbatically is to make ourselves available for God to redeem all the time and space of our lives. All seven days are holy because the eighth day is dawning.

See also FELLOWSHIP; HEALTH; HOBBIES AND CRAFTS; LEISURE; PLAY; PLEASURE; REST; SPIRITUAL DISCIPLINES; TIME; VACATIONS; WORSHIP.

References and Resources
S. Bocchiochi, *From Sabbath to Sunday: A Historical Investigation of the Rise of Sunday Obser-*

vance in Earliest Christianity (Rome: Gregorian University Press, 1977); M. J. Dawn, *Keeping the Sabbath Wholly* (Grand Rapids: Eerdmans, 1989); T. Edwards, *Sabbath Time* (New York: Seabury, 1982); Richard Foster, *Celebration of Discipline* (San Francisco: Harper & Row, 1982); A. D. Goldberg, "The Sabbath as Dialectic: Implications for Mental Health," *Journal of Religion and Health* 25, no. 3 (Fall 1986) 237-44; A. Heschel, *The Earth Is the Lord's and the Sabbath* (New York: Harper & Row, 1950); C. S. Lewis, *Christian Behaviour* (London: Geoffrey Bles, 1943); J. Moltmann, *God in Creation*, trans. M. Kohl (London: SCM, 1985); E. O'Connor, *Eighth Day of Creation: Gifts and Creativity* (Waco, Tex.: Word, 1971); E. Peterson, "The Pastor's Sabbath" *Leadership* 6, no. 2 (Spring 1985) 52-58; H. Rahner, *Man at Play* (New York: Herder & Herder, 1972); W. Rybczynski, *Waiting for the Weekend* (New York: Viking Penguin, 1991); W. Rordorf, *Sunday: The History of the Day of Rest and Worship in the Earliest Centuries of the Christian Church* (London: SCM, 1968); R. P. Stevens, *Disciplines of the Hungry Heart* (Wheaton, Ill.: Harold Shaw, 1993).

R. Paul Stevens

SACRAMENTS

The Christian faith is the most earthy of all religions: after all, it is rooted in the incarnation. Among other things, that supreme miracle insists that the physical matters a great deal. It matters so much to God that he expresses himself through it. He did it so uniquely when Jesus took human flesh. But the same principle of divine life through physical means remains central to Christianity. That is why the faith of the New Testament is unashamedly sacramental.

A lot of confusion gathers around the term *sacrament*. Some Christians are shy of it; others can speak of little else. Basic Christian usage is to see a *sacrament* as "a physical token that expresses a spiritual reality": as the old Anglican Catechism put it, "an outward and visible sign of an inward and spiritual grace." The catechism rightly goes on to say that Christians use this word *sacrament* of the two ordinances "ordained by Christ himself, as a means whereby we receive the same [that is, his grace] and a pledge to assure us thereof." The word derives from the Latin, where it was used of a soldier's oath of allegiance. All of this helps us to understand the normal Christian usage of the word.

Clearly the sacramental principle runs through the whole of life: a kiss, for example, or a handshake is an "outward and visible sign" that should, and normally does, convey the "inward and spiritual grace" of love* and friendship.* But depending on the attitude of the donor and the recipient, they may not do so. So the two great sacraments Christ left us, baptism* and the Lord's Supper, are outward and visible signs of the inward and spiritual grace of God, which enable us to begin and to continue the Christian life. They are meant to be channels of his unseen, but very real, grace to us. And we can certainly rely on the attitude of the donor. They are vehicles of God's grace and in the primitive church were not merely token signs but dynamic events—a real washing* and a real meal. But that may prove ineffectual if on our side there is no response: if we grasp the hand, so to speak, but not the friendship proffered; if we accept the kiss but reject the love.

The sacraments, then, like the incarnation whose influence they continue, are not only pledges of God's lasting grace to us but should be, and normally are, channels of that love. Most Christians restrict the word to describe the two great outward actions with inner meaning that Jesus himself inaugurated, namely, Communion* and baptism. Some denominations, rather unhelpfully it seems to me, add five more, which were not inaugurated by Christ and which are five among many other external acts with inward meanings. Other denominations (for example, the Quakers) observe no specific sacraments, arguing that all of life for the Christian is sacramental. They enshrine an important insight. In refusing to limit the number of sacraments to two or, with the Catholics, to seven, they insist that everyday life is shot through with gracious invitations from God to find him in the center of life rather than in the religious periphery. And that takes us to the heart of the sacramental principle.

See also BAPTISM; BODY; CHURCH IN THE HOME; COMMUNION; WORSHIP.

Michael Green

SELF-ESTEEM

The term *self-esteem* is often confused with other "self" terms such as *self-worth, self-love, self-image, self-acceptance* and, notably, *self-concept. Self-esteem* has a particular meaning: "how a person feels about who he or she is." The feelings may be positive or negative; the basis of assessment, varied. Self-esteem differs, for example, from self-concept. *Self-concept* is "what a person thinks he or she ought to be or could be." While self-concept affects self-esteem, the two terms refer to different processes.

A Recent Phenomenon

The study of self in academic psychology is a rather recent phenomenon. Even though the concept of self was introduced in the early 1900s, not much attention was paid to the study of self until the 1940s and 1050s in the writings of theorists such as Alfred Adler, Karen Horney and Eric Fromm. It is only since the advent of humanistic psychology that the study of self has taken center stage through the influence of theorists such as Carl Rogers, Abraham Maslow and Rollo May.

Currently in Western culture, positive self-esteem is considered essential to happiness. The self-esteem motto goes something like this: unless you value yourself and feel good about yourself, you will not be happy. Presently over thirty measures of self-esteem and self-concept exist, with the Tennessee Self-Concept Scale (Fitts) and the Piers-Harris Children's Self-Concept Scale (Piers) being the most highly recommended. Many of the measures still require more accurate definition of concepts and validation of data.

The Effects of Low and High Self-Esteem

Low or high self-esteem is *not* a cause or an effect of behavior. This means that self-esteem does not determine behavior. Low self-esteem does not make someone perform poorly. High self-esteem does not make someone more successful. Low self-esteem can in fact be a prod to higher accomplishment, as for the athlete who has to overcome physical difficulties or persons of small stature who became significant leaders. Low or high self-esteem cannot be tagged as the primary cause or effect of behavior.

While self-esteem is not a cause or an effect of behavior, it is associated with a variety of personal and interpersonal characteristics. For example, individuals who show anxiety,* neurosis or social inadequacy and report illnesses attributed to psychosomatic causes also tend to negatively assess their self-worth. Those who negatively assess their self-worth are more likely to be approval-oriented and sensitive to criticism, fear arguments, report that they are unable to overcome their disabilities, engage in dependent relationships and feel unlovable.

Individuals who are nonconformists, intellectually curious and goal-oriented, aspire to leadership* and generally find life more satisfying tend to positively assess their self-worth. Those who positively assess their self-worth also exhibit less defensiveness and more trust in relationships, are less likely to be depressed and report a more positive relationship with God.

The Development of Self-Esteem

Basic self-esteem is learned early in life in parent-child interactions. Because there is limited influence on a young child outside of parents, the parents' impact on the child's self-esteem is sizable and stems more from the emotional realm than verbal involvement. There are two primary building blocks in the development of self-esteem: acceptance and achievement. As two *I-statements,* these would be *I am loved* and *I am able.* Feelings of worth accompany the experiences of being loved and accomplishing tasks.

Parents express acceptance through gentleness, touch, time together, play and the meeting of appropriate needs and through encouraging and affirming positive behaviors with appropriate praise and affection. Parents validate achievements by noticing that the child is growing in the ability to do more things for himself or herself (for example, everything from feeding himself or herself and tying shoes to making decisions, creating things, forming relationships and living through failure and disappointment), communicating that recognition either verbally or nonverbally and giving the child increased opportunity to exercise age-appropriate skills.

Children learn basic self-esteem from parents because though they are not skilled interpreters of what they observe, they are excellent observers of their environment and their parents' responses. Children may learn low self-esteem from their parents' poor responses or from their "childish" interpretation of their parents' responses. If one parent validates the child's abilities while the other parent contradicts the validation, the child's sense of self-worth will manifest itself inconsistently. If a parent overly rewards or punishes a child, the child will reflect a more rigid I-am-good and I-am-bad sense of worth. If a parent repeatedly labels a child's actions as stupid, the child will believe he or she is stupid. If a parent pushes a child to compensate for the parent's low self-esteem, then the child will struggle with reaching high standards.

While these are negative examples, the same holds true for positive examples. If a parent gives and receives affection well, the child will learn the same. If a parent is appropriately proud of an accomplishment and can celebrate failures or setbacks with dignity, then the child learns how to live with a sense of worth in the world. As children enter the teen years and adulthood, they carry with them their basic self-esteem: their positive and negative experiences of love and achievement, their feelings and interpretations associated with these experiences and internalized values from parents, teachers, peers and culture.

The Ups and Downs of Self-Esteem

Self-esteem is never static. It is either growing positively or is decreasing negatively. The ups and downs of self-esteem stem from a comparison between one's ideal self and one's experience of reality. When the gap between ideals and experience is small, self-esteem increases. When the gap between ideals and experience widens, then self-esteem decreases. A person's ideal self is formed primarily from internalized values of parents and others (for example, hard work before play; it's better to be nice than to tell the truth) as well as from the culture through the media (for example, the rich and beautiful achiever is the ideal after which to strive). A person's experience of reality is formed from self-observation and through feedback from others (that is, the person's perceived self). The use of comparison between ideal and real as a basis for self-esteem means that people are constantly vulnerable to emotional ups and downs as they assess their worth. Adopting cultural values as the basis of ideals means that those who seek to compensate for low self-esteem will do so through seeking power, privilege, wealth or rights, which, as we will see, is not the biblical way to find self-worth.

The Christian and Self-Esteem

Taking our self-worth from values* in the culture,* feedback from others and comparison to others or to ideals is substantially different from basing one's worth upon what God thinks of us and how God acts toward us. Starting with God, rather than self or culture, yields a different basis for self-esteem. The *pursuit* of self-esteem could in fact be seen as an idolatrous pursuit for two reasons. Firstly, we are called to seek God above all else (Deut 5:7-8; Mt 6:33). Secondly, self-esteem, like happiness, is nearly impossible to achieve by pursuing it directly. Try to get self-esteem, and you are likely to fail. Self-esteem, much like blessedness, comes as a byproduct of seeking something else and someone other than self (Mt 5:6).

From a biblical viewpoint, positive self-esteem is based on the fact that God created us with the utmost care (Ps 139), in the divine image, nearly as angels (Ps 8), and has called his creation good (Gen 1:31). Further, God has chosen and redeemed his people, not on the basis of their being better than others, but simply as an expression of love toward them (Deut 7:7-9; 1 Jn 4:7-21). As those who are created, redeemed and justified (1 Cor 6:11) and who await heaven, God now calls us to love one another humbly in community (Jn 13) through servanthood. This frees us from a life of com-

parison (Gal 6:4; Col 3:1-7). Community in Christ is to be a place where we live out acceptance, confess sin and receive forgiveness and encouragement (Mt 18:21-35; 1 Thess 5:11; Jas 5:16). It is clear that one of the primary building blocks of self-esteem, acceptance, is woven throughout God's actions toward us and intentions for the church.

The other building block of self-esteem, achievement, is based biblically on the fact that part of God's image in us is creativity and part of God's call is to be vice-regents over creation. We are also called by God to make his name known and build the local church. Equipped by the Holy Spirit, we are called not only to the achievements of human growth but to creative and spiritual achievements— all for the glory of God. For the Christian, positive self-worth is the byproduct of life in Christ.

Developing Healthy Self-Esteem

Three primary steps to healing can be taken with adults who display low self-esteem. First, seek understanding of the factors, such as early childhood experiences, that may have contributed to low self-esteem. Once these are understood, it is time to move on. To move beyond blame and anger over the past is important, for there is no healing in blame and anger. Further, simply understanding the past does not in itself produce change and healing. We can prayerfully apply biblical truths to the understanding gained of the past. Then, it is time to get on with the primary task of taking responsibility for one's self-esteem in the present.

Second, address the cognitive distortions or the negative self-talk *learned* by the person from the internalized values, ideals and childish interpretations of experiences—from all the factors that have contributed to low self-esteem—and replace this negative self-talk with positive self-talk.

Third, develop relationships in which the person can give and receive acceptance and love.* With those in a pattern of abusive relationships, this third step may be possible at first only with a counselor or helper who is totally outside the circle of abuse and who can assist with the development of new behaviors of giving and receiving.

As an example of the work involved in these steps, I offer an exercise in replacing negative self-talk with positive self-talk. This exercise is based on Deuteronomy 7:7-9, which begins in verse 7 with these words: "The LORD did not set his affection on you and choose you because you were more numerous than other peoples."

1. Read aloud the following statements that reflect the identity, the self-talk, of God's chosen people. Add your own statements that you feel fit with the spirit of Deuteronomy 7:7-9.

It is not because I'm beautiful that God chose me and called me by name. It is not because I'm spiritually strong or sensitive that God chose me and called me by name. It is not because I'm great in comparison to others that God chose me and called me by name. It is not because of my accomplishments that God chose me and called my by name. Your statements

_____

_____

_____

_____

2. Now read aloud these positive statements that reflect the self-talk of God's chosen people:

God chose me because he desired to set his love upon me. God chose me because he is faithful to his promises. God chose me because he desired me to be part of his people who are set apart to serve him. God chose me because he desires to reveal his mighty power to me in delivering me from sin's bondage through Christ. God chose me because he wants me to know that he is God, the one who will bless my love for him for a thousand generations. Your statements:

_____

_____

_____

_____

_____

3. As you finish reading these statements, pay attention to the feelings that accompany this positive self-talk. List them. These positive statements represent the identity of a person chosen by God who knows to whom he or she belongs, from whence he or she has been brought by God and who he or she is as a chosen person and part of a chosen people. This identity cannot be bought or created—*it can only be accepted* (by one who is steeped in the truth of what it means to be chosen by God) *and lived out.*

If you have accepted this identity, what was important in doing so? If you have not yet accepted this identity, what makes accepting it difficult?

The quest for improved self-esteem has intensified in the last fifty years of the twentieth century due to the study of self put forward by humanistic psychology. The challenge for Christians is to base our self-worth on how God has created us, values us, acts for us and calls us to be increasingly like Christ. For the Christian, healthy self-esteem will always be a byproduct of redemption and redeemed relationships which await completion in God (Rom 8:18-21).

See also ADOLESCENT; ANXIETY; FRIEND-SHIP; LOVE; PARENTING; SUCCESS.

References and Resources

W. Backus and M. Chapman, *Telling Yourself the Truth* (Minneapolis: Bethany House, 1980); D. G. Benner, ed., *Baker Encyclopedia of Psychology* (Grand Rapids: Baker, 1985); D. K. Clark, "Philosophical Reflections on Self-Worth and

Self-Love," *Journal of Psychology and Theology* 13, no. 1 (1985) 3-11; W. Fitts, *Tennessee Self-Concept Scale: Manual* (Nashville: Counselor Recordings and Tests, 1965); E. Piers, *Manual for the Piers-Harris Children's Self-Concept Scale* (Nashville: Counselor Recordings and Tests, 1969); V. Satir, *Conjoint Family Therapy* (Palo Alto, Calif.: Science & Behavior, 1983); P. C. Vitz, "Leaving Psychology Behind," in *No God but God,* ed. O. Guinness and J. Seel (Chicago: Moody, 1992) 94-110.

Mike Nichols

SERVICE, WORKPLACE

In recent years there have been growing complaints about the weakening emphasis on service among workers. Jokes have long existed about what happened to the service promised by the description "civil servants." Tradespeople offering service seem to be less and less reliable in keeping appointments. In shops and department stores, banks and post offices, garages and government departments, customer service no longer seems to be as available as it used to be. Ironically enough, the type of work* which most often heads the list in complaints about service is the so-called service sector. Typical examples are restaurants whose waiters are untrained, airlines that overbook and auto-repair shops that do not undertake quality work and often overcharge in the bargain. Many now fear that the same kind of decline in quality that took place earlier in the industry field, and led to many of the present problems, is beginning to strike the service sector.

Understanding the Loss of Service

The reasons given for this are many. Some argue that younger people are no longer committed to the work ethic of the previous generation (*see* Work Ethic). Others point to an overemphasis on scale economies involving downsizing and cost-cutting that has affected both the private and the public domain. Some suggest that schools and colleges are no longer doing their job of training people satisfactorily for the work force. Others regard the deterioration of service as part of the broader weakening of morality and concern for others in society. There is some truth in all of these, but the reasons for the lack of service today go deeper.

It helps to approach the issue from another angle. In all our complaints we tend to lose sight of the fact that this is an issue concerning people. People care deeply about this, even if this is often for purely personal reasons, because we take for granted the association between work and service. This has not always been the case in the West and is still not the case in some cultures. In such settings when little service is forthcoming, people do not complain with the same degree of disappointment or indignation. For this is the way things are, always have been, and ever will be—just a fact of life. Our complaints are more intense precisely because we had hoped for more and want to see the situation changed. In this there is some promise.

Linking Work and Service

In large measure, the link between work and service is a consequence of the impact of the gospel on Western society. The key word used to describe the activities of early Christians was *service,* generally translated as "ministry."* This is occasionally used of activities in which people were engaged outside the church,* and in one place even non-Christians are described as God's servants when they do their work in ways congruent with the divine purposes (Rom 13:4). This attitude and language gradually permeated other kinds of work and at times even gave rise to new titles for the work people were doing. "Civil service" or "public service" is one such example. Another is the description given to the whole "service sector" which now accounts for some 75 percent of the economy in advanced industrial societies. In places influenced by British political practice even the word *ministry* is still used of the inner circle of parliamentarians around the prime "minister." The very frequency of the word *service* in the wider marketplace of ideas today is testimony to its continuing vitality. Almost five thousand books a year contain the word in their titles.

So we already have in the way we talk an unconsciously acknowledged theological connection between work and service. Improved service in the workplace begins with realizing more fully the link between the two. It will not be enough to try to push people into giving greater service, for unless they view work itself as a form of service and find the language to convey that, all the pep talks, prep courses and pop techniques to improve this will not take us very far. Service has more to do with how we view what we do and who we are ourselves than what we actually do and how we do it. The latter are certainly important but not in themselves sufficient, for without the former any improvements in service are built on rather shaky foundations. So a major part of the task is helping the whole culture of business and the workplace to embrace again a vision of service.

Recovering the Dignity of Service

One of the ways we can do this is to help bring the idea of vocation back into the workplace* (*see* Calling). Although our vocation touches all areas of life, not only our work, there is no doubt that those who see their work in some sense a calling or vocation are more likely to do it more in the spirit of service. This was one of the findings in the survey of senior managers conducted by William Diehl, as recorded in his book *In Search of Faithfulness*. It is partly because a sense of

vocation has been largely replaced by notions of a career, or just the job, that the quality of much of the work people do has also suffered (*see* Protestant Work Ethic).

But we must also find fresh, practical ways of bringing service and work back into closer connection with one another. This is already taking place in significant contemporary business literature. Much is said these days about the need for firms to place service at the center of what they do. In these highly competitive times, success will go to those who are perceived by the public as really delivering on their offers of service. Some companies make this point by offering to refund some or all of the cost of their product or service if it does not live up to expectations or if it is not supplied in the time promised. This means a lot to customers, who are mostly busy people who do not have time to wait around for deliveries or to keep chasing firms that have not done what they promised.

Another suggested way forward for businesses is to add some extra benefit to the customer on top of what is usually supplied. This is the so-called value-added factor, and customers, especially those who belong to the baby-boom generation, are increasingly looking for this. They realize that these days it is mostly a buyer's, not seller's, market and that since buyers are increasingly quality-conscious, they are primarily looking for the best deal they can get. Workplaces that are taking seriously "the search for excellence" (Peters and Waterman), "total quality management" (Deming), "total product concept" (Levitt) or the "principles of completeness" (Crosby) are seeking to equip themselves to do this. Going beyond this is the idea of offering "extraordinary" or "superlative" service (as exhibited in firms like Nordstrom or Federal Express). This means treating the client or customer as a partner in a lifelong relationship of giving and receiving which changes according to the needs and requirements of the person served as much as the challenges and developments in the serving organization.

Increasingly in this literature there is an emphasis on what the person of the worker, as well as the quality of the work, brings to the nature of the service offered. It is not just about the quality of products and services, it is about the quality of those producing them and serving customers. This is especially the case in those occupations that provide services rather than goods but all too easily focus on numbers, revenue or other measurable performance indicators rather than meeting both server and customer expectations. Unless there are internal changes taking place in the lives of the workers themselves, it is only a matter of time before the quality of what they do is affected; in some cases it is affected from the outset as their approach to customers or clients gets in the way of others wanting what they are making or offering.

Servant Leader and Serving Organization

This where the idea of the "servant leader" in the workplace comes in, for such a person can model to others the importance, meaning and practice of service connected with one's work. This idea was given particular currency in the 1970s by Simon K. Greenleaf (see Leadership; Leadership, Church). This has now undergone significant refinement at the hands of writers like Michael Maccoby, who distinguishes the different ways in which people serve depending on the type of contribution they offer. For *helpers* service means assisting people, valuing relationships above all and responding to specific needs. For *defenders* it means monitoring and protecting those who are disadvantaged. For *innovators* it means creating and implementing a more effective strategy. For newer-style *self-developers* it means facilitating a problem-solving process with customers and clients that includes an opportunity to learn and grow. These categories helpfully broaden the ways in which we should think of direct service to people. Too often we identify this mainly with the work of the first group. But even with these refinements, we need greater emphasis on such a person being a "leading servant" rather than just a leader—of whatever kind—with a service orientation.

In any case, the whole notion of leadership needs to be broadened to include a more collaborative approach and a recognition of the point at which everyone in the work force can take the lead in some respect or other. This means that we do not necessarily have to wait for designated leaders to take the lead in this or any other area. If they do, fine; if not, someone else can take the lead. But all of us—no matter how ordinary a position we might have or how ordinary our work might appear—can seek to fulfill our responsibility in a genuinely servant-like and service-oriented way. We can do this without seeking permission or affirmation.

We can exemplify service before those around us. We can make informal or formal suggestions about how our own work and the work around us can be improved. We can look for ways of generating discussion on how certain things might be done. We can both stand up for and stand up to our immediate overseers, for example, helping to conserve their energy, being responsible gatekeepers, defining them publicly, acting in their name, defending them, helping them focus. And we can buffer others from a leader, facing them with hard facts, presenting options and playing advocate when they are in danger of deciding unwisely. Though sometimes this will encounter opposition, forcing us to make some hard choices about how far we can go or whether we might have to change our work, at other times we will find a warm reception for our efforts.

Apart from what they can bring personally to the task, those in positions of leadership can go further and develop an organizational culture,* processes and training that will help others see their work as a service. The key here is for them to see themselves as stewards rather than controllers of the organization and everyone in it, exercising rank without privilege, developing partners rather than dependents and granting empowerment rather then entitlement. Practices that enhance service in their organizations include maximizing core workers' opportunity of designing and customizing policy; reintegrating the managing and doing of work; allowing measurements and controls to serve, not master, core workers; and supporting local solutions rather than consistency across all groups (Block, pp. 64-66). They should encourage people to put service before everything, and find appropriate ways of monitoring, rewarding and improving its quality, consistency and novelty, giving special attention and training to support and front-line service people on whom so much depends. Throughout the process, these leaders should be fully aware that service is not merely about giving someone a useful product or a service, but establishing a relationship with them that will encourage their looking to satisfy similar future needs from the same place.

See also INTEGRITY; LEADERSHIP; MINISTRY; ORGANIZATIONAL CULTURE; WORK; WORK ETHIC, PROTESTANT; WORKPLACE.

References and Resources
P. Block, *Stewardship: Choosing Service over Self-Esteem* (San Francisco: Barrett-Koehler, 1993);

I. Chaleff, *The Courageous Follower: Standing Up to and for Our Leaders* (San Francisco: Barrett-Koehler, 1955); P. B. Crosby, *Completeness: Quality for the Twenty-first Century* (New York: Penguin, 1994); W. Diehl, *In Search of Faithfulness: Lessons from the Christian Community* (San Francisco: Harper & Row, 1989); R. K. Greenleaf, *Servant Leadership: A Journey into the Nature of Legitimate Power and Greatness* (New York: Paulist, 1977); R. E. Kelley, *Power of Followership: How to Create Leaders People Want to Follow and Followers Who Lead Themselves* (New York: Double Currency, 1991); M. Maccoby, *Why Work: Motivating and Leading the New Generation* (New York: Simon & Schuster, 1988); B. Patterson, *Serving God: The Grand Essentials of Work and Worship* (Downers Grove, Ill.: InterVarsity Press, 1994).

Robert Banks

SEXUALITY

Contrary to the popular idea that God is in heaven shouting "Cut it out!" to any couple enjoying sexual intercourse within the covenant, God invented it, created it and blessed it saying, "It [is] very good" (Gen 1:31). It is good biologically—reducing tensions and creating new life (see Conception). It is good socially—strengthening the capacity for love.* It is good ethically—balancing fulfillment with responsibility. It is good spiritually—becoming a powerful experiential parable of Christ's will to bless his covenant partner, the church.* But crucial to the discussion of a theology and spirituality of sex is the simple observation that God says sex is good, not god! While modern people use sex, they also deify it. Their preoccupation with the genitals and the experience of sexuality betrays the fact they have made an ultimate concern out of something less than the Ultimate One. Such is the nature of idolatry. And sex makes a ready idol. In what follows, we explore what the Bible has to say about sex, its God-given purpose, how sex relates to prayer, and finally sex and singleness.

The Bible and Sex

The Bible contains references to almost every conceivable sexual experience, both healthy and sinful. Only a few references will be given here.

Divine intent. The purpose of God in creating humankind male and female is to create a community that reflects a God of love (Gen 1:27; Eph 5:22, 25), to end loneliness, to communicate love within marriage (Gen 2:18) and to continue the human race (Gen 1:28). Married love is dignified, holy and a joy to God (Gen 2:24; Song; Mt 19:5-6). Single people, nevertheless, may celebrate their appetite for covenant even while not experiencing its full expression in the covenant of marriage. Many do this within a covenant community.* Far from stigmatizing the single person, the New Testament offers singleness as a calling* and a gift (Mt 19:12; 1 Cor 7:17). Sexual restraint is, however, needed whether married or single (1 Thess 4:3-8; Heb 13:4) since promiscuous sex is harmful and alienates us from our Creator. Indeed sexual sins, more than most other sins, have a profound effect on our personality (1 Cor 6:18-20) and our spirituality (Rom 1:27). A life given over to sexual pleasure is profoundly empty as people seek ever more exotic thrills to titillate their satiated desires (Jude 7-13).

The emphasis of Scripture is not only on acts but on attitudes (Mt 5:28; 2 Pet 2:14). Sins of fantasy are as serious in God's sight as sins in body,* largely because the body is not the shell of the soul but part of the real person, as is the mind or emotions.* Some references bear on the question of pornography (Phil 4:8; 2 Tim 2:22; 2 Pet 2:14). But in God's sight, sexual sins are not worse or less forgivable than other sins, and there is hope of full forgiveness and substantial healing to those who have hurt themselves or others in this way (Jn 8:1-11; 1 Jn 1:9).

Covenant sex. Unquestionably sexual intercourse and its normal preparation (foreplay; Gen 26:8) are reserved for the full covenant experience of marriage* (Deut 22:13-29). Family planning, while not named directly in Scripture, must be considered in the light of Genesis 1:28, Psalm 127:3-5 and Hebrews 13:4. The reference in Genesis 38:9 is to failing to perform a marital duty; it is not a condemnation of contraception.* Premarital sex, understood biblically, is really misnamed. There is no such thing as premarital sexual intercourse. The act means marriage and is highly symbolic: the interpenetration of two lives in complete self-giving.

Sexual sin. The general word in the New Testament for unlawful and sinful sexual relationships (*porneia*) includes prostitution, unchastity and fornication (Gal 5:19; 1 Thess 4:3)—in each case the person is not treated with respect, indeed is treated rather as a sexual object. The desire is an evil desire (*epithymia;* Col 3:5) or a lustful passion (*pathos*), connoting a preoccupation with sexual pleasure and personal gratification (1 Thess 4:5). Several English words, including lewdness and lasciviousness, translate the word *aselgeia,* which means "sheer, shameless, animal lust to gratify physical desires" (Mk 7:22; 2 Pet 2:2). Obviously most of this sexual sin concerns sexual activity outside the marriage covenant, but it includes the possibility of married lust.

Prostitution treats sex as a commodity outside the covenant (Lev 19:29; Deut 22:21; Prov 6:23-35; 1 Cor 6:15-20), often leading to venereal disease, which is possibly mentioned in Leviticus 15:1 and Numbers 25:1-9. Extramarital sin, or adultery, while it does not reduce sexual activity to a commodity, breaks the marriage covenant and inflicts wounds on both persons (Ex 20:14; Lev 20:10-14; Prov 5:15-23; Mt 5:27-30), though some of these words also apply to distorted sexual expressions within marriage. While not directly dealing with sexual abuse, except in such passages as Deuteronomy 22:22-30, the Bible provides a theological context for the profound respect of women and the relational nature of sexual acts: in Christ a woman's body is not the exclusive possession of the husband (1 Cor 7:3-5), and the sex act is profoundly personal (1 Cor 6:18). Homosexual acts are an offense against the relational image of God (Gen 1:27; 19:5; Lev 18:22; Rom 1:24-27)—in all these cases Scripture deals with homosexual activity rather than the tendency to homosexuality.* Solo sex (see Masturbation) is not actually mentioned in Scripture, and the so-called sin of Onan (Gen 38:9-10) is an unrelated reference. Since the Bible reveals the communal purpose of sexuality (showing love and building communion) and the danger of an unhealthy fantasy life (Mt 5:28), solo sex must always be something less than God intended.

Sexual temptation. The Bible gives clear direction on handling sexual temptation (Gen 39:5-10; Job 31:1; 1 Cor 6:18; Eph 5:1-3) through fleeing, walking in the Spirit (Gal 5:16) and setting our hearts on things above (Col 3:1-14). Martin Luther once said that it is one thing to have a bird land on your head—just as sexual arousal is normal, one can hardly stop this from happening—but it is quite another thing to allow the bird to build a nest there. Becoming a Christian does not solve this problem. The power of the indwelling Christ does not anesthetize our sexual appetite. Just the reverse, new birth makes us fully alive in every conceivable way. But the cleansing love of God (2 Cor 5:14-21) drives out unworthy thoughts and attitudes, empowers us to love (Jn 15:13; 1 Jn 4:7-21) and releases us to become truly masculine or feminine.* Christians should be the sexiest people on earth precisely because their

natures are being conformed to the image of God (Rom 12:1-2), because their sexual experience within marriage is physical (union), social (intimacy) and spiritual (communion), and because they are lining themselves up with God's intended sexual design for us as human beings. Indeed there is growing empirical evidence for the fact that overall Christians are able to enjoy sex more than others and, within marriage, make better lovers!

Holy eroticism. One whole book of the Bible is devoted to the affirmation of passionate sexual love within the covenant: the Song of Songs. The Song can be considered an extended exposition of Adam's expectant delight when he first met Eve (Gen 2:23). Contrary to the usual interpretation that this is an allegory of Christ's love for the church—an approach taken by Bernard of Clairvaux, who devoted his whole life as a celibate monk to expounding this allegory—this book unashamedly celebrates sexual delight. But it does not celebrate lascivious sex. An old interpretation of this book argues that there is not a single male lover (Solomon, here adding one more beautiful woman to his harem) and the Shulammite woman (noted in the New International Version by the titles *Lover* and *Beloved*), but two lovers of the same woman (Solomon and a country man to whom the woman is betrothed and for whom she longs and dreams). The woman does not want to be aroused by Solomon, as noted in the frequent refrain, "Do not arouse or awaken love until it so desires" (Song 2:7). Solomon wants to "get" love and "make" love through flattery and self-gratification. The woman, in contrast, wishes to remain faithful to her true shepherd love to whom she is betrothed (Song 6:3; 7:10) and for whom she searches whether in dream or reality (Song 3:1-4). Following her rebuff of the king, this true lover affirms the exclusive and holy nature of their covenant love (Song 8:6, 12). So the Song exalts faithfulness within the security of covenant; it openly encourages bodily delight where there is such reverence and loyalty; it reveals the nature of holy eroticism.

Sexual spirituality. Precisely because complementarity and cohumanity are points of our godlikeness, sexuality is also the point of our greatest vulnerability—hence the many references in Scripture to sexual sin and perversion. Ultimately the solution for sexual sin is not psychological. As Jesus noted in the case of the woman with multiple relationships, healing is found in worshiping God in Spirit (or spirit) and in truth (Jn 4:23-24). Tragically, the church adopted the philosophy of Neo-Platonic dualism, teaching that spirit is holy and the body is either evil or inconsequential. In contrast, Paul says the body is for the Lord and the Lord is for the body (1 Cor 6:13), thus inviting theological reflection on our sexuality. What indeed does God have to do with genital activity, with sexual desire, with sexual differentiation as males and females, with the pleasure and playfulness of sexual activity within marriage and with the continuing sexual longings experienced by single people, whether that singleness* is chosen or involuntary?

The Purpose of Sex

Answering the question "Why is there sex?" the Bible tells us six things that are enough to start a social revolution, enough to leave us ashamed that we were ever ashamed of our sexuality.

Because we crave relationship. God has designed us to move beyond ourselves. The word *sex* comes from the Latin *secare*, which literally means "something has been cut apart that longs to be reunited." In Genesis 2:18 God says, "It is not good for the man to be alone." Adam discov-

ered soon enough that he needed another like himself—but different. So the male by himself cannot be fully in the image of God, nor can the female. The biblical phrase *the image of God* presupposes the idea of relationship. God is a Trinity, humankind a duality, of relationships. So part of our spiritual pilgrimage is to relate healthily to the opposite sex. The Roman Catholic writer Richard Rohr explains it this way:

> God seemingly had to take all kinds of risks in order that we would not miss the one thing necessary: we are called and even driven out of ourselves by an almost insatiable appetite so that we could never presume that we were self-sufficient. It is so important that we know that we are incomplete, needy, and essentially social that God had to create a life-force within us that would not be silenced! (p. 30)

To consummate covenant. In the Old Testament covenants were sealed and renewed by significant rituals and signs. This signing of the covenant emphasizes that it is not an idle promise but a solemn act with serious consequences. In the New Testament the Lord's Supper becomes the ritual of the covenant for those who belong to Jesus Christ. These rituals are like any sacraments*: God communicates a spiritual grace through a material reality. Sexual intercourse is the consummation and the ritual of the marriage covenant. Just as the bread and the wine offer us spiritual nourishment, so in marriage "sexual intercourse is the primary (though certainly not the only) ritual. It is an extension and fulfillment of the partners' ministry to each other begun during the public statement of vows" (Leckey, p. 17). Intercourse is to the covenant what the Lord's Supper is to salvation. It expresses and renews the heart covenant. If the symbol is not backed by a full covenant, it is merely a powerless, graceless act.

To keep us distinct in unity. At the candle-lighting portion of a wedding* ceremony the bride and groom, hands trembling, take the two lighted candles representing themselves and, with great solemnity, light a single central candle representing their marriage. But then they stoop down and blow out the two candles. Do they really mean to blow themselves out? Tragically, some do. One wag, hearing the familiar line "Two have become one," asked, "Which one?" In some cases that is a rather penetrating question. Community is com-unity. The word is made up of two parts. *Com* means "with" or "together." With *unity*, it means "unity alongside another." It is not the oneness of a drop of water returning to the sea: sexuality is not the urge to merge. Sexuality is the urge to be part of a community of two, symbolized by the act of intercourse: one person moves in and out of another. The differences and the uniqueness of both people are celebrated at the very moment of oneness and unity. God is the ultimate mystery of covenant unity. And every family in heaven and on earth is named (or derives its origin and meaning) from the Father (Eph 3:14-15). Reverently we may speak of the mystery of one God in three persons; we know they are not merged. Nor do we merge in the human covenant. Partners should find, not lose, their identity.

Because male and female are complements. In a covenant marriage, each calls forth the sexuality of the other. Eve called forth the sexuality of Adam. Until she is created, the man is just "the human" (*ha-adam*). Only after the woman is created is he "the man" (male person, *ha-ish*). His special identity emerges in the context of needing a suitable helper. Adam saw Eve as one called forth. His cry "At last!" (Gen 2:23 RSV) is an expression of relational joy. Now he has found a partner as his opposite, by his side, equal but different, his other half. C. S. Lewis compared our sexual unity to that of a violin bow and string. Both are needed, and neither can be fulfilled without the other. Speaking about the cellist Pierre Fournier, it was said that his "left hand [on the string] plays the notes and interprets the musical symbols of the score, but his right hand [on the bow] speaks, puts the emphasis, and is responsible for the interpretation" (Vancouver Symphony Orchestra). In our marriage I play the notes on the score, reading them sometimes very mechanically, while my wife, Gail, puts the emphasis, interpreting the notes. It may be different for another couple. All that matters is that bow and string together create one sound without trying to make each conform to the other.

It is important to note here that the Bible does not give us two parallel lists of qualities, one male and one female. That should be reason enough not to generalize on male and female stereotypes. The sexual act suggests that men and women are different in their sexuality. In intercourse woman receives the man, letting him come inside her. In this act she makes herself extremely vulnerable. The man, on the other hand, is directed outward. While the woman receives something, the man relieves himself of something. It means something different to the man. Perhaps it is less total for him (Thielicke, pp. 45-60). A woman needs to be psychologically prepared for this self-abandonment, not only by the public commitment of her husband to lifelong troth but also by her husband's ongoing nurture of the love relationship. This difference in sexual identity may also be the reason behind the common male complaint that their wives do not understand their need for sexual release and expression. It is a gross but instructive overstatement to say that men must have sex to reach fullness of love while women must have love to reach fullness of sex.

To create children. Thomas Aquinas believed adultery was wrong because people having sex outside marriage do not want to conceive a child (Aquinas 11.154.11.3). Most people today do not find this a convincing argument. But face-to-face intimacy, which in intercourse only humans enjoy, is very suggestive of the nature of the relationship. Similarly, natural sex gives the procreative process its own way (which adulterers are always determined to interrupt) and is a powerful statement of why we have this appetite. Lewis Smedes says that "sex and conception are the means God normally uses to continue his family through history until the kingdom comes on earth in the form of a new society where justice dwells" (1983, p. 168). It would be wrong to say that every act of intercourse must have procreation as its end. In the Genesis narrative the man and woman were in the image of God and enjoyed profound companionship before there were children. But to cut the tie between sex and children is to reduce sexuality. A childless marriage can be a godly community on earth. But a marriage that refuses procreation for reasons of self-centeredness is something less than the God-imaging community, male and female, that was called to "be fruitful and increase in number" (Gen 1:28). Our society treats babies as an inconvenience, an interruption to a blissful married life or a challenging career.* But the Bible says that babies are an awesome wonder. Even if the birth was unexpected and unplanned for—or perhaps even, humanly speaking, unwanted—it is the work of God, a lovely mystery. Healthy sexuality makes marriage the beginning of family.*

Because it incarnates the covenant. God wants us to have an earthly spirituality. These are carefully chosen words. Faith has to be fleshed out to be real. The Christian message is that God became a man. God didn't become just another spirit. The Word became flesh and dwelt among us (Jn 1:14). Spirit became body. In marriage, too, spirit must become body. Love must become incarnate. If in the church there are Word and sacrament, in a marriage there needs to be words and touch. Our society secularizes sex. It treats it as pure body, pure flesh—nothing more. There are no sins and no sexual perversions. The converse, just as wrong although sometimes thought to be Christian, is the problem of hyperspirituality. These Christians talk about God but either live uneasily with the physical or live a double life. Flesh (in the sense of the physical) and spirit have never been reconciled. Sex is looked down upon, almost as a necessary evil. Karl Barth once said that "sex without marriage is demonic." Now we must say that marriage without sex is demonic too. In contrast to the sacralizing and the secularizing of sex, the Bible sacramentalizes sex. It does this by putting it in its rightful place: in the covenant. That does not mean that single people cannot be whole without sexual intercourse. As Smedes puts it, "Although virgins do not experience the climax of sexual existence, they can experience personal wholeness by giving themselves to other persons without physical sex. Through a life of self-giving—which is the heart of sexual union—they become whole persons. They capture the essence without the usual form" (1976, p. 34).

Sex and Prayer

Sexual spirituality and *spiritual sexuality* appear to be oxymorons, but not to those who have been converted to a full biblical perspective on sexuality. There is a deep reason for this. The desire for sexual union and the desire for God are intimately related. God is a God of love.

God dwells in the covenant community of Father, Son and Holy Spirit, interpenetrating, mutually indwelling, living for and in one another, finding life in self-giving to the other—all ways of describing what the Orthodox fathers of the church in the fifth century described as *perichoresis*: the intercommunion of the Godhead in a nonhierarchical community of loving, mutual abiding. Made in the image of God (Gen 1:26), humankind was built male and female for communion, created to long for mutual abiding, destined to find fulfillment in self-giving. Commenting on how the sexual appetite is so closely related to worship and prayer, Alan Ecclestone notes:

> The primitive impulse to deify sexual love was not wholly misguided; it has all the features of great mystical experience, abandon, ecstasy, polarity, dying, rebirth and perfect union. . . . It prompts between human beings those features characteristic of prayer; a noticing, a paying attention, a form of address, a yearning to communicate at ever deeper levels of being, an attempt to reach certain communion with the other. (Wild, p. 23)

But there is an important corrective in Scripture: our sexuality arises from our godlikeness; our godlikeness does not arise from our sexuality. So this profound clue to our true dignity as God-imaging creatures, a clue written into our genetic code, our psychological structure and our spiritual nature, is an invitation to seek and worship God in spirit (truly in Spirit) and truth (Jn 4:23).

So prayer and sexuality are intimately related for both men and women, though differently so. Not surprisingly, many people find themselves sexually aroused when they pray, whether or not they are in the presence of someone of the opposite sex.

Sex and Singleness

Three biblical goals for our personal sexuality are (1) sexual freedom, (2) sexual purity and (3) sexual contentment. Sexual freedom does not mean freedom from constraint but freedom to express our sexuality fully and exclusively within the marriage covenant. When one is not yet married, or is called to the single life (*see* Singleness), sexual freedom allows us to appreciate the other sex and to welcome our sexual appetites but to refrain from full physical expression outside of the marriage covenant. What is seldom noted about self-control is that it is a byproduct of a prayerful life, the result of walking in the Spirit, and not something gained by steeling one's will or "trying."

Sexual purity is certainly not dull (read the Song of Songs). To live freely and with sexual purity, we must reduce the amount of stimulation we allow ourselves to receive from magazines, movies,* videos and mass media.* Job could say that he had made a covenant with his eyes not to look at a woman lustfully (Job 31:1), not an easy thing to do in a sexually saturated culture. Positively, we must increase our attention to God. In a shocking exposé in *Leadership* magazine, a onetime spiritual director anonymously confided his battle with pornography and perverted sexual behavior. While he found that his attempts at trying to become pure through self-determination and passionate prayers of repentance failed, he was delivered at last by the simple recognition that his addiction* to sex was shortchanging his intimacy with God. Love of God, that expulsive power of a new affection, purged lesser loves and even lust.

Sexual contentment, rather than sexual fulfillment, is a worthy Christian goal. The secret of contentment for Paul and ourselves is the practice of thanksgiving and continuing dependence on God

(Phil 4:6, 13). Thanksgiving is essential for single people who will be tempted to seek fulfillment mainly in themselves (*see* Masturbation) or in dating* relationships that are impure. Single people will find their sexual repose by directing their love with all of its passion to the loving community of Father, Son and Holy Spirit, through which literally we experience God as our spouse (Is 54:5).

In conclusion, sex is contemplative. This most down-to-earth daily stirring within us invites us heavenward. It does this by insisting through the very fibers of our being that we were built for love and built for the God who is love. It causes us daily to wonder at the mystery of complementarity, inviting us into a social experience in which there is more unity because of the diversity of male and female, just as God is more one because God is three. It demands of us more than raw, unaided human nature can deliver, a life of self-sacrifice and abiding contentment, qualities that can come only by practicing the presence of God. Finally, it invites us to live for God and his kingdom. As C. S. Lewis once said, if we find that nothing in this world and life fully satisfies us, it is a powerful indication that we were made for another life and another world. In some way beyond our imagination, human marriage will be transcended (Mt 22:30) and fulfilled. Indeed, we will not give or receive in marriage because we will all be married in the completely humanized new heaven and new earth, where God's people daily delight in being the bride of God (Rev 19:7; 21:2).

See also ABUSE; BODY; CALLING; CONTRACEPTION; FAMILY; HOMOSEXUALITY; LOVE; MARRIAGE; MASTURBATION; SINGLENESS.

References and Resources

D. Leckey, *A Family Spirituality* (New York: Crossroad, 1982); M. Mason, *The Mystery of Marriage* (Portland, Ore.: Multnomah, 1985); R. Rohr, "An Appetite for Wholeness," *Sojourners*, November 1982, 30-32; L. Smedes, *Mere Morality* (Grand Rapids: Eerdmans, 1983); L. Smedes, *Sex for Christians* (Grand Rapids: Eerdmans, 1976); R. P. Stevens, *Married for Good: The Lost Art of Remaining Happily Married* (Downers Grove, Ill.: InterVarsity Press, 1986, portions quoted with permission); H. Thielicke, "Mystery of Sexuality," in *Are You Nobody?* (Richmond, Va.: John Knox, 1965); Thomas Aquinas, *Summa Theologia*, trans. Fathers of the English Dominican Province, vol. 4 (New York: Benzigle Brothers, 1948); *Vancouver Symphony Orchestra Programme Notes*, March 13, 1983; E. Wheat, *Intended for Pleasure* (Old Tappan, N.J.: Fleming H. Revell, 1977); R. Wild, *Frontiers of the Spirit: A Christian View of Spirituality* (Toronto: Anglican Book Centre, 1981).

R. Paul Stevens

SHIFTWORK

In earlier times almost everyone worked during the day and rested at night. This practice is alluded to in Jesus' injunction regarding mission: "As long as it is day, we must do the work. . . . Night is coming, when no one can work" (Jn 9:4 NRSV). On occasions people did work at night: in two places we find reference to Paul's doing this (Acts 20:31; 1 Thess 2:9). The main exceptions to working during the day were those who were on watch or guard duty, servants at dinner parties or in taverns, traders bringing goods to market where there was a daytime curfew, or people dealing with an emergency situation. Even in these cases, working at odd hours or at night tended to be intermittent.

How Did Shiftwork Come into Being?

It was not until the Industrial Revolution that this pattern underwent serious change. What made the difference was the introduction of machines. Unlike humans, machines can run all night as well as all day, having to stop only when a problem develops or they break down. From an economic point of view, machines are more profitable if they are kept running. This development led to the formation of two, then three, shifts throughout a twenty-four-hour period. Generally workers rotated around these shifts, though in time some were compelled or chose to work a regular shift.

Minor variations of this occurred with the introduction of Morse code and then the wireless and with the creation of varying time* zones within large countries like the United States, Canada and Australia. This resulted in some people operating in the time zones of places other than where they lived and worked. As a result of the introduction of the telephone* and now the broader telecommunications revolution, people are able and at times required to operate according to the time zones of other countries. As larger numbers of people have become involved in shiftwork, there has been a corresponding increase in shiftwork among people in the service sector to cater to the workers' needs at the times they are available.

How Widespread Is Shiftwork, and What Are Its Effects?

Over the last few decades shiftwork has been increasing in most industrializing or industrialized economies. Overall in Western countries approximately one-third of all workers are employed at times other than standard working hours. Many of these are involved in rotating schedules, others in permanent shiftwork, including those who are operating according to the time zone of another region or country. Indeed the whole idea of normal working hours is becoming increasingly questionable. Many who work standard hours are now finding that sometimes they also have to work regularly at night or on a weekend.

There are some advantages in doing shiftwork. The pay is generally better. Time spent commuting* is often shorter.

The sense of camaraderie can be greater. But the disadvantages are serious, and awareness of them has grown over the years. Problems include (1) disrupted sleeping* patterns, (2) greater vulnerability to fatigue and depression,* (3) increased likelihood of physical illness, (4) more tensions with spouses and children, (5) less socializing and contact with friends,* (6) higher incidence of divorce* and (7) a tendency to die earlier. It is obvious that these are not minor difficulties.

How Can Shiftwork Be Handled More Responsibly?

For a long time the physical, psychological and social consequences of shiftwork were overlooked or viewed only as isolated cases. Now that they are well known, many employers and unions have begun to take steps to reduce them. Individual workers also need to know whether they should take on regular shiftwork at all or, if already doing so, how best to minimize its unfortunate consequences. Here are some major steps that can be taken:

1. Vary shiftwork with more normal work patterns. Though this involves adjustments to changing schedules, these are no greater than those experienced by someone traveling by air overseas.

2. With long-term shiftwork, avoid rotating shifts. Instead, have people work mostly the same hours.

3. As much as possible, it is best for people to work regular week-length rhythms, even if these do not always coincide with standard weekdays and weekends.

4. Shiftworkers need normal, generally long, weekends throughout the year so that their socializing patterns can coincide with those with whom they want to socialize.

5. Shiftworkers also need longer or more frequent holidays so that they can

make up time lost through shiftwork with their families.

There are other steps that can be taken, not only by individual shiftworkers but by those associated with them. First, spouses of shiftworkers can adjust as much as realistically possible to the latter's daily rhythm so that they can have more time together. Second, friends should be prepared to do the same from time to time so that they can maintain their relationship with shiftworkers and engage in common activities. It is lamentable that shiftworkers often lose long-standing friends and only develop relationships with others also working shifts; apart from the obvious relational loss, this tends to result in having too restricted a view of life and the world. Third, shiftworkers and their spouses, preferably children as well, need to be in a communal Christian group where they can gain support, find practical help for their special circumstances and forge long-term links with people living according to more normal time patterns. Fourth, congregations—whether acting in concert or on their own—should hold some groups, corporate worship* services and occasionally other activities at times shiftworkers can attend, sometimes late in the evening or early in the morning. Fifth, every so often permanent shiftworkers should try to rotate their jobs so as to have more normal employment or together with their families spend time with a counselor ensuring that habits,* tensions and ailments are not building up so as to create severe problems in the future.

Since surveys suggest that the trend toward shiftwork or other unusual work patterns is likely to continue, it is important that as Christians and as churches,* as employers and as unions,* further serious attention be given to this phenomenon. Since the debate has now moved beyond issues of salary and time off to issues of health and lifestyle, perhaps the time is now ripe to tackle issues of spirit and community.*

See also TIME; WORK; WORKPLACE.

References and Resources
W. P. Colquhoun and J. Rutenranz, *Studies of Shiftwork* (London: Taylor & Francis, 1980); T. H. Monk, *Making Shift Work Tolerale* (1992); A. J. Scott, ed., *Shiftwork* (Philadelphia: Hanley & Belfur, 1990).

Robert Banks

SHOPPING

Shopping has become the main activity for most people outside the home* and workplace.* This is a relatively recent phenomenon. In previous centuries, those at the top of the social pyramid were often engaged in what social critic Thorstein Veblen called "conspicuous consumption." But mass materialism became possible only in the wake of the Industrial Revolution and secularization.

The Rise of the Consumer Culture

For the consumer culture to arise, however, two other developments were necessary. One was the emergence of the mass media* and their offspring, advertising.* This provided the means for the wide-scale marketing of goods. The other development was the appearance of the therapeutic personality, defined according to unsatisfied needs and the desire for self-fulfillment. Previously, especially in Protestant countries, life revolved around personal self-denial in favor of a commitment to work* and thrift, family* and civic obligations. It was only when the external enticements of advertising connected with inner longings for physical and material well-being that the shift to a more individual, leisure-oriented, consumer culture took place. At the heart of this was the shopping mentality.

It was in newer Western societies, particularly the United States, that the consumer culture took root. One sign of this was the commercial co-option of the main annual celebrations of American Christianity—Easter,* Christmas,* Thanksgiving* and even Mother's Day—in the last quarter of the nineteenth and first quarter of the twentieth century. Another was the growth of increasingly large retail centers, from the department store to the shopping mall.* A further indication of this was the proliferation of road signs and billboards, catalogs and junk mail that have increasingly blanketed the country and filled mailboxes. The latest development is the appearance of home shopping TV* channels and shopping by computer.* While its members succumb to many of these developments, the church* as a whole body has increasingly turned itself into a marketing agency, advertising a shopping mall of religious services and meetings. Even God is often treated as a giant vending machine for religious consumption.

On average, Americans now spend about six hours a week in shopping-related activities, or around 6 percent of their waking hours. This is about 20 percent higher than twenty years ago. During that time, Sunday shopping has almost doubled and expenditure on consumer items has increased almost 50 percent in real dollar terms. While women devote more time to shopping than men, the difference amounts to only two hours a week. Better-educated people tend to shop more than others, though on the whole those with higher incomes do not spend more time shopping than those with lower ones. About half of people's shopping time goes toward buying groceries, clothing and other basic articles.

The Shopping Mentality

The spread of the consumer society has resulted in several noticeable changes in people's attitudes toward shopping.

As advertising becomes ever more sophisticated, we are more open to being manipulated and exploited by it. Advertisers imaginatively and emotionally cater to people's insecurities and lack of self-confidence. Particularly susceptible are the young and the housebound, and women more than men. Advertisers are also extremely successful in creating new needs* and in stimulating envy. But we cannot lay the whole blame on advertisers. Many people today go shopping partly to advertise themselves—to be seen by other shoppers and use their reactions as feedback for deciding whether they need to dress differently or have additional accouterments. All this helps create the consumer personality and the "shop till you drop" mentality.

Many people today rely on what they buy for telling them who they are or defining what they want to be. They look to shopping not just to get necessities or to feel pleasure, but to give them identity* and meaning. It is a case of "I shop, therefore I am." When feeling down about themselves or deciding to try to become someone different, they become prey to believing that buying new clothes, getting a new hairstyle or purchasing a new car will somehow miraculously bring this about. The attraction of the new is central here. Underlying this is often the desire to forge a whole new identity for themselves. Window-shopping provides literal "models" to look at. The way others are outfitted or housed supplies other models, as does the lifestyle of media, sports and fashion celebrities.

Shopping also appeals to certain quasi-religious longings. The experience can give a brief, if limited, sense of transcendence by helping people to "get out of themselves" and enter a different, almost magical, world. Shopping malls in particular seek to stimulate this through their expansive designs, exotic colors, lofty ceilings and uplifting music.* The quest for bargains also promises people the experience of a kind of material "grace." What could be more exciting than discovering something you really want that hardly costs anything? For some this is a reflection or substitute, however pale, for experiencing God's free offer of the gospel. Unfortunately it is one that never fully satisfies, for we cannot buy an identity or a purpose, intimacy or happiness.* Trying to do this only leaves us at the mercy of promises of more, better and newer versions of the same.

In these ways we have moved from being citizens to primarily consumers. This contains the risk that people themselves will become commodities to be bought by advertising, and sometimes even sold off through the sale of mailing lists. Like all commodities, from the point of view of the economist, producer, advertiser or salesperson, they are interchangeable, just numbers on a sales chart. In other cases people become compulsive or pathological spenders. For some women especially, shopping becomes a mood-elevating drug that feeds their poor self-image, makes them feel good and beautiful or restores a sense of excitement to their lives. This is a form of addiction* as powerful as dependence on alcohol or a chemical substance.

A Christian Perspective on Purchasing

How can we go shopping Christianly? In the first instance we should realize that we are not the first to search for a less material lifestyle. Others have traveled this route before, especially in the monastic tradition, early Anabaptist communities, the Quakers and Puritans, and most recently the Christian counterculture. All these people thought carefully about what, how much and when to buy, possess and consume.

The Bible also provides us with some basic perspectives. We need to remind ourselves that already, through Christ, we have been "bought at a price" (1 Cor 6:20), and therefore we do not have to buy our way to fullness of life. The model we should primarily seek to imitate is nothing less than Christ. As the Spirit transforms us into his image we become a "new creation," have a new identity and find a new direction. We should basically be content with whatever we have, knowing that God will at times lavish good things on us and at other times we may experience want (Phil 4:11). We ought to remember that since the form of this world is passing away, we should "buy something as if it were not [ours] to keep" (1 Cor 7:30). Indeed, freely giving away a generous proportion of what we earn is a responsibility (2 Cor 9:7-9). It is also important that we look to the Spirit to develop within us self-control, one of the prime fruits of the Spirit. If we "lack wisdom" in this or any other area, we are invited to ask God sincerely for it (Jas 1:5).

What follow are some general principles for resisting the consumer culture, refusing to be conned by manipulative advertising and distancing oneself from a consumer approach to life. These are designed to help us travel* in this world more lightly as resident aliens, whose prime loyalty belongs to a "better country" (Heb 11:13-16). First, as a family* or with other single friends or with your small group* in the church, begin to discuss the relationship between shopping and discipleship.* Through newspapers, magazines and books, investigate the facts about overconsumption and poverty* in your country and locality. Where you can do so reasonably and in a nonpressured way, make and grow things yourself rather than always being dependent on buying them. Collate your shopping trips into one or two a week, and where possible buy cooperatively rather than just for your individual or household needs. Discover places where prices are lower and packaging less wasteful. List specifically and budget carefully what you will buy, and resist the temptation to engage in impulse buying.

Many have found the following practical questions helpful in their shopping. If items are more than a certain price, ask the following questions:

☐ Why do you want the item, and are your reasons for doing so adequate?

☐ Do you have the budget to cover the cost, or will you have to put too much on credit*?

☐ Can you do without it, and what would you do with the money* if you didn't spend it this way?

☐ Would you be able to make the item, or would it be enough to get it secondhand?

☐ Do you need it now, or can it wait until you will use it more often?

☐ Have you, or those for whom you are buying it, made use of similar items already owned, or are you simply piling up items which will be little used?

☐ Can you borrow it or buy it with others so that several share a little-used, expensive product?

☐ If it is replacing something, do you have to replace it yet, or can you wait until it is worn out or broken?

☐ Is it fixable if it breaks, and is there an accessible, trustworthy repair center with reasonable prices?

☐ How much will it damage God's world, either by consuming scarce resources or by becoming nondisposable waste?

For those who are prey to impulse buying and overspending, here are further concrete suggestions about how to go shopping:

☐ Don't go shopping unless you have something specific in mind to buy.

☐ Go to the mall only with a definite purchase or fixed amount of money in mind.

☐ Wear a watch* or place a time limit

on how long you can "afford" to stay or shop.

☐ Take someone else with you, but not a person similarly vulnerable to the mall's enticements.

☐ Evade "sale traps" and query whether you really need the bargains on offer.

☐ Plan gifts for major holidays ahead so you do not run around in a last-minute panic.

☐ Delay big expenditures until you have had the opportunity to reconsider their necessity and check out others' prices.

☐ If in doubt about buying something, don't buy it. And every so often go without something significant.

☐ Develop an appreciation for the social aspects of the mall, or, if this is insufficient, don't meet others there.

☐ If married, promise yourself that you will tell your spouse everything you buy.

Above all, remember that God loves us just as much whether we have much or less, whether everything matches or not and whether we are in or out of fashion. All these suggestions are designed to help us shop "as to the Lord" rather than simply according to our own, others' or society's desires. In all this it is important to take just one step at a time rather than trying to change established patterns overnight. Keep in mind that the goal is not modesty or simplicity for its own sake, but for what it reflects of the values* of the kingdom. You can be open to occasionally buying freely and generously when this is appropriate in terms of God's purposes. Inexpensiveness or cheapness is not necessarily good in itself. Often it is more economical to buy for quality and durability. Also, emphasize the joyfulness and fun of a less consumer-oriented approach to life rather than laying heavy guilt trips on oneself or others.

See also CONSUMERISM; MONEY; SIMPLER LIFESTYLE; STEWARDSHIP; WEALTH.

References and Resources

R. W. Fox and T. J. Lears, *The Culture of Consumption: Critical Essays in American History, 1880-1980* (New York: Pantheon, 1983); M. Giordan, *The Great Consumer Con: How to Beat It* (London: Temple Smith, 1978); J. Kavanaugh, *Still Following Christ in a Consumer Culture* (New York: Orbis, 1991); L. Shames, *The Hunger for More: Searching for Values in an Age of Greed* (New York: Times Books, 1989); R. Shields, ed., *Lifestyle Shopping: The Subject of Consumption* (New York: Routledge, 1992); R. J. Sider, ed., *Living More Simply: Biblical Principles and Practical Models* (Downers Grove, Ill.: InterVarsity Press, 1980); M. Starkey, *Born to Shop* (London: Monarch, 1989).

Robert Banks

SHOPPING MALLS

Shopping malls have become a central fact of modern life. As the hub around which most people's purchasing revolves, they are at the center of commercial life. Their main predecessors were the late nineteenth-century luxurious arcades and emporia, or department stores, that appeared in Europe and America. In California during the twenties and thirties came the supermarket, or food mart equivalent of the department store. The first enclosed shopping mall was built in Southdale, Minnesota, in 1956, and many pedestrian malls were built in the decade that followed. The vertical galleries and or more spacious shopping plazas developed in the late seventies. By 1985 there were fifteen thousand enclosed shopping malls in the United States alone, with an annual turnover of around 5 billion dollars. Most recently we have seen the arrival of the giant megamalls or shopping worlds, comparable in size to older downtowns or suburban centers.

The typical suburban shopping mall has somewhere between one hundred and two hundred shops and several hundred thousand square feet of floor space. The megamalls are in a different category: the MetroCentre, Gateshead, outside Newcastle-on-Tyne in England, has its own specially constructed railway station; the Mall of America, in Bloomington, near Minneapolis, Minnesota, occupies seventy-eight acres; and the West Edmonton Mall in Canada, the world's largest, covers the equivalent of forty-eight city blocks. For all their similarities, however, there are national and regional differences between malls. Outside North America, shopping malls tend to include supermarkets as the main anchor stores. They also have more regular public transportation.* Malls are more numerous and in closer proximity in the United States, in some regions one for every 175,000 people. Where the climate is sunny and mild, malls may be partly or even wholly outdoors. More recently we have seen the construction of smaller, elitist malls for an upper-class clientele.

Popularity and Significance of Shopping Malls

Over the last fifty years shopping malls have become extremely popular. Why is this so? Due to the variety of shops there is greater choice. Since stores are closer together, shopping* itself is easier and more efficient. Direct public transportation, easy access by car and parking are convenient. Malls provide a safer, cleaner and more climate-controlled environment. In general they lend themselves to a more casual and egalitarian approach to shopping that fits our less formal and less elitist culture.* For all these reasons, people find shopping malls the most effective way to do their purchasing. The malls themselves are also designed from top to bottom to capitalize on this and induce impulse buying. This is why mall goers often have to walk considerable distances to reach elevators, cross upper-level galleries or find toilets and why anchor stores are placed at the extremities so that shoppers have to pass a range of smaller shops going to and from them. Old town centers, department stores, shopping centers, and minimalls have difficulty competing with the ambiance and convenience of malls.

This is not the whole story. Studies reveal that approximately 40 percent of mall goers do not go to buy. They have other reasons—symbolic, social, festive and religious—for spending time in malls. For example, malls appeal strongly to people's fantasies. They are shopping palaces in which people can indulge their material dreams, wishes and hopes. Even though people may not have the money to buy their dreams, there is always the substitute satisfaction of window shopping. In this way everyone can share the experience of royalty. Malls also appeal to people's desire to be with or even ahead of the times. The presence of futuristic architecture* is an example of this. Yet malls also appeal to nostalgia. They evoke this through reproducing in their galleries or atriums elements of small-town life: main street, the city park or the village square. This is attractive to those cut off from their roots who have longings for a more integrated and animated life.

Shopping malls also exercise a strong appeal to those wanting to socialize. "See you at the mall" is a very common expression. For teenagers—*mallrats* as they are sometimes called—it is a place to seek out or hang out with peers, particularly on Friday and Saturday evenings. For others visiting malls is a way of overcoming the loneliness of the suburbs. This is especially true for housebound mothers, who can join with each other in an expedition that is more an excuse for company than for buying anything. Older people, fearful for their safety on the streets, are also attracted to the mall. Many exercise and meet there, and some malls open up early to welcome them or

provide meetings rooms where they can hold functions. The social center of malls is the food court. This is generally a free and open space, with a picnic atmosphere, where people can come and go, eat and talk, in pleasant and upbeat surroundings. As malls add to their complexes hotels, conference facilities, libraries, other educational activities, professional services, civic functions and cultural functions, the social and communal significance of the mall is growing.

Malls appeal to those who are looking for fun and festivity. They are commercial fairgrounds or amusement parks, providing a variety of entertainments.* These include stage performances by musicians, dancers, variety acts, pantomimes, puppet shows and clowns, as well as visits by radio and television* celebrities. The spirit of a carnival and pleasure resort is enhanced by the bright lights, vibrant colors, echoing microphones and pervasive sound of music. Increasingly there are playgrounds, carousels, fun arcades, cinemas, zoos, fairground rides, pools and ice rinks. This tells us that shopping can be fun, a message the mall retailers hope we will hear. But this message is always on the edge of telling us that there is more to life than shopping, a risk they take in introducing so great an element of play.* In the most sophisticated malls, such as the Mall of America, the centerpiece is a large theme park, a small Disneyland. The whole mall revolves around this. This and other attractions have made megamalls huge tourist attractions, to which people travel* by charter bus or plane from hundreds and thousands of miles away.

Though many people do not realize it, part of the appeal of shopping malls is their religious dimension. Malls provide us with a sense of order and orientation: they are planned and purposeful environments, generally with a center, certain cyclical features and a quadrilateral shape echoing the four points of the compass. They create a miniature ordered cosmos, in which for a time we can "live and move and have our being" (Acts 17:28), and come away reenergized. It is no accident that malls often have the word *center* in their names nor that their actual center contains such mythical symbols of life as running water and trees. With their soaring ceilings, vaulting skylights, aerial walkways, echoing sounds and dizzying mezzanines, they provide a sense of transcendence. This a place where you can be taken out of yourself, experience a different world and come away uplifted. On the part of the designers, this is all quite intentional.

Malls not only exploit most of the main religious seasons of the year; their design and façade often reflect church architecture (*see* Church Building). The basic basilica model—a long rectangle with cross aisles—is central to the interior design of most malls. In some respects they are simply a collection of intersecting basilica-shaped galleries. Other malls go further and reproduce the outside look of the basilica. Newer malls even contain chapels, where people can meditate, spiritual counseling can be sought and, in some cases, church services are held. Many people regard the mall, whatever the architecture, as a sanctuary from the pressures and vicissitudes of the outside world. So the mall is not just a consumer marketplace, but it is in some sense a sacred space, a cathedral or temple to fulfill quasi-religious needs* and longings. Interestingly, the most influential figure in the early development of enclosed shopping malls was James Rouse, a lay Christian with an articulate theological understanding of malls' communal and religious character.

Given these factors, it not surprising

the mall plays such a central role in our culture. It is now the place where families* spend more time together than in any other activity, including the church.* For many people, shopping and visits to the shopping mall are at the center of both creating and expressing their lifestyle. Others have become so-called shopaholics, who are engaged in compulsive purchasing behavior, with the shopping mall the main place where they get their daily or regular fix.

Responsible and Spiritual Use of Shopping Malls

The question is twofold: How consonant with Christian values or how idolatrously opposed to them are the interests served, activities undertaken and atmosphere established in the shopping mall, and how can we approach them with Christian integrity? To find an answer, we need to ask a related question: Where exactly is God in the shopping mall? This is a good question to ponder in a shopping mall itself, while walking* around or sitting down and observing what goes on.

Some conclude, contradicting Psalm 139, that God is nowhere to be found. But God is always present in followers of Christ who work in or visit the mall, especially in their contact or fellowship* with one another. Since in some measure the image of God is reflected in all people, God is present in them and it. Any products or services provided by the mall that are necessary, or generally beneficial, also have God's endorsement. So too does anything that is done in God's name, according to the character of Christ and as an expression of the Spirit's creative gifts. The provision of employment to a wide range of people, with all that flows from that to others, including giving amongst other things to the church, has God's active imprint upon it and in it. The presence of shops with an overt religious commitment, such as

Christian bookstores, points to God's presence as well.

Still, there are negative and idolatrous influences in the mall. This is present whenever people look to the mall for more than can rightly be expected of it and when mall owners purport to offer more than they properly can. Malls also overstep the mark when they claim to be the new town center. This is true only in a limited way. They are very middle-class institutions, which are not generally located near or patronized by blue-collar people. Space in the mall is not open to all who wish to enter it but is policed by security staff, who ensure that undesirable people are asked to leave. In some malls young people are forbidden to walk around in groups over a certain number. Generally speaking public meetings cannot be held in a mall, literature cannot be handed out, movie* or film cameras cannot be used, and evangelism* cannot be overtly conducted.

In these and other ways, malls limit the democratic rights of citizens. Mall owners defend this by saying malls are private spaces and owners can set their own rules. Although this is true, malls pretend to be the new public spaces* as well. Also, there are now so many malls occupying such vast tracts of land where public rights* and privileges do not apply. For malls to become the democratic, multipurpose, public spaces they claim to be, many changes have to take place. Informally and formally, through the exercise of people power and legal sanctions, we need to encourage or, if necessary, force malls to move in this direction.

After the Mall?

Though they have dominated the retail scene for a generation, shopping malls themselves are now encountering strong competition from the newer discount power centers and factory outlet centers. These have increased several hundred percent in the last fifteen years. With prices often 20-50 percent lower than prices at normal retail outlets, power and outlet centers have business turnover that is often proportionally double that of malls. In a few places power centers and outlet centers are setting up alongside or with one another, providing even stronger competition. Some of the new festival marketplaces, with their less synthetic open-air character and more attractive natural or historical surroundings, are also intruding on the mall's dominance. In the short term, however, the mall's preeminence seems secure.

See also CITY; CONSUMERISM; MONEY; PUBLIC SPACES; SHOPPING.

References and Resources
J. Jacobs, *The Mall* (Prospect Heights, Ill.: Waveland Press, 1985); W. Kowinski, *The Malling of America: An Inside Look at the Great Consumer Paradise* (New York: Morrow, 1985); I. G. Zepp Jr., *The New Religious Image of Urban America: The Shopping Mall as Ceremonial Center* (Westminster, Md.: Christian Classics, 1986).

Robert Banks

SICKNESS

Strangely enough, not everyone believes that sicknesses are real. The philosopher Peter Sedgwick comments that "outside the significance that man voluntarily attaches to certain conditions, there are not illnesses or diseases in nature" (quoted in Beauchamp and Walters, p. 74). H. T. Engelhardt Jr. similarly remarks, "One draws a line between innocent physiological or psychological findings and pathological findings because of particular human values in a particular circumstance, not because of the discovery of an essential distinction" (quoted in Engelhardt, pp. 173-74). So, it is thought, disease, illness or sickness are creations of one's decision. This view has also been advocated by religious thinkers, notably by followers of Christian Science, although on entirely different grounds. They believe that God is the only reality and apart from God everything else, including sin, sickness and death, are mere appearances. Sickness is an illusion due to our forgetfulness of God. This produces fear, which is the true basis of all illnesses and is actually illness itself. "Take away fear, and at the same time you have also removed the soil on which sickness thrives" (quoted in Barth, p. 365). Jesus' task consists in freeing humanity from the illusion of sin, sickness and death.* This teaching does not stand up to the scrutiny of the Scriptures, which teaches that even though God is indeed the basis of all reality, God is not the only reality. Humankind is also a reality, a different one created by God and loved by him (Gen 1—2).

Sin, evil, sickness and death are real consequences of our willful disobedience of our Creator, a disobedience that ushers in broken relationships with God, each other and nature. These are tragic realities and certainly are not illusions. We believe with Karl Barth that "sickness is real . . . as an encroachment on the life which God has created" (p. 366). Jesus Christ actually died on the cross to conquer the realities of sin, sickness and death.

Another school of philosophy holds that disease, illness and sickness are not merely mental or social constructions but refer to conditions objectively found in nature. In this view, there is a single unifying characteristic that underlies all diseases and sicknesses: an interference with one or more normal functions. A disease or sickness is a deviation from the normal operation of the human species. This deviation may be the result of congenital malformations (for example, cleft palate, heart defects) or of a hostile environment (for example, bacteria, accident, pollution*).

The crux of the matter is to define what constitutes *normal*. In a relativistic culture, some want to deny an absolute standard of normalcy. Christopher Boorse, who holds an objective view of diseases and illnesses, cites C. Daly King as saying that "the normal is objectively, and properly, to be defined as that which functions in accordance with its design" (quoted in Beauchamp and Walters, p. 93). To Boorse, the human species *(Homo sapiens)* is designed to pursue a hierarchy of goals such as survival and reproduction; diseases and illnesses are malfunctions that do not conform to the designer's specifications towards achieving these goals. This root idea of design in relation to disease and illness is consistent with the doctrine of the image of God, which teaches that human beings are created to be God's image bearer with a definite purpose to glorify God (*see* Health). So with Barth we view sickness "as the forerunner and messenger of death" and therefore as "unnatural and disorderly": "It is an element in the rebellion of chaos against God's creation. It is an act and declaration of the devil and demons. . . . It is neither good nor is willed and created by God at all, . . . but is real, effective, powerful and menacing . . . to the man who has fallen from God and become his enemy" (p. 366).

Sickness as Disease and Illness

So far we have used the words *disease, illness* and *sickness* interchangeably. In fact, they are not fully identical. Illness and disease may be thought of as distinct, yet interrelated, aspects of that state of unhealth we may call *sickness*. We use the term *disease* to refer to the biological dimension of sickness that can be quantitatively measured through scientific laboratory tests or qualitatively observed through signs and manifestations. The term *illness* is reserved for the more subjective or psychological dimensions of sickness. In other words, disease is a malfunction or a maladaptation of biologic and psychophysiologic processes in the individual, whereas illness is a personal reaction to the experience of the disease. But this does not mean that they must coexist. Sometimes an individual may complain of feeling ill for which no anatomical, biochemical or physiological malfunction, that is, objective disease, can be identified, as, for example, with adjustment and aromatization disorders. Conversely, some diseases may also exist without the person feeling illness, for example, as with asymptomatic hypertension and atherosclerotic heart disease. Furthermore, an objective disease may, under certain circumstances, be induced by a subjective illness, for example, certain forms of peptic ulcer disease.

This distinction between the objective (disease) and subjective (illness) is particularly important in the treatment of sickness. Western physicians trained in a biomedical paradigm are better equipped to detect and treat diseases than to perceive and address the patient's experience of illness. While they focus their attention on the cure of the disease, they tend to overlook the patient's subjective needs entailed by the disease, thus not attending to the patient's illness. In some cases, the disease may have been cured, but the patient remains ill, sometimes even more ill because of the physician's failure to recognize the inner personal dimension of the sickness. When a person is afflicted by a disease, it involves more than the particular "dis-eased" part of the anatomy or physiology; rather, the whole person is affected.

The personal negative feelings may take the form of a sense of physical failure, mortality or despair due to loss of control over one's destiny. Furthermore, sickness includes an interpersonal and social dimension ranging from assuming a sick role, thus being freed from certain routine duties and responsibilities, to becoming disconnected and isolated from the world in which one lives. A diminished self-esteem is often experienced by the patient. In short, a "dis-eased" person experiences a loss of both individual autonomy and social interaction. Consequently, a person's disease may be cured, but unless these dimensions of life are regained, he or she may be unhealed and remain sick both at the personal and social level. It is for this reason we see in Jesus' healing ministry that he was concerned, not with physical restoration alone, but with restoration of relationships, especially with God (*see* Healing).

Sickness and Suffering
The distinction between disease and illness also helps us to understand suffering when we fall sick. In becoming ill, we suffer our disease. In the modern Western culture we are profoundly influenced by a utilitarian philosophy committed to maximize personal happiness. As a result we tend to see any sense of "ill-being" or disease as an unqualified evil that must be removed at all cost. But illness is not always as negative as it sounds; becoming ill often serves good purposes. Feeling pain alerts us to the accidental disease of injury and reminds us to attend to it. Without the sensation of pain or the feeling of becoming ill, we would be harmed further. So the illness of pain serves the most useful and necessary protective function for our body. Likewise, guilt may be considered as a form of mental/emotional illness, which warns us that something is wrong and makes us pause in what we may be doing. For many, it is precisely the painful experience of guilt that often is instrumental in leading to spiritual conversion.

In the Bible sufferings, including those associated with sickness, are not something good in itself (Lk 13:1-5; Jn 5:14). But it falls short of saying that suffering is an absolute disvalue. Suffering becomes an occasion in which people grow in perseverance and maturity leading to wisdom and obedience to God (Heb 5:7-9; Jas 1:2-8). In suffering, people are given the opportunity to cultivate the virtue of contentment, which is independent of the circumstances of life; they experience a joy of victory over the ill feeling (Rom 8:35-37; Phil 4:11-12). In our sickness we learn to trust and depend on God (2 Cor 12:9) and renew our appreciation of God's faithfulness. Often it is in our sickness that we are exposed to and overcome our own self-centeredness (Prov 3:11-12; Is 48:10; Heb 12:5-11; Rev 3:1) and gain the new capacity of "com-passion" to comfort others (2 Cor 1:3-5). Perhaps the greatest value of all is that our sickness reminds us of our creaturely limitation and finitude as a human reality, a reality not as an accident of evolution but a reality imposed by God. In our weakness and limitation we are forced to encounter God as our Creator, Lord and Judge, yet at the same time we are given the chance to experience a loving merciful Father, who has given up his Son as our healer. So our sickness is not only the "forerunner and messenger of death and judgment," but with Karl Barth we may affirm that it is also "the forerunner and messenger of the eternal life" that God has promised to humankind (p. 373).

To see positive value in our sickness and the suffering that comes with it is not to justify them, only to point out the redemptive possibilities in an otherwise unqualified evil. Once we see them from God's perspective, we may have an entirely different way to deal with our sickness and suffering. In fact, the real test of our commitment to a God-centered life is precisely in how we deal with suffering in our sickness. The supreme example is provided by Jesus in his obedience to God in dealing with life's sufferings (Heb 5:8) and the suffering of the cross (Mk 14:34). As disciples of Christ, we are called to suffer with our Master. As a slave of Christ, Paul considers that his sickness and suffering (2 Cor 11:23-25) are related to those of Christ (Col 1:24-26). In the light of the redemptive possibilities of sickness, we are better able to evaluate our experience of disease and illness and should be less inclined to want to get rid of them at all cost.

See also BODY; HEALING; HEALTH.

References and Resources

K. Barth, *Church Dogmatics* 3/4 (Edinburgh: T & T Clark, 1961); T. L. Beauchamp and L. Walters, eds., *Contemporary Issues in Bioethics* (Belmont, Calif.: Wadsworth, 1989); C. Boorse, "Health as a Theoretical Concept," *Philosophy of Science* 44 (1977) 542-73; H. T. Engelhardt Jr., *The Foundations of Bioethics* (New York: Oxford University Press, 1986); S. Hauerwas, *Suffering Presence* (Notre Dame, Ind.: University of Notre Dame Press, 1986); S. E. Lammers and A. Verhey, eds., *On Moral Medicine* (Grand Rapids: Eerdmans, 1987).

Edwin Hui

SIMPLER LIFESTYLE

The focus of what follows is the *simpler,* not *simple,* lifestyle. It is not an argument for the simplest possible lifestyle, as lived by monks and nuns in the past or by counterculture communities in the present, but for simplifying our lifestyle in an acquisitive and consumer-oriented culture (*see* Consumerism). Because our society is so shaped by such strong materialistic impulses, so permeated by powerful advertising* and so oriented to shopping* as a way of life, most of us need help in reducing our expectations and expenditure to more reasonable levels. We need to shift from "more" to "enough." This becomes even more necessary when certain basic Christian values* are taken into account. Some people's calling is to follow a *simple* lifestyle, and others have little choice in the matter. It is not these people but the bulk of us who are here in view.

Earlier Approaches to Simplifying Life
The desire to simplify life and major on essentials is not new to the modern world. The earliest Quakers aimed for simplicity in dress and life as well as in manners and worship, and even developed "sumptuary laws" to provide practical guidance for fellow "friends." The Puritans in both England and America did the same and placed a high value on thrift. We should not see either group as austere-minded or life-denying. Both maintained a real place for enjoying the basic good things of life, but they were also committed to putting their savings at the service of beneficial investment* or people in need. Other groups, such as the Moravians and Mennonites, and later Shakers, developed an even more distinctive and communal way of life, in which modesty and contentment were everywhere present.

Less shaped by Christian ideals, though still influenced by them, was the simplicity present in the best early republican circles in America, in the romantic simplicity focused on nature and domestic life of the English Lake poets such as Wordsworth and Coleridge, and in the related rustic simplicity sought by transcendentalists like Thoreau or Emerson. These ideals were followed by the naturalists, with their interest in handmade arts and crafts, who influenced the later counterculture and ecological* movements, both of which developed an anticonsumerist stance. Meanwhile those with a strong sense of vocation, including many Christians working among underprivileged groups or in overseas missions, developed a simpler form of life on the basis of their religious convictions and cultural circumstances.

Biblical Perspectives on a Simpler Lifestyle
Much could be said about simplicity from both the Old and the New Testament. The former grew out of a nomadic, later agrarian, way of life, some of whose values carried over into life in larger towns and cities. The Mosaic laws, prophetic injunctions and advice of the wise all inveigh against ostentatious wealth and indulgent luxury (see Wealth), as well as the self-centered and oppressive actions which tend to flow from these. Many laws in Exodus and Deuteronomy exist to prevent too great an inequity developing among the people, and to encourage the proper sharing of wealth and property so that the poor and weak are not disadvantaged (see Stewardship). The surrounding nations are frequently criticized for their quest for ostentatious wealth and displays of luxury in both the public and the private arena. The Israelites themselves are warned of the dangers of the too comfortable life of nice houses, growing herds, increasing income and abundance of food (Deut 8:11-19).

While in the public sphere there is a place for building a temple, a royal palace and other public works and, after the exile, for rebuilding parts of the city of Jerusalem and restoring the temple, in all these things a sense of proportion is generally maintained. Private wealth is not condemned if viewed and used properly, that is, seen as a blessing from God and regarded as a privilege to be shared generously with others. There are dire warnings against those who have the good things of life but ignore the poor on their doorstep (Amos 6:4-7) and strong endorsements of those who take the opposite attitude (Ps 112:1, 3-5, 9). The ideal woman, involved in business as well as raising her family, is depicted as opening her hands to the needy (Prov 31:20). Alongside these portraits there are also exemplary figures such as some of the prophets, or the divinely appointed "suffering servant" whose modest appearance and way of life may lead others to ignore him but who should not be overlooked by the faithful people of God (Is 53:2-3).

Throughout the New Testament we are presented with pictures and stories, principles and recommendations, that throw light on the importance of developing a lifestyle that is consistent with the purposes and character of God. We find these in the life of Jesus and the disciples in the Gospels, in the portraits of the early church in Acts and in the directions to churches in the apostolic letters. Jesus' way of life exemplifies perfectly the simple, though not austere, way of life foretold of the suffering servant (Mt 8:20), and his teaching encouraged an attitude toward possessions that was free of preoccupation and anxiety (Lk 12:22-32) and full of willingness to share them with those less fortunate (Lk 12:33-34). The early Christians in Jerusalem committed themselves to sharing some, though not all, of their resources with one another, especially with those in need (Acts 2:44-46; 4:32-35).

Paul has much to say about lifestyle. At the heart of his approach is the conviction that we have been "purchased" already (1 Cor 6:20) and that the basic "work" for our salvation has already been accomplished (Eph 2:8-9): no longer can our lives revolve around buying and consuming or around endless work and acquisition. We are also reminded that it is who we are and are becoming in the Spirit that is decisive, not what we own or achieve. This means that being or becoming is more important than having or doing. This involves developing self-control (Gal 5:23), one of the cardinal fruits of the Spirit, and generosity (2 Cor 8:8-9), one of the chief characteristics of Christ. We should also be aware that we are living "between the times" and therefore always sit somewhat loose to our acquisitions, never making them our chief focus (1 Cor 7:29-31).

In developing our way of life we should always have a view to the situation of our neighbors* (1 Cor 10:28) and the plight of those in need (2 Cor 8:1-5). On the other hand, we should not be overscrupulous about what we spend our money* on, lest we pay this too much attention and get caught up in casuistry (1 Cor 10:25-26). We should always be open to and grateful to God for the good things from God's creation* and providence that we enjoy (1 Tim 4:4-5). Central to our whole approach to life should be a willingness to accept whatever comes our way, whether it be much or little, on the principle that through Christ we can find contentment in all situations and that God will supply all that we need (Phil 4:11-13). Our life should be characterized by modesty in material things (1 Pet 3:3-4) rather than a greedy search for gain (1 Tim 3:8). We should be satisfied with the basic necessities of life, such as food and clothing, and grateful for anything extra that comes along (1 Tim 6:8).

General Principles for a Simpler Lifestyle

Before suggesting some practical guidelines for developing a simpler lifestyle, some clarifications and broader principles are worth noting.

A simpler lifestyle includes the way we spend our time and do our work as well as the amount of money we spend or goods we buy. It is about a total way of life, not just about living standards.

The issue at stake is not whether or not we should consume, but that we be producers as well as consumers. It is also about what and how much to consume.

We need to challenge the false views of those who are opposed to and those who are advocates of a simpler lifestyle. On the one hand, it is not true that maintaining present spending levels or increasing them is necessary for the health of the economy; the latter would just have to adjust to new spending habits and in the process could develop new enterprises and services. On the other hand, it is not true that a simpler lifestyle is less complicated: often the reverse is the case, as it sometimes takes more time, at least initially, to discover alternative sources of items or ways of doing things.

Related to the last point, it is important not to idealize greater simplicity. In some cases it is better to reckon with certain realities of life rather than retain unrealistic expectations or undertake extraordinary, sometimes exhausting, efforts to live according to them.

*Following a simpler lifestyle does not mean being opposed to technology.** Instead the right technology can be one of the agents for simplifying certain responsibilities.

Greater simplicity is a means, not an aim. Turning it into the latter gets it out of perspective with other important priorities, making it an idol to which they are sacrificed.

Developing a simpler lifestyle is a corporate as well as an individual challenge. Not just individuals but families, churches and organizations* need to consider their use of time and standard of life from this perspective. This is particularly important for churches not only because they are generally so preoccupied with putting up bigger and better church buildings* or in creating more and more time-consuming programs, but because what they do provides an influential model to their members of the key priorities and values of the kingdom.

Working out how to simplify life is something we need the help of others to do properly. It is too complex and large a task for us to do alone, even in our families, and we need to be held accountable by others for the choices we make. Central to this whole process is asking God for help in prayer and seeking the discernment that comes from the Spirit.

Practical Guidelines for a Simpler Lifestyle

Various groups have suggested guidelines for developing a simpler lifestyle. There are suggestions elsewhere for dealing with the pace of life (see Busyness) and the pressure of time.* One of the best known set of recommendations for dealing with goods and possessions was produced by the Central Committee of the Mennonite Church. Among its suggestions are recommendations for growing a vegetable garden as a family project, walking or cycling where possible instead of using a car, developing your own leisure activities alongside others that are available, using fewer disposables, lodging where feasible with friends when away from home, avoiding clothing fashions and fads, mending and reactivating old clothing instead of getting rid of it, buying used furniture, buying smaller cars, moving into a smaller house or sharing a house with someone, and refraining from shopping for recreation.*

Out of our own accumulated experience we have developed the following simple set of questions, considerations and recommendations to help maintain a simpler form of life. These are not intended to be prescriptive, but rather suggestive of possibilities that can be pursued.

In terms of living space, think carefully about what a house is for in God's purposes rather than what you would like to own, and let that guide your choice to buy or rent, as well as the location, size and furnishings that are appropriate. This may mean a larger house to accommodate frequent guests or Christian workers, or a smaller house in a disadvantaged neighborhood in which ministry is being undertaken. The issue of housing* also raises questions about how large a mortgage, or how much a proportion of our income, we wish to commit to our accommodation needs. Beyond these specific questions, considerations and guidelines, we should think about the wider configuration of our lives. Do we have to live singly, or as a separate family unit, or could we share an apartment with another single, live in or start up a community,* or look for some cooperative housing arrangement?

In regard to moving around, ask yourself if an automobile is really necessary or if public transportation* could do the job.* If we do need a car, what kind would be most suitable to the responsibilities we have to family, friends, visitors, church, work and other ministry? Are we better off getting one secondhand or new? How much of what we earn can we responsibly spend on acquiring, maintaining and insuring it? What policy should we have for loaning it to others who may not have a car or one suitable for their purposes? Given the amount of noise,* pollution* and injuries they cause, how many cars is it appropriate for a family to own, or how much can we share vehicles even if at times it is inconvenient for one family member?

With respect to purchasing habits, why not replace things only as they wear out, rather than beforehand, and only purchase certain items—such as compact disks and books—for special occasions? For the rest, we ask the following questions to help us decide whether or not to buy a particular item: Can we do without it, or what would we do with the money if we didn't spend it on what we are considering? Can we borrow it or (as we have done with cars, lawnmowers, gardening equipment and VCRs) own it jointly with someone else?

Do we need it now, or can we put off buying it till later? Have we fully used up similar items we have already bought, such as having read the books we already own? To what extent will it damage God's world, and if it causes too much, is there some alternative? There are also other important issues such as buying quality products, even if they cost more at the time, because of the longer life they will have overall.

Simplifying one's life raises a range of larger issues concerned with time as already mentioned, with calling* or vocation, with community and with our understanding and practice of ownership.* It is a complex issue in an already complex world, but one that is becoming increasingly important for citizens of the kingdom of God. At stake is nothing less than reflecting the values of the kingdom of God in the midst of a greedy and needy world.

See also OWNERSHIP; SHOPPING.

References and Resources

J. McInnes, *The New Pilgrims* (Sydney: Albatross, 1980); D. E. Shi, *In Search of the Simple Life: American Voices Past and Present* (Layton, Utah: Peregrine Smith, 1986); J. R. Shortney, *How to Live on Nothing* (New York: Pocket, 1971); R. J. Sider, ed., *Living More Simply: Biblical Principles and Practical Models* (London: Hodder & Stoughton, 1980); Simple Living Collective, *Taking Charge: Personal and Political Change Through Simple Living* (San Francisco: American Friends Service Committee, 1975); Smallternatives Working Group, *Smallternatives: Personal Guide to Saving Energy and Money* (Sydney: Second Back Row Press, 1979); John V. Taylor, *Enough Is Enough* (London: SCM Press, 1975).

Julie and Robert Banks

SINGLENESS

It could be said that there is no such thing as singleness. We all live out the joys and sorrows of our lives within a rich complexity of relationships. This is God's intention for all human beings. John Donne was right: "No man is an island."

Western culture, however, has a different perspective. It assumes marriage* and sexuality* as the prime context of intimacy, whereas Scripture assumes and exemplifies a much larger context. Modern approaches have understood human beings biologically, with the sexual drive as one of the dominant motivational forces. A biblical view understands human beings as created for intimacy with God and with one another. Marriage is often a significant framework for the outworking of intimacy, but it is not the only framework. These things are foundational for a true understanding of singleness.

Our concept of singleness has significantly changed in the past twenty years. Previously *single* referred to a person who had never married and implied virginity. Today the number of adults who are single by choice or circumstance has increased. It now encompasses not only the unmarried but also those who are divorced or widowed: "No longer does it imply virginity, merely the absence of a current sexual partner" (Foyle, p. 134).

In the quest for personal fulfillment so prevalent today, more people are looking for alternatives to the previously accepted social and sexual norms. They are deciding for themselves how they want to live their lives. In the West the single lifestyle is more accepted and more attractive than it has ever been. How does all this affect the Christian person who is single by choice or by circumstance?

Marriage is clearly a God-ordained institution, a context for sexual expression, child rearing and lifelong friendship.* It is a metaphor resonant of deeper spiritual realities, the foundational structure of most human societies. However, by focusing almost exclusively on marriage and the nuclear family* as the norm, as well as the prime context for intimacy, the church* has not told the whole truth and has, in some ways, bought into the prevailing culture.* The message conveyed by the church and by the culture is that to be single is to be unfulfilled, to be somehow not whole. What is needed is a much broader biblical understanding. It is important to consider the reasons why people are single, to put singleness in its true biblical context and to look realistically at some of the challenges and opportunities experienced by those who are single.

Reasons for Singleness

There are many different reasons why people are single. Singleness can be voluntarily chosen or involuntarily imposed; it can be temporary or long-term. All people are single at some point in their lives, either during early adulthood or, often, in old age.

Many people are single because of the death of a spouse. Unexpectedly they find themselves alone and having to face a complexity of tasks and feelings never before experienced. This kind of singleness is perhaps the one best understood by other people, for it fits fairly smoothly into society's attitudes and values.* Increasingly people end up being single because of divorce.* This is nearly always accompanied by emotional turmoil and is difficult for all involved. These two reasons for singleness, with their roots in loss, grief* and suffering, can make the adjustment to singleness prolonged and painful.

There are those who view marriage as normative but for a variety of reasons are not yet married. They may be postponing marriage until they are vocationally established; they may be caring for an elderly parent; or they may explain their singleness by saying that they have just never been at the right place at the right time for the right person to come along.

Some people have deliberately chosen a single life. There are those who have opted to focus time and energy on a challenging career. Others, observing those who unreflectively marry because somehow it is "the thing to do," decide to make a different choice. Those who go into religious orders voluntarily take a vow of celibacy and, although committed to a covenant community,* remain single. Others, by choosing to go overseas as missionaries, may circumstantially be eliminating marriage as an option. Still others, because of a homosexual* orientation, do not consider marriage as personally viable. Perhaps more than one is aware, the choice to remain single might be based on both conscious and unconscious psychological factors, such as a fear of intimacy, a strong desire for independence, unrealistic expectations of relationships or unresolved issues in one's family background.

For all of us, part of our being made in the image of God includes the capacity for love* and communication. This implies the desire for personal intimacy—the longing to be transparent and vulnerable within the context of relationships. Marriage and family are gifts from God and provide not only the stabilizing infrastructure of society but also a potentially rich context for relational intimacy. Most adults therefore long to find a place in such relationships. As the years pass and for one reason or another a person does not marry, doubts of different kinds set in. One looks inward, asking, *Is there something wrong with me?* or *Has God made a mistake?* Some of these questions can be healthy and can lead to constructive self-assessment, change and often a deeper level of trusting God.

Acceptance of Singleness

Adults who expect to marry do not always accept their single state immediately. Like many other experiences of life, the acceptance is often a gradual process. Each step is facilitated by a growing understanding of oneself as well as by God's grace.

Accepting reality is an important aspect of this process. As the awareness that one is single begins to take hold, there is often a genuine sense of loss. This is accompanied by grief as one acknowledges not only the lack of a marriage partner but also the loss of children and even grandchildren. The hope of creating and being part of a family unit fades. These losses are real, and grief is an appropriate response. Thus, it is important to acknowledge that acceptance is often initially accompanied by significant personal pain, which may recur at different ages and stages of life, and to acknowledge also that marriage has its pains and disappointments.

There is a further step in this process. Maturity comes when one is able to accept singleness in the present as from God and to trust that God is wise and loving and is well able to meet one's needs. At times this acceptance can be a catalyst enabling a person to embrace life in a new way and to understand and experience a broader context for intimacy. Instead of focusing on what has not been given or on what has been lost, one is able to see, and receive with thanks, the good gifts that have been given.

Some people will pass through these stages with a minimum of pain, but others will struggle deeply. The church as a place of community and compassion can be a great help for single people struggling to accept various aspects of their situation. In addition, a theology adequate to encompass these realities must be developed. It is the scriptural insights into singleness that will provide the needed comfort, strength and perspective.

Scriptural Insights

To have a true biblical understanding of singleness, we need to set it in a much larger context. We need to understand that first and foremost we are relational beings. We are created at the loving initiative of the triune God, who from before the foundation of the world experiences and expresses love and communication. We are created to be in relationship with God. And it is this relationship that uniquely gives us our deepest sense of identity. We are creatures of the Creator; we are sinners known and forgiven by the Redeemer; and we are loved children able to call God *Abba*.

We are also created to be in relationship with one another: "We are conceived in relationship; we are born into family relationship; we develop our sense of self in relationship and we know ourselves and are known in relationship" (McBride, p. 1). Being in relationship is the essence of what it means to be a human being, and God has provided for these relational needs in ways that are profound and wonderful.

Although sin has broken our relationship with God, ourselves, other people and creation, the glorious good news of the cross is that the way has been cleared for all of us to enter freely, by faith, into that relationship. There exists no Christian imperative to become married as soon as one can or to prefer marriage over singleness as more whole or wholesome (Collins, p. 11). Wholeness comes from relationship with God.

But there is more. God gives to us the gift of his family. He places us in relationship with one another, and we are called to listen,* to forgive,* to encourage one another. We are to love one another, bear one another's burdens and rejoice with one another. It is in the context of God's family that we develop our capacity for intimate relationship; we experience what it means to be sisters or brothers, mothers and fathers, to one another. It is in ever-deepening relationship with God and with one another in this family that our needs are met, that we discover that we know and are known, that we love and are loved, that we have the possibility of experiencing deep and long-lasting intimacy. As we grow in these relationships, we become more and more like the Lord Jesus (2 Cor 3:17-18).

Jesus clearly both taught about the permanence and dignity of marriage (Mt 19) and affirmed it by his presence at the wedding of Cana (Jn 2:1-11). He also taught the contrasting truth that marriage is not forever and will not be part of the way we relate in heaven (Lk 20:34). Moreover, from the biblical perspective it is clear that it is not marriage alone that provides the context of intimacy, but rather relationship with God and his family. And this is available to all people, whether married or single. A related resource and gift is friendship.

Jesus' singleness enabled him to focus on his messianic task; it also enables us to have insight into healthy ways of living as a single person. He lived out his life in close touch with his family and with a community of friends. He offered the men and women who knew him the love that he had experienced from the Father (Jn 15:9). He called them to care for one another with this same kind of love (Jn 13:34). We also see that Jesus was free to express love and care through human touch. He reached out and laid his hands on those who were in need of healing in both body and spirit. In loving humility he washed the feet of his friends and was quite comfortable to have John lean on him (Jn 13). He responded to the desperate touch of the woman with the hemorrhage (Mk 5) and the loving caresses of the woman known to all to be a sinner (Mk 14).

As well as forming committed, loving

relationships with the Twelve, Jesus also knew how to be alone. He spent forty days alone in the wilderness (Lk 4:2) and often withdrew from the crowds and even from his friends for times of solitude and prayer (Mk 1:35). In the last hours of his life he knew the anguishing aloneness of being forsaken by his friends and even by God. He is well able to understand us in our times of aloneness.

The events at the Garden of Gethsemane vividly illustrates that Jesus shared not only his thoughts but also his feelings with his friends. He was able to express his need for them to keep him company, to surround him and to stand with him as he faced not only death but separation from the Father (Mt 26:36-46). In both giving and receiving, Jesus models for us healthy, intimate interpersonal relationships.

The apostle Paul, who also was single, indicates that he had chosen this "better way" because it enabled him to focus on his primary calling to serve God. His logic is straightforward. Of necessity, married people must be most concerned with their spouses and children. Their interests are divided. However, those who are unmarried can be primarily concerned with serving God and others (1 Cor 7). He goes on to add, however, that both singleness and marriage are gifts from God. Ultimately we need to discover what our calling* is in this area. It is not simply a matter of choice. To choose marriage, or singleness, when we are not gifted for it could place us in a frustrating situation, though this does not rule out God's then supplying us with the gift.

Challenges and Graces

Singleness is described as a gift, but it must honestly be said that it is not always experienced as a gift. It can leave one feeling vulnerable and ill-equipped to deal with certain aspects of our humanity that are painful, such as loneliness, belonging and sexuality. It would be easy to think that these pains are unique to the single state, but they are not—they are human pains. Singleness provides a particular perspective for both experiencing and responding to these aspects of our humanity.

Loneliness. To speak of singleness is to imply aloneness; this is often equated with loneliness, which is what most people dread. Aloneness, however, is different from loneliness, and it is something we can choose, as Jesus did. It is crucial for our growth as Christians and need not be feared. It is often in times of aloneness that we can uniquely hear God. Loneliness, although painful, is at least a pain that we can do something about. It is often cured by focusing beyond ourselves and reaching out in love and hospitality* to someone else. Creating and sharing a home* with others can take the edge off loneliness, as can consciously developing loving relationships with both male and female friends of all ages.

Belonging. A poignant and often painful question of the single person is *To whom do I belong?* Married people have one another and their children, but a single person often has a sense of being adrift, not permanently anchored in relationships.

Here again the Scripture speaks strongly. We are called to worship because we belong: "O come, let us worship and bow down, let us kneel before the LORD, our Maker! For he is our God, and we are the people of his pasture, and the sheep of his hand" (Ps 95:6-7 NRSV). Ephesians reminds us that we are "no longer strangers," that we are "members of the household of God" (Eph 2:19 NRSV), belonging to one another in the community of faith. The bedrock truth for all of us is that in Christ we belong to him and to one another, and nothing "will be able to separate us from the love of God in Christ Jesus our Lord" (Rom 8:39 NRSV). We belong to God. We are his children, now and forever! This is the anchor that can bring comfort and steadiness when the belonging question rises. Further, we have friends. And in churches that offer real fellowship,* especially in small groups* and house churches, we can experience the grace of an extended Christian family.

Sexuality. Sex and *sexuality* are often used interchangeably and can thus be confusing. Both are God-given gifts. Sex is a biological drive oriented toward pleasure* and often procreation, whereas sexuality refers to the totality of our being, as reflected in the words in Genesis: "male and female he created them" (Gen 1:27 NRSV). Whether married or single, our sexuality impacts every aspect of who we are: our body* shape and functioning, our sense of self, our orientation to the world and to other people. The sexual drive is accompanied by a whole cluster of physical and emotional feelings that are part of being a healthy human being.

The Scripture is clear that sexual intercourse is to be expressed between a man and a woman within a covenant relationship of committed love and long-term faithfulness. In focusing on biological sex, society has removed it from this covenantal context and thus diminished its meaning and power. Single people are to wisely discipline their sexual thoughts and feelings while at the same time developing and appropriately expressing their sexuality. This requires personal and spiritual maturity. Failures of every kind occur, but God's kindness, forgiveness and restoration are real. In learning to responsibly handle all the dimensions of our sexuality, we learn many deep and important lessons about ourselves and God's grace.

Singleness then is to be understood and lived out in the broad biblical context of being relational beings, called into intimacy with God and others.

See also CALLING; DATING; FELLOWSHIP; FRIENDSHIP; HOSPITALITY; LOVE; MARRIAGE; SEXUALITY.

References and Resources

G. R. Collins, *It's O.K. to Be Single* (Waco, Tex.: Word, 1976); M. Foyle, "Overcoming Stress in Singleness," *Evangelical Mission Quarterly* 21 (April 1985) 134-41; A. Fryling, "The Grace of Single Living," in *HIS Guide to Sex, Singleness and Marriage*, ed. C. S. Board (Downers Grove, Ill.: InterVarsity Press, 1974) 74-79; S. Grenz, *Sexual Ethics: A Biblical Perspective* (Dallas: Word, 1990); J. McBride, "The Self in the Culture of the Therapeutic," unpublished lecture presented at Regent College, Vancouver, B.C., November 1994.

Thena Ayres

SLEEPING

We spend about a third of our lives sleeping but usually focus on sleep only when deprived of it. Since more and more people are suffering from sleep deprivation, at present it is the subject of much attention. There are various reasons for people's sleeping less than they should. Some are attempting to do too much (*see* Drivenness) and cut back on sleep to increase the time* at their disposal. Others are too uptight and preoccupied at the end of the day (*see* Stress) to rest* properly and therefore lose quality or quantity of sleep. Many carry their worries, plans and desires to bed with them and cannot relax enough to sleep well. Some live and work to an irregular rhythm and find their sleeping pattern sometimes disturbed (*see* Shiftwork).

One consequence of sleep deprivation is that insomnia has now become the major medical problem in newer Western societies. This lies at the root of the huge pharmacological industry in sleeping tablets and drugs for reducing stress.

When people do not get their proper sleep, they suffer more than a loss of physical energy. They have less psychological stamina, make poorer decisions and find it difficult to concentrate and think effectively. They also lose out on the equilibrium and, at times, insight that come from regular dreaming.*

Sleep in the Bible

While sleep is not a major topic in Scripture, the contexts in which it appears and the treatment Scripture gives it are instructive, both for sleep in itself and for the other activities that come with our bodies (eating,* staying warm or cool, etc.).

Job, in the midst of his arguments with his friends, provides a vivid description of his world—and ours:

Why are not times of judgment kept
by the Almighty,
and why do those who know him
never see his days?
Men remove landmarks;
they seize flocks and pasture them.
They drive away the ass of the father-
less;
they take the widow's ox for a
pledge.
They thrust the poor off the road;
the poor of the earth all hide themselves. . . .
They lie all night naked, without
clothing,
and have no covering in the cold.
(Job 24:1-4, 7 RSV)

It is a conflictive and dangerous world, a world in which those on the losing end can find themselves without the most basic of necessities. In our world at least one-sixth of the world's population lives in absolute poverty.* These poor, for whom even sleep can be problematic, form the constant background of this study.

For the world's actively literate the Preacher's observations may provide a more familiar starting point:

What has a man from all the toil and
strain with which he toils beneath the
sun? For all his days are full of pain,
and his work is a vexation; even in the
night his mind does not rest. This also
is vanity. (Eccles 2:22-23 RSV)

Life is hard, and this cuts into our sleep. Jacob, with Laban as his boss, would have agreed (Gen 31). Other texts witness to sleeplessness in different contexts (Job 7; Is 38).

Further, we are vulnerable during sleep, as the fates of Sisera (Judg 4), Samson (Judg 16) and Ishbosheth (2 Sam 4), the experience of Saul (1 Sam 26) and Job's portrait of the world (24:1-8) remind us. In summary, life itself is problematic and dangerous, and sleep increases our vulnerability on both counts. Things can go wrong while we sleep; people can do us wrong while we sleep.

Sleep as an Act of Faith

Given these threats, giving oneself over to sleep can be a basic expression of confidence, as, for instance, in Psalm 3:5-6:

I lie down and sleep;
I wake again, for the LORD sustains
me.
I am not afraid of ten thousands of
people
who have set themselves against
me round about. (RSV)

Because "he who keeps Israel will neither slumber nor sleep" (Ps 121:4 RSV), we can sleep. Psalm 127 reflects on this confidence, focusing on both God's protection and his gracious provision:

Unless the LORD builds the house,
those who build it labor in vain.
Unless the LORD watches over the city,
the watchman stays awake in vain.
It is in vain that you rise up early
and go late to rest,
eating the bread of anxious toil;
for he gives to his beloved sleep.
(vv. 1-2 RSV)

Jesus' sleep in the boat during the storm may be seen as an example of this confidence (Mt 8:24), a confidence that both natural processes and kingdom growth are accomplished by God even while we sleep. This possibility of sleep is shown in one of Jesus' parables:

The kingdom of God is as if a man should scatter seed upon the ground, and should sleep and rise night and day, and the seed should sprout and grow, he knows not how. The earth produces of itself. (Mk 4:26-29 RSV)

Because God provides, we can sleep. Sleep witnesses to a fundamental truth in the same way that keeping the sabbath* or the Lord's Day does: by God's grace we do not need to burn the candle at both ends to achieve prosperity or security. This witness has long found expression in vespers services and family prayers at night.

While sleep may be a gut-level expression of confidence, excessive sleep is simply an expression of folly:

How long will you lie there, O sluggard?
　When will you arise from your
　　sleep?
A little sleep, a little slumber,
　a little folding of the hands to rest,
and poverty will come upon you like
　a vagabond,
and want like an armed man.
　(Prov 6:9-11 RSV)

Both Jesus' sleep in the boat and Jonah's sleep in the boat (Jon 1:5-6) reveal character, but not the same character: one the sleep of faith, the other the sleep of a slothful escape from duty.

Forgoing Sleep

While trustful sleep may be the appropriate response in some situations, in others the appropriate response is to deprive oneself of sleep to pray or work.* God's watchfulness allows us to sleep securely, but we are also invited to participate in this watchfulness, forgoing sleep. Both biblical and extrabiblical evidence suggests that sleep was regularly broken for nighttime prayers, as witnessed in the Psalms: "When I think of thee upon my bed, and meditate on thee in the watches of the night" (Ps 63:6 RSV).

In more "acute" situations we find references to both prayer (2 Sam 12:16; Joel 1:13; Mt 26:36-46) and work through the night (2 Cor 11:27):

I will not give sleep to my eyes
　or slumber to my eyelids,
until I find a place for the LORD,
　a dwelling place for the Mighty
　　One of Jacob. (Ps 132:4-5 RSV)

These texts find a variety of contemporary liturgical expressions, in vigils before major feasts in the Christian year or periods of extended prayer in crisis situations. Jesus as he speaks of the urgency of the end times views sleeplessness as a metaphor for readiness: "Blessed are those servants whom the master finds awake when he comes" (Lk 12:37 RSV).

Because sleep needs to be broken off to participate in God's watchfulness, we need to find and follow an appropriate rhythm that expresses both our confidence in God's protection and our participation in God's watchfulness.

Sleep and Justice

Sleeping becomes an ethical issue largely when our conduct affects the sleep of others. Thus a proverb warns—only partly tongue in cheek—"He who blesses his neighbor with a loud voice, rising early in the morning, will be counted as cursing" (Prov 27:14 RSV).

More substantively, the Israelites were instructed not to take advantage of their neighbors' indebtedness to rob them of sleep:

If ever you take your neighbor's garment in pledge, you shall restore it to him before the sun goes down; for that is his only covering, it is his mantle for his body; in what else shall he sleep? And if he cries to me, I will hear, for I am compassionate. (Ex 22:26-27 RSV)

This theme also reappears in Job's declaration of innocence (Job 31:32).

Justice* is good news for the sleepless poor. It is striking that these texts do not start with sleep but offer a broad vision of justice in terms of loan guarantees or innocence. In that context the neighbor's sleep comes into the conversation. Our challenge, in a very different social setting, is to let our vision for justice be shaped by that vision so that our actions become good news for the poor in practical matters like sleep.

God's Sleep

What does God's watchfulness mean for the poor? Does God never slumber or sleep? The psalms—reflecting a liturgical tradition evidenced elsewhere in the ancient Near East—use sleep as a way of expressing God's absence:

Rouse thyself! Why sleepest thou, O Lord?
Awake! Do not cast us off for ever!
Why dost thou hide thy face?
Why dost thou forget our affliction and oppression? (Ps 44:23-34 RSV)

To have God asleep and the poor sleepless is an intolerable situation, theologically and existentially. Following the lead of the biblical witness, we should on the one hand learn from people like Job what our justice should look like and, on the other, cry out with the psalmist, with the poor, with Israel and with the church* until God does "wake up" and his kingdom come.

So faith not only gives us personal confidence to sleep but also compels us to cry out to God until we all can sleep securely. It is no surprise that secure sleep appears among the Old Testament's end-times promises, in Ezekiel 34:22-25 and Hosea 2:18:

And I will make for you a covenant on that day with the beasts of the field, the birds of the air, and the creeping things of the ground; and I will abolish the bow, the sword, and war from the land; and I will make you lie down in safety. (RSV)

Aids to Sleep

Sleeping properly, then, should be a regular part of our lives. It is honoring to God, beneficial to ourselves and advantageous for others. Apart from reliance on chemical aids to sleep, some nonmedical ways of dealing with insomnia to follow:

□ Wind down—don't go jogging just before sleep or watch television* until late in the evening.

□ Avoid caffeine and heavy meals just before going to bed, resorting if needed to warm milk or a light sandwich.

□ As much as possible, take only short naps during the day, so that you will sleep well at night.

□ Save the bedroom for sleeping and sex, not for other things like intense conversation,* working and squabbling.

□ Develop consistent sleep patterns, rather than ones that vary between cheating on sleep and desperately trying to make up.

□ Cast any burden you may have on God, and ask him to relax you and grant you the gift of sleep.

Sleeping pills may occasionally have their place, for example, in a time of great pressure or crisis when you are severely agitated, or when going on a long plane flight into a different time zone and it is important to be refreshed on arrival. Even then, however, adjusting your sleeping patterns two or three days ahead so that you begin to move into the time of the place to which you are going is a very effective nonmedicinal way of obtaining the sleep you need.

See also ANXIETY; DREAMING; REST; SAB-BATH.

References and Resources
J. A. Hobson, *Sleep* (New York: Scientific American Library, 1995); T. Jacobsen, *The Treasures of Darkness* (New Haven, Conn.: Yale University Press, 1976); P. Laxie, *The Enchanted World of Sleep* (New Haven, Conn.: Yale University Press, 1996); T. McAlpine, *Sleep, Divine and Human, in the Old Testament,* JSOTS 38 (Sheffield, U.K.: JSOT, 1987).

Thomas H. McAlpine

SMALL GROUPS

Small groups abound in our daily lives. They are variously described as teams, regular coffee klatches, task forces, study groups, committees,* working units, support groups and families.* Life would be empty without them. They function as the glue that helps to bond us with others in meaningful ways. Everybody knows that riding up to the seventh floor together in an elevator does not make the people therein a group. A group is characterized by intentionality in meeting on a regular basis over a period of time. Groups involve some commitment. They give us a sense of belonging.

The Need for Groups
Because they are so common, we often take groups for granted—as though they are part of our rights, a heritage (sometimes an albatross) of simply being alive. Actually the need for community* is God's way of marking us with the divine imprint. We were made to dwell in relatedness to others and to him.

Few, however, are prepared for the dynamics of maximizing experience in groups. Being in them is one of life's expectancies—because you exist you will spend a lot of time in groups. Recent studies indicate that around 40 percent of Americans meet weekly in small groups of one kind or another. Think of the number you have been involved in just this year. While we are immersed in groups as naturally as we are immersed in air, we seldom stop to think of the wisdom and uniqueness of being in such a relational network. And our responses are often set on automatic pilot, so we fail to change or grow but instead continue to repeat the conditioned responses to groups developed long ago.

But groups are meant to sustain and renew, to repair and bring new life. The challenge of differing opinions and dynamic interactions keep us stretching and adapting. Some groups become stuck because they try to nullify difference of opinion and refuse to risk openness to new ways of operating or thinking. The most helpful groups rock the boat, not just stick to the comfort zone. Just as the functioning cells cause our body to maintain life, so these people networks have been designed by our Creator to sustain and enhance life in our earthly existence.

The Benefits of Group Life
Relational networks make being an individual better. Sociologists tell us that three major needs are met through group involvement. (1) Groups give a person a sense of belonging, of inclusion, as reflected in, "I'm important; there is a place for me. I am needed." (2) Groups provide for our affection needs. Being a member yields an attitude of "I am lovable and valuable." Groups give us a place to love* and care for others, enabling us to give. (3) Groups provide spheres for influence, thus enabling members to communicate the idea that "I have something significant to pass on." And groups provide safe places to be influenced so members can be helped to think and act differently. All of the above (inclusion, affection and influence) are vital requirements for being a holistic person.

For the Christian, groups provide a healthy exchange between what a person experiences and does in life and what he or she believes. Groups give us permission to examine our faith as it relates to dilemmas of workplace, daily schedule, personal encounters, decisions, attitudes and so on. In sharing responses to these lifestyle circumstances, participants can find out what they believe, for we tend to reveal what we believe in the way we act every day. Thus small groups help us bridge from faith to life operations and back again.

Groups become forums for idea development, for they unconsciously mold and form convictions and understandings. In expressing yourself in a small group, you are cementing what you think. The feedback received helps reform that formational idea. Accountability is desired and feared, but progress demands it. A caring unit of persons comprising a group can help a person achieve desired outcomes simply by checking up and holding him or her accountable for commitments made.

Shared existence is richer. Good news is for sharing; burdens are lightened by others coming alongside; joy is enhanced by sharing it with another. Thankfulness, relief, achievements, disappointments and grief are greatly affected when a group is involved.

Christians in Groups

As the old hymn states about the perspective of the reborn on the natural world,

Skies above are softer blue,

Earth around is sweeter green,

Something lives in every hue

Christless eyes have never seen.

Likewise, the perspective on the world of small-group relatedness has a distinctively Christian dimension. As believers we approach groups differently from those in the world.

First, the Christian knows he or she is called to community. It is not an optional choice for those who make up the body of Christ. Each person is valuable. The composite of the many together makes possible the body. One alone cannot represent Christ effectively or adequately. As believers we have been designed for community, not solo sufficiency. We reflect the Godhead, each of whom carried out the ministry of the other and magnified the person of the other.

Though Christians are separated by many definitive factors, allegiance to our Head causes believers to find togetherness. That oneness comes from focused priority on God. It is sin that causes us to withdraw from relatedness. Dietrich Bonhoeffer states: "Sin demands to have a man by himself. It withdraws him from the community. The more isolated a person is the more destructive will be the power of sin over him and the more deeply he becomes involved in it, the more disastrous is his isolation" (p. 112).

Second, the Christian knows that fulfillment comes from both giving to and receiving from others. A characteristic of groups from a worldly point of view is that people come to get something and leave when they get what they need. Our self-centeredness tempts us to believe that groups exist for us, and our consumerism leads us to believe that if a group does not give us what we want, we will go to another group: "In general, Americans do not join groups for what they can contribute, but for what they can get out of them" (Dyrness, pp. 98-99). In contrast, Scripture calls disciples to ministry. There is no discipleship fulfillment without spending what is yours on the body for building it up. Persons are not to be used and then discarded. We are our brothers' and sisters' keepers. We do not mature alone. The apostle Paul states that we are to build up the body "until we all reach unity in the faith and in the knowledge of the Son of God . . . attaining to the whole measure of the fullness of Christ" (Eph 4:12-13).

Groups provide forums for Christians to build up faith and knowledge stores so all have as much as the most mature.

The Christian in groups finds ample opportunity to grow in response to persons and to reveal the dimensions of Christlike relatedness to other members. In small-group settings the reality of dying to yourself is evident. You have opportunity to give up your rights, to listen and to empower another. Groups provide arenas for putting to death passions to be right, to have the only answer, to fix everybody else's problems, to have everybody measure up to your expectations. They are laboratories for crucifixions. Perhaps that is one reason why Jesus selected the small-group format for equipping* the team he would leave behind to fulfill their mission of reaching the world with the gospel.

It is in groups that the reality of Christians loving and caring for one another can take place naturally. Of the early Christians who spent time in house churches and shared love in tangible ways, Tertullian said, "Behold how they love each other." The distinctions of Christianity are displayed in groups. Group evangelism is very biblical and probably one of the most natural ways of passing on the faith. Not only is it observable amid the community, but in groups persons are more likely to change beliefs because of openness to combined peer influence.

Everyday Implications

A Christian will view relational needs as reflective of who he or she is—a child of God, made to be relational by the Creator. Loneliness is therefore a gift that sensitizes us and drives us to God and to others so we become more holistic in our being. Small groups also have evangelistic implications (*see* Evangelism): work teams with unbelievers become stages to live out the lifestyle of the gospel in distinctively Christian responses.

We must do everything possible to resist the self-made, self-sustained image of secular humanism that promotes taking what we individually need to make us more sufficient individuals. Instead let us celebrate our uniqueness in what we have to contribute to the body of Christ. Let us exult over our need for others today by becoming involved in a group to give support and to hold us accountable or in a group where we can share and receive faith insights leading to the whole group's progressing in maturity.

Groups are sites for enrichment and health.* Pause to recall the benefits, achievements and growth points that have occurred in your pilgrimage through groups. Remember occasions when you have been able to connect the faith you profess with specific situations that have arisen in your life. How have groups helped you clarify your understanding and application of principles to life issues? Who are persons who have become like family to you, helping you to survive? Finally, rejoice that God has placed you among a select group called the body of Christ. What is your contribution toward its upbuilding and health?

See also CHURCH; CHURCH IN THE HOME; COMMITTEES; COMMUNITY; FAMILY; FELLOWSHIP.

References and Resources
D. Bonhoeffer, *Life Together* (New York: Harper & Brothers, 1954); W. Dyrness, *How Does America Hear the Gospel?* (Grand Rapids: Eerdmans, 1989); J. Gorman, *Community That Is Christian* (Wheaton: Victor Books, 1993); C. N. Kraus, *The Authentic Witness* (Grand Rapids: Eerdmans, 1979); M. S. Peck, *The Different Drum* (New York: Simon & Schuster, 1987); K. Smith and D. Berg, *Paradoxes of Group Life: Understanding Conflict, Paralysis and Movement in Group Dynamics* (San Francisco: Jossey-Bass, 1987); R. Wuthnow, *Sharing the Journey* (New York: Free Press, 1994).

Julie Gorman

SMALL TOWNS

"Jesus went about all the cities and villages, teaching in their synagogues, and proclaiming the good news of the kingdom, and curing every disease and every sickness" (Mt 9:35 NRSV).

When it comes to small towns, the Christian witness,* at least as recorded in Scripture, seems to overturn the common wisdom. Everyone knows that small towns are "a good place to raise children," which is often a reason people give for wanting to live in them. Cities,* on the other hand, are widely thought to be dens of iniquity. As the writer Ambrose Bierce once stated, tongue in cheek, "You can't stop the wicked from going to Chicago by killing them."

And yet the Christian vision of heaven is a city. Daniel speaks of Jerusalem as the city that bears God's name (Dan 9:18-19) and in Psalm 122, when we "go to the house of the LORD," it is Jerusalem we enter. Much of the Revelation to John of Patmos that draws the Bible to a close is devoted to a detailed description of the kingdom of God as a city, the New Jerusalem.

What does this mean? That God's ways are not our own, to be sure, and also that God has the power to transform even cities, which in our world are so often icons of human misery, into a paradise in which all our tears are wiped away. I also wonder if the vision of heaven as a city lets those of us in small towns know that the desire to use our towns as an escape from the problems of people in cities is an unholy thing, one that is ultimately self-defeating. People who flee the inner city for the suburbs soon find that they have taken the social problems of the city with them; if they flee the suburbs for small towns, the same thing happens. A city's grace, and its burden, is that it is open to humanity in all its diversity. Maybe God is trying to tell us that there is no escape from people whose color, faith, values* and lifestyle are not our own. No paradise on earth, no secure and perfect place, but we can begin to build the kingdom here by standing our ground, and trying to get along with people wherever we are.

Small towns represent many of the best things about America, the day-to-day honesty, trust and concern for the common good that seem at risk in the larger society. I treasure the luxury of not having to lock my doors and windows, of being known by the people I do business with and also of knowing them. When I shop downtown at the grocery store or the drugstore, the clerks are not impersonal workers in the "service economy," but my friends and neighbors.

In my small town, at least, there is no "bad neighborhood," a fact my city-dwelling teenaged niece found difficult to comprehend, when she was visiting and we told her that there was no place where it would be unsafe for her to jog. While there is a group of newer, more expensive homes on the west edge of town, most neighborhoods are mixed in terms of income and housing, and this has a stabilizing effect. It also blurs class distinctions, which I find appealing. My immediate neighbors are a retired trucker, a policeman, an attorney, a construction worker, a nurse (see Neighborhood).

At its best, small-town life encourages a sense of community,* the humble recognition that as mortals, as ordinary human beings, we have many needs and desires in common. At their worst, small towns turn this healthy commonality into a straitjacket of conformity. If the idol of "this is the way we've always done it" comes to prevail in small-town institutions, people with a different way, a fresh and possibly valuable new vision to offer, either leave or conform on the surface, while harboring bitterness within.

As Carol Bly notes in her provocative book *Letters from the Country*, "There is enormous pressure to conform and serve" in small towns. Often this leads to a frantic level of activity. When there are a few people and much community service* to be done, people can become overwhelmed, and the danger of burnout is as real as in fast-paced city life. As small-town people grow older, they often come to resent what Bly terms "the loss of selfhood which has taken place over all the years of community activity." They may take to making resentful remarks about the younger generation at the women's Bible study or grow unwilling to take on the duties that had seemed to give them pleasure: organizing a funeral luncheon, serving as treasurer for the deacons, reading a Scripture passage during worship.*

In my own book *Dakota,* I explore the dilemma of trying to discuss our weaknesses as well as our strengths realistically in a small town, where, "if a discouraging word is ever heard, it is not for public consumption." Our tendency, in small towns, to "make nice," can make a casualty of the truth. Jesus tells us that the truth will set us free, but in the small town that bit of gospel wisdom can get submerged in the desire to get along, to just get by.

The Gospels point to one of the worst problems that small towns have, which is to recognize, value and nurture the true gifts of the people in their midst. Gossip* is irresistible, adding spice to our everyday lives, which in a small town often unfold in quiet ways. But gossip can also be our enemy. Because we watch a family over several generations, we often pigeonhole people according to their family history, forgetting that we may not be allowing them to be the people God intends them to be.

Jesus found small towns a fruitful place for ministry.* In fact, in Luke 4:43 Jesus says that he was sent for the purpose of proclaiming the good news in the towns of Galilee. Mark and Luke tell us that immediately after his baptism by John and his trial in the desert, Jesus headed straight for the towns and villages, and quickly became known throughout the region for his preaching,* healing* and miracles. In his own hometown, however, the warm welcome for a local-boy-made-good soon turns into suspicion and even rage: How dare the son of the carpenter preach to us this way? I think the story reveals more about the low self-esteem of the townspeople than about Jesus's ministry, although in Mark 6:5-6 (NRSV) we are told that Jesus finds that he can do "no deed of power there" and is "amazed at their unbelief."

Perhaps it was this experience that led Jesus to give his disciples such harsh advice when he sent them out to preach and heal in small towns (see Mt 10). Those of us who live in such towns might reflect on these Gospel stories when we contrast the warm welcome that new preachers, doctors, lawyers, teachers, receive from us with the callous indifference, or bitter infighting, that so often colors their departures.

Small-town people might find great hope in the fact that in Luke's Gospel, at least, the disciples first recognize the risen Christ in the village of Emmaus. Significantly, it is in the offering of hospitality* to a stranger, and in the sharing of food, that Christ appears to them. We might remember that it is easy to "think small" in a small town, to be concerned only with our family,* friends and neighbors. But, as the old hymn says, "There's a wideness in God's mercy," and God wants us to think big. Christ may appear to us as a stranger, in the most unlikely encounters. Or Christ may appear as someone we thought we knew, who turns out to have needs we never dreamed of. We can resist—thinking it's only the grocer's daughter, the plumber's son—or we can let Christ reveal himself to us in each other.

See also CHURCH, SMALL; COMMUNITY, RURAL; GOSSIP; NEIGHBORHOOD; UNEMPLOYMENT.

References and Resources
C. Bly, *Letters from the Country* (San Francisco: Harper & Row, 1981); K. Norris, *Dakota: A Spiritual Geography* (New York: Ticknor & Fields/Houghton Mifflin, 1993).

Kathleen Norris

SOCIAL ACTION

Hannah Arendt made a distinction between "intellectual events" and "historic events." Often, she lamented, the two have little in common. Intellectuals toil away in the comfort of the academic peaks, while activists labor in the hurly-burly of the valley. It is essential, Arendt argued in *The Life of the Mind* (1971), to realize that thinking is as much a form of action as the busyness* of physical activity on the streets or in the marketplace. If we ever hope to probe the deeper significance of social action, heal the present culture wars and expose the ideology and inconsistencies of political correctness, we will need to know how and when to enter the fray. We will also need to know when to step out of it and reflect on the frenetic activism within it.

The Present Complexity
Our present social mood is characterized by polarization, divisiveness and ideology. J. Hunter's *Culture Wars: The Struggle to Define America* (1991) and T. Sine's *Cease Fire: Searching for Sanity in America's Culture Wars* (1995) use military metaphors to articulate a serious dilemma. The debate over whose values* should win the day has fragmented our cultural ethos into all sorts of warring tribes and clans. Single-vision chiefs have bullied their way to front stage (with their obedient tribes), convinced it is their sacred duty and responsibility to win the culture

war for their respective side.

If social action is ever going to be taken seriously in this environment, it must be nourished by substantive intellectual insights. This requires intellectuals and activists to work together and learn from one another. Thought and action must walk hand in hand once again. It is in this dynamic interplay that social action will take on significance.

We live in a period of intense and bitter polarization on many social issues. Political correctness and revolutionary politics* exist in all sorts of crude, subtle and sophisticated ways. High and cement-packed walls often, tragically, divide and insulate groups in our society that dare to define "values," and the need for them, in different ways.

One tribe tends to highlight traditional family values,* the war on drugs, the protection of the unborn and the need for anti-euthanasia* legislation. It abhors violence on our streets and in public media,* and welcomes a tougher policing system, retributive justice* and a return of the death penalty. This group also questions the public school system, encourages private or home schooling, challenges evolution, is opposed to homosexuality* and tends, to a significant degree, to justify its position by its interpretation of the Scriptures.

Another tribe tends to highlight environmental concerns, multiculturalism,* poverty* and the reasons for it, aboriginal issues, feminism, human rights, animal rights and the injustice of the world order, and questions the excessive expenditure on the military. Some members accept or encourage homosexuality and defend a woman's right to reproductive choice, including abortion; they may define the family* in different ways and view justice in more of a rehabilitative and restorative way. This group also tends to be less nationalistic and more open to immigrants and refugees, to ask questions about the virtues of free trade, big business and multinational corporations, and to view racism* as a disease in the marrow of our culture.

These brief sketches point to tendencies within different groups in our society. The sad thing is the way both groups often lack a rigorous sense of self-criticism. The other side is often caricatured by the use of all sorts of exclusionary language. Social psychologists call this the mote-beam syndrome. There is, in a very significant sense, the reality of excommunication for those who do not adhere to the credo of one of the groups.

The strong emotions* that often animate and sustain the "values debate" need to be diffused so that serious, sensitive and public dialogue can occur between their members. Authentic dialogue begins when each group can see the beam in its own eye and be hesitant about pulling out the mote in the eye of the other, and when attentive listening* begins to take place. This does not mean that agreement will necessarily occur, but such an approach creates the conditions for both groups to open their minds and chip away at the wall that divides.

Some Directions

First, it is crucial that we do not overly identify with any single cause or lobby group. One-dimensional groups frequently elevate their cause to the most important, subordinate or denigrate other social issues, then whip their devotees into an ideological frenzy. This approach to social action is problematic and, at worst, borders on the cultic. Not only is reality reduced to one issue, but the group usually insists that their interpretation of the issue is the only true one. Such a double reduction of reality is the breeding ground for fanaticism. Many of the issues raised by single-issue groups (abortion, poverty, family values, envi-

ronment) are crucial and must be addressed, but each group needs the intellectual humility to recognize that theirs is not the only organization contributing to the common good! A truly pluralistic* and multicultural society will respect the passions and interests of all concerned citizens.

Second, those who have the discernment to avoid single-issue lobby groups are often drawn to groups of the right or left around a cluster of issues. Just as it is questionable and intellectually naive to salute at the flagpole of single-issue groups, so it is intellectually shallow to uncritically bow before the cluster issues of the right or the left. The neoconservative worldview and the liberal worldview, like any worldview,* are usually articulating important insights but doing it in a limited and prejudiced way. The obstinate fact that neoconservatives and liberals rarely turn to one another to learn from one another in a conscious and deliberate way reflects the problem. Backs are often turned on one another, and little progress is made in learning how to deal with substantive conflict and difference.

If social action is going to get out of the thickets on these issues, we desperately need visionaries who will, as a matter of principle, refuse to become ethical tribalists. Visionaries are needed who have, on the one hand, the ability to see the validity and limitations in all positions and, on the other hand, the willingness to work as bridge builders and peacemakers. The Ethics and Public Policy Center (EPPC) and the important work of the Seamless Garment Network in the USA and Canada are good as primers in this area, but the vision must go much deeper and broader. Visionaries should take their red-heat zealousness and convert it into the much hotter white heat of wisdom. When passion and wisdom come together, a new vision will occur. We still await such an integrative, inclusive, whole and indeed holy outlook and practice. When social action is informed by a thoroughly critical yet interactive outlook, the fragmentary and tribal outlook of our era will be overcome. Such individuals and communities will inevitably be misunderstood and attacked by the ideologies of all tribes. Both clarity and charity are needed.

Understanding Social Action

Social activism can mean different things. There are those who see it as the taking of one or a few issues into the streets, doing marches, vigils, demonstrations and civil disobedience.* This is an important but not the only form of social activism. Some would argue that direct action is authentic education; others argue that the best form of social action is education.* Social action without a well-informed input can lead to the twisting of facts and figures to suit one's agenda. Social activism can also mean working on policy papers, presenting position papers to politicians, visiting politicians, organizing public forums for dialogue, presenting issues before the media, running for a political position (at various levels) or joining a nongovernment organization (NGO) or a government-assisted organization (GAO). Unfortunately, there is often a wide chasm between those who work at the grassroots level (and are suspicious of those in power*) and those whose activism is more from an intermediate or top-down level (and are hence in positions of power).

There is a real need for all levels to begin to work together in a more responsible way rather than in a mood of cynicism and mistrust. Just as in the world of ideas we need visionaries who can integrate the best of the insights of the left and the right, so we also need organizational visionaries who are nimble enough to work at various organizational levels. Ideas need organizations* and institutions to embody them in time and space. Social activists need those who think in a deep and inclusive manner; they also need people who can administrate, organize and carry the ideas institutionally over time. Unfortunately, many extreme idealists are so skeptical of organizations that they negate the very thing that could carry their vision. The church,* too, can become a self-serving and bureaucratic institution, but it can also be the vehicle for visionary social change. When the visionary turns against the church in the name of a purist idealism, animosity occurs and the vision of the visionary loses the opportunity to take substantive material form. But when vision and institution constantly, like sandpaper, rub against one another, much more is accomplished. This is not the easy way; it is simpler for visionaries and idealistic communities to head off in one direction and institutions to lumber along in another. But vision and institution need not hike in opposite directions. It is when they walk together that substantive social action can be affected.

Finally, we must exercise prophetic discernment. Arendt's *The Human Condition* (1958), Charles Taylor's *The Malaise of Modernity* (1991), Jean Bethke Elshtain's *Democracy on Trial* (1993) and James Skillen's *Recharging the American Experiment: Principled Pluralism for Genuine Civic Community* (1994) each highlight, in their different ways, the need for space to be provided in which substantive areas of disagreement and conflict can be heard and struggled through. Such insistence and passionate pleas by centrist and various types of communitarian liberals must be heard and acted upon if we are not going to create a society of ideological ghettos. But there are also limitations to this approach.

The ominous misuse of power is often camouflaged by seductive language and interest groups. This, then, is the dilemma of many social activists. When this directs the social and political scene, how can the "power elites" be challenged? In short, there are limits to dialogue in the search for change. When the Other refuses to listen, when unequal relationships and class structures are firmly maintained, when tyrants burst with "egophanic" fullness, the call for dialogue falls on deaf ears. The quest to dominate, control and manipulate by "power elites" such as corporations, the military-industrial complex, state bureaucracies and various liberationist groups presents a serious challenge. We need to ask ourselves, constantly, about those who have concentrations of power and wield it in an unjust way. We often go after the minnows but stroke the backs of sharks. The task of the intellectual activists is to know when the limits of dialogue and civility have been reached, and when prudence would move us from thought and dialogue to some form of responsible social protest.

Historically, the church was distinguished by its service to society.* Areas in which the church undertook practical neighbor-love include the care of infants and children, hospitality, the burial of the dead during plagues, the care of widows and orphans, the status of women and the establishment of hospitals and universities. Besides being the chief civilizing agency during the Middle Ages, the church was the chief instrument of social justice. During the revivals of the eighteenth and nineteenth centuries, the evangelists were often the leaders of social reform. Wesley said, "The Gospel of Christ Jesus knows . . . no holiness, but social holiness." In *The Social Achievements of the Christian Church* E. H. Oliver says the church has a fivefold function as servant: it must educate and inspire; it must pioneer new ministries; it must study to prevent rather than to cure; it must transform the helped into helpers. But the fifth is the function so desperately needed today: it must exercise its age-long prophetic vocation and serve as conscience to society (Oliver, p. 116).

See also CITIZENSHIP; CIVIL DISOBEDIENCE; MISSION; MULTICULTURALISM; POLITICS; VOTING.

References and Resources

H. Arendt, *The Human Condition* (New York: Harcourt Brace Jovanovich, 1978); H. Arendt, *Life of the Mind* (Chicago: University of Chicago Press, 1958); R. Beiner, *What's the Matter with Liberalism?* (Berkeley: University of California Press, 1992); N. Chomsky, *Deterring Democracy* (New York: Verso, 1991); N. Chomsky, *Necessary Illusions* (Montreal: CBC Enterprises, 1989); H. G. Gadamer, *Truth and Method* (New York: Continuum, 1975); J. Habermas, *Autonomy and Solidarity* (London: Verso, 1992); A. MacIntyre, *After Virtue* (Notre Dame, Ind.: University of Notre Dame Press, 1984); A. MacIntyre, *Whose Justice, Which Rationality?* (Notre Dame, Ind.: University of Notre Dame Press, 1988); E. H. Oliver, *The Social Achievements of the Christian Church* (United Church of Canada, 1930); E. Said, *Culture and Imperialism* (New York: Knopf, 1993); C. Taylor, *The Ethics of Authenticity* (Cambridge, Mass.: Harvard University Press, 1992; published in Canada as *The Malaise of Modernity*, 1991); D. Walsh, *After Ideology: Recovering the Spiritual Foundations of Freedom* (San Francisco: Harper & Row, 1990); S. Weil, *The Need for Roots* (New York: Harper & Row, 1971).

Ron Dart

SOCIETY

Society is such an everyday word that we seldom stop to think what it means. In fact, its meaning has changed quite radically over the past two hundred years and is changing again at the turn of the twenty-first century. This is not just an abstract question of semantics. How *society* is understood has implications for how human beings see themselves (identity) and the quality of human relationships (responsibility). The word *society* is an invention that may or may not be useful, depending on circumstances. That humans engage in social relationships seems clear. Whether any or all of those relations can helpfully be thought of as "society" is open to question.

Developing Views of Modern Society

The word *society* entered English usage in the fourteenth century, when it meant "companionship" or "fellowship."* By the seventeenth century, however, *society* had acquired a more abstract meaning; it was the entity to which all belonged, as distinct from the state, where power* lay. This is the idea of "civil society" (*see* Civility). The active sense of society declined, though action reappeared in "community"* and "individual."* By the later nineteenth century society was becoming synonymous with the new phenomenon of the nation-state.* The idea developed that those inhabiting a territory with a single governmental jurisdiction could be thought of as a single "people" or "society."

During the same period, the idea that human beings could be thought of as "individuals" took root, and thus an opposition was set up between "society" and "individual." The poet John Donne's famous "No man is an island" was decisively abandoned, and a strong streak of individualism appeared in social thought. It sometimes drew inspiration from a Protestant emphasis on "personal salvation" and personal interpretation of the Scriptures (and sometimes the influence was the other way around!). The Protestant stress on the personal was intended to counter false reliance on the authority of the church,* but it was easily co-opted for political and economic ends, and thus the assumption that Protestantism is necessarily individualistic was born.

Given this way of thinking, it is easy to see how leading social thinkers of the nineteenth and early twentieth centuries concluded that society was somehow "over against" individuals. Cities were growing rapidly in Europe and North America, and newcomers often felt overwhelmed when they arrived from the country, or as immigrants,* looking for work. However, some were relieved at the anonymity of city life; the sense of being a stranger was not always negative. Formal and contractual* relations seemed to predominate, leaving behind the closeness of (what was imagined to be) "community."

Not only were cities* growing. In the noisy factories and mills of early industrialism, individuals workers might feel alienated from their fellows, from their employers and even, according to Karl Marx's thought, from their real selves. Moreover, the unwritten rules of social life seemed to be changing, but it was not clear how people should go on in the new situation. Taken-for-granted assumptions about social relationships—deference, obligation—were swept aside, leaving people with a sense of uncertainty about "right" responses, what the sociologist Emile Durkheim called "anomie" or normlessness.

Even when rules did reappear, they were often the rules of the bureaucracy, where logical reasons were sought for every activity. Tasks had to be performed in the office, and these could be classified and streamlined for greater efficiency and productivity. Indeed, such rules seemed to predominate, even over values* such as love,* honesty or integrity. Max Weber foresaw the creation of "iron cages" of such "rational systems" of social organization, cages that would stifle the spirit and curb charisma. People in industrial societies felt more and more like "cogs" in a machine, especially with the advent of "scientific management" in the 1920s.

Some Christian Responses to Modern Society

During this period the most significant Christian contribution came from the so-called social gospel movement. The crying contrasts between wealth* and poverty,* especially in the great American cities, inspired attempts to show the compassion of Christ in practical ways. Some impetus for this movement came from leaders such as the Scotsman Thomas Chalmers or William and Catherine Booth's Salvation Army, which provided emergency relief and welfare by organizing private action and personal responsibility. But the social gospel tried to go beyond the individual to understanding corporate life, and it applied the Christian gospel to matters such as fair wages and urban poverty. It also deeply influenced the development of early American sociology.

While the social gospel made gains in showing the broader dimensions of the Christian message—sometimes obscured in a focus on individual salvation—it failed to break entirely with the thought forms of the day. In much of the movement, Jesus' good works were highlighted along with evolutionary optimism that harmony would come on earth through "progress" and human effort. Urban, industrial, bureaucratic society was thus recognized as having some distinct traits that called for Christian intervention. In a sense the social gospel faltered not because it was too radical but because it was not radical enough.

Later in the twentieth century, as the pitiful divisions between the "First" and "Third" worlds became painfully obvious, Christians again struggled to find a "social" dimension to the gospel. The result was "liberation theology," which originated among Latin American Catholics influenced by European ideas. Like the social gospelers, liberation theologians stressed the kingdom of God and the requirement to seek social justice in the face of grinding poverty and blatant inequity of resource distribution. But once again the movement was marginalized by many Christians because of its frequent use of Marxist categories (some of which seem to deny the work of God) and because of a residual humanist optimism (*see* Social Action).

Recent Interpretations of Modern Society

From the 1970s on, attention broadened to include several other responses to "modern societies," such as the environmental movement (*see* Ecology). Not only "society" but also "nature" had to be brought into the equation. For various reasons, Christian reflection and action regarding the environment succeeded better than some earlier efforts at social reflection.

Other very significant departures included feminism and peace movements. These drew attention to ways in which societies are internally and externally divided, and to the fact that "modernity" seemed to exacerbate rather than mitigate these divisions. Post-World War II feminist movements were galvanized above all by the massive integration of women into the paid labor force of the industrial societies. Questions were raised about work and domesticity, and also about production and consumption. Similar questions, from another angle, were highlighted by peace movements, which struggled especially against the stockpiling of nuclear armaments during and after the Cold War. This in turn was the product of the industrializing and globalizing of war—where bureaucracy, politics* and market economics also play a central role.

During the same period the "communications revolution" occurred (using, ironically, military-developed technologies* from the silicon chip to the Internet!), which also stimulated new consideration of what "society" might be. This, along with contemporary consumerism,* is a key factor. Marshall McLuhan's famous phrase about the "global village"* made possible by electronic technologies offered a new slogan that seemed to make sense of what was happening. At the same time, it would be mocked in the 1990s by the "virtual war" in the Persian Gulf, in which blood, maiming and destruction were deliberately drowned in a sea of electronic euphemisms.

Looking back, however, it becomes clear that the story of the modern world itself is one of steadily stretching social relationships. What began with the telegraph and the telephone* has been augmented by many new media from radio* and television* and now to the interactive multimedia of the Information Superhighway.* These make possible a myriad "actions at a distance." Many if not most relationships at the end of the twentieth century are remote ones. The global stock exchange is almost always open, shifting from New York to London to Frankfurt to Tokyo. People use telephones in cars, trains and planes as well as in offices and homes. Yet personal and intimate relationships still thrive, paradoxically, as never before.

Implications for Understanding Modern Society

What does this mean for "society"? It is by no means clear what the term should refer to. Transnational corporations span the globe, defying old national boundaries. Minorities and interest groups appear, appearing to some as a new tribalism. Politicians wring their hands, despairing of the "ungovernability" of their once-unified countries. To the most extreme observers, such as Jean Baudrillard, the social sphere—if it ever existed—has simply dissolved between the "masses" and the

"media." For him, society is a sociological invention, produced by surveys and opinion polls.

Without doubt, questions about society are raised in novel ways in a world of consumer markets and communications media. A society can no longer be defined by state authorities or by some central values that inform it. Rather, what used to be thought of as society is now better viewed as an arena of debates over such diverse matters from dress to waste disposal to life-support machines. The geographical-political or cultural-values definitions lose hold, and relationships and change become more significant. This stretching of social relations means that the global and the local interact constantly. Every cup of coffee consumed in North America tells a tale of communities in Latin America or Africa that connect the modern with the premodern. Every bottle of formula milk consumed in the latter continents tells a tale of companies in North America anxious to penetrate new markets. In each case, once again, issues of "society" and "nature" are inextricably linked together.

To speak of consuming suggests where the other crucial factor for understanding social relationships lies, and this again may mark off today's conditions from previous ones. In the era of early sociology, work* and employment provided the key clues about someone's identity and social position. Occupations, classes, life-chances all revolved around the work world. Now, suggests Zygmunt Bauman, in the "advanced" societies, consumption is the name of the game. Not just in the trivial sense that shopping malls* dominate urban planning or that commercials dominate TV (see Advertising), but in the sense that consumerism* dominates our understanding of morality (which comes down to choosing personal values), our approach to identity (what we consume tells us who we are and where we fit) and the managing of the economy (which revolves around advertising and consumption).

Future Directions of Modern Society

So *society*, the abstract term that seemed so attractive to the early sociologists, now seems to have been overtaken by events. The sense of structuring, of solidity and relatively rigid strata, may yet be superseded by something much more fluid. The random, the unexpected, unpredictable—yet still patterned, if playfully—appears more commonly than the stable and the structured. What social relationships are *becoming* rather than what they *are* may turn out to be the new focus of attention, though we should remember that early sociologists often *over*estimated the extent of change. Tradition still persists alongside (post)modern developments.

Curiously, these turns within our understanding of wider relationships may move social thought full circle to a much more *active* concept of the social, just as *society* once had the active connotation of "companionship." Perhaps, as Bauman suggests, *sociality* may be a better term to capture such relationships. This would put the accent on agency once more, on the *actions* that constitute social life within the limits of already existing social arrangements. But those arrangements would always themselves be seen as accomplishments, things produced by human activities, and subject to change.

As noted above, there is nothing sacred about the concept of society. It may blur understanding as much as lend clearer focus. Indeed, insofar as *society* is used as a counterpoint to the *individual* it is thoroughly misleading. At the very least, these concepts depend deeply on each other. As Marx observed, people make their own history but not in circumstances of their choosing. That which is perceived "out there" as "society" is the product of human activities, no less than is our immediate landscape. But like the landscape, it can, over time, and within certain limits, be altered, even transformed, by human endeavor, planned and unplanned.

What are those limits or conduits along which appropriate change may occur? For some contemporaries, the end of nation-state or cultural-values definitions of society is a welcome release. Following Friedrich Nietzsche, they see no particular limits or directions hampering social change. All voices get airspace; no minority, however bizarre, is excluded. In practice, of course, this breaks down. Needless to say, at the other end of the spectrum, fundamentalists of all stripes wish to reassert traditional codes of conduct and are even willing to forgo some gains of modernity—such as democracy—to reestablish them.

Christian Responsibility Within Modern Society

Christians cannot fall back on the Bible or the church to defend "society," or even, for that matter, social institutions such as "the family"* or "the state." Biblical sources reveal that humans form social relationships and that these include kinship and political relations involving legitimate authority, but this does not take us very far. When human beings are thought of in biblical terms as the "image of God," this cannot properly be divorced from the intrinsic sociality of God—three persons in one. Modern social thought never paid serious attention to this, but it is crucial.

Several features follow. God-as-Trinity is not gendered, but humans are created as male and female, with equal responsibilities to care for creation.* A concern for the natural environment is built into this notion of sociality. Moreover, these relations are normative; they are meant to be lived in particular ways. This relates back to Jesus' own teaching and practice of "neighborliness" (*see* Neighborhood)—to the person or persons, perhaps from a disadvantaged minority, who has a claim upon us by virtue of common humanness.

A major error made by early analysts of "society" was the belief that social relationships could somehow be abstracted from the real world of ethics and justice.* They cannot. From a Christian perspective, social relations may take myriad forms, and these often change over time. Given Jesus' own teaching, it is hard to defend the permanence of patriarchy and (elite) priesthood, and relatively straightforward to uphold heterosexual marriage* and the rule of (just) law.* But behind all these specifics lies a notion of human sociality that defines who we are—bearers of the image of a three-in-one God—and gives us a basic task—to relate responsibly to God, each other and the earth.

Jesus' teaching does not stop there, however. The church he founded is intended to pick up the ancient task given to Israel, to be a "light to the nations." Christ's reconciling work creates a reconciling community (*see* Church; Community), a place where harmonious difference—gender, class, ethnic—can be seen in practice, a colony, as Stanley Hauerwas puts it, of "resident aliens." This places a further question mark over present-day dominant social relations and points forward to a fulfillment of the God-people-land triad. It also invites the church to involvement, at every level of "society," to try to bring healing,* help and hope by bringing the justice and love of Jesus to all, "not in word only, but in deed and in truth."

See also CITIZENSHIP; COMMUNITY; STATES/PROVINCES.

References and Resources
S. Hauerwas, *Resident Aliens* (Nashville: Abingdon, 1989). David Lyon

SOUL

In everyday conversation the word *soul* can mean at least two things: (1) a precious human person (as in "Two hundred souls were lost in the plane crash") and (2) the eternal or immortal part of a human being, an incorruptible core (as in "We commit the body to the grave knowing that she still lives in her soul"). We will see that the first is actually closer to biblical truth than the second (compare Acts 27:37 KJV). In the Bible *soul* and *spirit* are sometimes used interchangeably to speak of the interior of persons, especially in their longings for relationship with God. Add to this confusion one more word: the universal word *heart* as a metaphor for the motivating center of a person. This complex use of words reflects the contemporary confusion about what makes human beings "tick" and what constitutes a spiritual person. Gaining a biblical view of *soul* is important for several everyday matters: a healthy and holy sexuality,* the nature of true spirituality, how we are to treat our bodies,* why we have spiritual conflict* and what happens at death.* The Old and New Testaments use a wide range of terms to describe the way human beings are made, and these must now be considered.

Soul Words in the Old Testament
In the Old Testament the word *spirit* (*ruah*) literally means "wind," "breath" or "moving air." *Spirit* normally means the "person empowered by God" (compare Num 11:26). Most commonly it refers to God and humankind in dynamic relation (Wolff, p. 39) rather than something innate to human beings that motivates persons to search beyond themselves.

Heart (*leb*) refers to the physical center of the body, both to the beating organ (the physical heart) and, more generally, to the breast enclosed by the rib cage (2 Sam 18:14). But *heart* is most commonly used metaphorically for the mental and spiritual center of the human person ("the secrets of the heart"; Ps 44:21). Heart life is expressed in (1) feelings ("A happy heart makes the face cheerful"; Prov 15:13), (2) longings and desires ("You have granted him the desire of his heart"; Ps 21:2), (3) thinking and reasoning* ("Teach us to number our days aright, that we may gain a heart of wisdom"; Ps 90:12) and (4) decisions of the will ("In his heart a man plans his course"; Prov 16:9). As Hans Wolff notes, "The Israelite finds it difficult to distinguish linguistically between 'perceiving' and 'choosing,' between 'hearing' and 'obeying,' " a difficulty that "comes from the factual impossibility of dividing theory and practice" (p. 51). Often the Old Testament uses *heart* where we would today commonly use *spirit*, that is, in passages that refer to relationship with God, where we would use *brain* as an organ of thinking and where we would use *will* for the power to make decisions.

Soul (*nephesh*) is a word complicated by its almost universal translation into the Greek *psychē*, from which we get English words like psychology. More often than not, however, *soul* in the Old Testament does not refer to the spiritual/emotional part of a person that can be disconnected from bodily life. *Soul* refers to the person as a longing person (Wolff, p. 10). After God breathed into Adam the breath of life, Adam "became a living being" (*nephesh;* Gen 2:7). Sometimes *nephesh* is used for the throat through which the breath of life passes, showing that the word in Old Testament usage does not mean the spiritual part of a person but rather a person with all kinds of longings—sensual and more-than-sensual. So the soul is often frightened, despairing, weak, despondent, disquieted and even bitter. It can also be satisfied, happy and at rest with God and itself.

As the organ of vital needs, the soul must be satisfied for a person to go on living. Satan, in the duel with God, must spare Job's *nephesh,* which simply means his life (Job 2:6). Life, for biblical persons, is total and cannot be segmented into two parts: a disposable shell (the body) and an indestructible spirit core (the soul). Thus the familiar psalm "Praise the LORD, O my soul; all my inmost being, praise his holy name" (Ps 103:1) could be simply and helpfully translated "Bless the Lord, O my life!"

It is impossible to have a fully biblical view of human personhood without taking this Old Testament perspective seriously. This is especially important because the church has historically been influenced by Greek philosophy in dividing the person into compartments. Biblically the soul is not a mere part of the person but an expression of the person as whole. *Nephesh* (soul), *ruah* (spirit) and *leb* (heart) refer to basic dimensions of our experience of life in relation to God (Pedersen, 1:102-6). This background is essential to the New Testament message about the dignity of human persons.

Soul Words in the New Testament

The New Testament assumed the Old and maintained the inspired view of the essential unity of the human person. Most significant of all, the New Testament hope is not for the immortality of the soul—an essentially Greek concept that involves disparaging the body as a useless encumbrance to the life of the spirit. Instead, the great hope in Christ after death is the resurrection of the body—full personal and expressive life in a new heaven and a new earth.

Tragically, much Christian theology

has relegated the body to the domain of this world. The body then is something intrinsically sinful, a prison for the soul. At the same time it is assumed that faith concerns the spirit, which is not of this world. Viewed this way, salvation and spirituality are escapes from bodily life: this diminishes such ordinary things as eating,* working* and sleeping.* The spiritual person is thus one who abandons sexual expression and lives the celibate life or spends his or her life in spiritual ministry. In contrast, the problem of humankind, according to the Bible, lies not in the body (*sōma*) but in the will. What we need is not to get rid of our bodies but to get a new heart (Ezek 11:19).

When we receive Christ, *we* get saved, not just our souls in the Greek sense. This is a two-stage process. First, our souls are substantially saved by being inseminated by God's Spirit, thus giving us new bodily and personal life on earth. Second, after death and when Christ comes again, we are given a new and perfect embodiment through the resurrection of our entire selves, bodies included.

Our passions do not come from the physical body (perceived as the source of sin) while ideas and moral convictions come from the soul (perceived as the center and source of righteousness). The body is not the prison house of the soul and its seducer into sin (Harder, p. 682; Dunn, p. 692). The soul is the seat of life, as indicated in the words of Jesus, "For whoever wants to save his life [soul] will lose it, but whoever loses his life [soul] for me and for the gospel will save it" (Mk 8:35).

A related word in the New Testament is *spirit*. Here again there is harmony with Old Testament thought. *Spirit* is that capacity in human beings that relates them to a realm of reality beyond ordinary observation and human control (Dunn, p. 693). God encounters people immedi-

ately through the spirit (Rom 8:16; 2 Tim 4:22). But it is, once again, a dimension of the whole person. So the popular debate as to whether human nature is two parts (soul-body) or three (spirit-soul-body), the latter based largely on one text (1 Thess 5:23), is unhelpful, a recent major scholarly work on the subject notwithstanding (Cooper). "The human person is a 'soul' by virtue of being a 'body' made alive by the 'breath' (or Spirit) of God" (Colwell, p. 29). The spirit is not one compartment of the Christian person—one boxcar in a three-car train (spirit-soul-body) in which each car could be uncoupled. The spirit is simply one dimension of personhood in a totally integrated personhood that is expressed in bodily activity, emotional* life and intellectual thought (soul).

Far from being three separate compartments, the human person is a psycho-pneuma-somatic unity. Touch a person's body and you have touched the person—a crucial Christian contribution to the matter of sexuality.* We never have sex with bodies but with souls, meaning persons! Touch the emotions and you touch persons. Touch the spirit and you have touched the whole person. In biblical anthropology we do not *have* a body or soul or spirit. We *are* a body, a soul, a spirit.

Soul and *spirit* are sometimes in Scripture used interchangeably to refer to the whole person seeking after God: "My soul thirsts . . . for the living God" (Ps 42:2). But sometimes the word of God penetrates "even to dividing soul and spirit" (Heb 4:12). When such a distinction is made, *soul* is normally used for the expressiveness of human personhood in emotions and thoughts: "My soul is overwhelmed with sorrow to the point of death" (Mt 26:38). The spirit is most commonly that inmost mysterious self, a self known mainly to God, though sometimes known through spiritual self-consciousness (1 Cor 2:11). It is characterized by our restless longing to know God for whom we were made. This distinction is further illustrated in 1 Corinthians 15. With an obvious play on words, Paul says that life in this world is characterized by our experience of a "soulish" body—a body expressive of emotions and thoughts and influenced by our environment. The actual words used are *sōma psychikcon* (natural body). After the resurrection of the body when Christ comes again, we will be raised a spiritual (or Spirit-ual) body *(sōma pneumatikon),* a body that expresses perfectly life in the Spirit (1 Cor 15:44). In the spiritual body we will perfectly conform to the image of Christ.

On Being a Soul Person
What does all this mean for everyday life? First, everyday spirituality looks toward a perfectly embodied soul life. The final end of the Christian life then is not a spirituality freed from body but a spiritual body; it is not an unencumbered angelic existence like that claimed by the superspiritual Corinthians but a fully embodied spirituality. The ultimate goal is not to be an immortal soul in heaven but a full-orbed person in the new heaven and new earth with all of its redeemed bodily existence: expressive worship,* creative activity, meaningful work and emotional freedom—the three-fold sabbath* rest of God, humankind and creation.*

Second, in view of our final end, everyday bodily life is hopeful. While in this life all healing* is partial, we anticipate the final healing in the resurrection of the body. Work in this life is meaningful, not only because it is an expression of our ensouled body and glorifies God by making God's world work, but also because it is, through faith, hope and love, a participation in the new heaven and the new earth. Sexual life is never merely physical but is a spiritual and "soulish" ministry within the marriage covenant anticipating the final day when all heaven is marriage (the wedding supper of the Lamb).

Third, ministry* touches whole persons. Psychosomatic medicine has recognized the relationship of bodily and emotional health. But ministry to people must go a step further and become psycho-pneuma-somatic, recognizing the whole person in relation (or out of relation) to God. Above all this has implications for spiritual growth* since Christian growth can never be an out-of-body holiness, an unemotional piety or anti-intellectual God-consciousness. Christian growth is growth as men and women—gender-related spiritual growth (see Femininity).

Fourth, being a soul person (and a whole person) means being relationally alive through love.* We are most godlike in relationships. Persons are not the same as individuals.* We are persons not in our individual life but in relationship to God and others. We were created male and female in the image of the triune God—built by love, in love and for love, called into existence by a personal God who *is* love within a triune community. So that which most links us with the living God—the soul—links us with our neighbor* and with the Christian community.*

Finally, Christian spirituality is not a human achievement (through disciplines and practices) but a response to the Spirit's initiative. *Soul* and *spirit,* as we have seen, refer to ways that people can be alive to God. It is a great mistake to consider Christian spirituality as the cultivation of our inbuilt desire for transcendence. Christian spirituality is essentially Spirit-uality—God's empowering presence calling human beings into dynamic relation and expressiveness. Many of the occasions in which *spirit* and *spiritual* are used in the New Testament should be capitalized, though few translations indicate this. Spiritual growth is Spirit-growth. Spiritual gifts* are gifts of the Spirit. Spiritual life is walking in the Spirit. God makes us fully alive as bodily persons, fully alive together and fully alive forever.

See also BODY; FAITH DEVELOPMENT; INDIVIDUAL; SEXUALITY; SPIRITUAL CONFLICT; SPIRITUAL DISCIPLINES; SPIRITUAL GROWTH.

References and Resources

J. E. Colwell, "Anthropology," in *New Dictionary of Theology,* ed. S. B. Ferguson and D. F. Wright (Downers Grove, Ill.: InterVarsity Press, 1988) 28-30; J. W. Cooper, *Body, Soul & Life Everlasting: Biblical Anthropology and the Monism-Dualism Debate* (Grand Rapids: Eerdmans, 1989); J. Dunn, "Spirit/Holy Spirit," in *New International Dictionary of New Testament Theology,* ed. C. Brown (Grand Rapids: Zondervan, 1979) 3:689-707; G. D. Fee, *God's Empowering Presence: The Holy Spirit in the Letters of Paul* (Peabody, Mass.: Hendrickson, 1993); G. Harder, "Soul," in *New International Dictionary of New Testament Theology,* ed. C. Brown (Grand Rapids: Zondervan, 1979) 3:676-86; J. Pedersen, *Israel: Its Life and Culture,* vols. 1-2 (Oxford: Geoffrey Cumberlege, 1964); H. W. Wolff, *Anthropology of the Old Testament,* trans. M. Kohl (Philadelphia: Fortress, 1981).

R. Paul Stevens

SPEAKING

The universal experience of speaking is not as simple as it once was. Words are now reduced to bits of information that can be digitalized, processed and transmitted. The net effect of this is the undervaluing of speech. In contrast, recovering a biblical view of speech and words can turn ordinary conversational* speech, as well as prepared public speeches such as sermons, lectures, introductions or annual reports, into a personal ministry that is evocative of faith for both the speaker and hearer.

The Mouth as an Organ of Human Expression

Speaking is humankind's distinctive privilege. Adam names the animals (Gen 2:18-23), though his speech is not recorded until his first poetic exclamation of joy in finding a suitable partner (Gen 2:23). Later in the Old Testament the mature person is pictured as meditating on God's Word (Ps 1:2) and continuously declaring in speech God's righteousness (Ps 71:24). The rich vocabulary of the Old Testament for the mouth (at least five different words) is matched by an even richer vocabulary for different kinds of speech (over twenty different words; Wolff, pp. 77-78). In the New Testament James bemoans the fact that the same tongue is capable of blessing* God or cursing men (Jas 3:9), giving an ambiguous personal expression that reflects the confused interior of the person so speaking. The tongue is hard to control (Jas 2:3-12) because persons are.

Words Express Persons

Every act of speech involves an unconscious revelation of the source of the words. Jesus said the mouth speaks for the heart (Mt 12:34; 15:18). Whether words are expressed in a casual remark or a carefully manuscripted speech, one's self is revealed. Even the attempt to conceal oneself, to give a message that is impersonal and disconnected with one's character, is a powerfully revealing message. One cannot stop up a water hose fully turned on by putting one's finger over the outlet. In biblical anthropology words are bodily expressions of a person's soul: "Behind the word stands the soul which created it" (Pedersen, 1:167). So the person comes out of the mouth, and our speech reveals the state of our inner integration or disintegration (Mt 15:18; Jas 1:26).

In one sense lying is impossible because the attempt to deceive, disguise or conceal something tells the truth about the speaker's personality (Pedersen, 1:411-12). So the indissoluble link between word and person is the source of the power of speech. This is especially true for God, whose word is utterly reliable (Num 23:19; 1 Sam 15:29) and incisively powerful (Heb 4:12). God's word will never return void (Is 55:11).

The Power of Speech

In the Hebrew language *word* (*dabhar*) is used both for the idea and the matter itself. Words are themselves neither abstractions nor representatives of abstractions. God speaks, and the world comes into being (Gen 1:3, 6, 11, 14, 20, 24; 2 Pet 3:5). In the same way, words and the events they cause are totally interconnected (Gen 15:1; 21:10; 22:15; 24:66; 44:7). A most revealing example is the act of giving a blessing; it cannot be recalled if it comes from the soul* (Gen 27:35-37). In the same way, weightless words ("empty talk"; 2 Kings 18:20) are not backed up with substance in the soul of the person. Normally the tongue has the power of life and death* (Prov 18:21) because people have such power.

Our words touch others—even God— powerfully, and the speech of a parent, child, brother, sister, enemy or friend can heal or wound, thus belying the ancient children's rhyme that "sticks and stones may break my bones, but names can never hurt me!" In a special sense those whose life is found in God will, like Samuel, be those whose words are not allowed to "fall to the ground" (1 Sam 3:19).

Sins and Graces of Speech

A spirituality of speech involves attending to the heart, not merely improving the technique of communication. The three vices of the tongue listed in Ephesians 5:4—*aischrotēs* (shamelessness),

mōrologia (silly talk or fishing for a laugh) and *eutrapelia* (facetiousness)—are expressions of inner disintegration. Instead, says the apostle Paul, let there be thanksgiving, that use of the tongue that is quite possibly the highest and holiest since it expresses the truth that a person loves God enough to be content (Rom 1:21). Thankful people live in joyful dependence on God (Eph 5:19-20), and their speech reveals this authentic godliness. Our speech should, indeed it will, reflect the new life planted in us by Christ (Col 3:9). A controlled tongue—so much a concern of James 3:1-12—comes from being a self-controlled person manifesting the fruit of the Spirit (Gal 5:23). That person has no fear of being manipulated by the controlling words of others and no need to control others by his or her words.

Speech as a Spiritual Discipline

Richard Foster says, "The tongue is a thermometer; it tells us our spiritual temperature. It is also a thermostat; it controls our spiritual temperatures" (p. 89). Speech is inescapably personal, experiential and substantial. Thus full human speech can only be partially expressed through a media experience or partially processed in a computer.* Human beings will always hunger both to receive and give interpersonal speech, face to face, in groups, congregations, classrooms and auditoriums. And "Christian" oratory that is not backed by authentic Christian character will be a dehumanizing experience. People will be most godlike when they use their words to build up, rather than tear down. Further true godliness is sometimes expressed in refraining from speech in order to attend to the speech of others. As the Old Testament preacher said, "There is . . . a time to be silent and a time to speak" (Eccles 3:7). Knowing when to speak (and not to speak) is one of the secrets of beautiful speech, which according to Proverbs is "like apples of gold in settings of silver" (Prov 25:11).

See also CONVERSATION; GOSSIP; LISTENING; PREACHING; PROMISING; STORYTELLING; TEACHING.

References and Resources
R. Foster, *Celebration of Discipline* (New York: Harper & Row, 1978); J. Pedersen, *Israel: Its Life and Culture*, 4 vols. (London: Oxford University Press, 1963); H. W. Wolff, *Anthropology of the Old Testament*, trans. M. Kohl (Philadelphia: Fortress, 1964).

R. Paul Stevens

SPIRITUAL CONFLICT

Why do I still experience lust? When I am criticized, I become deeply hurt and lash out in anger. What is the matter with me? There are some people I find almost impossible to love,* and they are some of the people I am closest to in this life! I feel continuous tension between the demands of home* and workplace.* Is my profession* too important? I desire to do good but seem unable sometimes to make it happen. Sometimes I seem almost driven to do wrong things. I feel a hateful fascination with what I see in the theater or on television*—wanting and not wanting at the same time. When I try to serve God in the world, it seems an invisible army contrives to make it impossibly difficult.

Contrary to the teachings of some, Christians struggle until the day they die. There is no experience of God that can usher one into sinless perfection free of the slightest twinge of difficulty. *Spiritual growth** is the progressive transformation of our persons into the likeness of Christ. But the transformation is not complete in this life. Some aspects of the conflict involve spiritual warfare with the principalities and powers.* There is an invisible backdrop to our struggle—a host of social, political and economic structures and invisible spiritual beings that frustrate the Christian's life and service* in the world (Eph 6:12). But part of the struggle *is* with flesh and blood, with human nature as it has become through sin, in opposition to life in the Spirit. This article will explore the tension between flesh and spirit—or more accurately, flesh and Spirit—in Paul's writings and will offer some practical help in dealing with spiritual conflict.

The Flesh Against the Spirit
In Paul's writing *sarx*, translated as "flesh," is a complex word not easily understood in English. Sometimes it merely means what is human about us. Once we regarded Christ "from a human point of view" (2 Cor 5:16 NRSV; compare 1:17). By human standards not many of the Corinthians were wise and educated (1 Cor 1:26). Sometimes *flesh* simply refers to one's bodily life (Rom 2:28) that is normally good or, at least, neutral. Paul did not agree with the Greek view of the body as a hindrance, but as a Jew he believed that people can glorify God with and in their bodies.* Our ultimate future is, not to be holy souls floating around eternity, but to be resurrected persons experiencing complete, personal, physical and communal life in the presence of God in a new heaven and a new earth (Rev 21—22). So *flesh* is not always pitted against life in Christ or the Spirit.

On this point it is remarkable that the works of the flesh Paul lists in Galatians 5:18 are largely nonphysical: "impurity; . . . idolatry and witchcraft; hatred, discord, jealousy, fits of rage, selfish ambition, dissensions, factions and envy" (NRSV). These are mostly psychological, spiritual and relational. The war is not mainly between our physical bodies and our human spirits but between something inside us that "desires what is contrary to the Spirit" (Gal 5:17 NRSV). Though four of the listed works of the flesh—sexual immorality, debauchery, drunkenness and orgies—involve the physical body, the root of these destructive activities is to be found in what Scripture calls the *heart* or *soul.**

While many modern versions translate *sarx* as "human nature," they must not be understood to communicate that there are two parts to us, one good and one bad, one higher and one lower, one given to God and the other given to sin. No, it is our whole person—body, soul and spirit—that struggles to live under the reign of Christ and in the Spirit. Biblically we do not "have" a body, "have" a soul and "have" a spirit, but are bodies, souls and spirits—integrated wholes. Touch someone's body in a sexual affair, and you have touched that person: such affairs arise not from an irrepressible instinct in our bodies but from something wrong in our persons. Idolatry and sorcery involve the secret tampering with the powers of evil through drugs or witchcraft. Enmity, strife, fits of anger, selfishness, dissensions, party spirit and envy are relational sins—in which persons are out of sync with others, seeking their own advantage or cherishing pain when someone else is honored. Even drunkenness and carousing are, in the end, not physical problems because they both involve the choice to give one's consciousness to a substance. So the works of the flesh are not to be located in our physical drives and appetites but in the fundamental orientation of our lives.

Sometimes Paul uses *flesh* in his letters to refer to that fundamental orientation, for example, in Romans 7:18 ("I know that nothing good lives in me, that is, in my sinful nature [*sarx*]"; NRSV) and Galatians 5:17 ("For the sinful nature [*sarx*] desires what is contrary to the Spirit"; NRSV). Here *flesh* stands for

flawed human nature as it has become through sin. It is life lived as though Christ had not come, died and been raised. It is life outside and against the Spirit. *Flesh* describes—but does not ultimately account for—the oft-repeated situation in which a person knows what to do but feels helpless to do it (Rom 7:8). There are many interpretations of Paul's striking confession in Romans 7:15: "For what I want to do I do not do, but what I hate I do" (NRSV). On one extreme, some argue that Paul was speaking of his pre-Christian state, and on the other, that he is confessing his present experience of struggle. Whatever the meaning, James Stewart offers a helpful pastoral comment on these words: "It is safe for a Christian like Paul—it is not safe for everybody—to explain his failings by the watchword, 'Not I, but indwelling sin. . . .' but a sinner had better not make it a principle" (p. 77). This is precisely the emphasis Paul brings in Galatians 5:16-26.

The Spirit Against the Flesh

Seldom noted in Paul's correspondence—sometimes because of the translation—is the fact that Paul's most common use of *Spirit* and *Spiritual* involves the use of a capital *S*. The war within is not between a lower nature (flesh) and a higher nature (spirit), but between the flesh and Spirit, between human nature as a whole turned inward and organized against God's purposes and the presence and power of God. Paul's point in saying that flesh and Spirit "are in conflict with each other, so that you do not do what you want" (Gal 5:17 NRSV) does not reflect a war over which the believer is helpless but speaks to people who are already "in the Spirit." These are reminded by Paul that just as they began their Christian life not by human effort but by receiving the Spirit (Gal 3:2-3), they cannot attain the goal of the Christian life by performance, religious or otherwise, but only through faith and Spirit. They can be taken triumphantly to heaven, but it is through the power of the gospel all the way.

So Christians are under obligation to live according to the Spirit and not to gratify the desires of the flesh (Gal 5:16). Walking in the Spirit precludes Christians from making provision for living according to the impulses of their former way of life: "Spirit people cannot do whatever they like. Freedom is not freedom for the flesh; it is freedom for the Spirit, so that they serve one another in love" (Fee 1991, p. 17). The possibility of a Christian's giving in to sin from time to time remains. Though the flesh has been crucified with the cross of Christ, a Christian might live as though he or she had not been redeemed, adopted, forgiven and indwelt by God's own Spirit. But it is inconsistent so to do. The fact that we continue to struggle makes it imperative not only to understand the nature of the conflict but also to learn how to deal with it.

Walking in the Spirit
In Galatians Paul teaches us how to live victoriously in the thick of battle, not how to live the victorious life. He starts with the fruit of the Spirit and gives an ad hoc list of benefits from being in Christ (Gal 5:22-23)—experiential (such as joy), attitudinal (such as patience) and behavioral (such as self-control). What is remarkable about this list is that Paul does not regulate the Christian life by a series of rules and behavioral requirements. For the Christian there can be no law (Gal 5:23) to regulate food, clothing, religious practices, entertainment and recreation. Human commandments have no value at all. What Paul proposes is letting the Spirit bear fruit in our lives. The contrast between works of the flesh and multiple fruits of the Spirit is often

noted. Works must be accomplished; fruit comes from irruption of life within. Ironically the first and foremost strategy for refusing to live by the flesh is indirect: to turn from concentrating on the flesh to concentrating on the Spirit.

In a shocking, anonymous article entitled "The War Within: An Anatomy of Lust," an American spiritual director revealed his long-standing struggle with pornography and voyeurism. He admitted that lust is fully pleasurable and has its own compelling rewards. He despaired that time after time when he repented in prayer and cried out to God to take away his desire, nothing changed. Then he chanced on a line from François Mauriac, stating that purity is the condition for a higher love—for a possession superior to all possessions: God. Whereas all the negative arguments against lust had failed and guilt had provided no power to change, "here was a description of what I was missing by continuing to harbor lust: I was limiting my own intimacy with God" ("The War Within," p. 43).

Fruit bearing is also the context for Paul's second strategy, a strategy that is also positively motivated. Crucifying the flesh is not first and foremost a negative work. It is like repentance. C. S. Lewis once remarked that repentance "is not something God demands of you before He will take you back and which He could let you off if He chose; it is simply a description of what going back is like" (quoted in "This War Within," p. 45). Paul's repeated exhortations in Galatians to the effect that "those who belong to Christ Jesus have crucified the sinful nature with its passions and desires" (Gal 5:24) should be understood this way. As with the fruit of the Spirit springing up from God's work within us, this experience basically springs from the ongoing effect of Christ's work for us and comes through in Paul's declaration, "May I never boast except in the cross of our Lord Jesus Christ, through which the world has been crucified to me, and I to the world" (Gal 6:14).

These statements are not appeals to self-crucifixion, mortification or self-hatred; such negative good works cannot accomplish anything more than positive good works. Paul appeals for a full and continuous awareness of and agreement with God's judgment on our autonomous, self-justifying life in the cross. John Stott reminds us that a crucifixion is pitiless (and we should not treat the flesh as respectable), painful (even though the pleasures of the flesh are fleeting) and decisive (as suggested by the tense in the Greek—fully accomplished) (pp. 150-51). Here, as everywhere in the Christian life, we move from the indicative (what exists) to the imperative (what ought to be done). Jesus *has* died for us, and the flesh *has* been substantially overcome; therefore, we should maintain a crucified perspective on the flesh. But mortification is less than half of living a victorious battle.

Once again Paul preaches good news. We do not have to live defeated lives: "So I say, live by the Spirit, and you will not gratify the desires of the sinful nature. . . . But if you are led by the Spirit, you are not under law. . . . Since we live by the Spirit, let us keep in step with the Spirit" (Gal 5:16, 18, 25). Here again we move from the indicative to the imperative. We *are* children of God and by the Spirit call God "Father" (Rom 8:15). We *are* led by the Spirit (an image used to describe a farmer leading cattle or soldiers escorting a prisoner to court). Because the Spirit leads us to *do* the walking, we have a continuous, gentle pressure toward goodness. Two words for walking are used—the ordinary word for "walk" and *stoikeō*, which means "to draw people up in a line," thus, "to line oneself up with the Spirit's initiatives." Both suggest an

action on our part, but that is responsive to the constant and creative initiative of the Spirit in our lives.

Negatively, walking according to the Spirit means not setting the mind on the things of the flesh (Rom 8:5) or doing the deeds of the flesh (Gal 5:19-21). We put these desires and deeds to death by the Spirit (Rom 8:13; Gal 5:16-18, 24-26). Involved in this is repudiating our boasting in human achievement, human wisdom or human law keeping as ways of achieving righteousness. Positively, walking according to the Spirit involves setting one's mind on the things of the Spirit (Rom 8:5), allowing the Spirit to produce character fruit (Rom 12—14; Gal 5:19-21) and receiving the Spirit's power for works of holiness (Rom 12:9-21; compare Is 58).

Until Christ comes again and introduces a new heaven and a new earth, we will never cease to experience tension and struggle. But we need not live defeated lives. As surely as Christ has come, has died and has risen, we are living in the age of the Spirit. And we can live by the Spirit. Indeed we will. New Testament spirituality is Spirit-uality. So Paul says, if translated literally, "Live by the Spirit, and you will not gratify the desires of the flesh" (Gal 5:16).

See also CONFLICT RESOLUTION; PRINCIPALITIES AND POWERS; SPIRITUAL DISCIPLINES; SPIRITUAL GROWTH.

References and Resources

D. L. Alexander, ed., *Christian Spirituality: Five Views of Sanctification—Reformed, Lutheran, Wesleyan, Pentecostal, Contemplative* (Downers Grove, Ill.: InterVarsity Press, 1988); W. Barclay, *Flesh and Spirit: An Examination of Galatians 5.19-23* (London: SCM, 1962); W. D. Davies, *Paul and Rabbinic Judaism: Some Rabbinic Elements in Pauline Theology* (Philadelphia: Fortress, 1980); G. D. Fee, *God's Empowering Presence: The Holy Spirit in the Letters of Paul* (Peabody, Mass.: Hendrickson, 1993); G. D. Fee, "Some Reflections on Pauline Spirituality," in *Alive to God,* ed. J. I. Packer and L.

Wilkinson (Downers Grove, Ill.: InterVarsity Press, 1992) 96-107; G. D. Fee, "The Spirit Against the Flesh: Another Look at Pauline Ethics," lecture at New Orleans Baptist Theological Seminary, November 7, 1991; M. Green and R. P. Stevens, *New Testament Spirituality: True Discipleship and Spiritual Maturity* (Guildford, Surrey, U.K.: Eagle, 1994; quoted with permission); J. S. Stewart, *A Faith to Proclaim* (London: Hodder & Stoughton, 1953); J. R. W. Stott, *The Message of Galatians* (Downers Grove, Ill.: InterVarsity Press, 1968). A. C. Thiselton, "Flesh," in *Dictionary of New Testament Theology,* ed. C. Brown (Grand Rapids: Zondervan, 1975) 1:671-82; E. Underhill, *The Fruits of the Spirit* (Wilton, Conn.: Morehouse-Barlow, 1989); "The War Within: An Anatomy of Lust," *Leadership* 3, no. 4 (Fall 1982) 30-48.

R. Paul Stevens

SPIRITUAL DISCIPLINES

Christian experience is transformational. The familiar story of the prodigal son in Luke 15 is suggestive of this. It took only a few hours to get the prodigal out of the far country, but undoubtedly it took many years to get the far country out of the prodigal. He was instantly forgiven* and justified, declared to be not guilty and given the tokens of acceptance: the ring, the robe and the reception. But almost certainly there were habitual thoughts to conquer, attacks of guilt for wasting the inheritance and the lingering censure of his brother. Salvation in Christ is both immediate and progressive—immediate in that we are instantly justified when we accept Christ's death as sufficient to take us to God just as we are; progressive in that we must then engage in a lifelong process of working out the implications of our justification in our thoughts, emotions, relationships, service and practices. This is where *spiritual disciplines* are crucial: they may be defined as Christian practices that encourage spiritual growth* and spiritual formation.* They are life patterns that direct us to God and disciple

us more fully into the likeness of Jesus Christ.

Everyday Disciplines

Both the Old and New Testaments reveal people being confronted with themselves, brought in touch with God and transformed in the context of everyday life. Abraham (Gen 18) met God in the context of hospitality.* Jacob (Gen 25—35) experienced his family* as a furnace of transformation as God kept reaching out to him through the mirrors provided by his family members—brother, mother, father-in-law and wives. Remarkably, the one event for which he was known to be a man of faith took place at the every end of his life: the blessing* of his children (Heb 11:21). Joseph (Gen 37—50) experienced his work* as the arena in which he was called to discover God's sovereign purpose for his life (Gen 50:20). He started with a career* (shepherding), found an occupation (as a slave in Potiphar's house and then a prisoner) and eventually through all discovered his calling* (to save the people of Egypt and Israel). (He was also the first futures trader, making investments* on the grain market.)

Moses was shaped by God and continuously drawn into a deeper life by the discipline of leadership.* Ruth found bereavement to be the context in which her life of faith was evoked and translated into practice. David and Jonathan experienced friendship* as a lifelong spiritual discipline, a discipline that led David to express his loyalty to his dead friend by caring for Jonathan's son Mephibosheth (2 Sam 9). The kings, good and bad, were tested by their experience of government, politics* and power.* Jeremiah discovered that his ministry* was the context in which he, and not just others, was being transformed.

The preacher of Ecclesiastes went through the discipline of success* and wealth.* Job found God and himself through suffering. Ezekiel, once a priest in Jerusalem, became a prophet when he went through the discipline of immigration* as an exile in Babylon. Jonah got "saved" by going on a journey (*see* Traveling) to people he did not love with a message he hardly believed. Hosea gained the heart of God when his own heart was broken and remade through a tragic marriage.* Daniel found encounter with advanced study and a foreign culture* the arena of faith and life building (Dan 1).

In the New Testament Mary and Joseph were shaped by an unexpected and unplanned conception* and birth.* Mary and Martha (Lk 10:38-42) were disciplined in the context of homemaking.* The man born blind (Jn 9) was transformed in the context of his illness and disability. James and John (Mk 10:35-45) were invited to grow by encountering their own ambition.* Peter (Acts 10) was challenged by encountering multiculturalism* and confronting his own ethnocentrism.* Paul found volunteer work as a tentmaking* missionary one of the "weaknesses" and hardships (2 Cor 11:27) that proved to be an arena of transforming grace. Philemon was invited to find the same thing through showing mercy to a former employee that had disappointed him bitterly.

Hardly any of these examples come from ecclesiastical contexts; they show that everyday life is inundated with opportunities to grow spiritually. Some of these everyday disciplines are *relational* (family, marriage, friendship, neighboring). Some are *vocational* (work, ministry, mission). Some are *societal* (culture, multiculturalism, government). Some are *existential* (suffering, relocation, relinquishment, success, death). And some are *personal* (ambition, ethnocentrism, calling). So we do not have to "get away from it all" to experience spiritual growth. Rather what we need to do is to explore the meaning of everyday life and live it fully for God—the very reason for this whole volume.

Christian Practices

There is another approach to spiritual disciplines—the classic approach—that considers Christian practices that help us make sense of everyday life. Some of these Christian practices, like the sacraments,* the Lord's Supper, fellowship* and sabbath,* are mandated in Scripture, give us perspective and help us become deep, rather than just busy, people.

Apart from these mandated practices, the Bible does not really emphasize disciplines in the way that has become trendy today. The Bible inspires us with a vision of a God who is continuously seeking us. In the light of this we find "our own way" of responding, which could include any of the following disciplines and some not even mentioned. These are offered as examples rather than as a plan. They are also offered with a caution. Disciplines are not the means of sanctification—that is God's work— but rather are ways of making ourselves available to God in spiritual growth. E. Stanley Jones says this magnificently:

Conversion is a gift and an achievement. It is an act of a moment and the work of a lifetime. You cannot achieve salvation by disciplines—it is the gift of God. But you cannot retain it without disciplines. If you try to attain salvation by disciplines you will be trying to discipline an unsurrendered self. You are sitting on the lid. The result will be tenseness instead of trust. . . . While salvation cannot be attained by discipline around an unsurrendered self, nevertheless when the self is surrendered to Christ and a new center formed, then you can discipline your life around that new center—Christ. Discipline is the fruit of conversion—not the root. (p. 210)

A handy way to survey these practices is to consider spiritual growth as a journey with three movements: the journey upward (to know and love God better), the journey inward (to know and love ourselves better) and the journey outward (to know and love others better). The order is significant. Self-discovery apart from God-discovery leads to dangerous egoism. Sometimes this egoism takes a disguised form of self-crucifixion or putting ourselves down emotionally as a way of ingratiating ourselves to God. In this case the cloak of pride is turned inside out, but it is still pride because "I" is still in the center (compare Col 3). No one is saved by either positive or negative works. Even a negative self-image does not commend us to God's favor. The journey outward in service depends on being real with God and ourselves. We cannot give bread to others if we do not have bread ourselves.

The Journey Upward

Solitude: planned availability. Silence does not guarantee solitude. And solitude is not the same thing as loneliness. When we are *lonely,* we reach out to other people to fill the void of our lives, and we cling to them to meet needs in ourselves. If people are not willing to do this for us, we may escape into busyness to avoid the further conversion of our own souls. *Solitude,* in contrast, is different from loneliness, for solitude is intentional isolation from others and planned availability to God. When we are lonely, we know we are alone. Solitude, in contrast, is the experience of silence in which we discover we are not alone. Loneliness is usually involuntary. But solitude is the grace of turning involuntary loneliness into a reaffirmation that we are in the presence of God and are positioned to experience God's friendship, even if it is dialogue about God's absence, as it was for the psalmist (Ps 22).

Thanksgiving: waging war on discontentment. The first movement of the soul toward God when we are alone should be gratitude. It was for lack of gratitude and reverence that the Gentiles, who "although they knew God . . . neither glorified him as God nor gave thanks to him" (Rom 1:21), were given over (Rom 1:24, 26, 28) to experience what we call *sins,* which in reality were symptoms of the fundamental sin of ingratitude (*see* Festivals, Thanksgiving). The original sin from the garden onward has been to turn away from simple love of God and to cease practicing continuous thanksgiving in the midst of ordinary life. John Calvin said, "We are surrounded by God's benefits. The best use of these benefits is an unceasing expression of gratitude" (*Institutes* 3.10.28). Being content in any and all circumstances (Phil 4:4-12) has almost nothing to do with the circumstances of our lives and almost everything to do with whether we refer everything to God in humble gratitude. There is nowhere else we can serve the Lord than where we are right now. Oswald Chambers put this in his deeply direct way: "Never allow the thought—'I can be of no use where I am'; because you certainly can be of no use where you are not" (p. 291).

Confession: being honest with God. We cannot be positive all the time any more than we can breathe out all the time. Sometimes in the psalms a person starts not with gratitude but rather with a lament. Gratitude often comes later, after the person has "told it like it is." Gratitude and confession are like the exhale and inhale of breathing. They belong together. Authenticity comes not by introspection but by yielding ourselves just as we are to the loving God who wishes to reside in us. Start with the Ten Commandments (Ex 20:1-17). Walk through each commandment slowly and leisurely and ask God to reveal to you what you must see in the light of his presence. Repentance, says C. S. Lewis, "is not something God demands of you before He will take you back and which He could let you off if you chose; it is simply a description of what going back is like" (quoted in "The War Within," p. 45).

Bible meditation: crawling through Scripture. Confession expresses the hunger of our hearts. God's Word feeds that hunger. But how are we to read the Bible? Reading* large passages of Scripture every day with a view to reading through the Bible each year is a wonderful discipline, and there are excellent lectionaries to assist you in this. But equally there is great gain in crawling through the Scripture, attending to each sentence and making it our own. Bible meditation is more than, though not less than, exegesis, which is the science of understanding the text in its context. Meditation helps us internalize what we have read and heard so that our fundamental longings and addictions are addressed by the inseminating Word of God. The words used in the Bible for *meditate* imply the use of both mind and heart. The Hebrew word *siach* means "to muse," "go over in one's mind," "rehearse" (Gen 24:63; Ps 119:15, 23, 27, 48, 78, 148). *Hagah* means "to mutter" or "meditate." It is used of the sound characteristic of the moaning of the dove (Is 38:14) or the growling of the lion over its prey (Is 31:4). The righteous ponder or brood upon the proper answer (Prov 15:28) and then talk about wisdom (Ps 37:30) or God's righteousness (Ps 35:28). *Promeletaō* in the New Testament means "to meditate before what you shall answer" or "to practice a speech" (Lk 21:14). In meditating we imbibe the word (Rev 10:10), chew on it as a cow chews its cud, make it our very own. It is a prayerful way of reading the Bible.

A central role in this is played by our imagination.* One way to make a beginning is to take an incident in the Gospels (such as Jn 5:1-15 or Jn 21:1-19) and put yourself into the story. Linger long enough on each detail until you have re-created the whole drama. Allow yourself prayerfully to identify with more than one character in the drama, and allow Jesus to minister to you as he ministers to the people in the story. This is one way in which the journey upward leads almost inevitably to confrontation of oneself. Another way is to focus on images in the Bible, its picture language for God, aspects of life, our own journey or the hope that lies before us. The Bible is rich in symbols, metaphors, similes and analogies that spur our minds and hearts as we imaginatively enter into them.

The Journey Inward

The lengths to which people will go to avoid self-confrontation are awesome. Work and leisure are the most common dodges. But by far the most dangerous are the diversions created when religion itself is used to escape self-discovery. Service to God and theologizing about God easily become a way of hiding, like Adam among the trees of the garden escaping from the voice and presence of the Lord. Some ministering people have what Eric Fromm called "market-oriented personalities"; they sell themselves to do whatever procures them signs of acceptance, so delaying the needed journey within. Fortunately our God is more willing to seek us than we are to be found.

Journal keeping. A discipline that encourages inner authenticity is keeping a journal. Psalm 42:5 is really a journal entry. In it David is talking to God in writing about his depression in the light of something greater than his own experience: "Why are you downcast, O my soul? Why so disturbed within me? Put your hope in God, for I will yet praise him, my Savior and my God." The psalms are an eloquent witness that outpourings of emotions, hurts, fears and resentments to God in prayer are not merely permitted; they are positively encouraged. One way of recognizing the word of God in the psalms is not merely to analyze their words but rather to allow God to be revealed through the psalmist's prayers. This is the metacommunication of the psalms that turns out to be more important than the messages communicated within the psalms. The God so revealed is one to whom we can bring the whole range of our experience, past and present, letting it pour right out just as it is.

Keeping a journal is like writing a letter to God or writing out our prayers or speaking to our own soul in the presence of someone greater than our own experience. Then our absence of experience of God or even our experience of the absence of God can become a cry for more reality with God. It is essential that we let our thoughts and feeling flow out without editing and self-criticism, for we have a God to whom we can pour out the darkest and deepest things within us.

Walking through life with Jesus. For many Christians the past is not in the past, except in the ultimate sense of being justified by faith. But in the day-to-day interchanges they are living out past hurts today, reacting in the light of unforgiven acts against them and repeating patterns that may have been handed down through many generations. Especially if we were rejected at birth, or our parents wished we were another sex, or our parents had attempted to abort us, or we were sexually or physically abused, or we witnessed a profound trauma, or we were profoundly hurt in romantic relationships from which we have never recovered, or we were scarred by failure at school, in the neighborhood, in the marketplace or in church ministry, we may be in need of soul healing (or the healing of memories, as it is sometimes called).

Deeply painful events in our past may have been suppressed merely to achieve survival, but they continue to affect us when we are touched by someone of the opposite sex or when a contemporary situation triggers some of the old feelings. Sometimes the violent anger that spills over, completely out of proportion to the triggering event, is a sign that there is an unhealed scar. Many Christian workers actually minister from this "hurt edge" and play the martyr or evoke pity as a way of gaining control of situations and people. True joy in the Spirit is lacking because joy is the overflow of the Spirit in all dimensions of our personhood and when our whole personal history has been redeemed.

So it is a good thing to engage in the discipline of walking through your life with Jesus, asking him to show you the happy as well as sad events and relationships that make up your personal story. Usually this takes several hours and may be done best in a retreat setting, because it takes action-oriented people several hours to stop long enough to get in touch with their own feelings. The theological reality behind this discipline is the statement of God to Jacob and Jesus to us: "I am with you" (Gen 28:15; 31:3). God is personally present through our entire lives from conception onward, even before we first felt the warmth of divine love. God is unconditionally present and does not require us or the other players in our lives to be worthy of his presence. God is omnipotently present, for there is no experience we have had, no matter how painful or violent, that cannot be transformed into an asset by divine grace. One reason why we so rarely experience full release and recovery of our past is that we are too theoretical and not specific enough in our desire to become whole. Our imaginations can serve us in this.

As we encounter situations in which we were hurt by others, we can prayerfully ask Jesus to show us his presence there, revealing his lordship and showing us what he will now do to that experience in the light of his victory on the cross. Far from leaving ourselves open to demons who come to us in the name of Jesus, this is a genuine act of worship and opens us up to the Spirit, provided that we do not reduce God to the picture we have of God, for this would be idolatry. When we have been profoundly sinned against, we can ask for grace to reach the point at which we can say to those who have wounded us, "I forgive them, for they did not know what they were doing." Sometimes with very painful events, such as the discovery of the sources of homosexual tendencies or the experience of sexual abuse, it is important to share this journey with at least one experienced counselor. Often hours of prayer and counseling become intertwined before there is complete and substantial healing of profound hurt.

Journey Outward

As we become increasingly real with God and ourselves, we are liberated to serve others. Often, however, the order is reversed. Our service to others raises crucial questions that inspire the inward and upward journeys. *Why am I so sensitive to criticism? Why do I work so hard?* So the three journeys are interdependent, as our suggested disciplines show.

Intercession. A remarkable passage in the book of Job shows Job praying for his grown children the morning after the party (Job 1:4-5)! Family life calls us to prayer. In marriage one of our most important ministries is to pray for our spouse—even more important than praying *with* him or her. Prayer for our enemies and the most difficult people in our lives is transformative *of ourselves* first and often of others. When we pray, we get in touch with God's mind about others. We piggyback on the Spirit's prayers. We touch people directly through Jesus the mediator. And we get changed.

Forgiveness. Family and work give us more than the average opportunity to practice the discipline of forgiveness.* Many people find repeating the Lord's Prayer one way of reminding themselves to keep this discipline. Forgiveness of others is at the heart of the prayer, but not merely forgiveness in our relationship with God. Once again the journeys are related: "Forgive us our debts, as we also have forgiven our debtors" (Mt 6:12). Augustine called this a terrible prayer because it says that what we desperately need ourselves can only be received when we extend it to others. We can only ask God to forgive us what we are willing to forgive others. (For other disciplines in the journey outward, *see* Hospitality; Ministry; Social Action; Spiritual Gifts; Stewardship.)

Spiritual disciplines like the ones we have already explored involve hard work: cultivating the soil, planting the seed, watering and fertilizing it, tearing out the weeds and removing the stones. Waiting for the harvest is itself hard work for the farmer. But, on the whole, the seed grows by itself. Spiritual disciplines, properly understood, are not attempts to merge ourselves with God, but ways of removing obstacles and creating new channels of response to the seeking Father. God does the finding, and our seeking is—even from the first movement within our souls—an active response to God's finding us. So disciplines are not the means of gaining godliness; they are the fruit of godliness. As we have seen, this involves both discerning God in everyday life and developing personal contemplative practices. As A. W. Tozer said, "To have found God and still to pursue Him is the soul's paradox of love, scorned indeed by the too-easily-satisfied

937

religionist, but justified in happy experience by children of the burning heart" (quoted in Hilton, p. xxviii).

See also SPIRITUAL FORMATION; SPIRITUAL GROWTH.

References and Resources
R. Banks, *Redeeming the Routines* (Wheaton, Ill.: Victor Books, 1993); G. Bernados, *The Diary of a Country Priest* (London: Fontana Books, 1956); D. Bonhoeffer, *Life Together* (San Francisco: Harper & Row, 1976); J. P. de Caussade, *The Sacrament of the Present Moment*, ed. K. Muggeridge (San Francisco: Harper & Row, 1982); O. Chambers, *My Utmost for His Highest* (New York: Dodd, Mead, 1956); R. Foster, *Celebration of Discipline* (San Francisco: Harper & Row, 1978); J. Houston, *The Transforming Friendship: A Guide to Prayer* (London: Lions, 1989); W. Hilton, *Toward a Perfect Love*, trans. D. L. Jeffrey (Portland, Ore.: Multnomah, 1985). R. P. Job and N. Shawchuck, *A Guide to Prayer for Ministers and Other Servants* (Nashville: Upper Room, 1983); E. S. Jones, *Conversion* (Nashville: Abingdon, 1959); H. Nouwen, *Creative Ministry* (Garden City, N.Y.: Image/Doubleday, 1971); D. Postema, *Space for God* (Grand Rapids: Bible Way, 1985); R. P. Stevens, *Disciplines of the Hungry Heart* (Wheaton, Ill.: Harold Shaw, 1993; portions quoted with permission); D. Willard, *The Spirit of the Disciplines: Understanding How God Changes Lives* (New York: Harper & Row, 1988); "The War Within: An Anatomy of Lust," *Leadership* 3, no. 4 (Fall 1982) 30-48.

R. Paul Stevens

SPIRITUAL FORMATION

There are three terms in current use that describe how Christians go about the growth and development of the spiritual life. These are discipleship* training, character development and spiritual formation. While they address the same general issue, each puts the emphasis at a different place in terms of the understanding and practice of Christian spirituality. By analyzing these three perspectives, we can identify the unique character of spiritual formation.

Discipleship training involves the transmission of the essential data of the Christian life from an older, experienced Christian to a younger (in spiritual years), newer Christian. This is a teaching relationship in which the discipler shows the disciple how to pray, study the Bible and share his or her faith with others. The aim of discipleship training is to produce a mature disciple, capable of engaging in ministry, knowledgeable about basic doctrine and committed to regular devotional practices (mainly Bible study and prayer, often called a daily quiet time). The Navigators, a parachurch organization that seeks to make disciples for Jesus Christ, has done much to popularize this method of spiritual growth (*The 2:7 Series*; Wilson). An updated version of discipleship training can be found in the writings of J. Robert Clinton and Paul Stanley, who describe a variety of mentoring-type relationships that have spiritual growth as their aim.

Character development is a term that describes the process whereby Christian men and women are exposed to regular, theologically nuanced teaching that, over time, produces a Christian lifestyle. Such a lifestyle is characterized by the Christian virtues* (though these are sometimes defined more by what one abstains from—taboos—than by what one engages in) and by good works. In this case, the pastor is the teacher, and the prime vehicle of instruction is the weekly sermon. The assumption is that when a person believes correct doctrine, a wholesome lifestyle follows. Within this perspective, psychology is sometimes greeted with suspicion, inner reflection and experience are suspect, and there is skepticism about the validity of other Christian communities not holding these views. This is a perspective that is found in some of the more conservative groups of the Reformed tradition.

Spiritual formation is the term with the

longest history (dating back to early monastic practices). It is the process whereby men and women who love and trust Jesus seek to take on the character of Christ guided by various spiritual practices. The central figure in spiritual formation is a spiritual director whose task is to help the directee discern the will of God for his or her life. The focus in their relationship is not so much teaching as it is prayer. The process of spiritual direction involves gentle encouragement, "holy listening" (Guenther), thoughtful questions and guidance in the practice of various spiritual disciplines.* Until recently, this perspective was found mainly in Roman Catholic and Episcopalian circles.

Clearly, each tradition touches upon issues of importance. It is important to master basic Christian ideas and to develop Christian habits.* It is important to become people of integrity, committed to strong and positive values.* It is important to discern the unfolding direction God has for our lives and to do so in a context of prayer that keeps us in touch with the presence of God. However, it is also necessary to see the limitations of each approach. Christian discipleship* can develop into an unhealthy dependence on a strong authority figure who makes decisions for us. Character development can lead to a harmful neglect of the interior life and to a superior attitude toward others whose doctrine and practice differ from our own. Spiritual formation can make the spiritual life into a matter of works, not grace, in which one's efforts and experience are what count, not the saving and sanctifying activity of the triune God.

The Biblical Foundation of Spiritual Formation

Three statements by Paul provide the biblical foundation for spiritual formation. The central word in each passage is *transformed* or *formed,* which is derived from the Greek root *morphē* (which is related to the English word *metamorphosis*). This is the word used in the Gospels to describe the change that took place in Jesus at his transfiguration (a complete change came over him; his body became translucent and so on; Mk 9:2). To be transformed is to undergo a deep-seated, all-encompassing change of character and conduct.

In Romans 12:2 Paul states: "Do not conform any longer to the pattern of this world, but be transformed by the renewing of your mind. Then you will be able to test and approve what God's will is —his good, pleasing and perfect will." The nature of the transformation is *from* the pattern or standards of the world *into* the image of Christ: "Here then are the stages of Christian moral transformation: first our mind is renewed by the Word and Spirit of God; then we are able to discern and desire the will of God; and then we are increasingly transformed by it" (Stott, p. 324). The process of spiritual formation makes great use of imaginative reflection on Scripture (for example, Ignatian contemplation) with the aim of discerning God's will so as to bring about genuine transformation (*see* Guidance).

In 2 Corinthians Paul asserts that "all of us, with unveiled faces, seeing the glory of the Lord as though reflected in a mirror, are being transformed into the same image from one degree of glory to another" (2 Cor 3:18 NRSV). There are three important insights from this passage. First, it is our experience of God's glory that brings about transformation. We are changed by beholding the divine. Second, the goal of this transformation is that we be made into the image of the Lord that we see, albeit dimly (as in a first-century polished metal mirror). Third, this process is gradual and progressive, moving from stage to stage. In this passage the goal and process of spiritual formation are defined.

The goal of this transformation is made even more explicit in Galatians: "My dear children, for whom I am again in the pains of childbirth until Christ is formed in you" (Gal 4:19). We are to be reshaped, molded, altered, changed from one form to another, until we reflect the image of Christ. In other passages Paul reminds us that we are in Christ and that Christ is in us (Rom 8:10; 1 Cor 1:30; 2 Cor 5:17; Col 1:27). The process of spiritual formation is the realization of this reality in everyday life.

What motivates us to pursue spiritual formation is one thing: the love of God. It is because we were grasped by God's love that we began this journey in the first place, it is because we experience God's love in our daily lives that we press on, and it is because we have a burning desire to love God that we give ourselves to these tasks.

Spiritual Disciplines and Practices

The spiritual disciplines lie at the heart of spiritual formation. They are the vehicles through which growth takes place. Certain disciplines are central to spiritual formation.

Spiritual direction. Christian spiritual direction is the

> help given by one Christian to another which enables that person to pay attention to God's personal communication to him or her, to respond to this personally communicating God, to grow in intimacy with God and to live out the consequences of the relationship. The focus . . . is on experience, not ideas, and specifically on religious experience, i.e., any experience of the mysterious Other whom we call God. (Barry and Connolly, p. 8)

Prayer is at the heart of spiritual direction. The director assists the directee to learn how to pray in such a way that there is genuine dialogue with God, not just a monologue of requests on the part of the directee. While this may involve some instruction in ways of prayer, it more often manifests itself in helping the directee to discern what God is saying to him or her.

Thus, discernment is an important aspect of spiritual direction. Discernment is the spiritual evaluation of specific experiences related to one's spiritual journey. Discernment is used in two (related) senses: discernment of God's will and desire in one's life and discernment between good and evil tendencies (or spirits). Discernment in the first sense involves developing a heightened sensitivity to the spiritual. It is learning to notice God in one's daily life. It is the development of a conversational relationship with the Lord. Discernment in the second sense alerts one to the various "voices" that assail a person: the voice of culture,* the voice of family* and friends, the voice of convention, the voice of appetite, the voice of addiction* and so on. It enables a person to distinguish the voice of the Holy Spirit in the midst of this inner cacophony. In both cases the question we ask of the choice we are making, of the feeling we are gripped by or of the voice we are hearing is whether such inner intuitions lead us godward or not. If they point us to God, in all likelihood they are from God. Experiences are evaluated by their fruits. Of course, it is not always easy (or possible) for a person to make such a judgment in the midst of the experience, which is where a spiritual director comes in.

There has been a revival of interest in spiritual direction in recent years. This is motivated, in part, by the deep interest in spirituality on the part of the baby-boom generation. Such interest can be very healthy, or it may be just a passing fad. (If "having a spiritual director" is made a sign of piety, the movement is in trouble.) One author suggests that if this current interest in spiritual direction follows the pattern of other recent movements in the church, it is apt to fade out in ten years' time. On the other hand, this renewed interest is leading to new approaches, new understandings and new depth to the ancient practice of spiritual direction. For example, as Protestants add their own distinct theological and practical insights (for example, insight into group spiritual direction drawing on traditions of spirituality in such groups as the Quakers) to the rich lore of understanding and practice from the liturgical churches, the movement will become healthier. A good example is the growth of discernment groups to help members resolve some personal, relational or vocational dilemma.

Lectio divina (or sacred reading). This is an approach to Scripture that seeks to read it with the heart as well as with the head. In *lectio divina* the focus is on Scripture as a way of hearing a word from God rather than on the study of Scripture with understanding as the aim (which is a crucial but different spiritual discipline). In fact, *lectio divina* is really a form of prayer because while it starts with the text, it ends in response to God.

The process is simple enough. We pick a text of Scripture. At first this will probably be a Gospel account or one of the psalms—material that has the power to move us in a deep way. The passage should be short—no more than ten verses or so. Then the passage is read slowly, repetitively, often aloud. We read until we are moved by a word or a phrase. Something causes us to pause. The reason does not matter, only that somehow our attention is captured by that word or phrase. We repeat it over and over again and let it sink and make connections with our life (this is an act of meditation).

Then we offer the word or phrase to God in prayer. We open ourselves to what God is saying to us by it. We ponder this message to us. We own it. We let it move us. We respond to it. We respond to God. When we find our mind wandering from that word or phrase, it is time to go back to the text and read further. Once again we listen for words that light up for us.

A spiritual director will often encourage a directee to approach Scripture in this manner, especially if that directee tends to come at faith via the mind only (or mainly). By discussing with the directee the outcome of *lectio divina,* the director helps that person get in touch with the dialogue God wishes to engage in with the directee.

Spiritual reading. While Scripture will always remain the central focus of meditation, it is also true that regular reading* of devotional classics is also deeply nurturing. By *devotional classics* I mean those writings forged out of deep spiritual quests. Books like *The Imitation of Christ* by Thomas à Kempis (which is certainly one of the greatest pieces of spiritual writing), *The Way of the Pilgrim* by an anonymous Russian pilgrim, *The Confessions of Saint Augustine, The Life of Saint Teresa of Ávila by Herself, The Revelations of Divine Love* by Julian of Norwich and *The Practice of the Presence of God* by Brother Lawrence have great power to instruct us, as do the books of certain contemporary authors such as C. S. Lewis, Thomas Merton and Henri Nouwen (see Muto).

Meditative prayer. This term is used to cover a variety of prayer practices in which the focus is on listening* to God as well as speaking* to God. This would include such activities as centering prayer, the prayer of examen, contemplative prayer, prayer of the heart and prayer of adoration (Foster).

Meditation is a form of reflection. It is a type of thinking. It is a way of mulling over an incident to discern its meaning;

it is puzzling out the meaning of a text; it is trying to process what God might be saying. This becomes prayer when the meditation is done in the presence of God and is offered to God. Contemplation is a related, though separate, term. Contemplation is a type of awareness. It is moving the focus from oneself (one's thoughts, concerns, needs) and giving attention instead to another (or to nothing in particular except a kind of open awareness that is attuned to God). As Ignatius of Loyola describes contemplation in his *Spiritual Exercises,* it involves focusing on Jesus as he appears in one of the Gospel stories, becoming absorbed in Jesus and then letting our experience with Jesus, in contemplation, unfold as it will. Properly speaking, meditation is not prayer but preparation for prayer; contemplation is prayer in that one connects with God.

It is not uncommon that one of the first tasks for the spiritual director or a formational group is to help teach the skills of meditation and contemplation. The director seeks to help the directee to "pay attention to God as he reveals himself" and to help the directee "recognize his reactions and decide on his responses to God" (Barry and Connolly, p. 46).

Retreats. We must also mention the use of retreats in the process of spiritual formation. These generally involve long periods of silence, liturgical services in which a meditation may be given to help direct the prayers of the retreatants, conversation with a spiritual director (but no one else) and a theme around which to focus prayer. Such a retreat contrasts sharply with the typical Protestant retreat, which features lots of activity and lots of input.

Spiritual journaling. In this form of reflection, one seeks to make sense of life as it unfolds on a daily basis and in terms of the overall patterns of one's life. This is a tool of great flexibility that allows us to engage life rather than just let it pass by and that gives us a perspective on how God has worked in our lives in the past (Peace 1995a).

Spiritual autobiography. This is the art of putting together the story of God's activity in one's life and presenting it to a small group of others similarly engaged in the same task. In this way we come to see the patterns of God's activity in our life over time, we learn to notice the presence of God in the ordinary and everyday, and we develop a sense of the trajectory that our life in God has been taking and so are better enabled to make choices about further directions (Peace 1995b).

Spiritual formation is, therefore, a healthy and holistic way of approaching spiritual growth. Its focus is more on experience than on information; it depends more on prayer than on study; it requires the help of a director or group rather than the guidance of an authority figure; it necessitates an inner desire to know God and not just an obligation to act and think like a Christian; it involves the cultivation of the inner life rather than the ordering of the outer life. As such, spiritual formation is more the activity of the mature believer who has mastered basic doctrine and who has allowed this knowledge and commitment to express itself in the everyday choices of life than the activity of a new believer who is engaged in the task of translating a newfound worldview into a consistent Christian lifestyle.

See also CHURCH MEMBERSHIP; DISCIPLESHIP; SPIRITUAL DISCIPLINES; SPIRITUAL GROWTH.

References and Resources
W. A. Barry and W. J. Connolly, *The Practice of Spiritual Direction* (San Francisco: HarperSanFrancisco, n.d.); J. R. Clinton and P. D. Stanley, *Connecting: The Mentoring Relationships You Need to Succeed in Life* (Colorado Springs: NavPress, 1992); R. Foster, *Prayer* (San Francisco: Harper SanFrancisco, 1992); K. O. Gangel and J. C.

Wilhoit, *The Christian Educator's Handbook on Spiritual Formation* (Wheaton, Ill.: Victor Books, 1994); M. Guenther, *Holy Listening: The Art of Spiritual Direction* (Boston: Cowley Publications, 1992); G. May, *Care of Mind/Care of Spirit: A Psychiatrist Explores Spiritual Direction* (San Francisco: HarperSanFrancisco, 1982, 1992); S. Muto, *A Practical Guide to Spiritual Reading* (Petersham, Mass.: St. Bede's Publications, 1994); R. Peace, *Spiritual Journaling: Recording Your Journey Toward God,* Spiritual Disciplines Series (Colorado Springs: NavPress, 1995a); R. Peace, *Spiritual Storytelling: Discovering and Sharing Your Spiritual Biography,* Spiritual Disciplines Series (Colorado Springs: NavPress, 1995b); R. Peace, *Contemplative Bible Reading: Experiencing God Through Scripture,* Spiritual Disciplines Series (Colorado Springs: NavPress, 1996); J. Stott, *Romans* (Downers Grove, Ill.: InterVarsity Press, 1994); *The 2:7 Series–Navigator Discipleship Training for Laymen Courses 1-3* (Colorado Springs: NavPress, 1974); C. Wilson, *With Christ in the School of Disciple Building* (Grand Rapids: Zondervan, 1976).

Richard V. Peace

SPIRITUAL GIFTS

Several prevailing misunderstandings make it difficult for us to come to the biblical data on their own terms without forcing on the material a grid of expectation formed by popular Christian teaching. It is popularly understood, for example: (1) that spiritual gifts are given at the time of conversion and do not change during one's lifetime; (2) that Christian maturation is hampered if we do not know what our gift is; (3) that our gift defines our identity ("I am a teacher"); (4) that gifts are primarily linked to roles and offices in the church; (5) that the more extraordinary gifts are indications of advanced spiritual life; (6) that gifts have little to do with our natural capabilities (sometimes called *talents**); (7) that gifts concern the spirit of a person (generally people talk of *spiritual gifts* but not of *Spirit gifts*); (8) that gifts define the character of the personal ministry of each Chris-

tian; (9) that emphasis on spiritual gifts may threaten the unity of the church and (10) that the lists of gifts in the New Testament are definitive and exhaustive.

In contrast, the biblical data affirm that gifts may be temporary or long-term; that being able to identify our gift is not as important as making sure our personal ministry edifies others; that our identity is found in relation to Christ and his people as a child of God rather than in what we do; that gifts are not usually related to specific roles and offices in church leadership (though sometimes they are); that the more visible gifts, while valuable, are not more valuable than less visible gifts since love (1 Cor 13) is the way gifts are best expressed; that the work of the Spirit in our lives turns persons-as-a-whole into gifts; that gifts are not properties of the human spirit but the gracious working of the Spirit through persons (and therefore are better described as *gifts of the Spirit* or *Spirit gifts*); that personal ministry is defined by service* and love* directed to the glory of God and the upbuilding of the saints; that instead of causing disunity, the diversity of Spirit expressions is necessary for the rich unity of the people of God; and that the various New Testament lists of gifts point to a great variety and to possibilities not even listed.

The Biblical Data

Since Paul uses "gift" language more than others in the New Testament, this overview of the data concentrates primarily on the Pauline letters (plus 1 Pet 4:10-11). First, despite frequent suggestions to the contrary, the word *charisma* does not mean "spiritual gift." Rather, it refers to "a concrete expression of grace," and only refers to "Spirit giftedness" when modified by the adjective *pneumatikon* (pertaining to the Spirit) or in a context in which such concrete expressions of grace are directly attributed to the Spirit. Thus, for example, *charisma* (gift) is used to describe eternal life (Rom 6:23), the special privileges of Israel (Rom 11:29), celibacy and marriage (1 Cor 7:7) and even an experience of personal deliverance from peril (2 Cor 1:11). On the other hand, the plural *charismata* is used primarily to describe gracious bestowments of the Spirit in the gathered community for the sake of building up the people of God.

The second word that is sometimes translated as "spiritual gifts" is *pneumatika* (1 Cor 12:1; 14:1), which literally means "the things of the Spirit," thus emphasizing the action of the Holy Spirit rather than the development of the believer's spirituality. Paul does use a word for "spirits" (*pneumata;* 1 Cor 12:10; 14:12, 32) seemingly in this sense: the believer's spirit is the place where the human and the divine interface in the believer's life (*see* Soul). There is one other word used: *dōrea*, the most common word for "gift" (Eph 4:7), which Paul uses in Ephesians to express how various persons who minister in the church (Eph 4:11) are God's gifts to the church. Thus it is almost impossible to organize Paul's teaching on gifts because the ad hoc nature of his letters presents us with considerable ambiguity both in the use of language and the nature of the listings.

1 Corinthians 12—14. Paul's purpose in this passage is primarily corrective, not instructive. Uninterpreted tongues in the gathered community is clearly the culprit (as 1 Cor 14 makes clear). True spirituality (in the sense of being a Spirit person) is most likely the issue, and Paul and the Corinthians are at odds on this matter (1 Cor 14:36-37). The result was inordinate zeal for tongues and consequent disorder in their assembly. In his effort to curb their misguided zeal, Paul

first argues for the necessity of diversity—if the community is truly to be "of the Spirit" (1 Cor 12:4-30). He then argues that no gifting counts for anything if love does not motivate (1 Cor 13:1-13), concluding that in terms of Spirit manifestations, love demands that we seek after intelligible utterances (1 Cor 14:1-25) and order (1 Cor 14:26-40) if the community is to be built up (1 Cor 14:1-19, 26-33) and outsiders are to be converted (1 Cor 14:20-25).

In the process Paul has occasion to list various *charismata*, ministries and forms of service at seven different points in his argument (1 Cor 12:8-10, 28, 29-30; 13:1-3, 8; 14:6, 26), no two of which are alike (not even 1 Cor 12:28 and 12:29-30). Not only is this so, but they appear in ways that make systematizing nearly impossible. Paul's concern is not with instruction about spiritual gifts as such—their number and kinds; rather he offers a considerable and diverse list so that they will stop being singular in their own emphasis (that is, on tongues). Thus, tailored to speak to their situation, the list in 12:8-10 is but representative of the diversity of the Spirit's manifestations.

In 1 Corinthians 12:27-30 after twice applying his analogy of the body, with emphasis on the need for diversity (1 Cor 12:15-26), Paul concludes with another list of gifts and ministries. The emphasis remains the same—the need for diversity. The list represents a whole range of ministries in the church, which were probably chosen for that reason. The first three (apostles, prophets, teachers) emphasize the persons who have these ministries, while the final five (miracles, gifts of healings,* helpful deeds, acts of guidance and tongues) emphasize the ministry itself. This probably suggests that the first three items are to be thought of, not as offices held by certain persons in the local church, but rather as ministries as they find expression in various persons; likewise, the remaining gifts are not expressed in the church apart from persons but are first of all gracious endowments, given by the Spirit to various persons in the church for its mutual upbuilding. "Helpful deeds" and "acts of guidance" occur only here in the New Testament. The gift of tongues is last, as always, because it is the problem child—included only after the need for diversity is well heard.

1 Corinthians 13:1-3, 8; 14:6, 26. For the most part the remaining lists in 1 Corinthians add little that is new, except for two things. First, we receive added insight into what Paul understands about knowledge, by his speaking in 1 Corinthians 13:2 of "knowing all mysteries and all knowledge." In 1 Corinthians 14:6 it appears alongside "revelation," which suggests Spirit-inspired understanding of the ways of God. Second, revelation, which first appears in 1 Corinthians 14:6, also is listed in 1 Corinthians 14:26 as one of the things that happens in the gathering for worship. Since the prophetic word in 1 Corinthians 14:24-25 also "reveals" the hidden secrets of the heart of the sinner and leads to conversion, it seems likely that this word indicates something of Paul's own understanding of prophecy.

Romans 12:6-8. The concern here is for a sober estimate of ourselves and the need for mutuality and diversity in the community.* This passage shares three things with 1 Corinthians 12—14: (1) the analogy of the body, (2) the fact that the members have *charismata* given to them and (3) the mention of prophecy as the first of the *charismata* and the inclusion of teaching as the third item. In contrast to 1 Corinthians, but in keeping with the issues in the Roman church, the seven items emphasize, not miracles and verbal utterances, but forms of service ("service" itself being one of the items listed). One further item (*paraklēsis,* "exhorta-tion," NRSV and NASB) is probably a verbal gift, but it might also be another form of serving ("encouraging," NIV). Furthermore, each item is qualified as to the manner in which the utterance or service is to be rendered ("according to the rule of faith," "with sincerity, earnestness, cheerfulness," etc.). The sixth item, *proistamenos,* can mean either "to manage/govern" or "to care for or give aid to" but its appearance here between "giving" and "showing mercy" suggests the latter even when leadership* is in view (as in 1 Thess).

Ephesians 4:11. This list is unique in the Pauline literature. Three ministries from 1 Corinthians 12:28 are mentioned (apostles, prophets, teachers); these are joined by "evangelists" and "pastors," the latter probably to be understood in very close relationship with "teacher." Although this list also occurs in the context of Spirit and body (Eph 4:4), these gifts are not referred to as *charismata,* nor are they suggested to be gifts of the Spirit. They are given to the church by Christ; they are people who function in these ways within the church for equipping the saints (*see* Equipping) so that they can do the "work of ministry, for building up the body" (Eph 4:12 NRSV). Are these people to be thought of in terms of their function or as holders of an office? The emphasis still seems to be on function. It is doubtful whether Paul ever considered an office in the church as a spiritual gift, either in terms of *charisma* or as a special endowment of the Spirit. That seems to be the reading of these texts from a later time (*see* Leadership, Church).

1 Peter 4:10-11. In this passage the Spirit is not mentioned but rather "God's grace." While Peter offers no gift list, or more accurately grace list (except *speaking* and *serving*), he emphasizes, as Paul did, the "various forms" (4:10) in which God's grace works among his people. He further calls believers to administer

God's grace faithfully as stewards with the purpose (implied from the context) of mutual enrichment and the goal "that in all things God may be praised through Jesus Christ" (4:11).

Gracious Endowments and Gifts of the Spirit

Despite the difficulties involved, the various items from these texts may be conveniently grouped under three major headings: Spirit manifestations within the worshiping community, deeds of service and specific ministries. The goal of all *charismata*, in all categories, is the building up of the community itself and individual members within the community. In its first two categories Paul makes a considerable point of the universality of such gifting within the Spirit-filled community.

Spirit manifestations within the worshiping community. There is a specific connection here between the Spirit and *charismata*. These appear chiefly to be supernatural manifestations of the Spirit within the community at worship. They can be further grouped into *miracles* and *verbal utterances*. Miracles include "faith" (the supernatural gift of faith that can "move mountains"; compare 1 Cor 13:2), "gifts of healings" (of the physical body; also 1 Cor 12:28, 30) and "workings of miracles" (all other such phenomena not included in healing; 1 Cor 12:10). The use of the plurals "gifts" and "workings" for the latter two probably mean that these gifts are not permanent, but each occurrence is a gift in its own right. Such phenomena were a regular part of the apostle's own ministry (Rom 15:18-19; 2 Cor 12:12) and the regular expectation of the Pauline churches (Gal 3:5).

Inspired utterances include "the message of wisdom" (1 Cor 12:8), "the message of knowledge" (12:8), "prophecy" (14:1), "the discernments of Spirits/spirits" (authors' trans. 12:10—we do not

know for sure which Paul means), "tongues" (12:10), and "the interpretation of tongues" from 1 Corinthians 12:8-10; "instruction" and "revelation" from 1 Corinthians 14:6; and (perhaps) "exhortation" (NRSV) from Romans 12:8—it might also include "singing" from 1 Corinthians 14:15 and 14:26 (compare Eph 5:19) and "speaking"* from 1 Peter 4:11. Attempts to distinguish some of these items from one another are generally futile, as is any distinction between their "charismatic" or "noncharismatic" expression (for example, teaching or singing). For Paul the "message of wisdom" is the preaching of the cross (see 1 Cor 1:18—2:16; the terminology occurs nowhere else). Knowledge, on the other hand, is closely related to mysteries in 1 Corinthians 13:2. Similarly, "prophecy" itself is closely connected to "revelation" in 1 Corinthians 14:25-26, 30. Probably these are to be understood as different emphases for the expression of the prophetic gift.

Outside of Paul's letters *prophecy* is mentioned as a crucial endowment of the Day of Pentecost by which Spirit-ministry has been universalized as proof that Joel's prophecy has been fulfilled (Joel 2:28-32; Acts 2:17-21). Thus prophecy in this present age of the Spirit and these "last days" (Acts 2:17) is a potential ministry for everyone since the Spirit has been poured out "on all people . . . both men and women" (Acts 2:17-18). Prophecy is the *charisma* most often mentioned in the Pauline letters (Rom 12:6; 1 Cor 11:4-5; 12—14; Eph 2:20; 3:5; 4:11; 1 Thess 5:20; 1 Tim 1:18; 4:14). In Paul such speech consisted either of spontaneous, intelligible messages, orally delivered in the gathered assembly and intended for the edification or encouragement of the people, or of "revelation" of some kind (Gal 2:2), which at times could expose the hearts of unbelievers and lead them to repentance (1 Cor 14:24-25). Those who prophesied were clearly understood to be in control (see 1 Cor 14:29-33). Although some people are called prophets, the implication of 1 Corinthians 14:24-25, 30-31 is that the gift is available—at least potentially—to all.

But it is also clear that prophecy does not have independent authority. It must be discerned by the charismatic community (1 Cor 12:10, 14:29; 1 Thess 5:21-22). People may believe themselves truly to be inspired of the Spirit, but in reality what is said may not come from the Spirit at all. Therefore, the community must test all things, holding fast to the good and dispensing with every evil expression. Some preaching ministries will have a prophetic dimension, and the need for testing in both listening to and delivering sermons is especially important.

Tongues. Paul's actual term is "different kind of tongues." (1) It is a Spirit-inspired utterance (1 Cor 12:7, 11; 14:2). (2) The speakers are not in ecstasy or out of control; they must speak in turn and remain silent if there is no one to interpret (1 Cor 14:27-28). (3) It is essentially unintelligible both to the speaker (1 Cor 14:14) and to the hearers (1 Cor 14:16), which is why it must be interpreted in the assembly. (4) It is directed basically toward God (1 Cor 14:2, 14-15, 28); one may assume, therefore, that what is interpreted is not speech directed toward others but the "mysteries" spoken to God. (5) As a gift for private prayer, Paul held it in the highest regard (1 Cor 14:2, 4-5, 15, 17-18). Since Paul does not envisage someone being present who might understand without interpretation, it is unlikely Paul viewed it as an actual earthly language.

Paul's concern was unquestionably for order and mutual upbuilding, which is the reason underlying his strong preference for prophecy over tongues *in the community.* It is in this context that we should understand Paul's injunction to "eagerly desire the greater *charismata*" (1 Cor 12:31). This most likely begins the argument on intelligibility and order in 1 Corinthians 14, which is then interrupted so as to place all these things in the context of love.

Gifts as deeds of service. This category includes "serving," giving, caring for (in the sense of leadership) and "showing mercy," from Romans 12:6-8 and helpful deeds and acts of guidance from 1 Corinthians 12:28 (these referring to serving the community as a whole, not simply other individuals). Similarly in Peter's correspondence, serving "with the strength of God provides" (1 Pet 4:11) is mentioned as an expression of God's grace at work in believers. Taken together these seem less obvious as expressions of corporate worship. In the Pauline context they seem to belong to Paul's ever-present interest in relationships within the church and fit with the Pauline understanding of ethics and community life (*see* Fellowship). As such they give visible expression to the fruit of the Spirit.

Specific ministries. Included here are such items as "apostles," "prophets" and "teachers" from 1 Corinthians 12:28 and Ephesians 4:11; "pastors" and "evangelists" from the latter passage and Timothy's own *charisma* of ministry in 1 Timothy 4:14. For the most part, these terms in Paul's letters seem to be primarily functional, rather than to denote office. In any case, the latter emerges from the former, not the other way about. Timothy's charism is clearly not an office: the *charisma* resides within him for the sake of his ministry.

Gifts and Everyday Life

What can we draw from all this by way of practical direction for daily living? First, Paul's churches regarded themselves as communities of the Spirit, and so should we, especially in our gathered worship services. The worship of the early church was far more "charismatic" than has been true for most of the church's subsequent history. Some indeed have tried to make a virtue out of this lack, arguing that the more extraordinary phenomena were relatively limited in the early church—that is, they belong to more "immature" believers like the Corinthians—and that they were no longer needed once the New Testament was canonized. But that quite misses the evidence in Paul, as well as his clear statement in 1 Corinthians 13:8-13 (see Fee 1987, pp. 641-52). One may as well argue that other Pauline churches did not celebrate the Lord's Supper since it is mentioned only in 1 Corinthians. On the contrary, a visible, charismatic dimension of life in the Spirit was the normal experience of the Pauline churches. Our lack of a full charismatic experience in our church life seems to be more a matter of our quenching the Spirit.

Second, we are not in control of the gifts and graces of God. This means that we should humbly welcome the manifestations of the Spirit and the graces of Christ as we find them in our brothers and sisters. Each local church is not an accidental collection of saints. The Spirit gives himself as he pleases (1 Cor 12:11). Our task is not to orchestrate the gifts but to welcome the mix of *charismata* given in every situation for mutual upbuilding and to "test all things" so as to "hold fast to what is good" (1 Thess 5:21). Indeed it is one way of discerning God's agenda for us. Since we might choose, if we could, other manifestations, this requires faith and humility.

Third, now that God's Spirit dwells among his people and in each believer, every member of the church is gifted for ministry. It does not matter if we can identify and label our gift. Questionnaires that enable us to identify our gift,

while often helpful, may discourage our remaining open to all the ways God's Spirit might choose to manifest through us while we keep trying to be the person described in the inventory. It is important to recognize that there is a great diversity of Spirit ministry in the body of Christ; it is not important to be definitive concerning the Spirit's work in us, a work that may change from time to time anyway. If we are confused about our gift, it is enough to serve one another in love (1 Cor 13). Gifts of the Spirit (and other gracelets) are given not primarily for personal enjoyment but for the upbuilding of others. There are no lack of opportunities to do this and no lack in the Spirit's provision for those who would depend on him.

Fourth, gifts are not possessions belonging to the believer. It may be misleading and possibly dangerous to speak of "my gift." At best the believer is a steward or trustee of the Spirit's work in his or her life (compare 1 Pet 4:10). Presumably, in the final evaluation, we will be held accountable for these Spirit/spiritual talents just as we will everything entrusted to us (Mt 25:14-30; compare 1 Pet 4:10).

Fifth, Scripture does not give any how-to plan for discovering one's gift. It does, however, hint that the special anointing of the Spirit may provide an extra dimension to very ordinary activities (such as serving, teaching, encouraging, contributing to the needs of others, leadership, and showing mercy), ways of serving that even those without faith may undertake (Rom 12:7-8). The Spirit's presence may be marked by generosity (in giving), diligence (in leading) and cheerfulness (in showing mercy; compare the emphasis in 1 Pet 4:10-11). The Romans passage offers the further suggestion that while not positively required, free experimentation in the various ways of serving others is permitted if we leave to God ways of enriching that service with his own presence, grace and power.

Sixth, the emphasis of Ephesians 4 on persons and the lack of definitiveness about the gift lists suggests that we should regard each brother and sister as a gift in his or her whole person (rather than simply "having" a gift). Further, in humility (Rom 12:3) we should accept ourselves as a gift from God to the people of God.

Seventh, gifts seem to be primarily associated with function rather than office. This is a healthy corrective to the widespread practice of designating officeholders by the appropriate gift even though the Spirit may not choose to work consistently in that way in this person. This encourages a greater depth of honesty and flexibility in church life.

Finally, God's people are the temple of God (the dwelling for his power and presence) not only when they are together but also when they are dispersed in family,* workplace,* neighborhood* and civic arenas often in ways that are not normally associated with spiritual gifts. While Paul and Peter both addressed the communal life of the people of God (by reason of the need in the community that generated the letter), their teaching does not contradict the larger context of Scripture—that God's people are endowed by his grace and Spirit for service in the world in the multitude of ways we can serve and show mercy (Rom 12:7-8) in the daily round, all for the praise of God's glory (Eph 1:12, 14). Love cannot and will not be contained in the church. As we have already seen, love demands that we seek after intelligible utterances (1 Cor 14:1-25) and order (1 Cor 14:26-40) if the community is to be built up (1 Cor 14:1-19, 26-33) and outsiders are to be converted (1 Cor 14:20-25). Love will also

demand that we do not contain gifts of the Spirit in the gathered life of the people of God.

See also FELLOWSHIP; MINISTRY; SPIRITUAL DISCIPLINES; TALENTS.

References and Resources
A. Bittlinger, *Gifts and Graces* (Grand Rapids: Eerdmans, 1967); G. D. Fee, *The First Epistle to the Corinthians,* New International Commentary on the New Testament (Grand Rapids: Eerdmans, 1987); G. D. Fee, *God's Empowering Presence: The Holy Spirit in the Letters of Paul* (Peabody, Mass.: Hendrickson, 1993); E. Käsemann, "Ministry and Community in the New Testament," in *Essays on New Testament Themes,* ed. R. P. Meye (London: SCM, 1964) 63-94; R. P. Martin, *The Spirit and the Congregation* (Grand Rapids: Eerdmans, 1984); R. P. Meye, "Spirituality," in *Dictionary of Paul and His Letters,* ed. G. F. Hawthorne, R. P. Martin and D. G. Reid (Downers Grove, Ill.: InterVarsity Press, 1993) 906-16; M. Volf, *Work in the Spirit* (Grand Rapids: Eerdmans, 1992).

Gordon D. Fee and R. Paul Stevens

SPIRITUAL GROWTH

Spiritual growth is a mystery. Trying to control it is as vain as telling a rose how to blossom or commanding a child to "grow up." Nonetheless, a reverent appreciation for the factors that inhibit or encourage spiritual growth is helpful for pastoral care,* both of others and oneself. *Spiritual growth* is that process by which the Christian person, in all aspects of his or her life, moves from the beginnings of life in the Spirit to full maturity.

Never a Solitary Matter
One of the great tragedies of the Western church today is that people read the Bible through the lens of Western individualism.* So passages like Ephesians 4:14 ("Then we will no longer be infants") and 4:15 ("We will in all things grow up into . . . Christ") are understood as descriptions of individual growth; in reality they are statements about the growth of

people together. Christian growth is growth in corporate, interdependent life through membership in the body of Christ. Passages such as Ephesians 5:18 ("Be filled with the Spirit") refer to the glorious gift of God's continuous Spirit-inundation to our life together, but they get reduced by Western readers to the cultivation of individual ecstasy.

So the marks of spiritual growth in Ephesians are relational and corporate: diverse and interdependent Spirit gifts (Eph 4:11), every-member ministry* (4:12), rich social unity (4:12), maturity (4:13), doctrinal discernment made by the people (4:14), speaking the truth and living in love* (4:15), dependence on Jesus rather than on leaders (4:15), interdependence rather than independence or codependence (4:16) and love (4:16). It is impossible for Christians to grow and build themselves up in love (Eph 4:16) as a collection of isolated individuals. So the context for spiritual growth is that gloriously synergistic combination of living simultaneously in the people of God and everyday life—in Christ together and in the world. But we must also explore what we mean by *spiritual*.

Spiritual or Spirit-ual?

Spirituality is one of those accordion words into which you can squeeze as much hot air as you wish. The word is often used to describe such diverse things as the inward, the demonic, the religious, the nonmaterial, experiences that are "out of body," and occasionally it describes prayer. But Christian spirituality is not merely human life expanded by disciplines and consciousness-raising practices. In Paul's correspondence the word *spiritual* should normally be capitalized (Fee 1992). *Spiritual gifts* * are Spirit gifts. They are not capacities that come out of our interior (*see* Talents) but rather energies, motivations and expressions of the life of the Spirit in the believing community.

Spiritual growth is primarily growth in

responsiveness and expressiveness of life in the Spirit. And life in the Spirit is not so much characterized by ecstasy (2 Cor 12:1-10) as by the empowering presence of God at work in our weakness for transformed ethical living in everyday arenas. The "unspiritual" person, according to James 3:15, has a devilish wisdom that harbors bitter envy and selfish ambition. Satan and the demons are "spiritual" and believe in God but do not have faith with deeds (Jas 2:18-19). In contrast, the person experiencing Spirit-growth is experiencing the transformation of her whole person "into [Christ's] likeness with ever-increasing glory" (2 Cor 3:18). All this, Paul says, "comes from the Lord, who is the Spirit" (2 Cor 3:18). But is Spirit-growth the exclusive interest of only one person of the Holy Trinity?

Growth into Trinitarian Love

All three persons of the Godhead are involved in development of Christian persons and the people of God to their intended maturity. The Father will equip us "with everything good for doing his will" (Heb 13:20-21). The Son invites his disciples to abide, or "remain," in him because "apart from me you can do nothing" (Jn 15:4-5). The Spirit brings people to spiritual birth so they can see and enter the kingdom of God (Jn 3:3, 5, 8), that is, the beginning of spiritual growth through which we are sealed (Eph 1:13) by the Spirit "who is a deposit guaranteeing our inheritance" (Eph 1:14). But Paul also prays that the Father will give "the Spirit of wisdom and revelation, so that you may know him better" (Eph 1:17). All three persons of the triune God are involved in spiritual growth.

Christian growth must be understood as growth *into* the love life and covenant community that are God. Jesus prayed to the Father that the disciples may be "in us" (Jn 17:21) so that "the love you have for me may be in them" (Jn 17:26). The goal is "that they may be one as we are one" (Jn 17:22). But living in the love of God (literally) involves a mutual abiding of God and believers. Not only do believers abide (corporately) in the triune God, but Father, Son and Spirit "make their home" in the obedient (individual) believer (Jn 14:23). A fully trinitarian approach to Christian growth has profound implications for relationships and community.* Most of all, a trinitarian approach to spiritual growth centers on the twin foci of love and humility—the supreme marks of the mature Christian.

Love characterizes the life of God in God's three-in-oneness. God is love (1 Jn 4:16), and we are most godlike when we love (1 Cor 13). Love involves sacrificial caring, secret generosity and social passion. If love characterizes the life of God, humility is the mark of a person truly in love with God. Humility is not preoccupation with self-depreciation (the cloak of pride turned inside out) but with God appreciation (Lk 14:11; 18:14), which liberates from self-criticism and addiction to the approval of others (Jn 8:29). When we are truly humble, we desire above everything the praise of God (Jn 5:44). We are becoming God-blinded people who, having looked at the sun, will see it everywhere. If we are most godlike when we love, we are most creaturely when we are humble. Spiritual growth aims at maturity of love and humility.

Metaphors of Growth

Because spiritual growth is a mystery that is beyond rational analysis or human technique, metaphors are needed—figures of speech providing sacred hints that express reality in ways that appeal to the imagination.* In the Bible there are four major metaphors of spiritual growth.

The seed—an agricultural metaphor. Growth includes germination, development, transitions, fruition and multipli-

cation. In his public teaching Jesus used the seed metaphor for the life of the kingdom sown into the soil of people's hearts (Mt 13:4) and for the sowing of the children of the kingdom into the world (Mt 13:38). Peter uses *seed* to express the awesome and inevitable life that is invested in believers when they receive Christ through the Word—that "imperishable" seed (1 Pet 1:23). Paul uses *seed* the same way: "I planted the seed, Apollos watered it, but God made it grow" (1 Cor 3:6). No one plants a seed without expecting a crop (Heb 6:7) or a harvest (Gal 6:9), the very thing God wants. The seed metaphor not only communicates the unfolding of the life contained within the seed but also suggests the pain and price of growth. Growth involves transformation—the changing of forms. Nothing happens unless the seed is sown and dies (Jn 12:24; 1 Cor 15:38, 44).

The child—a biological metaphor. In the New Testament we are portrayed as being born "a second time" (Jn 3:4) and becoming infants in Christ. Paul used this term for the Corinthians (1 Cor 3:1) because of their schismatic behavior and their infantile dependence on human teachers. In fact, he says, they are still "on the bottle" needing milk (1 Cor 3:2). The author of Hebrews uses the same metaphor for another community stalled in a no-growth life (Heb 5:12-13). Tragically many Christians run off to this and that conference being blown about by every wind of doctrine (Eph 4:14) and never learn to feed themselves or others (*see* Spiritual Disciplines). Just as infants learn to feed themselves, just as children move from total dependency to interdependency, just as young people move from a handed-down and secondhand faith to an adult faith of their own (*see* Faith Development), so we grow spiritually. Maturity, paradoxically, involves a recovery of true childlikeness (Mt 18:4;

19:14)—playfulness, spontaneity, whole-hearted trust.

The disciple—an educational metaphor. This metaphor is rich in meaning about direction and movement. In the ancient world disciples were learners who formed a deepening relationship with their master. The purpose was not merely the transmission of information. When the disciple is fully trained, Jesus said, the disciple "will be like the teacher" (Lk 6:40 NRSV)—an imitation process. Instead of creating uniformity, this results in a liberating interdependence because Jesus is determined to set us free: "I no longer call you servants. . . . Instead, I have called you friends" (Jn 15:15). So discipleship involves development from mere service to friendship with God—a transition that is parallel to one Paul explored frequently: from slavery to sonship and being an heir. In one sense we never move beyond obedience, but the obedience changes character from simply "doing what we are told" to doing God's will because we have increasingly the mind of Christ. This is the heart of guidance.*

The building—an architectural metaphor. The apostles often mixed their metaphors as they expressed the rich life of the believer. Paul moved back and forth from agricultural to architectural images: "You are God's field, God's building" (1 Cor 3:9). Once again he is thinking of the people of God and not merely a collection of individual saints. God's people is really the temple of God—a living building that grows increasingly into a sanctuary in which God's Spirit lives (1 Cor 3:16). Christ is the foundation of that building (1 Cor 3:11), and though Christ is the ultimate living stone, each of us is adding to the structure stone upon stone. Peter says we are being built "into a spiritual house" (1 Pet 2:5). We are like a medieval cathedral that is always being built and never quite finished. Who is doing the building? Who makes the house grow?

Cultivating Growth

The seed develops. The infant matures. The disciple learns. The building is being built. But all four metaphors show that growth requires human cooperation. In fact *both* God and the stones make the temple grow, but it is mainly God's continuing work of transformation. From first to last, from conception to resurrection, from germination to harvest, from laying the foundation to the completion of the temple, spiritual growth is primarily the achievement of God: "We are God's workmanship" (Eph 2:10). Paul is confident "that he who began a good work in you will carry it on to completion until the day of Christ Jesus" (Phil 1:6). The body of Christ "grows as God causes it to grow" (Col 2:19). The Christian life does not start as a human achievement, nor does it continue so. "Are you now trying to attain your goal by human effort?" Paul asks the Galatians who have slipped back into an achievement-oriented religiosity (Gal 3:3).

Growth, however, is not automatic. God seeks our cooperation. We are fellow workers with God (1 Cor 3:9). Paul thanks God that the faith and love of the Thessalonians are "growing more and more" (2 Thess 1:3). He warns Timothy that some have given up the good fight and "have shipwrecked their faith" (1 Tim 1:19). The author of Hebrews repeatedly warns his readers to be careful not to drift away from the faith (Heb 2:1) and not to fall short of true sabbath* rest in Christ (Heb 4:1). We must persevere in growth (Heb 10:36). It is literally grow or die!

Each of us, Paul argues, is striving as fellow workers with God and "each one should be careful how he builds" (1 Cor 3:10). Some people appear to be building with hay or straw, others with gold and silver. All will be revealed on the day of judgment. Some people's work on the building will not survive the fire; other people's work will last because their work was done with faith, hope and love (1 Thess 1:3).

How do we grow? There is personal cultivation to be done, removing the thorns and stones so the seed will grow. Spiritual growth involves crucifying the flesh (Gal 5:16-18), walking in the Spirit (Gal 5:25; 6:7-8), turning troubles into sacraments (Rom 5:2-5; Jas 1:2-4), engaging in spiritual disciplines,* thriving in church membership,* taking risks and keeping one's eye on heaven. All this happens in the thick of everyday life. One of the ultimate ironies of spiritual growth is related to the theme of this article: it is as we seek the growth of others that we grow ourselves. Equipping* is a mutual ministry. As we empower one another through loving, exhorting, serving, teaching, admonishing and praying for one another, we grow ourselves. The indirect way turns out to be the most direct.

But the growth is mainly God's work. Paul offers this final prayer to the Thessalonians: "May God himself, the God of peace, sanctify you through and through. May your whole spirit, soul and body be kept blameless at the coming of our Lord Jesus Christ. The one who calls you is faithful and he will do it" (1 Thess 5:23-24). God will do it, but we are God's coworkers. Simone Weil keeps this balance. She describes God crossing the infinity of time and space to knock at the door of our hearts, like a beggar, to possess us in love: "If we consent, God puts a little seed in us and he goes away again." The seed, she notes, encounters weeds and thorns, and rocks must be removed. Sometimes this gardening feels like a violent process, but "on the whole the seed grows of itself" (Weil, p. 91).

See also CHRISTIAN EDUCATION; DISCIPLESHIP; EQUIPPING; FAITH DEVELOPMENT; SPIRITUAL CONFLICT; SPIRITUAL FORMATION.

References and Resources

D. L. Alexander, ed., *Christian Spirituality: Five Views of Sanctification—Reformed, Lutheran, Wesleyan, Pentecostal, Contemplative* (Downers Grove, Ill.: InterVarsity Press, 1988); G. D. Fee, *God's Empowering Presence: The Holy Spirit in the Letters of Paul* (Peabody, Mass.: Hendrickson, 1993); G. D. Fee, "Some Reflections on Pauline Spirituality," in *Alive to God*, ed. J. I. Packer and L. Wilkinson (Downers Grove, Ill.: InterVarsity Press, 1992) 96-107; M. Green and R. P. Stevens, *New Testament Spirituality: True Discipleship and Spiritual Maturity* (Guildford, U.K.: Eagle, 1994); E. S. Jones, *Conversion* (New York: Abingdon, 1959); S. Weil, *Waiting on God*, trans. E. Craufurd (London: Collins, 1950); D. Willard, *The Spirit of the Disciplines: Understanding How God Changes Lives* (New York: Harper & Row, 1988).

R. Paul Stevens

SPORTS

A successful coach once said that sports were not a matter of life and death—they were much more important than that! The amount of time and energy expended by participants, the space given to sports by newspapers and broadcasters and the money paid by spectators and sponsors suggests that sports are among the most significant areas of human activity. On the surface, much of the activity appears inconsequential, even trivial: running, jumping, lifting or propelling a ball the length of a field, into a hole, over a net or between sticks. But the high level of interest taken by most people says much about the relationship of sports to basic human needs and their contribution to personal and social development.

History

Competitive team sports as we have them today are largely a legacy of the late nineteenth century. It was then that many rules became codified and games were incorporated into school curricula. Records in many of the current major leagues go back to this period. Horse racing probably goes back at least as far as the early sixteenth century, although, as with archery and fencing, many sports of this period are indistinguishable from military training. Individual athletic activity, however, was an ancient phenomenon. The original Olympics were founded around 776 B.C. The participants were the aristocracy with time for leisure,* and the prize was simply a laurel wreath. Gradually the interests of individual city-states took over, and rewards in kind, including tax exemptions and army deferments, were offered. In a frighteningly contemporary scenario, these Olympics folded in A.D. 394 amid cries of bribery, intimidation and cheating.

The reviver of the Olympics, Baron de Coubertin, emphasized the underlying ethic of the games: "The most important thing in the Olympic Games is not to win but to take part, just as the most important thing in life is not the triumph but the struggle." The ensuing hundred years have left their mark on sports in several key areas. Rampant commercialism and the demand for success at all costs have made amateurism increasingly unviable; Rugby Union, the last bastion, finally fell in 1995. Vibrant nationalism has replaced the Olympic ideal of *Jeux sans Frontiers,* (Games Without Borders). The pervasive influence of the media, which can dictate the timing and even rules of some sports—tennis tiebreakers were introduced because of television demands. This means that, in many people's eyes, sports are no longer their own masters. Sports that were once the domain of a particular subcultural group (horse riding, skiing and boxing, to name three) increasingly transcend those groups.

The Christian response to sports over

recent centuries has often taken its impetus from the Puritan reaction of the seventeenth century. To be fair, their opposition to many sports stemmed from either the cruelty involved (blood sports), the sport's association with gambling, the immorality and drunkenness among participants or the fact that much of the sport took place on the workers' only day off, Sunday. D. Brailsford is unfair when he says, "Puritans saw their mission to erase all sport and play from men's lives" (p. 141). Though some Puritans believed "any form of play took on the badge of time-wasting, idleness and, therefore, vice" (Brailsford, p. 127), others believed that enjoyment of good company, reading good books and appreciating God's creation were all legitimate and beneficial exercises. The contemporary sports scene is different in many ways from that of the seventeenth century, and there has been a welcome recovery of the doctrine of creation,* which encourages participation and enjoyment of leisure activities in moderation as gifts from God.

Biblical Data

Although sports and sporting contests were clearly part of life in the ancient Near East and in the Greco-Roman world, clear references to sporting activity are somewhat lacking in Scripture. Examples sometimes cited include Jacob's wrestling with the angel (Gen 32:24-26), the "contest" between David and Goliath (1 Sam 17), Jonathan's archery (1 Sam 20:20), the contest at Helkath Hazzurim (2 Sam 2:14-16), Paul's allusions to the athletic stadium and boxing ring (1 Cor 9:24-27) and the metaphor of the race with spectators (Heb 12:1-2). Most of these are tenuous and cannot act as a foundation for a theology of sports.

Jacob's experience was an earnest struggle, not a recreational diversion. The references in 1-2 Samuel deal with the realities of war and military engagement. Even Jonathan's archery fulfilled a military purpose and does not support the idea of archery as a form of recreation. The New Testament references allude to the existence of athletic contests (in Paul's case it is probably the Isthmian games, which involved the six basic disciplines of running, jumping, wrestling, boxing, javelin and discus), but the purpose of the illustrations is spiritual, and not much can be deduced from these passages about the writers' views of such sport per se. It is safe to assume that the biblical writers' attitude toward sports was governed by the extent to which core kingdom values were upheld or undermined by the activity in question.

Benefits of Sports

A major problem in generalizing on the theme of sports is the seemingly limitless variety of competitive sports. Any comprehensive encyclopedia of sports will contain statistics from over one hundred individual sports—from cricket to hanggliding, from skiing to snooker. It will include geographically limited sports such as baseball, bandy, shinty and the American, Australian and Gaelic codes of football, as well as minority sports such as real tennis, fives, pelota and petanque. While this diversity of sports and cultures makes generalized applications unhelpful, if not impossible, certain benefits and drawbacks can be highlighted that are applicable to most, if not all, sporting activities.

Physical. An obvious benefit of sports, and the most quoted reason for involvement, is physical exercise. The precise benefits will vary, but solo sports such as running, swimming and cycling will improve the participant's cardiovascular fitness, while other sports such as the various codes of football and hockey contribute more toward body toning, muscular strength and endurance. Regular participation in athletic sports maintains the body,* keeping it in good condition and counterbalancing more debilitating influences such as weight and aging.* Soccer and running develop the lower body more than the upper, while the reverse is true of some racket sports. Swimming has long been accepted as the simplest and most effective way of keeping all the body's muscles active, while, in contrast, a golf swing involves a series of subtle, rapid, unnatural body movements involving up to sixty-four muscles and lasting for less than two seconds. In this case the physical benefits are accrued more through the simple activity of walking than through anything integral to the game itself.

Mental and emotional. The possible connection between a disciplined and healthy body and a higher degree of mental astuteness and emotional stability cannot be ignored. It is common for psychiatrists to recommend sports for their emotional and social benefits. Temporary depressions* can be eased by physical exertion, and many can testify to receiving light on some complex problem while running or how mentally demanding work such as composition or written examinations* have proved much less taxing after engaging in some recreation.* From a spectator's perspective the emotions* involved tend to be more extreme, fleeting and unreliable and, for the partisan fan, are often completely dependent on the outcome of the game.

Sports have been regarded historically as an effective means of character building. The discipline of training, playing by the rules, coping with stiff opposition, striving to achieve the unthinkable and rebounding after disappointment or defeat are all useful attributes to develop in preparation for life. A healthy attitude to the above should result in an altogether more rounded and complete person.

Social and cultural. By their very nature team sports require cooperation and a high degree of interpersonal understanding and commitment. The esprit de corps experienced by team members is due to a combination of factors: an inherent enjoyment of the game, shared goals, a sense of achievement and shared sacrifices for the sake of the team. In many Western suburban societies where neighborhood* community* is decreasing, a sports club* can become a prime arena for the social interaction of like-minded people. Major spectator sports also play an important role in a city's* or country's sense of identity. In North America a city remains inseparably linked in the popular imagination with the name of its major-league team(s). In England the historical popularity of soccer is largely due to the loyalty felt by many to their local town* and the sense of corporate identity provided by its team. In Gaelic cultures sports such as hurling and shinty and their ancient precedents performed an important role in training young men of the clan for battle, and the resultant intertown and intercounty competition is still strong today. Over the years some sports have been unifying agents, bringing together participants of diverse backgrounds in places of conflict such as World War I Europe (with its famous Christmas Day soccer game), Northern Ireland, the Middle East and modern South Africa.

Spiritual. Organizations such as Athletes in Action in North America and Christians in Sport in the United Kingdom have played a part in ministering pastorally to those involved in professional and high-level sports, as well as giving the Christian message some street credibility among sports-obsessed youth. However, the spiritual dimension of sports is not limited to their usefulness as a medium for evangelism* but concerns the extent to which values* and morals are developed within the sporting arena. In particular, the Christian will be marked out by the way in which he or she responds to the clearly negative influences in contemporary sports, which are outlined below. Clear spiritual benefits can accrue from participation in sports as the Christian competitor grapples with the major issues of priorities, ambition,* temptation and discipleship.*

Problem Areas in Sports

Physical, emotional, cultural and spiritual abuses. Each of the benefits mentioned above can be lost through overindulgence or abuse. It could be argued that in some cases the physical benefits are nonexistent or even negative. Most notably there is the case of boxing: a sport whose sole object is to inflict physical injury and where the physical benefits by way of general fitness are clearly outweighed by the inherent danger. Furthermore, the body could be prematurely damaged if, in pursuit of commercial gain or fame, an athlete pushes too hard, indulges in performance-enhancing drugs,* or competes while injured—witness the common use of painkillers among American football players and the allegations of puberty-postponing steroids among East European gymnasts.

Similarly the emotional benefits of participation will be lost if the sport becomes an obsession and no comfort is derived simply from playing or achieving a "moral victory." During each World Cup there seems to be a report from some part of the globe about the suicide of a soccer fan whose country has just been eliminated. This took a shocking turn in Colombia in 1994, when the defender Andrés Escobar was murdered because of an unfortunate score on his own goal. The natural extremes of joy and disappointment must be kept in perspective, or all balance has been lost. It is worth noting that the demands of fame and success* have not always been kind to those who have reached the top. O. J. Simpson is the most celebrated example of a gifted sportsman with extreme domestic problems, but he is by no means alone. There is, sadly, the all-too-familiar sight of a gifted but socially inept and lonely "personality" who has sacrificed many of the normal activities of life in order to achieve a particular "corruptible crown" (1 Cor 9:25 KJV).

Socially, sport can also be used to reinforce boundaries. The Gaelic sports in Ireland were deliberately developed in ways that excluded the Protestant population, and the two codes of rugby derive from the late nineteenth-century class conflict in England. Issues of identity, loyalty and rivalry can also be overemphasized and corrupted and lead to intercommunity violence. The Stanley Cup riots in Montreal and Vancouver, hooliganism in Europe and the Honduras-El Salvadoran war of 1969 (sparked off by a soccer result) are extreme examples of the darker side of sport's appeal to nationalistic or tribal instincts.

Nor should we be blind to the mixed motives of even the most well-intentioned marriages of sports and spirituality. One commentator has remarked that the American athletic subculture is probably the most ministered-to segment in the world. Is such ministry undertaken purely out of need or because of its propaganda potential? Are lesser sports valued as much as high-profile ones? Are the big-name and less-famous stars treated equally? Are the theological opinions of sports personalities given greater authority than those of proven Bible teachers? How easily do worldly values creep into our assessments?

Commercialism. Increasing transfer fees, ludicrous wages, the advent of the player's agent, the high cost of admission to games, and strikes in ice hockey and baseball have all contributed to fan dissatisfaction and alienation. While it is partly true that the public's desire for success has contributed to the million-dollar merry-go-round, there is a limit to how much commercial exploitation even the most die-hard fan will tolerate. How ethical is it for soccer teams to exploit the loyalty of their millions of young (and often relatively poor) fans by bringing out a new uniform/strip every few months? How right is it that (in 1993) an NBA basketball star earned on average thirteen times the wage of a physician? What does it say about society when the U.S. Senate constitutes baseball an essential service by legislating the strikers back to work? Where is the morality in Mexico's spending millions on staging the Olympics when many of its inhabitants were starving? Or in Formula One motor racing, what are the ethics behind spending millions of dollars manufacturing machines that have no function outside the racetrack but burn up the earth's natural resources, pollute the atmosphere and endanger the lives of the participants?

All these have implications for the Christian, not least in the area of attachment to and stewardship* of money.* Christian professionals* must constantly examine their motives for being involved in a high-paying sport and seek to find ways in which their privileged financial situation can be turned to the advantage of others. If it is within their power to do so, will they remain loyal to one team and concentrate on building relationships within that community rather than seeking or accepting a more lucrative move elsewhere? How often do Christians witness to kingdom values by taking the less financially rewarding option? Christian fans also must continually assess the morality of paying upwards of $1000 for a good season ticket. Can the benefits of sports be enjoyed equally through supporting a Triple-A baseball or nonleague soccer team and keeping in touch with the professional scene through the more-than-adequate television coverage? Christians can play a strategic role in demonstrating that neither money nor sports dominate them and that if the whole edifice of the professional-sports scene were to collapse, life would continue.

Violence. All competitive sports require an element of mental or physical aggression, and most team sports require physical contact. The dilemma concerns the point at which such aggression is excessive, dangerous to the welfare of other players and damaging to the aggressor's own character and psyche. Should not Christians who regularly get red-carded in soccer recognize their weakness and take appropriate steps toward counseling and accountability? The New Zealand haka is a famous rugby ritual, but how many other pregame rugby and NFL warm-ups pander to an innately violent machismo and contribute to on-field violence? In high-contact sports the potential for fighting and brawling is ever-present, but Christianity aside, the true professional has always been regarded as the one who is able to take the knocks without retaliation (see Prov 14:29 GNB).

In ice hockey, fights by the players are expected at every venue, are treated by commentators as an interesting aspect of game strategy and are cheered by the crowd. Christians surely must go against the stream on this issue and refuse to accept that this form of aggression is essential to either the game or its entertainment.* In what way would this immensely skillful, exciting and highly physical sport be diminished by outlawing such fights? Since ring-related deaths in boxing continue at an alarming rate,

Christian involvement in this sport is becoming harder to justify. It is difficult to understand how an activity that would be a serious criminal offense outside the ring can be regarded as sport. It is argued that boxing is a way for the ghettoized to improve financially and socially. But at what price comes the improvement, and since when was social advancement more important than opposing institutionalized violence? The skill, fitness and opportunity to escape the ghetto that boxing offers are equally available through other sports. While, for example, motor racing and mountaineering can also be dangerous, the object of these sports is to conquer the danger through skill and technique. Of course, not all sport-related violence is even indirectly connected with the sport itself. Soccer hooliganism is a social malaise that would be unaffected by banning or changing the rules governing the game.

Competition. Many Christians struggle with competitiveness. They regard competitive instincts as part of their fallen human nature—a symptom of the desire to be best and to succeed at the expense of others. Some authors, such as A. Kohn, have put forward a radical case against competition.* This inevitably leads to a crisis of conscience when it comes to sports, for competitiveness is intrinsic to sports as participants compete against others, themselves, the clock or nature. The spur to improve and achieve is what motivates the participant, and the consequent excitement of the battle turns a sport into a spectacle worth watching. Removing the competitive element from sports emasculates them, stripping them of many of the benefits outlined above. The cut and thrust of competition and the discipline of performing within the confines of a strict code of rules sharpen the mental faculties, bond the members of a team together and lead to a higher level of physical achievement.

The problem is not the desire to compete but a temptation to win at all costs and to bend the rules and a distorted perspective that views all of life in terms of winners and losers. Competitiveness becomes tainted when it seeps into other areas, such as family life, church* or the workplace.* Competing for the affections of others, for status or power, springs from pride, and such jostling for position is explicitly condemned by Christ (Mk 10:35-45; Lk 9:46-50), who took the form of a servant (Jn 13:1-5; Phil 2:6-7) and submitted himself even to death. Professional sportspeople are usually gracious in victory, for every winner has experienced defeat, and it is accepted that the losers will have other chances to fight back. In other contexts, however, competitiveness can result in the systematic suppression of the disadvantaged and powerless. Competitive desires are no more sinful than sexual desires. To one God has given the gift of sports, to the other the gift of marriage, as the proper context for their expression. To cross the boundaries in either case is to court disaster.

Idolatry. Idolatry is the most common sin condemned in the Bible. The temptation to break the first command of the Decalogue (Ex 20:3) is so pervasive that every area of human activity has the potential to become an idol. It is not surprising, therefore, that something as fundamental to modern society as sport is vulnerable to it. For the spectator, the excitement of media-hyped events can be as seductive as any materialistic or sexual temptation. There is grave potential for addiction,* and we can become preoccupied with entertainment, which demands nothing of us physically, mentally or spiritually. For the professional participant, the quest for fame, money and social status, together with the increasing demands of coaches, sponsors, clubs and the general public, mean that 100 percent commitment to sports will lead to the exclusion of other relationships and the erosion of other loyalties. The Christian, in any field of life, has to work out the vocational implications of being totally committed to Christ alone. In the sports world where it is common to hear team owners speaking of "possessing" the players, these implications are particularly relevant.

One area where some prominent Christian sportspeople have displayed their priorities is Sunday sports. The infamous case of Eric Liddell in the 1924 Olympic Games, popularized by the film *Chariots of Fire*, has bolstered the sabbatarians' abstentionist case. However, the impressive list of Christian sportspeople who do compete on Sunday illustrates that it is not just biblical scholars who are divided on whether the strict requirements of the Jewish sabbath can be applied to the Christian community and would lead to the conclusion that this is a case of personal conscience. On one hand, the action of Liddell and Jones demonstrated in a powerful and tangible way that there was something more important in their lives than sports, and Sunday participants must decide what alternative ways are available for them to make similar proclamations. (German golfer Bernhard Langer's worship services for those on tour is one example.) On the other hand, it is symptomatic of a particularly introspective, myopic and almost pharisaic Christianity that more importance is attached to this legal issue than to many of the broader theological implications of sports (see Mt 23:23-24).

For those who are called to exercise their God-given gifts as professional athletes in a secular world, Sunday participation is probably inevitable, but alternative opportunities for worship and sabbath rest must be sought. For spectators and amateur participants who have more control over when and how often they play,* enough opportunities exist to participate on Saturdays and midweek, and Sunday participation could prove to be an unhelpful intrusion into time allocated for worship. Furthermore, the all-consuming nature of a competitive event physically and psychologically, with travel, emotional buildup, participation, unwinding and reflection all built into the experience, means that although the activity may in itself be recreational, participation may leave the player more drained than refreshed, and thus an essential benefit of sabbath* has been lost.

Conclusion

Christian professionals need to understand that a calling* to compete as an athlete is as high a calling as any other. Unique opportunities and unique difficulties will be theirs, but their gifts are God-given. Sports are to be enjoyed, and they must accept the consequent privileges and responsibilities. The church should encourage and support them in their calling and not hinder them through advocating a hierarchy of callings, perpetuating a disrespect for creative leisure or being sidetracked on minor issues such as sabbatarianism.

Christian sportspeople at all levels must also (1) refuse to be drawn into a win-at-all-costs philosophy, regardless of the demands of coaches, owners or the general public, thus obeying God rather than humans (Acts 4:19); (2) recognize the potential of fair play, sporting behavior and honesty (especially when infringements have gone unnoticed by the umpire) as a powerful witness to kingdom values, thus exhibiting Christian integrity (Tit 2:6-7); (3) constantly evaluate the time spent on training and participation, determining whether it is proportionate to time spent on their other callings of family,* church and community (Eph 5:15-16); (4) recognize the

essential transience of sporting pursuits, that is, athletic records rarely last more than a year, and trophy winners are often forgotten within a decade; (5) ensure that they experience the physical, emotional, social and spiritual benefits of sports and avoid the temptations of body abuse, obsessiveness and idolatry.

Likewise Christian spectators should (1) keep their sporting interests in perspective and avoid allowing the understandable and human responses of jubilation or disappointment to adversely affect other pursuits and relationships; (2) regularly reassess the money and time spent on sports events, determining whether they encourage the greed of players or owners, are being irresponsible in their personal budgeting regarding travel to overseas events, mindlessly buy the commercial products put out ad infinitum by the promoters, are passing on essentially materialistic values to their children and organize their lives around sporting schedules; (3) avoid adherence to the media-supported personality cult, recognizing that these people are sports stars and not role models; (4) ensure that their loyalty to city or country does not lead to racism* or ethnocentricity*; (5) enjoy sports for their own sake, appreciating the beauty* and skill involved, while recognizing their transience and the relative unimportance of what is at stake. This too shall pass (Eccles 3:20). It is not a matter of life and death.

See also AMBITION; BODY; COMPETITION; GAMES; LEISURE; PLAY; RECREATION; SUCCESS.

References and Resources

P. Ballantine, *Sport—The Opiate of the People*, Grove Ethical Studies 70 (Bramcote, U.K.: Grove Books, 1988); D. Brailsford, *Sport and Society: Elizabeth to Anne* (Toronto: University of Toronto Press, 1969); F. Inglis, *The Name of the Game* (London: Heinemann Educational Books, 1977); S. J. Hoffman, *Sport and Religion*

(Champaign, Ill.: Human Kinetics, 1992);
A. Kohn, *No Contest: The Case Against Competition* (Boston: Houghton Mifflin, 1992); J. W.
Loy and G. S. Kenyon, eds., *Sport, Culture and Society* (New York: Macmillan, 1969); R. D.
Mandell, *Sport: A Cultural History* (New York: Columbia University Press, 1984); M. Novak,
The Joy of Sports: End Zones, Bases, Baskets, Balls and the Celebration of the American Spirit (New York: Lanham, 1988).

David J. Montgomery

STATES/PROVINCES

Politicians in liberal democracies have rarely been held in lower public esteem than they are today. Governments seem remote, unresponsive, indifferent to our interests. It is understandable that in such circumstances people shut out politics* and simply get on with their private lives. To do so, however, carries a serious risk, for governments will always have a major influence on our daily environment. We need to recover a sense of the high calling* of government as one of the institutions established by God for human welfare. This happens on the level of the state or province.

What Is the State?

When we speak of *the state,* we refer to the whole system* of the national government of a country. This includes the lawmaking body (such as the U.S. Congress); the executive body, which implements the law* and determines national policy (such as the U.S. presidency); and the judiciary, which interprets and enforces the law (the U.S. Supreme Court, for example). In addition, federal states like the United States or Canada have two distinct territorial levels of government: the national or federal level and the state, provincial or regional level. The lower level has its own legislative, executive and judicial bodies, possesses powers to control certain areas of legislation and policy and plays a vitally important role. In this article *state* is explored both as

a national system and as a territorial region within a national state.

The State as a National System

Why do we have states? The purpose of the political institutions we have come to call *the state* is to secure a just public order—something every society and every individual citizen needs. Scripture testifies to this purpose and attributes it to divine providence (Rom 13:1-2). The Bible lays down no constitutional blueprint, but it does consistently teach that the task of the state is to establish a just public order in society (Judg 2:16; 1 Pet 2:13-14).

Interpreting the contemporary meaning of this biblical injunction is unavoidably controversial, yet the following can be suggested as broad tasks of government today: protecting the liberty of individuals, families and associations; guaranteeing the provision of basic needs,* especially those of the poor and vulnerable; preventing the undue domination of society by particular groups (such as corporations or unions*); punishing public wrongdoing; safeguarding the quality of the environment and promoting just international relationships.

Territorial Regions in the State

Among the just relationships that it is the duty of the state to safeguard are those that between different territorial units within a country. In some countries these territorial units may have long-standing historical, cultural or ethnic roots that may merit special legal (even constitutional) protection (such as the Province of Quebec in Canada or the communities of native peoples in the U.S.A. and in Canada). Here the case for a federal division of powers is particularly strong.

Such a division also comports well with powerful Old Testament warnings against the centralization of political power in ancient Israel (compare Deut

17:14-20; Num 2; 33:54-56; Josh 13—19; Neh 4:13). Indeed, the biblical material implies a general preference for federal-type or decentralized systems, even in medium-sized and smaller countries, in order to allow the people or their representatives to participate effectively in political decision-making.

A good place to begin the task of citizenship* is to try to influence what goes on in the available closer units of political decision-making: a school board, a neighborhood,* a city government, a state or provincial legislature. A national government characterized by justice* depends upon citizens, individually or corporately, taking small steps of justice in the immediate spheres within which God has called them to serve.

See also CITIZENSHIP; JUSTICE; POLITICS; POWER; PRINCIPALITIES AND POWERS.

References and Resources
P. Marshall, *Thine Is the Kingdom: A Biblical Perspective on Government and Politics* (Grand Rapids: Eerdmans, 1984); S. V. Monsma, *Pursuing Justice in a Sinful World* (Grand Rapids: Eerdmans, 1984).

Jonathan Chaplin

STEWARDSHIP

While *stewardship* is commonly used as a camouflaged appeal for funds for church and religious purposes, the term denotes a more comprehensive view of the Christian life affecting time,* work,* leisure,* talents,* money,* the state of one's soul and care for the environment. The Greek word for *steward* (*oikonomos,* from which we get our word *economy*) means "one who manages a household." Years ago persons called stewards, rather than huge financial institutions, were employed to manage the financial affairs and households of wealthy people. Their management included not only money

but everything that makes a household thrive, not unlike the vocation of homemaking* but on a large scale. A biblical example is Joseph's work as steward of Potiphar's house; his master did not "concern himself with anything in the house" (Gen 39:8).

Stewardship is a term theologically related to service or ministry* (*diakonia*). If *service* denotes the motivation for ministry—undertaking God's interests for the pleasure of God—*stewardship* suggests the purpose of ministry:* to manage God's world in harmony with the owner's mind. These two words, *service* and *stewardship,* taken together constitute the ministry of the laity* and are roughly equivalent to the much popularized term *servant leadership.* Because stewardship integrates many facets of everyday life, we begin with a summary indicating other articles that can be consulted. Then we will consider personal and church stewardship.

Managing God's Household
God is the ultimate owner of everything (Ps 24:1; 50:10) and has entrusted the nonhuman creation to the care of humankind. A good word to describe our double relationship with God and the world is *trusteeship:* we are entrusted with the care of the world and are accountable to God, who owns it and has declared his intended purpose. This trusteeship stems from the so-called creation mandate in Genesis 1:26-29. Humankind has "an accredited discretionary power" (Wright, p. 117) over everything except itself. The stewards are to take care of the earth (Gen 2:15) and develop it in response to the summons of God.

This far-reaching stewardship embraces (1) care of creation, so managing the resources of earth and sea (*see* Creation; Ecology); (2) expressing creativity in all of its forms, so developing God's aesthetic creation and bringing further beauty* into the world (*see* Art; Beauty; Craftsmanship); (3) maintaining the fabric of God's creation, so making God's world work (*see* Chores; Ministry; Service; Work); (4) enculturating the world and developing varieties of human expressions of values,* structures and lifestyles, so bringing distinctive meanings to the peoples of the world (*see* Culture); (5) harnessing the earth's potential by inventing tools and systems for making things, so bringing benefit to humankind (*see* Technology); (6) expressing dominion over time by ordering human life around patterns of time and by keeping one day a week for rest and reflection, so expressing dominion over time (*see* Sabbath; Time); (7) developing human society,* organizations and peoples/nations, filling the earth with peoples living in distinctive but harmonious communities and states, so creating structures as contexts for human life (*see* Organization; Politics; States/Provinces; Structures). Considered together, these are the ways we take care of God's household. This all-encompassing stewardship is the stewardship of every human being; every living thing and the whole material creation are not exempted from this stewardship in favor of something more "spiritual"; this is part of their spiritual ministry.

Caring for Creation

Some significant implications stem from this stewardship. First, God's calling* to humankind is not merely directed toward individuals but organizations and communities. Even corporations and nations have a call from God and should undertake stewardship.

Second, in defining humankind's relationship with the physical creation, stewardship keeps us from two extreme relationships with the earth: (1) reverencing and worshiping the earth (a trend toward which the ecology movement is moving) and (2) manipulating and ruthlessly exploiting the earth, which is still so common in industrialized countries. Unfortunately the Christian faith is accused of promoting the latter view, when it is precisely the loss of Christian stewardship that has caused the rape and pillage of the earth.

Third, in the Old Testament, God (the divine owner) gives "accredited discretionary power" to all humankind (Gen 1:26-29; Wright, p. 117) for the benefit of everyone. The first human ownership/stewardship implies the common ownership and shared use of the material resources of the world. The right of all is prior to the right of individuals or individual nations to accumulate personal wealth (*see* Justice; Money; Ownership; Poverty; Wealth). So there are severe limitations on personal or national ownership of the earth's resources; they are a divine gift entrusted to the race for the benefit of all. As John Chrysostom said in the fourth century, the rich are entrusted with wealth as stewards for the benefit of the poor (p. 50). What a gracious revolution would be incited by the application of this principle in the global village* today!

Israel as Exemplary Steward

Under the old covenant God's gift of trusteeship was especially directed to the nation Israel (Deut 10:14-15). There are three parts to the promise God gave to Israel: the presence (God will be with them), a people (he will be their God; they, his people) and a place (the land will be theirs, that is, entrusted to the people, not individuals).

The families (more like clans or extended families today) were the basic social, kinship, legal and religious structure under the old covenant. They were family-plus-land units, as is graphically illustrated by the redemption of Naomi's land-plus-family in Bethlehem (Ruth 4:9-

12). Thus in the Jubilee year (every fifty years) both God's ultimate ownership and the family's trusteeship were expressed by the return of the land to the original family, even if the land had been mortgaged or sold in the meantime to pay debts (Lev 25:4-18). The reason given is this: "The land is mine and you are but aliens and my tenants" (Lev 25:23). This has implications for the question of providing an inheritance for one's family (*see* Will, Last).

New Testament "Household" Responsibilities

Applying Old Testament legislation to people under the New Testament must be undertaken in a paradigmatic way— with the Old providing a structure for thinking of something greater that is fulfilled in the New. All the promises of God concerning God's presence, people and place find their "yes" in Christ (2 Cor 1:20). The Gentiles along with Jews in Christ become joint heirs (Eph 3:6) in a joint body so that "in Christ" answers to all that "in the land" meant to Israel— and even more! Fellowship* in Christ for the Gentiles as well as the Jews fulfills the analogous function for the Christian as the possession of the land did for the Israelite. But that does not eliminate the socioeconomic dimension of stewardship. Christian fellowship (*koinōnia*) is not merely "spiritual" communion. It is total sharing of life, not regarding possessions as absolutely one's own, bringing economic and social justice and peacemaking.

Christians share stewardship of the world with the rest of humankind, but they have three additional concerns: (1) the investment and proper use of our personal time, abilities and finances for the benefit of others, something for which we are held responsible by God (Mt 25:14-30; *see* Money; Spiritual Gifts; Talents); (2) the treasuring and distribu-

tion of the grace of God as proclaimed in the gospel (1 Pet 4:10), not only by apostles and church leaders (1 Cor 4:1; Tit 1:7) but by all believers' being stewards and witnesses of the gospel (*see* Evangelism; Laity; Ministry; Witness); (3) the full-fledged sharing of life (including material possessions) as a sign of being "in Christ." In the early church this meant sharing available assets over and above the normal (Acts 2:44-45; 4:32-35), engaging in relief missions to poor believers (Acts 11:27-3) and crosscultural giving to symbolize the mutual interdependence, equality and unity in Christ (1 Cor 16:1; 2 Cor 8:13).

Time, Abilities and Finances

It is unbiblical to relegate personal stewardship to merely the religious portion of our lives: to tithing, using our talents for the church or giving a percentage of our income to the Lord's work. All of us belong to God, and stewardship concerns the whole of everyday life.

The time of our lives. Instead of our squeezing yet one more Christian activity into our already overloaded schedule, stewardship of time might involve the opposite. We exercise stewardship of time in our daily occupations, fulfilling God's creational and providential calling to make the world work. We also invest time when we play* with our families or enjoy conversation* with friends. This everyday redemption of time springs from the sabbath,* which is one of the crucial signs that we take the stewardship of time seriously. We cannot lay aside our compulsion to work unless we believe that God is running the world and can be trusted with it while we rest.

Abilities for church and world. It is a sin not to use talents and gifts that God has given. Our gifts are on loan from God. They are to be used for the upbuilding of family, church, neighborhood* and society. In the end we are accountable for our use or disuse of them. Not all of this has to be organized through the local church; indeed, most of it will not be. Luther was eloquent on this subject. "How can you think you are not called?" he asked. He then reminded his hearers that they had more than enough to do in their homes, kitchens, workshops and fields:

> The idea that the service to God should have only to do with a church altar, singing, reading, sacrifice, and the like is without doubt but the worst trick of the devil. How could the devil have led us more effectively astray than by the narrow conception that service to God takes place only in church and by works done therein. . . . The whole world could abound with services to the Lord (quoted in Feucht, p. 80).

Finances, where your heart is. Contrary to the secular viewpoint—"If you don't own it, you won't take care of it"—being a steward should increase our care and diligence in the use of property and wealth. It is not ours; it will be taken back by God one day; God will hold us responsible for what we do with it. Our everyday stewardship—even maintaining a vehicle and doing chores*—links us with God, who maintains the world. God wants not just an intact creation but a "return" on his investment* (*see* Ownership).

It is tragic that Christian stewardship has been so often reduced to "tithing"—giving to the Lord's work one-tenth of one's income ("Is that gross or net after taxes?"). In the Old Testament tithes were like taxes paid to the temple; they were not discretionary gifts (for an exception, see Gen 14:20). This accomplished four things. It (1) celebrated the goodness of God (Deut 14:26), (2) acknowledged God's ownership of everything, (3) maintained places of worship (Num 18:21; Deut 14:27) and (4) cared for the poor (Deut 14:28-29). Even in the Old Testament tithing was only part of Israel's stewardship. The New Testament only once mentions tithing (Mt 23:23)—in the context of Jesus' calling the Pharisees to something more important. The New Testament principle is not one-tenth but "hilarious giving" (2 Cor 9:7), that is, cheerful and uncalculating. Since everything belongs to God, we should generously disperse what we can to help others. But the use of "should" destroys the very idea of Christian giving; it comes not from law, principle or obligation but from the spontaneous overflow of gratitude for Christ's blessing* on our lives (2 Cor 8:9).

The Grace of Giving

Many people give donations. The Bible calls us to stewardship. Donations imply that we are the owners and out of the generosity of our hearts we are giving some to others. Stewardship implies that it all belongs to God and is used for God's purposes. Donation spirituality is self-affirming and calculated for effect; stewardship spirituality is other-directed and wholehearted. Donation spirituality looks for a thank-you from the recipient; stewardship spirituality aims at "Well done" when the Lord returns.

Some questions to ponder are these: How much do we give that does not come from a sense of obligation or social expectation? Do we act as if the part we retain is actually ours? Do we regard whatever wealth we have as a stewardship on behalf of the poor? Does the disbursement of monies represented by our checkbook or credit-card* invoice reflect God's priorities for everyday life?

How does the grace of giving work out in practice? Of course, we should give to support Christian workers and causes as instructed in Scripture. But, in accordance with the Old Testament outlook, we should also see that we are stewards of money and assets in ways that benefit our families. To neglect family through sacrificing for the church is wrong. This is clearly something both Jesus (Mk 7:11) and Paul affirmed. Indeed not taking care of our families makes us worse than unbelievers (1 Tim 5:8). We should also heed Jesus' injunction to "use worldly wealth to gain friends for yourselves, so that when it is gone, you will be welcomed into eternal dwellings" (Lk 16:9). This means investing in people, giving money (anonymously, if possible) to the poor, showing hospitality.* As Thomas Aquinas so beautifully explained, this holistic stewardship is much more than handouts. He listed the seven corporal alms deeds—visit, quench, feed, ransom, clothe, harbor and bury (the dead)— and linked them with seven spiritual alms—instruct, counsel, reprove, console, pardon, forbear and pray (*Summa* 32.2.1).

In these matters mutual encouragement and accountability are needed. In the Western world we are modest about nothing except money. The fig leaf has slipped from the genitals to the wallet. Yet it is precisely in the way we spend time, abilities and especially finances that we reveal our true relationship to God and work out our salvation. Part of our problem is that we mostly think about and decide such matters on an individual basis or simply as families. Small groups* and spiritual friendships* can provide the fundamental contexts for sharing priorities, budgets and prayerfully supporting one another in becoming better stewards. In this matter the church as a whole needs to take the lead.

The Church's Stewardship

There is nothing in the Old or New Testaments to match or justify the present preoccupation of "stewardship" drives to raise money for Christian workers and church buildings.* Though some workers should be freed from common toil for a specific ministry, this is entirely exceptional and is a secondary form of Christian stewardship (*see* Financial Support). Most Christian workers throughout history have been self-supported tentmakers.* The primary understanding of Christian stewardship has to do with investing what God has entrusted to us, sharing the treasure of the gospel, demonstrating love, striving for economic justice and peace on earth, all of this starting with the Christian community* itself (Gal 6:10).

The church's time allocation, use of the gifts and talents of its members and allocation of financial resources are a graphic statement of its spirituality. If the local church consumes all the discretionary time of its members, not freeing them for family and neighbors, it is hoarding. If a church fails to release spiritual and natural gifts and allows people to "waste" themselves, it is squandering. If a church uses all its money on itself (staff and building), it is caring for itself rather than undertaking stewardship.

Some specific suggestions to be considered in light of this are the following: Spend half of the church budget beyond the local church. Apply simple-living guidelines to the church and not just to individuals. Invest time, abilities and finances in serving God's unity mission* by linking poor and rich churches, Third World and Western churches, fighting injustice and bringing peace, unity and equality as Paul did in the great collection (2 Cor 8—9). Devote leadership and resources to supporting people where God has placed them in the world, rather than enlisting them for the programs of the church. Send groups of people (and not just checks) to care for the poor at home and abroad (remember Aquinas's blend of corporal and spiritual alms).

Stewardship gives meaning to our

lives and helps us make sense out of everyday life. It captures all our energies, assets and creativity for God's grand plan of humanizing the earth and developing it as a glorified creation. It saves us from the twin dangers of despair (What will come of the earth?) and false messianism (If we do not save the planet, who will?) because we are cooperating with a God who is determined to bring the creation to a worthy end through its complete renewal (Rev 21:5). Stewardship is a thermometer of our spirituality and discipleship. Where our treasure is, there will be our hearts (Lk 12:34). Our response to a brother in need is a measure of our love for God (Jas 2:15-16; 1 Jn 3:17). But stewardship also provides an incentive to grow in Christ. If we give sparingly, we will live cramped, emaciated lives; if we give generously, we live expansively and deeply (Lk 6:38).

In the end what God wants back is not an untouched creation or an intact (but unused) human ability; God wants a "return" on his investment. Stewardship is the way God gets such a return. It is not simply giving things away or keeping them safely in trust, but wisely investing them in contexts in which they will do some good and multiply. On the judgment day God will be asking individuals, families, churches and nations what we did with what we had. How well will we have managed God's household in the time between Christ's first and second coming?

See also ENVIRONMENT; FINANCIAL SUPPORT; MONEY; SERVICE; SIMPLER LIFESTYLE; TALENTS; TIME.

References and Resources

J. Chrysostom, *On Wealth and Poverty*, trans. Catherine P. Roth (Crestwood, N.Y.: St. Vladimir's Seminary Press, 1984); Oscar E. Feucht, *Everyone a Minister* (St. Louis: Concordia, 1974); R. Foster, *Freedom of Simplicity* (New York: Harper & Row, 1989); D. J. Hall, *Stewardship of Life in the Kingdom of Death* (Grand Rapids: Eerdmans, 1988); L. T. Johnson, *Sharing Possessions: Mandate and Symbol of Faith* (London: SCM, 1981); M. MacGregor, *Your Money Matters* (Minneapolis: Bethany House, 1988); R. J. Sider, *Cry Justice: The Bible on Hunger and Poverty* (New York: Paulist, 1980); R. J. Sider, *Living More Simply: Biblical Principles and Practical Models* (Downers Grove, Ill.: InterVarsity Press, 1980); R. J. Sider, *Rich Christians in a Hungry World* (Dallas: Word, 1990); C. J. H. Wright, *God's People in God's Land: Family, Land and Property in the Old Testament* (Grand Rapids: Eerdmans, 1990).

R. Paul Stevens

STORYTELLING

Once upon a time, not so very long ago, stories were counted among the most treasured possessions in our homes.* To have known the stories of a family,* of a people, was to have held the key to the very heart of its being. To have spoken those stories in wise and timely ways was to have fulfilled a calling* esteemed by both paupers and kings. And to have heard those stories, to have truly listened to them with heart and mind, was to have participated in the oldest and perhaps most intimate of the human arts—*storytelling*.

The tradition of oral storytelling is common to every culture* the world over. Since the dawn of language, people have used the imagery and metaphor of stories to express their experience of life. We make stories as naturally as we make breakfast, or make love, says author Rudy Wiebe in his introduction to *The Story-Makers*. Through stories we make sense of that which we cannot face head on. Stories (by a means that cannot be fully explained) reach levels of the subconscious inaccessible to rational words alone (Bausch, p. 17). Stories are, simply and profoundly, the language of the soul.*

God created us to *story* together. The unfolding drama of the Creator's love for us opens with three engaging words: "In the beginning" (Gen 1:1). The stories of the Old Testament chronicle the lives of ordinary people who discover, daily, that spirituality is rooted in the earthy events of their lives (Is 25:6-9). God reaches out to us through stories. The new covenant was revealed through a Son who "has spoken to us" (Heb 1:2), "who unmasked eternal truths by telling homely stories of Palestinian life" (Bausch, p. 21). To return, as Christ calls us, to a childlike openness to mystery and love (Mt 18:3), we must restore and nurture a respect for the power of story and the place of storytelling in our lives.

The Story Stone

There is a story told among the Seneca people (in what is now New York State) of a boy who lived with his father, mother and sister on the edge of a great forest. Life was good for the people of the village. The men hunted, the women gathered, and the land provided everything they needed. But they were not quite human yet—they had no stories (Moore, p. 118).

One day, while hunting, the boy hears a large stone call out to him. The stone invites the boy to listen to a story but first requires a small gift. The boy gives to the stone the bird that he has caught, then sits in awe as the stone speaks this strange new thing. One by one, the other members of the family discover the boy's secret, each learning to give something in exchange for a story. Together the family decides to bring their stories back to the village. At once, upon hearing the tales, the loose gathering of people becomes a community.* The stories told become *their* stories, binding the people in ways that the common need of food and shelter never had. Then one day the stone announces that it will speak no more. The boy cries out, "That cannot be. I do not want to live without your stories!" To

which the stone replies, "You are now the storyteller. As long as one person remembers these stories, you will never be without them."

For some people, this ancient art of storytelling is as fresh and present as the morning. These are the friends, family members and strangers we all recognize as *natural storytellers*. With the gift of gab and a knack for just the right story at just the right moment, these characters are ready and willing to entertain, instruct and encourage us with their tales. But, are we always as eager to listen?*

Dramatic changes in society and technology* have, with startling speed, usurped the role of the storyteller as the "mirror and memory" of our lives (Yolen, p. 35). No longer do we look to our elders, or our story-keepers, for tales of heroes and heroines to model courage and morality. Instead, we grope for glimpses of celebrities whose private lives we love to covet (and criticize). Where once there was an extended family of grandparents,* adults and children living close to one another, sharing in a common folklore that told us who we were and how we were to live, there is now the nuclear or single-parent family often living a great distance from ancestral roots. For many of us the old stories and myths that once characterized our culture are now available only if we go searching for them on the library shelves.

Before television* took over the place of honor in our homes, families used to turn to each other for telling, listening and remembering (Deut 6:5-7; Rosenbluth, p. 2). Although we acknowledge readily that children love stories, we are only now beginning to recognize that as adults we need more than anecdotes in sermons or passing conversation (a kind of "fast food" for the soul). We are coming to understand that without storytelling we will, like the people of the Seneca legend, be living less than human lives. In key areas of knowledge—philosophy and ethics, anthropology and psychology, education* and communication—as well as in preaching and theology, an appreciation of story and the importance of storytelling is coming back into its own.

A Living Art

While it may be argued that there are stories everywhere around us (newspapers, books, television, film, video), none of these media fully embodies the art of storytelling. Storytelling is essentially an interactive experience. It requires an encounter between both storyteller and the story listener. It is a living, intimate and wonderfully unpredictable art. Stories may begin "a long time ago," but because they are heard and felt in the present, they always end with "right now" (Shea, p. 8).

A good storyteller is willing to be vulnerable, to *be* in the presence of the audience, to sense the mood of the listener and to respect the free will of each person to take what is needed from the story. This is the unique gift of respected elders among many aboriginal communities. When asked a direct question, the elders answer indirectly, with a story. The listener is left to reflect upon the possible meaning(s) of the story—an insight that often does not come for years (Cruikshank, p. 2).

The parables of Jesus reflect this same wisdom. Jesus knew that his listeners were at many different stages on their spiritual journeys. Rather than engage the crowd in an intellectual debate, he simply told stories (Mt 13:34). Those who had eyes to see and ears to hear understood (Mt 13:16). The Old Testament prophet Nathan was also gifted of God in telling the exact story needed to strike at the core of the matter. Instead of confronting David directly with his sins of adultery and murder, Nathan told a story: "There were two men in a certain town, one rich and the other poor" (2 Sam 12:1). David needed nothing more than the story to be enraged by the injustice revealed. The Scottish bard David Campbell says that stories are always the shortest distance to the truth.

Beginning to Tell

With models of great storytellers in Scripture and history, you may feel somewhat intimidated to follow in their footsteps. Like every good art, storytelling has masters to be admired, but at the heart storytelling has one simple rule: respect the story and your listener. Whether your story is a lively tale of fun and good humor or a mythic quest of courage, give the story all that it needs to be alive in the moment of sharing. See yourself as a finely tuned instrument upon which the story is played.

Choose to share only those stories that move you (to tears, laughter, wonder); then get to know the story inside out. Reflect carefully on the stages of the story: How does it invite the listener into the time of the story? How does it build? Where are the contemplative pauses? Does the story conclude with a sense of wholeness? Imagine the characters and the setting in your mind's eye. Choose (and pace) your language thoughtfully to give your listeners select sensory clues to re-create the story images in their own minds. Enjoy this as the greatest reward of the storyteller: the knowledge that within each imagination* lies a wholly unique version of the story; no two imaginings are ever entirely alike. Television cannot hold a candle to that.

Draw upon the many resources available to storytellers today. Subscribe to a national storytelling journal (addresses of two are noted in References and Resources). Associations of storytellers can provide a calendar of storytelling festivals, conferences and workshops. Immerse yourself in collections of folklore, myth and literary tales. Read stories and Scripture aloud (even if you are alone) to remind yourself that language was meant to be spoken.

Finally, be prepared to learn as much about yourself as you will about the stories. You will begin to see, hear and feel stories everywhere about you. You may begin to understand, as John Shea suggests, that ministry begins at the intersection between God and his people, as revealed in their stories. Be inspired along your journey by the words of the late Angela Sydney, beloved storyteller of the Tagish people in the southern Yukon, who once said, "I have no money to leave my grandchildren, my stories are my wealth" (Cruikshank, p. 36).

See also CONVERSATION; FAIRY TALES; GRANDPARENTING; MOVIES; PREACHING; TEACHING; TELEVISION.

References and Resources
W. J. Bausch, *Storytelling: Imagination and Faith* (Mystic, Conn.: Twenty-Third Publications, 1984); J. Cruikshank, *Life Lived like a Story: Life Stories of Three Yukon Elders* (Lincoln: University of Nebraska Press, 1990); C. P. Estes, *The Gift of Story: A Wise Tale About What Is Enough* (New York: Ballantine, 1993); D. Kossoff, *Bible Stories* (London: William Collins Sons, 1968); R. Moore, *Awakening the Hidden Storyteller: How to Build a Storytelling Tradition in Your Family* (Boston: Shambhala Publications, 1991); A. Pellowski, *World of Storytelling* (New York: Bowker, 1977); V. Rosenbluth, *Keeping Family Stories Alive: A Creative Guide to Taping Your Family Life and Lore* (Point Roberts, Wash.: Hartley & Marks, 1990); J. Shea, *Stories of God: An Unauthorized Biography* (Chicago: Thomas More, 1978); R. Wiebe, *The Story-Makers* (Toronto: MacMillan, 1970); J. Yolen, *Touch Magic: Fantasy, Faerie and Folklore in the Literature of Childhood* (New York: Philomel Books, 1981). *Appleseed,* Journal of the Storytellers' School of Toronto (412A College St., Toronto, Ontario, Canada M5T 1T3); *Storytelling Magazine,* Journal of the National Storytelling Association (P.O. Box 309, Jonesborough, TN 37659).

Susan Catherine Klassen

STRESS, WORKPLACE

Stress is as necessary to life as eating* and communicating. Without stress we would not be able to appreciate our limits or attain our objectives. Being under the right kind of pressure, whether self-induced or externally created, is integral to responding appropriately to the challenges of everyday life. To desire an existence that is stress-free is quite literally a death* wish.

The Universality of Stress
In the Bible we find many of its key figures under stress at various points in their lives: Moses feeling overwhelmed by the number of things he has to do (Num 11), Jeremiah voicing his personal and vocational frustrations to God (Jer 17) and Paul reconstructing the difficulties and anxieties* he faced (2 Cor 11). Most of these stressful experiences were constructive. Yet stress is a curse as well as a blessing, since it occurs in malignant as well as benign forms. It can be both constructive and destructive, opening up some possibilities in life and shutting down others. This negative side of stress is most devastating in modern Western societies.

Distinguishing between these two kinds of stress is relatively simple: if the situation generating stress requires no immediate physical response or if the stress response is greater than the need, then stress is inappropriate or wrong. This kind of stress is widely experienced and is more personally and socially injurious and causes more deaths than addictions* to smoking, alcohol and drugs* or the ravages of automobile* accidents. About 30 percent of adults in the United States say that they experience high stress levels nearly every day; an even higher percentage reports high stress once or twice a week. This is stress in its pathological rather than healthy mode.

Stress is problematic to us when, instead of occurring intermittently in stretching or threatening situations, it becomes a recurring or habitual phenomenon caused by overstimulation and hyperactivity. Stress creates difficulties when it does not let up and when it is triggered by ordinary, everyday events. In our society this kind of stress has reached epidemic proportions. People in earlier times may have worked harder than we do and may have become more physically fatigued, but no generation has ever been as psychologically hyped up, exhausted or stressed out. Nervous breakdowns, burnout and stress-related illnesses and deaths are common. In the past it was only in extreme situations, such as mass warfare, that large numbers of people underwent severe stress. Now it is found in everyday situations and especially in the workplace.*

Types and Degrees of Stress

The many general sources of stress have been documented: (1) continual busyness, the hectic pace of life and regulation by the clock; (2) constant noise, activity and movement, caused personally or by the immediate environment; (3) overly crowded and congested freeways, streets, shopping malls* and other settings in which considerable time is spent; (4) long-term demanding or threatening circumstances that stretch people beyond their normal limits; (5) unrealistic expectations or anxiety-creating deadlines, leading to overwork and sometimes workaholism; (6) repeated shock, confusion or conflict in unfamiliar social and cultural situations; (7) chronic tension in family situations or relationships that creates ongoing anxiety. These things in themselves are not stresses; it is how they are perceived that induces stress. So an important distinction is generally drawn between the sources of potential stress and an individual's perception or interpretation of them, making these sources into stressors.

When we are stressed, our bodies pump more adrenaline to help us cope. If this continues beyond a reasonable time, we suffer from stress disease, and our performance becomes adversely affected. When this happens, not only our nerves but our whole bodies are stretched. Stress then seeks out a weak link in our system. Connections have been established between stress and exhaustion, depression, insomnia, migraines, ulcers, colitis, high blood pressure, asthma, allergies, alcoholism, heart disease and divorce.* Chronic stress depletes both the brain's natural tranquilizers and the body's immune system, leading to a greater reliance on chemical tranquilizers, painkillers and antibiotics. The number of days lost to the workplace from all this and the indirect and direct cost to the individuals concerned are quite staggering.

Measuring devices like the Social Readjustment Rating Scale seek to quantify the amount of stress caused by various life events and then to analyze how vulnerable a person is to serious physical or psychological illness. At the top of the list of stressors are bereavement of a spouse or member of the family, divorce or marital separation, getting married and marital reconciliation, retiring* or being fired,* personal injury or illness. In the middle of the list are changing jobs or living conditions, taking out a heavy mortgage or facing foreclosure, an outstanding personal achievement or trouble with the boss, a son's or daughter's leaving home. Near the bottom of the list is a change in eating habits, having a vacation* or committing a minor violation of the law. When a person's score nears or overshoots 300 points, there is a 90 percent likelihood that he or she will experience some physical illness or psychological disturbance in the very near future.

Stress in the Workplace

One of the main settings in which stress occurs today is the workplace. For an increasing number of people a high level of abnormal as well as normal stress is created at work.* Conditions, practices, structures, attitudes, expectations, relationships, changes and systems in the workplace often produce strains that are higher than elsewhere. Given the grave consequences of long-term abnormal stress, working can be a risky affair. Since work or the lack of it is now the dominant reality in Western life, its contribution to the amount and degree of stress in contemporary society must be carefully examined. It has been estimated that up to 50 percent of workplaces in the country are overly stress-producing. This includes many religious organizations and churches.* It is little wonder that stress has become the greatest cause of job dissatisfaction and reduced productivity. Often complaints about conditions at work or about others in the workplace mask a deep stress over the character of the job itself. Sometimes this results in workers suffering from vague and undefinable sicknesses. Stress in the workplace can take many forms. Among the most serious forms of stress are the following.

Tensions with superiors. Bosses tend to generate stress if they love power, are overly ambitious, refuse to take responsibility for mistakes, cannot make decisions in a timely manner, do not maintain appropriate boundaries, tend to have unreal expectations of their employees and often display anger or fail to give affirmation. Superiors who have a need to control or intimidate are often uptight and overstressed themselves. Sometimes they try to minimize their own stress by provoking stress in others. Stresses further arise when employers do not give enough space for employees to use their full capabilities or expect more than some employees are capable of contributing. A supervisor's behavior toward subordinates is probably the single greatest contributor to stress in the workplace.

Problems with coworkers. This takes many forms. Examples include the clash of incompatible personalities and of conflicting beliefs or values, the lack of group cohesion and collaboration, failure on the part of some to pull their weight (especially when the performance of others is dependent on this), sexual harassment or abuse, racial prejudice or discrimination* and even having unresponsive and emotionless colleagues. On the other hand, relating too intensively in the workplace or having too much concern for sexual and political correctness can also give rise to tensions. Tragically, this stress sometimes leads to violence in the workplace. Around one thousand people in the United States are killed at work by colleagues each year.

The atmosphere of the workplace. Organizational culture* is largely shaped by workplace traditions and senior management. Workplace atmosphere is affected negatively by such internal factors as the inaccessibility of the ultimate decision makers, their lack of consultation with the rank and file, their inflexibility or incompetence, their being out of touch with current realities or unaware of the personal needs of the workers and their failure to establish adequate personnel policies or to provide proper staffing for an organization. Workplace atmosphere is also affected by external forces such as new technology,* downsizing because of competition* or the economic climate and the need for a more flexible and mobile work force. The attitudes and behaviors of workers themselves contribute to the atmosphere in such things as distrust of newcomers and outsiders, resistance to change or new ideas, an overly critical spirit or a passive-aggressive attitude toward the organization, fragmentation of the work force into competing interest groups or a tendency to find regular scapegoats for repeated workplace problems.

Personal struggles with work. Serious stress in the workplace is also caused by an employee's not fitting in a job, fear of unemployment,* sidelining or demotion and attempts to strike a healthy balance between work and family or leisure. Boredom* is also a major problem in the workplace.

As with the Social Readjustment Rating Scale, there are also instruments like the Job Stress Survey that measure occupational stress. People in different kinds of workplaces suffer from different kinds and levels of stress. Ranking highest in severity and occurrence is inadequate salary and lack of opportunity for advancement. After this comes problems related to superiors, such as those previously noted. Next comes problems relating to colleagues, such as others not doing their job properly. This is followed by matters relating to work conditions, such as meeting deadlines, excessive paperwork and inferior equipment.

What distinguishes stress in the workplace from stress elsewhere is its translation into dollars and cents. Given the central place financial reward plays in our society, this tends to heighten both the significance and level of stress there. Stress costs money* not only in lost earnings and profits but in claims and medical costs. For example, around one-sixth of all workers' compensation claims now appear to be stress related, and over the last decade and a half such claims have risen exponentially. The stakes are high in the search for healthy responses to stressors.

Ways of Handling Stress Constructively
One unhealthy response is simply to resign oneself to it, but this is filled with physical and psychological risk. Others desperately seek to control the situation so as to minimize stress, but this often places others under unfair strain. There are more constructive ways of handling stress, and it is incumbent on those who have the greatest chance of making changes to find these. This places a heavy responsibility on boards of directors, senior management, employers, heads of departments, union officials and coaches. Here we will focus on what we as workers can do to improve the situation.

First, we should discern how much stress we are under. Symptoms we will look for include personal ones such as the use of substances to escape problems, overdependence on distractions, general sense of unhappiness, conflict with or avoidance of significant others. Emotional symptoms include tension and anxiety, restlessness and irritability, panic feelings or periodic depression,* increased daydreaming* and fantasizing, a general lack of responsiveness, including sexual responsiveness. Stress has health indications as well: high blood pressure, headaches, constant fatigue, sleep* problems, ulcers, racing heart, muscle tension and aching and increased vulnerability to sickness or viruses.

Second, we should identify the source of the stress. This involves examining both external factors and our internal responses, the actions of others and our own perceptions of what is happening.

Third, we need to take responsibility for dealing with stress rather than expecting others to relieve us of stress. The two basic options here are fight or flight. Both are found in the biblical narratives. For example, Moses took up his leadership burden with God in prayer and was given a resolution to his problem; on the other hand, he ran from his God-given responsibility. Resistance can take several forms, among them thinking about the situation to get clarity on the key factors creating the stress, sounding out others by asking questions or sharing experiences that focus on your issues, owning up to your share in letting it get out of hand. The next stage is communicating this where it will do most good, generating discussion about the general issue of stress and setting individual or team priorities so that stressors can be minimized. Sometimes this involves saying no and seeing what the consequences are. A further stage is engaging in practices that will provide energy for this struggle until the situation improves: regular exercise, meditation and contemplation, listening to what our bodies are saying, eating a balanced diet and experimenting with ways to relax.

Sometimes, however, flight rather than fight is the best response. We find biblical examples of this even in the life of Jesus: stretched and exhausted by the number of people seeking his ministry, he withdrew into an isolated place for a time (Mt 4:23; 5:2). This was not avoidance but a recognition that the problem was too overwhelming to be fought successfully in his present condition. Flight can take a variety of forms: asking to be demoted or moved sideways to a less stressful and more enjoyable position. It might also entail resigning from one's present position and seeking similar work in a less stressful workplace or another kind of work altogether. Sometimes people need a period of withdrawal, perhaps without pay, so that the whole situation can be reviewed in a less-harassed way and strength can be built up to fight or pursue a new path.

Whatever tactic is taken up, fight or flight, it is imperative that some action be taken. The alternatives are either eventual burnout (the last desperate plea from our whole system that "enough is enough") or physical breakdown (the whole system that has been pushed too far seizes up). In all this we need to recognize that we cannot control all the events of life. Our attempts to handle stress responsibly will be successful only to a point. What we can gain with God's and others' help is some control over our own feelings and a stronger sense of identity.

See also ANXIETY; CONFLICT, WORKPLACE; HEALTH; OFFICE POLITICS; REST; SABBATH; TIME; WORKPLACE.

References and Resources
R. Crandall and P. L. Perewe, *Occupational Stress: A Handbook* (Washington, D.C.: Taylor & Francis, 1995); R. E. Ecker, *The Stress Myth: Why the Pressures of Life Don't Have to Get You Down* (Downers Grove, Ill.: InterVarsity Press, 1985); A. Hart, *The Crazy-Making Workplace* (Ann Arbor, Mich.: Servant, 1993); L. Levi, *Stress Sources: Management and Prediction* (New York: Liveright, 1967); J. Schor, *The Overworked American: The Unexpected Decline of Leisure* (New York: BasicBooks, 1991); F. C. Richardson, *Stress: Sanity and Survival* (London: Futura, 1979); J. C. Smith, *Understanding Stress and Coping* (New York: Macmillan, 1992); P. Tournier, ed., *Fatigue in Modern Society: Psychological, Medical, Biblical Insights* (Atlanta: John Knox, 1978).

Robert Banks

STRIKES

Strikes have been with us for a long time. In the eighteenth century they were called *turnouts*. The word *strike* was first used in connection with a work stoppage involving British sailors who struck (that is, lowered) their sails to bring their ship to a halt. The term was eventually used in contexts other than nautical ones to describe a cessation of work* by any group of employees.

The purpose of this article is to evaluate the strike on the basis of a Judeo-Christian understanding of justice* and conflict resolution.* To do so, we will first note the historical reasons that have made the strike dear to the hearts of labor unionists.* A brief look at the prevalence of strikes will allow us to put them into perspective as a part of overall economic activity. Finally, ethical perspectives on strikes will be considered.

Strikes and the Rise of Unionism

Early Canadian and American unions incorporated some biblical principles into their methods and objectives (*see* Unions), but they did not oppose the use of the strike to further their aims. Gradually the union movement became more secular in its orientation. Whether unions leaned more in a Judeo-Christian or secular direction, employer response to their efforts was universally the same—fierce, even ferocious, resistance. Unions learned to respond in kind. In 1910, for example, trade unionists bombed the *Los Angeles Times* plant. In 1914 National Guardsmen opened fire on striking miners in Colorado, killing many.

It was a series of highly successful strikes against four major U.S. employers in the 1930s that brought labor unions into the mainstream of economic life in North America. In 1936 Congress passed the Wagner Act, which not only recognized the right of workers to organize but compelled employers to engage in collective bargaining with their unions. It also forbade any employer interference or domination in the formation or administration of unions. Similar Canadian legislation followed in 1944.

The lesson that union leaders learned, more than any other, from their history was this: strikes work—whether legal or illegal, quiet or violent, however costly in terms of dollars, reputations, even lives. No other method works better. To this day unions are convinced that this highly successful weapon must be retained to accomplish their objectives of furthering the economic and social interests of workers and the general betterment of society as they see it.

Strikes and the Economy

Advocates of the strike weapon will point out that as a percentage of working time, person-days lost to work stoppages are minuscule and pale in comparison to the impact of illness, absenteeism, involuntary unemployment* and even weather.* In 1989, for example, time lost to strikes in Canada was 0.18 percent of working time, whereas person-days lost to illness were more than five times that figure. Strike opponents, on the other hand, note that Canada and the United States are conflict-ridden compared to most of their international competitors and trading partners. In the period from 1960 to 1984, for instance, time lost from strikes in Canada was forty times that in Japan and five hundred times that in Germany and Sweden. These sharp contrasts have not altered greatly in recent years.

Industrial relations scholars admit that very little is known about the costs to society of strikes and lockouts, largely because of the lack of research on the issue. Strictly in terms of direct dollar costs, it could perhaps be argued that the economic impact of strikes is not as great as is often believed. But whatever the costs are, strike supporters argue that they are inevitable given the adversarial foundation of our industrial relations system. Any substitute for the adversary system, in their opinion, would be far more costly than strikes. How else can workers get management to take them seriously and to bargain in good faith?

Opponents counter that such reasoning ignores the experience of other highly successful industrial nations that run much more collaborative industrial relations systems than our own. They also point out that the prevalence of strikes has built up a backlash of bad feeling against the union movement. As one commentator said, "Strikes help some unions. That is not the same as saying that they help all workers; but the costs are borne by society as a whole" (Stewart, pp. 41-42).

Ethical Perspectives

Business ethicists recognize the dilemma that strikes pose. On the one hand, they can cause financial injuries to employers and employees, inconvenience and worse to consumers and at times significant economic problems in society. On the other hand, many feel that workers can often obtain justice only through this means. Given these assumptions, business ethicists William Shaw and Vincent Barry have argued that a strike is justified when three conditions are met: (1) just cause, which refers to job-related matters such as inadequate pay and dangerous conditions; (2) proper authorization, meaning that workers must make the decision to strike without coercion or intimidation; and (3) last resort, which means that all other measures have been tried.

A basic moral principle is that one should always use the least injurious means available to accomplish one's objectives. There are many alternatives to the strike, such as mediation and arbitration, that can achieve workers' objectives. These avenues should be exhausted before a strike is called (Shaw and Barry, pp. 280-81).

The Christian is faced with a quandary. One can deplore the abuse of the strike while at the same time accept that there could be arguments for its legitimacy if it was employed to achieve biblically just objectives, assuming that other methods had proven to be fruitless. As Christian businessperson Fred Catherwood points out,

> The Christian faith teaches us respect for the individual, and if society respects the individual, he must be protected from the possibility of exploitation by those who employ him. . . . The right to withhold labor is usually the only sanction available to the working man. . . . It is natural and right for a Christian to deplore the use of force to settle a dispute. (Catherwood, pp. 74, 76, 80)

John Redekop notes the incompatibility between the strike ethic and the love ethic: "How can a Christian justify doing something as part of a group which he cannot accept as correct individual action for himself?" (p. 14). Christian union leader Ed Vanderkloet maintains, "Most of us agree that industrial conflict is an ugly thing and that we should try to eliminate strikes. But that is not as easy as it sounds. In fact, it is next to impossible" (p. 31).

A strike is never wholly private in its effects. Other people beyond the direct participants are bound to suffer some harm. Unfortunately, it is not always possible to determine the nature and extent of the harm. If one could be convinced that for many strikes the harm suffered truly amounted to mere inconveniences or that only the deserving suffered (such as an evil employer), the moral judgment would be a relatively easy one. But in many cases that assessment would be very difficult to make. Thus, I feel that the considerations leading up to the decision to strike should go beyond what the ethicists suggested to include the following:

1. Is the dispute a grave matter addressing a genuinely unjust situation? (I appreciate the difficulty in assessing this and the temptation to make the assessment in a highly subjective manner.)

2. Have all other avenues for resolving the dispute been thoroughly explored? (Many dispute-resolution strategies have proven to be more effective than is commonly held.)

3. Will innocent bystanders be hurt?

4. Will the legitimate moral rights* of others be violated?

Conclusions

Vanderkloet has noted that in medieval Europe trial by battle was the most common means of determining guilt and innocence and of settling disputes. The victor of the duel was assumed to be both morally and legally right. Gradually that system was discarded as people became more aware of the need for doing public justice. Now for virtually every kind of dispute other than industrial ones, our society has developed methods employing impartial judges, juries or umpires to settle them. Only in labor disputes do we still "slug it out on the picket line where ultimately the strongest wins" (Vander-kloet, p. 31).

The strike is to a large extent the major symptom of our adversarial industrial relations system here in North America. It is indeed a powerful instrument and has been used to good effect by organized labor in achieving its aims. But other international trading partners, including those lacking our Judeo-Christian heritage, have developed more just, collaborative industrial relations systems in which the use of the strike is a fraction of ours. Labor and management alike have tended to wave aside too easily the potential for alternative dispute-resolution strategies. The time has come for North Americans to decide whether the status quo represents either economic or ethical sense.

See also JUSTICE; TRADES; UNIONS; WORK; WORKPLACE.

References and Resources

F. Catherwood, *On the Job: The Christian 9 to 5* (Grand Rapids: Zondervan, 1983); J. H. Redekop, "Should Christian Teachers or Nurses Ever Strike?" (unpublished); W. H. Shaw and V. Barry, *Moral Issues in Business,* 5th ed. (Belmont, Calif.: Wadsworth Publishing, 1992); W. Stewart, *Strike* (Toronto: McClelland and Stewart, 1977); E. Vanderkloet, *In and Around the Workplace: Christian Directions in the World of Work* (Toronto: Christian Labour Association of Canada, 1992).

John R. Sutherland

STRUCTURES

Life is full of visible and invisible structures all of which are fundamental to making sense of life in this world. There are structures obviously made by human beings (such as buildings and bridges), structures of living things (such as the bone structure of animals and the organization of a microscopic cell) and invisible structures (of such things as time,* works of literature and the human psyche). In every aspect of everyday life—marriage,* work,* business, leisure,* church,* and social responsibility—we encounter structures for good or ill, often as a mixed blessing.

The word *structures* communicates two things: how the members of the whole are related to each other and how the whole achieves some purpose. The structure of a house expresses how the various building materials are put together so that the purpose of the architect is fulfilled. The structure of a poem describes how the words and lines are put together to create the impact intended by the poet. Structures help us to experience regularity, pattern, form and order. Without these there would be chaos, anarchy and confusion.

Intentional Order

The biblical account of creation describes God's bringing order out of chaos, the formless void mentioned in Genesis 1:2. God separated light from darkness (Gen 1:4), the sky from the waters (vv. 6-7), the sea from the land (v. 9) and the day from the night (v. 14), so bringing order to the formless void. In the ancient Near East the symbol of disorder was the sea (or the sea monster)— that unpredictable and uncontrollable domain whose saline substance could not be used by an agrarian society. But in a number of places in the Old Testament, Hebrew poets declare God's control over the sea. By setting a boundary for it, God made possible an ordered creation (Gen 1:5-9; compare Job 38:8-11; Ps 74:12-17; Ps 93; Prov 8:29).

Living things were also created in a structured way: vegetation of all kinds appears with seeds to reproduce (Gen 1:11-12); sea creatures, birds and land animals are all assigned their respective places to live and given the ability to reproduce (vv. 20-25). Finally, human beings were made in God's image so that they might have stewardship* over creation (vv. 26-28). Genesis 2:1 summarizes the work: "Thus the heavens and the earth were finished, and *all their multitude*" (NRSV, emphasis ours)—this last phrase often being translated as "host" or "army." Like an army, the creation consists of a diverse collection of objects, properly arranged and organized. So creation is literally a *kosmos,* an ordered world, which, as the apostle Paul says, continues to be held together in Christ (Col 1:17). But this world making, of which structures are so central, is not exclusively a divine work.

Genesis 2 suggests that part of the mandate God gave to Adam was also to bring order into the world. Adam was to take care of the garden (Gen 2:15), an activity that involved creating and maintaining order. Adam was invited to name the animals (vv. 19-20)—a work requiring insight into the nature of each one—thereby bringing order to the diversity among all the creatures. Part of the godlikeness of human beings is that people are invited to be cocreators with God, an activity that involves crafting structures.

To summarize, we live in a structured world; while God always remains free to do whatever he wants, there is an order to the world that God both creates and maintains. This structure is intelligible; we can discover something about this order by observing God's creation. Human activity involves creating structures, though not at the same level as God's creative activity.

Discerning Given Structures
Part of the human vocation is to discern and delight in the ordered way God has made the world in which we live and work. Even people who do not believe the biblical account of creation still assume the world is structured and that it is meaningful to ask questions about why things are the way they are.

Making the physical world intelligible. Scientific investigation would not be possible if the physical world were not structured (*see* Creation). Scientists try to explain the various patterns they observe in terms of laws. Johannes Kepler, for example, noted that planets travel in elliptical orbits. Isaac Newton then suggested that the reason for this was the gravitational force between a planet and the sun—an attractive force directly proportional to the product of their masses and inversely proportional to the square of the distance between them. This turned out to explain not only planetary orbits but also why apples fall to the ground. Newton's gravitational law helps us understand something about the structure of our world.

In chemistry Dmitri Mendeleev's periodic table of the elements demonstrates something of the internal structure of the hundred or so basic substances known to exist and explains family resemblances among them. In biology the process known as *photosynthesis,* whereby chlorophyll in a plant uses sunlight to combine carbon dioxide and water in the production of more complex compounds such as sugars,* is another description of the structure of the world. Gregor Mendel's observations regarding the breeding of peas has given us insight into the structure of heredity.

A dramatically new approach to exploring structures in the world is emerging from the field of chaos theory. Here the focus of attention is on how very complex and apparently random systems—systems too complex to be explained by the relationships among the various parts (that is, by natural laws)—can in fact be the result of very simple and well-defined causes. The structure of such things as clouds, coastlines and trees are of particular interest.

The term *fractal* was introduced to denote structures whose pattern repeats itself at different levels of magnification. Blood vessels, for example, are fractal. Beginning with the aorta of the heart, the blood vessels continuously branch and divide until in the capillaries the blood cells flow through single file. This structure has several advantages: (1) it is a very efficient way of transporting a limited supply of blood to each cell in the body; (2) the volume taken up by the blood vessels is only 5 percent of the body; and (3) the amount of information needed to encode this structure in the DNA is relatively limited since the pattern simply repeats itself over and over again. It turns out that many naturally occurring structures can be more easily understood in terms of fractal rather than Euclidean geometry, which limits itself to shapes such as squares, triangles, circles and so on. Concerning the latter, James Gleick suggests that Euclidean shapes "fail to resonate with the way nature organizes itself or with the way human perception sees the world" (pp. 116-17). The German physicist Gert Eilenberger comments on why we see beauty in natural landscapes but not in cityscapes: "Our feeling for beauty is inspired by the harmonious arrangement of order *and disorder* as it occurs in natural objects—in clouds, trees, mountain ranges, or snow crystals" (quoted in Gleick, p. 117, emphasis ours).

The structure of the physical world is wonderful—literally. It evokes wonder, as it did for the psalmist: "O LORD, how manifold are your works! In wisdom you have made them all" (Ps 104:24 NRSV). So the scientific exploration of structures in space is a holy occupation, but so is the study of structures in time.

Structured time. The regular movement of the earth structures our lives: days are divided into periods of light and darkness, a time to work and a time to rest. Years are divided into seasons, which are often celebrated in some way. In the biblical account of creation, the days are also gathered together into groups of seven with the seventh being a day of rest—a time to align oneself with the pattern God established in creation (Ex 20:8-11) and to reflect on God's work in bringing about liberation (Deut 5:12-15; *see* Leisure; Sabbath).

The Israelites, like most societies, celebrated various seasonal events (for example, new moon, harvest), but often combined these with the memory of significant events in their nation's history: Passover celebrated the exodus from Egypt at the time of the barley harvest; the Feast of Weeks (Pentecost), originally a celebration of the wheat harvest, later became a commemoration of God's giving of the law on Mt. Sinai; and the Feast of Tabernacles, coinciding with the olive harvest, was a celebration of God's preservation of the chosen people through the wilderness.

The teacher of Ecclesiastes, reflecting upon various rhythms of life, notes how various actions are appropriate at one time but not at another: at one time it is appropriate to weep, at another to laugh; at one time to tear, at another to sew (Eccles 3:1-8). So to discern the appropriate action for each day of our lives, we need wisdom.

The moral structure of the universe. According to the Bible the wise person has insight into the created order. Certain patterns of behavior are compatible with the way God intended; others conflict with it. Although freedom is often thought to be an escape from all structure, it is found by living within the boundaries of created structures.

The purpose of legal and Wisdom literature in the Bible is to make these structures clear, to instruct people on the way God intended life to be lived. The Ten Commandments are like a fence marking out an area in a field within which life will thrive. Breaking the law is like crossing the fence into forbidden territory; it is self-destructive behavior. In the Wisdom literature the field is divided, not so much into right and wrong, but into wise and foolish. Not only in morality but even in artistic expression, there are given structures.

Structure and the arts. Artists find avenues of expression by creatively working with the structure and content of their media: poets and storywriters crafting words into stanzas and plots, sculptors using hammer and chisel to create form from a piece of stone (often finding the structure in the stone itself), musicians transforming vibrations of strings, reeds or wind cavities into melody, harmony and rhythm (*see* Music). While human creativity is involved in all artistic expression, artists must respect the implicit structures and forms of their media.

Social and political structures. We were also created to live in families* and nations, these being ordained by God as fundamental social structures (Rom 13:1). These are not merely invented by humans but designed by the Creator as a social context for our good. Without them we would destroy ourselves in random promiscuous relationships (were there no family) and in anarchy (were there no government and no nation).

Politics* is essential to the human vocation and a service* rendered for the commonweal (the common good).

These contextual structures define a sphere for human activity and give people a sense of identity. The sin of Babel (Gen 11:1-9) was precisely the desire to create a homogenous, uniform world without national boundaries, without diversity as expressed in nations and people groups. God intended national structures to exist. "From one man he made every nation of men, that they should inhabit the whole earth; and he determined the times set for them and the exact places where they should live. God did this so that men would seek him and perhaps reach out for him and find him" (Acts 17:26-27).

Being World-Makers

But in all of the above areas, human beings are not only those who inherit an intentionally structured world that God could consider as "very good" (Gen 1:31); human beings are also world-makers. Human creativity involves making human structures: in the physical realm (through architecture,* technology,* science), in time (through planning* and sabbath*), in morality (through developing life patterns to express love* and justice*), in the arts (through making new things, which is the heart of creativity) and in society (through the art of government and politics).

In *The Sacred Canopy* Peter Berger has helpfully outlined the dynamic process in which we shape our world and in which our world shapes us. This involves three movements: (1) through cultural expression we relate to the world around us; (2) at some point we begin to experience the world, which has been shaped by our actions, as an object distinct from ourselves; and (3) this world then has the capability of acting back upon us and shaping our lives.

An example of this process is the creation of a nation. The founding fathers draft a constitution outlining the ideals (for example, equality of all people, democracy, freedom of speech) on which the nation will be built. Then they proceed to put in place people, institutions and laws to ensure that these ideals will be realized. But at some point the nation takes on a life of its own and is no longer dependent on the support of its founders. Finally the ideals expressed by the founders and protected and promoted by various means influence the lives of the citizens.

Every day we experience the influence of a wide variety of social structures—the nation, workplace, families, churches and so on. Each has been shaped by human activity, and each in turn shapes the lives of those living under them. But in world-making we face a double problem: we do not feel free to "make our worlds" the way we believe we should, and what we make turns out to be a mixed blessing, sometimes even a curse.

Fallen Structures and the Powers
Every day we encounter unjust and unloving structures, principles of conformity (for example, professionalism), negative cultural expectations, laws without moral foundations, technology as master and not mere servant, intractable institutions. With the growing awareness among social scientists of the role of social structures in shaping behavior, emotions and actions—often a detrimental influence—many theologians have begun to ask how the Bible addresses this reality. One approach has been to see a double reference in the phrase in Paul's letters "principalities and powers" (or more literally, "rulers and authorities")—one on a human level, another on a cosmic or spiritual level.

The background to this is in the Jewish belief that God assigned various angelic beings to rule over each of the nations (Deut 32:8-9; *Jub.* 15:31-32; compare Ps 82, where God chastises the members of the heavenly council for not extending justice to the poor). This idea seems to be reflected in Daniel 10, where Michael, the angel overseeing the affairs of Israel (Dan 12:1), is in conflict with the prince of Persia. Heavenly and earthly events paralleling and influencing each other (compare Rev 12:1-12) is typical of apocalyptic literature.

The fact that Paul uses words such as *rulers* and *authorities* to refer to cosmic powers—words that normally denote earthly figures—and the fact that he uses such words more than others that clearly refer to spiritual beings (for example, *Satan* and *demons*) suggest that he has both earthly and heavenly realities in mind when he speaks of rulers and authorities. Thus, when he writes in Colossians that all rulers and authorities have been created in, through and for Christ (1:16); that Christ is the head of every ruler and authority (2:10); and that Christ, by means of the cross, disarmed, exposed and triumphed over the rulers and authorities (2:15); he is referring not only to spiritual realities but also to structures of human existence.

Paul further expounds the relationship between spiritual powers and earthly structures in Ephesians, where he points out that believers struggle against rulers and authorities (6:12). This, however, is the conclusion to his section on the ethical implications of the gospel in which he appeals for unity within the church (4:1-16), godly living in the midst of a pagan society (4:17-5:20), husbands and wives loving each other (5:21-33), children and fathers relating properly (6:1-4) and slaves and masters showing mutual respect (6:5-9). When Paul talks about "spiritual" battles, he has in mind the very concrete situations of life: marriage, family, work, church, society. It is in these structures that spiritual forces are at work.

A further insight comes from the New Testament about the power of sin. The word *sin* normally refers to an act contrary to God's will. But Paul also uses the word to refer to a power that enslaves people to a life of self-centered activity (Rom 5—8). The significance of choosing the word *sin* to refer to such a power (rather than *Satan* or *demons*) appears to be that Paul saw an interrelationship between the acts and the power. Clearly, the power promotes the acts, but it is also true that the acts feed the power.

Recall Berger's description of world-building. Once again we can see how this applies. We are world-builders, but we are sinful ones. Therefore, everything we build in our world—institutions, culture and so on—is at least to some degree infected by sin. As this world takes on a life of its own and shapes the lives of people, it will also promote sin. How are we to relate to fallen existing structures or to the task of creating new ones?

Grappling with Structures

There are four historic approaches to relating to structures as powers, each one involving a view of reality (metaphysics) and an approach to the human vocation: (1) exorcism and intercession (dealing with the demonic in society), (2) suffering powerlessness (bearing witness to the kingdom of God as a redeemed society and refusing to resist evil), (3) creative participation (taking our part, to function as regents and stewards, in all the institutions of the world) and (4) engaging in a just revolution (overthrowing the existing structures, with violence if necessary).

In the way of exorcism, the assumption is that our role is to continue the liberation of individuals from bondage to Satan by preaching and prayer. The powers are much more than social structures. The social structures are merely fronts for Satan's grand plan to woo people away from God.

The way of suffering powerlessness is patterned after the way of the cross. Many in the Anabaptist tradition take this approach. Our role is not to change society directly but rather to witness. When we do this, even at the loss of our own lives, we expose the fallen state of all human rule and reflect God's action in the cross and the coming kingdom. The powers have been colonized by Satan and can only be overthrown by God. When the world is off center, it would take a lever with a fulcrum outside the world to move it. Christians, according to this approach, believe that the lever to move the world is the wooden cross.

The way of creative participation assumes that our role is to be stewards on earth. According to the creation mandate we are called to order and husband all the dimensions of societal and creational life. The structures have been colonized by Satan (according to some) or merely reflect the fallen condition of human beings (according to others). But it is possible, indeed it is our vocation, to bring these structures into conformity to the rule of Christ. We do this through our daily work, social action and mission. The danger in taking this approach exclusively is to minimize the demonic and the nonhuman forces and personages that we encounter in our public discipleship.

The final option is the way of the cleansed temple with Jesus as the model revolutionary. It has been promoted actively by liberation theologians, both Catholic and Protestant. One such Christian revolutionary, Dom Helder Cmara, summarized the dilemma implicit in taking this approach with these searching words: "When I give people food, they call me a saint. When I ask why there is no food, they call me a communist" (quoted in Brown, p. 86).

Which approach is right? Indeed all,

with the possible exception of the last, have strong support in Scripture and may be chosen in particular circumstances. The people of God as a whole must engage in a full-orbed approach. But discernment is needed.

Christ's complete victory over the principalities and powers, over Satan, sin and death, assures us that there is nowhere in the universe so demonized that a Christian might not be called to serve there. We fight a war that is already won. Therefore, as much as is now possible, Christians should Christianize the powers, to "peace" the powers through involvement in business, education,* government, politics and social action,* all the while knowing that the task of finally subjugating them is reserved for Christ alone (Eph 1:10; Phil 2:10-11). We work on the problems of ignorance, pollution, food distribution, injustice, genetic engineering and the proliferation of violence and weaponry, knowing that this work is ministry and holy. In the short run our efforts may seem futile, but in the long run this work will be gloriously successful because we are cooperating with what Christ wants to do in renewing all creation. In this we must live with heaven-mindedness, knowing that Christ said, "All authority in heaven and on earth has been given to me" (Mt 28:18). While the beast is master here for a moment (Rev 13:1-18), all dimensions of social unity will be restored according to God's design. And in the New Jerusalem the redeemed principalities and powers will provide structure for our common life and work (Rev 21:24).

See also JUSTICE; ORGANIZATION; POWER; PRINCIPALITIES AND POWERS; STRUCTURES, CHURCH; SYSTEM.

References and Resources
C. Arnold, *Ephesians: Power and Magic* (Cambridge: Cambridge University Press, 1989); P. L. Berger, *The Sacred Canopy: Elements of a* *Sociological Theory of Religion* (Garden City, N.Y.: Doubleday, 1967); H. Berkhof, *Christ and the Powers*, trans. J. H. Yoder (Scottdale, Penn.: Herald, 1962); R. M. Brown, *Spirituality and Liberation* (Philadelphia: Westminster, 1988); W. Carr, *Angels and Principalities: The Background, Meaning and Development of the Pauline Phrase "kai archai hai exousia"* (Cambridge: Cambridge University Press, 1981); J. Ellul, *The New Demons* (New York: Seabury, 1975); J. Gleick, *Chaos: Making a New Science* (New York: Penguin, 1987); H. Schlier, *Principalities and Powers in the New Testament* (New York: Herder & Herder, 1964); W. Wink, *Engaging the Powers: Discernment and Resistance in a World of Domination* (Minneapolis: Fortress, 1992); W. Wink, *Naming the Powers: The Language of Power in the New Testament* (Philadelphia: Fortress, 1984); W. Wink, *Unmasking the Powers: The Invisible Forces That Determine Human Existence* (Philadelphia: Fortress, 1986).

Gerry Schoberg and R. Paul Stevens

SUBURBIA

The most substantial thinking by Christians on urban life over the last fifty years has concentrated on the inner city.* This is understandable, since this aspect of urban life had been neglected for a long time. But the majority of people live in suburbs. Though suburbia has often come under criticism, it has received less than its proper share of serious attention. For a brief time in the sixties it looked as if this situation would be redressed (see Winter, 1961; Orr and Patrick, 1970), but since then there has been only occasional analysis of suburbia—mostly negative—from a Christian point of view. Where did suburbia come from, and how has it spread? What are its advantages and disadvantages? What changes are taking place in it, and how are we to handle them? How can its strengths be enhanced and its weaknesses be minimized?

The Meaning and Limits of Suburbia
There are several ways of defining suburbia, all of them now problematic. Once

it was relatively easy. Suburbs were the less densely populated areas that lay between the major cities* and the sparsely settled countryside (see Towns, Small; Community, Rural), whose primary economic activities were nonagricultural and whose political life was in the hands of independent local governments. But for some time now city governments have been merging city and country functions by expanding their boundaries, annexing suburban properties to capture more lucrative taxpayers, drawing people to work across adjoining county boundaries, and integrating inner urban and suburban planning services and political structures. This has made it more difficult to define where suburbia begins and ends.

Meanwhile, on the fringes of cities, country areas have been becoming more suburbanized as city people buy up rural properties and live there in a suburban-like way. Small towns in rural areas have even developed their own suburbs. With the possibility of telecommuting, a growing number of suburbanites are settling outside big cities, in some cases even in remote states. To complicate matters more, some inner-city areas have become gentrified, and some suburbs are becoming increasingly urban in character. There is also the complexity of suburbia itself. It is by no means a monolithic phenomenon. Suburbs may be older or newer, settled or transitional, ethnic or WASP, blue- or white-collar, growing or stagnant, affluent or low-income, dormitory or industrial, open or gated.

Although these changes and variables make it difficult to define suburbia or generalize about it, as long as we keep them in mind, the word still helps us identify a significant portion of any city. Suburbia also represents a state of mind or a way of life that can characterize someone living elsewhere. In each respect suburbia has become highly significant. It is where the largest proportion of people in most Western societies live, it has the strongest commercial and political clout, and it is the location for more churches* than anywhere else. Whether or not it is now in decline, as some are beginning to argue, it represents an important revolution in the way people live. It has made possible the democratization of comfortable and spacious accommodation, previously available only to the elite or new monied classes.

Origins and Development of Suburbia

How did this happen? Where did suburbia come from? To find out we have to go back to premodern times. In the Middle Ages the centers of larger cities contained a mixture of rich and poor housing, as well as of residences and workplaces.* The expansion of wealth* and increase in population in the seventeenth century led to the renovation of some city cores—with the building of squares for the wealthier and rebuilding of nearby homes for the poorer—and the establishing of spacious villas for the rich in agricultural settlements. The rise of the middle class was accompanied by a growing concern for the physical health of their families in the unclean city centers and for a better environment for nurturing children. This led to the creation of the suburb, a place adjacent to the city in which people who thought this way could build close to one another around a green space, such as a commons.

According to the historian Robert Fishman, the first example of this was the community of around seventy people set up around Clapham Common by William Wilberforce and others in the 1790s on the estate of one of their members. Though this new style of housing development separated work in the city from life in the home, the latter was a space in which discussion of public and private affairs took place in the company of spouse and children. For example, the movement against the slave trade was debated and organized in these homes, and women took responsibility for the general and spiritual education of their children. In other words, suburbia was preeminently an evangelical creation!

In the following century suburbia spread elsewhere in London and then to other parts of England such as Manchester—which developed the industrial suburb and became the world's first suburban city. It migrated to America, where, through Catherine Beecher and Andrew Jackson Downing, it was influenced by the English evangelical ideology of suburbia. In places like Riverside in New York State and then Philadelphia, whose railways opened up the first suburban sprawl, suburbia spread and became established. By the end of the nineteenth century, Australia had become the first country in which the majority of the population lived in suburbs.

This whole development in newer industrializing countries was in marked contrast to the urban growth of European cities like Paris, which exhibited an ongoing preference for intensive urban rather than expansive suburban development. In the former, suburbia was encouraged through the gradual relocation of industry to the suburbs and government lending schemes. Later critical growth points were the availability of automobiles for increasing numbers of people and the high number of postwar veterans' marriages. By the early 1970s in America too, the proportion of people living in suburbia edged ahead of that in city centers and rural areas. By the year 2000 it is estimated that 52 percent of the people in the world's cities will be living in suburbia.

Advantages and Disadvantages of Suburbia

Suburbia has always had its critics, particularly among the wealthy, academics and writers. More than one critic has spoken of the "quiet despair of the suburbs." People have attacked it for its lack of diversity and weaker sense of community,* for its conformity and being a cultural wilderness, for its isolation from reality and retreat from larger issues. It is said to encourage materialism, allow the rule of popular taste in architecture, turn the nuclear family too much in on itself and generate boredom* and alienation. For the young there is less to do and fewer job opportunities; the old are distanced from their relatives and peers. Separation of work* from home life and longer commuting times fragment people's lives and increase the pressure of time.* Upkeep of homes and property taxes become a heavier burden. Suburbs drain taxes* and resources from the inner city, create ethnic or working-class ghettos in their wake, and abandon the city center to public squalor and networks of freeways. In the suburbs themselves a strong civic core and even essential emergency services are often lacking.

Yet over the decades suburbia has attracted people partly because of its perceived advantages over earlier forms of urban living. There are more space and privacy,* less traffic and pollution,* greater safety and security. There are better schools and churches, lower housing costs and higher home ownership. There are more trees and gardens, public parks and children's play areas, sporting and recreational options. Clubs* and voluntary associations are in greater supply, and there are more activities for children. Suburbia is cleaner and quieter, more planned and orderly. It has more opportunity for private inventiveness; shops offer a wider range of goods and services; the countryside is more accessible. Even some intellectuals and writers, such as the Nobel Prize-winner Patrick Stewart, have issued strong defenses of suburbia against the criticisms of its despisers.

There is truth on both sides. There can be little doubt that the promoters of suburbia, especially those with a financial stake in its spread, and advertisers generally, have often idealized it. But many of the critiques of suburbia have come from an urban cultural elite who are often suspicious of desires to improve the family* and get closer to nature. Their perceptions are also colored by secondhand impressions rather than firsthand observation. Studies of suburbia show that moving to it often results in less change and more benefits than suggested. It is less homogeneous than is often thought, and time spent traveling to and from work is much the same as before. Interaction between husband and wife, parents and children, tends to increase. There is more visiting with neighbors, and people generally experience a reduction in boredom and alienation. It is well to remember that most suburbanites have chosen to live in suburbia rather than being forced to go there.

But suburbia is changing. More and more suburbs are becoming urbanized. As shopping centers emerge in the middle of suburbia, businesses move more and more jobs into it, local and regional cultural activities increase, and people prefer to live closer to their work, many suburbs are turning into genuine urban centers. In other cases new "edge" cities, often around high-tech industries, are being established on the boundaries of major conurbations, and smaller, decaying cities surrounded by suburbia are undergoing redevelopment. What qualifies a place for inclusion in these different forms of "ex-urbs" are their having five million square feet or more of leasable office space, at least 600,000 square feet of leasable retail space, more jobs than bedrooms, and their being per-

ceived by the population as one place. Though these new forms of city life have many attractions for those living nearby, they are also attracting the problems for which inner-city areas have become well known. The noise and pace of life, as well as crime* and drug* use, are increasing. But they are increasingly becoming the places where many people in newer Western societies live, work, play,* shop, learn and worship.*

Understanding and Living in Suburbia

Those who live in suburbia need to be more aware of its strengths and weaknesses, how it shapes them as persons, what it does to the larger city or adjoining countryside, and its impact on national and even international life. Since, as surveys show, churchgoers generally possess similar outlooks and adopt a similar lifestyle to others in suburbia, they particularly should be more aware of and troubled by their lack of distinctiveness. This is also true of the churches they attend, for mostly they do not reflect very much on how they are affected by their suburban context. They know something of the geography and demographics of their area, even of needy groups and social problems within it, but they rarely have a sense of suburbia as an enveloping culture, of the structural changes taking place within it and of the basic attitudes and values* that drive it. Though sometimes they may work at making some contribution to their local area, they do not often give thought to ways in which people and institutions living in suburbia can and should benefit the whole city and country.

There are various ways in which Christians and churches can gain this understanding. Some are very simple. For example, they could encourage small groups* in the church, educational programs and special occasions, to focus at some point each year on investigating their surroundings and looking for practical guidelines from Scripture, tradition, study and experience on how to respond to it. Resources to do this lie within the congregation itself. It begins by people reflecting on their own particular stories, specific settings and felt needs, as well as their common struggles, pressures and aspirations. Others in the congregation—because of their particular work, area of study or having lived for a time outside suburbia—have a more specialized contribution to make. Among these may be people who have had substantial involvement in civic affairs or in voluntary associations, have social science or theological qualifications, or have had crosscultural experience. There may also be access to others in the area who have made a special study of some aspect of suburbia.

Then it becomes a matter of working out practical strategies at the congregational, small group and family level that will maximize suburbia's strengths and minimize its weaknesses. In broader terms this will involve the members of the congregation and the congregation as a whole intentionally seeking first the welfare of the suburb in which it exists by bringing kingdom perspectives and values to bear upon it.

☐ How can they serve the suburb or cluster of suburbs or suburban city in which they live? What does this mean in terms of working within it where appropriate, supporting its economy, patronizing and improving its public transport,* taking an interest in civic affairs, encouraging its cultural life, investigating or writing up a local history, discerning its major social and psychological problems and collaborating with other churches to address these in a systemic way?

☐ How can they serve the immediate neighborhood* in which they live? What does this entail in terms of spending time and building relationships within it, de-

veloping a neighborhood watch or other neighborhood associations, holding block parties or celebrating local landmark events, supporting local shops and services, banding with others to assist those who are most needy or marginal in the area, seeking ways of intentionally and appropriately bringing the gospel to it?

☐ How can they serve the urban core and countryside of which they are a part? What does this involve in terms of maintaining awareness of significant changes in these areas and suburbia's contribution to them, developing partnerships with churches or Christian organizations* in these places to improve understanding and channel support, using the election process to serve the purposes of the wider region rather than just issues of suburban self-interest?

☐ How can the gospel be brought to bear more relevantly and powerfully to people in suburbia? What does this imply for the form discipleship takes so that the suburbanites will be able to avoid its temptations and build on its advantages, becoming truly "in" but definitely not "of" suburbia?

For most people in a suburban church this will be a matter of rethinking and changing their individual, family, communal or congregational lifestyle. For a few it will be a matter of reviewing and altering their employment or broader vocation. Those whose work, business or profession* directly affects the surroundings—as a manager of a corporation, public transport employee, town planner, member of an urban coalition, architect, worker in a citywide voluntary agency, or in any other way—have the added responsibility of considering how they could concretely help improve the suburb or wider city and region of which they are a part. For a few this may involve redesigning suburbia itself so that it is less vulnerable to what is presently ailing it and better equipped to enhance people's quality of life.

Along these lines, there are some exciting experiments under way to recapture some of the older urban-village or small-town virtues that earlier forms of suburbia left behind (Langdon, 1994). These, together with the urbanizing of the suburbia already referred to, if handled rightly, offer new and interesting possibilities for overcoming many of suburbia's liabilities. We should never regard any such developments as panaceas for what is wrong with people and the world and always recognize that the places we live in will be flawed and fail to live up to all our expectations. But our contributions in this area in tending the physical, economic, cultural and political environment in which God has placed us are one of the ways we serve the wider purposes of the kingdom of God.

See also CITY; INNER CITY; NEIGHBOR-HOOD; ZONING.

References and Resources

M. Baldassare, *Trouble in Paradise: The Suburban Transformation in America* (New York: Columbia University Press, 1986); P. Langdon, *A Better Place to Live: Reshaping the American Suburb* (Amherst: University of Massachusetts Press, 1994); D. Rask, *Cities Without Suburbs* (Baltimore: Johns Hopkins University Press, 1993); J. R. Teagrin, *The Urban Scene: Myths and Realities* (New York: Random House, 1973); A. T. Walter, *A Long Way from Home* (Grand Rapids: Zondervan, 1980); G. Winter, *The Suburban Captivity of the Churches* (New York: Doubleday, 1961).

Robert Banks

SUCCESS

Any decent dictionary can define success for you in an unexceptionable way. *Success* is attaining a desired result. Thus, a successful building project is one in which the building gets built, and a successful builder is one who can complete such projects. The problem comes when you stop talking about specifics like buildings and builders and begin talking in general. What does it mean for a *person* to be a success? The question does not ask about success at something in particular, like constructing a building. Rather, it asks about success as a person.

Here the dictionary definitions are not so helpful. It is difficult for a mere dictionary to tell you the desired result of being a person so that you can check to see if you have attained it. Dictionaries do try, however, to express dominant cultural values. A typical desktop dictionary gives this as a second meaning: "the attainment of wealth, position, honor, or the like."

Cultural Understandings of Success

Such a view of success has two strong variants in Western cultures. The first is the "crass" vision of success. A commonly seen poster embodies this meaning. It shows a pile of cars, jewelery, houses, and money.* At the bottom is the caption: "He who dies with the most toys wins." The poster is poking fun at the crass vision of success. But that understanding of success is around us and has its appeal. Yet when we actually think about living life compiling material goods, just so we can die at the end, it seems less compelling. The crass vision of success cannot seriously help determine whether a person has attained the desired result of life.

The second common variant of success avoids the excesses of the crass vision. It says that success in life means being materially comfortable and relatively independent. Attaining these goals allows you the possibility of attaining whatever other goals you might decide are worth pursuing. This vision is somewhat attractive. Being free from the immediate requirement of self-preservation and being safe, fed and warm do seem to be a good foundation for whatever particular success you might want to achieve. Yet there is a subtlety here. This common vision of success, for all its attractions, is what you might call *vertical*. It envisions success as being attained by an individual's climbing over adversity and attaining comfort. And the not-so-hidden assumption is that the measure of this success is still fundamentally economic. In the end this variant is not all that far from the crass vision of success.

Everyone wants to be successful, by which we mean attaining some set of life goals. But the economic description of success implicit even in the comfort-and-independence idea is far too limited to describe what we really mean by success. As a thought experiment, consider the following people who were undeniably successful in some sense but do not fit into the comfort-and-independence idea of success: Socrates, Jesus, Francis of Assisi, Søren Kierkegaard, Mahatma Gandhi, Martin Luther King Jr. This list could be extended arbitrarily, but the point it makes is simple. Many people have been successful in a way we find meaningful without having been either comfortable or independent. Some of them deliberately sacrificed both comfort and independence to attain their success. Furthermore, some of them attained success that was outside the scope of their own lifetimes: they died as failures but were clearly successful nonetheless.

We should call the people on this list (and others who could easily be added to their number) the *uncomfortable succeeders*. They make it clear that success is both broader and deeper than the simple definition of comfort and independence would lead us to believe. Success seems to be inextricably linked with attaining goals that are deep within a person but also far broader than a single individual. Whatever success as a person is, it is nei-

ther simple nor, apparently, easily attained.

Success and Character

Stephen Covey claims to have uncovered two divergent themes in two centuries' worth of American literature on success. The first dominated for the 150 years or so, and he calls it "the character ethic." This approach "taught that there are basic principles of effective living, and that people can only experience true success and enduring happiness as they learn and integrate these principles into their basic character" (Covey, p. 18). The character ethic includes virtues like integrity,* fidelity, patience, industry and simplicity, virtues* that can be attained only through sacrificing a certain amount of comfort and independence.

The past fifty years has, by contrast, been dominated by a vision of success that Covey calls "the personality ethic." In this vision "success became a function of personality, of public image, of attitudes and behaviors, skills and techniques, that lubricate the process of human interaction" (Covey, p. 19). Various schools of positive thinking and other popular approaches counsel that manipulating your own personality to maintain a particular attitude, or to "win friends and influence people," is the correct approach to success.

Covey and others have found this latter approach, however dominant it has been for the past two generations, fundamentally flawed and superficial. It thinks of success as something *added to* a person (like comfort and independence) rather than something that *grows out of* a person. Success understood in terms of a character ethic sees it as something that comes from the gradual unfolding of the best of what a person can be. But although success is rooted in a person's becoming a good person, exemplifying the virtues of that life, success is not limited to a kind of personal evolution and attainment, however good it might be. The uncomfortable succeeders may perhaps have been virtuous individuals, but that is not the measure of their success. Rather, they were successful in that they were successful *for others* regardless of what they attained for themselves.

The uncomfortable succeeders, and many like them, are successful just because they are not driven to attain success in its own right. Rather, they are driven to serve others, to make them successful, and so become successful themselves in the process. Kierkegaard's way of saying this is that it must be approached by means of indirection. To be successful, you must not try to find success directly. Instead, by trying to attain a different goal like helping others succeed, you discover that (lo and behold!) success has found you.

A Biblical Vision of Success

If we come to the Bible with one of the common understandings of success, it will provide us no help at all. Indeed, some analytical concordances show no uses of the word *success* at all in English translations. This, in itself, does not mean that the concept of success is absent; rather, it may imply that many translators believed that the common sense of success was not a good match for what the biblical writers were trying to express.

If the biblical writers believe in success, they do not think it is at all wrapped up in comfort and independence. On the contrary, they are often exhorting those who will listen to seek other goals. Success, for them, is measured by the attainment of other goals for the sake of other people. As good an example as any of this inversion of the idea of success comes in the letter to the Philippians. Quoting what was apparently a common Christian song of the time, the letter says,

Let the same mind be in you that was in Christ Jesus,
who, though he was in the form
of God,
did not regard equality with God
as something to be exploited,
but emptied himself,
taking the form of a slave,
being born in human likeness.
And being found in human form,
he humbled himself
and became obedient to the
point of death—
even death on a cross.

Therefore God also highly exalted him
and gave him the name
that is above every name,
so that at the name of Jesus
every knee should bend,
in heaven and on earth and
under the earth,
and every tongue should confess
that Jesus Christ is Lord,
to the glory of God the Father.
(Phil 2:5-11 NRSV)

This is a remarkable vision of the path to success. First, it is highly centripetal in its orientation. Far from concentrating on the self and arranging things so its goals are met, the orientation is spinning outward as hard as possible. Everything here is other-directed; nothing is oriented to self-attainment. Second, the vision of success finds its fulfillment not in success but in another state entirely: servanthood. The servant has no guarantee of comfort nor independence (compare Phil 4:10-13). Yet the way of the servant is, paradoxically, the way of success. In order to find success one cannot grasp after it but must accept and embrace its opposite. If you want with all your heart to be successful, that passion itself will make you fail; if you are willing to become a servant, you will find a different kind of success waiting for you there.

The uncomfortable succeeders all, in their own manners, went the way of the servant. Embracing service* gave them the freedom not to have to succeed and so allowed them to do so. Jesus and the other uncomfortable succeeders knew their efforts were doomed from the point of view of success measurement. By not concerning themselves with attaining success, but instead concerning themselves with being servants, they allowed success to surprise them and overtake their activities.

For this very reason, because Jesus humbled himself, God gave Jesus the name above all other names. Those around us who seek directly for success find that it eludes them. All they have in its place are the ambition* and self-involvement they used in their quest. The crass vision of success, according to which the one who has the most toys when he dies wins, has loftier neighbors, each of which is just as wrong. The goal may be the most friends or the most good deeds or the most converts or the most victories. In every case they are less crass than the materialistic version and no less wrong. All seek success directly and can be measured against their particular goals. All miss success, from the biblical point of view, because they are not willing to attain success on the way of the servant.

See also AMBITION; FAILURE; PROFESSIONS/PROFESSIONALISM; VALUES; VIRTUES.

References and Resources
S. R. Covey, *The Seven Habits of Highly Successful People* (New York: Simon & Schuster, 1989).

Hal Miller

SUGAR/SUGARY

Sugar consumption in North America is continually on the rise. We eat more than one hundred pounds annually, and most of us are not even aware of it. No one can escape sugar. It's in vitamins, peanut butter, canned vegetables, medications and even toothpaste. Soft drinks contain several teaspoons of sugar, and dry tonic water can have up to eighteen teaspoons. And of course we routinely add sugar to tea and coffee.

Sweet is good, but sweeter is better. And we do whatever we can to make our food "better." We take already naturally sweet fruit and bake it in pies, adding twelve to fourteen teaspoons of sugar. We dip fresh apples in caramel, camouflaging their already sweet flavor. To cakes, in which sugar is the main ingredient, we add frosting. And we delight in topping ice cream, already laden with sugar, with hot fudge, caramel or other syrups. Our snacks revolve around sugar and its quick highs.

Sugar and Health
Natural sugar, like honey, was made by God and does provide instant nourishment, as Jonathan experienced in 1 Samuel 14:24-30. But too much sugar can be dangerous. The pancreas, which regulates blood sugar by releasing insulin, can respond to a sudden surge of sugar with too much insulin. Hence, artificial sweeteners such as saccharine, cyclamate and the currently popular aspartame (marketed as NutraSweet) have been developed.

Sugar is the only food that can be directly absorbed into the bloodstream. Other foods, such as starch, must be broken down into sugar before the body can use them, and this involves time. Sweets shortcut the natural protection God designed in the human body. Earl Mindell observes that excessive sugar consumption has several potential negative side effects: tooth decay, obesity, aggravation of asthma, mental illness and other nervous disorders, changes in mood and personality, increased risk of heart disease, diabetes, hypertension, gallstones, back problems, arthritis, hypoglycemia and high blood pressure. The loss of necessary nutrients leads to an imbalance in the calcium-phosphorus ratio (Mindell, pp. 101-2).

Most commonly, sugar consumption robs people of healthy appetites. There are many children, junior couch potatoes, who avoid healthy foods and gorge on sweets. The overconsumption of sugar in children is promoted in Halloween trick-or-treating where children are actually encouraged to go from house to house gathering large bags full of candy. Candy, as most mothers will tell you, has a hyperactive effect on children.

For some people sugar is an addiction.* The first taste of sugar functions much like that first sip of alcohol. The person becomes out of control and is in a rage to find more sugar, even if that person has already eaten a filling and nutritious meal. Like alcohol, sugar can cause a surge of emotion and can make people feel both energetic and sleepy (Cauwels, p. 168). Quick highs are followed by deeper lows, and sugar addiction enslaves people in a ludicrous rut. An overdose of sugar hocks the body, and the pancreas tries to compensate by producing more insulin. The sugar is then lost to the bloodstream, and the person is left less energetic, less alert, and more hungry and irritable than before. The quick high is a downer in disguise.

Sugar and Partying

Sugar is often the most important ingredient in a social occasion. The sweeter the celebration, the sweeter the dessert menu. Cakes, candies and cookies are prominent on the dessert menu at birthdays,* weddings* and anniversaries.* The more important the occasion, the greater the effort to present sugar in an elaborate and stylish fashion. Inhibitions are lowered, and celebrants encourage one another to "sin boldly" and diet tomorrow. Further, participation in these sugar orgies is cross-generational; adults and children are allowed dispensations from normal dietary patterns.

As important as sugar is in celebrations, it is even more important when people find themselves in distress. Chocolate is the preferred antidepressant of millions of people. And although sugar may temporarily relieve pain, the subsequent low is even more devastating. Meanwhile, a permanent addiction to sugar takes hold.

Pain in all its forms is sugarcoated. We greet one another with the sugary "I'm fine, how are you?" We avoid people who do not present the appropriate sugary façade and who are genuine and natural in their responses to both the joys and the sorrows of life. It is all but impossible to share our painful experiences with sugar people. Instead, the painful aspects of life belong to the realm of the therapist, away from everyday interactions. And beyond being avoided, the nonsugarcoated message and the message bearer are devalued.

Collectively, sugarcoating values* results in a culture of thick denial which leads to various addictions. In fact our body is not created to deny pain. Pain increases when it is repressed. Pain leads to healing* when it is shared. Facing pain makes human beings real, creating authentic family and community relationships.

Sugar and Sex Stereotypes

Unhealthy and unfortunate stereotypes revolve around sugar. "Sugar and spice and everything nice—that's what little girls are made of." And those little girls grow up to be women suffering from the "nice lady" syndrome. When a woman deviates from this norm, she is labeled as aggressive and masculine; her sexual identity becomes an issue. Boys meanwhile are allowed to play more aggressively and even violently with toy guns, pretend warfare and real wrestling matches and fistfights. Men are not required to be nice. When they are violent, women are still supposed to be nice to them.

The nature and conditions of human life are anything but sweet. The cultural and theological stereotypes which push women to conform to the image of sweetness are in conflict with wholeness. Many women live with a false self-concept; an outer presentation of sweetness covers the internal bleeding and psychic numbness. Women are continuously tempted to abandon authenticity for social acceptance. Unless a woman has the courage to defy negative labels, her physical, emotional and spiritual homeostasis is at risk.

As opposed to the passivity and powerlessness of sugar niceness for women, sexual and economic power is the hallmark of the sugar daddy. The sugar daddy considers himself to be honorable, not deviant. In reality he leads a double life, victimizing two women, his wife and his mistress (Nelson, pp. 43-68). Many patriarchal societies justify male extramarital relationships while censuring female extramarital relationships—the old double standard.

Sugar imagery highlights the inequality in gender relationships. The resulting hypocrisy and denial diminish authentic relationships between men and women. Superficiality and pseudocommunity, rather than intimacy and authentic community, prevail. Meanwhile, both women and men are hungry for whole and wholesome relationships.

Sugar and Power

Most sugar consumers have no clue about the political, economic and cultural exploitations in the process of sugar production. Exploitation of labor on the sugar plantation under colonialism and capital-ism have had huge social ramifications (Schwartz, p. 313). The history of the sugar plantation is one wrought with inequality and coercive labor.

A pitfall in postindustrial society is the way we compartmentalize in the name of professionalism.* One hand does not know what the other hand is doing. We sprinkle the snow-white, sparkling sugar on our favorite desserts, but we do not witness the sweaty hands and feet of laborers who make our sweet tooths possible. We are disconnected from what we consume and how it is produced. The vicious cycle of injustice continues while we are preoccupied with our sugary lifestyles, which temporarily numb and deny the violence and pain in daily life.

This problem of denial originated with Adam and Eve, who first collaborated in the original sin and then sought to hide behind fig leaves. Such "sugarcoating" of sin produced a vicious cycle of denial throughout history in which powerful people continually deny the evils of violence and injustice they have woven into the social fabric.

Sugar and the Church

In the sugary church,* our sugar-oriented culture colludes with a triumphalist theology to prevent meaningful exchanges. People who come to church in search of healing* are driven into denial or hiding. While bleeding internally and starving for authenticity, they experience only a pseudocommunity. Like artificial sweeteners, pseudocommunity is full of artificiality. People do not feel free to speak the truth. That would be offensive. Conversation is superficial. Relationships are based on pretense and mirror the sugar effect of a quick high followed by emptiness. People leave the sugary church empty and starved for authenticity and transformation.

Sugar and Healing

Systems theory has closed some of the gaps between Western and non-Western ways of thinking by moving toward a more holistic paradigm that sees the natural and the spiritual worlds as deeply intertwined. In many non-Western cultures, bitter herbs are highly valued for their healing properties. The healing process begins with the person who prepares the bitter herb: one has to be virtuous and has to choose the right pot to boil herbs at the right temperature for the right time. These "bitter-herb cultures" accept suffering and pain as a natural part of life and consider them character-building opportunities, as Romans 5:3-4 indicates: "We also rejoice in our sufferings, because we know that suffering produces perseverance; perseverance, character; and character, hope."

As the Israelites journeyed to the Promised Land, they were commanded to eat a meal which included bitter herbs (Ex 12:8). The Passover meal portrays life as a journey, and the bitter herbs signify the necessary suffering that takes place on this journey. In the desert, there is no place for the luxury of sugar. There is no sugarcoating, no frostinglike coverup, no sugar substitute. There is no denial, only dealing with reality. In the most ordinary of human activities, in eating,* the providence of God shines through.

The Bible clearly indicates that the road toward healing involves brokenness. Jesus demonstrated this at the cross, and we remember this in another sugarless meal, the Eucharist. In breaking the bread and drinking the cup, the people of God are reminded of and participate in the obedience of Jesus to the will of God, his drinking of the bitter cup.

Bitter herbs and painful stories belong in the church. When the silence is broken and even the most shameful of stories are told, people are connected with the sacred. Even the most painful story turns into a sacred story. The bitter truth, like the bitter herb, is painful. Yet it leads to healing. In contrast to sweet sugarcoated talk, the identification of the community with the suffering of the individual leads to an authentic spiritual expression and real intimacy. As the suffering of Jesus at Gethsemane demonstrates, pain has within it the power of transformation if one is willing to confront it and break the silence.

References and Resources

J. M. Cauwels, *Bulimia: The Binge-Purge Compulsion* (New York: Doubleday, 1983); E. Mindell, *Unsafe at Any Meal* (New York: Warner Books, 1987); E. D. Nelson, "Sugar Daddies:'Keeping' a Mistress and the Gentlemen's Code," *Quantitative Sociology* 16 (Spring 1993) 43-68; S. B. Schwartz, *Sugar Plantations in the Formation of Brazilian Society* (Cambridge: Cambridbe University Press, 1985).

Young Lee Hertig

SUNDAY SCHOOL

The Sunday school has been an important educational and evangelistic ministry for many North American churches for over one hundred years. It has aided many Christians in their knowledge of Scripture, assisted many nonbelievers into faith and helped many churches in their desire to develop Christian community.*

History and Growth

Begun in 1780 by Robert Raikes in England, Sunday school was originally a tool to teach poor children how to read and write using the Bible as text. Sunday was chosen because it was the only day these children did not have to work in factories. Through the years Sunday school evolved into a teaching program of the church geared mainly to children.

When Sunday schools were introduced to North American churches in the early nineteenth century, denominational leaders debated as to whether it would interfere with the parents' responsibility of the faith education of the child at home. In spite of such protests, the Sunday school became established and grew throughout the late nineteenth and into the twentieth century. While theologically liberal churches began to see its decline around 1916, evangelical churches continued to experience growth through the middle of the century. During the early part of the century, the leadership of Sunday schools tended to pass increasingly into the hands of trained theological teachers. With the introduction of many evangelical publishing houses producing Sunday-school curriculum and the birth boom that came at the end of World War II, the Sunday school probably reached its pinnacle of acceptance and growth in North America by midcentury.

By the middle of the 1970s many churches were experiencing declining attendance in Sunday school, and changes began to take place in the format of this ministry. Today many churches have drastically altered its name, time, day, place and methods while still maintaining the purpose of sharing biblical truths in a teaching setting different from that of the worship service. Others have begun to see Sunday schools evolve into small groups* or house churches. For many churches, the Sunday school remains a vital component in the overall educational ministry. A wisely thought-through, planned and implemented Sunday school can still provide the church with a tool to promote an understanding of the Christian faith.

Dimensions of an Effective Sunday School

A tool to educate Christians about the truths of the faith. As such the Sunday school should not be seen as an end in itself. Too often the role of the Sunday school becomes confused with the function of education in the church (*see* Christian Education). The function of educating in the church existed long before the formation of the first Sunday school and will continue long after the last Sunday school closes its doors. However, as a tool for the education of a body of believers, Sunday school can be very effective.

The Sunday school can provide a format for an aspect of education that cannot occur in most worship services where preaching* is a main component. Whereas most listeners in a worship* service can only hear the proclamation of biblical truth, the Sunday school can provide a teaching setting in which interaction with that truth and with other believers can occur as part of the learning process. The Sunday school also deals with biblical truth with age appropriateness. Learning experiences in different classes or groupings can, when needed, be geared to the learning level of the participant and/or to the participants' spiritual maturity, something rarely possible when the church gathers as a whole body for learning. In the context of the Sunday school that important link between biblical truth and daily life can be reinforced, that is, how beliefs and values* can be lived out during the week.

An opportunity to develop community. It is often difficult, even in the smaller church, for people to develop a real sense of community (or *koinonia*) through attendance at a worship service. Community is formed through the interaction of lives in learning, sharing, caring and helping one another through our life experiences. The Sunday school can act as a catalyst for these qualities to occur. Many people have experienced the welcome of a Sunday-school class when moving to a different city and to a large, sometimes overpowering church. Often it is the warmth and acceptance of the members of the class that contributes to people becoming a part of the community.

This development of community must go beyond the mere acquaintance level of relationships. It should become a basis for encouragement and strengthening in the Christian's life. In 1 Thessalonians Paul states the importance of sharing lives with one another in the context of sharing the gospel; both are important (1 Thess 2:8, 12). Paul is indicating the importance of the community of believers in order to put the gospel into action (see Church; Community; Fellowship).

An opportunity for cooperative learning. In a society that promotes individualism* and competition even in the methodology of its educational institutions, the Sunday school can provide an environment in which people of all ages can learn from one another. In this setting laity* can teach laity and even help to overcome dependence upon professionals or formally trained theological teachers. This teaching can be enhanced when learners are working together in a climate of cooperation. And while small-group Bible studies offer a beneficial place for interaction about biblical truth, they can too easily become focused on the caring/sharing component of community at the expense of solid teaching. A healthy Sunday-school ministry will have a strong emphasis on a small-group ministry to encourage a developing of both heart and mind.

An opportunity for outreach. During this generation North American society has been pulling away from the truths of the Christian faith. Greater numbers of unchurched people are unfamiliar with or even distrustful of the local church. The Sunday school can be an entrance into the community of the church for those who initially may be hesitant to visit a church's worship service. A Sunday-school class can create an environment of warmth and acceptance, which can be difficult to develop in a worship service. Some Sunday-school classes even meet outside the church building in hotels, homes or restaurants and have an attraction to those who are more comfortable meeting with Christians in a neutral environment than in an unfamiliar religious setting. While the huge emphasis on evangelism that Sunday school had in the 1950s and before may be past, the Sunday-school ministry still can be creatively effective in presenting the gospel to a church's local community.

A supplemental tool for family learning. When Sunday school was being adopted by many churches in America in the early part of the nineteenth century, some denominational leaders feared this program would remove from the parents the responsibility to train their children properly in the home. Unfortunately, there is often a temptation for parents by default or intent to allow the Sunday school to have the major or sole role in the teaching of their children. Leaders in the Sunday school need to see themselves in partnership with parents and other leaders in the church in order to promote education and nurture throughout the life of the church and its members' lives.

The Sunday school has been and remains a valuable tool to assist the Christian's pilgrimage of faith and learning. This ministry,* however, needs to be viewed as only one part of the teaching* ministry of the church. The church will always have a need to educate its people, and the Sunday school can be an important and effective supplement in helping to achieve this goal.

See also CHRISTIAN EDUCATION; FAMILY GOALS; PARENTING; TEACHING.

Resources and References
E. A. Daniel, *Introduction to Christian Education*

(Cincinnati: Standard Publishing, 1987); K. O. Gangel and W. S. Benson, *Christian Education: Its History and Philosophy* (Chicago: Moody, 1983); M. Harris, *Fashion Me a People* (Louisville: Westminster/John Knox, 1989); W. Haystead, *The 21st Century Sunday School* (Cincinnati: Standard Publishing, 1995); W. R. Willis, *200 Years and Still Counting* (Wheaton: Victor Books, 1979).

James Postlewaite

SYSTEM

In everyday discourse we sometimes hear people say, "Blame it on the system!" or "You've got to know the system to get ahead." What do we mean by such language? And how are we to think in Christian terms about the experiences to which such talk refers?

A *system* is a number of things connected together as a whole. The whole is not a random happening but gives evidence of regularity and order in its organization and method, in its plan and operation. The human body* is a system of systems, and within the body we can identify a skeletal system, a circulatory system, a nervous system and so on. A machine, like an automobile* or computer,* is a system. Most of us have some kind of stereo system at home, an integrated whole composed of various electronic components. Schools and colleges are usually thought of as parts of an educational system. Nature and the environment form an ecosystem of interdependent parts. A system may be rigid or flexible, enduring or evolving, formal or informal.

To understand any individual thing, we need to attend to the systems of which it is a part. It is not enough simply to isolate something for study and reflection; we must also see its roles and relations within its systems. In the academic, business and professional worlds, there are now specialists in systems engineering and systems analysis.

A Christian Approach to Systems

God's creation* brought forth a kind of system. The individual parts of this created system (man and woman, animals, plants, the sun, moon, stars, etc.) each have a certain uniqueness, dignity, beauty and purpose (*see* Structures). But the individual parts are intended to flourish in relationships, not in isolation. As a whole, this created system displayed an equilibrium of freedom and order, innovation and constancy, individuality and community. The social system intended partnership and complementarity, meaningful work* and rest.* The broader ecosystem was characterized by beauty as well as utility.

The fall away from God and into sin brought disorder into God's created system. While the grace and providence of God have sustained the systems of our universe as a livable milieu, humankind's alienation from God is the fundamental cause of our problems in coping with the "systems questions" of our experience. Our social systems degenerated from partnership to competition,* oppression and exploitation. Our ethical and moral systems replaced reliance on God's judgment of what is good with a quest to know and declare autonomously what is good and what is evil. In place of God's system of partnership, we soon had a rigid separation in the roles of man and woman, polygamy, a violent competition between brothers and the creation of systems of war. Systems of idolatry and religion replace the living relationship with God.

Christians should not reject the notion of systems per se but should adopt a critical and redemptive stance toward them. We cannot live without systems of some kind—but systems can be better or worse, and they can help or hinder our pursuit of God's purposes for life. Our intervention into the various systems of nature is part of the human task. What is necessary, especially from a Christian point of view, is that these interventions (to fight disease, increase food production, explore the universe, acquire sources of energy, etc.) ought to be undertaken with respect for the value and integrity of God's creation. As stewards and caretakers of God's creation and as responsible keepers of our brother's and sister's life, we must be careful not to add to the disorder of the world through our interventions (*see* New Reproductive Technology). This is not an easy accomplishment in an era of great threats, great needs and a voracious appetite for technological* development.

Our social systems present us with other challenges. Some of these systems, for example, families* and households, tend to be informal. Traditions, habits* and unarticulated expectations and assumptions often form an invisible system within which we carry out our tasks. Even so, such systems for child rearing, decision-making and other activities can be better or worse. We cannot make every decision *de novo*. We need continuity, stability, tradition. But we must reflect critically on these patterns and systems. Are they promoting the partnership, dignity, growth, beauty and goodness of each member as God's creation intended? Are they redemptive, reconciling, healing* and life-giving as our Lord intends?

Businesses, churches,* schools, community groups and political organizations also have informal systems: customs, habits and traditions for decision-making and action. But they also, more than family and friendship,* create systems of formal structures* and policies. The organizational structure (administrative hierarchy, bureaucracy, committees,* job descriptions) might be thought of as the "skeleton" and "organs" of the system. Constitutions, laws, regulations, curricula, policy statements and employee handbooks describe the functional "circulatory system" in such social systems. Social systems, in short, have formal structures and processes as well as informal constraints.

The Challenge of Reforming Systems

We cannot live and work very well without such systems. No business or community or school will survive without adequate organization, without developing its system. Nevertheless, social systems can become unjust, repressive and even demonic. History gives us many examples of political structures whose laws were blatantly racist or discriminatory against women, religious and ethnic minorities, the landless or poor. Businesses, schools and churches have also been prone to systematic, structural and procedural evil and oppression.

Even when structural reforms have occurred, informal traditions and old-boy networks have kept many systems frozen to improvement. Reforming the system requires not only formal structural and procedural changes but changes in attitudes and values* in the organizational culture.* It is, of course, more difficult to reform the many than the few: the size and scale of organizations and systems present special problems. It is more difficult to reform the old and long-standing than the new and recent; old habits and traditions die hard. It is more difficult to reform the successful than the struggling; leaders and beneficiaries are resistant to upsetting the apple cart. It is difficult to bring about reforms without them being undergirded by powerful, shared values.

Part of the difficulty in reforming social systems arises because of the way responsibility is diffused in organizations. The "buck" gets passed around, and individuals find responsibility avoidable or unattainable: "It's not my fault." "That's the way we've always done things, and I can't change that." This resistance to change leads some to argue that at a fundamental level organizations and systems have been captivated by the principalities and powers* of evil. Well-intentioned individuals seem incapacitated by a demonic system.

Christians will recall that Paul "used the system" when he appealed to Caesar (Acts 22:25-29; 25:11). Peter urged subordination to human institutions and even to the economic system of slavery (1 Pet 2:13-25). On a personal level, however, Paul urged Philemon to set free his slave Onesimus (Philem 8-16). The New Testament suggests that (1) where possible, we create new, transformed systems bearing witness to the creative and redemptive purposes of God; (2) we speak up on behalf of those oppressed, challenging the masters of the system to be accountable to God; (3) we encourage those who are struggling under the weight of the system; and (4) when caught within an oppressive system, we exercise faithful servant leadership,* trusting God to use our faithful, alien presence to bring about divine purposes in due time.

In short, blaming our predicaments on "the system" may be true enough; evil and good are structural and systemic as well as personal. In fact it may be the system more than any individual's malice that is the source of our displeasure. But the assignment of blame hardly begins to describe the Christian calling* in the world. Rather than seek objects to blame, we should look for causes to address and create redemptive alternatives that bear witness to the goodness of God.

As Paul did, we may "use the system" but never in a self-serving, world-compromising way. We want to be "wise as serpents and innocent as doves" (Mt 10:16 NRSV), but this counsel to prudence must never justify an abandonment of our identity as the children of light, the citizens of God's kingdom, the ambassadors of the coming age of Jesus Christ. Because the weapons of our warfare are spiritual and because our battle with "the system" is not always with flesh and blood but rather with principalities and powers, with the cosmic powers of this present darkness, we must always be vigilant in prayer, and we must draw close to our fellow soldiers in the Christian community as we carry out our life in various systems (Eph 6:10-18).

See also ORGANIZATION; POWER; PRINCIPALITIES AND POWERS; STRUCTURES.

References and Resources

L. von Bertalanffy, *General System Theory* (New York: Braziller, 1968); L. von Bertalanffy, *Perspectives on General System Theory: Scientific-Philosophical Studies* (New York: Braziller, 1975); P. Collins and R. Paul Stevens, *The Equipping Pastor: A Systems Approach to Empowering the People of God* (Washington, D.C.: Alban Institute, 1993); E. H. Friedman, *Generation to Generation: Family Process in Church and Synagogue* (New York: Guilford Press, 1985); A. W. Schaef and D. Fassel, *The Addictive Organization* (San Francisco: Harper & Row, 1988); E. H. Schein, *Organizational Culture and Leadership: A Dynamic View* (San Francisco: Jossey-Bass, 1991); P. Senge, *The Fifth Discipline: The Art and Practice of the Learning Organization* (New York: Doubleday, 1990).

David W. Gill

T

TALENTS

Normally we use the word *talent* to describe an inborn ability such as an ear for music, organizational ability or effectiveness in public speaking. Talents are capacities for serving others given to us by God. But the term is forever associated with a famous parable of Jesus (Mt 25:14-30). One person was given five talents; another, two talents; and a third, one talent, "each according to his ability" (Mt 25:15). In the parable *talent* refers not to innate abilities but monetary currency like dollars or pounds. Strictly speaking, the parable is about how people invest money differently (*see* Investment). But few interpret this parable in terms of the stewardship* of money, and for good reason. What we do with money and assets is a metaphor for what we do with ourselves.

The parable of the talents raises a whole range of spiritual and theological questions. Are talents inborn abilities demanding fulfillment or God-given duties requiring faithful stewardship? Are we accountable not only to be true to ourselves but beyond ourselves to a significant Other? Why are some endowed with multiple talents and others with only one talent? Is our stewardship of talents (material or immaterial) directly related to our concept of God (Mt 25:24-25)?

The History of Talents

The idea of talents has a long history

starting with the Greek philosophers, then proceeding to the humanists like Erasmus and finally to the modern (and postmodern) human-potential movement. The ancient Stoic philosophers spoke of inherent aptitude and disposition, something expounded by Petrarch and others. Cicero, a contemporary of Jesus, urged each person to "cultivate that which is proper to himself" resolutely holding fast "to his own particular gifts," following "the bent of [his] own peculiar nature" (*De officiis*). By the time of the Reformation, the humanist theologian Erasmus and others were urging that people choose a lifestyle in harmony with their own nature. This stands in stark contrast to what Luther and Calvin taught.

Erasmus spoke of a deliberate human choice of a way of life; Calvin described a calling* from God. Erasmus argued from the irreversibility of each person's unique character, Calvin from the irresistibility of God's command. Erasmus became a scholar, renouncing his monastic vows, for which he felt unsuited, to follow his own nature. Calvin, on the other hand, denied himself the career he judged most natural and obeyed God's call "in spite of my natural inclination" (Douglas, pp. 262-63). While for Erasmus (and his modern counterparts in the human-potential movement) the one-talent man should be condemned for failing to maximize his life, for Calvin the one-talent man would be judged because he did not do what the master required. As we will see, a biblical spirituality of talents includes and transcends these two streams. Talents are in us, but they are also given to us for God's pleasure and the neighbor's good.

Talents as Subject of Contemplation

Calvin's contribution to the idea of talents is, not so much his repudiation of human choice (choice is bounded not eliminated by Calvin), but his emphasis on talents as pointing to the greatness of God: "The talents which we possess are not from ourselves . . . and our very existence is nothing but a subsistence in God alone" (*Institutes* 1.1.1). For Calvin, knowing God and knowing ourselves are completely intertwined, each leading to the other. Thus considering our talents and, at the same time, having "consciousness of our own infelicity" and "deformity" incite us to seek after God.

At the same time, only through knowing God can we know ourselves properly—viewing rightly our spiritual endowments, not attempting more than is compatible with our calling and not deeming any ordinary use of our talents in our calling as unimportant or lowly (*Institutes* 1.1.6). Luther also emphasized that what is important is not our natural endowment and self-chosen path of life but our being summoned by God from outside ourselves to serve God in both our spiritual and temporal vocation. The intersection of natural longing and aptitude and the call of God is a summons to live by faith. So both Calvin and Luther view talents as endowments from God to be used in service for the common good and for God's glory. In other words, we do not choose our vocation on the basis of our talents but rather dedicate our talents to the service of God in obedience to our calling.

But it was not long, a matter of decades, before Luther's and Calvin's emphasis on calling was moderated, largely by the English Puritans, into something chosen in the light of God's call and also in the light of one's own abilities (Douglas, p. 296). In this way the Puritans were the bridge between the Reformation and the modern world because they reflected theologically on calling and talent in the context of a society in which choice was increasingly possible.

The Importance of Talents

The idea of talents has been significant for remaking the Western world from the eighteenth century to the present, reconstructing society not on the basis of wealth,* privilege and lineage but affirming a natural equality based on the universal, though highly varied, talents of citizens (La Vopa, p. 172). Education* and parenting* have also been profoundly influenced by this outlook. Good teaching seeks to draw out what is innate to the student, reading his or her nature and transforming raw talent into ability. A crucial role of parents is to identify the particular life direction of each child, independent of lineage and social status. What the child should pursue is not the path that will bring honor to the parents but that for which the child is actually suited.

Supremely, the idea of talents is fundamental to the process of vocational guidance.* While Calvin felt summoned to a profession for which he felt unsuited and disinclined, this seems more the exception than the norm, though an exception to which we must remain reverently open. Normally God writes his will into our motivation, talents and spiritual gifts.* In fact there is no perfect "fit" in the occupational world, just as there is none in the church* and home.* So even when we choose an appropriate calling, we must still make God our portion and deepest joy. One crucial contribution of the Reformers on this matter is that our talents are given for the common good (commonweal), not merely for our personal joy. The Puritan William Perkins defined calling as a "certain kind of life, ordained and imposed on man by God, *for the common good* (Perkins, p. 750, emphasis mine).

Gifts and Talents

One final importance of talents relates to the matter of spiritual gifts. Talents and spiritual gifts both overlap, but they also can be distinguished. They overlap in that both talents and gifts are abilities given to us to serve God in specific ways: listening,* helping, communicating, organizing, edifying, entertaining. They can be distinguished in this way: talents are creational, that is, built into us by the sovereign work of God in our conception,* whereas spiritual gifts are inspirational, that is, workings and motivations by the direct action of the Spirit in us. Often spiritual gifts are not permanent but rather are temporary endowments of the Spirit for building others up. (Yet even this distinction may be overdrawn, as the parable of the talents suggests that if you don't use it you will lose it!)

Sometimes spiritual gifts seem to be a Spirit-anointing of a creational or providential talent, as is suggested by Romans 12:6-8. Giving is something many have the capacity or assets to do, but giving with generosity is an anointed "extra" of the Spirit. Often the preaching* gift is given to someone talented in public speaking—but not always!

It is often noted that Luther "secularized" spiritual gifts into talents used in all the roles and "callings" that make society work (magistrate, cobbler, husband and wife, teacher), removing them from the exclusivity of in-church ministry. The layperson's ministry* through talents is mainly in everyday life. In contrast, the modern Western church has largely spiritualized gifts as special supernatural endowments given exclusively for "ministry" in the gathered church (prophecy, healing, tongues, teaching, helps). The net result has been to downplay talents as though they were not "from God" and "for ministry," thus neglecting civil vocation, the neighborhood* and home as arenas for ministry. If Luther's approach dissolved gifts into talents, the modern evangelical separates gifts and talents, relegating talents to lesser vocational service in the world while placing greater worth on gift ministry in the church. In the latter we are not much better than the Corinthians who so prized certain gifts that they were neglecting their ministries in daily life (1 Cor 7:17, 20). A better approach is to see talents and gifts as overlapping—all from God, all for service in the church and the world, all for God's glory. Talents are needed in the church; gifts are needed in the world.

In conclusion we return to the parable of the talents (Mt 25:14-30). Our talents are endowments but not possessions; they are trusted to us on loan from God. We are evaluated not on the number of such talents we have but on what we do with what we have. It matters not whether we have one or ten talents. God intends us to be fruitful with our talents and not merely to preserve them. Probably our abilities will grow and multiply if we use faithfully what we have. What we actually do with our talents is related to our conception of God. If we have a restricted and negative view of a judging God, we, like the one-talent man, will likely have a pinched view of life, protecting ourselves from failure* and loss. If we view God correctly as generous and forgiving, we will take risks and flourish for the common good. In the end we are accountable to God for the use of our talents. According to Jesus the judgment day is not just about how we have loved our neighbor (Mt 25:31-46); it is also about what we have done with our talents

(Mt 25:14-30). The reason is sublimely simple. Talents are not "natural" but creational, deriving from the creative activity of God, who invites us through their use to be cocreators with God to make God's world work and to build up the body of Christ.

See also CALLING; CREATION; MINISTRY; SPIRITUAL GIFTS; VOCATIONAL GUIDANCE.

References and Resources

J. Calvin, *Institutes of the Christian Religion*, ed. J. T. McNeill, trans. F. L. Battles, 2 vols. (Philadelphia: Westminster, 1960); R. M. Douglas, "Talent and Vocation in Humanist and Protestant Thought," in *Action and Conviction in Early Modern Europe*, ed. T. Rabb and J. Seigel (Princeton, N.J.: Princeton University Press, 1969) 261-98; A. J. La Vopa, *Grace, Talent and Merit: Poor Students, Clerical Careers and Professional Ideology in Eighteenth-Century Germany* (New York: Cambridge University Press, 1988); W. Perkins, "A Treatise of the Vocations or Callings of Men," in *The Works of That Famous and Worthy Minister of Christ in the University of Cambridge* (London: John Legatt, 1626) 748-79; M. Volf, *Work in the Spirit* (New York: Oxford University Press, 1991).

R. Paul Stevens

TAXES

If the only two things of which we can be sure are death* and taxes, we might want to spend as much time and thought thinking about the latter as we do the former! Yet, while the Old Testament contains some references to the payment of tributes and Christ talks a little about appropriate attitudes to tax reform, it is very difficult to find modern writers who help us develop a deeper understanding of discussions about taxation. Engaging in thoughtful dialogue is made still more challenging because, despite the pervasiveness of taxation in everyday life, no area of public policy is more veiled from public understanding. The debate is focused on two issues: paying taxes and spending tax revenue.

Paying Taxes and Spending Tax Revenue

People resent paying taxes they perceive as unfair. In the literature of public finance, *tax fairness* has a very specific meaning, referring to the distribution of the burden of taxes among individuals. For the public, *tax fairness* is a multidimensional concept reflected in different ways in the tax system and in discussions of tax policy. *Tax fairness* encompasses the nature of what is taxed—property, sales, income or profit—overall levels of taxes, the individual's ability to pay, the question of exempting some from paying for reasons other than ability to pay (such as religious freedom or encouraging job creation) and the relative amounts of the tax burden we share with our neighbors.

People also raise questions of fairness when they see money raised from taxes being spent in ways with which they disagree. Our differences can be deeply philosophical, such as whether or not people should pay taxes when government intends to use the money* for the purchase or use of arms. Others question whether those who do not benefit from a service such as education* should be forced to pay for it. Still others ask if those (such as cigarette smokers) whose behavior means that they are more likely to require the use of a costly service (such as health care) should be required to pay for that service to allow those who alter their behavior (by refraining from smoking) to pay less. Others advocate the imposition of special taxes (such as *green taxes*) to be earmarked to resolve special problems (such as environmental degradation).

These questions become more and more pertinent as times get tougher. When paychecks are shrinking, people are much more conscious of the amount that comes off the top in taxes and more concerned about how that money is spent by governments. At the same time, decision-makers perceive that they face constantly increasing needs for services. The so-called experts in this field are often unable to talk about the issues without resorting to jargon. The vast majority of us who are trying to understand how best to balance issues of our own well-being and conscience with the real needs of others for support find we are unable to effectively participate in the debate unless we resort to oversimplification and add to the existing polarization. Tempers flare. Laws are passed in the heat of the moment, which create problems later. Communities are divided. People go without services they need because of perceived abuses by others.

What are appropriate answers to the issues surrounding taxes? What questions could we be asking to provide helpful leadership in this often divisive and sometimes destructive debate? Are there any "right" answers? What lessons was Christ trying to teach when he taught on the subject? Does the Old Testament provide any guidelines for contemporary policy?

Old Testament Perspectives

When Joseph began his rule over Egypt, he wisely set aside food from the years that yielded good crops for the famine years that followed. There is still a broad public consensus that the common good is served by setting aside provisions for a rainy day. But, as in biblical times, the consensus breaks down when people do not agree on the amount, the uses to which is it put and the degree to which they are consulted. One of the important factors that allowed Moses to persuade the Jews that they should leave Egypt was their resentment over taxation. When Bostonians expressed their resentment about taxation without representation by throwing boxes of tea into the harbor and declaring their independence from England, they were following in an age-old tradition (Gen 41:34; Ex 1:11; Deut 14:22-27)!

The Old Testament endorses rulers collecting taxes to prevent uprisings by providing services and anticipating future needs. Its stories also remind us that when rulers do not provide satisfactory explanations for taxation or fail to redistribute tax revenue in ways that are perceived to be fair, people will object, sometimes at great cost to both parties. It seems a lesson that the Judeo-Christian world is destined to learn over and over again (Gen 49:15; Neh 5:1-5).

Another theme is people signifying their subjection to a ruler through the payment of taxes or conversely signifying their independence by refusing to pay (Deut 18:1-5; 2 Sam 8:6; Ezra 4:13; *see* Civil Disobedience). These stories and teachings formed the foundation of thinking about taxation for those who encountered Jesus and his followers.

The Gospels

There are two passages in which Jesus focuses on taxes. The first concerns the Pharisees' query about paying taxes to Caesar (Mt 22:17-22). Some argue that this is a firm instruction to pay taxes no matter how distasteful. At first glance it could be taken to be such a statement, especially when it is combined with the following excerpt from Paul's statement about paying taxes in his letter to the Romans: "That is also why you pay taxes, because the authorities are working for God when they fulfil their duties. Pay, then, what you owe them; pay them your personal and property taxes, and show respect and honor for them all" (Rom 13:6-7 TEV). In Christ's time Jews hated paying taxes to the Romans for many reasons. They disliked paying in Roman coin because it meant they had to trade in the oppressor's currency in order to have the money to pay. They hated the symbolism of being forced to pay for the economic and military might that kept them subjugated. They resented that they did not have complete autonomy over their own communities. Their religious leaders taught that the empire was immoral and ungodly. Tax collectors were reviled as collaborators with the enemy. Income and other state taxes combined with religious and community taxes were heavy—about 40 percent of their income. In this context, these teachings seem firm indeed!

But might there not be other interpretations? Is it conceivable that Jesus was teaching the importance of strategic thinking? Might he be arguing that taxation is not symbolic of anything unless we choose to make it so? In the past much trouble had been caused by those who confused the payment of taxes with moral or spiritual obeisance. Perhaps Jesus reminds us that we can allow government to take our tax payments without giving it any authority over the realm that must be governed by our relationship with God. To refuse to pay taxes in his time would have been seen as sedition. Paul might have been reminding us of the importance Christ placed on picking our battles wisely.

The second passage (Mt 17:24-26) concerns the official query about paying the temple tax. This also speaks of strategy. Jesus is reminding us that we can make the payment of taxes into an issue or not as we choose. Whenever we have discerned real choices, God will provide the resources with which to carry them out. "Ask and it will be given to you" (Mt 7:7) applies to this instance as well.

If we accept that we do have a choice about whether to pay taxes, what principles should guide us as Christians in modern debates about tax policy? Jesus taught us several lessons here. He did not confront Peter in front of the tax collectors but waited until they were alone. He began with a quiet, affirming question— one to which he knew Peter would know the answer. His question assumed the right of common people to engage in discussion about tax policy and their capacity to do so thoughtfully. Finally, he asked Peter to find the resources to pay the tax without hardship and by doing what he did best—fishing.

We would do well to engage in debates about taxation respectfully, in community with others and with reference to resources for paying it stemming from the work they are called to do. We also learn the importance of not leaving this issue of public policy to the experts but rather owning it as our rightful domain. Because the question of fairness is so subjective, Christians and other morally concerned people have an important role to play.

When the payment of taxes threatens to cause hardship, we might well remember the lessons of the Old Testament and ask if the debate might become less heated in an atmosphere of real consultation. But hardship is relative. When we hear wealthy people stating their reluctance to encroach upon their children's inheritance so that they can remain in their large houses and pay property taxes, we might also remember Jesus' teachings about becoming anxious over money (Mt 6:19-20, 24-34) and about the difficulty rich people have in reaching a state of grace (Mt 19:23-24). When we hear people saying, "There is no such thing as a fair tax," we might ask a gentle question about what services they would like to see disappear first. When basic goods and services are taxed, we might remember that Jesus was a carpenter and that Christians are especially called to listen to the voices of all people in the discussion, including those of the poor and lowly. Indeed paying taxes is one way of exercising neighbor love* and of exercising personal partial impoverishment for the sake of less fortunate citizens (*see* Poverty; Wealth).

Conclusions

When the Pharisees asked Jesus about the greatest commandment, he answered: " 'Love the Lord your God with all your heart, with all your soul, and with all your mind.' This is the greatest and most important commandment. The second most important commandment is like it: 'Love your neighbor as you love yourself.' The whole Law of Moses and the teachings of the prophets depend on these two commandments" (Mt 22:37-40 TEV). To the extent that paying taxes has to do with neighborliness, we are called to address the issue of tax fairness in the context of our obligations to, and relationships with, God and people. In this regard we must ask what use is made of the taxes we pay. In a modern economy we delegate looking after our neighbors as we would be looked after ourselves. As Christians we know that God will feed, clothe, educate and heal us in the way we do this for our neighbors. We know that when we do it for one of God's smallest creatures, we do it for God. Taxes are the main method we have of transferring revenue from those who have to those who are in need.

But what if there is disagreement about the value of the chosen system of redistribution? What principles might we look to if we think that the welfare state encourages permanent and damaging dependency or that we do not love our neighbors if we allow our tax dollars to be used to purchase and employ weapons?

As in so many things, there are no easy answers. But if we allow ourselves to be guided by the two great commandments and leave the judgment of others to the Lord, there is some hope that we may influence the dialogue around us respectfully and critically as we struggle to arrive at meaningful answers.

See also POLITICS; PRINCIPALITIES AND POWERS; WEALTH; WILL, LAST.

References and Resources
Ontario Government's Fair Tax Commission, *Fair Taxation in a Changing World* (Toronto: University of Toronto Press, 1993).

Patricia Lane

TEACHING

Teaching is generally held in high regard in Christian circles. Pastors who provide clear and relevant teaching from the Bible are highly valued. Sunday-school* classes seek and hold on to excellent instructors. The largest proportion of small groups* in churches revolve around Bible studies. One of the first steps in the discipleship* of new Christians is to ensure they are grounded in "good teaching." When new forms of church* life appear, such as home churches, one of the first questions people ask about them is, What about the teaching? Many people aspire to become teachers in churches, Christian colleges or theological seminaries. In all these ways teaching comes before us as a central feature of contemporary Christian life. This is as it should be, the only difficulty being that however biblical the content of much teaching may be, there is often an unbiblical understanding of what teaching is, who should be doing it and how it ought to be carried out.

What Is Teaching?

Though they overlap, teaching may be distinguished from prophecy. Prophecy is primarily a direct word of God that illuminates something in the past, present or future; this can come through any source, from a vision or dream to a parable from creation* or a meditation on events. Teaching is primarily reflection on something God has already spoken or on the general revelation of God through creation and human life. The best preaching* tends to be a combination of prophecy and teaching. To understand teaching better, however, we do well to turn to the biblical writings.

The role of teachers and teaching is central to the Old Testament. Important religious leaders, such as Moses, taught the people to understand the meaning of God's covenant and law (Ex 19:25; 31:18). Instruction was provided by the wise men in Israel (see Proverbs, Ecclesiastes), who taught in the open air, at the city gates and at crossroads, as well as at the court (2 Sam 8:16-18; Prov 1:20-21; 8:1-3). They also gathered students around them to whom they gave more regular training (Prov 8:32; Is 8:16; 50:4). For these wise men there was a close connection between teaching and reflective life experience. In the home, parents also had the responsibility of teaching their children the basic elements of Israel's history and practices (Ex 12:24-28; Deut 6:4-9).

From all these sources it is clear that teaching was not primarily passing on what was studied in books. Learning important stories and sayings was certainly important, but this was not enough. To know something involved practicing as well as understanding what was being learned. It was a matter of the will as well as of the head. To know the truth was to have an intimate relationship with it, to become one with it and to live it out in a practical way.

In Jesus' time there were honored scribes and rabbis who knew and taught the Law. Although he took issue with their understanding of it, and at times criticized their practice, in his day learning and teaching the Law itself continued to involve more than book learning. Students of teachers observed them, followed them around, at times resided with them. They were not just students memorizing information but disciples learning a whole way of life.

Jesus approached teaching in the same manner, but with a greater inten-

sity. Although he is described as a prophet, Jesus is more frequently portrayed as a teacher (Mt 8:19; Mk 10:1; Jn 3:32), albeit an unusual one who, unlike the scribes and the Pharisees, speaks with authority (Mt 7:28-29). Jesus' instruction is occasioned sometimes by events (Mk 8:14), disputes (Mk 10:41-45), challenges (Mk 2:18-22), observation (Mk 12:41-44), questions (Mk 9:11-12) and others' comments (Mk 13). This suggests that almost anything can be the catalyst for it.

While sometimes Jesus teaches in a more structured way (Mk 6:8-11), at other times he does so less formally (Mk 9:33-37) or over a meal (Mk 14:17-21). As a teacher, Jesus gives special attention to his disciples and either explains or declares certain things only to them (Mk 4:11, 34; 8:27). His followers are not presented as students engaged in formal learning of the Old Testament or merely as memorizing and passing on what he says to them. They are to learn from his actions as well as his words, and live out as well as reflect on what he teaches. As his disciples, they are to go around with him and work alongside him on behalf of the kingdom of God (Mt 10). After his death he promises his disciples that the Holy Spirit will be with them to help them understand and implement what, by his words and life, he has taught them (Jn 14:15-17).

Teaching is also an important part of apostolic activity (Mt 28:20), and in the case of Paul this takes place with colleagues who travel around with him. Paul clearly regarded himself as a teacher in the church (Acts 20:21; 1 Cor 14:6) and values teaching extremely highly (1 Cor 15:3; 1 Thess 2:13; 2 Thess 3:6). His coworkers also learn from what he has taught them (2 Tim 3:14; compare 1:12). But they learn not only from his words but from his life, from his "purpose, faith, patience, love, endurance, persecutions, sufferings" (2 Tim 3:10-11). His colleagues are to teach others who will in turn pass on to others what they have learned (2 Tim 2:1-2).

Elsewhere in the New Testament we come across attacks against false teachers, who are more concerned with advertising themselves and deceiving or controlling their hearers than with passing on the message of God (2 Cor 11:19-21; 2 Peter 2:1). They have the capacity to influence whole churches in unhelpful directions and must be strongly resisted (Rev 2:20-25). In the letter of James we also find warnings against wanting to become a teacher without considering how large a responsibility it is, how much teachers will be held accountable for what they say and do, and how closely understanding is connected to character and behavior (Jas 3). We also find reference to how learners should be passing from an elementary stage in understanding and living out their faith to a more advanced level of knowledge and behavior (1 Cor 3:1-3; 14:20-21; Heb 5:11-14).

Teaching, then, is a far broader undertaking than we tend to think. As Parker J. Palmer (p. 31-32) says, we understand it better if we relate it to the original meaning of *truth* that is still preserved in the old word *troth* in some wedding* services. Knowing is more than gaining insight into the truth of something: it involves being betrothed to it so that it captivates us, our lives revolve around it and we serve it in very practical ways. So too in teaching we seek to bring others not just to an understanding but to an intimate love of the truth, so that they pledge themselves to it and devote themselves to its service. To succeed in this we need, as Palmer also puts it, to teach in such a way that we "create a space in which obedience to truth is practiced" (p. 69). The good teacher opens up a hospitable space in which

new ideas can receive a welcome, people's feelings and hesitations be acknowledged, discussion take place and friendship between teacher and learner be established.

Who Are the Teachers?

It is clear from the New Testament that some people have a special gift of teaching and others do not, and that this gift comes from the Holy Spirit. As Paul says, not all people are teachers (1 Cor 12:28). Most people have drawn the conclusion from this that teachers require formal qualifications before they can exercise their talent* and that only a few Christians can ever be involved in instructing others. Both conclusions are far from the truth. In the first place, Jesus frequently criticized the Pharisees though they had professional training in understanding the Law and divine authority to expound it, not only because their practice did not match their teaching but also because their teaching leads people astray (Mt 15:3-9; 23:1-4).

In the second place, already in the Old Testament the prophets looked forward to the time when, as God promised the people, "I will put my law in their minds and write it on their hearts. . . . No longer will a man teach his neighbor, or a man his brother, saying, 'Know the LORD,' because they will all know me, from the least of them to the greatest" (Jer 31:33-34). In line with prophetic revelation, the gift of the Spirit at Pentecost (Acts 2:17-18) falls on all people, young and old, women and men, servants and masters, so enabling the word of Christ to "dwell richly" in all, equipping* them all to "teach and admonish one another" in the church (Col 3:16). Although those who have a special gift along these lines should bring "a teaching" to the church when it gathers (1 Cor 14:26), it is also open to any member to share their understanding of God with others in the meeting when it is appropriate to do so.

So alongside, or included within, the "priesthood of all believers" is a "teacherhood" of all believers. It is because God shares the truth about the divine character and purposes among the people of God rather than to just a few people within them that the whole truth about God takes place only as all members of a church are playing their individual part in building up one another's understanding. Since it is difficult to make room for this in larger gatherings of the congregation, it is especially in small groups* and house churches (see Church in the Home) that such mutual instruction most effectively takes place. It is particularly in such settings—as members bring to the group situations, challenges, problems they are facing, and as members open the Scriptures, share their insights into them, and wrestle together to understand the will of God—that God builds up their understanding and directs their behavior. Such teaching and learning are always prepared to be augmented by whatever other understanding God may give through the practice of other spiritual disciplines* and the exercise of spiritual gifts* in the group.

Within such smaller groups and larger gatherings of the congregation there is a special place for those who have the ministry of teaching to a greater degree. Every group and congregation should be on the lookout for such people and encourage them to develop and refine their God-given ability. It is not formal theological education alone that qualifies such people to teach, though anyone who has a gift of teaching would only benefit from undergoing this. What primarily qualifies people to teach is long-term dwelling in the Scriptures—reading, pondering, praying and applying them—so that they begin to know

them from the inside and see connections between the diverse materials contained within them. What also qualifies them, as Luther said long ago, is experience of life itself, especially suffering. Through this they come to see and embody ever-deepening connections between Scriptures and everyday living. So it is people who come to know the mind, heart, imagination and will of God, who discern what this means for themselves, those around them and their wider world, and who live out what they have learned who are best equipped to provide the fundamental instruction in the church. Such people have a particular opportunity to share what God is teaching them when the whole congregation comes together. As in some earlier church traditions, for example, among the first Anabaptists, this could take the form of two or three spokespeople sharing with the congregation.

How Does Teaching Take Place?

Although something has already been said about Jesus' practice here, on this point Paul is once again a helpful guide. For him, though teaching sometimes included passing on a fresh understanding of God's written revelation in the Old Testament (for example, Rom 9—11), it goes far beyond that. He draws on what he observed about him in everyday settings (Acts 17:16-23), from his own experience of God and life (2 Cor 4:7-18), from the statements or writings of non-Christian writers (Acts 17:28; 1 Cor 15:33), and from some of the customs and conventions of his time (1 Cor 11:14). It is passed on in a range of settings, from formal lecture rooms at the regular scheduled times to conversation in the early hours of the morning in a home (Acts 19:8-9; 20:11). As a teacher he was more concerned with whether others were learning what he was saying, drawing proper conclusions from it and putting it into practice (Rom 6; 7:7-25; 15) than with instructing them in fancy and eloquent ways based on human performance rather than Holy Spirit depth (1 Cor 2:1-4).

Paul's teaching also took many forms, such as personal reminiscences (Gal 2:1-10) and testimony (Rom 11:33-36), discussion of struggles and humiliations (2 Cor 11:16-33), and advice on a wide range of matters from relating to God to various aspects of daily life (1 Cor 6—10). It took the form of asking questions as well as making statements, of giving praise as well as giving instruction, of speaking from the heart as well as from the head. It sought to argue and persuade rather than dogmatize and decree. And as the greetings on most of his letters indicate, instead of being only a solo effort, much of his teaching was a collaborative affair involving his coworkers as well.

All too often teaching is identified with one person standing up with the Bible or notes in front of them holding forth at length to an audience or group, perhaps with some time for questions and answers afterward. But there are a diverse range of ways in which teaching can take place. It can, and occasionally should in very large groups, occur in the form just mentioned. But most commonly it should take a more dialogical or conversational character. When Paul was speaking in the church at Troas we read that he "dialogued" with them (Acts 20:7) and then "conversed" with them during and after their common meal (Acts 20:11). This, as some translations bring out, is the force of the Greek words in these passages. In other words, during the early part of the meeting he had things to say but opened up opportunity for a serious discussion of these with the people whom he was addressing. In the later part of their meeting there was leisurely room to talk more informally about a whole range of issues connected with the Christian life. Paul's letters often betray his speaking practice, for they are full of questions that he imagines people asking or that he asks to an imaginary audience. He quotes from what they might have said if present or detours to clarify points where he suspects they will misunderstand. In all this Paul provides a good model for those engaged in teaching, especially in larger gatherings.

In smaller gatherings of the church there are many other ways of teaching. Teaching may take the form, as it so often did with Jesus, of sharing a parable or riddle for people to reflect on at length and in practical ways; it may take place through asking a profound question or stating a provocative thesis that forces people to explore some doctrine or issue in a way they have never done before; it could involve telling a personal or secondhand story about some formative experience so that others are stimulated to progress in their own spiritual or vocational journey; it might entail, as it did at times for the prophets, acting something out or getting the group to act out a story, so that learning takes place through seeing as well as hearing; it might mean, as sometimes happens among the wise in the Old Testament, composing an instructive song or poem, whose meaning the group then weighs and applies; or it could occur by leading people through a meditation on a particular passage or through an exercise in guided contemplation on some experience, followed by some sharing of their findings.

Broadening our understanding of how teaching takes place also broadens our appreciation of who can engage in it. Though not everyone has the gift of more directive instruction, many have abilities that would allow them to teach in one or more of the ways outlined. In all settings where teaching takes place—whether small or large, informal or formal, spontaneous or organized—it is important that those who receive it ask for discernment as to its truth and, when necessary, call upon those who have a special gift in this direction (1 Cor 12:10). This again demonstrates that teaching is not a solo activity but one requiring the involvement of others to have its full and proper effect. It only remains to add that those who are teachers remember that, strictly speaking, they, along with everyone else in the church, are only students themselves, for as Jesus said, "You are not to be called rabbi, for you have one teacher, and you are all brethren" (Mt 23:8 RSV).

See also CHRISTIAN EDUCATION; EDUCATION; LAITY; MINISTRY; PREACHING.

References and Resources
J. A. Grassi, *The Teacher in the Primitive Church and the Teacher Today* (Santa Clara, Calif.: University of Santa Clara, 1986); R. K. Greenleaf, *Teacher as Servant: A Parable* (New York: Paulist, 1979); H. Nouwen, *Creative Ministry* (New York: Doubleday, 1978); P. J. Palmer, *To Know As We Are Known: A Spirituality of Education* (San Francisco: Harper & Row, 1983).

Robert Banks

TECHNOLOGY

In the popular mind *technology* usually means things like machines. Technology is what engineers give us: telephones, fax machines, automobiles, electric lights, water purification plants, compact disk players and so on. We live in a high-tech world—a world of computers* and advanced technologies. While we might resist some aspects of modernity, it is very difficult to establish and live out a critical perspective on technology, the very thing we will explore in this article.

Defining Technology
Our word technology derives from the Greek roots *technē* and logos. As biology is the study of bios (biological life) and theology is the study of theos (God), so technology originally meant "the study of *technē*." *Technē* is the Greek word for an art,* skill or craft*—for a technique of making or doing something. In this basic sense, of course, we could say that birds have techniques for building nests, beavers have techniques for building dams, and flies have techniques for irritating us. Human beings also have always had techniques—various arts, skills and methods for meeting their needs* and desires—for building houses, making clothing, raising and preparing food (*see* Meal Preparation). We have had other techniques for making decisions, governing ourselves, communicating with others, raising children and worshiping God.

Some of our techniques are handed on by our traditions. Others are imposed by authorities: "This is the way we do this; period!" But what distinguishes our human (from animal) techniques is our capacity to revise or replace our various techniques through the application of our rationality. Human techniques are not just a product of our instincts or traditions but of our reason. We do not merely submit to nature but create artificial means; we develop tools to more effectively achieve our ends or goals. The difference between science and technology is that while science aims to know and understand things, technology aims to change things, to have a practical effect, to be useful.

Today, of course, we use the word *technology* not just for "the study of techniques" but for "tools" and "techniques" themselves ("Do we have the technology to do this or that?"). This subtle change in language highlights the fact that our modern techniques are now virtually all linked with study (discourse, *logos*), with research and rational analysis. There remain, of course, techniques that are handed on by long-standing tradition, socialization, religious faith and even biological instinct. But such techniques are in retreat because of the demonstrable, measurable success, the efficiency, of our rational technologies.

Technology in the Modern World

For most of human history, nature has been the primary milieu in which human life, including human technical development, proceeded. Specific techniques assisted life in remarkable ways, but choices were conditioned primarily by nature. For example, the length of one's workday was determined by when the sun rose and set. The range of one's movement was typically confined to the distance one could walk* or ride a horse. Learning was passed on from one person to another and depended on the presence of a living teacher.

Human life has also been conditioned by society and human culture.* Traditions placed constraints on what people did. Values,* embedded in customs and expressed in beliefs, constrained the development and use of techniques. Even if nature allowed the conditions for work, social or religious tradition might prevent you from working during certain times (for example, the institution of the sabbath day), at certain places (for example, sacred burial grounds or mountains) or in certain ways (for example, cruelty to animals, dietary prohibitions against pork, etc.). So too, the way one worked or played might be defined by social roles assigned to men and women, to old and young or to one social class or another.

But in the modern world, while neither nature nor human culture is a negligible factor, our primary milieu is technologically defined. We can work* as long as our electrical power keeps the lights on and our computers running. We can travel* as often and as far as our transportation technologies will take us. Our entertainment* is for the most part technologically constructed. Social taboos against shopping* or working on Sunday have disappeared. Socially determined roles for men and women, for old and young, have largely, though not entirely, disappeared. For the most part today, what we do, how we do it, where we do it, is determined by technology not by nature or social tradition. We live in a technological milieu.

How Technology Serves Us

For most of us most of the time, this change to a technological milieu is a good thing. Who would want to return to a time when the whims and constraints of nature were so confining? And who would want to return to a situation in which often irrational social traditions decided the possibilities of life for one's class or gender? In this sense technology has served and even liberated us.

Consider, for example, how technology has served us by creating tools that vastly extend our human powers: construction tools like hammers instead of rocks, then jack hammers instead of sledge hammers; medical tools like x-ray machines, prostheses and pharmaceuticals; transportation tools like planes, trains and automobiles*; communication tools such as television,* compact disc players, computers and fax machines. The list of technological tools is awesome. The ways these tools have served us is spectacular.

Technology has also served us by its development of methods. Technology is not just tools; it is a method of rational analysis, of quantification and measurement, of empirical testing, of innovation, of new ways of approaching problems. In the material world technology is the method of rationally analyzing how to move things from one place to another, how to multiply, divide, simplify or combine various elements and factors. As such, technology helps us break down a production and distribution process into its constituent parts and then restructure the process toward greater efficiency.

The method that works with automobile assembly lines and other material processes is also applied to human relations, as in the conduct of business meetings, the creation of effective advertising* and the development of psychotherapy. Technology is the creation of better means, in fact, of the "one best means" in every field of human activity. Modern bureaucracy, for example, operates under the rule of technological method—even if in practice it often is far less efficient than we would like.

How Technology Masters Us

Modern technology is not only our servant but our master in some important ways. It frees us in some ways; in others it constrains us and sets our agenda. This mastery has four characteristics.

Technology is ambivalent. This means that specific technologies always have both positive and negative aspects. It is common to say that technology is neutral and only its use or its users are good or bad. But technology is not neutral, nor is it exclusively evil or good; it is both good and bad. Certainly you can say that, for example, a gun in the hands of a crook will be put to bad use, and a gun in the hands of a good person can be put to good use. But it is the technology itself that makes possible these uses. One cannot simply invent guns without weighing these outcomes and deciding whether to proceed. So too, the development of automobiles not only results in freedom to travel but also in pollution, in serious injuries to people and in anonymity that facilitates social breakdown. The possibilities of television are accompanied by the loss of human conversation* and the

capacity to entertain oneself in a spectator era.

Our lives and choices are mastered and increasingly determined by both the positive and negative impacts of technology. Every benefit is accompanied by a cost. Often the positive and negative impacts of a technology are not fully seen by their inventors. Monks who invented the clock in the Middle Ages to add precision to their daily prayers in service of God did not realize that it would end up being a major instrument in the service of mammon by regulating work. The inventor of the stethoscope did not foresee that physicians would lose their capacity to listen to patients as they increasingly relied on technical instruments interposed between them and human beings. Inventors of computer networks did not foresee that pornography would be the major content traveling on their information superhighway.*

Technology has an almost deterministic force. Technological developments create technological problems that require further technological responses ad infinitum. There has been a qualitative shift from earlier eras in which specific tools and techniques were developed through the freely chosen creativity of human beings to meet specific, limited objectives. Technology now obeys its inner logic of development as rigorously as we used to think that nature obeyed its own laws. This necessity is especially visible in a larger view of the technological complex as a whole. "If it can be done, it will be done; indeed, it must be done": technology carries its own imperative to further development. Who today can oppose technological expansion and development?

Technology is universalistic. It invades every area of the world and every aspect of human existence. This is what Neil Postman calls "technopoly"—a monopoly over all human affairs. This includes the geographic universalization of technology. Every corner of the world is affected by technological intervention. Global development means technological development. Traditional ways of agriculture are replaced by technological ones. Traditional forms of governance must be replaced by bureaucracies. Those who resist are condemned to live at best as an underclass, at worst as the refuse dump of the globally dominant technological complex.

But technological universalism or technopoly also refers to the invasion of technology into every aspect of our lives. Politics* and campaigning are technicized; sport* and entertainment are dominated by technologies; public relations and fundraising obey technological laws; churches* employ public relations techniques to build their memberships; even prayer and spirituality are analyzed and taught as a set of rational techniques for manipulating God and the self. Sexuality,* the last domain of the truly wild and mysterious, has never been so technicized—not just in terms of reproductive or prophylactic technologies but in the technical analysis of the sex act itself. Our physical space is dominated by technological instruments; our psychic space is dominated by the method and values of technology: rationality, effectiveness, measurable success.*

Technology serves as the sacred. The sacred or the divine is whatever occupies the very center of our existence, giving our lives unity, direction and meaning. The traditional gods have been toppled and replaced by technology. Traditional gods may receive lip service in church or in private conversation, but in practice, on Monday morning if not before, it is technology that is served. Technology is our hope for the future and for our present-day salvation. When something is omnipresent, omnipotent and not subject to criticism, when it inspires and compels our sacrifices and praise, it is serving as a god. But is technology an adequate god? Or is it a bogus pretender to divinity that needs to be demythologized and desacralized? Is the technogod ultimately a liberating, redeeming god or an enslaving one?

Another way to express this is by saying we have moved from technology to *technologism.* Adding that *ism* is a way of saying that technological thinking and values have become the foundation, the worldview,* the criterion of all judgment. The potential goodness of technology is radically in question when it develops into technologism as an all-embracing intellectual, moral, cultural and spiritual identity.

The questions are these: Who or what is in control of our lives? Have we become mere tools of our tools? Have we made technology the god of our civilization? Gods always demand some kind of worship in return for the salvation, meaning and direction they offer. The worship demanded by technology has meant lives of frantic absorption into the latest technological development. Our lives are dominated by the products and the problems of technology. Our learning is dominated by the acquisition of technological literacy and competence.

We should evaluate this covenant with technology by asking what has been excluded. What has been lost is the value of the inefficient, the nonrational, the aesthetic, the spiritual and the traditional. Love and beauty, for example, are prostituted and lost when they are made to serve a technological calculus. Relationships with family members and colleagues are seriously distorted when rationality and efficiency are the criteria of value.

Four Basic Responses to Technology

Responses to this kind of critical questioning of modern technology usually take one of four forms.

Denial. Some will deny that there is a problem and protest that modern technology is more or less desirable and under control. This first response is partly a product of exhaustion. We simply do not have the time or energy to stop and take a critical look at the broader dimensions of what is happening to our human life. We are too busy. It is also true that our technological society provides innumerable distractions and opiates to its members. Denial is also a product of a lack of perspective. Most of our technologically trained population at large have little significant background in history, philosophy, theology and non-Western cultural attitudes. Yet these are precisely what we need for a critical perspective. We have much knowledge of a certain type, but little wisdom. Hence we tend to regard our Western technological perspective as the only legitimate one, though it is by no means the only perspective in the Western tradition, to say nothing of the rest of the world.

Love of technology. A second response allows that we have some serious dysfunctionality in our technological civilization, but we only need more and better technology to resolve these problems. This is the *technophile* response, the true believers. The priests and evangelists of technology want to get everyone on the information superhighway—with an integrated office system, linked to our home entertainment and work centers and to our portable cellular phone and powerbook computer. Thus the technological environment becomes essentially airtight, and everyone is technologically linked to everything at every moment. But where is this superhighway going?

Fear of technology. Opposite the technophiles are the third group, the *technophobes*. In the Industrial Revolution these were the Luddites, the band of protesters who wished to smash the machines and

maintain a more balanced existence. The hippies of the sixties made a somewhat similar call, but romanticism and adolescent anger make a flimsy foundation for resistance, as the subsequent absorption of the sixties generation into the yuppies has demonstrated. Technological reactionaries are doomed to be the colorful feather in the cap of the technological giant: a dash of color on a giant who moves forward unimpeded.

Resistance and revolution. This response calls first for a profound awareness and critical analysis of our reality: the reality of the technological main currents under the surface of the ocean of our existence and the reality of our flesh-and-blood neighbors. For such awareness we must stop relying on *USA Today* and on *CNN*-type news bites—and invest our time in broader, deeper works of cultural criticism, including historical and multicultural perspectives that will give depth and breadth to our own analysis of social and cultural reality. Along with this we will need to turn off the distractions and carve out time to develop human relationships with people around our living and working areas. This means learning how to listen,* how to be quiet, how to reflect deeply, how to care.

With this growing awareness, we need to resist, indeed, to refuse the necessity, universality and divinity of technology in our life and work, that is, "just saying no" to technology at decisive points. But gods do not easily vacate their thrones. To dethrone the old, we need to install a more appropriate one. To begin with, we can resist in the name of humanity. Our thinking, living, working and playing can revolve around the sacredness of human life, earth and universe in which, and with which, we flourish or come to grief. Concretely this means that people are not reducible to statistics, that intelligence is not reducible to IQ numbers or degrees held or genetic maps, that this living student or friend before me is sacred and is more important in his or her living wholeness and mystery than any rational calculation could ever account for. So we need to replace technologism with a robust humanism.

Christians, of course, would suggest that the strongest foundation on which to base such a humanism and to resist technologism is a theological one in which the transcendent God who created the universe and human beings is invited back into our sacred space. We would say that humanism is true and good because God has created humans in the divine image, whereas technological civilization tends to promote uniformity and reduce individuals to faceless atoms in a mass society. Biblical people would say that to mistreat or undervalue a person is to mistreat an irreplaceable child of God. To exploit and to abuse the earth and the universe are not merely a technological dysfunction but a serious sin against God and his creation.*

Resisting technology as a pretender to the place of God in our lives can thus proceed from resistance to a revolution in values that rebuilds authentic individuality and community*—a life in which we do not smash the machine, but we do question it, appraise it in reference to our human or religious values, and then sometimes say yes and sometimes no to its deployment as a servant in our lives.

The Impact of Technology on Theology and Religion

Without any doubt the development of certain technologies has served theology and the religious life in impressive ways. Communication techniques, most notably translation techniques and the printing press, have made possible a relatively inexpensive, massive diffusion of the Bi-

ble into the hands of the people, bringing new spiritual life to multitudes. It has also tended to move authority away from hierarchies and elites, who alone previously had access to Holy Scripture, into the hands of literate, popular masses. Better transportation has facilitated people's possibilities for gathering together for worship, witness, learning and service. Radio, television and other media have multiplied the potential exposure of large numbers of people to things theological and religious. Organizational, public relations and therapeutic techniques have contributed to the effectiveness of some aspects of religious life. Political techniques are now being used by various religious groups (for example, the "religious right") to increase their social impact, for better or worse.

But while noting the benefits, we must also ask how we respond to the lies, half-truths, manipulation and corruption that are technologically foisted on a gullible audience? Technology has vastly increased the potential impact of religious hucksterism and charlatanism. And how should we evaluate the impact of the technological medium on the life and message it is intended to serve? What is lost when the dynamic, personal character of the Christian gospel is replaced by the passive, depersonalized character of watching religious television (see Televangelism)? What is lost when pastoral searches, evangelistic campaigns, fundraising campaigns and pastoral care* are primarily structured by technobusiness models and methods?

Technology as a worldview and intellectual paradigm tends to progressively put in question and then marginalize the traditional, inefficient, unquantifiable, nonrational and transcendent. Individual techniques and technologies need not necessarily have this exclusionary impact. But we live in the era of technologism, of the global technological ensemble, of technology as infrastructure and intellectual/spiritual paradigm.

Towards a Theology of Technology

Any theological critique of technology must return to the biblical sources. There we find that technology is an expression of divinely created human creativity and imagination,* of doing and making good and helpful life-enhancing things. Technology and engineering are the expression of our human imagination and creativity in forming and transforming nature for practical purposes and uses. While there is plenty of biblical material emphasizing the spiritual and inward over the material and external, this is balanced by passages affirming the concrete, external world of things. For example, the Old Testament describes in detail the materials, dimensions and building techniques for Noah's ark, Moses' tabernacle and Solomon's temple. In a classic text, Moses says, "See, the LORD has chosen Bezalel . . . and he has filled him with the Spirit of God, with skill, ability, and knowledge in all kinds of crafts . . . to engage in all kinds of artistic craftsmanship" (Ex 35:30-33).

A major problem arises, however, when we treat technology as sacred, when it moves to the center of our lives, receives our sacrifices, bestows meaning, direction and significance on what we do. The root problems are idolatry and autonomy. What should be carried out in a living relationship to God, subordinate to the character and plans of God, is now autonomous, subject to nothing except its own internal imperatives. Such technology carries with it no respect for nature, social tradition, religious authority, the absurd or the paradoxical, the weak and the unproductive. And yet all of the foregoing are part of the world God has created and wishes to redeem. So it is essential for us to develop a theology of technology.

God's creativity as the source of human theological imagination. Recall the accounts in Genesis 1—2. God created; God made the heavens and the earth. God gave shape, order and design to what was without form, filled what was void or empty and illuminated the darkness. What God made was described as "good," "useful" and "pleasing to the eye." What God made was diverse, complex and awesome in scope. It was orderly and bounded but also set free.

We human beings are made in the image and likeness of this creating God. So the first and basic source of our own creativity is this fact of our nature. But human creativity and technology are not just an exhibition of our nature—they are also a response to the command and invitation of God. It is the freedom of obeying God's Word that underlies technological activity in a biblical worldview. God commands us: "Be fruitful and multiply," "Fill the earth and subdue it," "Have dominion," "Till and keep the garden," "Name the animals." At its best our technological creativity continues to bear witness to God's creation when it combines innovation harmoniously with what already exists as good, when it contributes both beauty* and utility to the world and when it allows both individual uniqueness and partnership/community to flourish.

Human creativity is bounded. Our technological and creative work is bounded in four ways. First, it is launched by the Word of God. Creation begins when God says, "Let there." Human work begins when God says, "Be fruitful . . . fill . . . subdue . . . till . . . keep . . . name." It doesn't begin out of idle curiosity, boredom,* greed or lust for power. Second, it is bounded temporally by the sabbath*: God rests on the seventh day and so do those made in God's image. There is a time to cease from technology. Third, it is bounded spatially in that there is a tree at the center of the garden that is not to be harvested for food; a limit is respected; it was a tree that could be harvested but must not be. There are limits that technology should not transgress. Finally, human creative work was bounded ethically in that the prohibited tree was the "ethics tree"—the tree of the knowledge of good and evil. Humans were to live and work in relationship to the God who sees and names the good; they were not to try to take this ethical knowledge for themselves outside of this relationship with God. All technology must be subjected to this fundamental ethical judgment of God.

Human technology now needs redemption. The Fall occurs when man and woman misuse their freedom, breech the boundaries and grab for the fruit of the ethics tree. The human situation changes dramatically. They are evicted from the garden and cannot go back. Technology is itself now fallen, sometimes perverse and violent, open to becoming idolatrous and autonomous.

Because of the Fall, the creativity motifs in a theology of technology must now be caught up within a theology of present and final redemption. Redemption means that in a fallen, broken world we are not able to act naively. Realism means we must take account always of the potential for deception and destruction in our work. Redemption means that our work (our technology) must aim at healing what is hurting, repairing what is broken, liberating what is in bondage, preserving what is degenerating, conserving what is disappearing. Creating, illuminating, ordering, filling, naming—these original motifs of creation continue, but the arena is no longer pure and innocent. Sacrifice, servanthood and humility will need to characterize a redemptive technology.

Human technology must keep the end in view. Technology is a development and perfection of means. But in our civilization the means have become ends in themselves and are developed without adequate attention to the proper ends of human life. Christian life is eschatological life: it is life lived in expectation of the coming end, the consummation of God's kingdom and purposes. The Holy Spirit is given as the pledge, the down payment, of our future inheritance. Christians lean toward the future (Rom 13:11-14). Thus, our technology needs a new, rigorous assessment of the true ends of human life. In the light of these ends, specific technologies can be assessed and evaluated. Our means must not be self-justifying. They must be justified by God's end, and then they must exhibit the character (not the contradiction) of that end.

Faithful Technology

Our challenge is to recover the notion of fidelity. The most important exercise of fidelity is toward God and his Word. After the Fall of Adam and Eve, God continues to speak to humankind. Often the word of God takes the form of questions: Where are you? What have you done? Where is your brother? Who do you say that I am? Faithful technology will hear God's commands and questions, seeking them not only as the starting point of our technological activity but as its boundary. It will aim to contribute to God's purposes for life in the world, trying to discern and respect appropriate limits and boundaries in space and time.

Fidelity to God means trying to hear God's ethical judgment on our projects instead of pronouncing our own and overcoming evil with the good. Fidelity to God means fidelity to our Creator and Redeemer. Faithful technology will not just be fruitful, fill, subdue, create, name, till and keep—but will go into all the world, love your neighbor, love your enemy, heal the sick, set free the captives, comfort the lonely, welcome the children.

Fidelity also must govern our relationships with others. Faithful technology will not subordinate people to technique. It will express faithfulness to partners, neighbors, friends, fellow humans. It will promote technology on a human scale. It will refuse to reduce people to technical categories, not try to adapt people to the requirements of technology. It will invite others to help rebuild the boundaries and discern and support good technological work.

Our modern choices with respect to technology are symbolically represented by the tower of Babel and Abraham's altars (Gen 11—12). The technology of Babel intends to make a name for the self, make security for the self, breech all limits, choose and occupy its own chosen place. But the technology of Abraham builds an altar for God and lets God care for our reputation, protect and guide us to the place he chooses. As Christians we know we cannot go back to Eden. We must go forward either to Babylon, where Babel's project is fulfilled, or to the New Jerusalem, where Abraham's project is fulfilled. The afterlife is depicted in the form of a city,* not a new garden, into which the nations bring their glory. We must pray and work that something of our own generation's technology might be worthy of a place in that city of God.

See also COMPUTER; COMPUTER GAMES; HOME VIDEO; INFORMATION SUPERHIGHWAY; TELEVISION.

References and Resources

I. Barbour, *Ethics in an Age of Technology* (San Francisco: Harper Collins, 1993); D. J. Boorstin, *The Republic of Technology* (San Francisco: Harper & Row, 1978); J. Ellul, *The Presence of the Kingdom* (London: SCM Press, 1951); J. Ellul, *The Technological Society* (New York: Vintage Books, 1964); S. C. Florman, *The Existential Pleasures of Engineering* (New York: St. Martin, 1975); G. P. Grant, *Technology and Justice* (Toronto: Anansi, 1986); C. Mitcham, *Thinking Through Technology* (Chicago: University of Chicago Press, 1994); S. V. Monsma, ed., *Responsible Technology* (Grand Rapids: Eerdmans, 1986); N. Postman, *Technopoly: The Surrender of Culture to Technology* (New York: Vintage Books, 1992).

David W. Gill

TELEPHONE

The telephone is one of the three most influential modern inventions (*see also* Automobile; Watch). It has played an extraordinarily pervasive role and had amazingly diverse effects in altering communication patterns between people and in modernizing society.* Telephones are the nerve ends of the modern world: like the body's central nervous system, they connect disparate members and channel messages from one to the other. Though occasionally we wish we could be as far away from it as possible and curse its intrusion on our lives, most of us use the telephone constantly and greatly appreciate all that it does for us. In the 120 years since its invention by Alexander Graham Bell, it has spread from the world of male-dominated business and government circles and the homes of the urban rich to the simplest dwellings in the most remote areas.

Ironically, when Western Union was first approached about setting up a telephone system it regarded the prospect of the telephone's being present in almost every home and business place as a fantasy and rejected the offer. In most places these days the phone system is a government utility, though in the United States and in many Third World countries it is run by private companies, often U.S. corporations. At present the telephone network is undergoing an interesting mixture of deregulation and reregulation, all the more confusing because the first is sometimes described as the latter.

Though in most Western countries more than 90 percent of the population have one or more phones in their residences, where there is more than a token cost involved in hooking up many people, the mobile young, more so than immigrants or the poor, are unconnected. We are also in the midst of significant changes in the world of telecommunications. With the coming of cellular models, the telephone is becoming ubiquitous: we can now take it with us virtually everywhere. When it is hooked up to a fax machine it can send documents quickly verbatim, and a video connection sets up the possibility of teleconferencing. Attached to a modem and computer,* it enables workers to engage in telecommuting and can send large amounts of material in the briefest amount of time.*

In all these ways the telephone has become an indispensable part of modern life. It has played a major role in maintaining cohesion as settlement spread and connected rural and urban areas in vital ways. It has changed the nature of how business operates, as well as how news is gathered, crime* investigated and law* enforced. It has changed the context and to some extent even the meaning of friendship* and neighborhood.* It helped pave the way for radio* and television,* and now for the fax and the Internet. It has altered patterns of leisure* activity and affected the handling of everyday crisis and routine. But what are its main uses, and who uses it most? How much has it destroyed face-to-face community,* and how much has it kept other forms of community alive? To what extent is it an accomplice of the consumer society and a primary cause of our pressured lifestyle? What role has it played in secularizing life or in furthering Christian ends? Until the last couple of decades there has been little discussion of these issues, largely because the telephone was taken for granted.

From a spiritual or theological point of view scarcely a thought has been given to the telephone, unless to see it as a way of directly advertising the gospel to people in their homes or providing them with valuable crisis counseling services. When it was becoming more widely available in the earlier part of the century, only groups such as the Amish debated its value. Some leaders warned of its dangers, arguing that it would subvert face-to-face community and allow the secular world to intrude too much into the life of discipleship.* There was a church split among the Amish over this, and Old Order Mennonites avoided this only by forbidding church leaders to own a telephone or members to enter hotels to use one. Quaint though this may seem to us, at stake was a vital issue: the extent to which such groups would permit the wider world to compete with established and highly symbolic patterns of communication centered in the shared life of the home* and congregation.

The Nature of Telephone Conversations
Telephone conversation takes place for a variety of reasons. The most common distinction is between what are termed *intrinsic* and *instrumental* purposes. The first has a social purpose, giving people opportunity to talk about their interests, concerns, experiences and relationships. The second has a task orientation, enabling people to further their work or make some arrangement. In homes the first kind of conversation dominates, especially among women, who use the telephone around seven times more for intrinsic purposes than instrumental. Even at home, however, men tend to use the phone in a task-oriented way. Instrumental conversation dominates in workplaces,* though the telephone is occasionally used for social ends. Many conversations are a mixture of the two.

The first kind of conversation is used

to build on and extend existing networks* of relationships. Women in particular, even though they do not talk as personally over the telephone as they do in each other's company, employ it to hold together the fabric of the family* and friends and to carry out important voluntary caregiving activities, often with those who are lonely, ill or in need. The telephone is especially important to those who do not have much face-to-face contact with others, such as the elderly, handicapped and infirm, and those for whom social contact is extremely important, such as single mothers, teenagers and troubled people. People moving into retirement homes use their telephones to keep in touch with friends and family, and sometimes for shopping.* Immigrants, especially women, use it to build a female support neighborhood* and also to bring language instruction within their reach.

There are other forms of communication by telephone. For example, it is commonly used, especially by teenagers, to play pranks. And it also can be a means of harassment.

Obviously, then, the telephone brings with it some difficulties. Those who have poor English depend on others to answer it and talk for them, those who are partly deaf cannot always hear properly, and those who have speaking problems cannot always make themselves understood. Most people feel guilty if they do not answer the telephone when it rings, or get frustrated when they call but succeed in reaching only an answering machine or voicemail. The telephone can make life too busy, intruding even on family meals, leisure times and periods of prayer and meditation. Salespeople can enter the home unannounced through it and take up time and energy. Children can get access to types of calls that are unfit for them or rack up large telephone bills by dialing out-of-state friends.

According to surveys, the things people particularly appreciate about the telephone, in order of importance, are its convenience, the way it saves time, ongoing contact with family and friends, opportunities for gossip, overcoming feelings of isolation and loneliness, reducing the tyranny of distance, saying things they could not say in person, accessing information without emotional consequences, avoiding small talk, the expression of feelings and a sense of security. What people especially dislike, again in order of importance, are its expense, interruptions at any time, intrusions on privacy,* calls from strangers, frustrations in getting through to people, uncertainty about what to say, overconvenience, its impersonal nature or its having brought bad news. Answering machines, it seemed, created as many difficulties as they resolved.

Putting the Telephone in Its Place
The telephone, then, plays a significant social role in the modern world. It has both significant relational and operational uses over a wide range of people and fields. Perhaps in the spiritual realm the closest analogue to the telephone is prayer, for it too is an extraordinarily wide-reaching, multipurpose, communally formative, yet individually valued, phenomenon. One of the unexpected findings of surveys that have been undertaken is the important psychological functions that telephone calls play: making people feel wanted, needed, included and involved, and in general the opportunity to be social and keep in touch. In other words, telephones seem to contribute to people's self-esteem* and experience of community. On the other hand, sometimes people feel that the telephone uses them, as when they sense they *must* answer it, are manipulated, encounter insensitivity, waste time on it or become addicted* to using it. In

these ways it turns people themselves into machines and leads them to feel insignificant.

All this suggests that the telephone is a two-edged sword, but one that is far more positive an invention than it is negative. As yet most people are only dimly aware of its complex impact and its wide realm of uses. Many don't even consider how to maximize its advantages and avoid its disadvantages. With regard to the latter, the following practical suggestions can help:

☐ Have only one phone for the family, and learn the art of sharing, self-discipline and sensitivity to other's needs.

☐ Use the phone only when necessary; visit rather than phone those working for or with you if they are in the next room.

☐ Tell people not to call you between certain hours. This helps both you and them establish boundaries for phone use.

☐ Don't answer the phone at mealtimes, even if you eat alone. When eating it is important to have time with others or to yourself.

☐ Preserve leisure time from intrusion by work-related calls. This means keeping cellular phones in their place.

☐ Interrupt politely and hang up immediately on all junk calls. This is your right, for they are invading your privacy.

☐ Give priority to people present with you over incoming calls from others. Answering machines can be a real help here.

☐ When necessary use answering machines to screen incoming calls. Or try providing family and friends with a recognizable signal.

☐ Fast from the phone occasionally for a day, a weekend or a holiday. This prevents addiction and keeps it in proper perspective.

Such guidelines will help you make the phone a servant rather than a master.

See also TECHNOLOGY.

References and Resources

S. Aronson, "The Sociology of the Telephone," *International Journal of Comparative Sociology* 12 (1971) 153-67; D. Bell, "Toward a Sociology of Telephones and Telephoners," in *Sociology and Everyday Life*, ed. M. Truzzi (Englewood Cliffs, N.J.: Prentice-Hall, 1968); G. Gumpert and R. Cathcart, eds., *Inter/Media: Interpersonal Communication in a Media World* (New York: Oxford University Press, 1979); J. Meyrowitz, *No Sense of Place: The Impact of Electronic Media on Social Behavior* (New York: Oxford University Press, 1985); I. de Sola Pool, *The Social Impact of the Telephone* (Cambridge, Mass.: MIT Press, 1977). Robert Banks

TELEVANGELISM

Televangelism is a loosely used term often applied to a broad range of religious, primarily evangelical, programming on broadcast and cable television. When used by evangelicals, it usually refers to programs with an evangelistic purpose, such as broadcasts of revivals and church services. As used by the mainstream media, however, *televangelism* is typically a pejorative term referring to any overtly religious TV fare, from talk shows to variety programs featuring musical performers. These contrasting definitions suggest the scope of public perceptions of television ministries, as well as the confusion about televangelism even within the church.

Clearly the church is of mixed minds about how to relate television to its overall mission and purpose in the contemporary world. The goal of evangelization* is certainly important (Mt 28:19-20), but it fails to justify much of what evangelicals do with the medium. Christian programs are often deeply anchored in the language and assumptions of religious subcultures; consequently, they do not appeal very effectively to those outside of the church. Some of the religious talk shows preselect the audience even more by espousing conservative political agendas. In addition, much of the television preaching,* although presented in biblical language, is based on secular self-help philosophies. Yet other shows are boring church services or high-energy religious songfests. All of this is televangelism.

Televangelism and the Local Church

Televangelism affects viewers' attitudes toward and perceptions of their local church,* especially congregants' expectations for preaching, liturgy and music. For example, there is little doubt that televangelism fosters entertainment-oriented liturgies in local churches. A growing number of churches are fashioning their worship services after the TV-styled variety show. Similarly, congregants often prefer a pastor who displays the type of charismatic persona developed by religious television celebrities, thus fostering the kinds of personality cults that divided even the early church (1 Cor 1:10-17).

Televangelism also affects the popular theology of many evangelicals. The so-called health-and-wealth theology, which emphasizes the power of individual believers to claim God's promise of financial prosperity and bodily health,* is spread extensively by some televangelists through their programs, literature, tapes and especially their best-selling books. Televangelists also help popularize various versions of biblical eschatology.

In spite of what many people believe, televangelism does not compete directly with local churches for financial contributions and members. Most viewers are active members of local churches who also support their churches. As the marketing business might put it, televangelism appeals to "heavy users" of religion for whom television is just one vehicle for expressing faith and practicing religion.

Televangelism and North American Culture

Televangelism is a product largely of North American culture, especially the United States. Its roots are deeply anchored in the history of popular American evangelicalism, especially revivalism. The vast majority of religious television programming around the world is either produced in the United States or based on American television production standards, popular American theology and pragmatic American business techniques. Non-American televangelists tend to imitate the programming of their colleagues from the United States.

Televangelism's business methods are probably its most characteristically American aspect. In spite of all the religious language used in televangelism, these programs are steeped in marketing and management techniques that are most evident in advanced capitalistic economies. Televangelists are usually talented fundraisers who sell various religious products in order to raise enough operating capital to pay the bills and expand the ministry. Moreover, the audience is often treated as an abstract market, not a congregation; many audiences exist only as a computerized mailing list or as a bank of demographic marketing data. Fundraising letters and on-air appeals create a sense of personal relationship when, in fact, the televangelist has never even met the vast majority of viewers and contributors.

Televangelism is also a product of American public rhetoric. Televangelists repeatedly speak of the medium in almost salvific terms, reflecting America's deep faith in technology* as a solution for nearly all personal and social ills. They also wax elegantly about the positive impact of their programming, much as American advertisers exaggerate the benefits of their products and services. Some televangelists even preach a polarized message that divides the world into two easily identifiable groups, righteous believers and wicked nonbelievers. The divisions are often ideological (for example, one's political affiliation or stand on a public issue), theological (for example, one's views of biblical inerrancy or matters such as creationism) or moral (for example, one's views on particular values or practices, such as gay sexuality or abortion). This kind of rhetoric reflects America's overarching moralism, which in the public arena typically oversimplifies complex issues through the use of glib stereotypes and victimization.

Contributing to Televangelists

In spite of all the difficulties involved in using television for evangelization, the medium is sometimes an effective means of spreading the gospel. Supported by a denomination, or at least under the purview of a board of discerning leaders, some televangelists preach the gospel without the corrupting influences of fundraising, market-driven theologies and personality cults. These televangelists should be encouraged and, when appropriate and feasible, supported financially. Before contributing to the work of any television ministry, however, potential givers should first find satisfactory answers to two essential questions.

First, how will the contribution be used by the ministry? Personal stewardship* of limited resources should lead contributors to support only those ministries that use the money wisely and effectively for the actual work of ministry. The easiest way to determine this is to request a copy of the annual financial report prepared by the ministry or, preferably, by the ministry's certified public accountants. Many TV ministries will supply such documents only to contributors. Some will not provide them under any circumstances. These kinds of secretive organizations may not merit support

(see Financial Support). Financial statements should be examined for the amount spent on administrative costs, or other questionable activities, versus the amount actually spent on direct ministry-related work.

Second, what does the ministry actually believe? As odd as it may seem for organizations claiming to spread the gospel, a considerable number of television ministries do not have a doctrinal statement to share with potential contributors. This is one of the reasons that these kinds of ministries can so easily slide into errant doctrine. Potential contributors should request a theological statement from the ministry under consideration. If they receive one, it is wise to examine it carefully, even to share it with a local pastor or discerning friends who might be able to assess its strengths and weaknesses.

Finally, it is very important that potential contributors compare the relative benefits of supporting a broadcast ministry against the benefits of helping other international and especially local evangelistic ministries. There is much evidence that the vast majority of lasting Christian conversions occur through interpersonal friendships,* not via mass-media evangelism. Local evangelism, including neighborhood and friendship evangelism, is crucial for the growth of the church. Televangelism should never be a substitute for personal evangelism. Nor should Christians use their support of televangelists as an excuse for not themselves witnessing to others.

Local Church Use of Television

Some of the larger, more progressive congregations use local broadcast or cable television to reach out to their communities. Although there are not many studies of the effectiveness of this kind of local ministry, it appears that local television can succeed under the right conditions. The overall technical quality of the program is very important; too many local religious broadcasts are embarrassingly amateurish. Also, the primary value of these programs, especially worship services, seems to be their role in encouraging the congregation to invite friends and acquaintances to worship services. A high-profile local broadcast creates congregational pride and community visibility, resulting in increased attendance by members and visitors. All of this encourages local evangelization.

See also EVANGELISM; HOME VIDEO; TELEVISION.

References and Resources
P. G. Horsfield, *Religious Television: The American Experience* (New York: Longman, 1984); Q. J. Schultze, *Televangelism and American Culture: The Business of Popular Religion* (Grand Rapids: Baker, 1991); L. I. Sweet, *Communication & Change in American Religious History* (Grand Rapids: Eerdmans, 1993).

Quentin J. Schultze

TELEVISION

Television is surely the most pervasive and influential mass medium of the late twentieth century. It is popular around the world, across social classes and among all ages. At the same time television is one of the most poorly understood media, eliciting both praise and superficial criticism. Moreover, the uses of television defy simple classification since the medium pervades every aspect of life. The merging of film, video and the computer* with television is making it even more difficult to define and evaluate the medium.

Television as Technology
Technologically speaking, television is a means of communicating a combination of moving image and sound. Sometimes the images and sounds are broadcast via the electromagnetic spectrum. Other

times they are transmitted via coaxial cable or projected from magnetic tape, laser disk or compact disk (CD). Television differs from film in the manner in which the sounds and images are both stored and played; film projects light through celluloid, whereas television relies on a cathode-ray tube to project the images, thus making it more difficult and more expensive to create large, high-quality images.

Television and video are increasingly difficult to distinguish. Many people use the term *television* to refer only to cable or broadcast television and *video* to refer to videocassette and computer-generated images. In the future, however, this kind of distinction will be challenged by new technologies* that combine such media. In any case, television will still be the major form of home entertainment, regardless of how the images are produced or transmitted.

The Appeal of Television
Television's appeal to humankind is apparently universal. Television lures viewers almost mysteriously, certainly more than the printed word, which requires literacy and greater mental and physical effort on the part of the user, and even more than radio,* which lacks the attractive images. From early childhood to the end of their lives, human beings will normally watch television if it is available and if they have the time.* Indeed, there is considerable evidence that television viewing is steadily eclipsing all other types of entertainment* and all other forms of leisure.* In North America, for instance, television viewing time is greater than that of all other forms of entertainment combined.

Probably the two most appealing aspects of television are its drama and persona. The most popular uses of the medium present messages as dramatic stories. This is true, for instance, not just of situation comedies, soap operas and police dramas, but even of many commercials, nearly all news stories, documentaries, sporting events (the drama of the game), movies,* animated children's shows and music videos.

Television's appealing use of persona similarly pervades the medium. In fictional programming, television *represents* all types of people, who are played by celebrities or stars. At the same time, television *presents* people who are more or less acting as themselves (for example, talk-show hosts and guests, news reporters and anchors, variety-show emcees, sports players and commentators, and televangelists*).

This combination of drama and persona creates a pseudorelationship between viewers and television personalities. Viewers feel as if they know various celebrities. In some cases this kind of pseudorelationship creates an uncritical, largely irrational trust (for example, trusting a TV preacher or a news reporter), an inability to distinguish between fact and fiction (for example, soap-opera viewers' emotional involvement in fictional weddings) and even a greater viewer commitment to televised characters than to real-life relationships.

Balancing Television with Real Life

Viewers should maintain a healthy balance between the medium's pseudorelationships and the viewers' real interpersonal relationships. Parents in North America on average spend over four hours daily watching television, a mere four minutes conversing with spouses and an unbelievable thirty seconds daily conversing with their children. Novelist and social critic Jerzy Kosinski in *Being There* has suggested that many solitary viewers are becoming "videots"—passive, nonthinking, solitary viewers incapable of normal social intercourse. Although this kind of thesis cannot be proven, there is abundant supporting anecdotal evidence from teachers, psychologists, social workers and other professionals.

For most families, a daily limit of one or two hours of television viewing would adequately control the tendency to overindulge, especially if the viewing is familial and not individual. In addition, regulating the number of personal television sets in the home can help enormously; too many parents try to solve the problem of deciding what to view by giving each family member his or her own set. Finally, the placement of the television set in the home is also important; if the living- or family-room furniture is organized around the set, for instance, television viewing, not conversing, will dominate in-home leisure time.

Viewing Versus Watching

It is important that Christians learn how to view television instead of only watching it. Viewing is an active, discerning response to televisual messages, whereas watching is passive and largely uncritical. Viewing requires the audience to look for the values and beliefs that animate television messages.

Neil Postman suggests that television tends inherently to eclipse critical thought by emphasizing image over word. Although there is undoubtedly some truth to this generalization, it wrongly assumes that viewers cannot be taught to think about the meaning of images, especially moving-image narratives. By equipping people to evaluate and reflect on programs, this type of visual literacy combats the tendency of the medium to trivialize subjects.

From a Christian perspective, viewing fosters spiritual discernment of the winds of secular doctrine (Eph 4:14) communicated through popular culture.* Viewing places all television programs in the context of God's Word, enabling viewers to identify and evaluate the worldviews* behind this popular entertainment.

Viewing can be fostered especially by parents, pastors and schoolteachers. Parents should view and discuss programs with their children. This is most effective as a regular, informal activity. Pastors have considerable potential to foster discernment by using popular TV characters and programs as illustrations in sermons and other Bible teachings. Schoolteachers have many opportunities to encourage discernment by integrating video segments into lectures and discussions across the curriculum. Students thereby learn to think about what they see, as well as to relate popular images to schoolwork.

Children and Television

Children often watch enormous amounts of television to relieve boredom.* Many parents encourage this by using the medium as a baby sitter, particularly before and after school, on Saturday mornings and during meal preparation.* Significant research suggests that this type of unsupervised use of television by children is not wise.

Until they reach about eight years of age, children are not capable of interpreting programs on their own with much critical ability. Younger children have difficulty separating television's fictional content from real life. Moreover, they cannot easily make sense of the meaning of televisual stories; their understanding of television is limited largely to describing dramatic action or events. Often children's understanding of a show is significantly different than the commonplace understandings of adults.

Therefore, it is essential that parents carefully monitor and supervise their children's use of the medium. This should include (1) wise selection of appropriate programs for young viewers, particularly shows that are slow-paced

and provide their own explanations of the stories; (2) parental viewing with children; and (3) parental discussion of programs with children, especially discussion of how each child is responding emotionally to programs.

Parents also need to balance their offspring's television time with other important activities. Reading* skills are often undeveloped in children because of excessive television viewing. Social skills are sometimes similarly retarded when a child does not spend adequate time interacting with other children. Children's normal patterns of sleep* are even interrupted in homes where parents do not adequately regulate viewing time.

Finally, television viewing can exacerbate a variety of childhood disorders, although the reasons are not precisely known. For example, television apparently worsens hyperactivity among some children. The medium also contributes to attention deficit problems in susceptible children. Because these links between television and childhood behavior are often idiosyncratic to specific children, it is essential that parents monitor the viewing of their offspring.

The Future of Television

Television is a rapidly evolving medium that will likely play a growing role in all areas of society, especially family life and education.* As computers merge with television, the medium will expand and specialize its content. This will further challenge Christians to use television wisely.

Television is shifting from a "broadcasting" system to various forms of "narrowcasting." The growth of cable television, with its specialized drama, sports and information, is only one step on the road to channel-free programming. Viewers will increasingly be able to select specific programs at any time from a broad menu of available options. So-called channel surfing (rapidly switching from one channel to the next, usually with a remote-control device) will be transformed into menu surfing. This technological revolution will change the television landscape into a cornucopia of specialized fare.

Televisual abundance of this kind offers positive opportunities as well as serious challenges to Christians. There will be many more worthwhile programs, including all kinds of instructional educational material and quality drama. But the new televisual landscape will also challenge the limits of Christian morality by providing specialized fare for people who practice unacceptable lifestyles or who believe in non-Christian religions.

It is imperative that Christians avoid a mindless adoption of the new television technologies. Parents need to establish in advance standards for familial use of new technologies. In addition, local congregations and Christian schools need to help individuals and families to live faithfully by cultivating critical viewing skills and sharing suggestions about worthwhile programs.

See also CULTURE; HOME VIDEO; INFORMATION SUPERHIGHWAY; MASS MEDIA; TELEVANGELISM; VIRTUAL REALITY.

References and Resources
J. P. Ferré, ed., *Channels of Belief: Religion and American Commercial Television* (Ames, Iowa: Iowa State University Press, 1990); T. Inbody, ed., *Changing Channels: The Church and the Television Revolution* (Dayton: Whaleprints, 1990); N. Postman, *Amusing Ourselves to Death: Public Discourse in the Age of Show Business* (New York: Viking, 1985); Q. J. Schultze, *Redeeming Television: How TV Changes Christians—How Christians Can Change TV* (Downers Grove, Ill.: InterVarsity Press, 1992); Q. J. Schultze, *Winning Your Kids Back from the Media* (Downers Grove, Ill.: InterVarsity Press, 1994); also available as a five-part video series with Gospel Films.

Quentin J. Schultze

TENTMAKING

The term *tentmaking* comes from the trade and practice of the remarkable New Testament couple Aquila and Priscilla, who were self-supporting Christian workers in three cities, Corinth, Ephesus and Rome. They sewed and sold tents that were made either from rough cloth woven from goats' hair or leather (Barnett, p. 926). The apostle Paul worked alongside this couple (Acts 18:1-3), supporting his own apostolic ministry by a trade, though from time to time he received financial support* and patronage from distant churches (2 Cor 11:9; Phil 4:10-20). *Tentmaking* is a pattern of relating work* and ministry* so that both are for God's glory, but the work supports the primary calling* of a person in some form of in-church or outreach ministry. The tentmaker thus has a second major arena of service in addition to the workplace. Over the centuries and especially today in the light of the global mission* of the people of God, tentmaking commends itself both theologically and strategically.

Relating Work and Ministry
In his classic work *The Case for the Voluntary Clergy,* Roland Allen notes the subtle distinction implicit in the tentmaking approach: "The distinction between the stipendiary (remunerated) and voluntary clergy is not a distinction between men who give their whole time to the service of God and His church and men who give part of their time to that service, but a distinction between one form of service and another" (1930, pp. 86-88). This form of service concerns the work-ministry mix, in which three patterns can be discerned: the supported Christian worker, the Christian professional and the tentmaker.

The supported (remunerated) Christian worker cannot distinguish between work and ministry, though the central idea behind financial support of Christian workers is not salaried employment with its contractual obligations but the receipt of a living. This apostolic right and privilege Paul defended vigorously from the examples provided by everyday life, the law, pagan and Jewish temples and the words of the Lord Jesus (1 Cor 9:1-14). While Paul defended his right to the patronage of the Corinthians, he refused that right at least in Corinth, Ephesus and Thessalonica for reasons we will explore. Peter is a biblical example of a person who accepted the privilege of financial support.

The Christian professional approaches a challenging career* or role in society as his or her primary arena for service in the kingdom of God. Service in the gathered church is normally related to discretionary time. Here again work and ministry are almost totally integrated. In the modern Western world these people are the least supported in the prayers, honor and equipping ministry of the church, especially in the case of homemakers* and volunteer workers* when their social service in society is unremunerated. Sometimes these people are lured from the ministry they have in the workplace into taking highly demanding church leadership* roles and, tragically, may give only leftovers to the workplace. Biblical examples of this option are found in Joseph, a professional politician in Egypt; Nehemiah, a personal assistant to the president; and Bezalel, a Spirit-inspired craftsman in the Old Testament (Ex 31:1-11). The reference in Philippians 4:22 to the church in Caesar's household is perhaps an indication of the Christian professional from New Testament times.

In the tentmaking option, work is for ministry. The great danger of this arrangement is that one will regard one's work as merely the means of making a livelihood rather than an arena of cocreativity, mission and caretaking of God's world (Gen 2:15). Tents (or some modern equivalent) should be made, not only to gain access to a closed society, but for God's glory and people's use. The Christian at work actually serves God and God's purposes even in the most mundane tasks (Col 3:22-25). So the true tentmaker witnesses in his or her work, not just works in order to be positioned to witness. The reasons are profoundly theological.

Theology of Tentmaking

Tentmaking raises important questions not only about the nature of work but about Christian vocation, ministry and mission.

The frequent use of the term *bivocational missionary* when describing a tentmaker is misleading and incorrect. There is one calling or vocation, not two. Paul says that all Christians are called (Eph 4:1) and that the call of God is all-embracing: it includes church,* family* and society (Eph 4:1—6:20). The idea of *vocation* is quite different from what is involved in an occupation or profession,* both of which are chosen by the person. To be a called person is to live one's life in response to the summons of Christ to discipleship, service and holiness. There is no hierarchy of calls within the people of God; there are only different expressions of the general calling to all according to gift, talent and temperament of the individuals.

Ministry is essentially an amateur matter in the true sense of the word—done for love rather than professionally. Tragically the church has allowed an amateur vocation to become something done by certain professionals. Roland Allen points out, "There is something in ministration in holy things which prevents certain men [*sic*] from receiving any material reward for such service. It is for them so essentially a service of God that they cannot bring themselves to receive any payment from men for doing it" (1930, p. 79). There is a long tradition for this, including, for example, Elisha (2 Kings 5:16, but see vv. 20-27), Amos and Nehemiah (Neh 5:14, 17). Jesus broke with the commercialism of the temple and cleansed it prophetically. We have no recorded instance of his receiving remuneration from the people he served though he did receive support from some of his disciples (Lk 8:3). Paul received support from the Philippians but not when he was serving them. Indeed, it appears Paul did not receive support from any church while he was with them (Everts, p. 297). To the Ephesians he could state he coveted no person's silver or gold and experienced the joy of giving rather than receiving (Acts 20:33-35). Paul's pattern is especially illuminating.

Tentmaking expresses not only biblical vocation and ministry but also biblical mission. God's first commission (Gen 1:26, 28) invites men and women to become world-makers through being garden-makers, structure-makers, culture-makers, homemakers, justice-makers, knowledge-makers, beauty-makers, communication-makers, image-makers, peacemakers and community-makers. All of these are dimensions of human work. But they also embrace the idea of mission: going forth and being sent. Implicit in the first commission is movement, so central to the biblical understanding of mission. The earth cannot be filled without moving, which is why the scattering that took place in Genesis 11 is both punishment and opportunity. Abraham and Sarah ministered on the move, God revealing himself to them as they did so. Joseph moved to Egypt, and in the movement from prison to palace he came to know God's sovereign purpose more fully, made the

economy work (the first futures trader on the grain market) and was reconciled to his brothers. Naomi was a homemaker who made her home on the move. She modeled God's character, and Ruth chose the God of Naomi, moving with her mother-in-law. Jesus was born on the move, grew up on the move and ministered on the move, modeling work and mission through relocation.

The Great Commission (Mt 28:18-20) does not replace the cultural commission (Gen 1:28-30). Rather it creates the context for its fulfillment and, by reconciling people to God, empowers them to become fully human and to humanize the world as world-makers. Tentmaking is a time-honored way of accomplishing the church's mission in the world. The church has never relied mainly on professionally trained and financially remunerated workers to accomplish its global agenda—until today.

History of Tentmaking
Over 75 percent of the major religious characters in the Bible were not full-time, supported workers. This is very obvious in the Old Testament, as the aforementioned figures demonstrate, but is also manifest in the New Testament. Paul and Barnabas left the international church in Antioch for Cyprus and this "traveling seminary" picked up Luke (Acts 16:11), Timothy (16:3), Aquila and Priscilla (18:18), Erastus (19:22), Sopater, Aristarchus, Secundus, Gaius, Tychicus and Trophimus (20:4). These early missionaries were constantly on the go and learned in transit. Priscilla and Aquila, our primary tentmaking models, were themselves mobile. They moved from Rome to Corinth when the Jews were persecuted under Claudius, then to Ephesus and back again to Rome, presumably in advance of Paul, who was delayed two years by being shuffled from court to prison. Much of the

Christian mission in the first century was undertaken in the context of movement. For example, Lydia, whom Paul met at Philippi, was a textile merchant from Thyatira and became the first church member in Europe. Churches, such as the one at Colossae, were planted along the trade routes in Asia through Paul's two-year marketplace mission in Ephesus (19:10) and without the benefit of financially supported workers. Today we should expect international travelers, people on overseas assignment and people doing business with multinationals to be frontline missionaries. They should be prepared, prayed for and recognized in local churches.

In the first three centuries, tentmaking church leadership was the norm, not the exception. Roland Allen cites the *Apostolic Constitution* and *Apostolic Canons* to show that bishops of large areas were shepherds (literal) and silversmiths. Even pastors of large churches, of six hundred or more people, were self-supporting in business. The major discussions in the church councils on this subject were not whether pastors should work but whether they should be prohibited from taking work in distant provinces managing estates, work that would take them away from the flock. More importantly, the early church conferences were concerned about the discipline of pastors who took work to make as much money as possible (Allen 1930, pp. 297-303). Allen argues that the cause of Christ can be advanced worldwide not by sending an army of trained professionals with a European education, dependent on their home country, but by mobilizing an army of volunteers, some of them like the apostle Paul and William Carey, paying the price of being crosscultural missionaries who support themselves in government work, international trade, education* or consulting. Allen was decades ahead of his time. Today we

are still not as radical in ministry and mission as the church was in New Testament times.

Many of the most influential figures in the modern Christian movement were tentmakers in the sense we have defined it: some Roman Catholic missionaries, Methodist lay preachers, William Carey (a shoemaker who became a manager of an indigo factory in India), other early Baptists who rejoiced that malsters and tinkers were pastoring churches, the Christian Brethren (including Rendle Short, a surgeon and preacher) and many nameless people in the former Soviet Union and other countries that are still closed (Wilson; Neill and Weber).

William Carey maintained that, whenever possible, practical missionaries should support themselves in whole or in part. Writing in 1792 he countered stock objections to service in distant parts:

> As to their distance from us, whatever objections might have been made on that account before the invention of the mariner's compass, nothing can be alleged for it, with any color of plausibility in the present age. Men can now sail with as much certainty through the Great South Sea, as they can through the Mediterranean, or any lesser Sea. Yea, and providence seems in a manner to invite us to the trial, as there are to our knowledge trading companies, whose commerce lies in many of the places where these barbarians dwell. (Carey, pp. 67-68)

The modern world is ripe for tentmaking missionaries. With ubiquitous travel,* urbanization as a global* phenomenon, a world economy, an international job market, rapid technology transfers and the pervasiveness of English, opportunities for sensitive tentmaking missionaries—for short or long periods of time—abound. But the reasons commending tentmaking are deeper than mere strategic expediency.

Why Tentmaking?

Paul's own case for tentmaking is the most illustrative. Though one could argue that this gifted church-planter, apostle and theologian could have accomplished more by being full time in supported ministry, Paul uses persuasive arguments to the contrary, arguments that carry weight today.

Tentmakers are determined not to be a burden to the people they serve. Undoubtedly Paul's work was arduous. It was not peripheral but central to his daily life (Hock, pp 558-59). He labored and toiled night and day (Acts 20:35; 1 Thess 2:9; 2 Thess 3:8). In Corinth especially this did not come easily. Paul's reason for accepting this hardship was simply not to be a burden (2 Cor 12:16; 1 Thess 2:6). In contrast to the desire of the Corinthians—that he might live under the patronage of some of their wealthy members (Barnett, p. 926)—Paul boasted to the Thessalonians that he did not "eat anyone's food without paying for it" (2 Thess 3:8).

Tentmakers set an example. Paul undertook a tentmaking lifestyle as an example to others of priorities and balance in ministry. In Ephesus his working from early dawn to midevening demonstrated his generosity: "In everything I did, I showed you that by this kind of hard work we must help the weak, remembering the words the Lord Jesus himself said, 'It is more blessed to give than to receive' " (Acts 20:35). Like Jesus, Christian leaders come not to be ministered to but to serve, not to receive but to give. Paul believed that his tentmaking approach helped the weak in faith, who frequently imagine that their next step in discipleship is to be supported financially by other Christians. In Thessalonica Paul faced a different problem. The people

there thought the Lord's coming was just around the corner. As they waited for the end, they sponged on the people who were working. Paul gave himself as a "model" (2 Thess 3:9) and commanded the idlers to work (2 Thess 3:12; see also 1 Thess 2:9; 4:11-12). A third modeling value, already mentioned, was to show the dignity of work, especially in contexts in which work was devalued. But the deepest reason for Paul's practice was the gospel itself.

Tentmakers are determined not to hinder the gospel. I return to the searching passage in 1 Corinthians 9 where Paul defends the right of Christian workers to be supported. He does this by appealing to the law, to the normal practice of paying people for work and to the words of Jesus. But Paul says, "We did not use this right. On the contrary, we put up with anything rather than hinder the gospel of Christ" (1 Cor 9:12). It is a strange statement. Normally we would think that Paul's having to spend eight to ten hours a day working kept him from doing the really important ministry of preaching the gospel and planting churches. But Paul believed that if he did receive a living from the Corinthians, he would probably hinder the gospel.

His reasons were related to the practice of ancient philosophers and missionaries who were supported by fees, patronage and begging as well as by working. The Corinthians were offended that Paul did not accept their patronage and thus questioned whether he was fit to be their apostle. Even worse was Paul's choice of a demeaning trade in a society that despised manual work (Fee, pp. 399-422; see also Hock, pp. 555-64). Paul's stance had to do with the nature of gospel ministry. The gospel is a free gift. Paul is not "free" to choose whether to proclaim this gospel. So he chooses to embody the essential nature of gospel ministry (as a free gift) by giving his own ministry "free of charge," thus ironically getting his pay by taking no pay (1 Cor 9:18). As the servant songs in Isaiah (42:1-9; 49:1-7; 50:4-9; 52:13—53:12) show, service rendered to God springs from a heart broken by God's loving invasion and freed from material motives or means. Tentmaking is one way of demonstrating the relation of ministry and reward. When disciples have only done their duty or have performed their contractual obligations of ministry for pay, they are still unprofitable servants (Lk 17:10).

Paul wanted to make it absolutely clear that he had no ulterior motive for sharing Jesus. He defends the rights of others to be supported but denies those rights himself. He thus gives a powerful motive for supporting others while refusing to raise one's own support by the kind of entrepreneurial activity now so generally required by Christian organizations. Just as a church has no right to demand that its leaders must all be tentmakers, so should a Christian worker not demand support. These are gifts of grace.

There are strategic reasons for tentmaking that relate to the advancement of the gospel by people whose primary employment is located in the world. As Roland Allen says,

> The hedge round the clergy is a very high and cultivated one . . . and consequently the restriction of ordination generally to men trained from youth within that hedge inevitably results in the clergy being more or less out of touch with the common experiences of common men. . . . The voluntary cleric carries the priesthood into the marketplace and the office. (1930, pp. 86-88).

For someone to minister as a gift is not only beautiful; it is expedient if we are to reach our generation for Christ. Quite possibly, the most expedient thing today to reach the pagan North American population is to have fewer supported missionaries and more self-supported ministers (Stevens, p. 141).

The Problems of Tentmaking

As already mentioned, tentmakers do not have an easy road to travel. But no form of Christian service, including that of the remunerated worker, is easy. Tentmakers usually find themselves with the equivalent of three full-time jobs: work, ministry and family (not in order of priority). It is impossible to contain Christian service within nine-to-five or after-six time frames. Not surprisingly Paul worked night and day. Work and sabbath* are essential for tentmakers to be more than survivors. But there will not be much time for work, sabbath and extensive leisure.* It is worth mentioning, however, that coping with multiple responsibilities may have a salutary effect in comparison with Christian service workers who have few natural rhythms built into their weeks. Few tentmakers burn out, perhaps because there is a healthier balance in their lifestyle.

Further, tentmakers rarely receive affirmation within the church unless they are ordained. Even then they may be treated as second class to the ordained and full-time workers. Tentmakers overseas have few support structures and are not treated on a par with full-time missionaries with their three-color glossy prayer cards and deputation schedules. Until such support structures are put in place, tentmakers will need to be entrepreneurial. They may also be forced, with surprisingly happy results, to find their support structure in the best place of all—the local churches where they serve. These difficulties notwithstanding, few tentmakers would have it any other way for reasons that are deeply inward and spiritual.

The Spirit of Tentmaking

In spite of the drift of our society toward

professionalism, the real future of the kingdom is with volunteers and amateurs. The spirit that motivates tentmaking takes us to the essence of Christian spirituality and gospel theology. Paul lived extravagantly because his Lord loved him extravagantly. In all religious systems the gods demand sacrifice, and the worshipers give it. But in Christianity God is the first to sacrifice, and God gives everything. Were this not the case, the Christian way would be a life of impossible burdens, including the burden of refusing to covet the silver and gold of others (Acts 20:33) and the burden of giving ministry free of charge. So even tentmaking must not become a duty. It is one way some of God's servants choose to love. The first love-worker or amateur is God, who is also the first volunteer worker. And the mystery implicit in the words of Jesus found only in Paul's quotation is that "it is more blessed to give than to receive" (Acts 20:35). In giving ministry free of charge we receive the Giver who impoverishes himself for our enrichment (2 Cor 8:9).

See also CALLING; FINANCIAL SUPPORT; MINISTRY; MISSIONS; MOBILITY; WORK.

References and Resources

R. Allen, *The Case for the Voluntary Clergy* (London: Eyre & Spottiswoode, 1930); R. Allen, *Missionary Methods: St. Paul's or Ours?* (Grand Rapids: Eerdmans, 1962); P. W. Barnett, "Tentmaking," *Dictionary of Paul and His Letters,* ed. G. F. Hawthorne, R. P. Martin and D. G. Reid (Downers Grove, Ill.: InterVarsity Press, 1993) 925-27; W. Carey, *An Inquiry into the Obligations of Christians to Use Means for the Conversion of the Heathens* (1792; reprint, London: Carey Kingsgate Press, 1961); J. Elliott, *Our Pastor Has an Outside Job* (Valley Forge, Penn.: Judson, 1980); J. M. Everts, "Financial Support," *Dictionary of Paul and His Letters,* ed. G. F. Hawthorne, R. P. Martin and D. G. Reid (Downers Grove, Ill.: InterVarsity Press, 1993) 295-300; G. D. Fee, *The First Epistle to the Corinthians,* New International Commentary of the New Testament (Grand Rapids: Eerdmans, 1987); M. Gibbs and R. T. Morton, *God's Frozen People* (London: Fontana Books, 1964); R. F. Hock, "Paul's Tentmaking and the Problem of His Social Class," *Journal of Biblical Literature* 97 (1978) 555-64; S. C. Neill and H. Weber, *The Layman in Christian History* (London: SCM, 1963); R. P. Stevens, *Liberating the Laity* (Downers Grove, Ill.: InterVarsity Press, 1985); C. J. Wilson, *Today's Tentmakers* (Wheaton, Ill.: Tyndale, 1979).

R. Paul Stevens

THEATER, LIVE

When the community gathers to witness words becoming flesh, when stories get up on-stage and live and move and be, something is happening that has a lot to do with the incarnational essence of the Christian faith. So it is a sad irony that for many centuries Christians have ignored, suspected and even opposed theatrical performance.

The Power of Theater

To this day I retain powerful sensory impressions of the first professional play I ever experienced some twenty-five years ago: an adaptation of *Great Expectations.* I had seen my share of television,* movies* and amateur plays, but nothing had prepared me for the transporting immediacy of the professional theater. A bookworm, I had no idea of the power of the senses to make a story live.

A man lights a pipe on-stage, and the blue-gray smoke unfolds and undulates upward through the stage lights, not a photograph* but a real, unhurried, three-dimensional dance, expanding and dispersing through the space until, most astonishingly and unmovielike of all, that sweet rich tobacco smell reaches my nostrils in the fourteenth row, aisle seat, house right. Six dark men in Victorian crepe brush by me, bearing an ornate coffin through the audience and onto the stage. I see them shake with the palpable weight of that terrible, heavy box, and I too feel the weight of its contents:

a human body, death.*

Two years later Christ brought the whole world alive to me in a way that was suddenly abundant with feeling, love, passion, sense. And in some ways I look back to that first encounter with the heightened reality of the theatrical world as a foretaste of the new life I was soon to experience in Christ.

The Contested Dignity of Theater

It is the very power of theater, and in particular its sensual power, that has led some Christians to be suspicious. This was strongly so in the first few centuries after Christ, though at that time theater was closely involved with pagan idolatry (and on occasion) immortality. But when a false dualism splits the spiritual from the physical and distrusts the body, when we forget that Scripture uses "the flesh" to refer not to our sensual selves but rather to our antispiritual tendencies, when a word-centered religion forgets that the Word became flesh and dwelt among us, then passion, feeling and the senses become suspect.

To the biblical Christian, however, our bodies* bear the image and likeness of our Maker, and they are to be celebrated and used to God's glory. The creation itself is God-made and should delight us as much as it did our Creator, who kept on saying, "Look at that! Isn't it great!" at the end of each day's creating. And so theater, that most physical, sensual, immediate and incarnational of arts, is to some Christians the most thrillingly divine of them all.

The theater artist is fascinated by the particularities of human life, with people and the dynamic of their relationships, with the human heart and the way it reveals itself in choices and action. By shaping this fascination into a story on stage, the artist performs a priestly act of oblation—a sanctifying act of thanksgiving, an offering up to God (Capon, p. 79).

Theater is an ultimately collaborative art form, welcoming every kind of artist to work together to make something greater. The storyteller, the composer, the visual artist, the dancer and the carpenter work together in an intentional community with a mission* of service to an audience—a simulacrum of any kind of community,* of the church,* of the body of Christ. The actor dare not say to the stage manager, "I don't need you." And unless the electrician runs the dimmer up on cue, who will see the truths conceived in the heart of the director and expressed in the bodies of the players?

When our God took on flesh and became a human being, it was as One who mostly told stories. And in this, theater artists have much in common with Jesus—because the art of theater is above all else the art of storytelling* elaborated.

In the twentieth century, literary fiction has shifted its emphasis away from plot toward point of view, narrative voice and other things. But that is one thing its crowd-pleasing cousin can never do: without story, what happens on a stage becomes something other than drama. It may be dance, it may be music,* it may be poetry or circus, but it is not a play. Like the stories of Christ or the prophet Nathan (2 Sam 12), which got inside people and revealed their hearts, stage stories too have a way of getting past rational defenses and straight to the listener's core. Hamlet knew it. When he needed to test his stepfather's soul, he hired a band of players to put on a show: "The play's the thing / Wherein I'll catch the conscience of the king."

The Paradoxical Service of Acting

In our world there has grown up a terrible misconception about the nature of the actor's task. We think it is all about ego, about putting the actor forward, about showing off, about wanting to be center stage. Is it not interesting how this mistrust of acting has crept into our language? We are paying no compliment when we say people are "making a spectacle of themselves," "feeding you a line," "doing their same old routine," "putting on an act," "acting up," "showing off," "making a scene," "playing a role" and so on. But many Christian actors find something profoundly spiritual in the discipline of setting their own persona aside, submitting themselves to the task of so identifying with another human soul* that they can take on that person's way of speaking, moving, feeling, thinking and wanting. Like John the Baptist they must diminish so that the other may be manifested.

Far more apt is the comparison to Christ himself, whom Paul describes in Philippians as One who, having the form and nature of God, did not consider equality with God a thing to be held on to, but emptied himself, taking on the character of a servant, the physicality of a human being. It is a poor actor indeed who simply pretends to be another character: who settles for seeming to be, rather than identifying with and imaginatively becoming that character. The actor builds this new person out of a miraculous confluence of two beings: the character who already exists in the script, created by the playwright and the actor's own self—feelings, desires, history, body and soul. The resulting character is neither fully fictional nor fully real, but mysteriously both fictional and real. The actor aspires to think the thoughts of the character while in the scene, not pretending to know more about the play than the character would in the moment: even so, the actor never actually "becomes the character"; always the actor remains himself, living out an expression of some aspect of his or her own self within different circumstances.

How reminiscent this is of Christ, fully man and yet still God. Not that actors do exactly what Jesus did in his incarnation: only that, in emptying themselves and taking the character of another, they taste at least a little of the divine humility of our Lord. And what a concrete lesson this is in our common humanity: knowing that, in different circumstances and with different choices, I could be a disciple, a Nazi, a hooker, a sage or an accountant. If you are going to embody someone, you cannot hold yourself above that someone or at arm's length: you have to climb into that body, taste the food, imagine the childhood, fear what he or she fears and want what he or she wants. It is a profoundly spiritual act, an act of identification, an act of love.*

Understanding Christian Theater

In recent decades there has been a tremendous explosion among Christians of interest in theater. When in the 1960s evangelical Christians became less separationist and began to experience the culture around them, that evangelical subculture began to realize that such a powerful medium might just as well be used for the kingdom of God as against it.

In recent years, as Christian theater artists grew in their craft and became more sophisticated in their understanding of it, many have turned from this utilitarian approach to a more incarnational, storytelling aesthetic, believing that the theater speaks most powerfully and is most transcendent when it is not harnessed to a pragmatic purpose. The Christian playwright who in her early career sets out to teach people things by using the stage eventually comes to the conclusion that her focus needs to be on telling a tale, not manifesting a moral. In the process of creating that story, the creator's image will be seen. In writing a play from the heart, the playwright's heart will be made known by the choices she makes, by the choices her characters make and by the consequences they experience. If that heart is filled with God's Spirit, then the play will be similarly filled even when the subject material is not overtly "Christian."

Why Go to the Theater?

We go to the theater to have experiences that are not our own, to be made larger. We identify with characters we might never otherwise meet; we see worlds we will never live in. In a highly concentrated, artistically rendered universe, characters strive and make choices and live out consequences before our eyes in the space of a couple hours, and sometimes that experience takes us outside ourselves so profoundly that we leave the theater changed: knocked off our "onotogical treadmill," we are suddenly open to new ways of seeing the world. And, possibly, we find ourselves in "a position where we may more easily contact God, or be contacted by him" (Baron, p. 34).

Some theater artists are quite intentional about this. By creating works that challenge our complacent and conventional assumptions, while refusing to "explain themselves away" by offering interpretation, they force us to do our own wrestling with fundamental assumptions. This can be a prophetic act in the Old Testament tradition. "If what art does is to reorient and repattern perception, creating the conditions for a new epistemology, then what the prophetic does is similar" (Fetcho, p. 19).

Humans learn, change and grow mostly through what they experience. In theater we experience vicariously a great deal that our own lives will never bring about. With the Holy Spirit working in us as we come to terms with these experiences, the theater affords an extraordinary opportunity to grow and become more human, to become wiser and more com-passionate as we are transformed by our experiences—whether actual or vicarious.

See also ART; CULTURE; LEISURE; PLAY; STORYTELLING.

References and Resources

G. Baron, "A Crisis Encounter: Can Art Make It Happen?" *Christianity Today* 6, no. 11 (June 6, 1980) 34-35; R. F. Capon, *An Offering of Uncles: The Priesthood of Adam and the Shape of the World* (New York: Harper & Row, 1967); D. Fetcho, "Art, Action, and Revival," *Radix* 17, no. 1 (Summer 1985) 16-23, 31.

—Ron Reed

TIME

The majority of people in Western societies complain about the pressure of time and the pace of life. About a third feel that they are too busy all the time, and another third too busy some of the time. This is particularly true of those in leadership positions, in business and the professions,* self-employed people, single parents and working women, especially those belonging to an ethnic minority. This even affects children, most of all in middle-class families. On the whole Christians, especially leaders, feel pressured and harried. They are often unable to accomplish all the significant things they would like to do and just as often do not have time to do these thoroughly. Overall most people find it difficult to keep up with what is going on, to maintain peace in the midst of activity, even to take pleasure in the work* they are doing.

As a result, we often feel frustration at having too much to do, guilt at not giving enough time to God or family* and anxiety* that we might not be successful in fulfilling all our goals. This sometimes leads to a high level of nervous tension, physical fatigue and emotional burnout. Learning how to handle schedules and priorities better through time-management strategies is helpful up to a point, but it is only a matter of time before the pressure of busyness and the pace of life reassert themselves. Indeed, part of the problem is our belief that busyness is a virtue. The reason for this is not difficult to find. Busyness reinforces our conviction that we are important, that we are achieving something and that we are really committed to the Lord's work. But this is an error. Both busyness and laziness—the first for doing too much, the second through doing too little—prevent us from giving our full attention and energy to doing what God wants us to do, no more and no less. In fact, busyness has traditionally been viewed as one of the forms that sloth—one of "seven deadly sins"—takes.

Biblical Principles for Time Use

This traditional suspicion of busyness has its roots in the biblical approach to time. Too often this is overlooked, both in Christian time-management discussions and by the countercultural Christian movement.

First, we should look at time as *a divine gift*. Its daily, weekly, seasonal and annual rhythms all stem from God (Gen 1:3—2:3; Lev 23; Ps 74:16) and reflect God's creative or historical activity. Time is not a human invention and is not under human control. Jesus condemns those who, like the rich fool, proudly think otherwise (Lk 12:16-20). Too often we act as if time were a commodity at our disposal rather than a daily present from God. Time is not a human resource for us to exploit but a precious offer to be handled carefully, wisely and appreciatively. Only God knows what the future contains, and frequently it is very different from what we plan (Prov 19:21).

The high value we place on busyness is actually a sign of how little we understand this. Though our desire may be to do God's will rather than satisfy our own

wants, our view of time is usually identical with that held by those around us: it is a commodity. Our language betrays us here: we talk about "spending," "investing," "buying" and "saving" time, words that are all drawn from the world of commerce. Instead of treasuring time as a gift from our Creator—a daily present to be opened with delight and treated as special—we treat it as a resource from which we should extract the maximum amount as fast as possible. This is similar to the way, until recently, we have tended to treat the environment, exploiting it for all it is worth and not worrying too much about the long-term consequences. Instead of seeing time as sufficient for whatever is important, we treat it as a scarce resource to be parceled out in small amounts, constantly regretting the fact that there is too little of it and that it passes too quickly. As a divine gift, time should be used playfully as well as energetically, big-heartedly and generously as well as carefully and thoughtfully, in people-oriented as well as task-oriented ways, with an eye to quality more than quantity and with a sense of wonder and adventure.

Second, according to the Bible *our time is limited*, in most cases to around seventy or eighty years (Ps 90:10). It is mainly lower mortality rates for children and more successful means of treating adult diseases that have changed since earlier periods, not the life expectancy of a healthy person. Even so our days seem too short, full and stressful, and we need discernment in order to handle responsibly the time God gives us. Our temptation is always to mortgage our time in advance in the same way we do with our unearned income. Consider the way we cram appointments into the weeks and sometimes months ahead and fill up our calendars and annual planners so far ahead. Despite our repeated prayers for God's guidance, we often behave like those referred to by the apostle James who say, "Today or tomorrow we will go to this or that city, spend a year there, carry on business and make money" (Jas 4:13). Yet as James told them, "You do not even know what will happen tomorrow.... Instead, you ought to say, 'If it is the Lord's will, we will live and do this or that.' As it is, you boast and brag. All such boasting is evil" (Jas 4:14-16).

The biblical injunction to number our days so that we use time responsibly is not identical with the kind of planning of time that we engage in. That planning, especially if "life planning" is involved, generally assumes two things over which we have no control: that our life is going to continue for a considerable time and that we have some control over the course it will take. Experience should teach us the error in assuming these. People's lives are often cut short, and few people can predict accurately what they will be doing five or ten years ahead, and the Bible warns us against operating this way. In fact, becoming too busy or anxious is a way of ignoring the temporary nature of this life. This is not to say that all planning* is wrong, but we should be more tentative about it and regard it as conditional, as did Paul in making his medium- and long-term plans (1 Cor 16:5-9). While he had desires and preferences, there is a modesty and flexibility to his approach. We should also be aware that the Bible's emphasis on recognizing the finite time at our disposal sits uneasily with our general tendency to ignore the passing of time, to work to keep ourselves youthful or to artificially extend the length of our lives. Instead we should preserve a sharp sense of our mortality and recognize that at any point God could remove us from the scene.

Third, according to the Bible, time can be measured but should be regarded as a *quality as well as a quantity.* We tend to use our watches* and clocks to divide time into the smallest mathematical units and then plan our schedule around these. Often we will do this down to the minute—in sports* down to the second. The Bible also speaks of *watches,* though like the watches on a ship these were several hours long. There is no Old Testament word for *hours,* only a Greek word later, and nothing corresponding to our *minutes.* Indeed, most time references in the Bible are fairly general. It is the event or experience someone is encountering that determines how long they will give to it, not a calculation of how much time is available for such things. This is the view of time expressed in Ecclesiastes, which says: "There is a time for everything, and everything on earth has its special season" (Eccles 3:1 NCV). This statement is followed by a list of common events and experiences, such as birth* and death,* laughter* and tears, mourning and dancing, embracing and withdrawing, searching and giving up, speaking* and keeping silence, going to war and making peace. Each of these should be given its appropriate timing and length of time, whether or not strictly speaking we have time for it when it occurs.

This is not to say that we should never organize our activities according to precise time measurements. Sometimes this is appropriate or necessary, especially when we are dependent on broader social schedules, when we are traveling* or when other people depend on our being somewhere at a precise time. But even then we should recognize that things may take longer than we had planned, either because of circumstances beyond our control or because there is a need for it. This is why as far as possible we should build a certain "elasticity" into our time. But it is also important to remember that the most important things we do each day, week and year can only rarely be scheduled specifically or may be strait-jacketed if we do. This is especially true of time with spouses and children (*see* Family Values), conversations* with friends, dealing with crises and suffering or getting our bearings from God for the future (*see* Vocational Guidance). Generally we approach such things by looking at how much time we have and working out what we can fit into it. Too often we allow what is important to be preempted by allegedly more pressing or immediate demands.

Fourth, *a balance should be struck* between different aspects of daily life. For example, there is a time to work and a time to rest* (Jn 9:4), a time to travel and a time to stay in one place (Deut 2:14), a time to meet with fellow believers and a time to share with those in need (Acts 20:7; Jas 2:15-17). Sleep* in particular is a nightly gift from God that we should fully enjoy, learning to entrust to God things we have not had time to do. If we steal time at either end of the day from the sleep we need in order to get more done, we are rejecting this loving provision of God, seeking to justify ourselves by our work rather than by our faith in God's ability to look after things and placing ourselves in the position of losing God's blessing* on our activities anyway (Ps 127:1-2). This does not mean that at no time is it appropriate for us to labor strenuously and even work into the night (Acts 20:31), but this should not become a permanent state of affairs. In particular we are to enjoy the benefits of having a regular sabbath* time when we are free from our usual responsibilities (Ex 20:8-11; 23:12-13). We should do this even when life gets busiest (Ex 34:21). Under the new covenant instituted by Christ we are no longer obliged to keep the Jewish sabbath as it is prescribed in the Old Testament (Rom 14:5-6; Col 2:16-17), but Jesus' movement between activity and withdrawal shows us the importance of regular rest from our labors.

Here is a prophetic word for all those who are too preoccupied with busyness and achievement. It is symptomatic that insomnia is the number-one medical problem today (*see* Dreaming; Sleeping). Though at times we may have to "burn the candle at both ends," this should never become habitual and should always be compensated for by more time for sleeping or recreation* afterward to make up what has been lost. As far as a weekly rest day is concerned, though we are not obliged to take one day a week as a sabbath, such is the general pace and regulation of life throughout the week that taking a weekly day of rest when possible becomes a virtual necessity. When, for whatever reason, this cannot be done, resting over a whole weekend every few weeks is an alternative. At such times we do not need to wear a watch or let the clock determine what we do. It is also good to celebrate special times in the year, whether traditional in the wider society, special to believers (for the Old Testament, compare Lev 23) or expressive of the life of our family, friendships or institution in which we work.

Fifth, we should live in the awareness that there are *special times* when we are called upon to set aside everything else either to receive something from God or to do something for God. Discerning when, where and how this is happening involves knowing the difference between what is really important and what is only seemingly urgent (Lk 10:38-42), between the clear call of God that must be obeyed and the unexpected opportunity that need not be taken up (2 Cor 2:12-13) and between our ordinary human plans and God's extraordinary purposes (Prov 19:21). Sometimes we find ourselves in an emergency time when we have to sit loose to our usual routines (1 Cor 7:29-30), knowing, however, that God will both provide for material (Mt

6:25-34) and spiritual (Is 55:10-11) needs.* We should also live in the conviction that the day of the Lord's coming is nearer than before (Rom 13:12) and will not be delayed forever (Rev 22:12). Though no one knows exactly when this will take place (Mk 13:32) and sometimes it might seem like a long time coming, God does not calculate time as we do (2 Pet 3:8). In the meantime, though sometimes God seems to act slowly, at other times God will act quickly to save, protect or honor us. Our task is simply to be prepared (Mt 24:36-51), resting in confidence that whatever happens, our whole life is in God's hands (Ps 31:15).

In general, then, we should follow Paul's advice and seek to use time wisely and responsibly, availing ourselves of whatever opportunities come our way to do good in the midst of predominantly evil times. Our motto should be: "Do not be foolish but learn what the Lord wants you to do" (Eph 5:15-17 NCV). This requires constant discernment and giving priority to constructive rather than wasteful activities. Among our closest circle of Christians, we should all encourage one another regularly to do this (Heb 3:13). Using our time wisely and responsibly does not mean developing a busy lifestyle that fills every moment with activities or seizes every possibility that comes our way. This is a misunderstanding of what is said in Ephesians 5:16, which only in the mid-twentieth century was translated as "making the most of every opportunity." In approaching time discerningly, we should reckon, as Paul did, with constant frustrations and delays in fulfilling our plans (Acts 13:49-51; 2 Cor 1:23—2:1), for this is simply a fact of life and of God's providence (1 Cor 16:7).

Conclusions

The subtitle of a popular time-management seminar is How to Get Twenty-Eight Hours out of Every Twenty-Four! This gets it completely wrong: the whole point is that for what God wants us to do, twenty-four hours is quite enough. Otherwise we are complaining that God is stingy and does not know the realities of life. There are other problems with the time-management approach. It tends to treat our difficulties with time as primarily individual and technical. If we can find the right strategies for dealing with it and get our personal lives in order, everything will be all right. But the pressure of time and pace of life today are also huge social and cultural problems, affecting everyone and every part of life. They stem from our deep-seated individualism* and belief that everything can be resolved by knowing the right techniques or having the latest technology* (such as laptop computer appointment books). In fact, only if we work at the problem of time together and help each other with our temptations to busyness, only if we develop a less harried approach to time in our personal lives and in our congregations, will we make much headway. This means reducing our hyperactive, program-oriented and committee-ridden church life in favor of more organic ways of operating and more shared leadership patterns.

The overall problem of most Christian time-management approaches is that they operate too much within a secular understanding. This is why, like everyone else, they tend to speak of time as a commodity (albeit a divine one), as an infinite resource rather than one that is daily renewable and as (disproportionately) a quantity to be filled or portioned out rather than also as a process or dimension of significant activities. Unless our organizing and prioritizing of time are accompanied by a paradigm shift in our attitude to and use of it, we are not getting to the root of the problem. When a paradigm shift does take place, all our questions about what we should be doing start to look different, for we find ourselves questioning some of our fundamental assumptions about what we should be doing and how we should be doing it. It is out of this that more creative and relevant, less busy and hectic, forms of lifestyle and ministry, even of congregational life, will begin to develop.

See also AGING; DRIVENNESS; LEISURE; PLANNING; SABBATH; WAITING; WATCH; WORK.

References and Resources
R. Banks, *The Tyranny of Time* (Downers Grove, Ill.: InterVarsity Press, 1983); L. Burns, *Busy Bodies: Why Our Time-Obsessed Society Keeps Us Running in Place* (New York: Norton, 1993); E. T. Hall, *The Silent Language* (New York: Doubleday, 1959); R. Keyes, *Timelock: How Life Got So Hectic and What You Can Do About It* (New York: Ballantine, 1991); S. B. Leas, *Time Management: A Working Guide for Church Leaders* (Nashville: Abingdon, 1978); G. G. Luce, *Body Time: The Natural Rhythms of the Body* (St. Albans, U.K.: Paladin, 1977); W. T. McConnell, *The Gift of Time* (Downers Grove, Ill.: InterVarsity Press, 1983); M. O'Malley, *Keeping Watch: A History of American Time* (New York: Penguin, 1990); J. Rifkin, *Time Wars: The Prime Conflict in Human History* (New York: Henry Holt, 1987); W. Rybczynski, *Waiting for the Weekend* (New York: Viking, 1991); J. B. Schor, *The Overworked American: The Unexpected Decline of Leisure* (San Francisco: Harper, 1991); D. Williams, ed., *Time to Live: Practical Ideas on Time Planning for Busy Christians* (London: SPCK, 1987).

Robert Banks

TRADES

At thirty-seven years of age, with two university degrees and a well-established professional career,* I became a tradesman and apprenticed to a carpenter in the home renovation business. Most of my ministerial colleagues thought I had temporarily lost my moorings. But I had several good reasons. My wife and I were called to plant a new church, and without a salary being volunteered, we needed to support ourselves financially (*see* Financial Support; Tentmaking). Further, I liked to work with my hands and have a natural talent* for making things out of wood. But finally I was convinced that I needed to see the work world of the ordinary Christian "from the bottom up." In the modern Western world professionals* are at the apex of the occupational pyramid, business and craftspersons* a notch down, with tradespeople and common laborers near the bottom. This is the case not only in so-called secular society but in the church,* where leadership positions on boards are normally filled by professionals and executives. It has not always been so and certainly was not so in the Bible. But every day, as I hammered and sawed and ate my lunch with drywall tapers and electricians, sharing their worlds and their loves, I was being educated in what could be called a blue-collar or denim-jeans spirituality.

Trades, as distinguished from professions, are occupations that employ primarily manual skills learned mainly in the context of apprenticeship on the job and result in making things, normally for pay. In contrast, *crafts*—personal skills employed in an artistic and aesthetic manner—are ways of making things that are intrinsically beautiful whether or not they are useful or sold. A craft may be undertaken as a hobby* for the sheer pleasure of enjoying oneself and God's creation or as a remunerated occupation, such as the work of a silversmith or perfumer. A trade may involve craftsmanship* but not necessarily so, as in the case of the electrician.

Trades in the Bible and Beyond
In contrast to the hierarchy of occupations in the modern world, the Bible

witnesses to a wide variety of ways of working without rating them on a scale of public importance or divine approval. For example, Deuteronomy prescribes that the king must not enrich himself through his position (Deut 17:16) and must "not consider himself better than his brothers" (Deut 17:20). In contrast to the view today that charismatic pastors and religious leaders are likely to be the most Spirit-filled persons, the only Old Testament saint who is specifically said to be "filled . . . with the Spirit of God" is a craftsman, Bezalel (Ex 31:3). The rich diversity of occupations named in Scripture, more than two hundred in all, has been researched by Walter Duckat in *Beggar to King*. The entries under *C* alone are indicative of the significance given by the Bible to trades and crafts: calker, camel driver, candymaker, captain, caravan chief, carpenter, carpetmaker, cattleman, census taker, charioteer, cheese maker, choirmaster, chorister, circumciser, clothier, cook, coppersmith, counselor, counterfeiter (not an approved occupation!), cupbearer, custodian and customs clerk.

Duckat notes that the life of the Hebrews in the Bible was similar to a medieval village, being largely agricultural and fairly self-sufficient. Farming* and shepherding were the fundamental occupations for men and homemaking* for women, something which in ancient times included crafts such as weaving. But specialists emerged in due course and guilds of craftspeople, merchants and even guilds of prophets were formed for common economic and cultural benefits (Duckat, p. xv). This was the beginning of the modern trade unions.* In biblical times people followed in the footsteps of their father or mother with little regard to *job satisfaction,* that relatively modern obsession.

By the time of Jesus and the birth of the church, there was a stunning contrast

between the Greek view of trades and the Jewish. In the Jewish world it was a duty to have a trade. So Jesus was a carpenter and Paul a tentmaker. The Talmud said, "He who does not teach his son a trade is as if he teaches him robbery" (*Tosepta Qiddušin* 1:11). Duckat notes, "The Hebrews were virtually the only ancient people who preponderantly viewed work as dignifying rather than demeaning" (p. xxi). In contrast, the Greek world into which the church was also born held laboring in contempt. The work of tradespeople was for slaves. Citizens should occupy themselves with contemplation and politics. The tension between these two views is with us to this day and is manifested in the hierarchical arrangement of "valuable work" within the Western Christian mind, even though this was temporarily corrected by Luther (Hardy). The professional minister and missionary are on the top, those in people-helping professions next, then business and then, near the bottom, trades. Someone really serious about serving God leaves the trade world and "goes into the ministry" rather than the reverse.

Trades as a Reflection of Society

With industrialization the world recovered the dignity of trades once again with the worker as the engine of economic development. Karl Marx took this a step further and made manual work, including the trades, as the primary means of finding the meaning in life, without, of course, any reference to a supreme being. This lopsided view of work made an idol rather than a curse of work. It failed to recover work as part of one's calling,* viewing it instead as the whole of one's calling. But with passing from the industrial society to the information society, trades have slipped once again, giving way to the omnipotent knowledge worker dealing everyday in computer* bytes rather than two-by-fours and pneumatic nailers. Routine manual work on assembly lines is being replaced by robots, and most of the trades are desperately trying to project an image of expertise as almost everything from rug cleaning to garbage collection gets "professionalized."

Duckat notes that "how work is viewed in any society casts important light on the prevailing thinking, social structure, and values of that people" (p. xx). The thought can be extended. What kind of work is praised casts a revealing light on the mindset of the church and what it really values. Further, it shows what we think of God and whether we are a people who resemble their God.

The gods of antiquity, and especially those of the Greeks, spent their time in debauchery or pleasures. The Hindu gods occupied themselves with everlasting repose. But the God of the Bible is a worker, a craftsperson, a tradesperson— the maker of things and people. Robert Banks's rich discussion of the metaphors of God as worker shows that almost every human activity imaginable that is for the common good is something God does. So the Talmud credits God with the origination of all trades (*Midrash on Genesis* 24:7).

How can we demean trades and worship God at the same time? Does our attitude to work* constitute a more direct way of "speaking rightly of God" (which is the heart of true theology; see Job 42:7) than our written theological tomes? If hymnology is sung theology (*see* Music, Christian), is work acted theology? So what can be done to recover the dignity of trades?

Recovering the Dignity of Trades

First, the church can become truly countercultural in treating every member of the body with equal dignity, refusing to estimate the value of people by degrees, income and social approval. This is part of empowering the whole people of God. Why do we interview visiting missionaries on Sunday and not tradespeople to find out how their faith makes a difference to everyday life? The relative absence of blue-collar workers in many churches is a simple reflection that they do not feel welcome or prized. But on a deeper level it is an indication that we are something less than the new humanity (Eph 2:15) characterized by a broken wall between formerly separated people. If people of the same "kind" gather together as they would anyway, Christian or not, Christ is not confessed. There is no new creation in evidence.

Second, we can help tradespeople revision their daily work as ministry. Tradespeople need to receive affirmation in ways other than good pay for their sometimes monotonous work. They are indispensable to the healthy functioning of society. A city* can manage without a mayor, at least for a while, but not without its trash collectors. As with all other forms of human work, tradespeople serve God (and therefore are "ministers") by meeting a genuine human need, by making God's world work, by providing for themselves and their families with some to give to others and by doing what they do for Jesus (Eph 6:5-9). Through working as a carpenter for five years, I discovered that tradespeople have many advantages. At the end of the day they can usually see what they have done and say to themselves, in unison with their Creator, "It is good" (Gen 1:31).

Third, we can explore the contemplative dimensions of being a tradesperson. I quickly discovered that at the end of a strenuous day I slept* well. Manual work is healthy and is less likely to kill a person than a stressful profession: "The sleep of a laborer is sweet" (Eccles 5:12). But there is more. While anyone doing business today must wrestle with the principalities and powers,* manual work possibly allows one to reflect and pray more "on the job" than in other careers, certainly so when the tools are laid down. As Paul knew so well, working "night and day" as a tentmaker-cum-apostle—visiting people, teaching in a public hall, meeting with churches and sharing the gospel—was invigorating and often challenging. In contrast, most professionals are spent forces when they finally close the office door and often take work home with them, to the neglect of their families, before they attempt a fitful sleep.

A negative note on this subject was sounded by Ben Sira (Ecclesiasticus) in the second century B.C. "Conversation with animals and the noise of the hammer and the anvil are not conducive to wisdom" (Sir 38:24-33), but this seems to be a criticism against work that consumed time that might be spent in the study of Torah. Indeed, most trades, with the exception of certain high-risk construction workers, allow for greater "leisure" on the job to reflect. An example would be the poems and songs written by David while a shepherd.

Finally, the life of a tradesperson is shot through with intimations of eternity and invitations to develop a denim-jean spirituality: forming things by hand, making the connection between bodily activity and mental creativity, creating something of benefit for others, working in teams, learning and teaching in an apprentice relationship life on life, talking with fellow workers about the stuff of everyday life (sports, food, family, play). Trades are like chores*; they are not just opportunities to practice spiritual disciplines,* but because of their somewhat tiresome nature and service role, they invite us Godward. Usually there is more laughter* and play

on a construction site than in a pastor's study. There might even be more prayer.*

See also CRAFTSMANSHIP; HOBBIES AND CRAFTS; PROFESSIONS/PROFESSIONALISM; UNIONS; WORK.

References and Resources

R. Banks, *God the Worker: Journeys into the Mind, Heart and Imagination of God* (Valley Forge, Penn.: Judson, 1994); R. Banks, *Redeeming the Routine: Bringing Theology to Life* (Wheaton: Victor Books, 1993); R. F. Capon, *An Offering of Uncles: The Priesthood of Adam and the Shape of the World* (New York: Crossroad, 1982); W. Duckat, *Beggar to King: All the Occupations of Biblical Times* (Garden City, N.Y.: Doubleday, 1968); L. Hardy, *The Fabric of This World* (Grand Rapids: Eerdmans, 1990); R. Hoppock, *Occupational Information: Where to Get It and How to Use It* (New York: McGraw-Hill, 1967); Jacob Neusner, trans., "Qiddushim," in *The Tosefta,* vol. 3 (New York: KTAV, 1979); Jacob Neusner, trans., *Genesis Rabbah, the Judaic Commentary to the Book of Genesis: A New American Translation,* vol. 1 (Atlanta: Scholars Press, 1985).

R. Paul Stevens

TRAVELING

Throughout history human beings have moved by walking* and by riding on donkeys, camels or horses. People have traveled on ships, steam engines, trains, buses, electric railways, streetcars, automobiles,* airplanes, rockets and space capsules. Now we can travel in virtual reality.* We can step into a simulator in a hotel in an exotic Pacific island and, without moving an inch, "experience the whole island" by "traveling" in an electronic helicopter. We can also surf on the information superhighway,* "traveling" around the globe looking for new relationships, experiences and above all information. What does it all mean? What are its effects? How does traveling relate to the purpose of God? In what follows we are focusing on forms of travel rather than general mobility.

Kinds of Travelers

Emigrants. The first travelers, Adam and Eve, were emigrants. They were thrust out of the Garden of Eden to fill and take care of the earth. This awesome vocation was to have been undertaken as an unspoiled calling.* But now, because of their revolt, it was forced upon them as a judgment. Yet there was grace in the judgment: the angel guarded the way back to the tree of life (Gen 3:24), thus preventing their perpetuating their fallen state (and the fallen world they were crafting) forever. The way forward takes them through history, through the cross and resurrection of Christ, until they once again eat of the tree of life (Rev 22:19). Adam and Eve started again, which is exactly what immigrants* throughout history have done.

This is travel for renewal. Seeking political and religious freedom and the opportunity to make a good life for themselves, immigrants leave one place and journey to another, often enduring great hardships both in traveling and in pioneering. In this way my grandfather traveled in 1903 from England to Toronto with six children and twenty dollars to start a new life as a baker. It was not long before he had his own business—Stevens Bread and Cakes—which he could never have done in England.

Fugitives. But not all who leave do so willingly. Some people travel as fugitives escaping from justice or injustice and come to a new place as refugees cast upon the mercy and goodwill of those who already live there. Cain was the first fugitive, the prototype of all who *must* travel but have nowhere specific to go (Gen 4:12-14), just anywhere except where they are. Fugitives travel for survival. Wanderers do not know where they are going, but they know they cannot stay where they are. They are not traveling *to* but *from.*

Nomads. These travel for sustenance and profit. Throughout history and even today nomadic clans and people groups move from place to place in search of better pasture or warmer places to winter. Gypsies make this a way of life, as do people in military service and pastors who work in denominational systems that routinely move their leaders before bonding can ever take place. In biblical times four special kinds of travelers were found: messengers (2 Sam 2:5), merchants (1 Kings 5:11; Ezek 27:17), government officials (2 Sam 10:2) and people on journeys for religious purposes (Lk 2:41-50; Dorsey, p. 891). The modern nomads are traveling salespeople, people in some of the arts,* and high-tech engineers who move from place to place, often at the will of their corporation. This is entrepreneurial travel. But such mobility* has its downside on families (for the downside, *see* Mobility). Some people upon retirement* sell their home and purchase a recreational vehicle to see the country, thereby using their automobile as their home and becoming upper- and middle-class nomads.

Explorers. One form of nomadic travel is for discovery. Now common in the West is the quest to find oneself by going on safari. As far back as the Middle Ages young knights made a grand tour, much as young people do today, as a way of achieving self-definition through testing. Accompanied by a tutor and keeping a diary, such young knights went to school in the world and in the process discovered who they were themselves. Today the journey to Europe with nothing but a backpack* is seen as the ideal "finishing school" for young adults emerging into the work world.

Tourists. The tourist, in contrast, travels for pleasure*: to see new things, meet new people, experience new foods and different cultures,* always with the intent of returning home.* While the rich and privileged have always been able to do this, the opportunity is now available to millions of middle-class people. The invention of the DC3 plane reduced per-mile passenger costs, radically opening up air travel (and long-distance travel) to almost everyone in the Western world. Guided tours, some of them directed to the young or economy-minded traveler (traveling and living in a huge refur-bished army vehicle), open up the world to the average person in the Western world, though not to the average person in the developing world. It is expected that by the turn of the twenty-first cen-tury $2.75 trillion will be spent by travel-ers taking at least one trip a year.

Touring is a privilege of the "haves" in this world. But tourism as a service indus-try has become a major industry, not only in rich Western countries such as Canada but in developing countries where tour-ism is one of the few remaining ways of gaining hard currency. Few people in such countries get to see the sights the tourists do—for example, wild animals in their natural habitat. It is sometimes ar-gued that tourist dollars provide these countries with the wherewithal to con-serve their natural resources, but the evidence seems to be on the other side. Tragically, entrepre-neurial tourism has, by and large, had a devastating effect on the natural environment and indigenous cultures. Worse still is the exploitation of the people, the case of young prostitutes in Thailand being one of the most tragic examples. At the sight of a tourist car Maasi herdsmen robed in flaming red clothes run from the cattle they are herd-ing to the tourists in order to be photo-graphed* for money. Most of the tourist money leaves the Third World. Few places on earth are now protected from the inquiring eyes and disposable cam-eras of tourists. But it is in the very nature of touring to want to go where there are few other tourists!

Pilgrim. If touring is a relatively mod-ern invention, more common through-out history is the *pilgrim,* the traveler who has a religious site as a destination (whether Canterbury, Jerusalem or Mecca). Pilgrims travel for spiritual en-richment to discover the roots of their faith. Such pilgrimages to Jerusalem three times a year in Old Testament times were fundamental to the rhythms of faith, as attested by the psalms of pil-grimage (Ps 120—134). These pilgrim-ages were communal and festive, accompanied by good food and just plain fun (Deut 24:24-26). Such travel was focused not primarily on the stimu-lation of going to new places but on going to places rich in spiritual tradition in order to go deeper with God and one another. In contrast to the tourist, who travels from the center of his or her world to an "other," the pilgrim journeys to the center. This distinction may be overstated, however, since tourism has become in many ways the functional equivalent of the pilgrimage—to the tourist attractions that are especially ad-mired and, in the case of the "serious" tourist, to find one's own authentic cen-ter by participating vicariously in other lifestyles and cultures (Cohen, pp. 49, 55).

Missionary. Finally there is the mis-sionary—a person away from home for Jesus, someone who crosses a cultural frontier for ministry. While all too often mission has been conceived as a one-way ministry (going there to give cross-cul-tural ministry), it is really a pilgrimage in which one discovers God and the gospel at a deeper level from the very people one is sent "to missionize." The story of Jonah is a classic example. Jonah was missionized by God through the very people he was sent to missionize. Paul himself, the archetypical missionary, hammered out the gospel of justification by faith in the context of his Gentile mission. Paul was a thoroughbred traveler but definitely not a tourist. His great skills in traveling, epitomized in his taking charge of the sinking ship on which he was traveling (Acts 27:13—28:10), were subordinated to the higher purpose of being an ambassador of God to the people through preaching the gospel and building bridges between Jews and Gentiles in Christ through facilitating mutual ministry.

Ecumenical travel for fellowship. This ecumenical travel builds unity among the people of God. In the New Testament people traveled (1) to proclaim Jesus as Messiah, (2) to visit God's people (Acts 15:36), (3) to bring news of what God had done elsewhere (Acts 14:27; 15:4), (4) to bring a matter of dispute to church leaders and communicate their decision (Acts 15:2, 22) and (5) to carry relief in times of famine and tragedy (Acts 11:28-30; Orchard, p. 483). Always it is a two-way process. This Scripture witness provides an important model for Christians traveling today: establishing contact on the basis of common allegiance to Jesus Christ, listening* before speaking, communicating their experiences of Christ and, where appropriate, putting questions to a local community's understanding of itself (Orchard, pp. 496-97).

This extensive list of images, many that apply to even a single person at different times of life, indicate that traveling is both "in our blood" (for some more than others) and our calling. Whether we travel because our business, trade* or profession* demands it, because we love it or simply because we want to be "home for the holidays," we need a theology of travel.

A Theology of Travel

The Bible witnesses to most of the ways of traveling mentioned above. Abraham was part of a great people migration out of Ur. But in Haran he became a pilgrim,

an unusual one. He knew he had a destination and clung to it by faith, but he could not see it. He died, as Hebrews says, not seeing the heavenly city to which he traveled, tenting as he went (Heb 11:8-10). Some of the itinerant prophets, like Elijah and Elisha, were religious nomads, moving from place to place in response to the leading of the Spirit. It is a good thing they were not married!

Even Jesus, with no place to lay his head, was a traveler and did his theological education with his twelve disciples on the move, not unlike Paul's traveling seminary with people he picked up along the way in his missionary journeys. The first Christians in Jerusalem were persecuted and thrust out as fugitives into the Jewish dispersion, but in God's providence they became missionaries and planted churches everywhere they went. Aquila and Priscilla were fugitives from Rome in the time of Claudius, immigrants to Corinth and missionary travelers to Ephesus and back to Rome in preparation for Paul's final visit, all the time paying their own way by making tents. Christians, then and throughout the ages, are people on the move. Examples abound of Christians joining great people movements and turning immigration into pilgrimage and mission, both for them and their traveling companions. The gospel spread in part throughout the world not only by intentional mission work but by those traveling for business. In a modern world with traditional mission work being constrained, international travelers have a unique opportunity to be ambassadors for Christ and should be commissioned to this by their local church.

Scripture takes up the theme of movement not only by describing individual saints in their travels but by considering the calling of the people as a whole. God's people are always on the move, first from Ur to Haran, into the Promised Land, down to Egypt, into the wilderness, into the Promised Land once again, into exile in Babylon and finally back to Canaan to restore the kingdom. Christians also are a people on the move, on a journey through this world and this life with the new heaven and new earth as our final destination.

However, according to the New Testament description, which is not always faithfully represented in translations, Christians should not view themselves in this world as *pilgrims* (just passing through) but as *resident aliens,* setting down roots even if they have no permanent entitlement. The theological meaning of *parish* is a company of resident aliens, domiciled but without civic rights. The people of God exist in a rhythm of gathering (*ekklēsia*) and dispersion (*diaspora*) like the gathering (for renewal) and dispersion (for energizing) of the blood in the body. The weekly rhythm of the church is both ecclesial and diasporal. The earliest mention of the Christian faith is one of movement: "the Way" (Acts 9:2). So travel touches something fundamental to our spirituality.

When we travel, perhaps on a vacation,* we leave the place where we normally experience the weekly cycle of work,* service* and rest* for another place—a hotel room in a foreign country or a tent by a lake. This process is spiritually evocative. The same is true for pilgrimage, immigration and missionary travel. It provides a life experience of the theological truth that this world is not our final home, that we live an exilic existence looking toward our final homeland and that our security is not bound up with our temporal residence but in God and a "world without end."

The Metaphor of Traveling

Not surprisingly, Scripture develops traveling as a metaphor of the spiritual life.

What we do on the outside often evokes something on the inside. Jacob ran away from home and his brother's murderous anger, but on the inside he was running away from himself and God. God wanted to bless him but could not do so until he admitted who he was, as symbolized in his enigmatic name, Heel-Grabber (the real meaning of *Jacob*). His whole journey to Haran and back again to Bethel, taking twenty years in all, was an exteriorization of what was going on inside. God threw up mirrors along the way (his father-in-law Laban, for example) and took him through a desperate reality therapy to stimulate the journey within. Not until Genesis 32 does Jacob say, "I am Jacob" and receive the blessing of God (32:27-29). His outer journey mapped his inner journey. Most of us can trace the geography of our interior life around the place names of our life story, the people we met and experiences we had.

The psychological life is a journey through passages from infancy to late maturity with transitions and crises, from infantile dependence through adolescent differentiation and finally to adult interdependence. Emotionally we journey from needing to be controlled from without to becoming self-controlled, from uncontrolled impulses to being able to delay gratification, from needing to be loved to being able to give love. Because we are naturally out of sync with God and ourselves, this journey is one from lust to pure desire and from addiction to freedom. The spiritual life can be pictured as a journey from a self divided by sin to a unified personality, from fear to faith, from idolatry to worship, from being externally directed by laws and principles to being internally inspired (2 Cor 3:7-18), from loving God for the benefits of doing so to loving God for God's sake. In terms of equipping,* the journey is from being sheep to becoming a shepherd, from being a consumer of ministry to being a minister.* It is a powerful and evocative metaphor. One of the most edifying activities to do in a small group* of a church is to have each person share his or her "journey." It is one way of speaking of spiritual growth* and a pattern that focuses not on "Are you there yet?" but on "What are you learning along the way?"

The Practice of Travel

Travel is not easy and is fraught with danger. In ancient times one exposed oneself to the risk of bandits, shipwreck and illness, and travelers were often not able to find an inn or home for hospitality.* In modern times there are thieves, plane and car crashes, amoebas and sometimes "No Vacancy" signs on hotels. Guided tours take much of the stress out of traveling for pleasure, but they also reduce the adventure. A further hazard in some traveling is isolation. Businesspeople and sometimes even missionaries are separated from spouse, children, friends, church and neighbors. The temptations to moral and sexual infidelity on long journeys are substantial and need to be wisely faced, not only by communicating home but also staying where possible with Christian people. People who travel a lot (and are rarely at home) have fleeting relationships and rarely experience community.* For some people travel is an addiction,* and like all addictions it is socially isolating. People who use travel as an escape are well advised to "stay put" long enough to get in touch with themselves. Otherwise, like Jacob, they may be taken through a desperate discipline in life until they find their restless hearts at rest in God.

Tourists are particularly disadvantaged in respect to experiencing community, and they seldom see the real condition of the country or meet the people of the land, except the well-groomed waiters in first-class hotels.

Here are some practical suggestions. First, do your own planning and read up on a country, rather than buying a packaged tour. Second, stay long enough in one place to meet the people, rather than having one-night stands in a country. Avoid Western hotels and stay where the people of the land stay. Third, be a respectful photographer, refraining from photographing any site the people regard as sacred. Fourth, drink in the experience, rather than videotaping it for future reference. Be there. Fifth, seek out God's people. Be an ecumenical traveler. One way of doing this is to engage in short-term mission projects as an alternative to an expensive tour; this will edify both the people and ourselves. Best of all we get to work with and live with the people.

Cross-cultural travel, especially in countries where we cannot speak the language, is both threatening and a privileged opportunity to be met by God. Immersion in another culture is like having layers of skin removed, by which we feel more than we normally do and learn more. Tourism becomes pilgrimage. Such travel allows us, especially when we meet with God's people, to know God better and deeper, since it is only "together with all the saints" (Eph 3:18) that we can know the height and depth of the love of God.

We were built for motion but not perpetual motion. God's design is actually a rhythm of travel and rest, movement and place. Indeed, Jesus used that double metaphor to describe the next life as either a journey with many resting places or a many-roomed resting place (Jn 14: 2). We do not know whether there will be journeying in the new heaven and the new earth. What we know is that the restlessness we feel in this life will find its perfect sabbath experience in the threefold harmony of God, humankind and creation in the new Jerusalem. Ever since

Eden we have been moving. The black spirituals captured this with sublime dignity: "I'm just a poor wayfaring stranger, traveling through this world of woe . . . my treasures are laid up somewhere beyond the blue." When Christ touches our lives, we begin an eternal journey. He promises to be with us along the way, as we was with Jacob (Gen 28:15) and to meet us when we finally cross the Jordan to the good land on the other side. So, in the end, God invites us in all the ways we travel—touring, immigrating, missionizing, visiting and even in escaping— to become pilgrims and to join all other pilgrims who long for "a better country—a heavenly one" (Heb 11:16). Then God will not be ashamed to be called "our God," for he has prepared a city for us.

See also BACKPACKING; COMMUTING; GLOBAL VILLAGE; HOSPITALITY; IMMIGRATION; LEISURE; MOBILITY; PUBLIC TRANSPORTATION; VACATIONS.

References and Resources
C. Aroney-Sine, *Survival of the Fittest: Keeping Yourself Healthy in Travel and Service Oversees* (Monrovia, Calif.: MARC, 1994); E. Cohen, "Pilgrimage and Tourism: Convergence and Divergence," in *Sacred Journeys: The Anthology of Pilgrimage*, ed. A. Morinis (Westport, Conn.: Greenwood, 1992) 47-61; D. A. Dorsey, "Travel," in *The International Standard Bible Encyclopedia* (Grand Rapids: Eerdmans, 1988) 891-97; M. Feifer, *Going Places: Tourism in History, from Imperial Rome to the Present* (New York: Stein & Day, 1986); E. J. Leed, *The Mind of the Traveler* (New York: BasicBooks, 1991); J. Murphy-O'Connor, "On the Road and on the Sea with St. Paul," *Bible Review* 1, no. 2 (1985) 38-47; "Off the Beach: Eight Awesome Alternatives to Sun, Sand and Surf," *The Other Side* 22, no. 2 (1980) 33-39; R. K. Orchard, "The Significance of Ecumenical Travel," *Journal of Ecumenical Studies* 15 (Summer 1978) 477-502; P. Rossman, "Tourism: An Issue for the Churches," *Christian Century* 98 (21 January 1981) 54-59; W. Rybczynski, *Waiting for the Weekend* (New York: Viking Penguin, 1991).

R. Paul Stevens

U

UNEMPLOYMENT

Many images are evoked by the term *unemployment:* children in rags, soup kitchens, fat employers, government inaction and movies of the Great Depression when men walked hours in search of a day's work. In these images, depending on one's values* and beliefs, the tendency is to want to blame someone or something, be it business, individuals or politicians. The fact is that many countries are plagued with high unemployment. In some countries the rate is as high as 12 percent, and in certain age groups, such as youth, it is 20 percent. In many countries on the African continent, where people struggle for basic survival, the category is not even considered.

In the early 1960s there were some who argued that the time was coming when the majority of people would not work; a minority would be employed and provide for the rest. What is happening? Is there a limit to the world's potential or need for work? Is the implication that a portion of the population is going to be chronically out of work? Or delightfully so?

Being unemployed is not simply being "out of work." When a company lays off, fires* or downsizes, the persons affected may continue to work doing chores* at home, doing volunteer service* in church* and community* and looking for a new job—a form of work

itself. Unemployment is the situation in which remuneration for one's labor is absent despite the desire and need for such pay. For people in the Western world, where identity* is tied deeply to occupation, the experience is usually devastating; they have become nobodies. But on a personal level unemployment is a time for reassessment and deep spiritual work. On a societal and national level unemployment is a stewardship* issue, since it reflects systemic sin and lack of social creativity in providing opportunities for all citizens to use their gifts and talents* for the common good.

The Reality Today

Once unemployment was considered a major sin. Now it is often regarded as inevitable. Many blue-collar jobs were lost or moved to different labor markets. While there used to be a safe haven in white-collar jobs, suddenly there is downsizing and reengineering of the firm or corporation. New terms such as *underemployment* are now part of the vocabulary. What does this mean? What is one to do? Does the Bible have something to say about all this?

In some parts of the world unemployment reaches astronomic proportions, such as the 30 percent unemployed in the city of Nairobi. In many Third World cities people may spend up to seven years looking for their first job when they move to the city, since the rural farmlands are now decimated into ever smaller, unproductive units that cannot sustain a family.* Unemployment in such areas is harder to define, since most people can provide some of their daily needs for food and shelter from the land unless there is drought, famine or war. Living as we do in a global village,* the problem is not merely "their problem" but ours. Robert Kaplan draws a disturbing picture of the disparities between countries:

> Think of a stretch limo in the potholed streets of New York City, where homeless beggars live. Inside the limo are the air-conditioned post-industrial regions of North America, Europe, the emerging Pacific Rim, and a few other isolated places, with their trade summetry and computer-information highways. Outside is the rest of mankind, going in a completely different direction. (p. 60)

In the industrial and postindustrial nations unemployment has taken on a new face. Instead of lifelong tenure with a corporation, school system or government office, most people increasingly face a lifetime of scramble from job to job. Changes in the work world are taking place faster than people can cope. Workers today are faced with unsettling trends: from production to service, from generalist to specialist, from repetitive tasks to intervention (especially by means of the computer*), from age-specific education* to lifelong learning, from working with tangibles to working with intangibles, and from hard work to stressful work. But one of the most threatening trends is the change from a lifelong career to multiple short-term assignments. This means that most people will experience some form of unemployment in their lifetime, even if the period of transition is brief.

The banking industry is a classic case study (see Aley). Layoffs in this industry, primarily through attrition, are not likely to lead to employment in the same field

but rather the use of one's experience of handling finances and people in a related field, usually at a lower salary. Vocational guidance* once was the "what am I going to be when I grow up" dilemma of young people. It is now a lifelong discipline. We must also learn to see unemployment itself as a spiritual discipline.

Unemployment and Idleness

How shall we regard unemployment? It does occur in Scripture. Jesus pictures workers waiting to be hired as day laborers without commenting on the morality of the men waiting to be hired or those who did not get hired (Mt 20:1). More commonly we find reference to the willfully unemployed or idle. This is clearly a sin (2 Thess 3:10-13). Even in retirement,* persons will continue to work doing chores and volunteering so long as they are able. For the independently wealthy or the recently retired, indulging perpetual idleness and leisure* is spiritually dangerous (Prov 6:9, 10-11; 10:5; 19:15, 24; 20:4).

While these texts are clear, surely there is a difference between sheer laziness and forced unemployment. If so, why do these texts not express it? One assumption is that there was no structural unemployment in Bible times. Another is that there was always work to be done. In an agrarian society of small farmers both assumptions were undoubtedly true. Most people were self-employed in a trade* or worked as farmers* in the context of an extended family structure in which kith and kin cared for each other, especially during times of famine, drought and economic difficulty. Also there were not carefully defined "jobs" as we know them, separate from the rest of life, but only "work" of various kinds in which everyone was involved, most of which was home-based and a family concern.

It is true that some people suffer unemployment because of poor performance and failure to keep learning in their job. These people may find in unemployment a challenge from God to work, to make a full-time job out of looking for work, to explore the reasons for their lack of really "getting into" their jobs or even their outright refusal to do more than the minimum required. Those suffering "outplacement," as it is euphemistically called, need to cultivate employment as an attitude. One key principle is to insist that the displaced person think of finding a job as being a job in itself.

One should have the same discipline in finding work as holding a regular job—starting time, ending time, dressing for work and so on. Maintaining a frame of mind of actively working to meet one's most important need—to be employed—is essential. There are always alternatives and choices. My father (Stevens), a business executive, worked in the shipping room for a time when the company had to become "mean and lean." My father (Mestre) was working for a company which fell on hard times. His work was designing, but for several weeks he was assigned to clean up the factory, as it was the only work available. Effort, skill level and attitude are key factors. "Whatever you do, work at it with all your heart, as working for the Lord" (Col 3:23). This is a text both for those looking for remunerated employment and for those who feel they are underemployed. But for many people the causes of unemployment are more complex. How are we to think and act when the whole economy is disrupted, when unemployment is clearly not the result of one's effort, attitude or performance?

Unemployment as a Structural Evil

When companies go bankrupt, when oversupply forces the government to reduce production until the situation has normalized, when the stock market in Japan crashes and the rest of the economic world suffers major reverses, when the economy of a country requires structural unemployment in order to sustain high salaries, we are dealing with a much more complex reality.

Echoing the view of many economists and sociologists, P. G. Schervitch argues that statistics of unemployment "elude any simple interpretation—the simple fact is that unemployment is not a unidimensional reality" (Schervitch, p. 2). Actually the redundant—people who lost their jobs because those jobs ceased to exist—represent only about one-quarter of the unemployed. Workers found their first jobs following redundancy surprisingly quickly. One-third found new jobs before becoming unemployed (Daniel, p. 3). Workers displaced by major redundancies tended to be more able and skilled, with good work records and substantial periods of service. They went straight to the head of the line. Those who suffered most were the less attractive job seekers, such as the longer-term unemployed already on the register, young people entering the job market for the first time and people returning to the labor market after a break for some reason (Daniel, p. 4).

How are we to respond to this? Part of our Christian ministry is not only to individual persons but to structures,* organizations,* nations and the principalities and powers.* Those of us who are employed should help individual unemployed persons to take appropriate creative initiatives to seek work, retrain and become productive again. We must also address the systemic factors that make unemployment a social problem. As someone said, "There, to the displeasure of God, go all of us." God's will is that a nation thrive in providing opportunities for all of its citizens to use their gifts and talents for the common good.

The earliest extant Christian writings contain admonitions for Christian communities to provide employment for the newly converted. Thomas Aquinas took this matter farther by regarding the efforts of employers in opening up remunerated work on a grand scale as an act of virtuous magnanimity (Gossé, p. 8). The contemporary activist William Droel calls for public discipleship:

All workers—the employed, the unemployed, homemakers, volunteers, business leaders and students—are called to exercise their voting franchise, their lobbying ability, their collective strength in unions and professional associations, and their wits on the job to affect company policies, to advance legislation, and to fashion other mechanisms aimed at building an economy in which all willing workers find employment. Economic structures do not arise by themselves. People establish them, set them in motion, and administer them. Therefore, people who are right thinking and acting can form and improve them. (Gossé, pp. 8-9)

The Spirituality of the Unemployed

Undoubtedly, for the unemployed there are difficult temptations to be overcome: to slip into self-pity, to wallow in being victimized by "the system," to conclude they have lost their self-worth, to feel shamed before family, friends, neighbors and church. Like most others this crisis is both danger and opportunity. There is the opportunity of reaffirming our identities in terms of Whose we are rather than what we do. There is the invitation to rediscover how God has made us with talents and personalities fitting us for occupations, possibly several. There is the discipline of vocational guidance and the growth that can come from exploring what can be learned about ourselves from the painful process of being "outplaced."

Being unemployed can drive a wedge into our family, church relations and community as the hurt person vents anger and frustration on others, or feels unable to face people. Being unemployed can be the occasion for a root of bitterness to grow in our relationship with God for denying us meaningful and remunerated employment. But being unemployed can also become the means of strengthening our relationships with God and others as we seek the prayers, help and advice of those closest to us. This interior work, alongside the exterior work of looking for a job, can be pleasing to God and work done to God himself (Col 3:23).

There are inevitably hard choices to be made if we are determined to find work. Should one relocate to a region where employment is increasing, or is unemployment insurance the safety net one needs? Is maintaining one's roots more important than being employed? Should we take any work just to be employed, even if we are unsuited or unmotivated? These are other questions that need to be considered in the context of a caring Christian community, such as a small group* in the church. Few people can gain perspective on their unemployment without the support of a nurturing community. Some churches and communities sponsor support groups for the unemployed to meet and share their pilgrimage. Books, especially those dealing with grief and unemployment, can be of substantial help, as can a day retreat for prayer and reflection (Gossé, pp. 37-41). While we are looking for work we are working and doing some internal work that may prove to turn the tragedy of unemployment into a discovery of the sufficiency of God's grace. Meanwhile the employed may pray for the forgiveness of society's sins and in whatever context God has placed us—teacher, neighbor, citizen, businessperson, government employee—to do our own work in such a way that we not only thrive ourselves but equip others, so humanizing the world in line with God's intention.

See also BUSINESS ETHICS; CALLING; CAREER; FIRING; LOYALTY, WORKPLACE; NETWORKING; PART-TIME EMPLOYMENT; SELF-ESTEEM; VOCATIONAL GUIDANCE.

References and Resources
J. Aley, "Where the Laid-Off Workers Go," *Fortune,* October 30, 1995, 45-48; D. D. Daniel, *The Unemployed Flow* (London: PSI Publishing, 1990); J. Gossé, *The Spirituality of Work: Unemployed Workers,* (Chicago: ACTA Publications, 1993); R. D. Kaplan, "The Coming Anarchy," *Atlantic Monthly,* February 1994, 44-76; P. G. Schervitch, *The Structural Determinants of Unemployment* (New York: Academic Press, 1983).

Michel Mestre and R. Paul Stevens

UNIONS

In response to a poll done by a Christian magazine, a retired clergyman who was also a long-time member of a union stated that "unions have done more to help the working[person] than our churches could ever do." But another pastor, who was also a former mechanic, was much less generous in his response: "Unions go to any extent to hold power" ("Christians on the Picket Line," p. 27). This diversity is typical of Christians today who, in spite of common principles and worldviews,* see trade unions in various lights and make decisions concerning their involvement with unions accordingly. To help Christians deal with this conflict, this article will evaluate the modern-union worldview, which union leaders claim is characterized by justice,* according to the biblical standard of justice.

Evolution of the Union Worldview
Unions are controversial bodies, as are the methods that they employ. The

worldview of the labor movement itself is shaped by its history of dealings with employers, governments and the courts; its perceived mandate as an agent of social change and its acceptance of the adversary system as its best form of protection.

In the 1860s American unions began to organize Canadian workers. Some of these groups attempted to base their objectives and practices on Judeo-Christian principles. The Knights of Crispin, for instance, drew their name and inspiration from a third-century nobleman, Saint Crispin, who gave up his privileged position to work among the boot makers of France and Italy. That union soon folded but was succeeded by the Knights of Labor, founded in 1869 by Uriah Stevens, who studied for the Baptist ministry. The Knights of Labor saw as their task to "Make industrial and moral worth, not wealth, the true standard of individual and national greatness." In the 1880s the Knights were one of the two dominant grassroots movements among the working class in Ontario, the other being the Salvation Army. Each organization was an outlet for strong religious convictions of members of the laboring class of the day. The editor of the Knight's principal newspaper, for instance, took the view that "the doctrines of Jesus Christ the carpenter—who would have been called a tramp and a Communist had he lived in these days—if applied to the present conditions would solve the question satisfactorily" (Marks, pp. 103-4). The Knights of Labor eventually disappeared from the North American scene, to be supplanted by more secular counterparts.

While early union leaders could be characterized more as social reformers than militant organizers with fat contracts in view, as idealists with lofty visions and compassion for the truly exploited and as fighters for changes that the most right-wing among us today would support, no corresponding chord of Christian charity could be discerned among the employers whose abuses they addressed or the legislatures and courts that rushed to the owners' aid. Unions eventually learned to respond in kind.

The history of unionism in the nineteenth and through much of the twentieth century in North America is marked by fierce, even ferocious, resistance on the part of employers to any attempts by unions to interfere with their preferred style of management* and employee relations. But in the mid-1930s in the U.S. a series of dramatic strikes against Ford and General Motors and against U.S. and Bethlehem Steel led to the arrival of trade unions as successful advocates for workers regarding wages, hours and working conditions. A boom in union membership ensued, although it has waned in recent years. It was only in 1936 in the U.S. and in 1944 in Canada that workers were finally granted the right to organize and bargain collectively without employer interference.

The Union Movement's View of Its Mandate

In describing its priorities and values, labor stakes out the moral high ground. In fact, many union leaders see themselves and their unions as taking the leadership in ensuring that justice is done in our society despite the best efforts of corporations and governments to subvert and exploit vulnerable individuals and groups. This concern goes well beyond bread-and-butter issues such as wages and working conditions. The Canadian Labour Congress (CLC), for instance, believes that such matters as child poverty,* health care, education,* equality of men and women, child care, unemployment* and other political and social issues fall within its mandate (White, p. 38). Its definition of a morally just soci-

ety, of course, does not necessarily employ a traditional Judeo-Christian understanding of morality. This is evident from CLC criticism of the largely Christian women's organization REAL (Realistic, Equal, Active, For Life) Women. The CLC attacked REAL Women because they "purport to represent the women of Canada although they wish to deny rights to lesbians, homosexuals, feminists, [and] pro-choice advocates" ("Canadian Labour Congress," p. 9).

Unions and Adversarialism

Beyond considerations of the proper mandate of the labor movement, trade unions see themselves as being in a disadvantaged position vis-à-vis the employer and the government. Unions fear that without the right to strike* as protection from the arbitrary use of employer power,* the individual worker is highly vulnerable to exploitation. The late Tommy Douglas, the first socialist to head a government in North America and a Baptist minister, defined the nature of the relationship of workers with their managers as follows: "The essence of industrial relations is conflict. It is a confrontation in which the workers through their collective power seek to wrest from the employer what they deem a fair share of the wealth they helped to create" (Douglas, p. 11). Industrial relations scholar Jack Barbash agrees: "Conflict in industrial relations, or more often the threat of it, far from being pathological or aberrant, is normal and even necessary. The principle is that the parties can be kept 'honest' only by countervailing checks and balances" (Barbash, p. 131).

Nevertheless, two schools of thought have developed in recent years within the union movement. One argues that the highly competitive international situation requires unions to work together with employers in a partnership that embraces teamwork, total quality management, even profit sharing and jointly managed retraining programs. The second and more dominant position rejects the notion of worker-initiated ways of improving the competitive capacity of employers. Such initiatives are viewed as ultimately requiring harder work for less pay and the concession of workplace rights.

A Biblical Critique of the Union Worldview

The early Christian influence on the labor movement has clearly waned to the point at which many Christians have a personal problem with any involvement with a union. Others have no difficulty with union membership and urge Christians to become more involved. What follows is an attempt to critique the union understanding of justice because it is on the basis of the pursuit of justice that unions chose many of their objectives and tactics.

Biblical justice. Biblical justice has a particular concern for those on the margins of society, the vulnerable and exploitable, and is not prepared to ignore them in the pursuit of some cause, however important to the person in a position of power (Jer 22:13-17). The biblical understanding of justice includes an extra component beyond dispassionate fairness. It is often characterized as *love in action.* Words such as righteousness, love* and compassion are often found together with justice in describing God's dealings with humanity (for example, Ps 89:14; Jer 9:24; Hos 12:6; Lk 11:42). The biblical perspective on economic life is shot through with the idea of just relationships and objectives. Economic pursuits are never to include the exploitation of another's weakness or ignorance. Material goods are to be viewed as gifts from God and to be used in the development of a society characterized by economic justice and balance. Life is not one of self-indulgence or self-interest but of concern for raising up the vulnerable, enabling them to live a meaningful life, even at the expense of one's own self-interest.

Unions and justice. On the surface justice would appear to be a major preoccupation of labor unions, especially in their many pronouncements about their concern for the vulnerable members of society, whom they feel are open to exploitation by either big business, big government or the courts. But while the trade union movement has to a certain extent included notions of justice within its stated objectives, it has ignored a number of other instances in which it could be accused of unjust practices of its own. Justice in reality is reserved for the union members themselves, too often without sufficient regard for those who might be exploited or ignored while the union is pursuing its objectives. This could include a weak employer whose livelihood is sacrificed by a powerful national union pursuing a *master contract* for a total industry, which many smaller employers in that industry could not afford. Innocent third parties are frequently inconvenienced and even genuinely harmed by such job action as strikes by teachers, health-care workers, postal workers and so on.

So-called fairness that only benefits union members in accord with the majority of the union, while ignoring others who might not benefit or who in fact may lose as a result of union success, is not justice at all, at least not in the biblical sense. Such justice lacks its sister values of love and reconciliation. What we are really seeing is a form of utilitarianism; that is, that which benefits the greatest number, with the minority, who are affected by the union's actions but not benefiting from them, losing out.

Justice and worker independence. It is precisely in this area of biblical justice, however, that a strong case can be made for one of the union movement's most important contributions—worker independence. Workers, if they are to realistically expect just treatment at the hands of employers, need the kind of protection that unions provide.

The Bible is quite realistic with respect to the issue of exploitation. It takes for granted that individuals in a more powerful position will inevitably exploit those weaker or more vulnerable than themselves, even within the ranks of the church. Thus, while the authority of church leaders* was to be acknowledged and respected by church members (1 Tim 5:17; 1 Pet 5:2), church leaders had to be warned not to take advantage of their positions to enrich themselves or to abuse their authority (1 Pet 5:2-3). Similar warnings of abuse were issued to husbands vis-à-vis wives (Eph 5:21-28; Col 3:18-19; 1 Pet 3:7), parents in their relationship with their children (2 Cor 12:14; Eph 6:4; Col 3:21) and masters as they supervised their employees or slaves (Eph 6:9; Col 4:1). In the Judeo-Christian tradition those in a dependent or vulnerable position have the right to expect just treatment and to be protected from exploitation, and those in a position of authority are never to exercise that authority in a self-interested fashion, but with a view to accomplishing just objectives.

Recent studies in the United States have clearly shown that workers lacking union membership have experienced exploitation that might not have occurred with the protection unions provide. Trends identified by the respected *Business Week* journal have included productivity rising faster than the wages of the increasingly productive employees; real wages of workers actually falling, especially in industries experiencing de-unionization; executive pay rising at a breathtaking clip; and owners of capital realizing gains on their investments triple that of wage increases during the same period (Bernstein, pp. 70-82). Consequently, even hard-line opponents of American labor such as Sen. Orrin Hatch (R-Utah) have said: "There are always going to be people who take advantage of workers. Unions even that out, to their credit. . . . If you didn't have unions, it would be very difficult for even enlightened employers to not take advantage of workers on wages and working conditions because of [competition from] rivals" (Bernstein, p. 70).

Conclusion

As I said at the beginning, unions are controversial bodies. Common criticisms cited are that unions abuse their right to strike and pursue their objectives without regard for their impact on vulnerable parties. Others praise union accomplishments when they parallel Christian objectives. From a Christian perspective one must be concerned with any organization* that claims to pursue just goals either through unjust means or with a corrupted view of justice. Involvement in such organizations presents the challenge of assessing both union means and ends from a thoroughly biblical worldview and deciding how one will respond.

See also CONFLICT RESOLUTION; MANAGEMENT; ORGANIZATION; POWER; STRIKES; TECHNOLOGY; TRADES; WORK.

References and Resources
J. Barbash, *The Elements of Industrial Relations* (Madison: University of Wisconsin Press, 1984); A. Bernstein, "Why America Needs Unions but Not the Kind It Has Now," *Business Week*, 23 May 1994, 70-82; "Canadian Labour Congress (CLC) Opposes REAL Women," *Reality* 10, no. 4 (1992) 9; "Christians on the Picket Line," *Faith Today* (September-October 1989) 27-32; T. C. Douglas, "Labor in a Free Society," in *Labor Problems in Christian Perspective*, ed. J. H. Redekop (Grand Rapids: Eerd-

mans, 1972) 11-13; L. Marks, "The Knights of Labor and the Salvation Army: Religion and Working Class Culture in Ontario," *Labour/Le Travail* 28 (1991) 89-127; R. White, "Labor's Political Goal: Defeat Corporate Agenda," *Canadian Speeches: Issues of the Day* 6, no. 5 (1992) 41.

John R. Sutherland

V

VACATIONS

The original meaning of *holiday*—holy day—contains a powerful suggestion: holiday making can become an experience of holiness in time.* But for many people, family or personal vacations, if they take them at all, are times of spiritual dryness or exhaustion. Often people say they must return to work* for rest!* Even with our huge vacation industry, people are either bored or stressed out on vacations. So far as its original meaning is concerned, the word *vacation* simply means "a vacancy" (from the Latin *vacatus*), that is, "doing nothing." But a vacation should have a more positive meaning than that. Getting out of our daily routines and working roles allows people to experience their individuality more fully and to be less programmed by what others expect.

A host of questions surrounds the practice of vacationing: Why do some people never take vacations or feel guilty if they do? In what ways do vacationing and sabbath* observance overlap? Is an expensive vacation in a luxurious setting ever justified? Does the process of trying to justify a vacation destroy the very idea of taking one?

The Difficulty of Doing Nothing

Understandably vacations are very stressful for workaholics (*see* Drivenness) who do not want to be, or feel they cannot be, freed from the compulsions of work.

One wife describes her husband on vacation in this way: The first day he calls back to work to cover what he forgot to do before leaving. Then he eats too much and gets sick, spending a day or two in bed. When he starts to come up from "under" his work, he seems to "get the bends" (like a diver returning too quickly to the surface). If we can get past the first week, he enjoys the second one but soon becomes preoccupied with all the work facing him when he returns to the office (Oates, p. 39). Christians are not exempt from such struggles. Often they feel they must justify the expenditure of money* or time on nonproductive and nonreligious inactivity. Justification by faith—that watchword of the Protestant Reformation—has not been sufficiently translated from Sunday faith to Monday faith, from weekend to workday, nor has it been translated into sheer enjoyment of time, place, people and experiences for their own sake. According to Bertrand Russell, the modern person thinks that everything ought to be done for the sake of something else, not for its own sake (Oates, p. 40). This instrumental or functional attitude is deeply ingrained in the thinking of church people and must be challenged for a person to be converted to vacationing, a conversion that is part and parcel of our conversion to Christ.

The idea of a paid annual leave from work is a relatively modern phenomenon, and it is by no means universal. It is unheard of in some Third World countries and by millions who work in the service sector of society. Many professionals* and self-employed people take vacations "at their own expense" with significant loss of revenue. Increasingly vacations in North America are becoming shorter, two or three brief times a year so work is not seriously interrupted (the European trend is somewhat different). Not surprisingly many choose not to take them at all or combine a short vacation with a professional conference in an exotic location. A whole industry has developed around *incentive trips,* which are designed to satisfy wanderlust and the work ethic* at the same time, all at the company's expense. It is argued that since they are offered to salespeople and managers whose performance has excelled, mornings in a conference and afternoons enjoying the amenities of a plush resort actually pay for themselves. This form of vacationing, if it may be called such, has been co-opted by capitalism to become a vital sales and marketing tool. Even without an incentive trip, travel* and work remain well connected for many people.

On such trips—whether for business or pleasure (there is rarely any difference)—business executives take their cellular phones, fax machines and computers,* even to the beach. The idea of vacationing loses its meaning if one takes along the infrastructure, seen or unseen, of normal stressful responsibilities. Many Christian academics and pastors have "working vacations" (an oxymoron) or "ministry trips." There is reason to think that in spite of the huge leisure* industry, the industrialized or postindustrialized information societies may have less restorative vacation experiences than older and less developed societies. So-called backward countries may be more advanced in some of the life patterns that really matter, such as visiting,* convers-

ing* and resting. All too often in the so-called developed countries vacations have been reduced to a commodity to be consumed* with the compulsiveness with which one must work in order to be "excellent." It has not always been this way.

Is Vacationing a Modern Invention?

Festivals* and holy days have been part of the annual rhythm of societies from time immemorial. They provided monthly or seasonal opportunities to engage in celebration, community events, religious ceremonies, feasting and revelry. Some of these were associated with the rhythms of the year in agricultural life (harvest or sheepshearing) or seasonal changes (solstice) and with annual migrations (for hunting, fishing or harvesting the orchards). Christianity often adopted and transformed these festivals into holy days, Christmas* and Thanksgiving* being conspicuous examples. The Jewish tradition is rich in holidays, such as Passover (Feast of Unleavened Bread; Deut 16:1-8), Feast of Tabernacles (Deut 16:13-17) and Ingathering (or Feast of Weeks; Deut 16:9-12; see also Ex 23:14-19). Three times a year the Israelites were required to set aside the normal rhythm of work and sabbath to undertake a pilgrimage to Jerusalem, often in a holiday mood, as the reference to Jesus' remaining behind indicates (Lk 2:41-52). These were far from being dull religious events, for Deuteronomy prescribes buying food, wine "and whatever you like" (Deut 14:26) with one's tithe to experience the joy of the occasion. But some of the righteous or unrighteous wealthy Israelites could do even more.

The references in Amos to summer and winter houses, to "houses adorned with ivory" and "mansions" (Amos 3:15), to lounging on your couches and dining on choice lambs and fatted calves, to strumming "away on your harps" and drinking "wine by the bowlful," (Amos 6:4-6) are a perceptive judgment on the rich Israelite playboys and playgirls who lived uncompassionate, self-centered lives and did not grieve over the fate of their nation (Amos 6:6; compare Gen 37:26). While it is true that until modern times only the rich could afford to travel extensively and stay in luxurious hotels and spas—with opportunities now opened to the middle class through inexpensive air fares (*see* Traveling)—almost all people in all ages have found or exploited something like vacations. Prior to the global trend toward urbanization most people possessed discretionary time in winter during what is still called in farm areas "fence-mending time."

In *Waiting for the Weekend* Witold Rybczynski traces the origin of the practice since the Industrial Revolution of staying home on Mondays, a practice that evolved into the institution of the weekend. The need for breaks in the routine of work is universal and is practiced even today, without calling them vacations, in the market days of Third World countries. The sabbath, which gets fuller treatment elsewhere (*see* Sabbath), was intended to be a weekly vacation to remember our roots, to celebrate creation* and to gain perspective for the coming week—all facets of personal and communal restoration. The lack of sabbath in contemporary Christian life is a tragic indication of the need for recovering a theology and spirituality of vacationing.

Thinking Christianly

The mandate to enjoy God's creation is an undertaking of grace that liberates us from judging our relationship to God and leisure in use-value terms and is an approach to the theology of time that delivers us from viewing time as a resource to be managed rather than a gift to be received (*see* Leisure). Great vacations, in one sense, can neither be planned nor managed. One further

theme warrants consideration in an article on vacationing: a theology of place.

A theology of place is foundational to Christian vacationing. God created the world to be inhabited and filled (Gen 1:28). Adam and Eve's priesthood in the garden involved turning raw space into place: a garden with borders, animals appropriately named, plants nurtured, musical instruments invented and gold mined. The so-called nesting instinct is not exclusively a maternal drive. Even on camping* trips men quickly turn raw space into a fire pit with a view, a "table and shelves," where pots can be hung up, and a drying area, where clothes can be set out to dry.

Travelers, whether backpacking* or riding the Concorde, long for resting places, an image Jesus used for his provision of a place (or places!) to experience in heaven (Jn 14:2; for movement as another theme taken up in Scripture, *see* Traveling). If some do not take vacations because they are taking themselves too seriously, others may not take them because they are taking their home too seriously—the house, garden and cat that cannot be left (for the opposite danger of not taking them seriously enough, *see* Mobility).

Taking a Vacation

In the light of the preceding theological reflection I offer some suggestions on how to take a vacation. First, plan to waste time rather than to fill up every hour with prearranged activity. Give God a chance to reach you! Second, find out what truly refreshes you (and your family) and do it: being beside a lake or sea (our chosen vacation for one month a year while the children were at home), visiting another culture* (our present preference), sleeping* a lot (something we do no matter how we "waste" time). Third, enjoy this leisure opportunity to pray, read Scripture and explore some of the spiritual disciplines* you normally practice in a hurried way. Fourth, keep a journal and reflect on what you have seen and heard, turning these into prayers. A friend of our family takes a sketchbook and records a year's worth of impressions later to be turned into paintings. I take my camera.

Fifth, avoid mixing work and vacationing, even working too hard at devotional things. Sixth, do things you normally "do not have time for," such as reading* books (if you are not reading for a living), refusing to read (if you read for a living), watching the clouds, visiting old friends or walking so slowly you actually see what is around you. Seventh, do not overdo vacations. People not accustomed to taking vacations should not start with a three-month trip with their family! In the same vein it is not wise to wait too long to have a vacation—until you are too exhausted to work and therefore, paradoxically, too exhausted to rest. Eighth, do not expect that some exotic place shown on a travel brochure will make you happy. You are responsible for your own happiness; it has little to do with how much money you have to spend. Ninth, take off your watch and live by the tides or the slant of the sun in the sky. Walk barefoot or fly a kite. Get in touch with God's creation. Finally, enjoy God. Flyn, in *Mister God, This Is Anna,* puts rest and creation in perspective:

"Why did Mister God rest on the seventh day?" she began.

"I suppose he was a bit flaked out after six days of hard work," I answered.

"He didn't rest cause he was tired, though."

"Oh, didn't he? It makes me tired just to think about it all."

"Course he didn't. He wasn't tired."

"Wasn't he?"

"No, he *made* rest." (quoted in Hansell, p. 115)

References and Resources
R. Banks, *The Tyranny of Time: When 24 Hours Is Not Enough* (Downers Grove, Ill.: InterVarsity Press, 1983); R. Capon, *An Offering of Uncles: The Priesthood of Adam and the Shape of the World* (New York: Crossroad, 1982); T. Hansel, *When I Relax I Feel Guilty* (Elgin, Ill.: David C. Cook, 1979); W. E. Oates, *Confessions of a Workaholic: The Facts about Work Addiction* (London: Wolfe Publishing, 1971); "Off the Beach: Eight Awesome Alternatives to Sun, Sand and Surf," *The Other Side* 22, no 2. (1980) 33-39; W. Rybczynski, *Waiting for the Weekend* (New York: Viking Penguin, 1991).

R. Paul Stevens

VALUES

Few words are used as frequently and with less clear meaning than the word *values*. The term has come to occupy a key position in all sorts of discussions, ethical, legal, political or religious. We speak of *personal values, family values,* *traditional values, Christian values, organizational values* and *societal values.* Yet it arose in its current usage only in the writings of German philosophers following Immanuel Kant (1724-1824) and particularly the philosopher Friedrich Nietzsche (1844-1900) and, influenced by him, the German sociologist Max Weber (1864-1920).

The Problem of Values Language
Of the many philosophers who have commented on the rise of values language, one of the most interesting is the late Canadian philosopher George Grant. Grant noted how values language was used by all sorts of people, whether religious or nonreligious, and that they took the term to be meaningful without realizing that it stems from a way of talking rooted in power and subjectivity rather than in objective virtue. So, he concluded, this language usurps "truth talk." A classic example of the subjectivity of values in contemporary society is the case of Sue Rodriguez. She narrowly

failed to get the Supreme Court of Canada to find a constitutional right to physician-assisted suicide. Rodriguez, suffering from a terminal illness, expressed the modern view succinctly in these words, "Why on earth would anyone want to impose their own value system on me? I've got mine, they've got theirs" (Birnie, p. 116).

C. S. Lewis was well aware of this shift from the objective to the subjective, from truth to opinion, in which the thing valued came to be less significant than the fact of the choice of the subjective valuer. This is what he called the inflation of the subject and the deflation of the object. We see the flowering of this language in moral debates in which the issue is *choice*. But, of course, the idea that the issue is choice is flawed because a choice can never be judged as moral or immoral unless one knows the moral framework in which it is being exercised. So when people write and speak on values today, it is virtually certain that their meaning will not be clear to modern readers or hearers who have been schooled to view values as expressions of merely personal judgment that make no claim on them at all.

Whatever else *values* signify, the use of this language is highly ambiguous. When a person speaks of family values, community values or Christian values, they usually assume that they mean something objective (that is, something in the nature of things, something that is good or true irrespective of what they may or may not think personally). However, it is very much in the nature of contemporary usage that "you have your values and I have mine" (that is, values are essentially subjective, one person's being inevitably different from another's). When a Christian speaks of Christian values in the contemporary debates, what is likely heard by the audience is "the values in which a Christian believes." Since values

language is, at best, ambiguous and, at worst, relative, it is the enemy of a language of objective goodness. It is no coincidence that this language of values is one language coined by the same philosopher who noted that "God is dead."

The Challenge of Value-based Education
The language of values raises a deep question about how we should approach education* and why in our time we have so readily lost our philosophical moorings. Why have certain segments of the Christian faith been so easily derailed? The earlier language of truth was based on a philosophical and theological framework in which the virtues* were known, discussed and learnt as true aspects of the human person, necessary for the proper formation of character. The virtues were moral (philosophical) and theological (the theological virtues being faith, hope and charity). That framework was maintained for many centuries but during the last few centuries has come under frequent attack. Fortunately, some recent philosophers have sought to restore the language and tradition of virtues, and their efforts are being taken seriously.

However, since the language of values dominates many Christian discussions, it is essential for us to renew our understanding of the objective language of truth and goodness in which valid principles are expressed as something more than personal or communal values. Instead of speaking in the muddied language of values, we should speak openly about good and evil, even though we may disagree as to what these are. As G. K. Chesterton once put it, "When you realize you are on the wrong road, the way to correct the error is to go back to where you went wrong." Our study and curriculum in churches and schools should provide a place for teaching these classical categories in the light of Christian revelation.

See also FAMILY VALUES; ORGANIZATIONAL VALUES; RIGHTS; VIRTUES.

References and Resources

M. Adler, *Reforming Education* (New York: Macmillan, 1988); L. H. Birnie, *Uncommon Will: The Death and Life of Sue Rodriguez* (Toronto: Macmillan, 1994); A. Bloom, *The Closing of the American Mind* (New York: Simon & Schuster, 1987); R. Guardini, *The Virtues* (Chicago: Regnery, 1963); S. Hauerwas, *Vision and Virtue: Essays in Christian Ethical Reflection* (Notre Dame, Ind.: University of Notre Dame Press, 1974); G. Himmelfarb, prologue "From Virtues to Values" to *The De-moralization of Society* (New York: Knopf, 1995); P. Kreeft, *Back to Virtue* (San Francisco: Ignatius, 1992); C. S. Lewis, preface to *The Hierarchy of Heaven and Earth* (London: Faber & Faber, 1952) 9-13; C. S. Lewis, "On Ethics," in *Christian Reflections,* ed. Hooper (London: Bles, 1967); C. S. Lewis, "The Poison of Subjectivism," in *Christian Reflections,* ed. W. Hooper (London: Bles, 1967) 72-81; J. F. Power, "George Grant's Critique of Values Language," in *George Grant in Process,* ed. Larry Schmidt (Toronto: Anansi, 1979) 90-98.

Iain T. Benson

VIRTUAL REALITY

Imagine that you are on trial. The prosecutor rises, and the judge instructs the bailiff to place helmets and gloves on the jury. The prosecutor speaks: "What you are about to experience, ladies and gentlemen of the jury, is the prosecution's reconstruction of the malicious behavior of the defendant on the night of the crime." You watch in horror as the jury gasps and groans at what they are experiencing. You can only imagine the sights, sounds, smells and touches—so real, and yet completely false—that will convince them you are guilty of a crime you did not commit.

Both the promise and the danger of virtual reality can be seen in its name. It is *virtual:* the set of sense experiences you have is contrived using computers* and output devices. What you experience is entirely synthetic. It can be changed subtly or dramatically by changing the programs that create it. Yet it seems to be *reality:* the experiences are so convincing that, in some cases, they seem really to be happening.

Basic Character

Virtual-reality systems work by providing sensory perceptions, to multiple human senses, that closely mimic those provided by "real" experience. Just as Renaissance artists worked to give the illusion of three dimensions to a flat canvas, so engineers of virtual-reality systems use computers to mimic our visual, auditory and tactile experience.

The most important factor in making virtual reality seem real is its ability to simulate the sensory results of movement on all six of the axes along which it might take place: forward/backward, left/right, up/down, pitch, roll and yaw. By manipulating visual and auditory input, virtual-reality systems can give the user a remarkably effective sense of moving "through" the world constructed by the computer.

By contrast, current graphical computer displays are quite flat in their aesthetic approach. They have no interest in portraying perspective or movement. It is instructive that the symbols such displays use are called *icons,* for they are very similar in intent to the iconic paintings of a millennium ago. Display icons intend to communicate a message rather than a rendering of reality. They are symbols, albeit only of 64 by 64 pixels.

Just as a Byzantine iconographer did not think Saint John "really" looked like the icon (halo and all), so conventional display designers do not think a wastebasket "really" looks like the icon in the corner of a Macintosh computer. Both are icons; the visual rendering is subordinate to the message they bear. Exact sensory correspondence to reality is of secondary importance.

Virtual-reality systems use a different set of criteria. Whereas ordinary graphic displays are highly stylized, virtual-reality systems try to look real. Fidelity to ordinary lived experience is crucially important. When you move in a virtual-reality system, your perspective must change as when you move in the world. When you hear something in a virtual-reality system, you must hear "normal" aurally complex sounds rather than single-frequency beeps and boops.

Creating such synthetic realities, however, is a technically difficult project. Human sensation uses redundant information provided by several of the senses to construct the picture we have of reality at any given time. When sighted people are blindfolded, for example, they naturally behave as blind people are accustomed to behaving. They attend more closely to sounds and smells and touch to fill up the information missing from the sense they normally rely upon.

The most effective virtual-reality systems try to provide synthetic reality to more than one of our senses. Merely providing visual reality is unconvincing because the ears and fingers are still in the normally experienced reality of whirs and clicking keys. The more virtual-reality systems can interact with multiple senses, the more effective they become.

Virtual-reality software tries to expand the monopoly of the visual to touch all the senses and make them part of the feedback loop between person and machine. To do so, they need capabilities that allow them to "fool" the senses into behaving as if they were receiving real stimuli. So, iconic and stylized visual displays give way to realistic ones in which perspective and shadow heighten the illusion of depth and movement.

This problem becomes a substantial engineering challenge, especially for the sense of touch, for the sense organ is distributed over the entire surface of the human body. The current state of the practice of virtual reality has concentrated almost entirely on visual and audio implementations. Only a few dedicated, and hence very expensive, systems have accepted the challenge of creating a true virtual reality that encompasses the senses. The *Star Wars* simulation at Disneyland or Disney World is, for many of us, as close to virtual reality as we will get.

Current Uses

At the moment most virtual-reality systems are toys or dedicated training devices. For example, training devices such as flight simulators allow airline pilots to experience flying an aircraft under emergency conditions without actually risking either an airframe or passengers to give them this experience.

These virtual-reality simulations are different from other computer modeling efforts (such as climate modeling or collision impact simulation) in that one of the important dimensions of the simulation is the opportunity people have to interact with what they perceive. Virtual-reality systems give their human participants a certain set of perceptions and let them respond to them. Pilots and others are happy to be able to learn from synthetic reality in such a way. Computer gaming* is the only other serious use of virtual reality at present. For a number of years gaming systems have been evolving toward greater and greater fidelity to ordinary perception.

Conventional computers involve their operators with one or two senses at most. Visual, and in the last ten years graphical, displays are the key intersection between current computers and people. Sound plays a smaller role at the moment, though audio interfaces have an enormous potential. Even though in the near future computer interfaces will doubtlessly become more "natural," that is, multisensory, virtual-reality techniques will probably have their most important impacts in two related areas.

The first is in simulation. Many military and commercial applications deal with situations that are either too dangerous to humans or too costly for personnel to train for directly. Airline pilots, for instance, should train for engine fires and emergency dives but shouldn't do so with real planes full of real people. In cases like these, virtual-reality simulations are currently very important and will become more important in the future. But simulations using virtual-reality systems need not be confined to military types of applications. Architects and facilities managers have for centuries used drawings and models to communicate their ideas to customers. Virtual-reality systems can allow clients to "walk through" buildings before they are built or allow facilities managers to experiment with various equipment and furniture layouts without actually creating them.

The second application area, gaming, will also be important for new virtual-reality systems. One trend in contemporary computer games is to increasingly involve the player's senses. The gaming situation takes on new excitement as more dimensions of sense are included in the game. In order to take increasing advantage of virtual-reality techniques, however, gaming will need increasingly to use specialized hardware, which will limit its market penetration.

Even apart from these two applications, simulation of the real world using virtual-reality techniques has some potential. Michael Chrichton's description of a virtual-reality database in the novel *Disclosure,* for example, shows some of the power that virtual-reality systems might give us. Mundane tasks such as file access and communication might end up being influenced by virtual-reality

techniques developed for other applications. But everyday tasks will probably benefit only from spin offs of virtual-reality programs created for and applied in other domains.

Reality and Virtual Reality

Virtual reality might seem to us as a perspective painting must have seemed to our pre-Renaissance forebears. When one's whole lived experience of representations of life has been flat, it is hard to express the effect of experiencing volume and color in a mere representation. Photography* created this same kind of transformed experience of representation in the nineteenth century. Virtual reality has brought the same transformation to us.

But though perspective painting and photography brought transformations of the representation of reality, they brought nothing inherently demonic with them. Each transformation had its detractors and even prophets who railed against it. Each might have seemed to be a violation of the sanctity of reality because its representation of reality was complete in a previously unparalleled way. Yet we now view the previous transformations of representation with equanimity. Now we are concerned about the capabilities we have to reengineer photographs so that they are *not* a close representation of reality. Computer retouching and enhancement have made a picture less than trustworthy evidence of reality in a profoundly new way.

Theologically, virtual reality is a new direction in our representation of reality. Like other representations, it will have both uses and abuses. We need to guard against attempts to substitute virtual reality for lived reality. But we need not be overly concerned that this new representation will undermine that reality. Any representation of reality—a novel or play, a painting or photograph, or virtual reality—can be pressed to become a substitute reality. In some ways virtual reality is more open to this abuse—partly because it involves multiple senses. But, at least at the current state of the practice, it is less open to this abuse because it requires highly contrived equipment and situations to be effective.

The transformation of a representation of reality into a substitute reality is a perpetual problem and a form of idolatry. This is the abuse of representation that the iconoclasts fought against. Their solution, however, was excessive. One need not destroy the representation to keep from worshiping it.

See also COMPUTER; COMPUTER GAMES; INFORMATION SUPERHIGHWAY; TECHNOLOGY.

Hal Miller

VIRTUES

Virtue is a term that is being recovered from Greek philosophy to become part of contemporary discussions on ethics. There is good reason for this: both in ancient literature and in the Bible, virtue is a fundamental dimension of ethical living and moral character development. While the concept of virtue predates Christianity, it has been greatly influenced and deepened by the Christian faith. It is also true to say that the thinking of Christians, especially in the Western church,* has been influenced by these Greek sources.

Few would deny that moral education is a pressing need today. Unfortunately the concept of virtue has, over the years, deteriorated and, like a host of other terms *(tradition, heritage* or even *right* and *wrong)* has lost its vibrancy. More commonly we now tend to speak of personal "values"* rather than virtues. And we create our own "values" rather than conforming ourselves to "virtues" as the

categorical "given" aspects of an overall (therefore shared) goodness. So the questions of what virtue is and how we can and why we should become virtuous are crucial considerations for everyday life.

Virtue in the Classical Tradition

For the Greek philosophers, virtues *(aretē)* related to the nature of the noble-minded, culturally developed person. For the Roman, virtue *(virtus)* signified the firmness and solidity that one who was noble maintained in public and private life. In the Middle Ages, virtue was the conduct of the chivalrous person.

The classical tradition (epitomized by Socrates, Plato and Aristotle) developed an understanding of the natural virtues that could be perceived by the exercise of natural reason. They had various lists of virtues. Aristotle, for example, divided all the virtues into those that were moral (having to do with character) and those that were intellectual (having to do with the mind). Crucial to this approach is the concept of the mean, sometimes called "the golden mean." All errors with respect to the virtues involve either an excess or a deficiency of the virtue in question. Thus the virtue of courage means that we ought to avoid the extremes of rashness or cowardice. Some of the difficulties of this pre-Christian understanding can be seen in such views as this: all virtue is knowledge and all vice is ignorance (Socrates). Along this line Socrates proposed that by attaining insight into the good we would be able to do it. In short, virtue could be learned.

While "What has Athens to do with Jerusalem?" has remained an abiding question throughout church history, there is no doubt that our understanding of Christian character has been profoundly shaped by these Greek influences. For example, the Christian thinker Thomas Aquinas grouped four key virtues together as the *cardinal virtues:* justice,* wisdom (prudence), courage (fortitude) and moderation (temperance or self-control). The term *cardinal* comes from the Latin word *cardio* (a hinge), because all the other virtues pivoted on these four. The fundamental assumption in much of this thinking is that "grace perfects nature." What is surprising, however, when we turn to Scripture, is the relative absence of preoccupation with virtues in the Greek sense.

Virtues in the Bible

There is no equivalent Hebrew word for the Greek *aretē* even though the so-called cardinal virtues are often mentioned as part of the righteous lifestyle of God's covenant people. Not surprisingly, in the Old Testament, the righteous do justice and live by wisdom.

In the New Testament the term *aretē* is used sparsely: once in the writings of Paul (Phil 4:8) and four times in Peter's letters (1 Pet 2:9; 2 Pet 1:3, 5), though it is usually not translated in English as "virtue." Nevertheless, it is indisputable that early Christians were aware of the good qualities found outside the family of God, and they interpreted the Christian life partly in the categories of Greek thought. The list of commendable virtues Paul gives in Philippians—true, noble, right, pure, lovely, admirable, excellent, praiseworthy—seems reminiscent of virtues commended by the Greek philosophers. This is no more surprising than the fact that Paul frequently uses the Greek concept of "conscience"* to communicate our moral responsibility and accountability in the Greek world when no such word was given him from his Jewish and biblical heritage.

So both Testaments contain many parallels with the Greek virtues. Wisdom (also called prudence) has been called the "charioteer of the virtues" because it, in a sense, steers our choices (Prov 14:15;

1 Pet 4:7). Justice is the moral virtue that consists in the constant and firm will to give one's due to God and neighbor* (Col 4:1). Courage is the moral virtue that ensures firmness in difficulties and constancy in pursuit of the good (Ps 118:14; Jn 16:33). Moderation is the moral virtue that tempers the attraction of pleasures and provides balance in the use of created goods. It ensures mastery by the will over instincts and keeps desires within the limits of what is honorable (Tit 2:12).

Nonetheless, three observations can be made of the biblical treatment of this subject. First, there is nothing in the Bible comparable to the cataloging of virtues, especially the four "cardinal" virtues. In fact other virtues are offered as the "hinges" of the spiritual life. Second, all the lists in the Bible are ad hoc—representative and exemplary but not definitive. And third, the discussion of theoretical versus practical virtues—fundamental to Greek philosophy—finds no place in the New Testament, where doing and being are fully united in the righteous life. The reasons for these differences are profoundly theological and stem from the distinctiveness of the Christian way.

The Three Theological Virtues: Faith, Hope and Love

In the New Testament the fundamental character virtues (if they may be called such) are faith, hope and love,* often mentioned singly and sometimes as a triad (1 Cor 13:13; 1 Thess 1:2-3; Col 1:5). These are sometimes called the "theological virtues," because they are gifts of God and have God as their primary object. These virtues dispose Christians to live in relationship with the Holy Trinity. They have the One and Triune God for their origin, motive and purpose. They are also the spiritual foundation for all other virtues: faith, hope and love are fundamental to being in right relation to God and neighbor. Or to put the matter in another biblical way, the other virtues are part of the manifold fruit of Spirit-living (Gal 5:22-23) that comes from faith in Christ and hope in God's purpose and through loving and being loved by God.

Thus Christian character is primarily, though not exclusively, a byproduct of living with faith, hope and love. For example, self-control (Gal 5:23) is not simply the result of reason or human volition but is dependent on God's primary act of creation. It is God who keeps us moment to moment by his grace, and for this reason charity, the supreme goal of all virtues, is not something of which we can boast but something within which we humbly cooperate with God's prior and gracious gifts to us (Gal 5:22; Eph 4:32—5:2; Col 3:12). The greatest is love itself (1 Cor 13:13).

Virtue in Past and Present Christian Thought

So we can understand why Christian writers after the first century did not accept the classical account of virtue as a complete view of the matter. Since the ultimate end of humanity is a supernatural one, it is necessary for us to be endowed with supernatural powers so that we may attain our destiny. A crucial issue in this matter is the way the revelation of virtues relates to the best of the pre-Christian tradition of virtues.

The understanding that grace perfects nature has been offered by Roman Catholic theologians such as Ambrose, Augustine, Aquinas, Catherine of Genoa and Philip Neri and such modern writers as Josef Pieper, Romano Guardini and Alasdair MacIntyre. In recent years and in the Protestant tradition, people such as Wesley, Wilberforce, Bonhoeffer, C. S. Lewis and Stanley Hauerwas have stressed the importance of virtue in rela-

tion to character. The Christian tradition of the virtues developed an understanding that grace (the gift of God) perfected what we could perceive with our unaided reason. As has been said by one current writer on the virtues: "Plato gives us virtue's grammar, Jesus gives us virtue's poetry" (Peter Kreeft).

C. S. Lewis understood the importance of understanding the virtues and said that "right actions done for the wrong reason do not help to build the internal quality or character called a 'virtue' and it is this quality or character that really matters" (*Mere Christianity*, III, chap. 2). Cardinal John Henry Newman noted that "the very problem which Christian duty requires us to accomplish is the reconciling in our conduct of opposite virtues."

Education in the Virtues

True education, as Augustine noted, is to learn what to desire. Since much of education* over the past hundred years or so has been marked by a jettisoning of the teaching about virtue, it is not surprising that so many are rather lost with respect to what the virtuous life entails. With God's help the virtues forge character and give facility in the practice of the good. The virtuous person is happy to practice them and gradually form good habits. Aristotle observed that an understanding of particular virtues was more helpful than simply being urged to "do good and avoid evil." Character is influenced by habits,* and habits are formed by choices. The virtuous life is a life in which the acquired habits are in harmony with one another.

Biblical revelation offers something substantially different that appears to be "foolishness" from the perspective of Greek philosophy (1 Cor 1:22-25). The gospel declares that God gives what he requires, that the grace of the new creation* accomplishes what never can be obtained by reason or moral effort alone. Virtues are not obtained solely by "pulling ourselves up by our own bootstraps." They are gifts of God.

But they are gifts that invite and even require human cooperation. That is surely what is behind New Testament exhortations to "think about such things" (Phil 4:8) in the context of a list of commendable character qualities, "get rid of" vices like slandering (Eph 4:31), "make every effort to add to your faith goodness" (2 Pet 1:5) and "live a life of love" (Eph 5:2). The virtuous life engages the whole person in what must be seen as active prayer. But it is not autonomous activity. Rather than simple human achievements, certainly not ones we might boast about having attained, Christian living is essentially responsive and always God-centered. Faith, hope and love keep us focused on the source—the God of all true virtue. Peter says that God's divine power "has given us everything we need for life and godliness through our knowledge of him who called us by his own glory and goodness [*aretē*]" (2 Pet 1:3). Paul reminds the Colossians that it is as "God's beloved" that they are to clothe themselves with goodness and patience (Col 3:12). What Athens requires, Christ inspires. All virtue depends upon charity and humility as the opposites of selfishness and pride. The virtues may be seen as the working out of love, for no one can be truly loving without being, at the same time, virtuous.

See also CHRISTIAN EDUCATION; CONSCIENCE; EDUCATION; FAITH DEVELOPMENT; JUSTICE; LOVE; SPIRITUAL FORMATION; SPIRITUAL GROWTH; VALUES.

References and Resources
M. Adler, ed., *Syntopicon*, in *Great Books of the Western World* (Chicago: Encyclopedia Britannica, 1952); R. Guardini, *The Virtues: On Forms of the Moral Life* (Chicago: Henry Regnery, 1967); S. Hauerwas, *Vision and Virtue: Essays in*

Christian Ethical Reflection (Notre Dame, Ind.: University of Notre Dame Press, 1974); P. Kreeft, *Back to Virtue* (San Francisco: Ignatius, 1992); C. S. Lewis, *The Abolition of Man* (London: Bles, 1943); C. S. Lewis, *Mere Christianity* (London: Bles, 1956); A. MacIntyre, *After Virtue* (Notre Dame, Ind.: University of Notre Dame Press, 1984); J. Pieper, *A Brief Reader on the Virtues of the Human Heart* (San Francisco: Ignatius, 1991); "The Virtues" and "The Moral Law" in *Catechism of the Catholic Church* (1993), para. 1803-45 and 1950ff.

Iain Benson

VISION

As the word itself suggests, *vision* generally refers to that upon which individuals, families or members of an organization* have "set their sights." It could be seen as a synonym for "overall goal." Some people keen on planning* might prefer terms such as *purpose* or *mission statement* to vision, though others delight in distinguishing a hierarchy: vision and values*; mission* or purpose; goals, objectives and tasks, each item down the list becoming more narrow, concrete and short-term. For our purpose, we will put vision at the top of the list and mainly confine the discussion to organizational vision (*see* Calling; Family Goals).

Thus *vision* is the overarching sense of direction in an organization such as a local church, what it sees itself being in the future. This vision may be mystical and universal, such as Abraham's anticipation of the heavenly Jerusalem: "For he was looking forward to the city with foundations, whose architect and builder is God" (Heb 11:10). Or the vision may be more immediate and even unique to a particular group, such as that which motivated the pioneering work among Gentiles by the nameless church planters in Acts 11:19-21.

The Necessity of Vision
The classic text is Proverbs 29:18: "Where there is no vision, the people

perish" (KJV). However, as the New International Version and other modern translations show, the vocabulary and context of this verse have more to do with obeying revealed moral law than with being faithful to something God has in store for us (Eph 2:10). If vision is no more than upholding virtues* or living out general biblical values such as the Great Commission (Mt 28:19-20), then there is little more to say. The very quality of these mandates as revelation establishes their central validity.

However, the Bible clearly shows that more particular visions are possible and useful and perhaps even essential. Admittedly, the evidence mostly relates to individual mandates, for example, Jesus' focusing on Jewish evangelism (Mt 15:21-28) and Paul's commissioning at his conversion (Acts 9). But there are hints that corporate visions also have a place. Jesus' disciples become involved in evangelizing the Jews (Mt 10:5-6, 23). The churches in Jerusalem and Antioch establish different ministries, for example, Antioch's commitment to giving (Acts 11:29); Paul's coworkers endorse his vision to take the gospel to Europe and accompany him to fulfill it (Acts 16:9-10).

A little reflection leads to the same conclusion about the need for group vision. No one organization can do everything, and consequently everyone cannot do the same thing (or something important will be neglected). The big question is, How do we find out what exactly we as a particular group are to be and do? Before attempting to answer this, we must address another question, Ought visions be highly focused or multifaceted? An argument could be made for a sharp focus, but there probably should be a place for the organization that casts a broad and varied net. To use Isaiah Berlin's imagery from his famous essay on Tolstoy's view of history, there is room for both hedgehogs and foxes in the kingdom:

> There exists a great chasm between those, on the one side, who relate everything to a single central vision . . . and, on the other side, those who pursue many ends, often unrelated and even contradictory. . . . The first kind of intellectual and artistic personality belongs to the hedgehogs, the second to the foxes. (Berlin, p. 3)

The Source of Vision

A strict denominational authority or a strong hierarchy in a parachurch organization might seek to *impose* a vision on a local group. Or, if not the vision itself, at least the components that shape a vision may be laid down by the "powers that be." But this is more like the blinders imposed on a horse drawing a cart rather than true vision. Vision, to be our own, needs to come from within the group (even if God is the ultimate source).

This leads us to the second possibility—that a vision will *impress* itself on a local church or parachurch group. This brings us close to the other major meaning of *vision:* a picture revealed to the mind or spirit by the Holy Spirit. We see this phenomenon many times in the book of Acts, for example, the church of Antioch being told by the Spirit to set Barnabas and Paul apart "for the work to which I have called them" (Acts 13:2; see also 16:9; 20:22). In verse 3 we also see the role that fasting and prayer might have in a vision for the church. Those who turn to God with a pure, seeking heart will see him (Mt 5:8) and also "see" the future he has for them.

Some would like to drive a wedge between the previous source of vision and the final one, *imagining* or constructing a vision with the creative mind of Christ given to us. However, the wedge is unnecessary: God works within the freedom he has risked providing to us. As with any human activity submitted to him, God is quite capable of shaping the planning process that leads to a sense of vision, and he is quite capable of making corrections if a group gets off track (*see* Guidance). This is especially true if that group is prayerful and open to more specific visions from the Spirit. Of course, every organization's vision should also be tested against God's supreme and enduring revelation in the biblical record. That being said, how does a group go about building a vision?

Gaining a Corporate Vision

The first step is to decide who will be involved in the process and how they will be involved. Such decisions are very much shaped by the leadership culture and official polity (government) of the organization. Some groups believe that a single visionary will receive direction, perhaps while on a personal prayer and planning retreat. Others will adapt this model to vest vision shaping in a group of leaders or members of a committee.* Still other groups will go for a bottom-up rather than top-down approach, looking for consultation, if not consensus, within the whole body. Here the leader becomes facilitator or equipper* rather than prophet or entrepreneur.

There are three components or raw materials that feed into the chosen process: the organization's location, congregation and tradition. First, as a general rule, a group's direction in mission and ministry* will be shaped by where they are placed in the world, both geographically and socially. It is true in this age of global travel* and communication that a group can have an impact well beyond its borders, but our prime responsibility still rests with our neighbors at home and at work. The concept of parish (a word derived from a root meaning "temporary colony") is a powerful one: penetrating the area where God has planted you,

meeting its needs and taking its people, institutions and culture captive for Christ.

The second component is the congregation, the resource of the body of Christ (always more important than your building or budget). What gifts are found among your people, and what burden has God laid on each heart? Is it a gift of preaching* and teaching, as seen in Timothy (1 Tim 4:13-14). Is there a leaning towards planting seeds or watering them (1 Cor 3:6)? Where do spiritual gifts* complement and the passions reinforce one another? When a vision is shared by many members, it is a good indication of its relevance to the whole organization. Wise elders, pastors or church boards will not ignore their flock as they attempt to identify their organization's direction. For example, with a bottom-up approach they may allow individuals with a passion and maturity to "vision-cast" before the congregation to see if anyone is drawn into the proposed cause.

The final raw material is the tradition of the group. It is fashionable to denigrate tradition today, to leave old wineskins behind. Though it is important to be open to change, abandoning past strengths and emphases too quickly may be unwise. Why not continue to make the unique contribution—theologically, spiritually and practically—that you have made in the past? There must be a very good reason to do otherwise. As with personality types, it is good to have different kinds of Christian organizations. We must be very certain before we assume God is asking us to specialize in radically new ways.

The Application of Vision

Having discovered or assembled a vision through a process of planning, we may ask, What is its value? First, a vision is the basis for further strategic planning. According to one planning paradigm, vision leads to a mission statement, which leads to goals and objectives. Second, it allows a group to be clear about what it is not doing. The selection of appropriate activities for the group must be accompanied by saying no to the many distractions that will come along. The negative here simply means concentrating group resources on projects that contribute to the particular vision of the group. Christians have a hard time saying no, especially to otherwise worthy projects. But even Jesus, the one who came to save the whole world, guarded his priorities.

Another function of a clearly articulated vision is to remind and reinspire. Visions can erode, perhaps as people become weary, or they can be corrupted, perhaps as people become cynical. Initial enthusiasm and idealism can give way to the caution and pragmatism of those with positions to protect. As with individuals, so with organizations: "Let's just do something, anything, and then let's lie down for a while." That is the time to pull out the vision statement and be reconnected to what was your pulse beat. Hezekiah learned the value of reconnecting to an original heart, in his case a vision of worship in the temple (2 Chron 29). Similarly, Josiah instituted renewal based on the vision of the rediscovered Book of the Covenant (2 Chron 34). Returning to roots, to original mandates, can be very life giving.

Josiah's action leads to one last question, Is an organizational vision static? It may be, but it is unlikely. Even if a church does not change location or a parachurch agency move to a new mission field, the target group may shift in composition. Many churches have had to struggle greatly with a changing parish profile; most of the struggle comes from not recreating their vision. Likewise, congregational makeup will change naturally (and sometimes unnaturally through schism). Further, as a matter of course, a group's tradition will evolve gradually with each new experience. Vision must move accordingly, though the change may not be dramatic. In fact, students of change agency maintain that dramatic shifts of vision are usually not wise. Finally, every vision must be held loosely, with open hands, for our God is one who makes all things new: God could have a few surprises in store for your group no matter how comprehensive your vision setting may be.

See also DAYDREAMING; IMAGINATION; LEADERSHIP; ORGANIZATIONAL CULTURE AND CHANGE; PLANNING; RENEWAL, CHURCH.

References and Resources
I. Berlin, *The Hedgehog and the Fox* (Chicago: Ivan R. Dee, Publisher, 1978); D. E. Galloway, *20 20 Vision* (Portland, Ore.: Scott Publishing, 1986).

Dan Williams

VISITING

The making and receiving of visits is a familiar aspect of life. Some people give more time to this than others; some seem to enjoy it more than others; some view it as more essential than others. How highly valued is visiting today? What kind of priority should we give it? Whom should we spend time visiting and why? What is supposed to come out of it?

Surveys and interviews suggest that in Western societies visiting others in a regular or leisurely way is decreasing. There are various reasons for this. First, more people are in the work force. These days, despite unemployment,* a larger proportion of people are working than previously. The clearest example of this is the two-career marriage: such people have less time for visits to neighbors, fellow Christians or the wider family. Second, working hours are longer (*see* Time). On average people have around twelve hours less free time per week than a decade ago. Third, urban sprawl and mobility* are increasing. Especially for middle-class single people and young marrieds without children, there are greater distances between them and others whom they might want or need to visit. Fourth, there is a devaluation of relationships. Except among some groups, such as the older "busters" (that is, twenty-five- to thirty-year-olds) relationships have come to be regarded in an increasingly instrumental fashion. More important is accumulating possessions and experiences. These four are not the only reasons for the decline in visiting but their combined force is significant.

What are we to make of this? Many people have begun to yearn for the days when they could visit others more easily, more regularly and in a more leisurely fashion. In non-Western cultures visiting others continues to be highly valued and practiced, and much time is given to it at least in rural areas. The Bible also has some things to say about this.

Visiting in Scripture

It is not difficult to see why Scripture gives a high priority to visiting others. Making a visit is just the reverse side of extending hospitality.* Since practicing hospitality is such a basic Christian obligation, so too is visiting, and for similar reasons.

First, visiting is important because it reflects the practice of God. Throughout the Bible God is described as one who visits us. It is not necessary for the word itself to be present to see this taking place. We have a vivid example of it taking place as early as the third chapter of Genesis, when God comes walking in the Garden of Eden looking for Adam and Eve (Gen 3:8-9). In passage after passage

God gets in touch with people, whether they are seeking to be in contact with him or not, and spends time with them in a wide variety of ways. He talks with them, gives them comfort, warns them against dangers, instructs them in various matters. In other places the word *visit* itself is used—in quite diverse ways. For example, God visits (or "comes to the aid of") people to provide food for them (Ruth 1:6), to fulfill a gracious promise (Jer 29:10), to take them to a new place (Gen 50:24), to offer them salvation (Ps 106:4), as well as to bring home to them the tangible consequences of generations of sinful behavior (Num 14:18). According to Job, God visits us daily to see how we are responding to all the divine things that come our way (Job 7:18).

Second, in the light of this it is not surprising that the Bible presents us with exemplars who made a practice of visiting others. So Paul frequently refers to his desire to visit or to revisit those who have responded to his message. He does this out of concern for them and to "see how they are doing" (Acts 15:36). While sometimes he can visit only for a week, on other occasions he wants to make more than just a "passing visit" (1 Cor 16:7). When his hopes of seeing them are dashed, he does not give up but continues to plan a visit (Rom 1:13). Where turning up at one of his churches is likely to cause conflict and distress, Paul refrains from making a "painful visit" so that when he comes, it will be a joyful rather than distressing occasion (2 Cor 2:1, 3). When he is torn away peremptorily from those with whom he is spending time, so intensely does he long to see them that he makes "every effort . . . again and again" to visit them (1 Thess 2:17-18).

Third, the Bible encourages us to give special preference in our visiting to those who are disadvantaged in some way. According to James the litmus test of genuine religion is to "look after orphans and widows in their distress" (Jas 1:27). Alongside talking about the importance of hospitality to the stranger or needy, Jesus points to the importance of visiting those who "are sick and in prison" (Mt 25:43 NRSV). One reason why these should have priority is evident. Because prisoners cannot get out, they are unable to enjoy the company of others by visiting them! The letters from prison written by the German theologian Dietrich Bonhoeffer remind us how much those in such a situation long for human contact with others at a distance. But more than human contact is at issue here. When we make such a visit, we visit not just the people but Christ himself (Mt 25:45)! In a quite literal sense we are engaged in a divine service. This should be of particular significance to hospital and prison chaplains whose main work this is.

Principles of Visiting
As mentioned above, visiting others seems to be in decline. This is a serious matter, for it means that something of the divine longing for fellowship is slowly going out of the modern world, even out of the church.* Such visiting seeks the presence of those whose company is enjoyable because there is much in common or because it could bring encouragement to them. It is part of the divine bringing of consolation or hope to others who are largely cut off from their normal sources of support, the divine giving or provision of guidance* for any who might be in need of material assistance or vocational guidance* and the divine association with people to whom something needs to be declared or restated. All of these are important aspects of ministry* among believers and to outsiders. We need to remedy the decline by imitating God's behavior towards us, learning from role models such as Paul

and heeding the instruction of Jesus and James.

If visiting is as important as the Bible suggests, we need to clear more time for it. Since it is a form of ministry that reflects the basic character of God and issues in a vital service of Christ, we ought to give it a high priority. This means making some hard choices: for example, searching for arrangements in the workplace that would allow greater job sharing for two-career couples, couples returning to only one partner working in a salaried position, refusing to work longer hours except when strictly necessary and being willing to take the consequences, lowering expectations about our standard of living so that we do not have to spend as much time earning and reducing involvement in other forms of ministry that may be regarded as important by the church but do not have as high a profile in Scripture. In some cases we should work to change the church's priorities so that ordinary members, rather than just the staff or pastoral-care team, visit members of the congregation and people outside the church as an expression of our genuine interest in them. In most cases this would result in more effective community-building pastoral care* and outreach by the church than does a reliance upon programs (see Equipping).

If we are to give more attention to it, we may need to relearn some of the art of visiting. This varies from place to place. In some societies visiting involves bringing particular kinds of gifts.* In others it is important to stay until the male or female host indicates that you are free to leave. Conventions vary as to dress, order of conversation* and how women and men relate. Depending on the culture,* paying a visit also involves greater or lesser spontaneity: in some cultures it is permissible to drop in on people unannounced at certain times, whereas in others this would be regarded as an intrusion. The secret to dropping in is to take some food along in case the hosts are unprepared, though only rarely is this likely to be the case. The secret to formally arranging a visit is to allow those invited to determine the time, style and length of stay.

The chief skills in visiting, which are also in diminishing supply, include not imposing on others, putting people at ease, asking the appropriate questions, listening* to what people say and appreciating the hospitality involved. These skills are not so much a case of learning certain techniques as developing a genuine interest in and concern for people, out of which other capacities flow.

We also need to rethink the rhythms of visiting. When it involves visiting someone in an institution, these are largely determined for us, but what is in our control is the regularity of and commitment to visiting a person over the long haul. When a visit is awkward and strained, there is a time beyond which little of value happens and preplanning that or sensing it during the visit is extremely helpful. When the person with whom we are in contact is obsessive about relationships, or the reverse of this and highly ambivalent, we need to realize that visits with the former must be limited and circumscribed and visits with the latter should be tailored to his or her wishes, rather than out of a sense of duty. When relationships are strong and developing, as with actual or potential friends, we need to visit regularly with an open time frame (*see* Friendship): a few hours every few weeks or months only allows us to catch up with each other, whereas what we need to go further and deeper is a whole day, sometimes a weekend and occasionally even a holiday together.

One thing is certain. If we wish relationships between families, friends and neighbors to deepen and the wider so-cial fabric to be strengthened, there will have to be a renewal of visiting in our day. As Christians we are well placed to do and demonstrate that. After all, we are the ones who know most of all the fundamental role of the divine visit Christ made to us when we were lonely, lost, estranged and at a distance from God. Since ours is the uniquely visited planet, we have a model before us that we should all energetically follow.

See also COFFEE DRINKING; CONVERSATION; FRIENDSHIP; PASTORAL CARE; TRAVELING.

References and Resources

R. Paul Stevens, *Disciplines of the Hungry Heart: Christian Living Seven Days a Week* (Wheaton, Ill.: Harold Shaw, 1993).

Robert Banks

VOCATIONAL GUIDANCE

Never before in history have so many people had the opportunity to change their lifestyles. Since many people no longer have to work "down in the mine," "take over their father's farm" or be "only a mother," they are faced with a myriad of choices. Because people bring to these choices fantasies and unconscious expectations, vocational decision-making today is less like fitting a peg into its proper hole and more like compressing an unruly spring into a container and wondering how long it will stay. It is an awkward and lifelong process, one substantially helped by being a Christian.

Definitions

Vocation is our divinely given life purpose embracing all dimensions of our human existence and the special dimensions of service Christians undertake in the church and world. *Vocational guidance* is the process of helping others, or receiving help oneself, to discover and persist in that life direction. It is more than finding the right job. It has a larger and deeper meaning: responding to God's purpose in marriage, singleness, family, neighborhood, church, political service and occupation. Vocational guidance is a modern concept that emerged principally from the Protestant Reformation. At a time when the rigid structures of society were breaking down, the idea of *calling** and the recovery of the dignity of work permitted people to make choices in occupations. Out of this the idea of vocational guidance was born.

Misunderstandings

The confusion surrounding this topic is illustrated by Barbara Zikmund. Vocation, she says, is presented as something that "(1) has little to do with our jobs, (2) has something to do with all jobs, (3) has more to do with certain jobs, (4) or has everything to do with on-the-job and off-the-job existence. No wonder good Christians get confused" (Zikmund, p. 328). So we must start by clearing away several misunderstandings.

The idea of choosing a calling is an oxymoron. The word *vocation* is derived from the Latin *vocatio* which means "to call." So vocation and calling are identical in meaning. It would be a good thing if we used *calling* more often since it invites the questions, By whom? and For what? Basic to the idea of vocation is a divine, not a human, choice. God has issued a summons to his creatures. This summons is all-embracing and includes work, family, neighborhood, civic responsibility and the care of creation. The basic structure is found in Ephesians 4:1, where Paul urges all Christians (and not just church leaders*) to "lead a life worthy of the calling to which you have been called" (RSV) and then in chapters 4—6 elaborates some of the contexts in which we are to live as called people: congregational life (4:1-16), marriage (5:21-33),

home (6:1-4), workplace (6:5-9) and society (6:10-18). Simply put, the Christian vocation is God's call to live for the praise of his glory (Eph 1:12, 14) and to serve God's purposes in every context of life. A career is chosen; a calling is accepted.

God does not have a wonderful plan for our lives. He has something far better—a wonderful purpose! For some Christians, concern "to be in the center of God's will" leads to guidance* anxiety. A plan, like a blueprint, must be followed in slavish detail, but a purpose is like a fast-flowing stream that carries a boat along and incorporates even mistakes into its ultimate direction. God's primary concern, according to the Bible, is not that we fit like pegs in their proper slots but that we become people who love God, neighbors and God's creation. To participate in God's grand purpose of renewing everything in Christ means to oppose evil, to do the work of maintaining a city, to build community, to create systems that bring dignity and value to human life. So John Calvin counsels that believers should "choose those employments which yield the greatest advantage to their neighbors" (*Opera*, XLI, 300). This does not mean, however, going into the ministry* or choosing a Christian service career or a "people" job.

Vocation is not the same as remunerated employment. Indeed, we do not need to have remunerated employment to have vocational contentment. Some fulfill their service to humankind through volunteer work* instead of or outside their remunerated occupation. Work,* occupations, careers* and professions* are important parts of our vocation in Christ, but they are not the whole. According to Scripture the first human couple was given three full-time jobs, not just one: first, to enjoy full-time communion with God; second, to build community on earth starting with the relationship of male and female and third, to take care of God's earth (Gen 2:15) and develop God's creation as coworkers with God (Gen 4:20-22). While sin marred this threefold human vocation, Christ has reclaimed us for this, and we enjoy substantial redemption until there is complete fulfillment of the human vocation in the New Jerusalem. So work in all its forms is much more than remunerated employment, though that employment may be located primarily in one of the three full-time jobs. Christians are required to seek gainful employment, to meet needs of their own (1 Thess 4:12; 2 Thess 3:12) and of others (Eph 4:28). But when we are technically unemployed* or retired,* we are still caught up in God's all-embracing summons.

Vocational decision-making is not a once-for-all event but a lifetime process. There is only one once-for-all vocational decision, and that is to yield to the gracious invitation of God in Christ and to welcome being caught up in his grand purpose. Within that purpose, life is full of adjustments, decisions, redirections, mistakes and even second chances. This has not always been recognized, as when vocation was identified with one's station in life. In fairness to Luther (who is often charged with promoting fixed callings understood as positions in life), he stressed the duties attendant on one's station as a means of fulfilling calling, not the location of that calling. Calvin and his followers developed this further: vocational living is using our gifts and talents* within our callings—thereby opening the door to "changing jobs" to fulfill calling. In a modern mobile society we must grasp the heart of vocational living as a continuous process of discerning God's will and purpose.

Vocational guidance is not simply an individual matter.

Gifts and talents are discovered and affirmed communally, and roles and responsibilities are defined communally.

While we should, as the Puritan William Perkins advised, explore our own affections, desires and gifts, we should also consult the advice of others because of our inherent tendency to be biased (p. 759). The Christian community should create an environment where people with a broad vision can encourage one another with the particularity of one's vocation (Fowler, pp. 115-25). Most people will find this possible in local churches, accountability groups and spiritual friendships.*

A Short Theology of Vocational Guidance

Amid the confusion surrounding vocational decision-making, there is nothing quite as comforting or constructively helpful as good theology. This brief summary will include Christian identity, personal vocation, God as vocational director, the will of God, the providence of God and knowing ourselves.

Our vocation comes out of our identity, not the reverse. In the secular world people are defined by what they do: She is a doctor; he is a business person. Guidance counselors speak of helping people gain a "vocational identity." But the Christian approach is the exact reverse. Our fundamental identity is to become children of God through Christ. So instead of developing a vocational identity, we should seek an identity-formed vocation. Being precedes doing. First we are called to Someone to become somebody. Then we are called to do something for that Someone. Vocation flows out of our essential identity in Christ. On this note Augustine insightfully recommended that someone wanting to find out who a person was should not ask what that person *does* but what that person *loves.*

Personal vocation particularizes God's general call to all humanity and his special call to his people. Unfortunately most discussions of vocation focus on the relative importance of two "doing" mandates: the creation (or cultural) mandate (Gen 1:27-29) and the Great Commission (Mt 28:18-20). Large parts of the contemporary church regard the Great Commission as the only mandate now in force and relegate the creation mandate to pre-Christian existence. The Reformers and Puritans had a better grasp of the breadth of God's call, arguing that God had diversified all the ways we fulfill the cultural mandate into all the occupations that keep the world running: homemakers,* blacksmiths, cobblers, teachers and farmers.*

A contemporary refinement of the Reformed view is supplied by Klaus Bochmuehl (p. 34). He asks us to imagine a three-tiered wedding cake. The bottom (and largest) layer is the *human vocation* of communion with God, building community and cocreativity (Gen 1—2). The second (and smaller) layer is the *Christian vocation* expressed in discipleship to Jesus, holiness in life and service in the world. This second layer is related to the first: becoming a Christian makes us more fully human (rather than angelic) and empowers us to fulfill the human vocation. Then we can imagine a third (even smaller) layer representing the *personal vocation*—that combination of human and Christian tasks to which a person is uniquely fitted by God and led by the Holy Spirit. Taken as a whole—all three layers of the wedding cake—we are not left guessing about who we are and what we are to do with our lives.

God is the ultimate vocational director. Robert Banks notes that God is also our vocational model dignifying all the ways God invites us to make the world work (p. 22). God is craftsperson, shepherd, weaver, farmer, architect, potter, host, homemaker, ruler and warrior, just to mention a few biblical metaphors. But God directs people providentially as he did with Adam and Eve in the garden,

Ruth gleaning in the field of Boaz, David in the court of Saul, Ezekiel among the exiles and Peter fishing just where Jesus needed to borrow a boat. Human freedom is real but limited. God is the only one who does "whatever he pleases" (Ps 115:3 NRSV). Our whole story, even parts that do not yet "make sense," is ordered and intended. Nothing can happen to us that cannot, by God's sovereignty, be turned into good (Rom 8:28).

God's will is not hard to find. Guidance is essentially a pagan concept. Outside the revelation of God to Israel and the church, people seek guidance by consulting mediums, casting spells and examining the entrails of animals and birds—all ancient equivalents to fortunetelling, reading the horoscope and looking for signs and portents. What Scripture offers is better than guidance; it offers the Guide. The Bible is more concerned with our relationship to the Guide than our being in "the center of his will," a concept not actually found in the Bible but promoted by popular Christianity. Perhaps 90 percent of our questions about what we are to do with our lives are answered by the teaching of Scripture. As Bochmuehl says, "If God does not call us to a particular task at a particular time, we must fall back on the creational and salvational tasks that have already been given: to sustain and to further physical and spiritual life in the family and in the community, in the neighborhood and in the nation" (p. 34).

Sometimes God will speak directly through an inner persuasion, a vision or a dream. Though normally it is bad advice to tell someone to do that for which he or she is disinclined or unqualified, Scripture witnesses to God's surprising and unwelcome summons, for example, to Moses, Jonah and Paul. Lee Hardy wisely comments, "When [God] does that, it is because he is about to give a special demonstration of his power. That is, he is about to perform a miracle—which is, by definition, a departure from the normal course of affairs" (p. 93). Lacking such supernatural direction, Christians are not powerless to move forward in their lives. They can do so confidently for good reason.

Vocational decisions are rarely irrevocable. We can trust God's providence in our lives. Calvin said God's hand is at the helm of both the universe and the life of the individual. Our lives are not a bundle of accidents. Family background, educational experiences and life experiences are a reflection of God's good purpose for our lives. Our personalities, spiritual gifts* and talents have been given by God. This can be overemphasized, as it sometimes was by the Reformers. But we should not reduce the hope and comfort implicit in a high view of God's providence by looking for God's leading mainly in supernatural signs and wonders. Even mistakes get incorporated into God's overall purpose though our life path may be temporarily revised as a result. Joseph is a stunning example of God's providence. He was able to say to his brothers, "So then, it was not you who sent me here, but God" (Gen 45:8) and "You intended to harm me, but God intended it for good" (50:20). Since career decisions, for example, are rarely irrevocable, we are saved from paralyzing fear of ruining everything by one bad choice. So we can do the thing at hand. We can laugh at ourselves because God is God. Indeed laughter* in face of a life decision may be an act of worship.* Trusting in God's providence, however, is not an alternative to knowing ourselves.

Self-knowledge is an important part of our spirituality. A study by the Marketing and Research Corporation showed that three or four out of every five people are in the wrong jobs (Jones, p. 30). Ralph Mattson and Arthur Miller have devoted themselves to making links between the central motivational thrust and its primary vocational expression in the workplace. Their approach, now systemized in the SIMA test, assumes that (1) God has made us with the capacity to enjoy working and serving in a particular way; (2) what brings joy to us is a powerful indication of what God has designed us to be and do; (3) our central motivating pattern is consistent through life—the boy that nurses a wounded bird at five drives an ambulance at thirty-five.

Sophisticated and popular tests are now available to measure interests, natural aptitudes, values, personality type, learning style and life changes, and many of these tests have been made available in self-help workbooks, such as *Naturally Gifted: A Self-Discovery Workbook* (Jones). These tests are useful and helpful in understanding ourselves, though they seldom acknowledge that much of the world does not enjoy the luxury of occupational choice or the privilege of a fulfilling career.

In some circles, knowing ourselves, especially if it involves loving ourselves, is considered antithetical to denying ourselves—taking up the cross and following Jesus (Mt 16:24). Sometimes it is. As John Stott reminds us, we are not commanded to love ourselves but our neighbor as much as we already love ourselves in a fallen state (Mt 22:39; Mk 12:31). Further, love (*agapē*) in the New Testament implies self-sacrifice. Finally, self-love as a form of idolatry is the essence of sin in the last days (2 Tim 3:2, 4; Stott, pp. 34-35).

Taking this warning seriously, we may nevertheless develop a biblical approach to self-affirmation. (1) We will never know ourselves as we really are apart from God's view of us, a view we gain primarily from Scripture and the inner affirmation of the Spirit. (2) It is safe and healthy to know ourselves when our primary focus is the glory of God and his will. (3) Neither self-confidence nor self-depreciation but true humility is the normal result of being in God's presence. C. S. Lewis put this aptly, "It is when I turn to Christ, when I give myself up to His personality that I first begin to have a real personality of my own" (p. 189). (4) Even our inabilities, flaws and weaknesses revealed to us in every vocational context become strengths for the person who lives by the grace of God (2 Cor 4:7; 11:30; 12:9). (5) Loving, or better affirming, ourselves in the sense of accepting and respecting ourselves as God does may be distinguished from God-excluding self-absorption (*philautos,* "lovers of one's own self"; 2 Tim 3:4). (6) Self-affirmation involves coming to a sane estimation of our own value and strengths (Rom 12:3) and agreeing with the priorities Scripture places on life purposes: maturity more than effectiveness, faithfulness more than success, character development more than skill development, being more than doing. Such God-inspired self-acceptance, unlike egotistical self-preoccupation, is marked by grace.

Since our capacity for self-deception is enormous, the process of knowing ourselves is lifelong. Action-oriented, task-oriented, high-energy people especially need spiritual disciplines* to get in touch with themselves. The choice of a career, a marriage partner or even a role in the church frequently is infused with internal fantasies, a wished-for self that becomes a means of gaining a psychosocial identity. All of this points to the process of vocational guidance as being central, rather than auxiliary, to our life in God.

Vocational Guidance as a Spiritual Discipline

The process of lifelong vocational decision-making *is* a discipline. It is not only helped by the use of spiritual disciplines, such as meditation and journaling, but it directs us to God for some of the following reasons.

Vocational guidance is concerned with both entering in and continuing in a calling in worthy manner (Eph 4:1). Vocational life is littered with idols: the idols of gain (being in it for the money), glory (seeking position in the church for human approval) and instant ecstasy (getting a "fix" or "high" from making a sale). All too easily a challenging profession or an all-consuming role like mothering can feed our addictions* and become idolatrous. *Idolatry* is defined simply as making something one's ultimate concern other than the One who is ultimate. The Puritan William Perkins reminds us that "walking worthy of one's calling" requires an ongoing process of sanctification of the worker and the works. He uses seventeenth-century examples of how not to walk worthy, examples that apply equally to today: for physicians, prescribing remedies without proper diagnosis; for booksellers, selling immodest and improper books; for the merchant and tradesman, having false weights and dressing up the wares so people are deceived; for the patron, making a public pledge of a large gift but following through with only part of it; and for the landlord, racking the rents (Perkins, p. 771).

The chief cause of a vocational mismatch is not being in the wrong location but yielding to the lust of the spirit. We should be living contentedly within our calling, but joy in service is not a matter of location as much as spirit. Drivenness* is a symptom of something wrong inside. The lust of the spirit is the desire for something other than what God deems best for us. If we do not judge that the particular calling in which God has placed us is the best of all callings for us, we will yield to discontentment, as did Absalom, the sons of Zebedee and Cain (Perkins, p. 756).

To counteract this pernicious lust, Perkins offers several practical measures: (1) discerning the initiative of God in our lives so that even in times of crosses and calamities we may rest certain that God has placed us in this calling (p. 760); (2) repenting if necessary for the wrong reasons we entered a calling (be it marriage, career or ministry) but refusing to forsake our place and so continuing with diligence and good conscience (p. 762)—a strategy that is crucial for those who feel they entered marriage for the wrong reasons. Further, Perkins advises (3) seeking sanctification both of the worker and the work by the Word of God and prayer (p. 766); (4) resisting the temptation to covetousness by laboring to see our particular situations as a providence of God no matter how difficult it may be and by resolving in our hearts that God—not a perfect situation—is our portion (Ps 16:6); (5) turning our affections from this world to better things by not seeking more in this world than we actually need and setting our mind on heaven (p. 770; compare Eph 1:18); (6) persisting in our calling by pruning our lives of ambition,* envy of others placed in "better" callings, and impatience, all of which incline us to leave our calling when trouble comes. On this last measure Perkins uses a medical image from the days before anesthesia that is superbly graphic. He says we must continue in our callings as the surgeon who continues to cut his patient even through the patient is screaming a lot (Perkins, p. 773)!

Hardship is not an indication of our being in the wrong calling. Run through all the callings, Luther pleaded, and you will find that every earthly occupation has a cross. We can suffer for the sake of others and identify in some small way with the suffering of Christ right where we are. This is entirely in line with a faithful interpretation of 1 Corinthians 7:20—

"Each one should remain in the situation which he was in when God called him"— namely that change, while permissible, should not be undertaken as though it had spiritual significance. Paul is a classic case. Though he was being stoned, dragged out of cities and suffered privations, not least of which was his day and night handwork to support himself as a tentmaker,* he knew he was doing God's will. Hardship can become a pruning experience, even a means of grace. Being in the will of God does not guarantee health, wealth and a creative, fulfilling career. Discovering that nothing in this world will ultimately satisfy us, as C. S. Lewis once pointed out, is a powerful hint that we were made for another life and another world. In the end what counts is that we are found in Christ.

We are accountable in the last day for what we have done with our lives. The supreme motivating factor in walking worthy of one's calling is the fact that we must all give account on the day of judgment for what we have done in our callings. Perkins asks, "How then can we give a good account of ourselves before God on that day? We must calculate our blessings, weigh all that was defective and then cleave to the surety of Christ, his death being all the satisfaction God needs" (p. 779). This strongly biblical note (Mt 25:19) is conspicuously missing in most Christian treatments of vocational guidance, as is the next.

We must walk by faith not sight. Walking by faith means that we cannot find the explanation of our lives in the circumstances in which we find ourselves but only by faith in God. This involves the daily discipline of seeking God's face, finding our satisfaction in God, affirming our acceptance in Christ—rather than finding the joy of our life in how well things are going. At the root of this—as Luther so wisely discerned—is our actual heart-level experience of the gospel.

A person who has gospel confidence, Luther stated, is like a man who feels completely comfortable and secure in the mutual love between his wife and himself. Such a person does not have to weigh which act or deed might bring about the maximum positive response: "For such a man there is no distinction in works. He does the great and the important as gladly as the small and the unimportant, and vice versa. Moreover, he does them all in a glad, peaceful, and confident heart, and is an absolute willing companion to the woman" (Luther, pp. 26-27). But if the man is insecure in his or her love, he will calculate and offer the largest and most impressive deed to gain what he thinks he can obtain by works. So too the person insecure in his or her relationship with God may choose to win approval by works, works that might include going into the monastery (in Luther's day) and going into the ministry (in our day). Without the foundation of divine approval, vocational decision-making will normally become a means of inventing personal meaning and satisfaction—a form of self-salvation for the unbeliever—or an attempt to win God's approval in the case of the believer.

In summary, we should regard the Christian life and service as a comprehensive and liberating summons of God. We already know what God's will in broad terms is for our life! Finding the best job is a minor part of this. We should do the thing at hand for God's glory until clearly led by God. We should affirm God's providence in our life. We are not a bundle of accidents, and even occupational—and other—mistakes can be incorporated into God's purpose for our life. This means we can live wholeheartedly and exuberantly in the present, not with our eye on the next (and more fulfilling) assignment. The heart of Christian vocation, and therefore the essence of vocational guidance, is not choosing to do something, but responding to the call to belong to Someone and because of that, to serve God and our neighbor wholeheartedly.

See also CALLING; GUIDANCE; MINISTRY; SERVICE; SPIRITUAL DISCIPLINES; TALENTS; WORK.

References and Resources

R. Banks, "The Place of Work in the Divine Economy: God as Vocational Director and Model," in *Faith Goes to Work: Reflections from the Marketplace,* ed. R. Banks (Washington, D.C.: The Alban Institute, 1993) 18-29; K. Bockmuehl, "Recovering Vocation Today," *Crux* 24, no. 3 (September 1988) 25-35; J. Calvin, *Institutes of the Christian Religion,* 2 vols., ed. J. T. McNeill, trans. F. L. Battles (Philadelphia: Westminster, 1960); W. Dumbrell, "Creation, Covenant and Work," *Crux* 24, no. 3 (September 1988) 14-24; J. W. Fowler, *Becoming Adult, Becoming Christian: Adult Development and Christian Faith* (San Francisco: Harper & Row, 1984); L. Hardy, *The Fabric of This World: Inquiries into Calling, Career and Choice, and the Design of Human Work* (Grand Rapids: Eerdmans, 1990); G. Jones and R. Jones, *Naturally Gifted: A Self-Discovery Workbook* (Downers Grove, Ill.: InterVarsity Press, 1993); M. Kolden, "Luther on Vocation," *Word and World* 3, no. 4 (1983) 382-90; C. S. Lewis, *Mere Christianity* (New York: Macmillan, 1952); M. Luther, *Treatise on Good Works,* vol. 44 of *Luther's Works,* trans. W. A. Lambert, ed. J. Atkinson, (Philadelphia: Fortress, 1966); R. T. Mattson and A. F. Miller, *Finding a Job You Can Love* (New York: Thomas Nelson, 1982); W. Perkins, *The Works of That Famous Minister of Christ in the University of Cambridge* (London: John Legatt, 1626); J. R. W. Stott, "Must I Really Love Myself?" *Christianity Today,* 5 May 1978, 34-35; B. B. Zikmund, "Christian Vocation—In Context," *Theology Today* 36, no. 3 (1979) 328-37.

R. Paul Stevens

VOLUNTEER WORK

Volunteers are ordinary people who have chosen to become involved in providing a needed service,* solving a problem or advancing a worthy cause, without thought of payment other than personal satisfaction. The history of volunteering is filled with people who set off on their own to create programs when no one else has had the vision—or the willingness—to act. As we will see, volunteerism has its roots not only in human altruism but in the divine mandate to love* one's neighbor. Further, it is implicit in the Christian gospel that those who have received the free gift of salvation will, in turn, give their service without obligation of recompense.

How Volunteerism Began

From the beginning of human experience, as modern sociology and anthropology show, human beings have striven to share and to cooperate just to survive in the face of hostile environments and strangers. As we read the pages of history, we find countless instances of individual effort to help others and promote the common good. These acts of kindness and goodwill are based on the Judeo-Christian principles of love, justice* and mercy. The command given to the Israelites by God through Moses to love your neighbor as yourself (Lev 19:18) was quoted by Jesus (Mt 22:39). Some of the Pharisees limited the meaning of the term *neighbor* but Rabbi Nahmanides took a wider view when he said, "One should place no limitations upon the love of neighbor, but instead a person should love to do an abundance of good for his fellow being as he does for himself." In telling the story of the good Samaritan, Jesus made it abundantly clear that *neighbor* means not merely "one who lives nearby" but "anyone with whom one comes in contact." Jesus' teaching has encouraged, even mandated, that we all are to be volunteers and reach out to those who need help. Further, the experience of acceptance by God and the gift of new life in Christ are a powerful motivation to serve others voluntarily, without restraint, obligation

or demand for payment. Jesus said, "It is more blessed to give than to receive" (Acts 20:35), a principle that Paul embodied in his practice of tentmaking.*

How Volunteerism Developed

People have always come together to get jobs done. Sharing equipment and labor at barn raisings or harvest, caring for a sick neighbor or friend, lending money* to help through a tough spot or being willing to listen are examples of ways people have endeavored to fulfill Jesus' mandate. The more primitive the society* or the more remote the community is from civilization, the greater will be the need to rally around one another in time of crises or stress.

"Modern associational forms of voluntary effort were stimulated by the Reformation's endorsement of freedom of association; they flowered with the urbanization of society during the industrial revolution, and experienced greater expansion during the twentieth century" (Manser and Cass, p. 19). The organizations that were formed as the result of these influences fulfill an incredible variety of purposes, some to serve the individual needs of their members, such as service clubs, Boy Scouts, Girl Guides and so on, and others to offer services to individuals and communities, for example, hospital auxiliaries, Red Cross, United Way and so on. Most often it was the voluntary effort of ordinary citizens, often working though their religious or cultural institutions, that led to the establishment of orphanages and homes for the aged as well as health and welfare agencies. Evangelical Christians have been especially prominent in the creation of such institutions.

A few examples will give some idea as to how widespread and diverse are the projects undertaken by volunteers: in Israel volunteers work closely with the military to provide grief counseling for families of soldiers killed in combat; in Ecuador volunteers run some of the major cemeteries and provide basic supplies, such as blankets, for hospitals; in Sri Lanka volunteers build wells.

Volunteerism Today

The need for voluntary action is as great today as it ever was, possibly even greater in our fast-paced, mobile society in which so many demands are placed on the family and the community. While the direct effects of volunteer work are felt at the individual or community level, the combined action of many millions of ordinary citizens from every region of the country has had a profound impact on virtually every aspect of society and has, in fact, fostered its growth and development. At the present time, informal volunteer work goes on every day as people occasionally help out neighbors, friends and others in a personal and spontaneous manner. More formal volunteer work is carried out within an organization or agency and is planned in advance.

Recent surveys have dispelled a number of widely held myths regarding volunteerism. One belief is that the great majority of volunteers are women, most likely middle-aged or older. Also there is the myth that they are from the more affluent strata of society and can afford to give away their time freely. According to a public opinion survey conducted in 1991, 71 percent of Canadian adults had done volunteer work at some point in their lives. According to a 1993 survey the volunteers were 33 percent male and 67 percent female, but this would not include all men who run sports programs as coaches and referees. Over 60 percent of volunteers were under 30 years of age, and 33 percent were unemployed. Only 12 percent were listed as being homemakers.* It is quite evident that the traditional profile of a volunteer has changed radically over the years.

Agencies and organizations using volunteers have had to become increasingly adaptable and more effective in managing a very valuable and often very scarce resource. The formula for successful volunteering appears to go something like this: provide opportunities for personal achievement, allow volunteers to make new discoveries about themselves and others and enable them to feel that they are forming social bonds and strengthening the community. Mix this with appropriate training, feedback and recognition, and you will have volunteers who feel energized by the assignment, see it as a fun endeavor and will complete it feeling better than when they started.

Some of the benefits volunteers bring to an organization are personal attention to one-to-one relationships; closer contact with the community; objectivity in the delivery of service; credibility, as volunteers have fewer vested interests; specialized skills, knowledge and contacts; refreshed energy; new ideas; a reservoir from which to recruit new paid staff; an opportunity to mix generations and cultures; a flexible transition stage for new services; freedom from experimentation; humanizing of services; consumer input and education. Yet these benefits are not without cost: there is considerable expense in paid-staff time and resources to organize and support an effective volunteer program. Nevertheless, the benefits the volunteer brings to the organization usually exceed these costs many times over.

Managing Volunteers

It is critical to consider the purpose of the volunteer program, how you plan to use the volunteers and to do everything possible to make the program work for volunteers, staff and organization. It is important to prepare the administration and staff of your organization for the introduction of the volunteer program as it is essential to have a positive attitude on their part and their full support. It is also necessary to have someone assigned to manage the program, whether presently on staff or newly hired. Many organizations today have job descriptions for their volunteers so that they have a clear understanding of what is expected of them.

The majority of volunteers expect to be treated with dignity and respect, to be given periodic evaluations of their work and to receive recognition of their contributions to the group. They may even expect and need to have out-of-pocket expenses such as bus fare, lunch money and even baby-sitter costs to make it possible for them to offer their time and services. Contrary to what is often said, "You cannot expect reliability from a volunteer but only from paid staff," volunteers that have a clear job description and are held accountable can be as reliable as those who serve for remuneration.

Those who manage volunteers need to understand the many possible motivations behind voluntary service, not all of which are purely altruistic. One pamphlet put out by a group called Parlay International listed forty-one reasons why people volunteer, including the following: to feel needed; to share a skill; to get to know a community; to demonstrate commitment to a cause or belief; to gain leadership skills; to act out a fantasy; to do your civic duty; because of pressure from a friend or relative; to keep busy for recognition; to repay a debt; to donate your professional skills; because there is no one else to do it; to have an impact; to learn something new; to fill up some free time; to help a friend or relative; for escape; to become an "insider"; because of guilt; to be challenged; to be a watchdog; to feel proud; to make new friends; to explore a career;

to help someone; as therapy (Parlay International, 1350.009).

In the church volunteering expresses the heart of Christian ministry.* As a spiritual discipline volunteering provides an arena for personal transformation and growth as we learn the blessing of giving without material reward and sometimes without intangible rewards.

See also MINISTRY; SERVICE, WORKPLACE; STEWARDSHIP; TALENTS; TENTMAKING.

References and Resources

W. H. Brackney, *Christian Voluntarism: Theology and Praxis* (Grand Rapids: Eerdmans, 1997); S. Ellis, *Focus on Volunteering* (Emeryville, Calif.: Parlay International, 1992); G. Manser and R. H. Cass, *Volunteerism at the Crossroads* (New York: Family Service Association of America, 1976); J. Lautenschlager, *Volunteering: A Traditional Canadian Value* (Ottawa: Voluntary Action Directorate, 1993); *Volunteers: How to Find Them, How to Keep Them* (Vancouver: Vancouver Volunteer Centre, 1990); Volunteer Centre of Ottawa—Carleton, *Why People Volunteer* (Ottawa: Voluntary Action Directorate, 1992).

Ruth Oliver

VOTING

There are many kinds of voting. In some churches* members elect their elders, deacons or other leaders. Many voluntary organizations elect officers and boards of directors. Labor organizations typically elect leaders. Mom and Dad may even ask their children to vote on where they would like to eat or go for vacation.* While all these forms of voting reflect the importance we attach to human expression, participation and responsibility, each represents a different meaning, depending on the nature of the institution or organization* in which the voting takes place. In this article we will primarily explore the significance of voting in a political election.

The History of the Popular Vote

In regards to politics the popular vote was a long time in coming. Not until the twentieth century did women win the right to vote (the franchise) in the United States. Not long before that only males who owned property were allowed to vote. The electoral process in political life arose as part of the movement toward accountable government. Autocratic monarchs and aristocrats, particularly when they claimed to rule by divine right, argued that their sovereignty required their independence. If they were restricted by others, their rule would not be the exercise of real authority. The monarchs who acknowledged God's supremacy argued that it was sufficient for them to be accountable to God. Under these aristocracies and monarchies the responsibility of the subject was to submit to the aristocrat's or monarch's rule, not to interfere with it.

Feudal lords and then monarchs of various kinds gradually found themselves hemmed in by lower magistrates and aristocrats who demanded (at times even voted) that the monarch meet certain of their requirements before they would pay taxes* or raise an army for the ruler. This process was extended to the point at which legislatures were eventually established to advise and give consent on the ruler's lawmaking. What, in fact, was happening was that the public realm (the *res publica*, from which we get our word *republic*) was gradually being distinguished from the private possessions of feudal lords, aristocrats and monarchs. The governance of all subjects was being recognized as a responsibility. Voting became one of the chief tools used by those who were governed to exercise responsibility in holding the executive authority accountable to the public and for the public good. That form of advice and consent eventually became the lawmaking responsibility of the governing process—the legislative branch of government.

Parliaments or congresses or legislatures were created even where monarchs continued to rule. In the United States the revolutionary patriots rejected a monarchy and set up a president (and, in the states, governors) to perform the executive duties of government. Legislative bodies became the primary locus of popular representation, and for that to work an electoral process was critical. The right to vote meant that a citizen was allowed to exercise some responsibility in the governing process by choosing representatives and holding them accountable.

The Meaning of the Vote

What happens, what power or authority is transferred, when a citizen votes for a representative? From the beginning of the modern electoral process this question of representation has been critical. One interpretation of the vote is that voters are acting to choose the persons most qualified to act independently as legislators or executives. Somewhat like elders or deacons in a church, the elected representatives are seen as entering an office that has a prior definition of responsibility. Once in office the representative is supposed to make his or her own decisions based on the best possible reasoning and deliberation, independent of any pressure from voters.

Another view of the electoral process is that the elected representative is chosen to stand in the place of the voters. The representative serves as the voice of the voters; he or she is supposed to reproduce the wishes of the voters, who would be governing themselves if they could all gather together to do so. Obviously, in this case the office of the representative is merely to speak for the voters, in contrast to the first view in which the representative holds an office of government that has its own requirements for deliberation and judgment independent of the voters.

Voting as Public Discipleship

While these details may sound insignificant and even unimportant to Americans, who are notorious for not voting at election time, Christians ought to take a different view of the matter. First, we ought to see political governance and representation as a process whereby officeholders are called to exercise an important God-given responsibility. Voters do not create the offices of government any more than they create the church offices of elders, deacons or bishops. It is not simply that self-governance is a practical impossibility for millions of citizens without representatives; more important is the fact that governance requires decisions that conform to standards of justice. Regardless of how people gain political office, their task is to perform the duties of government, not merely to do what someone else wants them to do or pays them to do.

Second, voting should serve as a means of connecting the government with the governed. The political community—the body politic—belongs to all citizens, not just to those who govern it. Everyone has a stake in it; all share responsibility, whether actively or passively, for its well-being. Voting is an act that fits into the wider meaning of representation, governance and citizenship. So how ought we to understand the importance of voting in this larger context?

An important distinction should be made at this point—one that is not always made in the American political setting. Electing representatives is a different kind of voting process than the one that takes place in a legislative body when laws* are being made by legislators. The purpose of voting within a legislative body is to pass laws by drawing the deliberative process to a close. Legislators debate the merits of a proposed law, and when they finally vote for or against a bill, they have to reach a single conclusion. A majority vote is typically required to decide either yes or no on a bill.

Citizens voting in an election to choose their representatives are not legislating or writing laws; they are merely selecting the people who will be empowered to do the legislating. There is no need at election time to reach a single winner-take-all conclusion, no need to reach a yes-or-no conclusion. The purpose of voting for representatives should be to allow the voters actually to choose the people they want to have as their representatives. For this reason I believe we should reexamine the American electoral system, which has a winner-take-all method of choosing representatives. Voting takes place in single-member districts, in which a single winner is chosen. The majority (or plurality) winner is made the representative of everyone who lives in the district. This turns out to be a strange way of choosing representatives because some voters will inevitably be represented by a candidate they opposed, not by the one they voted for. And if the candidate they vote for wins, then their choice cancels out the votes of those who voted for losing candidates. In other words, only the votes for the winner actually succeed in determining the representative. No wonder many people in the United States, Canada, Great Britain and other countries that use this system feel alienated as voters. Their votes often do not count.

A Proposal for the Reform of Voting

A different electoral system, which is used by most democratic countries in the world, does a better job of making votes count. Instead of creating single-member districts, they create multimember districts. Imagine, for a moment, that

Illinois has twenty seats in the U.S. House of Representatives. Instead of setting up twenty single-member districts, suppose Illinois were to make the whole state one district and allow many different political parties each to run twenty candidates. Voters would then vote for the party with which they identity. If 40 percent of the voters vote Republican, they would (and should) get 40 percent of Illinois' House seats—eight seats. If 30 percent vote Democrat, then the Democrats would get six seats. If the Green Party gets 5 percent of the vote, it would get one seat. If the Libertarians get 10 percent of the vote, they would get two seats. The point should be obvious. Citizens would actually be represented by the parties they vote for. Few, if any, votes would not count. Moreover, the election would be successful even if no party got more than 50 percent of the vote. An election need not have a majority winner. At the same time nothing prevents the voters from choosing a majority party. If 85 percent of the voters in Illinois vote Republican, then the Republicans would obviously hold a huge majority of Illinois' House seats. But that vote should not allow the Republicans to win 100 percent of the seats, as would probably happen under our present system. The purpose of an electoral vote is to give citizens the kind of representation they want in Congress or their state legislature, not to decide whether a bill wins or loses.

Voting in the system I just described (a form of *proportional representation* used for electing the Upper House in Australia) does a better job of connecting voters with their representatives. Voters get the representatives they want, rather than the ones they vote against. In this system it is typical for political parties to be stronger and to exercise more discipline over their candidates. This helps to overcome the power* of outside interest groups and the disintegrating effect of lone-ranger candidates winning elections without clear agendas or accountability to the voters.

Voting should be the means by which citizens gain representation and hold their representatives accountable. The best way to do that is to make it possible for voters to organize political parties that genuinely reflect their convictions. Elections should be events in which voters are doing more than choosing the lesser of evils among individual personalities; an election should be the time for voters to choose platforms, broad programs and principles according to which they want representatives to govern. Elections that do not offer this opportunity to voters will carry little meaning. That is one reason why half or more of the eligible voters in the United States do not turn out for elections.

A better electoral system of the kind I have described would also make it easier for voters to decide how to choose among candidates. Today a voter is usually confronted with just two choices—only one of whom will win the race. The Christian voter often faces the difficulty of choosing between the two: for example, what if one candidate is a Christian but his or her stance on many issues is weak or undeveloped or unjust from the Christian voter's point of view? What should the Christian voter do if the other candidate, though not a Christian, stands on a better platform and has a proven record of public service?

Responsible Voting

Obviously the voter must try to select the better of the two candidates as judged by how they will fill the office. The voter's decision might be little more than a choice for the lesser of evils, but a vote must be cast. This is where the importance of *office* comes in. Ideally the Christian voter would expect that Christian candidates should have the best political program, but that is not automatically the case. Imagine, for example, that I as a Christian were to go into farming* because I wanted to be a good steward of plants, animals and other resources in order to produce food for people. The problem is that I am not qualified to be a farmer. I know nothing about farming. Just because I am a Christian, I will not necessarily do what is right as a farmer—or as an artist, scientist or public official. Christian voters, in other words, must ask about more than the faith orientation of a candidate for public office; they have to ask how a candidate's faith orientation is related to his or her qualifications for the job as judged by experience, wisdom, political philosophy, an understanding of many different issues and more. If we had a different kind of electoral system, it would be easier for citizens to compare and judge each party, knowing that the candidates in each party would be bound by that party's platform and philosophy. Candidates would carry a larger banner and would be under stronger party discipline than is the case today.

Christians should be the kind of citizens who work for real governmental accountability, who become seriously involved in the election of representatives and who help push public officials (elected and unelected) to do justice. The voting system has a lot to say about how well citizens can achieve these aims. Electoral reform that can make voting more meaningful may be an urgent priority for Christians in the decades ahead.

See also CITIZENSHIP; JUSTICE; LOBBYING; POWER.

References and Resources
D. Amy, *Real Choices/New Voices* (New York: Columbia University Press, 1993); P. Marshall, *Thine Is the Kingdom* (Basingstoke, U.K.: Marshalls, 1984); J. W. Skillen, *Recharging the American Experiment: Principled Pluralism for Genuine Civic Community* (Grand Rapids: Baker, 1994); J. W. Skillen, "Toward Just Representation: A Proposal for Revitalizing Our System of Political Participation" (pamphlet published by the Association for Public Justice, Washington, D.C.).

James W. Skillen

W

WAITING

In the Western world waiting is a curse to be eradicated because it accomplishes nothing and wastes time. So almost everything gets instantized: food preparation, service, transportation, communication and leisure. In contrast, in the developing world waiting in long lines for service in a government office is a way of life, often being seasoned with lively conversations* with the people around you in the line. But most people in the developed world will do almost anything to avoid waiting. Waiting is boring.* To keep people waiting is a social sin. Forcing customers to wait is disastrous.

Instantizing Almost Everything

In response to this human demand for the eradication of waiting, technology* offers faster and more powerful computers (that "boot up" in seconds), automatic teller machines (that produce money without the time-consuming factor of dealing with people), microwave ovens (that reduce meal preparation time) and instant foods (that reduce ingestion time). The trend seems irreversible. To avoid waiting for the bus, people drive their cars to work, one person per vehicle. To avoid waiting for replies from letter writing,* people use e-mail. To avoid waiting for the repair of a toaster, people buy a new one. All this stems from the assumption that time is a commodity, a scarce resource that must be managed shrewdly.

Relationships are deeply affected by this instantizing trend. Intimacy takes time. Persons are mysteries. Friendship* cannot be rushed: there must be time for the ever deepening spiral of giving and receiving as layers of ourselves are unmasked progressively. No wonder so many people are lonely today. A good marriage is the product of a lot of waiting and cannot be instantized. No wonder there are so many divorces. Love cannot be given or received without waiting and listening*; instant sex, in contrast, is genital activity without waiting for the returns of love. No wonder there is so much preoccupation with sex in our society when there is so little sexual satisfaction.

Even death is affected. On one hand, when people find they have an incurable disease, they do everything possible to prolong life. Heaven can wait. On the other hand, when they get nearer to death and the quality of life has been drastically reduced, they cannot wait to die.

Religion gets sucked into this no-waiting vortex as preachers promise no-wait results from faith—instant health, wealth and happiness. Churches package their services into no-wait sound and sight bites without embarrassing silences. Starting a service late is a venial sin; ending late is a mortal sin. What would you do while waiting? People do not wait for God to speak, wait for spiritual gifts,* for maturity, for answered prayer, for the blessing* of God or for the Second Coming. They want it all now.

Paradoxically, the faster we go, the more it seems we must wait as we encounter technologically resistant zones in urban life: stalled traffic on freeways, delayed credit card transactions when the system is down, long waits for elective surgery, takeoff delays when air traffic control is overloaded. Some things seem to slow down when we try to speed them up. Family life is a case in point. Children, anxious to grow up as quickly as possible, wear adult clothes and savor adult experiences as early as possible. Yet people do not seem to be growing up as quickly as they once did. Adolescence has been prolonged indefinitely, and people delay having children themselves because they know intuitively that having children will force them to stop being children themselves.

Another example is spiritual growth.* There seems to be no effective way to force-feed Christians, to create an effective hothouse for fast growth, to package deeper spirituality in one short conference or to reduce spiritual disciplines to a how-to manual. As Jesus said, "The seed sprouts and grows, though he does not know how" (Mk 4:27). Try as we will, we cannot seem to eliminate waiting. Would it be a good thing if we could?

Waiting as Spiritual Discipline
Psychologists tell us that impulse control is a crucial life skill to be gained in the process of maturing. How can we learn to delay gratification if we live in an instantized culture? Sociologists claim the amount of leisure time is getting progressively reduced in the modern world as we squeeze ever more productivity out of the time we have. How as adults will we ever learn again to play if we fill up every gap in our date books with one more activity? Theologians proclaim that waiting for the blessing of kept promises is fundamental to living in hope—that crucial, though missing, dimension of Christian faith that enables us to live fully in the present without requiring everything now. How can we thrive in hope if we insist on instant sanctification, instant maturity, instant knowledge of God, instant heaven? The inspired apostles advise us that patience is crucial to spiritual maturity (Jas 5:7-11; Rom 5:4), and we learn patience in the most frustrating experiences of life (Rom 5:3; Jas 1:2-8). How can we ever become mature Christians if we eliminate the soil in which the fruit of the Spirit will grow?

In the Bible waiting is a metaphor for the life of faith. All the great heroes of faith in the Bible died without having it all: "They did not receive the things promised; they only saw them and welcomed them from a distance" (Heb 11:13). Adam and Eve had to wait for grace as they were thrust out of the garden with only a promise in their hearts. Abraham had to wait for a family. A generation of liberated slaves had to wait in the desert for the Promised Land. David had to wait for the throne. Job had to wait for God to speak. The exiles in Babylon had to wait for the restoration of the kingdom. The Jews in occupied Palestine had to wait for the messiah. Jesus waited thirty years to begin his ministry. Judas, in contrast, refused to wait for the kingdom and tried to make it happen. The wise virgins in the parable of Jesus were ready for a long wait; the foolish ones could not tolerate a delayed return of the Lord. The early disciples of Jesus had to wait for the promised Holy Spirit after Jesus rose from the dead. The converted Pharisee Saul had to wait fourteen years to be ready for his first short-term mission. All of us have to wait for heaven.

Waiting in the Psalms is a posture of focused expectation. "Wait for the LORD," the psalmist tells himself (Ps 27:14). "My soul waits for the Lord," he says to his friends (Ps 130:6 NRSV). "I wait for you, O LORD; you will answer, O Lord my God," he says to God himself (Ps 38:15). In the Lamentations of Jeremiah, written in the context of a social holocaust, the prophet calls to mind why waiting on God is so good: the never-failing compassions of God "are new every morning; great is your faithfulness. I say to myself, 'The LORD is my portion; therefore I will wait for him'" (Lam 3:23-24). God is utterly determined to give his presence, to bless his people and to provide a place for his people to dwell. Waiting for God is not like *Waiting for Godot,* Samuel Beckett's play about pointless, no-fulfillment waiting. Waiting for God is resultful—but not efficiently so.

The process of waiting is faith evoking, as Job found out. He wanted instant answers to his excruciating pain and loss, answers that his friends supplied with slick precision and impeccable orthodoxy. But in the process of waiting for God to speak—waiting persistently though not *patiently* (in the sense of passively)—Job discovered that he wanted God's presence even more than he wanted answers. What if God were to give us everything we prayed for immediately? (Would we not be sorry for asking—knowing so little about our real needs?) What if God revealed himself to us totally and instantly in our first encounter? (Would we cry out for the mountains to cover us?) What if Christian maturity were given in one transcendent moment and we never needed to grow? (Would not the Christian life be boring?) What if there were no bodily resurrection to wait for? (Would not all healing in this life be utterly disappointing?) What if Christ were not to come again? (Would not the world then end in a mere fizzle or a bang?) Refusing to wait is like turning to the last page of a novel to find out how it all ends. It spoils the whole story.

What Is the Good of Waiting?

Not all waiting is good. It is not good to wait another day to do the good we can do today or to wait for someone else to do what God has called you to do. It is not good to delay responding to the nuptial invitation of Christ or to wait for supernatural guidance* from God when you already know what to do from Scripture. Some waiting is not good because it has an unworthy object, or no object at all, or it is not good because the source is wrong—careless, apathetic, idle waiting without faith, hope and love. But Christian waiting, while hard, can be good and full of promise.

So opportunities to wait in everyday life can become a means of grace. Waiting in lines of people or cars gives us the opportunity to pray and meditate. If we cannot talk to the people around us, we can at least pray for them and our loved ones. Waiting relationally for the returns of love, for a long-awaited letter, for the answer to an important question, gives us the opportunity to go deeper with ourselves and God. Busyness and frenetic-paced living insulate us from getting in touch with ourselves, a vital dimension of Christian maturity. Waiting for late dinner guests can be a deliciously relaxing, leisure-full moment in the day. Waiting for the sabbath* each week can relativize our everyday work.

Reflecting on this matter, the Indian Christian Chandapilla once observed that there is always plenty of room at the end of the line. Up front, people are elbowing and pushing their way forward. But at the end of the line—a metaphor for the human factor in every situation whether business, church, family or neighborhood—there is no competition. You can find and be found by God, and you can find yourself waiting at the end of the line.

See also BOREDOM; COMMUTING; LEISURE; PROMISING; TIME.

References and Resources

D. Bonhoeffer, *Letters and Papers from Prison* (London: SCM, 1971); M. L. Raposa, "Boredom and the Religious Imagination," *Journal of the Academy of Religion* 53, no. 1 (1985) 75-91; W. Rybczynski, *Waiting for the Weekend* (New York: Viking Penguin, 1991); S. Weil, *Waiting on God*, trans. E. Craufurd (London: Collins, 1950).

R. Paul Stevens

WALKING

Walking is the basic way we get around. There is good reason for parents regarding a child's first step as a significant achievement. When in old age or through an accident our ability to walk is lost, we rightly view it as a major liability. The average person, living to seventy years of age, will walk between 100,000 and 150,000 miles during his or her lifetime.

The Nature and Practice of Walking

Despite its apparent ease, walking is a complex affair. It takes babies up to a year to begin to master it. If we are too self-conscious about it or feel too closely watched, it can become awkward. Actors must learn how to walk on to a stage or set so that the action does not look artificial. After a person has a prolonged sickness or suffers a bad accident, learning to walk again can be slow. Old people may find walking increasingly difficult and hazardous.

Generally, however, in comparison with other forms of movement, once we have mastered walking, we can do it instinctively. In terms of energy in relation to outcome, walking is highly efficient. Since reaction time is almost instantaneous and direction can be changed rapidly, walking has great flexibility. But walking does have its limitations. Its speed is not high, reducing the area we can cover in a given time. Over the long term walking consumes more strength than mechanical means of transport. The very young or old, the physically handicapped or disabled are at a decided disadvantage.

The Divine Benefits of Walking

Yet walking has some real advantages. These stem from its being specially designed and engineered by God as our most natural form of travel.*

Physical and psychological effects. In terms of keeping fit, a brisk twenty-minute walk several times a week is as effective as any other form of exercise except swimming. Studies show that walking can help reduce stress,* shifts in mood and addictive behavior. It can even increase self-esteem,* creativity and sense of control, as well as contribute to our alertness, ability to relax and positive attitude toward life. People who walk tend to have more effective immune functions and therefore remain healthier. Since about half of the decline normally associated with aging springs from underuse or disuse of the body, people who walk regularly also tend to live longer. Many medical professionals now endorse walking therapy for its preventive and rehabilitative effects, especially for those recovering from a heart attack or entering into old age. Even a ten-minute walk boosts energy four times longer than drinking coffee or smoking a cigarette, produces the energy equal to that resulting from eating a candy bar without generating fat or fatigue and uses stress in a positive way to exercise muscles and release tension.

Social and cultural effects. Walking with others, like eating* and drinking together, enhances social skills and relationships. It has often had a vital role in establishing—and also maintaining—friendships.* As the prophet says, "Do two walk together unless they have agreed to do so?" (Amos 3:3). Down through the centuries walking has also had significant cultural effects. For example, it played a part in the development of early Greek philosophy, especially among the so-called Peripatetics and Cynics. Music,* especially its more popular forms, has a debt to the wandering minstrels and troubadours of medieval times. The literary renaissance at the end of the eighteenth century, as embodied in poets like Wordsworth and Coleridge, owed much to the renewed practice of walking. Major essays on the pleasures of walking were written by notable figures of the period.

Spiritual and ministry effects. As many people have found, walking opens numerous possibilities for spiritual enrichment. This is already clear in Wordsworth's poetry, with its discovery and appreciation of the divine presence in the created world. As the kindred spirit John Findley said, it is not only "a joy in itself but . . . gives an intimacy with the sacred and primal things of earth that are not revealed to those who rush by on wheels." C. S. Lewis is one of many to have found Christ while taking a walk, for this activity opens up room for deep things to come to the surface. John Wesley found that walking twenty or thirty miles a day not only was health-giving but put "spirit into his sermon." Although he also traveled on horseback, Wesley would not have been able to carry the gospel to so many people had he not been prepared to walk, as did Paul, Francis and others before him.

Discerning When to Walk

Today walking tends to be a last resort. Faster mechanical means of transportation have lowered its status and pushed it into the background. For the majority of people walking is what you do when you have no other way of getting where you want to go or when another means is just too difficult or time consuming. People will sometimes drive a few hundred yards to shops, school or church,* rather than walk. In other words, walking takes place largely by necessity rather than as a proactive choice.

How do we know when we should use God's most available and natural form of transportation? We must begin by reversing our present attitude. Let us walk wherever we can appropriately do so and only use other means when we cannot. For example, we should walk to close destinations whenever we can conveniently and safely do so. Even if walking takes more time, there are the added physical, psychological and social benefits. When we experience a lot of tension in our lives or our physical capacities are declining, walking can help us relax and stay fit. Many older people find shopping malls* ideal for this because of their safety and opportunities for socializing. Also, we can intentionally set aside time to walk with friends and family as a way of building relationships and community.* We can also do this occasionally with our colleagues, neighbors* and small groups* in the church.

Since walking in the countryside or in the city* gives us a sense of scale with respect to our own importance, let us regularly make room for this. In doing so we gain a closer knowledge of our immediate and natural environment. Let us also consider how much walking may help us find solitude and opportunities to meditate and converse with God. The more attentive we become to what is around us, the more we shall also receive parables from God. When appropriate, walking around an area may open up ministry opportunities for us and for the congregations to which we belong. It enables people to begin to know who we are and enables us to begin to know them.

Walking as a Biblical Metaphor

The significance of walking appears in other ways, for example, as a metaphor describing some important aspects of life. It is interesting that God is depicted as walking in the Garden of Eden in the cool of the day (Gen 3:8). Even the Creator delights in taking an evening stroll! God also promises Israel, "I will walk among you and be your God" (Lev 26:12). Jesus not only walked all around Palestine—constantly encountering people on the streets and in their homes, places of business and worship centers—but also called people to follow his way of life. For his closest disciples this meant accompanying him wherever he went (Mk 3:14-16), and it was as he traveled that much of their training and much of his teaching and healing took place (Mk 8:31-33; 11:20-25; Lk 8:1-2; 24:13-32). Many of Jesus' parables also featured people who walked (for example, Lk 8:4-5; 10:30; 13:6).

The language of walking is used frequently in the Old Testament as a picture of the way the people should relate to God. Rather than "walk in the counsel of the wicked" (Ps 1:1) or "in pride" (Dan 4:37), they are encouraged to walk with the wise (Prov 13:20) and "humbly with your God" (Mic 6:8). In practice this means to "walk according to the law of the LORD" (Ps 119:1), in his ways (Ps 119:3) and paths (Is 2:3). For individuals the Lord's word is a lamp to their feet, which directs their footsteps (Ps 119:105, 133). To do this is to walk in freedom (Ps 119:45), uprightly (Is 57:2; compare Is 33:15) and securely (Prov 10:9). The model person is one whose "walk is blameless" (Ps 15:2; 84:11) and "in the light of [God's] presence" (Ps 89:15; compare Is 2:5). No greater compliment could be paid someone in the Old Testament than to say that he or she "walked with God" (Gen 6:9).

We find similar language in the New Testament. Here too walking is a key metaphor for depicting the way Christians should conduct themselves. John encourages believers to "walk in the light" (1 Jn 1:6-7; compare Jn 8:12; 11:9), as well as in truth, obedience and love (2 Jn 4, 6-7). For Paul walking is his major way of portraying the Christian life. Based on his own practice of walking, he even fashions a number of miniparables to throw light on different aspects of our pilgrimage. In general we walk in good works rather than worldly ones (Eph 2:2, 10), according to the Spirit rather than the flesh (Eph 5:8), in "newness of life" not death (Rom 6:4 NRSV), by faith not sight (2 Cor 5:7), in a proper way rather than a disorderly one (Rom 13:13). More picturesquely he exhorts us to "put shoes on our feet," that is, take the gospel wherever we go (Eph 6:15); to "walk a straight path," that is, have integrity (Gal 2:14); to "walk in the light," that is, be visible Christians (Eph 5:8); to walk "in another's steps," that is, follow good role models (2 Cor 12:18); and to "wash the dust off another's feet," that is, humbly serve others (1 Tim 5:10).

The Sacramental Character of Walking
It is clear from Scripture that God can speak to us as we walk so that we can communicate in recognizable ways with others. In view of the richness of the language, it is a pity that most modern translations of the Bible replace the image of walking with more prosaic descriptions such as "live," "behave" or "conduct yourselves." While not inaccurate, these translations cut off any imaginative associations that references to walking conjure up. As a result, the already weakened possibility of everyday activities becoming windows to divine realities is diminished even further.

Also affected is our ability to communicate effectively with others—not just because we are encouraged to talk in less concrete, vivid and familiar ways, but because the less we walk, the less contact we tend to have with other people. If we do not walk around our neighborhoods and our cities—Americans, as urban planners know, will generally not walk more than 600 feet from their driveway, parking space or office—we have less opportunity to get to know the people and places around us. One of the main reasons why many neighborhoods and parks have been taken over by gangs and criminals is that ordinary citizens do not walk around them. Most of these could be reclaimed for general, convivial use if we did.

See also BODY; CREATION; HEALTH; NEIGHBORHOOD; PUBLIC SPACES; SPIRITUAL GROWTH.

References and Resources
E. V. Mitchell, *The Pleasures of Walking* (New York: Vanguard, 1948); J.-J. Rousseau, *The Reveries of the Solitary Walker* (Indianapolis: Hackett, 1992).

Robert Banks

WASHING

Washing ourselves is one of the most basic human actions. Apart from eating* and drinking there is nothing more fundamental to our survival and association. Unless we wash regularly, we open ourselves up to sickness and disease; unless we wash, we also make it difficult for others to draw close to us and enjoy our company. For this reason washing has always been regarded as an important social as well as personal activity.

In many cultures,* as in biblical times, guests entering a home were provided with a pitcher of water to wash their hands and with someone to wash their feet. This was not only a Jewish but also an early Christian custom (Mk 7:3-4; 1 Thess 5:10). Such actions were viewed as an act of welcome and service, as well as a sign of holiness for some. Other ceremonies, such as the washing of one's hands as an expression of innocence (Ps

73:13), as a public sign of dismissing a situation (as did Pilate in Mt 27:24) or as an attempt to relieve guilt (compare Lady Macbeth), also came into being.

Some of these rituals still survive, if in a different form. For example, we do often ask visitors, especially if they have traveled some distance, whether they would like to use the bathroom (*see* Hospitality). We still use the language of "washing our hands" of something or someone. Obsessive people also sometimes wash themselves compulsively, and increasingly parents have become preoccupied with their children's cleanliness.

Across cultures and through the centuries, ways of washing and standards of cleanliness have varied. It is only in recent times that washing oneself has become a daily, or more than daily, affair. Until living memory in the West most people could only have a bath once a week. The general rise in living standards enabling every home* to have a bathroom, and in particular the invention of the shower, dramatically changed methods and expectations concerning washing. Modern advertising* elevates personal cleanliness to a position similar to that accorded it by the Pharisees in biblical times.

As a result cleanliness has tended to rank not "next to godliness" (as the popular saying puts it) but frequently above it. Many people daily spend more time washing themselves, especially their hair, than they do keeping their relationships with God or with significant others fresh and clear. Others value showers over baths because they are quicker, allowing them to pack more into each day at the expense of the reflective time and the relaxing effects a bath tends to provide.

Given the fundamental character of washing, it is not surprising that it should also become an important religious activity. Jesus' action of washing his disciples' feet exemplifies this and is the origin of the practice of foot washing that survives in some Christian traditions, such as among the Moravians (Jn 13:1-17). Jesus' practice of baptizing his followers and requiring his disciples to baptize converts reminds us that alongside eating and drinking, only washing has been given sacramental* significance (Mt 28:19). Water baptism* derives much of its force from being based on an everyday action that is indispensable to our well-being and preservation as well as to other's coming close to and becoming intimate with us.

Nor is it surprising that washing should become a metaphor for forgiveness and spiritual cleansing (Ps 51:7) or for experiencing the pouring out of the Spirit (Mt 3:11). In relation to water baptism, the more the connection between it and ordinary washing is understood, the more it takes place in a setting where washing publicly takes place, the more powerful an impression it creates on those who witness it. The more we allow our daily washing to remind us of the once-for-ever washing of forgiveness* that enables us to stand cleansed and fresh before God each day, the stronger a connection we will see between other daily actions and divine realities.

See also BAPTISM; BODY; CHORES; HEALTH.

References and Resources

D. Adam, *Tides and Seasons: Modern Prayers in the Celtic Tradition* (London: SPCK, 1989); J. Carroll, "The Soap Fetish," in *Sceptical Sociology* (Boston: Routledge and Kegan Paul, 1980) 106-29; M. Douglas, *Purity and Danger* (Boston: Routledge and Kegan Paul, 1966).

Robert Banks

WATCH

Time* has always been subject to measurement. In ancient times it was measured by comparison with how long a routine task or natural process took to complete, by observing the orbits of the sun and moon and by placing sticks in the ground and watching their shadows. In classical times came the more sophisticated hourglass and water clock. For them hours were still variable. Since twelve hours were attributed each to daytime and nighttime, they were longer in summer and shorter in winter.

In the thirteenth century the first mechanical clocks were installed in public buildings. They did not have minute hands and continued to mark variable hours. Much like the bells they replaced, they coordinated life generally rather than closely. By the fifteenth century domestic clocks were in evidence, though initially these had ornamental as much as practical value. By the seventeenth century scientists regarded the clock as the machine par excellence, and in the following centuries business people made it the pivotal machine in the Industrial Revolution.

Following the introduction of pocket watches in the late eighteenth century, the first wristwatch was made in Switzerland in 1865, and by 1880 these were being mass-produced for the middle class in North America. During the last two decades the digital watch has largely replaced the traditional analog version. Watches have become increasingly worn by everyone, including children. Meanwhile the spread of the watch into less-developed countries symbolizes and hastens the ongoing westernization of the whole world (*see* Global Village).

Impact and Significance

The spread of wristwatches introduced more personal habits of time keeping and made possible greater regulation of time in social life generally. People became more conscious of time, especially smaller units of time, and punctuality became a virtue or obsession. As long as we had analog watches with their circular hand movements—now enjoying something of a comeback—timepieces gave some sense of the sweep or flow of time. In the digital watch this evocation of daily rhythms is replaced by a mere succession of numbers. The advent of beepers on watches has only reinforced our awareness of passing time—whether we choose it or not—with hourly precision.

Particularly strange is the way the watch's mathematical or atomized view of time intrudes even upon our nonworking hours. This happens at night, even when sleeping,* and during weekends and vacation,* when strict knowledge of time is really unnecessary. These are periods when we could slip into a different mode of time. Our general failure to do this indicates how strong a hold the watch's view of time has upon us. Already by the eighteenth century Jonathan Swift, in his book *Gulliver's Travels,* foresaw this. After carefully observing Gulliver's behavior, the Lilliputians conclude that his pocket watch must be his god. Why? They ascribed divinity to his watch because Gulliver referred to it more than to anything else during the day in deciding what he should do! This forces us to ask how much our watches have become a kind of idol, dictating what we should do and on whose altar we sacrifice so many people and priorities.

Protest and Response

It is not surprising that some people have resisted the advance of mechanical timepieces. This began with the romantic poets and artists in the late eighteenth century who drew attention to the greater importance of inner, personal or subjective time over against its artificial objective measurement. When we are experiencing life deeply or fully, we are little conscious of the passing seconds, minutes and hours. Philosophers such as

Henri Bergson and Martin Heidegger also searched for a new sense of time far removed from the watch. In the sixties young people in the counterculture "dropped out" of the watch-driven society and opted for a style of life governed by more natural rhythms. These days many people pursue mystical experiences in the hope of entering into a different, timeless, state.

Yet the watch has its place, not always on our wrists perhaps, but in the general scheme of our individual and social lives. Despite its coming from a preindustrial time, the Bible contains time indicators of various kinds, for example, the parts of the day and night called *watches.* Today the watch is the literal heartbeat of the city,* and without it considerable chaos would reign. Without it we would be unable to effectively coordinate large movements of people across great distances into complex patterns of work* and play.*

The danger is that the watch too often becomes a master rather than a servant. We allow it to determine how much time we spend with spouses, friends and children; when we eat,* rest* and sleep; how long church lasts; what time we spend on various important activities; how much we can pack into a particular day. Generally it even dictates when and how long we give time to God!

Conclusion

There is a place for the watch, but it is a secondary one. In our watch-driven society we need to put the watch in its proper place. There are various ways we can do this. We should take off our watches when we don't need them and, when necessary, learn to judge the general passing of time by more natural means. We could do without the watch in church and in our communal small groups*; there we enter into God's time when, since God does not wear a watch, whatever happens should take its own appropriate divine length. This is something charismatic Christians are beginning to learn anew, though African-American Christians have known it all along.

As far as we can, we should also allow time given to relationships and responsibilities to be determined by how long they need rather than how much time the watch tells us we have. Let the watch take its cues from the significant events in our lives, not the other way round. One way of doing this is to put our watches into our pockets during such occasions, only taking them out when they are over or when we sense we must attend to another responsibility.

See also REST; STEWARDSHIP; TECHNOLOGY; TIME; WAITING.

References and Resources

R. Banks, *The Tyranny of Time* (Downers Grove, Ill.: InterVarsity Press, 1983); H. J. Cowan, *Time and Its Measurement from Stone Age to Nuclear Age* (Cleveland: World Publishing, 1958); D. S. Landes, *Revolution in Time: Clocks and the Making of the Modern World* (Cambridge, Mass.: Belknap, 1983); M. O'Malley, *Keeping Watch: A History of American Time* (New York: Penguin, 1990); K. Welch, *Time Measurement: An Introductory Essay* (Newtown Abbott, U.K.: David & Charles, 1972).

Robert Banks

WEALTH

Hardly anyone wants to be poor; most people would like to be rich. Wealth brings power, standing in the community, increased leisure and freedom from worry—so it is thought. Not surprisingly, in the richest part of the world many Christians are preaching a "prosperity gospel"—that faithfulness to Jesus will lead to personal wealth. Tragically, this distorted message is now taking root in some of the poorest countries of the world. Is wealth a sign of God's blessing? Is money* the main measure of wealth?

Why does money "talk"? Does the Bible endorse wealth, promote it or exclude it? How are we to respond in spirit and action? Our souls hang on our answers to these questions.

Wealth as Power

Principalities and powers* form an invisible background to our life in this world. One of those powers is money. *Mammon,* as it is sometimes called, comes from an Aramaic word, *amen,* which means firmness or stability. It is not surprising that a common English phrase is "the almighty dollar."

As an alternative god, mammon inspires devotion, induces guilt, claims to give us security and seems omnipresent—a godlike thing (Foster, p. 28). It is invested with spiritual power that can enslave us, replacing single-minded love for God and neighbor with buying-selling relationships in which even the soul can be bought (Rev 18:11-13). So money, wicked "mammon" (Lk 16:9 KJV), is a form or appearance of another power (Eph 1:21; Ellul, pp. 76-77, 81, 93). "The rich rule over the poor, and the borrower is servant to the lender" (Prov 22:7). Joseph, the righteous and Jesus are sold (Amos 2:6).

Money is not the only form of wealth, and not the first one named in Scripture. In ancient societies of Old Testament times, real wealth was associated with land. Even today in many Third World countries, land is the only permanent possession. Crops, cattle and houses could be destroyed by calamity, but the land will remain. So will the family.* In God's threefold promise to the descendants of Abraham (presence of God, peoplehood and a place to belong) the land figures prominently. Poised on the edge of Canaan, Israel was promised a good land to gain wealth. "Remember the LORD your God . . . gives you the ability to produce wealth" (Deut 8:18).

Land belonged to God but was trusted to families. When the land had been mortgaged or sold to pay debts, the Jubilee year (Lev 25) was the instrument of returning land to the original families.

How this applies to Christians today is a sensitive question. The meaning of "in the land" to Israel has now been encompassed by the phrase "in Christ" through which both Jews and Gentiles become joint heirs (Eph 3:6). This includes economic sharing and justice* but does not literally mean a common piece of geography (see Stewardship). So we are already seeing that Scripture appears to be ambiguous on this subject.

There are two voices of Scripture: one blessing the rich, the other cursing; one declaring that wealth is a sign of God's redemptive love to make us flourish on earth, the other declaring that wicked mammon (Lk 16:9), usually gained at the expense of the poor, is an alternative god (see Money). We need to look at each of these in turn.

Wealth as Blessing

The idea that wealth is a sign of God's blessing*(Deut 30:9; Prov 22:4) is illustrated by the lives of Abraham, Job and Solomon. In contrast to those who praised the Lord because they were rich (Zech 11:5) but were soon to be judged, it is noteworthy that each of these exemplars depended on God rather than their wealth (Gen 13:8-18; Job 1:21). The wise person in Proverbs is essentially a better-off person with servants—equivalent to our modern household machines—neither fabulously wealthy nor living in grinding poverty. Some wealth is a good thing; too much or too little would be alienating from God (Prov 30:9). So the wise person prays, "Give me neither poverty nor riches, but give me only my daily bread" (Prov 30:8).

The prosperity gospel now being preached worldwide is not satisfied with a comfortable existence or merely praying for our daily bread. We can critique it on at least three grounds. First, it encourages perverted motives: focusing on profitability. Second, it misinterprets God's deepest concerns for us: material well-being rather than total well-being. Third, it misinterprets God's promises to Israel as immediately applicable to Christians without being fulfilled and transfigured in Christ (compare 1 Tim 6:3-10). Nevertheless, the Old Testament clearly presents wealth as a means of God's grace.

Wealth as Sacrament

The Old Testament affirms that God is the true owner, proprietor and giver of wealth (1 Sam 2:7-8; Prov 3:16; Eccles 5:19; Hos 2:8). We are merely stewards (Prov 3:9). But the fact that God gives wealth, indiscriminately it seems, produces what Jacques Ellul calls "the scandal of wealth." God sometimes gives wealth to the wicked (Job 21:7-21; Ps 73:12-13). Why would God do this if wealth were a sign of being blessed? Contrary to the common argument that wealth is the result of "our hard-earned labor" or "our faithfulness," the Old Testament takes a more sacramental view.

Wealth is a free gift of God, a sign of God's grace given generously and without merit. Further, wealth points to the final consummation when our wealth will be taken into the Holy City (Is 60:3; Rev 21:24-26; see Ellul, p. 66). It is a gross and dangerous oversimplification to say the Old Testament endorses wealth as the blessing of God and the New Testament proclaims it is a curse.

Wealth as Temptation

Even the Old Testament warns that the pursuit of wealth for its own sake is vain and harmful, leading to self-destructive autonomy (Ps 49:6-7; Prov 23:4-5; 28:20; 30:8-9; Hos 12:8). Proverbs 10:15, for example, "The wealth of the rich is their fortified city," is illuminated by Proverbs 18:11, "They imagine it an unscalable wall." Wealth is an *illusionary* security. Wealth will not satisfy (Ps 49:6-7; Eccles 5:10). Several points need to be made here.

First, no one is made right with God (justified) by the fair acquisition of wealth (Prov 13:11) or by dispersing it on behalf of the poor. In the absence of a "principle" or "doctrine" about money, we are called to find our justification not in our use of money but in our relationship to God. We are accepted by faith through grace.

Second, instead of becoming stewards of wealth for the benefit of the poor (Prov 31:5, 8-9), we are tempted to use what wealth we have to dominate others (Amos 2:6)—a subject taken up by John Chrysostom in his sermons on Luke 16. Just as the brothers of Joseph enjoyed their fine meal and did not "grieve over the ruin of Joseph" (Amos 6:6; Gen 37:25), very few wealthy people have been able to resist becoming desensitized to the poor.

Third, especially reprehensible is yielding to the temptation to enlist God's Word to serve our lust for wealth (2 Kings 5:20-27; Mic 3:11), to "baptize" greed, a matter symbolized in the commercialized temple which Jesus cleansed.

When we turn to the New Testament we discover that "Jesus Christ strips wealth of the sacramental character that we have recognized in the Old Testament" (Mt 6:24; Lk 6:30; 12:33; Ellul, p. 70). The rich fool trusts in his barns and investments* and is not ready to meet God, nor is known by God. The rich already have their comfort (Lk 6:24); they have nothing to look forward to. The rich young man must give everything away and follow Jesus. True wealth is not the accumulation of houses, farms, jewels and money but something more.

Though these passages seem to argue for an antiwealth New Testament ethic, it is not that simple. Jesus affirmed the extravagant and wasteful display of love* when the woman poured perfume on him head: "She has done a beautiful thing to me" (Mk 14:1-11). And Jesus himself accepted the generous financial support of women with means (Lk 8:3). How are we to resolve this tension?

Heavenly Wealth

Unquestionably many of Jesus' negative statements about the rich and the wealthy are addressed to the spiritual malady fed by material abundance. "Be on your guard against all kinds of greed; a man's life does not consist in the abundance of his possessions" (Lk 12:15; compare Jas 5:1-6). As an alternative god wealth must be repudiated, if necessary by giving it all away (compare Lk 16:13). Ultimate security and blessing cannot be found in the accumulation of things (compare Mt 6:19).

At this point Scripture gives us a harmonious, though disturbing, single message. Possessions are solely and simply a matter of stewardship,* not ownership, and this life's assets are to be used with a heavenly orientation. What are these heavenly treasures, and how do they relate to everyday wealth, or the lack of it?

We gain an important paradigmatic perspective on this question from the Old Testament. There the inheritance received by Israel through the promise was a threefold blessing: the presence of God ("I will be with you"), the people ("you will be my people; I will be your God") and a place to belong ("the land will be yours"). As noted above, what we are given "in Christ" more than fulfills the promises made to Abraham and his descendants. God is with us in an empowering way through the Spirit. What greater treasure can there be than to belong to God and be known by him? In

Christ we experience peoplehood, a new family with hundreds of brothers and sisters, fathers and mothers, children and lands (Mt 19:29; Mk 10:29-30; *see* Church-Family). The promise of a place is fulfilled doubly: first in true fellowship* here on earth through a full sharing of life with other believers, and second in the place which Christ has prepared for us (Jn 14:2) in the new heaven and new earth, the city of God (Heb 11:13-16). Presence, peoplehood and a place—these are true wealth for the Christian. Money in the bank, ownership certificates of bonds and title deeds to properties are only an optional extra to this wealth. But what are we to do with the temporal wealth God has entrusted to us?

Stewards of Wealth

Stewardship is much more than giving money to the church or to charities. It is caring for God's creation,* managing God's household, bringing God's justice. Old Testament social legislation pointed to the coming (and present) kingdom of God with principles that were economically gracious: the provision for the gleaning of the poor by not harvesting everything one could (Ruth); the provision of the sabbath* for the land and for indebted people; the cancellation of debts* with Israelites and resident aliens in the seventh year—thus stressing neighbor love (Deut 15:1-6); the command to lend without interest to one's neighbor (Deut 15:7-11); the release of Israelite slaves on the seventh year (Deut 15:12-18); the provision of Jubilee, by which the hopelessly indebted could start again (Lev 25); the command that kings and leaders must not enrich themselves by that leadership but should live simply as brother-leaders (Deut 17:16-20).

While these commands are not to be slavishly followed under the circumstances of the new covenant, they reflect a minimum standard for economic life for people "in Christ." Christian stewardship cares for the earth, releases debts, empowers the poor, brings dignity to the marginalized and equalizes opportunity. But there is also direct giving.

Probably no other single factor indicates our true spirituality more than what we do with the wealth we have and in what spirit we share it. Christian giving is marked by hilarity (Lk 6:38; 2 Cor 9:7) that takes us beyond a calculated tithe and reflects the generosity of God. The Lord might well ask in this area as in others, "What more do you do than the pagans who know not God? And why?"

First, we are to invest primarily in people, especially the poor. The only treasure we can take from this life to the next is the relationships we have made through Jesus (Lk 16:9). The treasures in heaven are relationships that have been formed through the gracious use of money, the investment of the things of this life in a world without end, often in the context of everyday work.*

Second, we are to give wisely and carefully. It was John Wesley who advised: "Gain all you can, save all you can, give all you can." But the giving must take us beyond merely relieving the symptoms of people's distress through giving alms. Almsgiving may be a perversion of giving, because, as Ellul (p. 112) shows, it binds the recipient in an obligatory relationship, demands gratitude and does not usually address the reasons behind the person's poverty.* So individuals and churches should invest in people and causes grappling with the systemic powers that hold people in bondage to a cycle of poverty. There may be no greater area of discernment needed for the Christian in everyday life than to decide when, where and how to give money away.

Third, some form of voluntary impoverishment is required of all followers of

Jesus. It is not sufficient to say, as many do, "The rich young ruler was a special case" (see Mt 19:16-30). We are all in need of profaning the false god of Mammon and relativizing wealth in this life as something less than full treasure in heaven. There are several dimensions of voluntary impoverishment. We start by relinquishing ownership* to God. We practice continuous thanksgiving, which is the only way to become content whatever our circumstances (Phil 4:12-13). We should pay our taxes* with a generous heart, knowing that some of this is being used to provide services and care for the poor and disadvantaged. We should give directly to the poor with no strings attached as personally as possible (Lk 16:9; Stevens, pp. 159-65). We should give to God's global work (2 Cor 8—9). Finally we should be ready, if so commanded by Christ, to sell all.

Christian people do not have a monopoly on giving, any more than they have a monopoly on gifts of teaching* and administration or showing mercy. What makes giving a spiritual ministry, as Paul notes in Romans 12:7-8, is an extra anointing that God gives to people who are harmonizing themselves with God's Spirit. Then those who show mercy do it "cheerfully," and those contributing to the needs of others "generously." Throughout the New Testament it is the interiority of the matter that is emphasized: freedom from manipulation and covetousness, motivated by true love for God and neighbor. As Jacques Ellul notes, "Ultimately, we follow what we have loved most intensely either into eternity or into death" (Mt 6:21; Ellul, p. 83).

See also OWNERSHIP; POVERTY; POWER; PRINCIPALITIES AND POWERS; STEWARDSHIP.

References and Resources
J. M. Bassler, *Asking for Money in the New Testament* (Nashville: Abingdon, 1991); J. Chrysostom, *On Wealth and Poverty*, trans. C. P. Roth (Crestwood, N.Y.: St. Vladimir's Seminary Press, 1984); J. Ellul, *Money and Power*, trans. L. Neff (Downers Grove, Ill.: InterVarsity Press, 1984); R. Foster, *Money, Sex and Power* (San Francisco: Harper & Row, 1985); D. J. Hall, *Stewardship of Life in the Kingdom of Death* (Grand Rapids: Eerdmans, 1988); J. C. Haughey, *The Holy Use of Money: Personal Finances in the Light of the Christian Faith* (New York: Doubleday, 1986); L. T. Johnson, *Sharing Possessions: Mandate and Symbol of Faith* (London: SCM Press, 1981); R. J. Sider, *Rich Christians in an Age of Hunger* (Dallas: Word, 1990); R. P. Stevens, *Disciplines of the Hungry Heart* (Wheaton, Ill: Harold Shaw, 1993); C. J. H. Wright, *God's People in God's Land: Family, Land and Property in the Old Testament* (Grand Rapids: Eerdmans, 1990).

R. Paul Stevens

WEATHER WATCHING

I work in what is called a *climate-controlled building*—a euphemism for a structure in which the windows will not open. Theoretically I am protected from all the varieties of weather and can enjoy weatherless work, day in and day out. Frankly it is boring and sometimes downright oppressive. I find it invigorating just to walk outside my technologically designed cocoon and let the rain splash on my face or tramp in the snow. It is not good enough to turn on the radio and hear what the weather is supposed to be; I want to experience it—and for good theological reasons. It is part of my spiritual journey. But first, what is weather?

Weather refers to aspects of the atmosphere close to the earth. The consistent weather pattern of a region is called the *climate*. Weather is a complex phenomenon involving the interplay of temperature, air pressure, wind, moisture, precipitation and the rotation of the earth. The term *weather systems* indicates that the actual weather we experience is not the result of a single cause but many interdependent factors. Increasingly we are understanding weather as a global system in which changes in ocean currents in one distant part of the earth can affect daily weather here at home—sometimes called the *butterfly effect*. Forecasting how these many factors will affect the weather is a recently conceived science, originating in 1860 when data was first gathered in central locations by the newly invented telegraph. With advanced radar technology* weather forecasting will achieve a higher level of accuracy, especially in the prediction of floods, tornadoes, snowstorms and ice storms. It is seldom noted, however, that without weather there would be no life on earth at all. Weather is a gift of God. No matter how sophisticated the scientific analysis of weather becomes, weather will remain a mysterious thing. There are theological reasons for this.

Weather as Mystery

God not only makes weather; God is a weather person. God delights to make weather. Every day is a different day with different weather, a unique creation of God. God simply enjoys weather. The primary text for this truth is Job 38:22-37. In this extended speech God answers Job's gut-wrenching questions about the meaning of life and death with a weather forecast or, more accurately, a revelation of what is behind the forecast: "Have you entered the storehouses of the snow? . . . Who gives birth to the frost from the heavens? . . . Do you send the lightning bolts on their way?" (Job 38:22, 29, 35). All of this was intended to get Job to worship—the very thing weather is supposed to do. One crucial thing God tells Job about the weather as they discuss it from God's viewpoint is that it is not merely for humankind's benefit. God makes rain to fall "to water a land where no man lives, a desert with no one in it" (Job 38:26). How could we dare think it was all for us?

In modern life the mystery is almost lost. We scrutinize the effect of the thinning ozone layer on weather here on earth and even attempt to make weather by seeding clouds with frozen carbon dioxide. Generally we have an anthropocentric approach to weather—weather made by humankind for humankind. Increasingly we are becoming aware of the effect of human behavior on weather through automobile* pollution* (creating smog), urbanization (creating islands of heat) and industrial pollution (creating acid rain). On the one hand, weather is now a dismal revelation of humankind's stewardship* of the earth. On the other hand, weather always has been, and still can be, a mystery associated with the revelation of God's presence (2 Sam 12:17-18). "Peals of thunder, rumblings, flashes of lightning and an earthquake" (Rev 8:5) accompany all the great realities associated with the Second Coming of Christ, just as thunder and lightning, accompanied by thick clouds, expressed the mystery of God's first revealed covenant to Israel on Mount Sinai (Ex 19:16). Clouds indeed have a special place in holy revelation, generally connoting the presence of transcendent reality: "At that time men will see the Son of Man coming in clouds with great power and glory" (Mk 13:26). The greatest cloud of all, the rainbow, is a promise of God incarnated in light and moisture.

Mystery, however, is not what is usually associated with weather. Indeed, it is our fundamental conversation starter with both complete strangers and dearest friends: "It's hot (or cold) today." "Do you think it will rain (or warm up)?" "Have you heard the forecast (or temperature)?" Even in climates where there is virtually no change between summer and winter, bereft of seasons, where night temperatures are only slightly lower than day temperatures, people still revel in, or are disturbed about, the most minute weather changes. But small talk is not to be despised. Small talk is at least talk. It is a beginning at communication (*see* Speaking). If there were no weather, we might not talk to the gasoline station attendant or the postal carrier or the neighbor next door mowing her lawn. This fundamental everyday reality does perform this heavenly ministry of giving us something new every day to consider with our fellow human beings.

Jesus used people's interest in "reading" the weather when he was asked to provide a sign from heaven: "When evening comes, you say, 'It will be fair weather, for the sky is red,' and in the morning, 'Today it will be stormy, for the sky is red and overcast.' You know how to interpret the appearance of the sky, but you cannot interpret the signs of the times" (Mt 16:2-3). Today, of course, most people are far removed from reading the weather themselves and rely on professionals who use technology to forecast two and three days in advance—though even the professionals confess that this is as much an art as a science. We are still not able to predict accurately where a storm will hit, how high a flood will rise or where lightning will strike. Nevertheless we should thank God for the service rendered by the professional forecasters, especially the ministry they give in preventing airline and marine tragedies and enabling people to prepare for the onslaught of a destructive storm. But we should also continue to read the weather for ourselves, perhaps with even greater interest and reverence because with the help of technology we can get a satellite-eye view of it all.

Weather as Metaphor

Throughout Scripture weather is used figuratively as a way of expressing a truth that is better considered indirectly through metaphor and image. How does one speak of God and God's purposes?

Jesus communicated that God loves every human being unconditionally and without partiality. As he said, God "causes his sun to rise on the evil and the good, and sends rain [here as a blessing of God] on the righteous and the unrighteous" (Mt 5:45). How do you communicate to a theologian the surprise factor that is implicit in any real contact of a human being with God? "The wind blows wherever it pleases. You hear its sound, but you cannot tell where it comes from or where it is going. So it is with everyone born of the Spirit" (Jn 3:8). Spirit people are windlike. How can Jesus speak of the universal impact of his coming again at the end of time? "For as lightning that comes from the east is visible even in the west, so will be the coming of the Son of Man" (Mt 24:27). Therefore, says Jesus, do not let anyone fool you about his coming in secret (Mt 24:26). When the seventy disciples returned from their short-term mission* reporting that even demons were subject to them in Jesus' name, Jesus said, "I saw Satan fall like lightning from heaven" (Lk 10:18).

Paul also referred to weather for a higher purpose. Preaching in Lystra to people totally ignorant of the Bible, Paul spoke of the weather. This was no small talk: God "has shown kindness by giving you rain from heaven and crops in their seasons; he provides you with plenty of food and fills your hearts with joy" (Acts 14:17). Obviously people close to the land in an agricultural, preindustrial society would understand the analogy and might even be led to faith. Farmers* and landscape gardeners* today have this great privilege of being close to the elements. When I worked for five years as a carpenter, I was daily confronted with the challenges of searing heat and chilling drizzle, stimulating as it did thanksgiving for good clothes, warm and cold food and, above all, the shelter of home.* But what about people staring at a computer screen all day in a climate-controlled environment, traveling to and from work without even emerging into the weather, moving by subway, walking in covered malls or driving in air-conditioned vehicles? Does weather convince *them* of God? Can we speak of the ministry of weather?

Weather as Ministry

Proverbs declares, "By wisdom the LORD laid the earth's foundations . . . by his knowledge the deeps were divided, and the clouds let drop the dew" (Prov 3:19-20). More especially, the psalms are full of references to weather as a revelation of the goodness and glory of God: "You [God] drench its furrows and level its ridges; you soften it with showers and bless its crops" (Ps 65:10). In doing this, God calls "forth songs of joy" (Ps 65:8). Psalm 104 is really a catalog of all the kinds of weather that should cause us to praise God—which is all the kinds of weather there are—from the awesome sunset in which God "wraps himself in light as with a garment" (v. 2) to the pounding thunder. The key to all this is that "the heavens declare the glory of God; the skies proclaim the work of his hands" (Ps 19:1). Even the night eloquently and elegantly reveals the glory of God (Ps 19:2).

Why should we glorify God because of the weather? Because weather is something beyond our control (even though we may—tragically—influence great weather patterns by our sinful use of resources). Why? Because weather is a blessing; it reveals God's gracious care of creation, supplying all the world needs to thrive (even if it rains for the Sunday school* picnic). Why? Because weather is constantly changing; God is a God who loves innovation, creating every snowflake uniquely and delighting in the diversity of his creation. It is like God to

create weather—every day, every moment, something new. God is not a boring God, and life on earth is not either. Why? Because weather is in the end unpredictable, as is God who does "whatever pleases him" (Ps 115:3) and cannot be contained in liturgies, doctrines or anything humanly made.

Weather as Problem

But how should we view bad weather? What are we to think of tornadoes, hurricanes, tidal waves created by the awesome movements of tectonic plates, heat waves, droughts and hailstorms that decimate crops and pummel people? Occasionally Scripture says God has used such devastating weather as a judgment (2 Sam 12:17-18). Examples abound, including the bombing of the Amorites with huge hailstones when Joshua was busy occupying the Promised Land (Josh 10:11) and a prophetic drought (Amos 4:7) signifying a people that is living out of harmony with God (Rev 6:6). The worst famine, Amos prophesied, is the one that has now struck Western society: a famine of hearing the words of the Lord (Amos 8:11). But there is more than metaphor here. What are we to make of weather watching when it all seems bad? Is there "bad" weather or only weather that gives *us* bad experiences, which, were we to take a global perspective, is part of God's working out a sovereign purpose on a grand scale? And if it is bad for us, is God nevertheless calling us in it, inviting us to see whether there is a message in the weather, inviting us to depend on God and prayerfully cry, "Give us this day our daily bread"?

One human disease—seasonal affective disorder—is associated with living in a climate inhospitable to that person. The treatment is to move to a better climate. God heals* in many ways, according to a comprehensive list given by E. Stanley Jones: in direct answer to prayer, through medicine, through surgery, through suggestion and finally through the resurrection of the body. But one seldom-mentioned way included in the Jones list is this: through a change of climate (Jones, pp. 203-4). If some weather hurts, other weather heals.

Weather Wisdom

One thing not too clear to most believers is that we are not to be controlled by the weather. We are to be respectful, reverent, inquiring, investigative and prayerful, but not totally compliant. There is, of course, practical wisdom in closing down an outdoor meeting when the rain drizzles on, as Ezra did during the great national day of repentance (Ezra 10:13). One can hardly expect Jesus to work a miracle of calming a storm for the benefit of an evangelistic crusade (Mk 4:37). From time to time God does this, and we should not miss the faith-evoking truth of the disciples' confession: "Even the wind and the waves obey him!" (Mk 4:41), a reality I have known myself in turbulent sea voyages. And, if I may say this reverently, our God does not mind being asked to change the weather. Indeed, God enjoys almost any excuse for a conversation. Unlike the most "sophisticated" of his creatures, God seems to appreciate small talk. Prayer about anything gets us doing what prayer is all about: communion with God. My wife's earliest memory of God is a conversation about the weather. While she was raking the leaves in the backyard as a five-year-old, she said, "God, why do you make the wind blow the wrong way when you know I am raking the leaves?"

But in the end we are to live by faith, not by the weather: "Whoever watches the wind [that is, does nothing other than wait for the perfect day] will not plant; whoever looks at the clouds will not reap. As you do not know the path of the wind [an image Jesus used in Jn 3:8],

or how the body is formed in a mother's womb, so you cannot understand the work of God, the Maker of all things" (Eccles 11:4-5). Living by faith, not by weather, means bundling up when it is cold and rainy and going for that daily walk,* holding the marriage* seminar in the thick of a blizzard, teaching school in the middle of a heat wave and not staying at home because there is a cloud on the horizon. In the end all weather is God's weather, and God can be trusted with our lives, whatever the weather does to us.

See also BACKPACKING; CAMPING; FARMING; WALKING.

References and Resources

E. S. Jones, *Victorious Living* (Toronto: McClelland & Stewart, 1936).

R. Paul Stevens

WEDDINGS

Although the number of weddings taking place in church buildings* has declined over the last few decades, the traditional paraphernalia of weddings has diminished very little, and the amount of time* and money* spent on them has only increased. The wedding day, and all that goes with it, is often the major preoccupation for couples who wish to marry, churchgoers as well as others. A huge industry has grown up around it, providing invitations and cards, wedding rings and flowers, dresses and suits, wedding presents, flowers and bouquets, marriage celebrants and witnesses, reception places and services, food and music, and travel arrangements for the honeymoon. Not only wealthier but sometimes poorer families, especially ethnic and working-class ones, often spend large amounts of money to cover wedding expenses.

Most pastors ensure that couples getting married have some instruction and counseling to prepare for their life together. They also insist that wedding services themselves contain Christian instruction. But there is remarkably little Christian reflection on our current preoccupation with weddings, the forms they take or even the money spent on them. Consequently, weddings involving Christians may have a certain spirit or content which other weddings lack, but in most other respects they do not seem to be very different from other weddings. Here, as in so many other areas of life, we take our cues as much if not more from the culture* around us than from basic Christian principles.

Weddings Down Through the Centuries
Formal celebrations to mark the beginning of a marriage* exist in every society.* As far back as records go, they form an important rite of passage formalizing both the relationship of male and female and the family* as an institution. But it is difficult to trace the origin of wedding celebrations themselves. We can, however, note the appearance of certain marriage ceremonies. The Kiddish Jewish ceremony was present by the fourth century B.C., and the Christian wedding ritual of separating the betrothal from the nuptial service had formed by the ninth century.

We also can trace the origins of some specific elements or customs. The giving of consent, including that of the head of the household, goes back to Roman times. Wedding bands or rings, whose circular forms now express the eternal nature of love, developed out of ancient tribal customs in which women wore grass bracelets around their wrists or ankles. The placement of the ring on the third finger of the left hand has its source in ancient beliefs concerning the direct connection between that particular finger and the heart. Using white for bridal gowns is a Greek custom stemming from the association between that color and

purity or joyfulness. Other features, such as wearing a veil to symbolize purity or throwing rice to wish people the blessing of many children, are also long-standing traditions. From the Romans came the custom of eating a cake, which was originally offered to Jupiter.

Throughout the whole biblical period and well into the Middle Ages, weddings were arranged by the families concerned without any reference to professional religious people, such as priests, or to any official institutions. They were public and binding affairs, sometimes involving whole villages, but did not have the formal civic or legal status that marriages have today. That is why some Pharisees were able to divorce* their wives on the slightest of grounds just by drawing up a document to indicate their desire to be divorced (Mt 19:3-7). In the first millennium after Christ weddings continued to be arranged in much the same way. It was only to overcome certain abuses that during the Middle Ages priests were drawn into weddings, and later still that church legislation was passed requiring people to marry in a church building.

The earliest portrayals we have of marriages in the Bible provide little in the way of specific detail about wedding ceremonies. While some have tried to find the trace of an ancient liturgical blessing in God's words to the first couple to "be fruitful and multiply" (Gen 1:27-28 RSV), this is only a supposition. We do know a few concrete things about biblical weddings. Prior to the wedding came the betrothal; from that time on a couple was regarded as married, not simply engaged. This involved the negotiation of a dowry. For the wedding itself the bride wore a veil and wedding dress. When the Bible mentions wedding finery of rings, jewels and ornaments, this likely refers to marriages of wealthy families. The groom set out for the bride's house, at which her father pronounced a blessing. Then a procession of friends and neighbors came to the bridegroom's house, and they celebrated with a feast that could last up to a week or more (Judg 14:12). It was this procession that was the actual wedding ceremony. Though not too much weight should be placed on it, the first time marriage is referred to specifically as a covenant occurs in the last book of the Old Testament (Mal 2:14). A marriage license is mentioned for the first time only in the later inter-testamental book of Tobit.

A similar pattern for weddings lies behind several New Testament accounts. In passages like Matthew 25:1-12 their festive character (with loud acclamations), the scale on which they could be celebrated (ten attendants) and the flexible time frame for the occasion (no one is quite sure when the ceremonies will begin) also come through. As is often the case with proposals of marriage today, the date of weddings at this time appears to have been set by the groom and his family, and sometimes came as a surprise to the bride and her maids. Later Jewish writings, such as the Mishnah and the Talmud, prescribed other elements that might reflect earlier practice, such as the father's giving away of the bride. This was probably based on daughters' being the property of their father.

A Christian Perspective on Weddings

Developing a more thoughtful Christian perspective on weddings is not primarily a matter of separating out features that have pagan origins and discarding them in favor of others that stem from earlier Christian practice. Throughout history believers have taken up many things from their surrounding culture and then processed and woven them into meaningful Christian use. In any case, Christians themselves are as capable as anyone else of initiating practices that have a sub-Christian content or significance. But neither should we try to isolate elements of weddings that have some biblical parallel. The Bible was never intended to be a manual for wedding services, and the stories it contains about weddings reflect many agrarian Middle Eastern customs that would be artificial today. Instead, we need to reflect on the character and significance of the form weddings take today in light of a range of wider biblical principles and theological perspectives.

Here are a few guidelines we might consider.

While the wedding day and ceremony is one of the highlights of a person's life, we should not attribute so much importance to it that it takes away from more fundamental things. Sometimes planning* for a wedding takes up so much time and energy that couples put their relationship on hold while they go into business mode or, worse, find that this puts pressure on their relationship and causes serious tensions between them. It is sad when couples miss out on the benefits and pleasures of their engagement because organizing the wedding takes up most of their time and energy. While dealing with the complex and sensitive issues associated with planning a wedding can help a couple mature in their relationship, there is a point where the whole process becomes counterproductive. Sensitivity and common sense are required here.

While it is important that the wedding day go well, we must not give in to the temptations of perfectionism and professionalism. Perfectionism is the tendency to want every single aspect, every single item and every single person associated with the wedding to be "just so," without any blemish. Working toward this can be anxiety-producing and fatiguing—indeed exhausting for all concerned—and can take much of the pleasure and enjoyment away from the occasion. Professionalism* is nearly as bad. Increasingly couples hand over the planning and running of weddings to people who create an atmosphere that detracts from their essential family or friendly nature. Such people may be more polished and wittier, but often they make it more difficult for others to feel comfortable when it is their turn to contribute. If participants make a mistake, they feel they have committed a cardinal sin and let the whole wedding down. Too professional an atmosphere also tends to work against people relating to one another in a natural way. Instead, everyone begins to feel under pressure to perform.

While everyone wants a beautiful and memorable wedding, Christians have good reason to be concerned about the expense involved in even a moderately priced wedding in our culture. In North America it is not uncommon for people to spend $20,000 or more for a wedding and all the festivities before and after. Though we should not approach important occasions for celebrating with a miserly attitude, we do need to consider the biblical principle of simplicity (*see* Simpler Lifestyle). This applies to wedding showers as well. If in our culture at large there is a tendency to spend too much on externals and to fall prey too easily to the seductions of luxury, we should take care that even our celebrations bear witness to a different set of values.* An important part of our vocation as Christians today is to show that it is possible to have a good time without spending too much (*see* Partying). There are other factors too. The excessive amount of money spent on some weddings, or honeymoons, could if redirected actually give a young couple a more secure financial start in life by helping them put down a deposit on a house or apartment.

While we tend to think of weddings as separate from corporate worship, inviting our church family to actively participate in this God-honoring event is a way of worshiping together. Once upon a time weddings used to take place in the ordinary context of corporate worship.* Everyone would know about this in advance, and special guests would come from some distance. But weddings were an integral part of the ongoing communal life of a couple's, or at least one of the couple's, wider Christian family. The separation between these two that now takes place involves significant loss if also some gain. We are not proposing that all weddings between believers should take place in a normal corporate worship setting, but we should give careful thought as to how much of this can be preserved. One way of doing this today would be to place some of the responsibility for organizing and leading the wedding in the hands of the primary small group* or house church (*see* Church in the Home) where they are best known. Single friends should also be drawn into helping so that they do not feel too left out of the relationship. In some cases the reception (or even the wedding itself) could take place outside one of their homes,* or in some place closely associated with the life of the group.

While we are often told that the day belongs to the bride, the wedding ought to concentrate equally on the bride and the groom. There is no room in a Christian wedding for intentions or expressions based on the view that "this is the bride's day." Marriage is a genuine partnership, and this should be clearly symbolized from the beginning. This means as well that the couple could help create the service which will unite them, making it a very personal reflection of themselves. They need not discard, of course, all the long-standing traditions associated with weddings— many are long-standing because they have proven their value—but even these can be given creative or contemporary touches. Some changes should certainly be introduced, such as removal of the word *obey* from the wife's vow (or its introduction into the husband's as well) and presentation of the bride and groom by both sets of parents, instead of the father giving the bride away.

See also FESTIVALS; MARRIAGE; PARTY-ING.

References and Resources
A. C. Cardozo, *Jewish Family Celebrations* (New York: St. Martin's Press, 1982); J. P. Dever, "Marriage," *The New International Dictionary of the Christian Church* (Grand Rapids: Zondervan, 1974) 633-35; A. Fisher, "The Jewish Liturgy of Marriage," in *The Jewish Roots of Christian Liturgy,* ed. Eugene J. Fisher (New York: Paulist, 1990); D. Glusker and P. Misner, *Words for Your Wedding* (New York: Harper & Row, 1983); P. Lacey, *The Wedding* (New York: Grosset and Dunlap, 1969); D. Moore, *The Wedding Guide* (Seattle: IMS/Wedding Guide, 1993); J. M. Egan and M. Burbach, "Matrimony," *New Catholic Encyclopedia,* vol. 9 (New York: McGraw-Hill, 1967); K. Stevenson, *Nuptial Blessing: A Study of Christian Marriage Rites* (Nashville: Thomas Nelson, 1983).

Robert and Julie Banks

WHISTLE-BLOWING

Whistle-blowing can be defined as an employee's disclosing to the public illegal, immoral or unethical behavior of an employer or organization* that is likely to result in harm to others. Whistle-blowing should not be done without serious reflection on the part of the prospective whistle-blower. It presents a moral conflict of loyalty*—between one's employer and/or colleagues and the prevention of harm to third parties. Whistle-blowers, by calling attention to possible wrongdoing within their organizations, are the subjects of much controversy. Some see them as disgruntled employees who are tattletales, squealers and snitches. Others see them as noble characters or heroes who are willing to put themselves at risk to expose organizational practices that are wasteful, fraudulent or harmful to the public safety.

Purposes of Whistle-blowing
In an ideal organizational world whistle-blowing would be unnecessary. However, in those situations in which management has a myopic fixation on maximizing the bottom line at any cost, whistle-blowing may be needed. Some of the areas whistle-blowers have called attention to in recent years include price fixing, fraud, unsafe products, widespread embezzlement, insider trading and dumping of toxic waste. Frequently, these whistle-blowers have courageously put themselves at risk in the pursuit of bringing pressure on an organization to correct its wrongs.

Some whistle-blowers' actions, however, are ethically suspect. These individuals act out of selfish or egoistic reasons. Sometimes whistle-blowing suits are instituted by employees with an ax to grind. They may be blowing the whistle with the intent of getting even with the organization for recent decisions that affected them adversely or with the hope of getting a big financial payoff (for example, under the False Claims Act whistle-blowers can receive up to 25 percent of any money recovered by the government).

A Cost-Benefit Analysis of Whistle-blowing
The costs of whistle-blowing are high for both the company and the whistle-blower. Whether it wins or loses, the company "gets a black eye." It spends considerable time* and money* defending itself, and regardless of the outcome its reputation may be tarnished.

The potential costs to the whistle-blower are especially noteworthy. Unfortunately, many firms not only discourage but actually punish whistle-blowing.

Other than outright dismissal, retaliation often includes demotion, false complaints about job performance, relocation or reassignment, investigation of finances and personal life, and harassment of family and friends. Even if the whistle-blower ultimately wins, the costs can still be considerable: attorney fees, money spent for living expenses while the case drags on, mental anguish and possible ostracism by former coworkers.

Criteria for Whistle-blowing

To approach whistle-blowing from both a moral and rational perspective, certain criteria should be met:

1. The purpose of the whistle-blowing should have a moral base. The public interest should be the prime concern (for example, the desire to expose unnecessary harm, a violation of human rights or conduct counter to the defined purpose of the organization).

2. What is being protested should be of major importance, be carefully analyzed and be specifically articulated. Whistle-blowing requires that the wrongdoing is a *serious* breach of ethics (for example, a company engaged in the upcoming release of a product that does serious harm to individuals or society in general).

3. The prospective whistle-blower should have compelling evidence to substantiate the facts of the protest. It is also important for the employee to have tangible documentation of the practice or defect.

4. Before the whistle is blown, all internal avenues for change within the organization should be exhausted. The employee should report this concern or complaint to his or her immediate superior to provide an opportunity for rectifying the situation. If no appropriate action is taken, the employee should take the matter up the organizational hierarchy. Before he or she goes public, the resources for remedy within the company must be exhausted.

5. The whistle-blower should be above reproach. Specifically, the whistle-blower should not benefit from revealing the information. Whistle-blowing should be an act of conscience*—it should not be done principally from a selfish or vindictive orientation. To check for possible personal bias, the employee should seek considerable objective advice and then have the courage to personally accept responsibility for providing the information.

Some Final Thoughts

Sadly, legitimate whistle-blowing comes about too often because bureaucratic management blinds itself to shoddy products, environmental danger and questionable practices in order to maximize profit. Whistle-blowing may provide a signal that the organization is not performing well, has poor management or both.

It seems tenable to assume that three of the salient obligations that organizational members owe to the public it serves or to which it sells are truthfulness, noninjury and fairness. Therefore, when these crucial concomitants are willfully dashed, whistle-blowing may be necessary to bring this breach of trust to the public.

To avoid the costs of whistle-blowing for both the company and employee, some progressive organizations are attempting to provide ways for employees to report concerns and complaints. Some constructive avenues allowing employees to share their concerns include open-door policies, ombudspersons, confidential questionnaires and hot lines. While this is an encouraging sign, it would be naive to believe that there no longer will be a need for whistle-blowing. Paul Tillich in *The Courage to Be* suggests that following one's conscience and defying unethical and unreasonable authority is an act that entails considerable risk and great courage. As Christians we must not see our relationship with our employer as one of unilateral blind loyalty. Our ultimate responsibility and loyalty are owed to the Lord. We also have a responsibility to our neighbors, other employees, customers and the general public (Mt 22:34-40).

See also BUSINESS ETHICS; JUSTICE; LOYALTY, WORKPLACE; ORGANIZATIONAL CULTURE AND CHANGE.

References and Resources
S. Bok, *Secrets* (New York: Random House, 1983); N. Bowie, *Business Ethics* (Englewood Cliffs, N.J.: Prentice-Hall, 1982); G. F. Cavenagh, *American Business Values* (Englewood Cliffs, N.J.: Prentice-Hall, 1990); J. Richardson, ed., *Annual Editions: Business Ethics 95/96* (Sluice Dock, Guilford, Conn.: Dushkin, 1995); W. H. Shaw and V. Barry, *Moral Issues in Busi-ness* (Belmont, Calif.: Wadsworth, 1992); P. Tillich, *The Courage to Be* (New Haven, Conn.: Yale University Press, 1950).

John E. Richardson

WILDERNESS
In the words of legislation that first granted it in 1964 some protection in the United States, *wilderness* is a place where "mankind is a visitor and does not remain." In recent years places unmarked by human activity have come to seem increasingly valuable to human beings. Indeed, the popularity of wilderness-related activities—backpacking,* river rafting, tours to Antarctica and the Amazon—has become so great that it sometimes threatens to destroy the very thing people have come to admire.

Ambivalence About Wilderness
Despite our recent enthusiasm for wilderness, we have always been ambivalent about it, as is evident in expressions like "urban wilderness" and "lost in the wilderness." The word itself originally meant "a place of wild beasts," *wild* here meaning "will-ed"—that is, creatures which follow their own, not a human, will. Early settlers of the New World saw the wilderness condition of the continent as a situation to be remedied by human industry, and for nearly three centuries "progress" was understood to be the advance of civilization over wilderness.

But as wilderness became more rare, its value gradually increased. Nineteenth-century naturalists like Henry David Thoreau ("In wildness is the preservation of the world") and John Muir (founder of the Sierra Club) began to see spiritual values in wilderness. This idea that wilderness has spiritual value is widespread in our time. But just as important in arguments for protection have been the scientific arguments first advanced by American ecologist Aldo Leopold. Wilderness, he argued, is an example of "healthy land." Human activity almost always simplifies the extraordinarily complex balance of living and nonliving things that are part of an undisturbed ecosystem (*see* Ecology). Quite apart from their spiritual values, argue ecologists, we need wilderness areas, large and small, as places where the wisdom of the natural world may be preserved and studied.

Many contemporary attitudes toward wilderness are deeply rooted in Scripture. The biblical words commonly translated "wilderness" are usually descriptive of the desert: barren, uninhabited land, of no value for agriculture. Usually such land is portrayed negatively. The Israelites' forty years in the wilderness is, at least in part, a kind of punishment; a frequent threat of the prophets is that the land will become a wilderness. At the same time, wilderness came to be a place where, apart from the comfort and defenses of cities* and farms,* people came face to face with God: Moses, the children of Israel, David, many of the prophets, John the Baptist and Jesus all found the wilderness to be not only a place of hardship and trial but a place where they experienced God's voice and grace.

It would be more helpful for Christians to think of *wilderness* as simply "creation"—God's work, unshaped by human beings, good for its own sake, the result of the continuing love and sustaining care of the Creator. We are so used to seeing creation* in terms of the uses we make of it that we seldom see it in its own intrinsic power and beauty. One of the most instructive biblical glimpses we have of wilderness is God's answer to Job. The Creator answers his legitimate complaints by asking him to consider the vastness, intricacy and mystery of creation. In an increasingly human-centered civilization we also need to learn the lesson of our creatureliness, which wilderness can often teach us.

While it seems clear from the Bible (for example, in Rom 8:18-25) that creation waits to be brought into relationship with the human, it seems equally clear, from our dismal record of diminishing the richness of created life, that we have not yet learned to relate to creation in a way that does not silence its own voice. Till the day when we have so learned creaturely wisdom, there are good reasons to work for the preservation of, and the respectful experience of, those little bits of wilderness that remain, for they remind us, "The earth is the LORD's and everything in it" (Ps 24:1).

See also BACKPACKING; ECOLOGY; POLLUTION; TRAVELING; WEATHER WATCHING.

References and Resources
S. P. Bratton, *Christianity, Wilderness and Wildlife: The Original Desert Solitaire* (Scranton,

Penn.: University of Scranton Press, 1993); R. Nash, *Wilderness and the American Mind,* 3d ed. (New Haven: Yale University Press, 1982).

Loren Wilkinson

WILL, LAST

One of the most sensitive things we do in life is to write a last will and testament. Doing this confronts us with our own inevitable death*—an important and deeply spiritual ministry to ourselves. We are also forced to define who and what is valuable to us and how we wish our possessions to influence people after we die. A will can be a family blessing, a form of gift giving and a means of bringing peace and justice to our families. It can bless charitable organizations and encourage causes we embraced in this life. It can also be a hand extending from the grave to control, manipulate, divide and bring retribution for wounds not healed before we died. So the will reveals not only the state of our financial assets but the state of our souls.

Some people do not bother to make a will, not so much for "spiritual" reasons or even because their assets are comparatively small, but because they do not think it important. They do not survive, of course, to see people fighting over their possessions or the hurts caused because the people assumed to be the proper heirs did not actually receive the promised inheritance. Without a will your family's assets might be frozen for months; your nearest surviving kin may not have funds to continue normal life; provincial or state laws will determine the distribution of your assets without consideration of your wishes, sometimes ignoring the members of your family who should be the rightful heirs; more of your estate will be spent in administrative costs; and the process may be delayed for months, sometimes for years.

It is not the purpose of this article to

advise how a will should be written. Normally this should be done by a lawyer, though simple forms can be obtained in banks, which can be legal, if properly witnessed by two adults who are not beneficiaries, correctly signed and dated. Properly conceived wills name the executor (the person named to administer the will) and the beneficiaries (those who receive specific portions of the estate). They also need to be updated every five years or when there has been a change of residence, marital status or family circumstances. My purpose here is to explore the meaning of writing a will.

Before There Was a Will, There Was a Way

In ancient times the equivalent of the last will was the father's oral blessing of the family before he died (*see* Blessing, Family). Isaac's blessing Esau, his older son, in contradiction to God's revealed plan of maintaining the family leadership through Jacob (Gen 25:23) is a classic story of a last will gone awry. In giving his word even in the context of a ruse, Isaac could not recall his promise,* though he appointed the one he thought was the right person as leader of the family. God providentially arranged for Jacob to be the bearer of the promise. In Israel such final blessings included a double portion of the estate to the oldest male (Deut 21:15-17), since this person would be the responsible leader of the family. Job was conspicuously different from many of his contemporaries in giving his daughters an inheritance along with his sons (Job 42:15).

Sometimes the inheritance could be gained in advance, as witnessed by the younger son's request in the parable of the prodigal (Lk 15:11-32). Normally the issue was leadership in the family and the possession of the land owned by family (on the latter, *see* Stewardship). Behind the Old Testament legislation on inheritance is the principle that the land, ultimately owned by God but entrusted to clans, should be kept in the family.

In the ancient world, and in the Third World today, land is not only the most important possession (since it is the means of producing food) but very often is also the only possession. While once the passing of such lands to the surviving male heirs took place with the help of village elders, without a written will, today this has become a vexed matter as such estates are now hotly contested in Third World courts by second and third wives, by wives who were never legally married but cohabited and by legitimate and illegitimate children. So not only in the developed world, where the assets are primarily monetary and land recorded with proper title deeds, but even in the developing world, it is crucial today to attend to this important ministry of family love and neighbor love. It is not always, however, a loving ministry.

The Will to Curse

While the saying "You can't take it with you" is undoubtedly true, it is possible to extend a hand beyond the grave and wreak havoc on a family. Some people use their wills to control people they were unable to control in this life. In 1558 Michael Wentworth specified in his will that "if any of my daughters will not be advised by my executors, but of their own fantastical brain bestow themselves lightly upon a light person [deemed an unsuitable marriage partner], then that daughter was to have only sixty-six pounds instead of the one hundred pounds which was promised to the obedient" (Stone, p. 46). This has been rightly judged to be posthumous economic blackmail.

A son or daughter may be out of favor or has disgraced the family. Further wounds are inflicted posthumously by disinheriting that child, though the laws sometimes preclude totally excluding a near relative simply because they were not named in the will. Some states require that a spouse receive a mandated minimum share of the deceased spouse's estate, even though the deceased person intended to exclude the spouse totally. The Old Testament tried to regulate against such injustice based on personal favoritism rather than equality and fairness. If a man marries a second wife whom he loves more than the first, he may not give the rights of the first-born (the double portion) to the son of the second marriage (Deut 21:15-18).

No one dies with all the problems in his or her family fully resolved. Someone is loved less; someone is struggling with addiction and would squander an inheritance; someone is idle and lazy; someone has wounded and shamed the family. Not surprisingly some people use the will as their last chance to "get even," without remaining to assist in picking up the pieces. Rightly understood, making a will is an act of stewardship*—undertaking to manage one's household and appropriately transferring ownership* and responsibility. When a child is incompetent or foolish, a lawyer can assist in specifying a trust fund. Last wills cannot do much to solve family problems, but when poorly conceived, they can exacerbate the ones that already exist.

Will to Bless

Normally a will should express justice* and fairness in a family. This is not easy when there are great differences in economic strength among surviving members. It may be tempting to write a will based on perceived need rather than fairness: "James doesn't need my money since he has a professional income, but poor Martha has never had a chance." What the person cannot foresee is the reverses of life: James struggling with an incurable disease and unable to work; Martha divorced and remarried into a wealthy family. Further, it is impossible to regulate people's feelings. The elder son in the parable of the prodigal complained, "You never gave me"—when the father had given him everything (Lk 15:29, 31)! But what we can do in writing a will is to refuse to play favorites, to express mercy on those who have disappointed us, to provide as best we can for all kin who survive us and to trust that God will help them deal with such ongoing temptations of life as envy, greed and covetousness.

As a form of gift giving,* a last will can do a lot of good. First, if we have a surviving spouse, he or she will be able to continue a reasonably normal life. It is a practical way of loving our spouse. Second, we can continue our priorities in parenting* by naming a suitable guardian (with his or her permission) for our minor-aged children and providing for their maintenance. Third, we can bring positive delight to people by specifying the transfer of possessions that will bring joy to a particular relative or friend. For example, you can imagine that mahogany table, which Linda always loved, now in her living room. Fourth, we can empower the next generation to do things they would not otherwise be able to do, such as buying their own home. Fifth, we can see that all the outstanding debts* in this life, relational and financial, are forgiven. Sixth, we can bless charities and churches with a significant gift. Seventh, we can show impartial love like God's love to every member of the family, regardless of merit and performance, just as God makes the sun to rise on the just and unjust (Mt 5:43-47).

The Contemplative Will

Making a will helps us to prepare for our death and to begin the process of relinquishment, which is a spiritual work or discipline. This is both a ministry to ourselves (and not a selfish one) and a ministry to our survivors at the same time. But this spiritual work may encompass not only what happens *when* we die but also what happens *as* we die.

Many people today write a living will in addition to the one to be executed upon their death. A *living will* outlines how a person wants to be medically treated in the event of a terminal illness or a condition that requires life-sustaining procedures. It is normally a gracious thing to do this, as close members of the family, without such direction, may feel obliged to prolong life as long as possible, fearing accusations of disloyalty or lack of love. A living will too can be drawn up by a lawyer. While some people think this is a means of *causing* death, it really is a way of regulating the unnecessary delay of death through heroic medical interventions. Christians especially should be prepared to die (*see* Euthanasia).

Making a last will and testament recognizes several theological perspectives founded in Scripture. What God entrusts to us in this life is a multigenerational inheritance, not to be squandered in one single lifetime. The earth, the traditions of culture and family, the material treasures of one's family—these are not for ourselves alone but for our children and children's children (Prov 13:22; compare Ps 17:14). Further, we do not know how soon Christ will come and bring the whole human story to its consummate end. Wise stewards, like the wise virgins in the parable of Jesus, are ready for a long wait (Mt 25:4). Rather than living for the moment—which is a perversion of *parousia* or Second Coming readiness—Christians are called to be ready today but prepared for another thousand years.

Finally, providing for the next generation is an act of responsible Christian stewardship. But we must do this in a way that involves stewardship of life today. The gospel invites us to flourish in life now, not just to plan for the next life. Robert Louis Stevenson, always in poor health, was cheerfully working on a manuscript when his wife interrupted, "I suppose you will tell me that it is a glorious day." "Yes," he replied, "I refuse to permit a row of medicine bottles to block the horizon." (Quoted in Daly, p. 210.) Some people are so concerned to provide for their children that they refuse to enjoy life now; others, so anxious to squeeze everything they can out of today, leave nothing. Scripture properly understood provides the eschatological balance: living today because of tomorrow in the light of what God has done in the past.

As someone said, no one has ever seen an armored truck, laden with money, in a funeral procession. We cannot take it with us. But what we can take with us is faith, hope and love. We can take relationships we have made in Christ through the use of our money (Lk 16:9). And we can take the knowledge that our last determination on earth was that mercy and peace shall survive us as our true inheritance.

See also DEATH; EUTHANASIA; GIFT-GIVING; GRIEVING; PROMISING; STEWARDSHIP.

References and Resources
D. Clifford, *Plan Your Estate* (Berkeley: Nolo Press, 1990); E. J. Daly, *Thy Will Be Done* (New York: Prometheus Books, 1994); L. Stone, "The Rise of the Nuclear Family," in *The Family in History*, ed. C. E. Rosenburg (Philadelphia: University of Pennsylvania Press, 1975) 13-57.

R. Paul Stevens

WITNESS

A court of law is the most obvious place to find a witness. When a crime* has been committed, the prosecution bases its case on the evidence of those who witnessed it. The defense then probes the truthfulness and reliability of those witnesses, while also providing its own—usually people who did not see the alleged incident but who testify to the generally good character of the accused person. Authentic witness is essential for the judicial process (*see* Justice). The judge and jury discover the truth by listening to the evidence of the witnesses and deciding who can be believed.

Witness in the Bible

The Bible frequently uses the term *witness* for a person or thing giving testimony to the actions of God and for the truth claims of faith. In the Old Testament the ark of the covenant is also called "the ark of the Testimony" (Ex 25:22), while the structure that sheltered it is "the Tent of the Testimony" (Num 17:7). Together they bore witness to the special relationship between God and the people of Israel. When Joshua renewed that relationship, he placed a large stone in a prominent place to be a witness to the commitments that had been made by both God and people (Josh 24:27). This was a regular part of the legal process (*see* Law) in the ancient world, and the function of such artifacts was not only to remind people of the solemn vows that had been made but also to serve as witnesses in the legal sense should those promises be broken.

In the New Testament John's Gospel uses similar terminology to emphasize that what Jesus was saying and claiming was true. John the Baptist (Jn 1:7), the Hebrew Scriptures (5:39), Jesus' own deeds (5:36), even God (5:37) and the Holy Spirit (15:26)—all bore witness to the truth of Jesus' message. Later the apostles were commissioned to be witnesses to the gospel (Acts 1:8)—a mandate that they fulfilled, on the one hand, by reporting the words and deeds of Je-

sus and, on the other, by sharing their own personal stories of faith. They, in turn, encouraged all other Christians to be witnesses as well.

Christian Witness Today

The Greek word used in the New Testament for "witness" is *martys*, from which the word *martyr* is derived, reminding us that bearing witness can be a costly business. Bearing witness to Christ can take many forms, but it always incorporates two major elements.

First, there is the truth of the gospel. In the postmodern world Christian witness must begin by reaffirming the truth of the gospel (*see* Evangelism). Ever since the Enlightenment, the concept of absolute truth has been played down. What is true for one person is his or her "private truth," but it does not need to impinge on anyone else's life. Life has been divided into two spheres: the public world, dominated and directed by the scientific "truths" of mathematics, economics, politics* and so on, and the private world, within which values,* morality and faith have been confined. Those things that dominate the public world were generally believed to be true in some absolute sense (though even that is questioned today), but what went on in the private world was always a matter of individual choice and preference.

Dissatisfaction with this dualistic understanding of human experience is a major factor contributing to the collapse of modernity and, in the religious sphere, the rise of movements such as the New Age and the search for a new holistic paradigm of understanding. Historically, Christianity has accepted, if not actively promoted, the separation of public and private worlds. To regain credibility, Christians will need to return to their roots and rediscover the importance of bearing witness to the fact that if Christianity is "true," then its values and standards must impinge on the whole of life and must be just as true for economics and politics as for personal morality.

Second, there is the truth of Christian experience. Witnessing is not limited to claiming the high ground of intellectual debate. Indeed, because of today's widespread cynicism about the possibility of objective knowledge, a purely intellectual apologetic is unlikely to be particularly effective or relevant to Christian witness today. In the Old Testament both landscape and lifestyle embodied features that were specifically intended to provide an opportunity for subsequent generations to share the story of faith, as children and others asked about their meaning (for example, Ex 12:26-27; Josh 4:1-7; 1 Sam 7:12).

Christian Lifestyle

The Christian lifestyle should also be a witness by creating occasions for sharing personal stories of faith. The following aspects of Christian lifestyle are especially relevant in the postmodern situation.

Community. Writing in the late second century, the Christian Tertullian observed, "It is mainly the deeds of a love so noble that lead many to put a brand upon us. 'See,' they say, 'how they love one another'" (*Apology* 39). Jesus also made this central for Christian witness (Jn 13:34). Anyone can make grandiose truth claims, but if they do not match personal behavior, then a witness is judged unreliable. The earliest Christians were always publicly on show. In the great cities of the Roman Empire, the life of the Christian community,* with no church buildings,* centered on the home (*see* Church in the Home). But a Roman villa was not private space. It provided a home,* not only for its owner's family,* but also for the family's employees; it was as well a place of business. In today's world those who are not yet

Christians will need to feel they belong within the Christian community before they begin to consider what might be worth believing. When Christians offer a space in which people feel accepted for who they are, that is a significant witness to the gospel. Actions speak louder than words, and effective witness can only take place when there is a consistency between how Christians behave and what they claim to be true.

Honesty. An untruthful witness is of no value at all, and the Christian lifestyle should always be characterized by truthfulness and honesty. Such virtues are often regarded as old-fashioned and outmoded today, but without them no legal process would make sense, and there would be no justice* in the world. "Say only yes if you mean yes, and no if you mean no," Jesus counseled his disciples (Mt 5:37 NCV). Lies and dishonesty have no part in the work of God (Jn 8:44; Tit 1:2; Rev 21:8). If Christians are not truthful about things in everyday life, then why should they expect anyone to believe them on matters of faith? When church leaders* are engaged in corruption and scandal, it is not merely a personal tragedy: it is a denial of the gospel.

The home. Home and family life are an area of major concern throughout the world today (*see* Family Values). In the West increasing numbers of people experience home life as a source of tension, stress and breakdown. There are many reasons for this, most of them connected to the collapse of modernity and the emergence of new forms of family. In particular, the disintegration of patriarchy as women and children are given their proper value is leading to a backlash of domestic violence and abuse* almost unparalleled at any other time in history. The first page of the Bible affirms that both women and men are made "in the image of God" (Gen 1:27), while Jesus himself attached enormous significance to children, even inviting adults to learn from them (Mk 9:33-37). Christians are not perfect, of course, but they should always strive to aspire to those ideals in their own home relationships. Anything less—particularly an unbiblical perpetuation of patriarchy—will hinder any effective witness to the gospel.

The environment. This is another area in which, historically, Christians have often denied their own heritage. Wise stewardship* of the earth and a recognition of humankind as part of creation were always foundational in the Bible, but during the Industrial Revolution Christians, motivated by the Protestant work ethic,* lost sight of this. As a consequence, many people blame Christianity for all the ills of the environment. Of course, Christians are not the only ones who have polluted the planet. But when Christians allow and even encourage it as blatantly as some previous generations did, they do great harm to the witness to the gospel and make it much more difficult for genuine spiritual seekers to identify truth in the Christian way of life (*see* Creation; Ecology).

The Christian Difference

The gospel is distinctive, and our being noticeably different from other people is part of Christian witness. But being different does not mean being weird, or old-fashioned or withdrawn from the rest of the world. Jesus was often criticized for going to too many parties,* and he encouraged his disciples to engage fully with the whole of the life of the world, just as he did himself. But in the process, he told them to be "salt" and "light," by bearing witness to the values of God's kingdom (Mt 5:13-16). Witnessing in this sense means channeling God's blessing* into areas of life that otherwise might seem to be secular.

For instance, much modern art* is pessimistic in outlook; some of it even celebrates things that are depraved and inhumane. The mass media* can be the same. Being made in God's image involves sharing in the first of God's acts, which was creativity.* Christian witness here is not about denouncing art and the media but about recognizing that everyone is made in God's image and about encouraging the expression of different values, of hope and optimism and celebration: "We should give up the foolish task of trying to be saints, and get on with the more important task of trying to be human" (Dietrich Bonhoeffer). "Always be ready to answer everyone who asks you to explain about the hope you have, but answer in a gentle way and with respect" (1 Pet 3:15-16 NCV). Bonhoeffer and Peter both understood what Christian witness is all about.

See also EVANGELISM; MINISTRY; MISSION.

References and Resources
J. Drane, *Faith in a Changing Culture: Creating Churches for the Next Century* (San Francisco: HarperCollins, 1997); M. Green, *Evangelism Through the Local Church* (London: Hodder & Stoughton, 1990); B. Hanks Jr., *Everyday Evangelism: Evangelism as a Way of Life* (Waco, Tex.: Word, 1986); D. Innes, *I Hate Witnessing* (Ventura, Calif.: Regal, 1985); A. G. M. McPhee, *Friendship Evangelism* (Grand Rapids: Zondervan, 1978); R. M. Pippert, *Out of the Saltshaker and into the World* (Downers Grove, Ill.: InterVarsity Press, 1979).

John Drane

WORK

Work, whether in its presence or absence, is a pervasive part of everyday life. One of the first things we want to know about people is what they do. The waking time of most adults is taken up with work, and a person's passing is often noted in terms of their workplace* achievements. Work and worth, industry and identity, are very closely related in contemporary culture.* This article deals with work in this modern context. It will examine (1) a wider definition of work, (2) a biblically integrated view of work, (3) the disintegration of work and faith, (4) reintegrating spirituality and work and (5) redirecting Sunday towards Monday.

A Wider Definition of Work
Over the last two centuries work has become equated with a job.

This is a seismic shift in our understanding of ourselves, our world and even our God. It has had earthquakelike effects on people's emotional, family, social and spiritual life. The tremors have been felt hardest by the overworked, the unemployed,* housewives, the forcibly retired and the attention-deprived children.

Despite society's materialistic definition of work as what we are paid to do, work can include any positive productive activity. A helpful, wider Christian definition of work is this: "Work is the expenditure of energy (manual or mental or both) in the service of others, which brings fulfillment to the worker, benefit to the community and glory to God" (Stott, p. 162). On that definition many people in socially destructive jobs, for example, in a cigarette or armaments factory, might not be working. On the other hand, the unemployed person cleaning up the streets and recycling a cart full of soda cans, volunteers working for schools and churches or parents changing diapers or cooking meals are working. We need to revalue these tasks for both men and women by recognizing fundamental activities that keep the world going, even though they are unpaid and economically invisible.

But does this wider view of work have biblical backing? Unlike today, in biblical times work was not a separate sphere of life. Work was integrated with the home* (which was usually the workplace) and worship* (through sacrifice from God's gifts and one's produce). People were not primarily valued or identified in terms of their jobs as they are today. We need to develop a more integrated biblical view of work that does justice to the value of other vital activities and relationships.

A Biblically Integrated View of Work
There are several ways of developing a biblical approach to work. One is to do a concordance study of the word. Another is a creed-based approach in terms of God as Creator, Reconciler and Re-Creator—Father, Son and Holy Spirit (Preece). Here I will identify broad perspectives and principles that can help us place work within a scriptural framework of relationships—to God, humanity and the earth (Wright, pp. 89-90, 100).

God's work. The God of the Bible is a worker, in contrast to the ancient Near Eastern gods, who slept while their human slaves labored. Sadly, many of us forget that before we get up on Monday morning, God has already been at work: "He who keeps Israel will neither slumber nor sleep" (Ps 121:4 NRSV). Jesus said, "My Father is still working, and I also am working" (Jn 5:17 NRSV). The sabbath* is a reminder that we live by God's work, not our own (Gen 2:3; Mt 11:28; Heb 4).

Exploring the wide-ranging biblical imagery of divine work can give us a greater sense of being junior partners in God's work of creation, preservation and redemption. For example, God is an architect and a builder (Prov 8:27-31), a doctor-healer (Mk 2:12, 17), a teacher (Mt 7:28-29), a weaver (Ps 139:13-16), a gardener/farmer (Gen 2:8-9; 3:8; Jn 15:1-8), a shepherd (Ps 23; Jn 10), a potter/craftworker (Jer 18:1-9; Rom 9:19-21) and a homemaker (Lk 15:8; Banks). By seeing our work in the light of God's work, we can see God's hand in our everyday tasks. Unless we do so, we will underestimate the importance of God's work and either worship our work or think it worthless. But work can be an expression of worship or communion with God. It should not be confused with or replace our corporate worship, but it is an everyday offering of our whole selves, bodies and minds, to God (Rom 12:1-2). "Render service with enthusiasm, as to the Lord and not to men and women" (Eph 6:7 NRSV).

Human work and human relationships. Work is not only to provide for ourselves (2 Thess 3:10-13) and our families (1 Tim 5:8) but also "to have something to share with the needy" (Eph 4:28 NRSV). So work is one of the basic ways we fulfill our social responsibilities. Many things we make at work also provide the stage in which people can interact, for example, telephones and furniture. Making handheld video games largely does not. From a biblical view one question we can ask of our work is whether it furthers relationships or not.

While we should distinguish ourselves from what we do, we should not divorce the two. Being and doing flow into each other. A mother working in a shop does not stop being a mother while she is at work. Her homegrown experiences and skills are valuable (even if unrecognized) in her paid employment, and her experience on the job will be reflected at home.

The author of Ecclesiastes provides a balance between being and doing by emphasizing relationships. He has a word of warning for both the envious workaholic and the lazy shirkaholic who neglect relationships and lead meaningless lives. The alternative is that "two are better than one, because they have a good reward for their toil. For if they fall, one will lift up the other; but woe to one who is alone and falls and does not have another to help. . . . A threefold cord is not

quickly broken" (Eccles 4:9-12 NRSV). So, after communion with God "community building is every person's second full-time job" (Stevens, pp. 15-16).

The same writer provides a commentary on the fallen or cursed dimension of work or toil (see also Gen 3:17-19). Work done out of mere ambition* and selfishness and work neglected out of laziness are both vain. Even work with good motives will often be ignored or wasted. We all die, and our work will not last; it is transient. While we have opportunity, we should simply enjoy working, as well as the food and drink it puts on the table, as a gift from God. It is best to have modest expectations of work and not try to build lasting monuments (Eccles 2:18-26; Stevens, pp. 4-5).

Our groaning as we toil is part of creation's groaning, longing for liberation from the vanity to which it was subjected by God in hope (Rom 8:20-23). But *under the risen Son,* work done for God and others is not in vain, even if society may not value it. In the new heavens and new earth "my chosen shall long enjoy the work of their hands. They shall not labor in vain" (Is 65:22-23 NRSV). "Therefore, my beloved, be steadfast, immovable, always excelling in the work of the Lord, because you know that in the Lord your labor is not in vain" (1 Cor 15:58 NRSV).

Caring for the earth. According to Genesis 1:28 (NRSV), as those made in God's image, we are to "be fruitful and multiply, and fill the earth and subdue it." This is balanced by the direction in Genesis 2:15, in which Adam is to till and keep the garden, or serve and preserve it. This has not only agricultural but also cultural dimensions, as Adam's naming the animals shows. As God's representatives we are to care for the earth (*see* Ecology) and each other in the productive realm of work and the reproductive realm of family.* Women are involved in both realms. The wise woman of Proverbs 31 is involved in providing food, land and clothing, planting vines, trading and caring for the poor. Her work was publicly recognized, bringing her praise in the city gates (Prov 31:10-31). This needs to be heard in a world in which women are often paid less in jobs and work a second shift at home and in which many people receive no recognition for unpaid work done well.

In the divine economy, work is evaluated according to the way it fosters or retards relationships—between ourselves and God, our companions and the earthly resources we are called to develop.

The Disintegration of Work and Faith

Given the Bible's integrated view of spirituality and work, how did these two come apart, so that even many Christians do not feel the connection?

Historical reasons. In the Greek world work was seen as a necessity or curse for slaves to perform. The truly free and human pursuits were politics and philosophy: "Work was called 'unleisure,'. . . *ergon or ponos,* a burden and toil" (Stevens, p. 26). During the fifth century B.C. some cities issued a decree prohibiting their citizens from engaging in work!

This Greek influence appears in the apocryphal Wisdom book Ecclesiasticus, which, though more respectful of the trades* than the Greeks or the Egyptians, exalts the scribe over the tradesperson, contemplation and leisure* over material action. Only the one who is free from toil can become wise. Workers have to concentrate on their work rather than the wonders and mysteries of the world. The merchant or businessperson "can hardly remain without fault" (Sir 26:29) for "between buying and selling sin is wedged" (Sir 27:2).

Sadly, this is still the way many Christians see trades and business. In the hierarchy of vocations clergy* and missionaries (our equivalent of Ecclesiasticus' scribes of Bible scholars) are still near the top; the caring professions* (for example, social workers and doctors) are next, while business people and trades come last. Working with things such as technology,* money* and administration is often seen as inferior both by those who stress soul-winning and those who stress social activism. This stems from the division between spirituality and work, head and hand, wisdom and skill, people and things, which is not present in the more creation-centered canonical Wisdom literature (compare Prov 31) nor in the cultural mandate to rule the earth responsibly (Gen 1:26-28). Tradespeople and business people do not have to be social workers or evangelists to serve God at work.

Under the influence of Greek dualism the early church and the Middle Ages reinforced the distinction between spirituality and work. As a result the story of Mary and Martha (Lk 10:38-42) was reinterpreted to exalt the contemplative over the active life.

Martin Luther reacted against the medieval disparagement of ordinary work in favor of the work of priests or monks. He reclaimed the idea of vocation, or divine calling,* for the ordinary Christians as homemakers, paid workers or citizens. Luther saw all of these as providential ways in which Christians could serve their neighbor and worship God. The tools of one's workshop were constant reminders to do this: "In making shoes the cobbler serves God, obeys his calling from God, quite as much as the preacher of the Word." Luther could say, "God himself will milk the cows through him whose vocation it is!"

Unfortunately, around the time of the later Puritans (mid-17th century), the notion of vocation became secularized and narrowed down to the job. It became increasingly individualistic, losing the sense of worshiping God and serving the common good (*see* Calling). Through Benjamin Franklin (a Deist, not a Christian), the Protestant work ethic* became popularized through such maxims as "Early to bed and early to rise makes a man healthy, wealthy, and wise" and "Time is money." Through the concept of a career,* work increasingly became a means to the end of status and security rather than a means to the end of serving God and supporting self and others, which becomes a joy in itself.

For all its gains in living standards, the Industrial Revolution separated the spheres of work, home and church, institutionalizing working for a wage (something previously regarded as degrading compared with self-employment). Despite its considerable difficulties preindustrial life had a greater sense of integration between work, home and church. All were within sight of one another, and the church was the connecting link to the whole of life.

Contemporary reasons. Today many people are split between the Sunday and Monday, or private and public, areas of their lives. In a highly specialized society we play different roles according to different rules with different parts of our personalities, and our lives slowly disintegrate. Our name is truly "Legion."

Many of the pastoral and spiritual crises people face are a direct result of this disintegration of work, home and church. The absent-father syndrome has now been extended to include the absent-mother, as both parents struggle to keep jobs as well as maintain marriages* and families. There is often a direct clash between escalating demands on people by family, education, career and church that can be crippling unless an integrative spirituality sensitive to life stages is taught, modeled and nurtured.

Surveys indicate that in far-flung commuter suburbs low church attendance was due not to people there being less religious but to the long hours spent at, or going to and from, work. Some people want to attend church and small groups* but have too little time and energy. The church's mainly female pool of volunteer* labor is shrinking rapidly as the personal, social and financial rewards of working prove more attractive (although there are recent signs of a move back from this). In failing to shape and develop a spirituality for the workplace and neglecting to challenge its dehumanizing structures, the church has by default been (mis)shaped by it.

Reintegrating Spirituality and Work
To maintain spiritual integrity, we need a spirituality that integrates, not separates, our faith and work. The individualistic "Protestant prayer ethic," which gets the leftovers from the Protestant work ethic, fails to provide this. Under the pressures of modern work many Christians feel isolated and unsupported in the workplace and find it difficult to pray and reflect in a way that integrates their church and work lives. Some theological guidelines for developing a corporate spirituality of work follow.

Reemphasizing the importance of the church scattered as well as the church gathered. Both the vocational (the church scattered) and the worship (the church gathered) activities of Christians are important. On Sunday the latter equip and mobilize the scattered people of God for their mission and ministry on Monday. But also needed are small committed groups in which people can honestly share their struggles in faith, home and work.

We also need mission groups as well as Christian peers and mentors in the workplace. Without this our professional group unconsciously becomes our church, determining major life decisions concerning where to live, what car to drive, how to dress, where to school our children. This then determines our de facto spirituality, which is then used to justify our professional lifestyle.

Recapturing a sense of vocation. From the Bible and the Protestant Reformation emerges the understanding that all Christians have a ministry and vocation to serve in the working world, an understanding modeled on Christ as prophet, priest and king. This does not pit preaching* or evangelism* against ordinary work but sees kingdom work as healing creation and the Great Commission (Mt 28:19-20) as fulfilling the creation commission (Gen 1:26-28). So we do not unethically evangelize on the boss's time, trying to justify our job to the full-time preachers, but work, live and speak in a way that represents the rule of Christ over the whole of creation, including the working world.

Recapturing the idea of the "mixed life." We must not abandon Christian people to the totalitarian demands of many workplaces and the Martha life of unreflective activism. Nor should we forfeit the workplace and adopt the monastic, contemplative Mary life. The fourteenth-century monk Walter Hilton wrote letters to an English man of affairs, involved in commercial and political life, who wanted to enter contemplative life in a religious community. In his *Letters to a Layman* Hilton wisely counseled a third way, a mixed life combining the activity of Martha with the reflectiveness of Mary (Stevens, pp. xiv-xv). Such a spirituality needs to be consciously modeled and taught.

Reconnecting wisdom, virtue and skill. Developing a spirituality of competence and compassion is needed to overcome the split between Mary and Martha. Work is a major way we can cultivate and develop Christian virtues (Gal 5) and attitudes (Mt 5:1-13). It can develop either the fruit of the Spirit, making us

patient, gentle and self-controlled, or the opposite fruits of the flesh. These virtues do not spring up in a vacuum but emerge through much practice and, above all, grace. The "supernatural" virtues of faith, hope and love have particular significance for a spirituality of work. Paul commends the Thessalonians for their "work produced by faith, . . . labor prompted by love, and . . . endurance inspired by hope in our Lord Jesus Christ" (1 Thess 1:3). We carry these characteristics, and work characterized by them, all the way to heaven. This idea is captured in a painting of the Second Coming by Swiss artist Paul Robert in Neuchatel, Switzerland. It portrays the people rising to meet Christ, bearing the fruits of their callings: doctors having healed people, architects having built beautiful buildings and so on—each one eager to render an account to Christ of his or her work.

Redirecting Sunday Toward Monday

If we are to overcome the perceived gap between Sunday and Monday, the church will have to shift its pastoral and mission priorities toward Monday. Today the primary place where men and women meet others is the workplace. Evangelism in the marketplace was common in the New Testament (Acts 16:16-19; 17:17; 19:9-10, 23-29). While we should not be evangelizing on the boss's time, a truly integrated life and a willingness to speak in a wise and timely way tailored to the needs of others (Col 4:5-6) will attract questions and interest that can be explored during breaks and lunchtime and before or after work.

As Scripture imaginatively used workplace terminology to express aspects of the gospel message, so should we in sharing our faith. In early Christian times the terms *sacrifice* (of the work of one's hands), *redemption* (of slaves) and *debts** (of money) all had strong workplace connections. Moreover, teaching topics and illustrations should include work-related ones. Paul spoke at length of master-slave relationships (Eph 6:5-9; Col 3:22—4:1). In 2 Timothy 2:1-7 he draws from a range of working illustrations (athlete, farmer, soldier) for single-mindedness.

Corporate worship opportunities should be related to working life. Workers' testimonies—drawn from home-making,* volunteer work or the marketplace—can be a great encouragement to others and can be included in services during announcements, the offering (when we give the products of our work back to God) or at the conclusion of the service when we hear the call to mission. Prayers for people's working lives should be a regular part of intercession. Church rolls or address lists might include work roles to enable members to make connections and offer appropriate prayers. Special services, such as a faith-and-work Sunday or urban harvest festival with people bringing symbols of their work, are also a useful way of encouraging a more integrated spirituality.

Pastoral care should be extended to the workplace. Preventive pastoral care* will often involve standing for justice* with God's people and providing emotional and financial support if they face loss of employment for taking a Christian stand on an issue. Moreover, mutual confession, counseling and discipline need to be restored and related to workplace struggles and sins. Puritan manuals often dealt with issues of conscience in the workplace. Pastors, leaders' groups, church counseling ministries and small groups could provide appropriate supportive and accountable contexts.

The gap between Sunday and Monday can be narrowed further by creatively bridging the physical distance between churches and the workplace. The New Testament church met in homes that often had workplaces in the front room on the street. Masters and slaves shared the same living space and social life. While we cannot turn back the clock, we should bring our work, home and church life as close together as possible. We can use occasional fringe-work activities over meals or beverages to build relationships. Opening our homes in hospitality* to fellow workers can lead to a new level of relationship. Where possible, church buildings* should be located near the commercial center rather than be lost in suburban back streets.

These wide-ranging suggestions can begin to turn the tide of a war that has seen the workplace forfeited rather than lost. Together they can enable a greater integration of faith and work, Sunday and Monday, spirituality and activity.

See also CALLING; CAREER; HOMEMAKING; LEISURE; PROFESSIONS/PROFESSIONALISM; SERVICE, WORKPLACE; STRESS, WORKPLACE; UNEMPLOYMENT; WORK ETHIC, PROTESTANT; WORKPLACE.

References and Resources
R. J. Banks, *God the Worker* (Valley Forge, Penn.: Judson, 1994); R. J. Banks and G. R. Preece, *Getting the Job Done Right* (Wheaton: Victor Books, 1992); L. Hardy, *The Fabric of This World* (Grand Rapids: Eerdmans, 1990); G. R. Preece, "The Threefold Call," in *Faith Goes to Work*, ed. R. J. Banks (Washington D.C.: Alban Institute, 1993) 160-71; J. B. Schor, *The Overworked American* (New York: Basic, 1991); P. Stevens, *Disciplines of the Hungry Heart* (Wheaton: Harold Shaw, 1993); J. Stott, *Issues Facing Christians Today* (Basingstoke, U.K.: Marshalls, 1984); M. Volf, *Work in the Spirit: Toward a Theology of Work* (New York: Oxford University Press, 1991); C. J. H. Wright, *An Eye for an Eye* (Downers Grove, Ill.: InterVarsity Press, 1983).

Gordon Preece

WORK ETHIC, PROTESTANT

We hear frequent mention of the *Protestant work ethic*, sometimes positively but more often negatively. Except in some scholarly circles the phrase does not have a precise meaning, and even there not everyone is in full agreement. Generally it refers to some of the following attitudes and behavior: (1) believing that work* gives meaning to life; (2) having a strong sense of duty to one's work; (3) believing in the necessity of hard work and of giving work (even before the family) the best of one's time; (4) believing that work contributes to the moral worth of the individual and to the health of the social order; (5) viewing wealth* as a major goal in life; (6) viewing leisure* as earned by work and as preparation for work; (7) viewing success in work as resulting primarily from the amount of personal effort; (8) viewing wealth that accrues from work as a sign of God's favor. Though writers might single out one or two of these characteristics for special attention, everyone seems to be confident that he or she knows what the term means.

Individual reactions to the term and what it stands for tend to be all positive or all negative. Some regret the passing or weakening of this traditional understanding of work and would like to see it reinstated. Others regard the gradual demise of the Protestant work ethic as liberating, for it raises the possibility of a more open and flexible approach to work that is better suited to people's personal makeup and to current economic realities. An early depiction of conflict between these two attitudes is in the well-known play *Death of a Salesman* by Arthur Miller. Later examples may be found in such popular sitcoms as *All in the Family* and *Till Death Do Us Part*. As we shall see, present understandings of the Protestant work ethic contain a strange blend of authentic and inauthentic elements. It is by telling the story of how a focus on the Protestant work ethic arose that we can begin to distinguish between them.

Major Interpretations of the Protestant Work Ethic

In the middle of the nineteenth century, Karl Marx insisted that the modern middle-class ethic owed its existence to material factors, such as the spread of capitalist forces of production and the division and exploitation of labor. Shortly after the turn of the twentieth century, sociologist Max Weber acknowledged the role of these factors but argued that the root of the work ethic lay further back in religious beliefs about calling,* election and work stemming from John Calvin. These beliefs were further developed by such later Puritans as William Perkins and Richard Baxter and came to concrete expression in the approach of people like Benjamin Franklin. The unforeseen consequences of the Protestant perspective included a heightened sense of moral obligation to work, the conviction that a person's election by God was authenticated by his or her achievements at work and the perceived importance of living thriftily off the proceeds from work, with the remainder being saved, invested or given away. R. H. Tawney popularized a modified version of Weber's thesis. He argued that since the understanding of calling and pockets of capitalism had emerged before the Reformation, the work ethic was not a purely Protestant phenomenon. Also, it was not until the latter, largely post-Puritan, part of the seventeenth century that it developed the strong emphasis on individual success,* rather than social obligations, which we associate with it. From this point on, though more closely connected with Nonconformists and Methodists, the work ethic took hold. So Puritanism was only partially responsible for it. Since Tawney wrote, other historians have suggested that the story is even more complex. For example, even where Protestantism held sway, there were significant differences between regions in their attitudes toward work. Even climatic conditions appear to have played a part.

Key Criticisms of the Main Interpretations

There are good grounds for arguing that what most people have in mind when they refer to the "Protestant work ethic" would be more accurately described as the "post-Protestant work ethic." Calvin, following Luther, wrote in a time when ordinary work (when compared with monastic work) was devalued, and he was attempting to give work a new dignity before God, not insist on its centrality. In any case, his emphasis was on diligence in work and its usefulness to others, not on a preoccupation with work or on its personal significance. Calvin insisted on the importance of each person's finding a place through work for his or her God-given gifts (or talents,* a word whose meaning owes much to his influence) and of work as embodying and expressing the mutual dependence of people on each other, that is, as a concrete expression of human fellowship,* solidarity and community.* This also led Calvin to discern a connection between the general order of work in society and the provision of social justice* to those in need.

Weber lumped together the views of Calvin and later Puritans, but Calvin's followers began to move beyond his views in subtle ways. For example, many developed a greater interest in the use of time* at work and in the link between fruitful work and the doctrine of divine assurance. After the Restoration, when Puritanism again became a minority position, certain Nonconformists and eighteenth-century Methodists (on whom Tawney places the major weight) gave greater attention to the importance of getting the most financially that a person can through work, though with a view to saving and responsibly investing* it or giving it away (see Stewardship). Many also experienced solid work and its fruits as granting them upward social mobility, for which they were devoutly thankful to God.

The crucial differences in the development of the work ethic took place after this, occurring chiefly in the nominally religious, or early post-Protestant, attitudes that developed in the early days of the Industrial Revolution. In that period many people were gradually moving away from full dependence on the sufficiency of Christ's work for their salvation and sanctification. Requiring some other ground on which to justify themselves—before God, before others and sometimes most of all before themselves—they began to look around for a replacement. The burgeoning and increasingly dynamic field of work was nearest at hand, at least for the emerging middle class. So work began to become invested with new significance.

In pre-Reformation days many people had sought to justify themselves and gain acceptance with God and others through religious works. This road was largely closed to Protestants, but their ordinary work was still available to them as a substitute. As this happened, work moved into a more central place, being viewed less as a context for serving others than as a context for human achievement and less as a divine calling than as a personal career.* Work increasingly became the place where most of one's time and energy was invested, throwing out of balance the relationship between work, family and leisure. The degree of success in one's work, rather than a person's full acceptance by God, increasingly determined a person's status in the eyes of others. All of these attitudes are in basic conflict with the Protestant understanding of the gospel and vision of the Christian life.

Conclusion

In view of these criticisms, we cannot unreservedly regret the weakening of what is called the Protestant work ethic. Over the last two centuries it has become at best encrusted with, and at worst transformed into, something different from what it was originally. Also not everything said about the ethic by earlier Protestants was equally valid. For example, if Luther too rigidly tied people's work to their existing station in life rather than to the particular gifts God had given them to use, later Puritans too rigidly identified people's God-given vocation with work, at the expense of people's other involvements and responsibilities. Frequently, with some illustrious exceptions including Calvin and many early Puritans, the vocation of rest* alongside the vocation of work was not given its proper emphasis.

Even if we need to correct the earlier Protestant understanding of work and identify the secularized distortions that later crept in, the work ethic still preserves some genuine Protestant values. Among these we should include the virtue and dignity of work; the sanctity of all legitimate types of work; the importance of responsible work rather than slovenly work or idleness; the outcome of proper work—whether successful or not—as proceeding from a service to God and society. Other aspects of the original Protestant understanding of work need to be reclaimed: for example, its view of our work as part of our divine calling or vocation rather than as a personal career or just a job; its recognition of service* to others, rather than self-fulfillment or even our own gifts, as the main guide to our choice and conduct of work; its assurance that God is well able to supply such fulfillment if we put the purposes of the kingdom above our personal preferences (compare Mt 6:33); its refusal to regard work as what gives us our basic identity or meaning; its essentially communal, rather than individual, character; and its recognition of leisure as the foundation of work rather than requiring work for its justification. Taking all these characteristics into account, we can say, with the social commentator Daniel Yankelovich, that in some respects the work ethic is not so much overvalued as undervalued by too many people today. In other respects, far too much is made of it, and workaholic tendencies should be challenged wherever they arise.

See also CAREER; DRIVENNESS; LEISURE; PROFESSIONS/PROFESSIONALISM; SABBATH; SELF-ESTEEM; WORK.

References and Resources

S. N. Eisenstadt, *The Protestant Ethic and Modernization* (New York: Basic, 1968); A. Homes, "Wanted: A Work Ethic for Today," *The Reformed Journal* 28 (October 1978) 17-20; M. J. Kitch, ed., *Capitalism and the Reformation* (New York: Longman, 1967); H. Lehmann and G. Roth, *Weber's Protestant Ethic: Origins, Evidence, Contexts* (Cambridge: Cambridge University Press, 1995); P. Marshall et al., *Labor of Love: Essays on Work* (Toronto: Wedge, 1980); L. Ryken, *Work and Leisure in Christian Perspective* (Portland, Ore.: Multnomah, 1987); R. H. Tawney, *Religion and the Rise of Capitalism: A Historical Study* (London: Pelican, 1938); M. Weber, *The Protestant Ethic and the Spirit of Capitalism: The Relationship Between Religion and the Economic and Social Life in Modern Culture* (New York: Scribner's, 1958).

Robert Banks

WORKPLACE

Alongside work* itself, workplaces are undergoing significant changes today. There was a time, as during the biblical and classical periods, when work was largely undertaken in the field or open country, home or street, in small-scale factories or fishing enterprises. By late medieval and early modern times, open markets and guild-based businesses became more important. In the wake of the revolutions in industry and technology large mechanized factories and bureau-cratized offices came into being, and even farming,* ranching and fishing became big business. Now the context in which work takes places is changing substantially again.

In considering the workplace, I am thinking of the architecture and layout, the conditions and procedures, the dynamics and ethos, of the spaces in which we work. This whole environment should receive as much thoughtful Christian attention as what we do in it. Yet if work itself has often received little Christian reflection, this is even truer of the workplace. A main reason for this is that in many forms of Christianity, there is a dualistic tendency that separates the spiritual and the material, persons and structures,* the relational and cultural. Since the workplace is in part a physical context, in part a set of structures and in part an institutional culture, it easily falls victim to this dualistic way of looking at reality. Yet the total environment of the workplace is important, partly because as a human creation it tells us something about ourselves, our attitudes and values* and partly because our workplaces shape us, the work we do and the relationships we form at work.

The Changing Nature of the Workplace
Among the changes occurring in workplaces today, three-quarters of which are still small businesses, the following are particularly noteworthy. The majority of workplaces are becoming technologized. Nearly three-quarters of all jobs today require at least some elementary word-processing skills. Increasingly office work, retail work and even factory work are being mechanized and computerized. Though this replaces some monotonous jobs, it also tends to reduce the personal element in the workplace and creates a new class of mechanized workers who require special training or reeducation.

Another noticeable trend is the integration of smaller business enterprises into larger ones, or the more intentional collaboration of large and small businesses. The first is taking place even as many firms downsize and large public corporations are being broken up into more competitive units: this means we now have blended workplaces as well as blended families.

In most places the workplace is rapidly becoming more multicultural* and international. While affirmative-action practices have had their impact, the growing pluralism in modern societies has generated its own organic changes. In some sectors of the marketplace, links or business between firms in different countries is also forcing their work forces to be more cross-cultural.

With the breakdown in family* life and neighborhood* community,* workplaces have increasingly assumed some of the character of both. As a number of television sitcoms illustrate, many people now look to their workplaces for a sense of belonging, for quality relationships and for the experience of community. Sadly, sometimes Christians encounter these more in their workplaces than in their churches.* At the same time, workplaces have become more volatile contexts with respect to charges of sexual harassment and personal discrimination. Anxiety* has also increased about the incidence of workers with AIDS. Violence is also increasing as highly disgruntled and disturbed individuals are taking out their frustrations and pathologies on others in the workplace. Concern about injury, assault and even murder in the workplace is growing.

Other changes can be mentioned. For example, for a small but growing proportion of people, the home* is once again becoming their workplace, largely because of the personal computer.* In some cases this allows people to work in a different state or part of the country from where their company or firm is located. At present, approximately 4 percent of the population already work from home, and some predict that this will ultimately rise to around 20 percent. Others challenge this, arguing that most people will not want to give up the social benefits of working with others and that many jobs will require a mix of home- and office-based activity.

A Christian Perspective on the Workplace

All environments, whether human or divine, appealing or appalling, shape us in some degree or other. They affect what we are seeking to do and how we do it, our personal reactions and our relationships with others. We are built by the Creator in such a way that we are influenced not only by our bodies but by our physical surroundings. Because of this, we should become more aware of the changes that are occurring in the workplace. The more responsible our position, the more obligation we have to know and interpret such changes to others around us. But we need to evaluate as well as understand the changes in our workplaces. What are their positive and negative effects? How do we decide what has the character of one and what has the character of the other? We can look at these under the headings of architecture and layout, conditions and procedures, ethos and culture.*

The architecture and layout of a workplace raise questions about the atmosphere in which work is done, the comfort level of employees, the connection with the rhythms of the day or the natural world, the accessibility of leaders and the quality of communication with colleagues. It is important to create a setting that is as spacious and comfortable as possible. If, as is the case, most people are now spending more time at work than in any other activity, including sleep,* they should perform their tasks in conditions that are as congenial and conducive as possible. It is also important to create a setting that enhances the capacity for spontaneous as well as organized contact to happen between people. This is especially important for people whose work would be enhanced by it or, because of the repetitive nature of their jobs, would simply be made more enjoyable and less monotonous. Both lead to greater productivity and loyalty.* With workplaces becoming more technologized, care must be exercised lest they become as machine oriented as older mechanized factories did in the past. How to avoid the office becoming a kind of electronic assembly line is a real issue. Training people to use computers properly and exhibiting a concern for possible physical repercussions are useful as far as they go, but more attention needs to be given to the social consequences of the new technology* and its effect upon people's attitudes and general ways of thinking.

The conditions and procedures in workplaces are also important. It is still sadly the case that the majority of hours lost to the workplace is due to accidents—not to people taking illegitimate sick leave or wasting time on the job. Safety is still an important issue in the workplace, and we should have far more of it. Procedures also need to be developed to deal with the increasing possibility of violence in the workplace. Workers need to be informed about and prepared for the forms this takes, to learn how to handle it when it arises and to be helped to manage stress* and debrief after it takes place. On a different note, while gains were made earlier in the century by applying time-and-motion-study techniques to the workplace, these did not always take into account the differences between humans and machines.

The detailed timing of operations in some plants, financial institutions and fast-food outlets places workers under an extraordinary strain. After a while ongoing attempts to *kaizan,* that is, to increase time-and-motion efficiency of particular operations, become impractical or counterproductive. Too many workplaces are like a prison. This is not to say that everything should have a flexible character; ultimately that would be as frustrating and restrictive as its opposite.

While procedures for helping workplaces deal more responsibly with issues of harassment and discrimination are now fairly well in place, more organic ways of raising awareness and creating an inclusive culture still lag behind. So too does educating people into the differences between people of different ethnic groups or nationalities, so that, where appropriate, workplaces can develop a genuinely crosscultural way of operating. The dynamics and ethos of a workplace are crucial to its functioning well, mainly because they are vital to the well-being of its members. At work, as in all areas of life, being comes before doing, a fact that has often been forgotten. On the other hand, things can go too far in the opposite direction. Regarding the workplace as a surrogate family or community mistakes its proper purpose. If the workplace should never be an impersonal Fordian assembly line or Kafkaesque bureaucratic maze, nor should it be a kind of living room or community space. It is primarily a task-oriented, not person-oriented, affair. People are taken seriously because they are first and foremost persons, not functions, and because they perform tasks better when their personhood is respected, affirmed and developed. Some degree of community naturally arises as this is done, but it is not the main purpose of the workplace. The trick is to strike the right balance in the workplace between care for the task and care for the person.

A Christian perspective on the workplace cannot be summed up under any one phrase, such as enhancing its attractiveness or making it more congenial, improving its safety or bringing greater justice* into it, making it more humane or helping it to become more caring and compassionate. Any of these may be relevant at one time or another, often one more than another, sometimes several at once. All are important and at different times may have priority. The main thing is to have a good understanding of the total environment in which we are operating, along with a sharp sense of what is the most pressing concern at the present.

See also CONFLICT, WORKPLACE; DISCRIMINATION, WORKPLACE; LOYALTY, WORKPLACE; MULTICULTURALISM; ORGANIZATIONAL CULTURE AND CHANGE; STRESS, WORKPLACE; TECHNOLOGY; WORK.

References and Resources
J. F. Coates, J. Jarratt and J. B. Mahaffie, *Future Work: Seven Critical Forces Reshaping Work and the Workforce in North America* (San Francisco: Jossey-Bass, 1990); R. Flannery, *Violence in the Workplace* (New York: Crossroad, 1995); J. Renesch, ed., *New Traditions in Business: Spirit and Leadership in the 21st Century* (San Francisco: Berrett-Koehler, 1992).

Robert Banks

WORLDVIEW

A high-level discussion between the prime minister and premiers of Canada and the leaders of the aboriginal communities gets bogged down. The native leaders insist that the morning session begin with a prayer from one of their elders. And before the prayer can be sung, there needs to be a rather lengthy introduction describing the role of the elderly in native communities. After the prayer the leaders then want to pass the peace pipe amongst all the participants.

So far the prime minister's patience is being tried, but he remains gracious, though he is starting to worry about the time. But during the first speech of the morning (already forty-five minutes late!) one of the native leaders reminds his governmental discussion partners that the land of Canada was given to the aboriginal peoples as a gift of the Great Spirit and that they have a responsibility to care for this gift as an inheritance to their children and their children's children. At this point the prime minister's patience runs out. Interrupting the speaker, he exclaims that this interjection of religion into a political discussion about land and constitutional rights is totally out of order and will only serve to grind the discussion to a halt. The native leaders sit in silence for a moment, totally dumbfounded by this outburst.

In this vignette we see two conflicting worldviews at work. Involved in these worldviews are different understandings of community leadership and land, together with parallel views of the environment and economics. For the aboriginal leaders the elders are the source of wisdom and continuity who teach and remind the younger generation that the land is entrusted to them as a gift. Consequently, the aboriginal peoples judged that sacrificing the environment to narrowly defined economic interests is reducing the land to a commodity that can be sold to the highest bidder. They believe that to consider this "progress" is an odd and alien way to think and act. Just as odd to the prime minister that morning is the idea that the land is a gift of the Great Spirit.

Another vignette from modern urban life points out the powerful influence of worldviews. During a time of economic boom this sign is found in front of a downtown construction site: "Freedom for $999,000!" One is torn between thinking that this is a deal and that perhaps freedom is a tad too expensive. What could this sign mean? It is an advertisement* for a condominium tower that is being erected. You can buy a luxury downtown condo for this amount of money.* As you walk away, you know that you do not have that kind of money. But more importantly you are wondering whether any price can be put on freedom.*

The notions of land as a gift of the Great Spirit and freedom as purchasable for a mere $999,000 are literally worlds apart, indeed worldviews apart.

What Is a Worldview?

The term *worldview* comes from the German word *Weltanschauung* and connotes a global* perspective, an overarching view of the world that directs our life in the world. Worldviews are communally held frameworks of interpretation that provide the normative orientation of a community.* A worldview tells the community what the world is ultimately like and how they ought to comport themselves in that world. As such, worldviews are always incarnated; they take on cultural flesh. Far from being merely a system of thought, a worldview animates a culture's imagination, being the source of dreams, ethos and passion. It is the context in which the language of purchasing freedom for $999,000 or receiving land as a gift of the Great Spirit is deemed plausible or implausible. For the condo dweller this Great Spirit talk is nonsense. For the aboriginal leader, the language of buying freedom is inconceivable.

Worldviews are both visions *of* life and visions *for* life. They are both descriptive *of* the world, providing their adherents with the lens through which they can understand and interpret the world, and prescriptive *for* the world, providing the community with its most foundational values and norms. As such worldviews tell us both what the world *is* and what it *ought to be*. Never a matter of interesting speculation, a worldview, like the leaven of the gospel (Mt 13:33), permeates and flavors one's whole life.

Worldview Questions

Worldviews are religious in character. They provide their adherents with ultimate answers to ultimate questions, at least these four: (1) *Where are we?* or What is the nature of the reality in which we find ourselves? (2) *Who are we?* or What is the nature and task of human beings? (3) *What's wrong?* or How do we understand and account for evil and brokenness? and (4) *What's the remedy?* or How do we find a path through our brokenness to wholeness? Such ultimate questions require ultimate answers. Worldviews then are rooted in a faith stance—a stance in relation to that which is taken to be ultimate. Implied in the difficulties of communication in the story recounted at the beginning of this article are different sources of ultimacy.

Worldviews and Story

All worldviews entail a story, a myth that provides its adherents with an understanding of their own role in the global struggle between good and evil. Such a story tells us who we are in time and why we are here. For example, the way in which American history is taught to children and proclaimed on the political campaign trail is a good example of such a myth. The worldview of the "American dream" is the official and orthodox worldview of the United States and is proclaimed with equal conviction by both Democrats and Republicans. This worldview is rooted in the Enlightenment progress myth, which sees history as a story of cumulative development leading up to modern times and especially to America.

Therefore we can say that worldviews

are storied visions of and for life. The grounding story of a culture* provides it with its founding memories that serve as the source of its most hopeful visions.* It is only by knowing from where we have come that we can begin to discern where we are going. Again, this is amply illustrated by our opening vignettes. If a culture's story is one of conquest and progress defined in terms of economic growth and technological superiority, then the language of buying freedom for a price or negotiating land rights as if land were a commodity will make total sense. If, however, a community's story revolves around dependence on and harmony with nature (not conquest) and tells tales of the Great Spirit and the ancestors' wisdom, then that community will respond to contemporary life in a very different way.

Worldview Crises

A worldview is only sustainable as long as it serves to integrate and provide meaningful and normative direction for life. Just as worldviews provide an interpretive lens through which life is perceived and experienced, so also does the daily experience of life serve to confirm or undermine one's worldview. For example, some people actually have that $999,000 to buy freedom. And they spend that money, get that condo, fill it with expensive furnishings and engage in all of the activities that the dominant secular worldview says will secure freedom. But they still don't feel free. They continue to feel enslaved to the imperative to make even more money because this is the only way to guarantee their freedom. Or they continue to be plagued by past emotional crises. Or perhaps they are daily confronted with the poverty* of those who live on the street just a block away from their $999,000 piece of freedom, and the contradiction between these two lifestyles drives them to begin to question the justice* of their own affluence.

When a person (or a whole culture) begins to experience increased tension between his or her worldview and actual experience, then a worldview crisis begins to loom. For example, when the self-assured worldview of secular progress and unparalleled affluence is confronted with the realities of environmental breakdown, economic recession, international injustice and widespread personal and emotional brokenness, then that worldview is in crisis. Because the gap between the two is so great, the worldview begins to lose its grasp on the hearts and imaginations of its adherents. On a personal level a worldview crisis gives rise to the gravest sort of anxiety* because the very ground on which you stand is now uncertain and you become unsure who you are, what the meaning of life is and where you are going. When such a crisis occurs within the dominant worldview of a culture, then the very scaffolding on which the culture stands begins to collapse, and the masses are cast adrift, exposed and unprotected.

A Christian Worldview

A Christian worldview is only Christian in so far as it is biblical. The Bible answers for us the ultimate worldview questions: (1) *Where are we?* We live in the creation* that God calls into being, wisely structures and lovingly guides by his creative Word. (2) *Who are we?* We are special creatures called to love, worship and image God in our faithful stewardship* of this creation. (3) *What's wrong?* We are broken in our relationships with God, each other and the creation because we have fallen into sin and now serve false idols rather than the true God. (4) *What's the remedy?* God has lovingly chosen to redeem us and the whole creation by making a covenant with Israel and fulfill-

ing that covenant in the incarnation, cross and resurrection of Jesus Christ.

The Scriptures are a worldview book; they tell the story of God's relation to us and to all of creation—a dramatic story of creation, lostness and rescue—which becomes *our* story and the basis of our identity as the people of God when we turn to Jesus Christ in faith. Moreover, a biblical worldview understands creation, fall and redemption in comprehensive terms. *All* of reality is creaturely, *all* of creation is distorted by human disobedience, and Jesus Christ comes to restore *all* things. Consequently, the biblical worldview is truly a *world*view—all of reality falls within its compass.

See also CULTURE; ETHNOCENTRISM; MISSION; PLURALISM.

References and Resources
J. H. Olthius, "On Worldviews," *Christian Scholar's Review* 14, no. 2 (1985) 153-64; J. W. Sire, *The Universe Next Door: A Basic World View Catalog,* 2d ed. (Downers Grove, Ill.: InterVarsity Press, 1988); N. Smart, *Worldviews: Crosscultural Explorations of Human Beliefs* (New York: Scribner, 1983); B. J. Walsh, "Worldviews, Modernity and the Task of Christian College Education," *Faculty Dialogue* 18 (fall 1982) 13-35; B. J. Walsh and J. R. Middleton, *The Transforming Vision: Shaping a Christian World View* (Downers Grove, Ill.: InterVarsity Press, 1984).

Brian J. Walsh

WORSHIP

Originally to *worship* meant simply to "attribute worth"; worship could be directed to God or to a person to whom honor and respect should be given. In classical Christian writings it referred primarily to our chief goal in life, that is, rendering grateful homage and dedicating our lives to God rather than to any other person or object. This included a person's private religious devotions. The word has also been one of the main terms used for public religious services: many church notice boards list the hours for "divine worship." In charismatic circles the word has mainly come to signify the time of extended praise in church, generally led by a "worship team." In popular speech and song the word is frequently used of any extraordinary expression of devotion, for example, a person or group may "worship" a sports team or rock star, money* or power.* In some places the word is even used as a form of address, as to a judge in a law court or to an officeholder in a secret society. From a biblical point of view there are legitimate and illegitimate, acceptable and unacceptable, objects of worship (Gen 4:3-7; Is 1; Rom 14:17-18; Heb 12:28-29; 13:16). Discernment is necessary to distinguish true from false objects of worship.

People's feelings about what takes place in church services vary greatly. Some regard such corporate worship as primarily a duty; others as a delight. For some it is chiefly a matter of feeling inspired by or intimately connected to God, for others of being instructed or motivated to action. An increasing number of people today find traditional church services boring and irrelevant. This is particularly true of the younger baby-buster generation but also of many *seekers,* inquiring about or returning to church. Some find new styles of charismatic or contemporary worship appealing and uplifting. Disputes about appropriate and inappropriate styles of worship have divided many congregations, generally along age lines or according to different views of the Holy Spirit. Surveys of congregations across a wide denominational spectrum, such as those conducted by the Search Institute in Minneapolis some years ago, found that corporate worship is generally regarded as an oasis or refuge from workday demands, rather than as a base camp for equipping members to integrate faith and everyday life. This is why even many committed believers find church-

going disappointing and unempowering. Perhaps part of the problem is that our definition of worship is too narrow.

Biblical Worship: Acknowledging and Serving God Everywhere

In the Old Testament it is God who initiates the worshipful response of the people by revealing his divine name, rescuing Israel from its oppressors and establishing a covenant with them. The people acknowledge this by attending the temple, offering sacrifices and participating in the annual festivals. When they do this—as individuals, as families or as a nation—they do so preeminently at holy places (the tabernacle and later the temple), at holy times (annual festivals* and the sabbath*), with holy people (priests and Levites) and with holy sacrifices (clean and unclean animals). Whole sections and books of the Bible—especially from Exodus to Deuteronomy—are given over to instructions about these.

Yet the most important festival of the year, the Passover, takes place in homes and is presided over by the head of the household. Also, respect to God could be given by such ordinary actions as becoming silent or making a simple gesture. Meanwhile, reference to the whole people as "a kingdom of priests and a holy nation" (Ex 19:6) suggests that the whole of the people's life was to be brought into the service of God and offered as worship to God. To this end, God gave the Law, which contained social and civic as well as cultic provisions. Despite many prophetic criticisms of Israel's public and private worship of God and the exile of the people as a judgment for their disobedience, at the heart of their hope lies a restored temple in a purified land, one to which people from the whole earth will make worshipful pilgrimage (Ezek 40—48).

In the New Testament the sacrificial

system, temple and priesthood—which kept open the lines of communication between God and the people despite their disobedience—are replaced by the sacrifice, holiness and priesthood of Christ (Jn 2:19; Heb 10:1-18). The provisions of the Law, giving guidance on how the people can live obediently before God, are moved into the background, and their place is taken by the example of Christ and fruit of the Spirit (Mk 2:28; Gal 5:22-26). No longer is it necessary to worship God corporately in special places, for as Spirit God is present everywhere (Jn 4:23-24), and ordinary homes became the most common meeting places of the church (for example, Rom 16:5). No longer is it necessary to observe the annual festivals or the sabbath, for now all days and times are equally holy in God's sight (Col 2:16-19), even if it is particularly appropriate to gather on the first day of the week (1 Cor 16:1-2).

Many Old Testament words for the sacrificial worship in the temple also appear in the New Testament. But apart from a few references to the pagan cult (Rom 1:25) or to Jewish worship (Rom 9:4), these are used only metaphorically to refer to such things as proclaiming Christ (Rom 15:16), praising God (Heb 13:15), dedicating lives (Phil 2:17), exercising faith (Phil 2:17), sharing fellowship (Phil 2:25) and charitable giving (2 Cor 9:12). It is in performing such services in Christ's name and for Christ's sake that we please God and therefore worship God truly (Rom 14:18).

Worship is something anyone can do, anyplace and anytime. So we find words associated with worship are also used of people's service to society at large (even of the actions of unbelievers if they do what God wishes; Rom 13:7). Believers are encouraged to serve Christ and to please God in every setting, such as their daily work* (Col 3:22-24), family* life and marriage* (Col 3:18-20; Eph 5:21),

caring for the needy (Mt 25:45), providing hospitality* (Heb 13:2), acting justly and compassionately (Jas 1:27). Indeed, our spiritual worship involves nothing less than offering up our whole lives to God so that all we do is in conformity with God's character and standards rather than with the attitudes and values of the world (Rom 12:1-2). This means that we do not move in and out of worshiping God when we go to church on Sundays but are always worshiping God and just doing so well or badly, consciously or unconsciously.

The only thing that distinguishes our coming together in church* is that when we do so, we are worshiping God together as a body of God's people, whereas most of the time we are worshiping God on our own or with our families and friends. When we do meet together, it is, not only our singing together that is worship, but everything that we do—greeting* one another as we arrive, learning from the Scriptures, sharing news or announcements, singing praises or making prayers, sharing the Lord's Supper and visiting over coffee and cookies after the service. Indeed, for the early Christians having a common meal together was a regular part of their weekly corporate worship. When we are in church, the quality of our worship is not correlated to the intensity with which we focus upon God and feel God's presence. Instead of closing our eyes and concentrating upon God, as some do today, we are encouraged to keep our eyes open and actually "speak to one another with psalms, hymns and spiritual songs" (Eph 5:19), recognizing that encouraging and exhorting each other, receiving instruction and advice from one another (Col 3:16; Heb 10:24-25), are among the most worshipful activities. For in doing this, we discern the presence and communication of God in and through each person who is present.

Worship as Life Orientation: A Duty and a Delight

At the heart of the idea of worship is our relationship with God. All creation declares the glory of God unintentionally just by being itself (Ps 19:1). But human beings uniquely can choose to bless* God; indeed, we are obligated to do so. The fundamental way the Bible describes our relationship with God is the covenant, that binding personal relationship by which two parties (in this case God and people) belong together forever. The covenant starts with the promise* that God has selected, adopted and saved the people (Ex 19:4-6) making them a "treasured possession." God promises presence, community and a place to belong. The covenant itself is unconditional, founded as it is on the promise, but the blessings of the covenant (the land, the continuance of the people and the ultimate blessing of the Gentiles) are conditional upon obedience to its obligations. These obligations involve (1) a lifestyle of behavior appropriate for God's covenant people (embodied in the Ten Commandments) and (2) a lifestyle of blessing God (embodied in the temple worship and festivals). In other words, people in right relation to God live faithfully and bless God continuously. To live a holy life (as the Pharisees did in Jesus' time) but not to express love to God is to break the covenant, even though no grave breach of it is committed. This same failure to bless breaks the covenant of marriage: staying in it ungratefully (like a spouse remaining faithful in a difficult marriage but only complaining about it) still breaks the covenant because there is no blessing of the partner.

In the new, literally "renewed," covenant in Christ, the covenant is incarnated (in the life and ministry of Jesus), universalized (to include Gentiles) and internalized (through the indwelling Spirit that motivates us from within). All this was foretold under the old covenant but has now become a reality. This renewed covenant still carries the twin obligations of faithful living and grateful blessing. But these are no longer obligations imposed from the outside; they are inspired from the inside as God gives us the power to fulfill them and does so in a way that makes obedience a pleasure. In Jesus' reflection on John 17 we gain a glimpse of the internal worship life of the triune God. Father, Son and Spirit bring glory to each other, go out of themselves in love for each other and eternally delight in one another. During Christ's earthly ministry we have a sacred hint of this in his spontaneous worship when "full of joy through the Holy Spirit" (Lk 10:21), Jesus thanked and blessed the Father. So for God's people worship is not a desperate effort to cross the infinity of time and space and bring honor to God; it is being taken into the continuous worship that goes on within the Godhead. It is modeled and inspired from above, not created and worked up from below.

Some people have trouble blessing God because they feel that God has not blessed them. Like Naomi, they feel that "the Almighty has made my life very bitter" (Ruth 1:20). The roots of this go very deep, as deep as the original sin in the Garden of Eden. That first sin was not eating the forbidden fruit but turning away from our fundamental posture of gratitude to and reverence of God (compare Rom 1:21) to allow a root of bitterness to slip in. This had its source in the serpent, who insinuated that God was holding back some blessing from the man and the woman (Gen 3:1). Bitterness is not caused by circumstances but by a spiritual choice. Do we trust and love God enough to be content? Further, lapsing into self-pity often comes from a shortsighted faith; God is able to bring good out of all things and turn even the curses experienced in this life into blessings. If not in this life (as happened with Naomi), God will ultimately bless us totally through the resurrection of our bodies and our living in the new heaven and earth. It is here that God's promises of presence, community and place reach their full consummation.

"Count your blessings" is an ancient saying containing a crucial insight: being blessed is a matter of perspective, of worldview,* of spirituality. So the frequent self-exhortation the psalmist utters—"Bless the LORD, O my soul, and all that is within me, bless his holy name" (Ps 103:1 NRSV)—is exactly what people need to do in their covenantal relationship with God. If there is no blessing, there is no faith and no joy. When we worship, we literally enjoy God, delight in God, play with God, relish God, bring pleasure to God. C. S. Lewis once said that in commanding us to worship, God is inviting us to enjoy him. Paradoxically, while worship, like play, is a "waste of time" because it does not accomplish anything, worship does actually affect God. It is a truly awesome thing that worship makes a difference to God, actually blesses God.

But worship, as we have already seen, is much more than worship services. We also bless God by transforming all aspects of everyday life into a spiritual ministry to others for God, seeking to live according to God's priorities and values, doing this in God's Spirit and for God's benefit. This means that we are also worshiping God when we are seeking to bring benefit to others, often so concentrating on this that we are not intentionally focusing on God at all. It is precisely when we are giving ourselves away to whatever calling,* ministry,* opportunity or need God has given us, that we are reproducing that total commitment to others exemplified in Christ, God's

Son. Perhaps at times when we, like Christ on the cross, experience more what seems like our abandonment by God than intimacy with God, we may be worshiping God in the most profound way. The devoted mother, the servant employee, the committed volunteer are worshiping God as much in their parenting,* working and serving as in their times of intimate personal prayer or joyful corporate praise to God.

Heavenly Worship

In the last book of the Bible we are given an empowering vision of worship in the new Jerusalem. All earthly worship should be inspired by the worship that is already going on in heaven and that we will experience more fully when Christ comes again. In this sense our present worship is like "playing heaven," as when little children invite each other to "play house," looking forward to the day when they are grown up and have their own home. So in our worship now we are anticipating the joy of the final redemption of matter and time in one continuous, everyday life expression of joy and pleasure in God.

Far from being dull and stereotyped (playing the same old songs on our harps sitting on gold streets) worship in heaven is exquisitely beautiful, continuously spontaneous and totally enjoyable. The picture given to us in Revelation 21—22 has several characteristics that can inspire our worship now.

The worship is responsive. It is caused by God and God's actions rather than "worked up" by human effort. God awakens a desire for worship (Rev 3:20; 5:2) in the same way he awakened a desire in Adam for a wife.

The worship is reverent. God-pleasing and for God's benefit, it is inspired by the mercy of God and directed to the pleasure of God. The alternatives promoted today—relational, charismatic or contemplative worship—focus on what we get out of corporate worship. But the royal priesthood (Rev 1:6; 5:10) is focused on blessing God.

The worship is inclusive. Revelation gives us a picture of all nations, tribes and peoples together worshiping God. The global village* has become the global garden city.* The synergism of this is far more than the sum of individual privatized worship.

The worship is intelligent. The mind is engaged fully in heaven. Worship is not a "touchy-feely" affair but reflects (as does John himself) on the great themes of God as Creator and Redeemer (Rev 4—5). Worship is evoked by the qualities and actions of God: power, wealth, wisdom, strength, honor, glory, blessing and sovereignty (Rev 4:11; 5:11, 13; 7:12; 19:1).

The worship is theological. Revelation is a christocentric commentary on the whole Old Testament explaining how Christ is the goal toward which the whole drama has been moving. This great theological theme provides the framework for the dominant mood of the book: worship. The original covenant reaches its consummation in the marriage supper of the Lamb, when we commune with Christ forever.

The worship is aesthetic. Worship in heaven appeals to our senses in a spiritual way. There are sounds (trumpets, shouting in a loud voice, silence), motions (falling down prostrate, casting our crowns before the throne), light (rainbows and exquisite emerald), rhythm (antiphonal, sequential and total groupings of praise; Rev 5:9, 12-13; 19) and patterns (the encircling throne; Rev 5:11). Heavenly worship appeals to the sanctified imagination.*

The worship is holistic. This worship does not only comprise times of direct focus upon God but the whole of life in the garden city of God, so full of divine creativity,* beauty and wonder. Into this all the delightful things people have made from every nation will be brought and enjoyed.

The worship is prophetic. A balance of awe and intimacy, adoration and access, with respect to God is our destiny and should shape our worship in the here and now. In the same way our present earthly worship prepares us for life in the heavenly city. Perhaps in some way beyond our imaginations, but hinted in Hebrews 12:22-24, our present worship contributes to the ongoing worship in heaven.

What does worship accomplish? The question seems inappropriate because worship is not utilitarian: it does not accomplish anything. We do not make more money by it or get instant healing. Yet, worship "works" precisely because it lifts us above the compulsion to make everything useful and restores what we earlier called our true human posture: continuous reverence and thanksgiving.

By worshiping we are kept in touch with the really real, not the fake imitations that surround us and cry out for our ultimate loyalty. By worshiping we are challenged to live by kingdom priorities. Our society inundates us with messages to buy, consume and experience. Along with sabbath, worship helps us meet at the center of everything so that life is not lived eccentrically. Eugene Peterson says that a "failure to worship resigns us to a life of spasms and jerks, at the mercy of every advertisement, every seduction, every siren" (p. 60). Finally worship prepares us for heaven. Worship in this life is like one grand rehearsal for the real thing—holiness in space and time* with God at the center of everything. So in the deepest sense we do not keep the discipline of worship; worship keeps us.

See also BLESSING; CHURCH; CHURCH IN THE HOME; COMMUNION; MINISTRY; MU-

SIC, CHRISTIAN; PRAYER, CORPORATE; PREACHING; SACRAMENTS; SPIRITUAL GIFTS.

References and Resources

R. Corriveau, *The Liturgy of Life: A Study of the Ethical Thought of St. Paul* (Brussels: Bellarmin, 1970); F. Hahn, *Worship in the New Testament* (Philadelphia: Fortress, 1973); G. Kendrick, *Learning to Worship as a Way of Life* (Minneapolis: Bethany House, 1985); T. M. Lindsay, *The Church and the Ministry in the Early Centuries* (London: Hodder & Stoughton, 1902); C. F. D. Moule, *Worship in the New Testament* (London: Lutterworth, 1961); D. Peterson, *Engaging with God: A Biblical Theology of Worship* (Grand Rapids: Eerdmans, 1992); E. H. Peterson, *Reversed Thunder: The Revelation of John and the Praying Imagination* (San Francisco: Harper & Row, 1988); H. Rowley, *Worship in Ancient Israel* (London: SPCK, 1967); E. Schweizer, "The Service of Worship," in *Neotestamentica* (Zurich: Zwingli, 1964) 333-43; H. W. Turner, *From Temple to Meeting Place: The Phenomenology and Theology of Places of Worship* (The Hague: Mouton, 1979).

Robert Banks and R. Paul Stevens

Z

ZONING

Zoning in its simplest form is the segregation of publicly and privately owned land into zones which separate commercial and industrial uses from residential uses. As such, zoning bylaws have a profound impact on our daily lives and shape the face, if not the very soul, of our cities.*

Through these regulations our civic governments enshrine the widely held belief that neighborhoods* must be sanctuaries from the dual pressures of industry and traffic. Since these values* are so common, neighborhoods often fight emotional battles to preserve the status quo. While the values which zoning legislation protects are seldom a matter of dispute, modern social and environmental problems are forcing urban planners to question the many assumptions that are woven deeply into the fabric of existing legislation.

The Rise of Zoning Legislation

Before examining some of these assumptions, we might well look at the rise of zoning legislation in North America and Europe.

Genesis 1 (RSV) is an account of how the Spirit of God brought order and design to an earth that was "formless and empty." Since we are created in the image of God, it is not surprising that we should strive to impose order on that which we perceive to be chaotic. Possibly the first encoded housing code is found in the requirement to build a railing around a roof deck to keep people from falling off (Deut 22:8).

The history of Western civilization is the history of mighty rulers building well-planned cities as monuments to their power* and ingenuity. With the rise of democracy and land ownership,* modern zoning bylaws have replaced the decrees of monarchs as the vehicle with which to create ordered cities.

The first modern zoning bylaw was enacted in Frankfurt, Germany, in 1891. The success of the well-ordered German cities so impressed American planners that in 1916 the city of New York adopted the first zoning bylaw. Within twenty years federal model zoning bylaws were enacted throughout the United States. Similar legislative initiatives spread to Great Britain and Canada. The Canadian and British legislations developed broad discretionary powers to use such bylaws to distribute wealth* created through the rezoning process for the purpose of providing public amenities. In contrast, in the United States the emphasis on property rights was reflected in court decisions, which often operated to restrict the redistribution aspect of zoning bylaws in favor of individual property rights.*

Prior to the advent of zoning legislation, land use was regulated by restrictive covenants which were registered against the land by a developer to control the quality of the buildings constructed and the manner in which the land was used. Alternatively, the common-law doctrine of nuisance operated to allow land owners to sue one another when noxious or industrial uses were conducted in residential areas. While these devices produced a degree of segregation, many neighborhoods still had a wide diversity of business and residential uses. The diversity of types of housing also led to a broader socioeconomic diversity of residents.

Zoning and the Modern City
With the success of the motor vehicle, North Americans were provided with the means to escape the limits of the traditional small lot of the cities. Cheap land allowed the creation of spacious subdivisions. The desire to create truly separate residential neighborhoods pushed neighborhood stores and services to the periphery of the residential subdivisions and eventually into large malls* where economies of scale could operate to produce attractive pricing. In the process, neighborhood pedestrian traffic and street life declined as the automobile* further insulated residents from the daily encounters which are so essential to the creation of a sense of community. Largely lost in this process were the small family businesses unable to compete with national chains, and with them was lost a sense of stability and community.

The creation of the suburban subdivision also served to limit the ethnic and economic diversity of residents which is more frequently found in older areas of the city. The high cost of large suburban homes ensured that the residents would be homogenous in their economic status and indirectly their race. The strict definition of areas as "single-family" limited the opportunities for boarding rooms and in-law suites. This had the further effect of limiting the diversity of the population to the nuclear family. The institutionalization of senior citizens also removed seniors from residential areas and limited their traditional role in providing family support.

Zoning and the Gospel
The gospel of Jesus Christ is a message of inclusion and a call to reject position, privilege and the institutions which protect them. Jesus' unconditional love of the sick, the tax collector, the prostitute and the child is an invitation to understand ourselves and the spiritual emptiness which drives us to perform. Like the good son in the parable of the prodigal son (Lk 15), we explode in anger as we realize that the achievements for which we have toiled to define ourselves are unimportant to our Father's love for us. Our sense of control and order is lost as grace extinguishes our pride and places us as an equal in the company of the prodigal.

Zoning bylaws reflect our need to segregate ourselves through pride and fear. Changes to these rules will not change people's deepest fears. Those changes will, however, provide us with the opportunity to grow in spiritual understanding as we know and relate to our neighbors. In doing so, we will sow the seeds of community* and allow our children to see glimpses of God's unconditional love.

Planners throughout the world have been experimenting with regulatory mechanisms which attempt to create the social diversity and sense of community which existed in the traditional town* setting. Effective zoning, while recognizing the traditional rights of ownership, also recognizes the biblical principles of stewardship* that demand that our use of the land be accomplished in a manner that minimizes the negative impacts on our physical and social environment. The challenge for Christians is to be thoughtful participants in our civic governments. Our challenge is to recognize that the status quo has robbed our neighborhoods of their traditional diversity and to pursue creative choices which will once again open our communities to the old, the disabled and the poor. Locating daycare centers, senior facilities and schools together to create shared programs would be a small step to bridge the generational isolation. More liberal regulations regarding extending families, student housing and small family-based community care homes would be effective steps to renewal.

In opening the doors of our communities we also open our hearts to experience God's grace. Let us be mindful of this as we take small daily steps toward that goal.

See also ARCHITECTURE, URBAN; CITY; COMMUNITY; COMMUTING; INNER CITY; NEIGHBORHOOD; PUBLIC SPACES; SHOPPING MALLS; SMALL TOWNS; SUBURBIA.

References and Resources
M. Goldberg, *Zoning: Its Cost and Relevance for the 1980's* (Vancouver: Fraser Institute, 1980); H. J. M. Nouwen, *The Return of the Prodigal Son* (Toronto: Doubleday, 1992); S. M. Peck, *The Different Drum* (New York: Simon & Schuster, 1988); W. Rybczynski, *City Life: Urban Expectations in a New World* (Toronto: HarperCollins, 1995); F. S. So, *The Practice of Local Government Planning* (Washington, D.C.: International City Management Association, 1959).

Derek Creighton

LIFE ACTIVITIES, INTERESTS & CONCERNS INDEX

The Life Activities, Interests and Concerns Index lists subject categories associated with six major domains of everyday life: (1) the individual and relationships; (2) home and family; (3) work, money and marketplace; (4) neighborhood, city and society; (5) leisure, culture and environment; and (6) church and mission.

Each domain includes an introductory paragraph exploring its theological relevance to everyday Christian living. Within each of the six domains, subjects are arranged alphabetically; many of the subject headings also contain cross-references. To find articles related to a particular topic, choose one of the domains and check the alphabetical listing within that domain. A subject with a *See* cross-reference (for example, Borrowing. *See* Debt) indicates that there is no article by that title (Borrowing) but directs you to a similar article (Debt) within which you will find relevant information. A subject with a *See also* cross-reference (for example, Conversation. *See also* Gossip) indicates that there is an article by that title (Conversation) and also directs you to a related article (Gossip).

1. The Individual and Relationships

At every stage of human life—from conception to resurrection—we are invited by God to find meaning and purpose in everyday life. The ordinary "daily round"—from washing our faces in the morning to slipping into bed at night—is full of hints of God's purpose and invitations to grow in faith. In addition, life is full of significant transitions—from leaving home to leaving this life—each of which is a moment of personal and spiritual growth. The articles in this section explore the theology and spirituality of everyday life in the experience of individual persons and their relationships.

Abortion

Abuse

Accountability. *See* Accountability, Relational; Accountability, Workplace

Addiction

Admonishing. *See* Preaching

Adolescence

Adornment

Affirming. *See also* Blessing, Family

Aging. *See also* Discrimination, Workplace; Retirement

Anniversaries

Anxiety

Bereavement. *See* Death; Grieving

Birth. *See also* Conception; Pregnancy

Body

Boredom

Busyness. *See* Time

Circumcision

Civility

Cleaning. *See* Washing

Clothing. *See* Adornment; Dress Code, Workplace

Conception. *See also* New Reproductive Technology

Conflict, Church. *See* Church Conflict; *see also* Conflict Resolution

Conflict Resolution

Conflict, Spiritual. *See* Spiritual Conflict

Conscience

Contraception

Conversation

Cooking. *See* Eating; Meal Preparation

Creativity. *See* Art; Beauty; Craftsmanship

Dating

Daydreaming

Death. *See also* Grieving; Miscarriage

Debt. *See also* Credit

Depression

Dreaming. *See also* Daydreaming

Dressing. *See* Adornment; Dress Code, Workplace

Driving. *See* Automobile;

Commuting; Mobility
Drunkenness. *See* Addiction
Dying. *See* Death

Eating. *See also* Chocolate;
  Meal Preparation; Sugar/
  Sugary
Eating Out. *See* Eating
Emotions
Euthanasia
Examinations

Faith Development
Farewell
Feelings. *See* Emotions
Festivals—Christmas
Festivals—Easter
Festivals—Thanksgiving
Forgiveness. *See also* Conflict
  Resolution
Freedom
Friendship

Gift-Giving
Gossip
Gratitude. *See* Festivals—
  Thanksgiving
Greeting
Grieving
Growth, Spiritual. *See* Spiri-
  tual Growth
Guidance. *See also* Voca-
  tional Guidance

Habits
Hairstyle. *See* Beauty; Body
Happiness. *See* Pleasure
Hate
Healing
Health
Health Insurance. *See* Insur-
  ance
Heart. *See* Emotions; Reason-
  ing; Soul
Homosexuality

Hospitality

Illness. *See* Sickness
Individual. *See also* Freedom
Insomnia. *See* Rest; Sleeping
Insurance

Letter Writing
Life Insurance. *See* Insur-
  ance
Listening
Love

Masturbation
Menopause and Male Cli-
  macteric
Menstruation
Midlife Crisis. *See* Life
  Stages; Menopause and
  Male Climacteric
Mind. *See* Reasoning
Miscarriage

Need
New Reproductive Technol-
  ogy. *See also* Conception

Oaths. *See* Promising
Ownership, Private. *See also*
  Stewardship

Person/Personhood. *See*
  Abortion; Body; Concep-
  tion; Euthanasia; Soul
Pets
Planning
Pregnancy
Privacy
Promising. *See also* Contract

Reasoning
Reproductive Technologies.
  See New Reproductive
  Technology
Rest. *See also* Leisure

Resurrection. *See* Body
Retirement
Rights

Saving. *See* Gift-Giving; In-
  vestment; Stewardship
Self-Esteem
Senses. *See* Body; Listening
Sexual Abuse. *See* Abuse
Sexuality
Sickness
Sleeping
Soul
Speaking
Spirit. *See* Soul
Spiritual Conflict
Spiritual Direction. *See* Spiri-
  tual Formation
Spiritual Disciplines. *See also*
  Spiritual Formation
Spiritual Formation. *See also*
  Spiritual Growth
Stress, Workplace

Talents
Thinking. *See* Reasoning
Time

Values
Virtues
Visiting
Vows. *See* Promising

Waiting
Waking. *See* Sleeping
Walking
Want. *See* Need
Washing
Watch
Welcome. *See* Greeting
Wellness. *See* Health
Will. *See* Soul
Will, Last

2. Home and Family

Family is one of those notoriously hard words to define. But in this section we explore family as a community of belonging which one enters by birth, adoption or the marriage covenant. In the "Church and Mission" section there are additional important articles in which the thought of the church as the Christian's "first family" is explored. Both home and church are meeting places with God. Many people think that finding God at home—sometimes called "domestic spirituality"—is a matter of bringing God into the home through family devotions and religious ritual. But the whole of family life itself is a spiritual discipline inviting us Godward. God made human beings to live in family because God—in Father, Son and Holy Spirit—dwells in family. Created human beings reflect that image on earth. So the most mundane as well as the most exalted family experiences—from reading a story to your children to planning a family wedding—and all the family transitions—from adolescence to empty-nesting—are designed by God to be faith-evoking and life-affirming. Even family problems and domestic crises are opportunities as well as dangers.

3. Work, Money and Marketplace

Work has become for many people the central reference point in their lives and the main consumer of their time and energy. Whether people have much or little, money is what much of life today revolves around. There is an implicit theology in everyone's attitude to and handling of work. The following entries look at the relationship between God and the marketplace, at work as a spiritual discipline, and at how to handle some of the main pressures and dilemmas that arise in a work setting.

Unemployment
Unemployment Insurance.
  See Insurance
Unions

Values, Organizational. *See*
  Organizational Values

Vocation. See Calling/Vocation
Vocational Guidance
Volunteer Work

Wealth
Whistle-Blowing

Work. *See also* Calling; Career; Professions/Professionalism
Workaholism. *See* Drivenness
Work Ethic, Protestant
Workplace

4. Neighborhood, City and Society

Neighborhoods, towns, cities and society as a whole are undergoing significant changes. The following entries discuss these and examine how we should evaluate what is happening and respond with integrity to it. Central to our attempt to seek the welfare of the city is the struggle to redevelop or build greater community and to strengthen and enlarge the quest for justice. Doing this requires both practical theological discernment and an authentic everyday spirituality.

Anonymity. *See* City; Community; Loneliness
Architecture, Urban
Automobile. *See also* Commuting; Traveling

Borrowing. *See* Debt
Buying. *See* Consumerism; Ownership, Private; Shopping

Capital Punishment. *See* Death; Justice
Car. *See* Automobile; Commuting
Change, Organizational. *See* Organizational Culture and Change
Citizenship
City
Civil Disobedience
Civility
Clubs
Committees
Community
Community, Rural
Community, Urban. *See* City; Community
Commuting
Consumerism
Country Living. *See* Community, Rural
Culture, Organizational. *See* Organizational Culture and Change
Credit. *See also* Debt
Credit Card
Crime
Crowds

Discrimination. *See* Discrimination, Workplace; Multiculturalism; Pluralism
Dissent. *See* Civil Disobedience; Social Action
Driving. *See* Automobile; Commuting; Mobility
Drugs

Ecology
Education
Education, Christian. *See* Christian Education
Elections. *See* Justice; Lobbying; Voting
Ethnocentrism
Examinations

Farming
Fences
Freedom
Freeways. *See* Automobile; Commuting; Suburbs
Friendship

Global Village
Government. *See* Politics

Homelessness. *See* Mobility
Hospitality
House. *See* Home

Immigration
Inner City
Institutions. *See* Organization; Organizational Culture and Change

Joining Political Parties. *See*

Political Parties, Joining
Justice
Justice System. *See* Justice

Law. *See also* Justice; Law Enforcement
Law Enforcement. *See also* Crime
Leadership
Lobbying
Loneliness. *See* City; Community

Malls, Shopping. *See* Shopping Malls
Marketing. *See* Advertising
Mobility
Money
Multiculturalism. *See also* Pluralism

Nation. *See* Nationalism
Nationalism
Need
Neighborhood
Neighboring. *See* Neighborhood
Noise

Organization
Organizational Culture and Change
Organizational Values

Parks. *See* Public Spaces
Peacemaking. *See* Conflict Resolution; Social Action
Planning
Playgrounds. *See* Public

5. Leisure, Culture and Environment

We are surrounded by opportunities for leisure, cultural enjoyment or advancement. We are also influenced by our humanly constructed and divinely created environment. Understanding how, where and when each of these fits into God's purposes is at the core of the following entries. Pervading them is a sense of God's being the ultimate source and embodiment of rest and artistry, and of our need to reflect these in our own spirituality.

6. Church and Mission

At the heart of Christian experience is community. In one sense, the "individual" Christian does not exist, since we are designed by God to live the Christian life as a people; solitary discipleship is not an option. The articles in this section explore many of the dimensions of church life in both theory and practice. But they also include entries on our mission in the world—at home, next door and in faraway places. Both in gathering as believers and in dispersing into the world, there is much in what follows to help live in this world in a Christian way.

LIFE
EXPERIENCE
INDEX

The articles in the Life Experience Index are divided into two major categories. The Life Stages and Passages category has six subdivisions; the Life Experiences and Responsibilities category has thirty subdivisions. Within each subdivision the topically related articles are arranged alphabetically. To find articles related to a particular topic (for example, Finances), choose one of the two major categories (in this case, Life Experiences and Responsibilities) and browse through its subdivisions until you find the desired topic (Finances). The entries under the topic will help you explore the theological significance of one facet of everyday Christianity.

SUBJECT INDEX

This subject index is a cross-referenced alphabetical listing of all of the articles and related topics of *The Complete Book of Everyday Christianity*. To find an article or articles related to a particular topic, simply look it up in the subject index. A subject with a *See* cross-reference (for example, Borrowing. *See* Debt) indicates that there is no article by that title (Borrowing), but you are directed to a similar article (Debt) in which you will find pertinent information. A subject with a *See also* cross-reference (for example, Conversation. *See also* Gossip) indicates that there is an article by that title (Conversation), and you are also directed to a related article (Gossip).